MATTHEW

Baker Exegetical Commentary on the New Testament

ROBERT W. YARBROUGH
AND ROBERT H. STEIN, EDITORS

Volumes now available

Matthew *David L. Turner*

Luke *Darrell L. Bock*

John *Andreas J. Köstenberger*

Acts *Darrell L. Bock*

Romans *Thomas R. Schreiner*

1 Corinthians *David E. Garland*

Philippians *Moisés Silva*

1 Peter *Karen H. Jobes*

Revelation *Grant R. Osborne*

David L. Turner (ThD, Grace Theological Seminary; PhD cand., Hebrew Union College–Jewish Institute of Religion) is professor of New Testament at Grand Rapids Theological Seminary, where he has taught for more than twenty years.

MATTHEW

DAVID L. TURNER

Baker Exegetical Commentary on the New Testament

Baker Academic
a division of Baker Publishing Group
Grand Rapids, Michigan

©2008 by David L. Turner

Published by Baker Academic
a division of Baker Publishing Group
P.O. Box 6287, Grand Rapids, MI 49516-6287
www.bakeracademic.com

Printed in the United States of America

Library of Congress Cataloging-in-Publication Data
Turner, David L.
     Matthew / David L. Turner.
        p.   cm.   — (Baker exegetical commentary on the New Testament)
     Includes bibliographical references (p.) and indexes.
     ISBN 978-0-8010-2684-3 (cloth)
     1. Bible. N.T. Matthew—Commentaries. I. Title.
     BS2575.53.T87 2007
     226.2′077—dc22   2007031941

To Beverly

Contents

Series Preface ix
Author's Preface xi
Abbreviations xiii
Transliteration xviii
Map xx

  Introduction to Matthew *1*
 I. Prologue/Introduction: Origin of Jesus the Messiah (1:1–2:23) *52*
   A. Title and Genealogy of Jesus the Messiah (1:1–17) *54*
   B. Birth of Jesus the Messiah (1:18–25) *63*
   C. Visit of the Magi (2:1–12) *76*
   D. Escape to Egypt (2:13–15) *88*
   E. Massacre at Bethlehem (2:16–18) *92*
   F. Return to Nazareth (2:19–23) *96*
 II. Early Days of Kingdom Word and Deed (3:1–7:29) *101*
   A. Narrative 1: John and Jesus and the Kingdom of God
      (3:1–4:25) *102*
   B. Discourse 1: Sermon on the Mount (5:1–7:29) *141*
III. Galilean Ministry Continues (8:1–11:1) *226*
   A. Narrative 2: Three Cycles of Miracles and Discipleship
      (8:1–10:4) *227*
   B. Discourse 2: Mission and Suffering (10:5–11:1) *266*
 IV. Growing Opposition to the Kingdom of Heaven (11:2–13:52) *285*
   A. Narrative 3: Three Cycles of Unbelief and Belief
      (11:2–12:50) *286*
   B. Discourse 3: Parables of the Kingdom of Heaven
      (13:1–52) *332*
  V. Opposition to the Kingdom Continues (13:53–19:2) *356*
   A. Narrative 4: Various Responses to the Son of God
      (13:53–17:27) *357*
   B. Discourse 4: Values and Relationships in the Kingdom
      Community (18:1–19:2) *431*

VI. Opposition Comes to a Head in Judea (19:3–26:2) *455*
   A. Narrative 5: Ministry in Judea (19:3–23:39) *456*
   B. Discourse 5: Judgment of Jerusalem and the Coming of Christ
      (24:1–26:2) *565*
VII. Epilogue/Conclusion: Passion, Resurrection, and Commission
     (26:3–28:20) *613*
   A. Preliminary Events and Preparation of the Disciples
      (26:3–46) *616*
   B. Arrest and Trial (26:47–27:26) *634*
   C. Crucifixion (27:27–56) *657*
   D. Burial of Jesus (27:57–66) *673*
   E. Resurrection of Jesus (28:1–15) *679*
   F. Commission by the Risen Lord (28:16–20) *687*

Works Cited *693*
Index of Subjects *763*
Index of Authors *769*
Index of Greek Words *780*
Index of Scripture and Other Ancient Writings *781*

Series Preface

The chief concern of the Baker Exegetical Commentary on the New Testament (BECNT) is to provide, within the framework of informed evangelical thought, commentaries that blend scholarly depth with readability, exegetical detail with sensitivity to the whole, and attention to critical problems with theological awareness. We hope thereby to attract the interest of a fairly wide audience, from the scholar who is looking for a thoughtful and independent examination of the text to the motivated lay Christian who craves a solid but accessible exposition.

Nevertheless, a major purpose is to address the needs of pastors and others involved in the preaching and exposition of the Scriptures as the uniquely inspired Word of God. This consideration directly affects the parameters of the series. For example, serious biblical expositors cannot afford to depend on a superficial treatment that avoids the difficult questions, but neither are they interested in encyclopedic commentaries that seek to cover every conceivable issue that may arise. Our aim, therefore, is to focus on those problems that have a direct bearing on the meaning of the text (although selected technical details are treated in the additional notes).

Similarly, a special effort is made to avoid treating exegetical questions for their own sake, that is, in relative isolation from the thrust of the argument as a whole. This effort may involve (at the discretion of the individual contributors) abandoning the verse-by-verse approach in favor of an exposition that focuses on the paragraph as the main unit of thought. In all cases, however, the commentaries will stress the development of the argument and explicitly relate each passage to what precedes and follows it so as to identify its function in context as clearly as possible.

We believe, moreover, that a responsible exegetical commentary must take fully into account the latest scholarly research, regardless of its source. The attempt to do this in the context of a conservative theological tradition presents certain challenges, and in the past the results have not always been commendable. In some cases, evangelicals appear to make use of critical scholarship not for the purpose of genuine interaction but only to dismiss it. In other cases, the interaction glides over into assimilation, theological distinctives are ignored or suppressed, and the end product cannot be differentiated from works that arise from a fundamentally different starting point.

The contributors to this series attempt to avoid these pitfalls. On the one hand, they do not consider traditional opinions to be sacrosanct, and they are certainly committed to do justice to the biblical text whether or not it supports such opinions. On the other hand, they will not quickly abandon a long-standing view, if there is persuasive evidence in its favor, for the sake of fashionable theories. What is more important, the contributors share a belief in the trustworthiness and essential unity of Scripture. They also consider that the historic formulations of Christian doctrine, such as the ecumenical creeds and many of the documents originating in the sixteenth-century Reformation, arose from a legitimate reading of Scripture, thus providing a proper framework for its further interpretation. No doubt, the use of such a starting point sometimes results in the imposition of a foreign construct on the text, but we deny that it must necessarily do so or that the writers who claim to approach the text without prejudices are invulnerable to the same danger.

Accordingly, we do not consider theological assumptions—from which, in any case, no commentator is free—to be obstacles to biblical interpretation. On the contrary, an exegete who hopes to understand the apostle Paul in a theological vacuum might just as easily try to interpret Aristotle without regard for the philosophical framework of his whole work or without having recourse to those subsequent philosophical categories that make possible a meaningful contextualization of his thought. It must be emphasized, however, that the contributors to the present series come from a variety of theological traditions and that they do not all have identical views with regard to the proper implementation of these general principles. In the end, all that really matters is whether the series succeeds in representing the original text accurately, clearly, and meaningfully to the contemporary reader.

Shading has been used to assist the reader in locating the introductory comments for each section and concluding summaries, where these appear. Textual variants in the Greek text are signaled in the author's translation by means of half-brackets around the relevant word or phrase (e.g., ⌜Gerasenes⌝), thereby alerting the reader to turn to the additional notes at the end of each exegetical unit for a discussion of the textual problem. The documentation uses the author-date method, in which the basic reference consists of author's surname + year + page number(s): Fitzmyer 1992: 58. The only exceptions to this system are well-known reference works (e.g., BDAG, LSJ, *TDNT*). Full publication data and a complete set of indexes can be found at the end of the volume.

Robert Yarbrough
Robert H. Stein

Author's Preface

I would be remiss if I failed to acknowledge that in God's providence numerous individuals have contributed in various ways to the completion of this project. I thank all of them, especially those mentioned below.

The editors at Baker Academic provided much help and encouragement while enduring my many delays in producing this manuscript. I especially thank Jim Kinney and Wells Turner. Robert Yarbrough's work as BECNT editor was thorough and competent. His suggestions greatly improved this commentary. Former Baker editor Jim Weaver and former series editor Moisés Silva were of much help in the early stages of this project.

My professors at Cedarville University, Grace Theological Seminary, and Hebrew Union College–Jewish Institute of Religion (Cincinnati) provided me with the tools for biblical studies and modeled the competent use of those tools.

Numerous scholars have helped form my understanding of Matthew. Those to whom I am most indebted include Dale Allison, Craig Blomberg, Dale Bruner, John Calvin, D. A. Carson, W. D. Davies, Robert Gundry, Donald Hagner, Jack Kingsbury, Andrew Overman, and Anthony Saldarini.

The administration of Cornerstone University/Grand Rapids Theological Seminary supported this project over the long haul. University president Rex Rogers encourages academic excellence and faculty publications. Provost Robert Nienhuis approved release time from classroom duties. GRTS president Doug Fagerstrom provided constant and enthusiastic encouragement. Former and current GRTS deans James Grier and John VerBerkmoes supported release time from my other duties so that more time could be spent on this project.

My faculty colleagues at Grand Rapids Theological Seminary, David Colman, Joe Crawford, and Carl Hoch Jr. (all deceased), Steve Argue, Byard Bennett, David Kennedy, Mark Lamport, John Lawlor, Robert Lehman, David Livermore, Gary Meadors, Catherine Mueller-Bell, Peter Osborn, Noē Palacios, Robert Rapa, and Michael Wittmer provided encouragement and a community conducive to the ongoing study of Scripture.

The Dead Theologians' Society, a motley crew of GRTS alumni, irreverently yet consistently calls me to intellectual honesty and spiritual accountability.

Four friends, Michael Forrest, John Lillis, Richard Sharpe, and James Van Stensel Jr., have helped me understand and live according to the spirituality of the Sermon on the Mount. Two special couples, Nate and Myrna Price and David and Denise Van Stensel, have encouraged and prayed for my wife, Beverly, and me for years.

It is a matter of course for authors to thank their spouses for patiently bearing with them during the long hours needed to complete a book manuscript, but the contribution of my wife, Beverly, vastly exceeds mere patience. At every significant point in my career she has believed in my dreams more deeply than I have, and her commitment to helping me accomplish my goals has been amazing.

Soli Deo gloria!

Abbreviations

Bibliographic and General

ABD	*The Anchor Bible Dictionary,* edited by D. N. Freedman et al., 6 vols. (New York: Doubleday, 1992)
BCE	before the Common Era
BDAG	*A Greek-English Lexicon of the New Testament and Other Early Christian Literature,* by W. Bauer, F. W. Danker, W. F. Arndt, and F. W. Gingrich, 3rd ed. (Chicago: University of Chicago Press, 2000)
BDB	*A Hebrew and English Lexicon of the Old Testament,* by F. Brown, S. R. Driver, and C. A. Briggs (Oxford: Clarendon, 1907)
BDF	*A Greek Grammar of the New Testament and Other Early Christian Literature,* by F. Blass and A. Debrunner, translated and revised by R. W. Funk (Chicago: University of Chicago Press, 1961)
Byz	reading of most Byzantine manuscripts
CAH	*Cambridge Ancient History,* edited by S. A. Cook, F. E. Adcock, and M. P. Charlesworth, 12 vols. (Cambridge: Cambridge University Press, 1923–39)
CE	Common Era
Eng.	English
ESV	English Standard Version
frg(s).	fragment(s)
Gk.	Greek
GKC	*Gesenius' Hebrew Grammar,* edited by E. Kautzsch, revised by A. E. Cowley, 2nd English ed. (Oxford: Clarendon, 1910)
Heb.	Hebrew
Institutes	John Calvin, *Institutes of the Christian Religion*
KJV	King James Version
L&N	*Greek-English Lexicon of the New Testament: Based on Semantic Domains,* by J. P. Louw and E. A. Nida, 2nd ed., 2 vols. (New York: United Bible Societies, 1989)
Lect	reading of most lectionaries in the Synaxarion and the Menologion when these agree
LSJ	*A Greek-English Lexicon,* by H. G. Liddell, R. Scott, and H. S. Jones, 9th ed. (Oxford: Clarendon, 1968)
LXX	Septuagint
MS(S)	manuscript(s)
MT	Masoretic Text
NA^{27}	*Novum Testamentum Graece,* edited by [E. and E. Nestle,] B. Aland et al., 27th rev. ed. (Stuttgart: Deutsche Bibelgesellschaft, 1993)
NAB	New American Bible

NASB	New American Standard Bible
NIDNTT	*New International Dictionary of New Testament Theology*, edited by C. Brown, 4 vols. (Grand Rapids: Zondervan, 1975–85)
NIV	New International Version
NJB	New Jerusalem Bible
NJPS	*Tanakh: A New Translation of the Holy Scriptures according to the Traditional Hebrew Text* (Philadelphia: Jewish Publication Society, 1985)
NKJV	New King James Version
NLT	New Living Translation
NRSV	New Revised Standard Version
NT	New Testament
OG	Old Greek
OT	Old Testament
OTP	*The Old Testament Pseudepigrapha*, edited by J. H. Charlesworth, 2 vols. (Garden City, NY: Doubleday, 1983–85)
REB	Revised English Bible
RSV	Revised Standard Version
TDNT	*Theological Dictionary of the New Testament*, edited by G. Kittel and G. Friedrich; translated and edited by G. W. Bromiley, 10 vols. (Grand Rapids: Eerdmans, 1964–76)
TNIV	Today's New International Version
UBS[4]	*The Greek New Testament*, edited by B. Aland et al., 4th rev. ed. (Stuttgart: Deutsche Bibelgesellschaft and United Bible Societies, 1994)
v.l.	*varia lectio* (variant reading)

Hebrew Bible

Gen.	Genesis	Ezra	Ezra	Hos.	Hosea
Exod.	Exodus	Neh.	Nehemiah	Joel	Joel
Lev.	Leviticus	Esth.	Esther	Amos	Amos
Num.	Numbers	Job	Job	Obad.	Obadiah
Deut.	Deuteronomy	Ps(s).	Psalm(s)	Jon.	Jonah
Josh.	Joshua	Prov.	Proverbs	Mic.	Micah
Judg.	Judges	Eccles.	Ecclesiastes	Nah.	Nahum
Ruth	Ruth	Song	Song of	Hab.	Habakkuk
1 Sam.	1 Samuel		Songs	Zeph.	Zephaniah
2 Sam.	2 Samuel	Isa.	Isaiah	Hag.	Haggai
1 Kings	1 Kings	Jer.	Jeremiah	Zech.	Zechariah
2 Kings	2 Kings	Lam.	Lamentations	Mal.	Malachi
1 Chron.	1 Chronicles	Ezek.	Ezekiel		
2 Chron.	2 Chronicles	Dan.	Daniel		

Greek Testament

Matt.	Matthew	1 Cor.	1 Corinthians	1 Thess.	1 Thessalonians
Mark	Mark	2 Cor.	2 Corinthians	2 Thess.	2 Thessalonians
Luke	Luke	Gal.	Galatians	1 Tim.	1 Timothy
John	John	Eph.	Ephesians	2 Tim.	2 Timothy
Acts	Acts	Phil.	Philippians	Titus	Titus
Rom.	Romans	Col.	Colossians	Philem.	Philemon

Heb.	Hebrews	2 Pet.	2 Peter	3 John	3 John
James	James	1 John	1 John	Jude	Jude
1 Pet.	1 Peter	2 John	2 John	Rev.	Revelation

Other Jewish and Christian Writings

'Abot R. Nat.	'Abot de Rabbi Nathan
Apoc. Abr.	Apocalypse of Abraham
Apoc. El.	Apocalypse of Elijah
Apoc. Mos.	Apocalypse of Moses
Apoc. Pet.	Apocalypse of Peter
As. Mos.	Assumption of Moses
Bar.	Baruch
2 Bar.	2 Baruch (Syriac Apocalypse)
3 Bar.	3 Baruch (Greek Apocalypse)
4 Bar.	4 Baruch (*Paraleipomena Jeremiou*)
Barn.	Barnabas
1 Clem.	1 Clement
Did.	Didache
Eccl. Hist.	Eusebius, *Ecclesiastical History*
1 En.	1 Enoch (Ethiopic Apocalypse)
2 En.	2 Enoch (Slavonic Apocalypse)
3 En.	3 Enoch (Hebrew Apocalypse)
1 Esd.	1 Esdras
2 Esd.	2 Esdras (4 Ezra)
Gk. Apoc. Ezra	Greek Apocalypse of Ezra
Gos. Pet.	Gospel of Peter
Gos. Thom.	Gospel of Thomas
Haer.	Irenaeus, *Against Heresies*
Hom. Matt.	John Chrysostom, *Homiliae in Matthaeum*
Ign. *Eph.*	Ignatius, *Letter to the Ephesians*
Ign. *Magn.*	Ignatius, *Letter to the Magnesians*
Ign. *Phld.*	Ignatius, *Letter to the Philadelphians*
Ign. *Smyrn.*	Ignatius, *Letter to the Smyrnaeans*
Ign. *Trall.*	Ignatius, *Letter to the Trallians*
Jdt.	Judith
Jos. Asen.	Joseph and Aseneth
Jub.	Jubilees
L.A.B.	*Liber antiquitatum biblicarum* (Pseudo-Philo)
Let. Aris.	Letter of Aristeas
Let. Jer.	Letter of Jeremiah
Liv. Pro.	Lives of the Prophets
1–4 Macc.	1–4 Maccabees
Marc.	Tertullian, *Against Marcion*
Mart. Ascen. Isa.	Martyrdom and Ascension of Isaiah
Midr.	Midrash
Paed.	Clement of Alexandria, *Paedagogus*
Pol. *Phil.*	Polycarp, *Letter to the Philippians*
Pr. Azar.	Prayer of Azariah
Prot. Jas.	Protevangelium of James
Ps. Sol.	Psalms of Solomon

Ques. Ezra	Questions of Ezra
Rab.	Rabbah
Sib. Or.	Sybilline Oracles
Sir.	Sirach (Ecclesiastes)
Strom.	Clement of Alexandria, *Stromata* (*Miscellanies*)
Sus.	Susanna
T. Ash.	Testament of Asher
T. Benj.	Testament of Benjamin
T. Dan	Testament of Dan
T. Gad	Testament of Gad
T. Iss.	Testament of Issachar
T. Jac.	Testament of Jacob
T. Job	Testament of Job
T. Jud.	Testament of Judah
T. Levi	Testament of Levi
T. Mos.	Testament of Moses
T. Naph.	Testament of Naphtali
T. Reu.	Testament of Reuben
T. Sim.	Testament of Simeon
T. Sol.	Testament of Solomon
Tob.	Tobit
Wis.	Wisdom of Solomon

Josephus and Philo

Abraham	*On the Life of Abraham*
Ag. Ap.	*Against Apion*
Ant.	*Jewish Antiquities*
Contempl.	*On the Contemplative Life*
Decalogue	*On the Decalogue*
Drunkenness	*On Drunkenness*
Embassy	*On the Embassy to Gaius*
Flaccus	*Against Flaccus*
Flight	*On Flight and Finding*
Good Person	*That Every Good Person Is Free*
Heir	*Who Is the Heir?*
J.W.	*Jewish War*
Life	*The Life*
Migr.	*On the Migration of Abraham*
Moses	*On the Life of Moses*
Planting	*On Planting*
Posterity	*On the Posterity of Cain*
Sacrifices	*On the Sacrifices of Cain and Abel*
Spec. Laws	*On the Special Laws*
Virtues	*On the Virtues*
Worse	*That the Worse Attacks the Better*

Rabbinic Tractates

The abbreviations below are used for the names of the tractates in the Babylonian Talmud (indicated by a prefixed *b.*); Palestinian, or Jerusalem, Talmud (*y.*); Mishnah (*m.*); and Tosefta (*t.*).

'Arak.	*'Arakin*	*Ma'aś. Š.*	*Ma'aśer Šeni*	*Šabb.*	*Šabbat*
B. Bat.	*Baba Batra*	*Mak.*	*Makkot*	*Sanh.*	*Sanhedrin*
B. Meṣi'a	*Baba Meṣi'a*	*Meg.*	*Megillah*	*Šeb.*	*Šebi'it*
B. Qam.	*Baba Qamma*	*Menaḥ.*	*Menaḥot*	*Šebu.*	*Šebu'ot*
Bek.	*Bekorot*	*Mid.*	*Middot*	*Šeqal.*	*Šeqalim*
Ber.	*Berakot*	*Mo'ed Qaṭ.*	*Mo'ed Qaṭan*	*Ta'an.*	*Ta'anit*
'Ed.	*'Eduyyot*	*Ned.*	*Nedarim*	*Ṭohar.*	*Ṭoharot*
'Erub.	*'Erubin*	*Neg.*	*Nega'im*	*Yad.*	*Yadayim*
Giṭ.	*Giṭṭin*	*Nid.*	*Niddah*	*Yebam.*	*Yebamot*
Ḥag.	*Ḥagigah*	*'Ohol.*	*'Oholot*	*Zebaḥ.*	*Zebaḥim*
Ker.	*Kerithot*	*Pesaḥ.*	*Pesaḥim*		
Ketub.	*Ketubbot*	*Qidd.*	*Qiddušin*		

Qumran / Dead Sea Scrolls

CD	Damascus Document
1QapGen	Genesis Apocryphon
1QH	Thanksgiving Hymns/Psalms (*Hodayot*)
1QM	War Scroll (*Milḥamah*)
1QpHab	Commentary on Habakkuk
1QS	Rule of the Community (*Serek Hayaḥad*)
1QSa	Rule of the Congregation (1Q28a)
1QSb	Rule of Benedictions (1Q28b)
4QFlor	Florilegium (4Q174)
4QMMT	*Miqṣat Ma'aśê ha-Torah* (4Q394–99)
11QT	Temple Scroll (11Q19–20)

Greek Papyri

BGU	*Aegyptische Urkunden aus den Königlichen/Staatlichen Museen zu Berlin, Griechische Urkunden* (Berlin, 1895–)
CPR	*Corpus papyrorum Raineri archeducis Austriae* (Vienna, 1895–)
P.Cair.Preis.	*Griechische Urkunden des Ägyptischen Museums zu Kairo,* edited by F. Preisigke, Schriften der Wissenschaftlichen Gesellschaft zu Strassburg 8 (Strassburg: Trübner, 1911)
P.Mich.	The University of Michigan Papyrus Collection, University Library, Ann Arbor, MI
P.Wisc.	*The Wisconsin Papyri,* edited by P. J. Sijpesteijn, Papyrologica Lugduno-Batava 16 (Leiden: Brill, 1967–77)

Classical Writers

Ann.	Tacitus, *Annales (Annals)*
Hist.	Tacitus, *Historiae (Histories)*
Nat.	Pliny the Elder, *Naturalis historia (Natural History)*

Transliteration

Greek

α	*a*	ζ	*z*	λ	*l*	π	*p*	φ	*ph*
β	*b*	η	*ē*	μ	*m*	ρ	*r*	χ	*ch*
γ	*g/n*	θ	*th*	ν	*n*	σ/ς	*s*	ψ	*ps*
δ	*d*	ι	*i*	ξ	*x*	τ	*t*	ω	*ō*
ε	*e*	κ	*k*	ο	*o*	υ	*y/u*	‛	*h*

Notes on the Transliteration of Greek

1. Accents, lenis (smooth breathing), and *iota* subscript are not shown in transliteration.
2. The transliteration of asper (rough breathing) precedes a vowel or diphthong (e.g., ἁ = *ha*; αἱ = *hai*) and follows ρ (i.e., ῥ = *rh*).
3. *Gamma* is transliterated *n* only when it precedes γ, κ, ξ, or χ.
4. *Upsilon* is transliterated *u* only when it is part of a diphthong (i.e., αυ, ευ, ου, υι).

Hebrew

א	ʾ	בָ	*ā*	*qāmeṣ*
ב	*b*	בַ	*a*	*pataḥ*
ג	*g*	חַ	*a*	furtive *pataḥ*
ד	*d*	בֶ	*e*	*sĕgôl*
ה	*h*	בֵ	*ē*	*ṣērê*
ו	*w*	בִ	*i*	short *ḥîreq*
ז	*z*	בִ	*ī*	long *ḥîreq* written defectively
ח	*ḥ*	בָ	*o*	*qāmeṣ ḥāṭûp*
ט	*ṭ*	בוֹ	*ô*	*ḥôlem* written fully
י	*y*	בֹ	*ō*	*ḥôlem* written defectively
ךְ/כ	*k*	בוּ	*û*	*šûreq*
ל	*l*	בֻ	*u*	short *qibbûṣ*
ם/מ	*m*	בֻ	*ū*	long *qibbûṣ* written defectively
ן/נ	*n*	בָה	*â*	final *qāmeṣ hēʾ* (בָה = *āh*)
ס	*s*	בֵי	*ê*	*sĕgôl yôd* (בֶי = *êy*)
ע	ʿ	בֵי	*ê*	*ṣērê yôd* (בֵי = *êy*)
ףְ/פ	*p*	בִי	*î*	*ḥîreq yôd* (בִי = *îy*)
ץ/צ	*ṣ*	בֲ	*ă*	*ḥāṭēp pataḥ*
ק	*q*	בֱ	*ĕ*	*ḥāṭēp sĕgôl*
ר	*r*	בֳ	*ŏ*	*ḥāṭēp qāmeṣ*
שׂ	*ś*	בְ	*ĕ*	vocal *šĕwāʾ*
שׁ	*š*			
ת	*t*			

Notes on the Transliteration of Hebrew

1. Accents are not shown in transliteration.
2. Silent *šĕwā'* is not indicated in transliteration.
3. The spirant forms ב ג ד כ פ ת are usually not specially indicated in transliteration.
4. *Dāgeš forte* is indicated by doubling the consonant. Euphonic *dāgeš* and *dāgeš lene* are not indicated in transliteration.
5. *Maqqēp* is represented by a hyphen.

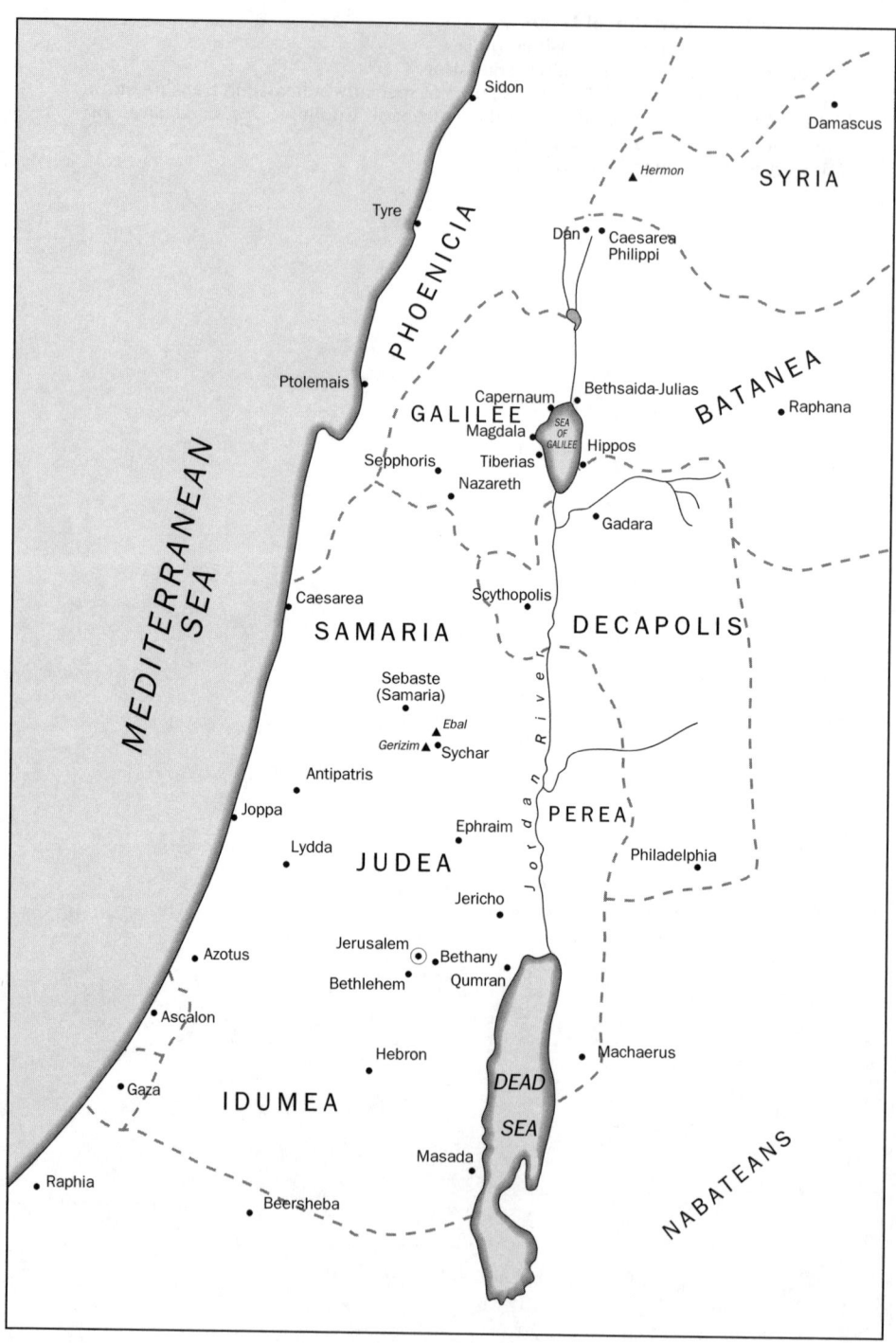

Introduction to Matthew

Overview

Matthew's Unique Message

The Gospel according to Matthew equipped its original Christian Jewish readers with the teaching of Jesus the Messiah so that they might effectively spread the message of God's reign to all the nations. Matthew's story of Jesus sets the scene by presenting Jesus's ancestral background and linking him to the ministry of John the Baptist. Jesus's baptism by John is the occasion of his empowerment with the Spirit for ministry. Matthew presents this ministry in five "chapters," each with a narrative about Jesus's works and a discourse containing Jesus's words. The story ends in Jerusalem, where God raises Jesus from the dead, reversing Jesus's unjust crucifixion and empowering him to commission the disciples for world mission.

God's reign is first announced by John the Baptist, whose message and fate anticipate that of Jesus. Jesus receives the Father's endorsement and the Spirit's empowerment at his baptism and begins his ministry of demonstrating the kingdom in Galilee by proclaiming the words of God and performing the works of God. Jesus's ethical teaching is presented in the Sermon on the Mount as fulfilling that of the law and the prophets. His ongoing ministry of word and work in Galilee reaches out to marginalized persons of society but raises the hackles of some religious leaders. Jesus then teaches his disciples to expect serious opposition and persecution in their own ministries. As the Galilean ministry continues, opposition escalates, and Jesus is accused of collaborating with Satan. He then teaches his disciples through parables that reception of the kingdom message will be mixed. As the ministry continues, opposition becomes clearer, and Jesus again teaches his disciples. He promises to build his church but also speaks clearly of his upcoming death in Jerusalem. Despite his emphasis on self-denial, his disciples are preoccupied with greatness, so Jesus teaches them about values and relationships in their community. Jesus now turns toward Jerusalem, enters the city, and meets intense opposition from the religious establishment. After several heated arguments, he denounces Israel's leaders and teaches his disciples how they must live in light of the destruction of the temple and his coming. One of his own disciples then betrays him to the leaders, who bring him before the Roman governor. Pilate crucifies Jesus and seals his tomb, but God raises him. Jesus meets his disciples in Galilee and commissions them to make disciples from all nations.

Matthew equips his Christian Jewish community with the Torah-fulfilling teaching of Jesus on righteous living, on opposition during mission, on the mixed external reception of the message, on the internal values that characterize his community, and on how to live in light of his coming. This teaching along with Jesus's powerful presence will enable the community to continue kingdom ministry to Israel and begin discipling the Gentiles.

Matthew's Influence on the Church

As the first Gospel in the canon, Matthew has received a great deal of attention through the centuries (Kealy 1997; Luz 1994). Matthew is the NT book that influenced the early church most (Massaux 1990–93), leading to a rich reservoir of patristic commentary (tapped by Simonetti 2001, 2002). This prominence is mainly due to Matthew's unique structure, which focuses the reader's attention on the Sermon on the Mount and the other four major discourses of Jesus. The history of the interpretation of Matthew is outside the scope of the present volume, but it is clear that through the centuries the First Gospel has occupied the minds of many great expositors. The work of U. Luz has especially emphasized *Wirkungsgeschichte*, the history of Matthew's influence on, and reception by, the church (1989: 95–99). Allison (2005b: 117–31) speaks appreciatively of the strengths and ongoing relevance of the patristic exegesis of Matthew.

Yet during the twentieth century, Matthean studies became somewhat passé, mostly because of the dominance of the Markan-priority view of synoptic origins. Many scholars who took this view held that Mark embodied an earlier and more authentic version of the historical Jesus. More recently, however, Matthew has begun to receive more attention, as evidenced by such commentaries as Beare (1981), Benoit (1972), Blomberg (1992a), Bonnard (1970), Bruner (1987, 1990), W. Davies and Allison (1988, 1991, 1997), France (1985), Garland (1993), Grundmann (1975), Gundry (1994), Hagner (1993, 1995a), Hare (1993), Harrington (1991), Hauerwas (2006), Keener (1999), LaGrange (1948), Limbeck (1986), Luz (1989, 2001, 2005), G. Maier (1979–80), Meier (1979, 1980b), Morris (1992), Nolland (2005), Overman (1996), Sand (1986), Schnackenburg (2002), Schweizer (1975), and Witherington (2006). In addition, numerous important works have addressed various themes related to Matthew's provenance and theology; they include Allison (1993b, 2005b), Aune (2001), Balch (1991), Bauer (1988), Bornkamm, Barth, and Held (1963), Broer (1980), Didier (1972), Gaechter (1963), Gerhardsson (1979), Kingsbury (1988a, 1989), Marguerat (1981), Overman (1990b), Saldarini (1994), Schenke (1988), Shuler (1982), Sim (1998b), Stanton (1992b, ed.

1995), Westerholm (2006), and Wilkins (1988). This renewed interest in Matthew is mainly due to the rise of the disciplines of redaction and narrative criticism and to the increasing awareness of Matthew's Jewish roots. (See Hare 1998, 2000.)

Distinctive Aspects of This Commentary

The availability of so many fine works on Matthew means that a new project must add something to what is already available (Engelbrecht 1995; Hagner 1995b). The distinctive aspects of this project are as follows. First, many treatments of Matthew assume that Matthew is rewriting and expanding Mark. Be that as it may, the original readers of Matthew most likely did not hold it in one hand and Mark in the other, assuming that Matthew could not be understood apart from Mark. The present commentary therefore approaches Matthew in its own right, utilizing what has come to be known as narrative criticism (Fokkelman 1999; Powell 1990; Resseguie 2005). This method relates the parts of a Gospel to its whole instead of reading Matthew as an adaptation of Mark.

Second, this commentary attempts to explain Matthew in the context of Second Temple formative Judaism(s). It is written from the perspective argued by Overman (1990b), Saldarini (1994), and Sim (1998b) to the effect that Matthew was written to a group of Christian Jews who were still in contact with non-Christian Jews in the synagogue. This view avoids the anachronistic reading of Matthew as promoting Christianity as a new religion for Gentiles in opposition to Judaism, a monolithic old religion for Jews. Matthew and his community were part of a process in which Pharisees, Sadducees, Essenes, followers of Jesus, and others were presenting somewhat diverse competing versions of Judaism. Judaism had not yet become unified by the ascendancy of the Jabneh (Jamnia; cf. Lewis, *ABD* 3:634–37; Lewis 1999–2000) rabbis after the 70 CE destruction of Jerusalem. Matthew should not be read from a perspective that reflects the result of this diversification—the second-century parting of the ways between Christianity and Judaism. Rather, Matthew should be read as the voice of "Jews for Jesus," as it were, during a time of much diversity within Judaism. (See Hare 2000 for another view.)

Third, in keeping with the objectives of the Baker Exegetical Commentary on the New Testament series, this commentary provides both analysis and synthesis. Some treatments of Matthew excel in historical and exegetical analysis, notably W. Davies and Allison's three-volume commentary in the International Critical Commentary series. Others provide exceptional theological depth, such as F. D. Bruner's profound two-volume work. The present commentary does not have the depth of these two works in their respective areas but instead weaves analysis and synthesis together to provide comprehensive yet concise discussions of both historical-exegetical and literary-theological matters. The amount of interaction with current scholarship will not always satisfy academics, but bibliographic notes will at least point the way to additional recent studies.

Fourth, the theological perspective of the present work reflects a recent discussion among evangelicals that has led to a view known as progressive dispensationalism (Blaising and Bock 1992, 1993; Saucy 1993). While affirming such central dispensational tenets as the imminence of Jesus's coming and a future national conversion of the Jews, this approach takes a much more sanguine approach to the continuity of Scripture than did classical dispensational approaches. Although full rapprochement with covenant theology is not likely, progressive dispensationalism has much in common with this approach, especially premillennial versions. The interpretation of Jesus's Sermon on the Mount (Matt. 5–7) and Olivet Discourse (Matt. 24–25) is directly affected by this approach, as is the exegesis of such cruxes as Matt. 11:12; 19:28; 21:43.

Fifth, this commentary provides both a readable dynamic-equivalence, or functional-equivalence, translation[1] and numerous comments on Matthew's Greek syntax. Since translation is the briefest sort of commentary, the translation here reflects the views supported in the exegesis of the Greek syntax. Any translation by a single individual is bound to be somewhat idiosyncratic, and so readers should compare the translation found here with the Greek text and standard translations. The translation consistently attempts to avoid male language when the exegesis has determined that humans in general rather than males in particular are meant by the author. Although the noun "man" and pronouns "he," "his," and "him" have been used elsewhere for humans in general, such inclusive use of male language does not appear in this translation for the simple reason that it does not reflect sound exegesis to the current generation. Admittedly, this may at times lead to unfamiliar, even awkward phrasing (cf. Matt. 7:24; 16:24–26), but this is preferable to conveying the impression to some readers that Jesus is only concerned with males.[2]

Literary Matters

Gospel Genre: The Question of History and Theology

Due to apologetic concerns over the historicity of the Gospel traditions, conservative evangelicals have at times been reluctant to view the Gospels as theologically motivated. At the other end of the spectrum are liberal scholars who tend to view the Gospels as imaginative documents

1. "Dynamic" and "functional" describe a translation that is based on the ideas (deep structure) of a text and sensitive to its idioms as opposed to a translation that attempts a formal equivalence by reproducing as much as possible the words and phrasing (surface structure) of a text. Cf. Nida and Taber 1982.
2. On recent controversies in Bible translation, see Carson 1998; Grudem et al. 2006; Poythress and Grudem 2004; Ryken 2003; Scorgie et al. 2002; Scorgie and Strauss 2003; Strauss 1998; Ware 2002.

produced to meet the church's needs rather than to transmit reliable Jesus traditions. Such scholars think the Gospel stories frequently reflect the situations and controversies of the post-70 CE church rather than the historical Jesus (e.g., Beare 1981: 13–15). Evangelicals have rightly responded in defense of the historical reliability of the Gospels (e.g., Blomberg 1987b; E. Ellis 1999), but their stress on historicity may neglect the theological import of the Gospels.

Others have argued, at times from misguided dispensational views, that the church derives history from the Gospels and theology from the epistles of the NT, especially those of Paul. This history-versus-theology dichotomy is false, whether in a conservative detheologizing context or in a liberal dehistoricizing context. The Gospels narrate what really happened but do so in part for theological reasons. According to Luke's prologue, Luke did careful research in order to ascertain the reliability of oral and written traditions so that Theophilus might be taught reliable truths about Jesus (Bock 1994: 51–67). If one may extrapolate from Luke to the Gospels in general, their procedure was to transmit the Jesus traditions they had received, with a view toward meeting the spiritual needs of their audiences, which included the historical grounding of their faith.

The Gospels are theological interpretations of selected traditions that the authors accepted as reliable accounts of historical events that occurred during the life and ministry of Jesus. Some scholars argue that the Gospels are examples of the ancient genre of laudatory biography or encomium (e.g., Shuler 1982; Talbert 1977, critiqued by Aune in France and Wenham 1981: 9–60). Others hold that they constitute their own genre (e.g., Guelich in Stuhlmacher 1991: 173–208). Be that as it may, most if not all would agree that the Gospels are not comprehensive biographies or exhaustive histories of Jesus. A perusal of any Gospel synopsis or harmony dispels that notion. But each Gospel's Jesus stories are calculated to meet the needs of its respective audience. There is overall continuity in the Synoptic Gospels' accounts, but there is a great deal of individual freedom as the authors tailor their traditions for their respective communities. If John 20:30–31 provides a model, the theological purposes of the evangelists guided their editing of tradition, leading to literary narratives, not historical chronicles. Their purpose was not to satisfy intellectual curiosity by compiling historical data but to disciple their respective communities by bringing selected episodes from the life of Jesus to bear on the communities' needs. The Gospels continue to teach the church by narrating reliable words and deeds of Jesus. The Gospel authors faithfully present story as history and creatively interpret history as story (Byrskog 2000; cf. 1994; G. Osborne 2005; J. W. Scott 1985).[3]

3. On the genre of the Gospels, see Burridge 2004; Frickenschmidt 1997; Guelich in Stuhlmacher 1991: 173–208; Nolland 2005: 19–22; Shuler in Dungan 1990: 459–83; Stanton in van Segbroeck et al. 1992: 1187–1201; Vorster 1981.

Source Criticism and the Synoptic Problem

A cursory reading of the Gospels reveals the fundamental difficulty known as the synoptic problem—why are the first three Gospels so similar in some respects and so different in others? Conservative evangelicals may attribute such matters solely to divine leading of the authors, but reflection on Luke 1:1–4 should lead one beyond such naive pietistic solutions. Luke researched earlier written "accounts" (singular διήγησις, *diēgēsis*, Luke 1:1; cf. Let. Aris. 1, 8, 322; Josephus, *Ant.* 11.68) and oral traditions emanating from eyewitnesses (αὐτόπτης, *autoptēs*, Luke 1:2; cf. Josephus *J.W.* 3.432; *Ant.* 18.342; 19.125; *Ag. Ap.* 1.55). Theories of synoptic origins can be divided into two main groups: those that posit the literary independence of each Gospel and those that see some sort of literary interdependence between the Gospels.

Literary independence. Certain scholars argue from the prevalence of oral transmission of sacred tradition in the ancient Near East that each Gospel author edited the available oral tradition without borrowing from another Gospel (Farnell in R. Thomas 2002: 226–309; Linnemann 1992; Rist 1978; Westcott 1895: 165–212; Ingolfsland 2006). In this approach, assuming the traditional view of apostolic authorship, Matthew reflected on his experiences as an eyewitness of Jesus's ministry and augmented his own recollections with oral traditions. This approach accounts for the differences between the Synoptics with some plausibility, but it does not adequately account for the extensive and often verbatim agreements between the synoptic accounts (e.g., Matt. 3:7–10 and Luke 3:7–9; Matt. 9:14–17 and Mark 2:18–22).

Literary interdependence. Most scholars conclude that some sort of literary interrelationship is necessary to explain the phenomena of the Gospels.[4] In fact, such a view was held by Augustine and many of the church fathers, who believed that the canonical order of the Gospels represented their order of literary dependence.[5] In the late eighteenth century the Griesbach hypothesis, which posited that Mark used both Matthew and Luke, revised the patristic approach to Matthean priority.[6] Although some scholars still hold to Matthean priority (cf. Tuckett 1983b, 1984), the scholarly consensus today favors Markan priority, with Mat-

4. For detailed discussions of source criticism and the synoptic problem, see D. Black and Beck 2001; Dungan 1990; Hawkins 1909; Longstaff and Thomas 1988; Neirynck 1974; Orchard and Riley 1987; Reicke 1986; Sickenberger in Schenke 1988: 655–72; Stein 2001: 29–169; Streeter 1924; Tuckett 1984; J. Wenham 1991.

5. Augustine, *Harmony of the Gospels* 1.1.1–4; 1.3.6; 1.4.7; 4.10.11. Modern advocates of the Augustinian hypothesis include Butler 1951 and J. Wenham 1991. Although Augustine anticipated most modern scholars in positing a literary-dependence theory, his view that the Gospels are the result of eyewitness testimony is not shared by most today (e.g., R. Brown 1997: 109).

6. Griesbach 1789–90. Modern advocates include Dungan and Peabody 1996; Farmer 1964; Neville 1994; Orchard and Riley 1987; Peabody 2002.

thew and Luke composing their Gospels in dependence on Mark and the hypothetical source Q (Tuckett 1996; M. Williams 2006), which purportedly contained a collection of the sayings of Jesus. This view is known as the two-source theory (Mark and Q), but it has been further developed into the four-source theory, in which Mark and Q are supplemented by the additional hypothetical sources M, for unique Matthean tradition, and L, for unique Lukan tradition (Streeter 1924). (For critiques of this consensus, see Butler 1951 and Stoldt 1980.)

The Markan-priority theory tends to reduce Matthean studies to distinguishing between tradition and redaction by locating Matthew's sources (Mark, Q, and M) and discerning Matthew's editorial refinements as an indication of his unique theological interests. It is commonly assumed that Matthew's redactional departures from his tradition are historically less reliable. Yet many evangelical scholars utilize this approach without diminishing the historicity of Matthew (e.g., Blomberg 1992a; Carson 1984). If one accepts the traditional view of apostolic authorship, one may wonder why an eyewitness of Jesus's ministry would base his Gospel on the account of Mark, who was not an eyewitness. Yet patristic tradition places Peter's recollections and authority behind the Gospel of Mark (Eusebius, *Eccl. Hist.* 3.39.15; cf. Gundry 1994: 621). It has been argued that Mark would be rendered superfluous had Matthew been written first, but this overlooks the presence of vivid narrative details in Mark that are not found in Matthew. Ultimately, whether Mark abbreviated Matthew's discourses and expanded Matthew's narratives (minority view; cf. S. E. Johnson 1991; Kingsbury in Farmer 1983: 331–61) or whether Matthew adapted Mark's narrative to his discourses derived from Q (consensus view; cf. Dermience 1985; Huggins 1992), what matters most to the church is the meaning of the Gospels as literary and theological wholes.

Narrative Criticism

The impossibility of arriving at certainty in solving the synoptic problem and the atomizing tendencies of source-critical studies have led some to adopt a more holistic approach commonly known as narrative criticism. Narrative criticism draws conclusions about meaning and theology by comparing the parts of each Gospel to the whole Gospel instead of its putative sources. According to Powell (1990: 20), in order to read the Gospels in this way, "it is necessary to know everything that the text assumes the reader knows and to 'forget' everything that the text does not assume the reader knows." This approach seems fitting if the Gospels are viewed as theologically interpreted history, written for the edification of Christian communities. One would think that the Gospels functioned as wholes within those communities, not as overlays to be spread upon previous Gospels or other sources. Modern scholars have been understandably preoccupied with uncovering the history of the traditions they find in the Synoptics, but such an approach was hardly that of ancient Christian communities. It seems unlikely that such communities read one Gospel as an overlay of a previous Gospel, and it is difficult even today to utilize source-critical methodology for Gospel studies in the context of church ministry.

Narrative criticism seems much more appropriate than source criticism for the study of the Gospels in a church context, given the genre of the Gospels as theologically interpreted history and the canonical function of the Gospels as Holy Scripture. Therefore this commentary will be a narrative-critical study, although source-critical matters will occasionally be noted (see the plea for methodological eclecticism in W. Davies and Allison 1988: 1–4). A weakness of literary criticism in general and of narrative criticism in particular is that the historical referents of the literary documents are usually ignored as being beside the point. But when Holy Scripture is studied within an evangelical context, the historical events interpreted by the literary sources retain high value.[7]

Literary Structure

In the narrative-critical approach utilized by the present study, one attempts to articulate the role of the parts in framing the whole of the First Gospel. Grasping the structure of Matthew is crucial to this approach.[8] Although some scholars (e.g., Gundry 1994: 10–11; Harrington 1991: 4) despair of outlining Matthew, the following approaches are commonly found.

Markan outline. One regularly encounters analyses of Matthew along the chronological and geographical lines that work well with Mark (e.g., Hendriksen 1973: v–vi; Morris 1992: v–ix). Such an approach yields something similar to the following:

    I. Infancy narrative (1:1–2:23)
    II. Preparation for ministry (3:1–4:11)
    III. Public ministry in Galilee (4:12–15:20)
    IV. Public ministry outside Galilee (15:21–18:35)
    V. Journey to Jerusalem (19:1–20:34)
    VI. Final days in Jerusalem (21:1–27:66)
    VII. Resurrection and the Great Commission (28:1–20)

In some cases an outline like the above is used but with topical themes, such as "King" or "Messiah" (e.g., Toussaint 1980: 25–27). All such out-

---

7. On narrative criticism, see Alter 1981; Berlin 1983; R. Edwards 1985, 1989; Fokkelman 1999; Kingsbury 1988a: 1–42; Powell 1990, 1992b; Powell in Kingsbury (ed.) 1997: 9–15; Resseguie 2005; Rhoads and Syreeni 1999; J. W. Scott 1985.

8. On the structure of Matthew, see Allison 1992b; D. Barr 1976; Bauer 1988; Carter 1996: 149–75; Combrink 1982, 1983; Gaechter 1963; Humphrey 1977; Kingsbury 1989; Krentz 1964; Matera 1987; Neirynck 1988; Powell 1992a; Slater 1980; K. Smyth 1982; Standaert in van Segbroeck et al. 1992: 1223–50; M. Thompson 1982; Weren 2006.

lines are more or less artificially superimposed upon Matthew rather than derived from it. This approach has some value in clarifying the biographical and geographical flow, but it does not engage Matthew's distinctive pattern of alternating narrative and discourse blocks of material.

"From then on Jesus began. . . ." Some scholars (e.g., Kingsbury 1988a; 1989: 7–25; Bauer 1988) have called attention to the phrase ἀπὸ τότε ἤρξατο ὁ Ἰησοῦς (*apo tote ērxato ho Iēsous*), which occurs at two pivotal points. In 4:17, just after the account of John the Baptist's arrest, Matthew announces the beginning of Jesus's public ministry with the words "from then on Jesus began to preach." In 16:21, just after Peter's confession that Jesus is the Messiah, Matthew characterizes Jesus's messianic ministry as one of suffering with the words "from then on Jesus began to tell his disciples plainly that he would go to Jerusalem . . . and be killed." In this approach Matthew's structure appears as follows:

I. Preparation of Jesus the Messiah (1:1–4:16)
II. Proclamation of Jesus the Messiah (4:17–16:20)
III. Passion of Jesus the Messiah (16:21–28:20)

Although it is significant that Matthew inserts ἀπὸ τότε ἤρξατο ὁ Ἰησοῦς at two critical points in his narrative, this phrase seems to be more of a biographical or chronological marker than a literary device. This second approach to Matthew is not all that different from the previous approach, and it does not handle Matthew's alternating narrative/discourse pattern, which is the most obvious structural difference between Matthew and the other Synoptics. For this reason, the following approach is preferable (but see Bauer 1988: 129–34).

"When Jesus had finished. . . ." Students of Matthew have long noticed the unique juxtapositioning of narrative and discourse materials. What is more, Matthew marks each of the five transitions from discourse back to narrative with the phrase καὶ ἐγένετο ὅτε ἐτέλεσεν ὁ Ἰησοῦς (*kai egeneto hote etelesen ho Iēsous*, when Jesus had finished; 7:28; 11:1; 13:53; 19:1; 26:1; C. R. Smith 1997). Acknowledging this structural pattern does not necessitate accepting Bacon's view (1918, 1928, 1930) that Matthew contains five books of Jesus that correspond to the five books of Moses in the Pentateuch. This third approach has difficulties in that certain discursive materials occur in narrative sections, most notably the warning to the disciples and the woes to the religious leaders in Matt. 23. But all things considered, this approach has the most to commend it.[9] A detailed outline based on this insight is found at the end of this introduction, but a condensed version is as follows:

9. Among those who adopt this approach are Benoit 1972: 7–12; Bonnard 1970: 7, 110; Carson 1984: 50–57; W. Davies and Allison 1988: 61; Gaechter 1963: 16–17; Hill 1972: 44–48; LaGrange 1948: lxxxv; Meier 1980b: vii–viii; Scaer 2004: 21–29; Schlatter 1963: 125–28;

I. Prologue/introduction: Origin of Jesus the Messiah (1:1–2:23)
II. Early days of kingdom word and deed (3:1–7:29)
    A. Narrative 1: John and Jesus and the kingdom of God
       (3:1–4:25)
    B. Discourse 1: Sermon on the Mount (5:1–7:29)
III. Galilean ministry continues (8:1–11:1)
    A. Narrative 2: Three cycles of miracles and discipleship
       (8:1–10:4)
    B. Discourse 2: Mission and suffering (10:5–11:1)
IV. Growing opposition to the kingdom of heaven (11:2–13:52)
    A. Narrative 3: Three cycles of unbelief and belief (11:2–12:50)
    B. Discourse 3: Parables of the kingdom of heaven (13:1–52)
V. Opposition to the kingdom continues (13:53–19:2)
    A. Narrative 4: Various responses to the Son of God
       (13:53–17:27)
    B. Discourse 4: Values and relationships in the kingdom com-
       munity (18:1–19:2)
VI. Opposition comes to a head in Judea (19:3–26:2)
    A. Narrative 5: Ministry in Judea (19:3–23:39)
    B. Discourse 5: Judgment of Jerusalem and the coming of
       Christ (24:1–26:2)
VII. Epilogue/conclusion: Passion, resurrection, and commission
    (26:3–28:20)

Some scholars attempt a synthesis of this approach with the second approach discussed above (e.g., Blomberg 1992a: 22–25, 49; McKnight in J. Green and McKnight 1992: 530–32). Derickson 2006 attempts to construe the narrative-discourse sections chiastically centering on Matt. 13 (cf. Lohr 1961).

Literary Style

Scholars generally view Matthew's Greek style as aesthetically adequate if not exceptional. The author was relatively fluent in Semitic languages as well as Greek, which led to frequent Semitisms (W. Davies and Allison 1988: 80–85). These Semitisms emanate from Matthew's sources, the Hebrew Bible, the LXX, and Matthew's own personal writing style. They are incorporated into Matthew's syntax in a way that avoids awkward or harsh expressions and retains acceptable Greek style (see Engelbrecht 1990).

Another matter of style is Matthew's purported use of sources, primarily Mark, Q, and M. Those who scrutinize Matthew from the Markan-priority perspective conclude that Matthew regularly abbreviates Mark's

---

Stendahl 1968: 21–27. This view is critiqued by Bauer 1988: 27–35; Kingsbury 1989: 2–7. Allison 2005b: 135–55 defends the view and develops its implications of Matthew as a biographical account that enjoins Jesus's disciples to imitate him.

account of Jesus's deeds and expands Mark's account of Jesus's words. From a narrative-critical perspective, this phenomenon indicates that Matthew features Jesus's words more than his deeds. However one solves the synoptic problem, there are certain words and expressions that Matthew uses much more frequently than Mark and Luke (W. Davies and Allison 1988: 74–80; Gundry 1994: 674–82; Luz 1989: 52–73).

Matthew seems to be fond of various numerical patterns, such as the seven petitions in the Lord's Prayer (6:9–13), the seven parables (13), and the genealogy's format of fourteen (double-seven) generations (1:1–17). Matthew is fond of threefold structures (W. Davies and Allison 1988: 61–72). Additional features include repetition of contrast and comparison, particularization and climax, *inclusio*, and chiasmus.[10] Such features will be noted in the body of this commentary.

Historical Origins

The origins of the Gospel of Matthew are not easily ascertained. One can only read between the lines of the Gospel itself in search of historical implications and evaluate the patristic traditions about the book.

Authorship

The Gospel of Matthew is technically anonymous, as are the other Gospels, although the Gospel of John hints at its authorship (John 21:24; cf. 13:23; 19:26; 20:2; 21:7, 20). Hengel's (1985: 64–84; 2000: 48–53, 77) plausible argument that the titles of the Gospels are very early, perhaps even original with each Gospel, has positive implications for traditional views of the Gospels' authorship. Hengel shows that ancient custom tended to identify books by their authors (cf. Tertullian, *Marc.* 4.2). One should not assume (as does Hagner 1993: lxxvi) that the Gospels originally circulated anonymously and that their titles were added in the second century. The nearly unanimous attribution of the Gospels to their traditional authors by about 150 CE better supports the theory that their titles were original rather than the theory that they originally circulated anonymously.

Any view of authorship depends upon inferences drawn from the book itself (internal evidence) and upon assessment of the credibility of the patristic testimony that Matthew the apostle wrote the Gospel (external evidence).[11]

Internal evidence. Matthew's grammar, syntax, literary style, and distinctive themes lead most scholars to conclude that he was a Jew who

10. See J. C. Anderson 1994; Bauer 1988; S. Black 2002; Hermant 1999; Howell 1990; Luz 1989: 36–39; Nolland 2005: 23–29; Schenk 1987.

11. On the authorship of Matthew, see Abel 1971; Carson and Moo 2005: 140–50; K. Clark 1947; W. Davies and Allison 1988: 7–58; France 1989: 50–80; Gundry 1994: 609–22; Petrie 1967; Stonehouse 1979: 19–47.

understood Hebrew and Judaism.[12] This conclusion allows for the traditional view of authorship but does not prove it. Some look at these details and take them differently—that Matthew was a Gentile who used Jewish terminology but often misunderstood it. Others argue that Matthew's Jewish trappings amount to a literary ploy to advance a polemic against Judaism.[13] This is extremely unlikely.

External evidence. This Gospel was ascribed to Matthew the apostle by the first quarter of the second century CE. The titles of notable ancient MSS (e.g., ℵ, B, D, L, W, f^1, f^{13}, *Byz*, L) ascribe the book to Matthew (W. Davies and Allison 1988: 129n90). Patristic tradition agrees with this ascription. Eusebius, *Eccl. Hist.* 3.39; 6.14; 6.25.4 (early to mid–fourth century CE), cites Papias (early second century CE; cf. Meredith in Tuckett 1984: 187–96), Clement of Alexandria (early third century CE), and Origen (mid–third century CE) to this effect. The words of Irenaeus (late second century CE) agree (*Haer.* 3.1.1; cf. Eusebius, *Eccl. Hist.* 5.8.2; Köhler 1987). Additional fourth-century CE testimony is found in Cyril of Jerusalem (*Catechesis* 14), Epiphanius (*Refutation of All Heresies* 30.3), and Jerome (*Prologue to Matthew*). This tradition generally affirms the priority of Matthew (Farnell 1999). The patristic tradition that Matthew was originally written in Hebrew will be discussed later under "Canonicity and Textual History." Although the patristic testimony to the apostle Matthew as the author of the First Gospel is early and unanimous, many current scholars discount the value of this testimony and prefer to think that authorship by Matthew the apostle is "most unlikely" (Nolland 2005: 4).

Matthew the tax collector. The traditional author of the First Gospel is mentioned five times in the NT (Matt. 9:9; 10:3; Mark 3:18; Luke 6:15; Acts 1:13; cf. *b. Sanh.* 43a). The name in Hebrew means "gift of Yahweh." The reference to Jesus's calling Matthew in Matt. 9:9–13 is paralleled by Mark 2:13–17 and Luke 5:27–32, both of which have Levi, not Matthew. There are several explanations for this (Gnilka 1986–88: 1.330–31). Some Jews had two names (Acts 4:36; Josephus, *Ant.* 12.285; 18.35, 95; 20.196), and Jesus gave Simon the name Peter (16:18). On the assumption of Markan priority, the author of Matthew was aware of the reference to Levi in Mark and of the name Matthew, not Levi, in the list of apostles in Mark 3:16–19 (cf. Matt. 10:2–4; Luke 6:14–16). And if the author of Matthew is assumed not to have been Matthew the tax collector, the author may have conformed the name he found in Mark 2:14 (Levi) to the name he found in Mark 3:18 (Matthew). On the contrary assumption of the traditional view of authorship, it is plausible

12. E.g., W. Davies and Allison 1988: 17–58; Luz 1989: 77–78; Segal in Balch 1991: 3–37.

13. Advocates of the minority view include K. Clark 1947; M. Cook 1983b; Fox 1942; Meier 1979: 17–25; Nepper-Christiansen 1958.

that Matthew the apostle was also called Levi. It is also plausible that the name Μαθθαῖον (*Maththaion*) is used because of its assonance with μαθητής (*mathētēs*, disciple), since discipleship is a key theme in the First Gospel (Kiley 1984).

Sources

On the assumption of Markan priority, Matthew's narrative framework came from Mark. It is commonly stated that approximately 90 percent of Mark is also found in Matthew. Carson and Moo (2005: 96) affirm that 97 percent of Mark's words are paralleled in Matthew (cf. Stein 2001: 52; Tyson and Longstaff 1978: 169–71). Yet this may overestimate the degree of Matthew's putative dependence on Mark, since others as diverse as Streeter and Linnemann estimate the percentage of parallels to be in the fifties (Yarbrough 1997: 163–65).[14] The teachings of Jesus found in both Matthew and Luke are viewed as originating in Q, which may not have been a written document (Tuckett 1996: 83–106). Uniquely Matthean material derives from M (Streeter 1924). Synopses of the Gospels include charts that display Matthew's putative Markan source, and scholars have also compiled a critical text and concordance of Q (J. M. Robinson et al. 2000). Yet a minority of scholars are not persuaded by the Q hypothesis (cf. Goodacre 2002). On the assumption of Matthean priority, the question of sources must be addressed with a very different paradigm (Farmer 1964: 199–286).

Date

It is very likely that there are allusions to Matthew in Ignatius (late first or early second century CE) and in the Didache (early second century CE).[15] When these allusions are taken in conjunction with Papias's testimony cited in Eusebius (see above), it seems clear that Matthew was well known by the early second century. Accordingly, the Gospel must have been written by the turn of the first century CE at the latest. The current scholarly consensus, based on the Markan-priority view of Gospel relationships, places Matthew's origin in the eighties or nineties CE. In some cases this view is buttressed by the idea that Matt. 24–25 constitutes a *vaticinium ex eventu* (prophecy after the event), written after the destruction of Jerusalem in 70 CE. (See Nolland 2005: 14 for a critique of this line of thinking.) Additionally, it is sometimes argued that the historical situation reflected in Matthew is the conflict of the developing church with the formative rabbinic Judaism that emanated from Jamnia (Jabneh) after the destruction of Jerusalem.

---

14. Part of the difficulty is the elusiveness of the term "parallel," which may refer to three types of agreement: of consecutive words, of nonconsecutive words, or even of equivalent words (Tyson and Longstaff 1978: 11).

15. Ignatius, *Eph.* 19; *Smyr.* 1. See Massaux 1990–93: 1.94–135; Schoedel in Balch 1991: 129–77; Smit Sibinga 1966; Trevett 1984.

On the other hand, if one accepts the patristic testimony to apostolic authorship, the date will probably need to be set earlier. Additionally, if one takes Matt. 24–25 as an authentic dominical logion, not as prophecy after the event, there is no need to date the Gospel after 70 CE (Nolland 2005: 16). And if one is not convinced of Matthew's dependence upon Mark, this is another reason for an earlier date. Noteworthy scholars who favor a pre-70 CE Matthew include C. Blomberg, D. A. Carson, R. H. Gundry, G. Maier, J. Nolland, B. Reicke, and J. A. T. Robinson. But these scholars are generally not dogmatic.[16]

Recipients and Occasion

Matthew's characteristic fulfillment formula quotations from the Hebrew Bible and his presentation of a Jesus who came not to destroy but to fulfill the law and the prophets are but two of the reasons every student of Matthew must come to some conclusion about the relationship of this Gospel's recipients to Judaism. Scholars are divided on this issue, with some convinced that Matthew's community contains many Gentiles and has already separated from the synagogue (Gundry, Stanton), and others holding the opposite view that Matthew's community is largely Jewish and is still connected with the synagogue (Harrington, Overman, Saldarini, Sigal, Sim). Yet others occupy a middle ground between these poles, arguing that Matthew can be satisfactorily explained only when it is viewed against the background of an embattled minority in the process of leaving the synagogue (Hagner 1993: lxxxi; 2003). This commentary has adopted the view that Matthew's community is still engaged with the synagogue.[17]

Although many theories have been proposed, the location of Matthew's community will likely never be known with anything approaching certainty. The city of Antioch is most frequently advocated.[18] Witherington (2006: 26–28) favors Capernaum or, perhaps, Sepphoris. Others suggest Phoenicia (Kilpatrick 1946: 130–34), Galilee (Overman 1990b: 158–59), Alexandria (Brandon 1951), Caesarea Maritima (Viviano 1979), or even Pella in Transjordan (Slingerland 1979). Grasping the message of the book does not depend on knowing the location of its original recipients.[19]

16. On the date of Matthew, see W. Davies and Allison 1988: 127–38; Gundry 1994: 599–609; J. A. Robinson 1976: 86–117.

17. On the *Sitz im Leben* and occasion of Matthew, see Balch 1991; S. Brown 1980; W. Davies 1964; Hagner in McKnight and Osborne 2004: 263–82; Hare 2000; Hummel 1966; McIver 1999; O'Grady 2001; Schweizer in Stanton 1995: 129–55; Senior 1999; Sim 1998a, 2001; Stanton 1984, 1985, 1992a, 1996; Vledder 1995; Vledder and Van Aarde 1994; Wansbrough 2000; White in Balch 1991: 211–47.

18. On Antioch, see W. Davies and Allison 1988: 143–47; Farmer 1976; Stark in Balch 1991: 189–210; Streeter 1924: 500–23; Zumstein 1980.

19. On the local origin of Matthew, see Kennard 1949; R. Osborne 1973; Viviano 1979. The arguments of Bauckham (in Bauckham [ed.] 1998: 9–48) in favor of an intended original wide audience for Matthew are not to be taken lightly. Cf. Keener 1999: 45–51.

The occasion of the Gospel's writing and its purposes can only be approximated in hypotheses inferred from the text. Assuming that the audience is a Christian Jewish community (or multiple communities in various locations), it is evidently a community that needs to understand how the life of Jesus the Messiah "fulfilled" the Hebrew Bible and how Jesus's teaching interpreted the Torah of Moses (Matt. 5:17–48). The community also needed to know why the entrenched non-Christian religious leaders were no longer to be emulated (Matt. 23). And the community evidently needed to expand its horizons toward gentile mission. Matthew regularly portrays Gentiles in a positive light, as when the gentile women are mentioned in Jesus's genealogy (1:3, 5, 6) and the faith of certain Gentiles is stressed (8:10; 15:28; 27:54). Such details from the narrative prepare the reader for the climactic commission that the community take Jesus's message to all the nations (28:19). The discussion below of Matthew's theological emphases provides additional implications about the occasion and purpose of the Gospel.

Textual History

The testimony of Papias. A foundational question in the textual history of Matthew is its possible origin as a Semitic text later translated into the present Greek Matthew. Patristic sources that take this position have been cited in the previous discussion of authorship. The key patristic text is Eusebius (260–340 CE), *Eccl. Hist.* 3.39.16, which cites Papias to the effect that "Matthew collected the oracles [*logia*; sayings of or about Jesus] in the Hebrew language [*Hebraidi dialektō*, perhaps "Hebraic style"] and each one interpreted [*hērmēneusen*, perhaps "translated"] them as best he could."[20] Papias is dated variously from about 100 to 140 CE, and so his testimony is important for the date of the First Gospel.

At first glance this text implies that any Greek editions of Matthew have been translated from an original Hebrew document. But the present Greek Matthew does not read like a translation of a Hebrew original. Some scholars have argued that Matthew wrote both a Hebrew Gospel and a Greek Gospel. Others think that Papias's *logia* were sayings of Jesus that modern source critics call Q or were even Jesus's discourses that are found in canonical Matthew. No MSS, however, exemplify the putative Hebrew Matthew mentioned by Papias (G. Howard 1986, 1995; cf. W. L. Peterson 1998). For these and additional reasons, others (e.g., Gundry 1994: 619–20; Kürzinger 1983) propose that *Hebraidi dialektō* does not mean the Hebrew language but Semitic rhetorical style and that

---

20. Ματθαῖος μὲν οὖν Ἑβραΐδι διαλέκτῳ τὰ λόγια συνετάξατο, ἡρμήνευσε δ' αὐτὰ ὡς ἦν δυνατὸς ἕκαστος. Additional references to a Hebrew Matthew include Irenaeus, *Haer.* 3.1.1; Origen, cited by Eusebius in *Eccl. Hist.* 6.25.4; and Eusebius, *Eccl. Hist.* 3.24.6; 5.10.3. An analogy may be Josephus's *Jewish War*, which was apparently written first in Aramaic and later in Greek.

hērmēneusen does not refer to translation but to interpretation. If this is the case, Papias speaks of Matthew's Jewish style of composition, which subsequent readers interpreted to the best of their ability. Perhaps such features as Matthew's genealogy and stress on "fulfillment" are indicative of his Jewish compositional style.[21]

Greek Manuscripts

The textual history of Matthew is represented by a great number of Greek MSS.[22] More than twenty uncial MSS contain complete or nearly complete texts of Matthew, among them ℵ and B (fourth century); C, D, and W (fifth century); O, Z, 042, 043 (sixth century); 0211 (seventh century); L (eighth century); F, K, M, U, V, 037, 038, 041, and 045 (ninth century); and G, S, 036 (tenth century). The fifth-century uncial A contains Matt. 25–28. The ninth-century uncial H (013) contains Matt. 15–28. Sixth-century uncials N, O, and P (022, 023, 024) contain parts of Matt. 1–4; 6–24.

About twenty early and often fragmentary papyri MSS contain portions of Matthew, including $\mathfrak{P}^{103}$ (Matt. 13–14, second century); $\mathfrak{P}^{104}$ (Matt. 21, second century); $\mathfrak{P}^{64+67}$ (Matt. 3; 5; 26, ca. 200);[23] $\mathfrak{P}^{77}$ (Matt. 23, second–third centuries); $\mathfrak{P}^{1}$ (Matt. 1, third century); $\mathfrak{P}^{45}$ (Matt. 20–21; 25–26, third century); $\mathfrak{P}^{53}$ (Matt. 26, third century); $\mathfrak{P}^{70}$ (Matt. 2–3; 11–12; 24, third century); $\mathfrak{P}^{101}$ (Matt. 3, third century); $\mathfrak{P}^{102}$ (Matt. 4, third century); $\mathfrak{P}^{110}$ (Matt. 10, third century); $\mathfrak{P}^{37}$ (Matt. 26, third–fourth centuries); $\mathfrak{P}^{25}$ (Matt. 18–19, fourth century); $\mathfrak{P}^{35}$ (Matt. 25, fourth century); $\mathfrak{P}^{62}$ (Matt. 11, fourth century); $\mathfrak{P}^{71}$ (Matt. 19, fourth century); $\mathfrak{P}^{86}$ (Matt. 5, fourth century); $\mathfrak{P}^{19}$ (Matt. 10–11, fourth–fifth centuries); and $\mathfrak{P}^{21}$ (Matt. 12, fourth–fifth centuries).

In addition to its presence in the above papyri and uncial MSS, hundreds of additional minuscules of the Byzantine or Majority text-type testify to the text of Matthew. Matthew is also abundantly cited in patristic sources, widely used in church lectionaries, and translated into other languages by the early ancient versions.[24]

21. On Papias and Gospel origins, see M. Black 1989; A. Baum 2001; W. Davies and Allison 1988: 8–17; Körtner 1983; Kürzinger 1983; Meredith in Tuckett 1984: 187–96; Munck 1962: 249–60; Yarbrough 1983.

22. The MSS cited here were culled from Aland and Aland 1989 and UBS⁴. Cf. Comfort and Barrett 2001.

23. $\mathfrak{P}^{64}$ is the controversial Magdalen papyrus, affirmed by Thiede 1995 to date from ca. 60 CE. It had been purchased in Luxor in 1901 by C. B. Huleatt, who gave it to Magdalen College, Oxford. It had been previously dated to ca. 200 by C. Roberts 1953. Thiede's arguments and dating would revolutionize Matthean studies, but his views have not proved persuasive to other scholars. See Grelot 1995a, 1995b; Head 1995; Parker 1999; Thiede 1996; Thiede and D'Ancona 1996.

24. R. Swanson 1995 is a helpful general tool for Matthean textual studies. See also D. Black 1989a; J. K. Elliott 1999; Martini in Didier 1972: 21–36; and the sources cited in W. Davies and Allison 1988: 147–48.

Canonicity

There was no doubt about the canonicity of Matthew, the most popular Gospel of the early church, among the orthodox in either the eastern or western regions of the church. The heretic Marcion (second century) and his followers, however, held to a canon that did not include Matthew, not to mention the Hebrew Bible, Mark, John, and the General Epistles. Marcion affirmed a sort of gnostic dualism between the Hebrew Bible and the NT as revelations of two different gods, and so Matthew's insistence on the fulfillment of the Bible by Jesus was unacceptable. Marcion accepted only an edited version of Luke's Gospel and the Pauline Epistles as his canon. Evidently, his attack on the incipient orthodox canon was a major factor leading to the formalization of the canon.

In addition to the patristic sources already cited, the so-called Anti-Marcionite Prologues to Luke and John (date uncertain) and the Muratorian Fragment (probably late second century) both speak of the undisputed fourfold Gospel tradition of the church (cf. Irenaeus, *Haer.* 3.11.8; Cyprian, *Epistles* 73.10; Clement of Alexandria, *Strom.* 3.13; Origen, cited by Eusebius, *Eccl. Hist.* 6.25.3ff.; Eusebius, *Eccl. Hist.* 3.25.1; Athanasius, *Festal Letters* 39; and many others [see further Bellinzoni 1992]).

Theological Emphases

It is difficult to select and briefly summarize the major themes of this Gospel, but the following themes are at the heart of Matthew's distinctive presentation of Jesus the Messiah and his rule.

Matthew and the Hebrew Bible

Matthew's pervasive use of the Hebrew Bible is one of the major reasons many interpreters note the Jewish orientation of this Gospel.[25] Indeed, the prevalence of this intertextuality calls into question the very notion of an "Old Testament" in Matthew's theology. If Matthew's Jesus came not to abolish but to fulfill the law and the prophets (Matt. 5:17), it is doubtful that Matthew conceived of the Jewish Scriptures as "old," at least in the connotative senses of "antique, outmoded, quaint." Instead, Matthew viewed both the historical patterns and the prophetic oracles of the Hebrew Bible as filled with ultimate significance through the ministry and teaching of Jesus.

In addition to numerous informal allusions, which are difficult to count, there are about fifty formal quotations. These may be categorized in various ways, such as by introductory formula ("in order that it might

25. On Matthew's use of the Hebrew Bible, see France 1980–81; 1982; 1989: 166–205; Gundry 1967; Hartman 1972; Moo 1983; Nolland 2005: 29–36; Rothfuchs 1969; Soarés-Prabhu 1976; Stanton 1992b: 346–63; Stendahl 1968; Van Aarde 1997; van Segbroeck in Didier 1972: 107–30.

be fulfilled," "for it is written," etc.) or speaker (Jesus, Matthew, etc.). This commentary will deal with each of Matthew's biblical citations individually, but here is a convenient summary based on the index in UBS[4] (pp. 889–99), followed by a key to the symbols.

Matthew's Use of the Hebrew Bible

Matthew	Bible reference	Subject
1:23 (M)	*Isa. 7:14; 8:8, 10	The virgin will conceive
2:6 (M/chief priests and scribes)	#Mic. 5:2	The ruler from Bethlehem
2:15 (M)	*Hos. 11:1	God's Son called from Egypt
2:18 (M)	*Jer. 31:15	Wailing for murdered children
2:23 (M)	*?	Jesus called a "Nazarene"
3:3 (M)	Isa. 40:3	John a voice in the wilderness
4:4 (J)	#Deut. 8:3	People live by more than bread
4:6 (M/Satan)	#Ps. 91:11–12	Angelic protection
4:7 (J)	#Deut. 6:16	Do not test God
4:10 (J)	#Deut. 6:13	God alone to be worshiped
4:15–16 (M)	*Isa. 9:1–2	Galilee sees the light
5:21 (J)	Exod. 20:13/Deut. 5:17	Do not murder
5:27 (J)	Exod. 20:14/Deut. 5:18	Do not commit adultery
5:31 (J)	Deut. 24:1	Letter of divorce
5:33 (J)	Lev. 19:12/Num. 30:2	Vows must be carried out
5:38 (J)	Exod. 21:24/Lev. 24:20/ Deut. 19:21	Eye for an eye
5:43 (J)	Lev. 19:18	Love your neighbor
8:17 (M)	*Isa. 53:4	He took our sicknesses
9:13 (J)	Hos. 6:6	God wants mercy
10:35–36 (J)	Mic. 7:6	Enemies within the household
11:10 (J)	#Mal. 3:1	Messenger prepares the way
12:7 (J)	Hos. 6:6	God wants mercy
12:18–21 (M)	*Isa. 42:1–4	The beloved servant
12:40 (J)	Jon. 1:17	Jonah in the fish's belly
13:14–15 (J)	*Isa. 6:9–10	Hearing without understanding
13:35 (M)	*Ps. 78:2	Mysterious speech in parables
15:4 (J)	Exod. 20:12/Deut. 5:16; Exod. 21:17	Honor your father and mother
15:8–9 (J)	Isa. 29:13	Hypocritical worship
18:16 (J)	Deut. 19:15	Two or three witnesses
19:4–5 (J)	Gen. 1:27/5:2; Gen. 2:24	God made male and female
19:7 (M/Pharisees)	Deut. 24:1	Letter of divorce
19:18–19 (J)	Exod. 20:12–16/Deut. 5:16–20; Lev. 19:18	Do not murder
21:5 (M)	*Isa. 62:11/Zech. 9:9	The king comes on a donkey
21:9 (M/crowds)	Ps. 118:25–26	Blessings for the son of David
21:13 (J)	#Isa. 56:7	A den of thieves
21:16 (J)	Ps. 8:3	Praise from children

Matthew	Bible reference	Subject
21:42 (J)	Ps. 118:22–23	The cornerstone
22:24 (M/Sadducees)	Deut. 25:5	A man dies without children
22:32 (J)	Exod. 3:6, 15	I am the God of Abraham
22:37 (J)	Deut. 6:5	Love the Lord your God
22:39 (J)	Lev. 19:18	Love your neighbor
22:44 (J)	Ps. 110:1	Sit at my right hand
23:39 (J)	Ps. 118:26	Bless the one coming
24:30 (J)	Dan. 7:13	The Son of Man arrives
26:31 (J)	#Zech. 13:7	The shepherd struck
26:64 (J)	Ps. 110:1; Dan. 7:13	The Son of Man coming back
27:9–10 (M)	*Jer. 32:6–9; Zech. 11:12–13	Thirty pieces of silver
27:46 (J)	Ps. 22:1	Forsaken by God

Key
M = cited in a Matthean authorial comment
M/. . . = cited by a character in the narrative
J = cited by Jesus
* = introductory formula referring to fulfillment
# = introductory formula "it is written"

Since Matthew's use of the Bible frequently includes the concept of fulfillment, special attention to this theme is necessary.

Fulfillment

Matthew's distinctive use of the Hebrew Bible revolves around his ten fulfillment formula quotations, which utilize the verb πληρόω (*plēroō*, fulfill). These are especially prominent in Matt. 1–2. This discussion surveys introductory formulas, biblical passages cited, and the nature of fulfillment in Matthew. Specific questions such as the OT text-form cited (whether close to that of the LXX or the MT, for example) will be discussed as the commentary encounters the individual passages.[26]

Introductory Formulas

The introductory formulas for the quotations are as follows:

1:22   ἵνα πληρωθῇ τὸ ῥηθὲν ὑπὸ κυρίου διὰ τοῦ προφήτου λέγοντος,

       hina plērōthē to rhēthen hypo kyriou dia tou prophētou legontos,

       in order that what was said by the Lord through the prophet might be fulfilled, which says,

26. For further discussion of fulfillment in Matthew, see Beaton 2002: 86–121; France 1980–81, 1982; Gundry 1967; Hagner 1993: liii–lvii; Hartman 1972; Luz 1989: 156–64; F. Martin 1988; Miler 1999, 2001; Moule 1968; M. Müller 2001; Senior in Tuckett 1997: 89–115; Soarés-Prabhu 1976; Stanton 1992b: 346–63; Stendahl 1968; van Segbroeck in Didier 1972: 107–30.

2:15	ἵνα πληρωθῇ τὸ ῥηθὲν ὑπὸ κυρίου διὰ τοῦ προφήτου λέγοντος,
	hina plērōthē to rhēthen hypo kyriou dia tou prophētou legontos,
	in order that what was said by the Lord through the prophet might be fulfilled, which says,
2:17	τότε ἐπληρώθη τὸ ῥηθὲν διὰ Ἰερεμίου τοῦ προφήτου λέγοντος,
	tote eplērōthē to rhēthen dia Ieremiou tou prophētou legontos,
	then what was said by the prophet Jeremiah was fulfilled, which says,
2:23	ὅπως πληρωθῇ τὸ ῥηθὲν διὰ τῶν προφητῶν
	hopōs plērōthē to rhēthen dia tōn prophētōn
	so that what was said through the prophets might be fulfilled
4:14	ἵνα πληρωθῇ τὸ ῥηθὲν διὰ Ἠσαΐου τοῦ προφήτου λέγοντος,
	hina plērōthē to rhēthen dia Ēsaïou tou prophētou legontos,
	in order that what was said through the prophet Isaiah might be fulfilled, which says,
8:17	ὅπως πληρωθῇ τὸ ῥηθὲν διὰ Ἠσαΐου τοῦ προφήτου λέγοντος,
	hopōs plērōthē to rhēthen dia Ēsaïou tou prophētou legontos,
	so that what was said through the prophet Isaiah might be fulfilled, which says,
12:17	ἵνα πληρωθῇ τὸ ῥηθὲν διὰ Ἠσαΐου τοῦ προφήτου λέγοντος,
	hina plērōthē to rhēthen dia Ēsaïou tou prophētou legontos,
	in order that what was said through the prophet Isaiah might be fulfilled, which says,
13:35	ὅπως πληρωθῇ τὸ ῥηθὲν διὰ τοῦ προφήτου λέγοντος,
	hopōs plērōthē to rhēthen dia tou prophētou legontos,
	so that what was said through the prophet might be fulfilled, which says,
21:4	ἵνα πληρωθῇ τὸ ῥηθὲν διὰ τοῦ προφήτου λέγοντος,
	hina plērōthē to rhēthen dia tou prophētou legontos,
	in order that what was said through the prophet might be fulfilled, which says,
27:9	τότε ἐπληρώθη τὸ ῥηθὲν διὰ Ἰερεμίου τοῦ προφήτου λέγοντος,
	tote eplērōthē to rhēthen dia Ieremiou tou prophētou legontos,
	then what was said through the prophet Jeremiah was fulfilled, which says,

All ten of the preceding formulas have the verb πληρόω with the substantive participle τὸ ῥηθέν (*to rhēthen*, what was spoken) as its subject and the preposition διά (*dia*, through) expressing the means of the speech. Five of the formulas are introduced by ἵνα (*hina*, so that, 1:22; 2:15; 4:14; 21:4), three by ὅπως (*hopōs*, so that, 2:23; 8:17; 13:35), and two by τότε (*tote*, then), which takes the indicative ἐπληρώθη (*eplērōthē*) instead of the subjunctive πληρωθῇ (*plērōthē*, 2:17; 27:9). Ἵνα and ὅπως are synonyms, so nothing should be made of this word difference. Soarés-Prabhu's argument (1976: 50–52) to the contrary is unconvincing. There is some debate over whether τότε provides a distinct nuance to the formulas it introduces. Some think that τότε is used to introduce quotations that describe calamities, so that divine intention is not implied as it would be with ἵνα or ὅπως (Soarés-Prabhu 1976: 50–52), but it is debatable whether Matthew was so concerned with theodicy.

Two of the formulas (1:22; 2:15) use the prepositional phrase ὑπὸ κυρίου (*hypo kyriou*, by the Lord) to underline the divine agency implicit in the participle τὸ ῥηθέν, which should be understood as a "divine" or "theological" passive (Zerwick 1963: §236; BDF §§130.1; 342). This may be an Aramaism, reflecting sensitivity to the mention of God's name. Be that as it may, the presence of both prepositional phrases (ὑπὸ κυρίου and διὰ τοῦ προφήτου, *dia tou prophētou*, through the prophet) in these formulas points to a dual-authorship view of Scripture where the human prophet is the channel through which the divine agency speaks (cf. Matt. 15:4, 7; 22:43; Acts 1:16; 4:25; 28:25; Rom. 1:2; 2 Tim. 3:16; 2 Pet. 1:19–21). Passages such as these are foundational for evangelical views of biblical inspiration and authority.

References to the prophet vary. In four instances reference is made to a single unnamed prophet (Matt. 1:22; 2:15; 13:35; 21:4), and in five instances reference is made to a single named prophet (Jeremiah in 2:17; 27:9; Isaiah in 4:14; 8:17; 12:17). The important uncial MS Sinaiticus (א*) and a few other MSS support reading Isaiah in 13:35 also. The most troublesome passage is 2:23, where unnamed plural prophets are cited but there is no unambiguous biblical text to the effect that the Messiah will be called a Nazarene. The fulfillment of the words of unnamed plural prophets is also mentioned in a rhetorical question by Jesus at his arrest and in a subsequent comment by Matthew (26:54, 56).

Although there is some debate over 1:22, all of these fulfillment-formula quotations occur in Matthean narrative contexts. In addition to these ten passages, three others should be noted:

13:14 καὶ ἀναπληροῦται αὐτοῖς ἡ προφητεία Ἠσαΐου ἡ λέγουσα,
kai anaplēroutai autois hē prophēteia Ēsaïou hē legousa,
and for them the prophecy of Isaiah is being fulfilled, which says,

26:54 πῶς οὖν πληρωθῶσιν αἱ γραφαὶ ὅτι οὕτως δεῖ γενέσθαι;
pōs oun plērōthōsin hai graphai hoti houtōs dei genesthai?
How, therefore, would the Scriptures be fulfilled that say it must happen this way?

26:56 ἵνα πληρωθῶσιν αἱ γραφαὶ τῶν προφητῶν
hina plērōthōsin hai graphai tōn prophētōn
in order that the writings of the prophets might be fulfilled

These passages, with the possible exception of 26:56, occur in Matthew as the words of Jesus. A different verb (ἀναπληρόω, *anaplēroō*, fulfill) is used in 13:14, which cites Isa. 6:9–10; Matt. 26:54, 56 alludes to the events surrounding Jesus's arrest as fulfilling "the Scriptures of the prophets" without citing a specific passage.

Biblical passages cited. Turning from the introductory formulas to the biblical passages themselves, the summary below may be helpful. Of the ten passages, seven are relatively straightforward references to individual biblical texts. The other three, however, are not so simple. Two of the quotations (21:4–5; 27:9–10) are composites of two or more biblical texts, and one (2:23) does not seem to refer clearly to any biblical passage. Most of the passages cited are from the prophets, although there are two notable exceptions. The question of the text form used by Matthew is complicated. These complexities will be handled as the individual passages are discussed in the body of the commentary.

Biblical Texts Cited in Matthew's Fulfillment Citations

Matthew	Bible reference	Subject
1:23	Isa. 7:14	A virgin will conceive and bear a son called Immanuel.
2:15	Hos. 11:1	God called his Son from Egypt.
2:18	Jer. 31:15	In Ramah, Rachel unconsolably mourned her murdered children.
2:23	Judg. 13:5, 7?; Isa. 11:1? (Unclear)	The Messiah will be called a Nazarene.
4:15–16	Isa. 9:1–2	Dark Galilee of the Gentiles sees the light.
8:17	Isa. 53:4	The servant bears the nation's diseases.
12:18–21	Isa. 42:1–4	Gentiles will hope in the Spirit-empowered servant.
13:35	Ps. 78:2	The psalmist speaks parabolically of deep things.
21:5	Isa. 62:11; Zech. 9:9	Zion's king appears meekly, riding a donkey's colt.
27:9–10	Jer. 32:6–9; Zech. 11:12–13	Thirty pieces of silver are used to buy the potter's field.

Fulfillment in Matthew. The notion that fulfillment entails a specific biblical prediction being "fulfilled" (occurring) in a NT event is simplistic at best. This is mainly due to mistakenly equating prophecy with prediction. But the discussion that follows shows that fulfillment in Matthew has as much to do with historical patterns as with prophetic predictions. Prophetic prediction contains the prophet's revelational foresight of a future event (cf. 2:4–6), but Matthew's fulfillment quotations more often contain Christian hindsight in which a historical event from the Hebrew Bible serves as a pattern for a NT event that it anticipated. Historical events, whether past, present, or future, are viewed as the providential outworking of God's plan. Also, biblical prophecy is primarily not prediction but covenantal admonition, which utilizes the rehearsal of past events as well as the prediction of future events to motivate present covenant loyalty. Fulfillment in Matthew includes ethical and historical matters as well as predictive prophecy.

Matthew uses the verb πληρόω (*plēroō*, fulfill) sixteen times (1:22; 2:15, 17, 23; 3:15; 4:14; 5:17; 8:17; 12:17; 13:35, 48; 21:4; 23:32; 26:54, 56; 27:9), the verb ἀναπληρόω once (13:14), the adjective πλήρης (*plērēs*, filled, full) twice (14:20; 15:37), and the noun πλήρωμα (*plērōma*, fullness) once (9:16). Four of these twenty instances do not speak of theological fulfillment and are irrelevant to this discussion (9:16; 13:48; 14:20; 15:37). The remaining sixteen are briefly discussed below.

One passage presents the legal experts and Pharisees as fulfilling the measure of the sin of their ancestors (23:32). The gist of 23:29–36 is that Jesus's enemies are the culmination of previous enmity against God's messengers the prophets (cf. 5:12; 21:34–39). Just as the prophets anticipate the Messiah, the prophets' enemies anticipate the Messiah's enemies. Biblical redemptive history provides a pattern that leads up to climactic fulfillment in the NT. But the fulfillment is the climax of a historical pattern, not a predictive oracle.

Two passages present Jesus as the one who fulfills "all righteousness" at his baptism (3:15) and who teaches that he comes not to destroy but to fulfill the law and the prophets (5:17). Strictly speaking, messianic prediction alone is not the focus of the baptism. The point is that Jesus's identification with repentant Israelites in his baptism amounts to an obedience that fulfills the uprightness required of kingdom disciples. As the servant of Yahweh, Jesus does fulfill biblical prediction, but the point here is that the Messiah's uprightness will please the Father. Jesus's affirmation that he came to fulfill "the law and the prophets" should be viewed as fulfillment of the Bible as a whole, not merely of its predictive portions. And it is clear from the ensuing context (5:18–20) that ethical concerns are preeminent, not mere predictions.

The remaining thirteen passages (ten in Matthew's narrative comments, three in the words of Jesus) speak of biblical fulfillment in some fashion. Of the ten passages in Matthew's narrative, four occur in the infancy narrative of Matt. 1–2. Matthew 1:22–23 cites Isa. 7:14, a passage that probably is misunderstood if it is viewed as a strict prediction of a future virgin-born Messiah. Rather, Isa. 7:14 speaks of a sign given to King Ahaz in his own lifetime, and Matthew views it as an event that anticipates the virgin birth of the Messiah, an ultimate sign to the nation of Israel. Matthew 2:15 cites Hos. 11:1, which speaks of the historical exodus of Israel from Egypt. Matthew capitalizes on the metaphor of Israel as God's son to speak of a much greater exodus of God's unique Son in a recapitulation of redemptive history. Matthew 2:17–18 cites Jer. 31:15, which personifies the nation of Israel at the Babylonian exile as Rachel weeping for her children who were dead. A similar yet much more significant weeping for dead children occurred when Herod ordered the slaughter of the babies in the region of Bethlehem. But it is significant that the sorrow in both the Hebrew Bible and Matthew occurs in the context of hope. Matthew 2:23 significantly speaks of the fulfillment of plural prophets in Jesus's move to the obscure village of Nazareth. In the commentary on Matt. 2:23, it is argued that this passage plays on the similar words "Nazareth" and "Nazarite" (נְזִיר, *nĕzîr*, Num. 6; Judg. 13:5–7). It is also possible that Matthew has the branch (נֵצֶר, *nēṣer*) of Isa. 11:1 in mind. If it is correct that Matt. 2:23 is essentially a Messianic pun, it fits with the other biblical fulfillments cited in the infancy narratives, which are not primarily predictive in nature.

Matthew 4:14 places the return of Jesus to Galilee after his baptism in the context of biblical fulfillment. Isaiah 9:1–2 speaks of a deliverer who will bring salvation to Galilee after the Assyrian attack and exile. No doubt Matthew connected this with Jesus because of the stress on sonship and the throne of David in Isa. 9:6–7. Matthew 8:17 views Jesus's ministry of healing and exorcism as fulfillment of Isa. 53:4, where the servant vicariously removes the infirmities of the nation by bearing them himself. It is difficult to relate the physical and spiritual implications of this passage. In the context of growing opposition from the Pharisees, Matt. 12:17–21 cites Isa. 42:1–4 to substantiate Jesus's forbidding those whom he had healed from telling who he was. In Isa. 42 the Spirit-empowered servant proclaims justice to the Gentiles with mercy and gentleness. In keeping with this model, Jesus does not brashly confront his opponents with examples of spectacular healing. Instead he opts for strategic withdrawal in his mission of bringing hope to the Gentiles. Matthew 13:35 connects Jesus's use of parables to the deep sayings of the psalmist in Ps. 78:2. Although no predictions are made in the verse cited, Matthew nevertheless describes the psalmist as "the prophet." Matthew 21:4–5 describes Jesus's plan to ride a donkey's colt into Jerusalem as fulfilling what seems to be a composite of Isa. 62:11 and Zech. 9:9. Both biblical passages speak of the future deliverance of Jerusalem. Matthew 27:9–10 finds fulfillment of Zech. 11:12–13 (with similarities to motifs in Jer. 18:2–6; 19:1–13). Apart from the obvious difficulty that a passage from Zechariah is cited as Jeremiah, the connection to the thirty pieces of silver is hermeneutically challenging as well. It seems best to view this as Matthew's application of a biblical situation to Jesus's betrayal because of explicit verbal parallels (thirty pieces of silver, etc.) and implicit theological parallels (Israel's apostasy and rejection of God's messengers).

Three references to the fulfillment of the Bible occur in the words of Jesus. In his parabolic discourse Jesus speaks of God's sovereignty and finds the unbelief of his audience to be in keeping with Israel's unbelief at an earlier stage of redemptive history (Matt. 13:13–15). In answer to his disciples' question about why he speaks in parables to the crowds, Jesus first alludes to Jer. 5:21 (and/or other similar biblical texts) and then speaks of the fulfillment of Isa. 6:9–10. In its original context this passage spoke of the rebellion and unbelief of Israel in the days of the prophet Isaiah, but it also suits Israel's rebellion in the days of the Messiah Jesus. The other two instances where Jesus speaks of biblical fulfillment occur in the same context in Matt. 26:54–56. With his arrest imminent, one of his disciples prepares to fight for him. Jesus says to this disciple that the Father can give him power to avoid arrest, but then he raises the question "How then would the Scriptures be fulfilled which say that it must happen like this?" He then addresses the crowd and states that these things happened so that the writings of the prophets might be fulfilled. Although no biblical text is introduced here, Jesus probably has in mind Zech. 13:7 (introduced in Matt. 26:31). The arrest of the shepherd leads to the scattering of the sheep. But evidently Jesus sees his arrest as the beginning of fulfillment of other biblical passages as well, since he speaks of the prophets in the plural. Thus the reader is sensitized to note biblical fulfillment in Jesus's trials, crucifixion, and resurrection.

In summary, biblical fulfillment in Matthew includes ethical, historical, and prophetic connections. These categories are not discrete but overlapping; individual fulfillments may contain elements of all three aspects. At times the ethical element is preeminent (3:15; 5:17). At other times fulfillment of biblical prediction is primary (4:14; 8:17; 12:17; 21:4; 26:54, 56). But probably the most prevalent aspect of fulfillment in Matthew concerns historical patterns (1:22; 2:15, 17, 23; 13:14, 35; 23:32; 27:9). Events in biblical history anticipate events in Jesus's ministry in that Jesus fills them with new significance. Even Jesus's opponents have their precursors in the Bible. By recapitulating these biblical events, Jesus demonstrates the providence of God in fulfilling his promises to Israel. As implied in the genealogy, biblical history is fulfilled by Jesus the Messiah, who is Abraham's son and David's son.

Matthew's understanding of the Bible is also reflected in his unique genealogy of Jesus, a portion of the book that also requires special emphasis.

Matthew's Genealogy of Jesus

Three issues in Matthew's genealogy merit discussion: (1) the discrepancy with the number fourteen, (2) the reason Matthew included the women in the genealogy, and (3) the relationship of Matthew's genealogy to Luke's.[27]

The number fourteen. The following table shows that only the second set of "fourteen" generations actually has fourteen. The first and third sets actually have thirteen generations.

---

27. Additional studies of Matthew's genealogy include Abadie 1999; Bauer in Bauer and Powell 1996: 129–60; R. Brown 1993: 57–92; C. Davis 1973; M. Johnson 1988; Masson 1982; G. Moore 1921; Nineham 1975–76; Waetjen 1976; and R. Wilson 1977.

Three Sets of "Fourteen Generations" in Matt. 1:1–17

	Matt. 1:1–6a	Matt. 1:6b–11	Matt. 1:12–16
1	Abraham–Isaac	David–Solomon (Bathsheba)	Jeconiah–Shealtiel
2	Isaac–Jacob	Solomon–Rehoboam	Shealtiel–Zerubbabel
3	Jacob–Judah	Rehoboam–Abijah	Zerubbabel–Abiud
4	Judah–Perez (Tamar)	Abijah–Asaph (v.l.)	Abiud–Eliakim
5	Perez–Hezron	Asa–Jehoshaphat	Eliakim–Azor
6	Hezron–Ram	Jehoshaphat–Jehoram	Azor–Zadok
7	Ram–Amminadab	Jehoram–Uzziah	Zadok–Akim
8	Amminadab–Nahshon	Uzziah–Jotham	Akim–Eliud
9	Nahshon–Salmon	Jotham–Ahaz	Eliud–Eleazar
10	Salmon–Boaz (Rahab)	Ahaz–Hezekiah	Eleazar–Matthan
11	Boaz–Obed (Ruth)	Hezekiah–Manasseh	Matthan–Jacob
12	Obed–Jesse	Manasseh–Amon	Jacob–Joseph
13	Jesse–David	Amon–Josiah	Joseph (Mary)–Jesus
14		Josiah–Jeconiah	

Scholars have responded to this discrepancy in different ways. Augustine, for example, viewed the genealogy to be presenting forty generations and compared it to other significant biblical uses of the number forty (*Harmony of the Gospels* 2.4.9). Whatever the merit of his approach, it seems to omit what Matthew emphasized, the number fourteen.

One can derive three sets of fourteen names in the following way. The first set of fourteen runs from Abraham to David (1:2–6a). The second set runs from Solomon to Jeconiah (1:6b–11). The third set runs either from Shealtiel (Salathiel in NRSV) to Jesus (including Mary) or from Jeconiah to Jesus (excluding Mary; 1:12–16). The first option for the third set is more plausible, since Jeconiah has already been counted once as the last name in the second set. R. Brown (1993: 82) notes that there are indeed fourteen names in the first set, so perhaps Matthew intended that Abraham (1:2) be viewed as a generation. This will not work in the third set, however, where the first name (Jeconiah) represents the last generation of the second set. But all this may be irrelevant, since Matthew is speaking of generations (1:17), not of individual persons.

Blomberg (1992: 53) remarks that ancient literary convention often alternated between inclusive (first and third sets) and exclusive (second set) reckoning. If this is true, the shift between thirteen and fourteen is understandable. It has been suggested that names were omitted because of errors in the transmission of the text, but there is no MS evidence for any such omissions. Gundry (1994: 19) solves the problem in the third set by suggesting that Matthew counts Joseph and Mary as separate generations, but this breaks the literary pattern in 1:16 and seems to count the "nongeneration" of Jesus by Joseph as a generation. There are many other suggestions that are even less convincing.

However one handles this problem, Carson's point (1984: 68) is noteworthy: "The symbolic value of the fourteens is of more significance than their precise breakdown." Matthew certainly knew basic arithmetic as well as modern scholars do, but Matthew's literary conventions are ancient, not modern. By modern standards, Matthew's linear genealogy is artificial because it is not exhaustive. Matthew has omitted three names that are found in 1 Chron. 3:10–14 between Solomon and Josiah, and other omissions can also be noted (R. Brown 1993: 81–84). But it is not that Matthew has erred, since he did not intend to work exhaustively and precisely. The fact that David is the fourteenth name in the genealogy and the symbolic significance of fourteen as the numerical value of David's name explain the artificiality of the genealogy (cf. Nolland 2005: 86–87).

The women in Matthew's genealogy. A second feature of the genealogy calls for comment: the inclusion of women.[28] It is generally acknowledged that women are seldom included in Jewish genealogies, which are usually patrilineal. For some exceptions, see Gen. 11:29; 22:20–24; 35:22–26; 1 Chron. 2:18–21, 24, 34, 46–49; 7:24. Several explanations have been proposed, but none of them is totally convincing. (See the discussion in R. Brown 1993: 71–74.)

Since the days of the church fathers, it has been proposed that Matthew includes the women as prototypical sinners whom Jesus came to save. Thus the women take their place in the narrative alongside the magi, the Roman centurion, the Canaanite woman, and others in Matthew who bear testimony to the grace of God. A similar view has it that all these women were guilty of scandalous sexual union. Tamar and especially Rahab were indeed guilty of heinous sins, but this is not the case with Ruth and Bathsheba. The biblical account of Bathsheba's adultery with David (2 Sam. 11) appears to characterize her as the passive victim of his aggression. Ruth's nocturnal contact with Boaz (Ruth 3:13–18) is not a steamy scene of seduction but includes a marriage proposal to a kinsman as enjoined in the Torah. Another problem here concerns Matthew's intent in listing these women alongside Mary, whose virtuous character is stressed. Unless Matthew intended to contrast these women with Mary, it makes little sense to mention them.

Another popular approach to this question asserts that all these women were Gentiles who typify Matthew's intent to stress that the gospel is for all the nations (Keener 1999: 78–81; Hauerwas 2006: 31–33). This is shown repeatedly in the narrative and climactically at the conclusion of the book. Tamar and Rahab were Canaanites, Ruth was a Moabite, and Bathsheba was evidently a Hittite like her husband, Uriah. Against this

---

28. For additional studies of the women in the genealogy, see Bauckham 2002: 17–46; Blomberg 1991; Freed 1987; Heil 1991c; Hutchinson 2001; G. Jackson 2002: 86–99; Nolland 1997a; Weren 1997.

position, it is argued that Jewish tradition generally viewed these women as virtuous proselytes, but their gentile origins would not be thereby denied, and this would make them even better prototypes of Matthew's stress on gentile mission. The problem of relating these women to Mary remains, however, and if this view is adopted, it must be assumed that Matthew did not intend for these women to be typical of Mary.

Blomberg (1991), interacting with Schaberg (1987) and R. Horsley (1989), argues that all these women bore illegitimate children and thus pave the way for the suspicion that Jesus was also illegitimately conceived by Mary. Thus Matt. 1–2 implies that God liberates people from the stigma of illegitimacy through the virgin birth of the Messiah. This view has the strength of tying these four women to Mary with a common thread, something lacking in the preceding views. But this view can only presume that the prostitute Rahab had an illegitimate child, since the Bible is silent on this. And Ruth's union with Boaz seems to be legitimate also. In these two cases, only the suspicion of illegitimacy can be implied.

Matthew's inclusion of four noteworthy, even notorious, women in his genealogy has not yet been fully explained. Certain elements of all the views have merit. Perhaps all that can be said is that the presence of these women in the genealogy implies Matthew's later stress on the universal world mission of the gospel and his later focus on genuine piety. God's grace in Jesus the Messiah reaches beyond Israel to Gentiles, beyond men to women, beyond the self-righteous to sinners. In saving his people from their sins, Jesus is not bound by race, gender, or scandal.

Matthew's genealogy and Luke's. A third area of discussion in Matthew's genealogy concerns its relationship to Luke's genealogy (Luke 3:23–38; see the discussion in R. Brown 1993: 84–94). Whereas Matthew's genealogy selectively and thus somewhat artificially traces Jesus's ancestors from Abraham on, Luke more comprehensively covers this ground from Jesus all the way back to Adam. Luke has twenty-one pre-Abrahamic generations and fourteen generations between Abraham and David, one more than Matthew's "fourteen." Between David and Shealtiel, Luke has twenty-one generations to Matthew's fifteen. From Shealtiel to Jesus, Luke has twenty generations to Matthew's twelve. The syntax of the genealogies differs in that Matthew follows the "A was the father of B" pattern whereas Luke utilizes the genitive of relationship (BDF §162; Wallace 1996: 83–84): "A was [the son] of B." Context differs as well: Matthew's genealogy is placed at the outset of the Gospel whereas Luke's is sandwiched between his accounts of Jesus's baptism and temptation. Matthew's 3 × 14 structure is a transparent feature of his genealogy, but there is much debate over the possibility of an 11 × 7 structure for Luke's Gospel.

The table (cf. R. Brown 1993: 76–79) displays the similarities and differences between these genealogies. Note that the table arranges Luke's

Comparison of Matthew's and Luke's Genealogies

Luke 3:23–38 (Adam–Jesus)	Matt. 1:2–17 (Abraham–Jesus)	Luke 3:23–38 (Adam–Jesus)	Matt. 1:2–17 (Abraham–Jesus)
God (3:38)		Menna	
Adam		Melea	
Seth		Eliakim (3:30)	Rehoboam (1:7)
Enosh		Jonam	Abijah
Kenan (3:37)		Joseph	Asaph
Mahalaleel		Judas	Jehoshaphat (1:8)
Jared		Simeon	Jehoram
Enoch		Levi (3:29)	Uzziah
Methuselah		Matthat	Jotham (1:9)
Lamech (3:36)		Jorim	Ahaz
Noah		Eleazar	Hezekiah
Shem		Jesus	Manasseh (1:10)
Arphaxad		Er (3:28)	Amon
Cainan		Elmadam	Josiah
Shelah (3:35)		Cosam	
Eber		Addi	
Peleg		Melchi	
Reu		Neri (3:27)	Jeconiah (1:11)
Serug		Shealtiel	Shealtiel (1:12)
Nahor (3:34)		Zerubbabel	Zerubbabel
Terah		Rhesa[c]	Abiud (1:13)
Abraham	Abraham (1:2)	Joanam	
Isaac	Isaac	Joda (3:26)	
Jacob	Jacob	Josech	
Judah (3:33)	Judah	Semein	
Perez	Perez and Zerah (Tamar; 1:3)	Mattathias	
Hezron	Hezron	Maath	Eliakim
Arni	Ram	Naggai (3:25)	Azor
Admin[a]		Esli	Zadok (1:14)
Amminadab	Amminadab (1:4)	Nahum	Akim
Nahshon (3:32)	Nahshon	Amos	Eliud
Sala	Salmon	Mattathias	Eleazar (1:15)
Boaz	Boaz (Rahab; 1:5)	Joseph (3:24)	Matthan
Obed	Obed (Ruth)	Jannai	
Jesse	Jesse	Melchi	
David (3:31)	David (1:6)	Levi	
Nathan[b]	Solomon (Bathsheba)	Matthat[d]	
Mattatha		Heli (3:23)	Jacob
		Joseph[e]	Joseph (1:16)
		Jesus	Mary–Jesus

[a]A difficult textual problem complicates the presence of Admin and Arni in the genealogy. UBS[4] rates the problem as C, indicating that the editors have a considerable degree of doubt about which is the superior reading. (For discussion, see Metzger 1994: 113 and the exegetical commentaries.)

[b]Here Luke's David–Nathan diverges from Matthew's David–Solomon. There is no agreement again until Shealtiel in Luke 3:27/Matt. 1:12.

[c]Once again the genealogies diverge after a brief convergence with Shealtiel–Zerubbabel. Luke's Rhesa is not otherwise known from the Bible.

[d]It is uncertain whether Luke's Matthat is the same person as Matthew's Matthan.

[e]According to Luke, Joseph's father was Heli, but according to Matthew, it was Jacob. (For discussion of this difficulty, see Carson 1984: 64–65.)

genealogy in reverse order. Persons mentioned by Luke who are not in Matthew (more than sixty people) are in italics. Luke provides twenty-one generations between God and Abraham and fifty-six generations between Abraham and Jesus. These are in the left column. The right column displays Matthew's forty-two generations between Abraham and Jesus. This column has gaps where Luke lists more generations than Matthew. In Matt. 1:3 Ram comes between Hezron and Amminadab, but in Luke 3:33 Arni and Admin intervene between Hezron and Amminadab. A major difference occurs in Matt. 1:6/Luke 3:31, where Matthew puts Solomon after David and Luke puts Nathan after David. From this point the genealogies diverge totally until they converge briefly with Shealtiel–Zerubbabel in Matt. 1:12/Luke 3:27. Then they diverge again until Joseph in Matthew 1:16/Luke 3:23. In other words, the genealogies converge in Matt. 1:2–6/Luke 3:32–34 (with one difference); Matt. 1:12/Luke 3:27; and Matt. 1:16/Luke 3:23. But they diverge much more often in Matt. 1:3/Luke 3:33; Matt. 1:6–16/Luke 3:24–31 (with one agreement). Between Abraham and Jesus, Luke has fifty-six generations, and only twelve of these converge with Matthew's forty-two generations. Convergence occurs during the premonarchical period, divergence elsewhere.

Theological problems. There are difficulties on three levels. Both genealogies have their individual problems, and additional issues arise when they are compared. People are mentioned in the genealogies who do not appear in the Hebrew Bible or anywhere else. And people in one genealogy do not match up with people in the other. At this point one's overall theological perspective informs exegesis. Scholars who are skeptical of the historical accuracy of the Gospels tend to deprecate the historicity of the genealogies and totally despair ever reaching anything like a solution to the problems. They see the genealogies as theological constructions with dubious historical moorings. Others prefer to remain in ignorance of the difficulties while proclaiming a faith that does not wish to be confused by facts. There is good reason, however, to accept the historical reliability of the Gospels, and those who are committed to it (see Blomberg 1987b) point to solutions that are plausible though certainly not totally satisfying. The faith commitment of the scholar is decisive. The problem is that there is simply insufficient information to reach convincing conclusions. More than sixty years ago Machen (1930: 202–9, 229–32) presented plausible answers to many of these questions, but his solutions are often overlooked today.

Another line of theological discussion is the question of the differences in the genealogies and their respective purposes. The fourth-century author Hilary of Poitiers believed that Matthew presented Jesus's royal succession and Luke his priestly (*On Matthew* 1.1). It has been argued by many older commentators (e.g., Broadus 1886: 6, though disputed by Barnes 1868: 2 and Calvin 1972: 1.54–55) that Matthew gives Joseph's genealogy whereas Luke gives Mary's. Although it is possible that Mary was a descendant of David (Luke 1:32), she is not mentioned in Luke's genealogy; instead Joseph is (3:23). This theory arises not from reading Luke but as an expedient to relieve a difficulty (Carson 1984: 64).

Another approach sees both genealogies as Joseph's but with the nuance that Matthew provides Jesus's royal succession to the throne and Luke provides his real genealogy. In this approach Joseph's real father was Heli (Luke 3:23), and Jacob (Matt. 1:16) was Heli's full brother, who died without an heir. Heli carried out a levirate marriage (Deut. 25:5–10) with Jacob's widow. But this theory raises many other questions too numerous to be discussed here (S. Brown 1977: 86–90; Carson 1984: 64–65; Machen 1930: 207–9).

Masson (1982) presents an elaborate and creative synthesis of both approaches, but when all is said and done, it is clear that the overall theological perspective of the interpreter is decisive. Evangelicals must admit that there are insuperable difficulties in fully resolving all the problems in the genealogies. But this does not amount to capitulation of biblical authority. Although there is not sufficient evidence to solve the difficulties, there is likewise insufficient evidence to demonstrate that the biblical record is false. No doubt both genealogies are based on traditions available to Matthew and Luke, which they passed on in good faith (Albright and Mann 1971: 5–6). No doubt Matthew and Luke also had distinct purposes in composing their genealogies, and neither intended to summarize exhaustively the biological lineage of Jesus (R. Brown 1993: 85). With this in mind, many of the difficulties are more understandable if not solvable. Difficulties and distinct purposes aside, both Matthew and Luke affirm Jesus's Abrahamic and Davidic ancestry as well as his miraculous conception by the virgin Mary.

Another area of theological concern is the respective purposes of the genealogies in their literary contexts. Matthew uses his genealogy primarily for christological purposes, to demonstrate the Abrahamic and Davidic ancestry of Jesus the Messiah while showing him to be the fulfillment of God's promises. Additionally the presence of the women, who are evidently Gentiles, hints at Matthew's agenda for universal mission to all the nations.

The situation is quite different with Luke's genealogy, which occurs not at the beginning of his Gospel but between his accounts of Jesus's baptism and temptation. It seems significant that both the baptism pericope that precedes the genealogy and the temptation pericope that follows it stress the divine sonship of Jesus. At the baptism the Father affirms this unique sonship (Luke 3:22), and at the temptation the devil unsuccessfully tests it (4:3, 9). The genealogy, tracing Jesus's ancestry back to Adam and indeed to God (3:38), leads one to the same conclusion: Jesus is the Son of God. The first Adam was also a son of God, but he failed under satanic testing. Endued with the Spirit (3:22; 4:1, 14, 18), the second Adam is victorious over Satan. Thus at the beginning of his ministry Jesus is viewed as the representative person for all human beings (Marshall 1978: 161). Luke, like Matthew, mentions Abraham and David, but Luke's purpose is not to relate Jesus to Abraham and David. Rather, it is to relate all mankind to the God of Abraham, of David, and, preeminently, of Jesus (Bock 1994: 348, 60).

Christology

Matthew uses the Hebrew Bible to demonstrate to his readers that the person, ministry, and teaching of Jesus are rooted in the history, ethics, and prophecies of Israel's Scriptures. The following major titles or descriptions of Jesus are presented in the order in which one encounters them in Matthew.[29]

Messiah/Christ. Jesus is called "the Messiah" in the very first verse of Matthew, at the end of the genealogy (Matt. 1:16–17), and at the beginning of the description of the circumstances of his birth (1:18). This cluster of references to Jesus as the Messiah strongly links Jesus to Israel's history and hopes. It is certainly the key to the identity of Jesus in Matthew. A messiah is literally one anointed by God for special service or office (1 Sam. 9:15–16; 10:1; 16:3, 12–13; Exod. 28:41; 1 Chron. 29:22; Isa. 45:1). Most significantly for Matthew, the term occurs as a royal title in some biblical texts (1 Sam. 24:6; 2 Sam. 1:14; Ps. 2:2). But the Christian notion of a lowly, suffering, eventually crucified Messiah was evidently foreign to the Judaism of Jesus's day. Even John the Baptist had doubts about whether Jesus was the Messiah (Matt. 11:2–3), but through divine revelation Peter was enabled to affirm it strongly (16:16). Jesus then told (16:20) the disciples not to tell others that he was the Messiah, evidently to forestall the growing opposition to his ministry.

Another cluster of references stressing Jesus as Messiah occurs in Matthew's description of the passion week in Jerusalem. Jesus's clashes with the religious leaders culminate in an episode that stresses his Davidic messianic connections (22:41–42). Contrasting his own view of spirituality with that of the religious leaders, Jesus affirms that no one except the Messiah should be called "master" (23:10). In his answer to the disciples' question about the signs of his return, Jesus warns them not to believe in counterfeit messiahs (24:23–26). At his hearing before the Jewish council, Jesus's affirmative answer to the high priest's question as to whether he is the Messiah takes the language of Dan. 7:13 (Matt. 26:63–64), but this only leads to mockery (26:68). Later, when he offers to release Barabbas (27:17, 22), Pilate alludes to the fact that some call Jesus Messiah.

In Matthew the Messiah is crucified, but he is raised and given all authority (28:18), an allusion to Dan. 7:13–14 that recalls Jesus's use of the

---

29. For additional studies, see Carson in Rowdon 1982: 97–114; France 1989: 279–317; Hill 1980, 1984, 1986; Kingsbury 1981; 1984; 1985; M. Müller 1999; Quesnel 1991.

language of that text in Matt. 26:64. It is this exalted Messiah who sends the disciples out to disciple the nations. Perhaps the key to Matthew's distinct view of Jesus as Messiah is the linkage of "Messiah" to "Son of God" in two key passages (16:16; 26:63–64). This will be discussed below under the heading "Son of God."

Son of David. This title occurs more frequently in Matthew than in the other Gospels. Matthew identifies Jesus as the son of David immediately after identifying him as the Messiah in 1:1, and Matthew quickly establishes and emphasizes Jesus's Davidic lineage in the infancy narrative (1:6, 17, 20). Subsequent uses of the title occur on the lips of those who call on Jesus to heal them (9:27; 15:22; 20:30–31). On another occasion a healing leads the crowds to wonder whether Jesus is the son of David, the Messiah (12:23). Here one title seems to be tantamount to the other. The texts that connect Jesus's Davidic lineage with healing demonstrate that Jesus uses his royal authority to help, not to oppress, the needy. At Jesus's triumphal entry (21:9), the crowd shouts praise to God for Jesus the son of David, echoing the language of Ps. 118:25–26. Later that day Jesus's acceptance of this praise becomes the occasion for the religious leaders' indignation against Jesus (21:15). When the conflict between Jesus and the religious leaders escalates during the passion week, Jesus's final disputation with those leaders is cast in terms of the identity of the Messiah as the son of David. Jesus cites Ps. 110:1 to the effect that David's son is also David's Lord (22:41–45), asserting that the son of David is also the Son of God. Matthew's use of the son-of-David motif stresses Jesus's messianic credentials to heal and to rule. This stress seems to be rooted in such biblical texts as 2 Sam. 7:14–16; Pss. 2; 89; Isa. 9:6–7; 11:1–5; Jer. 23:5–6. Jesus as the Davidic Messiah inherits the promises God made to David and brings God's rule to bear upon Israel. (See Duling 1978; 1992; J. M. Gibbs 1963–64; Levin 2006; Loader 1982; Novakovic 1997; 2003; Paffenroth 1999.)

Son of Abraham. Jesus's title "son of Abraham" occurs immediately after his identification as the Messiah, the son of David, in 1:1. In itself the title evidently does not have messianic implications. The ensuing genealogy stresses this Abrahamic lineage in 1:2, 17 not simply to show Jesus's Jewish roots but also to portray Jesus as the one who culminates God's plans that originated in Abraham. One should also note John the Baptist's warning that the Pharisees and Sadducees who came to his baptism should not rely on their Abrahamic origins (3:9). For John, repentance, not descent from Abraham, was required to avoid the coming judgment (3:8–10). This theme is furthered by Jesus's response to the remarkable faith of the Roman officer (8:10–12). Gentiles like this officer (not Jews like the leaders who came to John) would share in the great eschatological banquet with Abraham, Isaac, and Jacob. Again, ethics, not ethnicity, is the issue. It is not that Matthew was excluding Jews as a whole from God's eschatological blessings but that Matthew was stressing the need of all humans, Jew and Gentile alike, to believe in Jesus. Matthew's mentions of Abraham remind us of God's call of Abraham, the promise that in Abraham all nations would be blessed (Gen. 12), and the near sacrifice of Abraham's only son (Gen. 22). Evidently, the promise to Abraham would not be totally fulfilled in the present world, because Jesus took this promise to imply that there would be a resurrection of the dead (Matt. 22:32; cf. Exod. 3:6).

Immanuel. The significance of Jesus as "God with us" is developed through the citation of Isa. 7:14 in Matt. 1:23 (cf. Isa. 8:8, 10). This crucial passage looms large in Christian theology of the virgin birth (actually conception) of Jesus. Matthew's closing portrayal of Jesus's promise to be with the disciples until the end of the age (Matt. 28:20) forms a literary *inclusio* with 1:23, in which the presence of God in the person of Jesus is stressed at both the beginning and the end of the narrative. Another instance of this motif is 18:20. (See Kupp 1996.)

King. The arrival of the wise men in Matt. 2 in search of the newborn King of Israel sets in motion a story of conflict between God's true ruler and the evil pretender Herod. Matthew understands Jesus's triumphal entry into Jerusalem near the end of his life as the act of a king (21:5), since he cites Isa. 62:11 to this effect. Jesus's prediction of future judgment portrays him as the enthroned Son of Man (Matt. 25:31), a King who separates the blessed from the cursed (25:34, 40–41). Later, at his hearing before Pilate, Jesus accepts Pilate's question as a true statement of his kingship (27:11). Then he endures the soldiers' mocking use of the title (27:29) and Pilate's evidently sarcastic reference to it on the signboard placed over his head on the cross (27:37). Even the religious leaders mock Jesus's kingship (27:42), but after his resurrection he is given all authority and sends his apostles out into the world as their exalted king (28:18; cf. 26:64; Dan. 7:13–14).

Son of God. Some scholars argue that "Son of God" is the preeminent title of Jesus in Matthew (Kingsbury 1989: 89; cf. Hill 1980 for a response). With such biblical texts as Pss. 2:7; 89:27 as likely background, Matthew presents Jesus as the virginally conceived Son who uniquely signifies the presence of God with his people (Matt. 1:23; cf. Isa. 7:14; J. M. Gibbs 1968; Nolland 1996b). Jesus's sojourn in Egypt recapitulates the history of Israel (Matt. 2:15; cf. Hos. 11:1). At his baptism, Jesus is endorsed as the Father's beloved Son and endowed with the Spirit for ministry (Matt. 3:17; cf. Isa. 42:1). Soon Satan challenges this endorsement when Jesus is led by the Spirit into the wilderness, but by relying on the Scriptures, Jesus is enabled to vanquish Satan and victoriously recapitulates Israel's wilderness wanderings (Matt. 4:3, 6). He does not succumb to the temptation to manifest his unique sonship by spectacular acts. Rather, he shows divine sonship by submission to the will of the Father.

Jesus's divine sonship is also shown in Matthew through his authority over evil spirits and the weather (8:29; 14:33). Only the Father and the

Son, who is the sole agent through whom people may come to know the Father (11:27), share this authority. This is recognized by Jesus's apostles, who through Peter acknowledge that he is "the Messiah, the Son of the living God" (16:16). This linkage of the titles "Messiah" and "Son of God" is quite significant, although Peter still has much to learn about divine sonship as submission to the Father (16:22–23). Soon afterward Jesus's transfiguration demonstrates to his disciples that as God's Son, his word alone must be heeded.

As Jesus's conflict with the religious leaders worsens, Matthew portrays through parabolic imagery the religious leaders' rejection of God's unique Son (21:33–41; 22:2–14). At the end of their disputes, Jesus's allusion to Ps. 110:1 indicates, to their chagrin, that his sonship is both Davidic and divine (22:45). At Jesus's trial before the high priest, Caiaphas asks him whether he is "the Messiah, the Son of God," echoing ironically the testimony of Peter (26:63; cf. 16:16). Jesus's reply ominously cites the words of Dan. 7:13 about the coming of the Son of Man. The irony continues at Jesus's crucifixion, where the mockery of the criminals and the religious leaders contrasts with the confession of the Roman soldiers—both the mockers and the confessors refer to Jesus's claim to be the Son of God (27:40, 43, 54). (See Mowery 1990, 2002; Verseput 1987.)

Lord. Matthew uses the title "Lord" for Jesus against the background of its use in Greco-Roman times, ranging from a polite greeting of a human superior (like "sir" in English) to a term for the Roman emperor, who was thought to be divine. The term occurs about six thousand times in the LXX as a translation of the Hebrew *Yahweh*, the sacred Tetragrammaton, the name of God. Matthew is not at all hesitant to apply the term "Lord" (*kyrios*) to Jesus. Matthew 3:3 cites Isa. 40:3, applying to Jesus a passage originally referring to Yahweh. In Matt. 7:21–22 (cf. 25:37, 44), Jesus is addressed as "Lord" in his capacity as eschatological judge. Frequently those desiring to be healed address Jesus as Lord (8:2, 6, 8; 15:22, 25, 27; 17:15; 20:30–31, 33), as do the disciples (8:21, 25; 14:28, 30; 16:22; 17:4; 18:21; 26:22).

At times Jesus calls himself Lord, as when he warns his disciples that if he as their Lord is called prince of demons, it will be worse for them as his servants (10:24–25). Jesus expresses his authority over Sabbath law by referring to himself as Lord of the Sabbath (12:8). He describes himself as Lord when he sends the disciples to obtain a donkey and its colt for the triumphal entry into Jerusalem, instructing them to tell objectors, "the Lord needs them" (21:3). He describes his return as the coming of the Lord (24:42).

The ambiguity of the term "Lord" means that we must carefully look at each of its usages in context. At times it carries contextual overtones of Jesus's divinity, but at other times it is merely a respectful way of addressing Jesus.

Teacher. In Matthew the disciples never call Jesus "teacher." Rather, this term is nearly always reserved for addresses to Jesus by those who do not follow him, such as the teachers of religious law, the Pharisees, the tax collectors, the supporters of Herod, and the Sadducees (8:19; 9:11; 12:38; 17:24; 19:16; 22:16, 24). On three occasions, Jesus calls himself teacher (10:24–25; 23:8; 26:18), so it must be noted that, for Matthew, there is nothing necessarily sinister in the use of the term. But for Matthew, Jesus is so much more than a teacher that those who refer to him this way are guilty of damning him with faint praise.

Son of Man. The Gospels use this expression more that any other to refer to Jesus, and it is found with only one exception (John 12:34, in response to a saying of Jesus) in sayings ascribed to Jesus. The expression appears more than one hundred times in the Hebrew Bible, more than ninety times in Ezekiel alone. It most often describes frail, finite humanity in contrast to the awesomeness of God and often occurs in synonymous parallelism with "man" (e.g., Num. 23:19; Ps. 8:4). It is the term used throughout Ezekiel when God addresses Ezekiel (cf. Dan. 8:17).

Matthew uses "Son of Man" thirty times, but with three primary nuances. First, "Son of Man" occurs in passages that stress Jesus's suffering and humility. As Son of Man, he has no place to lay his head (Matt. 8:20), he is called a drunk and a glutton (11:19), and he will be in the heart of the earth for three days and nights (12:40). While he is on earth, people think he is merely a prophet (16:13–14), and the story of his glorious transfiguration will not be told until after his resurrection (17:9). He will be mistreated and suffer just like John the Baptist (17:12), even to the extent of being betrayed by a close associate (17:22; 20:18; 26:2, 24, 45). Despite this treatment, he will serve others and give his life as a ransom for many (20:28; cf. the textually dubious 18:11). The biblical background for this use of the term seems to be the many passages that employ it to describe humanity in general and a prophet in particular.

Second, "Son of Man" occurs in certain passages that stress Jesus's present power and authority. Thus he has authority on earth to forgive the paralytic's sins, and Jesus heals him in order to demonstrate this authority (9:6). He is the Lord of the Sabbath (12:8), and yet his authority is so controversial that he is slandered by his enemies (12:32). His ministry plants the seed of the authoritative kingdom message (13:37).

Third, the term occurs in passages that focus on Jesus as the glorious coming King. He will send his angels to remove sinners from his kingdom (13:41) as he comes in the glory of his Father to judge all people (10:23?; 16:27–28; 24:27, 30, 37, 39; 25:31; 26:64). At the time of his glorious kingdom, his followers will also be abundantly rewarded (19:28), but they must first be on constant alert for his unexpected return (24:44).

The background for the second and third uses of the term to stress Jesus's present authority and glorious return is no doubt Dan. 7:13, to which Jesus alludes in Matt. 26:64. The context of Dan. 7:13 includes a judgment scene in which God, pictured as the "Ancient of Days," delivers the rule of the earth to the son of man, who with his people prevails over his enemies and rules the earth. There are also overtones of Dan. 7:13–14 in the language of the Great Commission, Matt. 28:18–20. This duality of present and future nuances, referring to both the authority exercised by Jesus during his earthly ministry and the glorious authority he will exercise at his return, is crucial for one's understanding of Matthew's "kingdom of heaven."[30]

Additional titles. Matthew applies other, less significant titles to Jesus. Among them are "shepherd" (2:6; 9:36; 25:32; 26:31), "bridegroom" (9:15; 25:1), "the coming one" (11:2; 21:9; 23:39), "servant" (12:18; cf. Isa. 42:1), "prophet" (13:57; 16:14; 21:11, 46; cf. Deut. 18:15), "stone" (21:42–44; cf. Ps. 118:22–23; Dan. 2:44–45), and "rabbi" (26:25, 49).

Kingdom of Heaven

The kingdom of God/heaven is undoubtedly at the center of the message of Matthew.[31] It is a complex matter, and this discussion will summarize only (1) the use of "kingdom," (2) the relationship of the kingdom of heaven and the kingdom of God, and (3) the presence and future of the kingdom.

The kingdom in Matthew. The expression "kingdom of heaven" is literally "the kingdom of the heavens" (ἡ βασιλεία τῶν οὐρανῶν, *hē basileia tōn ouranōn*). This expression occurs thirty-two times in Matthew and nowhere else in the NT (3:2; 4:17; 5:3, 10, 19 [2x], 20; 7:21; 8:11; 10:7; 11:11, 12; 13:11, 24, 31, 33, 44, 45, 47, 52; 16:19; 18:1, 3, 4, 23; 19:12, 14, 23; 20:1; 22:2; 23:13; 25:1).[32] Matthew also uses the more common expression "kingdom of God," ἡ βασιλεία τοῦ θεοῦ (*hē basileia tou theou*) four or five times, depending on which text is followed (6:33 *Byz*; 12:28; 19:24; 21:31, 43). It is difficult to grasp why Matthew uses "kingdom of God" in these texts instead of "kingdom of heaven."

The word "kingdom" occurs nineteen other times in Matthew. Two of these instances refer to human kingdoms (4:8; 24:7), and two refer to Satan's kingdom (12:25, 26). The remaining fifteen refer to the kingdom of God. Of this group, eight use the word βασιλεία absolutely, that is, without grammatical modifiers (4:23; 6:33, though there are modifiers

---

30. On Jesus as Son of Man, see BDAG 1026–27; M. Black 1969; Caragounis 1986; M. Casey 1979, 1987; A. Collins 1987; J. Collins 1992; Coppens 1981, 1983; Donahue 1974; Geist 1986; Häfner 1994; Hampel 1990; Higgins 1980; Kim 1983; Lindars 1983; Luz 1992b; Martin de Viviés 1995; Marshall 1994; Pamment 1983; Tödt 1965; Vermes 1978; Wink 2002.

31. See M. Bailey 1999a; Beasley-Murray 1986; Beasley-Murray in Green and Turner 1994: 22–36; Caragounis in Green and McKnight 1992: 417–30; Carter 1997a; Chilton 1984; France 1990; Mowery 1994; Pamment 1980–81; Perrin 1963; Ridderbos 1962; J. Thomas 1993; du Toit 2000; and W. Willis 1987, esp. Farmer, 119–30.

32. Some MSS include a second occurrence of the term in 7:21. If this variant is accepted as authentic, the total number of occurrences increases to thirty-three.

in variant readings; 8:12; 9:35; 13:19, 38; 24:14; 25:34). Four texts use βασιλεία with nouns or pronouns refering to the Father (6:10, 13 *Byz*; 13:43; 26:29), and three with nouns or pronouns referring to Jesus (13:41; 16:28; 20:21). In addition to speaking sometimes of the kingdom as the Father's or Jesus's, these texts also speak significantly of the gospel or word of the kingdom (4:23; 9:35; 13:19; 24:14) and of those who respond to this message as the sons of the kingdom (8:12; 13:38).

The word βασιλεύς (*basileus*, king) occurs twenty-two times in Matthew. In eight instances the word describes human kings, one referring to David (1:6), three referring to Herod (2:1, 3, 9) and four referring to others (10:18; 11:8; 14:9; 17:25). The other fourteen instances refer to the Father or to Jesus. The Father is in view six times: 5:35 (alluding to Ps. 48:2); 18:23; 22:2, 7, 11, 13 (in Jesus's parables). Jesus is described as King eight times: at birth (2:2), at the triumphal entry (21:5; citing Zech. 9:9), at the Son of Man's return and judgment of the nations (25:34, 40), and in connection with the trial and crucifixion (27:11, 29, 37, 42). In addition, the references to Jesus as the son of David have regal overtones (1:1, 6, 16, 17, 20; 9:27; 12:3, 23; 15:22; 20:30, 31; 21:9, 15; 22:42–43, 45).

Matthew's use of kingdom terminology occurs in several important connections in his gospel. The kingdom is at the heart of John's, Jesus's, and the church's proclamations (3:2; 4:17; 10:7; 13:19; 24:14). Jesus's miracles demonstrate the authority of the kingdom (4:23–25; 8:9–13; 9:6–8; 12:28; 20:30–34). His teaching on the ethical life of disciples prominently features the kingdom (5:3, 10, 19, 20; 6:10, 33; 7:21). His parables picture the work of the kingdom in redemptive history (13:11, 19, 24, 31, 33, 38, 43–45, 47, 52; 18:23; 22:2; 25:1). As King, he judges the world (25:34, 40).

The kingdom of heaven and the kingdom of God. Although Matthew occasionally speaks of the "kingdom of God" (12:28; 19:24; 21:31, 43), his unique term "kingdom of heaven" occurs thirty-two times. Occasionally scholars argue that there is a distinction between the kingdom of heaven and the kingdom of God (e.g., Pamment 1980–81). Dispensationalists have frequently promoted this distinction, although not all dispensationalists support it (e.g., Toussaint 1980: 65–68; Toussaint in Toussaint and Dyer 1986: 23). The *Scofield Reference Bible* (Scofield 1909: 1003) posits five distinctions between the kingdom of heaven and the kingdom of God. In this view, the kingdom of heaven is mediatorial but the kingdom of God is universal. The kingdom of heaven is the realm of outward profession, but the kingdom of God is entered only by internal regeneration (cf. Walvoord 1974: 30). The kingdom of heaven merges into the kingdom of God at Christ's return. This view of the kingdom of heaven as the sphere of external profession separates the kingdom of heaven from the church. It also effects the interpretation of Jesus's parables of the kingdom in Matt. 13. Dispensationalists often view the leaven and the mustard seed (13:31–33) as symbols of evil within the sphere of profession rather than as symbols of genuine growth in God's work on earth (Gaebelein 1910: 282–93; Kelly 1911: 280–84; Scofield 1909: 1016; Toussaint 1980: 181–82; Walvoord 1974: 101–4).

The purported distinction between "kingdom of God" and "kingdom of heaven," is untenable for at least three reasons. First, Matt. 19:23–24 uses both expressions in a synonymous fashion. Second, a comparison of parallel synoptic texts indicates that Matthew often uses the expression "kingdom of heaven" when Mark and/or Luke use the expression kingdom of God (compare, e.g., Matt. 13:31 with Mark 4:30; Matt. 19:14 with Mark 10:14 and Luke 18:16). Third, Matthew's terminology is likely due to the association of heaven as God's realm with God himself (cf. the prominence of this association in Dan. 2:18–19, 28, 37, 44; 4:34–35, 37; 5:23; 12:17; Pennington 2003). Such an association is called metonymy, and it is likely occasioned by reverence for the name of God in Matthew's Christian Jewish community (cf. Luke 15:18, 21). Matthew's four kingdom-of-God texts are probably just stylistic variations for literary purposes.

The distinction of "kingdom of heaven" as the sphere of external profession versus "kingdom of God" as the realm of genuine spirituality is flatly contradicted by Matt. 5:20; 7:21; 18:3–4. This major supposed distinction is, then, untenable. Additionally, despite various arguments to the contrary, there is ample evidence that the kingdom of heaven and the kingdom of God are identical. This evidence can be drawn from synoptic parallels and from the use of the word "heaven" as a semantic substitution for the word "God." First the evidence from the synoptic parallels.

The word βασιλεία (basileia, kingdom) occurs fifty-five times in Matthew if the variant reading in 6:13 is included. It occurs twenty times in Mark, forty-six times in Luke, and four times in John (3:3, 5; 18:36 [2x]). The following table displays the use of βασιλεία in Matthew, showing any synoptic parallels to Matthew's usages. When only the reference appears, it signifies ἡ βασιλεία τῶν οὐρανῶν in Matthew (thirty-three times, counting the variant reading at 7:21) or ἡ βασιλεία τοῦ θεοῦ in Mark or Luke. Brief explanations accompany other references.

The Use of βασιλεία in Matthew

Matthew	Mark	Luke
3:2		
4:8: "all the kingdoms" + τοῦ κόσμου (tou kosmou, of the world)		4:5: "all the kingdoms" + τῆς οἰκουμένης (tēs oikoumenēs, of the world)

Matthew	Mark	Luke
4:17	1:15	
4:23: "gospel of the kingdom"		
5:3		6:20
5:10		
5:19 (2x)		
5:20		
6:10: "your kingdom"		11:2: "your kingdom"
6:13 v.l.: "the kingdom"		
6:33: "the kingdom (of God [v.l.])"		12:31: "his kingdom"
7:21		
7:21 v.l.		
8:11		13:29
8:12: "sons of the kingdom"		
9:35: "gospel of the kingdom"		8:1: "gospel of the kingdom of God"
10:7		9:2
11:11		7:28
11:12		16:16
12:25: "every kingdom"	3:24: "a kingdom"	11:17: "every kingdom"
12:26: "his kingdom"		11:18: "his kingdom"
12:28: "kingdom of God"		11:20: "kingdom of God"
13:11	4:11	8:10
13:19: "the word of the kingdom"		
13:24	4:26	
13:31	4:30	13:18
13:33		13:20
13:38: "sons of the kingdom"		
13:41: "his kingdom"		
13:43: "their father's kingdom"		
13:44		
13:45		
13:47		
13:52		
16:19		
16:28: "his kingdom"	9:1: "kingdom of God"	9:27: "kingdom of God"
18:1		
18:3		

Matthew	Mark	Luke
18:4		
18:23		
19:12		
19:14	10:14	18:16
19:23	10:23	18:24
19:24: "kingdom of God"	10:25: "kingdom of God"	18:25: "kingdom of God"
20:1		
20:21: "your kingdom"	10:37: "your glory"	
21:31: "kingdom of God"		
21:43: "kingdom of God"		
22:2		
23:13		
24:7: "kingdom against kingdom"	13:8: "kingdom against kingdom"	21:10: "kingdom against kingdom"
24:14: "the gospel of the kingdom"		
25:1		
25:34: "the kingdom"		
26:29: "my Father's kingdom"	14:25: "kingdom of God"	22:16: "kingdom of God"

Note: Other Markan kingdom texts are 6:23; 9:47; 10:15; 11:10; 12:34; 15:43. Other Lukan kingdom texts are 1:33; 4:43; 9:11, 60, 62; 10:9, 11; 12:32; 13:29; 14:15; 17:20 (2x), 21; 18:17, 29; 19:11, 12, 15; 21:31; 22:18, 29, 30; 23:42, 51.

From this table, we can conclude that twenty-nine of Matthew's fifty-six kingdom texts have no parallel in Mark or Luke. Thirty-three of these fifty-six kingdom texts are kingdom-of-heaven texts. Of these, twenty-one are not paralleled by kingdom-of-God texts in the other Gospels. Of the twelve that are paralleled, two occur in Mark alone, six occur in Luke alone, and four occur in Mark and Luke combined. Thus it is clear that in multiple passages Matthew's "kingdom of heaven" is Mark's and Luke's "kingdom of God." In these passages Matthew portrays Jesus as speaking of the "kingdom of heaven" where Mark and Luke portray him as speaking of the "kingdom of God." Additionally, Matt. 19:23–24 uses the two terms synonymously. This would certainly indicate that "kingdom of heaven" in Matthew should not be viewed as substantially different from "kingdom of God" in the other Gospels. The concept does not differ; only the expression does. Why the difference in expression?

"Kingdom of heaven" in Matthew is usually explained as a circumlocution that avoids mentioning the name of God by containing a word that is readily associated with God. This would fit with Matthew's Christian

Jewish audience, since it would reflect special piety for the divine name (see G. Howard 1977: 63–83). In this metonymy, God's abode (see, e.g., Dan. 2:19, 28, 37, 44; 4:26, 31, 37; 5:23; 6:27) is substituted for God's person or name. The metonymy can be found elsewhere in the Bible (e.g., Dan. 4:26; Luke 15:18, 21) and is natural for Matthew's thought. He frequently speaks of the "Father in heaven" (5:16, 45, 48; 6:1, 9; 7:11, 21; 10:32, 33; 12:50; 16:17; 18:10, 14, 19; 23:9). At times "from heaven" or "in heaven" seems to mean "from God" or "in God" (3:17; 5:12, 34; 6:20; 16:1, 19; 18:18; 21:25; 23:22). So the expression "kingdom of heaven" is part of a general pattern centering on Matthew's conception of the earth as humanity's abode and the heavens as the abode of God and God's angels (18:10; 22:30; 24:30–31; see Pennington 2003). Eschatological hope in Matthew includes heaven's rule coming to earth (6:10; 11:25; 28:18). Additional explanation for "kingdom of heaven" in Matthew is offered by Carson (1984: 100–101), Gundry (1994: 43), and Schweizer (1975: 47). They suggest that Matthew uses "kingdom of heaven" to allow room for both the Father and Jesus as King, but this is overly subtle and unnecessary in view of the fact that Matthew speaks elsewhere of both the Father and the Son as King.

One final matter needs to be addressed: Matthew's four (five?) kingdom-of-God texts (6:33 v.l.; 12:28; 19:24; 21:31, 43). If avoidance of the divine name causes him to speak of the "kingdom of heaven," why does he ever speak of the "kingdom of God"? Perhaps "kingdom of God" is used in 12:28 because of the previous mention of the Spirit of God in the verse. It would seem from 19:23–24 that Matthew saw no problem with using the two terms together as synonyms, and so perhaps he was not overly scrupulous about avoiding God's name. The Matthean kingdom-of-God texts are not readily explained as some sort of special emphasis. W. Davies and Allison (1988: 391–92) conclude that this is merely a stylistic variation, and this seems to be the better part of wisdom on the question.

The presence and/or future of the kingdom. The question of the presence and future of the kingdom is closely tied to the question of its nature. It seems that a kingdom requires a ruler, those who are ruled, the exercise of that rule, and a realm in which the rule occurs. Those who prefer to think of the kingdom as present focus on the dynamic "rule" aspect of a kingdom whereas those who prefer to think of it as future focus on the concrete "realm" aspect. The modern debate in its larger context has been between advocates of "consistent eschatology" (*konsequente Eschatologie*) and "realized eschatology." As advocated by J. Weiss, A. Schweitzer, and current exponents, consistent eschatology holds that Jesus was a prophet who predicted imminent apocalyptic catastrophe that would usher in the reign of God. In this view, then, the kingdom of God is future. On the other hand, realized eschatology (Dodd 1961) tends to view Jesus as a teacher of ethics whose ministry inaugurated the kingdom on earth, where it will always be. In American evangelical circles a similar debate occurs between dispensationalists, who tend to think of the kingdom as the future millennium on earth, and amillennialists, who tend to think of the kingdom as the present rule of Christ within believers through the Spirit. But these are not mutually exclusive categories.

Ladd (1974) puts to rest any notion that the kingdom is only present or only future. He demonstrates that a comprenhensive treatment of the kingdom can only conclude that it is both present and future, and nearly all contemporary NT scholars agree.[33] Although some would still argue that the kingdom of God is exclusively present (e.g., Crossan 1973) or future (e.g., Toussaint in Toussaint and Dyer 1986), their positions are exegetically dubious. The use of βασιλεία (*basileia*) in the NT as well as the use of מַלְכוּת (*malkût*, rule, dominion) in the Hebrew Bible connotes dynamic rule more than concrete realm, although the two concepts should not be separated. Insistence that the kingdom is essentially a concrete realm leads inevitably to viewing it as strictly future as well, and this will not do in Matthew. John, Jesus, and the disciples announce the dawning of the kingdom (3:2; 4:17; 10:7). Those who repent at this message of God's rule already possess the kingdom (5:3, 10). The royal power of God is dynamically present in Jesus's words and works (esp. Matt. 12:28). The church is endowed with this dynamic power for ministry through its confession of Jesus as the Son of God (16:18–19; 28:18–20).

But this stress on the kingdom as the present dynamic rule of God exists alongside eschatological hope for a full manifestation of God's rule on earth (6:10). Those who have already experienced the kingdom's power (5:3, 10) will someday receive it in full measure (5:3–9). In the meantime their quest is for a greater approximation of kingdom righteousness on earth (6:33). At the return of Jesus the Son of Man, the entire world will come under God's rule (7:21–23; 25:31, 34). So it is not that the kingdom does not involve a concrete realm. It is, rather, that the kingdom exists as a microcosm today and as a macrocosm when Jesus returns. Today the rule of God is shown in the lives of believers individually and corporately and as they relate to the world. In that day God's rule will be extended to all mankind in judgment or redemption.

Generally, the kingdom of heaven refers to the nearness or even presence of the rule of God in the person, works, and teaching of Jesus (3:2; 4:17; 10:7; 11:12; cf. 12:28), but there are times when it implies (5:19; 7:21; 13:24, 47; 25:1) or clearly describes (8:11; cf. 6:10; 13:38–43; 25:34; 26:29) the future reign of Jesus upon the earth. Perhaps the best way to describe the dynamic nature of God's reign is to say that it has been inaugurated at Jesus's first coming and will be consummated when he returns.

---

33. For helpful discussions of Jesus's teaching about the kingdom and for additional bibliography, see Allison 1985b; Beasley-Murray 1986; Caragounis in Green and McKnight 1992: 417–30; and W. Willis 1987.

Matthew characterizes the preaching of Jesus, John, and the apostles as being centered on the kingdom (3:2; 4:17; 10:7). References to the present experience of the kingdom (Matt. 5:3, 10) frame the Beatitudes, which otherwise speak of future kingdom blessings. Jesus's kingdom includes a radical righteousness greater than that of the legal experts (5:19–20); it requires disciples to seek it first, before their daily needs (6:33). Even John's greatness as a prophet of the kingdom is eclipsed by the least one who experiences eschatological kingdom realities (11:11–12). The parables of the kingdom in Matt. 13 present figuratively the preaching of the kingdom and responses to it, and the keys of Matt. 16:19 further symbolize its authority. Entrance into this kingdom requires childlike humility (18:3–4; 19:14), and the unknown time of its future arrival mandates constant alertness (25:1–13).

Conflict over Authority

The key motif in Matthew that moves the plot and portrays the struggles (cf. Matt. 11:12) involved in the advance of the kingdom is conflict. The outset of Matthew's story includes conflict between Herod the Great and the infant Messiah just born in Bethlehem (Matt. 2). Divine intervention preserves Jesus, but the male babies in Bethlehem perish. As John announces Jesus, conflict arises between John and the religious leaders over genuine righteousness (3:7–12). Later John's prophetic denunciation of Herod Antipas's illegal marriage to the former wife of his brother results in his imprisonment and grisly execution (14:1–12), and Jesus likens the treatment he receives to that of John (17:12). Satan himself tries to tempt Jesus to gratify his human needs and accomplish his messianic mission in ways that are disobedient to the Father (4:1–11).

Once Jesus's public ministry begins, his teaching about righteousness in the Sermon on the Mount clashes with that of the religious leaders (5:20–6:18), and the people are quick to pick up on the contrast (7:28–29). This leads to further, more intense controversies about the forgiveness of sins (9:1–8) and Jesus's association with sinners (9:9–13). His ministry of exorcism leads to the Pharisees' charges that he is collaborating with the devil (9:34; 12:22–32). Soon he must warn his followers that much opposition will attend their ministries (10:16–42; cf. 24:9). Many of the people who hear Jesus's teaching and see his miracles do not repent and follow him, and he denounces them for their unbelief (11:16–24). The rules of Sabbath observance occasion a heated dispute (12:1–14), after which skeptical religious leaders with evil motives ask Jesus for a sign (12:38–42; cf. 16:1–4). Jesus's parables of the kingdom of heaven also speak of conflict engendered by varying responses to the message of the kingdom (13:19–21, 38–39). Even the people in his own synagogue in Nazareth do not believe in his message (13:53–58). Jesus's teaching about inner purity clashes with the Pharisaic tradition of ritual purity through the washing of hands before meals (15:1–20; cf. 16:5–12). Later, as he moves toward Jerusalem, he debates the matter of divorce with the Pharisees, contrasting their relatively liberal view of it with his own stricter view based on God's original design for marriage (19:3–9).

When Jesus enters Jerusalem, the conflict enters its most intense phase. The Jerusalem leaders are offended at the crowds who shout Ps. 118:25–26 during the entry and at Jesus's cleansing of the temple (21:8–17). Matthew's narrative then presents a conflict over the source of Jesus's authority (21:23–27). This leads to Jesus's confrontation with the leaders over their refusal to recognize his authority (21:28–44), and they wish to arrest him (21:45–46). Additional conflicts occur in Matt. 22, leading to Jesus's indictment of the leaders (23:1–12) and his pronouncement of woes upon them (23:13–36). All that remains is for them to plan (26:3–5) and carry out his arrest (26:47–56), trials (26:57–68; 27:11–26), and crucifixion (27:32–44). Even the resurrection of Jesus does not end the enmity: the religious leaders conspire with the Roman soldiers to spread the lie that Jesus's disciples stole his body from the tomb, a lie that still circulated when Matthew wrote his Gospel (28:11–15).

Why did these controversies with the religious leaders occur? Jesus claimed that his mission was not to destroy the law and the prophets but to fulfill them. His interpretations of the Bible conflicted with those of the religious leaders, who were committed to the oral traditions that had been passed on to them from previous teachers. And so it came down to this: Who was the authoritative interpreter of Moses, Jesus or the religious leaders? For Matthew and his Christian Jewish community, Jesus's teaching about the law of Moses (halakah) was authoritative, and this brought his followers into conflict with the leaders of the synagogues with which they continued for a time to be associated. This commentary assumes that Matthew's community was still associated with the synagogues at the time the Gospel was written.[34]

Anti-Semitism? Does Matthew's emphasis on the conflict between Jesus and the religious leaders contain and incite anti-Semitism? There can be no doubt that Christian anti-Semites have used Matthew to promote their agenda. But this was certainly not Matthew's purpose. Most likely Matthew was a Jew and was writing to Jews who believed that Jesus was the Jewish Messiah. These Christian Jews were evidently in a heated religious conflict with non-Christian Jews, but sectarian conflict was common during the time of Second Temple Judaism. No doubt Matthew's agenda was to refute the non-Christian Judaism of the Jewish establishment, whether Matthew is placed before or after the 70 CE destruction of Jerusalem and whether that establishment was the Jerusalem lead-

34. On the conflict in Matthew and between early Christianity and formative Judaism, see Deutsch 1992; Dunn 1991, 1992; Freyne 1988b; Horbury 1982, 1998; Hultgren 1979; Kingsbury 1987a; Pantle-Schieber 1989; Repschinski 2000; Saldarini 1992b; Saldarini in L. Levine 1992: 23–38; Saldarini in Balch 1991: 38–61; Saldarini 1995, 1997; Vledder 1997.

ers whom Jesus opposed or the protorabbinic movement that evidently came to be centered in Jabneh (Jamnia) after 70 CE. The situation was a religious dispute between Jews, not a gentile polemic against the Jewish race. Christians must acknowledge with shame the fact that anti-Semites have misused Matthew, but it is anachronistic to interpret Matthew as a (gentile) Christian polemic against the Jewish race.[35]

The Church and Gentile World Mission

The Gospel of Matthew, though often and truly described as the most Jewish of the Gospels, is also the only Gospel to use the word "church" (*ekklēsia*, 16:18; 18:17). As in Dan. 7, so in Matthew, the Son of Man has his community of saints, which confesses his identity and maintains its own unity. We can glean the identity of this community by reading Matthew from the beginning and noting the hints dropped by Matthew concerning the type of people who are followers of Jesus. Or we can ascertain it by taking note of the final triumphant commission Jesus leaves with his disciples (Matt. 28:18–20).

From the beginning Matthew makes it clear that the community of the Messiah is formed from unexpected sources. The mention of Tamar, Rahab, Ruth, and Bathsheba (1:3, 5, 6), all evidently Gentiles with overtones of scandal in their backgrounds, prepares the reader for Jesus's association with the sinners of his own day. The inexplicable arrival of the mysterious wise men from the east who wish to worship Jesus (2:1–12) augurs the power of the message of the kingdom to summon followers in surprising ways. Jesus's amazement at the faith of the Roman officer (8:10–12) and his acknowledgement of the faith of the Canaanite woman (15:28) encourage the readers of this Gospel to believe that the message of the kingdom is able to engender faith from unlikely sources in their own day. The Roman soldier's amazed confirmation of Jesus's true identity at the crucifixion (27:54) has a similar effect. All of these episodes from the narrative collectively influence Matthew's original Jewish readers to expand their vision of the people of God. It is not that they are to abandon their fellow Jews, but the message of the kingdom must be taken to *"all* the nations" (28:19; cf. Schnabel in Green and Turner 1994: 37–58; J. J. Scott 1990; Sim 1995; Smillie 2002).

Jesus's final commission of his disciples is based on his now exalted status. Having received all power, he sends the Eleven to all the nations to make disciples who will obey all his commands, and he arms them with the promise that he will be with them all the days until the end of

35. On Matthew and anti-Judaism, see Broer 1996; Burnett 1992; M. Cook 1983a, 1983b; Freyne in Neusner and Frerichs 1985: 117–44; Garland 1979; Ingelaere 1995; L. Johnson 1989; A.-J. Levine, P. Shuler, and W. Carter in Farmer 1999: 9–62; Luz 1992a; Marguerat 1995; McKnight in C. A. Evans and Hagner 1993: 55–79; Niedner 1989; Pawlikowski 1989; Przybylski 1986: 181–200; Russell 1982, 1986, 1989; Russell in Aune 2001: 166–84; Saldarini in Aune 2001: 166–84; Sandmel 1978: 49–70; H.-F. Weiss 2001.

the age (28:18–20). The universal scope of this commission is daunting, but it can be accomplished if the disciples remember that their Messiah, like the victorious son of man in Dan. 7, has received universal authority (Tisera 1993). As they complete the arduous task of teaching future disciples to obey all of Jesus's commands, he will constantly be with them until the end.[36]

Outline

I. Prologue/introduction: Origin of Jesus the Messiah (1:1–2:23)
  A. Title and genealogy of Jesus the Messiah (1:1–17)
  B. Birth of Jesus the Messiah (1:18–25)
  C. Visit of the magi (2:1–12)
  D. Escape to Egypt (2:13–15)
  E. Massacre at Bethlehem (2:16–18)
  F. Return to Nazareth (2:19–23)
II. Early days of kingdom word and deed (3:1–7:29)
  A. Narrative 1: John and Jesus and the kingdom of God (3:1–4:25)
    1. Ministry of John the Baptist (3:1–12)
    2. Baptism of Jesus (3:13–17)
    3. Testing of the Son of God (4:1–11)
    4. Withdrawal to Galilee (4:12–17)
    5. Calling four fishermen (4:18–22)
    6. Summary of the early ministry (4:23–25)
  B. Discourse 1: Sermon on the Mount (5:1–7:29)
    1. God's approval: The Beatitudes (5:1–16)
    2. Jesus and the Bible (5:17–48)
    3. Religious duties (6:1–18)
    4. Kingdom values: God or money? (6:19–34)
    5. Dealing with people (7:1–6)
    6. Prayer encouraged (7:7–11)
    7. Summary of biblical ethics (7:12)
    8. Exhortation and warning: True and false religion contrasted (7:13–27)
    9. Narrative conclusion: Amazement at Jesus's authority (7:28–29)
III. Galilean ministry continues (8:1–11:1)
  A. Narrative 2: Three cycles of miracles and discipleship (8:1–10:4)
    1. Cycle 1: Three healing miracles and two would-be disciples (8:1–22)
      a. Three healing miracles (8:1–17)

---

36. On mission in Matthew, see S. Brown 1977, 1980; Hare and Harrington 1975; LaGrand 1995; A.-J. Levine 1988; Schnabel in J. Green and Turner 1994: 37–58; 2004.

       b. The accompanying teaching on discipleship (8:18–22)

    2. Cycle 2: More miracles with a focus on discipleship (8:23–9:17)

       a. The three miracles (8:23–9:8)

       b. The focus on discipleship (9:9–17)

    3. Cycle 3: Additional miracles with a focus on mission (9:18–10:4)

  B. Discourse 2: Mission and suffering (10:5–11:1)

    1. The commission proper (10:5–8)

    2. Instructions on support (10:9–15)

    3. Warnings about opposition to the mission (10:16–39)

    4. The reward for supporting the mission (10:40–11:1)

IV. Growing opposition to the kingdom of heaven (11:2–13:52)

  A. Narrative 3: Three cycles of unbelief and belief (11:2–12:50)

    1. Cycle 1: Jesus and John rejected (11:2–30)

       a. The identity of Jesus and John (11:2–19)

       b. Jesus denounces unrepentant cities (11:20–24)

       c. Gracious revelation in the midst of opposition (11:25–30)

    2. Cycle 2: Sabbath conflicts and Jesus's response (12:1–21)

       a. Picking and eating grain (12:1–8)

       b. Healing in the synagogue (12:9–14)

       c. The servant's response to escalating opposition (12:15–21)

    3. Cycle 3: Confrontation with the Pharisees (12:22–50)

       a. The unforgivable sin (12:22–37)

       b. Some legal experts and Pharisees ask for a sign (12:38–45)

       c. The true family of Jesus (12:46–50)

  B. Discourse 3: Parables of the kingdom of heaven (13:1–52)

    1. Parables to the crowds (13:1–35)

    2. Parables to the disciples (13:36–52)

V. Opposition to the kingdom continues (13:53–19:2)

  A. Narrative 4: Various responses to the Son of God (13:53–17:27)

    1. Rejection in Nazareth (13:53–58)

    2. Herod the tetrarch, Jesus, and the death of John the Baptist (14:1–12)

    3. Jesus feeds the five thousand (14:13–21)

    4. Jesus walks on the water (14:22–33)

    5. Jesus heals many at Gennesaret (14:34–36)

    6. Conflict over the tradition of the elders (15:1–20)

    7. Exorcism of the Canaanite woman's daughter (15:21–28)

    8. Another miracle meal (15:29–39)

    9. The second request for a sign (16:1–4)

10. Warning against the Pharisees and Sadducees (16:5–12)
11. Peter's confession and Jesus's promise (16:13–20)
12. Jesus's suffering and a model of discipleship (16:21–28)
13. The transfiguration and its aftermath (17:1–13)
14. An epileptic boy healed (17:14–21)
15. The second passion prediction (17:22–23)
16. The question about the temple tax (17:24–27)
B. Discourse 4: Values and relationships in the kingdom community (18:1–19:2)
   1. Humility and the value of the little ones (18:1–14)
     a. Authentic spiritual greatness (18:1–5)
     b. Warnings against causing believers to sin (18:6–9)
     c. Parable of the lost sheep (18:10–14)
   2. Rebuke and forgiveness in the community (18:15–35)
     a. Rebuking a fellow disciple who sins (18:15–20)
     b. The necessity of forgiveness (18:21–35)
   3. Narrative conclusion (19:1–2)
VI. Opposition comes to a head in Judea (19:3–26:2)
A. Narrative 5: Ministry in Judea (19:3–23:39)
   1. Family values and sacrificial service (19:3–20:34)
     a. Marriage and divorce, singleness, and children (19:3–15)
     b. Wealth and the kingdom: Three conversations on sacrificial discipleship (19:16–20:16)
       i. The conversation with the wealthy young man (19:16–22)
       ii. The conversation with the disciples (19:23–26)
       iii. The conversation with Peter (19:27–20:16)
     c. The third passion prediction (20:17–19)
     d. A dispute over greatness in the kingdom (20:20–28)
     e. Jesus heals two blind men (20:29–34)
   2. Approaching Jerusalem: The triumphal entry (21:1–11)
   3. Cleansing and controversy in the temple (21:12–17)
   4. Cursing the fig tree (21:18–22)
   5. Increasing controversy with the leaders in the temple (21:23–22:46)
     a. Three questions about authority (21:23–32)
     b. Parable of the tenant farmers (21:33–46)
     c. Parable of the wedding feast (22:1–14)
     d. The Pharisees' question: Paying taxes to Caesar (22:15–22)
     e. The Sadducees' question: Marriage in the resurrection (22:23–33)
     f. The Pharisee lawyer's question: The greatest commandment (22:34–40)

g. Jesus questions the Pharisees: David's son is David's Lord (22:41–46)
6. Warnings to the disciples and woes to the Pharisees (23:1–39)
a. Warning the disciples (23:1–12)
b. Denouncing the Pharisees (23:13–36)
c. Conclusion: Jesus's lament over Jerusalem (23:37–39)
B. Discourse 5: Judgment of Jerusalem and the coming of Christ (24:1–26:2)
1. Narrative introduction: A question while leaving the temple (24:1–3)
2. The discourse proper (24:4–25:46)
a. Exposition: What will happen (24:4–35)
   i. The beginning of birth pains (24:4–14)
   ii. The abomination of desolation (24:15–28)
   iii. The coming of the Son of Man (24:29–31)
   iv. Parable of the fig tree (24:32–35)
b. An exhortation to alertness (24:36–25:46)
   i. Comparison to the days of Noah (24:36–42)
   ii. Parable of the thief (24:43–44)
   iii. The faithful and the evil slave (24:45–51)
   iv. Parable of the wise and the foolish virgins (25:1–13)
   v. Parable of the talents (25:14–30)
   vi. The final judgment (25:31–46)
3. Narrative conclusion and the fourth passion prediction (26:1–2)
VII. Epilogue/conclusion: Passion, resurrection, and commission (26:3–28:20)
A. Preliminary events and preparation of the disciples (26:3–46)
1. The plot to kill Jesus (26:3–5)
2. Anointing at Bethany (26:6–13)
3. Judas agrees to betray Jesus (26:14–16)
4. The Last/Lord's Supper (26:17–30)
5. The disciples' denial predicted (26:31–35)
6. Deep distress in Gethsemane (26:36–46)
B. Arrest and trial (26:47–27:26)
1. The arrest of Jesus (26:47–56)
2. Jesus appears before the Sanhedrin (26:57–68)
3. Peter's three denials (26:69–75)
4. The Sanhedrin's formal decision (27:1–2)
5. The remorse and suicide of Judas (27:3–10)
6. Jesus appears before Pilate (27:11–26)
C. Crucifixion (27:27–56)
1. Jesus is mocked and led away to Golgotha (27:27–32)
2. Jesus is crucified (27:33–37)

3. Mockery by observers (27:38–44)

4. The death of Jesus (27:45–56)

D. Burial of Jesus (27:57–66)

1. Joseph of Arimathea buries Jesus (27:57–61)

2. Jewish and Roman leaders secure the tomb (27:62–66)

E. Resurrection of Jesus (28:1–15)

1. Mary Magdalene and another Mary encounter the angel (28:1–7)

2. Jesus appears to the women (28:8–10)

3. The "cover-up" (28:11–15)

F. Commission by the risen Lord (28:16–20)

➤ I. Prologue/Introduction: Origin of Jesus the Messiah (1:1–2:23)
II. Early Days of Kingdom Word and Deed (3:1–7:29)
III. Galilean Ministry Continues (8:1–11:1)
IV. Growing Opposition to the Kingdom of Heaven (11:2–13:52)

I. Prologue/Introduction: Origin of Jesus the Messiah (1:1–2:23)

Matthew's infancy narrative begins with a title (1:1), which refers primarily to 1:2–25 but secondarily to themes found throughout the Gospel. Following this title are the genealogy (1:2–17), the birth of Jesus (1:18–25), the visit of the magi (2:1–12), the sojourn in Egypt (2:13–15), the massacre of the children (2:16–18), and the return to Nazareth (2:19–23). The literary structure and theological import of this material are matters of no little discussion.

In his influential study *"Quis et unde?"* (reprinted in Stanton 1995: 69–80), K. Stendahl argues that Matt. 1–2 explains who Jesus is and whence he comes. Matthew 1 demonstrates Jesus's identity as the Messiah, son of David and son of Abraham, who will save his people from their sins. Matthew 2 focuses on geography in order to draw theological implications, such as Jesus's Davidic connections (born in Bethlehem). R. Brown (1993: 50–54), adapting and expanding Stendahl's work, presents the following analysis:

Quis (Who?) Jesus's identity as son of David, son of Abraham (1:1–17)

Quomodo (How?) Jesus is son of David through virginal conception by the Holy Spirit and by adoption into a Davidic family (1:18–25)

Ubi (Where?) Jesus the son of David is born in David's city, Bethlehem, yet as son of Abraham he is visited by the gentile magi (2:1–12)

Unde (Whence?) Opposition to Jesus the son of David from King Herod leads him from Bethlehem through Egypt to Nazareth (2:13–23)

Both of these studies are quite helpful in unfolding the literary structure and theological motifs of Matt. 1–2. However one outlines this material, several motifs must be noted. Matthew 1 and 2 both end with Jesus receiving a "name," "Immanuel" in 1:23 and "Nazarene" in 2:23. It is also clear that each pericope in Matt. 1–2 contains a biblical citation (Matt. 1:23/Isa. 7:14; Matt. 2:6/Mic. 5:2; Matt. 2:15/Hos. 11:1; Matt. 2:18/Jer. 31:15; Matt. 2:23/Isa. 11:1?). For Matthew, Jesus is the one in whom biblical messianic promises and patterns are fulfilled. The biblical citations in Matt. 2 all contain geographical themes: Bethlehem, Egypt, Ramah, and Nazareth. Angelic dream appearances to Joseph recur (1:20; 2:13, 19), and two pericopes stressing Herod's hostility (2:1–12, 16–18) are interspersed among these three dream appearances. The following analysis is adapted from R. Brown (1993: 53–54):

Jesus the Messiah is David's and Abraham's son

Genealogy: Jesus the Messiah culminates Israel's history (Matt. 1:2–17)

> *Dream 1:* Jesus is Immanuel. His virginal conception fulfills Isa. 7:14 (Matt. 1:18–25)

Magi: In David's city, Bethlehem, Jesus fulfills Mic. 5:2 and is shown to be Abraham's son by blessing Gentiles in spite of hostile, deceptive King Herod (Matt. 2:1–12)

> *Dream 2:* Jesus, God's Son, recapitulates the exodus, fulfilling Hos. 11:1 (Matt. 2:13–15)

Massacre: King Herod murders the boys of Bethlehem, fulfilling Jer. 31:15 (Matt. 2:16–18)

> *Dream 3:* Jesus moves to Nazareth, again fulfilling biblical prophecies (Matt. 2:19–23)[1]

---

1. Additional studies of Matthew's infancy narrative include France in France and Wenham 1981: 239–66; Freed 2001; Hultgren 1997; Kingsbury in Aune 2001: 154–65; Schaberg 1997; Weaver 2000.

I. Prologue/Introduction: Origin of Jesus the Messiah (1:1–2:23)
➤ A. Title and Genealogy of Jesus the Messiah (1:1–17)
    B. Birth of Jesus the Messiah (1:18–25)
    C. Visit of the Magi (2:1–12)

A. Title and Genealogy of Jesus the Messiah (1:1–17)

It is obvious even to the casual reader that each of the four Gospels has a unique beginning. Mark commences in the most concise fashion and places the reader at the outset of Jesus's ministry by 1:9. Luke commences with a carefully crafted preface, which links his Gospel to previous narratives and traditions (Luke 1:1–4; Bock 1994: 51–67). Matthew and Luke alone contain material about Jesus's infancy and early years, but this material seldom overlaps. John's unique prologue (John 1:1–18) concerning the "Word" (λόγος, *logos*) who became flesh sets the tone for many of the themes of John's Gospel. All four Gospels, however, stress the preparatory ministry of John the Baptist before they launch into the ministry of Jesus.

Matthew's story of the origin of Jesus begins with a title (1:1) and a genealogy (Matt. 1:2–17; cf. Luke 3:23–38). The title stresses Jesus's connection to the archetypal patriarch, Abraham, and to King David. Both Abraham and David received covenantal promises from God that Matthew views as culminating in Jesus, who will reign over Israel and extend God's blessings to all the nations (cf. Gen. 12:1–3; 2 Sam. 7:8–16). The genealogy also prominently features David (Matt. 1:6, 17). Matthew makes it clear in a summary (1:17) that he structures his genealogy into three sections of fourteen generations (1:2–6a, 6b–11, 12–16). It seems clear from this structure that Matthew views the history of Israel as being fulfilled through Jesus, Abraham's and David's son, in whom Israel finds both relief from the judgment of the exile and renewal of the promises made to the ancestors.

The unit can be outlined as follows:

1. Title (1:1)
2. Genealogy of Jesus the Messiah (1:2–17)

Exegesis and Exposition

[1]An account of the origin of Jesus the Messiah, the son of David, the son of Abraham:

[2]Abraham was the father of Isaac,
and Isaac was the father of Jacob,
and Jacob was the father of Judah and his brothers,

[3]and Judah was the father of Perez and Zerah, whose mother was Tamar,
and Perez was the father of Hezron,
and Hezron was the father of Ram,
[4]and Ram was the father of Amminadab,
and Amminadab was the father of Nahshon,
and Nahshon was the father of Salmon,
[5]and Salmon was the father of Boaz, whose mother was Rahab,
and Boaz was the father of Obed, whose mother was Ruth,
and Obed was the father of Jesse,
[6]and Jesse was the father of King David.

David was the father of Solomon, whose mother had been Uriah's wife,
[7]and Solomon was the father of Rehoboam,
and Rehoboam was the father of Abijah,
and Abijah was the father of ⌜Asaph⌝,
[8]and ⌜Asaph⌝ was the father of Jehoshaphat,
and Jehoshaphat was the father of Joram,
and Joram was the father of Uzziah,
[9]and Uzziah was the father of Jotham,
and Jotham was the father of Ahaz,
and Ahaz was the father of Hezekiah,
[10]and Hezekiah was the father of Manasseh,
and Manasseh was the father of ⌜Amos⌝,
and ⌜Amos⌝ was the father of Josiah,
[11]and Josiah was the father of ⌜ ⌝ Jeconiah and his brothers at the time of
the exile to Babylon.

[12]After the exile to Babylon, Jeconiah was the father of Shealtiel,
and Shealtiel was the father of Zerubbabel,
[13]and Zerubbabel was the father of Abiud,
and Abiud was the father of Eliakim,
and Eliakim was the father of Azor,
[14]and Azor was the father of Zadok,
and Zadok was the father of Achim,
and Achim was the father of Eliud,
[15]and Eliud was the father of Eleazar,
and Eleazar was the father of Matthan,
and Matthan was the father of Jacob,
[16]and Jacob was the father of Joseph, ⌜the husband of Mary, from whom was
born Jesus⌝ who is called the Messiah.

[17]So there were fourteen generations from Abraham to David,
and fourteen generations from David to the exile to Babylon,
and fourteen generations from the exile to Babylon to the Messiah.

1. Title (1:1)

1:1 This verse provides a sort of title for what follows, but for how much of what follows? Matthew's account or record (βίβλος, *biblos*; BDAG 176) of Jesus's origin or beginnings (γένεσις, *genesis*; BDAG 192; Nolland 1996c) may be intended to headline (1) just the genealogy (Nolland 2005: 71), (2) the genealogy and virgin birth narrative that follows, (3) the entire account of Jesus's origin and early years in Nazareth, (4) all of the above and also John's ministry and Jesus's baptism and temptation, or (5) even the entire Gospel. If γένεσις is translated narrowly as "genealogy," only 1:2–17 is characterized as the record of Jesus's origin, but then it is hard to explain the occurrence of γένεσις again in 1:18, describing the miraculous details of Jesus's birth. Thus it seems that at least 1:1–25 should be viewed as the account of Jesus's beginnings. Blomberg (1992a: 52), Carson (1984: 61), and others wish to extend this from 1:1 to 2:23, but this depends on whether the contents of 2:1–23 qualify as a record of Jesus's origin or birth.

W. Davies and Allison (1988: 150) argue from the LXX usage of the expression βίβλος γενέσεως (*biblos geneseōs*, Gen. 2:4; 5:1) that this is the title for Matthew's entire book. They point out that the LXX most frequently uses a different formula, "these are the generations" (αὗται αἱ γενέσεις, *hautai hai geneseis*), to introduce genealogies (e.g., Gen. 6:9; 10:1; 11:10, 27; 25:12, 19; 36:1, 9; 37:2; Num. 3:1), and that the term βίβλος most naturally refers to a "book," not merely a portion of it. Additionally, they note that the first book of the Bible was already known as Genesis in the first century CE, and that Matthew seems to view Jesus as a new beginning of God's creation (cf. Nolland 1996a). Thus they interpret 1:1 as "Book of the New Genesis wrought by Jesus Christ, Son of David, Son of Abraham" (W. Davies and Allison 1988: 153; cf. Allison 2005b: 157–62).

When Matthew is read as a literary whole, it is clear that the terminology of 1:1 is indicative of themes to be developed extensively throughout the entire book. Thus, from a literary-theological standpoint, it is difficult to limit the title to the genealogy (Waetjen 1976). Matthew's emphasis on Jesus the Messiah as son of Abraham and of David is not limited to the genealogy. This literary continuity may provide a basis for Fenton's view (1963: 36) that the title has a "telescopic" reference not only to Jesus's early days but also to his entire ministry as the historical demonstration of the implications of his miraculous birth. Although this is true, the account of Jesus's origin (1:2–25) is primarily in view. (These matters are discussed at some length in Bourke 1960; Krentz 1964; and Milton 1962.)

Whereas the word "Jesus" (see the discussion at 1:21) is no doubt meant to be viewed as a personal name, Χριστός (*Christos*, Christ; 1:1, 16, 17, 18; 2:4; 11:2; 16:16, 20; 22:42; 23:10; 24:5, 23; 26:63, 68; 27:17, 22) should be viewed as a title that indicates Jesus's supreme role and office in God's plan. Both Χριστός and its Hebrew equivalent, מָשִׁיחַ (*māšîaḥ*, Messiah), are related to the ceremony of anointing a king or priest for office in recognition of God's approval (Exod. 28:41; 1 Sam. 9:15–16; 10:1; 16:3, 12–13; 1 Chron. 29:22). In some biblical passages the term "the lord's anointed" is a title for the divinely endorsed king (1 Sam. 24:6; 2 Sam. 1:14; Ps. 2:2; Dan. 9:24?). During intertestamental times messianic speculation flourished as Israel reflected on the prophetic hope of a restored Davidic monarchy. Messianic hope was tied to Israel's longing for God's eschatological vindication and Israel's resulting freedom from gentile domination. In Matthew, Χριστός is a key christological title that portrays Jesus as the one who fulfills the biblical-historical pattern and eschatological hope. (For additional discussion of this title and bibliography, see Hurtado in Green and McKnight 1992: 106–17.)

When "Christ" is joined with "the son of David, the son of Abraham," Jesus's messianic status is even more strongly stressed. "Son of David" is frequently a messianic title (Matt. 1:1, 6, 17, 20; 9:27; 12:23; 15:22; 20:30, 31; 21:9, 15; 22:42, 45; cf. Rom. 1:3), drawing from such biblical material as 2 Sam. 7:11–16; Ps. 91; Jer. 23:5; 33:15. "Son of Abraham" occurs in Matthew only in 1:1, but Abraham is mentioned elsewhere (1:2, 17; 3:9; 8:11; 22:32; cf. 4 Macc. 6:17, 22; 18:1) as the prototypical Israelite whose eminent status in God's kingdom is unquestionable. This close connection of Jesus with Abraham, along with John's and Jesus's severance of the religious leaders from any connection with Abraham (Matt. 3:9; 8:11), coheres well with the Pauline emphasis on Christians as the genuine children of Abraham (Rom. 4:9–17; Gal. 3:6–14, 29). Perhaps Matthew's stress on Gentiles (e.g., Matt. 2:1; 4:15; 8:5; 15:22; 27:54) implies that in Jesus the promise is fulfilled that all nations would be blessed through Abraham (Gen. 12:1–3). In any event, Jesus is positioned here as the representative of Israel, the epitome of Israel's history (Keener 1999: 74).[1]

2. Genealogy of Jesus the Messiah (1:2–17)

After mentioning the Messiah, David, and Abraham in his title (1:1), Matthew continues chiastically in his genealogy to mention Abraham (1:2), David (1:6), and the Messiah (1:16). The structure of the geneal-

---

1. The biblical-theological foundation of Matthew's Christology is presented in just a few words here. The sonship of Jesus as Χριστός is a major theme in Matthew. Jesus is the son of Mary (1:21, 23, 25; 13:55), and legally he is the son of Joseph (13:55) and the son of David through Joseph (1:1, 20; 9:27; 12:23; 15:22; 20:30, 31; 21:9, 15; 22:42, 45). He is the son of Abraham (1:1), the Son of God (2:15; 3:17; 4:3, 6; 8:29; 14:33; 16:16; 17:5; 21:37–38; 22:2; 26:63; 27:40, 43, 54), the Son of Man (8:20; 9:6; 10:23; 11:19; 12:8, 32, 40; 13:37, 41; 16:13, 27, 28; 17:9, 12, 22; 18:11; 19:28; 20:18, 28; 24:27, 30, 37, 44; 25:13, 31; 26:2, 24, 45, 64; cf. Dan. 7:13), and simply "the Son" (11:27; 28:19). For a discussion, see Kingsbury 1989: 40–127.

ogy is made clear by its summary in 1:17. It traces fourteen generations from Abraham to David, fourteen generations from David to the exile in Babylon, and fourteen generations from the exile to the Messiah. Modern readers should beware a tendency to dismiss the genealogy as a boring, irrelevant way to begin a book about Jesus. If Jesus is to be the Messiah, he must be connected to David and Abraham as 1:1 affirms, and the genealogy develops this connection (Overman 1996:29–31). It is clear from 1:17 and from a comparison with Luke 3:23–38, however, that this genealogy is not an exhaustive or chronologically exact record of Jesus's family tree. Although genuine historical information is provided, the purpose is primarily theological, not chronological.

The three sections of the genealogy pivot on King David and the exile to Babylon. David represents one of the highest points of the biblical narrative, and the exile represents one of the lowest. It is likely that in Jesus the son of David, Matthew sees one who will restore a new Israel from an exile even more deplorable than the Babylonian exile. Matthew has evidently chosen fourteen generations to structure his genealogy because David is the fourteenth name in the genealogy and fourteen is the numerical value of "David" in Hebrew. Consonantally, דוד (dwd) is 4 (d) + 6 (w) + 4 (d) when the places of the consonants in the numerical order of the Hebrew alphabet are added together. This gematria, which assigns numerical values to letters, stresses the centrality of David in Jesus's background as well as the centrality of great David's greater son, Jesus, for Matthew's readers.[2]

The aorist active verb ἐγέννησεν (egennēsen, begot, was the father of) occurs thirty-nine times in 1:2–16 before the abrupt shift to the aorist passive form ἐγεννήθη (egennēthē, was born) in 1:16, describing Jesus's birth. Although Matthew purports to list three sets of fourteen generations, ἐγέννησεν occurs fourteen times only in the second set (1:6b–11). It occurs thirteen times in the first set (1:2–6a) and twelve times in the third (1:12–16). Evidently, Matthew realized that he had omitted some names from the genealogy and wished ἐγέννησεν in these cases to be understood as "was the ancestor of," not "was the father of." This would be in keeping with biblical precedent where ancestors were sometimes called "fathers."

Departures from the simple "A was the father of B" pattern occur in several places. In 1:2 the phrase "and his brothers" is added to "Jacob was the father of Judah." This reference to Judah's brothers seems to be well explained as an allusion to the twelve tribes who form the locus of the people of God and the pattern for the twelve apostles (Carson 1984: 65; cf. 8:11; 19:28). In 1:3 Zerah is mentioned along with his twin, Perez. In 1:3, 5, 6 the genealogy unconventionally includes the women

2. See Hagner 1993: 6–7 for arguments against the Davidic gematria view and discussion of other approaches to the prominence of the number fourteen in the genealogy.

Tamar, Rahab, Ruth, and Bathsheba, although the latter is mentioned as "the one who had been Uriah's wife" instead of by her name.[3] In 1:6, where David is described as "king," there is again stress on his centrality. In 1:11 there is a reference to the brothers of Jeconiah and to the time frame of the Babylonian exile. Evidently, Jeconiah had only one brother, Zedekiah (1 Chron. 3:16), so this reference may be to his cousins or to the other Jews who accompanied Jeconiah to Babylon. The most obvious and important break from the "*A* was the father of *B*" pattern is found in 1:16, where the switch from an active to a passive verb occurs in describing the birth of Jesus.[4]

a. From Abraham to King David (1:2–6a)

It is important to read 1:2 in light of 1:1. Mention of Abraham concludes 1:1 and begins 1:2, initiating the chiasmus that continues with David (1:6) and the Messiah (1:16). Abraham stands at a decisive point, the origin of the nation of Israel (Gen. 12:1–3), and is also at the root of the new people of God (3:9; 8:11). Genesis 12–50 comprises the biblical patriarchal narrative alluded to here. Judah's prominence among his brothers is due to the fact that his tribe bears the scepter (Gen. 49:10; cf. Matt. 2:6; Heb. 7:14). In view of Matthew's willingness to mention women later, it is noteworthy that the matriarchs of Israel are not mentioned here alongside the patriarchs.

1:2

In 1:3–6 Matthew may be drawing from 1 Chron. 2:3–15 and Ruth 4:18–22. See Hendriksen (1973:111–13) for a helpful chart of the biblical background of the genealogy. Tamar, the wife of Judah's son Er, is the first woman mentioned in the genealogy. Genesis 38:6–30 relates the story of her incestuous liaison with her father-in-law, Judah, after he failed to fulfill his obligation to provide a levirate husband for her.

1:3–4

Rahab is well known to readers of the Bible (Josh. 2:1–21; 6:17, 22–25; Heb. 11:31; James 2:25). According to Josh. 2, Rahab the prostitute of Jericho protected the Israelite spies because of her fear of the God of Israel. Her family was spared from the destruction of that city and lived among the Israelites. The Bible does not otherwise indicate that Rahab married Salmon and was the mother of Boaz. There are chronological

1:5–6a

---

3. In 1:6 the prepositional phrase ἐκ τῆς τοῦ Οὐρίου is an example of what BDF §162 calls "the genitive of origin and relationship" to "identify a wife by her husband." In the genealogy, Matthew consistently expresses the agency of the mothers with ἐκ (1:3, 5, 6, 16). BDAG 296 indicates that ἐκ may express male agency in conception as well. Cf. 1:18, 20; 3:9; 19:12.

4. See the introduction to this commentary for a discussion of the lack of precision in the use of the number fourteen, the purpose of mentioning the women, and the differences from Luke's genealogy. See also Abel 1973–74; S. Brown 1977: 57–95; C. Davis 1973; M. Johnson 1988; J. Jones 1994; Nettelhorst 1988; Nineham 1975–76; Ostmeyer 2000; Van Elderen in Vardaman and Yamauchi 1989: 3–14; Waetjen 1976; and R. Wilson 1977.

problems if Rahab was the immediate mother of Boaz; perhaps all that is implied is that Rahab was a female ancestor of Boaz. The story of Ruth the Moabitess coming to Bethlehem with her mother-in-law, Naomi, and marrying Boaz is told in the book of Ruth. Ruth 4:18–22 is likely a source of Matt. 1:3b–6. If so, it is instructive to note Matthew's addition of the names Rahab and Ruth as well as the description of David as king, which likely anticipates the description of Jesus as Messiah.

b. From David to the Exile (1:6b–11)

1:6b–11   "The one who had been Uriah's wife" is a curious way to refer to Bathsheba. Perhaps it is a euphemism, or perhaps it calls attention to David's sin in having Uriah killed in battle. More likely it hints that Solomon's mother was a Gentile (since Uriah was a Hittite). Second Samuel 11–12 relates the sad story of Bathsheba's adultery with David, the ensuing intrigue and death of her husband, Uriah, the death of her son by David, and finally the birth of Solomon. With the mention of Bathsheba, Matthew has now included in Jesus's genealogy the names of four women, all of whom were evidently Gentiles with somewhat tawdry pasts. The names of the men in 1:7–10 are evidently drawn from 1 Chron. 3:10–14. A comparison of 1:8 with biblical passages (2 Kings 8:24; 1 Chron. 3:11; 2 Chron. 22:1, 11; 24:27) indicates that Matthew has omitted Ahaziah, Joash, and Amaziah between Joram and Uzziah. With the mention of the exile in Matt. 1:11, 1:6b–11 has covered both the beginning and the seeming end of David's line (cf. Nolland 1997b).[5]

c. From the Exile to Jesus the Messiah (1:12–16)

1:12–15   The final set of "fourteen" generations moves from the abyss of the exile to the apex of the Messiah. A comparison of 1:12 with 1 Chron. 3:19 uncovers a difficulty: was Shealtiel (Matthew) or his brother Pedaiah (Chronicles) the father of Zerubbabel? Other biblical texts agree with Matthew against 1 Chronicles (Ezra 3:2, 8; 5:2; Neh. 12:1; Hag. 1:1, 12, 14; 2:2, 23). Perhaps the solution is that Shealtiel died and Pedaiah entered a levirate marriage with Shealtiel's widow to raise up children for his brother. The nine names from Abiud to Jacob in 1:13–15 evidently span a time period of about five hundred years, but none of them is mentioned in the Hebrew Bible.

1:16   The line of Jesus from prototypical Abraham through royal David now comes down to unpretentious Joseph. In 1:18–2:23 Joseph's obedient care for his adopted son is stressed, but here in 1:16 he is described only as

---

5. When used with the genitive, the preposition ἐπί may mean "at the time of" (BDAG 367). The word μετοικεσία occurs only here (1:11, 12, 17) in the NT, although it is also used in the LXX to describe the exile to Babylon (2 Kings 24:16; 1 Chron. 5:22; Ezek. 12:11). BDF §166 views Βαβυλῶνος as a genitive of direction ("to Babylon").

Mary's husband. His brief appearance in Matthew underlines his modeling of obedience and his Davidic descent even as a humble carpenter (1:16, 18, 19, 20, 24; 2:13, 19; 13:55). His wife, Mary, is not mentioned frequently either (1:16, 18, 20, 24; 2:11–13; 12:46–50; 13:55). At this point the chain of thirty-nine occurrences of the active verb ἐγέννησεν (egennēsen, was the father of) is broken by the passive ἐγεννήθη (egennēthē, was born), and "we encounter the biggest surprise of the genealogy" (Hagner 1993: 12). The passive seems to imply the divine activity made clear in 1:18–25.[6] The prepositional phrase ἐξ ἧς (ex hēs, from whom) strengthens this implication, since the relative pronoun ἧς is feminine in gender. Thus it is already stated that Joseph was not the biological father of Jesus—he did not "beget" Jesus. Jesus was born from Mary in the supernatural manner about to be explained in 1:18–25.

d. Summary (1:17)

As noted previously, this verse provides the structure for the genealogy and reveals its theological implications. The conjunction οὖν (oun, then, therefore) introduces the summary as an inference to be drawn from 1:2–16. In the "fourteen" generations from Abraham to King David, Matthew demonstrates Jesus's sonship and aligns Jesus as Messiah with the historical outworking of the promise of God. In the "fourteen" generations from David to the exile, Matthew recounts the decline of Israel under the judgment of God. And in the "fourteen" generations from the exile to the Messiah, Matthew traces the faithful purpose of God in fulfilling his promise despite the rebellion of his people. Bruner's suggestion (1987: 4) that the genealogy may be visualized as a leaning capital *N* is helpful in laying out the structure and theological implications of the genealogy.

1:17

This summary of the genealogy underlines its crucial turning points: Abraham to David, David to the exile to Babylon, and the exile to the Messiah. Matthew organizes the material under the number fourteen, which is argued above to be a gematria for David. Some scholars (e.g., Hendriksen 1973: 110) think that Matthew chose fourteen because it is twice seven, the number of fullness or perfection. In this view, there are six sets of seven generations, and the Messiah inaugurates the seventh seven.

Bruner (1987: 19) is no doubt correct that the genealogy is not a simple historical list but a work of theological craftsmanship. Nevertheless his assertion (1987: 14–17) that Matthew has made errors in the genealogy is debatable. It can be argued that Matthew made errors only if it can be demonstrated that Matthew intended to construct a comprehensive and exhaustive genealogy. Matthew's "errors" are theologically motivated

6. For discussion of the "divine passive" in Greek grammar, see Wallace 1996: 437–38. This understated way of referring to God is sometimes called the "theological passive."

omissions, not mistakes in simple arithmetic. Matthew could evidently count to fourteen as well as his interpreters can.

Additional Notes

1:7–8, 10. The names Asaph and Amos both have textual variants, which are discussed in Metzger 1994: 1–2. In both cases the more ancient Egyptian MSS support the names as given above, but the more numerous though relatively recent Byzantine text and other MSS support the names Asa and Amon. Some assume that Matthew erred by confusing the psalmist Asaph (Pss. 50; 73–83) with king Asa or that Matthew's source contained this error. Some MSS of 1 Chron. 3:14 LXX do read Amos, not Amon, and this may account for the textual variant in 1:10. Gundry 1994: 15 believes that for subtle theological reasons Matthew intentionally used the wrong spelling. Others assume an early scribal error in the transmission of Matthew's text. There is some evidence for Carson's point that ancient spelling conventions were not as strict as modern standards (1984: 69–70). In any case, Matthew certainly knew the difference between the psalmist Asaph and the king Asa. Borland's attempt (1982: 501–3) to uncover an anti-inerrancy conspiracy here is misguided.

1:11. In 1:11, several of the later uncials and minuscules have Joachim as the son of Josiah and father of Jeconiah. This variant evidently was motivated by the desire to conform Matthew's genealogy to that of 1 Chron. 3:15–16 (Metzger 1994: 2). The external evidence for the insertion of Joachim is weak in comparison with that supporting the shorter reading, which includes early uncials, the Byzantine text, the Vulgate, and other ancient versions. Additionally the insertion is suspect from the standpoint of internal evidence because it amounts to a fifteenth generation in the second section of the genealogy.

1:16. This theologically crucial verse has some textual variants, which are discussed at length in Metzger 1972; 1994: 2–7. Nearly all the Greek MSS as well as the early versions support the reading reflected in the translation that begins this unit, to the effect that Joseph was Mary's husband and that Jesus was born through Mary. This reading is an abrupt shift from the pattern of the genealogy in 1:2–16a and is certainly implicit support for Matthew's high Christology; Jesus is not merely the natural son of Joseph. Two other principal variant readings exist. Some Caesarean text Greek MSS and Old Latin MSS read, "Jacob was the father of Joseph, to whom being engaged, the virgin Mary bore Jesus, who is called Messiah." External support for this reading is weak, and it seems to inject information from 1:18–25 back into the genealogy. More controversial is the reading of the Sinaitic Syriac MS: "Jacob was the father of Joseph; Joseph, to whom was engaged the virgin Mary, was the father of Jesus who is called the Messiah." This reading conceivably allows for a denial of the virgin birth, but this is debatable, since Mary is still described as the virgin and Joseph's "fatherhood" may only be a legal fatherhood by adoption (Machen 1930: 176–87). At any rate, the external evidence for this third reading is very weak. In terms of transcriptional probability, it is much more likely that these other two variant readings arose from the well-attested reading than vice versa. In terms of intrinsic probability, the author of 1:18–25 certainly did not mean to communicate in 1:16 that Joseph was the biological father of Jesus.

I. Prologue/Introduction: Origin of Jesus the Messiah (1:1–2:23)
   A. Title and Genealogy of Jesus the Messiah (1:1–17)
➤ B. Birth of Jesus the Messiah (1:18–25)
   C. Visit of the Magi (2:1–12)

B. Birth of Jesus the Messiah (1:18–25)

The miraculous birth of Jesus, hinted at in 1:16, is now explained. Thus 1:18–25 is a sort of commentary on 1:16. Joseph discovers that his fiancée, Mary, is pregnant, and he plans to divorce her quietly. But his plans are radically changed by an angelic visitor, who explains the miraculous origin of her pregnancy and commands Joseph to take a very different course of action. He is to take Mary as his wife and name her son Jesus, which befits the child's special mission to "save his people from their sins" (1:21). Matthew adds editorially that all this fulfills the prophetic word about Immanuel. Joseph responds to the angel with unquestioning obedience. He takes Mary as his wife but does not have sexual relations with her until she bears her son, whom he names Jesus.

The structure of 1:18–25 is shown by the outline below. The circumstances are explained in 1:18–19, but this setting is interrupted by the angelic visit and command (1:20–21). The citation of Isa. 7:14, perhaps an editorial aside, is featured at the center of the pericope in order to explain the prophetic significance of this situation (Matt. 1:22–23). The pericope concludes with Joseph's obedient response to the angel's command (1:24–25). As W. Davies and Allison (1988: 196–97) note, this same structure is also found in later angelic visits to Joseph (2:13–15, 19–21) and in various biblical stories of angelic visits (Gen. 16:1–16; Judg. 13:2–25; Luke 1:5–25). It is crucial to note that here in 1:18–25 Matthew begins to stress his theme of fulfillment (1:22–23). The one who is born from the line of the patriarch Abraham and King David is the one in whom the promises of God are realized (cf. 2 Cor. 1:20).

The unit can be divided as follows:

1. Mary's embarrassing circumstances (1:18)
2. Joseph's plan (1:19)
3. The angel's surprising announcement (1:20–21)
4. The basis in biblical pattern (1:22–23)
5. Joseph's obedience (1:24–25)

Exegesis and Exposition

[18]Now the ⌐birth⌐ of ⌐Jesus the Messiah⌐ happened like this: His mother Mary was engaged to be married to Joseph, but before they began

to live together, she was found to be pregnant through the Holy Spirit. [19]Though he was a righteous man, Joseph her husband did not wish to expose her to public disgrace. So he decided to divorce her privately. [20]But after he had considered this, suddenly an angel of the Lord appeared to him in a dream and said, "Joseph, son of David, don't be afraid to take Mary home as your wife, because the child conceived in her is through the Holy Spirit. [21]She will have a son, and you must name him Jesus because ⌜he⌝ will save his people from their sins."

[22]Now all this occurred to fulfill what the Lord had spoken through ⌜ ⌝ the prophet:

[23]"Look! The virgin will become pregnant and will bear a son, and they will call him Immanuel" (which means "God with us").

[24]And when Joseph woke up, he did what the angel of the Lord had said. He took Mary home as his wife, [25]but he was not intimate with her until she had borne a ⌜son⌝, and he named him Jesus.

1. Mary's Embarrassing Circumstances (1:18)

1:18   Matthew has announced that he is giving a record of the birth of the Messiah (1:1), and he has provided an overview of the Messiah's Abrahamic and Davidic ancestry (1:1–17). Now that the Messiah has been firmly rooted in the context of redemptive history, Matthew goes on to provide the specifics of his birth.[1] The word γένεσις (genesis, birth) is repeated from 1:1. The Greek word order places the genitive construction "of Jesus Christ" before the noun γένεσις (cf. 10:2), placing more emphasis on the genitive and connecting 1:18 more closely with 1:17. Two details provided in 1:18 are crucial for understanding Joseph's dilemma in 1:19. Mary is engaged to Joseph (cf. Luke 1:27; 2:5),[2] but before their marriage is consummated, she is discovered to be pregnant. The Holy Spirit is mentioned here for the first time in Matthew. The Spirit is involved in Jesus's conception (cf. 1:20), empowerment (3:16; 12:18, 28), and leading (4:1). In Jesus's view, the Scriptures come from the Spirit (22:43). John spoke of the day when Jesus would baptize in the Spirit (3:11), and Jesus promised his disciples that the Spirit would supply their testimony during persecution (10:20). The world mission of the disciples would include baptism in the name of the Father, Son,

---

1. The conjunction δέ is probably not adversative ("but, yet"), contrasting Jesus's birth to that of the others in the preceding genealogy (so Carson 1984: 81). Rather, the sense is explanatory ("now, so"), and the logical movement is general to specific (BDAG 213).

2. The phrase μνηστευθείσης τῆς μητρὸς αὐτοῦ Μαρίας τῷ Ἰωσήφ is a genitive absolute (see BDF §§417, 423; Wallace 1996: 654–55). This use of the adverbial or circumstantial participle occurs about forty-nine times in Matthew (1:18, 20; 2:1, 13, 19; 5:1; 6:3; 8:1, 5, 16, 28; 9:10, 18, 32, 33; 11:7; 12:46; 13:6, 19, 21; 14:15, 23, 32; 16:2; 17:5, 9, 22, 24, 26; 18:24, 25; 20:8, 29; 21:10, 23; 22:41; 24:3; 25:5; 26:6, 7, 20, 21, 26, 47; 27:1, 17, 19, 57; 28:11). The aorist tense is most frequent (27 times), but the present (20 times) and perfect (twice) are also used. Most (43) occur in Matthew's narrative sections, but Jesus's discourses contain six.

and Holy Spirit (28:19; cf. Schaberg 1982; on the Spirit in Matthew, see Charette 2000).

Engagement or betrothal frequently occurred when girls were twelve years old. When the groom had completed his obligations to the bride's father according to the marriage contract, the bride came under the authority of her husband, but she did not necessarily move to her husband's house at that time. It was evidently common for a year or so to pass between the betrothal and the marriage proper, when cohabitation began (*m. Ketub.* 5.2; *m. Ned.* 10.5). Apparently, the situation in 1:18 includes all but the final stage of the process (cf. 25:1–12; R. Brown 1993: 123–24). Joseph has become engaged to Mary and has assumed authority over her. He is already her husband (ἀνήρ, *anēr*) and plans to divorce Mary to solve his problem (1:19; cf. Deut. 22:23–24). But 1:18 adds that Joseph and Mary have not yet "come together" (συνελθεῖν, *synelthein*; see LSJ 1712); they were not yet living together as husband and wife.

2. Joseph's Plan (1:19)

Joseph's plan to quietly divorce Mary is explained here. The plan emanates from Joseph's character as a just man who does not wish to publicly disgrace Mary. This is expressed in the Greek text with two circumstantial participles whose logical relationship to each other and to the main verb of the sentence is a matter of some debate. Joseph's righteousness is of the experiential, practical sort. Matthew is saying that Joseph is an upright, devout man who obeys the law of Moses (cf. Luke 1:6 and Tosato 1979).[3] A Protestant notion of imputed forensic righteousness is not taught here. Some suggest that "righteous" here is equivalent to "merciful" and that Joseph's reticence to disgrace Mary publicly is due to his kindness toward her. But this is dubious lexically. It is better to take "righteous" in its normal sense as "law-abiding" and thus to handle the participial phrase as concessive (BDF §417; Wallace 1996: 634–35, against Carson 1984: 81): "though he was righteous." If so, the conjunction καί (*kai*, and), which connects the two participles, should be viewed as a mild adversative ("yet"), which is not unlike Matthew's use of καί elsewhere (e.g., 3:14; 6:26; 10:29; 12:43; 13:17; 26:60; cf. BDAG 495; BDF §442). Then the meaning is that even though Joseph is a law-abiding man, he does not wish to use the law in all its rigor against Mary (R. Brown 1993: 125–28; Hagner 1993: 18). Instead he plans a quiet divorce. If this interpretation is correct, Joseph becomes something of a model of one whose high standards are balanced with compassion.

1:19

3. For Matthew's approach to righteousness as obedience to the law, see 3:15; 5:6, 10, 20, 45; 6:1, 33; 9:13; 10:41; 12:37; 13:17, 43, 49; 20:4; 21:32; 23:28, 29, 35; 25:37, 46; 27:19. For general discussion of righteousness in Matthew, see Przybylski 1980; Yri in Carson 1992: 96–105. For discussion of Joseph's righteousness, see Tosato 1979.

Instead of a public trial, which would result in disgrace as well as divorce (Deut. 22:23–27), Joseph opts for a private divorce, which evidently could be achieved if he merely drew up a divorce statement himself and gave it to Mary in the presence of two or three witnesses (Num. 5:11–31; Deut. 24:1; *m. Giṭ.* 9.10; cf. S. Brown 1977: 128).

It seems necessary to assume that Joseph is planning to divorce Mary because he does not yet know the cause of her pregnancy. The reader of Matt. 1:18 knows that the pregnancy was caused by the Holy Spirit, but Joseph knows only that he is not the cause of it. Thus in 1:20 the angel's explanation of the miraculous cause of the pregnancy provides the reason Joseph should take Mary home as his wife. A different approach is taken by Gundry (1994: 21–22), who assumes that Joseph hesitated to take Mary home as his wife precisely because he did understand that she was pregnant by the Holy Spirit and was afraid to approach her. But this does not explain why Joseph has evidently decided to divorce Mary, and it seems to disregard the causal force of the angel's revelation in 1:20.

3. The Angel's Surprising Announcement (1:20–21)

1:20   Joseph's plans are suddenly changed by the angelic visitation and revelation.[4] Revelation through dreams occurs repeatedly in Matthew (2:12, 13, 19, 22; 27:19; cf. Joel 2:28; Acts 2:17; Gnuse 1990; Keener 1999: 95–96). Matthew's "angel of the Lord" should not be identified with the biblical theophanic angel (Gen. 16; Exod. 3; Judg. 6). The absence of the article ("the") is noteworthy in 1:20. The presence of the article in reference to the angel in 1:24 is anaphoric (BDF §252; Wallace 1996: 217–20, but see also 252). This angel is merely a messenger of God, not God's very appearance.[5] Revelation in dreams is not uncommon in the Bible (Gen. 37:5–7; Job 33:15–17; Dan. 2; 7). The fact that Joseph is a son of David may be deduced from the genealogy. When Joseph is called a son of David by the angel, this pericope is tied to the genealogy

---

4. The particle ἰδού occurs here for the first of 62 times in Matthew. It frequently introduces divine intervention or something else that is surprising or remarkable. At times its occurrence is hard to explain and translate. See also 1:23; 2:1, 9, 13, 19; 3:16, 17; 4:11; 7:4; 8:2, 24, 29, 32, 34; 9:2, 3, 10, 18, 20, 32; 10:16; 11:8, 10, 19; 12:2, 10, 18, 41, 42, 46, 47, 49; 13:3; 15:22; 17:3, 5 (2x); 19:16, 27; 20:18, 30; 21:5; 22:4; 23:34, 38; 24:23, 25, 26 (2x); 25:6; 26:45, 46, 47, 51; 27:51; 28:2, 7 (2x), 9, 11, 20; and Pryke 1968.

5. As is common in Matthew, the angel's message is introduced as a direct quotation with the participle λέγων. At times λέγων occurs "redundantly" alongside another finite verb of speech (BDF §420; Wallace 1996: 649–50). In some occurrences it is followed by ὅτι, which introduces the quotation (9:18; 10:7; 14:26; 16:7). It occurs in Matthew's fulfillment formulas (1:22; 2:15; 3:3; 4:14; 8:17; 12:17; 13:35; 21:4; 22:31; 27:9). See also 2:2, 13, 20; 3:2, 14, 17; 5:2; 6:31; 8:2, 6, 25, 27, 29, 31; 9:14, 18, 27, 29, 30, 33; 10:5, 7; 12:10, 38; 13:3, 24, 31, 36; 14:15, 27, 30, 33; 15:1, 7, 22, 23, 25; 16:13, 22; 17:5, 9, 10, 15; 18:1, 26, 28, 29; 19:3, 25; 20:12, 30, 31; 21:2, 9, 10, 15, 20, 23, 25, 37; 22:1, 4, 16, 23, 24, 42, 43; 23:2; 24:3, 5; 25:9, 11, 20, 37, 44; 26:8, 17, 27, 39, 42, 48, 65, 68, 69, 70; 27:4, 11, 19, 23, 24, 29, 40, 46, 54, 63; 28:9, 13, 18.

and Jesus's Davidic roots are further underlined. This is the only time in Matthew that "son of David" does not refer to Jesus. Joseph is commanded not to fear taking Mary as his wife,[6] because[7] her pregnancy is induced by the Holy Spirit.[8] Now Joseph knows what the narrator has told the reader in 1:18. The following narrative shows how well Joseph heeds this command.

The angel's annunciation to Joseph continues. He should take Mary home because her pregnancy is from the Holy Spirit, and she will bear a son whom Joseph will name Jesus because of his mission to save his people from their sins. Future indicative verbs express not only the prediction of Mary giving birth to a son but also the command (BDF §362; Wallace 1996: 569–70; cf. 5:43; 21:3; 27:4) that Joseph should name him Jesus. The angelic annunciation has a form that is common to other biblical birth announcements (Gen. 16:11; 17:19; Luke 1:13, 31). **1:21**

The name Jesus ('Ιησοῦς, *Iēsous*) fits the predicted mission of Jesus. It is a Greek form of the biblical name Joshua (יְהוֹשֻׁעַ, *Yĕhôšūaʿ*). The word יְהוֹשֻׁעַ, sometimes shortened to יֵשׁוּעַ (*Yēšûaʿ*), was a common name among Jews. It was popularly related to the Hebrew verb "save" and understood to mean "Yahweh saves." In the NT, Moses's successor Joshua is viewed as a type of Christ (Heb. 3–4). By naming Mary's son, Joseph will be accepting legal paternity. By naming him 'Ιησοῦς, Joseph will be making a statement about Jesus's redemptive mission: "He will save his people from their sins." A similar play on words (paronomasia) with a personal name occurs with Simon Peter in 16:18 (cf. 1 Sam. 25:25).

The angel here alludes to Ps. 130:8, where Israel is exhorted to trust in Yahweh's unfailing love because Yahweh would redeem Israel from all their sins. Thus Jesus, already shown to be the miraculously conceived Son of God and about to be revealed as "God with us," is portrayed as Yahweh's agent in effecting this eschatological salvation. Salvation in Matthew can refer to deliverance from physical danger, illness, and death (Matt. 8:25; 9:21–22; 24:22), but salvation from sins is the focus of the angel's announcement here. In Matthew, sin (ἁμαρτία, *hamartia*) is confessed by those whom John baptizes and is forgiven by Jesus (3:6; 9:2, 5, 6; 12:31; 26:28). Forgiveness is accomplished by Jesus's gift of

6. The command of the angel to Joseph is a prohibition clause with the aorist imperative, μὴ φοβηθῇς. Some grammarians assert that such a construction prohibits the initiation of action, as opposed to μή with the present imperative, which supposedly prohibits the continuance of an action. This distinction is valid in some instances, but it does not work here. It is clear from the context that Joseph is already concerned about the situation and is afraid to take Mary home, so this grammatical "rule" has exceptions. See Wallace 1996: 714–25.

7. This explanatory clause is introduced by γάρ, which is frequently used in Matthew. Its narrative implications are examined in R. Edwards 1990.

8. The agency of the Spirit of God in Mary's miraculous conception and also in events related to it is featured in Luke's narrative (Luke 1:35; cf. 1:15, 41, 67; 2:26).

himself as a ransom for sinners in sacrificial death, as exemplified in the elements of the Last Supper (20:28; 26:26–30).

It is perhaps significant that the allusion to Ps. 130:8 substitutes "his people" for "Israel." Luz (1989: 121) believes that "his people" stands for Israel, the biblical people of God, but it is more likely that this expression implies the biblical-remnant concept of a genuine Israel within national Israel. In Matthew λαός (*laos*, people) occurs in contexts that refer to the nation in general (2:4; 4:23; 21:23; 26:3, 5, 47; 27:1, 64), but it also occurs in citations of the Bible and in other spiritually significant contexts (1:21; 2:6; 4:16; 13:15; 15:8; 27:25). Jesus's saving ministry of word, deed, and sacrificial death creates a division within Israel. Those who admit they are sick come to Jesus as their physician, but most Israelites will not admit their sickness (9:9–12). Thus Jesus begins to build his church (16:18–19), "a people who will produce [the kingdom's] fruit" (21:43). Israel as a nation is not abandoned, but only Jews who will repent and turn to Jesus the Messiah will receive the forgiveness of their sins and experience the fullness of biblical eschatological blessings (19:28–30). See Repschinski 2006 for a discussion of the Christology of 1:21.

4. The Basis in Biblical Pattern (1:22–23)

1:22 There is some question whether 1:22 continues the angel's announcement to Joseph or whether that announcement concludes in 1:21, with 1:22 beginning Matthew's explanation of the prophetic significance of the situation. Carson (1984: 76, following Fenton 1980: 79–80) argues that the angel's words continue through 1:22–23 because 1:22–23 corresponds closely with 21:4 and 26:56, where Jesus rather than Matthew is viewed as the speaker. Additionally, it is argued that the perfect-tense verb γέγονεν (*gegonen*) is more naturally rendered as the angel saying, "now all this *has happened*," than as Matthew's editorial explanation, "now all this happened." On the other hand, there is better reason to take 1:22–23 as Matthew's comment. First, although 26:56 is likely the words of Jesus, 21:4 is more likely Matthew's comment. And 26:56 is not strong evidence in this discussion because no Scripture is introduced by the statement. Rather, it describes Jesus's arrest as fulfilling the prophets (note the plural). So the evidence from 21:4 and 26:56 does not convince. Second, the perfect-tense verb γέγονεν may be interpreted as an "aoristic perfect" (BDF §343) and translated simply "happened," which fits the interpretation that it is a Matthean editorial comment. Third, it makes more sense to view 1:22 as the first of Matthew's nine fulfillment formula introductions of biblical passages (see the introduction to the commentary for a discussion of these introductory formulas, the biblical passages cited, and the nature of "fulfillment" in Matthew). The other eight formulas are best interpreted as Matthew's editorial comments, and so it is most likely that 1:22 is also.

Whoever the speaker is, it is crucial to grasp the meaning of the fulfillment concept mentioned in 1:22. All the events that have transpired concerning Mary's miraculous conception fulfill what was spoken "by" the Lord (ὑπό, *hypo*, plus the genitive with the passive verb describes the agent of the action) "through" the prophet (διά, *dia*, plus the genitive expresses the means the Lord used). Passages such as this (cf. 2:15; 15:4, 7; 22:43), together with 2 Pet. 1:19–21 and 2 Tim. 3:16, are foundational for the evangelical doctrine of biblical authority.

Isaiah 7:14 is now cited as the text fulfilled by Mary's virginal conception of Jesus. Matthew follows the LXX, which is a literal translation of the Hebrew, with one exception. The LXX has καὶ καλέσεις (*kai kaleseis*, and *you* will call), but Matthew has καὶ καλέσουσιν (*kai kalesousin*, and *they* will call); the Hebrew Bible has וְקָרָאת (*wĕqārā't*, and *she* will call). Variant LXX readings and possible repointing of the MT further complicate the matter. The third-person plural in Matthew may simply be an impersonal plural (cf. 5:15; 7:16; 9:17), but it is more likely that, for Matthew, it implies that the people whom Jesus saves from their sins will call him Immanuel. (On the textual form of the quotation, see Menken 2001a.)

1:23

There has been a great deal of discussion concerning the Greek and Hebrew words for "virgin" in these texts, discussion going all the way back to Justin Martyr's *Dialogue with Trypho* (43.5–8; 84.1–4) in the second century. An extended treatment of this matter here is necessitated not only by this text's prominence in theological controversy but also, more important, by its prominence as Matthew's first formula quotation. Isaiah 7:14 speaks of "the virgin" (הָעַלְמָה, *hā'almâ*), a word that describes a young woman who is old enough to be married. It has been reported that fundamentalists burned RSV (1952) Bibles because the RSV translated הָעַלְמָה as "young woman" instead of "virgin." The NRSV (1989) has retained this translation. Although the normal denotation of this word is female adolescence, it usually also connotes virginity, the lack of sexual experience (Gen. 24:43; Exod. 2:8; Ps. 68:26 MT [68:25 Eng.]; Song 1:3; 6:8; but Prov. 30:19 is debatable). Another Hebrew word describing such a young woman is בְּתוּלָה (*bĕtûlâ*; see Gen. 24:16; Lev. 21:3, 13, 14; Deut. 22:14, 19, 20; Judg. 19:24; 2 Sam. 13:2, 18). At times conservatives who take Isa. 7:14 as strictly predictive make much of the word עַלְמָה because they believe the word implies sexual inexperience more strongly than בְּתוּלָה does, but the evidence is not convincing. The fact that the LXX translated עַלְמָה as παρθένος (*parthenos*, virgin) is not decisive for exegesis because the LXX of Isaiah is known to be a rather loose translation (Seeligmann 1948). Be that as it may, there is no doubt that, for Matthew, Mary was a virgin, a sexually inexperienced young woman. This is certain not only from the usually unambiguous word παρθένος (Matt. 1:23; cf. 25:1, 7, 11; Luke 1:27; 2:36; Acts 21:9; 1 Cor.

7:25, 28, 34, 36, 37; 2 Cor. 11:2; Rev. 14:4; but cf. Gen. 34:3 LXX) but also from the details of the narrative (Matt. 1:16, 18, 20; cf. Luke 1:34–35).

Even more crucial exegetically is the question of Matthew's hermeneutical use of the Hebrew Bible (cf. Huat 2000). The three general approaches to this question may be categorized as typological, predictive, and multiple fulfillment. The *typological* view stresses the immediacy of the sign to Ahaz in Isa. 7:14a, 16 and the possible fulfillments of Isa. 7:14 in the near future of the biblical context (8:3–4, 8, 10, 18). Thus Isa. 7:14 is viewed as a sign to Ahaz that was fulfilled during his days, and Matthew sees in the passage a historical pattern that comes to climactic fulfillment with Jesus. A young woman in Isaiah's day conceived a significant son who served as a sign of deliverance to Ahaz and the house of David (Isa. 7:2, 13). But much more significantly, a young woman in Matthew's day who was literally a virgin conceived by the Spirit a son of ultimate significance to the house of David, the nation of Israel, and all the nations of the earth. In Isaiah's day the son was a token of divine presence and deliverance. In Matthew's day the son was himself "God with us," the deliverer of his people (Barnes 1868: 7–8; Broadus 1886: 12).

The *predictive* view takes Isa. 7:14 as foreseeing the eventual miraculous birth of the Messiah from a woman who was literally a virgin. Matthew interprets this predictive prophecy literally and views it as predicting the birth of Jesus and him alone. Thus the prophecy transcends the contemporary difficulties facing King Ahaz and points to a sign in the future. Nevertheless, the overwhelming significance of the sign transcends its temporal distance. Proponents of this view (e.g., Barbieri in Walvoord and Zuck 1983: 20; Calvin 1972: 165–69; Carson 1984: 78–79; H. Fowler 1968: 1.38–42; Hendriksen 1973: 134–41; Machen 1930: 288–91) argue that the normal birth of a son from a young woman (as required in the typological view) would have little or no force as a sign to King Ahaz. Additionally, they believe that only the predictive view does justice to the son's name, Immanuel.

The strength of the typological view is its focus on the historical context of the original prophecy, and the strength of the predictive view is its focus on the NT fulfillment.

The third view, *multiple fulfillment*, attempts to draw from both of these strengths. In this approach the prophecy foresees not only a partial fulfillment in the days of Ahaz but also a climactic fulfillment in NT times (Blomberg 1992a: 60; Gundry 1994: 24–25; Hagner 1993: 20; Ridderbos 1987: 29–30; Toussaint 1980: 44–46). The human prophet Isaiah may not have fully grasped this, but after all, the prophecy is the Lord's and Isaiah is merely the messenger. Such a *sensus plenior* (fuller meaning) was intended by the divine author if not fully understood by the human author.

One should hesitate to be dogmatic on this matter, since each position has its credible advocates and arguments. The typological view, however, seems best for several reasons. First are the weaknesses of the other views. The multiple-fulfillment view introduces an unwarranted distinction between what the prophet predicted and what God intended to reveal by the text. Even Kaiser's attempt (1988: 66–67) to handle this as "generic fulfillment" is lacking here because he does not demonstrate the connection between the near and the far elements in Isaiah's intent. Additionally, the double-fulfillment view assumes that the esoteric connection between the near and the far fulfillments of the prophecy is available only to one who is divinely inspired. But if the christological significance of the Hebrew Bible is accessible only from such a revelatory stance, the organic unity of the Bible is compromised and made inaccessible to ordinary believers (cf. Luke 24:27, 44–45; John 5:39). Instead of this view, which posits an enigmatic double entendre and subsequent divine inspiration to recognize it, one does much better to assert a typological connection in which the biblical historical events contain theological motifs that anticipate the Christ event when seen with Christian hindsight. Such hindsight is not limited to those who wrote the NT but is available to all who will search the historical events and theological motifs of the Bible. The dynamic that connects Isa. 7:14 with Matt. 1:23 is not two levels of foresight, one on the surface of the text and the other beneath it. Rather, Matthew reads the events of the Bible from a Christian perspective and from a belief in divine providence. Thus he discovers events and motifs that come to climactic fulfillment in Jesus the Messiah, who is David's son and Abraham's son.

The predictive view has problems with its relevance to the immediate historical context, and the original context must be primary in any sound exegesis. It seems clear from Isa. 7:15–17 that the son to be born signals the demise of Ahaz's enemies, for they will be forsaken before the son comes to the age of moral discretion. It is difficult, if not impossible, to relate this to the birth of Jesus several hundred years later. Some scholars argue that only a miraculous event such as Jesus's virgin birth could have value as a "sign" (אוֹת, 'ôt) to Israel, but a study of Isaiah's use of אוֹת elsewhere (Isa. 7:11, 14; 8:18; 19:20; 20:3; 37:30; 38:7, 22; 55:13; 66:19) shows that this is not always the case. Additionally, such a study shows that the אוֹת in Isaiah is an event that is contemporaneous with the time frame of the prophecy, not distantly removed from it. This would indicate that signs in Isaiah are "present persuaders," not "future confirmation" (contra Carson 1984: 79, who follows J. Motyer 1970: 118–25). Even more problematic to the predictive view, it is doubtful that Isa. 7:14 should even be translated as a prediction of the future, since it is a verbless clause, which, depending on the context, is normally translated as a present or a past tense (Walton 1987: 290–91). Thus the translation should likely be "a young woman is pregnant, and is about to bear a son."

Although some believe that Isa. 7:14 describes the birth of Maher-shalal-hash-baz (8:3–4, 10, 18), Walton (1987: 289–97; cf. J. Willis 1972: 1–18 for a similar approach) has plausibly argued that Isa. 7:14 originally described the coming birth of a son to a nameless young woman in Ahaz's harem. Perhaps this son was Hezekiah himself (Kaiser 1988: 64), a common Jewish view, but this is conjecture. The issue is not *who* the child was but *what* the child signified. The point is that even though times were bad at the moment, judgment would soon fall on the enemies Pekah and Rezin. Thus the young woman should give her son the name Immanuel, since God was still with his people and would deliver them from this situation.

When Matthew, as a disciple of Jesus the Messiah, read Isa. 7, Isaianic motifs acquired new significance. He did not create the virgin birth narrative as an imaginative midrash on Isa. 7. Neither did he view Isa. 7 under inspiration as an intended prediction of Jesus's virgin birth. Rather, he saw the motifs of the oracle of Isa. 7–9, particularly its stress upon the house of David (7:2, 13; 9:7), a young girl giving birth to a son (7:14–16; 8:3–4), and the presence of God with his people (7:14; 8:8, 10), in light of the miraculous birth of the Messiah. Matthew was obviously aware of these Isaianic motifs as well as Isaiah's specific future predictions of the Messiah in the following context (Isa. 9:1–7, cf. Matt. 4:15–16; Isa. 11:1–5, cf. Matt. 2:23 [possibly]; 3:16; Isa. 42:1–4, cf. Matt. 12:18–21). The motifs in Isa. 7–8 anticipated and thus supported the message of Jesus the Messiah as Matthew understood it and wished to communicate it. In Jesus the Messiah, the house of David was culminated. Mary's virginal conception of Jesus the Messiah amounted to an infinitely greater sign to Israel. And Jesus the Messiah was himself God with the nation of Israel.[9]

The preceding extended discussion is necessary for this *crux interpretum*, but it runs the risk of missing the forest for the trees. Whatever position one takes on the matter of Matthew's characteristic understanding of the Bible, one must not miss the most crucial matter, that Mary's son Jesus is Immanuel, God with us. This is Matthew's main concern here, and we risk missing it if we pay attention only to the preceding controversy. Matthew's Christian Jewish audience would evidently already know the Hebrew name עִמָּנוּ אֵל (*'immānû 'ēl*; Greek transliteration, Ἐμμανουήλ, *Emmanouēl*), but for added emphasis he also supplies the Greek equivalent in words identical to Isa. 8:8 LXX, μεθ' ἡμῶν ὁ θεός (*meth' hēmōn ho theos*; cf. Isa. 8:10 LXX). This "name" is more of a title signifying the character and mission of Jesus as God with his people to save them from their sins. It is not just that God is present in Jesus to

---

9. For additional discussion of the exegesis of Isa. 7:14 and its use in Matt. 1:23, see Beecher 1975: 354–58; Jensen 1979: 220–39; Kaiser 1988: 55–70; J. Motyer 1970: 118–25; Rice 1978: 220–27; Walton 1987: 289–306; J. Willis 1978: 1–18; and Wolf 1972: 449–56.

help his people (Hill 1972: 80; Nolland 2005: 102). Such an approach implies a mere cyclical pattern between the biblical testaments, not a full typology where the NT antitype transcends the biblical type by bringing it to climactic fulfillment. Judging from the implications of his previous material (Matt. 1:1, 16, 18, 20) and his overall high Christology (e.g., 3:17; 11:27; 28:18–20), it is likely that Matthew intended this in the fullest sense: Jesus as God's Son is also God himself with his people, effecting their deliverance. This is the ultimate manifestation of God's presence. The significance of Isaiah's typical Immanuel, though great in itself, pales in comparison with Matthew's antitypical with-us-God, Jesus.

That Jesus is God with his people is a recurring theme in Matthew. Jesus is with his disciples when the storm strikes, and he saves them from it (8:23–27). He is with them as they are received or rejected while preaching his kingdom (10:25, 40; 17:17). He is with them as they solemnly handle intractible offenders in his new community (18:15–20). He is so identified with their experiences that he views them as his own (25:40, 45). In fact, the final reference to the Immanuel theme concludes the Gospel and creates an *inclusio* enveloping the entire Gospel with this motif. As the church obeys its mandate to disciple all the nations, Jesus promises to continue his presence with his followers all the days until the end of the age (28:18–20; cf. Kupp 1996).

5. Joseph's Obedience (1:24–25)

In Matt. 1–2, three times Joseph models quiet obedience (Bruner 1987: 35–36) to angelic revelation in dreams (cf. 2:13–15, 19–21 for similar syntax). He gets up and does exactly as he is told without hesitation or question. Given his previous perplexity and plan (1:19–20a), this is nothing less than remarkable and compares to Mary's humble obedience in Luke 1:38. Joseph takes Mary to his house as his wife.

1:24

Matthew adds another detail to underline Jesus's miraculous birth: Joseph has no sexual relations with Mary before Jesus is born. The euphemism involved in Joseph's not "knowing" Mary is common in the Bible (BDAG 200; cf. Gen. 4:1, 17, 25; 38:26; Judg. 11:39; 19:25; 1 Sam. 1:19; 1 Kings 1:4; Luke 1:34).[10] (See Feuillet 1990.)

1:25

Although to say that Joseph had no sexual relations with Mary "until" (ἕως, *heōs*) Jesus was born is not necessarily to say that he had such rela-

10. The imperfect verb οὐκ ἐγίνωσκεν describes the period between Joseph's taking Mary home and Jesus's birth as a time when Joseph and Mary were not sexually intimate. The imperfect frequently portrays past action as continuing or repeated, but it may also portray action as attempted but not achieved ("conative"; cf. Matt. 3:14) or action at its inception ("ingressive"; Matt. 3:5; Wallace 1996: 544–45, 551–52). Thus it is possible that Matt. 1:25 implies that Joseph did not attempt to initiate sexual intimacy with Mary during this time. The inceptive concept could imply that Joseph did begin sexual relations with Mary after Jesus's birth (W. Allen 1912: 10).

tions afterward, it would seem that he did.[11] The syntax of ἕως is generally unremarkable, but its use in 1:25 affects the question of Mary's perpetual virginity, a tradition most frequently associated with the Roman Catholic Church, although the doctrine is also held by the Orthodox Church. Does this sentence imply that Joseph was intimate with Mary after Jesus's birth (so Boring 1995: 136)? In Matt. 1:25 ἕως occurs with a negative main verb and the genitive relative pronoun. This type of construction occurs nowhere else in Matthew. The closest parallel is 17:9, but there the negative verb is an imperative, not an indicative as here. On eight occasions there is a negative verb, but it is in a clause of emphatic negation (5:18 [2x], 26; 10:23; 16:28; 23:39; 24:34; 26:29; cf. BDF §431(2); Zerwick 1963: §444) and there is no genitive relative pronoun. In four cases there is a genitive relative pronoun but no negative main verb (13:33; 14:22; 18:34; 26:36). In 12:20 there are negative future verbs but no genitive relative pronoun. In 24:39 there is a negative aorist verb but no genitive relative pronoun.

A perusal of these passages indicates that there is no *grammatical* reason to assume that Joseph was intimate with Mary after the birth of Jesus. The question of Mary's perpetual virginity cannot be settled on grammatical grounds (against McNeile 1915: 10). Yet her perpetual virginity is doubtful on other grounds, such as the existence of Jesus's brothers and sisters (Matt. 13:55–56; see R. Brown et al. 1978: 65–72, 273–75; Meier 1992). Nevertheless, Protestants should take note of the ancient origins of this dogma (e.g., Prot. Jas. 9.2; Chromatius, *Tractate on Matthew* 3.1; John Chrysostom, *Hom. Matt.* 5.3) and of the reticence of none other than Calvin to critique it (1972: 1.70).

Mary was engaged to be married to Joseph, and Joseph was commanded to take Mary home as his wife. The most natural reading of Matt. 12:46; 13:55, 56 (cf. Mark 3:31–32; 6:3; Luke 8:19–20; John 2:12; 7:3, 5, 10; Acts 1:14) would indicate that Jesus had full brothers and sisters, not step-brothers and step-sisters or cousins. This renders the following overstatement of McKenzie (1968: 67) dubious: "The NT knows nothing of any children of Mary and Joseph." Harrington (1991: 191) is closer to the facts when he says, "It is doubtful that Matthew knew the tradition about the perpetual virginity of Mary" (cf. R. Brown 1993: 132; Viviano 1990b: 635).

The dogma of Mary's perpetual virginity is found as early as the second-century Protevangelium of James (19.3–20.2), where her intact hymen after Jesus's birth is described quite graphically. Matthew's reserved account reads rather differently from this somewhat sensationalized version of Jesus's birth although the latter is based on Matthew and Luke. Many

11. Matthew uses the word ἕως forty-nine times: 1:17 (3x), 25; 2:9, 13, 15; 5:18 (2x), 25, 26; 10:11, 23; 11:12, 13, 23 (2x); 12:20; 13:30, 33; 14:22; 16:28; 17:9, 17 (2x); 18:21, 22 (2x), 30, 34; 20:8; 22:26, 44; 23:35, 39; 24:21, 27, 31, 34, 39; 26:29, 36, 38, 58; 27:8, 45, 51, 64; 28:20.

considerations outside the purpose of this commentary play a part in this discussion, but the genuine humanity of Jesus as well as the sanctity of marital sexual relations are perhaps diminished if Mary remained a virgin during and after his birth. What Matthew stresses is the miraculous nature of Jesus's conception, not the miraculous preservation of Mary's virginity during his birth or her perpetual virginity afterward. Mary is best honored as a model believer if she is given the normal role of wife and mother (Bruner 1987: 36–40; see the additional note on 1:25).[12]

Matthew 1 has two major sections, the genealogy and the virginal-conception story. This chapter reveals who Jesus is and what he has come to do. He is the Messiah, son of David and son of Abraham. In fulfillment of God's plan for redemptive history, he has come as "the-with-us-God" (Bruner 1987: 28) who will save his people from their sins. In Matt. 1, then, we have in seed form the two doctrines that are widely acknowledged to be Matthew's chief concerns, Christology and ecclesiology.[13]

Additional Notes

1:18. There are two textual variants in 1:18. First are four variations on "Jesus the Messiah": Ἰησοῦ Χριστοῦ, Χριστοῦ Ἰησοῦ, Ἰησοῦ, and Χριστοῦ. The first of these has the lion's share of the external evidence but raises concerns on internal grounds because it is quite rare for the article τοῦ to precede Ἰησοῦ Χριστοῦ. Although the editors of UBS[3] had difficulty in deciding which reading was original (C rating), the editors of UBS[4] view the first reading as almost certainly original (B rating). In any event, the meaning is not substantially changed.

In the second variant, the reading γένεσις exists alongside the similar word γέννησις in the Byzantine text and other MSS. It would be easy for copyists to confuse these words. Since γένεσις also occurs in 1:1 but with a different nuance, internal evidence can be argued both ways on this question, but external evidence favors γένεσις, which has early broad support (Metzger 1994: 7).

1:21. The use of the nominative-case personal pronoun αὐτός probably adds emphasis to the subject, Jesus, in the angel's pronouncement: "*He* will save his people from their sins" (Wallace 1996: 321–23). Other examples of nominative αὐτός in Matthew are 3:4, 11; 8:17, 24; 11:14; 12:50; 14:2; 16:20; 21:27; 26:48; 27:57.

1:22. A few Greek MSS and ancient versions include the name "Isaiah" with "the prophet." The absence of the name from the preponderance of MSS leads Metzger 1994: 7–8 to conclude that it is a scribal explanation. See "Theological Emphases: Fulfillment" in the introduction for an extended discussion of Matthew's fulfillment formula quotations of the Bible.

1:25. A variant reading expands υἱόν to τὸν υἱὸν αὐτῆς τὸν πρωτότοκον. This reading is found in the Byzantine text and other MSS, but it may simply be an interpolation from Luke 2:7. Without the expansion it is still clear in Matthew's narrative that Jesus is Mary's firstborn.

---

12. Allison 2005b: 163–72 argues that Joseph's conduct is intended as exemplary in light of 5:32; 19:9, where Jesus arguably prohibits divorce except in the case of adultery. Joseph's chastity with Mary after they came together is also viewed as exemplary in light of a common ancient view that intercourse during pregnancy was unseemly at best.

13. Additional studies of Matt. 1:18–25 include Allison 1993a; R. Brown 1987; Derrett 1997a; Erickson 2000.

I. Prologue/Introduction: Origin of Jesus the Messiah (1:1–2:23)
  B. Birth of Jesus the Messiah (1:18–25)
➤ C. Visit of the Magi (2:1–12)
  D. Escape to Egypt (2:13–15)

C. Visit of the Magi (2:1–12)

The RSV and Fenton (1963: 44–49) divide Matt. 2 into five sections, each containing a biblical allusion. This scheme places a break between 2:6 and 2:7 due to an unwarranted stress on the minor biblical allusions in 2:11. It is better to stress the four major biblical quotations and posit four sections (1–12, 13–15, 16–18, 19–23). The chapter can also be profitably viewed as a drama in two acts comprising 2:1–12 and 2:13–23 respectively (S. Brown 1977: 178–79). The worship of the magi in the first act contrasts with the treachery of Herod in the second. There is also the strange indifference of the chief priests and legal experts (2:4–6), who quickly display biblical knowledge but do not act on it. Through it all, God protects the nascent Messiah by angelic appearances in dreams to the magi and especially to Joseph, who obeys at each juncture. Matthew tells this story in language that tends to parallel that of the description of Pharaoh's attempt to kill Jewish male babies in the early chapters of Exodus (cf. Exod. 1:22; 2:15, 23; 4:19–20). Herod amounts to a new pharaoh and Jesus is the new Moses (Allison 1993b: 140–65).

Matt. 2:1–12 can be displayed chiastically. This helps place the focus of the pericope on the citation of Mic. 5:2 and thus on Matthew's characteristic emphasis on Jesus's continuity with biblical patterns and predictions.

Magi arrive from the east (2:1)
  Magi have seen a special star and seek to worship Jesus (2:2)
    Herod is terrified of the one born king of the Jews (2:3)
      Herod questions the religious leaders (2:4)
      Religious leaders answer Herod (2:5–6; cf. Mic. 5:2)
    Herod plots against the one born king of the Jews (2:7–8)
  Magi see the star again and are enabled to worship Jesus
    (2:9–11)
Magi depart to their own country (2:12)

The events of Matt. 2 hint at two motifs that are stressed as Matthew's story of Jesus develops further. First, the worship of the magi implies that God's redemptive purposes extend beyond the nation of Israel.

Second, the treachery of Herod and the indifference of the religious leaders demonstrate that many within Israel will not believe in Jesus. Herod's unbelief is particularly blatant yet also instructive. He uses his newly acquired knowledge of Jesus the Messiah to plot against Jesus, but as the chapter closes, Herod is dead but Jesus is alive, still fulfilling the patterns and predictions of the Bible. Further occurrences of these motifs may be found in 8:10; 15:28; 21:31; 22:8–10.

The unit can be outlined as follows:

1. The magi's arrival and question (2:1–2)
2. Herod's response (2:3–4)
3. The biblical prediction (2:5–6)
4. Herod's deceptive plot (2:7–8)
5. The magi in Bethlehem (2:9–11)
6. Departure of the magi (2:12)

Exegesis and Exposition

[1]Now after Jesus had been born in Bethlehem of Judea during King Herod's reign, some men from the east who studied the stars arrived ⌜unexpectedly⌝ in Jerusalem [2]and started asking, "Where is the one who was born king of the Jews? We saw his star when it arose, and we have come to worship him."
[3]When King Herod heard about this, he was alarmed, as was all Jerusalem. [4]So he summoned all the chief priests and legal experts of the people and inquired from them where the Messiah was to be born. [5]"In Bethlehem of Judea," they told him, ⌜"for so it is written by the prophet⌝:

[6]"'And you, Bethlehem of Judea,
      You are by no means least among the rulers of Judea.
   For from you will come a ruler
      who will shepherd my people Israel.'"

[7]Then Herod secretly summoned the men who studied the stars and found out from them exactly when the star had appeared. [8]He sent them to Bethlehem with these orders: "Go and carefully search for the child. When you find him, report to me so that I can come and worship him too." [9]When they had heard the king, they left, and suddenly the star that they had seen in the east went ahead of them until it stopped over the place where the child was. [10]And when they saw the star, they were overwhelmed with joy. [11]When they went into the house, they saw the child with Mary his mother, and they knelt down and worshiped him. They opened their baggage and offered gifts to him of gold, frankincense, and myrrh. [12]Later they were warned in a dream not to return to Herod, so they withdrew to their own country by another route.

1. The Magi's Arrival and Question (2:1–2)

2:1 The new pericope begins with a genitive absolute (see footnote 2 of the comments on 1:18), which sets the time of the arrival of the magi as some time after the birth of Jesus.[1] The passive genitive participle γεννηθέντος (*gennēthentos*, was born) is consistent with passive verb forms in 1:16, 20. A comparison of 2:1 with 2:7, 16 indicates that the magi evidently arrived about two years after the birth. Luke 1:26; 2:1–7 mentions Joseph and Mary's origins in Nazareth and their trip to Bethlehem in response to the decree of Caesar Augustus. Matthew says nothing about this background, simply mentioning that Jesus was born in Bethlehem and connecting this with Mic. 5:2. Readers of Matthew who were familiar with the Bible would recognize Bethlehem as David's city and connect it with Matthew's earlier stress on David (Matt. 1:1, 6, 17, 20). Luke 2:4, 11 explicitly stresses Bethlehem as the city of David (cf. John 7:42). It is clear that Matthew is not interested in historical, chronological, and geographical details for their own sake. Rather, these details are mentioned to the degree that they serve Matthew's theological interests. This is not to say that Matthew invents "history" to serve theology but that Matthew selects historical details that support his theological ends and omits other details.

Jesus was born during the reign of Herod the Great, and various modern scholars place the date of the birth from 7 to 4 BCE (see Vardaman and Yamauchi 1989). The puzzling BCE dating of Christ's birth is due to mistakes made when the Christian calendar was instituted in 525 CE by Dionysius Exiguus. Herod the Great ruled from 37 to 4 BCE. Half-Jewish and half-Idumean, he was known for his shrewd diplomacy and his public works program, the remains of which may be seen yet today: the western retaining wall (the Wailing Wall) of the Temple Mount in Jerusalem, the city of Caesarea, the Masada and Herodion (near Bethlehem) fortresses, and the enclosure at Machpelah (the traditional burial site of Sarah; cf. Gen. 23) in Hebron. But Herod's personal life was a shambles, and palace intrigue was rampant. He had several wives and sons, some of whom he ordered murdered because of his fear that they were plotting against him. The Bethlehem atrocity (Matt. 2:16) was in keeping with Herod's usual manner of guarding his throne from any potential usurpers. In this connection, Macrobius's (ca. 400 CE) report rings true: the emperor Augustus spoke of Herod in a pun, saying that it was safer to be Herod's sow (ὗς, *hys*) than his son (υἱός, *huios*). However, this report is probably not historical (*Saturnalia* 2.4.11).[2]

1. Once again ἰδού introduces a startling new development in the story. See footnote 4 of the comments on 1:20 for discussion.

2. Josephus, *Ant.* 14–18, is the primary ancient source for the life of Herod. For a helpful summary of the life of Herod the Great and the Herodian dynasty and for a bibliography,

In light of later developments, it is significant that Matthew refers to Herod as king and specifies that the magi arrive in Jerusalem. Herod's kingship is merely a political office, and he will go to great lengths to guard against any potential rival. Jesus's kingship, like David's (1:6), is genuine and legitimate, given to him by God at birth (2:2). It is appropriate that the magi arrive in Jerusalem, David's capital city, the city of the great king (5:35; Ps. 48:2). It is the city of Solomon's temple, but Jesus is greater than Solomon and his temple (12:6, 42). He must cleanse the temple when he enters the city as its rightful king (Matt. 21), only to be crucified there a few days later (Matt. 27).

According to popular tradition, the magi (μάγοι, *magoi*), often called the wise men (cf. Powell 2000), were three kings named Balthasar, Caspar, and Melchior, whose relics now reside in the cathedral at Cologne. Beyond the fact that one might deduce that there were three men from the number of the gifts they gave Jesus, there is no basis in Matthew for this tradition. The magi were not kings but more likely were prominent priestly professionals who studied the stars and discerned the signs of the times.[3] They may have come from Arabia, Babylon, or Persia (cf. Maalouf 1999). Perhaps there are historical connections between them and the "Chaldeans" mentioned in Daniel (1:4; 2:2; 4:7; 5:7), who were adept in the interpretation of dreams. Elsewhere in the NT μάγοι are viewed quite unfavorably (Acts 8:9; 13:6, 8). One hesitates to call them astrologers because of the unsavory connotations of the term today (thus the translation above, "men who studied the stars"), but perhaps this is the best one-word translation. How these men came to interpret the star as an indication of the birth of the Messiah is a mystery, but some speculate that they were somehow aware of the prophecy of Balaam in Num. 24:17. The inclusion of the pericope about the magi does not amount to a sanction of astrology, which is condemned and forbidden in the Bible (e.g., Isa. 47:13–15; Jer. 10:1–2). Rather, Matthew includes the incident to contrast the mysterious insight of the magi with the obtuseness of Herod and the religious leaders.

The historicity of the magi's visit is frequently denied (Schnackenburg 2002: 20). Beare (1981: 74–75) explains the magi as a Christian reflection on the visit of an Armenian king to the emperor Nero in AD 66. Gundry (1994: 26–27) views the account of the magi as an imaginative midrash on Luke 2:8–20, the story of the annunciation to the shepherds. Others take the story as a midrash on the biblical account of Balak enlisting

---

see H. Hoehner in Green and McKnight 1992: 317–26. The classic studies of Herod and his dynasty are Perowne 1973, 1974.

3. For a study summarizing the historical background of the magi and affirming the historicity of Matthew's account, see Yamauchi 1989: 15–39. See also Allison 2005b: 17–41; Böcher in Schenke 1988: 11–24; Delling, *TDNT* 4:356–59; Ferrari d'Occhieppo in Vardaman and Yamauchi 1989: 41–53; Hoehner 1977: 11–28; R. Horsley 1989: 53–60; Keener 1999: 99.

Balaam to prophesy against Israel, only to have Balaam bless Israel instead (Num. 22–24). Another similar biblical story is the Queen of Sheba's visit to Solomon (1 Kings 10; 2 Chron. 9). It is likely that Num. 24:17 ("a star will come out of Jacob, a scepter will rise out of Israel") is echoed in this story, but this does not necessarily bring the historicity of the story into question. (See Yamauchi 1989: 18–23 for a critique of these positions.)

2:2   The magi come from the east (cf. Matt. 8:11; 24:27) and inquire where the king of the Jews was born because they have seen his star[4] ἐν τῇ ἀνατολῇ (*en tē anatolē*, when it arose). This phrase should not be translated "in the east" (NASB) because points of the compass occur without the article in the NT (as in 2:1; cf. BDF §141.2; 253.5). Additionally, this might imply that the magi came from the west toward an eastern star, which would contradict 2:1. Rather, the phrase describes the rising of the star (BDAG 74; NIV margin; NLT, NRSV). Modern readers wonder whether the rising of the star may be explained scientifically as a comet, a planetary conjunction, or a supernova providentially arranged by God. Whether these modern explanations have merit or not, Matthew would evidently view the occurence as a miracle.[5]

In some mysterious manner, the rising star has led the magi to Jerusalem to worship the one born king of the Jews (ὁ τεχθεὶς βασιλεὺς τῶν Ἰουδαίων, *ho techtheis basileus tōn Ioudaiōn*). The participle τεχθείς functions as an attributive adjective that portrays Jesus as the "born-king" of the Jews. This contrasts with Herod's kingship, which is merely the result of shrewd political manipulation. Jesus's genuine kingship is due to his Davidic sonship, as made clear in the genealogy. Yet Jesus is also the Son of God, as implied in 1:18–25 and made more explicit as the narrative proceeds. As the born-king of the Jews, Jesus will be able to resist Satan's test in offering him all the world's kingdoms (4:8). He will be able to affirm his superiority to King Solomon (12:42) and promise a glorious future return to the earth (16:28; 19:28; 20:21; 25:34). Yet he will be able to enter Jerusalem humbly (21:5) and endure the unspeakable mockery leading to his crucifixion (27:11, 29, 37, 42). The resurrection will vindicate his claims and validate him as the born-king of the Jews, to whom all power has been given (28:18).

The wise men come to "worship" (προσκυνῆσαι, *proskynēsai*) Jesus. This word is not limited to religious contexts and may simply signify bowing or kneeling to pay homage or respect to a superior, such as a king (18:26). Thus it is often translated "kneel down" in the NIV, even in contexts that describe Jesus (8:2; 9:18; 15:25; 20:20). In other contexts,

4. For discussion of the position of the possessive pronoun αὐτοῦ before the definite noun τὸν ἀστέρα, see BDF §284.
5. On the star, see Allison 1993c; Aveni 1998; Boa and Proctor 1985; Ferrari d'Occhieppo 1994; Humphreys 1992; Kidger 1999; Parpola 2001.

the NIV does translate the word as "worship" (2:2, 8, 11; 14:33; 28:9, 17). Given Matthew's high Christology, however, it seems that religious worship is at least implied in every passage (Carson 1984: 86, 90 cautions otherwise). Although reverence for a fellow human being is all that is indicated in 18:26, Jesus's exchange with Satan indicates in the strongest terms that worship is to be given only to God (4:9–10). This implies that when Jesus is the object of "worship," more than mere respect for a superior is meant. Comparison of Matthew's stress on such worship with the relative absence of this theme in the other Gospels (Mark 5:6; 15:19; Luke 4:7, 8; 24:52; John 4:20–24; 9:38; 12:20) also supports this point. Throughout Matthew, Jesus is presented as the Son of God, Immanuel. Thus it is not surprising that Jesus is frequently worshiped as God the Son. Just how much of this the magi understand is debatable, but on a literary level more than homage to a king is implied.

2. Herod's Response (2:3–4)

The conjunction δέ (*de*) introduces this verse with a note of explanation   2:3
or perhaps mild contrast. The magi have come to worship the newborn king, but when King Herod hears of it, he becomes quite disturbed at this threat to his own rule. The aorist passive verb ἐταράχθη (*etarachthē*, was troubled) should be viewed as ingressive or inceptive (BDF §331; Wallace 1996: 558–59), indicating that when Herod hears (ἀκούσας, *akousas*, a temporal or causal participle) the wise men's inquiry, he becomes disturbed. For similar syntax, see 8:10; 14:13; 17:6; 19:22, 25; 20:24. A genuine king of Israel would have rejoiced at the prospect of the Messiah's birth and would have known where the Messiah would be born. Instead, Herod's response is anxiety and fear, and this fear is shared by all Jerusalem.

Jerusalem's fear is variously explained. It seems unlikely that "all Jerusalem" would fear the born-king of the Jews for the same reason King Herod would. Thus Carson (1984: 86) believes that Jerusalem was afraid that this news would provoke Herod to further violence and cruelty. Beare (1981: 77) thinks that this may refer only to popular messianic excitement over the rumors of Jesus's birth. W. Davies and Allison (1988: 238–39) and R. Horsley (1989: 49–52) believe that "all Jerusalem" refers to the Jerusalem establishment that controlled the politics, economics, and religious activities of the rest of the nation. Many of the leaders of the Jerusalem establishment would be Herod's political bedfellows whose fears would closely parallel Herod's if a potential rival was on the horizon. This last suggestion seems preferable. As Matthew's story proceeds, this same Jerusalem establishment will unite in diametrical opposition to the born-king of the Jews (see 15:1; 16:21; 20:17–18; 21:1, 10; 23:37).

Because he fears the news brought by the magi, Herod gathers the chief   2:4
priests and legal experts (also paired in 20:18; 21:15) of the people (cf.

21:23; 26:3, 47; 27:1) to find the answer to the their question about the place of Jesus's birth. This reveals Herod's ignorance of the Hebrew Scriptures as well as his quick response to a potential rival. He assembles a meeting of the chief priests, which evidently would include the present and former high priests, the heads of the twenty-four main divisions of priests (cf. Luke 1:5, 8), and temple officers. Along with the Sadducean priestly hierarchy, Herod summons the scribes (γραμματεῖς, grammateis) of the people.[6] These men were not primarily professional copyists of the Bible but teachers of its meaning and application to Jewish life. Such legal experts were often Pharisees, and Matthew links the two terms several times (5:20; 12:38; 15:1; 23:2, 13, 15, 23, 25, 27, 29). This mention of the chief priests and legal experts at Jesus's birth tends to anticipate their active involvement in his death (16:21; 20:18; 21:15; 26:57). Herod will soon die (2:19), but the religious leaders remain to oppose Jesus.[7]

Herod asks the religious leaders where the Messiah will be born. The imperfect verb (ἐπυνθάνετο, epynthaneto) could be viewed as appropriate for the incomplete action inherent in asking a question (BDF §328), or it may have just an inceptive nuance ("he started asking"). Herod's question equates the magi's "king of the Jews" with "the Messiah." The linkage of Messiah with king also appears in the passion narrative (26:63, 68; 27:11, 17, 22, 29, 37).

3. The Biblical Prediction (2:5–6)

2:5   The Sadducean high priests and the Pharisaic legal experts do not always agree on matters of doctrine, but they univocally answer Herod's question and cite Mic. 5:2 (combined with 2 Sam. 5:2) in support. They believe that the Messiah will be born in Bethlehem of Judea, which was also the home of Jesse and David (1 Sam. 16:1; 17:12, 15). It has been so written by the prophet (οὕτως γὰρ γέγραπται διὰ τοῦ προφήτου, houtōs gar gegraptai dia tou prophētou). This introductory formula recalls that in 1:22 but differs from it in that a form of the verb πληρόω (plēroō, fulfill) does not appear. The leaders cite the Bible here as a text that proves their

---

6. Cf. Josephus, *Ant.* 6.120; 7.110, 293, 319, 364; 9.164; 10.55, 58, 94, 95, 149; 11.22, 26, 29, 128, 248, 250, 272, 287; 12.142; 16.319; 20.208–9; *J.W.* 1.479, 529, 532; *Ag. Ap.* 1.290.

7. For further discussion of the high priests and legal experts, see Jeremias 1962: 160–81, 233–45. Matthew mentions the chief priests in 2:4; 16:21; 20:18; 21:15, 23, 45; 26:3, 14, 47, 59; 27:1, 3, 6, 12, 20, 41, 62; 28:11 (the high priest himself is mentioned in 26:51, 57, 62, 63, 65) and the legal experts in 2:4; 5:20; 7:29; 8:19; 9:3; 12:38; 13:52; 15:1; 16:21; 17:10; 20:18; 21:15; 23:2, 13, 15, 23, 25, 27, 29, 34; 26:57; 27:41. Another group connected at times to the high priests and legal experts is the elders (πρεσβύτεροι). See Jeremias 1962: 222–32 and 15:2; 16:21; 21:23; 26:3, 47, 57; 27:1, 3, 12, 20, 41; 28:12. The three groups are portrayed together plotting against Jesus in 16:21; 26:57; 27:41. Evidently, these three groups made up the high court, or Sanhedrin. The phrase "the people's legal experts" occurs only here in Matthew, but "the elders of the people" occurs in 21:23; 26:3, 47; 27:1. See also Gale 2005; Klijn 1959: 259–67; Schwartz 1992: 89–101; and Twelftree in J. Green and McKnight 1992: 728–35.

answer to Herod. This would make little sense unless they understood Mic. 5:2 as a direct prediction of the Messiah's birthplace. The abiding authority of the Bible as God's revelation is implied by the force of the perfect-tense verb γέγραπται, which presents the ancient text as something that stands written contemporaneously with the NT situation (cf. BDF §340; Wallace 1996: 574–76). The passive verb should be viewed as a divine, or theological, passive, implying God's agency (Zerwick 1963: §236; Wallace 1996: 437–38). The prepositional phrase διὰ τοῦ προφήτου expresses the human means used by the divine agency.

Micah 5:2 LXX is an accurate translation of the Hebrew Bible, but the form of the text appearing in Matthew differs from both MT and LXX in four obvious ways. Three of these are relatively inconsequential. First, Matthew has "Bethlehem in the land (γῆ, $g\bar{e}$) of Judah" whereas the MT has "Bethlehem Ephrathah" and the LXX has "Bethlehem house [οἶκος, *oikos*] of Ephrathah." It may be that Ephrathah (cf., e.g., Gen. 35:19; 48:7; Ruth 4:11; 1 Chron. 4:4) is an archaic term, unfamiliar to Matthew's audience (Carson 1984: 87), and that Matthew wishes to highlight Jesus's ancestor Judah (Matt. 1:2–3; cf. Gen. 49:10). Or perhaps Bethlehem of Judah anticipates the mention of Judah in the next line of Mic. 5:2. At any rate, Bethlehem of Judah is also found in the Bible (Judg. 17:7–9; 19:1–2, 18; Ruth 1:1–2; 1 Sam. 17:12) to distinguish it from another Bethlehem of Zebulon in Galilee (Josh. 19:15).

2:6

Another difference between Matthew and the text of both MT and LXX is Matthew's use of the word ἡγεμών (*hēgemōn*, ruler) to describe Bethlehem's insignificance among the rulers (*hēgemones*) of Judah instead of the "clans" (lit. "thousands") of Judah in MT and LXX. This may again be due to anticipation of the participial cognate ἡγούμενος (*hēgoumenos*, ruler) in the next line, or perhaps Matthew understood the MT word translated "thousands" as "princes," which is possible if the consonants are repointed (W. Davies and Allison 1988: 243). Another minor difference is Matthew's insertion of γάρ (*gar*, for) in the third line of the quotation, "*for* from you will come forth a ruler." The reason for this addition becomes clear when the next change Matthew makes in the verse is discussed.

The key difference between Matthew and MT/LXX is his addition of the word οὐδαμῶς (*oudamōs*, by no means) to the second line of the quote. Whereas MT and LXX make a simple assertion to the effect that Bethlehem is insignificant among the clans of Judah, Matthew's addition asserts the contrary: "You by no means are least among the rulers of Judah." But this contradiction is only superficial. In MT and LXX the geographical insignificance of Bethlehem is implicitly contrasted with its theological significance in a concession-result semantic pattern. The same contrast is present in Matthew but is expressed in a negation-reason semantic pattern. One could interpretively translate the MT as follows: *"Even though* you are insignificant among the clans of Judah, *nevertheless* from you one will go forth for me to be ruler in Israel."* Micah foresees that the Messiah will rise from a geographically insignificant town. As Matthew looks back to Micah's prophecy, he notes in hindsight that the birth of Jesus has transformed the significance of Bethlehem. From Micah's view, Bethlehem has prospective significance. From Matthew's retrospective view, Bethlehem is not at all insignificant. In the flow of redemptive history, Bethlehem's theological significance has finally overcome its geographical insignificance. Thus Matthew also adds the particle γάρ in line 3 to identify the birth of Jesus as the event that brings Bethlehem from the wings to center stage in the drama of redemptive history.

The biblical quotation is actually a combination of Mic. 5:2 and 2 Sam. 5:2. Matthew omits the end of Mic. 5:2, "whose origins are from long ago, from ancient times." Instead, he appends a line from 2 Sam. 5:2 (cf. 1 Chron. 11:2) to the effect that Jesus will shepherd God's people Israel. Whereas the last line of Mic. 5:2 is certainly compatible with Matthew's high Christology, the material from 2 Samuel fits Matthew's Davidic emphasis. In 2 Sam. 5 Saul had died (2 Sam. 1:1) and David had been anointed king over Judah in Hebron (2:3–4). After seven and a half years there (2:11), representatives from Israel came to Hebron and anointed David king of Israel as well. To consolidate his reign, David conquered Jebus/Jerusalem and reigned there for thirty-three years (5:5–10). The words Matthew includes from 2 Sam. 5:2 were originally spoken by the representatives from Israel who were recounting God's earlier promises to David (cf. 1 Sam. 18:5, 13, 16; 25:30; Ps. 78:70–72). The image of Jesus as shepherd fits into Matthew quite well (Matt. 9:35–36; 14:14; 15:32; 25:31–46; 26:31; cf. Golding 2006) and is based on the Hebrew Bible (cf. Ps. 23; Jer. 23; Ezek. 34; Mic. 2:12–3:3). There is also an implicit contrast between Jesus as the genuine Davidic shepherd of Israel and Herod, who with his religious leaders is a false shepherd (Matt. 9:36; John 10:11–16) and a counterfeit successor of David. (On the biblical citation, see Heater 1983; Jenson in Satterthwaite et al. 1995: 189–211; Lust in Tuckett 1997: 65–88; Petrotta 1985, 1990.)

4. Herod's Deceptive Plot (2:7–8)

2:7–8   By the time Herod secretly summons the magi, he has already concocted his scheme to murder Jesus. He needs to ascertain from them the time when the star that marked the birth of Jesus first appeared (cf. 2:16).[8] In their naïveté, the magi unwittingly give Herod the information he needs. Herod also deceptively asks them to search carefully for the child and

---

8. The verb ἠκρίβωσεν occurs only here and in 2:16. The related adverb ἀκριβῶς occurs in 2:8.

report his whereabouts so that Herod can also go and worship him.[9] Then he sends them off to Bethlehem, only about five miles to the south. As the unknowing magi eagerly press on in the last leg of their long journey, Herod knows when the helpless baby was born and where he evidently is living. If the magi report back to him as he has requested, he will know exactly who the child is, and his plot will be absurdly easy to accomplish.

From a literary standpoint, this is a remarkable situation. Matthew the narrator knows all about Herod's duplicity, but the magi as characters in the story have not yet even a clue of it. The perceptive reader might gradually pick up on this, perhaps with previous knowledge of Herod's character (2:3), with possible suspicion of Herod's ignorance of the Messiah's birthplace (2:4), and with probable suspicion of Herod's conspiratorial, if not sinister, secret meeting with the magi (2:7–8). The reader's suspicions are confirmed as the story unfolds in 2:12–23.

5. The Magi in Bethlehem (2:9–11)

After learning from the king that they should go to Bethlehem and becoming unwitting accomplices in his plot to murder Jesus, the magi set out on the short journey. As they go, the star they originally saw unexpectedly reappears and miraculously leads[10] them to the vicinity of Jesus, perhaps to his exact location. This astral guarantee of God's guidance exhilarates the magi. Whatever the merit of positing a providential basis for what the magi saw earlier (2:1), no comet, supernova, or planetary conjunction would exhibit the phenomena observed here by the magi. It is ironic that the birth of Jesus produces only anxious fear in the leaders of Israel (2:3) whereas it is the occasion of overwhelming joy in the mysterious gentile magi.[11] The devotion of the magi is in stark contrast to Herod's treachery and the seeming apathy of the chief priests and legal experts. Why are the magi the only ones who travel to Bethlehem?

2:9–10

9. For other constructions with the participle πορευθέντες and the aorist imperative (here ἐξετάσατε), cf. 9:13; 11:4; 28:19. This use of the participle is sometimes styled "pleonastic" (BDAG 853; BDF §419.2; Moulton and Turner 1963: 154; Moulton 1908: 230), "graphic" (Zerwick 1963: §363), or even "redundant" (Wallace 1996: 649–50) because, strictly speaking, it is unnecessary, since its meaning is implied by the imperative. This is generally spoken of as a Semitic idiom. Such a participle takes on an imperatival flavor because of its association with the imperative.

10. The imperfect verb προῆγεν should probably be viewed as inceptive (Moule 1959: 9), describing the beginning of a process: the star "began to go before" or "started going before" the magi. Similarly the aorist verb ἐστάθη, following the aorist participle ἐλθών, indicates the point when the star arrived and "came to stand" or "began to stand" over the place where Jesus was (BDF §331). Cf. Viviano 1996.

11. The emphatic construction ἐχάρησαν χαρὰν μεγάλην σφόδρα utilizes the cognate accusative (BDF §153; Wallace 1996: 189–90) with the adverb σφόδρα (cf. 17:6; 21:5; 27:54) to doubly stress the extent of the magi's joy.

2:11 Led by the miraculous star, the magi arrive at the house where Jesus resides. Matthew's "house" is not a contradiction to the "manger" of Luke 2:7 (contra W. Davies and Allison 1988: 248), since perhaps as much as two years have passed since Jesus was born (Matt. 2:16). The focus of the magi is on the child Jesus, not his mother, Mary, who is mentioned, or his adoptive father, Joseph, who is not. They fall before Jesus and worship him. In this commentary at 2:2 it was argued that the worship of the magi implies more than mere homage to a superior, and here is an additional reason to see in their worship insight into a high Christology (Keener 1999: 105). If the aorist verb προσεκύνησαν (*prosekynēsan*, they worshiped) implies only a kneeling down in obeisance to a king, the aorist participle πεσόντες (*pesontes*, having fallen down) is superfluous (cf. 4:9 but 18:26). After worshiping Jesus, they open their treasures (cf. 6:19–21; 19:21) and give Jesus gifts appropriate for a king: gold, frankincense (Exod. 30:34–38; Lev. 2:1–2, 14–16; 6:14–18; 24:7; Neh. 13:5, 9; Isa. 60:6; Jer. 6:20), and myrrh (Gen. 37:25; Exod. 30:23; Esth. 2:12; Ps. 45:8; Song 1:13; 3:6; Mark 15:23; John 19:39). Frankincense and myrrh were both aromatic gum resins derived from trees and bushes and imported from the east (cf. Kruse 1995; Kügler 1997; Van Beek 1960).

Commentators from Origen (*Contra Celsum* 1.60) to Hendriksen (1973: 171–76) have found symbolic significance in these gifts: gold for a king, frankincense for Jesus's divinity, and myrrh for death (W. Davies and Allison 1988: 249–50). It is much more likely that 2:11 alludes to biblical passages such as Pss. 72:10–12; 110:3; Isa. 60:1–6. Solomon received gifts from gentile visitors, and the prophets foresaw glorious days when gentile tribute would be brought to Zion (Rev. 21:24–26; cf. Sim 1999a).

6. Departure of the Magi (2:12)

2:12 Before they unwittingly participate in Herod's monstrous scheme, the magi are warned by God in a dream not to go back to Herod. Dreams occur frequently in Matthew's infancy material (1:20; 2:12, 13, 19, 22), but angelic visitation is not mentioned here or in 2:22. The magi return by another route, evidently bypassing Jerusalem entirely and following trade routes through the wilderness of Judah to the east. They could have traveled either north or south of the Dead Sea, but it seems that the southern route would have promised more secrecy.[12]

---

12. The departure of the magi is expressed by the verb ἀνεχώρησαν. In Matthew this verb usually (9:24 and 27:5 are exceptions) expresses what might be called "strategic withdrawal" from those who oppose Jesus and the message of the kingdom. Thus the magi, along with Joseph, Mary, and Jesus, withdraw at crucial times to a place of safety (2:12, 13, 14, 22). When John is imprisoned, Jesus withdraws to Galilee and begins his ministry there (4:12). Aware of the murder plot of the Pharisees, Jesus withdraws from their company and forbids those he has healed from making him known, evidently to lessen publicity that would provoke further opposition (12:15). When John is executed by Herod the tetrarch, Jesus withdraws to a remote place (14:13). After the confrontation

How the magi originally understood that an astral phenomenon signaled prophetic fulfillment and the birth of the Messiah is shrouded in mystery. Numbers 24:17 was evidently understood messianically by the Jews, but how the magi might have come to associate a particular star with that prophecy is unclear. Dispersed Jews in the east may have influenced the magi, but in the final analysis the worship of the magi is nothing less than a miracle of divine grace. Matthew 11:25–27 explains the divine initiative active when anyone comes to faith in Jesus the Messiah, and Matt. 11:28–29 supplies Jesus's invitation for others to emulate the example of the magi. This incident well illustrates the truth that has become something of a cliché: God works in mysterious ways, his wonders to perform. The religious leaders, replete with scriptural knowledge, react with apathy here and with antipathy later. The magi, whose knowledge is quite limited, nevertheless offer genuine worship to the born-king of the Jews.[13]

Additional Note

2:5. The introductory formula used by the religious leaders (οὕτως γὰρ γέγραπται διὰ τοῦ προφήτου) generally occurs on the lips of Jesus in Matthew, with the exception of Satan's use of it in 4:6. Uses of this formula are as follows:

Matthew	Speaker	Bible reference	Formula
2:5	Leaders	Mic. 5:2/2 Sam. 5:2	οὕτως γὰρ γέγραπται διὰ τοῦ προφήτου
4:4	Jesus	Deut. 8:3	γέγραπται
4:6	Satan	Ps. 91:11–12	γέγραπται γὰρ ὅτι
4:7	Jesus	Deut. 6:16	πάλιν γέγραπται
4:10	Jesus	Deut. 6:13	γέγραπται γάρ
11:10	Jesus	Exod. 23:20/Mal. 3:1	οὗτός ἐστιν περὶ οὗ γέγραπται
21:13	Jesus	Isa. 56:7/Jer. 7:11	γέγραπται
26:24	Jesus	No specific text	καθὼς γέγραπται περὶ αὐτοῦ
26:31	Jesus	Zech. 13:7	γέγραπται γάρ

Perhaps 26:24 should not be included in this table, since no specific biblical text is cited (but cf. 2:23). The hermeneutical use of the Bible varies in these passages. Some seem to evince a prediction/fulfillment dynamic (2:5; 11:10; 26:24, 31), others supply ethical authority (4:4, 6, 7, 10), and one seems to involve a typological pattern (21:13).

---

with the Pharisees over washing hands before meals, Jesus withdraws to the region of Tyre and Sidon and encounters the remarkable faith of a Canaanite woman (15:21). As opposition increases, however, there is no further withdrawal. Jesus must go to his death in Jerusalem (16:21). On ἀναχωρέω, see Good 1990.

13. On Matt. 2:1–12, see R. Brown 1993: 165–201, 607–15; Buetubela 1994; Cuvillier 1999b; Nolland 1998; Raimbault 1998.

I. Prologue/Introduction: Origin of Jesus the Messiah (1:1–2:23)
   C. Visit of the Magi (2:1–12)
➤ D. Escape to Egypt (2:13–15)
   E. Massacre at Bethlehem (2:16–18)

D. Escape to Egypt (2:13–15)

Though the analysis here divides the rest of the chapter into three sections (13–15, 16–18, 19–23) coinciding with three formula quotations, Matt. 2:13–23 as a whole should be viewed as a unit containing the withdrawal and return of the Messiah (cf. Erickson 1996). The three dream units concerning Joseph (1:18–25; 2:13–15; 2:19–23) are interlocked with the two units concerning Herod's treachery (2:1–12; 2:16–18):

> *Dream*: Joseph should marry Mary and name the child Jesus
>   (1:18–25)
>   *Treachery*: Herod enlists magi to find Jesus (2:1–12)
> *Dream*: Joseph should take Jesus and Mary to Egypt (2:13–15)
>   *Treachery*: Herod murders the male infants of Bethlehem
>   (2:16–18)
> *Dream*: Joseph should return to Israel (2:19–23)

Joseph's role of protecting Jesus is contrasted with Herod's role in attempting to murder Jesus. Through it all, divine intervention in the form of repeated angelic visitations ensures the safety of the born-king of the Jews, the Son of God, Jesus the Messiah.

The unit can be outlined as follows:

1. Joseph's dream (2:13)
2. Joseph's obedience (2:14–15a)
3. The biblical pattern (2:15b)

Exegesis and Exposition

[13]After they had departed, unexpectedly an angel of the Lord appeared to Joseph in a dream and said, "Get up, take the child and his mother, and flee to Egypt. Stay there until I tell you, because Herod is going to search for the child to kill him." [14]So Joseph got up, took the child and his mother at night, and departed to Egypt. [15]He stayed there until Herod died, so that what the Lord said by the prophet might be fulfilled:

"Out of Egypt I called my son."

1. Joseph's Dream (2:13)

After the magi have withdrawn (ἀναχωρησάντων, *anachōrēsantōn*; the same verb used in 2:12 is repeated here in participial form), the divine intervention to thwart Herod's plot takes another step. For the second time (cf. 1:20) Joseph unexpectedly (ἰδού, *idou*) receives revelation from an angel in a dream. This time the historical present φαίνεται (*phainetai*) describes the appearance of the angel, perhaps indicating that the appearance coincides with the magi's withdrawal (BDF §321; cf. S. Black in Porter and Reed 1999: 120–39).[1] Joseph is to take Jesus and Mary to Egypt and stay there until he receives further notice, because Herod is going to try to murder Jesus.[2]

2:13

2. Joseph's Obedience (2:14–15a)

Joseph again responds to the angel with prompt, unquestioning obedience (1:24). Under cover of darkness,[3] Joseph, Mary, and Jesus withdraw to Egypt and remain there until Herod dies and they receive another angelic revelation (2:19). Egypt was a natural place to flee to because Herod had no jurisdiction there and many Jews lived there. Perhaps Matthew wants his readers to remember the family of Jacob sojourning in Egypt to avoid famine in Palestine (Gen. 46). On the level of the infancy story, the withdrawal to Egypt preserves Jesus from Herod's plot, but Matthew has a deeper purpose in mind as well.

2:14–15a

Gundry (1994: 32) believes that Matthew created the story of the flight to Egypt as a midrash on Luke's pericope concerning the Jerusalem visit of Joseph, Jesus, and Mary (Luke 2:22). This is highly unlikely for several reasons. (See Carson 1984: 71–91.)

1. Φαίνεται is the first use of the "historical present" in Matthew. Grammarians generally view this use of the present in a past time context as a stylistic effort to portray certain past events with added vividness. No doubt colloquial conversational speech commonly resorted to a similar style. According to Moulton and Turner 1963: 60–62, the historical present is very common in Mark (151 uses) and John, though rare in Luke. They claim 93 examples in Matthew, of which I have found more than 80. Most of these (65) are forms of verbs of speech (e.g., λέγω) introducing direct quotations: 4:6, 10, 19; 8:4, 7, 20, 22, 26; 9:6, 9, 28, 37; 12:13, 44; 13:28, 51; 14:8, 17, 31; 15:12, 33, 34; 16:15; 17:20, 25; 18:22, 32; 19:7, 8, 10, 18, 20; 20:6, 7 (2x), 8, 21, 22, 23; 21:13, 16, 19, 31 (2x), 41, 42; 22:8, 12, 20, 21, 43; 26:25, 31, 35, 36, 38, 40, 45, 52, 64, 71; 27:13, 22; 28:10. Another use introduces a new pericope or a change of character within a pericope (e.g., 3:1). Historical presents are also found in 2:13, 19; 3:1, 13; 4:5, 8, 11; 9:14; 15:1; 17:1; 22:16; 25:19; 26:36, 40 (2x), 45. It is difficult to discern patterns or consistency in this usage. For further general discussion, see Wallace 1996: 526–32, and for the historical present in Matthew, see S. Black in Porter and Reed 1999: 120–39.

2. The angel's words to Joseph (ἐγερθεὶς παράλαβε) again combine participle and imperative in a "graphic" circumstantial-participle construction (cf. 2:8). The imminence (BDF §356) of the danger facing Jesus is underlined by the use of the verb μέλλει with the infinitives ζητεῖν and ἀπολέσαι. No wonder Joseph left immediately for Egypt.

3. Νυκτός without a preposition is an adverbial genitive of time (BDF §188.2; Wallace 1996: 122–24).

3. The Biblical Pattern (2:15b)

2:15b   The sovereignty of God achieves not only the immediate welfare of the
infant Jesus but also the ultimate fulfillment of a well-known biblical
pattern. Matthew's second fulfillment formula quotation (see "Theological
Emphases: Fulfillment" in the commentary introduction) alludes to the
new significance of the event described in Hos. 11:1: "Out of Egypt I
called my son." The introductory formula is identical to the one that
occurs in 1:22 and denotes the accomplishment of God's purpose in his
word through the prophetic channel. Matthew cites only the last clause
of Hos. 11:1, and his text form is nearly a word-for-word equivalent of
the MT. The LXX has the compound aorist verb μετεκάλεσα (*metekalesa*)
whereas Matthew has ἐκάλεσα (*ekalesa*). More significantly, the LXX has
God summon "his children" (τὰ τέκνα αὐτοῦ, *ta tekna autou*), not "my
son" (τὸν υἱόν μου, *ton huion mou*) from Egypt (cf. Menken 1999a). No
doubt this concept of sonship is the reason Matthew was attracted to
Hos. 11:1 in the first place. The initial words of Hos. 11:1, though not
cited by Matthew, are also crucial for the sonship theme. The verse as a
whole affirms that God loved Israel and called him/it from Egypt when
he/it was a child.

There are essentially two approaches to Matthew's use of Hos. 11:1.
Some scholars believe that Matthew, perhaps mistakenly, saw in the
passage a prediction of Jesus's sojourn in Egypt and departure from
there. But most would agree that in its original context, Hos. 11:1 is
not a prediction of the future but a reference to the exodus, God's past
redemptive act of bringing the nation of Israel out of Egypt.

Those who think that Matthew saw a prediction of Jesus in Hos. 11:1
must either disparage Matthew's hermeneutic (Barclay 1975: 1.35–36;
Boring 1995: 153–54; Luz 1989: 146n24; T. Robinson 1928: 9) or attribute
to Matthew revelatory insight into the *sensus plenior* of Hosea (Fee and
Stuart 1993: 185; H. Fowler 1968: 1.83). Neither of these views is satis-
factory. The first attributes error to Matthew, and the second attributes
inscrutable hermeneutics to the Holy Spirit.

There is a better way, one affirming that Matthew's application of Hos.
11:1 to Jesus does not distort Hosea (Calvin 1972: 1.101). It is that in its
original context, Hos. 11:1 is not a prediction of Jesus but a reminiscence
of the exodus. This was at least as clear to Matthew as it is to modern
interpreters (Hare 1993: 15). But Hos. 11:1 alludes to a theological motif
that was dear to Matthew: divine sonship. The exodus demonstrated
Israel's unique status as God's firstborn son. What was true of Israel on a
metaphorical level is more profoundly true of Jesus the Messiah. Matthew
has already shown the uniqueness of Jesus's sonship from the perspective
of his Davidic genealogy and miraculous conception. Matthew will go
on to show how Jesus's baptism and temptation demonstrate his divine
sonship even more fully. In Hos. 11:1 the exodus provides a historical

pattern of God's loving preservation of his son Israel from Pharaoh's wrath. From a Christian perspective, this past event is recapitulated by God's loving preservation of his Son, Jesus, from Herod's wrath. In the Hebrew Bible the nation is the son of God (Exod. 4:22–23; Jer. 31:9, 20; Hos. 1:10), and the Davidic kings are sons of God (2 Sam. 7:14–15; Pss. 2:6–7, 12; 72:1; 89:26–37). God's special love and covenant loyalty are promised to both the nation and the kings. For Matthew, these themes are consummated in Jesus, whose individual life is an antitypical microcosm of macrocosmic typological Israel.

Matthew certainly noted Hosea's stress on God's love and loyalty to his people (Hos. 1:6–7; 2:1, 23; 11:1, 8). And he was aware of Hosea's repeated mention of Egypt (7:11, 16; 8:13; 9:6; 11:5; 12:1; 13:4). Both Hosea and Matthew believed that God's true people would turn to God and God's Davidic king in the last days (Hos. 3:5; Matt. 1:21). Hosea 11:1 is not a prediction of Jesus but is part of an emotional appeal for Israel to turn from apostasy to its loving God. For Matthew, this return would be accomplished through faith in Jesus the Messiah, whose life typologically repeats crucial events of biblical redemptive history. (For further discussion of this approach, see W. Davies and Allison 1988: 261; Kaiser 1985: 47–53; Hagner 1993: 36–37; and esp. T. Howard 1986.)

This typological approach (Nolland 2005: 123) is preferable to the *sensus plenior* view because it focuses on a theme dear to Matthew: redemptive history. Jesus really does fill biblical-historical patterns and prophetic predictions with their ultimate significance. Matthew's approach to the Bible is not the product of mysterious revelations that give him license to ignore the original meaning of the text and assert new meanings by divine fiat. Rather, Matthew looks at biblical history with the conviction that it is organically related to Jesus the Messiah as the seed is to the harvest.

It is unusual that Matthew places this fulfillment quotation before the departure of Jesus from Egypt, to which it refers. Generally, fulfillment formulas are inserted after the narration of the events to which they refer. But Matthew did not place the formula before the event here because he intended to stress God's care for Jesus while he was in Egypt (Gundry 1994: 34). Rather, the geographical orientation of 2:13–15 and 2:19–20 as a whole is Egypt. Interspersed in 2:16–18 is an orientation to Bethlehem and Ramah. In 2:21–23 the orientation is toward the destination Nazareth, not the point of origin, Egypt. If Matthew had cited Hos. 11:1 at 2:21 when Jesus left Egypt, this would have spoiled this orientation to Nazareth (S. Brown 1977: 219–20; Carson 1984: 91; W. Davies and Allison 1988: 262).[4]

4. For more on Hos. 11:1 in Matt. 2:15, see R. Brown 1993: 202–30; France 1980–81; Sailhamer 2001; McCartney and Enns 2001; Soarés-Prabhu 1992.

I. Prologue/Introduction: Origin of Jesus the Messiah (1:1–2:23)
   D. Escape to Egypt (2:13–15)
➤ E. Massacre at Bethlehem (2:16–18)
   F. Return to Nazareth (2:19–23)

E. Massacre at Bethlehem (2:16–18)

In 2:16–18, Matthew returns to the story of Herod and the magi, which was suspended briefly from 2:1–12 by 2:13–15. After a short amount of time passes, Herod realizes that the magi are not coming back, and so he uses the information he has previously received from the chief priests and legal experts and the magi. He knows from the religious leaders *where* Jesus was born (2:5–6), and he knows from the magi *when* Jesus was born (2:7). With this information he launches the atrocity of murdering all the male children in the Bethlehem area who are under two years of age. This section of Matt. 2 stands in sharp contrast to the previous section, 2:13–15, which stresses the divine protection of Jesus. That God protects Jesus from the rage of Herod but permits Herod to slaughter other innocent children is another of many instances of the problem of evil as part of divine providence. The narrative of the massacre of Bethlehem's male infants first describes the atrocity and then interprets it in light of a significant previous atrocity.

The unit can be outlined as follows:

1. Herod's atrocity (2:16)
2. The biblical pattern (2:17–18)

Exegesis and Exposition

[16]Herod was filled with fury when he realized that he had been deceived by the men who studied the stars. So he sent men to murder all the boys in Bethlehem and in all its region who were two years old or younger, in keeping with the exact time he had learned from the men who studied the stars. [17]Then what was spoken by the prophet Jeremiah was fulfilled:

[18]"A voice was heard in Ramah,
⌜Wailing⌝ and great grief;
Rachel wailing for her children,
and she refuses to be consoled,
because they are no more."

1. Herod's Atrocity (2:16)

2:16   Since Bethlehem is only about five miles from Jerusalem, Herod would soon realize that the magi are not coming back. Perhaps only two or three days have passed since the magi left Jerusalem for Bethlehem.[1] Although Herod believes that the magi have tricked him, their lack of complicity in his plot was due to divine intervention. Herod's rage is not in reality directed against the magi; it is against God, who directed them not to return to Herod. Thus his fury is pathetic and futile, like that of the kings whom God warned in Ps. 2 (cf. Acts 4:24–28). Since Bethlehem was a small village, the loss of life was relatively low, but the innocence of the victims underscores the outrageous nature of this heinous act. Matthew does not concoct this story out of meditation on Jer. 31:15 (Beare 1981: 82). Nor does he change Luke's pericope about the sacrifice of doves when Jesus was presented in the temple (Luke 2:24) into the story of the slaughter of Bethlehem's male babies (Gundry 1994: 34–37). Although there is no record of these events outside this pericope, this atrocity fits well into what is known from extrabiblical sources about the ruthless nature of Herod's rule. (See France 1979: 98–120; in Livingstone 1980: 83–94.)[2]

2. The Biblical Pattern (2:17–18)

Herod's heinous act fulfills his own rage and paranoia, but Matthew is more interested in how it fulfills Scripture. He introduces Jer. 31:15 with a fulfillment formula similar to those used earlier in 1:22 and 2:15 (see "Theological Emphases: Fulfillment" in the commentary introduction). There are, however, three minor differences. First, Matthew uses τότε (*tote*, then) instead of ἵνα (*hina*, in order that) to introduce the quotation (cf. 27:9). This may be due to a desire to lessen the implication that God's purpose was fulfilled by the atrocity. Second, Matthew omits the phrase "by the Lord," which appeared in 1:22 and 2:15; he thereby makes the divine origin of the text less explicit here. Third, Matthew mentions here for the first time the name of the prophet he is citing. Jeremiah is named only by Matthew in the NT (2:17; 16:14; 27:9). (For studies of Jeremiah in Matthew, see Knowles 1993; Law 1997; Menken 1984; Winkle 1986; Zucker 1990.)

2:17

1. For the second time (cf. 2:7) Matthew introduces Herod's activity with the particle τότε. This temporal particle, which introduces subsequent events, occurs 158 times in the NT, and 90 of these are in Matthew. In contrast, Mark uses it 6 times, Luke 15 times, and John 10 times. The temporal force of the word is not always clear in Matthew. For its use, see Matt. 2:7, 16, 17; 3:5, 13, 15; 4:1, 5, 10, 11, 17; 5:24; 7:5, 23; 8:26; 9:6, 14, 15, 29, 37; 11:20; 12:13, 22, 29, 38, 44, 45; 13:26, 36, 43; 15:1, 12, 28; 16:12, 20, 21, 24, 27; 17:13, 19; 18:21, 32; 19:13, 27; 20:20; 21:1; 22:8, 13, 15, 21; 23:1; 24:9, 10, 14, 16, 21, 23, 30, 40; 25:1, 7, 31, 34, 37, 41, 44, 45; 26:3, 14, 16, 31, 36, 38, 45, 50, 52, 56, 65, 67, 74; 27:3, 9, 13, 16, 26, 27, 38, 58; 28:10 and McNeile 1911: 127–28.

2. According to Josephus, Herod had his wife Mariamne and his sons Alexander, Aristobulus, and Antipater executed. To ensure mourning at the time of his own death, he ordered that representatives of every Jewish family be executed after he died, but this reprehensible order was not carried out (*Ant.* 15.231; 16.392–94; 17.180–87, 193; *J.W.* 1.551). Keener 1999: 110–11 nicely summarizes this material.

2:18   There are several differences in the text form of Jer. 31:15 as found in MT, LXX, and Matt. 2:18, but none seem significant for exegesis. If the text is arranged in five lines as in the translation above, lines 1 and 5 are nearly word for word equivalent. In lines 2, 3, and 4, there is variation in the number of words and a difference in word order, but the meaning is unaffected. Overall Matt. 2:18 is a bit closer to the MT than the LXX. (See Menken in Moyise 2000: 106–25.)

Jeremiah 31:15 occurs in an oracle of joy and hope to those who are about to be exiled, probably to Babylon because of Nebuchadnezzar's conquest of Judah in 587 BCE. Indeed, Jer. 31:15 is "the only gloomy verse in all of Jer 31" (W. Davies and Allison 1988: 269). Although captivity is unavoidable, the captives must go on with their lives for seventy years until God restores them to the land God promised to their forefathers (Jer. 29:4–14). God is punishing Israel and Judah for their apostasy but will restore them to himself and to the Davidic dynasty (30:8–9; 33:14–15, 17). Israel is viewed as a virgin (31:4, 13, 21) whom God loves as his special people (30:3, 22; 31:1, 2, 7, 33) and will save as a remnant (31:7). God yearns for Israel because God is Israel's father and Israel is his firstborn (31:9, 20). Thus there is hope that Israel's children will return (31:17), because God will make a new covenant with the nation and forgive their sins (31:31, 34). Nevertheless, there is presently great mourning by Rachel, who personifies the mothers of Israel, for her children who have died in the ravages of war.[3] This oracle contains numerous themes that resonate with Matthew's own theological interests.

In light of this background, it seems that "fulfillment" here should not be viewed simplistically as the eventuation of a prediction. Kaiser's attempt (1985: 56) to view the verse as generic rather than specific prediction is only marginally helpful. Jeremiah 31:15 is not a prediction but a present lament in the context of hope for future blessing. There are other connections between Matthew and Jeremiah. First are the motifs summarized above (e.g., exile, God's people, David, sonship), which are likely the contextual reasons Matthew cites the passage. Then there is the geographical connection with Rachel and Bethlehem-Ephrathah (Gen. 35:19; 48:7; 1 Sam. 10:2). Ramah does not figure directly in Matt. 2 but is mentioned in Jer. 40:1, where it is described as the place where the exiles were gathered before departure for Babylon. Evidently, Ramah was north of Jerusalem near Bethel, although its exact location is still debated. There is also the obvious connection of mourning for innocent children who have been unjustly murdered. A case can be made here for an analogy or typology being drawn between the two incidents. Also, Jer. 31 refers to Egypt (31:32) and to Israel as God's son (31:9, 20), themes that perhaps tie it to Matthew's previous biblical citation in 2:15.

---

3. On ancient Jewish interpretation of Rachel's lament, see Zatelli 1991.

But the setting of Jer. 31:15 in the context of hope is probably the area where Matthew's main theological interest is centered (Carson 1984: 95; Tasker 1961: 44). In Jeremiah's view of the future, Rachel's mourning for her children would be consoled by Israel's return to the land and the making of a new covenant. The similar mourning of the mothers of Bethlehem also occurs in the context of hope, but the hope here is now about to be actualized through the sacrificial death and resurrection of the Messiah (Matt. 26:27–28). God comforted the exiles with the hope of restoration and the new covenant, and this hope is about to be actualized through the Messiah. Thus the mourning mothers of Bethlehem were anticipated by the mothers who lost children at the time of the exile. In view of all these connections between Jer. 31 and Matt. 2, Schnackenburg's characterization of this citation as "forced" (2002: 26) is puzzling. (On Matt. 2:16–18, see Becking 1994; France in Livingstone 1980: 83–94; Knowles 1993: 33–52; Mans 1997; Niedner 2002.)

Additional Note

2:18. For convenient discussions of the differences in text form between MT, LXX, and Matt. 2:18, see W. Davies and Allison 1988: 268–70; Gundry 1967: 94–97. These differences do not appear to be exegetically or theologically significant. In line 2 (see the arrangement in the translation above), where Jer. 38:15 LXX has three nouns expressing Rachel's sorrow (θρήνου καὶ κλαυθμοῦ καὶ ὀδυρμοῦ), Matthew has two nouns with an adjective stressing the second (κλαυθμὸς καὶ ὀδυρμὸς πολύς). Here Matthew is closer to the construct state of the Hebrew syntax of the MT. The textual variant in the Majority text (adding θρῆνος to the other two nouns of mourning) is similar to the LXX. This leads Metzger (1994: 8) to view the variant as assimilation to the LXX. In lines 3 and 4, the LXX and Matt. 2:18 diverge in word order and in the words used for Rachel's mourning, comfort, and children. But in these three instances, the words seem to be generally synonymous and the meaning is not appreciably changed.

I. Prologue/Introduction: Origin of Jesus the Messiah (1:1–2:23)
    D. Escape to Egypt (2:13–15)
    E. Massacre at Bethlehem (2:16–18)
➤ F. Return to Nazareth (2:19–23)

F. Return to Nazareth (2:19–23)

This unit picks up again the narrative of 2:13–15, which was briefly interrupted by the story of the murder of Bethlehem's male infants. It contains the fourth and fifth dreams and the third appearance of an angel of the Lord in the infancy narratives. The death of Herod permits the safe return of Jesus to Israel, but Joseph deems it wise to live in Nazareth of Galilee, not in Judea, where Herod's son Archelaus rules in the place of his father. The unit briefly describes Joseph's response to another dream and interprets it in light of Scripture. The structure is as follows:

1. Joseph's dream (2:19–20)
2. Joseph's obedient response (2:21–23a)
3. The biblical pattern (2:23b–c)

Exegesis and Exposition

[19]But when Herod died, an angel of the Lord appeared unexpectedly in a dream to Joseph in Egypt [20]and said, "Get up, take the child and his mother, and go to the land of Israel, for those who were trying to murder the child are dead." [21]So Joseph got up, took the child and his mother, and traveled to the land of Israel. [22]And when he heard that Archelaus was ruling Judea in his father Herod's place, he was afraid to return there. But after he was warned in a dream, he went away to the region of Galilee [23]and settled in a town called Nazareth, so that what was said by the prophets might be fulfilled, "He shall be called a Nazarene."

1. Joseph's Dream (2:19–20)

2:19 The syntax of 2:19 repeats the pattern of 2:13. A genitive absolute, providing background, is followed by the particle ἰδού (*idou*), which introduces an unexpected development, the angel's appearance in a dream to Joseph. In this case, the genitive absolute communicates the death of Herod. Herod has been the antagonist of Jesus throughout Matt. 2 and has just attempted to annihilate any potential rivals to his throne. But because of divine intervention, Jesus is still alive when Herod dies. Josephus, *Ant.* 17.168–81, describes Herod's final illness and death in gruesome detail.

2:20 The words of the angel commanding Joseph to take Mary and Jesus and return to Israel repeat verbatim the instructions given in 2:13 that they

should leave Israel. In both 2:13 and 2:20, there is also a clause introduced by γάρ (*gar*, for) explaining why the instructions must be followed.
It is ironic that Herod's attempt to murder Jesus is the occasion of the
withdrawal to Egypt and that Herod's death is the occasion of Jesus's
return to Israel. The plural "those who were trying to murder the child
are dead" is curious since it is Herod alone who died. W. Davies (1964:
78; cf. Baxter 1999; W. Davies and Allison 1988: 271) takes this as an
echo of Exod. 4:19, indicating a Moses typology. The parallel to Exodus
is striking, extending even to the Semitic idiom for attempting murder,
"seeking the life [ψυχήν, *psychēn*]." Harrington (1991: 45) takes it as a
description of the religious leaders who assisted Herod's opposition
and who later conspire to kill Jesus (cf. 26:3–4). But Herod died, not
the leaders, so the best explanation is probably to regard it as a generalizing or allusive plural. In this construction (BDF §141; Moulton and
Turner 1963: 25–26; Wallace 1996: 403–6) an important individual may
be described with the plural.

2. Joseph's Obedient Response (2:21–23a)

By now Joseph's pattern of immediate response to angelic instructions is
expected (cf. 1:24; 2:14). Joseph evidently planned to settle in Bethlehem,
perhaps because he assumed that Herod's son Antipas would succeed
his father as ruler there. But he changes his plans when he learns that
Herod's son Archelaus rules Judea.[1] According to Josephus (*Ant.* 17.188),
Herod made a late change in his will, appointing Archelaus his successor
as king. Archelaus received Judea, Samaria, and Idumea. Antipas was
to rule Galilee and Perea, and Philip received Iturea and Trachonitis
(cf. Luke 3:1). But Caesar Augustus apparently appointed Archelaus as
only ethnarch of Judea, Samaria, and Idumea, not king. Archelaus had
a reputation for ruthlessness and scandal, and he was banished to Gaul
about 6 CE (Suetonius, *Tiberius* 8; Josephus, *Ant.* 17.311–17, 342–44;
Hoehner 1972: 103–5). Joseph's fear of Archelaus is confirmed by yet
another angelic dream revelation, which warns him to avoid Judah and
Archelaus. The interplay here between Joseph's responsible decision
making and God's leading is intriguing. The warning of the angel underlines the fear Joseph already feels and evidently leaves it up to him
where to settle. The text does not indicate that Joseph feared Archelaus
or moved to Nazareth because of the angel's warning. As it turned out,
Joseph's fears were justified. The withdrawal to Egypt was due to specific
angelic revelation, and now similarly the decision to withdraw to Galilee
is influenced by a more general angelic warning.

2:21–23a

---

1. The two circumstantial aorist participles in 2:22 (ἀκούσας . . . χρηματισθείς) are
causal (Moule 1959: 102–3; Moulton and Turner 1963: 157), explaining why Joseph acted
as he did.

Galilee becomes very important in Matthew's portrayal of Jesus as the one who fulfills Isa. 9:1–2 (Matt. 4:12–16; Freyne 1980; 1988a; in McKnight and Osborne 2004: 21–35). After John's imprisonment, Jesus withdraws there and begins his kingdom ministry in "Galilee of the Gentiles" (4:15). Other important events occur there, but it is from this same Galilee that Jesus sends his successors to disciple all the nations (28:7, 16). Many have noticed the difference between Matthew and Luke regarding Galilee. According to Luke 1:26–27; 2:1–7, Mary and Joseph originally lived in Nazareth. Although one would not gather this from Matthew, nothing said by Matthew contradicts it. Matthew simply picks up the story after Joseph and Mary have arrived in Bethlehem to register for Augustus's census. Another difference is the sojourn in Egypt, mentioned by Matthew but not by Luke. Still, Luke's account does not contradict Matthew's Egyptian visit, which may be fitted into Luke 2 at some time prior to the return to Nazareth, described in Luke 2:39. Evidently, the presentation of Jesus in the temple (Luke 2:21–38; cf. Lev. 12:2–8) should be viewed as historical background for the arrival of the magi some time later. Popular messianic speculation would likely be stirred by both events. At any rate, both of these difficulties are examples of the selectivity of the Gospel authors in omitting material that does not fit their individual literary and theological interests.

Because of political danger, common sense, and the angelic warning, Joseph decides to settle in Nazareth. One does not learn from Matthew what readers of Luke would know; it was only natural for Joseph and Mary to return to their hometown. Nazareth was an obscure village, not mentioned anywhere in pre-Christian literature, about fifteen miles west of the southern tip of the Sea of Galilee. It sat on the northern rim of the Megiddo valley just south of the thriving city of Sepphoris.

3. The Biblical Pattern (2:23b–c)

2:23b–c   Joseph's decision to settle in the unremarkable hamlet of Nazareth has one result that is remarkable to Matthew: the fulfillment of the prophetic word. The introductory formula is like those used earlier in 1:22; 2:15, 17 (see "Theological Emphases: Fulfillment" in the commentary introduction). The conjunction ὅπως (hopōs, so that; cf. 8:17; 13:35) begins the introductory formula on a note similar to its synonym ἵνα (hina). It indicates that Joseph's decision to settle in Nazareth is a matter of God's purpose. Matthew uses the plural "through the prophets" (διὰ τῶν προφητῶν, dia tōn prophētōn; cf. 26:54, 56) and omits the "redundant" participle λεγόντων (legontōn, saying), which occurs in other introductory formulas. Both of these features may be significant clues to solving the difficulty of the quotation "He will be called a Nazarene."

The difficulty here is simple: no biblical texts refer to Jesus as a Nazarene, let alone explicitly say, "He shall be called a Nazarene." Gundry

(1967: 97–104) has a thorough discussion of the various approaches to this problem.[2] There are only two major ways to solve the difficulty. One posits a paronomasia (pun) in which Matthew is associating the place name Nazareth (Ναζαρέτ, *Nazaret*) and the word for a resident of Nazareth, "Nazarene" (Ναζωραῖος, *Nazōraios*) with either the Hebrew word for "branch" (Isa. 11:1) or the biblical "Nazirite," one especially dedicated to God (Judg. 13:5, 7; 16:17). The other views the pun theories as overly subtle and posits instead that Matthew is drawing together the obscure geographical origins of the Messiah and the biblical-theological theme that the Messiah will be humble and despised. Yet a third approach believes that Matthew's words are intentionally open-ended and allusive and that a combination of the above approaches is indicated (R. Brown 1993: 218–19; Schnackenburg 2002: 27–28).

Some proponents of paronomasia believe that Matthew connects Nazareth with the reference to the Messiah as a "branch [נֵצֶר, *nēṣer*] from Jesse's roots" in Isa. 11:1 (cf. synonyms in Isa. 4:2; 53:2). The Davidic emphasis of this passage and the fact that Matthew has already cited Isa. 7:14 in 1:23 are points in favor of this wordplay. If it is correct, Matthew connects the sound of the place name Nazareth with the messianic term נֵצֶר, which fits into Matthew's Davidic stress (Luz 1989: 150; Nolland 2005: 130). As mentioned, other proponents of wordplay connect Nazareth with "Nazirite" (נָזִיר, *nāzîr*), an individual whose total dedication to God was marked by ascetic practices (Num. 6:2, 13, 18–21; Judg. 13:5, 7; 16:17; 1 Sam. 1:11; Lam. 4:7 MT; Amos 2:11–12; cf. Luke 1:15; Acts 18:18; 21:23–24). (This approach is favored by Hill 1972: 87 and W. Davies and Allison 1988: 276–77.) Menken (2001a) supports the view by arguing that Matt. 2:23 depends specifically on Judg. 13:5, 7. For Matthew, Jesus's dedication to God was no doubt total, yet Jesus, unlike John the Baptist, did not follow an ascetic lifestyle (Matt. 11:18–19). The studies, however, that attempt to debunk this view by reviewing the technical etymology of these terms seem to be beside the point, since wordplays are based on popular associations, not on philological sophistication.

A second approach is favored by those who believe the wordplay approaches are overly subtle and thus weak as indications of how Jesus fulfills the Hebrew Bible. Proponents note the obscurity and humility of the Messiah in Matthew and connect this with the general tenor of the Bible that the Messiah will be despised and rejected (Pss. 22:6–8, 13; 69:8, 20–21; Isa. 11:1; 49:7; 53:2–3, 8; Dan. 9:26). Matthew's mention of the transformation of obscure Bethlehem by Jesus's birth (Matt. 2:6) and his stress on Jesus's humility (11:29; 12:19; 21:5) and rejection (8:20; 11:16–19; 15:7–8) are cited by advocates of this position (Carson 1984: 97; Gundry 1967: 103–4; Morris 1992: 49; Tasker 1961: 45; Tous-

2. See also R. Brown 1993: 217–19, 223–25; W. Davies and Allison 1988: 274–81; Hagner 1993: 39–42; Menken 2001a; Soarés-Prabhu 1976: 193–216.

saint 1980: 56–57). Other references to Nazareth in Matthew imply its unsavory gentile connections and obscurity from the perspective of urban Jerusalem (4:13; 21:11; 26:71). Additional support is found in the evidence elsewhere in the NT that Nazareth was a despised place (John 1:46–47; 7:41–42, 52) and that "Nazarene" was a term of derision for early disciples of Jesus (Acts 24:5). It may well be that Matthew's reference to Nazareth should be taken in light of his previous reference to Bethlehem as a place whose political insignificance is overshadowed by its theological significance (Matt. 2:6).

Although it is difficult to rule out the first approach as a possible secondary allusion, the second approach is preferable. Matthew's introductory formula cites the prophets in general and does not use the participle λέγοντος, which frequently introduces a direct quote (e.g., 1:22; 2:15, 17; 3:3; 4:14). Thus it seems that he is alluding to the general teaching of the prophets, not to a wordplay on a specific word in a single passage. Matthew repeatedly echoes the general tenor of the prophets that the Messiah would be lowly and despised, although it evidently cut against the grain of first-century messianic speculation.[3]

In retrospect it is clear that the message of the so-called infancy narratives in Matt. 1–2 has little to do with Jesus's infancy. Rather, they trace his ancestry, miraculous conception, early worship and opposition, and residence in Nazareth. All this is interwoven with biblical-historical patterning and prophetic prediction. Jesus is the Messiah, the son of David, the son of Abraham. He is the culmination of biblical history and prophecy. As the son of David, he is the genuine King of Israel, contrasted with the wicked usurper Herod. As the son of Abraham, he brings the blessings of God to the gentile magi. W. Davies and Allison (1988: 282) put it deftly: "Jesus culminates Israel's history in chapter 1; in chapter 2 he repeats it."

As Matthew's story of Jesus continues, both of these themes are developed. The contrast between Jesus and the false leaders of Israel erupts into full-fledged hostility leading to his death. But his outreach to the Gentiles culminates with his resurrection and mandate to the disciples to take the gospel to all the nations.

---

3. On the difficulties of Matt. 2:23, see Berger 1996; Menken 2001a; V. Wagner 2001; Zolli 2001.

I. Prologue/Introduction: Origin of Jesus the Messiah (1:1–2:23)
➤ II. Early Days of Kingdom Word and Deed (3:1–7:29)
III. Galilean Ministry Continues (8:1–11:1)
IV. Growing Opposition to the Kingdom of Heaven (11:2–13:52)

II. Early Days of Kingdom Word and Deed (3:1–7:29)

If Matt. 1–2 describes Jesus's origin, Matt. 3:1–4:25 firmly grounds the ministry of Jesus in the work of Jesus's forerunner, John the Baptist, predicted in Isa. 40:3. The story of Jesus's preparation for ministry begins with the ministry of John the Baptist and ends with John's imprisonment. Only when John is imprisoned does Jesus's ministry begin (Matt. 4:12). His early ministry in word and deed meets with much success in Galilee (4:12–25), leading to his first discourse, the Sermon on the Mount (5:1–7:29).

The Sermon on the Mount presents the ethics of the kingdom inaugurated by the words and deeds of Jesus. The body of the sermon (5:17–7:12) is an *inclusio* formed by references to obedience to, and thus fulfillment of, the law and the prophets. The introductory Beatitudes (5:3–12) and metaphors of salt and light (5:13–16) express the values of the kingdom and the witness to it. The sermon concludes with three metaphorical reminders that response to Jesus's inauguration of the kingdom will have eternal consequences (7:13–14, 15–23, 24–27). The mention of the crowd's amazed response to Jesus's authoritative words (7:28–29) leads naturally into the ensuing narrative block, where the authoritative deeds of Jesus are emphasized (8:9; 9:6; 10:1). The overlapping *inclusio* formed by the nearly identical summaries of Jesus's ministry in 4:23 and 9:35 enhances this portrayal of Jesus's holistic ministry of authoritative words and deeds. This structure leads the reader to note the continuity between the words of Jesus that conclude the first narrative-discourse block (3:1–7:29) and the deeds of Jesus that begin the second narrative-discourse block (8:1–10:42).

II. Early Days of Kingdom Word and Deed (3:1–7:29)
➤ A. Narrative 1: John and Jesus and the Kingdom of God (3:1–4:25)
   B. Discourse 1: Sermon on the Mount (5:1–7:29)

A. Narrative 1: John and Jesus and the Kingdom of God (3:1–4:25)

John's ministry in the desert of Judea, predicted in Isa. 40:3, results in many Judeans coming to him for baptism (Matt. 3:1–6). But when his ministry attracts Pharisees and Sadducees, he rebuffs them and warns them of judgment (3:7–12). He hesitates to baptize Jesus but performs the baptism at Jesus's insistence that it is necessary to fulfill all righteousness (3:13–15). At this point the Spirit comes upon Jesus, and a voice from heaven expresses the Father's approval of his beloved Son (3:16–17). Jesus's divine sonship is then put to the test by Satan, but Jesus emerges victorious (4:1–11). Then Jesus hears that John has been imprisoned. He withdraws to Galilee and begins his ministry there in fulfillment of Isa. 9:1–2 (Matt. 4:12–25). With the presentation of the ministry of John, Matthew for the first time parallels the other Synoptics (Mark 1:1–11; Luke 3:1–22) and also John (John 1:19–34).

The story of Jesus's preparation in Matt. 3:1–4:16 focuses on John's ministry. John prepares the way for Jesus. His baptism of Jesus is the occasion of the Spirit's coming and the Father's approval of his beloved Son. This sonship, affirmed by the Father at Jesus's baptism, is immediately tested by Satan. After this testing, the imprisonment of John leads to the beginning of Jesus's ministry in Galilee. Although John is mentioned later in Matthew (cf. 9:14; 11:2–19; 14:1–12; 16:14; 17:9–13; 21:23–32), it is clear that his role is secondary and preparatory whereas Jesus's role is primary and climactic. This is made clear especially in 11:2–14, which describes the redemptive historical significance of John's ministry. Although John is the apex of the old order of promise, those who participate in the new order of fulfillment in the kingdom of heaven are greater than he (11:11–13). There are several parallels between Jesus and John in Matthew (W. Davies and Allison 1988: 289).

A transition from John's to Jesus's ministry is signaled in Matt. 4:17. Many interpreters of Matthew believe that the phrase "from that time" at Matt. 4:17 (see also 16:21) signals the beginning of the second major section of Matthew. In this approach, 1:1–4:16 is preparatory, 4:17–16:20 narrates Jesus preaching of the kingdom, and 16:21–28:20 presents Jesus's Passion. One may grant that the phrase "from that time" plays a role in Matthew's presentation of major periods in the life and ministry of Jesus. However, an alternative to this approach is to take Matt. 3–4 as a narrative block preceding Jesus's first discourse in Matt. 5–7 (see, e.g., Carson 1984: 50, 98 and Meier 1980b: 1, 21). In this view, Matt. 1–2 is a prologue or introduction, with Matt. 3–7 as the first narrative/discourse block. Matthew 3:1–4:25 provides the narrative component that leads up to the Sermon of the Mount (5:1–7:29), the first discourse. The question of Matthew's structure has been discussed more thoroughly in the introduction to this commentary, which argues that both approaches draw legitimate conclusions and supply helpful insights into Matthew's message. But both fall short as wholly satisfying global solutions to all of Matthew's features because they are, after all, modern approaches to Matthew that cannot exactly reproduce the original author's thought. All in all, the second of the two approaches has more merit, and it will be utilized in this commentary.

1. Ministry of John the Baptist (3:1–12)

Matthew 3:1–12 includes a summary of John's message (3:1–2), its basis in the Bible (3:3), his ascetic way of life (3:4), and the results of his preaching (3:5–6). Then attention is focused on his confrontation with the religious leaders who come to him for baptism (3:7–12). Their imminent judgment (3:7, 10) can be avoided only by personal repentance (3:8), not by reliance on Abrahamic ancestry (3:9). John's water baptism pales in comparison with that of the Coming One's Spirit-fire baptism (3:11), which will once and for all purify Israel (3:12). The unmistakably vivid metaphorical language of John's denunciation cannot be missed: snakes (3:7), stones (3:9), an ax, trees, and fire (3:10), and the harvest with its threshing floor, wheat, chaff, and barn (3:12). John's stark negativity toward the religious leaders contrasts with his respect for Jesus in the next section, especially 3:14.

This unit can be outlined as follows:

    a. The origins of John's baptism of repentance (3:1–6)
    b. John warns the Pharisees and Sadducees of the coming
       judgment (3:7–12)

Exegesis and Exposition

[1]Some years later, John the Baptist appeared preaching in the desert of Judea.

[2]He said, "Repent, for the kingdom of heaven has come near. [3]For this is what was spoken of by Isaiah the prophet:

> "A voice of one shouting in the desert:
> 'Prepare the way of the Lord,
> Make straight paths for him.'"

[4]Now this John was wearing clothes made of camel's hair, and he had a leather belt around his waist. His food was locusts and wild honey. [5]People started coming out to him from Jerusalem and all Judea and all the region around the Jordan, [6]and they were being baptized by him in the Jordan River when they confessed their sins.

[7]But when he saw many of the Pharisees and Sadducees coming for his baptism, he said to them, "You offspring of vipers! Who warned you to flee from the coming wrath? [8]Bear fruit showing repentance then! [9]Don't even think to

say to yourselves, 'We have Abraham as our father.' I tell you that God is able to raise up children for Abraham from these stones. [10]The ax is already being swung at the root of the trees. Every tree that is not bearing good fruit is being cut down and thrown into the fire. [11]I am baptizing you with water in reference to your repentance, but after me is coming someone who is greater than I. I am not fit to carry his sandals! He will baptize you with the Holy Spirit and fire. [12]His pitchfork is in his hand, and he will clean out his threshing floor. He will gather ⌐his wheat into the barn,⌐ but he will burn up the chaff with fire that cannot be extinguished."

a. The Origins of John's Baptism of Repentance (3:1–6)

Nearly thirty years (Luke 3:23) have evidently transpired between Matt. 2:23 and 3:1. Although the apocryphal gospels contain many fanciful stories about Jesus's childhood, the NT is mostly silent on this theme. The only scriptural information on this period is found in Luke, who indicates that Joseph and Mary returned to Nazareth amazed at the revelations given about Jesus in the temple (Luke 2:25–38). Jesus's childhood and early adolescence are described in Luke 2:40, 52, two similar statements that frame the incident at the temple during Passover when Jesus was twelve years old (2:41–51). Two general observations may be made about this time in Jesus's life. First, his childhood development was indeed a normal human development. Luke 2:40, 52 indicates that Jesus "grew up" physically, socially, intellectually, and religiously. Second, this normal child possessed paranormal insight into his identity and religious heritage. This is indicated by Jesus's interchange with the teachers in the temple (2:46–47) and his understanding of the temple as his Father's house (note the wordplay with "father" in 2:48–49).

But Matthew says nothing directly about the years between Jesus's coming to live in Nazareth as a small child and his coming to John for baptism as an adult (Matt. 2:22; 3:13). One can draw a few inferences from 13:54–58 about Jesus's upbringing in Nazareth, but the fact is that Matthew's theological purposes are not furthered by biographical details of this period. Matthew is interested in telling the story of Jesus's origins (Matt. 1–2) and his preparation for ministry (3:1–4:16).

The prepositional phrase ἐν δὲ ταῖς ἡμέραις ἐκείναις (*en de tais hēmerais*   **3:1** *ekeinais*, in those days; cf. 13:1; 24:22, 29, 36; 26:29) is intentionally somewhat vague. There is no basis here for precise chronological placement as in Luke 3:1–2 (Hoehner 1977: 29–44). Evidently, the time frame is 27–29 CE. Matthew does not mention the circumstances surrounding the birth of John the Baptist as Luke 1 does. He vividly describes the arrival of John the Baptist with the historical-present verb παραγίνεται (*paraginetai*, appears; cf. 3:13 and footnote 1 of the comments on 2:13).[1] Proclamation characterizes John's arrival. Although he is known as "the Baptizer," he arrives "preaching" (κηρύσσων, kēryssōn; cf. 4:17, 23; 9:35; 10:7, 27; 11:1; 12:41; 24:14; 26:13).[2] The description of John as "the Baptist" (ὁ βαπτιστής, ho baptistēs) is a *nomen agentis* that characterizes him as one who performs the action of baptism (Moulton and Howard 1920: 364–65).

John's ministry was carried out in the desert of Judea, the barren area just west of the Dead Sea. This mostly uninhabited area is characterized by a dry climate and a topography featuring valleys (wadis) running from the hills in the west to the geological rift valley of the Jordan River and the Dead Sea in the east. During the rainy season, these wadis become swift streams, but they are mainly dry the rest of the year (cf. 7:26–27). Some English-language versions of the Bible refer to the desert (ἔρημος, erēmos; cf. 3:3; 4:1; 11:7; 15:33; 23:38; 24:26) as the "wilderness," but this can be misleading, since this term may connote to English-language readers a forest or jungle. The role of the desert in redemptive history as a place of refuge or testing and as the site of the exodus, the giving of the law, and renewal movements may be significant here (cf. 24:26; 1 Kings 17:2–6; 2 Kings 6:1–2; Acts 7:44; 21:38; Heb. 11:38; Rev. 12:6; Ps. Sol. 17.17; Josephus, *Ant.* 20.189; *J.W.* 2.259–62; Funk 1959; Mauser 1963), but these theological overtones do not put the historicity of this pericope in doubt.

3:2 John's message is characterized as having two aspects: (1) an ethical imperative (μετανοεῖτε, metanoeite, repent) based on (γάρ, gar, for) (2) an eschatological reality (ἤγγικεν ... ἡ βασιλεία τῶν οὐρανῶν, ēngiken ... hē basileia tōn ouranōn, the kingdom of heaven has come near). This is the first occurrence of the message that echoes throughout Matthew's Gospel (cf. 4:17, 23; 9:35; 10:7; 13:19; 16:19; 21:43; 24:14). Repentance is not limited to the emotional (sorrow for sin), etymological-intellectual (change of mind), temporal (initial conversion), or volitional (doing penance) dimensions often stressed in popular definitions. Although all of these contain elements of truth, repentance (cf. 3:8, 11; 4:17; 9:13 *Byz*; 11:20, 21; 12:41) is more than the combination of all of them. It is the turning of the whole person from sin to God in obedience to the message of the kingdom. This entails recognition of need, sorrow for sin, a decision to turn from sin to God, and a subsequent obedient lifestyle. The

---

1. Studies of John the Baptist include Guyénot 1999; Häfner 1994; Kazmierski 1996; Krentz 1983; Meier 1980a; Murphy-O'Connor 1990; Schlatter 1956; Scobie 1964; J. Taylor 1997; Trilling 1959; in Lange 1980: 273–95; R. Webb 1991b; Wink 1968; Yamasaki 1998: 81–95; Bauckham 1995; Frankemölle 1996; D. Smith 1982; and Wainwright 2000. Hutchison 2002 provides several reasons to doubt the popular notion that John was an Essene from the Qumran community.

2. The circumstantial participle κηρύσσων should be viewed as modal (Moulton and Turner 1963: 154; Wallace 1996: 527–28). That is, it describes the manner of John's arrival: its key feature was proclamation.

background for this understanding of repentance is found in the biblical themes expressed by נָחַם; (*niham*, be sorry; e.g., Job 42:6; Jer. 8:6) and שׁוּב (*šûb*, turn; e.g., Ezek. 18:21, 23, 27, 28, 30–32). Keener (1999: 120) points out that John is not calling his Jewish audience to regular turning from specific sins but to a radical conversion from an old to a new way of life, a repentance of the sort that they as Jews might associate with Gentiles converting to Judaism.

The demand for repentance is based on the reality of God's eschatological rule: the kingdom of heaven is near. "Kingdom of heaven" is a distinctively Matthean expression for the kingdom of God. There is little doubt that Matthew uses it in order to avoid mentioning the name of God, which was held in awe by pious Jews. Heaven stands for God by metonymy, the substitution of one word for another with which it is naturally associated (cf., e.g., Dan. 4:26; Matt. 21:25; Luke 15:18, 21). Instead of thinking of the kingdom as a concrete entity that is either present or future, one should view it as gradually and dynamically exerting its power through the words and works of God's messengers.

The perfect-tense verb ἤγγικεν expresses the urgency of the demand for repentance. This verb is used elsewhere in Matt. 4:17; 10:7; 21:1, 34; 26:45–46. God's reign has drawn near in redemptive history—it is imminent. But as a reason for repentance, one could say that God's rule is now morally present. Since this same message is preached by John, Jesus, and the disciples (3:2; 4:17; 10:7), static geographical conceptions of the kingdom should be resisted. John is not speaking primarily of a concrete realm but of a dynamic, life-changing reign. Although there is historical progression in the manifestation of this reign, as a moral motivation it has already arrived. In this sense ἤγγικεν does not differ a great deal from ἔφθασεν (*ephthasen*, has come) in 12:28. The stress here on the presence of the kingdom as God's eschatological dynamic for moral change does not in any way contradict its use elsewhere as the future earthly realm or domain of Jesus (e.g., 7:21–23; 25:31, 34; 26:29). Jesus's kingdom is both present and future, now and not yet.

For an extended discussion of Matthew's use of βασιλεία, the relation of the kingdom of heaven to the kingdom of God, and the presence and future of the kingdom, see "Kingdom of Heaven" in the introduction to this commentary.

3:3   Having summarized John's message (3:1–2), Matthew now turns to his characteristic motif of biblical support. John's origins in the obscurity of the desert and Jesus's origins in the small village of Bethlehem are both grounded in the Hebrew Bible. The characteristic fulfillment formula does not occur here. Gundry (1994: 44) believes that this is because Matthew reserves it for pericopes about Jesus, but this seems to be contradicted by 2:17. Instead of the usual formula, Matthew simply says, "This is the one spoken of by Isaiah the prophet." This formula is similar to the one used by Peter in Acts 2:16. Although the fulfillment formula is not used here, it seems clear that the formula used here points to John as the eschatological fulfillment of Isa. 40:3.[3] Isaiah is mentioned elsewhere in 4:14; 8:17; 12:17; 13:14; 15:7, frequently in connection with Jewish opposition and gentile openness to Jesus.

Synoptic comparisons are interesting here. Matthew quotes Isa. 40:3, and Luke 3:4–6 quotes Isa. 40:3–5. Both quote the Scripture after introducing John. Mark 1:2–3 quotes it before introducing John and conflates Mal. 3:1 with Isa. 40:3 in the quotation. The text forms of MT, LXX, and Matthew are quite similar, but Matthew agrees more with the LXX. There are three differences. First, in the MT the phrase "in the desert" describes the verb "prepare," not the "voice" as it does in the LXX and Matthew.[4] Second, the MT refers to the desert twice with different Hebrew words whereas the LXX and Matthew refer to it only once. Third, Matthew diverges from MT and LXX at the end of the quotation. Whereas MT and LXX have straight paths "for our God," Matthew has "his paths" or "paths for him." The topographical changes mentioned here allude to the ancient custom of building or repairing roads to honor the visit of a king, but Matthew pictures the moral changes demanded by the preaching of John.

In its immediate context, Isa. 40:3 comforts the exiles in Babylon with the hope of return to the land. But in the larger context of Isa. 40–66, the prophecy of Isaiah describes the eschatological restoration of Israel with worldwide consequences experienced by all humankind (40:5). Matthew has a better grasp of this material than Beare (1981: 90), who derides Matthew's supposed unhistorical mishandling of Scripture. The overall perspective of Isa. 40–66 includes the Spirit-endowed Messiah (Isa. 42:1–4/Matt. 12:18–21) and the Suffering Servant (Isa. 52:15/Matt. 28:19; Isa. 53:4/Matt. 8:17; Isa. 53:7/Matt. 26:63; 27:14), envisioning nothing less than new heavens and a new earth (Isa. 65:17; 66:22/Matt. 19:28). Blomberg (1992: 75) correctly speaks of foreshortened prophetic perspective and views the ministry of John as heralding the beginning of this great eschatological vision. From a Christian perspective, the fulfillment that began with John and Jesus continues today through the preaching of the gospel and awaits consummation at Jesus's second advent. For Matthew, Isaiah's "way of our God" is the "way of the Lord"

---

3. Matthew's identification of John the Baptist with Isaiah's voice is not unlike the pesher hermeneutic of the Qumran sect (Carson 1984: 101). This approach views contemporary people and events as the fulfillment of biblical prophecy. It is found in Dead Sea Scrolls such as the commentaries on Nahum (4Q169) and Habakkuk (1QpHab).

4. In Isa. 40:3 פַּנּוּ בַמִּדְבָּר (in the wilderness prepare) is parallel with יַשְּׁרוּ בָּעֲרָבָה (make straight in the desert). The Qumran Community understood this text as the reason for its withdrawal from sinners and its location in the desert. See 1QS 8.14; cf. 9.19–20. At Qumran, making straight paths for the Lord was interpreted to mean correctly interpreting and obeying God's law.

Jesus. If Jesus is Immanuel, "God with us" (Matt. 1:23), then his way is "the way of our God." The deity of Christ is implied here.

After summarizing John's message as that promised in Isaiah, Matthew now describes his austere clothing and diet.[5] According to W. Davies and Allison (1988: 295–96), bedouin still wear camel's hair garments and eat locusts today. A camel's hair garment bound with a leather belt might suggest poverty in another context, but here it is suggestive of John's prophetic role and stern message of repentance. Indeed, John is much like Elijah in this respect (2 Kings 1:8; Zech. 13:4; cf. Mal. 4:5; Matt. 11:7–9, 14; 17:10–13; Heb. 11:37). Eating locusts was permitted by Scripture (Lev. 11:20–23), and wild (uncultivated) honey is mentioned several times (Gen. 43:11; Exod. 3:8; Deut. 32:13; Judg. 14:8; 1 Sam. 14:25; Ps. 81:16; Ezek. 27:17; cf. Kelhoffer 2005a, 2005b). All in all, John's clothing and diet model the message he preaches. He is unconcerned with the niceties of wardrobe and food (Matt. 11:8, 18; cf. 2 Macc. 5:27; Josephus, *Life* 11), and he calls Israel away from preoccupation with such things and toward the kingdom.

3:4

Now Matthew turns to the response to John's message. People from all over Jerusalem, Judea, and the Jordan region are going to John and being baptized by him in the Jordan River as they confess their sins. The imperfect verbs ἐξεπορεύετο (*exeporeueto*, were going out) and ἐβαπτίζοντο (*ebaptizonto*, were being baptized) indicate that this response was widespread and regular. Either inceptive ("started going out . . . began to be baptized) or iterative ("kept on going out . . . kept on being baptized") nuances are possible (Moulton and Turner 1963: 67; Wallace 1996: 544–47). The personification of the place names (i.e., the text reads, literally, "Jerusalem [etc.] was coming out") adds to the impression that the response to John is truly sensational. This is corroborated by Josephus (*Ant.* 18.118).

3:5–6

The meaning of the word "baptize" and the detail that the baptisms are being done in (ἐν, *en*) the Jordan River indicate the probablity that John immerses those who repent (cf. BDAG 164–65; Did. 7). Jewish ritual baths in this time period likewise included immersion. The present adverbial participle ἐξομολογούμενοι (*exomologoumenoi*, confessing) implies that the confession occurs at the same time as the baptism. In light of 3:7–8, there is the additional implication that John does not baptize those whom he deems unrepentant. This is consistent with Josephus's understanding of John's baptism in *Ant.* 18.117. There is no reason to think that the baptism itself effects repentance in an automatic fashion.

---

5. The imperfect verb εἶχεν shows that camel's hair garb was John's customary wardrobe. The pronoun αὐτός that begins this verse is somewhat emphatic, implying a translation such as "now this John" or "now John, he." Moulton and Turner (1963: 41) and M. Black (1967: 96) view as proleptic the use of the pronoun followed by the resumptive noun "John," reflecting an Aramaic idiom.

Rather, this baptism is a sign of repentance and a seal of forgiveness. Perhaps the custom was for repentant baptismal candidates to confess their sins publicly as they were being baptized.

The implications of 3:6 for a theology of John's baptism must be compared with similar statements in 3:11, especially the difficult phrase εἰς μετάνοιαν (*eis metanoian*, for/in reference to repentance; see Beasley-Murray 1962: 1–44).

John's baptism should be understood in connection with biblical ritual cleansings, Jewish proselyte baptism, and the cleansing rituals of the Qumran community (see Badia 1980; Gnilka 1961–62; Pusey 1984: 141–45; D. Smith 1982; J. Taylor 1997: 49–100). It seems best to view it against a broad background of similar acts rather than attempt an explanation that draws from only one of the possible backgrounds. The Hebrew Bible itself frequently alludes to water cleansing as a picture of forgiveness, spiritual purity, and eschatological blessing (Ps. 51:6–9; Isa. 4:4; 44:3; Jer. 4:11–14; Ezek. 36:24–27; Zech. 13:1). But there are three important contrasts between John's baptism and these possible backgrounds. First, John insists on repentance and baptism for Jews, not gentile proselytes. This would have countered the current view that Israel's problems were due only to gentile oppression and that the Messiah's mission was merely to set Israel free from this oppression. Descent from Abraham was no guarantee of God's favor (3:9). Second, John's baptism was a single act of confession, not a repeated ritual as in the Hebrew Bible and in the Qumran community. Third, John's ministry and baptism were directed toward the nation of Israel as a whole, not toward a sectarian monastic community as at Qumran. W. Davies and Allison (1988: 299) may be correct that John's baptism was a creative reapplication of biblical and cultural motifs in keeping with his prophetic insight into God's will.

b. John Warns the Pharisees and Sadducees of the Coming Judgment (3:7–12)

3:7   Although the popular response to John's ministry is sensational, Matthew has yet to indicate what the religious establishment thinks of it. The conjunction δέ (*de*, but) expresses the contrast between this popular response and that of the Pharisees and Sadducees. Earlier (2:4) the high priests and legal experts appeared to help Herod discern where the Messiah would be born. Now the Pharisees and Sadducees appear in the context of John's ministry and are soundly rebuked by John (3:7–12). Matthew thus lays out the opposition of the religious leaders as a foil to the magi and the popular response to John. The syntax of the phrase τῶν Φαρισαίων καὶ Σαδδουκαίων (*tōn Pharisaiōn kai Saddoukaiōn*, the Pharisees and Sadducees) employs a single article with the two nouns joined by "and" (the so-called Granville Sharp construction; Wallace 1996: 270–90). This implies that the two groups are one in some sense, but when this construction occurs with plural nouns, as here, the connection should not be overdrawn. Since the two groups were theologically disparate, their unity here and elsewhere in Matthew may be only in opposition to Jesus, an enemy of the religious establishment (Wallace 1996: 279). Both groups come to the baptism of John, and both are rebuked by John. This anticipates the unified opposition that these two groups will later levy against Jesus (cf. 16:1, 6, 11, 12).[6]

According to Josephus (*Ant.* 17.42), there were more than six thousand Pharisees.[7] It is plausible that they arose as the Hasidim during the revolt against the Seleucid kings in the second century BC. The name "Pharisee" is probably derived from a Hebrew word meaning "separatists" (פְּרוּשִׁים, *pĕrûšîm*; A. Baumgarten 1983; Jastrow 1971: 1222). Their chief characteristic was rigorous adherence to the law, which in their view encompassed both their written Bible and the oral traditions that had grown up as a "fence around the law" (*m. 'Abot* 1.1). In Matthew their preoccupation with the "traditions of the elders" as rules of conduct (halakoth) puts them at loggerheads with Jesus. Their views of such matters as Sabbath observance and ritual washings were determined by the oral law. But this was viewed by Jesus as a pedantic and burdensome addition to the genuine (written) law of God (cf., e.g., 15:1–20; 23). Blomberg (1992: 77) rightly points out that not all Pharisees were hypocrites. Later the Talmud would acknowledge that some Pharisees were hypocritical (*b. Soṭah* 22b).[8]

Much less is clearly known about the Sadducees, since the limited evidence often comes from anti-Sadducean sources.[9] Josephus spends

---

6. Matthew speaks of the Pharisees twenty-nine times. On eleven occasions they are mentioned alone: 9:11, 14, 34; 12:2, 14, 24; 15:12; 19:3; 22:15, 41; 23:26. They are linked with the legal experts (scribes) ten times: 5:20; 12:38; 15:1; 23:2, 13, 15, 23, 25, 27, 29. Five times they appear (as here) with the Sadducees, although the other four times occur in one pericope: 3:7; 16:1, 6, 11, 12. In 21:45 and 27:62, the Pharisees also appear with the chief priests, who were Sadducees. In 22:34–35, one of the Pharisees is described as a lawyer (νομικός), although there is some doubt as to the genuineness of this reading. Mark speaks of the Pharisees twelve times and Luke mentions them nineteen times.

The Sadducees are mentioned much less frequently in Matthew, seven times in three pericopes. They appear with the Pharisees in the context of John's ministry (3:7) and later join with them in an attempt to put Jesus to the test by asking for a heavenly sign (16:1, 6, 11, 12). Once Jesus has entered Jerusalem, they unsuccessfully attempt to question him on the resurrection (22:23, 34). Mark and Luke each mention the Sadducees only once.

7. Substantive discussions of the Pharisees include Bowker 1973; Carson 1982; de Lacy 1992; Deines in Carson et al. 2001: 443–504; Deines and Hengel 1995; Finkelstein 1938; Goodblatt 1989; Kampen 1988; Mason in C. A. Evans and Porter 2000: 782–87; Neusner 1973; Pelletier 1990; Rivkin 1978; Saldarini 2001; Stemberger 1995; and Westerholm in J. Green and McKnight 1992: 609–14.

8. Additional rabbinic references to the Pharisees include *t. Šabb.* 1.15; *y. Ber.* 14b; *y. Soṭah* 19a, 20c; *b. Qidd.* 66a; *b. Šabb.* 13a; *b. Soṭah* 20a–22b.

9. Mainly because of the limited evidence, many studies approach the Sadducees as a foil to the Pharisees rather than in their own right. See G. Baumbach in J. Maier and

some time describing them in *J.W.* 2.164–66 and *Ant.* 13.171–73, 297–98; 18.11, 16–17. Their name likely identifies them as sympathizers with the Zadokites, descendants of Zadok, high priest during the days of the Davidic monarchy (2 Sam. 8:17; 15:24; 1 Kings 1:34; 1 Chron. 12:29). A smaller group than the Pharisees, they evidently were well-to-do priests who had no use for the oral law of the Pharisees. They tended to be more pro-Roman than the Pharisees, and they stressed human freedom more than the Pharisees did. Their denial of the resurrection and afterlife is well known (cf. Matt. 22:23–33). Perhaps this was due to preoccupation with literal interpretation of the five books of Moses and neglect of the rest of the Hebrew Bible, although W. Davies and Allison (1988: 302–3) doubt this. Pharisaic Judaism lived on after the destruction of the temple in Jerusalem in 70 CE, but this event evidently marked the end of the Sadducees for all practical purposes. References to the Sadducees in rabbinic literature are often negative and frequently contrast their views of ritual purity with those of the Pharisees (e.g., *m. Yad.* 4.6–7; *m. Parah* 3.7; *m. Nid.* 4.2). Some scholars point to interesting parallels between Saducean legal positions and those at Qumran.[10] This probably points to the common Zadokite origins of both the mainline Sadducees and the sectarian Essenes, who are the most likely founders of the separatist Qumran community.

It is difficult to know exactly why the Pharisees and Sadducees come to John's baptism. They are probably not motivated simply by curiosity. Perhaps they are there in an official capacity to investigate the furor in the desert. John's rhetorical question ("Who warned you to flee . . . ?") makes it more likely that they are there as candidates for baptism. The NASB, NLT (note), and RSV take it this way ("coming for baptism"), but the Greek phrase ἐρχομένους ἐπὶ τὸ βάπτισμα αὐτοῦ (*erchomenous epi to baptisma autou*) is less precise and may simply indicate that they have come to the place where John is baptizing (NIV). At any rate, John does not view their motivation as genuine. His vivid accusatory description of the Pharisees and Sadducees as the "offspring of vipers" is twice echoed by Jesus (12:34; 23:33, cf. Ps. 58:4; Gen. 3:1; Isa. 14:29; 30:6; Jer. 46:22; Keener 2005). This is meant to accuse the Pharisees and Sadducees of evil character. They view themselves as children of Abraham (Matt. 3:9), but John has a very different idea of their spiritual ancestry.

John's sarcastic question "Who warned you to flee . . . ?" indicates that he does not believe that the Pharisees and Sadducees are genuine

---

Schreiner 1973; Le Moyne 1972; Porton in C. A. Evans and Porter 2000: 1050–52; Saldarini 2001; and Stemberger 1995.

10. E.g., the Qumran text 4QMMT, which delineates some of the works of the Torah, appears to be a communication from Qumran leaders to the high priest in Jerusalem that promotes Qumran legal rulings (halakoth) over against rulings that appear, in later rabbinic literature, to be mainline Saducean teachings. See Schiffman in Schiffman and VanderKam 2000: 1.559.

converts. If the emphasis is placed on "Who," John is disclaiming any connection with their spiritual pilgrimage to the Jordan. *He* certainly has not warned them to flee the coming judgment. If the emphasis is placed on "you," the implication is that *they* are unrepentant and thus are not fit candidates for baptism. Those who do not repent when they hear the message of God's eschatological rule will face imminent judgment, "the coming wrath." This eschatological wrath is vividly pictured as the harvest of genuine fruit and the incineration of nonproductive trees and chaff in 3:10, 12 (cf. 23:33).

John's observation of the Pharisees and Sadducees leads him to believe that they are unrepentant, and so he demands that they produce fruit (3:8) and then responds to an anticipated objection (3:9). The conjunction οὖν (*oun*) that introduces 3:8 is left untranslated by the NIV and is taken emphatically ("really bear fruit . . .") by Morris (1992: 58). More likely it should be taken in its normal inferential sense. John does not believe that the religious leaders are genuine converts, but if they wish to be viewed as such, *then* they must produce fruit (W. Davies and Allison 1988: 305). Producing fruit as a metaphor for a repentant lifestyle occurs elsewhere in Matthew (3:10; 7:16–20; 12:33; 13:8, 23, 26; 21:19, 33–44; cf. James 3:18) and is common in the Bible (Ps. 1:3; Prov. 1:31; 11:30; Isa. 3:10; 5:1–7; Hos. 10:1, 12–13; cf. 2 Esd. [4 Ezra] 3:20; Sir. 23:25). John now and Jesus later both affirm that the lifestyle of converts must fit or correspond to their profession of repentance. A change in lifestyle will never occur if confidence is placed in descent from Abraham (3:9).[11] Such descent and the blessings it brings are admirable but do not merit salvation (cf. Rom. 3:1–4:15; 9:1–11:32).[12] If John is speaking Hebrew, the irony of his words is underlined by a play on words between son (בֵּן, *bēn*) and stone (אֶבֶן, *eben*; cf. Matt. 21:37, 42; Kazmierski 1987). Even if John is speaking Aramaic, where son is בַּר (*bar*) rather than *bēn*, the indirect wordplay would likely still be noticed by those familiar with both languages.

A vivid picture of judgment underlines John's demand for proof of repentance (3:8). The picture likens unrepentant hearers of the kingdom

3:8–9

3:10

---

11. Jesus's Abrahamic origin has been demonstrated clearly in the genealogy (1:1–17) but the Pharisees and Sadducees may make no such claim without bearing the accompanying fruit. Here another prohibition clause with the aorist subjunctive apparently forbids the continuance of an act already in progress (μὴ δόξητε). John's audience is to stop thinking that descent from Abraham is salvifically meritorious. According to some grammars, the present subjunctive as a rule expresses this notion, with the aorist subjunctive forbidding the initiation of action. But this text does not fit the "rule." Cf. 1:20 and the discussion in Wallace 1996:723–25.

12. Keener (1999: 125–27) provides a helpful summary of personal and ancestral merit in Jewish texts. Here the matter of ancestral merit is the issue, since descent from Abraham is evidently regarded by some in John's audience as the basis of their present status before God. M. Elliott (2000) argues that many Second Temple Jewish texts stress a purifying judgment in which the salvation of a righteous remnant, not Israel as a whole, is achieved.

message to trees that do not bear fruit—they are cut down and thrown into the fire (cf. 7:19; 12:33; Isa. 10:15–19; Jer. 11:16). Jesus's cursing the unfruitful fig tree in Matt. 21:19 is a similar image. The burning of unfruitful trees is also related to the punishment of evildoers in the fires of hell (5:22; 13:42, 50; 18:8–9; and 25:41). The adverb ἤδη (*ēdē*, already) heightens the vividness of the picture, and the present-tense verb κεῖται (*keitai*, is being laid) depicts the chopping down of unfruitful trees as a present process. As the kingdom message is preached, those who reject it are already being marked out for judgment, even though the full force of that awful judgment has not yet been felt. This stress on the present ongoing nature of kingdom judgment indicates that the other two present-tense verbs in the verses should not be viewed as merely futuristic. Immediacy and certainty are implied (W. Davies and Allison 1988: 311). The cutting down and burning of the fruitless trees begins with the proclamation of the urgent message of God's rule. Those who do not repent are already under judgment. The issue is not the root of descent from Abraham (3:9) but the fruit of obedience.

3:11–12   John now contrasts his ministry with that of the one who is coming after him. John's water baptism for repentance prepares Israel for Jesus's more powerful Spirit-and-fire baptism.[13] John is not even fit to perform the menial task of carrying Jesus's shoes. Jesus's powerful ministry is likened to a harvest, in which the grain is gathered (cf. 6:26; 13:30) and the chaff is burnt. Jesus, the mighty one who comes after John, is the eschatological harvester who saves or judges. Thus it is now clear that the indefinite passive verbs of 3:10 find their subject in Jesus. He lays the ax to the trees, chops them down, and throws them into the fire. The imagery of 3:12 is similar to that of biblical texts such as Ps. 1:4; Isa. 5:24; Dan. 2:35; Hos. 13:3.

The contrast between John and Jesus is expressed strongly by the conjunction tandem μέν . . . δέ (*men . . . de*, on the one hand . . . on the other hand) and by the use of the personal pronouns ἐγώ . . . αὐτός (*egō . . . autos*, I . . . he). John's description of Jesus as the one who comes after him is noteworthy in that this phrase usually describes a lesser disciple who "comes after" a teacher (cf. 4:19; 10:38; 16:24). In a sense Jesus does indeed "come after" John as his disciple to be baptized by him, but John quickly notes the incongruity of the situation (3:13–14). So, in a more profound sense, the greater one comes after the lesser one in redemptive history (cf. Frankemölle 1996).

13. The Holy Spirit has been mentioned as the miraculous agent behind Jesus's conception (1:18, 20). Now, as John speaks of the future, he asserts that Jesus will baptize in the Holy Spirit. But even though he will eventually dispense the Spirit to others (3:11), Jesus presently needs the empowerment of the Spirit for his messianic mission (4:1; 12:18, 28). For a perceptive study of the ministry of the Spirit to Jesus, see Hawthorne 1991.

There is no little controversy over the relationship between John's baptism and repentance. The phrase εἰς μετάνοιαν (eis metanoian) is unique to Matthew and is translated "for repentance" in the NASB, NIV, NJB, and NRSV. This might imply that the baptism accomplishes repentance (H. Fowler 1968: 1.104–5) or, in contrast, that the baptism is occasioned by repentance. The former view seems to attribute a sacerdotal power to John's baptism that is denied by Josephus (Ant. 18.117) and is foreign to Matthew's emphasis on the necessity of repentance. The latter view seems to fit the contextual fact that John requires repentance in candidates for baptism (Matt. 3:7–9), although arguments for a causal meaning for εἰς (eis, to) (Dana and Mantey 1955: 104; BDAG 291; Moulton and Turner 1963: 266–67; Wallace 1996: 369–71; cf. Matt. 12:41) are not persuasive. Perhaps the meaning is simply that the baptism is in reference to, or in connection with, repentance (Blomberg 1992a: 79; Harris, NIDNTT 3:1208–9; cf. BDAG 291). This connection is threefold in that baptism assumes repentance, expresses repentance, and through God's grace issues in ongoing repentance (Calvin 1960: 2.1313–15 [Institutes 4.13–15]).

John's baptism utilizes water (ἐν ὕδατι, en hydati), but Jesus's baptism will include the Holy Spirit and fire (ἐν πνεύματι ἁγίῳ καὶ πυρί, en pneumati hagiō kai pyri). The preposition ἐν used in both expressions can be translated "in, with, by," and it is difficult to know which is best here. Since John's baptism was probably "in" water, not merely "with" water, it may be best to preserve the analogy by understanding Jesus's baptism as being "in" the Holy Spirit and fire. Although some scholars (e.g., Bruner 1987: 79–80; Luz 1989: 171; Ridderbos 1987: 55) see two baptisms here, one in the Spirit indicating salvation and the other in fire indicating judgment, it is preferable to see only one purifying baptism. The grammar of the passage supports this, since the verb "will baptize" occurs once and the preposition ἐν occurs once with "Holy Spirit and fire" as a compound object. Thus a single baptism with ostensibly two aspects is indicated (cf. R. Campbell 1996; Tavardon 2002). And even this duality of aspects is questionable, since the Holy Spirit and fire may be a hendiadys where the two words communicate a single meaning (W. Davies and Allison 1988: 317). This seems to be indicated also by texts that associate the eschatological outpouring of the Spirit with both cleansing water (Isa. 32:15; 44:3; Ezek. 36:25–27; 37:14, 23; 39:29; Joel 2:28–29) and refining fire (Isa. 1:25; 4:4; 30:27–30; Zech. 13:9; Mal. 3:1–3; 4:1; cf. 2 Esd. [4 Ezra] 13:8–11; Acts 2:3).[14] So it is best to conclude that the one eschatological outpouring of the Spirit through Jesus will purify and judge. This is pictured as a harvest in 3:12, where the threshing or winnowing process separates the wheat from the chaff (cf. Ps. 1:4; Prov. 20:26; Isa. 41:14–16;

---

14. 1QS 3.7–9 (cf. 4.21; 1QH 8.21) speaks of the purifying work of the holy spirit in humbling members of the community so that they would obey the law of God. This work of the spirit prepares the community for the ceremonial washings practiced by the sect.

Jer. 15:7; 51:33; Dan. 2:35; Hos. 6:11; 13:3; Joel 3:13; Mic. 4:12–13; Rev. 14:14–20). A fork or shovel was used to toss the harvested and threshed grain in the air, and the wind dispersed the chaff while the heavier grain fell to the floor. The grain was gathered, but the chaff was swept up and burnt. It is exegetically and theologically suggestive that the wheat is described as "his," but there is no such qualification for the chaff. (For further study of this harvest imagery, see R. Webb 1991a.)

Matthew's capsulized portrayal of John's kingdom message stresses the judgment of God upon the unrepentant. The image of the ax already at the tree's root shows that the judgment is already in process. The image of unquenchable (ἄσβεστος, *asbestos*) fire underlines the severity of the punishment in a way that does not fit the concept of annihilationism but rather is tantamount to the Christian doctrine of eternal punishment. Taken together, these images present a very different picture of God and his rule than is often presented in pulpits today, where the stress is on God's provision of goods and services to meet people's felt needs. One wonders whether John would even recognize this "gospel" of self-actualization as an authentic interpretation of the message of God's kingdom.

Additional Note

3:12. There are several minor variant readings on the phrase that describes the gathering of the wheat into the barn. These concern the genitive-case personal pronoun αὐτοῦ, which variously occurs with one, both, or neither of the nouns "wheat" and "barn."

2. Baptism of Jesus (3:13–17)

The oxymoronic character of Jesus's baptism has always challenged interpreters. John is baptizing those who repent and confess their sins (3:6). John refuses to baptize those who bear no fruit indicating that they have repented (3:8). In contrast, Jesus is initially refused baptism because he evidently does not need to repent and bring forth fruit (3:14).[1] "John had difficulty baptizing the Pharisees and Sadducees because they were not worthy of his baptism. Now he has trouble baptizing Jesus because his baptism is not worthy of Jesus" (Carson 1984: 107). W. Davies and Allison (1988: 324) put it into redemptive-historical perspective: "If John's baptism only foreshadows an eschatological baptism, how can the dispenser of the latter submit to the authority of the former?" Matthew alone among the Gospels mentions John's hesitation to baptize Jesus.

This unit divides as follows:

a. Arrival of Jesus (3:13)
b. Discussion and baptism (3:14–15)
c. Approval from heaven (3:16–17)

Exegesis and Exposition

[13]Then Jesus arrived at the Jordan from Galilee. He came to John to be baptized by him, [14]but John tried to prevent him. John said, "I need to be baptized by you, yet you are coming to me?" [15]Jesus replied to him, "Let it be done right now, for it is proper for us to do this to fulfill all righteousness." Then John permitted it.
[16]And when Jesus was baptized, as soon as he came up out of the water, the heavens were suddenly opened ⌜to him⌝, and he saw ⌜the⌝ Spirit of God descending like a dove ⌜and coming⌝ upon him. [17]And suddenly a voice from the heavens was saying, ⌜"This is my Son, whom I love; with him I am very pleased."⌝

a. Arrival of Jesus (3:13)

Jesus's arrival at the Jordan (cf. 3:6) to be baptized by John (3:13; cf. Mark 1:9–11; Luke 3:21–22)[2] leads to a brief debate between John and

3:13

---

1. The καί that introduces John's incredulous question "and you are coming to me?" is clearly adversative in force and should be translated "but" or "and yet" (BDAG 495; Zerwick 1963: 153; cf. 1:19; 6:26; 10:29).

2. The infinitive with genitive article τοῦ βαπτισθῆναι (*tou baptisthēnai*) expresses Jesus's purpose in coming to John at the Jordan. A similar infinitival purpose clause is found in 2:13. See Wallace 1996: 590–92.

Jesus before John acquiesces (Matt. 3:14–15). The historical-present verb παραγίνεται (*paraginetai*, arrived) recalls 3:1 and parallels the arrival of Jesus with that of John. John has come on the scene, and now Jesus also enters to be baptized by John. The statement that Jesus has come from Galilee connects with 2:22–23 and resumes the narrative of Jesus's preparation for ministry after an interval of at least twenty-five years. Jesus went to Galilee as a young child but comes from Galilee to John as an adult. According to Luke 3:23, Jesus is about thirty years old now. The intervening narrative of John's ministry in Matt. 3:1–12 sets the stage for Jesus's baptism (3:13–15), which itself is the setting for his reception of the Spirit and endorsement from the Father (3:16–17). The Father's endorsement is immediately challenged by Satan's testing of Jesus (4:1–11).

b. Discussion and Baptism (3:14–15)

3:14   John's attempt to deter Jesus is expressed by the imperfect verb διεκώλυεν (*diekōlyen*), which should be viewed as conative ("tried to prevent"; BDF §326; Wallace 1996: 550–52). John expresses his incredulity at Jesus's request by noting that their roles should be reversed: Jesus should baptize John. Emphatic personal pronouns in the Greek further stress the incongruity of the situation. It is unclear how John came to his convictions about Jesus. It seems likely that John would have learned from his mother, Elizabeth, about the remarkable circumstances of his own birth (Luke 1:5–25) and of his role as Jesus's forerunner (Luke 1:39–56), but Matthew's narrative omits these details.

3:15   Jesus commands John to perform the baptism immediately because it is appropriate for them to fulfill all righteousness in this way. This statement features two key Matthean themes, fulfillment (see "Theological Emphases: Fulfillment" in the commentary introduction) and righteousness (see the discussion at 1:19). Of the many approaches to the exegesis of this statement, only three will be briefly discussed here. Some scholars (e.g., Bruner 1987: 84–85) suggest that Jesus is referring to Christian baptism, but this view is anachronistic and does not adequately handle the two distinctive Matthean themes mentioned above. Additionally, ἡμῖν (*hēmin*, us) does not refer to Jesus and Christians but to Jesus and John. Cullmann (1950: 15–17) has argued from Isa. 53:11 that Jesus's baptism prefigures his death, through which righteousness and forgiveness are accomplished. But this view is overly subtle. It again seems foreign to Matthean theology and smacks of a Pauline emphasis. Some argue that fulfilling all righteousness means that Jesus is taking upon himself the obligation to obey the law that has been stressed by John (e.g., Harrington 1991: 62; Hill 1972: 96; cf. 21:32). This is closer to Matthew's theology but still does not adequately handle the fulfillment theme in Matthew.

Therefore it seems best to conclude with others (e.g., Carson 1984: 105–8; W. Davies and Allison 1988: 325–27) that Jesus fulfills all righteousness by fulfilling biblical patterns and predictions about the Messiah. In Jesus's baptism he and John fulfill the Scriptures by introducing the Messiah to Israel. This baptism, as the inauguration of Jesus's ministry to Israel, leads immediately to biblical fulfillment in that the Spirit as a dove comes upon the Messiah (Isa. 11:1–2; 42:1; cf. Matt. 12:18, 28) and the Father endorses his Son in the voice from heaven (Ps. 2:7; Isa. 42:1; cf. Matt. 17:5). In baptism Jesus, as the Suffering Servant, proclaims and exemplifies the righteousness envisioned by the prophets. Fulfilling *all* righteousness implies that Jesus's baptism is a key event in unfolding everything that will eventually be entailed in rightly relating the world to God (Nolland 2005: 154). Additionally, Jesus identifies in baptism with the repentant righteous remnant within the nation of Israel (cf. Matt. 3:5–6). Although he has no sin to confess, his baptism nevertheless demonstrates his humility and anticipates his ministry to lowly but repentant people (cf. 2:23; 11:19; 12:20; 21:5). This humility is immediately tested by Satan, who puts worldly splendor before Jesus to tempt him to renounce the pattern of lowliness begun in the baptism. But Satan fails.

Matthew says nothing about the baptism itself. He merely records that John immediately permits Jesus to be baptized when he hears why it is appropriate. Here John's prompt obedience effectively models discipleship in a manner much like that of Joseph in Matt. 2.

c. Approval from Heaven (3:16–17)

Matthew passes over the baptism of Jesus quickly in order to stress two attesting events that pertain to biblical fulfillment: the heavenly vision (3:16) and the heavenly voice (3:17). The former relates to the coming of the Spirit upon Jesus (cf. Isa. 11:1; 42:1; 61:1), and the latter relates to the Father's endorsement of Jesus (cf. Ps. 2:7; Isa. 42:1). Taken together, the two events augur two key interrelated features of Jesus's ministry. He is empowered by the Spirit (cf. Matt. 12:18, 28) and approved by the Father (cf. 17:5). Theologians often look at this text as an anticipation of the Christian doctrine of the Trinity (cf. 28:19).

3:16–17

In 3:16 Matthew stresses the immediacy of the dramatic attesting events that follow the baptism. Jesus leaves the water promptly (εὐθύς, *euthys*, immediately), suddenly (καὶ ἰδού, *kai idou*, and behold; see the first footnote of the comments on 1:20) receives the vision of the heavens standing open, and suddenly (καὶ ἰδού is repeated) sees the Spirit descending as a dove upon him. The opening of heaven is a regular feature of biblical apocalyptic visions (cf., e.g., Isa. 64:1; Ezek. 1:1; John 1:51;

Acts 7:56; Rev. 4:1).[3] The Spirit's dovelike descent to Jesus may remind the reader of other appearances of doves in redemptive history (cf. esp. Gen. 1:2; 8:10).[4] Matthew may not stress the relationship of the Spirit and Jesus in the same way and to the same extent as Luke (cf. Luke 1:35; 4:1, 18; 24:49; Acts 1:2, 5, 8; 2:4, 33, 38–39; 10:38) and John (John 1:32–34; 3:34; 20:22), but he does indicate that the Spirit led Jesus into the desert to be tempted and that Jesus's miraculous powers were due to the power of the Spirit (Matt. 4:1; 12:18, 28).

In 3:17 the heavenly voice suddenly confirms and interprets the import of the heavenly vision of the Spirit's descent. This voice is no doubt related to the intertestamental concept of the בַּת קוֹל (*bat qôl*, daughter of a voice) by which God spoke to his people after the cessation of prophecy. But W. Davies and Allison (1988: 335–36) point out an important difference in the Gospel account. In rabbinic conception the voice is something of an indirect echo of God's speech, but in Matthew the voice directly communicates the Father's endorsement of the Son. Probably the point here is that God has now broken his silence and is speaking directly to his people again in his beloved Son, Jesus, upon whom the Spirit has come (cf. 17:5).

The words of the heavenly voice express the Father's approval of the Son in words that allude to Ps. 2:7 and Isa. 42:1 (cf. Gen. 22:2; Exod. 4:22–23). As explained in the additional note on 3:17, it appears that the primary text is Isa. 42 and that Ps. 2 is secondary (cf. Nolland 2005: 157). The allusion blends the Suffering Servant motif from Isaiah with the sonship motif of Ps. 2. The servant motif interprets the baptism, by which Jesus identifies with the righteous remnant of Israel. The sonship motif recalls the unique circumstances of Jesus's conception and infancy (Matt. 1:16, 18–25; 2:15) and sets the scene for Satan's tests (4:3, 6). The sonship motif also implies Jesus's Davidic connections (1:1; cf. 2 Sam. 7:13–14; Ps. 89:27). These prior references to Jesus's sonship make it clear that his baptism is not the occasion of his adoption into this relationship. Rather, the baptism is the occasion of Jesus's recognition or ordination into his ministry as Israel's Messiah.

The Father's pleasure in such a servant-Son is notably expressed by the aorist εὐδόκησα (*eudokēsa*; cf. 12:18; 17:5). Perhaps the usual historical sense of the aorist should be understood here. If so, the pretemporal election of Jesus may be implied (Carson 1984: 109), but more likely the baptism of Jesus is the specific event that pleases the Father (Gundry 1994: 53) and the translation should be something like "with him I have become pleased" (ingressive aorist, Moulton and Turner 1963: 71;

---

3. The opening of the heavens is expressed by the aorist passive verb ἠνεῴχθησαν, which in an understated fashion speaks of the activity of God. This "divine," or "theological," passive is also found in 3:10. See Wallace 1996: 437–38; Zerwick 1963: §236.

4. For further discussion of the dove symbolism, see W. Davies and Allison 1988: 331–34; Gero 1976; Keck 1970; and Telfer 1928.

Wallace 1996: 558–59). Other interpreters (Broadus 1886: 59), however, seem to view the aorist as gnomic, or timeless (Moulton and Turner 1963: 73), reflecting the Father's eternal intratrinitarian relationship with the Son. Whatever implications one may draw from and for systematic theology, Jesus's baptism, for Matthew, is a crucial occasion for the Father's pleasure (cf. 17:5). In Christian theology this baptism is the historical actualization of a pretemporal election, and it manifests the Father's ongoing relationship with the Son. This should not, however, obscure Matthew's focus on Jesus's baptism as the event that fulfills all righteousness and pleases the Father.[5]

A brief word on synoptic relationships is appropriate at this point. After his unique material on Jesus's genealogy and infancy in the first two chapters, Matthew's narrative of John's ministry and baptism of Jesus in chapter 3 parallels the other Gospels to some extent. All three of the Synoptics cite Isa. 40:3 as speaking of John's ministry. Mark's account is briefest; Mark 1:2 alludes to Mal. 3:1 along with Isa. 40:3 as the basis of John's ministry. Luke's account is the most lengthy, detailing the rulers who were on the scene when John arrived (Luke 3:1–2), citing a lengthier section of Isa. 40 than Matthew does (Luke 3:5–6), and giving a brief summary of dialogue between John and his audience (Luke 3:10–15). Luke and Matthew both speak of Jesus baptizing in the Spirit and fire (Matt. 3:11; Luke 3:16) whereas Mark mentions the Spirit only (Mark 1:8).

Compared with Mark and Luke, Matthew's account presents two unique features. He alone presents the dialogue between Jesus and John in which John hesitates and Jesus ties the necessity of his baptism to the fulfilling of all righteousness (Matt. 3:14–15). This section highlights the distinctive Matthean themes of fulfillment and righteousness. The other unique feature is Matthew's account of the Father's endorsement of the Son (3:17). Here Matthew couches the Father's words in the third person ("*this* is my son . . . with *him* I am pleased") instead of the second person ("*you* are my son . . . with *you* I am pleased"). As frequently noted by interpreters, this has the effect of making the endorsement more public in Matthew, although Matthew may intend the endorsement to be only for John's benefit. Also this form of the endorsement brings it into conformity with the Father's words at the transfiguration (17:5). Perhaps the third-person language is also intended to confront Matthew's audience more directly with the truth of Jesus's sonship. Luz (1995: 36) is correct in pointing out that "Matthew . . . links Jesus's divine sonship with his obedience." The Father endorses the Son after the Son in baptism fulfills all righteousness. If this is true of Jesus, how much more should it be true of those who call Jesus Lord.

5. On Matt. 3:13–17, see Allison 1992a; Capes 1999; A. Fuchs 1999; Uprichard 1981; Vigne 1992; R. Webb 2000; Yamasaki 1998: 95–100.

A concluding word about the function of chapter 3 in Matthew's narrative is needed. Gardner (1991: 68) is correct in pointing out that the story of John's baptizing Jesus serves two main purposes: it provides the basis for the transition from John to Jesus, and it attests Jesus's unique identity as the servant-Son of God. John, as the forerunner, now passes from center stage so that the spotlight may shine on Jesus. Although John will appear again in the story, there can be no doubt about his subservience to Jesus in redemptive history. Jesus will proclaim the same message as John (3:2; 4:17) and will eventually suffer a fate similar to John's (17:12), but John's great redemptive historical significance pales in comparison with that of Jesus (11:11). W. Davies and Allison (1988: 343) also point out how John's ministry serves to introduce Matthew's definition of the genuine people of God and Matthew's dualism of those who respond correctly and incorrectly to the message of God's rule. The genuine people of God are not merely Abraham's descendants but those who also show their repentance by their changed lifestyles. Those who show no repentance are in danger of imminent judgment.

The concluding pericope of Matt. 3, on Jesus's baptism, is most fecund in its christological implications. Suggestions for biblical theology and typology are many and profound. Several trajectories should be mentioned. In 3:17 Jesus is described in terms that clearly represent the Isaianic Suffering Servant, whom Yahweh has chosen (cf. esp. Isa. 42:1). Related to this is the sonship typology metaphorically applied to Israel as a nation (Exod. 4:22; Jer. 3:19; 31:9, 20; Hos. 11:1) and to David as the ideal king who serves Yahweh (2 Sam. 7:5–16; Pss. 2:7; 89:3, 20, 26–27). The fulfillment of biblical covenantal promises to the nation and to the king is found in Jesus, who recapitulates Israel's history as he sojourns in Egypt and passes through the waters before being tested in the wilderness. Additionally, the emphasis on Jesus as the Father's *beloved* Son may be intended to recall Isaac's relationship to Abraham (Gen. 22:2). More likely are the creation overtones found in the dovelike Spirit who descends on Jesus in a manner that calls Gen. 1:2 to mind. Thus, in Jesus God has begun nothing less than the renewal of the entire creation (cf. Matt. 19:28). It remains for the rest of Matthew's narrative to develop the distinctive understanding of Jesus and the new people of God that has been introduced here.

Additional Notes

3:16. Several textual variants present themselves here. If αὐτῷ is omitted (as in א*, B, Old Syriac, and others; cf. Luke 3:21), the opening of the heavens is not as much of a personal experience of Jesus as it is a public event. But there is adequate testimony to the genuineness of αὐτῷ in א¹, C, D, *Byz*. The possible omissions of τό before πνεῦμα and τοῦ before θεοῦ are rather inconsequential for exegesis. The omission of καί before ἐρχόμενον (as in א*, B, and others) would refer to the dove's coming upon Jesus instead of the Spirit's coming upon Jesus as a dove. But καί is adequately supported by a variety of witnesses.

3:17. It is widely recognized that the Father's endorsement of the Son alludes to Ps. 2:7 and Isa. 42:1, although scholars differ on the relative prominence given to these two biblical texts in Matthew's mind. If Matthew intends to allude primarily to Ps. 2, then Jesus's baptism takes on overtones of Davidic sonship and messianic office. If Isa. 42 is primary, the baptism speaks of Jesus's humbly identifying himself with God's repentant people as the servant of the Lord. As the following discussion will demonstrate, Matt. 3:17 is a composite allusion to both texts, and the resulting significance of Jesus's baptism is similarly a conflation of messianic office and servant function. It is precisely by serving that Jesus's messianic office is demonstrated (cf. 12:18–21).

The first assertion of 3:17 ("This is my Son") is quite similar to the second clause of Ps. 2:7 in both MT and LXX, although the word order is reversed and the demonstrative pronoun and third-person verb are used instead of the second-person personal pronoun and verb. It is more difficult to determine the source of the adjective ἀγαπητός. Genesis 22:2 may be implicated here, but it is more likely that Matthew has in mind Isa. 42:1. In the first place, the third-person statement of Matt. 3:17 may be due to the similar pronouncement "Behold my servant" in Isa. 42:1. Second, the word "servant" in Isa. 42:1 dovetails with the "son" of Ps. 2:7. But most important, ἀγαπητός is similar to the word "elect" in Isa. 42:1 MT and LXX. Indeed, the Targum on Isa. 42:1 uses the word "beloved" instead of "elect," as does the LXX in the similar passage, Isa. 44:1. In addition, the formula quotation of Isa. 42:1 in Matt. 12:18 speaks of the servant as beloved, not elect. Certainly the concepts of love and election are intricately interwoven in biblical theology.

The final phrase of Matt. 3:17 ("with him I am very pleased") has no connection with Ps. 2:7. It is semantically similar to the phrase "in whom my soul delights" in Isa. 42:1 and may even be Matthew's paraphrase of Isa. 42:1. Indeed, Symmachus's and Theodotion's translations of Isa. 42:1 are the same as Matthew's. Additionally, Matthew's formula citation of Isa. 42:1 in 12:18 speaks of the Father's approval of the servant in words nearly identical to Matt. 3:17. The prepositional phrase ἐν ᾧ occurs in 3:17 whereas the phrase εἰς ὅν is used in 12:18. But the same verb εὐδοκέω occurs in both passages. Finally, Matthew's primary dependence on Isa. 42:1 seems certain because of that text's reference to the Spirit being put on the servant.

Therefore, it seems clear that Matthew has Isa. 42:1 in mind even more than Ps. 2:7. W. Davies and Allison's conclusion (1988: 338) seems to be required: "The first line of our text is from or has been influenced by Ps. 2:7 (LXX?) while the next two lines are derived from a non-LXX version of Isa. 42:1." Although Ps. 2:7 may appear to be primary from a quick perusal, Isa. 42:1 is actually the primary text on which Matthew is reflecting. Jesus's sonship (Ps. 2:7) is crucial for Matthew, but Jesus the Davidic Messiah functions as a humble servant, not a proud despot. This is implied in the baptism and made clearer in the citation at Matt. 12:18–21.

3. Testing of the Son of God (4:1–11)

Matthew 4 leads the reader from the final preparatory episode (the temptation, 4:1–11) to the beginning of Jesus's public ministry in Galilee (4:12–25). Jesus authenticates the Father's baptismal endorsement in his victory over Satan's triple test. As John's ministry ends, Jesus begins his own ministry in fulfillment of biblical prophecy. The theme of his preaching is the kingdom of heaven, and his message is authenticated by powerful works. There are two hinge verses in this unit, 4:12 and 4:17. The end of John's wilderness ministry and the beginning of Jesus's Galilean ministry are marked by 4:12, and Jesus's continuation of John's message of repentance in light of the inaugurated kingdom is flagged by 4:17.

The testing narrative itself (4:1–11; cf. Mark 1:12–13; Luke 4:1–13) consists of three incidents wrapped in an introduction, where Satan arrives (4:1–2), and a conclusion, where Satan departs (4:11). Matthew's temptation pericope differs significantly from both Mark's and Luke's. Mark's short summary of the temptation (Mark 1:12–13) does not mention Jesus's fasting or that there were three distinct episodes of temptation. With the active voice of ἐκβάλλω (ekballō, impel), Mark expresses the Spirit's agency in leading Jesus, whereas Matthew uses the passive of ἀνάγω (anagō, lead up) with the preposition ὑπό (hypo, by). Neither Mark nor Luke indicates that the Spirit's leading was for the express purpose of Jesus's temptation, as Matthew does in 4:1. Mark alone mentions the presence of wild animals in the wilderness, and his description of the angels' ministry does not specify, as Matthew's does, that this ministry began at Satan's departure. Luke does not mention the angels at all. Luke 4:1–13 agrees with Matthew in describing Jesus's fast and the three distinct episodes of temptation, but Luke's order differs. Matthew and Luke agree in placing the turning of stones into bread as the first temptation but differ in the order of the other two. Matthew puts jumping from the temple pinnacle second and worshiping the devil third, but Luke reverses this order, perhaps in keeping with Luke's stress on Jesus's orientation toward Jerusalem (Bock 1994: 365–66). Only Luke has the ominous remark that Satan's departure at the end of the temptations is only temporary.

Expositions of Jesus's temptation tend to read it in light of either Adam and Eve's temptation in Eden or Israel's testing in the wilderness. Some scholars focus on how the temptation defines what type of Messiah Jesus will be. Another, more psychological, approach stresses how the temptation narrative provides a foil to negative temptation experiences found in Scripture and throughout human history. All of these approaches have merit, but Nolland (2005: 162) correctly observes that the temptation narrative highlights key aspects of the value system that undergirds Jesus's ministry.

The outline of this unit is as follows:

a. The setting of the tests (4:1–2)
b. The first test and biblical response (4:3–4)
c. The second test and biblical response (4:5–7)
d. The third test and biblical response (4:8–10)
e. The departure of Satan and the ministry of the angels (4:11)

Exegesis and Exposition

[1]Then Jesus was led away into the desert by the Spirit to be tempted by the devil. [2]After he had fasted forty days and forty nights, he was hungry.

[3]Then the tempter came and said to him, "If you are the Son of God, order these stones to become loaves of bread." [4]But Jesus answered, "It is written:

'People do not live by bread alone,
but by every word that comes out of the mouth of God.'"

[5]Then the devil took him to the holy city and had him stand upon the highest point of the temple. [6]He said to him, "If you are the Son of God, throw yourself down, for it is written,

'He will put his angels in charge of you,
and they will carry you along with their hands,
so that you don't even strike your foot against a stone.'"

[7]Jesus said to him, "But it is also written,

'Do not put the Lord your God to the test.'"

[8]Again the devil took him to a very high mountain and showed him all the kingdoms of the world and their glory. [9]He said to him, "I will give all these things to you if you will kneel down and worship me." [10]Then Jesus said to him, "Get away ⌜ ⌝, Satan, for it is written:

'Worship the Lord your God,
and serve only him.'"

[11]Then the devil left him, and suddenly angels came and began to help him.

a. The Setting of the Tests (4:1–2)

4:1 Matthew's τότε (*tote*, then) places Jesus's testing temporally and logically after his baptism. Jesus must first be attested by the Father before he may be tested by the devil.[1] The place of testing is the desert, earlier the scene of John's ministry (see comments on 3:1). Although the desert may have been viewed as a place of danger and evil spirits (Matt. 12:43), its chief import here is redemptive-historical. Jesus as God's obedient Son recapitulates the history of Israel, God's disobedient son. This seems clear from the parallel features of the accounts and the repeated citations of Deut. 6–8. It is striking that the Spirit leads Jesus to the desert for his testing. The Spirit is already known to be the agency behind Jesus's virginal conception (Matt. 1:18, 20) and empowerment for ministry (3:16–17). But the Spirit's active involvement in Jesus's testing is still surprising at first glance. Yet the text clearly indicates that although the Spirit is the agent who leads Jesus, the devil is the agent who tests him. This agency is expressed in both cases by the preposition ὑπό (*hypo*, by, cf. BDF §232). Additionally, the verb πειράζω (*peirazō*, test) may express both the nuance of testing to achieve approval (cf. Gen. 22:1; Exod. 20:20) and that of tempting to achieve disapproval (cf. 1 Cor. 7:5), depending upon the motive from the context. Both nuances are pertinent here in that the Father through the Spirit leads Jesus to be tested in order to confirm him in his role as messianic Son and servant, yet the devil tempts Jesus to achieve messianic status by using his prerogatives self-ishly in disobedience to the Son-servant paradigm. The Father's aim is to accredit Jesus, the devil's to discredit Jesus (Calvin 1972: 1.136). It is clear that the testing/tempting occurs as the Father's purpose through the Spirit's leading. This is expressed grammatically by the telic infinitive (BDF §390) πειρασθῆναι (*peirasthēnai*, to be tested). Although the devil possesses superhuman powers, he is a fallen creature and merely reacts to the plan and purpose of God, the holy Creator (cf. Job 1).

4:2 Jesus's testing occurs during a fast of forty days and forty nights, which echoes Israel's forty years of wilderness wandering (Exod. 16:35; Num. 14:33; Deut. 2:7; 8:2, 4; 29:5; Josh. 5:6; Neh. 9:21; Ps. 95:10; Amos 2:10; Acts 7:36; cf. 1 Cor. 10:5).[2] Such a fast might involve abstention from food

---

1. There are several references to the devil in Matthew. Six times he is described as ὁ διάβολος (4:1, 5, 8, 11; 13:39; 25:41). He is also referred to as σατανᾶς (adversary) in 4:10; 12:26 (cf. 16:23 referring to Simon Peter), as Βεελζεβούλ in 10:25; 12:24, 27, as ὁ ἐχθρός in 13:39 and, if the substantive adjective refers to a person, as ὁ πονηρός in 5:37, 39; 6:13; 13:19, 38.

2. The number forty is pregnant with theological implications because of its appearance in such contexts as Noah's flood, Moses's receiving the law, Elijah's walk, Jonah's preaching, Israel's wilderness wanderings, Jesus's wilderness fast, and the period between his resurrection and ascension. Cf. Gen. 7:4; Exod. 16:35; 24:18; 34:28; Num. 14:33; 32:13; Deut. 2:7; 8:2; 9:9–10:10; 29:5; Josh. 5:6; Judg. 3:11; 5:31; 8:28; 13:1; 1 Sam. 4:18; 17:16; 2 Sam. 5:4; 15:7; 1 Kings 2:11; 11:42; 19:8; Neh. 9:21; Ps. 95:10; Ezek. 4:6; 29:11–13; Amos 2:10;

but not from water, as may be implied in Luke 4:2 (but see Exod. 24:18; Deut. 9:9), and it might entail abstention during the day but not at night (cf. Wimmer 1982). In the Bible the number forty is frequently connected with times of hardship or punishment (cf., e.g., Gen. 7:4; Ezek. 4:6; Jon. 3:4; Acts 1:3). Moses fasted forty days and forty nights on Mount Sinai before receiving the law (Exod. 24:18; 34:28; Deut. 9:9; cf. 1 Kings 19:8). But here the most prominent biblical echo is certainly the forty years of Israel's wilderness sojourn. Although one would assume that Jesus became hungry during the forty days of his fast, this verse stresses his hunger after it. The aorist participle, in this case νηστεύσας (nēsteusas, having fasted) normally refers to action prior to the aorist verb, in this case ἐπείνασεν (epeinasen, he hungered). The adverb ὕστερον (hysteron, afterward) also supports this notion, which places Jesus's testing after, not during, his forty-day fast.

b. The First Test and Biblical Response (4:3–4)

Matthew describes the devil (4:1) as ὁ πειράζων (ho peirazōn, the tempter).   **4:3** Perhaps this description anticipates the similar activity of the religious leaders as Matthew's story develops (Gundry 1994: 55; cf. 12:38; 16:1; 19:3; 22:15, 18, 35).[3] Although πειράζω does not occur in 16:21–28, it is clear from 16:23 that Peter's unwitting attempt to deter Jesus from the cross is also a temptation. As the tempter, Satan refers to Jesus's divine sonship as the pretext to solicit Jesus to perform an act that would sever his filial relationship to the Father. The Greek construction of Satan's words uses the particle εἰ (ei, if) with the indicative mood of the verb in what grammarians call a first-class condition or a condition of reality (BDF §371–72). Some scholars believe that this construction tends to assume the reality of the idea it expresses and should be translated "since . . ." If this approach is adopted, Satan does not doubt Jesus's sonship but instead assumes it to deceive Jesus into exercising his filial prerogatives in a selfish manner. Jesus is not tempted to doubt his sonship but to exercise it in a manner contrary to the servant model implied at his baptism (Gundry 1994: 55). Many commentators seem to agree with this point (e.g., Blomberg 1992a: 84; Carson 1984: 112; W. Davies and Allison 1988: 361), and it is favored here (but see Bruner 1987: 104–5).

Two cautions are in order, however. First, Boyer's study (1981) of the approximately three hundred instances of the first-class condition in

5:25; Jon. 3:4; Matt. 4:2; Acts 1:3; 7:30–42; 13:18, 21; Heb. 3:9, 17. Poelman 1964 probes several of these contexts.

3. The arrival of Satan is expressed by the participle προσελθών. The verb προσέρχομαι occurs more than fifty times in Matthew, often describing the arrival of Jesus's disciples or opponents at the beginning of a pericope. See 4:3, 11; 5:1; 8:2, 5, 19, 25; 9:14, 20, 28; 13:10, 27, 36; 14:12, 15; 15:1, 12, 23, 30; 16:1; 17:7, 14, 19, 24; 18:1, 21; 19:3, 16; 20:20; 21:14, 23, 28, 30; 22:23; 24:1, 3; 25:20, 22, 24; 26:7, 17, 49, 50, 60, 69, 73; 27:58; 28:2, 9, 18. See J. Edwards 1987.

the NT demonstrates that it frequently does not include assumption of reality. Matthew uses this construction twenty-eight times, and in Boyer's view eight of them are obviously true conditions, four are obviously false conditions, and sixteen are difficult to determine.[4] For example, "reality" is assumed in the first-class condition of Matt. 12:28 only for the sake of argument, and the argument proves the absurdity of the "reality" that is assumed. Thus interpretation should be developed from the context, not merely from a grammatical rule. Second, even though Satan may not have doubted Jesus's divine sonship in principle, his evil career of rebellion against God denies Jesus's sonship in practice and epitomizes the ultimate irrationality of sin. Jesus's baptism evoked the Father's approving words concerning his sonship; now those approving words evoke Satan's command for Jesus to relieve his hunger by turning stones into loaves of bread. At issue here is the type of Son Jesus will be. Will he utilize his endowment with the Spirit in a selfish fashion, or will he humbly depend on his Father to meet his needs? As God's servant, how will he fulfill his mission? Satan's mention of rocks echoes John's words in Matt. 3:9. If God is able to make disciples out of stones, should not God's Son have the right to make bread out of stones? Satan doubts Jesus's sonship, so recently announced by the Father. It is as if Satan were saying again, "Indeed, has God said?" (that is, "Can God's word be trusted?"; cf. Gen. 3:1).

4:4 Jesus's response simply cites the second half of Deut. 8:3 with an introductory formula that stresses the abiding authority of the Hebrew Bible: "It is written" (NLT: "The Scriptures say"). In context, this passage rehearses God's care for Israel during its forty-year wilderness experience. The first half of Deut. 8:3 alludes to God's purpose in permitting Israel's hunger in the wilderness: it was so that the people might learn that they needed not only bread but also God's word to survive (cf. John 4:34; 6:35).[5] This purpose of God in Deut. 8:3 is similar to the statement of purpose in Matt. 4:1. Deuteronomy 8:5 likens the wilderness wandering to a father's discipline, and this terminology finds its full implications in the testing of Jesus. Satanic temptation is the setting for divine testing, and Jesus no doubt recalls the earlier test, which was not passed with flying colors.

---

4. This is the first occurrence of the first-class condition in Matthew. Boyer (1981) studied the nuances of the construction and categorized the twenty-eight uses in Matthew as follows:
1. Condition obviously true (4:3, 6; 6:30; 7:11; 10:25; 12:28; 18:28; 22:45)
2. Condition obviously false (12:26, 27; 27:40, 43)
3. Condition undetermined (5:29, 30; 6:23; 8:31; 11:14; 14:28; 16:24; 17:4; 18:8, 9; 19:10, 17, 21; 26:33, 39, 42)

5. The future verb ζήσεται may be taken as gnomic (NIV, NLT, NRSV, TNIV; cf. Wallace 1996: 571) or imperative (KJV, NASB, Harrington 1991: 65; cf. Wallace 1996: 569–70). Both are plausible here and in Deut. 8:3 (יִחְיֶה), but the former view is more likely because of the aphoristic nature of the statement.

He is aware of the daily need to depend on the Father for bread (Matt. 7:9), and he will not use his power as some sort of magician.

c. The Second Test and Biblical Response (4:5–7)

Matthew and Luke differ in the order of the second and third temptations. **4:5** The scene now shifts from the isolation of the desert to the political and religious center of Israel. The phrase "the devil took him" most likely describes a visionary experience rather than physical movement, as does 4:8–9. Jerusalem is also described as "the holy city" in 27:53. Satan shows Jesus the perspective from "the highest point" (πτερύγιον, *pterygion*) of the temple. The word πτερύγιον, related to the word for "wing," has a range of meanings including "tip," "end," "peak," and "turret." It may refer to the southeastern corner of the temple complex, overlooking the Kidron valley (cf. Josephus, *Ant.* 15.411–12; T. Sol. 22.8; Eusebius, *Eccl. Hist.* 2.23.11), but any elevated location could be in view (see Schwarz 1992c).

The second temptation again doubts Jesus's sonship but with a new twist: **4:6** biblical support. Satan cites Ps. 91:11–12 with the same introductory formula ("for the Scriptures say") Jesus has just uttered. Satan seeks to have Jesus jump off a high pinnacle of the temple and assures him that Scripture says that God will protect him. In the previous temptation, Jesus has just proclaimed his dependence on the word of God, citing Deut. 8:3, and so Satan now cites a word from God, Ps. 91, which speaks beautifully of the security of those who depend on the Lord (cf. Kähler 1994). Will Jesus take this "leap of faith"?

Jesus counters Satan's use of Ps. 91 with Deut. 6:16, which refers to **4:7** Israel's doubting God's provision of water in Exod. 17:7 (cf. Ps. 95:7–11; 1 Cor. 10:9; Heb. 3:7–19). It is not that Deut. 6:16 contradicts the psalm but that Satan has misapplied it. Satan tempts Jesus to capitalize on his unique messianic status as a way out of self-induced mortal peril, perhaps as a stunt to appeal to the masses. But since Jesus receives the Father's approval by serving as an obedient Son, the proposed leap from the pinnacle of the temple would amount not to trusting God but to testing God. Once again Jesus recapitulates an event from Israel's history but with better results. He did not use his status as the beloved Son to satisfy his hunger, and he will not now put God to the test as Israel did.

d. The Third Test and Biblical Response (4:8–10)

This scene may be intended to recall God's promise to Abraham (Gen. **4:8–9** 13:14–15) or Moses's looking at the promised land from Mount Pisgah (Deut. 3:27; 34:1–4). The third temptation, like the second, is probably a visionary experience. Jesus is taken to a high mountain, presented with the glory of all the world's kingdoms, and promised that he will receive it all if he will only worship Satan. This temptation is unlike the first two in at least two ways. First, it does not address Jesus as the Son of God because it does not concern a misuse of his messianic prerogatives. Second, it blatantly asks Jesus to break the first commandment, instead of appealing to Jesus's hunger (the first temptation) or to Scripture (the second temptation). In keeping with the recapitulation theme in Matthew, Jesus's being asked to bow down and worship Satan recalls Israel's idolatrous worship in the desert (Exod. 32). Will Jesus attempt to begin his messianic rule by disobeying his Father?

4:10   Jesus's response to this temptation is an authoritative command—"Get away, Satan." Satan's opposition to the Father's first commandment receives only a blunt rejection by the beloved Son, who pleases the Father, on the basis of Deut. 6:13, which is only three verses before the verse cited in the second test. Deuteronomy 6, perhaps the greatest chapter in the Torah, proclaims the exclusivity of Israel's God and Israel's responsibility to love God exclusively (6:4–5). Israel's people are warned not to forget God when they come into their land but to fear him and not to fear false gods (6:12–14). By not worshiping Satan, Jesus avoids repeating the sin of Israel when it worshiped the golden calf. If he is to rule the world, it will be by the path of obedience to the Father. Later in Matthew, it becomes clear that this path leads to the cross, a fact that is difficult even for Peter to grasp (Matt. 16:21–26).[6]

e. The Departure of Satan and the Ministry of the Angels (4:11)

4:11   Satan can only depart in response to Jesus's authoritative rebuke. But Matthew does not thereby imply that Satan's evil activity is finished (cf. 5:37; 6:13; 12:28–29; 13:19, 38). Luke 4:13 makes this clear: "He left him until the next opportunity came." The ministry of angels to Jesus is referred to again in Matt. 26:53. Jesus mentions other angelic ministries in 13:39, 41, 49; 16:27; 18:10; 22:30; 24:31, 36; 25:31, 41. The mention here recalls Satan's previous use of Ps. 91:11–12 in Matt. 4:6. If Jesus were to jump off the pinnacle of the temple, Satan promised that angels would protect him. Ironically, Jesus does receive angelic ministry, but only after he obeys the Father.

Additional Notes

4:4. Scripture citations introduced by γέγραπται occur nine times in Matthew:

6. On Jesus's temptation, see Baudoz 2001; Carré 2000; T. Donaldson 1985: 87–104; Fitzgerald 1972; Gerhardsson 1966; Gibson 1995: 25–118; Grelot 1989, 1995c; Hasitschka in Tuckett 1997: 487–90; Murphy-O'Connor 1999b; Neugebauer 1986; Stegemann 1985; Stegner in Evans and Sanders 1997: 98–120; N. Taylor 2001; W. Wilkens 1981–82.

Matthew	Speaker	Hebrew Bible
2:5	Religious leaders	Mic. 5:2
4:4	Jesus	Deut. 8:3
4:6	Satan	Ps. 91:11–12
4:7	Jesus	Deut. 6:16
4:10	Jesus	Deut. 6:13
11:10	Jesus	Mal. 3:1
21:13	Jesus	Isa. 56:7; Jer. 7:11
26:24	Jesus	None
26:31	Jesus	Zech. 13:7

4:10. C², D, *Byz*, and many ancient versions and patristic sources add ὀπίσω μου after ὕπαγε. But it is easier to understand ὀπίσω μου as an interpolation from Matt. 16:23; Mark 8:33 than to understand how it could have been omitted, resulting in the shorter reading found in א, B, and others.

4. Withdrawal to Galilee (4:12–17)

After successfully resisting Satan's tests, Jesus begins his ministry in Galilee in fulfillment of Isa. 9:1–2 (Matt. 4:12–17). In the phrase "Galilee of the Gentiles," both the geographic and the ethnic elements are significant for Matthew's theology. Jesus brings light to a dark place, and his message is ultimately for all the nations (24:14; 28:19). Jesus's message is summarized with the exact words that previously described the message of John the Baptist (4:17; cf. 3:2). The continuity between Jesus and John will also be seen later in Matthew's narrative (cf. 4:12; 11:18–19; 13:53–14:13; 17:9–13).

The unit divides as follows:

    a. The occasion and setting (4:12–13)
    b. The biblical pattern (4:14–16)
    c. The kingdom preaching begins (4:17)

Exegesis and Exposition

¹²When Jesus heard that John had been arrested, he returned to Galilee. ¹³He left Nazareth and went to dwell in Capernaum, which was by the lake in the area of Zebulun and Naphtali,¹⁴to fulfill what had been said through the prophet Isaiah:

> ¹⁵"Land of Zebulun and land of Naphtali,
> the way of the sea, along the Jordan, Galilee of the Gentiles—
> ¹⁶the people living in darkness have seen a great light;
> and on those living in the land and shadow of death, a light has dawned."

¹⁷From that time Jesus began to proclaim the message, "⌜Repent, for⌝ the kingdom of heaven has come near."

a. The Occasion and Setting (4:12–13)

4:12–13   Jesus left Judea and "returned to Galilee" when he learned that John had been imprisoned. "Returned" translates a word (ἀναχωρέω, *anachoreō*) that is used several times in Matthew to describe a strategic withdrawal in the face of danger (2:12–14, 22; 4:12; 12:15; 14:13; 15:21). The arrest and imprisonment of John will lead to his grisly execution (14:1–12), which in turn will lead to another strategic withdrawal by Jesus (14:13). These two withdrawals by Jesus may anticipate the close connection made later between the fate of John and the fate of Jesus (11:18–19; 17:12). Jesus first goes to Nazareth, where he grew up (2:23). At the triumphal entry, Nazareth will still be known as his hometown (21:11). Matthew does not dwell on Nazareth (but cf. Luke 4:16–30), preferring to stress Capernaum because its location has prophetic significance. Capernaum (cf. Matt. 8:5; 11:23; 17:24) is on the northwest shore of the Sea of Galilee, roughly two miles west of the Jordan River. Matthew's description of Capernaum in 4:13 anticipates the citation of Isa. 9:1 in Matt. 4:15 by stressing Capernaum's location by the sea in the territory of Zebulun and Naphtali (cf. Josh. 19:32–39). Capernaum is not mentioned in the Hebrew Bible, but for Matthew its obscurity signifies a dark place on which the light is about to shine.

b. The Biblical Pattern (4:14–16)

For Matthew, Jesus's residence in Capernaum, located in the territory of Zebulun and Naphtali, has prophetic implications. With his characteristic fulfillment formula (cf. 1:23; 2:15, 17, 23 and "Theological Emphases: Fulfillment" in the commentary introduction), Matthew introduces a quote from Isa. 9:1–2. Originally Isa. 7–9 promised deliverance from the threat of Assyria. Matthew has already connected the birth of Jesus with the sign promised to Ahaz (Matt. 1:23; cf. Isa. 7:14; 8:8, 10). Here he connects the political darkness facing Israel in the days of Isaiah to the spiritual problem that caused it. Israel's defection from the Mosaic covenant led to her oppression by other kingdoms, Assyria in this case. But for Matthew, Israel's dark political prospects were symptomatic of her need for the redemption from sin available through Jesus the Messiah.

The stress of Isa. 9:6–7 upon a son who will rule David's kingdom fits nicely with the Matthean theme that Jesus is the son of David. But the mention in Isa. 9:1–2 of the scorned Galilee and its association with despised Gentiles repeats the idea that God rejects the proud and receives the most unlikely sinners into fellowship with himself. Matthew repeatedly stresses the mission to the Gentiles, either by implicit details (Matt. 1:3, 5–6; 2:1; 5:47; 6:32; 15:28; 22:9) or by the explicit teaching of Jesus (8:10–12; 21:43; 24:14; 28:19). Jesus's Galilean ministry prepares the reader for his Galilean commission, that his disciples should disciple all the nations (28:16–20). Galilee was evidently looked down upon by the "enlightened" Jerusalem establishment and those who supported it. Its population appears to have been mixed Jews and Gentiles (see mention of gentile Sidonians in Galilee: Judg. 18:7, 28; 2 Kings 15:29; 17:24–27; 1 Macc. 5). It is to this darkened place (cf. Ps. 107:10; Luke 1:79) that Jesus brings the light of the kingdom of God. Jesus will not minister directly to Gentiles during these early days (10:5–6; 15:24), but the beginnings of his ministry in a remote, despised place largely populated by Gentiles foreshadow the expansion of the mission to all the nations at the end of Jesus's ministry (24:14; 28:19).[1]

c. The Kingdom Preaching Begins (4:17)

4:17   Jesus's early message is portrayed here with the same language used to portray John's message in 3:2. The ethical imperative (μετανοεῖτε, *metanoeite*, repent) is grounded in the inaugurated eschatological reality of the nearness of kingdom (cf. this commentary's introduction; the comments on 3:2; Marcus 1988a). The linkage between the messages of John and Jesus lays a foundation for the similar fates of the two messengers (14:2; 17:12–13).

Many interpreters of Matthew think that the phrase ἀπὸ τότε (*apo tote*, from that time; cf. 16:21) signals a transition to the second major section of Matthew (Bauer 1988: 73–108; Kingsbury 1989: 89). One may grant the role this phrase plays in Matthew's presentation of the stages of Jesus's life and ministry. But it is not nearly as prominent as Matthew's unique literary structure, which alternates discourse and narrative material by inserting the phrase καὶ ἐγένετο ὅτε ἐτέλεσεν ὁ Ἰησοῦς (*kai egeneto hote etelesen ho Iēsous*, and it happened when Jesus had finished; cf. 7:28; 11:1; 13:53; 19:1; 26:1) at the end of each major discourse. The latter phrase is taken as determinative of Matthew's structure in this commentary.

Additional Note

4:17. Although a few ancient versions have μετανοεῖτε, ἤγγικεν or simply ἤγγικεν instead of μετανοεῖτε· ἤγγικεν γάρ, this last wording is overwhelmingly attested in the Greek MS tradition and agrees with Matt. 3:2.

1. On Galilee, see Freyne 1980; 1988a; Giesen 2001; Habbe 1996; Hertig 1998; L. Levine 1992. On the use of Isaiah, see Carter 2000a; Menken 1998b; Tisera 1993: 79–100. On the citation of Isa. 9:6–7, see Carter 2000a; Menken 1998b. On the kingdom of heaven in Matthew, see "Theological Emphases: Kingdom of Heaven" in the commentary introduction and Carter 1997b; Farmer in W. Willis (ed.) 1987: 119–30; J. Thomas 1993.

5. Calling Four Fishermen (4:18–22)

This paragraph contains two similar stories about Jesus's calling two fishermen. The story about the call of Simon (Peter) and Andrew (4:18–20) is very similar to the subsequent story (4:21–22) about the call of James and John. Both stories are similar to the story of Elijah's call of Elisha (1 Kings 19:19–21) and contain a fourfold structure (W. Davies and Allison 1988: 392–93): (1) the appearance of Jesus (Matt. 4:18, 21), (2) comment on the work of the prospective disciples (4:18, 21), (3) the call to discipleship (4:19, 21), and (4) obedience to the call (4:20, 22). In both narratives it is Jesus who sees the prospective disciples and takes the initiative in calling them to follow him (cf. John 15:16). This is an important factor in distinguishing Jesus as a charismatic or prophetic figure, after the model of Elijah, from the later rabbinic model, in which disciples took the initiative in attaching themselves to the rabbi (cf. *m. 'Abot* 1.6). In the Bible, God's call regularly comes to people while they are working—to Gideon while threshing (Judg. 6:11–12), to Elisha while plowing (1 Kings 19:19), to Amos while herding (Amos 7:14–15), and to Matthew in his tax collector's booth (Matt. 9:9). All such stories emphasize that God's call demands a decisive break with business as usual (W. Davies and Allison 1988: 397).

The unit outline is as follows:

a. Call of Simon (Peter) and Andrew (4:18–20)
b. Call of James and John (4:21–22)

Exegesis and Exposition

[18]Now as Jesus was walking by the Sea of Galilee, he saw two brothers, Simon, who was called Peter, and Andrew his brother. They were casting a net into the sea, for they were fishermen. [19]And he said to them, "Follow me, and I will make you fish for people." [20]Immediately they left their nets and followed him. [21]Going on from there, he saw two other brothers, James, the son of Zebedee, and John his brother. They were in the boat with Zebedee, their father, mending their nets, and he called them. [22]Immediately they left the boat and their father and followed him.

a. Call of Simon (Peter) and Andrew (4:18–20)

4:18   The name Simon (cf. 10:2; 16:16–17; 17:25) appears much less often in Matthew than the nickname Peter, which Jesus gives Simon in 16:17–18.[1] It is not coincidental that Peter is the first disciple who responds to the call of Jesus, since Peter is prominent throughout Matthew, especially in 16:13–28. Andrew, on the other hand, is mentioned only once after this (10:2; but cf. John 1:35–42). The final clause of 4:18 may seem redundant, but it is intended to show that Peter and Andrew are commercial fishermen, not casual anglers. It also prepares the reader for Jesus's play on words in 4:19. The net was a circular device, weighted with stones, that was thrown into the water. When pulled up, it tightened around the fish.

4:19   The call to discipleship (δεῦτε ὀπίσω μου, *deute opisō mou*, follow me; BDAG 220) is an unconditional, unexplained demand, not a polite, reasoned invitation. For the first disciples, the following of Jesus entails both literally traveling with him and ethically obeying his teaching and modeling of God's will, which leads to hardship and peril (8:19, 22; 10:38; 16:24; 19:21). Fishing for people is an expression found elsewhere in the NT only in Mark 1:17. It is possible that fishing here is an allusion to Jer. 16:16, but it is much more likely, in view of Matt. 13:47–50, that fishing for people has implications of eschatological judgment.

4:20   Peter and Andrew's response to the call is immediate sacrificial obedience. They walk away from their families, homes, and livelihood and follow Jesus in a life of homelessness (8:20). For the similar story of the call of Matthew, see 9:9. Following Jesus is a common theme in Matthew.[2] This expression can describe the activity of the Twelve and of other close disciples, but it is also used for the crowds, whose shallow "following" of Jesus should not be viewed as genuine discipleship.

b. Call of James and John (4:21–22)

4:21–22   The call of James and John follows the pattern just discussed. These brothers are mentioned later in the narrative, sometimes by name (10:2; 17:1) and sometimes as "the sons of Zebedee" (20:20; 26:37; 27:56). They

---

1. Πέτρος appears here for the first of twenty-three times in Matt.: 4:18; 8:14; 10:2; 14:28, 29; 15:15; 16:16, 18, 22, 23; 17:1, 4, 24; 18:21; 19:27; 26:33, 35, 37, 40, 58, 69, 73, 75. For further study of Peter, see Allison 1992c; R. Brown et al. 1973; Caragounis 1989; Cullmann 1962b; Dschulnigg 1989; Fornberg 1995; Kingsbury 1979; Nau 1992; Syreeni in Rhoads and Syreeni 1999: 106–52; D.Turner 1991.

2. Ἀκολουθέω occurs in Matt. 4:20, 22, 25; 8:1, 10, 19, 22, 23; 9:9, 19, 27; 10:38; 12:15; 14:13; 16:24; 19:2, 21, 27, 28; 20:29, 34; 21:9; 26:58; 27:55. For further study of discipleship in Matthew, see J. Brown 2002; Deutsch 1987; R. Edwards in Segovia 1985: 47–61; 1997; Hagner 1998a; Hartin 1998; Kingsbury 1988b; Luz in Stanton 1995: 98–128; Morris in J. Green and Turner 1994: 112–27; Patte 1996; Trainor 1991; Westerholm 2006; Wilkins 1995.

too are commercial fishermen and are mending their nets in preparation for another voyage on the lake. At the summons of Jesus, they
likewise immediately walk away from their maritime career. In this case
it is added that they also leave their father behind, unlike a would-be
disciple later in the narrative (8:21–22). Their sacrifice entails the loss
not only of finances but also of family. In Matthew, following Jesus is
repeatedly put in tension with family relationships (cf. 8:21–22; 10:21,
34–37; 12:46–50; 19:29).

Matthew 4:18–22 narrates the obedience of Jesus's first disciples, who
immediately left family and livelihood to follow him. But Matthew's
purpose goes beyond providing a narrative of the past, to provide a
challenge for the future. Jesus's ministry is a model for our own ministries, and the obedience of the first disciples challenges all disciples to
similar obedience. The immediate, unquestioning, sacrificial response
of the first disciples to Jesus's absolutely authoritative call to discipleship is a model for today. Discipleship is incumbent upon all Christians,
whether or not they are called to vocational ministry. The unquestioning
obedience of Peter and Andrew[3] and of James and John condemns any
delay or ambivalence in responding to Jesus. The obedience of Jesus's
first disciples contrasts with the excuses of the later would-be disciples
who will not make the requisite sacrifice (8:18–22; cf. 19:16–26). Even
true disciples who have responded to the call need to have their faith
strengthened (8:23–27). Their task is daunting (10:5–42), but their reward
is great (19:27–30).[4]

3. Cf. John 1:35–42, where Andrew and Peter are presented as disciples of John before
their contact with Jesus.
4. On Matt. 4:18–22, see Carter 1997a; R. Edwards in van Segbroeck et al. 1992: 1305–24;
1997: 19–27; Knowles 1993: 194–97; Murphy-O'Connor 1999a.

6. Summary of the Early Ministry (4:23–25)

The final section of Matt. 4 encapsulates the ministry of Jesus (Hagner 1993: 78). It may be viewed as it is construed here, as a concluding summary of Jesus's early ministry in Galilee (cf. Mark 1:14–20, 39; Luke 4:14–15, 44), or, as W. Davies and Allison (1988: 410) take it, as the introduction to the Sermon on the Mount. Matthew 4:23 is repeated almost verbatim in 9:35. Both 4:23 and 9:35 are located just before major discourses of Jesus, and they serve to summarize his deeds as the context for his words. But there is likely more to the repetition than this. Taken together, 4:23 and 9:35 are an *inclusio*, a pair of literary bookends, summarizing Jesus's words and deeds at the beginning and end of two sections that present his words (Matt. 5–7) and deeds (Matt. 8–9) in detail (see the outline below). Significantly, both the words (7:29) and the deeds (8:9; 9:6) demonstrate Jesus's kingdom authority, an authority that he passes on to his disciples in 10:1. As his words and deeds proclaim and demonstrate the kingdom, so will the words and deeds of his disciples (10:7–8).

Inclusio in Matt. 4:23–9:35

A Summary of Jesus's teaching, preaching, and healing (4:23)
B Jesus's authoritative words (5:3–7:27; see 7:29)
B′ Jesus's authoritative deeds (8:1–9:34; see 8:9; 9:6)
A′ Summary of Jesus's teaching, preaching, and healing (9:35)

Exegesis and Exposition

²³Jesus was going throughout all Galilee, teaching in their synagogues and proclaiming the good news about the kingdom and healing every kind of disease and sickness among the people. ²⁴The news about him spread throughout all Syria; and people brought to him all who were ill, those suffering from various diseases and pains, demon-possessed, epileptics, paralytics; and he healed them. ²⁵Large crowds followed him, people from Galilee and the ten cities and Jerusalem and Judea and from east of the Jordan River.

4:23 Jesus's ministry is presented in a threefold fashion here: synagogue teaching, public preaching of the kingdom, and powerful healings. Synagogues (cf. 6:2, 5; 9:35; 10:17; 12:9; 13:54; 23:6, 34) evidently developed after the exile to Babylon. They were gatherings for prayer and the study of Scripture, primarily the Torah (cf. Luke 4:16–28). They apparently also functioned as community courts, especially with the rise of the rabbinic movement after the destruction of the temple in 70 CE.[1] The central theme of the proclamation of the nearness of God's kingdom or rule through the Messiah has already been stressed in 3:2 and 4:17 and will continue to be featured in Matthew's narrative (cf. 9:35; 10:7, 27; 11:1; 13:19; 24:14; 26:13). In addition to the verbal aspect of Jesus's ministry, Matthew also shows that Jesus's powerful acts of mercy demonstrate the reality of the rule of God (cf. 8:7, 16; 9:35; 10:1, 8; 12:10, 15, 22; 14:14; 15:30; 17:16, 18; 19:2; 21:14). Matthew's comment that Jesus heals *every* kind of sickness and disease stresses the extent of Jesus's kingly power (cf. Giesen in Schenke 1988: 79–106; Heil 1979; Twelftree 1999). See Twelftree in McKnight and Osborne 2004: 191–208 for a historical survey of the scholarly study of Jesus's miracles.

It is also clear from Matt. 4:23–25 that Jesus's ministry is holistic. He deals with both physical and spiritual needs, the former sometimes evidently preceding the latter. Although he demands repentance, he does not make repentance the prerequisite for healing. Jesus has compassion on the needy crowds and acts to help them, evidently in many cases before they hear him preach. W. Davies and Allison put it well: "The first act of the Messiah is not the imposition of his commandments but the giving of himself" (1988: 427). And in narrating the gracious ministry of Jesus, Matthew surely intends it as a model for the ministry of the disciples. They too are not only to preach the kingdom (4:17; 10:6) but also to do works of compassion that demonstrate its power and grace (4:24; 10:1).

It is also the mission of Jesus to defeat the devil. As soon as Jesus emerges victorious from his testing (4:1–11), he is presented at the outset of his ministry as one who cures not only physical diseases but also demonic possession. Jesus's power over the forces of darkness is made clearer after the Sermon on the Mount as Matthew narrates Jesus's Galilean ministry (8:16, 28–34; 9:32–34; 12:22–32; 15:22–28; 17:18). One incident in particular (8:29) shows that the demons intuitively recognize Jesus's messianic identity and his ultimate eschatological authority over them. In another (12:22–32), Jesus counters the false accusation that he is in league with the devil (cf. 9:34) with the affirmation that his Spirit-empowered exorcism ministry amounts to the binding of a strong man and the removal of his property. Thus the kingdom has already en-

---

1. For convenient summaries of the synagogue in NT times and for bibliographies, see Chilton and Yamauchi in C. A. Evans and Porter 2000: 1145–53; J. Dunn in Charlesworth 2006: 206–22; J. Kloppenborg in Charlesworth 2006: 236–82; Meyers and Hachlili, *ABD* 6:251–63; B. Viviano in Charlesworth 2006: 223–35; and Yamauchi in J. Green and McKnight 1992: 781–84.

croached upon Satan's territory, and Satan will ultimately be defeated. Additional NT teaching makes this even clearer (John 12:31; 16:11; Heb. 2:14; 1 John 3:8; Rev. 5:5; 12:7–10; 20:1–10; cf. Kampling 1986).

4:24–25 These verses describe the far-reaching results of Jesus's kingdom ministry of word and deed and should be viewed as the narative context of the Sermon on the Mount. Jesus's reputation spreads north from Galilee into Syria, and soon people from all over are coming to Jesus for healing. Matthew 4:24 describes in more detail than 4:23 the diseases healed and adds that Jesus also deals with demonic possession (cf. 8:16, 28; 9:32–34; 10:8; 12:22, 24, 27–28; 15:22–28; 17:18; E. Eshel in Charlesworth 2006: 178–85; Trunk 1994). The "paralytics" mentioned here do not correspond exactly to what is known by modern medicine as paralysis. The point is that the people were lame, unable to walk, whatever the underlying reason for that symptom (BDAG 768; D. Peterson 2006). All who are brought to Jesus are healed, and this leads to crowds of people following Jesus. People not only from Galilee but also from the regions surrounding Galilee are "following" Jesus, which here does not have the strict ethical sense of 4:19, 21.

Matthew's first use of the term "crowds" is noteworthy, since it will often portray those who are attracted to Jesus because of his sensational deeds (cf. 8:1, 18; 11:7; 12:46; 15:30; 17:14; 19:2). The crowds are, as it were, "in the middle," between Jesus and his disciples on the one hand, and the hostile religious leaders on the other. At times the crowd seems favorable to Jesus (9:8; 12:23; 15:31; 22:33), and he to the crowd (9:36; 14:14; 15:32). But as time wears on, under the influence of the leaders, the crowd ultimately assents to Jesus's death (26:47, 55; 27:20, 24). In this context, the presence of the crowds leads Jesus away to the mountain where he delivers his first discourse (5:1). (See Carter 1993; Cousland 2002; Doyle 1984.)

The Decapolis (literally, the "ten cities") was a group of Hellenistic cities southeast of Galilee administered from Syria by the Romans (cf. Mark 5:20; 7:31; Josephus, *Life* 341; *J.W.* 3.446). Nearly all of them were east of the Jordan River.[2] "East of the Jordan River" is literally "beyond the Jordan," which refers to the region farther south, east of Jerusalem and the Jordan River. This phrase appears about twenty-five times in the Hebrew Bible and several times in the NT (Matt. 4:15, 25; 19:1; Mark 3:8; 10:1; John 1:28; 3:26; 10:40). Matthew's geographical language covers the whole land of Israel, moving from northwest (Galilee) to northeast (the Decapolis) to Jerusalem (probably to be understood as the center of the land) to southwest (Judea) to southeast ("beyond the Jordan"). (Cf. Krieger 1986.)

---

2. For a helpful summary of the ten cities, see R. Ciampa in C. A. Evans and Porter 2000: 266–68.

II. Early Days of Kingdom Word and Deed (3:1–7:29)
    A. Narrative 1: John and Jesus and the Kingdom of God (3:1–4:25)
➤ B. Discourse 1: Sermon on the Mount (5:1–7:29)

B. Discourse 1: Sermon on the Mount (5:1–7:29)

Historicity

The Sermon on the Mount does not appear as such in Mark and appears only partially in Luke 6:17–49 (cf. Bock 1994: 548–628).[1] Scholars have propounded several theories to explain this variation among the Synoptic Gospels. Some believe that Matthew has created the sermon from traditions, documentary sources, and his own ingenuity, so that the sermon should not be attributed to the historical Jesus. This approach tends to take the Gospels as unhistorical fabrications, concocted for strictly theological reasons. A second view holds that Matthew created the structure of the sermon but genuine Jesus traditions make up its content. In this view, Matthew collated various teachings of the historical Jesus that were originally uttered at different times in different locations and placed them here in his narrative. Many evangelicals hold this view (e.g., France 1985: 105–6; 1989: 162–63; Hagner 1993: 83; Keener 1999: 162; Witherington 2006: 115). Matthew, however, clearly brackets the sermon with indicators of a specific time and place when the sermon occurred (5:1–2; 7:28–8:1), and so these historical markers must be ignored or viewed as fictional for the second view to be adopted.

A third view is that Matthew accurately records the gist (*ipsissima vox*, "the very voice," of Jesus) of a historical sermon that Jesus uttered. Some may go even further to affirm that Matthew gives an exact and complete word-for-word (*ipsissima verba*, "the very words," of Jesus) transcription of the sermon Jesus uttered. Although the second and third views are both held by conservative evangelicals, the third view is highly preferable because of the genre of the Gospels and the historical transmission of the teachings of Jesus. Authentic reporting of a historical event need not be word-for-word transcription. It is difficult to conceive how such a transcription could have been compiled in the first place, let alone transmitted to the likely author, Matthew, who may not yet have been a disciple (9:9). Rather, the sermon is a reliable summary of what Jesus said, an account that bears the marks of an editor. The fact that certain of the sayings of Matthew's sermon occur in other contexts in Mark and Luke is evidently due to Jesus's repeating key themes in his itinerant ministry (Carson 1984: 123–25). Calvin (1972: 1.168) thinks that

1. See France 1989: 161 for a simple chart of synoptic parallels to the sermon.

the sermon incorporates teaching both from the occasion represented in 5:1–2 and from other, later discourses of Jesus. (On the larger question of the authenticity of the words of Jesus in the Gospels, see Bock in Wilkins and Moreland 1995: 73–99.)[2]

Literary Structure

The introduction to this commentary argues that the bulk of Matthew (Matt. 3–25) consists of five blocks of narrative/discourse material (Matt. 3–7; 8–10; 11–13; 14–18; 19–25). These five sections of Jesus's works and words are divided by the key phrase "and it happened when Jesus had finished" (7:28; 11:1; 13:53; 19:1; 26:1). The Sermon on the Mount should be seen as the representative ethical teaching of Jesus, developing the summary statement of 4:23, which presents a word/deed complex. Accordingly, 4:23 and the similar summary in 9:35 provide a frame, or "bookends," for Jesus's ministry of teaching and doing miracles. Both the words (Matt. 5–7) and the works (Matt. 8–9) demonstrate the authority of the kingdom of heaven (7:28–29; 8:9; 9:6–8).

There are many approaches to the structure of the sermon.[3] Patte (1987) presents a chiastic approach, but its elements are disproportionate, and it is unconvincing. W. Davies (1964: 304–15; 1966: 88–89) finds the pattern for the sermon's structure in words attributed to Simon the Just (*m. 'Abot* 1.2), which posit the Torah, temple worship, and kind deeds as three things that sustain the world.[4] Davies views them as corresponding to Matt. 5:17–48; 6:1–18; and 6:19–7:27. This connection between a mishnaic saying and the structure of the sermon seems a bit arbitrary, but Davies's scheme is adopted by Boring (1995: 173) and W. Davies and Allison, who demonstrate numerous triadic structures in the sermon (1988: 62–64; cf. Allison 1987c). It seems clear that 5:17–48 and 6:1–18 are discrete sections, but it is more difficult to view 6:19–7:12 (or 7:27) under one heading. Another approach views the Lord's Prayer (6:9–13) as the center of the sermon, with the material preceding the prayer expounding the first three "your" petitions and the material following the prayer expounding the three "our" petitions (Bornkamm 1977–78; Grundmann 1968; Guelich 1982: 324–25). The analysis proposed below is

2. Thorough, exegetically based treatments of the sermon as a whole include H. Betz 1995; Carson 1978; Dumais 1995a; Guelich 1982; Lambrecht 1985; Lloyd-Jones 1981; Scaer 2000; Stott 1978; Strecker 1988; Talbert 2006; Zeilinger 2002.

3. Additional studies include Allison 1987; 2005b: 173–215; H. Betz 1995: 44–66; Bornkamm 1977–78; J. Brooks 1992; Kingsbury 1987b; Kodjak 1986; Luz 1989: 218–23; B. Scott and M. Dean in Bauer and Powell 1996: 311–78; Smit Sibinga 1994; Stanton 1992b: 285–306.

4. On the larger question of the Jewish context of the sermon, see W. Davies 1964, 1966; Draper 1999; Flusser 1987; Ginzel 1985; Hengel 1987; Massey 1991; Songer 1992; Worth 1997.

based on the clear *inclusio* formed by the references to the righteousness of the law and the prophets in Matt. 5:17 and 7:12:

Analysis of the Sermon on the Mount

- *Introductory narrative framework (5:1–2):* **Jesus is prompted to teach by the crowds, and his disciples gather around him to hear his teaching.**
  - *Introduction to the sermon (5:3–16):* The Beatitudes (5:3–12) describe the divinely approved lifestyle of those who have repented at the arrival of the rule of God in Jesus's words and works. Those who live by Jesus's ethical teaching manifest the values of the rule of God to the world as salt and light (5:13–16).
    - *Body (5:17–7:12):* Jesus announces (5:17–20) and then explains (5:21–48) his relationship to the law with six contrasts. Then he turns to hypocritical versus genuine religious practice (6:1–18), materialism and anxiety (6:19–34), spiritual discernment (7:1–6), and prayer (7:7–11). A summary reference to the law (7:12) completes the theme of obeying the law and the prophets that began in 5:17.
  - *Conclusion to the sermon (7:13–27):* By three stark contrasts (two ways, two fruits, two foundations) Jesus challenges his listeners to make a correct response to his teaching. They are to take the narrow way (7:13–14), to avoid the bad fruit of the false prophets (7:15–23), and to build their lives on the words they have heard (7:24–27).
- *Concluding narrative framework (7:28–29):* **The crowds are amazed at Jesus's uniquely authoritative teaching.**

Major Interpretive Approaches

Here only a few major interpretive approaches to the sermon can be mentioned.[5] Dispensational interpreters have traditionally tended to view the sermon as Jewish law for the kingdom, not gracious teaching directly relevant for the church (Gaebelein 1910: 108–11; Scofield 1909: 999–1000; Walvoord 1974: 45–46).[6] This kingdom teaching may relate to the time of Jesus's earthly ministry or to the future tribulation or millennium. This view tends to assume mistakenly that Matthew was written to Jews who did not believe in Jesus. Lutheran interpreters similarly tend to view the sermon as law, not gospel, but think that its high legal standards will show people their sinfulness and draw them to the cross for forgiveness. A. Schweitzer viewed the sermon as an *Interimsethik* for the supposedly short interim that Matthew conceived between the advents

---

5. For the plethora of approaches, see esp. Kissinger 1975. H. Betz (1995: 3) opines that no complete bibliography on the sermon or the history of its interpretation has been or ever will be written, since such a work would have to engage the entire history of biblical exegesis, theology, and even secular philosophy. Nevertheless, H. Betz (1995: 6–44) does offer a summary of the history of interpretation. On the history of interpretation, see also L. Allen 1992; Bauman 1985; Berner 1985; Beyschlag 1977; Carlston 1985; Carter 1994b; Dumais 1995b; Durston 1988; Grant 1978; Guelich 1982: 14–22; Luz 1989: 218–23; Stanton 1992b: 289–97; Strecker 1988: 15–23. For bibliographies on the sermon, see Cranford 1992; Dumais 1995b; Kissinger 1975; Luz 1989: 209–11; Mills 2000; Nolland 2005: 186–90.

6. There are exceptions to this tendency. See, e.g., Lawlor 1974: 11–13; J. Martin 1986: 35–48.

of Jesus. Other interpreters, across the spectrum of denominations and views of eschatology, take the sermon as an ethic for today but differ on whether the sermon is personal ethics or a public-policy agenda to be implemented through political processes. Calvinists, Anabaptists, and advocates of the so-called social gospel all take the sermon as directly applicable to believers today.[7]

The view taken here is that the sermon amounts to personal ethics for followers of Jesus. This does not amount to privatism—followers of Jesus are to be salt and light in this world. The Sermon on the Mount is Jesus's authoritative teaching about the way believers should live today. Those who repented when they heard the gospel preached by John and Jesus (3:2; 4:17) needed to know how to live under God's saving reign. As Jews, they especially needed to know how Jesus's teaching related to Moses and the Hebrew Bible. Fulfilling biblical values is the framework of the sermon (5:17; 7:12), and Jesus's disciples are those who long for the time when these values will be fully realized on earth (6:10).

7. On the ethics of the sermon, see Allison 1999; Cahill 1987; Dumais 1998; Greenfield 1992; Hagner 1997b; Johner 1998; G. Lohfink 1988; Lohse in Oberlinner and Fiedler 1991: 131–40; Matera 1989; Pathrapankal 1997; Römelt 1992; Wink 1992.

1. God's Approval: The Beatitudes (5:1–16)

Structure

The structure of the Beatitudes is a matter of no little debate (Hagner 1993: 88–91). The following structure (with the grammatical details that demonstrate it) is explained more fully below.

The Structure of Matthew's Beatitudes

5:3 Poor in spirit are blessed because *theirs is the kingdom of heaven*
(The present tense ἐστιν [*estin*] in the promise, identical to 5:10)

    5:4 Mourners are blessed because *they will be comforted*
(A future passive[1] promise [παρακληθήσονται, *paraklēthēsontai*] as in 5:9)

        5:5 Meek are blessed because *they will inherit the earth*
(A future transitive verb [κληρονομήσουσιν, *klēronomēsousin*] with direct object as in 5:8)

            5:6 Hungry are blessed because *they will be filled*
(A future passive promise [χορτασθήσονται, *chortasthēsontai*] as in 5:7)

            5:7 Merciful are blessed because *they will be mercied*
(A future passive promise [ἐλεηθήσονται, *eleēthēsontai*] as in 5:6)

        5:8 Pure are blessed because *they will see God*
(A future transitive verb [ὄψονται, *opsontai*] with direct object as in 5:5)

    5:9 Peacemakers are blessed because *they will be called sons of God*
(A future passive promise [κληθήσονται, *klēthēsontai*] as in 5:4)

5:10 Persecuted are blessed because *theirs is the kingdom of heaven*
(The present tense ἐστιν in the promise, identical to 5:3)

Expansion:

5:11–12 Persecuted are blessed with the prophets because of Jesus
(Shift to second person, triple description of persecution, double command to rejoice, continuity with the prophets)

---

1. Here and in 5:6–7, 9 the passive implies divine agency. See Wallace 1996: 437–38.

Altogether there are nine beatitudes in Matt. 5:3–12, but the ninth (5:11–12) is really an expansion of the eighth (5:10).[2] Although some (e.g., W. Davies and Allison 1988: 430–31) opt for a structure with three sets of three, the first eight exhibit such a tightly knit parallel structure that it is preferable to understand them as two sets of four with an expanded conclusion (Gundry 1994: 73; Luz 1989: 226; Nolland 2005: 196–97; D. Turner 1992b). The first set emphasizes the disciple's vertical relationship to God; the second emphasizes the disciple's horizontal relationship to people. Both relationships occur in the midst of oppression. The first and eighth beatitudes bracket the set with stress on the present partial experience of the kingdom. The remaining pairs symmetrically stress the future full experience of the kingdom.

Meaning

A beatitude, or macarism (from μακάριος, *makarios*, blessed), consists of a pronouncement concerning who are blessed, often followed by a promise as to why they are blessed (here introduced by ὅτι, *hoti*, for, since, because). To be blessed is to be the happy recipient of divine favor or approval (BDAG 611). The focus, however, is not on the subjective feelings of the blessed person but on the objective reality of the inauguration of the rule of God in Jesus. The opposite of "blessed" is not "unhappy" but "cursed" (Boring 1995: 177). There are about forty-five macarisms in the Hebrew Bible[3] and thirty-seven in the NT.[4] The NT beatitudes often carry eschatological overtones similar to beatitudes in apocalyptic literature.[5] Beatitudes are also found in the Dead Sea Scrolls.[6]

There are two contrasting views of the meaning of the Beatitudes. One sees them as indicative pronouncements of gracious kingdom blessings. The other sees them as ethical exhortations about entrance

2. Luke 6:20–26 symmetrically balances four beatitudes with four woe oracles. See Bock 1994: 571–86.

3. These expressions typically begin with something like אַשְׁרֵי־הָאִישׁ אֲשֶׁר. See Deut. 33:29; 1 Kings 10:8 (2x); Isa. 30:18; 32:20; 56:2; Pss. 1:1; 2:12; 32:1, 2; 33:12; 34:9; 40:5; 41:2; 65:5; 84:5, 6, 13; 89:16; 94:12; 106:3; 112:1; 119:1, 2; 127:5; 128:1, 2; 137:8, 9; 144:15 (2x); 146:5; Job 5:17; Prov. 3:13; 8:32, 34; 14:21; 16:20; 20:7; 28:14; 29:18; Eccles. 10:17; Dan. 12:12; 2 Chron. 9:7 (2x). Another fifteen beatitudes are found in the LXX: Sir. 14:1, 2, 20; 25:8, 9; 26:1; 28:19; 31:8; 34:15; 48:11; 50:28; Tob. 13:15–16 (13:14 Eng. [2x]); Wis. 3:13; Isa. 31:9.

4. In addition to Matt. 5:3–11 (9x), see 11:6; 13:16; 16:17; 24:46; Luke 1:45; 6:20, 21 (2x); 22; 7:23; 10:23; 11:27, 28; 12:37, 43; 14:15; 23:29; John 20:29; Rom. 4:7, 8; 14:22; James 1:12; Rev. 1:3; 14:13; 16:15; 19:9; 20:6; 22:7.

5. See, e.g., 1 En. 58.2; 81.4; 82.4; 99.10; 103.5; 2 En. 41.1; 42.6–14; 44.4; 48.9; 52.1–14; 61.3; 62.1; 66.7; Sib. Or. 3.371–72; 4 Macc. 4:17–18.

6. 4Q525 2.2.1–6 is the most frequently cited text. Cf 1QH 6.13–16; 1QS 9.15. Similarities to Ps. 15 and Sir. 14:20–27; 15:1–10 are noted. See Brooke 1989; Charlesworth 2000; Puech 1988, 1991; Viviano 1992; in Schiffman and VanderKam 2000: 1.89–90.

requirements (Guelich 1976). If the latter view is correct, human effort must produce the characteristics mentioned here so that one might earn God's approval. If the former view is correct, one can only thankfully acknowledge these characteristics as evidence of God's gracious working in one's life and cultivate them as one lives as a disciple of Christ. Certainly the view that regards them as blessings rather than requirements is correct. Those who repent at the message of the kingdom (3:2; 4:17) acknowledge their own spiritual bankruptcy and rejoice in God's blessings of salvation.

The Beatitudes reveal key character traits that God approves in his people. These character traits are gracious gifts indicating God's approval, not requirements for works that merit God's approval. Those who repent receive these character traits in principle but must cultivate them in the process of discipleship. The qualities that God does approve are explained in two sets of four that respectively describe relating to God and relating to other people (see also 22:37–40). God approves those who relate to him by admitting their spiritual poverty and mourning over sin and oppression, humbly seeking spiritual fullness (5:3–6). God approves those who relate to others mercifully and purely as peacemakers, even though they may be persecuted for their righteous behavior (5:7–12). At first this may sound like a sadistic joke, appealing only to those who enjoy pain. Jesus appears to be saying that those who are unhappy are happy. But in reality Jesus is showing the error of superficial, self-centered living. His biblical realism establishes the values that lead to true bliss and ultimate comfort for his followers.

The radical spirituality of the Beatitudes directly confronts several cultural views of God's approval. One of these is that popularity with one's peers indicates divine approval, but this is plainly contradicted by the statement that those who are persecuted by their peers have God's approval (5:10–12; 7:13–14). Another mistaken viewpoint is that one may have divine approval if one simply keeps a prescribed set of rules, but Jesus states that only a righteousness that surpasses mere rule keeping will suffice for his kingdom (5:20). Some would say that an abundance of material possessions is an indication of divine favor, but according to Jesus, preoccupation with such possessions is antithetical to the values of the kingdom (6:19–21, 33). Ability to perform miraculous displays is commonly associated with divine approval, but on the last day some miracle workers will learn that Jesus does not acknowledge them as his people (7:22–23). In much of the world, there is a premium on education for those who preach the gospel, but according to Jesus, one must obey his words, not simply know what they are (7:26).[7]

7. For further study of the Beatitudes, see Broer 1986; W. Davies and Allison 1988: 431–42; Di Lella in M. Morgan and Kobelski 1989: 237–42; Dupont 1969–73; Eigo 1995;

The outline of this exegetical unit is as follows:

a. Narrative introduction: The setting of the sermon (5:1–2)
b. Approval in relating to God (5:3–6)
c. Approval in relating to people (5:7–10)
d. Expansion: Approval during persecution (5:11–16)
  i. Understanding persecution (5:11–12)
  ii. Witness during persecution (5:13–16)

Exegesis and Exposition

[1]When Jesus saw the crowds, he went up on the mountain; and when he sat down, his disciples came to him. [2]He opened his mouth and began to teach them, saying,

> [3]"Blessed are the poor in spirit, for the kingdom of heaven is theirs.
> [4][Blessed are those who mourn, for they shall be comforted.
> [5]Blessed are the gentle, for they shall inherit the earth.]
> [6]Blessed are those who hunger and thirst for righteousness, for they shall be satisfied.
> [7]Blessed are the merciful, for they shall receive mercy.
> [8]Blessed are the pure in heart, for they shall see God.
> [9]Blessed are the peacemakers, for they shall be called children of God.
> [10]Blessed are those who are persecuted because of righteousness, for the kingdom of heaven is theirs.

[11]"Blessed are you when people insult you and persecute you, and [falsely] say all kinds of evil against you because of me. [12]Rejoice and be glad, for your reward in heaven is great; for in the same way they persecuted the prophets who were before you.

[13]"You are the salt of the earth; but if the salt has lost its saltiness, how can its flavor be restored? It is no longer good for anything, except to be thrown out and trampled under people's feet.

[14]"You are the light of the world. A city built on a hill cannot be hidden; [15]Neither does anyone light a lamp and put it under a basket. Rather, they set it on its stand, and it gives light to everyone in the house. [16]In this way let your light shine before people so that they may see your good works and praise your Father who is in heaven."

Fitzmyer in van Segbroeck 1992: 509–15; Genuyt 1997; Gourges 1998; H. Green 2001; Guelich 1976; Hanson 1994; Kessler 1997; McEleney 1981; Powell 1996; Schweizer 1972–73; J. Thompson 1999; Trites 1992; D. Turner 1992b; Zimmerli in Bammel et al. 1978: 8–26. For challenging expositions, see Bruner 1987: 133–59; Carson 1978; Lawlor 1974; Lloyd-Jones 1981: 32–148; Stott 1978: 30–56.

a. Narrative Introduction: The Setting of the Sermon (5:1–2)

These verses along with 7:28–8:1 provide the narrative setting for the ser-   **5:1–2**
mon (cf. Baxter 2004; Keegan 1982). Once again Matthew presents Jesus
doing something significant on a mountain (cf. Ito 1994), which probably
reflects an intended typological relationship between Jesus and Moses
(compare the following verses in Matthew with Exod. 19–20; 34: Matt. 4:8;
14:23; 15:29; 17:1; 24:3; 28:16; see also Allison 1993b: 172–80; Baxter 1999;
T. Donaldson 1985: 105–21). Jesus evidently retires to the mountainside
to teach his disciples more privately, but it is doubtful that the crowd is
entirely absent from this discourse. More likely, the disciples, as the inner
circle, closely listen to Jesus while a throng of people gathers around the
periphery of the scene and exhibits varied levels of interest and comprehension. Teaching while sitting was evidently customary (cf. 13:1–2; 23:2; 24:3),
but in other contexts, sitting is the posture for pronouncing eschatological
judgment (19:28; 20:21, 23; 22:44; 25:31; 26:64). Allison (1993b: 176–80)
argues that pre-Christian Jewish tradition portrayed Moses as enthroned
upon Sinai. Matthew often speaks of various people "gathering around"
Jesus to hear him teach or to ask him for something (e.g., 8:2, 5, 19).

b. Approval in Relating to God (5:3–6)

The word "beatitude" is related to the Latin *beatus*, which means "blessed."   **5:3**
To be blessed (μακάριος, *makarios*) is to receive God's approval, favor,
endorsement, congratulations. To be "blessed" is to be so much more
than "happy," since the word "happiness" conveys only a subjective,
shallow notion of serendipity, not the conviction of being a recipient of
God's grace. God initiates blessing by graciously condescending to save
people. They respond to God's initiative by blessing God with praise and
obedient living. Their present experience of God's reign in Jesus motivates
them to live in light of its future intensification (6:10). The pattern of the
Beatitudes is to highlight the character of the blessed person and then
to explain the promise of God to such a person.

The first beatitude concerns authentic spirituality. God's approval
does not come to those who boast of their spiritual riches. Rather, God's
endorsement is for those who admit their spiritual poverty (cf. 11:5; Isa.
61:1). To be "poor in spirit" is to acknowledge one's total dependence
on God for everything, for righteousness (contra Keener 1999: 168; cf.
Matt. 5:6) as well as sustenance. The Bible contains repeated references
to the עֲנָוִים (*ănāwîm*, afflicted), people whose economic distress left
them with nothing to rely upon except God (Nolland 2005: 198–201).[8]
Their distress was due to problems such as death in the family, phys-

---

8. See, e.g., Lev. 19:9–15, 32–33; Deut. 15:4, 7, 11; Ps. 37:10–17; Prov. 16:18–19; Isa.
61:1–2; Jer. 22:15–17; Amos 2:6–8; cf. James 2:5. For rabbinic use, see Jastrow 1971:
1094.

ical handicap, advancing age, military defeat, social injustice, and alien status. But spiritual poverty should be acknowledged by everyone, not just those who have adverse circumstances. Material prosperity should not deaden our sensitivity to our spiritual poverty.

Matthew 5:3 and 5:10 have identical promise statements ("for theirs is the kingdom of heaven") and thus frame the entire section. Also, the promise statements of 5:3 and 5:10 both use the present tense whereas the promise statements of the intervening verses 4–9 all use the future tense. Scholars debate the significance of the present tense in 5:3, 10. Some opt for the futuristic use of the present (e.g., Gundry 1994: 68; Keener 1999: 166), and others stress the present realization of kingdom blessing (e.g., Carson 1984: 132; Hagner 1993: 92). The latter view of a presently inaugurated kingdom that will be consummated in the future is highly preferable. The oppressed poor presently experience the blessing of the kingdom only partially.

Matthew's phrase is "poor in spirit" (cf. Isa. 57:15), but Luke's version of this beatitude has only "blessed are you who are poor" (Luke 6:20). Although some scholars believe that Matthew has spiritualized Luke's more accurate version of a saying originally about material poverty (e.g., Beare 1981: 128; Hare 1993: 36), it is much more likely that Matthew has only clarified the original intent of Jesus by focusing on the inner disposition of those in poverty (Hagner 1993: 91). There is also here a likely allusion to Isa. 66:1–2, similar to the allusion to Isa. 61:1–2 in Matt. 11:5 (cf. Matt. 25:31–46). The Hebrew equivalent to the phrase "poor in spirit" is used in 1QM 14.7 to describe the Qumran community, whose members took a vow of poverty in dependence upon God for righteousness and sustenance.[9] For other texts that stress internal disposition over external conditions, see "pure in heart" in Matt. 5:8 and "meek and lowly in heart" in 11:29. In Scripture, those who are poor are often the pious and the persecuted.[10]

5:4 Here Jesus indicates that those who mourn receive God's approval. The grammar of 5:4 is mirrored by that of 5:9. People mourn over many different misfortunes, but the most likely reasons for mourning here are sin or persecution. Some interpreters argue that mourning over one's own sin and that of the world in general is in view (Bruner 1987: 138–39; Carson 1984: 133; Hendriksen 1973: 270–71). This fits with Matthew's emphasis on repentance (3:2; 4:17) and with the testimony of such great saints as Isaiah (Isa. 6) and Job (Job 42). But probably the focus is more on those who mourn over afflictions and persecutions that arise because of their allegiance to the kingdom (Hagner 1993: 92; cf. Matt. 5:10–12, 38–48; 10:16–42; 13:21; 23:34; 24:9; Tob. 13:14). Matthew 5:3–4 seems

9. The phrase is וּבְעָנְיֵי רוּחַ, "among the poor in spirit." See also 1QH 5.13–14.3; 1QM 11.9, 13; 13.14; 14.7; 1QpHab 12.3, 6, 10; 4Q171 col. 1, frg. 1.1.21 (on Ps. 37:6); col. 2, frg. 1.2.10 (on Ps. 37:11); Flusser 1960.

10. On "poor in spirit," see Bock 1994: 552, 571–75; Guelich 1982: 109–11; Kellenberger 1997; Meadors 1985; R. Smith 1998.

to be alluding to the themes of affliction and mourning found in Isa. 61:1–2 (cf. Matt. 11:5b), and the eschatological reversal portrayed here is likewise found in Isa. 61:3–11. But in fact, it is impossible to separate mourning over sin and mourning over affliction, since those who mourn over sin turn away from it and those who turn away from sin face affliction from sinners. In any event, those who mourn now will receive future comfort through the anointed servant of Isa. 61.

God's inaugurated reign will eventually result in humble disciples, not arrogant tyrants, inheriting the earth. The grammar of 5:5 is mirrored by that of 5:8. The language here clearly alludes to Ps. 37:9, 11, which speaks of the oppression of the godly by the wicked. Such oppression is also implicit in Matthew, and so Hagner (1993: 92) is likely correct that this beatitude does not speak of those who are humble in an abstract sense but of those who have been humbled, "bent over by the injustice of the ungodly." Authentic meekness (πραΰς, *prays*, meek) is an unassuming humility that rests in God (Ps. 37:7) and renounces self-effort to relieve one's oppression and to achieve one's desires. Jesus perfectly models this humility (Matt. 11:29; 12:18–21; 21:5). This kind of person will inherit the earth. Once again Jesus goes against the grain of human culture and experience by asserting that the meek—not those well stocked with wealth, armament, or status—will inherit the earth. Matthew often stresses the theological significance of the earth (5:13, 18, 35; 6:10, 19; 9:6; 10:34; 11:25; 16:19; 18:18–19; 19:28–29; 23:9; 24:30, 35; 25:34; 28:18). (See N. Lohfink 1997; Talbot 2002.)

5:5

Those who are famished for righteousness will be satisfied. The grammar of 5:6 is mirrored by that of 5:7. This verse probably alludes to Ps. 107:5, 9. The righteousness spoken of here must not be reduced either to personal piety or to social justice. In Matthew, righteousness language speaks of right behavior before God.[11] Protestant Christians who are used to reading Paul may think that Matthew is speaking of the imputed righteousness of Christ (cf., e.g., Rom. 5:1–2), but this forensic sense is not a Matthean nuance. Here the emphasis is on the practical side, the upright lifestyle (see also Matt. 1:19; 3:15; 5:10, 20, 45; 6:1, 33). Those who realize their lack in attaining right behavior before God, rather than those who boast of their righteous accomplishments, will receive what they long for. Those who repent in view of the nearness of the kingdom long not only for personal righteousness but also for righteous living to permeate society as a whole (cf. Isa. 51:1–5). Only when God's will is done on earth as it is done in heaven (Matt. 6:10) will social justice be fully achieved.

5:6

---

11. The vocabulary of righteousness is often found in Matthew, including the noun "righteousness" (δικαιοσύνη, 3:15; 5:10, 20; 6:1, 33; 21:32), the verb "justify" (δικαιόω, 11:19; 12:37), and the adjective "righteous" (δίκαιος, 1:19; 5:45; 9:13; 10:41; 13:17, 43, 49; 23:28, 29, 35; 25:37, 46; 27:4, 19, 24). See Przybylski 1980 for a full discussion of this language.

The first four beatitudes show that divine approval means that one has been humbled under God's mighty hand through the kingdom message, so that one admits one's spiritual poverty, mourns over sin and the oppression of God's people, rests in God's care in the face of oppression, and hungers for greater righteousness on earth (5:3–6). Thus humility is the basic trait of authentic kingdom spirituality (see also Mic. 6:6–8; Matt. 11:25–30; 18:1–5; 19:13–15). A humble person who acknowledges sin—not a smug one who congratulates himself on his goodness—receives God's endorsement (see also Matt. 9:12–13).

c. Approval in Relating to People (5:7–10)

5:7 This verse begins the second set of beatitudes, which describe the pattern of divine approval in relating to people (5:7–10). It is first stated that God's approval comes to those who relate to others with mercy, which includes pity plus action. An allusion here to the language of Prov. 14:21 and/or Prov. 17:5 LXX seems likely. The crucial importance of the theme of mercy for the disciple is repeatedly modeled in Jesus's life and teaching (Matt. 6:2–4; 9:27, 36; 15:22; 17:15; 18:33; 20:30). By contrast, Jesus finds a lack of mercy in the Pharisees (9:13; 12:7; 23:23; cf. Hos. 6:6; Mic. 6:8). Those who have experienced God's mercy will show it to others (Matt. 18:21–35) and so demonstrate their destiny as those who will yet receive mercy at the last day. The proximity of mercy to justice (5:6) shows that these character traits are not mutually exclusive but complementary (cf. 1:19).

5:8 The promise that the pure in heart will see God may be an echo of Ps. 24:3–4 (cf. Pss. 51:10; 73:1). Purity of heart amounts to an internal integrity that manifests itself behaviorally. Matthew presents certain Pharisees as modeling an external, rule-oriented purity that Jesus rejects because it masks inner corruption (cf. Matt. 15:1–20; 23:25–28; 27:6). His disciples are characterized by inner piety and purity that flow from single-minded devotion to God (cf. 6:22–24; 13:45–46; 22:37; James 3:17–18) and surpass mere externally acceptable behavior (Matt. 5:20–22, 27–28). The power of God's reign inaugurated by Jesus purifies from the inside out, and so the disciples must cultivate integrity in their private and public lives (cf. 5:28; 6:21; 9:4; 11:29; 12:34; 13:15, 19; 15:8, 18, 19; 18:35; 22:37; 23:26). Seeing God is impossible in this life (Exod. 33:20), but prophetic visions describe seeing God as a part of the blessings of the world to come (Isa. 52:6; 60:16; Jer. 24:7; 31:31–34; 1 John 3:2; Rev. 22:4). Allison (2005b: 43–63) provides a thorough exegetical and theological study of seeing God.

5:9 This beatitude is not about being a passively peaceful person but about being an active reconciler of people (cf. NLT's "those who work for peace"; Luke 2:14; 19:38; Acts 10:36; Eph. 2:14–18; James 3:18; *m. 'Abot* 1.12). Those who are truly called God's children will bear a filial likeness to their heavenly Father, who treats enemies well (Matt. 5:43–48).[12] Their experience of peace with God enables them to seek the cessation of hostilities and the ultimate welfare of the world. Although the kingdom message itself may offend some people and lead to hostility (10:34), Jesus's disciples actively seek harmonious relationships with others (10:13). In a world full of all sorts of aggression, Jesus's reminder that peacemakers (not warmongers) have God's approval is sorely needed. Peacemakers will be recognized as authentic members of God's family when ultimate eschatological *shalom* finally dawns on earth.

With the second mention of the phrase "Theirs is the kingdom of heaven"   **5:10**
(see 5:3), the Beatitudes have come full circle. The chief marks of those who already live under God's rule are humility toward God and mercy toward people. One might expect such humble, merciful people to be valued highly by their fellow humans, but such is not the case. Jesus's disciples should expect not praise but persecution for their righteous behavior. Jesus himself preeminently displayed these righteous characteristics, and he was persecuted to the point of death (23:31–32). He warns his disciples that their upright behavior will receive similar treatment (cf. 2 Macc. 7:9; 14:38; 4 Macc. 9:29; 18:3; 2 Bar. 52.6; Matt. 5:44; 10:16–42; 13:21; 24:9–14; 1 Pet. 3:14; Hare 1967). This beatitude is expanded in Matt. 5:11–12, where persecution for righteousness is explained as persecution because of the disciples' affiliation with Jesus.

d. Expansion: Approval during Persecution (5:11–16)

i. Understanding Persecution (5:11–12)

W. Davies and Allison (1988: 430) make a strong case against the approach followed here, which construes 5:11–12 with 5:13–16 instead   **5:11–12**
of 5:3–10. It is clear that 5:11–12 is related to 5:3–10, since 5:11–12 is another beatitude, and 5:11–12 relates to persecution, as does 5:10. But the differences justify viewing 5:11–12 as literarily distinct from 5:3–10. These chiefly relate to the departure from the tightly knit pattern of 5:3–10, which has been previously shown. The beatitude in 5:11–12 uses the second person whereas those in 5:3–10 all use the third person. Also, the beatitude in 5:11–12 is considerably longer than those in 5:3–10, with a triple description of the oppression (5:11b), its reason (5:11b; cf. 10:18, 39; 16:25; 19:29), and two commands on how to deal with it (5:12a), all of which intervene before the promise of reward appears (5:12b). An additional explanation connecting the disciples with previously persecuted prophets comes after the promise (5:12c). Overall 5:3–10 amounts to a backward glance and 5:11–12 to a forward glance toward future

---

12. "Children of God" is literally "sons of God' (υἱοὶ θεοῦ), but the text is speaking inclusively of male and female disciples alike who are related to God as followers of Jesus. Cf. 5:45; 8:12; 13:38; 23:15, 31; 27:9; BDAG 1024–25.

persecution for Jesus's sake (Nolland 2005: 208). Therefore, although there is an obvious conceptual unity of 5:11–12 with 5:3–10, there is also good reason to take this expanded beatitude with 5:13–16 as a distinct description of the life of a disciple in the world.

The followers of Jesus must not simply endure persecution in a stoic fashion. Rather, they are to experience it with deep joy, since in it they are identified with their Messiah, Jesus (cf. 10:22, 25; 24:9), and continue in the train of the prophets who have been previously persecuted (cf. 23:29–39).[13] What is more, they will experience great future reward (cf. 5:46; 6:1–18; 10:41–42). (On 5:11–12, see Stenger 1986.)

From the Beatitudes, Christians learn that the character traits reflecting God's reign are chiefly humility toward God and mercy toward people. By God's grace these traits are present in principle in the lives of God's people. Yet these traits must be cultivated so that they become more dynamically present in fact. Believers develop maturity in discipleship as they grow in their understanding of, and obedience to, Scripture as they face the tests of life. The resource of the Spirit and encouragement from the Christian community are necessary. In a world that values pride over humility and aggression over mercy, Jesus's disciples are the "Christian Counter-culture" (Stott 1978). As they maintain this countercultural witness to the world, they may look to their master, who perfectly exemplified the character traits of the Beatitudes (Keener 1999:172). Jesus was meek (11:29). He mourned (26:36–46). He "fulfilled all righteousness" (3:15; 27:4, 19). He was merciful (9:27; 15:22; 17:15; 20:30–31). And above all, he was oppressed and persecuted. Thus, as disciples cultivate the countercultural graces of the Beatitudes, they are in reality cultivating likeness to the Master. Living in the present by the values of the future kingdom marks Jesus's disciples as out of step with their contemporaries and equips them for witness, to which the sermon now turns.

ii. Witness during Persecution (5:13–16)

5:13   The image of salt (cf. Mark 9:50; Luke 14:34) is somewhat difficult to interpret because of its wide usage in the ancient world (W. Davies and Allison 1988: 472–73). In addition to its use as a seasoning for food (Job 6:6; Col. 4:6), salt was added to sacrifices (Lev. 2:13; Ezra 6:9; Ezek. 43:24), connected with purity (Exod. 30:35; 2 Kings 2:19–22), a sign of barren wasteland (Judg. 9:45; Job 39:6; Ps. 107:34; Jer. 17:6; Zeph. 2:9), a sign of loyalty (Num. 18:19; Ezra 4:14; 2 Chron. 13:5), and used in fertilizer (Luke 14:34–35) and in cleaning newborn infants (Ezek. 16:4). In the Mishnah salt is associated with wisdom (*m. Soṭah* 9.15). The Roman historian Pliny the Elder describes uses for salt in his *Natural History*

---

13. On the theme of Israel's persecution of the prophets, see, e.g., 10:41; 21:34–36; 22:6; 23:29–36 in light of 1 Kings 18:14; 19:10; Jer. 26:11, 23; 2 Chron. 36:15–16; Neh. 9:26; along with Acts 7:52; 1 Thess. 2:15; James 5:10; see also O. Steck 1967.

(31.73–92). The purifying use of salt could be intended here, given 5:8, but perhaps the multiple ways in which salt benefits the world is the point of the metaphor (Hagner 1993: 99). Attempting interpretive precision is not wise here (Nolland 2005: 212). The image of salt should be viewed contextually as in some way analogous to the more accessible image of light.[14] Salt is thus a metaphor for one's exercising a beneficial influence on the world, in a manner analogous to the way light is beneficial in illumining darkness. Salt that has lost its saltiness, however, is good for nothing. Evidently, salt in the ancient world was not always pure, and the presence of other minerals in it could result in the loss of its distinctive flavor. Such loss of saltiness symbolizes the sort of spiritual decline against which Jesus explicitly warns elsewhere (e.g., 7:26–27; 13:20–22; 24:10–12). It also reinforces the kingdom value of inner purity (5:8). (See Latham 1982; Minear 1997; L. Porter 1995.)

5:14   Light is a prominent and univocal image in the Bible, especially in the Pauline and Johannine literature. In Qumran texts light and darkness stand for the ethical forces of good and evil respectively (e.g., 1QS 3.3, 19–22; 1QM 13.5–6, 14–15; cf. Sir. 50:6–7; *L.A.B.* 51.4). Matthew 4:16 (citing Isa. 9:2) has already associated light with Jesus and the kingdom ministry in dark Galilee. Isaiah 42:6 speaks of Israel's role in the world as a "light to the Gentiles" (cf. Isa. 49:6; 51:4–5; Dan. 12:3; John 1:4–5; 3:19–21; 8:12; Acts 26:18; Rom. 2:19; Eph. 5:8; Phil. 2:15; Col. 1:12–13). The image of the city on the hill is clear even if no particular city is intended, but it is plausible, in view of biblical prophecy, that Jerusalem is intended (contra Schnackenburg 2002: 51).[15] Jesus's statement that it is his disciples who illumine the world for God is mildly polemical, since it implies that Israel and especially its leaders are not fulfilling this lofty role (Boring 1995: 182). The polemic is stronger if the city is an allusion to Jerusalem, since it would imply that's God's illumining presence in the world flows from Jesus's disciples, not a place. (See M. Fowler 2001.)

5:15–16   The second image that develops the metaphor of light is an oil lamp, which would often be placed high on a stand, never covered with a basket. Thus common sense shows that it would be ridiculous for the disciples to hide their good deeds from the world. Matthew frequently stresses that good deeds are the mark of discipleship. The grace-induced character traits just highlighted in the Beatitudes are seminal good deeds. Previ-

---

14. The expressions "salt of the earth" (γῆ; cf., e.g., 5:18, 35; 6:10, 19; 9:6; 10:34; 11:25; 16:19; 23:9; 24:35; 28:18) and "light of the world" (κόσμος; cf., e.g., 4:8; 13:38; 16:26; 18:7; 24:21; 25:34; 26:13) are parallel (cf. Pöttner 1997). A study of Matthew's use of these words shows that although Matthew is fully aware of the fleeting, temporary nature of the present age (αἰών; cf., e.g., 12:32; 13:22, 39–40, 49; 24:3; 28:20), he does not view it as intrinsically evil but as God's creation, the province of present ministry and future reward.

15. E.g., Isa. 2:2–5; 42; 49; 54; 60; cf. Heb. 11:16; 12:22; Rev. 3:12; 21:2–27; K. Campbell 1978: 346.

ously John had demanded "fruit" as a condition of his baptism (3:8, 10), and Jesus returns to this metaphor for good deeds later in the sermon (7:16–20; cf. 12:33; 13:8, 26; 21:41).

Without good works one simply is not a disciple of Jesus (7:24–27; 13:23, 38; 10:22; 24:13). A so-called disciple without good works is of no more value than tasteless salt or an invisible lamp,[16] but an authentic disciple affects people, especially through the character traits of Matt. 5:7–10, bringing glory to the heavenly Father (cf. Matt. 9:8; 15:31; John 15:8; 1 Pet. 2:12).[17] Perhaps the dual images of salt and light are intended to portray two aspects of witness that are not easy to balance: engagement and distinctiveness. As salt, Jesus's disciples must engage the world, but as light, they must never allow their engagement to lead to the compromise of kingdom values and their assimilation to the world. Jesus perfectly and harmoniously models both images.

Additional Notes

5:4–5. A relatively few ancient sources reverse the order of 5:4–5, the second and third beatitudes, resulting in an antithesis between heaven in 5:3 and earth in 5:5. Metzger (1994: 10) reasons that the reversal is secondary, done to produce the antithesis, whereas had 5:3 and 5:5 originally stood together, no copyist would have inserted 5:4 between them.

5:11. A relatively few ancient sources in the Western tradition omit the word ψευδόμενοι, translated here "falsely" (cf. Luke 6:22). Even if the word is omitted, one would assume that the persecutors' charges against Jesus's disciples would be false (cf. 1 Pet. 4:15–16), but perhaps this was not clear enough to an ancient scribe, who added ψευδόμενοι. The word is viewed as suspect by the UBS[4] editors, who place it in brackets. See Metzger 1994: 11.

---

16. The rhetorical question in Sir. 41:14 makes the same point: "What is the value of concealed wisdom, any more than that of treasure that is invisible?"
17. On God as Father, see the comments on 6:9a.

2. Jesus and the Bible (5:17–48)

Literary Structure

Matthew 5:17–48 includes a general introduction (5:17–20) followed by two sets (5:21–32 and 33–48)[1] of three specific contrasts between traditional understandings of the Bible and Jesus's ultimate authoritative understanding. The basic point of the introductory section is to prohibit disciples from thinking that Jesus has come to destroy the law. Rather, he has come to fulfill the law (5:17), since the entire law is eternally valid (5:18; cf. Byrskog 1997). His disciples must obey him as its ultimate interpreter and teach his interpretations of it (5:19) in order to have a moral uprightness that exceeds that of the scribes and Pharisees and that is fitting for the kingdom (5:20). The first set of specific contrasts contains the teaching of Jesus on anger (5:21–26), adultery (5:27–30), and divorce (5:31–32). The second set contains the teaching on vows (5:33–37), retaliation (5:38–42), and the attitude toward enemies (5:43–48). The last verse of the section may be viewed as a generalizing summary of Jesus's fundamental teaching on the fulfillment of the law: disciples are to emulate the character of God (5:48; cf. Lev. 11:44–45; 1 Pet. 1:16).

Jesus and the Law: Continuity and Discontinuity

What does it mean when Jesus prohibits his disciples from thinking that he has come to destroy (καταλῦσαι, *katalysai*, abolish, do away with, BDAG 522) the law or the prophets and affirms that he has come to fulfill (πληρῶσαι, *plērōsai*; 5:17)? Possible shades of meaning include carrying out the law, showing forth its true meaning, and completing it (BDAG 829). But if Jesus has come simply to carry out what Moses said, his finality is compromised, continuity is overemphasized, and the six contrasts of 5:21–48 are rendered superfluous. On the other hand, the notion that Jesus completes the law overstates discontinuity and is tantamount to saying he has come to abolish the law. It seems clear that there is an essential continuity of the teaching and mission of Jesus with the redemptive ethical intent of the Hebrew Bible. But accomplishing the purpose of the law should not be taken to mean

---

1. The division of the six contrasting teachings into two sets of three is based not so much on Matthew's tendency toward triadic structures as on the insertion of the particle πάλιν at the beginning of the fourth contrasting teaching (5:33).

that Jesus has come only to establish or confirm the law. His teaching is not contradictory to anything in the Hebrew Bible, although it must in some sense transcend it. So both extremes must be ruled out, which leaves the remaining alternative as most likely: Jesus has come to show forth the true, transcendent meaning of the law by reaffirming it without merely repeating it. How should this view be articulated?

First, interpreters must allow Matthew himself to define the term "fulfill," by paying close attention to how he uses the term throughout his Gospel and by carefully noting the relationship between Jesus's teaching and the law of Moses in the six specific examples that occur immediately after 5:17–20.[2] Matthew's Jesus is the ultimate goal of the law and the prophets, the one to whom they point. His mission of kingdom word and deed fulfills the ethical standards and eschatological promises of the law and the prophets. Thus he becomes the sole authoritative teacher of the law, and his interpretations take on the character of new law for his disciples. His teachings are not brand new in the sense of having no root in the Hebrew Bible but new in the sense of transcending the traditional understanding of the law promulgated by the religious leaders. It is not Moses, much less the religious leaders, who authoritatively teach Jesus's disciples. Jesus alone fills that role. The six examples in 5:21–48 do not amount to Jesus's merely confirming Moses or bluntly contradicting Moses but to Jesus's unfolding the implications that were in Moses all along, although undetected by the current religious leaders of Israel. In this respect Jesus's "fulfillment" of the Hebrew Bible is not unlike the interpretations of the Bible found in the later rabbinic literature. These rabbis maintained that their seemingly innovative rulings were all along contained by implication in the Torah revealed to Moses at Sinai. But Jesus claims far more than this, as will be seen. (See Snodgrass 1992 and Snodgrass in Bauer and Powell 1996: 99–128.)

The Disciples and the Law: Law and Grace

In a passage characterized by high-impact statements, the words of Jesus in 5:19–20 about the disciples' obligation to the law may be nothing less than astonishing to Christians who believe they are under grace, not law. Those accustomed to interpreting certain sections of Paul's Epistles (e.g., Rom. 6:14; 7:1–6; 10:4) in ways that deprecate the

---

2. For a discussion of fulfillment in Matthew and in Matt. 5:17–20 specifically, see this commentary's introduction. Among the voluminous literature on Matthew and the law, see Banks 1974, 1975; Charles 1992; J. Grier in Meadors 1991: 165–77; Houlden in S. Porter et al. 1994: 115–31; Ljungman 1954; Loader 1997; Luomanen 1998b: 69–92; Luz 1978; B. Martin 1983; McConnell 1969; Meier 1976; Moo 1984; Moule 1968; M. Müller 1992; O'Rourke 1962; Snodgrass 1992; Snodgrass in Bauer and Powell 1996: 99–128; Westerholm 1992.

law will have difficulty with the perpetual binding authority of the law, as interpreted by Jesus, on his disciples (Overman 1996: 77). But Paul spoke positively about the law in ways similar to Jesus's teaching. He affirmed the holiness, justness, goodness, and spirituality of the law (Rom. 7:12, 14). He taught that the law's righteous standards could be fulfilled by Christians who relied on the Spirit (Rom. 8:4). He viewed Jesus as the end or goal (τέλος, *telos*) of the law (Rom. 10:4; cf. Gal. 3:23–25; BDAG 998–99) and spoke of love as the fulfillment of the law (Rom. 13:8–10; Gal. 5:13–14; cf. Matt. 22:35–40).

Yet Paul's situations, audiences, and problems were very different from Matthew's. As Paul labored to extend the gospel from Christian Jewish communities like Matthew's to Gentiles, he spoke out strongly against the notion that Christian Gentiles, in order to be assimilated into the Christian Jewish communities, must obey the law as traditionally interpreted (Galatians; cf. Acts 10:44–11:18). Paul's uncompromising opposition to requiring that Gentiles become Jewish proselytes in order to follow Jesus resulted in no little tension with Christian Jews (Acts 15:1–5; 21:20–21) and was misunderstood by non-Christian Jews (Acts 21:21, 28). Yet during his mission to the Gentiles, Paul continued to affirm his Jewish identity and loyalty to the law (Acts 24:14–18; 25:8; 28:17, 23). He insisted that his message was based on the promises of the Hebrew Bible.[3] Paul participated in synagogue worship and other Jewish practices throughout his ministry.[4] As an evangelist to Gentiles, however, his strategy included flexibility in areas he deemed expedient (1 Cor. 9:19–23). His seemingly negative teaching on the law was not directed against the law per se but against teachers who erroneously wished to bring his gentile converts under the law (Gal. 1:6–9; 3:1; 4:17; 5:12; 6:12–13). Though insisting that such converts were not obligated to the law as a rule of life (Gal. 3:1–3; 5:1–4; 6:15; cf. Acts 15:19–29), he also stated that their obedience to Jesus through the Spirit would "fulfill" the law's righteous requirements (Rom. 8:1–4). Paul's identification of the "weightier matters" of the law with love (Rom. 13:8–10; Gal. 3:14) is consistent with the teaching of Jesus (Matt. 22:34–40).[5]

This unit can be outlined as follows:

3. See Acts 13:26, 32, 46–47; 21:39; 22:3, 14; 23:5–6; 24:11–21; 26:4–8, 22–23; 28:17, 19–20, 23; cf. Rom. 1:1–2; 9:3; 11:1; 15:7–13. For a helpful summary of Paul's ongoing Jewish identity and practice, see McRay (2003: 47–52) and the literature cited there.

4. Acts 13:5, 15; 17:1, 10; 18:4, 18; 20:17–26; 22:3, 17; 23:1–6; 24:11–21; 25:8; 26:20–23; 28:20.

5. On the law in Matthew and Paul, see Dodd 1953: 53–66; Hagner 1997a; Mohrlang 1984. For various views of the wider theological question of the relationship of the law and the gospel for the Christian, see Strickland 1996; Thielman 1999; D. Wenham 1995: 219–30. Calvin's discussion of "third and principle use" of the law (1960: 1.360–66 [*Institutes* 2.7.12–17]) is still valuable.

a. General relationship (5:17–20)
b. Specific ethical application: Six examples (5:21–48)
   i. Anger and abusive speech (5:21–26)
   ii. Adultery and lust (5:27–30)
   iii. Divorce and adultery (5:31–32)
   iv. Vows (5:33–37)
   v. Retaliation (5:38–42)
   vi. Loving one's enemies (5:43–48)

Exegesis and Exposition

[17]"Do not suppose that I have come to abolish the law or the prophets; I have not come to abolish but to fulfill. [18]For truly I tell you, until heaven and earth pass away, not even the smallest letter or stroke of the pen will pass from the law until all things are accomplished. [19]Therefore, whoever does away with one of the least of these commandments and teaches people accordingly will be called least in the kingdom of heaven; but whoever practices and teaches them will be called great in the kingdom of heaven. [20]For I tell you that unless your righteousness surpasses that of the legal experts and Pharisees, you will surely never enter the kingdom of heaven.

[21]"You have heard that it was said to the people of old, 'You shall not murder' and 'Whoever murders shall be liable to judgment.' [22]Yet I tell you that everyone who is angry with his brother or sister ⌐ ⌐ shall be liable to judgment; and whoever says to his brother or sister 'Empty head!' shall be answerable to the council, and whoever says 'Fool!' shall be deserving of hellfire. [23]Therefore, if you are presenting your offering at the altar and there remember that your brother or sister has something against you, [24]leave your offering there before the altar. First go and be reconciled to your brother or sister, and then come and present your offering. [25]Settle promptly with your legal adversary while you are still with him on the way, or your adversary will hand you over to the judge, and the judge to his assistant, and you will be thrown into prison. [26]Truly I tell you, you will never get out of there until you have paid back the last cent.

[27]"You have heard that it was said, 'You shall not commit adultery.' [28]Yet I tell you that everyone who looks at a woman in order to lust for her has already committed adultery with her in his heart. [29]And if your right eye makes you sin, gouge it out and throw it away, since it is better that you lose one of your body parts than for your whole body to be thrown into hell. [30]If your right hand makes you sin, amputate it and throw it away, since it is better that you lose one of your body parts than for your whole body to go into hell.

[31]"And it was said, 'Whoever divorces his wife must give her a certificate of divorce.' [32]Yet I tell you that everyone who divorces his wife, except for sexual infidelity, makes her commit adultery; ⌐and whoever marries a divorced woman commits adultery⌐.

³³"Furthermore, you have heard that it was said to the people of old, 'You shall not break an oath but shall keep your oaths to the Lord.' ³⁴Yet I tell you, swear no oath at all, either by heaven, because it is God's throne, ³⁵or by the earth, because it is his footstool, or by Jerusalem, because it is 'the city of the great King.' ³⁶And do not swear an oath by your head, because you cannot make one hair white or black. ³⁷Rather, let your affirmative word be 'Yes' and your negative word be 'No'; anything beyond these is from the evil one.

³⁸"You have heard that it was said, 'An eye for an eye and a tooth for a tooth.' ³⁹Yet I tell you, do not resist an evil person; but if anyone hits you on your right cheek, turn the other cheek to him also. ⁴⁰And if anyone wants to sue you and take your shirt, let him have your coat also. ⁴¹And if anyone forces you into service for one mile, go two miles with him. ⁴²If anyone asks anything of you, give it to him, and if anyone wants to borrow from you, do not turn away from him.

⁴³"You have heard that it was said, 'You shall love your neighbor and hate your enemy.' ⁴⁴⌜Yet I tell you, love your enemies and pray for those who persecute you,⌝ ⁴⁵so that you may be children of your Father who is in heaven, because he makes his sun rise on the evil and the good and sends rain on the righteous and the unrighteous. ⁴⁶For if you love only those who love you, what reward do you have? Do not even the tax collectors do the same? ⁴⁷And if you greet only your brothers and sisters, what are you doing more than others? Do not even the ⌜Gentiles⌝ do the same? ⁴⁸Therefore you shall be perfect, as your heavenly Father is perfect."

a. General Relationship (5:17–20)

Matthew 5:17–20 first describes the relationship of Jesus to the law and the prophets and then speaks of the permanence of the law and the resulting obligation of disciples to obey and teach it in order to demonstrate the higher righteousness required by the kingdom. This paragraph can be analyzed as follows:

1. Prohibition: Do not think that Jesus has come to abolish the law (5:17a).
2. Antithetical clarification: Jesus has come not to abolish but to fulfill (5:17b).
3. Explanation 1:[6] Even the smallest parts of the law are permanently valid (5:18).
4. Implication:[7] Spiritual status is measured by conformity to the law (5:19).

---

6. The expression ἀμὴν γὰρ λέγω ὑμῖν, introducing 5:18, and the similar λέγω γὰρ ὑμῖν, introducing 5:20, both serve as emphatic explanations of the respective preceding statements. In 5:17–18, the axiomatic permanence of the law renders unthinkable the notion that Jesus has come to abolish it. In 5:19–20 the eschatological necessity of a higher righteousness underlines the necessity of obeying and teaching even the least of the law's commandments.

7. The antithetical statements ὃς ἐὰν οὖν λύσῃ and ὃς δ' ἂν ποιήσῃ καὶ διδάξῃ draw contrasting implications from the premise of the law's permanent validity.

> 5. Explanation 2: Righteousness greater than that of the religious leaders is required to enter the kingdom (5:20).

5:17   To Matthew's Christian Jewish audience, "good works" (5:16) would imply righteous works (מִצְוֹת, *miṣwôt*) enjoined by the law and the prophets.[8] Thus Jesus's relationship to the Hebrew Bible must not be misunderstood. Jesus's relationship to the law and to the prophets is a watershed issue for the interpretation of Matthew and for biblical theology in general. The antithetical terms καταλῦσαι (*katalysai*, abolish) and πληρῶσαι (*plērōsai*, fulfill) set the agenda for a general statement (5:17–20) that is expanded in six contrasting teachings (5:21–48) that take up the rest of the chapter. The mention of the law and the prophets here and in the summary statement of 7:12 is an *inclusio*, or framework, that brings the main body of the sermon full circle. The metaphorical use of καταλύω may be illustrated by its literal use in 24:2; 26:61; 27:40. The meaning of πληρόω must be examined in light of its frequent usage in biblical introductory formulas (1:22; 2:15, 17, 23; 4:14; 8:17; 12:17; 13:35; 21:4; 26:54, 56; 27:9). Other significant uses are 3:15 and 23:32. Jesus does not contradict or abrogate the law and the prophets, but neither does he merely reaffirm them. He fulfills them or brings them to their divinely intended goal, because they point to him (Boring 1995: 189; W. Davies and Allison 1988: 485–87).

The way in which the relationship of Jesus to the law is phrased here is significant. Jesus's disciples are forbidden to think that he has come to abolish the law. One wonders, then, whether the notion that Jesus came to abolish the law has already become a charge levied against Jesus by the religious leaders. He will later be charged with planning to destroy the temple (26:61; 27:40). Nolland (2005: 17) notes that the preceding narrative has not prepared the reader for 5:17, and he takes it as a lens for viewing 5:21–48. Some scholars locate the setting for this charge not with the historical Jesus but in the later days of Matthew's community (e.g., Overman 1996: 78–80). Perhaps such later difficulties over the ongoing role of the law (cf. Acts 15; 21:21; Galatians; Rom. 3:1–8, 31; 6:14–15; James 2) led Matthew to recount this genuine dominical saying. In any event, Matthew affirms that Jesus himself warned against the idea that his teaching was antinomian, although it is not altogether clear whether the warning was preventative or curative.[9]

---

8. The phrase τὸν νόμον ἢ τοὺς προφήτας refers to the Hebrew Bible in its entirety, as in 2 Kings 17:13; Neh. 9:26; Zech. 7:12; Matt. 7:12; 11:13 (reverse order); 22:40; John 1:45; Acts 13:15; 24:14; 28:23; Rom. 3:21. Luke 24:44 adds the Psalms to the phrase. The prophets were viewed as reaffirming the archetypal prophet Moses (Deut. 18:15–19). In 5:18 the word νόμος as well likely refers to the Hebrew Bible as a whole, as in Luke 10:26; 16:17; John 10:34; 12:34; 15:25; Rom. 3:19; 1 Cor. 14:21; cf. BDAG 678.

9. The prohibition μὴ νομίσητε utilizes the aorist subjunctive. Traditionally, Greek grammars have viewed such prohibitions as forbidding the beginning of an action, and prohibitions using the present imperative as forbidding the continuance of an action.

Matthew 5:18 serves as an affirmative and authoritative[10] explanation   **5:18–19**
of 5:17. Far from abolishing the law, Jesus brings it to its desired goal
because not even its slightest detail will go unaccomplished. The two
phrases "until heaven and earth pass away" and "until all things are accomplished" (cf. 24:34–35) are essentially synonymous references to the
end of the present world and the beginning of the eschaton (cf. 12:32;
13:30, 39, 40, 49; 19:28; 24:3, 14; 28:20). Until that time the law is valid.
Matthew 5:19 draws two contrasting inferences from 5:18 to the effect
that it is absolutely essential that disciples of the kingdom obey and
teach the law. Punishment and reward are determined by one's stance
with respect to the law. It would be hard to make a stronger statement
about the ongoing authority of the Torah than that made in 5:18. Jesus
refers to the smallest letter of the Hebrew alphabet (׳, *yod*; Greek *iota*)
and the smallest stroke of the pen (cf. Luke 16:17), sometimes called a
serif, by which two similar letters are distinguished. For example, *kaf*
[כ] and *resh* [ר] have no such stroke but *bet* [ב] and *daleth* [ד] do. The
argument is from lesser to greater: by affirming that God will bring
to pass even the most trivial parts of the law, Jesus implies that its
weightier matters are absolutely certain to be accomplished. Therefore
Jesus's disciples must not disobey or do away with (λύω, *lyō*; Josephus
Ant. 11.140) any part of the law, however trivial it may seem (cf. 23:23;
m. 'Abot 2.1; 3.18; 4.1). This calls into question the tendency in Christian
theology to divide the law into civil, ceremonial, and moral aspects to
which are attributed differing levels of authority for the church. (On
5:19, see Sim 1998a.)

The inference of 5:19 on the necessity of obeying and teaching the law   **5:20**
is followed here by a further explanation. Jesus fulfills the law and de-
clares it to be perpetually authoritative for his disciples. As its ultimate
authoritative interpreter, he demands a higher righteousness (cf. Eckstein

---

But it seems likely that the aorist-subjunctive prohibition in Matt. 1:20 forbids Joseph
to keep being afraid to take Mary as his wife. See Wallace 1996: 723–25 for discussion
and examples. The question in 5:17 is whether the false notion that Jesus has come to
abolish the law is already prevalent and needs to be corrected or whether Jesus forbids
his disciples to even consider such a notion. The latter nuance is evidently more likely,
given the grammar.

10. The word ἀμήν adds emphasis and solemnity to Jesus's assurance of his continuity
with Moses. This is the first of thirty-one occasions in Matthew where ἀμήν occurs with
λέγω, always on the lips of Jesus: 5:18, 26; 6:2, 5, 16; 8:10; 10:15, 23, 42; 11:11; 13:17;
16:28; 17:20; 18:3, 13, 18, 19; 19:23, 28; 21:21, 31; 23:36; 24:2, 34, 47; 25:12, 40, 45; 26:13,
21, 34 (cf. the frequent double ἀμήν in John). This use of ἀμήν to *preface* Jesus's sayings
is striking in light of its common liturgical use as an affirmative congregational *response*
to the reading of Scripture or a doxology. Probably the only clear Second Temple parallel
to this prefatory ἀμήν is T. Abr. A 8.7 (God speaks); 20.2 (death speaks). Cf. Deut. 27:15;
Ps. 106:48; 1 Esd. 9:47 LXX; Neh. 5:13; 8:6; Tob. 8:8; 3 Macc. 7:23; 4 Macc. 18:24; 2 Cor.
1:20; Rev. 3:14; 7:12; 22:20; *m. Soṭah* 2.5. See further the discussions and literature cited
in W. Davies and Allison 1988: 489–90; Nolland 2005: 219.

2001) than that taught and followed by the religious leaders. Since their practice of the law does not regard him as its fulfillment, it is deficient (Boring 1995: 186). Christology is the foundation of ethics. Jesus, the one to whom the law points, emphasizes the higher righteousness that is the true ethical intent of the law and that enables the disciples to enter the kingdom.[11]

The higher righteousness enjoined here is developed in the six contrasts of 5:21–48. As Jesus's disciples live by this teaching, their righteousness will surpass that of the religious leaders, and their good deeds will be like a shining light that causes people to glorify their heavenly Father (5:16). As the six concrete examples that come next are examined, it will be determined whether Jesus is replacing, intensifying, or simply expounding the Hebrew Bible.

b. Specific Ethical Application: Six Examples (5:21–48)

In 5:21–48 Jesus unpacks the higher righteousness required of his disciples in light of his mission not to abolish but to fulfill the law and the prophets. He presents six specific ethical examples in two sets of three (Boring 1995: 188; Nolland 2005: 228). The six examples contain:

1. Traditional teaching (5:21, 27, 31, 33, 38, 43)
2. Jesus's contrasting teaching (5:22, 28, 32, 34a, 39a, 44)
3. A concrete application or further explanation of Jesus's teaching (5:23–26, 29–30, 34b–37, 39b–42, 45–47)[12]

The symmetrical and repetitive structure of this section is unmistakable, as shown in the table below:

The Structure of Matt. 5:21–48

Ἠκούσατε ὅτι ἐρρέθη τοῖς ἀρχαίοις (v. 21)	ἐγὼ δὲ λέγω ὑμῖν ὅτι (v. 22)
Ēkousate hoti errethē tois archaiois	*egō de legō hymin hoti*
You have heard that it was said to the people of old	but I say to you that
Ἠκούσατε ὅτι ἐρρέθη (v. 27)	ἐγὼ δὲ λέγω ὑμῖν ὅτι (v. 28)
Ēkousate hoti errethē	*egō de legō hymin hoti*
You have heard that it was said	but I say to you that
Ἐρρέθη δέ (v. 31)	ἐγὼ δὲ λέγω ὑμῖν ὅτι (v. 32)
Errethē de	*egō de legō hymin hoti*
And it was said	but I say to you that

11. The phrase "entering [εἰσέρχομαι] the kingdom" repeatedly describes salvation in Matthew (5:20; 7:21; 18:3; 19:23–24; 23:13), as does the similar expression "entering into life" (18:8–9; 19:17). Cf. 7:13; 24:38; 25:10, 21, 23; Luomanen 1998b.

12. The third example, on divorce (5:31–32), lacks a specific application of Jesus's teaching. Boring (1995: 191) takes the exception clause in 5:32 as a situational application, but this is doubtful.

Πάλιν ἠκούσατε ὅτι ἐρρέθη τοῖς ἀρχαίοις (v. 33)	ἐγὼ δὲ λέγω ὑμῖν (v. 34)
Palin ēkousate hoti errethē tois archaiois	*egō de legō hymin*
Again, you have heard that it was said to the people of old	but I say to you
Ἠκούσατε ὅτι ἐρρέθη (v. 38)	ἐγὼ δὲ λέγω ὑμῖν (v. 39)
Ēkousate hoti errethē	*egō de legō hymin*
You have heard that it was said	but I say to you
Ἠκούσατε ὅτι ἐρρέθη (v. 43)	ἐγὼ δὲ λέγω ὑμῖν (v. 44)*
Ēkousate hoti errethē	*egō de legō hymin*
You have heard that it was said	but I say to you

*The symmetry of the section is not exact in that 5:43 has ἠκούσατε ὅτι ἐρρέθη (cf. 5:27, 38) instead of ἐρρέθη δέ (cf. 5:31). Also, whereas Jesus's contrasting teaching is introduced with a recitative ὅτι (Wallace 1996: 454–55) in all three of the examples in the first set, the ὅτι is not to be found in the second set.

Antitheses or Contrasts?

Although it is common for interpreters to speak of the six examples in 5:21–48 as antitheses (e.g., Boring 1995: 188 reluctantly; Hagner 1993: 110, although qualified on p. 112; Hare 1993: 49–51; Harrington 1991: 90; Nolland 2005: 228), this is certainly a mistake (Broer 1993a; Flusser 1992–93; Garland 1993: 63–64; Keener 1999: 181; Overman 1996: 80–81). An antithesis is not merely a contrasting statement, it is a contradictory statement. If Jesus had intended to teach antithetically to the law and the prophets, he would have come to abolish the law and the prophets. If Jesus had been speaking antithetically, he would have said the unthinkable: "You have heard that it has been said, 'You shall not murder,' but I say unto you, 'You shall murder.'"

Some urge that the use of the milder conjunction δέ (*de*, and, but, yet) instead of ἀλλά (*alla*, but) to introduce each of Jesus's teachings lightens the contrast (Keener 1999, 181; Overman 1996, 81). But δέ is not necessarily a milder adversative than ἀλλά—it is just more versatile. The transcendent teaching of Jesus contrasts not with that of Moses but with that of the traditional legal experts because it restores the original divine intention of the law (Garland 1992: 62–63). For this reason the terms "hypertheses" and "epitheses" have been suggested instead of antitheses (Boring 1995: 188).

In all six of the contrasts, there are two crucial matters to keep in mind. First is the contrasting parallel in audiences, the people of old (Israel) versus "you" (Jesus's disciples), implying that disciples, not the Jews as a nation, are the locus of Jesus's revelatory ministry. Second and even more noteworthy is the contrast between the agency of what was said and what is now being said. The text emphasizes that Jesus himself is speaking with authority that transcends that of the previous divine revelation through Moses.[13] Jesus does not deny that God spoke through Moses (cf. 15:4, where Jesus introduces a quote from the Mosaic law by saying, "For God said . . ."), but in strong language he affirms his own transcending revelatory agency. This authoritative way of speaking is not lost on those who hear him (7:29; 8:8–9; 9:6; 10:1; 15:4; 28:18). Boring's explanation (1995: 189) of all six of the contrasts as specific expressions of the great commandment (22:34–40) is theologically attractive but exegetically unsupported.

The Contrast: Jesus versus Moses or Jesus versus the Pharisees?

It must be asked whether Matthew in 5:21–48 intends to set Jesus against Moses or against the ostensible contemporary experts on Moses, the Pharisees. In other words, is Jesus presented as contesting Moses, or is he contesting those who speak for Moses (cf. 23:2–36)? The question is perhaps impossible to answer because it is too complex to be put in so reductionist a manner. It seems that in some instances Jesus deals with contemporary paraphrases of the implications of the law and in others more directly with the law itself. In the former category would be contrasts one, three, four, and six (5:21, 31, 33, 43), where the biblical text is cited with additional material appended (5:21, 43) or cited in a modified manner (5:31) or where a summary of several texts is given (5:33). In the latter category, contrasts two and five, the Bible is cited word for word and no additions are made to it (5:27, 38). Thus most of the contrasts contain evidence that contemporary construals of Moses are meant. And this is inevitable, since the ancient text of Moses had been subject to hundreds of years of interpretation and developing oral tradition.

Matthew presents Jesus as coming not to abolish but to accomplish the purpose of the law and the prophets (5:17). Thus one would expect the contrasting teaching of Jesus to transcend the Bible in a manner that does not formally violate its ethical authority. Yet at the same time, Jesus warns his disciples that their righteousness must exceed that of the religious teachers (5:20), and so one would expect his teaching to expose the inadequacies and mistakes of those teachers as he expounds Moses in an ultimate manner. In other texts (e.g., 9:10–13; 15:1–9; 19:1–9) Jesus explicitly rebukes the religious leaders for their mistaken views of the law and the prophets, and so one should not be surprised to find similar confrontations occurring implicitly here. This model of exposition plus exposure is clearest in examples three and six (5:31, 43), but it is present to some extent in each example. For example, in 5:33–37, on vows, Jesus first alludes to biblical texts as revealed to the ancestors and then proceeds to refute contemporary casuistry in the use of vows. To illumine the ulti-

---

13. The words λέγω ὑμῖν have already been seen in 5:18, 20, and now they are repeated with ἐγώ added in 5:22, 28, 32, 34, 39, 44 (cf. 19:24).

mate goal of Moses and the prophets, Jesus must show the darkness that clouds the teaching of the religious leaders. (See Kampen 1994.)

The Hermeneutic of Jesus

The relationship of Jesus to the Scriptures is a theological watershed. Jesus's general statement about accomplishing the biblical purpose, not abolishing it, and his six specific contrasting situations have been variously understood along a spectrum of continuity and discontinuity. The view of some scholars that Jesus's life and teaching simply established or confirmed the law understates the legitimate discontinuity between Jesus and the Hebrew Bible. Others have stressed that Jesus's own personal obedience to the law completed its role in redemptive history. This view correctly stresses Jesus's obedience to the law but is mistaken on the implications of this obedience. A third group of scholars have argued that Jesus, as a new Moses, brought a new law that superseded the old law, but this errs on the side of excessive discontinuity. Theologians commonly stress the "moral law," not the law's civil or ceremonial aspects. But Jesus fulfills the whole law, not anachronistic categories that suit its modern readers (Hauerwas 2006: 65–67). Yet other scholars conclude that Jesus reveals or intensifies the true inner meaning of the law. This view has some merit, but at best it is only a partial answer.

Jesus is the end or goal of the law, and therefore he is its ultimate, definitive interpreter. He alone is the authoritative eschatological teacher of the law and the prophets. The life and teaching of Jesus fulfill the law just as NT events fulfill biblical predictions and patterns. On the one hand, Jesus does not contradict the law, but on the other hand, he does not preserve it unchanged (cf. Röhser 1995). He reveals the ultimate meaning of the law of God for those whose righteousness must exceed that of the legal experts and the Pharisees (5:20; cf. 22:34–40; 23:23–24). Jesus brings the law to its intended goal in the following ways:

1. He teaches that the prohibition of murder implicitly prohibits the anger and abusive speech that lead to murder. Although the Scriptures do not condone anger, Jesus's transcendent teaching links it to a capital crime. Anger and angry words are tantamount to murder (5:21–26).[14]
2. He teaches that the prohibition of adultery implicitly prohibits the lust that leads to adultery. Although the Scriptures do not condone lust, Jesus's direct linkage of lust to adultery is a more stringent standard of sexual ethics, which interprets the seventh command-

14. The act of murder may seem far worse than angry thoughts. Yet in these six contrasts Jesus warns against the view that one can tolerate wicked thoughts as long as one does not act on them.

ment by the tenth commandment (Exod. 20:17). Lust is tantamount to adultery (Matt. 5:27–30).

3. He teaches that marriage is a sacred union, inviolable except when infidelity occurs. Although the Scriptures do not condone divorce (esp. Mal. 2:14–16), there is reason to believe that it was condoned by many of Jesus's contemporaries. But he teaches that divorce and remarriage (except in the case of infidelity) are tantamount to adultery (Matt. 5:31–32). Divorce is merely a temporal concession to human sinfulness, but permanent marriage is the original model for humans (19:8).

4. He teaches that use of vows would be unnecessary if disciples consistently took to heart the biblical admonitions to tell the truth. Although the Scriptures do not condone the misuse of vows, Jesus criticizes their use. He forbids (although the prohibition may not be absolute; cf. Blomberg 1992a: 112; W. Davies and Allison 1988: 536; Hagner 1993: 129) what the letter of the Scriptures permits, but he does so to uphold the spirit of the Scriptures against the bearing of false witness. For Jesus, casuistry in the taking of vows is tantamount to bearing false witness (5:33–37; cf. 23:16–22).

5. He teaches that the law on retaliation was designed primarily to limit conflict and only secondarily to endorse it. The Scriptures do not condone unjust punishment for crimes and damages, but Jesus teaches that instead of retaliating in kind to wrongdoing, his disciples should respond with grace. Insistence on taking one's own vengeance is tantamount to denying that God will avenge his people (5:38–42).

6. He teaches that all humans, not only one's friends, are to be loved. Although the Scriptures do not condone hatred of one's enemies, Jesus makes love of enemies the preeminent evidence of one's filial relationship to the heavenly Father. Hating one's enemies is tantamount to paganism (5:43–48).

i. Anger and Abusive Speech (5:21–26)

5:21–22 The introductory words "You have heard that it was said to the people of old"[15] appear again in the fourth example (5:33), introduced there by πάλιν (*palin*, again, furthermore, BDAG 752–53).[16] This implies that the six examples are intended to be viewed as two groups of three. This first example of how Jesus definitively interprets the law (5:21–26) develops the biblical teaching on murder. Matthew 5:21b refers to Exod. 20:13;

---

15. "People of old" translates τοῖς ἀρχαίοις, which refers to those who lived in ancient times (cf. Sir. 39:1; 1 Kings 5:10 LXX [4:30 Eng.]; Philo, *Heir* 181; Josephus, *Ant.* 7.171; Did. 11.11; Eusebius, *Eccl. Hist.* 3.39.1). In light of the use of the expression in Luke 9:8, 19 (cf. Josephus, *Ant.* 12.413), it might be understood here as a dative of means (KJV).

16. The same nuance of πάλιν as a marker of related items in a discourse appears in Matt. 13:45, 47; 18:19; 19:24.

Deut. 5:17 (cf. Ruzer 1996), but 5:21c, "Whoever murders shall be subject to judgment," is probably a summary of texts such as Exod. 21:12 and Deut. 17:8–13 (cf. Deut. 16:18; 2 Chron. 19:5).

Jesus's contrasting teaching in 5:22 lists three hypothetical instances in which anger or angry speech will lead to judgment as surely as murder. It is likely that the three descriptions of judgment ("liable to judgment," "answerable to the council,"[17] "deserving of hellfire") are not ascending in severity but are progressively more vivid descriptions of the consequences of anger and abusive speech. Jesus's view of anger as tantamount to a capital crime is shocking, to say the least.[18] Anger against one's "brother or sister" likely means another person in one's religious community rather than another human being in general.[19] The second and third instances of anger and abusive speech both move from a furious attitude to abusive speech, calling a person an idiot or a fool.

Jesus now speaks of the consequences of anger and abusive speech by posing a concrete situation in which personal reconciliation takes precedence over religious duty. Significantly, the situation here does not pertain to one's own anger but to the anger or grudge of another. Disciples are thus not only to rein in their own anger but also to take steps to reconcile with others who are angry at them. It is not a question of arguing about who offended whom but of taking responsibility and initiating reconciliation. Jesus's concern for harmonious relations within the community of disciples is underlined in Matt. 18:6, 10, 12–17, 21–35. Here reconciliation with a fellow disciple must be addressed before one offers a sacrifice in the temple. Jesus's stress on the priority of reconciliation and justice over sacrificial worship is in keeping with such biblical texts as 1 Sam. 15:22; Isa. 1:10–18; Hos. 6:6; Mic. 6:6–8. As in the model prayer (Matt. 6:12, 14–15; cf. 18:15–17), divine forgiveness is linked with human forgiveness. The temple imagery is interesting in light of the extreme likelihood that Matthew is addressing a Christian

5:23–24

---

17. It appears that συνέδριον here refers to a local council, as in 10:17, rather than the high council in Jerusalem, as in 26:59. On the difficult matter of terminology, local councils versus the supreme council in Jerusalem, and whether there were separate religious and civil councils, see Twelftree in C. A. Evans and Porter 2000: 1061–65 and in J. Green and McKnight 1992: 728–32. Important ancient texts include all of *m. Sanh.*; *m. Soṭah* 9.11; Josephus, *Ant.* 14.89–91, 167–80; *Life* 62.

18. There is not a word here about justified anger or righteous indignation (cf. similarly James 1:20). Luz prefaces his discussion of the history of interpretation of this passage (1989: 286–88) with the comment that the history of its influence "is largely a history of mitigating its harshness." On permissible anger, see Jer. 6:11; 15:17; Sir. 1:22; 1 Macc. 2:44; 2 Macc. 10:35; Philo, *Spec. Laws* 3.31; Eph. 4:26 (Ps. 4:4); *b. Meg.* 6b.

19. In this passage, Jesus speaks against anger toward a "brother" (ἀδελφός). But here and elsewhere in Matthew (cf. 5:47; 7:3–5; 12:48–50; 18:15, 21, 35; 23:8; 25:40; 28:10), this word does not describe a male sibling (as in 1:2, 11; 4:18, 21; 12:46–47; 13:55) but a fellow disciple or, less likely, a fellow human, one's neighbor (BDAG 18–19). The translation reflects this use of ἀδελφός as meaning "brother or sister."

Jewish community. According to Acts, the Christian Jews in Jerusalem continued to participate in the temple cultus (Acts 2:46; 3:1; 5:12, 42; 21:26; 22:17; 24:12, 18; 25:8; 26:21).

5:25–26 Another hypothetical situation shows that the obligation to seek reconciliation applies not only to relations within the community of disciples (5:23–24) but also to relationships outside that community. Unless adversarial legal situations are settled out of court, serious judicial consequences will result. In the judicial system assumed here, debtors were evidently incarcerated until payment was made. Perhaps these verses speak metaphorically to the matter of averting the wrath of God, but this is not so obvious as some (e.g., Blomberg 1992a: 108) think. The last contrast in 5:38–48, where disciples are enjoined to love their enemies, should be read alongside 5:25–26. Luke 12:57–59 presents this saying in a different context. On Matt. 5:21–26, see Wick 1996. Allison (2005b: 65–78) defends Cyprian's intertextual reading of Gen. 4:1–16 with this passage.

ii. Adultery and Lust (5:27–30)

5:27–28 The second example of how Jesus definitively interprets the law moves from the sixth to the seventh commandment and develops the biblical teaching on adultery (Exod. 20:14; Deut. 5:18; cf. Matt. 5:32; 19:9, 18; cf. Cuvillier 1998). In contrast to the biblical commandment, Matt. 5:28 condemns the adulterous thoughts that lead to overt adulterous acts, not just the behavior itself. Although the Hebrew Bible and Second Temple Judaism certainly did not condone lust,[20] Jesus's direct linkage of lust to adultery is a more rigorous standard of sexual ethics. By stressing the lustful intention over the act itself, Jesus apparently interprets the seventh commandment by the tenth commandment, which forbids coveting in general and specifically coveting one's neighbor's wife. But Matt. 5:28 is speaking of women in general, not just married women. Second Temple writings warned men of the dangers of women (e.g., Sir. 25:21; 26:9; Ps. Sol. 16.7–8; Josephus *J.W.* 2.121; *Ant.* 7.130), but Jesus puts the onus on men. And Matt. 5:28 may not be simply about looking with lust at a woman but about looking at a woman in such a way as to entice her to lust (Carson 1984: 151).

5:29–30 These two verses speak hyperbolically in parallel fashion to underline the gravity of Jesus's teaching on lust in 5:28 (cf. 18:7–9 for similar hyperbolic language). Sin must be avoided even if radical sacrifice is required. Lust must be treated with the utmost seriousness because it can cause a person to be thrown into hell. The right eye (5:29; cf. 1 Sam. 11:2; Zech. 11:17; 2 Pet. 2:14; 1 John 2:16) and the right hand (5:30; cf. Gen. 48:14; Ps. 137:5) are respectively the means through which lustful

---

20. E.g., Sir. 9:8; 23:6; 41:21; Sus. 8; 1 En. 67.8; Jdt. 12:16; 1QS 1.6–7; 4.10; CD 2.16.

thoughts are initially engendered (Josh. 7:21; 2 Sam. 11:2; Ezek. 6:9) and subsequently carried out. If these bring one into an occasion of sin,[21] they must be dealt with by radical surgery (cf. Col. 3:5–8). Since evil arises in the heart (cf. Matt. 15:19; Gen. 6:5; 8:21; Jer. 17:9), amputation cannot cure it, and so it should go without saying that these two commands are hyperbolic. But the hyperbole shocks the reader with the real point: it is better to deal decisively with lust than be thrown into hell because of it. (See Deming 1990.)

iii. Divorce and Adultery (5:31–32)

Jesus's third example of his definitive interpretation of the law develops the biblical teaching on divorce. Matthew 5:31 (cf. Mark 10:11–12; Luke 16:18) refers to Deut. 24:1–4 (cf. Matt. 19:7), which in its original context prohibits a man from remarrying a woman he has previously married and divorced if she has subsequently been married to another man who has died or divorced her. The detail of the Deuteronomy passage most relevant to then-current views of divorce was evidently the existence of a written legal document (Deut. 24:1, 3).[22] Apparently, many teachers of Jesus's day had taken this passage as carte blanche for divorce. According to the Mishnah (compiled from earlier oral tradition ca. 200 CE), Hillel (first cent. BCE) permitted divorce if a wife had spoiled a meal, and Akiba (second cent. CE) permitted it if a more beautiful woman was available (Deut. 24:1; *m. Giṭ.* 9.10).[23]

5:31–32

Jesus's strict view of divorce is evidently similar to that of Rabbi Shammai (first cent. BCE), who is also cited by the above text from the Mishnah.[24] According to Jesus, a man who divorces his wife for any reason other than sexual infidelity causes her and her potential future spouse to commit adultery. If there has been no sexual infidelity, there can be no real divorce. If there has been no real divorce, there can be no remarriage, and additional sexual unions are adulterous. There is much debate on the word πορνεία (*porneia*, sexual infidelity), but it seems most likely that Jesus has in mind any sort of sexual activity not involving one's

---

21. The verb σκανδαλίζω vividly describes serious spiritual downfall (BDAG 926), even final apostasy, using the imagery of a trap. See Matt. 11:6; 13:21, 57; 15:12; 17:27; 18:6–9; 24:10; 26:31, 33. Cf. the noun σκάνδαλον in Matt. 13:41; 16:23; 18:7.

22. The term in Matthew is ἀποστάσιον (cf. Matt. 19:7; Mark 10:4), similar to the LXX expression βιβλίον ἀποστασίου, used to translate the Hebrew phrase סֵפֶר כְּרִיתֻת in Deut. 24:1, 3 (cf. Jer. 3:8). The rabbis called it a גֵּט, the plural of which is גִּטִּין, the name of the Mishnah tractate (*Giṭṭin*) that deals with divorce (Jastrow 1971: 233).

23. The debate in *m. Giṭ.* 9.10 is over the interpretation of the phrase עֶרְוַת דָּבָר in Deut. 24:1. Hillel and Akiba took this rather loosely as a reference to anything in the wife deemed unseemly by the husband. Josephus evidently agreed (*Ant.* 4.253).

24. According to *m. Giṭ.* 9.10, Shammai viewed עֶרְוַת דָּבָר in Deut. 24:1 as דְּבַר עֶרְוָה, evidently a matter of sexual impropriety. Matthew's Greek phrase λόγου πορνείας is roughly equivalent to דְּבַר עֶרְוָה. Texts from Qumran also take a rather strict view of divorce. Cf. 11QT 57.17–19; CD 4.21–5.2.

spouse (W. Davies and Allison 1988: 529–31).[25] Jesus prohibits what the Bible was understood to permit in the area of divorce. As the definitive eschatological teacher of the law, his interpretation is based on the original divine intent for marriage, not the expediency of the moment. The Pharisees' overly permissive interpretation capitalized on a concession to human sinfulness (cf. the commentary on Matt. 19:3–9).

Why do Matt. 5:32 and 19:9 alone among the synoptic divorce sayings (cf. Mark 10:11; Luke 16:18) provide an exception to the prohibition of divorce?[26] Answering this vexing question is not properly part of the exegesis of Matthew. Those who hold to Markan priority tend to view the exception clause as Matthean redaction, not authentic historical Jesus tradition (e.g., Hagner 1993: 123; Stein in J. Green and McKnight 1992: 194–95). Others wish to take Mark 10:11 and Luke 16:18 as proverbial statements offering an ideal general principle, with Matthew providing a contextual qualification (Keener 1999: 190–91). Another line of interpretation seems preferable, if not convincing, one related to the respective communities for which the Synoptic Gospels were written. In this view, Matthew retains the authentic dominical exception clause for his Christian Jewish audience because of the connection with Deut. 24:1–3 whereas it is omitted by Mark and Luke, who are writing for mainly gentile audiences.[27]

iv. Vows (5:33–37)

5:33–34a Matthew 5:33–48 comprises the second set of three examples of Jesus's definitive interpretation of the Hebrew Bible. The matter of vows or oaths is addressed in 5:33–37, the fourth example, which begins in the familiar pattern of first alluding to the Bible (5:33; cf. Exod. 20:7; Lev. 19:12; Num. 30:3–15; Deut. 23:21–23; Ps. 50:14; Zech. 8:17; Wis. 14:28; James 5:12) and then giving the contrasting teaching of Jesus (Matt. 5:34a). Matthew 5:33 is not a direct quote of a single biblical passage but a summary of several passages (cf. 5:21c). The Hebrew Bible contains positive examples of oaths (Gen. 14:22; 21:24; 47:31; Josh. 2:12), and punishment was threatened for false oaths or oaths not carried out (Exod. 20:7; 1 Kings 8:31–32; cf. Wis. 12:21). Reservations about oaths

25. The view that πορνεία in Matt. 5:32 refers to incest or marriage within the prohibited degrees of kinship in Lev. 18:16–18 (cf. 1 Cor. 5:1; possibly Acts 15:20–29) is overly subtle and goes against the overall tenor of Jesus's contrasting interpretations of the law in Matt. 5:21–48. For discussion and bibliography, see BDAG 854; Carson 1984: 413–18; Crouzel 1988; D. Janzen 2000; Luz 1989: 298–310; Stein in J. Green and McKnight 1992: 192–99.

26. Treatments of this question include A. Guenther 2002; D. T. Smith 1989; Warren 1998; Weibling 2001; Wiebe 1989; Witherington 1985.

27. It is, sadly, not surprising that the literature on 5:31–32 is extremely voluminous. See esp. Bockmuehl 1989; Instone-Brewer 2002: 133–88; Kampen in Brooke and García Martínez 1994: 149–67; Keener 1991; W. Luck 1987; Nolland 1995; Scharbert 1997; Sigal 1986: 83–118; Warden 1997. See further this commentary at 19:9.

are found in many places, including Deut. 23:23; Eccles. 5:4–5; 9:2; Sir. 23:9; Philo, *Decalogue* 84; *Spec. Laws* 2.1; *m. Demai* 2.3; *b. Ned.* 22a. The Qumran community evidently required an entrance oath (cf. Josephus, *J.W.* 2.139, 142; CD 15.5–6; 1QS 5.7–8) but had reservations about other oaths (Josephus, *J.W.* 2.135; CD 15.1–5; 1QS 6.27; 11QT 53–54). Their reservations seem to have been prompted by reluctance to use God's name in an oath (cf. 1QS 6.27–7.2).

Herod's frivolous oath (motivated by lust, cf. Matt. 5:31–32) will lead to the beheading of John the Baptist (14:7, 9). Sadly, Peter will take an oath in his third denial of Jesus (26:74). Jesus evidently does not take an oath when he is charged to do so by the high priest (26:63). This section on oaths has no synoptic parallel; Matt. 23:16–22 also takes up oaths from a negative perspective (cf. 12:34–37). (See also W. Davies and Allison 1988: 532–38; Garland in J. Green and McKnight 1992: 577–78.)

After the general statement in 5:34a, Jesus forbids four specific vows, each **5:34b–36** time because the one who takes a vow assumes prerogatives that belong solely to God (5:34b–36).[28] The first two prohibited oaths call respectively upon heaven and earth, and both are inappropriate because heaven and earth are God's created domain and are under God's control, not that of human creatures (cf. Isa. 66:1; Acts 7:49). The third oath calls upon Jerusalem, which is also inappropriate because it is the city of the great King (cf. Ps. 48:2), the place where the God of the covenant chooses to make his presence visible on earth (cf. Duling 1991). The fourth oath, swearing by one's head, is similarly out of place because it arrogates to the one who makes the vow power that belongs only to God. According to Deut. 6:13; 10:20, oaths were to be taken in the name of God, but by the time of Jesus, pious Jews evidently would not utter that name. The oblique terms "heaven," "earth," and "Jerusalem" were used in oaths as metonymies, circumlocutions associated with God. Such vows are mentioned in the Mishnah (e.g., *Šeb.* 4.13; *Ned.* 1.3; *Sanh.* 3.2). But Jesus shows that "an oath is an oath regardless of how oblique the reference to God" (Garland in J. Green and McKnight 1992: 578).

This negative teaching is balanced with a positive command enjoining **5:37** simple verbal integrity. One's word alone ought always to be reliable without being supported by an oath. The tendency to take oaths concedes to prevarication and thus originates in evil, which may subtly refer to Satan, the originator of deception (John 8:44).[29] If one's heart is right with God, upright speech will transparently represent what is in one's heart. Perjury and false witness will not occur. In the Hebrew

28. Repetitive rhetorical patterns are again found in 5:34b–36, where each of the four specific examples of prohibited vows begins with μήτε and the reason for each prohibition begins with a causal ὅτι.
29. The expression τοῦ πονηροῦ can be masculine or neuter. Cf. 6:13; 13:19, 38; John 17:15; Eph. 6:16; 1 John 2:13; 5:18–19.

Scriptures, oaths were permitted as long as irreverence and falsehood were not involved. They were intended to ensure the truthfulness of one's word and of one's resolve to follow through on obligations. But ironically, vows could result in two classes of utterances, one with a vow committing the speaker to veracity and the other without a vow, implying no such commitment. By the time of Jesus, subtle casuistic distinctions between binding and nonbinding vows had further muddled things (cf. Matt. 23:16–22). In response, Jesus forbids what the Scriptures permit, but truth is the goal of both the biblical permission and Jesus's prohibition. Here Jesus comes close to contradicting the Bible, but he views the traditional biblical interpretation as permitting a double standard on verbal integrity. So, although on one level Jesus may be said to contradict "the letter of the law," he does so in order to uphold its "spirit" on a more profound level, and he thereby upholds the commandment against false witness (Exod. 20:16).[30]

v. Retaliation (5:38–42)

5:38–39a The fifth example (5:38–42; cf. Isa. 50:4–9; Luke 6:29–30) refers to Exod. 21:24; Lev. 24:20; and Deut. 19:21. Here Jesus qualifies the application of the biblical principle of retribution in kind, or *lex talionis* (cf. Broer 1993c, 1994). In 5:38 Jesus alludes to the "eye for an eye, tooth for a tooth" legislation, and in 5:39a he contrasts his own teaching, that disciples should forsake the idea of retribution altogether by not resisting an evil person.[31]

The biblical insistence on punishment matching the crime might seem harsh at first glance, but matching punishment to the crime prevents excessive punishment. Although an eye must be taken for an eye, two eyes or a life may not be taken for an eye. Thus the Hebrew Bible is already concerned with the matter of retaliation, and it prohibits disproportionate revenge (Lev. 19:18; but see Gen. 4:23–24; 34:1–31). Here Jesus goes even further and teaches that godly kindness should transcend retaliation in personal disputes (cf. Rathey 1991). As in the case of divorce (5:31–32; 19:3–12), Jesus's teaching transcends a biblical regulation that arose as a concession to the hardness of the human heart. Yet Jesus's transcendent teaching is not totally unanticipated in the Hebrew Scriptures (cf. Lev. 19:18; Deut. 32:35; Prov. 20:22; 24:29; 25:21–22; Isa. 50:6; Lam. 3:30).

This teaching would obviously be at odds with the cause of the Jewish "Zealots," who favored armed rebellion against Rome,[32] but it is primarily a personal ethic that does not contradict the legitimate role of the state in protecting its citizens from lawlessness and aggression.

30. On 5:33–37, see Brant 1996; Garlington 1995; Ito 1991; Kollmann 1996.
31. Both the Hebrew Bible and Second Temple Jewish texts advocated kind treatment of enemies in certain contexts. See Exod. 23:4–5; Job 31:29–30; Prov. 24:17–18; Sir. 28:1–8; 1QS 10.17–19; CD 9.3–6; 2 En. 50.3–4.
32. For more on the Zealots, see the second footnote to the comments on 22:19–22.

These verses list five hypothetical concrete situations in which Jesus's **5:39b–42**
general teaching on nonretaliation applies (cf. Luke 6:29; Did. 1.4–5).[33]
The first (Matt. 5:39b) probably pictures a personal dispute that leads to
an insulting backhand slap by a right-handed person to the right cheek
of another person (cf. Job 16:10; Ps. 3:7; Isa. 50:6; Lam. 3:30; Matt. 26:67;
Acts 23:2–3; 2 Cor. 11:20; *m. B. Qam.* 8.6). The second (Matt. 5:40) speaks
of a legal dispute in which one is ordered to forfeit one's shirt (χιτών,
chitōn, an inner garment evidently like a nightshirt; cf. Matt. 10:10) as
collateral for a debt (cf. Exod. 22:25–27; Deut. 24:12–13) or to satisfy a
claim for damages. The third situation (Matt. 5:41) envisions an occupying
Roman soldier conscripting a Jewish person to carry his equipment (cf.
Matt. 27:32; Mark 15:21). In each situation Jesus commands disciples to
go beyond the expected response. Instead of angrily slapping the aggres-
sors back, disciples are to allow themselves to be slapped again on the
other cheek. Instead of standing up for their rights by filing a countersuit,
disciples are to give up their coat (ἱμάτιον, *himation*, outer garment or
cloak; Matt. 9:20; 24:18; cf. the reverse in Luke 6:29) as well as their shirt.
Biblical law forbids this practice as overly harsh (Exod. 22:25–26; Deut.
24:12–13). Instead of resisting occupying military forces, the disciples are
to help them by carrying their equipment two miles instead of one. The
point of the first three situations is that the disciples are not to be a part
of furthering the typical cycle of evil action and escalating evil reaction
in this fallen world (Blomberg 1992a: 113).

The fourth and fifth examples (5:42) take the disciple in a more positive
direction. Not only is the disciple to avoid evil by nonretaliatory reaction
when oppressed by a more powerful person; the disciple is also to promote
good by a generous, benevolent response to those who are less powerful
(cf. Luke 6:34–35). This teaching is in keeping with biblical law (cf. esp.
Deut. 15:7–11; also Lev. 25:35–55). At his own arrest and trials, Jesus will
exemplify what is taught here (Matt. 26:67; 27:11–13, 35; cf. Mark 14:65;
John 18:22–23; 19:3; 1 Pet. 2:23). But these five examples should not be
taken in a pedantic fashion that would limit their intended application.
One may never need to literally turn the other cheek, give up one's coat,
or go the extra mile, but one must be willing to selflessly suffer personal
loss with faith that the loving heavenly Father will meet one's needs and
deal with the injustice in his own time. This concept was not unknown
to Second Temple Judaism (1QS 10.19–20; 11.1–2; Josephus, *J.W.* 5.377;
2 En. 50.4). Paul was evidently familiar with this tradition (Rom. 12:14–21,
quoting Deut. 32:35 and Prov. 25:21–22; 1 Cor. 6:7–8; 1 Thess. 5:15).[34]

33. Grammatically, the five illustrations are introduced alternately by indefinite relative clauses (ὅστις) in 5:39, 41 and by substantive participles that take on a conditional
nuance in 5:40, 42.
34. On nonretaliation, see Daly in Culliton 1982: 34–62; Donelson 1988; Gill 1991;
R. Horsley 1986; Klassen 1984; Lambrecht 1987, 1994; Rathey 1991; Wink 1992; Zerbe
1993.

vi. Loving One's Enemies (5:43–48)

5:43–44 The sixth and final example of Jesus's transcendent teaching refers to Lev. 19:18. Jesus states that one should love and pray even for one's enemies and persecutors (Matt. 5:43–44; cf. Luke 6:27–28). Such behavior will emulate the actions of the heavenly Father (Matt. 5:45) and transcend typical human practice (5:46–47). A concluding word commands that the disciple compare his or her behavior not to cultural norms but to transcendent norms—one is to be perfect as the heavenly Father is perfect (5:48). Evidently, the traditional view of the Scriptures mistakenly restricted the scope of the word "neighbor" in order to legitimize hatred of enemies (cf. Bergmeier 1998). Jesus rejects this approach and insists that disciples of the kingdom emulate the King.

Leviticus 19:18 commands love for neighbors, not hatred for enemies (cf. Mathys 1986). Perhaps hating enemies was taken as a logical corollary of loving neighbors or as a legitimate conclusion from texts such as Deut. 7:2; 20:16; 23:3–6; Pss. 26:4–5; 137:7–9; 139:19–22 (cf. Mekilta on Exod. 21:35; Sipra on Lev. 19:18; 1QS 1.3–4, 10–11; Josephus, *J.W.* 2.139). In Lev. 19:18 one's neighbor is evidently a fellow Jew, and perhaps the traditional teaching in Jesus's day read the text restrictively as applying only to Jews. But certain biblical texts also speak of humane treatment for non-Israelites (e.g., Lev. 19:33–34; Deut. 10:18–19; cf. Exod. 22:21–22; 23:9; Deut. 1:16; 27:19; Pss. 94:6; 146:9; Jer. 7:5–6; 22:3; Ezek. 22:7, 29; 47:22–23; Zech. 7:9–10; Mal. 3:5). Certain texts include non-Israelites under the general heading of "neighbor" (Jer. 7:5–6; Zech. 7:9–10). As the parable of the good Samaritan (Luke 10:25–37) shows, Jesus would not have accepted a restrictive reading of the word "neighbor." Praying for one's persecutors is a striking demonstration of one's love for them (cf. Luke 23:34; Acts 7:60). But this too is anticipated in the Scriptures (Gen. 20:17; Exod. 23:4–5; Num. 12:13; 21:7; 1 Sam. 24:17–19; 2 Sam. 19:6; 1 Kings 3:11; Job 31:29; Ps. 7:3–5; Prov. 24:17–18, 29; 25:21–22; Jer. 29:7; Jon. 4:10–11).[35]

5:45–47 The purpose (ὅπως, *hopōs,* in order that) of loving our enemies is to emulate the benevolent character of our heavenly Father.[36] Loving one's enemies is first compared to God's love and beneficence for people (5:45). Then two rhetorical questions call on disciples to practice a higher righteousness than the tax collectors and pagans do (5:46–47). There is no reward in being like tax collectors[37] who merely reciprocate the love

35. On loving enemies, see Jahnke 1988; Kuhn in Frankemölle and Kertelge 1989: 194–230; Milavec 1995; Reiser 2001; Ruzer 2002.

36. The word υἱοί here implies that the relationship between the Father and his children defines the children as taking on the character of the Father. Perhaps there is a bit of the Hebraic idiomatic use of בֵּן here. See BDAG 1024–25; Eph. 4:31–5:2

37. Tax collectors (τελῶναι) were local people, likely Jews, who worked for politically connected foreigners who had contracted with the Romans to collect taxes and had then often exacted more than was due, keeping the overage for themselves (BDAG 999). When

shown to them. Neither is there anything praiseworthy in reciprocating the greetings that come from one's fellows (ἀδελφοί, *adelphoi*, brothers), as the Gentiles do.

It is clear that action, not emotion, is called for here, since disciples are not only to pray for enemies (5:44) but also to do them good (since God does; 5:45; cf. Luke 6:35; Ps. 145:9; Acts 14:17) and to greet them respectfully (Matt. 5:47). This last action may imply a wish for their welfare (Gen. 43:27; Exod. 18:7 LXX). Jesus's words contradict a Zealot mentality, since the "enemies" of Jewish disciples would certainly include the Romans. Matthew 5:9 has already spoken of how the disciples' role as reconcilers in the world manifests their filial resemblance to the heavenly Father. Other NT texts stress how Christians' love for people, especially enemies, marks them as members of God's family (Eph. 4:31–5:2; 1 John 4:7–12; 1 Pet. 1:14–25). Loving one's enemies is imitating God.

This verse draws a conclusion (οὖν, *oun*, therefore) based on verses 45–47. Disciples are to model their lives after the universal benevolence of their heavenly Father, not after the mutual admiration practiced by the tax collectors and pagans. The language of this verse is similar to that of Lev. 19:2: "You must be holy for I, the LORD your God, am holy" (NLT). But the language and emphasis of Deut. 18:13 on blamelessness is probably echoed here as well.[38] To be perfect (τέλειος, *teleios*) in the immediate context is to be complete or mature in one's approximation of God's benevolence. In the narrative flow of Matt. 5, "perfection" is uprightness and blamelessness in consistently obeying God's law as ultimately interpreted by Jesus. Relatively few Christians hold the idea of perfection as absolute sinlessness; such a view would evidently not be acceptable to the one who taught his disciples to pray for forgiveness (Matt. 6:12; cf. 1 John 1:8). The surpassing righteousness of which Jesus began to speak in 5:20 is summarized here not as sinlessness but as imaging the Father's characteristic of universal benevolence (cf. Borchert 1992; E. Brown 1998; Hartin 1996).

Matthew 5:48 draws a conclusion not only to the sixth and final example of Jesus's teaching but also to 5:21–48 as a whole (Boring 1995: 195). All six of the areas addressed by Jesus call for perfection or modeling of the Father's character. One can do no better than imitate the Father.

5:48

Jews worked for these "tax farmers," they were generally regarded as ritually impure, thieves, and traitors, which may explain Jesus's pairing of tax collectors (5:46) with pagans (5:47; cf. 18:17). For Jesus's association with tax collectors, see 9:10–11; 10:3; 11:19; 21:31–32; Luke 18:9–14; 19:1–10.

38. Deuteronomy 18:13 enjoins God's people to be תָּמִים, which can mean "blameless, complete, having integrity" (BDB 1906, 1071). See Gen. 6:9; 17:1; Josh. 24:14; 2 Sam. 22:24; Amos 5:10; Pss. 15:2; 119:1; Prov. 11:20; 28:18, which speak of God's people being תְּמִימִם, and Deut. 32:4; 2 Sam. 22:31; Ps. 18:31 MT (18:30 Eng.), which speak of God being תָּמִים. Texts from Qumran tend to equate perfection with fully obeying the Torah as the community interprets it. See, e.g., CD 2.15; 7.5; 1QS 1.8; 2.2; 8.1, 20–21.

What more could be said? This is the surpassing righteousness of which Jesus spoke in 5:20. As Jesus's disciples are transformed by the rule of God and obey Jesus's definitive interpretation of Moses's Torah, they model God's character and become salt and light in this world.

It has been argued here that 5:21–48 is in continuity with the law and the prophets to an extent greater than is commonly held. Be that as it may, there is no doubt that much in 5:21–48 is antithetical to fallen human culture. Jesus's ethic contradicts the fallen human aggressiveness that seeks to dominate other people. His words against the misuse of women by adultery and divorce ought to resonate with contemporary sensibilities. His stress on integrity in speech is much needed in the Christian community, where it is not uncommon for prominent believers to be caught in lies. The teaching against retaliation is important but more difficult to apply in a society where Christians have religious liberty. Finally, there is no doubt that Christians have much to learn about loving their enemies when there are numerous occasions in which they find it very difficult to love one another.

The six examples that contrast Jesus's ultimate transcendent teaching of the Hebrew Scriptures with the traditional understandings of it amount to pointers in the direction of the righteousness that is greater than that of the religious leaders (5:20). Now Jesus will turn from relationships with people to religious activities (6:1–18) and attitudes toward material things (6:19–34). The message of the kingdom dynamically transforms the disciple's conduct in this area also.

Additional Notes

5:22. As it stands, this verse unconditionally censures anger against a fellow disciple, but a variant reading adds the word εἰκῇ after τῷ ἀδελφῷ αὐτοῦ, yielding the translation "everyone who is angry with his brother or sister *without cause* shall be liable to judgment." This makes the rigorous stricture against anger more palatable but in so doing renders the variant less likely, although it is preserved in sources as ancient as the second century. The more difficult shorter reading easily explains the presence of the easier longer reading, not vice versa.

5:32. The last phrase of 5:32 contains two variant readings. The entire phrase is omitted by D and a few other witnesses, perhaps because it was viewed as superfluous (Metzger 1994: 11). B and a few other witnesses read ὁ ἀπολελυμένην γαμήσας instead of ὃς ἐὰν ἀπολελυμένην γαμήσῃ, which is found in ℵ, *Byz*, and others. This variant may have arisen to make the construction more parallel to ὁ ἀπολύων in the first part of the verse. In any event, the meaning is not appreciably changed.

5:44. Two sets of variants (found in *Byz* and others) lengthen the shorter text reflected in the translation. Since it is difficult to understand why the longer readings would have been omitted by ℵ, B, and others, it is more likely that the longer readings were interpolated from Luke 6:27–28.

5:47. Instead of ἐθνικοί (found in ℵ, B, D, and others), *Byz* and others have τελῶναι. It seems likely that ἐθνικοί is original and that τελῶναι was substituted to conform 5:47 to 5:46.

3. Religious Duties (6:1–18)

Analysis

Matthew 6:1–18 presents the teaching of Jesus on three religious duties that would be basic for a Christian Jewish community such as Matthew's. Jesus first enunciates the general principle that informs these duties (6:1) and then addresses alms (6:2–4), prayer (6:5–15), and fasting (6:16–18). The teaching here is closely related conceptually and literarily to the preceding section, 5:21–48. Conceptually, 6:1–18 presents another area in which Jesus, as the ultimate teacher of the law and the prophets, explains the greater righteousness (5:20) by which disciples emulate the perfection of the Father (5:48). Literarily, 6:1–18 resembles the structure of 5:21–48 by its logical movement from a general principle (6:1; cf. 5:20) to specific examples (three examples in 6:2–18; cf. six examples in 5:21–48).[1] Another literary similarity is the repeated statement "Truly I tell you, they have their reward," which clearly demarcates the structure of the material (6:2, 5, 16; cf. 5:21, 27, 31, 33, 38, 43). Throughout 6:1–18 contrasting statements are used to show the difference between the greater righteousness required of Jesus's disciples and the practice of the religious leaders.

Brief Analysis of Matt. 6:2–18

Situation	"Whenever you . . ."	6:2, 5, 16
Prohibition	"do not . . ."	6:2, 5, 7–8, 16
Reason	"Truly I tell you . . ."	6:2, 5, 16
Command	"but when you . . ."	6:3, 6, 7, 17
Result	"your Father . . ."	6:4, 6, 18

The general principle enunciated by 6:1 connects righteousness with the disciples' intention.[2] The disciples must above all avoid doing religious acts in order to impress people, since the heavenly Father will not reward such acts. When each of the three specific practices is singled out for attention, a similar pattern occurs in which Jesus first forbids hypocritical religious practice and then commands genuine

---

1. W. Davies and Allison (1988: 577–78) find this pattern in several biblical and Second Temple texts.

2. On intention in Jesus's ethical teaching, compare the infinitival purpose clause πρὸς τὸ θεαθῆναι αὐτοῖς in 6:1 with πρὸς τὸ ἐπιθυμῆσαι αὐτήν in 5:28 and πρὸς τὸ θεαθῆναι τοῖς ἀνθρώποις in 23:5. Cf. 13:30; 26:12.

religious practice. In each of the three situations, Jesus gives a reason for prohibiting a behavior and indicates a positive result of the commanded behavior.

A more detailed analysis indicates the symmetrical manner in which each facet of Jesus's prohibition of hypocritical religion has a counterpart in his commendation of genuine religion (Boring 1995: 200):

The Symmetrical Constrasting Structure of Matt. 6:2–18

Hypocritical Religion Prohibited:
1. The occasion: "Whenever you . . ." (6:2, 5, 6, 7, 16)[3]
2. The prohibited ostentatious activity: "do not . . ." (6:2, 5, 7, 16)[4]
3. The prohibited motivation: "to be admired by others" (6:1, 2, 5, 16)[5]
4. The solemn affirmation: "they have their reward" (6:2, 5, 16)[6]

Genuine Religion Commanded:
1. The contrasting occasion: "but when you . . ." (6:3, 6, 9, 17)[7]
2. The commanded secret activity (6:3, 6, 9–13, 17)[8]
3. The commanded motivation: to be seen only by the Father (6:4, 6, 18)[9]
4. The solemn affirmation: "your Father will repay you" (6:4, 6, 18)[10]

The Proper Audience for Religious Performance

The goal for disciples of Jesus is to be perfect as the heavenly Father is perfect (5:48). The disciple's *character* is to be modeled on the Father's character, and the disciple's *performance* is to be done for the Father's

---

3. Indefinite temporal clauses introduced by ὅταν, except for a temporal present participle in 6:7. For ὅταν, see also 5:11; 6:2, 5, 6, 16; 9:15; 10:19, 23; 12:43; 13:32; 15:2; 19:28; 21:40; 23:15; 24:32, 33; 25:31; 26:29.

4. The syntax of the prohibitions is μή + aorist subjunctive in 6:2, 7–8; οὐκ + future indicative in 6:5; and μή + present imperative in 6:16.

5. The hypocritical intention is expressed by the infinitive in the general statement of 6:1 (πρὸς τὸ θεαθῆναι αὐτοῖς) and by a purpose clause with ὅπως in 6:2, 5, 16.

6. The threefold affirmation ἀμὴν λέγω ὑμῖν, ἀπέχουσιν τὸν μισθὸν αὐτῶν corresponds to μισθὸν οὐκ ἔχετε παρὰ τῷ πατρὶ ὑμῶν τῷ ἐν τοῖς οὐρανοῖς in 6:1. But the general statement in 6:1 contains nothing else that anticipates the contrasting teaching developed in 6:2–18.

7. The contrast is expressed by a genitive absolute construction σοῦ δὲ ποιοῦντος in 6:3, by the indefinite temporal clause σὺ δὲ ὅταν in 6:6, by a present imperative in 6:9, and by an adverbial participle and aorist imperative in 6:17.

8. As might be expected, each of these is expressed by an imperative.

9. The genuine motivation for religious activities is expressed by a purpose clause with ὅπως in 6:4, 18. Note the same construction expressing the hypocritical intention in 6:2, 5, 16. The genuine motivation for prayer is implicit in 6:6.

10. The expression ὁ πατήρ σου ὁ βλέπων ἐν τῷ κρυπτῷ ἀποδώσει σοι occurs in 6:4, 6, and in 6:18 the statement is identical except that κρυπτῷ becomes κρυφαίῳ.

approval. "Disciples must impress God alone" (Keener 1999: 206). This cuts against the grain of popular cultures that value exhibitionism and ostentation. The "If you've got it, flaunt it" principle can perversely infiltrate the modern church as it had the Judaism of Jesus's day (cf. *b. Soṭah* 22b). But Jesus would have his disciples do the right thing in the right way.

The tendency in Christian circles to publicize those who give large sums surely violates the central principle of this passage and forgets the lesson of the widow's mite (Mark 12:41–44; Luke 21:1–4). In prayer, eloquence and length are confused with effectiveness, as if God were ignorant of the disciples' needs and reluctant to meet them. Fasting tends to be ignored altogether, but similarly rigorous pious activities are widely heralded. In all three areas mentioned in Matt. 6:1–18, gaining the fleeting applause of one's peers amounts to forfeiting the Father's eternal approval. Disciples must be content to be noticed by the Father, realizing that temporary human approval is insignificant in the light of eternity. Giving to the needy in order to receive publicity is not *giving* at all—it is *paying* for human approval, and it forfeits divine approval (Plummer 1915: 91). (On 6:1–18, see Agnew 1995; Syreeni 1994; Wick 1998.)

The unit outline is as follows:

a. General principle (6:1)
b. Three specific practices (6:2–18)
   i. Charity (6:2–4)
   ii. Prayer (6:5–15)
       (1) Two contrasts: Publicity and verbosity versus privacy and simplicity (6:5–8)
       (2) The model prayer (6:9–15)
           (a) Priorities: Three Petitions for the Father's glory (6:9–10)
           (b) Problems: Three petitions for the disciples' needs (6:11–13)
           (c) The principle: The attitude in which God is approached (6:14–15)
   iii. Fasting (6:16–18)

Exegesis and Exposition

[1]"Make sure you do not practice your righteousness before people in order to be noticed by them; otherwise you have no reward with your Father who is in heaven.

[2]"So whenever you give to the poor, do not sound a trumpet before you, as the hypocrites do in the synagogues and on the streets so that they may be praised by people. Truly I tell you, they have their reward. [3]But when you give to

the poor, do not let your left hand know what your right hand is doing, [4]so that your giving will be in secret; and your ⌜Father⌝ who sees what is done in secret will reward ⌜you⌝.

[5]"And whenever you pray, do not be like the hypocrites, because they love to stand up and pray in the synagogues and on the street corners so that people may see them. Truly I tell you, they have their reward. [6]But you, whenever you pray, go into your inner room, close your door, and pray to your Father who is in secret, and your Father who sees what is done in secret will reward ⌜you⌝. [7]While you are praying, do not babble as the Gentiles do, for they think they will be heard because of their many words. [8]So do not be like them; for ⌜your Father⌝ knows what you need even before you ask him.

[9]"Therefore you should pray like this:

'Our Father who is in heaven,
May your name be honored.
[10]May your kingdom come.
May your will be done,
On earth as it is in heaven.
[11]Give us our necessary food for today.
[12]And forgive us of our debts, as we also have forgiven our debtors.
[13]And do not lead us into temptation, but deliver us from the evil one. ⌜For yours is the kingdom and the power and the glory forever. Amen.⌝"

[14]"For if you forgive people of their transgressions, your heavenly Father will also forgive you. [15]But if you do not forgive ⌜people⌝, neither will your Father forgive your transgressions.

[16]"And whenever you fast, do not be like gloomy hypocrites, for they disfigure their appearance so that they will appear to people to be fasting. Truly I tell you, they have their reward. [17]But you, anoint your head and wash your face while you are fasting, [18]so that you will not appear to people to be fasting but to your Father who is in secret; and your Father who sees what is done in secret will reward ⌜you⌝."

a. General Principle (6:1)

6:1   This verse enunciates the general principle behind the three specific activities in this section: charity (6:2–4), praying (6:5–15), and fasting (6:16–18).[11] This principle concerns intention in religious duties (cf. *b. Meg.* 20a). Disciples must guard against the perverse tendency to do good deeds in order to receive human admiration, because this forfeits divine reward (cf. Matt. 10:41–42; 19:27–29). Matthew's term for religious

---

11. Tobit 12:8 links these three activities and prioritizes giving, whereas Gos. Thom. 5, 14 rejects all three.

activity is δικαιοσύνη (*dikaiosynē*, righteousness), which refers to practical or functional godliness, obedience to God's laws.[12] It has already been made clear that Jesus's standard of righteousness is higher than that of the religious leaders (5:20). This verse correlates with 5:16: if the disciples are to do good deeds to the Father's glory, they cannot do them for their own glory. References to reward in this context recall 5:12, 46 and anticipate 10:41–42; 16:27; 19:29; 20:8; 25:21–29, 34.

b. Three Specific Practices (6:2–18)

i. Charity (6:2–4)

The three concrete examples presented here are central to Second Temple Judaism (cf. Tob. 12:8). The first concrete application of the principle of Matt. 6:1 is that of giving to the needy, a crucial duty for pious Jews.[13] Keener (1999: 207) overstates the matter when he says that the three examples are random, but he is correct that they are intended to be suggestive of how the principle of 6:1 is to be applied to all religious activities. Although trumpets were used in Jewish religious activities (Joel 2:15; CD 11.21–22; Josephus, *Ant.* 3.294; *m. Taʿan.* 2.5; *b. Šabb.* 35b; *b. Ber.* 6b; *b. Sanh.* 35a), there is no rabbinic text that connects blowing trumpets with giving to the poor. The meaning is metaphorical and hyperbolic (cf. Nolland 2005: 274; Isa. 58:1; Joel 2:1); it describes drawing attention to oneself (like the modern expression "blowing your own horn"). It might refer to a trumpet-shaped collection box that resounded when coins were thrown into it (*m. Šeqal.* 1.3; 2.1; 6.1–5; W. Davies and Allison 1988: 579; Lachs 1987: 112–13; McEleney 1985). "Hypocrites" occurs here for the first time in Matthew (cf. 6:5, 16; 7:5; 15:7; 22:18; 23:13–15, 28; 24:51). A hypocrite is an actor (BDAG 1038),[14] and religious activity is not for those who love (cf. 6:5) to put on a show for people but for those who sincerely love to serve God. Instead of giving in a flashy public manner to attain self-aggrandizement, disciples are to give secretly so that the Father, who is aware of secret actions, can reward them. The emphasis on secrecy is underlined by the hyperbolic "Do not let your left hand know what your right hand

6:2–4

---

12. See BDAG 248 and the discussion of righteousness in this commentary on 1:19. Cf. Matt. 3:15; 5:6, 10, 20; 6:33; 25:37. The Hebrew Bible anticipates this meaning of righteousness in texts such as Ezek. 3:20; 33:13; Dan. 9:18. Cf. Tob. 4:5–6; 12:8; CD 1.1, 16; 4.17; 1QS 1.5; 3.1; 4.2; 8.2; 9.5; 1QH 5.9; 15.14, 17; 4Q174 3.17; 4Q184 frg. 1.16.

13. Cf. Deut. 15:7–11; Ezek. 16:49; Prov. 29:7; CD 14.13–16; Matt. 26:11; Luke 3:11; John 9:8; Acts 3:1–10; 4:35; 6:2–3; 9:36; 10:2; 11:29; 20:35; 24:17; Gal. 2:10; Eph. 4:28; Did. 1.6; Sir. 3:30; 4:1–8; 12:1–3; 17:22; 29:8; Tob. 1:3; 2:2, 14; 4:7–11; 12:8–9; *m. ʾAbot* 1.5; 5.13; *m. B. Qam.* 10.1.

14. Batey 1984 speculates that Jesus's use of the term "hypocrite" comes from his contact with the theater in Sepphoris near Nazareth. But the term is used for ethical pretense in other Jewish texts (e.g., Sir. 1:29; 32:15; 33:2; Ps. Sol. 4.6, 20; not to mention Gal. 2:13). Cf. J. Barr in P. Davies and White 1990: 307–26; Oakley 1985; van Tilborg 1972b.

is doing." Disciples are to seek eventual permanent divine reward (cf. Tob. 4:10; 12:8; 14:10) rather than immediate temporary human praise. This emphasis on authentic inner religion (ἐν τῷ κρυπτῷ, *en tō kryptō*; cf. Rom. 2:28–29; Deut. 30:6) is not absent from rabbinic literature.[15] Jesus's critique is aimed at abuse of Pharisaic practice, not against Pharisaism per se.

ii. Prayer (6:5–15)

Jesus's teaching on prayer in 6:5–15 is the centerpiece of 6:1–18 and perhaps of the Sermon on the Mount as a whole. This teaching is more detailed than that on alms and fasting. It consists of two warnings on how not to pray, each balanced by positive teaching (6:5–6; 6:7–8), followed by the model prayer (6:9–15). First Jesus contrasts publicity to privacy (6:5–6) and verbosity to simplicity (6:7–8) in prayer. Certain Jews sought publicity, and the pagans were known for verbosity, but the disciples were to pray privately and simply. These two contrasts lead naturally into the model prayer, which balances three petitions for the Father's glory (6:9–10) with three petitions for the disciple's needs (6:11–13). The phrase "on earth as it is in heaven" (6:10c) characterizes the first set of petitions, and the attitude of forgiveness (6:14–15) characterizes the second set.

One may think of 6:9–10 as indicating the *person* to whom prayer is addressed (6:9b) and the *priorities* by which prayers are formed (6:9c–10). This person to whom prayer is addressed is characterized as "Father," a term inevitably colored by one's relationship to one's human father. This human relationship may help or hinder one's perception of God as heavenly Father. One may think of 6:11–15 as concerning the *problems* about which disciples pray (6:11–13) and the *principle* that governs their prayers (6:14–15). As they pray about their provisions (6:11), pardon (6:12), and protection (6:13), they remind themselves that if God had not forgiven them, they would not be praying at all, and they respond to God by forgiving others (6:14–15).[16]

---

15. Cf. *m. 'Abot* 1.13; 5.13; *m. Šeqal.* 5.6; *y. Ber.* 14b; *y. Soṭah* 20c, 22b; *b. Pesaḥ.* 113a; *b. B. Bat.* 9b, 10a–b; *b. Yebam.* 79a; *b. Ned.* 62a; *b. Mo'ed Qaṭ.* 16b; *b. Soṭah* 22b, 41b–42a; *b. Ber.* 28a; T. Job 9.7–8; Ps. Rab. on Pss. 12:3; 52:1; Eccles. Rab. on Eccles. 4:1; 5:5.

16. For bibliographies of the enormous literature on the prayer, see H. Betz 1995: 382–86; W. Davies and Allison 1988: 621–24; Carmignac 1969: 469–533; Dorneich 1988; Luz 1989: 367–68. The following studies are noteworthy: Abrahams 1967: 2.94–108; Bahr 1965; Bradshaw 1982: 1–46; Brocke et al. 1974; R. Brown 1965: 217–53; Byargeon 1998; Carmignac 1969; Charlesworth 1992b; Crosby 2002; C. F. Evans 1963; Finkel in Finkel and Frizzell 1981: 131–70; Garland 1992; Genuyt 1998; Gibson 2001; Jeremias 1967; Lanier 1992; Lapide 1991; Lochman 1990; Migliore 1993; Oakman in Chilton and Evans 1999b: 137–86; O'Neill 1993b; Petuchowski and Brocke 1978; Philonenko 2001; Stritzky 1989; van Tilborg 1972a; Zumstein 2001. Theological exposition is provided by Bruner 1987: 233–57; Hinkle 2002; Minear 2000, 2002; N. Wright 1997.

(1) Two Contrasts: Publicity and Verbosity versus Privacy and Simplicity (6:5–8)

Jesus forbids his disciples to pray hypocritically on the street or in the synagogue (cf. 23:5–7). Instead, they are to pray privately in an inner room (6:5–6; cf. 24:26; Luke 12:3, 24; BDAG 988). This is an allusion to Isa. 26:20 (cf. the LXX: Gen. 43:30; Exod. 7:28 [8:3 Eng.]; 2 Kings 4:33), which in its context speaks of Israel hiding from judgment in anticipation of blessing. Although Jesus is portrayed as praying privately in the Gospels (Mark 1:35; 6:46; 14:32–42; Luke 5:16; 6:12; 9:18, 28–29; cf. 2 Kings 4:33), here he forbids hypocrisy, not sincere prayer in public or in religious services (cf. Matt. 11:25; Mark 6:41; Luke 11:1; John 11:41–42; 1 Tim 2:1–2, 8). This critique addresses insincere Jewish practice and may have in mind hypocrisy in reciting the Amidah—or Eighteen Benedictions (to be uttered three times a day)—the Shema (to be done twice daily), and various other blessings. (See also the remarks on 6:9a.)

6:5–6

In 6:7–8 Jesus critiques the prayers of non-Christian Gentiles or pagans (cf. 5:47; 6:32), which evidently could include long-winded babbling to obtain the attention of the gods, or perhaps even the utterance of repeated magical incantations.[17] But Jesus reminds his disciples that their Father already knows what they need before they ask (cf. 6:32; Isa. 65:24; Dan. 10:12; Luke 12:30; Acts 10:31). Jesus was not the first to command an economy of words in prayer (cf. Eccles. 5:2; Isa. 1:15; Sir. 7:14; 2 Bar. 48.26; *m. Ber.* 3.5; 4.4; but contrast *y. Ber.* 4.7b, which counsels multiplied prayers). It is appropriate to recall Elijah's prayer contest with the prophets of Baal in connection with this verse, especially 1 Kings 18:26–29. Ancient Greek authors also spoke out against loquacious prayers (cf. the examples cited by H. Betz 1995: 365–67).

6:7–8

(2) The Model Prayer (6:9–15)

(a) Priorities: Three Petitions for the Father's Glory (6:9–10)

As form-critical scholars note (e.g., H. Betz 1995: 350; van Tilborg 1972a), the model prayer of 6:9–15 (cf. a shorter version in Luke 11:1–4 and a nearly identical one in Did. 8.2) tends to interrupt the repeated pattern of Matt. 6:2–4; 6:5–8; 6:16–18. But this does not necessarily bring the prayer's authenticity or the literary unity of 6:1–18 into doubt. The model prayer provides a balancing positive example that offsets the preceding

6:9a

---

17. The prohibition of "babbling" utilizes an extremely rare word, βατταλογέω. In the NT it occurs only here and in Codex D of Luke 11:2. It may occur only once outside the NT in literature that is not dependent on the NT. Evidently, it describes an intentionally repetitive speech pattern similar to the involuntary repetitions of a person who stutters. See BDAG 172; H. Betz 1995: 364–67; W. Davies and Allison 1988: 587–88; and Delling, *TDNT* 1:597–98. Its meaning is clarified by πολυλογία in 6:7b, but this too is a rare word (cf. Prov. 10:19 LXX).

critique of hypocritical prayer, and it exemplifies the kingdom values inculcated in the Beatitudes. The similarity of this prayer to the Kaddish, a postsermon synagogue prayer, is noted by many (e.g., Abrahams 1967: 2.98–99; Baumgardt 1991; W. Davies and Allison 1988: 595–97; Hagner 1993: 147).[18] Possible connections with the prayer known as the Amidah, Tefillah, or Eighteen Benedictions (Shemoneh Esreh) have also been investigated.[19] Although the content of Jesus's prayer reveals basic Jewish values and concerns, it differs from typical Jewish prayers in its simplicity, brevity, and eschatological orientation (W. Davies and Allison 1988: 595; but see Flusser 1990: 53–62).

Although Jesus said that his disciples were to pray "like this" (οὕτως, houtōs), Did. 8 enjoins that this prayer be repeated three times a day (cf. Bahr 1965). From ancient times Christians have placed the prayer on amulets, charms, and wall hangings. This is more than a little ironic. The "Lord's Prayer" is in fact the model prayer for his disciples. It is not a mantra to be repeated mindlessly or superstitiously but an example of a prayer informed by kingdom values, the kind of prayer a disciple should pray. In such prayer, doxology (exemplified by the first three "your" requests) precedes and permeates requests for human needs (exemplified by the last three "us" requests).

Prayer is to be addressed to "our Father in heaven" (cf. 3:17; 5:9, 16, 45, 48; 6:1, 4, 6, 8, 14–15, 18, 26; 7:11, 21).[20] The family imagery speaks of the intimacy of the disciples' relationship to God, but the qualifier "in heaven" reminds one that God is not a pal. Rather, this God is the awesome God of heaven who has come near in the person of his beloved Son and counts disciples of the kingdom as his dear family (cf. 12:46–50; Isa. 57:15). God is "*our* Father in heaven" because God has come near to his children by his grace, establishing a covenant relationship of intimacy and community. Yet God is at the same time "our Father *in heaven*"; he remains distant from his children because of his glory, which leads his disciples to approach him with awe.[21] This God deserves the utmost

18. A common translation of the prayer is as follows: "Exalted and hallowed be his great name in the world that he created according to his own will. May he let his kingdom rule in your lifetime and in your days and in the lifetime of the whole house of Israel, speedily and soon. Praised be his great name from eternity to eternity. And to this say, Amen." For a discussion of Jewish prayers in the time of Jesus, see Charlesworth 1992.

19. See W. Davies and Allison 1988: 595–97; Lachs 1987: 117–24; Overman 1996: 94–97. For the content of Shemoneh Esreh, see Schürer 1973: 2.455–63.

20. On the vexing question whether Jesus's reference to God as Father was unparalleled in his day (as proposed by Jeremias 1967: 29, 54–57, 89–98), see the contrary arguments of D'Angelo 1992 and Vermes 1973: 210. Keener's balanced discussion (1999: 216–18) and citation of ancient texts are quite helpful. Jesus's view of God as Father was distinctive if not absolutely unique. See further J. Barr 1988; Feneberg 1988.

21. Cf. Dan. 4:26; Luke 15:18; Rom. 1:18 and extrabiblical texts such as 1 Esd. 4:58; Tob. 10:13; Jdt. 6:19; 1 Macc. 3:18, 50, 60; 4:24; 3 Macc. 4:21; 7:6; 1 En. 6.2; 13.8; 83.9; 91.7; 1QM 12.5; *m. 'Abot* 1.3, 11; 2.2, 12.

devotion flowing from love and reverence for the one who perfectly and harmoniously possesses goodness and greatness, grace and power, immanence and transcendence. When prayer is made, God's goodness and greatness must be carefully balanced to achieve intimacy without sentimentality, on the one hand, and reverence without austerity, on the other.

The three "your" requests should be understood as three ways of asking   **6:9b–10** for essentially the same thing. God's name[22] represents his person and character (BDAG 712), God's kingdom is the earthly imposition of his character, and God's will flows from his character (cf. Metzler in Chilton and Evans 1999b: 187–202). To a certain extent, God's character is revered as he rules on earth through people who do his will, but the main focus of these requests is on the future full manifestation of God's reign on earth (cf. 1 Cor. 16:22; Rev. 22:20).

Since the three "your" petitions are essentially one, the final phrase of Matt. 6:10, "on earth as it is in heaven," describes all of them, not just the third. Disciples long for the realities of heaven to be realized on earth (cf. Schneider in Schenke 1988: 283–97). All three requests imply that certain aspects of the kingdom are yet future, entailing the progressive actualization of God's character, reign, and will on earth, that is, universally. Such requests come from one whose hunger for righteousness on earth will not be satisfied with a snack, as it were, but only with the eschatological banquet associated with the age to come (5:6; cf. 8:11). The Father is the Lord of heaven and earth (11:25), and he has given the resurrected Jesus universal authority in heaven and on earth (28:18). In the meantime, as disciples are engaged in the gradual extension of the kingdom by their words and deeds, their utmost desire is for the ultimate realization of God's reign on earth at the end of the age (13:37–43; 24:14; 28:20).

Matthew 6:9–10 convincingly shows that one should not pray primarily in order to receive goods and services from God but to render service to God. Prayer is not first and foremost an exercise to vindicate the disciple's causes, meet the disciple's needs, fulfill the disciple's desires, or solve the disciple's problems. Rather, one's priority must be the promotion of God's reputation, the advancement of God's rule, and the performance of God's will. These three petitions are essentially one expression of burning desire to see the Father honored on earth as he is already honored in heaven (cf. Rev. 4–5). The disciples' hope is not escapism—they do not look to leave the earth for an ethereal heavenly existence. Rather, they look for a concrete existence in which heaven comes to earth, and they seek heaven's interests on earth today as they

---

22. On the setting apart of God's name, see Lev. 22:32; Isa. 29:23; Ezek. 36:23; 1 En. 61.12. For the opposite, see Lev. 18:21; Ezek. 36:20. God's name is a revelation of himself (Gen. 32:28–29; Exod. 3:13–14; Isa. 52:6).

anticipate a time when God's reign on earth will be consummated (Matt. 13:40–43; 16:27–28; 19:28–30; 25:34).

(b) Problems: Three Petitions for the Disciples' Needs (6:11–13)

6:11   Three petitions for the disciples' needs now balance the three previous theocentric petitions. Whatever one's wants, one's deepest human needs are found in these requests: daily sustenance (6:11), forgiveness (6:12), and avoidance of sin (6:13). In 6:11 the key word in the expression translated "our necessary food for today" is the obscure adjective ἐπιούσιος (*epiousios*), which may be a coined term (Origen, *Prayer* 27.7); it does not occur outside Christian literature dependent on this text (cf. Luke 11:3; Did. 8.2; Metzger 1957; Hemer 1984). Educated guesses at its meaning include "daily," "necessary," and "for tomorrow," understood by some as a reference to the eschatological "tomorrow" that follows "today," this age.[23] Whatever the precise meaning, the point seems to be that the disciple prays for immediate day-to-day necessities rather than for long-term luxuries. In Matt. 6:25, disciples are told not to worry about such necessities, and in 6:34 they are told not to worry about tomorrow. Rather, they are to trust their Father implicitly for everything. The fact that in biblical times manual laborers were paid on a daily basis (20:8) seems to reinforce the perspective taught here.

6:12   Prayer for ongoing forgiveness (6:12) implies that the disciple has made the decisive turn from sin to God demanded by the message of the kingdom (3:2; 4:17). This request shows that authentic disciples on a regular basis have obligations to God that remain unfulfilled (cf. Lachs 1975a). The word "debts" (ὀφειλήματα, *opheilēmata*) occurs only one other time in the NT (Rom 4:4; cf. a cognate word in Matt. 18:32; Did. 8.2), and there it describes financial obligation (cf. LXX: Deut. 24:10; 1 Esd. 3:20; 1 Macc. 15:8). The parallel in Luke 11:4 uses the common word for "sin," ἁμαρτία (*hamartia*). Here in Matthew the idea is moral obligations owed to God that have not been met (cf. the cognate terms in Matt. 23:16, 18; Rom. 13:7–8; 1 Cor. 7:3 and the discussion in H. Betz 1995: 400–404). This nuance of sin as unfulfilled obligation paves the way for the expansion of forgiveness in terms of unmet human obligations in Matt. 6:14–15. When disciples pray for pardon, they recognize that they are not yet perfect—their attitudes and activities often fall short of kingdom standards (cf. 5:3, 6). Receiving this pardon is an amazing privilege, but it comes with a

---

23. For a survey of views and literature, see BDAG 376–77; Boismard 1995; Hemer 1984; Hill 1983; Hultgren in Hultgren and Hall 1990: 41–54; Nijman and Worp 1999; Orchard 1973; H. Betz 1995: 397–99.

corresponding responsibility, extending pardon to others. A forgiven person is a forgiving person.

The third request (6:13) is stated in two contrasting ways, negatively ("Do   **6:13** not lead us into temptation"; cf. Luke 11:4; Mark 14:38) and positively ("but deliver us from the evil one"; cf. John 17:15; 2 Thess. 3:3; 2 Tim. 4:18; Rev. 3:10; Grelot 1989). Since the Spirit led Jesus into a time of testing (4:1), this petition is not so much for God not to lead the disciple into a moral test as it is for the disciple to be delivered from Satan so as not to yield to temptation. Some argue that the testing spoken of here is the eschatological woe before the arrival of the bliss of the kingdom (Meier 1980b: 62; Tasker 1961: 74), but this is overly subtle in view of the frequent use of πειρασμός (*peirasmos*) for present trials. (For another overly subtle view, see Houk 1966.)

The justice of God as it relates to temptations faced by humans is one aspect of the complex theological problem of theodicy (cf. H. Betz 1995: 313–14, 406–10; Carmignac 1969: 236–319; Houk 1966; Moule 1974). God permits evil to exist in the world and indeed permits his people to be tested, yet God is not to be blamed when humans fail the test, succumb to evil, and fall into sin (cf. 1 Cor. 10:13; Heb. 2:18; 4:15; James 1:12–18; 2 Pet. 2:9; Sir. 15:11–20; Origen, *Prayer* 29–30; *b. Ber.* 60b).

When disciples pray for protection from temptation to sin, they pray for God to break the cycle that so often plagues them (cf. Josh. 7:20–21; James 1:13–15). Temptation leads to sin, and sin leads to the necessity of praying for forgiveness. Prayer for protection from temptation and deliverance from the evil one's strategies breaks the cycle (cf. Matt. 4:1–11). (See Tournay 1998.)

The doxology found as the second half of Matt. 6:13 in the KJV is not found in many of the most ancient MSS and is probably not a part of the original version of this Gospel (cf. the additional note on 6:13). It interrupts the continuity between the petition in 6:13 and the explanation in 6:14–15. Nevertheless, it provides a fitting conclusion to the prayer and may have been added for liturgical purposes (cf. 1 Chron. 29:11–13). (See M. Black in P. Davies and White 1990: 327–38.)

(c) The Principle: The Attitude in Which God Is Approached (6:14–15)

Just as the phrase "on earth as it is in heaven" (6:10) related to all three   **6:14–15** of the previous petitions, so also here the words of 6:14–15 on the necessity of an attitude of forgiveness relate not just to 6:12 but also to all three requests for human needs. Disciples are hereby warned not to ask for their needs to be met in a spirit that is unwilling to meet the needs of others. Rather, disciples will realize that their experience of God's forgiveness enables them to forgive others (cf. 5:23–24, 38–48; 18:21–25). This has been misunderstood by some classic dispensationalists as "legal ground," which teaches that our forgiving others merits God's forgiving us, as some classic dispensationalists implied (Gaebelein 1910: 143). Rather, the point is that God's initiative in graciously forgiving us should motivate us to forgive others. Forgiving others demonstrates that we have been forgiven by God. Forgiven, we have been freed to forgive. This is not the reverse of what Paul taught (cf. Matt. 5:23–24; 9:2, 5, 6; 12:31–32; 18:32–35; Eph. 4:31–5:2; Col. 3:13; contra Walvoord 1974: 53).

Disciples today must reflect on the extent to which their prayers correspond to the Lord's model prayer. Probing questions must be asked. Are their prayers motivated by the vision that God's will must be done on earth as it is in heaven? Do their prayers for personal needs arise from hearts reconciled with their neighbors as well as with God? As prayer for personal needs is considered, anxiety over material things inevitably surfaces. Matthew 6:19–34 presents Jesus's teaching on this topic.

iii. Fasting (6:16–18)

6:16–18   Fasting is the third area of religious activity now addressed with the same pattern found in the previous teaching on giving and praying. While fasting, we should not neglect our appearance in order to draw attention to ourselves.[24] Rather, we should maintain personal grooming so that God alone notices the fast and rewards us. Of the three activities treated in 6:1–18, fasting is certainly the least important to many Christians today. Indeed, it is not commanded in any of the NT Epistles. Yet it was an important part of Jewish religious practice in the days of Jesus. Fasting was a prescribed part of various Israelite community activities involving public repentance (Joel 1:14; 2:15), and pious Jews fasted voluntarily during times of religious devotion, especially prayer.[25] It is primarily voluntary fasting that is in view here. Jesus himself fasted (Matt. 4:2; cf. Moses and Elijah, Exod. 34:28; 1 Kings 19:8) and spoke metaphorically of the appropriateness of fasting for his disciples after his death (Matt. 9:14–15). The Pharisees fasted (9:14; cf. Luke 18:12), and Jesus does not criticize them for the practice. In Acts the disciples fasted before selecting church leaders (Acts 13:2–3; 14:23).

The prophetic critique of fasting not accompanied by just behavior (Isa. 58:3–7; Jer. 14:11–12; Zech. 7:4–14; 8:19; cf. Sir. 34:31; Gos. Thom. 14, 104) is not unlike Jesus's condemnation of hypocritical fasting here. Although genuine external signs such as sackcloth, ashes, and torn garments could accompany genuine fasting (Dan. 9:3; Jon. 3:5; Jdt. 8:5;

24. Ἀφανίζω can mean "to destroy or ruin." Here it may mean "to neglect personal grooming" or "to disfigure" (LSJ 286b) one's face. BDAG 154 connects the idea to the theatrical imagery suggested by hypocrisy (cf. Matt. 6:5): ancient actors wore masks that portrayed their character's disposition.

25. See 1 Sam. 7:5–6; Neh. 1:4; Dan. 9:3; Jon. 3:5; Tob. 12:8; 2 Macc. 13:12; Matt. 4:2; 9:14–15; Mark 2:18–20; 9:29; Luke 2:37; 18:12; Acts 13:2–3; 14:23; 23:21; Philo, *Spec. Laws* 2.203; *m. Ta'an.* 1.4–7; 2.1, 9; *b. B. Bat.* 60b; Did. 1.3; 7.4; 8.1. Cf. Wimmer 1982.

1 Macc. 3:47; Josephus, *J.W.* 3.47), Jesus was not impressed with fasting advertised by an artificially haggard demeanor (Matt. 6:16; cf. Luke 24:17) or with a theatrically altered appearance. Such behavior may have been the norm for actors who sought the crowd's applause, but it is singularly inappropriate for disciples who seek the Father's approval. They should wash themselves and anoint their heads normally so that only the Father knows about their fast.[26] This seems to portray fasting during affliction as a time of genuine inner joy rather than of counterfeit outward pain.

The focus of Matt. 5:21–48 was on Jesus as the authoritative interpreter of the law. The focus in 6:1–18 is on Jesus as teacher of the community cultus. But these two sections are similar in two ways. First, the structure of both sections includes an initial general statement (5:17–20; 6:1) followed by a series of specific examples that feature repetition, contrast, and symmetry. There are three contrasting examples in 5:21–32, 33–48 and three in 6:2–4, 5–15, 16–18. Second, both sections stress a higher righteousness in which internal intention leads to external activity (5:8, 16, 20, 22, 28, 37, 48; 6:1, 4, 6, 13–15, 18).

Additional Notes

6:4. With the reading αὐτὸς ἀποδώσει σοι or ἀποδώσει σοι αὐτός, the Textus Receptus and other MSS stress the Father's role in rewarding the disciples. These additions of the personal pronoun αὐτός are not likely to be original, but they correctly emphasize the truth that genuine reward comes from God alone. Another variant reading in this verse, found in the Byzantine text and other later witnesses, has the phrase ἐν τῷ φανερῷ at the end, producing a contrast with ἐν τῷ κρυπτῷ in the first half of the verse (cf. 6:6, 18). This results in the debatable idea that God will openly reward those who secretly give, pray, and fast (cf. 7:21–23; 16:27; 19:28).

6:6. The phrase ἐν τῷ φανερῷ is added again here by some MSS. See the note on 6:4 (cf. 6:18).

6:8. A few early sources have ὁ θεὸς ὁ πατὴρ ὑμῶν instead of ὁ πατὴρ ὑμῶν, but this variant has a Pauline flavor (cf., e.g., Rom. 1:7) that occurs nowhere else in Matthew. Some late sources conform 6:8 to 6:14 (not 6:9, *pace* Metzger 1994: 13) by adding ὁ οὐράνιος to ὁ πατὴρ ὑμῶν. Scribal error evidently accounts for the variant ὁ πατὴρ ἡμῶν instead of ὁ πατὴρ ὑμῶν in other sources.

6:13. The shorter rendering of this verse, found in most recent translations, is due to the rejection of a longer doxological ascription that appears in various forms. A few sources simply add ἀμήν to ῥῦσαι ἡμᾶς ἀπὸ τοῦ πονηροῦ. The Byzantine text-type supports the words enclosed in half-brackets (⌐¬) in the above translation. Other sources further augment the words in half-brackets (⌐¬) with a trinitarian formula. Since the longer versions of this verse are not found in many early Greek MSS and patristic sources, they most likely result from liturgical adaptation. See Bandstra 1981, 1982; Metzger 1994: 14; van Bruggen 1982.

---

26. The practice of anointing the head was a customary part of grooming the hair. See 2 Sam. 12:20; 14:2; Pss. 23:5; 104:15; Eccles. 9:8; Dan. 10:3; Jdt. 16:7–8; Matt. 26:7; Luke 7:46. Also, *m. Taʿan.* 1.4–5 shows that rabbinic halakah did not necessarily forbid anointing during times of fasting.

6:15. The words τὰ παραπτώματα αὐτῶν are found after τοῖς ἀνθρώποις in many MSS representing different text-types. Since these words are also found in 6:14 and at the end of 6:15, the debate over their genuineness is a matter of omission of a supposed redundancy versus addition of a balancing phrase. In any event, the meaning of the verse is not changed.

6:18. See the notes on 6:4 and 6:6 for discussion of the variant at the end of this verse.

4. Kingdom Values:
God or Money? (6:19–34)

Structural Analysis

Matthew 6:19–34 is closely tied to the human-needs portion of the model prayer, most specifically to the request for daily provision (6:8b, 11, 25, 31). There is also probably a connection between the ostensible persecution to be endured (5:10–12, 39–42, 44; 6:13–15) and worry over material needs (6:11, 19, 25, 28, 31, 34). Persecution would greatly exacerbate anxiety over material needs. The passage centers on three kinds of statement:

1. *Prohibitions* of materialistic activities and anxious thoughts (6:19, 25, 31, 34a)
2. *Exhortations* enjoining kingdom priorities in activities and attitudes (6:20, 33)
3. *Motivations* (statements, proverbs, illustrations, and rhetorical questions) that move disciples toward obedience (6:21–24, 26–30, 32, 34b–c)

These three types of statements are woven together in a repetitive manner, forming an aggregate that reinforces Jesus's teaching. There are also several bipolar structures in this section, including earth and heaven (6:19–20), temporary goods and enduring reward (6:19–20), good and bad eyes (6:22–23), light and darkness (6:22–23), service to God and possessions (6:24), and what Gentiles seek and what disciples seek (6:32–33). These opposites paint a clear picture of antithetical orientations to human existence, life with or without God (Boring 1995: 209–10).

Some (e.g., Carson 1984: 176–82) divide the passage into two units, the first on materialism (6:19–24) and the second on anxiety (6:25–34). Others (e.g., W. Davies and Allison 1988: 625) agree that 6:25–34 is a unit but view it as the last in a series of four units, preceded by 6:19–21; 6:22–23; 6:24. The unequal length of the units is a weakness of this scheme. The most difficult part of this passage is 6:22–23, which contains a saying (on the eye as lamp of the body) that is difficult to understand both in itself and in its relationship to the context. Overall, 6:19–34 may not yield as easily to structural analysis as preceding parts of the sermon despite W. Davies and Allison's attempt (1988:

625–27) to diagram it and point out a strong structural resemblance to 7:1–12.

Despite these difficulties, it is possible to discern an *inclusio* in the passage if not a clear chiasmus. The pair of negative and positive commands at the outset of the text (6:19–21) is answered by the pair of positive and negative commands (reversing the order) at the conclusion of the text (6:33–34). The segment 6:25–31 is also tightly structured, beginning and ending with a prohibition of anxiety about food, drink, and clothing (6:25, 31) and with its middle containing interspersed illustrations from nature (birds in 6:26 and plants in 6:28) and rhetorical questions (6:25, 26, 30). The diagram below seeks to display this structure:

Inclusio and Chiasmus (?) in Matt. 6:19–34

Prohibition of earthly treasure (6:19)[1]
  Command to lay up heavenly treasure (6:20–21)[2]
    First pair of illustrations (eye and slave; 6:22–24)
      Two eyes, good and bad (6:22–23)
      Two masters, God and money (6:24)
    Second pair of illustrations (birds and flowers; 6:25–31)
      First prohibition of anxiety over food, drink, clothes
        (6:25a–b)[3]
        First rhetorical question (6:25c)[4]
          First illustration: God cares for birds (6:26a–c)
        Second and third rhetorical question (6:26d–27)
          Second illustration: God's care for flowers (6:28–29)
        Fourth rhetorical question (6:30)
      Second prohibition of anxiety over food, drink, clothes
        (6:31–32)
  Command to seek God's kingdom first (6:33)
Prohibition of anxiety about the future (6:34)

Message

In Matt. 6 Jesus addresses two matters, hypocrisy in religious activity (6:1–18) and covetous anxiety (6:19–34). The first part of the chapter explains and enjoins the proper practice of religious duties, and the

---

1. The two prohibitions use μή plus the present imperative and the aorist subjunctive respectively in 6:19 and 6:34.

2. The two positive commands in 6:20, 33 both use the present imperative with δέ.

3. This text prohibits anxiety by the use of μή plus a form of μεριμνάω three times—the present imperative in 6:25 and the aorist subjunctive in 6:31, 34.

4. The first, second, and fourth rhetorical questions (6:25c, 26d, 30) begin with οὐχί, οὐχ, and οὐ respectively and thus expect a positive answer (BDF §220; Moulton and Turner 1963: 282–83). Each of these three questions contains a type of lesser-to-greater logic. The third (6:27) is more of a direct question and expects the negative answer "no one."

second part stresses the proper priorities in caring for one's worldly needs (Blomberg 1992b). Both parts of the chapter call upon disciples to put God first. W. Davies and Allison (1988: 648) ask, "Having prayed the prayer of Jesus, how could one remain anxious?" Disciples are taught in 6:1–18 to live for the Father's approval, not their peers' applause. Disciples are taught in 6:19–34 that their heavenly Father's care for them is much greater than his care for birds and flowers. If disciples seek the Father's kingdom first, their needs will be met (cf. Lev. 25:18–22; Ps. 127:2; Isa. 32:17; Phil. 4:6–7; 1 Tim. 6:6–10; Heb. 13:5; 1 Pet. 5:7). They will receive that for which they did not seek. But ironically, if they seek first to meet their own needs, they will not be different from the pagans, who do not have a God who knows what they need. They will never have enough.

The unit may be outlined as follows:

a. God or greed? (6:19–24)
   i. Earthly and heavenly treasures (6:19–21)
   ii. Necessity of a clear perspective (6:22–23)
   iii. Incompatibility of discipleship and greed (6:24)
b. Kingdom or anxiety? (6:25–34)
   i. Anxiety and God's care for birds (6:25–27)
   ii. Anxiety and God's care for flowers (6:28–30)
   iii. Incompatibility of discipleship and anxiety (6:31–34)

Exegesis and Exposition

[19]"Do not store up for yourselves treasures on earth, where moth and rust destroy and where thieves break in and steal. [20]But store up for yourselves treasures in heaven, where neither moth nor rust destroy, and where thieves do not break in and steal; [21]for where your treasure is, there your heart will be also. [22]The lamp of the body is the eye; so, then, if your eye is healthy, your whole body will be full of light. [23]But if your eye is bad, your whole body will be full of darkness. If, then, the light that is in you is darkness, how great is the darkness! [24]No one can serve two masters; for either he will hate the one and love the other, or he will be loyal to one and despise the other. You cannot serve both God and wealth.

[25]"For this reason I tell you, do not worry about your life, about what you will eat ⌜or what you will drink⌝, nor about your body, about what you will put on it. Is not life more than food, and the body more than clothes? [26]Look at the birds of the air, that they do not sow or reap or gather into barns, yet your heavenly Father feeds them. Are you not worth much more than they? [27]And who of you by worrying can add even one hour to his life? [28]And why are you worried about clothing? Notice how the flowers of the field ⌜grow; they do not toil or make clothes⌝, [29]yet I tell you that not even Solomon in all his glory clothed himself

like one of these. [30]But if God so clothes the grass of the field, which is alive today and tomorrow is thrown into the furnace, will he not much more clothe you? You of little faith! [31]So do not worry, saying, 'What will we eat?' or, 'What will we drink?' or, 'What will we wear?' [32]for the Gentiles seek all these things. For your heavenly Father knows that you need all these things. [33]But seek first ⌜the kingdom of God and his righteousness⌝, and all these things will be added to you. [34]Therefore do not worry about tomorrow; for tomorrow will care for itself. Each day has enough trouble of its own."

a. God or Greed? (6:19–24)

i. Earthly and Heavenly Treasures (6:19–21)

6:19–21   These verses (cf. Luke 12:33–34) contain a prohibition against the hoarding of earthly treasures (6:19), followed by a positive command for the accumulation of heavenly treasure (6:20), backed up by an explanation that one's heart will inevitably be devoted to what one treasures (6:21). Heavenly treasure (cf. 13:44) is not susceptible to destruction by moths (cf. Isa. 50:9; 51:8; Job 4:19; James 5:2–3) or to other decay (βρῶσις, brōsis, eating; cf. Isa. 51:8 again) or to theft (cf. Ezek. 12:5, 7; Matt. 24:43) as earthly treasure is.[5] The "eating" spoken of here probably refers to insects, but rust, dry rot, or some other type of decay cannot be ruled out. The point is that heavenly treasure alone should be the focus of our heart, since it alone can provide genuine security and permanence (Matt. 13:52; 19:21; cf. Luke 12:16–21; 1 Tim. 6:18–19). Our heart (cf. Matt. 5:8, 28) is our inner intellectual and volitional core, the source of our deeds (cf. 15:17–20). Human finiteness alone, not to mention the exacerbating effects of sin, makes it very difficult to focus our heart solely on God and not on our possessions (cf. 6:24). Our heart is inevitably drawn to what we value most, and if kingdom values (cf. 5:3–10) are the priority, we are indeed laying up treasure in heaven. Seeking heavenly treasure, however, does not amount to avoidance of earthly involvement. Treasure in heaven is probably metonymy for treasure with God (cf. Luke 15:18). Disciples of Jesus long for the eventual rule of heaven's values on earth, and in the meantime they work to implement those values "on earth as it is in heaven" (Matt. 6:9–10).

5. Βρῶσις commonly means "eating" (Rom. 14:17; 1 Cor. 8:4; 2 Cor. 9:10; Col. 2:16) and even what is eaten, a meal (John 4:32; 6:27, 55; Heb. 12:16). But here it evidently refers to a process of decay or deterioration by uncertain means. There may be hendiadys of βρῶσις and σής, implying insect consumption. Or perhaps the inevitable eventual decay of material goods is in view. See BDAG 184–85. But in Isa. 51:8 the verbal cognate of βρῶσις appears twice, as does the noun σής. It is likely, then, that Matt. 6:19–20 alludes to Isa. 51:8 and that insect infestation is the cause of the decay. The context of Isa. 51 concerns the pursuit of righteousness (51:1) and the law (51:7), the comfort of Zion (51:3), and the function of Israel as a light to the Gentiles (51:4). These themes are certainly part of Matthew's theological agenda. Finally, Isa. 51:8 contrasts God's righteousness and salvation with transient human enemies of Israel, who will become moth-eaten. This contrast (cf. Isa. 51:6) is compatible with that of Matt. 6:19–20.

ii. Necessity of a Clear Perspective (6:22–23)

The metaphor of the eye (cf. Luke 11:34–36) is difficult. This proverbial   **6:22–23**
statement about the eye being the body's lamp is followed by two opposite
scenarios that result from good or bad eyesight. Good eyesight illumines
one's whole life whereas poor eyesight is a great hindrance.[6] In ancient
times it was believed that the eye was a source from which light emanated, interacted with objects illumined by the sun, and then returned
to the person (Allison 1987a; H. Betz 1985: 71–87). But Jesus is speaking
metaphorically. Matthew 6:23 may allude to the "evil eye," a source of
greed and avarice according to ancient Near Eastern culture (Bridges
2001; Hagner 1993: 158; R. Roberts 1963; cf. Deut. 15:9; 28:54, 56; Prov.
23:6; 28:22; Matt. 20:15; Mark 7:22; *m. 'Abot* 2.12, 15; 5.16, 22).

Given what precedes (the heart is where the treasure is) and what
follows (the dilemma of two masters), this difficult saying means that a
proper view of possessions is basic to kingdom values. An evil eye will
hoard earthly possessions only to see them decay. A "healthy" (ἁπλοῦς,
haplous, single, sincere; BDAG 104; Syreeni 1999) eye will not look
with envy upon others' decaying wealth but will clearly see kingdom
values and store up undecaying treasures in heaven. Matthew 6:23b is
an exclamation about the perversely ironic situation in which one's eye,
which should provide light (metaphorically, proper values), provides
only darkness (metaphorically, greed and envy). This last comment is a
call to self-examination (W. Davies and Allison 1988: 640). (See Zöckler
2001.)

iii. Incompatibility of Discipleship and Greed (6:24)

The practice of slavery underlies this verse (cf. Luke 16:13), which is   **6:24**
an example of chiasmus, or introverted parallelism.[7] A slave cannot
wholeheartedly serve two masters, since slavery demands the undivided
attention of the slave to the master. If there are two masters, their demands will be incompatible. Similarly, Jesus's disciples cannot divide
their loyalties between heavenly and earthly values. The use of the polar
opposites "love" and "hate" reflects a Semitic idiom that should not be
unduly pressed (cf. Luke 14:26). The point is that the slave will inevitably
love and be devoted to one master more than the other (cf. Matt. 10:37).

6. Allison 1987a argues that whereas modern people view the eye as a receptor of light,
ancient people viewed it as a projector of light. This may make better sense of 6:23.
7. The parallel structure is as follows, with a literal translation in brackets:

   A Οὐδεὶς δύναται δυσὶ κυρίοις δουλεύειν [No one is able two lords to serve;]
      B ἢ γὰρ τὸν ἕνα μισήσει καὶ τὸν ἕτερον ἀγαπήσει, [for either the one he will hate
         and the other he will love,]
      B′ ἢ ἑνὸς ἀνθέξεται καὶ τοῦ ἑτέρου καταφρονήσει. [or to one he will be devoted
         and the other he will despise.]
   A′ οὐ δύνασθε θεῷ δουλεύειν καὶ μαμωνᾷ. [You are not able God to serve and
      wealth.]

Divided loyalty is impossible—a disciple cannot be the loyal slave of both God (producing heavenly treasure) and wealth (producing earthly treasure).[8] God's kingdom demands exclusive loyalty, as Jesus reminded Satan (4:10, citing Deut. 6:13). One's devotion to it must be single-minded. This is emphasized further by the switch from the third person to the second person in the last clause of 6:24. (See Brennecke 1997.)

b. Kingdom or Anxiety? (6:25–34)

There is a subtle transition from greed in 6:19–24 to anxiety in 6:25–34 (Gundry 1994: 115). These verses begin with a general prohibition against worrying about life. Two (or perhaps three; see the additional note on 6:25) staples of everyday life are singled out to explain what is meant by "life"—what one eats and what one wears (6:25). God's provision of food is then stressed in 6:26–27, and of clothing in 6:28–30, before the general prohibition against worry is restated in 6:31 and again in 6:34 (cf. Luke 12:22–31). Rhetorical questions underline the incompatibility of anxiety with faith (Matt. 6:25, 26, 30) and stress its impotence (6:27). For an analysis of the structure of this section, see the structural-analysis chart in the introduction to 6:19–34, above.

i. Anxiety and God's Care for Birds (6:25–27)

6:25–27 If one cannot serve God and money (6:24), then one cannot be anxious for the material things that money can buy. The first of three prohibitions[9] sets the agenda for the entire paragraph of 6:25–34—the disciple must not be anxious over "life." This general term stands for the material goods that support life: food, drink (see the additional note on 6:25), and clothing.[10] Food and drink appear separately in 6:25a and 6:31, but in 6:25b–26 food alone is mentioned. The prohibitions here are about undue anxiety that does not take note of the Father's loving care for his

---

8. Wealth is μαμωνᾶς, from מָמוֹן, used for "wealth" or "property." See Luke 16:9, 11, 13; *m. 'Abot* 2.17; CD 14.20; 4Q266 frg. 10.1.14; 1QS 6.2; 1Q27 frg. 1.2.5; and Jastrow 1971: 794 for rabbinic use. Second Temple Judaism could acknowledge wealth as a divine blessing (Let. Aris. 204–5; *m. 'Abot* 4.9) but was also aware of its dangers for God's people. See Matt. 19:22–26; Sir. 31:8–11; 1 En. 63.10; 94.8; 96.4; 97.8; 1QS 10.18–19; 11.2; CD 4.17; 8.7. Serving wealth is just as incompatible with serving God as is serving idols (Nolland 2005: 304; cf. Exod. 20:5; 34:14; Deut. 4:23–24; 5:8–9; 6:14–15).

9. As noted in the footnotes to the structural-analysis chart, the first prohibition uses the present imperative and the second and third use the aorist subjunctive. In cases such as this, it is difficult to maintain the simplistic distinction (as in Dana and Mantey 1955: 301–2; Moulton and Turner 1963: 74–78) between present imperative as forbidding the continuance of action and aorist subjunctive as forbidding the initiation of action. Wallace's discussion (1996: 723–25) is more nuanced, but one still wonders whether there is any semantic difference between these three prohibitions.

10. The word translated "life" is ψυχή, which here of course describes not the soul but life or living itself, as enhanced by food and clothing. Cf. 2:20; 20:28; Luke 12:22–23; and BDAG 1098–99.

disciples (cf. 10:19; Luke 10:41; 12:11, 22, 26; Phil. 4:6), but believers should have a proper concern for one another (1 Cor. 7:32–34; 12:25; Phil. 2:20)

Three rhetorical questions underline the prohibition against worrying. The first (Matt. 6:25d) queries whether life is more than food and clothing. The implication is that the God who gives life can easily supply the means to sustain it (cf. 4:4; Prov. 30:8–9).[11] The second question (6:26) is based on a command to observe the birds and calls on the disciple to reflect on God's providential care for birds, which do not work to grow their food, let alone grow anxious over it (cf. Matt. 8:20; 13:32; Job 38:41; Pss. 104:27–30; 147:9; Ps. Sol. 5.9–10). The argument is *a minori ad maius*, from the lesser to the greater, a common pattern in rabbinic texts, where it is called *qal wahomer* (light and heavy; cf. Matt. 6:30).[12] Evidently assuming the Genesis narrative of humanity's creation in God's image, Jesus asks whether humans are not of more value than birds (cf. Matt. 10:31; 12:12). This reasoning is even more striking if Jesus has in mind unclean birds such as ravens (Lev. 11:15; Deut. 14:14). The third question (6:27) is stated bluntly without an accompanying illustration. It highlights the obvious: worry is impotent to lengthen one's life.[13] This question's power lies in its absurdity—of course worry cannot add an hour to one's life. Worrying may actually shorten life. It is not likely that this question speaks of adding a cubit to one's stature (BDAG 812; Luz 1989: 406). The word ἡλικία (*hēlikia*), here translated "life," usually refers to length of days or age rather than the height of one's stature (BDAG 435–36). Πῆχυς (*pēchys*, literally, forearm), here translated "hour," does indeed refer to a cubit, which was about eighteen inches long, but this does not seem to make sense in this context, even as hyperbole. Words for space measurements can be used metaphorically as time measurements (Ps. 39:5; cf. Sir. 30:24; BDAG 812), and this makes better sense here (H. Betz 1995: 475; W. Davies and Allison 1988: 652–53).

ii. Anxiety and God's Care for Flowers (6:28–30)

These verses turn from worry about food to worry about clothing (cf. 6:25) by using a lesser-to-greater argument as in 6:26. Disciples are commanded to learn from God's providential care for flowers (cf. Gos. Thom. 36), which, apart from even a moment of work, are more beautiful than

6:28–30

---

11. W. Davies and Allison (1988: 648) describe the logic here and in 6:26 (cf. 6:30) as from the lesser to the greater. But here in fact it is the opposite, from the greater to the lesser. God, who gives life and a body to the disciples, has no problem with supplying food and clothes.

12. Rabbinic tradition ties the formulation of this method of legal reasoning to Rabbi Hillel, who flourished just before the time of Jesus. Hillel's seven exegetical rules begin with קַל וָחוֹמֶר. See Mielziner 1968: 123–41.

13. More accurately, it is humans who are impotent to lengthen their lives "by worrying." The participle μεριμνῶν is instrumental.

King Solomon in all his royal splendor (Matt. 6:28–29; cf. 1 Kings 3:13; 4:20–34; 7:1–51; 10:14–29; Carter 1997c). The rhetorical question in 6:30 leads disciples to reflect on God's wonderful providence. If God so clearly cares for plants,[14] which have such a short life span (cf. Pss. 37:2; 90:5–6; 102:11; 103:15–16; Isa. 40:6–8; James 1:10–11; 1 Pet. 1:24–25), will God not care much more for the disciples of his beloved Son?[15] Hesitation in responding positively to this question is due to "little faith." This expression (ὀλιγόπιστοι, oligopistoi) occurs in other challenges to the disciples in Matthew (8:26; 14:31; 16:8; 17:20). It shows that the disciples need to strengthen their genuine though insufficient commitment to the values of the kingdom.

iii. Incompatibility of Discipleship and Anxiety (6:31–34)

6:31–32 These verses repeat the prohibition from 6:25, summarize the reasons of 6:26–30, and draw a conclusion (οὖν, oun, therefore). Disciples must not ask what they will eat, drink, or wear (6:31),[16] since these questions are like those of pagan Gentiles, who do not realize that they have a heavenly Father (cf. 5:45, 48; 6:1, 4, 6, 8, 9, 15, 18, 26) who knows their needs (cf. 6:8; 7:11). The Greco-Roman deities were notorious for capricious actions. Devotees of these gods had to wonder whether their gifts and offerings had appeased the gods and rendered them benevolent (cf. Acts 14:8–18; 28:1–6). This is not the case with the disciples' heavenly Father, whose love and concern are trustworthy and unchanging. Previously Jesus stated that the practice of loving only one's friends was unacceptable for his disciples, since it was acceptable pagan conduct (5:47). He also contrasted the proper way for his disciples to pray with the prayers of pagans who thought they needed to pray verbosely in order to obtain their gods' attention (6:7). Now he points out similarly that worry over food and clothing is similarly unacceptable. The point is that "worry is practical atheism and an affront to God" (Mounce 1985: 58). The heavenly Father who loves even his enemies certainly also cares for his disciples, and they must respond by loving their enemies and trusting their Father to meet their needs.

6:33–34 The positive command in 6:33 balances the prohibition in 6:31. In contrast (δέ, de) to the anxieties of the pagans, Jesus's disciples must have

14. The word in 6:30 is not κρίνα (flowers) as in 6:28 but χόρτον (grass; cf. Isa. 40:6–8), since the point is not now the beautiful "clothing" of plants but their short existence. See Dillon 1991.

15. קַל וָחֹמֶר (lesser to greater) reasoning has already been explained in the comments on 6:27 (for reasoning from greater to lesser, see the third footnote to the comments on 6:25–27). Here it is explicitly expressed by πολλῷ μᾶλλον, which occurs several times in Pauline arguments. See Rom. 5:10, 15, 17; 1 Cor. 12:22; 2 Cor. 3:9, 11; Phil. 2:12; and also Heb. 12:25.

16. These are genuine deliberative questions that seek information (Wallace 1996: 465–68), not rhetorical questions like those Jesus uses in this context.

as their primary concern God's kingdom and the upright lifestyle (Yri in Carson 1992: 96–105) that accompanies it. Paradoxically, if the disciples put God's interests first, God will give[17] them all the food and clothing they need (cf. Schmidt 1988 and an even more profound paradox in 16:25). On the other hand, worrying does nothing except marginalize God and his kingdom. Prayer for the realization of God's kingdom and will on earth (6:10) must be linked with the disciple's own efforts to realize its greater righteousness (5:20). Whereas the disciples' needs may be met only partially during the present life (5:3–10; 6:11), they will receive an abundant reward when the kingdom comes in its fullness (19:28–29). On 6:25–33, see Dillon 1991; Steinhauser 1990.

The conclusion of this section (οὖν, *oun*) returns to the previous prohibitions of anxiety (6:25, 31): tomorrow's food and clothing are not the disciple's concern (6:34). Disciples must address themselves to today's concerns (cf. 6:11) while believing that tomorrow is in the hands of the loving heavenly Father (cf. Prov. 27:1; James 4:13–15). This passage does not teach that the disciple will receive food and clothing automatically without planning and work. Rather, such planning and work must not be motivated by, or lead to, the anxiety that distracts from first things—God's kingdom and righteous standards. When God's disciples put first things first, God will meet their needs for sustenance and clothing.

According to Matt. 6, religious duties are to be performed in secrecy (6:1–18), and devotion to kingdom values is to be carried out in singleness of mind (6:19–34). Human applause is fleeting and worry is futile. Kingdom life must be lived in the audacious belief that it simply does not matter whether anyone but God knows and cares about the disciple's devotion and needs. Without such belief and the lifestyle that flows from it, hypocrisy and anxiety will be the rule.

The Father expects his children to put him first, but he delights in meeting their needs. Disciples must not permit their needs to dominate their prayers, their thoughts, and their activities. That is immaturity. But neither must disciples think that God does not care about their needs. That is unbelief. Disciples must prioritize their allegiance to God, his rule, and his righteous standards. In so doing, they will receive all they need to eat and wear as fringe benefits. But if they prioritize their own needs in their prayers and activities, they will never experience the joy of resting in the Father's care and provision. As the translator of the familiar hymn by Carolina Sandell Berg puts it,

Children of the heavenly Father safely in his bosom gather;
Nestling bird nor star in heaven such a refuge e'er was given.

17. The future passive is a divine or theological passive, an understated way of expressing God's agency. See Wallace 1996: 437–38.

God's care for his own does not necessarily guarantee an easy life filled with luxuries (cf. 5:10–12; 10:16–39; 24:9–13). God's care for his own may entail poverty for some and wealth for others. Wealthy Christians are not necessarily greedy, and poor Christians are not necessarily free of anxiety about possessions.

Additional Notes

6:25. The words ἢ τί πίητε (B and many other witnesses) are omitted by ℵ and a few other witnesses, evidently to bring this verse into conformity with Luke 12:22. But the shorter reading is unlike 6:31 (contra Metzger 1994: 15). *Byz* and many other witnesses begin the debatable phrase with καί instead of ἤ. The lack of preponderance of either internal or external evidence renders a decision on these questions very difficult.

6:28. The third-person plural verbs in this verse (αὐξάνουσιν . . . κοπιῶσιν . . . νήθουσιν, attested by ℵ¹, B, and others) are found as third-person singular verbs in L, W, *Byz* (cf. Luke 12:27), probably because of the neuter plural subject κρίνα. Evidently, ℵ originally read οὐ ξένουσιν οὐδὲ νήθουσιν οὐδὲ κοπιῶσιν, which would result in the translation "They do not comb, they do not spin, they do not toil" (Metzger 1994: 15). The variant readings do not alter the general idea of the verse.

6:33. The textual tradition contains several variations on the wording of τὴν βασιλείαν [τοῦ θεοῦ] καὶ τὴν δικαιοσύνην αὐτοῦ, but the meaning of the verse is not appreciably altered by any of them. See Metzger 1994: 15–16 for further discussion.

5. Dealing with People (7:1–6)

Analysis

The connection of Matt. 7:1–11 (cf. Luke 6:37–38, 41–42) to the preceding context is not easy to discern. Carson (1984: 182) thinks that Matt. 7:1–5 is intended to prevent judgmentalism, which could come from the high standards previously laid out in the sermon. Matthew 7:6 then has a balancing effect on 7:1–5 (cf. France 1985: 143). Against some scholars (e.g., Boring 1995: 211; Calvin 1972: 1.227; Hagner 1993: 171), 7:6 should be understood, then, not as a detached unrelated saying but as a warning against gullibility, the opposite of judgmentalism (Carson 1984: 185; Gundry 1994: 122). Keener (1999: 240) aptly points out that this prohibition of judgmentalism is related to the previous command for forgiveness (6:12–15). Bruner (1987: 272–76) develops this idea more fully, noting the thematic unity between the warning against judgmentalism in 7:1–5 and previous teaching on mercy and nonretaliation in 5:7, 21–26, 38–48; 6:12, 14–15.

W. Davies and Allison view the connection as a transition from the proper use of money to the proper treatment of one's neighbor, both being social issues (1988: 688). They attempt to demonstrate a parallel structure between 6:19–34 and 7:1–12 as follows:[1]

1. Instruction:
   Exhortation (6:19–21; 7:1–2)
   Parable concerning the eye (6:22–23; 7:3–5)
   Second parable (6:24; 7:6)
2. Encouragement: The Father's care (6:25–34; 7:7–11; argument from lesser to greater)
3. Golden Rule (7:12)

Although the above analysis is not convincing, it does show a degree of structural connectedness between 6:19–34 and 7:1–12. In this approach, the body of the Sermon on the Mount contains instruction on the law (5:17–48), on duties related to the religious community (6:1–18), and on life in the wider world (6:19–7:12). The difficulties in understanding the connection of 7:1–6 to 7:7–11 and 7:12 will be discussed in the next section of the commentary.

---

1. W. Davies and Allison 1988: 626. The display of the text here differs from theirs but the substance of the analysis is the same.

Jesus's teaching on how to deal with people in 7:1–6 implicitly contrasts two extremes. First comes a warning against judgmentalism in 7:1–5. Then there is a brief warning against gullibility, the opposite of judgmentalism (7:6).

The unit outline is as follows:

a. Warning against judgmentalism (7:1–5)
b. Warning against naïveté (7:6)

Exegesis and Exposition

[1]"Judge not, so that you will not be judged. [2]For the way you judge others will be the way you are judged, and the evaluation you give will be the evaluation you get. [3]And why do you look at the speck that is in your fellow disciple's eye, but you do not notice the beam that is in your own eye? [4]Or how dare you say to your fellow disciple, 'Let me take the speck out of your eye,' when, look, there is a beam in your own eye? [5]You hypocrite, first remove the beam from your own eye, and then you will see clearly to remove the speck from your fellow disciple's eye. [6]Do not give what is holy to dogs, and do not throw your pearls to pigs, or they will trample them under their feet, and turn on you and tear you to pieces."

a. Warning against Judgmentalism (7:1–5)

This warning contains an initial prohibition (7:1) supported by eschatological motivation (7:2) and a humorous hyperbolic illustration (7:3–5) that points up the necessity of self-examination preceding any attempt to discern a fellow disciple's weaknesses.

7:1   This verse consists of a prohibition symmetrically balanced by a negative purpose clause stating what the prohibition intends to avoid, that not judging results in not being judged. One cannot assume that the use here of the present imperative in a prohibition is a command to cease what is already in progress rather than a command that forbids the future occurrence of something.[2] It may be, as W. Davies and Allison (1988: 668) suggest, that this teaching is intended to warn the disciples against being like certain Pharisees who are presented as being judgmental (9:10–13; 12:1–8; cf. Luke 15:1–2; 18:9–14). "You will not be judged" refers to God's judgment on the last day.[3] God alone can make ultimate judgments about people, and he does so through his agent Jesus, the Son of Man (cf. Matt. 7:21–23; 13:36–43, 47–50; 16:27–28; 19:28; 24:30;

---

2. The dual prohibitions in 7:6 use the aorist subjunctive, but one cannot assume that the prohibitions there are solely against future acts. See the discussion on 1:20, the first footnote at 6:25–27, and Wallace 1996: 723–25.

3. All three passive verbs in 7:1–2 (κριθῆτε . . . κριθήσεσθε . . . μετρηθήσεται) clearly imply divine agency and should be viewed as instances of the divine or theological passive (Wallace 1996: 437–38).

25:31; 26:64). This prohibition is closely related to previous commands that the disciples must seek reconciliation (5:21–26), love their enemies (5:43–48), and forgive those who injure them (6:12, 14–15; cf. 18:21–22). It amounts to a specific instance of the practice of the Golden Rule (7:12). But this prohibition of judgmentalism does not rule out the need for spiritual discernment (7:6).

Matthew 7:1 is certainly one of the most misquoted verses in the NT. The cause of ethical relativism is often supported by this text (cf. Nolland 2005: 317–18). But the Jesus of the Sermon on the Mount clearly would not deny the existence of moral absolutes from which one can make absolute statements about right and wrong, good and evil. Depending on the context, the words "judge" and "judgment" connote either analysis and evaluation or condemnation and punishment.[4] Discipleship inevitably requires discerning "judgments" about individuals and their teachings (e.g., 3:7; 5:20; 6:24; 7:6, 16, 20; 10:13–17; 13:51–52; 18:15–20). Jesus himself makes such judgments (e.g., 4:10; 6:2, 5, 16; 7:21–23; 8:10–12; 13:10–13; 15:14; 23:1–7). Jesus does not forbid here what he has commanded and exemplified elsewhere (Overman 1996: 99).

What is forbidden is a rigid, censorious judgmentalism that scrutinizes others without even a glance at oneself (7:3; cf. Ps. 18:25–26; Rom. 2:1; 14:10; 1 Cor. 4:5; 5:12; James 4:11–12; 5:9). Such a draconian standard will return to haunt the one who condemns others by it (Matt. 7:2; cf. 5:43–47; 6:14–15; 18:12–20, 32–35; cf. 2 Sam. 12:1–15; Sir. 18:20; *m. 'Abot* 1.6; 2.5; *m. Soṭah* 1.7). Jesus teaches that honest introspection is absolutely necessary for clear discernment and just moral judgments. Christian interpersonal judgments must be constructive, not retributive, since Jesus's disciples will not demand an eye for an eye and will love their enemies (Matt. 5:38–48; 18:15–20; cf. Gal. 6:1).

This verse explains (γάρ, *gar*, for) why judgmentalism is prohibited (cf. Mark 4:24; Luke 6:37–38). The two clauses of this verse are in synonymous parallelism. The motivation for stopping such judgmental activity (Matt. 7:2) is the prospect of *lex talionis*, punishment in kind (cf. 5:38; James 2:13). God will judge people by standards no less strict than those they use in judging other people. If one does not wish to be judged and punished harshly by God, one will not judge and punish fellow humans harshly. Therefore the behavior of Jesus's disciples is to be constantly oriented to the prospect of standing before divine judgment at the end (Strecker 1988: 143). **7:2**

The motivation provided by the warning of harsh divine judgment is here augmented by a pair of rhetorical questions that humorously present an absurd situation in which a disciple whose vision is obscured by a log[5] **7:3–5**

---

4. The verb κρίνω and the related noun κρίμα are used here. Cf. BDAG 567–69.
5. A δοκός is a massive timber beam used to support a roof or to bar a large door. Cf. BDAG 256.

attempts to remove a speck[6] from a fellow disciple's eye (7:3–4; cf. Luke 6:41–42a). The two questions stress the perverse tendency of humans to critique in others what they excuse in themselves. These questions are followed by a charge of hypocrisy (cf. Matt. 6:2, 5, 16; 15:7; 22:18; 23:13–15, 23, 25, 27, 29; 24:51) and a command to look honestly at oneself before one looks judgmentally at another (7:5; cf. Luke 6:42b).[7] The word ἀδελφός (adelphos, brother) evidently refers to a fellow member of the community of disciples, regarded as a family (cf. Matt. 5:22–24; 12:50; 18:15, 21, 35). Jesus's hyperbolic metaphors of the log and the speck refer respectively to blatant sins and minor shortcomings. How can someone whose vision is totally obscured render a just assessment of another person's minor vision problems (7:3), let alone attempt the delicate task of correcting the problem (7:4)? Jesus labels this absurd situation as hypocrisy and teaches that just judgment of others can be rendered only when one has first judged oneself (7:5; cf. 18:15–20; 1 Cor. 11:31; Gal. 6:1; James 4:11–12).

b. Warning against Naïveté (7:6)

7:6   This unique Matthean verse is enigmatic (Boring 1995: 212) unless viewed as a foil to 7:1–5 (cf. Nolland 2005: 321–23 for a discussion of various interpretations). It guards against gullibility, an attitude that is the very opposite of the one addressed in 7:1–5. The warning takes the literary form of chiasmus, or introverted parallelism (Moulton and Turner 1963: 345–47), since it seems likely that it is the swine that trample the pearls and the dogs that turn and bite.[8] Jesus's disciples must not be censorious (7:1–5), but neither must they be oblivious to genuinely evil people. It is quite unlikely that this verse concerns secret teachings that should be held back from outsiders (Gos. Thom. 93). The setting of this warning is not so much the Eucharist service (contra van de Sandt 2002; cf. Did. 9.5) as mission activity, which could pose grave dangers (Matt. 5:10–16; 10:16–39; 13:28, 39 [the devil is the enemy]; 23:34–35; 24:9). As in the parable of the pearl, the message of the kingdom is "what is

---

6. A κάρφος is an insignificant piece of foreign matter, perhaps a bit of straw or a splinter of wood. Cf. BDAG 510–11.

7. A chiastic structure appears in 7:3–5. Matthew 7:3 and 7:4 both speak first of a brother's speck and then of one's own log, but 7:5 reverses the order, speaking first of the log and then of the speck. The literary device points up the necessity of reversing the human tendency to focus on others' shortcomings rather than on one's own.

8. Matthew 7:6 may be displayed as follows, with a literal translation in brackets:

    A μὴ δῶτε τὸ ἅγιον τοῖς κυσίν [Do not give what is holy to dogs]

        B μηδὲ βάλητε τοὺς μαργαρίτας ὑμῶν ἔμπροσθεν τῶν χοίρων, [nor throw your pearls in front of pigs,]

        B′ μήποτε καταπατήσουσιν αὐτοὺς ἐν τοῖς ποσὶν αὐτῶν [lest they trample them with their feet]

    A′ καὶ στραφέντες ῥήξωσιν ὑμᾶς. [and turning around they may tear you in pieces.]

holy" (13:45–46; cf. Exod. 29:37; Lev. 2:3). Disciples must realize that the sacred message of the kingdom must be handled with discernment, since there are malicious people who will respond to the message with violence against the messengers.

In first-century Palestine most dogs were wild scavengers (Matt. 15:26–27; cf. 1 Sam. 17:43; 1 Kings 21:19; Ps. 22:16; Gal. 5:15; Phil. 3:2; 2 Pet. 2:22; Rev. 22:15; 1 En. 89.42), and pigs were viewed as unclean beasts (Matt. 8:32; cf. Lev. 11:7; Deut. 14:4–20; Acts 10:12–14). Their use here is as striking metaphors of those who contemptuously and viciously reject the message of the kingdom. This warning does not forbid evangelization of Gentiles (the gentile mission had not yet been mandated [Matt. 10:5; 15:24]). That would be in tension with the hints that Matthew repeatedly drops into his narrative about gentile receptivity to the kingdom (e.g., 1:3, 5–6; 2:2–12; 8:10; 15:28; 27:54) and would directly contradict the concluding pericope of the Gospel, 28:19–20. Rather, disciples are to be wary while preaching the message of the kingdom, since it is volatile truth that may polarize those who hear it (cf. 5:10–16; 10:16; 24:9; Acts 5:33–40; 6:8–8:3; 13:44–51; 16:19–40; 18:12–17; 19:23–41; 21:27–44; Titus 3:10–11; Heb. 10:32–34).

Jesus's disciples should be neither inquisitors (Matt. 7:1–5) nor simpletons (7:6). Neither censoriousness nor naïveté helps the church (cf. Kollmann 1997). Yet unless one has removed the log from one's own eye, one will not be able to discern the difference between a fellow disciple with a relatively minor problem and an enemy who will do great harm to the kingdom. If genuine introspection does not occur, a disciple may blunder on the side of judgmental hypocrisy or naive gullibility. Ignorance of oneself is often mixed with arrogance toward others (W. Davies and Allison 1988: 673), with disastrous results.[9]

---

9. For further studies of Matt. 7:1–6, see T. Bennett 1987; Couroyer 1970; Derrett 1988a; Lips 1988; Llewelyn 1989; Rüger 1969; von Lips 1988.

6. Prayer Encouraged (7:7–11)

The flow of thought between 7:1–6 and 7:7–11 (cf. Luke 11:9–13) is difficult to understand. None of the following approaches to the relationship between 7:7–11 and the preceding context is totally convincing. Discernment in dealing with people is stressed in 7:1–6 by warnings against two extremes, judgmentalism (7:1–5) and gullibility (7:6). Hagner (1993: 173) is right that on the surface, 7:7–11 is about prayer and has no obvious connection to the preceding or following contexts (cf. Hill 1972: 148; McNeile 1915: 91). Other scholars (e.g., Gundry 1994: 119, 123; Keener 1999: 245; Schweizer 1975: 172), however, attempt to find a connection in the common theme of how to treat people. If this is the case, the passage teaches that one must treat people with discernment—not judgmentally (7:1–5) or gullibly (7:6) but with the same generosity exhibited by the heavenly Father in answering prayers (7:7–11). In so doing, they must remember the Golden Rule and treat others as they would like to be treated (7:12). (See McEleney 1994.)

Perhaps the return to the theme of prayer (cf. 6:9–13) is intended to encourage the disciples about the Father's care for them despite the difficulties inherent in discipleship, both those previously mentioned and those, just mentioned, related to dealing with people (Carson 1984: 186). In this case, prayer is the disciples' resource as they aspire to the greater righteousness taught by Jesus from 5:21 to 7:6. Guelich (1982: 322–25, 77–79, following Bornkamm 1977–78) views all of 6:19–7:12 as an exposition of the life of prayer that sequentially treats the various petitions of the Lord's Prayer (6:9–13). Although this construal of the literary structure of 6:19–7:12 is dubious, the thematic unity of 7:7–11 (and, to a lesser extent, 6:19–7:6) is clear (cf. Luke 11:9–13; John 16:23–24).

An *inclusio* brackets Matt. 7:7–11 with the command "Ask, and it will be given to you" in 7:7 being answered by the promise "Your Father . . . [will] give to those who ask" in 7:11. As a whole, 7:7–11 is similar in structure to 7:1–6, with initial commands and promises containing divine passive future verbs (7:1–2; 7:7–8), followed by rhetorical questions that pose absurd illustrations (7:3–4; 7:9–10), and concluding with a resolution of the absurdities that provides the lesson to be learned by disciples (7:5; 7:11). There is a clear symmetry in the triple command and promise language of 7:7–8.[1]

Exegesis and Exposition

[7]"Ask, and it will be given to you; seek, and you will find; knock, and the door will be opened to you. [8]For everyone who asks receives, and the one who seeks finds, and to the one who knocks, the door is opened. [9]Or is there any man among you who will give his son a stone when he asks for a loaf of bread? [10]Or will he give him a snake when he asks for a fish? [11]If you, then, even though you are evil, know how to give good gifts to your children, how much more will your Father who is in heaven give good things to those who ask him!"

Each of the three commands of 7:7 is followed immediately by an appropriate promise. The three words "ask" (cf. 6:8; 18:19; 21:22), "seek" (cf. Acts 17:27; Deut. 4:29; Ps. 105:4; Prov. 1:28; 8:17; Isa. 65:1; Jer. 29:13), and "knock" collectively refer to prayer. The three commands use present imperatives that should be viewed as enjoining habitual, iterative prayer (Wallace 1996: 722). The three promises use future passive verbs that imply divine activity in answering the prayers (Wallace 1996: 437–38). The three additional promises of Matt. 7:8 repeat the language of 7:7 and stress the readiness of the heavenly Father to meet the needs of the disciples.[2] The paired triple constructions of 7:7–8 emphasize the reality of answered prayer. There are no exceptions—everyone who asks receives, albeit the Father determines how to answer the requests. Although verbose prayers are not appropriate (6:7), regular prayers are central to the spiritual discipline taught by Jesus.

The paired triple-command/promise structure of 7:7–8 is now supported by two rhetorical questions (7:9–10; cf. Luke 11:11–12) that lead to a lesser-to-greater argument (Matt. 7:11). Both rhetorical techniques have been used previously in the sermon: rhetorical questions in 5:13, 46, 47; 6:25–27; 7:3–4 and lesser-to-greater arguments in 6:26–30. Family imagery is the key to 7:9–11 (cf. 6:9). The questions of 7:9–10 vividly point out that human parents would not give their children a stone (cf. 4:3)

7:7–8

7:9–11

---

1. The following displays the step parallelism (Keener 1999: 244) of 7:7–8, with a literal translation in brackets:

7:7 Αἰτεῖτε καὶ δοθήσεται ὑμῖν, [Ask and it will be given to you,]
    ζητεῖτε καὶ εὑρήσετε, [seek and you will find,]
    κρούετε καὶ ἀνοιγήσεται ὑμῖν· [knock and it will be opened for you;]

7:8 πᾶς γὰρ ὁ αἰτῶν λαμβάνει [for everyone asking receives]
    καὶ ὁ ζητῶν εὑρίσκει [and the one seeking finds]
    καὶ τῷ κρούοντι ἀνοιγήσεται. [and for the one knocking it will be opened]

2. The first two of the three verbs expressing the promises in 7:8 (λαμβάνει and εὑρίσκει) should be understood as futuristic presents that emphasize the certainty of answered prayer (Wallace 1996: 535–37).

and a snake when they are hungry and ask for dietary staples such as bread and fish.[3] The if-then argument of 7:11 builds on the assumption of universal human sinfulness. Even though human parents are sinful, they nevertheless generally know how to meet their children's basic needs. How much more will the heavenly Father (who is not sinful) give his disciples good gifts! So prayer is encouraged all the more by the force of Jesus's *a minori ad maius* (lesser to greater) logic, which augments the threefold promise of 7:8.

The positive, gracious tone of 7:7–11 provides a welcome change from the many prohibitions that have preceded it. Commands have led to reassurance. Although kingdom standards are high, disciples should not be discouraged or anxious in pursuing them. Prayer is a strenuous quest. But God is not unaware of the disciples' needs and does not need to be persuaded to answer. God is infinitely better than the best of human parents, and God promises to supply the needs of his children when they habitually acknowledge their dependence upon him. A similar argument with feminine imagery is found in Isa. 49:15.

Matthew 7:7–11 is a sort of postscript to the model prayer in 6:9–13. The prayer teaches the right way to pray, and this passage inspires confidence that prayer will be answered. The model prayer builds on the truth that religious duties are to be performed for God's eyes only (6:4, 6, 18). Jesus has also assured the disciples that their heavenly Father knows what they need even before they can ask him (6:8, 32). The additional point of 7:7–11 is that the God who knows his disciples' needs will certainly answer their prayers (7:7–8) from the depths of his goodness (7:11; Strecker 1988: 148). Disciples are often tempted to think that God is unaware of their trials and needs. This absolutely mistaken notion is put to rest by 6:8, 32—"Your heavenly Father knows." Even when disciples realize that God knows their needs, they may still wonder whether God is able to answer their prayers. But 7:7–8 makes it clear that an answer is certain: "You will receive." And even when disciples believe that God knows and will answer, they may doubt that the answer is good. But a comforting affirmation of God's benevolence is provided by 7:9–11—"Your heavenly Father will give good gifts."

---

3. The language here (cf. 12:11) probably refers to a father (ἄνθρωπος) and his son (υἱός) in 7:9 but to children in general (τέκνα) in 7:11. Another approach would take ἄνθρωπος in 7:9 as generic or pleonastic (BDAG 82). Nevertheless, the analogy in 7:11 portrays God as πατήρ, the heavenly Father, as in the model prayer (6:9).

7. Summary of Biblical Ethics (7:12)

This verse (cf. Luke 6:31) should be understood as a conclusion to everything said since 5:17. The conjunction οὖν (*oun*, therefore) indicates that 7:12 draws a conclusion from the preceding thoughts. In a narrow sense, 7:12 can be understood to conclude from God's benevolent response to the wishes of his disciples that they should likewise do for others whatever they would like to be done for them. But in a wider and much more profound sense, 7:12 forms an *inclusio* with 5:17 and concludes the entire body of the sermon, which began there with Jesus's statement of his mission (W. Davies and Allison 1988: 685–86, 688–89). Jesus did not come to cancel but to accomplish the purpose of the law and the prophets, and so his disciples must live according to a scriptural ethic (Boring 1995: 213). The encapsulation of this ethic in 7:12 summarizes how Jesus wishes his disciples to fulfill the law and the prophets. Later the Great Commandment (Matt. 22:36–40) will similarly encapsulate the law by linking Deut. 6:5 and Lev. 19:18.

Exegesis and Exposition

[12]"Therefore, whatever you want people to do for you, do the same for them, for this is the law and the prophets."

The essence of the law and the prophets is that one should treat other humans just as one would like to be treated by them (cf. 19:19; 22:34–40; Luke 6:31). All of Jesus's teaching since Matt. 5:21 about the greater righteousness necessary for his kingdom (5:20) is summarized here by the Golden Rule. Similar "rules" may be found in Jewish and Greco-Roman literature of the period (W. Davies and Allison 1988: 686–88 provide examples) and in most other major world religions. The most famous Jewish parallel is attributed to Rabbi Hillel (*b. Šabb.* 31a). In an interview with a would-be proselyte, Hillel puts the matter similarly but in a negative fashion: "What is hateful to you, do not do to your neighbor: that is the whole Torah, while the rest is commentary on it. Go and learn it" (cf. Jospe 1990). The difference between Hillel and Jesus is not so much that Jesus positively transforms a negative Jewish saying, since some Christian sources (e.g., Acts 15:20 v.l.; Did. 1.2; Gos. Thom. 6) have a negative formulation and some Jewish sources have a positive formulation (Strecker 1988: 152; cf., e.g., Sir. 31:15; Let. Aris. 207; T. Naph. 1.6; 2 En. 61.1; cf. the negative formulation in Tob. 4:15). Rather, Jesus

7:12

sets this rule in the unique eschatological context of his own words and deeds, which manifest the nearness of the kingdom. The wellspring for Jesus's teaching is the Hebrew Bible (Lev. 19:18, 34; Exod. 23:4–5), and he brings it to its intended goal by setting its teaching in the context of his own definitive eschatological message.[1]

From 5:21 through 7:11, Matthew has summarized the definitive teaching of Jesus on several key areas of ethical and religious life. Matthew construes this definitive teaching as climactic in nature (5:17–20); a more profound ethical standard could not be conceived, in Matthew's view. The ethic is explained in the concrete contexts of obeying the Torah (5:21–48), practicing religious duties (6:1–18), dealing with material possessions (6:19–34), relating to people (7:1–6), and praying (7:7–11). If they have been inspired by the beneficence of their heavenly Father, disciples of the kingdom will be like him. And as their Lord Jesus has come not to abolish but to accomplish the purpose of the law and the prophets, so the disciples must be like him. These two themes meet in 7:12, where doing good to others (as the heavenly Father does; cf. 5:45–48) is identified as the quintessence of biblical ethics. The general statement of 7:12 condenses the thirty-nine books of the Hebrew Bible into fifteen Greek words (cf. Ricoeur 1990).[2]

With the summarizing statement of the Golden Rule in 7:12, the sermon's main body has concluded. Jesus has come not to abolish but to fulfill the law and the prophets (5:17), and he requires that his disciples do no less. The summation of the law as loving one's neighbor or doing for others whatever one would like them to do to oneself is therefore not a higher law that replaces the Torah but the true goal of the law (W. Davies and Allison 1988: 689–90). Paul's view is similar to that of the Matthean Jesus on this point: loving one's neighbor is the fulfillment of the law (Gal. 5:14; Rom. 13:8–9). Johannine texts also underline the centrality of love (John 13:34; 14:21–24; 17:26; 1 John 2:4–11; 3:11–18; 4:7–12, 19–21). The sermon now concludes with solemn warnings on the necessity of obedience to his teaching (Matt. 7:13–27).

1. On Hillel and Jesus, see Charlesworth and Johns 1997, esp. Alexander, pp. 363–88.
2. On the Golden Rule, see J. Fuchs 1991; Ricoeur 1990; Theobald 1995; Topel 1998.

8. Exhortation and Warning: True and False Religion Contrasted (7:13–27)

Matthew 7:13–27 presents an ethical dualism that vividly and repeatedly contrasts discipleship with antinomianism.

Ethical Dualism in Matt. 7:15–23

Matthew 7	Discipleship	Lawlessness
Two gates/ways (7:13–14)	Narrow gate	Wide gate
	Difficult way	Broad way
	Life	Destruction
	Few	Many
Two trees/fruits (7:15–23)	True prophets (implied)	False prophets
	Sheep	Wolves
	Good trees	Bad trees (thorns, thistles)
	Good fruit (grapes, figs)	Bad fruit
	Life (implied)	Judgment (fire)
	Doing the Father's will	Saying "Lord, Lord . . ."
Two builders/foundations (7:24–27)	Wise person	Foolish person
	Hears/obeys Jesus	Hears/does not obey Jesus
	House built on rock	House built on sand
	House stands during flood	House falls during flood

This contrast has roots in the Hebrew Bible (e.g., Deut. 11:26; 30:15, 19; Jer. 21:8; Pss. 1:1–6; 119:29–32; 139:24; Prov. 14:2; 28:6, 18). It is found in Second Temple Jewish literature (e.g., Wis. 5:6–7; Sir. 2:12; 15:11–17; 21:10; T. Ash. 1.3–5; 2 En. 30.15; 42.10; 2 Esd. [4 Ezra] 7:3–9; 1QS 3.13–4.26), early Christian literature (Did. 1.1; 2.2; 5.1,

Barn. 18.1), and rabbinic literature (*m. 'Abot* 2.9, 12–13; Sipre on Deut. 11:26; *b. Ber.* 28b).[1]

Matthew 7:13–27, the conclusion to the sermon, is divided by some scholars into four paragraphs: 13–14, 15–20, 21–23, and 24–27 (e.g., France 1985: 146; Hagner 1993: 181, 185; Lambrecht 1985: 184–85; Strecker 1988: 158, 164). But the judgment scene in 7:21–23 is clearly tied to the parabolic language of 7:15–20, since both paragraphs speak of false prophets (7:15, 22; cf. 24:5, 11, 24; Boring 1995: 217), whose evil deeds (7:17–19, 22) are known (7:16, 20, 23) and judged (7:19, 22–23). Therefore 7:15–20 (actions of the false prophets) is linked to 7:21–23 (words of the false prophets), and there are really only three sections in 7:13–27 (Guelich 1982: 384–85). W. Davies and Allison (1988: 693) demonstrate this in detail. As a whole, 7:13–27 constitutes a stern warning that presents two contrasting responses to the sermon in the form of three metaphors: (1) two gates/paths (7:13–14; cf. Luke 13:24); (2) two trees/fruits (Matt. 7:15–23; cf. Luke 6:43–46); and (3) two builders/foundations (Matt. 7:24–27; cf. Luke 6:47–49). The upshot of this section is that there is no middle ground, no third alternative between the obedience to Jesus that brings life and the disobedience that brings death.

The unit may be outlined as follows:

a. Two gates/ways (7:13–14)
b. Two trees/fruits (7:15–23)
c. Two houses/foundations (7:24–27)

Exegesis and Exposition

[13]"Enter through the narrow gate because ⌜the gate⌝ is wide and the way is broad that leads to destruction and there are many who are entering through it. [14]⌜How⌝ small ⌜the gate⌝ and how narrow the way that leads to life, and there are few who find it!

[15]"Beware of the false prophets, who come to you in sheep's clothing but on the inside are ravenous wolves. [16]You will recognize them by their fruit. People don't gather grapes from thornbushes or figs from thistles, do they? [17]Similarly, every good tree bears good fruit, but the worthless tree bears worthless fruit. [18]A good tree cannot bear worthless fruit, nor can a worthless tree bear good fruit. [19]Every tree that does not bear good fruit is cut down and thrown into the fire. [20]So, then, you will recognize them by their fruit. [21]"Not everyone who says to me, 'Lord, Lord,' will enter the kingdom of heaven. Only those who do the will of my Father who is in heaven will enter. [22]Many will say to me on that day, 'Lord, Lord, did we not prophesy in your name, and in your name cast out demons, and

---

1. For discussion of the background of the "two ways" theology, see Suggs in Aune 1972: 60–74; Rordorf 1972.

in your name perform many miracles?' ²³And then I will declare to them, 'I have never recognized you; get away from me, you who practice lawlessness.'

²⁴"Therefore everyone who hears these words of mine and carries them out ⌜will be like⌝ a wise man who built his house on rock. ²⁵And the rain fell, and the flood came, and the winds blew and beat upon that house; yet it did not fall, for its foundation was on rock. ²⁶But everyone who hears these words of mine and does not carry them out will be like a foolish man who built his house on sand. ²⁷And the rain fell, and the flood came, and the winds blew and beat upon that house; and it fell—and great was its collapse!"

a. Two Gates/Ways (7:13–14)

The statement of the quintessence of kingdom ethics in 7:12 has con-   **7:13–14**
cluded the body of the sermon. The only command remaining to be
obeyed is the threefold warning against disobedience. This section begins
with a command to enter by the narrow gate (7:13a; cf. Luke 13:24).
Then there are two symmetrical contrasting statements that support
the command. The first (Matt. 7:13b) explains that many (those who are
spiritually complacent) take the wide gate and broad road to destruction, evidently because this looks like the easy way. The second (7:14)
contrasts the few (those who are spiritually committed) who opt for
the narrow gate (cf. Ps. 118:19–20; Isa. 60:11, 18; 3 Macc. 5:51; 2 Bar.
51.10; 2 Esd. [4 Ezra] 7:6–9; Rev. 21:12–13, 15, 21, 25; 22:14) and difficult road to life (cf. Matt. 19:24).[2] The narrow gate and the difficult
road are metaphors for repentance and kingdom ethics, and the relative
few who find this route are the disciples. The difficult road may allude
to persecution (cf. 5:10–12; 10:16–23; 13:21; 24:9, 21, 29). "Finding" the
gateway to life pictures discipleship as an active search for the kingdom,
the opposite of the passive complacency that takes the easy way. "Life"
is the experience of eschatological fellowship with God in the future
kingdom (19:16–17, 23–24; cf. 18:8–9; 19:29; 25:46). "Destruction" is
the polar opposite, separation from God, which is hell (cf. 7:23, 27). On
7:13–14, see Denaux in Delobel 1982: 305–35; Derrett 1982.

It is difficult to know exactly how to picture the contrasting gates and
roads of 7:13–14 (W. Davies and Allison 1988: 697–98). It is possible that
the respective terms are simply parallel metaphors and refer to the same
thing (Guelich 1982: 388; cf. Isa. 62:10). Nevertheless, one need not press
the metaphors unduly to imagine that one travels the road and then comes
to the gate, but this reverses the order of the terms as they occur in the
text. It may be more helpful to picture a wall with a narrow gate and a
wide gate. One can easily enter the wide gate, and once one is inside,
the path (of antinomianism; cf. 7:19, 23, 26) is smooth. But suddenly, as

---

2. As discussed in the additional notes below, 7:14 begins with either ὅτι or τί. If ὅτι,
the symmetry between 7:13b and 7:14 is complete. If τί, the exclamation of 7:14 contrasts
with each point of 7:13b. See D. Black 1989b; G. Horsley 1990.

if a bridge has disastrously collapsed, one arrives in hell. The wide path that promised freedom has ended in separation from God. But when one takes the difficult step of entering the narrow gate, although the path of discipleship is very arduous, suddenly one is ushered into eternal life. The rugged path that threatened to destroy has ended in one's sharing in the life of God and his kingdom. Those who take the easy road find to their horror that it leads to the most difficult destination imaginable. But those who take the difficult path of the kingdom arrive joyously in the kingdom to experience life with the Father. Exegetical nuances aside, the contrast of the many and the few in 7:13–14 is sobering, to say the least. It motivates disciples to strive first to enter the narrow gate themselves and then to help others enter it by making disciples from all the nations of the earth (9:37–38; 28:18–20).

b. Two Trees/Fruits (7:15–23)

The second and most complex picture of contrasting responses to the kingdom is found in 7:15–23 (cf. Luke 6:43–46). The vivid imagery of this section is drawn from both animal (Matt. 7:15) and plant (7:16–20) life and is meant to portray the false prophets who endanger the journey of the disciples. These false prophets will not be recognized by Jesus, the eschatological judge (7:21–23).

The Chiastic Structure of Matt. 7:16–20

A ἀπὸ τῶν καρπῶν αὐτῶν ἐπιγνώσεσθε αὐτούς. (v. 16)
From their fruit you will recognize them.

B μήτι συλλέγουσιν ἀπὸ ἀκανθῶν σταφυλὰς ἢ ἀπὸ τριβόλων σῦκα;
They don't gather from thornbushes grapes or from thistles figs, do they?

C οὕτως πᾶν δένδρον ἀγαθὸν καρποὺς καλοὺς ποιεῖ, (v. 17)
Similarly, every good tree good fruit bears,

D τὸ δὲ σαπρὸν δένδρον καρποὺς πονηροὺς ποιεῖ.
and the bad tree evil fruit bears.

C′ οὐ δύναται δένδρον ἀγαθὸν καρποὺς πονηροὺς ποιεῖν (v. 18)
It is not able a good tree evil fruit to bear

D′ οὐδὲ δένδρον σαπρὸν καρποὺς καλοὺς ποιεῖν.
neither a bad tree good fruit to bear.

B′ πᾶν δένδρον μὴ ποιοῦν καρπὸν καλὸν ἐκκόπτεται καὶ εἰς πῦρ βάλλεται. (v. 19)
Every tree not bearing good fruit is cut down and into the fire it is thrown.

A′ ἄρα γε ἀπὸ τῶν καρπῶν αὐτῶν ἐπιγνώσεσθε αὐτούς. (v. 20)
So, then, from their fruit you will recognize them.

This section includes a clear *inclusio* with the warning of 7:16 repeated verbatim in 7:20. It is also likely that a symmetrical chiasmus can be detected, as the preceding display indicates. The initial command[3] A and the identical concluding A' (introduced by the inferential ἄρα γε, *ara ge*, so then) frame the passage. The rhetorical question B and iterative statement B' both express the worthlessness of plants that do not produce good fruit. The pairs CD and C'D' express positively and then negatively the inevitable connection between the quality of a tree and its fruit.

To stay on the straight and narrow way, disciples must exercise discernment   **7:15**
between the true (cf. 10:41; 23:34) and the false (cf. 24:11, 24) prophets who come to them. This section begins with the warning in 7:15a to beware of (cf. 6:1; 10:17; 16:6, 11–12) false prophets. The danger and deceptiveness of the false prophets are emphasized by comparing them to vicious wolves (7:15b–c; cf. Ezek. 22:27–28; Jer. 5:6; 23:2; Zeph. 3:3–4; John 10:12; Acts 20:29) that somehow appear as harmless sheep (Matt. 9:36; 10:6, 16; 25:33; 26:31; cf. Num. 27:17; Pss. 78:52; 100:3; 1 En. 89–90; John 10:1–30; 1 Pet. 5:2). Past false prophets would have been well known to Matthew's community from the Hebrew Bible.[4] Scholars have identified these false prophets as Jewish opponents, such as the Pharisees (Hill 1976: 343–48; Lagrange 1948: 152), the Essenes (Daniel 1969), or the Zealots (Cothenet in Didier 1972: 281–308). Strecker (1988: 161–62) argues that the warning is hypothetical and general, with no specific historical referent, but these false prophets are clearly involved in the Christian community. They are described as itinerants who come to Christian communities (7:15; cf. 10:11, 41; 23:34; 2 John 10; 3 John 7), and they claim to have done miracles in the name of Jesus their Lord. But their lives are characterized by lawlessness (ἀνομία, *anomia*; cf. Matt. 13:41; 23:28; 24:12; Davison 1985). Lawlessness is also the likely result of the teaching of future false prophets predicted by Jesus in 24:11–12 (cf. Jude 4). Matthew takes pains to portray Jesus as the ultimate teacher of the law rather than as one who came to destroy the law (Matt. 5:17–48). Therefore the false prophets who are warned against here should probably be viewed as libertines or antinomians. By the time of the writing of Matthew, such false prophets may have falsely invoked Paul as their patron.[5]

3. The future indicative ἐπιγνώσεσθε should probably be understood as imperatival, or less likely as gnomic. See BDF 183; Wallace 1996: 569–71.
4. Deut. 13:1–18; 18:14–22; Num. 22; 1 Kings 18:19; 22:6; Jer. 6:13; 8:8–12; 23:13–22; 28:15; 29:31; Lam. 2:14; Ezek. 13:2–16; 22:28; Mic. 3:5–7; Zech. 13:2–4; cf. 2 Bar. 66.4; Mart. Ascen. Isa. 2.12–15; Josephus, *Ant.* 8.236, 318; *J.W.* 6.285; 1QH 4.16; 11QT 54.8–18; 61.1–5; Matt. 24:11, 24; Mark 13:22; Luke 6:26; Acts 13:6; 2 Cor. 11:12–15; 1 Thess. 5:20; 2 Pet. 2:1, 15–16; 1 John 4:1; Rev. 2:20; 16:13; 19:20; 20:10; Did. 11–12; 16.3–4; Aune 1983: 222–29; Luomanen 1998b: 93–100.
5. The various views are briefly summarized in Hagner 1993: 182–83. The view that the false prophets were antinomian, which is the view I accept, is argued by G. Barth in Bornkamm, Barth, and Held 1963: 73–75, 159–64. Guelich (1982: 402–3), Gundry (1994:

7:16 The warning is followed by the basic instruction on how to detect the marauding wolves (7:16a). The notion of detecting the false prophets by their fruit entails an abrupt shift of metaphor from the animal kingdom to that of plants (cf. Luke 6:43–44).[6] The plant metaphor continues in 7:16b with a rhetorical question that highlights the folly of attempting to harvest grapes from thornbushes and figs from thistles (cf. Judg. 9:7–15). But even though the false prophets are pictured as thornbushes and thistles, they are found, as it were, in the vineyard, the community of the disciples, since they call Jesus Lord and minister in his name (Matt. 7:21–22; cf. 10:16; 24:11, 24).

7:17–19 Οὕτως (houtōs, thus; cf. 5:12, 16, 19; 6:9, 30; 7:12) indicates that 7:17 draws a comparison with 7:16. The imagery of 7:16 is the basis for the developed imagery of 7:17–19, where "good fruit" corresponds to the grapes and figs and the "bad tree" corresponds to the thornbushes and thistles. The same idea is stated first positively and then negatively in the parallel clauses of 7:17–18. Both good and bad (worthless, BDAG 852, 913) trees inevitably produce corresponding fruit (7:17);[7] it is impossible for them to do otherwise (7:18; cf. James 3:12). The fate of the worthless trees is explained in Matt. 7:19—they are chopped down and burned (cf. Ezek. 31:12; Dan. 4:14; Luke 13:6–9).[8] This imagery reminds the reader of John the Baptist's stern words about eschatological judgment (Matt. 3:8–10; cf. 13:40, 42, 50; 18:8–9; 25:41; John 15:6). Disciples (good trees) repent and obey Jesus (good fruit). Others (worthless trees) turn away from God and God's kingdom and live accordingly (worthless fruit).[9] Matthew 7:19 serves to connect the plant metaphor of 7:16–18 to the eschatological judgment scene in 7:21–23 (W. Davies and Allison 1988: 710).

---

133), and Hill (1976: 340) disagree. H. Betz (1995: 547–48) thinks that the theological position taken here is similar to that of the Torah-observant Jerusalem "pillars" against Paul's doctrine of justification by faith (cf. Gal. 2:1–10). Yet there is reason to think that Paul himself was slandered by antinomians (Acts 21:20–26; Rom. 3:8, 31; 6:1, 15; Phil. 3:17–19; James 2:14–26) and that there is an essential unity between the sermon and Paul on ethics (Carson 1984: 193; Gundry 1994: 133; Hagner 1993: 191–92).

6. On fruit as a metaphor for discernible behavior, see Isa. 5:2, 4, 7; Jer. 2:21; Matt. 3:8, 10; 12:33; 13:8, 26; 21:19, 34, 41, 43; John 15:2–8, 16; Rom. 7:4; Gal. 5:22; Eph. 5:9; Phil. 1:11; Col. 1:6, 10; Heb. 13:15; James 3:10–12, 18. Cf. Sir. 27:6; 2 En. 42.14; Gos. Thom. 45.

7. In 7:17–18 the generalization about two kinds of trees is expressed in three ways. The adjective πᾶς describes the category of good trees in 7:17a, but the generic article (Wallace 1996: 227) is used in 7:17b to make the categorical statement about bad trees. In 7:18 neither πᾶς nor the article is used; the construction is anarthrous and indefinite (Wallace 1996: 244).

8. The present tense verb ἐκκόπτεται is more likely gnomic than futuristic (Wallace 1996: 523).

9. The "bad" tree is σαπρός, which can mean spoiled or rotten. But here the point is that both the tree and its fruit are of inferior quality, unwholesome, or even evil, since the worthless fruit is described as πονηρός in 7:17b, 18a. Cf. Matt. 12:33; 13:48; Eph. 4:29; BDAG 852, 913.

This conclusion (ἄρα γε, *ara ge*, accordingly; cf. 17:26; Acts 8:30; 17:27)   **7:20**
repeats verbatim the words of Matt. 7:16a. The *inclusio* structure of
7:16–20 includes the initial statement of a thesis (7:16a) followed by supporting argument (7:16b-19) that brings one full circle back to the initial
statement, restated as a conclusion (7:20). The false prophets' sheeplike
appearance need not deceive the disciples because their true identity
can be ascertained by examining their deeds or works, metaphorically
described as "fruits." One's spiritual identity is determined not by what
one says but by what one does, because what one does inexorably reveals
one's heart. The truism holds: actions speak louder than words. The latter are empty and hypocritical when the former are missing. What one
does reveals who one is.

Jesus now turns from the works of the false prophets to their words (cf.   **7:21**
Luke 6:46; 13:25–27). The works must be discerned in the present by the
disciples (Matt. 7:15–20), but the words will be examined by Jesus at the
final judgment (7:21–23; W. Davies and Allison 1988: 711). The unique
sonship of Jesus (cf. 3:17; 17:5) will one day be exercised in his unique
role as the Father's eschatological judge.[10] This is the first of several times
in Matthew where Jesus refers to God as "my Father" (cf. 10:32–33; 11:27;
12:50; 15:13; 16:17; 18:10, 19; 20:23; 25:34; 26:29, 39, 42, 53).

On "that day,"[11] many (cf. "many" in 7:13; 24:11) will call Jesus "Lord,   **7:22**
Lord" (7:21; cf. 25:11; LXX: Esth. 4:17b; Pss. 108:21; 140:8) and claim
that they have prophesied (cf. Jer. 14:14; 27:15; 29:9), cast out demons
(cf. Matt. 4:24; 8:16, 31; 9:33–34; 12:24–29), and done many miracles in
his name (cf. 4:24; 8:3, 13; 9:6, 22; 10:1, 8; 11:4–5). Their problem is not
inactivity: there is fruit, but the fruit is not good or genuine (cf. 13:24–30,
36–43, 47–50). Only those who do the Father's will (6:10; 12:50; 21:31;
26:42; cf. CD 3.15–16; Jub. 21.2–3, 23) will enter the kingdom, and doing
that will cannot be identified with lawless behavior, even when it is accompanied by charismatic gifts.[12]

This verse applies the general principle of judgment (obedience to the   **7:23**
Father, 7:21) to the specific claim of charismatic activity (7:22). Jesus's
chilling response is that despite their claim, he never "knew" (cf. 25:12)

---

10. The agency of Jesus as divinely authorized eschatological judge is found in many NT
texts, e.g., Matt. 10:32–33; 11:27; 13:41–43; 16:27; 19:28; 24:29–31; 25:31–46; 26:64; 28:18;
cf. John 3:35; 5:19–29; Acts 10:42; 17:31; Rom. 2:16; 2 Cor. 5:10; Phil. 2:9–11; 2 Tim. 4:1, 8;
1 Pet. 5:4; Rev. 19:11. Perhaps Dan. 7, esp. 7:9–14, 22, 27, is the background for all this.

11. See this expression in 7:22; 24:19, 22, 29, 36, 38; 26:29; cf. 10:15; 11:22, 24; Isa.
2:20; 10:20; Hos. 1:5; Amos 8:9; 9:11; Zeph. 1:10, 15; Zech. 12:3; 13:1; 14:4; 1 En. 45.3;
Luke 17:31; 21:34; 2 Thess. 1:10; 2 Tim. 4:8.

12. It is clear from many biblical texts that supernatural phenomena must not be equated
with genuine faith and divine endorsement. Cf. Matt. 24:23–26; Exod. 7:11, 22; 8:7, 18;
Deut. 13:1–5; Acts 8:9–24; 13:6–12; 19:13–17; 2 Thess. 2:9–10; Rev. 13:13–15; Josephus,
Ant. 20.167–72. Other texts subordinate charismatic activities to humility and the exercise
of character-building gifts (Luke 9:51–55; 10:20; 1 Cor. 12–14).

the false prophets. He does not accept their addressing him as Lord, and he utterly renounces them as his followers. His lack of recognition or acknowledgment is akin to biblical passages where God's knowledge of his people implies a personal relationship, not merely an awareness of facts.[13] In terms of systematic theology, this is election (BDAG 201), not omniscience.

The last clause of 7:23 is an allusion to Ps. 6:8 (6:9 MT; cf. Pss. 119:115; 139:19; Matt. 25:41; Luke 13:27; 1 Macc. 3:6). Despite the cautions of W. Davies and Allison (1988: 718–19; cf. Davison 1985), the last phrase of Matt. 7:23 seems to be a key to the identity of the false prophets. It describes them as those who do iniquity or lawlessness (ἀνομία, *anomia*; cf. esp. 24:11–12 as well as 13:41; 23:28), which means that they take a lax view of the law and the need for obedience to it. Jesus came to fulfill the law (5:17–20), and so antinomians who disregard the law are not genuine disciples no matter how many spectacular deeds they perform. Jesus's disciples must be on guard against such counterfeit prophets, who would lead them away from the narrow road of repentance to the wide boulevard of lawlessness (cf. Davison 1985).

The plain words of 7:15–23 clearly distinguish between two kinds of fruit and two kinds of trees. This rejects any sort of "cheap grace," which teaches that the many who luxuriate on the broad path will somehow after all end up in the kingdom with those who make the rigorous trek of discipleship. The metaphor of fruit indicates that only an upright lifestyle is compatible with discipleship. Paul also frequently stressed the necessity of perseverance and good works (e.g., Rom. 2:13; 3:8; 8:25; 11:22; 13:14; Gal. 5:6; Eph. 2:10; 4:17; Col. 1:23; Titus 2:7, 14; 3:8, 14). But this teaching against antinomianism must not be distorted by legalistic and perfectionistic accretions.

One should not conclude from this warning against antinomian prophets that Matthew takes a consistently negative view of prophets and charismatic activities. Jesus himself is the prophet par excellence, and he commissions his disciples to prophetic word and deed (Matt. 10:1, 6, 8). Disciples should support such ministry, since reception of the prophets will bring them a reward equivalent to that of the prophets themselves (10:41). Jesus promises to send future prophets (23:34) whose destiny is to share in the persecution that their master and his other disciples would experience (cf. 5:12). Thus Jesus in Matthew repudiates antinomianism, not prophets per se (cf. Deut. 13:1–5; 18:14–22; Did. 7.8). The spiritual gift of charismatic activity is no substitute for the spiritual fruit of righteousness.[14]

13. Cf. John 10:14; 1 Cor. 8:3; Gal. 4:9; 2 Tim. 2:12, 19. See the use of יָדַע in such texts as Gen. 18:19; 2 Sam. 7:20; Pss. 1:6; 37:18; Jer. 1:5; Hos. 13:5; Amos 3:2; Nah. 1:7; 1 Chron. 17:18.

14. For further studies of Matt. 7:15–23, see H. Betz 1985: 125–57; Böcher 1968; Cothenet in Didier 1972: 281–308; Daniel 1969; Hill 1976; Légasse 1968; Marguerat 1981: 175–211; Minear in Gnilka (ed.) 1974: 76–93; Trites 1992.

c. Two Houses/Foundations (7:24–27)

In this concluding section of the sermon, the third picture of contrasting responses to the kingdom presents opposite approaches to home construction (cf. Luke 6:47–49). House building as a metaphor is found elsewhere in Scripture.[15] In light of Matt. 13:55 and Mark 6:3, it is plausible that Jesus had personal experience in house construction. As in the previous two pictures, the reality portrayed by the vivid language of the storm is the final judgment,[16] not the "storms of life's trials" (contra Augustine, *Sermon on the Mount* 2.24.87; H. Betz 1995: 566; Hendriksen 1973: 381). The picture of the two gates/ways portrays the end of life's journey as either life or destruction (Matt. 7:13–14). The picture of the two trees/fruits portrays the bad trees (false prophets, 7:15, 22) as thrown into the fire (repudiation on the last day, 7:19, 23). Here in 7:24–27 judgment is portrayed as a storm (cf. Prov. 10:25) and resulting flood where lives/houses either withstand or succumb to the scrutiny of divine justice.

This section is not unlike the covenantal blessings and curses that conclude the Torah (Meier 1980b: 75; Schweizer 1975: 190). These are conditioned upon obedience to Moses (Deut. 28:1–2, 15, 45, 58). Among the many curses are destructive rain and building a house but not dwelling in it (Deut. 28:24, 30). The rabbinic text 'Abot R. Nat. 24a has an antithetical parable that is remarkably similar to Matt. 7:24–27. This text was not compiled until 400 CE at the earliest, but it purports to transmit the teaching of a second-century CE sage.

Antithetical Parables of Divine Judgment (Matt. 7:24–27)

7:24–25

Prosaic Subject: Person who hears and does what Jesus taught (7:24a–b)

　Parabolic Predicate: Wisely builds house on bedrock, which withstands the storm and flood (7:24c–25)

7:26–27

Prosaic Subject: Person who hears and does not do what Jesus taught (7:26a–b)

　Parabolic Predicate: Foolishly builds house on sand, which is destroyed by the storm and flood (7:26c–27)

The parallel language in 7:24, 26 is an implied invitation to obey as well as a warning to those who refuse to obey.[17] As a whole, these verses

---

15. See Deut. 28:30; Ps. 127:1; Prov. 10:25; 12:7; 14:11; 24:3; Jer. 22:13–14; and esp. Ezek. 13:8–16, which denounces false prophets as those who build a defective wall that falls down during a storm. Sirach 22:16–18 uses building metaphors for wisdom, among them a wooden beam that will not be shaken by an earthquake. Contrast the metaphorical builders of shoddy walls in CD 4.19; 8.12, 18; 19.24, 31. See also 1 Cor. 3:10–15.

16. Cf. Gen. 6–7; Matt. 24:39; Ps. 66:10–12; Isa. 28:2, 17; 29:6; 30:27–30; Ezek. 13:10–16; 38:22; 1QH 3.14; 2 Bar. 53.7–12.

17. The syntax of this language differs slightly, but there is little, if any, semantic difference between the indefinite relative pronoun with indicative verbs in 7:24 (πᾶς οὖν ὅστις ἀκούει . . . καὶ ποιεῖ) and the participles in 7:26 (καὶ πᾶς ὁ ἀκούων . . . καὶ μὴ ποιῶν).

contain symmetrically antithetical statements alternating prose (7:24a–b, 26a–b) and poetry (parable; 7:24c–25, 26c–27) as shown above.

The conjunction οὖν (*oun*, therefore; cf. 5:19, 23, 48; 6:2, 8, 9, 22, 23, 31, 34; 7:11, 12) that introduces 7:24 makes sense as drawing an inference from the immediately preceding section about lawless false prophets. In this reading 7:24–27 contrasts discipleship, as hearing and wisely doing Jesus's teaching (7:24–25), with lawlessness, as hearing but foolishly not doing Jesus's teaching (7:26–27). Yet it may be that 7:24–27 is intended to draw a final inference from the entire concluding warning section of the sermon (from 7:13 on) or even from the body of the sermon as a whole (from 5:17 on).

7:24–25 In 7:24–25 the wise (cf. 10:16; 24:45; 25:2, 4, 8, 9) response of hearing and doing the words of Jesus (7:24; cf. 12:50; Luke 8:21; John 12:47; 13:12–17; James 1:22–25) is pictured as building a house on bedrock (Matt. 16:18; 27:51, 60; cf. 13:5, 20; Deut. 32:4, 18, 31; 1 Sam. 2:2; Pss. 18:2, 31, 46; 27:5) that withstands a storm (Matt. 7:25).[18] Elsewhere in Matthew hearing alone is not necessarily portrayed favorably (10:14; 13:19, 22; 15:12; 19:22), but doing is clearly approved (1:24; 3:8, 10; 5:19; 7:12; 12:50; 13:23). The rain, flood, and wind of the storm portray the rigor of divine judgment, but disciples who obey the sermon need not fear, since their lives are founded upon the bedrock of Jesus's words (cf. Prov. 12:7; 14:11).[19]

7:26–27 In 7:26–27 the foolish (cf. 5:22; 23:17; 25:2, 3, 8) response of hearing but not obeying the norms of the kingdom is pictured as building a house on sand, which collapses during a storm and a flash flood (cf. Job 8:15; Pss. 11:6; 83:15; Prov. 14:11; Isa. 28:15–18; Dan. 9:26; 1 En. 94.7). When the rains, floods, and winds (eschatological judgment) beat upon the house built on sand, it falls with a great crash. Sand is regularly used elsewhere as a metaphor not of instability but of innumerability (e.g., Rom. 9:27; Isa. 10:22; Rev. 20:8; cf. Gen. 22:17; Pss. 78:27; 139:18; 1 Macc. 11:1; Sir. 1:2). The obvious danger of building a house on such an absurdly unsuitable foundation underlines the horror of coming to total ruin at the final judgment. This unspeakable disaster can be avoided only by obeying the sermon.

Both the wise and the foolish builders hear the teaching of Jesus, which fulfills the law and the prophets not only as the present standard of ethics but also as the future standard of judgment. But hearing the teaching of Jesus is regarded as genuine only when it is accompanied by doing what Jesus says. The false prophets, whatever their appearance, are

18. The verb ὁμοιόω is regularly used to introduce parables (Matt. 11:16; 13:24; 18:23; 22:2; 25:1). Cf. the adjective ὅμοιος in 11:16; 13:31, 33, 44, 45, 47, 52; 20:1; 22:39.

19. "Flood" translates ποταμοί (rivers); the imagery here most likely portrays a flash flood in which a ravine (today called a wadi) that is dry in the summer becomes a raging torrent during a heavy winter rain (BDAG 856).

lawless. The wide gate, though attractive, leads to destruction. Houses built on sand collapse utterly under divine judgment, but houses built on rock withstand it. This metaphor rings true even today, since extreme weather regularly exposes shoddy craftsmanship and inferior building materials. But in Jesus's metaphor, the difference between wisdom and folly in building a life rests in simply obeying Jesus. Wise disciples act on what they hear from their master; foolish people complacently hear but do nothing. The former build an enduring house on rock; the latter, a doomed edifice on sand. Neither the ancient crowds who originally heard the sermon from Jesus nor the modern readers of Matt. 5–7 can dare to walk away unchanged, complacent. To do so is ultimately to not weather the storm, to be eternally separated from Jesus, to arrive in hell.[20]

Additional Notes

7:13. The words ἡ πύλη are absent from ℵ* and other witnesses, but external evidence overwhelmingly attests them. Some think that the words are interpolated here from 7:14, where they are better attested. But Metzger 1994: 16 is probably correct that the picture in both verses is of a road leading to a gate.

7:14. The first word of the verse includes a variant. It is hard to understand why ὅτι would be altered to τί if it were original. Despite strong external evidence for ὅτι, it is more likely that the verse is not an explanation of 7:13 but a contrasting exclamation in which τί stands for the Semitic exclamation מָה (cf. Luke 12:49; Pss. 133:1; 139:17). See BDF §299; BDAG 1007; Metzger 1994: 16. Another variant is the omission of ἡ πύλη again, as in 7:13, but in this verse Codex Sinaiticus includes the questionable words.

7:24. In some MSS, including the Majority Text, ὁμοιώσω αὐτόν (cf. 11:16; Luke 7:31; 13:18, 20) appears instead of ὁμοιωθήσεται (cf. Matt. 7:26; 25:1). The meaning is the same with either reading, but ὁμοιωθήσεται is better attested.

20. For further studies of Matt. 7:24–27, see Flusser 1981: 98–105; Heil in Carter and Heil 1998: 23–35; Hultgren 2000: 130–37; I. Jones 1995: 173–89; Knowles in Longenecker 2000: 285–305.

9. Narrative Conclusion: Amazement at Jesus's Authority (7:28–29)

The alternation of narrative and discourse blocks throughout Matthew is signaled at the end of each discourse with the recurring words "and after Jesus finished . . ." (rendered with some variation in our translation).[1] As is argued in the introduction to this commentary, this is probably the most distinctive structural element of Matthew's approach to telling the story of Jesus. The crowd's amazed response to Jesus's authoritative words in Matt. 5–7 anticipates their amazed response to his authoritative works contained in the following narrative (8:1–9:34; esp. 8:9; 9:6–8). The effect of this structure of alternating narrative and discourse is heightened by the "bookends" in 4:23 and 9:35.

Matthew 7:28 narrates the crowd's amazement, and 7:29 explains it. Their amazement at the authority of Jesus evidently came not so much from his clarity or bluntness as from his juxtaposition of his own views with statements from the Torah in the contrasts of 5:21–48. Jesus's teaching includes more than strict exegesis of Torah. He does not cite human authorities in support of his views. It is also clear from the immediately preceding context that Jesus speaks of himself as the agent (7:21–23), and of his words as the standard (7:24–27), of eschatological judgment. Such staggering claims indicate an authoritative mode of communication that puts Jesus above even Moses, who received the Torah from God on Mount Sinai. God's revelation of his ultimate law through the definitive eschatological teaching of Jesus the Messiah was even more astonishing than the awesome revelation to Moses (cf. Heb. 12:18–29).

Exegesis and Exposition

[28]Now when Jesus had ended these sayings, the people were astonished at his teaching, [29]for he was teaching them as one having authority and not like their legal experts.

7:28–29   Just as 4:25–5:2 led the reader from the narrative into the discourse, so 7:28–8:1 leads the reader out of the discourse back into the narrative. Both passages mention large crowds following Jesus and his respective ascent or descent of the mountain. The response of the crowd (cf. 4:25; 5:1) is amazement (7:28; cf. 13:54; 19:25; 22:33; cf. also 9:33;

1. Καὶ ἐγένετο ὅτε ἐτέλεσεν ὁ Ἰησοῦς occurs in 7:28; 11:1; 13:53; 19:1; 26:1.

15:31; 22:22); they are overwhelmed not by the rhetorical niceties of the teaching but because Jesus's uniquely authoritative way of teaching is so different from what they are used to hearing from their legal experts (7:29; cf. the commentary on 2:4). Evidently, scribal authority was tied to traditional sources: one's views were authoritative when tied to convincing citations of previous teachers (*m. 'Abot* 1.1; *y. Pesaḥ.* 6.1.33a). Jesus's teaching assumes a transcendent authority that their teachers rightly do not claim to possess. The pronoun "their" evidently distinguishes Jewish legal experts in general from Jewish legal experts who believe in Jesus (13:52; 23:34). Matthew does not mention whether the crowd engages Jesus with questions. Their mute amazement further underlines the unique authority of Jesus as the definitive teacher of the law (cf. 17:1–8), who expects a righteousness that is greater than that of the religious leaders (5:20).

This amazing authority of Jesus has only begun to impress the reader of Matthew. Matthew has yet to show that the deeds of Jesus are likewise authoritative (8:9; 9:6, 8) and that the disciples will soon receive similar authority for their early ministries (10:1). The source of Jesus's authority will become a major controversy between Jesus and the religious leaders (21:23–24, 27). An even fuller authority will ultimately be given to the exalted Jesus, and he will exercise it in commissioning his disciples for worldwide ministry (28:18–20).

I. Prologue/Introduction: Origin of Jesus the Messiah (1:1–2:23)
II. Early Days of Kingdom Word and Deed (3:1–7:29)
➤ III. Galilean Ministry Continues (8:1–11:1)
IV. Growing Opposition to the Kingdom of Heaven (11:2–13:52)

III. Galilean Ministry Continues (8:1–11:1)

Matthew presents the authoritative words of Jesus in chapters 5–7 and the authoritative deeds of Jesus in chapters 8–9. This sets the scene for the commissioning of the disciples in Matt. 10 for their own ministry of word and deed. Jesus's miracles have already been generally noted (4:23–24; cf. 8:16; 9:35), and now Matt. 8–9 presents selected specific miracles in order to demonstrate Jesus's authority (8:9; 9:6–8; Kingsbury 1978a). Matthew's tendency toward topical arrangement and the location of the parallel passages in Mark and Luke make it likely that some of these miracles actually occurred before the Sermon on the Mount.

Matthew 10 presents the second featured discourse of Jesus, the discourse on mission. The Twelve have seen Jesus's mighty words and deeds; now their own itinerant ministries to Israel begin as Jesus continues his ministry (11:1). The Twelve extend Jesus's ministry by announcing the kingdom and demonstrating its power. Their task will not be easy, since opposition will be fierce. But the reward for supporting the mission will be great.

A. Narrative 2: Three Cycles of Miracles and Discipleship (8:1–10:4)

The stories included in Matt. 8–9 are presented not haphazardly but carefully as key examples (Keener 1999: 258) of Jesus's authoritative deeds.[1] These instances of healing flesh out the summary statement of 4:23–24 (Nolland 2005: 348). In Matt. 8:2–9:34, three sets of three miracle stories[2] are interwoven with two sets of two discipleship stories. This is followed by a pericope stressing the need for more messengers of the kingdom (9:35–38). The overall emphasis is on faith, discipleship, and gentile mission. Scholars have noted that there are actually ten miracles in this section, since the story of the healing of the synagogue official's daughter in 9:18–26 has embedded within it the story of the healing of the hemorrhaging woman (9:20–22). Some have argued for an intended comparison between Jesus's ten miracles and Moses's ten plagues on Egypt (Teeple 1957: 82). The arguments for this are not at all convincing, but it is intriguing that the book of Exodus arranges the ten plagues as three sets of three leading up to the tenth climactic plague (Allison 1993b: 211). In any event, the structure of three cycles—each containing alternating stories about miracles and discipleship—remains, as the following analysis shows:

IA. Miracles: Three healing miracles (8:1–17)
IB. Discipleship: Two would-be disciples confronted (8:18–22)

IIA. Miracles: Three miracles (storm, demons, paralytic; 8:23–9:8)
IIB. Discipleship: Association with sinners, newness (9:9–17)

IIIA. Miracles: Three miracles (daughter/woman, blind men, demons; 9:18–34)
IIIB. Summary/transition: Plentiful harvest yet few workers (9:35–10:4)

---

1. Among the many helpful studies of this section are Burger 1973; Gatzweiler in Didier 1972: 209–20; Gerhardsson 1979; Heil 1979; Held in Bornkamm, Barth, and Held 1963: 165–299; Kingsbury 1978a; Légasse in Léon-Dufour 1977: 227–49; Luz in Hawthorne and Betz 1987: 149–65; Stewart-Sykes 1995; W. Thompson 1971; van der Loos 1965; Vledder 1997.

2. For a helpful summary of miracles in Matthew and suggestions for interpreting the miracle stories, see Boring 1995: 241–51. See further Held in Bornkamm, Barth, and Held 1963: 211–46; Hendrickx 1987; H. Kee 1983; Theissen 1983; van der Loos 1965.

1. Cycle 1: Three Healing Miracles and Two Would-Be Disciples (8:1–22)

Matthew 8–9 interweaves miracle stories with discipleship stories. In this first cycle, three healing miracles (8:1–17) lead into two stories about discipleship (8:18–22). Jesus's words have previously shown his authority (7:29). Now three therapeutic deeds involving the leper, the centurion's servant, and Peter's mother-in-law (8:1–17) confirm this authority (8:9; 9:6). Jesus's abrupt dismissal of the pair of would-be disciples at the end of the section (8:18–22) is in keeping with his authoritative teaching on the rigors of authentic discipleship.

a. Three Healing Miracles (8:1–17)

The three miracle stories that compose Matthew's first set are about a leper (8:1–4), a Roman centurion (8:5–13), and a woman (8:14–17).[1] The first and third stories are both about Jewish people, and both conclude with Scripture citations (Lev. 13:49; 14:2 in Matt. 8:4, and Isa. 53:4 in Matt. 8:17). Although the second story does not include a Scripture citation, it is nevertheless the featured story in this set because (1) it is longer than the other two; (2) it stresses the key theme of Matt. 5–9, the authority of Jesus (7:28–29; 8:9; 9:6; 10:1); and (3) it emphasizes the faith of a Gentile (8:10–12), another key Matthean motif.

The unit outline is as follows:

i. The leper (8:1–4)
ii. The centurion's servant (8:5–13)
iii. Peter's mother-in-law (8:14–15)
iv. Summary and biblical fulfillment (8:16–17)

Exegesis and Exposition

¹After Jesus had come down from the mountain, large crowds followed him. ²And suddenly a leper came to him and bowed down before him, and said, "Lord, if you are willing, you can make me clean." ³Jesus reached out his hand and touched him, saying, "I am willing; be cleansed." And immediately his leprosy was cleansed. ⁴Then Jesus said to him, "Make sure that you tell no one; but go, show yourself to the priest, and present the offering that Moses commanded for a testimony to them."

⁵And after Jesus had entered Capernaum, a centurion came to him, imploring him ⁶and saying, "Lord, my servant is lying paralyzed at home, terribly tormented." ⁷Jesus said to him, "I will come and heal him." ⁸But the centurion said, "Lord, I am not worthy for you to come under my roof, but only say a word, and my servant will be healed. ⁹For I am also a man under authority, with soldiers under my command. I say to one, 'Go!' and he goes, and to another, 'Come!' and he comes, and to my slave, 'Do this!' and he does it." ¹⁰Now when Jesus heard this, he was astonished and said to those who were following, "Truly I tell you, ⌜I have

1. Each of the three pericopes in this section has a similar introduction describing Jesus's activity. The first two begin with genitive absolutes, καταβάντος δὲ αὐτοῦ in 8:1 and εἰσελθόντος δὲ αὐτοῦ in 8:5. The third pericope begins in 8:14 with a similar adverbial participle construction, καὶ ἐλθὼν ὁ Ἰησοῦς.

found such great faith with no one in Israel." ¹¹I tell you that many will come from the east and the west and recline for a meal with Abraham, Isaac, and Jacob in the kingdom of heaven; ¹²but the sons of the kingdom will be cast out into the outer darkness, where there will be weeping and gnashing of teeth."

¹³Then Jesus said to the centurion, "Go; let it be done for you just as you believed." And the servant was healed that moment.

¹⁴And when Jesus came into Peter's house, he saw Peter's mother-in-law lying in bed with a fever. ¹⁵He touched her hand, and the fever left her; and she got up and began waiting on him. ¹⁶When evening came, they brought to him many who were demon-possessed; and he cast out the spirits with a word and healed all who were ill. ¹⁷He did this to fulfill what was spoken through Isaiah the prophet: "He himself took away our diseases and removed our illnesses."

i. The Leper (8:1–4)

8:1   The reference to the mountain recalls 5:1 and frames the intervening discourse. Mountains are repeatedly mentioned in Matthew at theologically significant junctures (4:8; 5:1; 8:1; 14:23; 15:29; 17:1, 9, 20; 21:21; 24:3, 16; 26:30; 28:16). This may imply a comparison between Jesus and Moses.[2] The reference to the crowds similarly frames the Sermon on the Mount by recalling 4:25; 5:1. The crowds will be frequently mentioned as Matthew's narrative proceeds.[3] They contain individuals whose comprehension of Jesus's identity and message often proves to be superficial and fickle (compare 21:9, 11 with 27:24–25). The leper in 8:2 is evidently a notable exception to this rule.

8:2   The first of three sets of three miracle stories concerns individuals who were at the margins of Israelite society. Matthew's first story is about a leper who is healed by Jesus (8:2–4; cf. Mark 1:40–44; Luke 5:12–14).[4] Leprosy in the Bible can refer to a variety of skin problems and should not be equated with the dreaded malady known today as Hansen's disease. Even garments could become "leprous" (Lev. 13:47–59). In all such cases, the priests were responsible for ruling on matters of ritual purity. Questionable individuals were quarantined until their status became clear. Lepers were not permitted social contact with other Jews and were to shout warnings to those who might come near

2. The similarity of the Greek text of Matt. 8:1 to that of Exod. 34:29 LXX A is striking. Cf. Allison 1993b: 179–80; T. Donaldson 1985.

3. Cf. 4:25; 5:1; 8:1, 18; 9:8, 33, 36; 11:7; 12:15, 23, 46; 13:2, 34, 36; 14:5, 13–15, 19, 22–23; 15:10, 30–33, 35–36, 39; 17:14; 19:2; 20:29, 31; 21:8–9, 11, 26, 46; 22:33; 23:1; 26:47, 55; 27:15, 20, 24.

4. This first story is introduced by ἰδού, which is equivalent to the frequent expression הִנֵּה in the Hebrew Bible. This particle is used most often in narrative to draw attention to what follows as something noteworthy or unusual. It is difficult to translate, but perhaps "suddenly" or "Look!" is appropriate. It occurs more than 60 times in Matthew alone and more than 190 times in the NT. See BDAG 468.

them (Lev. 13:45–46).[5] With such strictures, the leper in Matt. 8:1–4 is rather audacious even to approach Jesus (contrast Luke 17:12) for cleansing, although his posture, his calling Jesus "Lord" (see "Lord" under "Christology" in the introduction to this commentary), and his confidence in Jesus's power all indicate great respect. Although this leper's faith is striking, the next story portrays even greater faith.

Jesus's willingness, not his touch, is all that is necessary for the healing **8:3–4** (cf. 8:8), but the touch is probably the first human contact the leper has had throughout the duration of his illness. Touching the leper is even more audacious than the leper's approaching Jesus, since Jesus would also become ritually unclean when he touches the leper (Lev. 5:3). But the touch, instead of defiling Jesus, immediately cleanses the leper. Jesus instructs the cleansed leper to tell no one about his cleansing. This surprising command may be due simply to the priority of going to a priest to certify the cleansing and to offer a sacrifice (8:4; cf. Luke 17:14; Lev. 13–14, esp. 14:2–57). Jesus intends the cleansing of the leper to be a testimony to the power of the kingdom (cf. Matt. 10:18; 24:14), not simply a testimony to the cleansed leper's fitness to rejoin society (as Hagner 1993: 200 maintains). Jesus will commission his disciples to cleanse lepers (10:8), and he will mention the cleansing of lepers as a messianic sign when he is asked by John's messengers whether he is the Messiah (11:5).[6]

Jesus's command for silence about the healing remains somewhat puzzling (cf. 9:30; 12:16; 16:20; 17:9). One need not resort to W. Wrede's theory of a "messianic secret" (cf. Tuckett 1983a), however applicable this notion may be to the Gospel of Mark. More likely the silence enjoined here is due to Jesus's reluctance to stir up the crowds. At times Jesus found it necessary to withdraw from the scene when the notoriety due to his miracles reached near-riot proportions (e.g., 4:23–5:1; 8:18; 13:2; 21:11). At other times he seemed simply to need respite from the press of the multitudes (14:23). Also, the hostility of the religious leaders seemed to grow in direct proportion to Jesus's popularity with the masses (9:32–34; 12:22–24; 15:12, 21; 16:1, 4, 6, 20). So it was prudent for Jesus to keep a low profile and to avoid inflaming the messianic speculations of the crowds (9:30; 14:13; 17:9), but it was more important for Jesus to fulfill messianic prophecy (Matt. 12:15–21; cf. Isa. 42:1–4), even if this brought unwanted attention.

---

5. For the background on leprosy in the Hebrew Bible, see Lev. 13–14; Num. 12:10–15; 2 Kings 5 (cf. Luke 4:27); 2 Chron. 26. In the Gospels, see Matt. 8:2–3; 10:8; 11:5; 26:6; Mark 1:40–42; 14:3; Luke 4:27; 5:12–13; 7:22; 17:12. See also *m. Nega'im* and Pilch 1981.

6. On leprosy, see further the summary and bibliography of Wright and Jones, *ABD* 4:277–82. On the problems of translating the biblical language about leprosy, see J. G. Anderson 1980; Hulse 1975.

ii. The Centurion's Servant (8:5–13)

8:5–6   Matthew's second story is about the healing of a Roman centurion's servant at Capernaum (cf. Luke 7:1–10).[7] A centurion commanded about a hundred soldiers (a "century") and was subordinate to a tribune.[8] Capernaum has already been mentioned as Jesus's hometown in Matt. 4:13 (cf. 9:1; 17:24). Its unbelief (emphasized later in 11:23) is in marked contrast to the officer's faith. As did the leper, the officer also seeks out Jesus and calls him "Lord." His servant is bedridden with severe pain and paralysis (cf. 4:24).[9]

8:7–9   Jesus's immediate offer to go and heal the servant is the occasion for the officer's amazing faith. He acknowledges his unworthiness (cf. 3:11),[10] which may imply both perception of Jesus's lordship and awareness that coming to a Gentile's house is not an acceptable Jewish practice (cf. Acts 10:28; 11:3). He has addressed Jesus as "Lord" twice (Matt. 8:6, 8), and now he compares Jesus's authority (cf. 7:29; 9:6–8) to his own place in military command. He realizes that Jesus can heal his servant with only a word (8:8; cf. 8:16). Such healing from a distance is unprecedented in Matthew to this point and was quite unusual in the ancient world.

8:10–11   Since the officer is a Gentile, his astonishing faith (cf. 9:2, 22, 29; 15:28; 17:20; 21:21; 23:23; contrast "little faith" in 6:30; 8:26; 14:31; 16:8) becomes an opportunity to teach (cf. 15:21–28). Jesus turns to those who are "following" him, which likely includes both the inner circle and others who are less committed to Jesus (cf. 8:1). He tells these followers the shocking news that he has not encountered faith such as this gentile officer's anywhere in Israel.[11] He then speaks of the future kingdom as a time when many from the east and the west will recline with Abraham and the patriarchs, enjoying the great eschatological feast (8:11; cf. 22:1–14; 25:10; Luke 14:15–16; Rev. 19:9). Jesus's prediction is reminiscent of biblical teaching on the gathering of Israel from all over the earth (Isa. 43:5–6; 49:12; 65:13–14; Ps. 107:3; cf. Bar. 4:37) and the future worship

---

7. The semantic range of the Greek word παῖς includes either a young person under the age of puberty or one who is committed to serve another as a slave or servant (cf. 2:16; 8:13; 12:18 [describing Jesus's relation to God; cf. Acts 3:13, 26; 4:27, 30]; 14:2; 17:18; 21:15; BDAG 750–51). The latter is probably intended here although some believe that the term should be translated "boy" or "son" (e.g., Hagner 1993: 204). See also R. P. Martin in Guelich (ed.) 1978: 14–22.

8. For the generally positive portrayal of centurions in the NT, see 27:54; Luke 7:2, 6; 23:47; Acts 10:1, 22; 21:32; 22:25, 26; 24:23; 27:1, 6, 11, 31, 43; 28:16; cf. Josephus, *Ant.* 14.69; 17.282; *J.W.* 2.63; 3.124.

9. The passive of βάλλω indicates that the servant is prostrate with physical disability. Cf. 8:14; 9:2; Mark 7:30; Luke 16:20; Rev. 2:22; Josephus *Ant.* 9.209; *J.W.* 1.629.

10. The syntax of the expression οὐκ εἰμὶ ἱκανὸς ἵνα contains a nonfinal epexegetical use of ἵνα. See Wallace 1996: 476.

11. The introductory phrase λέγω δὲ ὑμῖν adds emphasis and solemnity to this teaching. Cf. 6:29; 12:6, 36; 17:12; 19:9; 26:29.

of God by Gentiles all over the earth, often portrayed as occurring in Jerusalem (Isa. 2:2–3; 25:6–9; 45:6; 59:19; 60:3–4; Mic. 4:1–2; Zech. 8:20–23; Mal. 1:11). (See the discussion in Gundry 1967: 76–78.)

In striking contrast to the eschatological bliss shared with the patriarchs,   **8:12** the "sons of the kingdom" will be excluded and punished (cf. Marguerat 1981: 243–57; Reiser 1997: 230–41).[12] "Sons of the kingdom" (13:38; cf. 9:15; 23:15; Luke 16:8; 1QM 17.8) is a Semitic idiom referring to those who would be the expected heirs to God's eschatological blessings. "Outer darkness"(cf. Matt. 22:13; 25:30; Apoc. Pet. 78.23; T. Jac. 5.9) refers to the removal of sinners to a place very far from the light of God's gracious presence (cf. Matt. 4:16).[13] "Weeping and the gnashing of teeth" (cf. 13:42, 50; 22:13; 24:51; 25:30; Luke 6:25; 1 En. 108.3; 2 En. 40.12) vividly portrays the unspeakable anguish of separation from God. This frightening imagery marks one of the most sobering moments of Matthew's story of Jesus. The motif of eschatological reversal is present here, since God's people who presently mourn and weep will do so no longer when they inherit the kingdom (Matt. 5:4; cf. Luke 6:21, 25; Rev. 21:4).

Most interpreters (e.g., Beare 1981: 209; France 1985: 156; Hagner 1993: 206; Luz 2001: 11) understand Jesus to teach here that the centurion is a harbinger of the future salvation of Gentiles, a theme related to Matthew's stress on the universal mission of the church (Matt. 28:20). But this theology of the reversal of the roles of Israel and the Gentiles in redemptive history is not as absolute as some maintain. Only the "many" Gentiles who believe are to be included, and only Jews who do not believe will be excluded. The biblical texts (cited above) to which Jesus's words allude speak of both Jews and Gentiles worshiping God in Jerusalem in the future. Jesus and his twelve disciples are Jewish, and Jesus will later speak of them as ruling the twelve tribes of Israel in the world to come (19:28). Although the healing of the gentile centurion's servant is given the most narrative space by Matthew, it is surrounded by two other healing stories involving Jews, that of the leper (8:1–4) and that of Peter's mother-in-law (8:14–17). W. Davies and Allison (1991: 27–29; cf. Allison 1989) oppose the usual view of Gentiles usurping Jews by arguing that the reversal here is that of dispersed or unprivileged Jews versus privileged Jews rather than Gentiles versus Jews. Although this interpretation is doubtful, the concern to avoid reading a later Christian theology of supersession back into Matthew is commendable.[14]

---

12. The divine passive ἐκβληθήσονται expresses God's agency in this action. See Wallace 1996: 437–38.

13. The place of perdition is often pictured as dark. See 2 Pet. 2:17; Jude 13; Wis. 17:21; Tob. 14:10; 2 Esd. (4 Ezra) 7:93; 1 En. 63.6; 108.14; Ps. Sol. 14.9; 15.10. This is the case even in texts that speak of perdition as fiery, e.g., 1 En. 103.7; 2 En. 10.2; 1QS 4.13.

14. For the inclusion of believing Gentiles in God's plan, see Matt. 1:3–5; 2:1–12; 3:9–10; 4:15–16; 15:21–28; 24:14; 27:54; 28:19. For the exclusion of unbelieving Jews, see 3:9–10; 21:31, 43; 23:13, 15, 37. Cf. Aurelius 2001; M. Elliott 2000; Overman 1996: 117–19.

8:13   Jesus now turns from addressing his evidently stunned followers to the centurion, whose surprising faith led to the shocking teaching of 8:10–12. He tells the man to go home since his request will be granted just as he believed (cf. 9:29; 15:28). At this moment, as he expected, his servant is healed,[15] not by touch, as in the case of the leper, but at a distance. As in a similar story in John 4:46–53, the precise timing and the distance are noted to underline the supernatural authority of Jesus (cf. Landis 1994).[16]

iii. Peter's Mother-in-Law (8:14–15)

This brief story is chiastic in structure (Hagner 1993: 209), with the touch of Jesus transforming the situation from one in which Jesus serves Peter's mother-in-law to one in which she serves him:

    A Jesus sees Peter's mother-in-law

      B She is sick in bed

        C She has a fever

          D Jesus touches her

        C′ The fever stops

      B′ She gets up

    A′ She serves Jesus

8:14–15   The third and final healing story in Matthew's first set is the shortest. Peter's mother-in- law (cf. 1 Cor. 9:5) is bedridden with a high fever at Peter's house (cf. Mark 1:29–31; Luke 4:38–39). Excavations in Capernaum have uncovered the foundations of what some believe may be this very house (W. Davies and Allison 1991: 33–34; Strange and Shanks 1982). The leper took the initiative for his own cleansing, and the centurion took the initiative for his servant's healing, but here Jesus alone initiates the healing. As in the case of the leper, this healing includes touching (cf. Matt. 9:29; 20:34; Lalleman 1997; Schwarz 1994b). The authority of Jesus is underlined by the immediacy and totality of the healing. As soon as Jesus touches her, the woman gets up and starts serving him,[17] perhaps by preparing a meal.

iv. Summary and Biblical Fulfillment (8:16–17)

8:16   The leper was healed during the journey between the mountain and Capernaum, the centurion's servant upon arrival in Capernaum, and

---

15. The dramatic aorist (Wallace 1996: 564–65) passive ἰάθη subtly expresses the immediacy of the healing through the authoritative agency of Jesus.

16. On 8:5–13, see Burchard 1993; Catchpole in van Segbroeck et al. 1992: 517–40; Jennings and Liew 2004; Lindars in van Segbroeck et al. 1992: 1985–2000; Saddington 2006; Tisera 1993: 101–29.

17. The verb διηκόνει should be taken as an inceptive imperfect. See Wallace 1996: 544–45.

Peter's mother-in-law in Peter's house. Evidently, this series of healings encourages the residents of the region to bring many more afflicted people to Jesus later that evening (cf. Mark 1:32–34; Luke 4:40–41). Jesus casts out the demons (literally, "spirits"; cf. Matt. 10:1; 12:43–45) by a mere command (literally, "by a word"; cf. 8:8), which indicates his authority. This authority is further stressed by the statement that Jesus healed all who were ill.

This summary of healings and exorcisms (cf. 4:23–24; 9:35) leads into another biblical-fulfillment formula in 8:17, which cites Isa. 53:4. Isaiah 53, a passage rich in messianic significance,[18] describes the servant (Isa. 52:13; 53:11) as a despised person who bears the sins (53:4–6, 8, 11–12) of others without complaint (53:7). Matthew has evidently made his own rather literal translation of two lines of synonymous parallelism in Isaiah.[19] The two words Matthew uses for human affliction (ἀσθένεια, astheneia, disease; νόσος, nosos, illness) usually refer to physical illness and pain but can also serve as metaphors for sin. Matthew obviously takes them in the physical sense here.

8:17

The use of Isa. 53:4 in Matt. 8:17 has led to much debate over the relationship of Jesus's ministry and death to physical healing (cf. Mayhue 1995). A broad, biblical-theological view of sickness and death helps to resolve this question. Pain, illness, and death were originally rooted in sin (Gen. 3), and redemption from sin will ultimately result in the redemption of the body (Rom. 8:23) and the end of pain (Rev. 21:4). Matthew views the healings and exorcisms performed by Jesus as evidence for the presence of God's reign, which anticipates a glorious future reality (Matt. 11:2–6; 12:28–29; 19:28). Therefore Matthew links Jesus's healing of physical illnesses to his substitutionary death for sinners (1:21; 20:28; 26:28). As indications of kingdom authority, the healings are tokens of the ultimate eschatological results of Jesus's redemption. Some Christians have made too much of this, taking it as supporting the notion that Christians need never be sick, that physical healing is in the atonement. Yet this must be qualified by pointing out that such healing is universally

18. Isaiah 53 is formally cited elsewhere in the NT: Isa. 53:1 in John 12:38 and Rom. 10:16; Isa. 53:7–8 in Acts 8:32–33; Isa. 53:9 in 1 Pet. 2:22; and Isa. 53:12 in Luke 22:37. Several less-formal allusions occur in Matthew: Isa. 53:2 possibly in Matt. 2:23; Isa. 53:5 in Matt. 26:67; Isa. 53:7 in Matt. 26:63 and 27:12, 14; Isa. 53:9 in Matt. 26:24; Isa. 53:12 in Matt. 27:38. Additional allusions are too numerous to be listed here. Nickelsburg (2003: 17–20, 105–7) shows from Jewish Second Temple literature that the NT understanding of the servant is not totally unique.

19. Matthew's αὐτὸς τὰς ἀσθενείας ἡμῶν ἔλαβεν καὶ τὰς νόσους ἐβάστασεν literally renders חֳלָיֵנוּ הוּא נָשָׂא וּמַכְאֹבֵינוּ סְבָלָם. The LXX (οὗτος τὰς ἁμαρτίας ἡμῶν φέρει καὶ περὶ ἡμῶν ὀδυνᾶται) evidently translates חֳלָיֵנוּ metaphorically (in keeping with its biblical use in Isa. 1:5; Hos. 5:13; Jer. 6:7; 10:19) with ἁμαρτίας and renders the second line of the verse rather loosely (cf. Menken 1997). Nickelsburg (2003: 17–20, 105–7) summarizes the interpretation of the servant of Isa. 53 in Second Temple literature in comparison and contrast to NT interpretation. See Bellinger and Farmer 1998.

and fully experienced only during the future aspect of the kingdom, when God's will is done on earth as it is in heaven. There are individual instances of healing in the present age, but these are only temporary and do not warrant the teaching that Christians can simply name and claim their healing because it has already been guaranteed by the atonement. Matthew 8:17 connects Isa. 53:4 to Jesus's earthly ministry, not to his atoning death. The point of the miracles is to stress Jesus's unique messianic authority, not the theapeutic blessings he brings to his people.

The role of faith varies in the three healings in Matt. 8:1–15. Faith was clearly involved in the first two healings, but in the second case, it was not the faith of the servant but of the centurion. In the third case, concerning Peter's mother-in-law, there is no indication of anyone's faith precipitating the healing. The leper's words best imply an appropriate view of healing. He knows that Jesus *can* heal him if he *wishes* to heal him (8:2). This puts the power and providence of God side by side. There is no doubt about the power of God, but the leper does not presume upon Jesus's sovereign providence, which would be putting the Lord to the test (cf. 4:7). Followers of Jesus cannot dictate that God be willing to heal, but they can rest in God's love and sovereign providence, which makes no mistakes (Bruner 1987: 299–300). The leper is not deficient in faith; he is amazingly proficient in spiritual wisdom.

Jesus and the Outsiders

Matthew selected from the many healing stories available to him these three stories about a leper, a Gentile, and a woman in order to show Jesus's compassion for those who were powerless in Jewish society (cf. 9:36). The leper was ritually impure and would thus have been an outcast from all social and religious functions. The Roman centurion had power over the Jews whose land his empire occupied, but as a Gentile, he had no religious status. Peter's mother-in-law had no ceremonial or ethnic limitations, but her gender would preclude her from many privileges available only to males.[20] None of the three could enter the Court of Israel in the temple, where Jewish males presented their offerings to the priests (Bruner 1987: 307–8). Yet these people from the margins of society are featured by Matthew because they were often surprisingly receptive to the message of the kingdom. The tawdry women in Jesus's genealogy (Matt. 1), the bizarre astrologers (Matt. 2), those healed in Matt. 8, and others throughout this Gospel indicate not only that Jesus will save his people from their sins but also that his people are an amazingly diverse group.

It was crucial for Matthew's Christian Jewish community to take up their mission to disciple not only their own nation (10:5–6) but also all

---

20. For a feminist perspective on Jesus's dealings with women in Matthew, see Kitzberger 2000; A.-J. Levine and Blickenstaff 2001; Wainwright 1988, 1991, 1998.

the nations (24:14; 28:19). Matthew therefore presents Jesus not only as the Messiah of all nations but also as the model for ministry that brings the Messiah to all the nations. Scruples about ritual purity, ethnic exclusivism, and gender stereotypes must not hinder this mission. Followers of Jesus must love and minister to outsiders as he did (Bruner 1987: 308; Keener 1999: 273).

Additional Note

8:10. Instead of the text of UBS[4], παρ' οὐδενὶ τοσαύτην πίστιν ἐν τῷ Ἰσραὴλ εὖρον (found in B, W, et al.), many other MSS (including ℵ, C, L, f[13], *Byz, Lect*) have the similar words οὐδὲ ἐν τῷ Ἰσραὴλ τοσαύτην πίστιν εὖρον. But this is likely assimilation to Luke 7:9 (Metzger 1994: 17).

b. The Accompanying Teaching on Discipleship (8:18–22)

Two interviews with would-be disciples (8:18–20 and 8:21–22; cf. Luke 9:57–60) appear between the first (8:1–17) and second (8:23–9:8) sets of three miracle stories. These two interviews illustrate the nature of Jesus's ministry and show by contrast what type of disciples he is seeking (see 6:33; R. Edwards in van Segbroeck et al. 1992: 1305–24; Kingsbury 1988b).

This unit can be divided as follows:

    i. The enthusiastic legal expert (8:18–20)
    ii. The hesitant disciple (8:21–22)

Exegesis and Exposition

[18]Now when Jesus saw ⌜a crowd⌝ around him, he gave orders to cross to the other side of the sea. [19]Then a legal expert came and said to him, "Teacher, I will follow you wherever you go." [20]Jesus said to him, "The foxes have dens and the birds of the air have nests, but the Son of Man has nowhere to lay his head." [21]Another of ⌜his⌝ disciples said to him, "Lord, first let me go and bury my father." [22]But Jesus said to him, "Follow me, and let the dead bury their own dead."

i. The Enthusiastic Legal Expert (8:18–20)

8:18   Because of the increasing press of the crowd at Capernaum,[1] Jesus commands the disciples to make a boat trip to the other side of the Sea of Galilee (8:18). This command is important for interpreting the ensuing narrative, since it sets the interviews with the would-be disciples in the context of the story of the stilling of the storm, encouraging the reader to view the historical storm also as a metaphor of discipleship (Bornkamm, Barth, and Held 1963: 52–57). Matthew's narrative itself implies that 8:18 is a call to discipleship, not just a command to get away from the crowd by taking a boat trip.

8:19–20   As the trip to the other side is being contemplated, one of the Jewish legal experts ("scribes") addresses Jesus as "teacher" and promises to follow

1. The adverbial participle ἰδών is used here and elsewhere in Matthew (5:1; 9:4, 22, 23, 36; 21:19) to indicate that Jesus's perception of situations leads him to take various actions. For the same use with other people, see 2:10, 16; 3:7; 8:34; 9:8, 11; 12:2; 14:26; 18:31; 21:15, 20, 32, 38; 26:8; 27:3, 24, 54; 28:17.

him wherever he might go (8:19). Thus far in Matthew, the legal experts have not been presented positively (2:4; 5:20; 23:13, 15, 23, 25, 27, 29; but see 13:52; 23:2–3, 34). In Matthew those who call Jesus "teacher" are not disciples (12:38; 19:16; 22:16, 24, 36). The legal expert evidently makes his promise solely on his own initiative, and Jesus takes a dim view of it. He starkly alludes to his itinerant form of ministry, which leaves him with not so much as a place to sleep (8:20). Even the animals have that (cf. 6:26). Matthew's readers can only conclude that the legal expert's enthusiasm is superficial and that he has not counted the cost of discipleship. Perhaps his enthusiasm is due to witnessing the many miracles Jesus is performing. Be that as it may, his promise is hasty and unreliable.

Matthew 8:20 is the first time the title "Son of Man" occurs in this Gospel. Here it stands in place of the pronoun "I." This much-debated title, derived from Dan. 7:13–14, as a whole stresses the exaltation of Jesus (cf. Matt. 9:6; 19:28; 25:31; 26:64). Here it tends to express a very strange situation in which, even though Jesus is the exalted miracle-working Messiah, he is also a homeless itinerant, deprived of basic creature comforts. When he stays in a house, it is someone else's, such as Peter's in this context.[2]

ii. The Hesitant Disciple (8:21–22)

A second individual makes an excuse to delay his itineration with Jesus (cf. 1 Kings 19:19–21).[3] Matthew's use of the phrase "another of his disciples" in 8:21 shows that both the teacher in 8:19 and the person who is concerned about his father here are followers of Jesus in some sense of the word. Matthew uses the term "disciple" approximately seventy-five times, and the precise nuance of the term must be picked up in each context (cf. Deutsch 1987; R. Edwards 1997; Patte 1996; Wilkins 1988, 1995). This second individual purports that his father's funeral takes priority over following Jesus. Honoring one's parents (Exod. 20:12; Deut. 5:16; Matt. 15:4; cf. 1 Kings 19:19–21) would presumably include seeing to their proper burial (Gen. 50:5; Tob. 4:3; Sir. 38:16; *m. Ber.* 3.1).

8:21–22

High priests and Nazirites were exempt from burial responsibilities (Lev. 21:11; Num. 6:6–7), although priests were allowed to touch dead family members (Lev. 21:2). Some scholars think that such Jew-

---

2. See the additional discussion of the title "Son of Man" under "Christology" in the introduction to this commentary, and the convenient summaries in W. Davies and Allison 1991: 43–53; Hagner 1993: 214–15. Detailed discussions are found in Caragounis 1986; M. Casey 1979, 1987; A. Collins 1987; J. Collins 1992; Donahue 1986; Fitzmyer 1997: 143–60; Higgins 1980; Kim 1983; Lindars 1983; Tödt 1965; Vermes 1978.

3. This disciple's request to bury his father πρῶτον may be intended to contrast with Jesus's command to seek the kingdom πρῶτον (6:33). For other texts that use πρῶτον to speak of kingdom priorities, see 5:24; 7:5; 12:29; 13:30; 23:26. Cf. 19:30; 20:16, 27; 21:28, 31; 22:38. See also Hengel 1981: 3–15.

ish customs as extended mourning or eventual secondary burial of the deceased's bones in an ossuary are implied here,[4] but such conjectures may only distract the reader from the rigor of Jesus's words. Although there may be hyperbole here (cf. Matt. 5:29–30), Jesus demands immediate loyalty to the kingdom and states that those who are not loyal to it can care for the burial. Jesus's pun that the dead can bury their own dead means that those who will bury the would-be disciple's father are dead to the kingdom, not alive to its rigorous eschatological demands, which supersede even one's duty to parents.

The two individuals who speak to Jesus about discipleship in 8:18–22 illustrate opposite problems. The first (8:18–20) is carried away with emotional enthusiasm but has not rationally considered the sacrifice demanded in an itinerant ministry. Perhaps he is impressed with Jesus's miracles and wants to participate in such glorious events. But miracles are not at the heart of kingdom ministry (7:21–23), and true disciples must be willing to be deprived of life's basic necessities. The second individual has a more realistic understanding of the sacrifice entailed in discipleship. His reason for postponing following Jesus seems legitimate (Gen. 50:5; Exod. 20:12; Deut. 5:16). Jesus himself reaffirms the Torah on honoring one's parents (Matt. 15:4–6; 19:19). But harsh as it may seem, Jesus teaches that the paramount demands of his kingdom revise one's notions of family (cf. 10:37; 12:46–50).

Both individuals are disqualified as disciples. The first's enthusiasm arises from his ignorance of the cost of discipleship, and the second's timidity is due to his awareness of that cost. Jesus's followers must count the cost of discipleship and temper their faith with a realism that considers the deprivations that come to those who follow Jesus (cf. 10:34–39; 16:24–25; 19:29; 20:26–27). One can hope that both individuals were led to authentic discipleship by Jesus's rebukes, but Matthew's silence is sobering.

Additional Notes

8:18. The difficulty of sorting out the several variant readings regarding the word ὄχλος results in the editors of UBS[4] giving their preferred reading ὄχλον a C rating. These variants chiefly relate to whether ὄχλος should be singular (B and some Cop^{sa} MSS) or plural (ℵ*, f[1], and others), and whether the word πολύς should be read as modifying the singular (W and others) or plural (ℵ[2], C, Byz, Lect) form of ὄχλος. Many scholars prefer the UBS[4] reading because it is the shorter reading that arguably best explains the origin of the rest (Metzger 1994: 17), but πολλοὺς ὄχλους is the reading attested by the most MSS and text-types, and it is a Matthean expression (cf. 14:14; 21:8).

8:21. The word αὐτοῦ is absent from ℵ, B, and others but is found in C, L, W, Byz, Lect, and others. It is placed in brackets in UBS[4] because the editors could not agree on its authenticity due to conflicting plausible arguments about the internal evidence (Metzger 1994: 17–18). Does the absence of the word indicate copyists' reluctance to admit that the legal expert was a disciple of Jesus?

4. Cf. Bockmuehl 1998: 553–81; W. Davies and Allison 1991: 56–58; Luomanen 1998b: 100–109; McCane 1990.

2. Cycle 2: More Miracles with a Focus on Discipleship (8:23–9:17)

With the abrupt dismissal of the pair of would-be disciples in 8:18–22, the first cycle of miracle stories and discipleship ends. Now the genuine, yet flawed, disciples follow Jesus as the story continues with a second cycle, which likewise focuses on miracles (8:23–9:8) and discipleship (9:9–17). The three miracle stories expose the disciples to the weakness of their own faith (8:26) and to the presence of opposition (8:34; 9:3). The two discipleship stories feature Jesus's outreach to sinners (including Matthew; cf. 21:31–32) and the reason for his distinctive teaching on fasting (cf. 6:16–18).

a. The Three Miracles (8:23–9:8)

The second set of three miracles includes the calming of the storm (8:23–27; cf. Mark 4:35–41; Luke 8:22–25), the exorcism of two demon-possessed men (Matt. 8:28–34; cf. Mark 5:1–20; Luke 8:26–39), and the healing of a paralyzed man (Matt. 9:1–8; cf. Mark 2:1–12; Luke 5:17–26). The three miracles demonstrate, respectively, Jesus's authority (cf. Matt. 7:29; 8:9; 9:6) over nature (cf. 14:19–20, 22–33; 15:36–37; 21:19), evil powers, and disease.

This unit may be outlined as follows:

    i. Calming of the storm (8:23–27)
    ii. Exorcism of the Gadarene demoniacs (8:28–34)
    iii. Healing of a paralytic (9:1–8)

Exegesis and Exposition

8:23When he got into the boat, his disciples followed him. 24And suddenly a severe storm came up on the sea, so that the boat was being swamped by the waves; but Jesus himself was asleep. 25And they came to him and woke him and said, "Save us, Lord; we are perishing!" 26And he said to them, "Why are you afraid, men of little faith?" Then he got up and rebuked the winds and the sea, and it became perfectly calm. 27The men were astonished and said, "What kind of man is this, that even the winds and the sea obey him?"

28When he came to the other side, to the region of the ⌜Gadarenes⌝, two men who were demon-possessed encountered him as they were coming out of the tombs. They were so extremely violent that no one could pass through that way. 29And suddenly they cried out, "What do you have to do with us, Son of God? Have you come here to torment us before the time?" 30Now there was a herd of many swine feeding at a distance from them. 31So the demons began to beg him, saying, "If you are going to cast us out, send us into the herd of swine." 32And he said to them, "Go!" So they came out and went into the swine, and suddenly the whole herd rushed down the steep bank into the sea and drowned in the waters. 33The herdsmen ran away, and went to the city and reported everything, including what had happened to the demon-possessed men. 34Then immediately the whole city came out to meet Jesus; and when they saw him, they implored him to leave their region.

9:1Getting into a boat, Jesus crossed over the sea and came to his own town.

2And right away they brought to him a paralytic lying on a bed. And when he saw their faith, Jesus said to the paralytic, "Take courage, child; your sins are forgiven." [3]Immediately some of the legal experts said to themselves, "This fellow blasphemes." [4]Now Jesus ⌜knew⌝ their thoughts, so he said, "Why are you thinking evil in your hearts? [5]For which is easier to say, 'Your sins are forgiven' or 'Get up and walk'? [6]But so that you may know that the Son of Man has authority on earth to forgive sins"—then he said to the paralytic, "Get up, pick up your bed and go home." [7]And he got up and went home. [8]But when the crowds saw this, ⌜they were filled with awe⌝ and glorified God, who had given such authority to human beings.

i. Calming of the Storm (8:23–27)

This pericope must be understood as an interpreted historical event. This means not only that a miracle did happen but also that the miracle teaches theological truth that Matthew wishes his readers to understand. These theological implications pertain both to the authority of Jesus and to the nature of genuine discipleship (Bornkamm in Bornkamm, Barth, and Held 1963: 52–57; Feiler 1983). The latter is just as clear as the former when the context of the story is analyzed. W. Davies and Allison (1991: 68) point out a chiastic structure that places the key interaction between Jesus and the disciples in 8:25–26 at the center of the pericope. Jesus has issued orders to depart to the other side (8:18), but the departure is delayed by interviews with two would-be followers (8:19–22). Then Jesus leads the disciples into the boat and they follow him (8:23).[1] When they encounter the storm, their faith is tested (8:25–26), and they learn that Jesus's authority is sufficient to overcome any trial that may come their way. The encounter with the storm is the occasion for the more important encounter with Jesus, which prepares them for further encounters with the trials of life. (On biblical sea storm scenes, see Aus 2000; Thimmes 1992.)

The story of the calming of the storm (cf. Mark 4:35–41; Luke 8:22–25) begins the second set of three miracle stories (Matt. 8:23–27; 8:28–34; 9:1–8). The previous narrative has shown Jesus's authority over sin, disease, and demons, but this passage demonstrates Jesus's authority over nature. Jesus's plan to go to the other side of the lake (8:18) has been delayed by the interviews with the two would-be disciples. But now Jesus gets into the boat, with his disciples following his initiative.[2] This is another indication that this nature miracle is also a test of discipleship.

8:23

---

1. The first would-be disciple rashly promises to follow Jesus anywhere (8:19), but the second wishes to postpone following Jesus (8:21). Genuine disciples are followers: 8:23; cf. 4:20, 22; 9:9; 10:38; 16:24; 19:21, 27, 28; 27:55. Yet even the crowds "follow" Jesus around (4:25; 8:1; 14:13; 19:2; 20:29; Kingsbury 1978b), and many in the crowd evidently do not have a clear grasp of his identity and message.

2. The syntax of 8:23 (καὶ ἐμβάντι αὐτῷ εἰς τὸ πλοῖον ἠκολούθησαν αὐτῷ οἱ μαθηταὶ αὐτοῦ) is sometimes described as containing a dative absolute (A. Bruce 1957: 143). R. Young

8:24–25 Suddenly a dangerous storm threatens to capsize the boat (cf. 14:24). Matthew uses the word σεισμός (*seismos*) for the storm, which is an unusual meaning for a word that generally refers to earthquakes (cf. 24:7; 27:51; 28:2; Schwarz 1994a). But Jesus is oblivious, taking a nap, which may have implications of trust in God's protection (Job 11:18–19; Ps. 3:5–6; Prov. 3:24–26; Acts 12:6). Biblical texts in which God seems to have gone to sleep and forgotten Israel during trials may also be relevant here (Pss. 35:23; 44:23–24; 59:4; Isa. 51:9). The disciples frantically plead for deliverance from imminent drowning (cf. Matt. 14:30). The intensity of the storm is underlined when one remembers that four of the disciples were commercial fishermen who were used to the weather on the Sea of Galilee (cf. 4:18–22).

8:26 One would expect Jesus to respond immediately to the plea for deliverance from imminent death, but he first rebukes the disciples for their lack of faith (cf. 14:31). Only after this does he rebuke the storm, and the sudden squall is over as quickly as it began. Jesus's calming of the storm is similar to God's actions in the Hebrew Scriptures (Jon. 1–2; Pss. 65:7; 89:8–9; 104:7; 107:23–32; Isa. 51:9–10). His rebuke of the wind and waves strikingly personifies these supposedly natural forces by utilizing language found at times in exorcisms (cf. Matt. 17:18). This may imply that this nature miracle is at the same time a victory over evil supernatural forces.

8:27 The disciples marvel at Jesus's power over the storm (cf. 9:33; 21:20). Their amazement recalls 7:28 and anticipates 9:8, 33; 12:23. Jesus's authority over nature produces the same result with the disciples as his authoritative teaching did with the crowd (7:29). Their question about what sort of man Jesus is leads the reader to remember Matt. 1–4, where Jesus's unique birth, early experiences, baptism, and temptation all augur the sort of man he has become. From these narrated details the reader knows more about Jesus than the disciples do at this point.

By calming the storm, Jesus has shown himself to be the Lord of nature. But this nature miracle is intended to teach about discipleship. The "little faith" (ὀλιγόπιστος, *oligopistos*; cf. 6:30; 14:31; 16:8; 17:20) of the disciples is exposed. It is genuine faith, but it is limited in its awareness of Jesus's power. After the challenge of the storm and the rebuke of Jesus, their faith is ostensibly strengthened. The most critical concern that faces Jesus's disciples is not potential persecutions or disasters. Rather, it is the quality of their faith, which is directly proportionate to the accuracy of their perception of Jesus, the object of their faith. In the middle of

---

(1994: 45) even describes αὐτῷ as the subject of ἐμβάντι. It is better to understand the syntax as emphasizing Jesus's initiative (W. Davies and Allison 1991: 71) by placing ἐμβάντι αὐτῷ pendently at the beginning of the clause. The second αὐτῷ is resumptive and the direct object of ἠκολούθησαν. The participle ἐμβάντι is adjectival. Similar constructions occur in 9:27, 28.

the storm, as the boat is about to go under, Jesus addresses the disciples' weak faith before he rebukes the storm. This means that the first priority of disciples must be to focus on the power of Jesus, not the power of life's storms that threaten to overcome them.

Blomberg (1992a: 150) makes the valid point that this pericope is more about Christology than about discipleship, but Matthew's narrative does not bifurcate the two. The interplay of Christology and discipleship is especially apparent in 8:25, where the disciples call Jesus "Lord" in the face of imminent death but evidently do not clearly grasp the authority their Lord possesses. To overcome anemic faith, disciples must trust in the power of Jesus. Unless they are saved from little faith, they will indeed perish. One need not follow patristic allegorization of the boat into the church (e.g., Tertullian, *On Baptism* 12) to come to this conclusion. (On 8:23–27, see Heil 1981: 84–103; S. Park 2000.)

ii. Exorcism of the Gadarene Demoniacs (8:28–34)

This account of exorcism in the land of the Gadarenes (8:28–34; cf. Mark 5:1–20; Luke 8:26–39) is the second miracle story in the second set of three such stories in Matt. 8–9. The story of the healing of the paralytic (9:1–8) will conclude this second set. As Jesus has planned (8:18), he and the disciples arrive on the other side of the lake despite the storm. Geographical details are unclear, but the boat crosses the Sea of Galilee from Capernaum on the northwest to the eastern shore. The city of Gadara was five or six miles from the Sea of Galilee, but according to Josephus (*Life* 9.42), the region of Gadara was adjacent to the sea. See Blomberg (1987b: 149–50) for discussion of the geographical questions that arise from a comparison of Matt. 8:28 with Mark 5:1 and Luke 8:26. See the additional note on Matt. 8:28 for a discussion of the vexing textual question regarding the Gadarenes.

The somewhat unprecedented keynote of this pericope is opposition. That Jesus is opposed by the fierce demoniacs is not surprising, but his exorcism leads not to adulation but to further opposition. Thus the pericope presents two episodes of hostility toward Jesus, the first (8:28–32) longer than the second (8:33–34), but the second more striking than the first.[3] This pericope begins with the activity of Jesus, as do nearly all the pericopes in this context (cf. 8:1, 5, 14, 18, 23, 28; 9:1, 9, 10, 18, 27, 35; but see 9:14, 32).

Demon "possession" appears frequently in Matthew (4:24; 7:22; 8:16, 28, 31, 33; 9:32–34; 10:8; 11:18; 12:22, 24, 27, 28; 15:22; 17:18), but the details of this particular incident are remarkable. Jesus has already cast out demons, and he has just calmed a storm, but here his single word "Go!" demonstrates his authority not only over demons but also over

---

3. The parallel hostile encounters that make up this pericope (W. Davies and Allison 1991: 85) are implied by the cognates ὑπήντησαν (8:28) and ὑπάντησιν (8:34).

animals and the Sea of Galilee. The authority of Jesus's words (7:28–29) and deeds (8:9; 9:6) continues to be a key theme in all of Matt. 8–9. But this episode shows that the authority of Jesus operates alongside his mercy (W. Davies and Allison 1991: 116). Jesus relates compassionately to these dangerous demoniacs (cf. 4:23; 9:36) as a model for his disciples' own mission (10:1, 8). (See Keener's helpful excursus on exorcism [1999: 283–86] and, on this pericope, Craghan 1968; Derrett 1979a; and W. Pesch 1972.)

8:28–29   In the region of Gadara (see the additional note on 8:28), Jesus encounters two fierce demoniacs who live in the macabre environs of a cemetery and menace anyone who ventures near. The pair immediately recognize Jesus as the Son of God (1:23; 2:15; 3:17; 4:3, 6; 14:33; 16:16; 17:5; 27:54; cf. James 2:19) and ask what he has in common with them (cf. Maynard 1985). They wonder whether Jesus has come to torture them prematurely, before the appointed time of judgment (cf. 13:30; 16:3; 1 En. 10.4–6, 12–13, 15–16; 19.1; 69.28; Jub. 5.6, 10; 10.8–9; *L.A.B.* 60.3). Their awareness of Jesus's identity as the Son of God, a key Matthean theme (Matt. 1:23; 2:15; 3:17; 4:3, 6; 14:33; 16:16; 17:5; 27:54), and of the future judgment of demons (25:41; cf. 1 Cor. 4:5) is striking. Their question reflects Matthew's "inaugurated" eschatology, in which the future reign of God is already encroaching on Satan's domain (cf. Matt. 12:28; Keener 1999: 286).

8:30–32   A large herd of pigs grazing nearby provides a way for the demons to escape the presence of Jesus. The demons themselves request that Jesus send them into the pigs if he casts them out of the men (cf. 12:43–45).[4] Both the pigs and the cemetery residence would be ritually impure for Jews. Up to this point, the demoniacs have done all the talking, and Jesus's reply is only one word: "Go!" Jesus permits their wish and they enter the pigs, precipitating a stampede down a steep hillside into the lake, where the entire herd drowns.[5] This dramatic result from just a single word of Jesus underscores his authority. But his authority is not yet universal, since he permits the demons to destroy the pigs and presumably to continue their nefarious activities (cf. 12:43–45) until their ultimate judgment (25:41; cf. 1 En. 15–16; Jub. 10.8–9). The herding of pigs (cf. Luke 15:15) and the eating of pork were forbidden to Jews (Lev. 11:7; Deut. 14:8; Isa. 65:4; 66:3, 17; Acts 10:10–14; 1 Macc. 1:47;

4. Their request is an instance of the imperative mood (ἀπόστειλον) being used not for a command but for an entreaty by a subordinate to a superior. See Wallace 1996: 487–88.

5. The view that ἀπέθανον describes the death of the demons more than that of the pigs (Gundry 1994: 160; Luz 2001: 25; Schweizer 1975: 223) is grammatically possible but theologically doubtful. In this view, the demons, contrary to their expectations (8:29), are immediately sent to hell. More likely the manner of the pigs' death contains imagery of eschatological punishment (Schnackenburg 2002: 86; cf. Matt. 25:41; Rev. 20:3, 10, 14–15).

2 Macc. 6:18–23; *m. B. Qam.* 7.7). This implies that Gadara is gentile or mixed-race territory, since it is east of the Sea of Galilee and supports pig herding. One wonders whether the demoniacs are Gentiles, since the mission to the Gentiles has not yet begun (10:5–6, 18), but this, after all, is a chance encounter, not a sustained mission (Luz 2001: 24).

The result of the exorcism is that the pig herders spread the news to the people of the nearby town, who come to Jesus en masse to ask him to go away. Their reasoning is not explained, but they may have mistaken Jesus for a dangerous magician (Hagner 1993: 228). It is also plausible that they are Gentiles whose livelihood depends on the drowned pigs. If so, economic concerns outweigh the freeing of the demoniacs from Satan's dominion (Keener 1999: 287–88). Matthew's Christian Jewish readers would probably take the opposite view, that the destruction of a herd of unclean pigs was appropriate and even humorous. At any rate, this negative response to a miracle is quite a contrast to the previous positive responses to Jesus's miracles. 8:33–34

The Gadarenes' rejection of Jesus anticipates 10:13–15, where the disciples are warned that some households and villages will reject their mission. The rejection of Jesus teaches his disciples that they are not above their Master. They must face rejection and persecution realistically—with faith, not fear (7:6; 10:24–33). Those who do not know Jesus often make it clear that they do not want to know about Jesus. Carson's wry comment (1985: 219) about the Gadarenes puts it well: "They preferred pigs to persons, swine to the Savior." But the grace of God still today turns those who reject Jesus into his followers when the gospel is faithfully proclaimed by the words and deeds of Jesus's followers. On 8:28–34, see Adna in Chilton and Evans 1999a: 279–301; Loader 1982; Merklein in van Segbroeck et al. 1992: 1017–38.

iii. Healing of a Paralytic (9:1–8)

Matthew 9:1–8 completes the second set of three miracle stories with the account of the healing of a paralyzed man. In the alternating sets of three miracle stories with pairs of discipleship stories, this second set of three miracle stories in 8:23–9:8 corresponds to 8:1–17, and the second pair of discipleship stories in 9:9–17 corresponds to 8:18–22. The healing of the paralytic (cf. Mark 2:1–12; Luke 5:17–26) occurs after a return to Capernaum (Matt. 9:1), where Jesus stresses his authority to forgive sins (9:2). This leads to the charge of blasphemy from the legal experts who are present (9:3). These legal experts evidently think that he has pronounced forgiveness because he is unable to heal (9:4–5). Knowing these thoughts, Jesus heals the man to demonstrate his authority to forgive sin (9:6–7), and the crowd responds in awe and glorifies God (9:8).

This incident demonstrates the most crucial aspect of Jesus's authority, the forgiveness of sins. Jesus has taught with authority in the Sermon on the Mount (7:28–29), and he has authoritatively healed people, even from a distance (8:9). But authority to forgive sins is much greater than authoritative words and actions, since it gets to the root of the problems and illnesses that are symptoms of sin. Teaching against sin does not cause sin to stop, let alone secure its forgiveness. Sick people may be healed, but sooner or later they will get sick again, and ultimately they will die. As great as Jesus's authority in these domains is, it pales in comparison with his authority to forgive sins. Such authority is at the heart of Jesus's mission to save his people from their sins (1:21) by giving his life as a ransom for them (20:28), thereby inaugurating the new covenant (26:28; cf. Jer. 31:31). As God's beloved Son, Jesus acts with a divine prerogative. He does not blaspheme (Matt. 9:3); he saves.

9:1–3   After his rejection in a gentile area (Gadara), Jesus travels back across the Sea of Galilee "to his own town" (Capernaum, not Nazareth; cf. 4:13; 8:5), where he heals a paralyzed man (cf. 4:24; 8:6) in the synagogue. Comparison of this account with the synoptic parallels (Mark 2:1–12; Luke 5:17–26) indicates that Matthew probably places this story here for topical and theological, rather than chronological, reasons. This healing receives a mixed response, showing that the theme of opposition is escalating. Jesus heals in response to "their" faith (9:2), which may include that of the paralytic as well as of those who carried him to Jesus. His tender reference to the paralytic as "child" (τέκνον, teknon; cf. 9:22) shows that Jesus's authority is exercised with compassion. The forgiveness of sins reminds the reader of the angel's prediction that Jesus would save his people from their sins (1:21; cf. 3:6; 6:12; 9:13; 11:19; 12:31; 26:28). The response of the legal experts is not compassionate but accusatory: they think Jesus has blasphemed (cf. 26:65; John 10:33). But ironically, Jesus is not blaspheming; they are. Later, the legal experts themselves ascribe his miracles to Satan (cf. Matt. 9:34; 12:24, 31). Blasphemy is the slandering of God by reviling his name or by pretending to do what he alone can do. Jesus's forgiving the paralyzed man is no pretense, but the legal experts' words slander the Son of God.

9:4–6   Jesus's knowledge of the legal experts' thoughts (cf. 12:25; 21:2–3; 22:18) should be attributed to the ministry of the Holy Spirit, not simply to his divinity (3:16; 4:1; 12:28; cf. 10:20; John 3:34; Acts 2:22; 10:38). Jesus's knowledge leads to his asking them why they think evil of him and to posing a second question that gets to the root of their evil thoughts (9:4–5). Evidently, the legal experts think that Jesus pronounced forgiveness of sins because it was easier to do that than to heal. But Jesus tells them that the imminent healing will demonstrate his authority to forgive sins. He then turns to the paralyzed man and tells him to get up, grab his mat, and go home. The man's immediate healing and sudden departure underline the central point of Matt. 8–9: Jesus's works confirm his authority as the Son of Man to forgive sins (cf. 8:20; Dan. 7:13–14; see further the discussion of "Son of Man" under "Christology" in the introduction to this commentary). Both his teaching and his miracles demonstrate the authority of God's rule on earth (Feuillet 1954). When these verses are taken with other Matthean texts (6:10; 16:19; 18:18; 28:18), Jesus's future universal authority is implied (Nolland 2005: 382).

One result of this healing is the opposition of the legal experts (9:3). But **9:7–8** two additional results are explained here. First, Matthew simply states that the man got up and went home exactly as Jesus said (9:7). Second, Matthew describes the emotional response of the crowd, a reverential fear (cf. 14:30; 17:6; 27:54) coupled with praise to God for giving such authority to humans. This means either that the authority given to Jesus benefits humankind in general or, more likely, that the authority has been given to Jesus and his disciples viewed as human beings (Boring 1995: 235; Schnackenburg 2002: 88; cf. 16:19; 18:19).

Reflection on Matt. 9:1–8 includes the complex relationship of sin and sickness. Humans do not have the requisite insight to diagnose whether sin is the cause of sickness in individual cases (Job; Luke 13:1–5; John 9:2–3; James 5:15; but cf. Paul's apostolic insight in 1 Cor. 11:30). Yet it is possible that Jesus through the Spirit knows that this man's illness is due to sin (Bruner 1987: 329–30). Psychosomatic illness is another possibility, and in this plausible scenario, forgiveness of sins frees the paralytic of guilt and thereby heals him (Barclay 1975: 1.327–28). In any case, Matthew does not focus on the reason for the paralysis but on the authority of Jesus to forgive sins. Throughout history humans have suffered many physical maladies due to the maelstrom of sickness and death ensuing from Adam's sin (Gen. 3). But through the obedience of Jesus, who is portrayed as the last "Adam" (Rom. 5:12; 1 Cor. 15:22), the new humanity can find immediate release from sin's bondage and ultimate physical healing as well (cf. Ps. 103:3 and the comments on Matt. 8:17). Jesus's healings signify that the ultimate defeat of sin and Satan has begun.

Matthew's portrayal of Jesus's response to the Jewish teachers here is not conciliatory but confrontational. The accusation of blasphemy contradicts Jesus's unique standing as the Son of God, and no gentle compromise is possible in this case. Sadly, things are only going to become worse (cf. 9:34; 10:16–17; 11:20–24; 12:2, 10, 14, 24, 38).[6]

Additional Notes

8:28. The destination of the boat trip presents a difficult textual question, not only in Matthew but also in Mark 5:1 and Luke 8:26. All three Synoptics have textual variants for three similar words. The editors of UBS[4] prefer the reading Γαδαρηνῶν in Matthew because of its early MSS support

---

6. On 9:1–8, see Dupont 1960; A. Fuchs 1990; Greeven in Lange 1980: 205–22; Reicke in J. K. Elliott 1976: 319–29; Vargas-Machuca 1969.

(א* [with a minor spelling difference], B, C, and others). The city of Gadara, modern Um Qeis, was a Decapolis city five miles southeast of the Sea of Galilee. Two other readings are possible: Γεργεσηνῶν and Γερασηνῶν. Γεργεσηνῶν is read in א^c, L, W, *Byz, Lect*, and so on but may be assimilated from Mark 5:1 (א^c, L, Δ, and others) and Luke 8:26 (א, L, and others). Γερασηνῶν is read only in ancient versions of Matthew (e.g., It, Vg, Cop^{sa}), although it has Greek MS support in Mark 5:1 and Luke 8:26. Assuming the historicity of the pericope, Γερασηνῶν is least likely, since Gerasa (modern Jerash), a city of the Decapolis, was more than thirty miles southeast of the Sea of Galilee. Γεργεσηνῶν (alluding to Gergesa, modern Kursi) was suggested by Origen (*Commentary on John* 5.41). This city was located on the shore of the Sea of Galilee and is evidently the only place where there are cliffs overlooking the water (Eusebius, *Onomasticon*, 74.13). Since Matthew refers to the *region* of the Gadarenes, Γαδαρηνῶν can be harmonized with Γεργεσηνῶν. Josephus (*Life* 9.42) seems to say that Gadara's region bordered the Sea of Galilee, and coins from Gadara often portray ships. The region of Gadara may have included Gerasa/Kursi. (See T. Baarda in E. Ellis and Wilcox 1969: 181–97; Z. Safrai 1996.)

9:4. The most likely reading, καὶ ἰδών (well attested in א, C, D, L, *Byz, Lect*, and so on), also found in 9:2, 22, 23; 21:19, raises the difficulty of "seeing" others' thoughts and has evidently given rise to the easier expression καὶ εἰδώς (B, E^c, *f*¹, and others), which speaks of Jesus's "knowing" their thoughts.

9:8. The most likely reading, ἐφοβήθησαν (attested in א, B, D, W, *f*¹, and others), evidently gave rise to ἐθαύμασαν (attested in C, L, Δ, Θ, *Byz, Lect*, and others) because of the perception that amazement rather than fear was the appropriate reaction to Jesus's forgiveness of sin. But ἐφοβήθησαν properly describes the awe and reverence that would be fitting for the solemnity of Jesus's words.

b. The Focus on Discipleship (9:9–17)

The second set of three miracle stories is now complete, and the narrative turns again to a pair of discipleship stories (9:9–17; cf. Mark 2:14–22; Luke 5:27–39). Having read the legal experts' thoughts in Matt. 9:1–8, Jesus now responds to indignant questions from the Pharisees (9:9–13). This pericope clarifies the mission of Jesus by recounting what transpires after the call of Matthew (9:9). Evidently, Matthew throws a dinner party for his previous and new associates (9:10). Perhaps it is a farewell party for Matthew's former associates (Schnackenburg 2002: 88). The teaching about Jesus's mission flows from the controversy resulting from the Pharisees' indignation over Jesus's association with known sinners (9:12–13; cf. Hos. 6:6).

Jesus's response to the question from John's disciples about fasting (Matt. 9:14–17) is similar to the previous pericope in that in both stories Jesus's disciples do not follow the traditional meal practices of the Pharisees. They enjoy table fellowship with undesirables, and they do not fast. The underlying issue in both 9:9–13 and 9:14–17 is the relationship of Jesus, his teaching, and his disciples to Moses, his law, and his disciples (the Pharisees).

The outline for this unit is as follows:

  i. The call of Matthew (9:9)
  ii. The meal with sinners (9:10–13)
  iii. The question from John's disciples about fasting (9:14–17)

Exegesis and Exposition

[9]And as Jesus was passing by from there, he saw a man called Matthew, sitting at the tax collector's booth; and he said to him, "Follow me!" And he got up and followed him. [10]As Jesus was reclining at the table in the house, soon many tax collectors and sinners arrived and were reclining with Jesus and his disciples. [11]Now when the Pharisees saw this, they said to his disciples, "Why is your teacher eating with the tax collectors and sinners?" [12]But when Jesus heard this, he said, "Those who are healthy do not need a physician, but those who are sick. [13]Now go and learn what this means: 'I desire compassion, and not sacrifice,' for I did not come to call the righteous but sinners ⌜ ⌝."

[14]Then the disciples of John came to him and asked, "Why do we and the Pharisees ⌜fast often⌝, but your disciples do not fast?" [15]And Jesus said to them, "The attendants of the bridegroom cannot mourn as long as the bridegroom is

with them, can they? But days will come when the bridegroom is taken away from them, and then they will fast. [16]Now no one sews a patch of unshrunk cloth on an old garment; for the patch pulls away from the garment, and a worse tear happens. [17]Neither do people put new wine into old wineskins; otherwise the wineskins would burst, and the wine would pour out and the wineskins would be ruined. Rather, they put new wine into fresh wineskins, and both are preserved."

i. The Call of Matthew (9:9)

9:9   Near Capernaum Jesus encounters Matthew working at a tax collection office (cf. 5:46; 10:3; *b. Sukkah* 30a; BDAG 999). Matthew is called Levi in both Mark 2:14 and Luke 5:27, and it is not clear why the name differs here (Kiley 1984). Jews could have two Semitic names (Acts 4:36; Josephus, *Ant.* 12.285; 18.35, 95; 20.196). Perhaps Jesus gave Levi the name Matthew as he did Simon the name Peter. In any event, there is no reason to think Levi and Matthew were two different people (contra Luz 2001: 32). The collection booth may have been situated near the sea to facilitate collection of taxes on fish or of duties on goods brought into Herod Antipas's domain by boat. The call of Matthew echoes the call of four other disciples in Matt. 4:18–22 and anticipates the list of the Twelve in 10:1–4. As in 4:18–22, Jesus takes the initiative and Matthew follows immediately and unquestioningly.[1] The radical character of Matthew's obedience is not lessened by the plausibility that he has already heard of John the Baptist's ministry and Jesus's words and deeds.

ii. The Meal with Sinners (9:10–13)

9:10–11   Evidently soon after his call, Matthew invites Jesus and the disciples to a dinner at his house (cf. Luke 5:29). Many tax collectors (cf. Matt. 5:46) and sinners, probably Matthew's friends and colleagues, are invited to the dinner along with Jesus and his disciples (cf. 11:19; 18:17; 21:31–32). Tax collectors would likely be unacceptable to the Pharisees not only because of their oft-deserved reputation for extortion (cf. Luke 3:12–13) but also because of their frequent association with Gentiles. The term "sinners" (Matt. 9:11, 13; 11:19; 26:45; cf. Mark 2:14–22; Luke 5:27–39) may designate those whose behavior was egregiously ungodly, but from the Pharisaic viewpoint, it would also include those who did not observe the traditional interpretations of the Hebrew Bible (15:2) on such matters as ritual purity, food laws, and Sabbath observance (cf. E. Sanders 1983; N. Young 1985). The Pharisees would not attend this sort of dinner, and they are offended that Jesus and his disciples do attend. Fellowship around a table was taken seriously in Jesus's time as implying a deeper unity, and his participation in table fellowship prob-

---

1. Following Jesus is mentioned in 4:19–25; 8:1, 10, 19, 22–23; 9:9, 27; 12:15; 14:13; 16:24; 19:2, 21, 27–28; 20:29, 34; 21:9; 26:58; 27:55.

ably should be viewed as a foretaste of eschatological festivities (Boring 1995: 235; cf. 8:11; 22:1–14; 25:1–13; 26:29).

Jesus's answer to the accusation, disguised as a question, assumes a   **9:12–13**
common cultural association of sin with disease (cf. 8:16–17; 9:1–8).
Metaphorically speaking, the sinners with whom he associates are "ill"
and need a "physician." His recommendation that the Pharisees reflect
on Hos. 6:6, "I desire compassion, not sacrifice," focuses attention on
a prophetic critique of the mentality that prioritizes the performance
of religious ritual over the maintenance of personal integrity and social
justice (cf. Matt. 5:7; 12:7; 1 Sam. 15:22; Jer. 7:22–23; Ps. 40:6–8; Heb.
10:4–9; Hill 1977–78).[2] Jesus's command that they "go and learn"[3] suggests that they are ignorant of a fundamental biblical teaching. Hosea
puts compassion and sacrifice as either-or alternatives, but this is a
hyperbolic way of saying that God desires ethical loyalty more than
mere participation in the sacrificial system (cf. Isa. 1:10–17; Jer. 7; Edin
1998). The prophets did not wish to abolish the temple but to reform it
by stressing inner purity over ritual purity. Neither does Jesus repudiate
the temple here (contra Meier 1980a: 94). Jesus's final words apply the
metaphorical language to the reality of his mission: the "healthy" are
those who think they are righteous, like the Pharisees, and the "sick"
are those who realize that they are sinners in need of Jesus's medicine.
To these sinners Jesus is sent, and he calls them to repentance (Matt.
3:2; 4:17).[4]

As the ultimate and definitive teacher of the law (5:17–48), Jesus exemplifies Hos. 6:6 in calling Matthew the tax collector to be his disciple and
in associating with outcast tax collectors and sinners (cf. Matt. 8:1–17;
Luke 19:1–10). The Pharisees do not grasp the relevance of Hos. 6:6 to
this situation.[5] Jesus's ministry is not circumscribed by ritual impurity,
ethnicity, gender, or social stigmas. God relates primarily to sinners in
mercy, and his primary desire is for his people to show mercy, not to offer
sacrifices. Jesus epitomizes this ideal. Jesus does not downplay the law

---

2. The context of Hos. 6 fits the context of Jesus's ministry in that Hosea also speaks against religious acts without inner piety (Hos. 4:4–10; 6:9; 8:11–13; 10:1–2), alludes to prophetic confrontation (6:5; 12:10), and calls for repentance (2:14; 3:5; 6:1–3; 10:12; 11:8–11; 12:6; 14:1). Hosea 6:6 fits the general pattern of synonymous parallelism in which compassion, or covenant loyalty (חֶסֶד; 6:6a; cf. 2:21; 4:1; 6:4; 10:12; 12:6), is paired with recognition of God (דַּעַת אֱלֹהִים; 6:6b; cf. 4:1; Prov. 2:5) as traits desired by God, rather than mere sacrifice (זֶבַח; 6:6a; cf. 3:4; 4:13–14, 19; 8:13; 9:4; 11:2; 12:12) or burnt offering (עֹלוֹת; 6:6b; cf. Isa. 1:11; Jer. 6:20; 7:21–22; Amos 5:22; Mic. 6:6).

3. There are later rabbinic parallels to this phrase, including Seder Eliyahu Rabbah 18; Num. Rab. 149a. A similar expression occurs in *m. 'Abot* 2.9.

4. The phrase "to repentance" is textually dubious here, but it is found in the parallel text, Luke 5:32. See the additional note on 9:13.

5. *'Abot R. Nat.* 4 cites Hos. 6:6 in a lament by Rabbi Johanan ben Zakkai over the destruction of the temple; he teaches that sacrifice will be continued by compassionate deeds after the temple's destruction (cf. *m. 'Abot* 1.2). See also *b. Sukkah* 49b.

or the sacrificial system, but for him, adherence to the law starts with a compassionate heart. W. Davies and Allison (1991: 105) put it well: "Cultic observance without inner faith and heart-felt covenant loyalty is vain." Matthew presents the religious leaders' opposition to Jesus as becoming more and more pronounced. Here the Pharisees question Jesus indirectly through his disciples, but later (excepting Matt. 17:24) the leaders' questions will be addressed to him directly (cf. 15:1–2; 16:1; 19:3; 21:16, 23; 22:16, 23, 35). Ultimately Jesus turns the tables and asks them a question they either cannot or will not answer, which effectively ends the pattern of interrogation (22:41–46).

Jesus's social interaction with notorious sinners scandalized the Pharisees of his own day, and it likewise tends to embarrass those in our day whose views about separation from worldliness stress externals rather than personal integrity. Association with unbelievers must be handled with wisdom so that ethical compromise is avoided, but fear of such compromise cannot become an excuse for isolation from those who most need the message of the kingdom (cf. 1 Cor. 5:9–10). (On 9:9–13, see Landmesser 2001.)

iii. The Question from John's Disciples about Fasting (9:14–17)

9:14–15 The question from John's disciples regarding fasting (cf. 6:16, 18; Mark 2:18–22; Luke 5:33–39; Cremer 1965; A. Kee 1969, 1970; Ziesler 1972–73) indicates that they and the Pharisees regularly fast but that Jesus's disciples do not. John's ascetic lifestyle is mentioned elsewhere in Matthew (3:4; 11:18; cf. Luke 1:15). His disciples evidently feel that this absence of fasting is inconsistent with loyalty to God and the law. The fasting in question here is perhaps the voluntary twice-weekly fast alluded to in Luke 18:12 (cf. Did. 8.1), not the obligatory fast commanded in connection with the Day of Atonement (Lev. 16:34; Num. 29:7–11), which Jesus and his disciples evidently keep. Jesus's answer metaphorically employs wedding (Matt. 9:15), garment mending, and winemaking (9:16–17) practices. Just as it would be wholly inappropriate for the groomsmen[6] to fast while they are with the groom, so it is inappropriate for Jesus's disciples to fast while he is with them.[7] The arrival of the Messiah is hardly the time to fast, but in the future, Jesus will be taken away from them and they will indeed fast. Wedding banquet imagery is used in the Bible to describe eschatological blessings (8:11–12; Isa. 25:6–10; cf.

---

6. The phrase οἱ υἱοὶ τοῦ νυμφῶνος literally means "sons of the wedding hall" but is an idiom for those attending the groom at the ceremony. The word υἱός is a metaphor for one closely associated with the groom (BDAG 1025; cf. Mark 2:19; Luke 5:34; and similar usage in Ps. 149:2 LXX and 1 Macc. 4:2).

7. The view that the groomsmen are an image of unrepentant Jews (Schnackenburg 2002: 89) seems to be mistaken.

2 Bar. 29.3–8; 1 En. 62.14; 1QSa 2.17–22). God is sometimes pictured in the Bible as a bridegroom (e.g., Isa. 54:5–6; 62:4–5; Hos. 2:16–23). John the Baptist used this image to describe Jesus (John 3:29; cf. 2 Cor. 11:2; Eph. 5:25–32; Rev. 19:7; 21:2, 9; 22:17). The mention of the bridegroom's being taken away (cf. Isa. 53:8) is a veiled prediction of Jesus's being arrested and crucified (cf. Matt. 10:16–33, 38; 12:38–40; 16:21; 17:9–13, 22–23; 20:28; 26:11).

The second part of Jesus's response to their question is more difficult. **9:16–17** Two metaphors image the incompatibility of the new with the old, the first about patching garments (9:16) and the second about wine and wineskins (9:17). One would never patch an old garment with new cloth, since the new cloth would shrink when washed and the old garment would be ripped worse than before. Similarly, one would never put new wine in old wineskins, since the fermentation pressure would burst the old, brittle skins (cf. Job 32:19). Rather, one would always put[8] new wine into new, flexible skins.

How do these two metaphors connect with the bridegroom metaphor of 9:15, and what is the answer to the question from John's disciples? Scholars (e.g., Blomberg 1992a: 159; Hagner 1993: 244–45) regularly take the three metaphors to describe the incompatibility of the old age, exemplified by the traditional Pharisaic piety, with the new age, exemplified by the definitive climactic teaching of Jesus. The way of life inculcated in Jesus's life, words, and works cannot coexist with the old ways (e.g., fasting) of Pharisaic Judaism. But Jesus is answering John's disciples, not the Pharisees, and he teaches his disciples how to fast in Matt. 6:16–18. He also indicates that his disciples should fast when he is gone.

A more nuanced approach to this question takes due note of the temporary presence of the bridegroom with the wedding guests. A wedding celebration obviously calls for a feast, not a fast. While Jesus is with his disciples, messianic jubilation is appropriate, not fasting. But Jesus will not be with the disciples for long (26:18), and so extraordinary joy and devotion must characterize this brief period of time. After Jesus is taken away, his disciples will once again fast, but in the way he teaches, not in the Pharisaic fashion (6:16–18).

Matthew 9:14–17 is, by any interpretation, a key text on continuity and discontinuity in biblical theology. Although the text does not teach a blunt supersessionism in which Jesus replaces Moses, it is clear that when the disciples fast after Jesus has been taken away, they do not go back to fasting as if he had never come. The final clause of 9:17, "and both are preserved," is crucial. Does Jesus mean to say that the *new* wineskins and new wine are both preserved (Hagner 1993: 244) or that the *old* wineskins and new wine are both preserved (Boring 1995: 236;

---

8. The self-evident nature of the two metaphors is expressed by the gnomic-present verbs ἐπιβάλλει and βάλλουσιν in 9:16–17. See Wallace 1996: 523–24.

W. Davies and Allison 1991: 112, 115)? In view of 5:17–20 and Matthew's overall teaching, the second option is preferable. Jesus, as the ultimate teacher of Israel, preserves the law and the prophets by fulfilling them, not merely by reiterating past teaching (which overstates continuity) or by bluntly jettisoning past teaching (which overstates discontinuity). Fasting is preserved, but in the new context of the righteousness of the inaugurated kingdom, not in the old context of Pharisaic tradition. (See Derrett 2000; I. Jones 1995: 364–68.)

Additional Notes

9:13. Although it is not even included in the UBS[4] text or apparatus, a final phrase of this verse, εἰς μετάνοιαν, is arguably original. It is found in the parallel Luke 5:32 and in many MSS, including C, L, Θ, and the Majority text. It finishes the thought of the infinitive καλέσαι and is consistent with Matthean theology (Matt. 3:2; 4:17). But the shorter reading tends to be preferred because it is well attested (ℵ, B, D, and others) and best explains the longer reading.

9:14. Three readings compete here: νηστεύομεν πολλά (attested in ℵ[2], C, D, L, W, *Byz*, *Lect*, and others), νηστεύομεν πυκνά (Luke 5:33; attested in ℵ[1], many Old Latin MSS, and so on), and νηστεύομεν (similar to Mark 2:18; attested in ℵ, B, and others). The external evidence is relatively even, although weakest for the second reading. The question of interpolation from Mark and Luke exacerbates the difficulty. The UBS[4] editors accept the first reading but put πολλά in brackets because it is not found in ℵ and B.

3. Cycle 3: Additional Miracles with a Focus on Mission (9:18–10:4)

Matthew now presents the third and final set of three miracles stories (9:18–34), followed by a focus on discipleship in mission (9:35–10:4). This prepares the reader for Jesus's mission discourse (10:5–42). In this section Jesus again responds to faith by healing people in physical need. But the familiar theme is reiterated here in an unusual fashion, with one miracle story (9:20–22) embedded within the framework of another (9:18–19, 23–26). Both stories stress the action of faith leading to touch as the means of healing. In comparison with Mark 5:22–43 and Luke 8:41–56, Matthew's version of the complex or double pericope is highly condensed. The intercalation of the story of the woman's healing with the story of the raising of the official's daughter delays the outcome of the initial story and heightens the suspense.

The unit can be outlined as follows:

a. Three miracles (9:18–34)
   i. Jesus raises the synagogue official's daughter (9:18–19, 23–26) and heals the hemorrhaging woman (9:20–22)
   ii. Jesus heals two blind men (9:27–31)
   iii. Jesus exorcizes a mute man (9:32–34)
b. The focus on mission (9:35–10:4)
   i. Summary of Jesus's ministry and appeal for more workers (9:35–38)
   ii. Jesus commissions the twelve disciples (10:1–4)

Exegesis and Exposition

9:18While he was saying these things to them, suddenly a certain official came and began bowing down before him and said, "My daughter has just died; but come and lay your hand on her, and she will live." 19So Jesus got up and followed him, as did his disciples. 20Then suddenly a woman who had been suffering from hemorrhages for twelve years came up behind him and touched the fringe of his cloak; 21for she was saying to herself, "If I can only touch his cloak, I will be healed." 22Jesus turned around and saw her and said, "Daughter, take courage; your faith has made you well." And from that moment, the woman was made well.

23Then Jesus came into the official's house and saw the flute players and the disorderly crowd. 24He said, "Go away, for the girl did not die but is sleeping."

And they began laughing at him. ²⁵But when the crowd had been put outside, he went in and took her by the hand, and the girl was raised up. ²⁶And this news spread throughout the whole region.

²⁷Then as Jesus was passing on from there, two blind men began to follow him, crying out, "Have mercy on us, son of David!" ²⁸When he had gone into the house, the blind men approached him, and he said to them, "Do you believe that I am able to do this?" They answered him, "Yes, Lord." ²⁹Then he touched their eyes and said, "Let it be done to you according to your faith." ³⁰And their eyes were opened. Jesus sternly warned them, "See that no one knows about this!" ³¹But they went out and spread the news about him throughout all that area.

³²And as they were leaving, just then a mute, demon-possessed man was brought to Jesus. ³³After the demon had been cast out, the mute man spoke; and the crowds were amazed and were saying, "Nothing like this has ever been seen in Israel." ³⁴⌐But the Pharisees began saying, "He casts out the demons by the ruler of the demons."⌐

³⁵Then Jesus was going through all the cities and villages, teaching in their synagogues and proclaiming the gospel of the kingdom and healing every disease and every sickness. ³⁶Now when he saw the crowds, he felt compassion for them because they were distressed and dejected, like sheep without a shepherd. ³⁷Then he said to his disciples, "The harvest is plentiful, but the workers are few. ³⁸Therefore beseech the Lord of the harvest so that he might send out workers into his harvest."

¹⁰:¹Then Jesus summoned his twelve disciples and gave them authority over unclean spirits, to cast them out, and to heal every kind of disease and sickness.

²Now these are the names of the twelve apostles: first, Simon, who is called Peter, and Andrew his brother; and James the son of Zebedee, and John his brother; ³Philip and Bartholomew; Thomas and Matthew the tax collector; James the son of Alphaeus, and ⌐Thaddaeus⌐; ⁴Simon the Zealot; and Judas ⌐Iscariot⌐, the one who betrayed him.

a. Three Miracles (9:18–34)

i. Jesus Raises the Synagogue Official's Daughter (9:18–19, 23–26) and Heals the Hemorrhaging Woman (9:20–22)

9:18–19 As the "sandwich story" (T. Shepherd 1993) of the official's daughter begins, the official[1] expresses the hope that Jesus can reverse the recent death of his daughter if he lays his hands on her (9:18). Although touch is included in other healings in Matthew (e.g., 8:3, 15), this is the only

---

1. Mark 5:22 and Luke 8:41 describe him as a synagogue ruler, but Matthew's ἄρχων εἷς is indefinite. This is probably a Semitism, since אֶחָד can be used as an indefinite pronoun or article (e.g., 1 Sam. 1:1; 6:7; 24:15). Cf. Matt. 8:19; 21:19; 26:69; BDAG 292; BDB 25; BDF 129–30.

healing specifically described as including the laying on of hands. The ruler's strong faith in Jesus is shown not only by his words but also by his worshipful posture before Jesus (cf. 2:2, 8, 11; 8:2; 9:18; 14:33; 15:25). Jesus does not respond by saying anything; instead, accompanied by his disciples, he rises and follows the official (9:19). At this point (9:20) the intercalated story of the healing of the hemorrhaging woman begins.

The woman's twelve-year chronic hemorrhage evidently was due to a uterine disorder. In faith (9:21) she touches the fringe of Jesus's cloak (9:20; cf. 14:36; 23:5).[2] In 9:22 Jesus encourages her (cf. 9:2; 14:27) and points to her faith as the means of her healing. This is the most direct statement in Matthew on the agency of faith in healing. It is the power of the woman's faith that delivers her, not some magical power residing in Jesus's garment. Jesus would technically contract ritual impurity when the woman touched him (cf. 8:2–4; Lev. 13–14; 15:25–33; Ezek. 36:17; CD 4.12–5.17; 11QT 48.15–17; Josephus, *J.W.* 6.426; *m. Nid.* [all]; *m. Zabim* 5), but instead she contracts deliverance, her hemorrhage immediately vanishing. Matthew uses the verb σῴζω (*sōzō*) to describe her healing as divine deliverance. This word may describe physical (e.g., Matt. 8:25; 14:30; 24:22; 27:40, 42, 49) as well as spiritual (1:21; 10:22; 16:25; 19:25; 24:13) deliverance, since the two are deeply intertwined (see comments on 8:17; 9:6).[3]

9:20–22

Now the intercalating story of the official's daughter resumes. Jesus encounters a disorderly crowd of mourners at the official's house. Flute playing was customarily heard as a sign of mourning, and hired musicians were often used in wakes (cf. 11:17; Ezek. 24:17, 22; Jer. 9:17–22; 16:7; 48:36; Hos. 9:4; Amos 5:16; 2 Chron. 35:25; Rev. 18:22; Josephus, *J.W.* 3.437; *m. Ketub.* 4.4, *m. Šabb.* 23.4). Jesus dismisses the mourners with the statement that the girl is merely sleeping, not dead (cf. John 11:11–14; Acts 20:9–12). "Sleep" can be a euphemism for death (Dan. 12:2; Matt. 27:52; John 11:11–12; Acts 7:60; 13:36; 1 Cor. 11:30; 15:6, 18, 20; 1 Thess. 4:13), and just possibly the language of 9:18 means only that the girl is at the point of death. But most likely Jesus does not so much deny the fact of her death as its finality; he affirms that she will be raised (Boring 1995: 238; W. Davies and Allison 1991: 131–32; Hagner 1993: 250). In any event, the skeptical laughter of the crowd (Matt. 9:24) underlines the greatness of the miracle that Jesus is about to perform.

9:23–24

2. This "fringe" (κρασπέδου) probably refers not simply to the hem but especially to the required tassels (צִיצִת) on the corners of the cloak (Num. 15:38–39; Deut. 22:12; Zech. 8:23). See BDAG 564.

3. On this pericope, see Hutter 1984; Robbins 1987; Trummer 1991. On Jesus's healing women, see Fonrobert in C. A. Evans and Sanders 1997: 121–40; A.-J. Levine in Bauer and Powell 1996: 379–98; Love in Stegemann et al. 2002: 85–101; Rosenblatt in Kitzberger 2000: 137–61; Wainwright in Kitzberger 2000: 224–44.

9:25–26 After the crowd has been put out (cf. 7:6?), Jesus enters the girl's room and takes her hand (cf. 8:15); amazingly, she is raised. News of the miracle immediately spreads throughout the entire area (cf. 4:24; 9:31). The simplicity of this story should not detract from the fact that raising the dead is probably the most spectacular of all Jesus's miracles, reminiscent of similar miracles by Elijah and Elisha (1 Kings 17:17–24; 2 Kings 4:17–37).[4] W. Davies and Allison (1991: 125) raise an intriguing question about the placement of the most spectacular miracle here instead of at the end of this section. They conclude that the exorcism story placed at the end furthers the theme of the religious leaders' increasing animosity toward Jesus and their attribution of his miracles to the prince of the demons (Matt. 9:32–34; cf. 12:24).

The two miracles in this double story address two basic issues of human existence: the depths of parental love and the pain of chronic disease (in this case, resulting in social ostracism due to ritual impurity). The synagogue ruler's love for his little girl confronts the power of death when he takes the initiative to plead for Jesus to touch and heal her. Jesus defeats death, and a family is spared the shattering loss of a child. In light of Matthew's already/not-yet conception of the kingdom, the raising of the little girl points to the ultimate resurrection of the dead by Jesus's power (cf. Dan. 12:2; Matt. 13:43; 27:52; John 5:25–29; Acts 17:31).

The hemorrhaging woman takes the initiative to touch Jesus's garment to rid herself of chronic disease with its resulting ritual impurity. She is freed not only from the physically debilitating effects of the disease but also from its social stigma. Now she may live vigorously and experience normal human social relationships again. Her condition is not as hopeless as that of the official's daughter, but her despair must be deep after twelve years without relief. As noted above in the comment on 9:22, her "deliverance" implies an even greater deliverance from the sin that is the root cause of the physical infirmity.

As touching as these human needs are, the major stress of Matthew's narrative is christological, not anthropological. Jesus is presented once again as the one whose authority on earth to forgive sins is demonstrated by his powerful deeds of compassion (Matt. 9:6, 36). This presentation continues in the next two incidents, as blind and mute men are healed. (On 9:18–26, see Kalin 1988.)

ii. Jesus Heals Two Blind Men (9:27–31)

9:27–28 This story of the healing of the two blind men (cf. 20:29–34; Isa. 35:5–6) is without parallel in Mark and Luke. The remarkable initiative and the faith of these two men are demonstrated by their following Jesus right

---

4. Cf. 10:8; Luke 7:11–17; John 11:43–44; Harris in D. Wenham and Blomberg 1986: 295–326; Rochais 1981: 39–112.

into a house. Following Jesus implies discipleship at some level. The blind men address Jesus as "son of David," which implies his messianic authority to heal.[5] As Jesus moves on toward Jerusalem in Matthew's narrative, his Davidic origins become an occasion for controversy (Matt. 12:3; 21:9, 15; 22:42, 43, 45). Jesus asks the men if they believe he can heal them (cf. 8:2; 17:16, 19), and they readily affirm their faith in him.

This healing, like that of Peter's mother-in-law (8:14–15) and the official's   **9:29–31**
daughter (9:23–25), occurs in the relative privacy of a house. The role of faith in healing is repeated here (cf. 8:13; 9:2, 22). Jesus's command for silence once more raises the vexing question of the "messianic secret" (cf. 8:4; 12:16; 17:9). As the citation of Isa. 42:1–4 in Matt. 12:15–21 shows, Jesus, as God's servant, did not wish for his spectacular works to result in a mob mentality that would eclipse his authoritative words and incite the religious leaders and the Romans to view him as politically subversive. But one is not surprised when the two men disobey Jesus and spread the story all over that region (cf. 4:24; 9:26). (On Jesus's healing the blind, see Trummer 1998.)

iii. Jesus Exorcizes a Mute Man (9:32–34)

Like the preceding story, this account of the healing of the demon-   **9:32–34**
possessed (cf. 8:28–34) mute man is without parallel in Mark and Luke. Matthew distinguishes here between the symptom of muteness (cf. 12:22, 24; Isa. 35:5–6) and its supernatural cause, demon possession (cf. Matt. 4:24; 8:16, 28, 33; 9:32; 12:22; 15:22). The agency of others bringing the mute man to Jesus is similar to other healings in the narrative (4:24; 9:2; 12:22). This relatively unremarkable exorcism has two remarkably antithetical results (Boring 1995: 240): the crowds view this amazing exorcism as unprecedented, but the Pharisees attribute it to Jesus's being empowered by the ruler of the demons. This scurrilous charge appears in Jesus's mission discourse (10:25) and reaches its ugly climax in relation to the unpardonable sin (12:22–37; cf. Stanton in J. Green and Turner 1994: 164–80). Although faith is implied here, it is not explicitly mentioned. (On exorcism in Matthew, see E. Eshel in Charlesworth 2006: 178–85; Trunk 1994; Twelftree 1993.)

With these two miracle stories, the third set of three miracle stories (9:18–34) comes to an end. The narrative section that contains this pattern began in 8:1, and it is now complete except for a concluding summary in 9:35–38 (cf. 4:23–25) and a transition to the second discourse on mission (10:1–4). Since 8:1 Jesus has been portrayed as a healer of leprosy, paralysis, fever, demon possession, blindness, and muteness.

---

5. Cf. 1:1; 11:5; 12:22–23; 15:22; 20:30; 21:9, 15; 22:42, 43, 45; cf. Mark 10:47–48; Luke 18:38–39; Duling 1978; 1992; J. M. Gibbs 1963–64; Loader 1982; Luz 2001: 47–48; Mullins 1991; Nolan 1979: 145–215; Suhl 1968. See also the discussion of Jesus and "son of David" under "Christology" in the introduction to this commentary.

He has even raised a little girl from the dead. These acts not only model the compassion that is about to be highlighted in 9:35–38; they also demonstrate Jesus's authority on earth to forgive sin (9:6). Miracles therefore are not so much about immediate human felt needs as they are about God's ultimate deliverance from the sin that is at the root of disease. (On the eschatological significance of Jesus's Spirit-empowered miracles, see Charette 1996.)

b. The Focus on Mission (9:35–10:4)

Matthew 9:35–10:4 is transitional: 9:35–38 concludes the narrative of selected miracles stories that began in 8:1, and 10:1–4 introduces the mission discourse of Matt. 10. The stress in Matt. 8–9 on the authoritative deeds of Jesus (8:8–9; 9:6) corresponds to the stress in Matt. 5–7 on the authoritative teaching of Jesus (7:28–29). Matthew 5–9 presents Jesus as the authoritative Messiah of Israel, whose words proclaim and whose actions actualize the rule of God. The nearly identical summaries in 4:23 and 9:35 serve as an *inclusio*, bookends that bracket the two "books" of Jesus's words and deeds within a missional perspective (Nolland 2005: 406). At the same time, 4:23–5:2 and 9:35–10:4 set the narrative contexts for the discourses in Matt. 5–7 and Matt. 10 (W. Davies and Allison 1991: 143). After summarizing the words and deeds of Jesus, Matthew now presents Jesus's mandate that his disciples increasingly share in Jesus's mission (Schnackenburg 2002: 92–93).

i. Summary of Jesus's Ministry and Appeal for More Workers (9:35–38)

9:35 This pericope is without parallel in Mark and Luke. The summary of Jesus's ministry in 9:35 repeats verbatim the summary of 4:23 except for its replacement of "all Galilee" with "all the cities and villages" and its omission of the final phrase of 4:23, "among the people." Here Matthew begins to draw to a close the narrative of Jesus's miracles that began in 8:1. (For discussion of Matthew's presentation of Jesus's miracles, see Kingsbury 1978a; Légasse in Léon-Dufour 1977: 227–49; and Luz 2001: 52–58.)

9:36 The needs of the multitudes are not the only reason for Jesus's compassion (cf. 14:14; 15:32; 18:33; 20:34). His pity for the crowds is heightened because their state of distress is exacerbated by a lack of leadership; they are likened to sheep without a shepherd (cf. 1 Kings 22:17; Ezek. 34:5; Zech. 10:2; Mark 6:34). The language suggesting the imagery of a predator mangling the sheep and throwing them to the ground recalls many passages in the Hebrew Bible that speak of Israel as God's flock and Israel's leaders as shepherds.[6] Matthew himself uses this imagery

---

6. E.g., Num. 27:17; 2 Sam. 5:2; 1 Kings 22:17; 2 Chron. 18:16; Isa. 56:11; Jer. 3:15; 10:21; 12:10; 23:1–4; Ezek. 34:5; Zech. 10:2–3; 11:16; cf. Jdt. 11:19; Golding 2006.

elsewhere (2:6; 25:32; 26:31). The imagery implies that the religious leaders of Israel are not faithful shepherds of Israel but vicious predators. On this point Jesus only reiterates the prophetic critique of the Jerusalem establishment. This prepares the reader for the sustained polemics against the leaders that are yet to come when Jesus arrives in Jerusalem.

Jesus's compassion for needy Israel is now expressed by another meta-phor, that of the harvest. Israel's situation is likened to a bountiful harvest without sufficient workers (cf. Luke 10:2; Charette 1990; Legrand 1965). If the shepherdless-flock imagery expresses the desperation of Israel's situation, the harvest imagery expresses the urgency of this desperation (Garland 1993: 109). The ministry of the disciples is vitally needed at this crucial time, and they should pray so that God will send even more workers into the field (see Venetz 1980). Matthew's harvest imagery (3:8–10, 12; 6:26; 13:30, 39; 21:34; 25:24, 26; cf. 20:1–16) is also thoroughly biblical.[7] The words about the paucity of laborers for the abundant harvest provide a transition into the mission emphasis of Matt. 10 (Blomberg 1992a: 165–67).

9:37–38

The most important theme of Matt. 5–9 in general and of 9:35–38 in particular is christological. As Immanuel, God-with-us, Jesus's words and deeds epitomize the character and compassion of his Father in heaven. His ethical teaching and his compassionate acts exemplify the values and power of the kingdom of heaven. But Jesus speaks of the need for additional workers for the harvest. The previous emphasis on discipleship (8:18–22; 9:9–17) indicates the kind of workers for whom the disciples are to pray in 9:38. Judging from the sobering instructions in the mission discourse in Matt. 10, these workers will need to endure much opposition.

The opposition that is ahead for the disciples as shepherd-harvesters is also implied in Matt. 5–9. Jesus has taught that his disciples' righteousness must surpass that of the current religious leaders (5:20). His authoritative teachings transcend the influence of these current leaders (7:28–29). At the eschatological banquet, many of these leaders will evidently be displaced by those who acknowledge Jesus's authority (8:11–12). Certain of these leaders accuse Jesus of blasphemy and of being in league with the ruler of the demons when he casts out demons (9:3, 34). So it is no wonder that Jesus pictures Israel as sheep without a shepherd (9:36) and calls for more harvesters (9:37–38). And it is not surprising that the current leaders will oppose the disciples' mission (10:14–42).

---

7. E.g., Job 4:8; 5:5; 24:6; Isa. 9:3; 17:5; 18:4; 24:13; 27:12–13; Jer. 2:3; 8:20; 12:13; 51:33; Hos. 2:9; 6:11; Joel 3:13; Amos 9:13–15; Mark 4:29; John 4:35–38; 2 Cor. 9:10; Rev. 14:15. Cf. 2 Esd. (4 Ezra) 4:26–40; 2 Bar. 70.2. It is sobering that harvest is often a picture of judgment, not restoration.

ii. Jesus Commissions the Twelve Disciples (10:1–4)

Jesus has just emphasized to his disciples the need for his mission and commanded them to pray for workers for the harvest (9:37–38). Now his commission (cf. Mark 6:7–13; Luke 9:1–6) lays out their own contribution. The needy multitudes of Israel must be reached with the redeeming power of God's rule, and the disciples here receive the authority to minister as Jesus has ministered in words and deeds. In the following discourse, the disciples are repeatedly reminded that their future is inescapably linked to their allegiance to Jesus. As they continue his kingdom ministry, they will experience a mixed response. Whether they are rejected and persecuted (Matt. 10:14, 18, 22, 24–25) or received (10:11, 40), it will be due to their identification with Jesus and his teaching (10:18, 22, 24–25, 32–33, 39). The dual references to the twelve disciples in 10:1 and 11:1 provide an *inclusio* that transitions from the preceding narrative to the discourse of 10:5–42 and then back to the ensuing narrative (Garland 1993: 110).

The apostles who are mentioned elsewhere in Matthew are not always portrayed in a positive light. Jesus will construct his church despite imperfect building materials (cf. 2 Cor. 4:7). Yet the Twelve are crucial for the continuity between the pre- and postresurrection ministries of Jesus (W. Davies and Allison 1991: 151), and they will be the eschatological rulers of Israel (Matt. 19:28; McKnight 1986).

10:1   Matthew has previously mentioned the call of only five of Jesus's disciples (4:18–22; 9:9), but Jesus now commissions twelve disciples to extend his ministry of kingdom word and deed (cf. Mark 3:13–19; Luke 6:12–16). Jesus takes the initiative in calling (Matt. 4:18–22) and commissioning his disciples, and he extends to them his authority. This inner circle of Jesus's disciples is first called the Twelve here (cf. 10:2, 5; 11:1; 20:17; 26:14, 20, 47), and the number twelve occurs in several other contexts in Matthew (9:20; 14:20; 19:28; 26:53). Jesus's choice of twelve disciples is intended to correspond to the twelve tribes of Israel (19:28), who are currently without godly leaders (9:36).[8] Matthew presents these twelve disciples as Israel's new leaders (19:28; 21:33–44; D. Turner 2002). The authority of the kingdom is a crucial theme in Matthew (7:28–29; 8:9; 9:6–8; 21:23–27; 28:18; cf. 12:22–29). The disciples are here given authority over evil spirits and disease, the same domains encountered previously by Jesus's authority (4:23–24; 9:35).

10:2–4   This is the only time in Matthew where the Twelve are described more technically as apostles, not disciples as in 10:1 (cf. 11:1; 20:17; 26:20). Other lists of the Twelve appear in Mark 3:16–19; Luke 6:14–16; Acts 1:13 (displayed in Boring 1995: 254 and Carson 1984: 237). Simon (Peter),

---

8. For studies of the Twelve, see Cullmann 1962a; Geyser 1978; Horbury 1986, Klein 1961; McKnight 2001; Meier 1997; Rigaux in Ristow and Matthiae 1963: 468–86.

Andrew, James, and John have been mentioned previously (Matt. 4:18, 21), and so it is appropriate that they are first on the list. Simon Peter appears many times in Matthew,[9] but Andrew is not mentioned again (cf. Mark 1:29; 13:3; John 1:35–44; 6:8; 12:22). In view of Matt. 4:18 and 16:16–19, it is fitting that Peter is "first" at the head of the list. The brothers James and John, the sons of Zebedee, along with Peter will experience Jesus's transfiguration (17:1). They will also seek to sit at Jesus's right and left in the kingdom (20:20; cf. Acts 12:2). Of the apostles listed in Matt. 10:3–4, Philip (cf. John 1:43–48; 6:5–7; 12:21–22; 14:8–9), Bartholomew, Thomas (cf. John 11:16; 14:5; 20:24–28; 21:2), Thaddaeus, and Simon the Zealot are not mentioned elsewhere in Matthew. Matthew has already been mentioned in 9:9. James the son of Alphaeus may be the James mentioned in 27:56. Simon is described as ὁ Καναναῖος (*ho Kananaios*), but this word is probably not a toponym alluding to Cana or Canaan. Rather, it reflects an Aramaic term for an enthusiast or zealot (BDAG 507; Mézange 2000; Nolland 2005: 412; cf. Num. 25:11; 1 Kings 18:40; 19:10). Judas Iscariot, the betrayer, looms large toward the end of the Gospel (Matt. 26:14, 25, 47, 49; 27:3; cf. John 6:70–71; 12:4; 13:2, 26, 29; Acts 1:16, 25), and it is fitting that he is mentioned at the end of the list.

Additional Notes

9:34. Certain scholars (e.g., W. Allen 1907: 98) argue that this verse is assimilated from Matt. 12:24; Mark 3:22; or Luke 11:15 and ought to be omitted. But the external evidence for omission consists of relatively few Western text MSS (D, some Old Latin MSS, and so on). The evidence for including the verse is very strong (ℵ, B, C, L, W, *Byz, Lect,* and others). See Birdsall in Dunn 1992: 117–22.

10:3. The last disciple named in 10:3 is Θαδδαῖος (ℵ, B, *f*[13], and others), but there are three other readings of note. Λεββαῖος is poorly supported by D and some Old Latin MSS, and a weak conflated reading, Θαδδαῖος ὁ ἐπικληθεὶς Λεββαῖος, also exists in the medieval minuscules 13 and 828. More impressively supported is the conflation Λεββαῖος ὁ ἐπικληθεὶς Θαδδαῖος (C[2], L, W, *Byz, Lect*). The choice appears to be between the text (Θαδδαῖος) and this last conflated reading; Θαδδαῖος is more likely because of its strong external support and the fact that it explains the conflated reading better than vice versa. See Metzger 1994: 21.

10:4. Although not mentioned in UBS[4], a variant occurs here on "Iscariot." The text reading, ὁ Ἰσκαριώτης, and the variant, ἀπὸ Καρυώτου in John 6:71 (ℵ*, Θ, *f*[13], and others), both support the traditional view that Judas is identified as אִישׁ־קְרִיּוֹת (man from Kerioth). The weakly attested reading Σκαριώτης, which is found in D, has given rise to several creative etymological interpretations. See Metzger 1994: 21–22.

---

9. See 4:18; 10:2; 14:28–29; 15:15–16; 16:16, 18, 22–23; 17:1, 4, 24, 26; 18:21; 19:27; 26:33, 35, 37, 40, 58, 69, 73, 75; Kingsbury 1979; Nau 1992; D. Turner 1991. Cf. Peter's prominence in John 1:35–44; 6:68; 13:6–37; 18:10–27; 20:2–6; 21:2–21; Acts 1:13–15; 2:14–38; 3:1–12; 4:8–19; 5:3–29; 8:14–20; 9:32–43; 10:5–46; 11:2–13; 12:5–18; 15:7; Gal. 2:7; 1 Pet. 1:1; 2 Pet. 1:1.

B. Discourse 2:
Mission and Suffering (10:5–11:1)

This discourse follows the previous focus on Jesus's compassion (9:35–38). In 10:1 Jesus commissions the disciples, and this commission continues in 10:5b–8 after the insertion of the list of the names of the Twelve in 10:2–5a. The discourse concludes with the characteristic transitional formula at 11:1 (cf. 7:28; 13:53; 19:1; 26:1). The Twelve have seen Jesus's words and works; now it is they who begin their own itinerant ministries (10:1, 5–8) as Jesus continues his (11:1). They will extend Jesus's ministry by announcing the kingdom and demonstrating its power to Israel through mighty works (10:1, 7–8). Certain portions of this discourse parallel material in Mark and Luke.[1] Many scholars believe that Matthew has composed this discourse from sayings of Jesus that were originally uttered in different settings. As with the Sermon on the Mount, however, Matthew presents this material as a discrete discourse at a specific occasion, with narrated historical brackets (9:35–10:5a; 11:1). See the previous discussion of the historicity of the Sermon on the Mount.

The many different views of the literary structure of this discourse (Barta 1988; Combrink 1977; Genuyt 1991; Weaver 1990) imply that its structure is not as clear as that of the first discourse, the Sermon on the Mount. W. Davies and Allison's chiastic approach (1991: 160–62) is not totally convincing (cf. Boring 1995: 255 for a different chiastic layout), but there is a certain symmetry in that after the initial instructions (10:5–10), the emphasis falls upon kingdom reception or rejection:

Reception: Blessings for worthy homes and villages (10:11–13)

Rejection: General warning—unworthy homes and villages
       (10:14–15)

Rejection: Specific warnings—synagogues, governors, kings, family
       (10:16–39)

Reception: Rewards for receiving Jesus's followers (10:40–42)

---

1. The most notable parallels are as follows:
     Matt. 10:5–16 and Mark 6:8–11; Luke 9:3–5; 10:5–15
     Matt. 10:17–25 and Mark 13:9–13; Luke 21:12–19; cf. Matt. 24:9–14
     Matt. 10:26–42 and Mark 9:37–41; Luke 12:2–12

How the mission limited to Israel in Matt. 10 relates to the universal world mission mandated in Matt. 28:18–20 has been much discussed.[2] The mission discourse is intended primarily for the ministry of Jesus's original disciples to the cities of Israel (9:36; 10:5–6), but there are indications that it speaks to situations beyond this original mission that anticipate the ongoing world mission of the church at large. It contains references to appearing before gentile rulers and to the necessity of perseverance until the day of judgment (10:18, 22, 26, 28). Matthew has previously hinted that Gentiles will be included in his community (esp. 8:11–12), and this becomes clearer as the narrative proceeds. The expanding mission will lead to expanded opposition from both Israel and other nations (23:34–36; 24:9, 14). Thus the discourse has an open-ended relevance beyond its original audience. It presents an initial stage of mission that later expands to all the nations after the resurrection (28:18–20).[3] The fact that the modern Western church has not yet experienced widespread persecution of the sort mentioned in the discourse should not blind Western Christians to the profound truths presented here.[4]

The discourse itself contains:

1. The commission proper (10:5–8)
2. Instructions on support (10:9–15)
3. Warnings about opposition to the mission (10:16–39)
4. The reward for supporting the mission (10:40–11:1)

---

2. For further studies of mission in Matthew, see S. Brown 1977, 1978, 1980; Frankemölle in Kertelge 1982: 93–129; Hooker 1971; Jeremias 1966b; Manson 1964; Schnabel 2004; J. J. Scott 1990. Wilkinson 1974 explores the relationship between 10:1, 8 and modern medical missions.

3. See the comments on 10:5–6 and also the helpful synthesis of Carson (1984: 240–43). Cf. A.-J. Levine 1988; Tisera 1993: 131–58.

4. For further studies of the mission discourse, see Beare 1970; S. Brown 1978; Combrink 1977; Grassi 1977; McKnight 1986; Morosco 1979, 1984; E. Park 1995; Uro 1987; Weaver 1990.

1. The Commission Proper (10:5–8)

The listing of the Twelve by name in 10:2–4 is a sort of digression, and in 10:5–8 the commissioning of the Twelve resumes. In 10:1, Matthew only summarizes what Jesus said, but in 10:5b–42 he narrates the instructions of Jesus as a direct quotation. These instructions begin with the narrow focus of the mission (10:5–6), the gist of the message (10:7; cf. 3:2; 4:17; 24:14), and the works the disciples should do to demonstrate the authority (10:1) Jesus has given them (10:8).

The unit may be outlined as follows:

a. Audience (10:5–6)
b. Message (10:7)
c. Miracles (10:8)

Exegesis and Exposition

[5]These twelve Jesus sent out after he had given them the following orders: "Do not go in the direction of Gentiles, and do not enter any Samaritan village; [6]but go rather to the lost sheep of the house of Israel. [7]And as you go, preach, 'The kingdom of heaven is at hand.' [8]Heal the sick, ⌜raise the dead,⌝ cleanse the lepers, cast out demons. Freely you received, freely give."

a. Audience (10:5–6)

10:5–6 Matthew now narrates the instructions Jesus gives the disciples before he sends them out. The discourse begins with an abrupt prohibition: the disciples must not go to Gentiles or Samaritans (cf. 15:24). The destination of the mission is to be limited to the people of Israel,[1] who are again likened to lost sheep needing a shepherd (cf. 7:15; 9:36; 10:16; 12:11–12; 15:24; 18:12; 25:32–33; 26:31; Isa. 53:6; Jer. 23:2–3; 50:6; Ezek. 34:11–12, 16, 31; Zech. 13:7). Gentiles and Samaritans are excluded at this point, yet before his death Jesus anticipates mission to all nations (Matt. 8:11; 10:18; 21:43; 22:9; 24:14), and after his resurrection he commands it (28:19; cf. Sim 1995). Despite this, gentile mission remains controversial during the early postresurrection period (e.g., Acts 8:14–15; 11:1–18; 15). This stress in Jesus's ministry underlines the priority of Israel in redemp-

---

1. The expression "house of Israel" occurs more than 140 times in the Hebrew Bible, ca. 80 times in Ezekiel alone (e.g., Exod. 16:31; Lev. 10:6; 1 Sam. 7:3; Isa. 5:7; 63:7; Ezek. 3:1), and 6 times in the NT (Matt. 10:6; 15:24; Acts 2:36; 7:42; Heb. 8:8, 10). The expression οἴκου Ἰσραήλ is appositional to πρόβατα, not partitive (Wallace 1996: 84–86, 94–100).

tive history (A.-J. Levine 1988; cf. Anno 1984). This is the only time the Samaritans (see R. Anderson, *ABD* 5:940–47), who occupied territory between Judah and Galilee, are mentioned in Matthew.

Matthew 10:5 prohibits what 28:18–20 commands. How should this striking contrast be understood? The priority of Israel in God's covenant plan cannot be minimized (Hare 1993: 111). Matthew presents Jesus as the son of Abraham, through whom all the nations will be blessed (1:1; cf. Gen. 12:2–3). Although physical descent from Abraham in itself does not merit God's favor (Matt. 3:9; 8:12), the Jews remain the foundational covenant people of God, and eschatological blessing amounts to sharing in the promises made to the patriarchs (8:11; 19:28). Gentile world mission does not replace the foundational mission to Israel but supplements and broadens it (Gnilka 1986–88: 1.112).

Christianity must not be separated from its roots in the Hebrew Bible and Second Temple Judaism. The particularistic phase indicated by 10:5 is necessary for Jesus to be the fulfillment of Israel's history and hope. His disciples become the nucleus and foundational leaders of the nascent church (cf. 16:28; 19:28; 21:43). In God's mysterious plan, most Jews have not believed that Jesus is their promised Messiah, but a messianic remnant of Christian Jews remains to this day. Therefore gentile Christians must always acknowledge the priority of Israel in redemptive history (Gen. 12:2–3; Luke 2:32; John 4:22; 10:16; Acts 15:12–18; Rom. 11:16–24; 15:7–13; Eph. 2:11–13; Rev. 21:12–14). There is a sense yet today in which "to the Jew first" still rings true (Rom. 1:16).

b. Message (10:7)

The central message from the disciples should be what John and Jesus have already been depicted as preaching: repentance in view of the presence of God's rule, the kingdom of heaven (cf. 3:2; 4:17; 9:35; 13:19; 24:14). The anticipated church that will be built by Jesus is also to preach this message of the eschatological rule of God (24:14).

10:7

c. Miracles (10:8)

As Jesus said in 9:6, the authority of the ministry of word is to be demonstrated by the ministry of deed. The disciples are to heal, cast out demons, and even raise the dead. As Matt. 8–9 shows, they have already seen Jesus do all these things. They have received the gracious blessings of the kingdom without paying for them, and they are to extend these blessings to others without any expectation of remuneration. Seeking financial gain will inevitably discredit the kingdom mission (cf. Acts 3:6; 4:32–5:11; 8:18–20; 18:1–3; 20:33–35; 1 Cor. 9:18; 2 Cor. 11:7; 12:14–18; Phil. 4:10–18; Did. 11.3–12; *m. 'Abot* 1.3, 13; 4.5; *m. Bek.* 4.6). Attachment to this present world is singularly inappropriate for

10:8

those who seek a kingdom that is not of this world (W. Davies and Allison 1991: 171).

Additional Note

10:8. Although not noted in UBS[4], several variants surround the clause νεκροὺς ἐγείρετε (well supported in ℵ, B, C*, D, and others). Most consist of differences in word order, but the clause is omitted in the Majority text.

2. Instructions on Support (10:9–15)

The second section of the discourse (cf. Mark 6:8–11; Luke 9:3–5; 10:4–12) begins as the first did (Matt. 10:5), with a prohibition. The disciples are told not to make extensive preparations for their journey. They are to take no additional money or clothing (10:9–10). Instead, those who receive them and their message will care for them (10:11). The disciples' greeting of peace should go out to every household and village, but sadly, many will not receive them or their message (10:12–14). Judgment day will be less tolerable for them than for Sodom and Gomorrah (10:15; cf. 11:22–24). This first section of the discourse anticipates the detailed description of conflict (10:34) and persecution that follows.

Exegesis and Exposition

⁹"Do not acquire gold or silver or copper for your money belts, ¹⁰or a bag for your journey, or two coats, or sandals, or a staff; for the worker is worthy of his support.

¹¹"And whatever town or village you enter, inquire who is worthy in it, and stay there until you leave. ¹²As you enter the house, greet it. ¹³If the house is worthy, let your greeting of peace come upon it. But if it is not worthy, let your greeting of peace return to you. ¹⁴And whoever does not receive you or heed your words, as you go out of that house or that town, shake the dust off your feet. ¹⁵Truly I tell you, it will be more bearable for the land of Sodom and Gomorrah in the day of judgment than for that town."

The Twelve are not to take extra money or clothes with them on the mission. Their needs will be met by the anticipated support of those who receive their message (cf. 10:11–13a, 40–42). The message of the kingdom is not for sale (cf. Acts 8:20), but those who receive its gifts freely should also give freely to its messengers (Matt. 10:8b, 11). The proverbial saying about the worthiness of the worker probably distills biblical principles regarding day laborers and priests (Lev. 19:13; Num. 18:31; Deut. 24:15; 25:4; cf. Luke 10:7; 1 Cor. 9:9, 14; 1 Tim. 5:18). Hospitality to God's messengers was viewed as a sacred duty (cf. Did. 11–13). The instructions in Matt. 10:9–10 are difficult to reconcile with Mark 6:8–9 and Luke 9:3 (but see Blomberg 1987b: 145–46 for suggestions).

Even though John the Baptist's and Jesus's ministries may have prepared the countryside to receive Jesus's disciples, one is still struck by

10:9–10

the relative lack of funds and equipment the disciples are to take. This reminds believers today that their ultimate ministry resource is the Lord's power, not their own provisions. This simplicity of provisions tends to reflect negatively on the aggressive fund-raising and lavish accoutrements that are observed in certain ministries today. "Jesus' agents live simply" (Keener 1999: 317; cf. Bruner 1987: 375–76).

10:11–13 Contrasting responses to the kingdom message are anticipated here (cf. Mark 6:10–12; Luke 10:5–6). The disciples should seek those who are purported to be "worthy" people and stay with them.[1] This worthiness is evidently shown by acceptance of the kingdom message. Jesus's disciples are to accept hospitality and to give a greeting of peace to worthy homes.[2] Those who reject the kingdom message are unworthy of his messengers. The disciples are to retract their blessing as they leave such a home. This bifurcated response to the messengers of messianic peace prepares for the sobering teaching of Matt. 10:34.

10:14–15 Reception of the disciples is linked to the response to their message (cf. Mark 6:11; Luke 9:5; 10:10–11). Refusal to heed the message is rejection of the messenger. The disciples are to demonstrate the gravity of such rejection by a symbolic act of renunciation, shaking the dust of such homes or villages off their feet as they leave. Some take this as shaking from one's outer garment the dust stirred up by one's feet (Gundry 1994: 190; cf. Neh. 5:13; Acts 13:51; 18:6), but more likely it is the dust on one's feet (cf. Luke 10:11). In any case, the action symbolizes the severance of relationship: the disciples reject those who have rejected the kingdom message and leave them to their inevitable judgment (cf. Matt. 7:6). The rejection of the disciples is more egregious than Sodom and Gomorrah's outrageously shameful treatment of God's angels (Gen. 18–19). Judgment more severe than that of those two notorious cities awaits those who reject Jesus's messengers.[3]

---

1. For other texts that speak of someone being worthy (ἄξιος) in the context of hospitality, see 10:37–38; 22:8; Luke 15:19; Rom. 16:2; 3 John 6; Did. 13.1.

2. For such a greeting that wishes well-being (לָכֶם שָׁלוֹם or εἰρήνη ὑμῖν), cf. Judg. 6:23; 19:20; Luke 10:5; 24:36; John 20:19, 21, 26; Tob. 12:17. For similar farewells, cf. Gen. 26:29; Judg. 18:6; Mark 5:34; Luke 7:50; Acts 15:33; 16:36; 1 Cor. 16:11; James 2:16; Jdt. 8:35; Josephus, *Ant.* 1.179. The greeting of peace should be viewed as a wish for the realization of God's rule on earth, since the essence of God's messianic rule is peace in such texts as Isa. 9:7; Matt. 5:9; Luke 1:79; 2:14; 19:38; Rom. 14:17; 16:20; Eph. 2:17. See BDAG 288.

3. The judgment of Sodom had already attained proverbial status. Cf. 11:24; 2 Pet. 2:6; Jude 7; Gen. 18–19; Deut. 29:23; 32:32; Isa. 1:9–10; 3:9; 13:19; Jer. 23:14; 49:18; 50:40; Lam. 4:6; Zeph. 2:9; Ezek. 16:46–56; 3 Macc. 2:5; 2 Esd. (4 Ezra) 7:106.

3. Warnings about Opposition to the Mission (10:16–39)

The central section of the discourse on mission is a solemn warning of coming persecution, with appropriate encouragement for faithful confession of Jesus and the promise of reward. Although the structure is not explicit (Hagner 1993: 262), this section can be viewed as a more detailed elaboration of the rejection previously summarized in 10:13–15. It can be divided into three sections:

1. Warnings and encouragement (10:16–23)
2. Reasons not to fear persecution (10:24–33)
3. Jesus and peace (10:34–39)

Matthew 10:16–23 consists of two cycles of warning and encouragement. The first (10:16–20) warns of persecution from religious courts and civil rulers (10:16–18) but encourages the disciples with the work of the Spirit, who will speak through them during these dire circumstances (10:19–20). The second cycle (10:21–23) warns of what is almost unthinkable, betrayal by one's own family (10:21), and encourages the disciples by stressing the coming of Jesus, who will save those who remain faithful to the end (10:22–23).

Matthew 10:24–33 provides three reasons disciples should not fear persecution. First, disciples are reminded that, as Jesus's servants, they are not above him and are to be like him. They will share in his treatment by the persecutors (10:24–25). The disciples will presumably grasp this teaching more fully as the opposition to Jesus gradually intensifies and culminates in Jerusalem. Second, they should not fear, since, although they share Jesus's persecution, they will also share in Jesus's vindication (10:26–27). Later, they will share the postresurrection perspective of Matthew the narrator and grasp that the resurrection vindicated Jesus and that his return will vindicate them. Third, the disciples should not fear persecutors but the one to whom both they and the persecutors will give account on judgment day (10:28–33). The ordeal of persecution is only temporary, but the persecutors will suffer eternal punishment. Jesus, the eschatological judge, will respond in kind to both confessors and deniers.[1] The disciples can deal with

---

1. Jesus as the agent of God's eschatological judgment is a prominent theme in Matthew. Cf. 7:21–23; 8:11–12; 11:20–24; 12:32, 41–42; 13:41–43; 16:27; 18:8–9; 19:28–29; 22:43–44; 23:39; 24:30–31, 50–51; 25:14–46.

fear by reflecting on their shared identity with Jesus, by focusing on his return, and by maintaining their awe of God.

In 10:34–39 Jesus's second discourse moves toward its conclusion with the stark warning that he will not automatically bring peace to the earth. His message will sever the most intimate human relationships. The disciples' most basic values will be tested; even their own families cannot take precedence over their allegiance to Jesus. This difficult teaching is only exacerbated when one considers the importance of the family in the Hebrew Bible (Exod. 20:12; 21:17; Lev. 20:9; Deut. 5:16) and in the teaching of Jesus elsewhere (cf. Matt. 15:4–6; 19:8–9, 19). One's allegiance to Jesus can cause such dissension that one's family relationships must be severed. This will no doubt bring excruciating anguish, but this temporary trauma must be compared with the horror of eternal separation from Jesus. Jesus's own example shows that one's ultimate loyalties must lie with the new family of his followers (12:46–50; cf. John 7:3–9). He promises that the blessings of the future kingdom will somehow offset the angst of lost present relationships (cf. Matt. 19:29).

The outline of this unit is as follows:

a. Two cycles of warning and encouragement (10:16–23)
  i. Official persecution and the Spirit's ministry (10:16–20)
  ii. Family division and the coming of Jesus (10:21–23)
b. Three reasons not to fear persecution (10:24–33)
  i. Disciples share in their master's persecution (10:24–25)
  ii. Disciples must not fear persecutors (10:26–27)
  iii. Disciples must fear only the ultimate judge (10:28–33)
c. Jesus and peace (10:34–39)
  i. The divisive mission of Jesus (10:34–36)
  ii. The ultimate loyalty of Jesus's disciples (10:37–39)

Exegesis and Exposition

[16]"Behold, I send you out as sheep in the midst of wolves; so be shrewd as serpents and innocent as doves. [17]But beware of people, for they will hand you over to the courts and flog you in their synagogues; [18]and you will even be brought before governors and kings for my sake, as a testimony to them and to the Gentiles. [19]But when they hand you over into custody, do not worry about how to speak or what you will say; for what you are to say will be given to you in that hour. [20]For it is not you who are speaking but the Spirit of your Father who speaks in you.

[21]"Brother will betray brother to death, and a father his child; and children will rise up against parents and have them put to death. [22]And you will be hated by everyone because of my name, but the one who has endured to the end—this one

will be saved. ²³But whenever they persecute you in one town, flee to ⌜another⌝, for truly I tell you, you will not finish going through the towns of Israel until the Son of Man comes.

²⁴"A disciple is not above the teacher, nor a slave above the master. ²⁵It is enough for a disciple to be like the teacher, and for a slave to be like the master. If they have called the master of the house Beelzebul, how much more the members of his household! ²⁶Therefore do not fear them, for there is nothing concealed that will not be revealed, or hidden that will not become known. ²⁷What I tell you in the darkness, speak in the light; and what you hear whispered in your ear, proclaim upon the housetops.

²⁸"Do not fear those who kill the body but cannot kill the soul; but rather fear him who can destroy both soul and body in hell. ²⁹Are not two sparrows sold for a penny? And yet not one of them falls to the ground apart from your Father. ³⁰But even the hairs of your head are all numbered. ³¹So do not fear; you are more valuable than many sparrows. ³²Therefore I will also confess before my Father who is in heaven anyone who confesses me before people. ³³But I will also deny before my Father who is in heaven anyone who denies me before people.

³⁴"Do not think that I have come to bring peace on earth; I have not come to bring peace but a sword. ³⁵For I have come to turn a man 'against his father, and a daughter against her mother, and a daughter-in-law against her mother-in-law, ³⁶and a man's enemies will be the members of his household.' ³⁷Whoever loves father or mother more than me is not worthy of me; and whoever loves a son or daughter more than me is not worthy of me. ³⁸And whoever does not take the cross and follow after me is not worthy of me. ³⁹The one who has found life will lose it, and the one who has lost life for my sake will find it."

a. Two Cycles of Warning and Encouragement (10:16–23)

i. Official Persecution and the Spirit's Ministry (10:16–20)

The disciples are warned that those who reject the kingdom message will not be content with passive unbelief. They will actively oppress the messengers of the kingdom. The disciples are likened to sheep among wolves (cf. 7:15; Acts 20:29; John 10:12; Ezek. 22:27) and then encouraged to be shrewd as snakes (cf. Gen. 3:1) and harmless (cf. Rom. 16:19; Phil. 2:15) as doves. This inculcates wisdom accompanied by integrity, combining intellectual and ethical characteristics. The disciples will be among wolves as they minister only in Israel: their fellow countrymen will pose significant danger for them. The wolves of Matt. 10:16 point to the religious leaders whose opposition to Jesus mounts as the narrative unfolds.   **10:16**

The persecution by the "wolves" is described in detail in the following verses (cf. Mark 13:9–13). Both Jews and gentile rulers will engage in it, with Matt. 10:17 probably alluding to religious persecution from Jewish courts (cf. Acts 5:27; 6:12) and Matt. 10:18 to negative treatment at the hands of provincial rulers and kings, usually Gentiles (cf. Acts 25:23;   **10:17–18**

27:24). Punishment in the synagogues will include the same excruciating flogging that will be inflicted upon Jesus (cf. Matt. 20:19; 23:34; 27:26; 2 Cor. 11:23–25). But persecution for the sake of Jesus and his kingdom is, ironically, an opportunity for further testimony to Jesus and his kingdom. Jesus himself will be brought before both Jewish and gentile authorities (cf. Matt. 26:57, 59; 27:2, 11), but these verses look beyond the immediate mission to Israel to the disciples' mission to all the nations after the resurrection of Jesus (cf. 24:14; 28:18–20; Acts 4:1–22; 5:17–41; 6:12–8:3; 12:1–19; 16:19–40; 21:27–28:31; Phil. 1:12–18).

10:19–20   The disciples need not worry (cf. 6:25, 31, 34) about what they will say during the coming duress, because God will give them[2] the appropriate words through "the Spirit of your Father" (cf. Mark 13:11–13; Luke 21:12–17).[3] Up to this point in Matthew, the Spirit has been mentioned solely in connection with Jesus and his kingdom ministry (Matt. 1:18, 20; 3:11, 16; 4:1; cf. 12:18, 28, 31–32). But as the disciples extend the message of Jesus, they too will experience the similar work of the Spirit in their lives (cf. John 14:15–31; 15:26–16:31). Eventually the risen Jesus will baptize the postresurrection church with the Spirit (Matt. 3:11), and it will be led by the Spirit in responding to ongoing persecution (Acts 4:8, 13, 29, 31; 5:32; 6:5, 10; 7:51, 55; 13:9).

ii. Family Division and the Coming of Jesus (10:21–23)

10:21–22   The kingdom message will be excruciatingly divisive, severing the most cherished human relationships. In this, the most heartbreaking moment of the discourse, it is predicted that the disciples will be betrayed to death even by their own family members (10:21). This alludes to Mic. 7:6, which is cited more directly in Matt. 10:35–36. The prospect of such betrayal is extremely distressing, but it is mollified somewhat by the growing new family of disciples, with God as the Father (10:20; 12:46–50; 23:8–11). This is a difficult teaching, to say the least, but it underscores the reality that the primary allegiance of disciples must be to Jesus and to their new family of fellow disciples, not to their natural families (10:34–39; 12:46–50).

10:23   During this horrible scenario, endurance is the mark of the true disciple (cf. 7:21, 24; 13:21; 24:13). During persecution, only those whose perseverance demonstrates their authentic faith will be saved. Disciples who encounter persecution in one village are to flee to the next village (cf. 10:14; 23:34;

---

2. God's agency is implied by the divine passive δοθήσεται. This is common in Matthew. See Wallace 1996: 437–38.

3. This phrase continues the frequent references in Matthew to God as the Father of Jesus's disciples (5:16, 45, 48; 6:1, 4, 6, 8, 9, 14, 15, 18, 26, 32; 7:11; 10:20, 29, 33; 13:43; 23:9). But God is the Father of Jesus's disciples because he is foremost the Father of Jesus (7:21; 10:32–33; 11:25–27; 12:50; 15:13; 16:17, 27; 18:10, 14, 19, 35; 20:23; 25:34; 26:29, 39, 42, 53).

Acts 17:13; 1 Thess. 2:15), with the assurance that Jesus will come before they have finished going through the villages of Israel (Matt. 10:23).

The reference to the coming of the Son of Man in 10:23 is one of the more difficult passages in Matthew.[4] There are several plausible explanations:

1. Jesus will soon follow up on the ministry of the disciples. In this view, the coming is not eschatological but simply refers to Jesus's rejoining the disciples before they complete their immediate ministries.
2. Jesus's resurrection amounts to a coming, since by it the new era of the church is inaugurated (Albright and Mann 1971: 125; Stonehouse 1979: 240).
3. The coming of Jesus is a process beginning with the resurrection, continuing through Pentecost, and culminating in his return to earth (Hendriksen 1973: 467–68).
4. The destruction of Jerusalem in AD 70 amounts to a coming in judgment upon Israel (Carson 1984: 252–53; Hagner 1993: 279–80).
5. Jesus will return to the earth before the disciples complete their mission to Israel (W. Davies and Allison 1991: 192; Blomberg 1992a: 176; Garland 1993: 112; Gnilka 1986–88: 1.379; Gundry 1994: 194–95; Harrington 1991: 147–48; Keener 1999: 324–25; Schnackenburg 2002: 98–99).[5]

Choosing between the various views is not easy. A consistent picture should emerge as we interpret other Matthean "coming" texts (16:28; 24:30, 44; 25:31; 26:64). At least some of these texts depend on Dan. 7:13. One must also decide whether Jesus's mission discourse in Matt. 10 describes only the original mission of the Twelve or whether it in some places anticipates the later mission of the postresurrection church. All things considered, it seems best to conclude that the coming of Jesus mentioned here is his return to earth. This verse anticipates a continuing mission to Israel until the second coming of Christ. Jesus's mission discourse anticipates the mission of the church throughout the period between the first and second comings of Jesus (W. Davies and Allison 1991: 179–80), and this mission includes ongoing mission to Israel during the outreach to all the nations.

4. The many studies of Matt. 10:23 include Bammel 1961, Bartnicki 1987; Boring in MacRae 1976: 127–33; R. Clark 1963; Dupont 1958; Giblin 1968; Hampel 1989; McDermott 1984; McKnight in K. Richards 1986: 501–20; Nepper-Christiansen 1995; J. A. Robinson 1979; Sabourin 1977; Schürmann 1968: 150–56. Luz (2001: 91–94) nicely summarizes the history of interpretation.

5. Calvin's comments (1972: 1.302) on this issue are somewhat droll. He thought the destruction-of-Jerusalem view (4 above) was "rather forced" but admitted that the second-coming view (5 above) was "tolerable." His personal view was that the coming here had reference to Jesus bringing comfort and relief through the Spirit to believers who were in desperate straits.

b. Three Reasons Not to Fear Persecution (10:24–33)

i. Disciples Share in Their Master's Persecution (10:24–25)

10:24–25 The disciples are no doubt chagrined at the bleak prospects for their mission, and so Jesus reminds them of their place as his servants. The student-disciples should not expect better treatment than their teacher-master has received (cf. 23:8; Luke 6:40; John 15:20). Their identity is inextricably linked to his. Jesus's opponents have gone so far as to call him Beelzebul, so why should his disciples expect to be praised? The epithet Beelzebul is probably intended to link Jesus with evil spirits, as in Matt. 9:34.[6] The greater-to-lesser argument posits that if the persecutors are bold enough to call the master and head of the house (cf. 13:27, 52; 20:1; 21:33; 24:43) Beelzebul, much more certainly they will call his servants Beelzebul. The point is that the disciples will share in the malfeasance directed against Jesus.

ii. Disciples Must Not Fear Persecutors (10:26–27)

10:26–27 The natural fear of persecutors is forbidden in 10:26–33 three times (10:26, 28, 31; cf. Luke 12:2–9; 1 Pet. 3:14; Rev. 2:10; Allison 1988a). Both Matt. 10:26 and 10:27 contain Hebraic synonymous parallelism. Recognizing that they share their master's fate should release disciples from fear (cf. 5:11–12). They should be emboldened by realizing that they are following in the footsteps of Jesus. Additional motivation is found in eschatological reversal, in which present secrets, evidently the hidden sins of the persecutors, will be revealed on judgment day. Therefore the disciples must not fear but must proclaim openly what Jesus teaches them privately, in spite of persecutors (Pappas 1980). (Cf. McKnight in Chilton and Evans 1999b: 363–83.)

iii. Disciples Must Fear Only the Ultimate Judge (10:28–33)

10:28 The sovereign care of the Father for the disciples is highlighted in 10:28–31. Disciples are not to fear those whose powers are merely temporal and physical but God, whose power is eternal (cf. Ps. 33:18–19; Wis. 16:13–14; 2 Macc. 6:30; 4 Macc. 13:13–15; Marshall 1970). The persecutors can cause only physical death, but God will punish eternally in hell.

---

6. In terms of etymology, Βεελζεβούλ (בַּעַל זְבוּל) may be "lord of the household" or "lord of the heights" (cf. 1 Kings 8:13; Isa. 63:15; Hab. 3:11; Ps. 49:15 MT [49:14 Eng.]). If so, there is a wordplay with οἰκοδεσπότην in 10:25 (Aitken 1912: 51; Maclaurin 1978: 156–60). But probably the term as used here alludes to the libel that Jesus is Satan, master of evil spirits (cf. Matt. 12:24, 27; Mark 3:22; Luke 11:15, 18, 19). A textual variant (see Matt. 10:25 in the apparatus of NA²⁷) has Beelzebub, evidently "lord of flies" (בַּעַל זְבוּב; cf. 2 Kings 1:2, 3, 6, 16, where perhaps זְבוּב replaces זְבוּל, expressing Jewish derision toward the Canaanite god). See Aitken 1912; BDAG 173; Gaston 1962; Lewis, *ABD* 1:638–40. Limbeck in Feld and Nolte 1973: 31–42; Maclaurin 1978.

Disciples are not only to draw near to God as a loving Father (cf., e.g., Matt. 10:20, 29) but also to be in awe of God's authority as their eschatological judge (Heb. 10:31; James 4:12; Rev. 14:7). The temporary peril of persecution and martyrdom is daunting, but it pales in comparison with eternal punishment in hell.

The language of this verse assumes a sort of dualism of body and soul. "Hell" is γέεννα (*geënna*), the valley of Hinnom southwest of the old city of Jerusalem.[7] This was a dreaded place where human sacrifice was at one time offered to the god Molech (2 Kings 23:10; 2 Chron. 28:3; 33:6; Jer. 7:31–32; 19:2–9; 32:35). The notion that a constant fire burned there, incinerating the city's garbage, seems to be without ancient support. Γέεννα in Matthew is the place of fiery punishment following the last judgment (Matt. 18:8; 25:41; cf. 25:46; Dan. 12:2; Milikowsky 1988). It is distinguishable from ᾅδης (*hadēs*), the place where the dead wait for the final judgment.[8]

Matthew 10:28 is frequently cited in theological debates over annihilationism or conditional immortality, the view that unbelievers cease to exist at the final judgment. This is contrary to the orthodox Christian teaching of the conscious eternal punishment of unbelievers. The issue hinges on 10:28b, where God is described as the one who can destroy both body and soul in Gehenna (Milikowsky 1988). Annihilationists take the word "destroy" (ἀπόλλυμι, *apollymi*) as teaching a final judgment where unbelievers are annihilated or cease to exist. This "destruction," however, is a state of punishment for the whole person (cf. 5:22, 29–30; 18:9; 23:15, 33) that is as eternal as the blissful life in God's kingdom (25:41, 46; cf. Dan. 12:2; John 5:29; Acts 24:15; 2 Thess. 1:9; Rev. 14:10; 20:10, 15; 21:8). Eternal punishment is, to say the least, a fearful doctrine, but it is precisely the motivation given here for faithful discipleship in the face of persecution (Matt. 10:22, 28, 33). To put it bluntly, if there were no hell to avoid, there would be one less reason to be faithful to Jesus and one more reason to deny him. (On Jesus's teaching about hell, see Yarbrough in C. Morgan and Peterson 2004: 67–90.)

This section provides welcome reassurance with a lesser-to-greater **10:29–31** argument to the effect that disciples are more valuable to God than sparrows (10:29–31; Allison 1990; J. Cook 1988). A rhetorical question invites disciples to reflect on the matter (10:29a) and conclude that they need not fear persecutors (10:31). The monetary worth of two sparrows was insignificant, since an ἀσσάριον (*assarion*) was a copper coin worth about one-sixteenth of a denarius, the normal wage for day laborers (cf. 20:2; MacDonald 1989). God's awareness of a comparatively worthless

---

7. Cf. 5:22, 29, 30; 18:9; 23:15, 33; Josh. 15:8; 18:16; 2 Chron. 28:3; Jer. 7:32; Neh. 11:30; Mark 9:43, 45, 47; Luke 12:5; James 3:6.

8. On hades, cf. 11:23; 16:18; Luke 10:15; 16:23; Acts 2:27, 31; Rev. 1:18; 6:8; 20:13; Bar. 3:11, 19; Tob. 3:10; 1 En. 102.5; 103.7; Josephus, *J.W.* 1.596; *Ant.* 6.332.

sparrow's death provides much incentive for trusting that God is aware of the persecution of his people.[9] God is aware of even the number of hairs on their heads (cf. 1 Sam. 14:45; 2 Sam. 14:11; Luke 21:18; Acts 27:34), and so they are of more value than a whole flock of sparrows (cf. Matt. 6:26; 12:12; Derrett 1997a). Disciples may never fully grasp why God permits persecution, but they can be certain that God knows their travail and will deal justly with their persecutors (10:26, 28b, 33). Hagner (1993: 286) puts it well: "God has the knowledge, the power, and the concern to protect the disciples from any *ultimate* harm or injury" (cf. Allison 1988a).

10:32–33 Awareness of one's value to God is a powerful motivation in withstanding persecution.[10] Persecutors will try to force Jesus's disciples to join them in denying God. Confessing Christ before persecutors is a specific instance of endurance (cf. 10:22). Facing up to persecutors is put antithetically, with the confession of 10:32 contrasting with the denial of 10:33 (cf. Luke 12:8–9; 2 Tim. 2:12). Denial is the rejection or disowning of Jesus. If a person confesses Jesus before persecutors, Jesus will confess that person before his Father on judgment day (cf. Matt. 7:21). But if a person joins the persecutors in denying Jesus, that person and the persecutors will be denied by Jesus. A person's public recognition or denial of Jesus in this life anticipates Jesus's recognition or denial of that person at the judgment. Loyalty to Jesus may result in persecution now, but it will result in the loyalty of Jesus on judgment day.

c. Jesus and Peace (10:34–39)

i. The Divisive Mission of Jesus (10:34–36)

10:34–36 Here is a shockingly counterintuitive statement: the presence of the kingdom will not mean the absence of hostility. Far from it (10:34; Barta 1979; Tannehill 1975: 140–47). This unsettling teaching is supported by Mic. 7:6 (Matt. 10:35–36; cf. 10:21; Luke 12:51).[11] Jesus disabuses the

---

9. The future verb πεσεῖται should be taken as gnomic: "falls" (cf. Wallace 1996: 571). Jesus is speaking proverbially.

10. Matthew 10:31 and 32 both begin with the inferential conjunction οὖν. This probably indicates that the disciples' value to God (10:29–30) is intended to motivate them not to fear persecution (10:31) and as a result not to deny Jesus when they are being persecuted (10:32). It also implies that 10:32–33 is to be viewed as the conclusion of the preceding line of thought rather than the beginning of a new one.

11. Micah 7:6 is cited here in a text form similar to the LXX. The use of this passage should be viewed in the context of Micah's frequent criticisms of the social injustice that would lead to the exile (Mic. 2:1–3, 8–9; 3:1–4, 9–12; 6:9–12; 7:3). This maltreatment of vulnerable people was such that one could not trust even neighbors, friends, and family members (Mic. 7:5–6). The use of Mic. 7:6 in Matt. 10:35 predicates intrafamilial betrayal of the mission of Jesus with the introductory words ἦλθον γὰρ διχάσαι ἄνθρωπον. The lack of harmony within families is due not to social injustice, as in Micah, but to rejection of the kingdom message. But the use of Mic. 7:6 here may penetrate behind the surface of

disciples of euphoric thoughts about the immediate results of his mission with a prohibition that reminds the reader of the programmatic text in Matt. 5:17. His ministry will not bring instant universal serendipity to the world. Jesus's purpose is division before harmony.[12] Peace on earth (cf. Luke 2:14) will not be attained apart from Jesus's work of reconciling people to God. People reconciled to God have the capacity to be reconciled to each other and are equipped to work for peace (cf. 5:9; 10:13). But those who refuse to acknowledge Jesus as God's agent for peace may view the kingdom message as another reason for division and alienation, even from their own families. The alternative to peace is a sword (26:47, 51–55), which may symbolize conflict and death.[13] The kingdom message of repentance is confrontational (cf. 11:12), and conflicting responses to this message can fracture even the dearest human relationships (cf. Jub. 23.16, 19; 1 En. 56.7; 100.1–2; 2 Esd. [4 Ezra] 5:9; 6:24; 2 Bar. 70.3; *L.A.B.* 6.1; Gos. Thom. 16; *m. Soṭah* 9.15). It is not yet the time of reconciliation between parents and children envisioned in Mal. 4:6 (cf. Matt. 17:10–13).

ii. The Ultimate Loyalty of Jesus's Disciples (10:37–39)

In light of potential family strife due to opposite responses to the kingdom message, disciples are warned against misplaced loyalties. To love one's family more than Jesus is to be unworthy of him (cf. 22:8; Luke 15:19, 21; John 1:27; Acts 13:25; Heb. 11:38; Derrett 1999). Such misplaced loyalties constitute a refusal to take up one's cross and follow Jesus. Paradoxically, the attempt to avoid the cross and preserve one's life inevitably results in the loss of one's life. But accepting the cross and giving up one's life results in gaining it. The reference to taking up the cross may allude to the Roman custom of forcing a condemned man to

10:37–39

---

social injustice to the basic problem: rejection of God's law and reign. Micah also speaks of the absence of peace and the presence of the sword (3:5; 4:3; 5:5–6; 6:14). He inveighs against the lack of integrity and compassion in the practice of the temple sacrifices (6:6–8; cf. the use of the similar text Hos. 6:6 in Matt. 9:13; 12:7). Perhaps Jesus should be viewed in Matt. 10:37 as a Micah redivivus, another prophet whose radical message comes from the Spirit in contrast with that of false leaders (Mic. 3:8–12). Micah and Jesus both foresaw that a time of conflict would occur before God's *shalom* ultimately prevailed (Mic. 4:1–8). See Cope 1976b: 77–81; Grelot 1986.

12. Viewing the unsavory aspects of 10:34–35 as the effect rather than the purpose of Jesus's coming (Hagner 1993: 292) is not helpful. Although the stark antithesis of peace and sword may be somewhat hyperbolic, it remains true that Jesus intends it to be this way. The infinitives in the three ἦλθον statements in 10:34–35 (βαλεῖν and διχάσαι) express purpose, not result (Wallace 1996: 590–94). For this use with ἦλθον, cf. 2:2; 5:17; 9:13; 12:42; 20:28; cf. 6:1.

13. The sword is often mentioned in texts about eschatological tribulation: e.g., Isa. 66:16; Wis. 5:20; Sir. 39:30; Jub. 9.15; 1 En. 62.12; 63.11; 90.19; 91.11–12; 2 Bar. 27.5; 40.1; Luke 21:24; Rom. 8:35; Rev. 6:4.

carry his own cross to his crucifixion (cf. Matt. 27:32).[14] The paradox here is similar to that found in Jesus's warning to Peter and the disciples in 16:24–25. Only when we are willing to sacrifice our life and the relationship to our family for the sake of Jesus do we begin to live. But if the prospect of martyrdom or alienation from family leads us to renounce Jesus, we lose our life even while trying to save it.[15]

Additional Note

10:23. It is difficult to resolve the questions posed by the variants at the end of the second clause of this verse, but in any case, there is little change in meaning. Two shorter readings posit only one cycle of persecution and flight. These diverge over the synonyms ἑτέραν (ℵ, B, W, 33, and others; read by UBS[4]) and ἄλλην (C, Δ, *Byz, Lect,* and others). Several other readings present a longer text with an additional cycle of persecution and flight to yet another (ἑτέραν or ἄλλην) city that will not exhaust the villages of Israel before the coming of Jesus. Perhaps the longer readings better explain the last clause about not exhausting the villages of Israel, but that may reveal their secondary status. Be that as it may, they are much more weakly attested.

---

14. Contrary to the popular image of a person carrying an entire cross, it is much more likely that only the horizontal beam (the *patibulum*) was carried to the site of crucifixion and there affixed to the vertical beam (the *stipes* or *staticulum*). For ancient descriptions of the horrors of crucifixion, see Josephus, *J.W.* 5.449–51; Tacitus, *Ann.* 15.44.4; Plato, *Gorgias*, 473b–c; Seneca, *Ad Lucilium* 101. See the helpful summaries by O'Collins, *ABD* 1:1207–10; Fitzmyer 1978; Hengel 1977.

15. Among the many studies of Jesus's profound word on self-denial and cross bearing, see Beardslee 1979; Fletcher 1964; George 1968; M. Green 1983; Griffiths 1970; Seccombe in O'Brien and Peterson 1986: 139–51. Luz 2001: 113–15 concisely discusses historical and exegetical matters.

4. The Reward for Supporting the Mission (10:40–11:1)

The discourse ends much more positively with the prospect of reward for those who hospitably receive Jesus's disciples. It takes more than missionaries to accomplish Jesus's mission—the whole community of disciples must be actively involved. Those who support the missionaries will receive a reward equivalent to that of the missionaries. After the extremely sobering words about persecution and alienation from one's own family, the conclusion provides a note of balance that encourages the disciples for their mission.

Exegesis and Exposition

¹⁰:⁴⁰"The one who receives you receives me, and the one who receives me receives the one who sent me. ⁴¹The one who receives a prophet in the name of a prophet shall receive a prophet's reward; and the one who receives a righteous man in the name of a righteous man shall receive a righteous man's reward. ⁴²And whoever in the name of a disciple gives to one of these little ones even a cup of cold water to drink, truly I tell you, that person will certainly not lose a reward."

¹¹:¹When Jesus had finished instructing his twelve disciples, he went from there to teach and preach in their cities.

The solemn words of 10:37–39 about one's deepest loyalties in the face of persecution are now balanced somewhat by these concluding words of the discourse, which stress reward.[1] God will reward those who receive the messengers of the kingdom, because receiving Jesus's messengers amounts to receiving Jesus, and receiving Jesus amounts to receiving the Father. The disciples are the agents of Jesus, and Jesus is the agent of the Father. Similarly, those who receive a prophet (cf. 5:12; 7:15–17; 11:9; 23:34; 1 Kings 17:9–24; 2 Kings 4:9–37) or a righteous person will receive a reward equivalent to the prophet or righteous person's reward (Matt. 10:41; cf. 13:17).[2] Such people should receive hospitality because

10:40–42

---

1. The phrase οὐ μὴ ἀπολέσῃ in 10:42 contains the double negative with the future tense. This "emphatic negation" absolutely denies the possibility of the loss of reward for anyone who receives a disciple of Jesus. See Wallace 1996: 468–69, 571.

2. Contra Hill 1964, a "righteous person" is simply another word for a disciple, not a quasi-technical term for a developing class of Christians.

prophets stand for the message of God and righteous people stand for the character of God.[3] Even a seemingly insignificant cup of cold water given to a disciple meets a very basic human need and will bring reward to the person who gives it (10:42). Jesus's disciples are characterized here as "little ones" (cf. 18:6, 10, 14; 25:40, 45).

Despite the potentially horrific difficulties to come, the disciples will find people who respond positively to the message of Jesus and treat them hospitably. But the conclusion of this discourse is not unlike that of the Sermon on the Mount. Both discourses present loyalty to Jesus and his kingdom in blunt either-or language. One's "house" is built either on rock or on sand (7:24–27). One's life will be either lost or found (10:39). Inevitably, some try to find a way of compromise in which they may have both family and Jesus, their own lives and Jesus's mission, but there is no such middle ground in his teaching. Matthew 11 will make this even clearer as it narrates the imprisonment of John and the increasing opposition to Jesus.

11:1   The mention of the twelve disciples here at the end of the discourse forms an *inclusio* with their mention at the beginning (10:1). With his characteristic formula ("When Jesus had finished"; cf. 7:28; 13:53; 19:1; 26:1) Matthew turns from Jesus's mission discourse to Jesus's mission action itself, teaching and preaching (cf. 4:23; 9:35).[4] Matthew 11:1 mentions only that Jesus instructed the disciples before setting out again on his own ministry. Neither Jesus's sending out the disciples nor their later return are mentioned, although they are with him later (12:1). Evidently, Matthew does not describe the mission of the disciples because his purpose centers on Jesus and his teaching for the church.

---

3. The phrase "in the name of" means "for the sake of" or "in the capacity of" and refers to reception on the merits of the person's identity or classification as a messenger of Jesus. See BDAG 714.

4. The compound articular infinitive construction τοῦ διδάσκειν καὶ κηρύσσειν expresses the purpose of the verb μετέβη. Cf. BDF §400; Moulton and Turner 1963: 141–42; Matt. 2:13; 3:13; 4:1; 13:3; 21:32; 24:45.

III. The Galilean Ministry Continues (8:1–11:1)
➤ IV. Growing Opposition to the Kingdom of Heaven (11:2–13:52)
   V. Opposition to the Kingdom Continues (13:53–19:2)
   VI. Opposition Comes to a Head in Judea (19:3–26:2)

IV. Growing Opposition to the Kingdom of Heaven (11:2–13:52)

Matthew 11:2–13:52 is the third block of narrative (11:2–12:50) and discourse (13:1–52) in the first Gospel. In the narrative section, opposition to Jesus comes to a head with the accusation that Jesus relies on the devil to cast out demons (12:24) and his counter-accusation that his opponents have blasphemed the Holy Spirit (12:31–32). The parables contained in the discourse section emphasize the sovereignty of God (13:10–17) over the mixed response to the kingdom message (13:19). The discourse concludes with a challenge to Jesus's disciples to understand his teachings as scribes of the kingdom of heaven (13:51–52).

IV. Growing Opposition to the Kingdom of Heaven (11:2–13:52)
➤ A. Narrative 3: Three Cycles of Unbelief and Belief (11:2–12:50)
  B. Discourse 3: Parables of the Kingdom of Heaven (13:1–52)

A. Narrative 3: Three Cycles of Unbelief and Belief (11:2–12:50)

Just as the narrative of Matt. 8–9 follows the Sermon on the Mount, so the narrative section of Matt. 11–12 follows the discourse on mission. Overall these two chapters stress Israel's unbelief (esp. 11:16–24; 12:41–42) and the escalating opposition to Jesus from the religious leaders (esp. 12:2, 10, 14, 24, 38). But there are more-positive sections that respond to unbelief and opposition with trust in God's sovereignty (11:25–30), fulfillment of prophecy (12:17–21), and commendation of discipleship (12:46–50). Schnackenburg (2002: 103) describes Matt. 11–12 as "conversations and confrontations." (See Lategan 1977 on structural interrelations in these chapters and Verseput 1986 for a detailed discussion of Matthew's purposes in composing this narrative.)

Blomberg (1992a: 183) takes Matt. 11 to be about implicit opposition and Matt. 12 to be about explicit opposition. But although Matt. 11:1–16 might be rightly viewed as about implicit opposition, Matt. 11:12, 18–24 must be understood as about explicit animosity. A preferable analysis is suggested by Hagner (1993: 298) in general terms and by W. Davies and Allison (1991: 233–34) in more detail. This approach identifies three collections of passages, each containing three elements, the first two stressing unbelief and the third, belief:

The Structure of Matt. 11–12

I. Sayings Collection 1
  1. Unbelief: John the Baptist (11:2–19)
  2. Unbelief: The towns of Galilee (11:20–24)
  3. Belief: "Come unto me" (11:25–30)
II. Sayings Collection 2
  1. Unbelief: Sabbath controversy (12:1–8)
  2. Unbelief: Sabbath controversy (12:9–14)
  3. Belief: "The hope of the Gentiles" (12:15–21)
III. Sayings Collection 3
  1. Unbelief: The unforgivable sin (12:22–37)
  2. Unbelief: An evil generation (12:38–45)
  3. Belief: Jesus's true family (12:46–50)

The seven parables of Matt. 13 provide Jesus's interpretation of the intensifying opposition to the kingdom message (13:19–23). This opposition is presented as originating from the archenemy, the devil (13:19, 25, 28,

39). Although superficial followers of Jesus will come and go (13:19–22, 30, 40–42, 49–50), authentic followers will sacrificially embrace Jesus's teaching and bear fruit (13:23, 30, 43–46, 48–49). Ultimately the Son of Man will judge the world, punishing the unbelievers and rewarding his disciples (13:39–43, 49–50). The disciples must digest this new teaching of Jesus and grasp its relationship to previous teaching so that they will be able to carry out their own ministries effectively in the future (13:51–52). The structure of the parabolic discourse in 13:3–52 will be discussed in the commentary on that chapter.

1. Cycle 1: Jesus and John Rejected (11:2–30)

Israel's unbelief is stressed in 11:2–19 with a focus on the identity of Jesus (11:2–6) and John (11:7–15), followed by a complaint that neither John nor Jesus has been welcomed by his contemporaries (11:16–19). Israel's unbelief is also stressed in 11:20–24, this time with two parallel denunciations. Jesus first rebukes Chorazin and Bethsaida, which will receive greater punishment than the notorious Tyre and Sidon (11:20–22). Then he turns to Capernaum (4:13; 9:1) and warns that its hopes of exaltation will not be realized; it will receive punishment even worse than Sodom (11:23–24). The heavy atmosphere of unbelief and opposition is lightened in 11:25–30, where Matthew narrates a remarkable prayer and invitation. Jesus responds to unbelief by referring to his role as the sole revelator of the sovereign Father (11:25–27). Then he reiterates the call for repentance, urging weary people to come to him for ultimate Sabbath rest (11:28–30).

a. The Identity of Jesus and John (11:2–19)

Matthew 11:2–19 (cf. Luke 7:18–35) is an *inclusio* formed by the Messiah's works in Matt. 11:2 and wisdom's works in 11:19. The passage contains three sections, each beginning with a question (W. Davies and Allison 1991: 233). In the first section, John asks about Jesus's messianic vocation (11:2–6). In the second section, Jesus asks and answers a question about John's epochal significance (11:7–15). In the third section, Jesus sadly asks and answers the question of what his contemporaries' lack of repentance can be compared to (11:16–19). Despite dramatic messianic works and the preparatory ministry of an epochal divine messenger, both with biblical credentials (11:5, 10), Israel by and large does not repent.

The outline of the unit is as follows:

   i. Jesus answers John's question about the Messiah (11:2–6)
     (1) John's question (11:2–3)
     (2) Jesus's answer (11:4–6)
   ii. Jesus's teaching on John's epochal significance (11:7–15)
     (1) John's identity (11:7–10)
     (2) John's unique role (11:11–15)
  iii. Jesus reproaches unbelief (11:16–19)

Exegesis and Exposition

²Now when John was in prison, he heard of the works of the Messiah, and so he sent word ⌜by⌝ his disciples ³and said to him, "Are you the one who is to come, or should we look for another?" ⁴So Jesus answered and said to them, "Go and report to John what you are hearing and seeing: ⁵the blind receive sight, and the lame walk, the lepers are cleansed and the deaf hear, the dead are raised up, and the poor have the good news preached to them. ⁶And blessed is anyone who does not take offense because of me."

⁷As these were leaving, Jesus began to speak to the crowds about John, "What did you go out into the desert to see? A reed swaying in the wind? ⁸But what did you go out to see? A man dressed in soft clothing? Those who wear soft clothing are in kings' palaces! ⁹But what did you go out ⌜to see? A prophet?⌝ Yes, I tell you, more than a prophet! ¹⁰This is the one about whom it is written,

'Behold, I am sending my messenger before your face,
who will prepare your way before you.'

[11]Truly I tell you, among those born of women no one greater than John the Baptist has arisen! Yet the one who is least in the kingdom of heaven is greater than he is. [12]From the days of John the Baptist until now, the kingdom of heaven suffers violence, and violent people take it by force. [13]For all the prophets and the law prophesied until John. [14]And if you are willing to accept it, John himself is Elijah who is to come. [15]Anyone with ⌜ears⌝, listen!

[16]"But to what shall I compare this generation? It is like children sitting in the marketplaces who call out to the other children [17]and say,

> 'We played the flute for you, and yet you did not dance;
> ⌜we sang a dirge⌝, and yet you did not mourn.'

[18]For John came neither eating nor drinking, yet they say, 'He has a demon!' [19]The Son of Man came eating and drinking, yet they say, 'Behold, a gluttonous man and a drunkard, a friend of tax collectors and sinners!' But wisdom is vindicated ⌜by her deeds⌝."

i. Jesus Answers John's Question about the Messiah (11:2–6)

John's question (11:2–3) about whether Jesus is the "coming one"[1] is really about what kind of Messiah Jesus is.[2] Matthew has highlighted the mixed response to Jesus's ministry since 4:23. Increasing opposition from the religious leaders (5:20; 7:29; 9:3, 11, 34) threatens to outweigh popular acclaim (4:25; 7:28; 8:1, 18; 9:8, 33). John's question is crucial for the reader of Matthew because it focuses on the significance and ultimate denouement of the conflicting responses to Jesus. John's doubts should not be downplayed but given full force. John had ample reason to believe in Jesus (3:13–17), but the delay of judgment of sin (3:10–12), John's imprisonment (4:12), and the increasing opposition to Jesus would inevitably shake his confidence. Jesus's answer to John (11:4–6) reminds him of the fulfillment of biblical salvation promises, not judgment promises. John's doubts and the way Jesus deals with them are exemplary for all disciples. Those who focus on the messianic works of Jesus will be blessed and will not lose faith (11:6).

(1) John's Question (11:2–3)

11:2–3   Jesus has just taught his disciples about the difficulties of kingdom mission, and now John in prison sends his disciples to ask Jesus a related

---

1. For this messianic title, cf. 3:11; 11:14; 21:9; 23:39; Heb. 10:37; Rev. 1:4, 8; Acts 19:4. The biblical background is evidently found in Ps. 118:26; Dan. 7:13; 9:25–27; Mal. 3:1. The title uses the futuristic sense of the present-tense participle (Wallace 1996: 535–37).
2. Detailed studies of this pericope include Augustine in Dupont 1989: 283–301; Brunec 1967; Dupont 1961; Kümmel 1978: 2.177–200; Lambrecht 1980; Schönle 1982; Vögtle 1971: 219–42.

question.[3] Although his disciples were mentioned in 9:14, John has been absent since his imprisonment marked the beginning of Jesus's Galilean ministry (4:12). Here the redemptive-historical significance of the "beginning" of Jesus's ministry is explained (cf. Luke 7:18–35). Although John clearly knows Jesus's identity (Matt. 3:13–17), the limited outward effects of Jesus's ministry prompt his question. John is aware of what Jesus is doing,[4] but he evidently expects a more immediate judgment of the religious and political establishment (cf. 3:7–12; Luke 7:18–23).[5] Perhaps the use of the word ἕτερος (heteros, another) here indicates that John is pondering whether to look for another Messiah of an entirely different kind from Jesus (Gundry 1994: 205; Keener 1999: 335).

(2) Jesus's Answer (11:4–6)

Jesus's answer calls John's messengers' attention to what is heard (words) as well as to what is seen (works). Six specifics are enumerated in 11:5:

11:4–5

1. Blind people see (cf. 9:27–28; 12:22; 20:30; 21:14; Isa. 29:18b; 35:5a; 42:7a, 18b).
2. Lame people walk (cf. 15:30–31; 21:14; Isa. 35:6a).
3. Lepers are cleansed (cf. 8:2; 10:8).
4. Deaf people hear (cf. 9:32–33; 12:22; 15:30–31; Isa. 29:18a; 35:5b; 42:18a).
5. Dead people are raised (cf. 9:18–26; 10:8; Isa. 26:19).
6. Poor people hear the good news (cf. 4:14–17, 23; 5:3; Luke 4:18; Isa. 61:1c).

This description of Jesus's ministry is drawn heavily from the Hebrew Scriptures (Isa. 26:19; 29:18; 35:5–6; 42:7, 18; 61:1), although this material is not quoted but only alluded to in its general sense. Isaiah 35:6b also speaks of mute people speaking, but this is passed over here although Jesus has performed such miracles (Matt. 9:32; 12:22). In the Hebrew Bible, there is no prophecy of lepers being cleansed. The clear biblical echoes found in this list of messianic works performed by Jesus provides much for John to ponder. (On messianic works in the Dead Sea Scrolls, see J. Collins 1994; Kvalbein 1997, 1998; Niebuhr in Tuckett 1997: 637–46.)

---

3. The extent of John's cognitive dissonance should not be minimized. The subjunctive verb προσδοκῶμεν (cf. 24:50; 2 Pet. 3:12–14) represents genuine deliberation. See Wallace 1996: 465–67.
   4. The phrase τὰ ἔργα τοῦ Χριστοῦ reveals the narrator's confident perspective on Jesus's identity despite John's doubts. On this phrase, see J. Collins 1994.
   5. On John the Baptist, see 3:1–15; 14:1–12; 17:9–13; Dupont 1961; Hutchinson 2002; Meier 1980a; Schlatter 1956; Scobie 1964; J. Taylor 1997; Trilling 1959; R. Webb 1991b; Wink 1968.

11:6 If John focuses on these words and works of Jesus, he will not take offense at Jesus but will be blessed.[6] Taking offense, literally, "stumbling" (σκανδαλίζω, *skandalizō*), refers to a serious loss of faith, spiritual defeat, or apostasy (cf. 5:29–30; 13:21, 41, 57; 15:12; 16:23; 17:27; 18:6–9; 24:10; 26:31, 33). This language both comforts and warns. It comforts by encouraging John to reflect on Jesus's messianic works, and it warns that he must not allow doubt to defeat him. John's imprisonment and the delay in the judgment he predicted (3:10–12) are outweighed by Jesus's miraculous works.

Matthew 11:2–6 interprets all of Matt. 4–10 (W. Davies and Allison 1991: 242). As the coming one whom John announced, Jesus's words and works bring the saving rule of God to bear on human sin and suffering, fulfilling Isaiah's prophecies. If one as great as John could doubt this, what of Jesus's other followers? They too must focus on Jesus's messianic words and works in the face of increasing opposition. If the followers of Jesus focus on opposition and the delay in God's judgment, doubts will arise. Their focus must be on the presence of salvation, not the absence of judgment (cf. 2 Pet. 3:8–9, 15a). For the doubts and difficulties of other great servants of God, see 1 Kings 19:4; 1 Sam. 25:21–35; Jer. 20:14–18; Acts 18:9; 2 Cor. 1:8; 4:8; Heb. 5:7–8; James 5:16–18.

ii. Jesus's Teaching on John's Epochal Significance (11:7–15)

John's doubts (11:2–6) do not indicate that he is a weak, vacillating person. To the contrary, no human being ever lived who is greater than the one spoken of in Mal. 3:1, who would prepare the way for the Messiah (Matt. 11:7–10). John lives at the crucial conclusion of the prophetic era, but he will be martyred just before Jesus's redemption inaugurates the new covenant (cf. 26:28). John's Elijah-like ministry heralded the kingdom that is violently opposed, and he has become a victim of this violence (11:11–15). Neither John nor Jesus, whose lifestyles are quite opposite, is acceptable to their evil contemporaries (11:16–19). "John is too holy; Jesus is not holy enough" (Hagner 1993: 311). But ultimately, Jesus, perhaps personified as wisdom, will be vindicated by his deeds (11:19). Matthew 11:7–19 sets the scene for the blatant slander raised against Jesus in Matt. 12.

(1) John's Identity (11:7–10)

11:7–10 The inquiry by John's disciples leads to a minidiscourse to the crowd on John's redemptive-historical significance (cf. Luke 7:24–35). As John's disciples depart, Jesus seizes the moment to teach about John's epochal significance. His teaching first poses a rhetorical question three times—

---

6. See the introduction to the Beatitudes (5:3–12) for discussion of the beatitude form.

"What did you go out into the desert to see?" (Matt. 11:7–9).[7] The first two questions (11:7–8) are a bit sarcastic and expect a negative answer: John is not a reed blowing in the breeze—the picture of a weak and wavering person. Nor was he dressed in soft clothes suitable for a king's palace (cf. 3:4; 2 Kings 1:8). The third rhetorical question (Matt. 11:9) reaches the heart of the matter and expects a positive answer: John is neither a vacillating weakling nor a dapper gentleman but a prophet, even a superprophet (cf. 14:5; 21:26; Luke 1:76), whose crucial role prepared the way for Jesus in fulfillment of Mal. 3:1 (cf. Matt. 3:3; Isa. 40:3).

(2) John's Unique Role (11:11–15)

Jesus's testimony to John's greatness continues with a striking contrast.   **11:11**
No one greater than John has ever lived, but surprisingly, John's greatness pales in significance when compared with that of the least person in the kingdom of heaven (cf. 13:17; Dan. 4:17; Viviano 2000). This statement is sometimes understood to teach that John did not experience the inauguration of the kingdom but only came to its borderline (e.g., Boring 1995: 268; Toussaint 1980: 150). But this view contradicts Matt. 11:12a (cf. 8:11) and Matthew's parallel presentation of John and Jesus (3:2; 4:17). John is included in the inauguration of the kingdom, but he does not live to experience its ongoing encroachment of Satan's domain or its future consummation. His epochal ministry marks not only the

---

7. The layout below indicates the repetitive and climactic structure of 11:7–9. The wrong answer (*A*) to the first question (*Q*) is so obvious that there is no comment (*E*) on it (11:7). Jesus makes a sarcastic comment on the second wrong answer (11:8). The correctness of the third answer is explicitly affirmed, strengthened, and then explained from the Scriptures (11:9–10). The use of ἀλλά in 11:8, 9 to introduce the second and third questions is somewhat unusual. Winer (1882: 552) spoke of ἀλλά in these verses as absorbing the expected negative after a negative question. BDAG 45 takes it as indicating that the preceding is to be regarded as settled, and as transitioning to new material.

 Q[1] τί ἐξήλθατε εἰς τὴν ἔρημον θεάσασθαι; (v. 7)
  What did you go out into the desert to see?
 A[1] κάλαμον ὑπὸ ἀνέμου σαλευόμενον;
  A reed by wind shaken?
 Q[2] ἀλλὰ τί ἐξήλθατε ἰδεῖν; (v. 8)
  But what did you go out to see?
 A[2] ἄνθρωπον ἐν μαλακοῖς ἠμφιεσμένον;
  A person in soft clothes dressed?
  E ἰδοὺ οἱ τὰ μαλακὰ φοροῦντες ἐν τοῖς οἴκοις τῶν βασιλέων εἰσίν.
   Look, those soft clothes wearing in the houses of kings are.
 Q[3] ἀλλὰ τί ἐξήλθατε ἰδεῖν; (v. 9)
  But what did you go out to see?
 A[3] προφήτην;
  A prophet?
  E ναὶ λέγω ὑμῖν,
   Yes, I tell you,
  καὶ περισσότερον προφήτου.
   and more than a prophet.

apex of the old era but also the outset of the new (W. Davies and Allison 1991: 251–52; Verseput 1986: 85–90).

11:12   Violence has been related to the inauguration of the kingdom since the days of John (cf. Luke 16:16). Lexical problems seriously hinder the exegesis of this verse, and the history of its interpretation is extremely complicated (Cameron 1984; Luz 2001: 140–44). The most difficult issue is the ambiguity of the word βιάζεται (*biazetai*, "use force" [when active or middle voice] or "be treated forcefully or oppressed" [when passive]) in 11:12a. The force or violence connoted by the word can have a positive or negative nuance, depending on the context. Thus 11:12a could describe either enemies' forceful attack upon the kingdom or the kingdom's powerful encroachment of Satan's domain. A second difficulty arises with the cognate βιασταί (*biastai*, violent or impetuous people), used in 11:12b. A third complexity occurs from use of the verb ἁρπάζω (*harpazō*, grab or plunder), which could refer to violent men oppressing the kingdom or to impetuous disciples eagerly entering it.

There are any number of interpretations of this verse, but three major approaches must suffice for this discussion:

1. Both 11:12a and 11:12b should be understood as positive statements about the advance of the kingdom (NIV). The verb βιάζεται is interpreted as a middle voice reflecting the dynamic advance of God's rule (12:28). The forceful grabbing of the kingdom in 11:12b is viewed as enthusuastic converts pressing into the kingdom (Calvin 1972: 2.7; Hendriksen 1973: 488–90; Keener 1999: 339–40). This approach was popular among Greek patristic sources (e.g., Clement of Alexandria, *Paed.* 3.7.39; Irenaeus, *Haer.* 4.37.7).
2. Both 11:12a and 11:12b should be understood as negative statements about the oppression of the kingdom by its enemies (KJV, NAB, NASB, NJB, NRSV, REB; Boring 1995: 268; W. Davies and Allison 1991: 256). The verb βιάζεται is interpreted as a passive, reflecting the persecuting activity of opponents upon the kingdom. The βιασταί are enemies such as Herod the Great (2:1–12, 16–18), the religious leaders (9:34; 10:17; 12:14; 21:35–39), and Herod the Tetrarch (14:1–12), who plunder the disciples (5:10–12, 38–48; 10:16–39; 23:34; 24:9).
3. Matthew 11:12a and 11:12b contrast the forceful advance of the kingdom with the violent attack upon it (NLT; Carson 1984: 266–67). The verb βιάζεται is interpreted as a middle in a positive way, but βιασταί is taken negatively. John's ministry marks the beginning of both these trends, growth and opposition.[8]

8. See BDAG 175–76; Carson 1984: 265–68; W. Davies and Allison 1991: 254–56; Verseput 1986: 92–99 for surveys of various views of this crux. For more detailed studies, see Barnett 1977; Braumann 1961; Cameron 1984; Catchpole 1981; Chilton 1979: 203–30; W. Moore 1975; 1989; J. Shepherd 2004; Thiering 1979.

The first view above can tend toward triumphalism, not to mention its lexical deficiencies. The third view is attractive because it appears to capture the spirit of 12:28 and the dramatic encroachment of evil by God's rule. It also has some lexical credibility. But the case for taking βιάζεται positively as an intransitive middle has not been made; there are no clear examples of it in ancient literature (W. Moore 1975, 1989; Schrenk, *TDNT* 1:609–14; J. Shepherd 2004). It is best to understand this difficult passage according to the second view, as teaching the difficult truth that John in prison is learning: the kingdom will not immediately judge God's enemies but will itself be oppressed by them for a time until God vindicates himself and his people (6:9–10; 10:40–42; 16:21–27; 25:31–40).

John's epochal role is the climax of the prophets and the law. This expression reverses the usual order[9] and views the entire Hebrew Bible as prophetic, connecting with the theme of 11:9. Perhaps the reversed order views Torah from the perspective of the prophets and implies that all of Scripture is prophetic in a sense similar to that expressed in Luke 24:44. All scriptural prophecy culminated in John, who fulfills the role of Elijah. **11:13**

In this role John functions as Elijah, whose return is prophesied in Mal. 4:5–6 (cf. Matt. 17:9–13). The citation of Mal. 3:1 in Matt. 11:10 anticipates this reference to the coming of Elijah. Interpreters differ on whether this prophecy requires the literal return of the person Elijah or merely speaks of a person whose powerful ministry is like that of Elijah (cf. Luke 1:17; Kaiser 1982). The latter view seems best, but in any event, here the citation of Mal. 3:1 in Matt. 11:10 and the allusion to Mal. 4:5–6 both stress the prediction of John's preparatory ministry in the Hebrew Bible. But John's Elijah-like ministry hinges on whether the crowd will accept it. The warning formula "anyone with ears . . ." (cf. Matt. 13:9, 43; Rev. 2:7, 11, 17, 29; 3:6, 13, 22; Gos. Thom. 8, 21, 24, 64, 65, 96) underlines the urgency of John's ministry and the tragedy of rejecting it. **11:14–15**

Jesus's solemn words in Matt. 11:15 underline the importance of grasping his identification of John the Baptist with Elijah (11:14). These words have been the occasion of much discussion. A first reading of Mal. 4:5–6 seems to indicate a future return of Elijah the prophet to the earth to herald the day of the Lord. That Mal. 4:5–6 was taken at face value may be seen from John 1:21 and Matt. 16:14; 17:10; 27:47, 49 (cf. Sir. 48:10). Jesus himself seems to affirm a future role for Elijah in Matt. 17:11, and some commentators believe that Mal. 4:5–6 will yet be literally fulfilled (e.g., Toussaint 1980: 211). But in what sense is John said to be Elijah? In other passages, John, on the one hand, denies that he is Elijah (John

---

9. Cf. ὁ νόμος καὶ οἱ προφῆται in 7:12; 22:40; Luke 16:16; Acts 13:15; Rom. 3:21 and similar expressions in Matt. 5:17; Luke 24:44; John 1:45; Acts 24:14; 28:23.

1:21), but on the other hand, he is said to minister in Elijah's spirit and power (Luke 1:17), which may remind the reader of the manner in which Elisha succeeded Elijah (2 Kings 2:9–15). John is not Elijah reborn, but he fulfills a role similar to that of Elijah. Sadly, his contemporaries are, for the most part, not willing to accept this (Matt. 11:14; 21:32), and his martyrdom (14:1–12) ominously hints at a similar end for Jesus (17:12). Whether there is yet to be a literal return of Elijah to fulfill Mal. 4:5–6 must be left an open question.

iii. Jesus Reproaches Unbelief (11:16–19)

Jesus turns from explaining John's significance to confronting the unbelief of "this generation" (cf. 12:39, 41–42, 45; 16:4; 17:17; 23:36; 24:34). The parable of 11:16–19 is applied in 11:18–19 to the contemporary situation (cf. Luke 7:32–35).[10] The parable is chiastic in form, since John, as it were, sings a dirge and Jesus plays a flute:

> A   Flute playing but no dancing (11:17a)
>   B   Dirge singing but no mourning (11:17b)
>   B′ John's abstinence slandered as demon possession (11:18)
> A′ Jesus's participation slandered as excess (11:19)

11:16–19   The rejection of John and Jesus by "this generation" (Lövestam 1995) is compared to the behavior of childish brats who will not play either a wedding game or a funeral game. Neither John's abstinent lifestyle (compared to mourning or singing a dirge at a funeral) nor Jesus's enjoyment of food and drink (likened to dancing at a wedding feast) could satisfy their contemporaries.[11] John was slandered as a demon-possessed person, Jesus as a glutton and drunkard because of his association with tax collectors and sinners (Donahue 1971; H. Kee 1996). Clearly Jesus did associate with such people (cf. 9:10), but the charge of drunkenness and gluttony was a lie, evidently circulated by those who objected to table fellowship with sinners (9:11). The statement that wisdom (cf. 12:42; 13:54) is vindicated by deeds (11:19) probably refers to the righteous activities of both John and Jesus. Their deeds prove their wisdom.[12] The use of wisdom language to describe Jesus's mission does not justify the

---

10. The introductory words τίνι δὲ ὁμοιώσω τὴν γενεὰν ταύτην; ὁμοία ἐστίν are formulaic before parables. Cf. ὁμοιόω in 7:24, 26; 13:24; 18:23; 22:2; 25:1; and ὅμοιος in 13:31, 33, 44, 45, 47, 52; 20:1.

11. The adversarial responses to both Jesus and John as well as the concluding proverb in 11:17–19 are all expressed with καί, not a more commonly used adversative conjunction. For this use of καί, perhaps due to the wide usage of the ו conjunction in Hebrew, see BDAG 495; BDF §442; Moule 1959: 178; Moulton and Howard 1920: 469; Zerwick 1963: §455. Cf. Matt. 3:14; 6:26; 10:29; 12:43; 13:17; 26:60.

12. Moulton and Turner 1963: 73 is probably correct that ἐδικαιώθη is a gnomic aorist, expressing timeless truth. For additional studies of this passage, see Deutsch 1987: 46–54,

identification of Jesus with wisdom hypostatized (as in Burnett 1981: 88–91; Suggs 1970: 33–34). Wisdom is not used metaphysically but as a metaphor for Jesus's and John's credible ministries (M. Johnson 1974; Laansma 1997: 167–70; Verseput 1987:115–17). (See Pregeant in Bauer and Powell 1996: 197–232; Witherington 2000.)

Additional Notes

11:2. The original reading is most likely that of UBS[4]: διά (well supported in ℵ, B, C*, D, P, W, f^{13}, 33), not δύο (L, f^1, *Byz*, *Lect*, and others), which is likely assimilated from Luke 7:18.

11:9. The choice here is between ἰδεῖν; προφήτην (UBS[4], ℵ[2], B*, C, D, L, f^1, f^{13}, *Byz*, *Lect*) and προφήτην ἰδεῖν; (ℵ*, B[1],W, Z, and others). The external evidence favors the former reading, but this textual question is further complicated by options in punctuation and the meaning of τί ("what . . . ?" or "why . . . ?"). The former reading is also more likely when these additional factors are considered. See Metzger 1994: 22–23.

11:15. The UBS[4] reading ὦτα is found in B, D, and others, and the longer reading ὦτα ἀκούειν in ℵ, C, L, W, f^1, f^{13}, *Byz*, *Lect*. The external evidence is stronger for the latter reading, but the former reading better explains the latter than vice versa. The same question arises in 13:9, 43. The longer reading is undisputed in Mark 4:9, 23; 7:16 (omitted in UBS[4]); Luke 8:8; 14:35 and may have been assimilated to Matt. 11:15 from those texts.

11:17. The choice here is between the UBS[4] reading ἐθρηνήσαμεν (ℵ, B, D, f^1; cf. Luke 7:32) and ἐθρηνήσαμεν ὑμῖν (C, L, W, Δ, Θ, f^{13}, *Byz*, *Lect*). The latter reading better parallels the first line of 11:17, but for that reason it is more likely to have been added than omitted.

11:19. The UBS[4] reading ἀπὸ τῶν ἔργων is supported by relatively few MSS (ℵ, B*, W, and others), but it is evidently preferred because of the editors' estimate of the weight of those MSS and their view that the main competing reading (ἀπὸ τῶν τέκνων, found in B[2], C, D, L, f^1, *Byz*, *Lect*) is an attempt at harmonization with Luke 7:35.

117–19; 1990; Hultgren 2000: 202–12; I. Jones 1995: 266–69; Linton 1976; Mussner 1959; Völkel 1978; Zeller 1977.

b. Jesus Denounces Unrepentant Cities (11:20–24)

After a general introductory statement (11:20), the parallel structure of these denunciations is shown in the following layout:

The Parallel Structure of Matt. 11:21–24

A οὐαί σοι, Χοραζίν, (v. 21)
Woe to you, Chorazin,
οὐαί σοι, βηθσαϊδά·
woe to you, Bethsaida;
B ὅτι εἰ ἐν Τύρῳ καὶ Σιδῶνι ἐγένοντο αἱ δυνάμεις αἱ γενόμεναι ἐν ὑμῖν,
because if in Tyre and Sidon had occurred the miracles that occurred in you,
πάλαι ἂν ἐν σάκκῳ καὶ σποδῷ μετενόησαν.
long ago in sackcloth and ashes they would have repented.
C πλὴν λέγω ὑμῖν, (v. 22)
However, I tell you,
Τύρῳ καὶ Σιδῶνι ἀνεκτότερον ἔσται ἐν ἡμέρᾳ κρίσεως ἢ ὑμῖν.
for Tyre and Sidon more bearable it will be on the day of judgment than for you.
A′ καὶ σύ, Καφαρναούμ, (v. 23)
And you, Capernaum,
μὴ ἕως οὐρανοῦ ὑψωθήσῃ;
not to heaven you will be exalted, will you?
ἕως ᾅδου καταβήσῃ·
To hades you will descend;
B′ ὅτι εἰ ἐν Σοδόμοις ἐγενήθησαν αἱ δυνάμεις αἱ γενόμεναι ἐν σοί,
because if in Sodom had occurred the miracles that occurred in you,
ἔμεινεν ἂν μέχρι τῆς σήμερον.
it would have remained until today.
C′ πλὴν λέγω ὑμῖν (v. 24)
However, I tell you
ὅτι γῇ Σοδόμων ἀνεκτότερον ἔσται ἐν ἡμέρᾳ κρίσεως ἢ σοί.
that for the land of Sodom more bearable it will be on the day of judgment than for you.

1. Cycle 1: Jesus and John Rejected
   b. Jesus Denounces Unrepentant Cities
                                            Matthew 11:20–24

The denunciation first of Chorazin and Bethsaida in 11:21–22 and then of Capernaum in 11:23–24 is expressed in a symmetrical structure that includes the denunciation (A and A′, not parallel in form), the reason (B and B′, parallel second-class conditionals), and the eschatological verdict (C and C′, parallel πλήν [*plēn*, nevertheless] statements).

The reproaches of 11:20–24 are the most severe words of Jesus to this point in Matthew (but see 23:13–39). Any questions on the part of the reader as to how Jesus's ministry was being received are put to rest here. Although Matthew has stressed that multitudes followed Jesus because of his healing miracles, evidently the majority of these crowds did not grasp the point of the miracles: Jesus's authority on earth to forgive sins (9:6). Many had observed and personally experienced the blessings of the miracles, yet sadly, relatively few had grasped the significance of the miracles as authenticating the kingdom message of repentance (cf. John 6:14–15, 26–27). Many readily received the eschatological blessings of the kingdom, but relatively few accepted the ethical imperative of repentance (cf. Matt. 7:13–14; see Comber 1977).

This unit can be outlined as follows:

   i. Rebuke of Chorazin and Bethsaida (11:20–22)
   ii. Rebuke of Capernaum (11:23–24)

Exegesis and Exposition

[20]Then he began to denounce the cities in which most of his miracles had been done, because they did not repent. [21]"Woe to you, Chorazin! Woe to you, Bethsaida! For if the miracles that were done in you had been done in Tyre and Sidon, they would have repented long ago in sackcloth and ashes. [22]Nevertheless I tell you, it will be more tolerable for Tyre and Sidon on the day of judgment than for you. [23]And you, Capernaum, ⌜you will be exalted to heaven, will you?⌝ ⌜You will descend⌝ to hades; for if the miracles that were done in you had been done in Sodom, it would have remained to this day. [24]Nevertheless I tell you that it will be more tolerable for the land of Sodom on the day of judgment than for you."

i. Rebuke of Chorazin and Bethsaida (11:20–22)

11:20–22 The general reproach of Jesus's contemporaries in 11:16–19 leads to the sharp denunciation of specific towns in 11:20–24. The general introductory statement of 11:20 underlines the guilt of those who saw Jesus's miracles but refused to repent (cf. John 12:37). Then Jesus first singles out Chorazin and Bethsaida (cf. R. Arav in Charlesworth 2006: 145–66; Pixner 1985; Strickert 1998), towns near Capernaum at the northern end of the Sea of Galilee. The pattern is charge, reason (Matt.

11:21), and verdict (11:22), as laid out above. Their unbelief is even worse than that of Tyre and Sidon, important coastal cities that were ancient enemies of Israel.[1] Tyre and Sidon would have shown their repentance with sackcloth and ashes (cf. Esth. 4:1–4; Ps. 69:11; Jon. 3:5) had they seen Jesus's miracles,[2] but[3] Chorazin and Bethsaida will fare worse than Tyre and Sidon on judgment day (cf. Matt. 15:21–28). These two Galilean towns are not mentioned elsewhere in Matthew, but they evidently experienced the ministry of Jesus summarized in 4:23; 9:35; 11:1. The pronouncement of woe here balances the beatitude spoken to John's followers in 11:11. Additional pronouncements of woe are found in 18:7; 23:13–16, 23–29; 24:19; 26:24 (cf. Num. 21:29; Isa. 3:9–11; Ezek. 24:6–9). (See D. Turner 2004.)

ii. Rebuke of Capernaum (11:23–24)

11:23–24   The second reproach follows the same pattern of charge, reason (11:23), and verdict (11:24). Sodom will fare better on judgment day than will Jesus's own town, Capernaum (cf. 4:13; 9:1). Its unbelief is described in scriptural language (Isa. 14:13–15; Ezek. 26:20; 31:14; 32:18, 24) that compares Capernaum's arrogance to that of the pagan king of Babylon. Far from being exalted to heaven, Capernaum will be punished in hades, the place of the dead (see the comments on 10:28). Its punishment will be worse than that of Sodom, the most notoriously wicked city in the entire Bible. Jesus has already spoken similarly about Sodom in 10:15.[4]

These three Galilean towns will face such severe judgment because they received such clear and sustained revelation. Greater access to truth brings greater accountability. This passage seems to assume a principle of proportionate accountability that results in degrees of reward and punishment (cf. Luke 12:47–48; Keener 1999: 345). The wicked towns of Tyre and Sidon, along with Sodom, had not received as much revelation as had Chorazin, Bethsaida, and especially Capernaum, Jesus's adopted hometown (Matt. 4:13; 9:1). Thus the judgment of Tyre, Sidon, and even Sodom will be more tolerable than that of Chorazin, Bethsaida, and Capernaum. These Galilean towns serve as a warning to nonchalant

1. On Tyre and Sidon, see 15:21; Acts 12:20; 2 Sam. 5:11; 1 Kings 5:1; 9:11–12; 1 Chron. 14:1–2; 2 Chron. 2:3, 11; Pss. 45:12; 87:4; Isa. 23:1–8; Jer. 25:22; 27:3; 47:4; Ezek. 28:2, 12, 21; Joel 3:4–8; Zech. 9:1–4; 1 Macc. 5:15; Jdt. 2:28; Josephus, *Ant.* 8.320; 15.95.

2. This is expressed with the second-class, or contrary-to-fact, conditional construction. See Wallace 1996: 694–96; Matt. 11:23; 12:7; 23:30; 24:22, 43.

3. The particle πλήν here and in 11:24 evidently expresses contrast with the preceding hypothesis regarding Tyre and Sidon. Their fate aside, the severe judgment of Chorazin and Bethsaida is assured (BDAG 826). Thrall 1962: 73–74 poses the possibility that πλήν is equivalent to ἀμήν. Cf. 10:15; 26:39, 64.

4. Among the many texts on Sodom, see Gen. 13:13; 18:20–19:28; Deut. 29:23; 32:32; Isa. 1:9–10; 13:19; Jer. 23:14; 49:18; 50:40; Ezek. 16:46–56; Amos 4:11; 2 Pet. 2:6; Jude 7; Rev. 11:8; cf. Jub. 16.5; 20.6; Mart. Ascen. Isa. 3.10; 1 Clem. 11.1; Gk. Apoc. Ezra 2.19; 7.12.

people whose familiarity with Christianity has bred contempt of it. Being born into a Christian family, being a member of a church, or even being a citizen of a country where Christianity is prominent are blessings from God but do not take the place of personal repentance. Judas Iscariot is sad testimony to the fact that those who are nearest to the means of grace are sometimes the furthest from its end. (See Bruner 1987: 424–29; Marguerat 1981: 259–64; Reiser 1997: 221–30.)

Additional Note

11:23. Two problems arise here. The first, in 11:23a, is evidently due to a transcriptional accident. UBS[4] prefers the reading μὴ ἕως οὐρανοῦ ὑψωθήσῃ; (ℵ, B*, C [τοῦ οὐρανοῦ], D, W, most Latin MSS). Most likely two other readings, ἡ ἕως τοῦ οὐρανοῦ ὑψωθεῖσα (33, *Byz*[pt], *Lect*) and ἡ ἕως τοῦ οὐρανοῦ ὑψωθής (13, 180, *Byz*[pt]), occurred during transcription from oral reading of the exemplar. After Καφαρναούμ the first letter of μή was accidentally dropped, and the remaining η was viewed as a relative pronoun or article. See Metzger 1994: 24–25.

A second problem, in 11:23b, is more difficult. UBS[4] reads the more common active verb καταβήσῃ (B, D, W, most ancient versions), but there is ancient support for the less-common passive verb καταβιβασθήσῃ (ℵ, C, L, *f*[1], *f*[13], *Byz*, *Lect*). The former reading can be viewed as an authorial allusion to Isa. 14:15 LXX or as an editorial assimilation to that text (cf. Luke 10:15 for the same problem). The latter reading is the more difficult and presents the same idea as the former, yet more vividly. External evidence is not decisive.

c. Gracious Revelation in the Midst of Opposition (11:25–30)

In this passage Jesus responds[1] in two ways to growing opposition. He first finds comfort and strength in the sovereignty of God his Father and in his role as the exclusive revelator of the Father (11:25–27). Then he continues to invite people to follow him (11:28–30). This response is in striking contrast to the announcement of doom upon the unrepentant towns.[2]

The unit outline is as follows:

    i. Gracious election (11:25–27)
    ii. Gracious invitation (11:28–30)

Exegesis and Exposition

[25]At that time Jesus said, "I praise you, Father, Lord of heaven and earth, that you have hidden these things from the wise and intelligent and have revealed them to infants. [26]Yes, Father, for this was pleasing to you. [27]All things have been handed over to me by my Father; and no one knows ⌜the Son except the Father; nor does anyone know the Father except the Son⌝, and anyone to whom the Son chooses to reveal him. [28]Come to me, all who are weary and loaded down, and I will give you rest. [29]Take my yoke upon you and learn from me, for I am gentle and humble in heart, and you will find rest for your souls. [30]For my yoke is easy and my burden is light."

i. Gracious Election (11:25–27)

11:25   Here things take a striking turn from rebuke to a prayer, not of lament but of public thanksgiving. During increasing conflict and rejection, Jesus rests in the Father as Lord of heaven and earth (cf. Luke 10:21; Acts 7:49 [Isa. 66:1–2]; Tob. 7:17 LXX; Jdt. 9:12 LXX; 1QapGen 22.16, 21; Shem-

---

1. The words ἐν ἐκείνῳ τῷ καιρῷ ἀποκριθεὶς ὁ Ἰησοῦς εἶπεν are puzzling since no one has asked Jesus a question. The "answer" may be viewed as a response to the difficulties Jesus faced at that time (Calvin 1972: 2.20; cf. 12:1; 14:1). A similar "answer" is found in 22:1. For another view, stressing the Semitic idiom, see BDAG 114; BDF §140; W. Davies and Allison 1991: 273.

2. This remarkable passage has led to many studies, including Allison 1988b; Bacchiocchi 1984; H. Betz 1967; Cerfaux 1954–55; Charette 1992a; W. Davies 1962: 119–44; Deutsch 1987; Hunter 1962; Légasse in Coppens 1976: 245–74; U. Luck 1975; Luomanen 1998b: 109–21; Sabbe in Delobel 1982: 363–71; Stanton 1982; K. Steck 1955; Suggs 1970.

oneh Esreh, benediction 1). The Father sovereignly hides "these things" (perhaps the eschatological significance of the miracles) from those who "think themselves wise and clever" and reveals himself to the "childlike" (cf. Matt. 13:10–17; Luke 10:21–22). A similar contrast was made previously between those who thought themselves to be healthy and those who were ill (9:12–13). Here the contrast is not literally between intellectuals and children but between those who are proud and those who are humble. The former refuse to repent when they are confronted with the words and works of the kingdom. The latter respond to the kingdom message in repentance, acknowledging their childlike dependence upon the heavenly Father. Several times Matthew speaks of Jesus's disciples as poor, little, or childlike (cf. 5:3; 10:42; 18:6; 21:16; 25:40; Luke 10:21–22; Grundmann 1959). This concealment from the proud is "the dark side of grace" (Gundry 1994: 216; cf. Calvin 1972: 2.21–23).

Jesus affirms that the basis of the Father's concealing and revealing activity is the Father's own desire. Nothing outside the Father has determined this course of action. The word translated "pleasing" is εὐδοκία (*eudokia*; cf. Luke 2:14; Eph. 1:5, 9; Phil. 2:13; and רָצוֹן [*riṣôn*] in CD 3.15; 1QH 4.32–33; 1QM 18.14; 1QS 11.18; 4Q400 frg. 1.1.16), which refers to God's pleasure, goodwill, or favor. **11:26**

Jesus turns from prayer to affirmation of his unique messianic status as the exclusive revelator of the Father. The Father has delegated all things to the Son (cf. 28:18), with whom he shares a unique relationship of intimate reciprocal knowledge. This is not unlike the relationship of God and wisdom in Hellenistic Jewish texts that reflect on Prov. 1:20–23; 8:1–36 (e.g., Sir. 1:6–9; 24:19–22; 51:23–30; Bar. 3:32; Wis. 8:4; 9:1–18; 10:10). Only through the Son can humans receive the knowledge of the Father (W. Davies 1953). The high Christology here is similar to that of the Gospel of John (e.g., John 1:14, 18; 3:35; 14:6–9; 17:1–8; cf. 1 Cor. 15:20–28; Eph. 1:9–10; see Grundmann 1965–66; Pryor 1991a; Sabbe in Delobel 1982: 263–71). Here the trinitarian basis of Jesus's messianic mission, previously seen at Jesus's baptism, is reiterated and developed (cf. Matt. 3:17; 12:18; 17:5; 28:18–19). The unique relationship of the Father and the Son in redeeming God's people is clearly described in 11:25–27. **11:27**

Previous details in Matthew's narrative have prepared the reader for this quintessential statement. Immanuel, the Son miraculously born to Mary, signifies the unique saving presence of God with his people (1:23). Jesus's baptism demonstrates the pleasure the Father takes in the Son (3:17; cf. 17:5; Isa. 42:1). Satan is unable to shake the Son from his resolve to please the Father (Matt. 4:1–11). Jesus's miracles show that the Father has given Jesus authority to forgive sins (9:6). In times of persecution, disciples must confess the Son if they wish the Son to confess them to the Father (10:32–33, 40). Further development of the Son's grandeur will occur, culminating in the postresurrection Great Commission, predicated on the exalted Jesus's universal authority (28:18–20). But one would be hard pressed to speak of the Son in more exalted language than that used in 11:27, which bluntly yet beautifully teaches that the saving knowledge of God the Father comes only through the electing revelation of Jesus, the exclusive mediator of salvation.

ii. Gracious Invitation (11:28–30)

Matthew 11:28–30 is one of the most memorable passages in all of Scripture. Again the literary structure of these verses is clearly parallel. There are two somewhat symmetrical sets, each containing an appeal, a description/motivation, and a promise. In the twofold appeal (A and A'), the second statement uses the fitting metaphor of the yoke of discipleship. Following each appeal is a description, first of the weary ones whom Jesus is inviting (B) and second of Jesus himself (B'). These descriptions are really motivations for responding to the appeal: Israel is burdened and Jesus is gentle. Those who respond to the appeal will experience the promised rest (C and C'). Here the second statement is more vivid, alluding to Jer. 6:16. Finally, only the second set has an additional line that describes Jesus's yoke as easy and his load as light (D). This last line develops the idea of Jesus as gentle and contrasts with Israel's present burdened state of weariness. (See Motte 1981.)

The Structure of Matt. 11:28–30

A Δεῦτε πρός με (v. 28)
   Come to me
   B πάντες οἱ κοπιῶντες καὶ πεφορτισμένοι,
      all who are tired and burdened,
      C κἀγὼ ἀναπαύσω ὑμᾶς.
         and I will rest you.
A' ἄρατε τὸν ζυγόν μου ἐφ᾽ ὑμᾶς καὶ μάθετε ἀπ᾽ ἐμοῦ, (v. 29)
    Take my yoke on you and learn from me,
    B' ὅτι πραΰς εἰμι καὶ ταπεινὸς τῇ καρδίᾳ,
       because gentle I am and humble in heart,
       C' καὶ εὑρήσετε ἀνάπαυσιν ταῖς ψυχαῖς ὑμῶν·
          and you will find rest for your souls;
          D ὁ γὰρ ζυγός μου χρηστὸς (v. 30)
             for my yoke [is] easy
             καὶ τὸ φορτίον μου ἐλαφρόν ἐστιν.
             and my burden light is.

11:28–30   Here Jesus turns from taking solace in God's sovereignty to an appeal for people to come to him (cf. Gos. Thom. 90). This verse is thoroughly and strikingly christocentric. If people come to know the Father only through Jesus, it is only fitting for Jesus to invite them to come to *him* and to promise that *he* will give them rest as they take *his* yoke upon themselves.[3] Jesus takes on the role of God in fulfilling the promises of rest,[4] based on God's rest after creation as the model for Israel's rest on the Sabbath (Gen. 2:2; Exod. 20:10–11; 31:15; 35:2). The appeal is stated in a twofold manner: Jesus invites people (1) to come to him (cf. Matt. 4:19; 22:4) and (2) to take his yoke upon them (Maher 1975) and learn from him. Both invitations are followed by promises of rest (with allusion to Jer. 6:16 in Matt. 11:29d), and there is additional incentive provided in the description of Jesus's yoke and burden in 11:30. In short, the invitation is to a life of following Jesus's teaching and example of humility and gentleness (cf. 5:5), symbolized by the yoke.

Jesus's promise of rest is likely an allusion to Exod. 33:14b. The language of rest and an easy yoke is similar to the way wisdom (cf. Matt. 11:19; 23:34) was spoken of in Sir. 6:23–31; 24:19; 51:23–27, which develops the personification of wisdom found in Prov. 8:1–21, 32–36; 9:4–6. There may be an implied contrast to the yoke (cf. Acts 15:10; Gal. 5:1) and burden (cf. Matt. 23:4; Luke 11:46) of Pharisaism here. The written Torah is not a heavy burden, but the Pharisaic oral traditions have encumbered those who wish to obey the Torah (cf. Matt. 15:3–9). As the ultimate interpreter of Torah (5:17–48), Jesus fulfills the role of wisdom and is the sole agent to provide rest for the people of God. (See Laansma 1997: 6–9, 159–208.)

It is oxymoronic, if not paradoxical, to speak of an easy yoke and a light burden. Jesus did not endorse the oral traditions of the Pharisees, which could obscure the weightier matters of the law (cf. 15:3–20; 23:16–24). But Jesus's yoke is not less rigorous than that of the Pharisees, since the righteousness he requires surpasses that of the Pharisees (5:20). Jesus is the sole revealer of the Father, and he, not the Pharisees, is the definitive teacher of the Torah (5:17–48). He is gentle and humble (Good 1999) whereas they are proud and ostentatious (6:1–18; 23:1–12). Their traditions obscure and even transgress the obligations demanded by the Torah (15:3, 6), but Jesus gets to the heart of the Torah by stressing its weightier matters. The heart of the oxymoron is that his focus on weightier matters leads to a lighter yoke (cf. 1 John 5:3). (See H. Betz 1967; Deutsch 1987; Janzen 1987; Maher 1975; Stanton 1992b: 364–77.)

The way in which Jesus links the sovereignty of God (Matt. 11:25–27) to an appeal for human decision (11:28–30) is striking. In the history of the church, polarization on these two areas of its doctrine has occurred regularly. Some teachers emphasize the sovereignty of God and

---

3. For the yoke as a reference to the Torah of God's kingdom, see Jer. 5:5; Ps. Sol. 7.9; 2 Bar. 41.3; *m. 'Abot* 3.5; *m. Ber.* 2.2. Similar texts appear in later rabbinic literature.

4. On rest, see Exod. 33:14; cf. Deut. 12:10; 25:19; Josh. 1:13; 22:4; 23:1; 2 Sam. 7:1, 11; 1 Kings 5:4; 8:56; Esth. 9:16; Isa. 14:3; 28:12; Heb. 3:11, 18; 4:1; Laansma 1997: 17–158, 209–51. On rest in light of biblical prophetic expectation, see Charette 1992a.

others stress human responsibility. But since biblical texts often speak of these matters side by side (e.g., Gen. 50:20; Acts 2:23; 13:48; 2 Tim. 2:10), it seems foolish to attempt to separate them. Ultimately, it is due only to the sovereign grace of God that sinners repent and believe in Jesus. This grace operates only through the message of the gospel of Jesus. When the gospel is rejected, followers of Jesus can only reaffirm God's sovereignty and continue to offer the gospel. People come to faith for two reasons: ultimately, because of God's purpose in election and, instrumentally, because they have heard the gospel. The missional church must continue to rest in the sovereignty of God and the sufficiency of the gospel to bring people to faith.

Matthew 11 is the first of three passages contrasting belief and unbelief. Here, two examples of unbelief (11:2–19; 11:20–24) are followed by an example of belief (11:25–30). Opposition to Jesus and his messengers has been increasing throughout Matthew's narrative (2:16; 3:7; 4:1; 5:10–12; 7:6; 8:20, 34; 9:3, 11, 34; 10:14–39). But as Matt. 11 concludes, the situation has become unmistakably grim. The kingdom is being violently attacked by people who obstinately refuse its authority (11:12, 16–24). Nevertheless, the Son has revealed the Father to certain "childlike" people whose weariness has compelled them to find rest in assuming Jesus's yoke (11:25–30; cf. 10:42; 18:1–10; 25:40). Those who are wise in their own eyes will all the more reject this humbling message as Matthew's narrative unfolds the second (12:1–21) and third (12:22–50) sets of unbelief and belief passages (cf. 9:12; 12:2, 10, 24; 18:6; 25:45).

Additional Note

11:27. There is overwhelming external evidence for the UBS[4] reading τὸν υἱὸν εἰ μὴ ὁ πατήρ, οὐδὲ τὸν πατέρα τις ἐπιγινώσκει εἰ μὴ ὁ υἱός ($\mathfrak{P}^{62\text{vid}}$, $\mathfrak{P}^{70\text{vid}}$, ℵ, B, C, D, f[1], f[13], Byz, Lect, most ancient versions). A variant (N, several patristic sources) arranges the wording to state reciprocally that only the Son knows the Father and only the Father knows the Son.

2. Cycle 2: Sabbath Conflicts and Jesus's Response (12:1–21)

The narrative of Matt. 11–12 stresses increasing opposition to Jesus's kingdom mission. The threefold structure of this passage has been discussed above (see the introduction to 11:2–12:50). Each of the three sets of passages contains two passages stressing unbelief followed by a passage stressing belief. Matthew 12:1 is the beginning of the second of these three sets, with 12:1–8 and 12:9–14 stressing unbelief and 12:15–21 stressing belief.

a. Picking and Eating Grain (12:1–8)

Matthew 12:1–8 (cf. Mark 2:23–28; Luke 6:1–5) describes a controversy over Jesus's disciples picking and eating grain as they walk through a field (Matt. 12:1–2; cf. Deut. 23:24–25). Jesus's response to this objection mentions King David, the temple, and the Sabbath (Yang 1987) to demonstrate the disciples' innocence and to show that he is greater than each of these items (12:3–8).[1] The argument from David's activities (12:3–4) would be problematic enough for the Pharisees, but Jesus's claim to be greater than the temple and to be Lord of the Sabbath would be viewed as outrageous.

The unit outline is as follows:

    i. The accusation of unlawful activity (12:1–2)
    ii. The answer from Scripture (12:3–8)
        (1) David's "unlawful" activity (12:3–4)
        (2) The priests' "unlawful" activity (12:5–6)
        (3) A basic hermeneutical problem (12:7–8)

Exegesis and Exposition

[1]At that time Jesus went through the grainfields on the Sabbath, and his disciples became hungry and began to pick heads of grain and eat. [2]But when the Pharisees saw this, they said to him, "Look, your disciples are doing what is unlawful on the Sabbath." [3]But he said to them, "Have you not read what David did when he and his companions became hungry, [4]how he entered the house of God, and ⌜ate⌝ the consecrated bread, which was not lawful for him or his companions to eat but was only for the priests? [5]Or have you not read in the law that on the Sabbath the priests in the temple desecrate the Sabbath yet they are innocent? [6]Now I tell you that something greater than the temple is here. [7]But if you had known what this means, 'I desire compassion and not sacrifice,' you would not have condemned the innocent. [8]For the Son of Man is Lord of the Sabbath."

---

1. For further study of 12:1–8, see Cohn-Sherbok 1979; Genuyt 1993; Harrington in Eskenazi et al. 1991: 45–56; Hicks 1984; Leitch 1966; E. Levine 1975–76; Lohse in Eltester 1960: 79–89; Repschinski 2000: 94–107; Robbins in Mack and Robbins 1989: 107–41; Schweizer in Kiilunen et al. 1983: 169–79. Verseput 1986: 153–294 provides an excellent discussion of all of Matt. 12. See Hultgren 1979 and Keener 1999: 351–53 for discussion of the form and function of controversy stories.

i. The Accusation of Unlawful Activity (12:1–2)

Matthew places the events of 12:1–8 "at about that time," that is, during   **12:1–2**
the days of opposition narrated in chapter 11. It was not against the law
of Moses to pick a few heads of grain if one became hungry as one walked
through a field, but one was not allowed to use a sickle (Deut. 23:25; cf.
Lev. 19:9–10; 4Q159; Josephus, *Ant.* 4.231–39; *m. Pe'ah* 2.7–8; P. Casey
1988).[2] The Pharisees apparently view the disciples' picking a few heads
of grain by hand as work that desecrates the Sabbath day.[3] There is irony
in Matthew's intentional placement of these Sabbath controversy stories
right after the promise of Jesus to give his disciples rest.

ii. The Answer from Scripture (12:3–8)

Jesus's response to this accusation includes questions about two relevant
biblical precedents, David (12:3–4) and the priests (12:5–6). He then returns
to Hos. 6:6 (cf. Matt. 9:13) to underline a basic hermeneutical conflict between himself and the Pharisees (Matt. 12:7–8). Jesus makes crucial statements about his identity and stature in 12:6 and 12:8 (cf. 12:41–42).

(1) David's "Unlawful" Activity (12:3–4)

Jesus's two questions (12:3, 5) imply that he is surprised at their bibli-   **12:3–4**
cal ignorance. Both questions turn the tables and put the burden on the
Pharisees. They have no doubt read, but they have not understood and
obeyed.[4] Jesus's first question alludes to 1 Sam. 21:1–6 (cf. Lev. 24:8),
the account of the sad incident where David, while fleeing from Saul,
lied to the priest Ahimelech. This resulted in Saul having all the priests
at Nob murdered. The argument is implicitly from lesser to greater, as
becomes clear in Matt. 12:6 (cf. 12:8, 41, 42; 22:41–46). The Pharisees
do not object to David's technically illegal behavior of eating the sacred
bread (the "bread of the presence" or "showbread"; cf. Lev. 24:5–9) with
the permission of the priest Ahimelech, but they object to Jesus's hungry
disciples doing what was permitted by Deut. 23:25. According to Jesus,
the activity of his disciples is a permissible exception to the general rules
of Sabbath observance.[5] Although Jesus's argument may not fit typical

---

2. The nuance of the aorist ἐπείνασαν is ingressive. Cf. 12:3; Wallace 1996: 558–59.
3. Matthew mentions the Sabbath in this controversy story (12:1–12) and in 24:20;
28:1. Other key texts include Exod. 20:10; 34:21; Deut. 5:12–15; Neh. 13:15–22; Isa. 56:2,
4, 6; Ezek. 20:13; Jub. 2.17–23; 50.12; 1 Macc. 1:43, 45; 2:32–41; CD 10.14–11.18; *m. Šabb.*
7.2; Philo, *Moses* 2.22. See McIver 1995b; Neirynck in Dupont 1989: 227–70; Sigal 1986:
119–53; H. Weiss 1990; Wong 1991; Yang 1987: 139–95.
4. The question οὐκ ἀνέγνωτε (12:3, 5; 19:4; 22:31; cf. 21:16) implies incredulity that
they have not grasped the Scriptures.
5. Ancient sources acknowledge that special circumstances sometimes modified the
nature of Torah observance. See Num. 28:9–10; 1 Macc. 2:39–41; Jub. 50.10–11; Mekilta
on Exod. 31:14; *m. Yoma* 8.6; *m. Pesaḥ.* 6.1–2; *m. Šabb.* 16.1–7; 18.3; 19.1–3.

rabbinic methods (Cohn-Sherbok 1979), his hermeneutic is based on his authoritative stance (Matt. 5:17–48; 12:6, 8) and his prioritization of human need over oral legal tradition (9:13; 12:7; 15:3; 22:36–40; 23:23). (For further discussion of Jesus's appeal to 1 Sam. 21, see Banks 1975: 114–18; W. Davies and Allison 1991: 310–12.)

(2) The Priests' "Unlawful" Activity (12:5–6)

12:5–6   Jesus's second question relates to the priests' "working" in the temple on the Sabbath. Technically, this breaks the law, but the priests are guiltless because their cultic obligations override the general Sabbath law (Lev. 24:8; Num. 28:9–10; 11QT 13.17; Josephus, *Ant.* 14.63; *m. Ned.* 3.11; *m. Pesaḥ.* 6.1–2; cf. John 7:23). Temple "work" takes precedence over Sabbath "rest." The Pharisees are inconsistent because they do not object to such priestly Sabbath breaking but they object to Jesus, who is greater than the temple and its sacrificial ministry.[6]

(3) A Basic Hermeneutical Problem (12:7–8)

12:7–8   The concluding verses of this section get to the heart of Jesus's differences with the Pharisees. Two major problems surface: the Pharisees do not interpret the Bible as Jesus does, and they do not recognize his authority as Lord of the Sabbath. Jesus again cites Hos. 6:6 (cf. Matt. 9:13; Lybaeck in Tuckett 1997: 491–99) to prove that the Pharisees' harsh approach to the Sabbath contradicts God's compassionate purposes for God's people. Counting what is implicit in 12:3 and explicit in 12:6, Jesus's assertion that the Son of Man is Lord of the Sabbath in 12:8 is the third such superiority statement (cf. 22:41–45).

Crucial to Jesus's differences with the Pharisees are their contrasting ways of interpreting the Hebrew Bible. The Pharisees seem to begin with the institution of the Sabbath and view it as of utmost importance. Their oral tradition on proper Sabbath observance overrides the humanitarian concerns behind Deut. 23:25, which permits hungry people to pick and eat grain as they walk through a field.[7] Jesus, on the other hand, begins with God's concern for his people, which takes precedence over the institution of the Sabbath on certain occasions (Keener 1999: 354–56). "The Sabbath was made to benefit people, and not people to benefit the Sabbath" (Mark 2:27 NLT). Jesus's argument is both haggadic (the analogy drawn from a narrative passage about David) and halakic (the precept

---

6. Evidently, the neuter μεῖζον is used instead of the masculine in order to emphasize the general quality of greatness rather than the specific individual, Jesus. Cf. 12:41–42. See BDF §138; Moulton and Turner 1963: 21; Winer 1882: 222; commentators such as W. Davies and Allison 1991: 314; Gundry 1994: 223; LaGrange 1948: 233.

7. Sabbath observance at Qumran was even more rigorous; there it was forbidden to speak secular words on the Sabbath or to talk about work to be done after the Sabbath. Cf. CD 10.14–11.18, esp. 10.18–19.

drawn from a legal passage about the priests; Hagner 1993: 328). As Lord of the Sabbath (Matt. 12:8), Jesus provides the ultimate interpretation of its role in the life of God's people (cf. 5:17–48). His approach to the Sabbath is a clear example of how his promise of rest, an easy yoke, and a light burden (11:29–30) is fulfilled. But Jesus's interpretive prowess is due to his supreme position as one greater than David, the temple, and the Sabbath. Davidic promises, priestly activities, and Sabbath rest all find fulfillment in him.

Additional Note

12:4. The UBS[4] reading of this verse (ἔφαγον; ℵ, B, 481) may be seriously doubted. The reading ἔφαγεν is much more widely supported (𝔓[70], C, D, L, f[1], f[13], Byz, Lect, and others; cf. Mark 2:26; Luke 6:4) and makes better sense of the passage. UBS[4] adopted ἔφαγον on the assumption that a scribal change from the difficult -ον ending to -εν is more likely than the reverse (Metzger 1994: 26). No doubt ἔθαγον is more difficult than ἔφαγεν, but it results in the unlikely statement that *they* (David and his men) ate what was not lawful for *him* to eat. It seems more likely that ἔφαγον is a transcriptional error.

b. Healing in the Synagogue (12:9–14)

Another Sabbath controversy follows on the heels of the previous one (cf. Mark 3:1–6; Luke 6:6–11). The conflict is again about whether certain activity is permissible. Jesus enters a synagogue and is asked whether it is lawful for him to heal a man with a deformed hand (Matt. 12:9–10). He then explains why it is indeed lawful to do this (12:11–12). He heals the man's hand, but this leads to a plot against his life (12:13–14; cf. 2:16; 16:21; 17:12, 22–23; 20:18–19; 21:38–39; 22:15; 26:4, 59; 27:1, 20, 62–66; 28:11–15). Keener (1999: 357) points out that this healing can be viewed as a divine endorsement that validates Jesus's previous teaching on Sabbath observance.

The outline of this unit is as follows:

   i. The occasion (12:9–10)
   ii. Jesus's teaching (12:11–12)
   iii. The healing and its result (12:13–14)

Exegesis and Exposition

⁹Departing from there, he went into their synagogue, ¹⁰and a man was there whose hand was withered. And they asked Jesus, "Is it lawful to heal on the Sabbath?"—so that they might accuse him. ¹¹So he said to them, "If any of you has a sheep and if it falls into a pit on the Sabbath, will you not take hold of it and lift it out? ¹²How much more valuable, then, is a person than a sheep! So then, it is lawful to do good on the Sabbath." ¹³Then he said to the man, "Stretch out your hand!" So he stretched it out, and it was restored, as good as the other hand. ¹⁴But the Pharisees went out and conspired against him so that they might destroy him.

i. The Occasion (12:9–10)

12:9–10   The Sabbath conflict intensifies when Jesus heals a man's deformed (ξηράν, *xēran*, literally, "dried up, withered" or paralyzed) hand in the synagogue (cf. 1 Kings 13:1–6; T. Sim. 2.11–14). The Pharisees' question about whether it is lawful to heal on the Sabbath does not stem from a sincere desire to discuss halakah but from their wish to have something with which to accuse Jesus, probably in formal court proceedings (Matt. 12:10; cf. Luke 13:14; John 5:7–9). The penalty for profaning the Sabbath was death (Exod. 31:14; cf. Sipre on Num. 15:33), and so their question may be linked to the plot in Matt. 12:14. If the tradition later codified in the Mishnah about 200 CE was current in Jesus's day, the Pharisees themselves would have evidently permitted healing on the Sabbath if human life was in immediate danger (*m. Yoma* 8.6; cf. *m. Šabb.* 22.6; Mekilta on Exod. 22:2).

ii. Jesus's Teaching (12:11–12)

Jesus responds that it is lawful to do good on the Sabbath. Perhaps the point is that such a response to an emergency constitutes a technical, not a real, violation. But it is not clear that the minimal activity involved here was "work." Jesus cites a situation the Pharisees might have permitted: removing a sheep from a pit (possibly a cistern; cf. Deut. 22:4; Prov. 12:10; Matt. 15:14).[1] The argument is again from lesser to greater, since healing a diseased person is more necessary than lifting a sheep out of a pit (cf. Matt. 6:26–30; 7:11; 10:31). Doing good on the Sabbath is equivalent to prioritizing compassion over sacrifice (12:7). This is an instance of Jesus not annulling the law but fulfilling it (5:17) by loving a neighbor (7:12; 19:19; 22:39–40). Accordingly, Jesus and his disciples should not be viewed as Sabbath breakers (cf. 24:20).

12:11–12

iii. The Healing and Its Result (12:13–14)

Jesus concludes his argument by doing what the Pharisees consider to be unlawful: he commands the man to stretch out his hand, and it is restored to normal as he does so. The Pharisees respond by walking out and hatching a murder plot (cf. 22:15; 27:1, 7; 28:12). Their conspiracy to kill Jesus does not surprise the attentive reader of Matthew (cf. 3:7; 9:11, 34; 12:24; 15:7, 12; 16:6, 21; 17:9, 12, 22; 20:18; 21:38, 46; 22:15, 34; 23:30–32; 26:2–5, 14–16).

12:13–14

This passage reinforces the basic impasse that is evident in 12:1–8. Jesus and the Pharisees are at loggerheads over the relationship of Sabbath law to compassionate deeds. The Pharisees' strict tradition evidently makes little exception for instances of compassion such as Jesus's healings. But the Pharisees' approach is inconsistent. It is assumed that they have no problem with a sheep's being rescued from a pit on the Sabbath, yet they condemn Jesus for healing a person. They might have responded to Jesus that the healing of the man's hand is not a matter of life or death and can wait until the next day, but Matthew's narrative is silent about any possible surrejoinder from them. As the ultimate interpreter of Torah (5:17–48), Jesus properly relates Sabbath law and human need. The written Torah is not violated by this healing.

The legal dispute aside, the Pharisees take steps to eliminate Jesus. This seems to be a rather draconian solution to a halakic dispute. Perhaps in

---

1. But even if the Pharisees would have permitted the removal of the sheep (cf. *m. Beṣah* 3.4), the residents of Qumran evidently would not have. See CD 11.12–14.

their own minds, the Pharisees are only planning to enforce Exod. 31:14, but baser motives are probably at work. Jesus is perceived as a threat to the status quo: an increase in his popularity and influence would inevitably mean a decrease in that of the Pharisees (cf. Matt. 27:18). Also, the Pharisees may fear that Jesus's followers will become a mob that the Romans will view as a threat to their rule over Judea (cf. Luke 23:1–14; John 19:12). At any rate, it is not a little ironic that a dispute over the finer points of Sabbath law leads the Pharisees to plan to break the sixth commandment. (On 12:9–14, see Hendrickx 1987: 149–67; Repschinski 2000: 107–16; Yang 1987: 195–214.)

c. The Servant's Response to Escalating Opposition (12:15–21)

Jesus leaves the area where the previous two conflicts have occurred and continues his ministry of healing. He warns those healed not to make him known (12:15–16). This seemingly strange warning is explained as the fulfillment of Isa. 42:1–4 (Matt. 12:17–21; cf. 3:17; 17:5).

The unit can be outlined as follows:

i. Withdrawal and many more healings (12:15–16)
ii. Biblical fulfillment: The Lord's servant (12:17–21)

Exegesis and Exposition

[15]But Jesus, aware of this, withdrew from there. ⌜Many⌝ followed him, and he healed them all [16]and warned them not to make him known, [17]in order to fulfill what had been spoken through Isaiah the prophet:

> [18]"Look at my servant whom I have chosen,
>   my beloved in whom my soul is well pleased.
> I will put my Spirit upon him,
>   and he will proclaim justice to the Gentiles.
> [19]He will not quarrel or cry out,
>   nor will anyone hear his voice in the streets.
> [20]A bent reed he will not break,
> And a smoking wick he will not put out,
>   until he leads justice on to victory.
> [21]And in his name Gentiles will hope."

i. Withdrawal and Many More Healings (12:15–16)

By some means[1] Jesus becomes aware of the Pharisees' plot and makes a strategic withdrawal to another area (cf. 2:12–14, 22; 4:12; 9:24; 14:13; 15:21). As usual, there are many following Jesus and many healings (cf. 4:23; 9:35). He warns those he heals not to make him known (cf. 8:4; 9:30; 16:20; 17:9), evidently because he will not pander to those who

12:15–16

---

1. Some commentators would automatically attribute Jesus's awareness in situations such as this (cf. 16:8; 22:18; 26:10) to his divinity, but if there is a supernatural source for Jesus's knowledge, it is the Spirit of God (cf. 3:16; 12:18; Hawthorne 1991).

want only to see spectacular feats. Such a frenzied response to Jesus would clearly intensify Pharisaic opposition. (See Tuckett 1983a on the "messianic secret.")

ii. Biblical Fulfillment: The Lord's Servant (12:17–21)

12:17-18 Jesus's wish to keep a low profile in the face of Pharisaic opposition and popular enthusiasm fulfills Isa. 42:1–4, the longest biblical passage cited in Matthew. Matthew's version of the passage does not exactly follow either the Hebrew MT or the LXX and is likely his own translation of a Hebrew original.[2] This text, already alluded to at Jesus's baptism (Matt. 3:17; cf. 17:5), speaks of the Lord's beloved servant as one who is enabled by the Spirit to proclaim justice to the nations (12:18).[3] This significant reference to the Gentiles anticipates their positive responses to Jesus that follow as the story proceeds (cf. 15:28; 27:54).

12:19-21 The Spirit leads the servant away from the kind of ministry that would please the carnal desires of the crowd. The servant is not characterized by quarreling,[4] shouting, or rhetoric calculated to incite the mob. He will handle weak people, pictured as bent reeds and flickering lamps, with compassion and gentleness. In the end he will cause justice (cf. Beaton 1999) to be victorious,[5] and the Gentiles will hope in his name.[6] His ultimately victorious ministry will be characterized by compassionate deeds rather than inflammatory words.

The citation of Isa. 42:1–4 here serves three purposes. First, it explains why Jesus withdraws from conflict with the Pharisees and why he urges the people whom he has healed not to reveal who he is. Due to the Spirit's enablement, Jesus's ministry is not characterized by acts and words calculated to incite the masses. Instead, he proves to be gentle and merciful in his ministry to the weak (cf. Matt. 5:5, 7; 11:29). Second, Isa.

---

2. See W. Davies and Allison 1991: 323–24 for a summary of major textual issues. More-detailed treatments are found in Gundry 1967: 110–16; Menken 1999b; Stendahl 1968: 107–15.

3. Matthew's version of the last clause of Isa. 42:1 says that Jesus will *proclaim* (ἀπαγγελεῖ) justice to the Gentiles, whereas the Hebrew text says that the Lord's servant will *cause* justice to go forth (יוֹצִיא) to them. The LXX's ἐξοίσει (he will carry out) is closer to the Hebrew.

4. The basis of Matthew's οὐκ ἐρίσει is not clear, since both MT (יִשָּׂא) and LXX (ἀνήσει) simply say that the servant will not lift up (his voice?). Perhaps Matthew took יִשָּׂא in a reflexive sense. At any rate, the idea that the servant will not quarrel fits the picture of humility found in Isa. 42:2–3.

5. The idea of victory (εἰς νῖκος) in Matt. 12:20c is not directly derived from either MT or LXX. Matthew has evidently omitted two lines from Isaiah (Isa. 42:3c–42:4a) and derives Matt. 12:20c from Isa. 42:4b (or 42:3c), but both MT and LXX have the servant bring forth justice on earth (or faithfully in 42:3c) instead of bringing justice to victory.

6. The last line of the citation (Matt. 12:21) is nearly identical to Isa. 42:4c LXX (καὶ ἐπὶ τῷ ὀνόματι αὐτοῦ ἔθνη ἐλπιοῦσιν), lacking only the LXX's ἐπί before τῷ ὀνόματι. Isaiah 42:4c MT speaks of the coastlands waiting (or hoping) for his teaching (לְתוֹרָתוֹ).

42:1, 4 indicates that the servant would minister to the Gentiles (Overman 1996: 181). As Jesus is being increasingly rejected by many Jews (cf. 8:12), Matthew is gradually making it clear that certain Gentiles are receptive to him (cf. 1:3, 5–6; 2:1–2, 11; 4:15–16; 8:10–12; 15:28; 27:54) and that the followers of Jesus must widen their horizons for a worldwide ministry to all the nations (8:11–12; 10:18; 15:22–28; 22:9; 24:14; 25:32; 28:18–20).[7] Third, Isa. 42:1 stresses that the servant's ministry will be Spirit-empowered. This provides the background for Jesus's response to the slander that his powers are demonic. The Pharisees' charge in Matt. 12:24 is found to be an antiscriptural and unforgivable slander of the Spirit of God (12:31–32). (See Menken 1998b; Neyrey 1982; Tisera 1993: 159–85.)

It is ironic that the power of Jesus and the kingdom is manifested by humble compassionate service (cf. 5:5, 7; 11:29; 2 Cor. 4:7–10; 12:9–10). The Messiah uses his power not to manipulate people but to serve them. Jesus does not extend his influence by selfish quarrels and inflammatory rhetoric. His ministry will eventually bring justice to victory (Matt. 12:20), but even John the Baptist has doubts about how this is being accomplished. Christians today have a great deal to learn from their Lord on this matter. Their course of life is likewise to be that of sacrificial service (cf. 16:21–25; 20:25–28). (On 12:15–21, see Beaton 2002.)

Additional Note

12:15. On the strength of ℵ, B, and most of the Latin tradition, the UBS[4] editors read πολλοί as original, but they defer to a wide range of support (C, D, L, W, f^1, f^{13}, *Byz*, *Lect*, and others) and insert ὄχλοι in brackets, resulting in [ὄχλοι] πολλοί (cf. 4:25; 8:1; 13:2; 15:30; 19:2).

---

7. Although a minority, some ancient Jewish sources viewed the servant of Isa. 42 as the Messiah. See Targum Jonathan on Isa. 42:1; 43:10; 52:13; 'Abot R. Nat. 43, 121B; 2 Bar. 70.9. More frequently the servant was interpreted as being the nation of Israel.

3. Cycle 3: Confrontation with the Pharisees (12:22–50)

Pharisaic opposition to Jesus comes to a head here. The healing of a blind, mute, demon-possessed man (12:22) results in three antithetical responses (12:22–37). The crowd, responding to Jesus (12:23), wonders whether Jesus is the Messiah (12:23), but the Pharisees, evidently alarmed by the miracles and the crowd's openness to Jesus, respond by slandering Jesus (and, more important, the Spirit) with the charge of collaborating with the prince of the demons (12:24). The rest of the passage narrates Jesus's response to this slander (12:25–37). Jesus argues against the Pharisees' view of his ministry and affirms that it can only be understood as the arrival of the kingdom by the power of God's Spirit (12:25–28). He compares the advance of the kingdom into Satan's domain to binding a strong man in order to loot his household and warns his listeners that neutrality regarding the kingdom is impossible (12:29–30). The Pharisees' slander is an unforgivable blasphemy not only of Jesus but also of the Spirit who empowers Jesus (12:31–32). Their slanderous words betray their evil hearts and portend their eschatological doom, just as worthless fruit proves that a tree is worthless (12:33–37; cf. 3:10; 7:16; 13:38). The antithetical response to Jesus narrated here provides a clear illustration of 11:25–27.

The next pericope continues the stress on unbelief (12:38–45). The previous strong words provoke a request for a sign (12:38). Jesus's answer (12:39–45) is threefold. First, he refuses to give a sign other than that of Jonah (12:39–41). Then he makes a similar point with his reference to the queen of the South (12:42). Finally, a story about an unclean spirit emphasizes the increased accountability of Jesus's contemporaries (12:43–45).

The final section of the cycle (12:46–50) focuses on genuine community. The arrival of Jesus's mother and brothers provides an opportunity for teaching (12:46–47), and Jesus uses this moment to explain the basis of true family relationships (12:48–50). Although this ends the bleak cycle on a positive note, the divisiveness of the kingdom message is again stressed here (cf. 10:34–39).

a. The Unforgivable Sin (12:22–37)

Matthew 12:22–37 contains one of the more ominous warnings in this Gospel. It comes as no surprise in light of the increasing opposition to Jesus's ministry just narrated in 11:7–24. A previous exorcism has already led to Jesus's being accused of collaborating with the devil (9:32–34), and now the accusation resurfaces (12:24) after Sabbath controversies (12:1–14) and another exorcism (12:22). Jesus responds to the accusation by showing its absurdity (12:25–27) and explaining the real source of his authority over demons (12:28–29). The passage concludes with solemn words about the eternal consequences of this accusation (12:30–37).

The outline of this unit is as follows:

i. The occasion (12:22–23)
ii. The accusation (12:24)
iii. Jesus's response (12:25–37)
    (1) Jesus refutes the Pharisees' explanation (12:25–27)
    (2) Jesus provides the real explanation (12:28–30)
    (3) Jesus warns of the unforgivable sin (12:31–37)

Exegesis and Exposition

²²Then a demon-possessed man who was blind and mute was brought to Jesus, and he healed him, so that the mute man spoke and saw. ²³So all the crowds were amazed and started saying, "Could this man be the son of David?" ²⁴But when the Pharisees heard this, they said, "This man casts out demons only by Beelzebul the ruler of the demons." ²⁵And ⌜knowing⌝ their thoughts, he said to them, "Every kingdom divided against itself is laid waste; and every city or house divided against itself will not stand. ²⁶If Satan casts out Satan, he is divided against himself; how, then, will his kingdom stand? ²⁷And if I cast out demons by Beelzebul, by whom do your sons cast them out? Therefore they will be your judges. ²⁸But if I cast out demons by the Spirit of God, then the kingdom of God has come upon you. ²⁹Or how can anyone enter the strong man's house and carry off his possessions if he does not first tie up the strong man? Then he will plunder his house. ³⁰Whoever is not with me is against me; and whoever does not gather with me scatters.

³¹"Therefore I tell you, every sin and blasphemy shall be forgiven people, but blasphemy against the Spirit shall not be forgiven. ³²And if anyone speaks a word against the Son of Man, this shall be forgiven; but if anyone speaks against the Holy

Spirit, this shall not be forgiven, either in this age or in the age to come. [33]Either make the tree good and its fruit good, or make the tree worthless and its fruit worthless; for the tree is known by its fruit. [34]You brood of vipers, how can you who are evil speak what is good? For the mouth speaks from what overflows from the heart. [35]The good person brings what is good out of a good treasure; and the evil person brings what is evil out of an evil treasure. [36]But I tell you that on judgment day people shall give an account for every careless word they speak. [37]For by your words you will be vindicated, and by your words you will be condemned."

i. The Occasion (12:22–23)

12:22–23   The healing of a blind and mute man who is demon-possessed produces antithetical results (cf. Mark 3:20–30; Luke 11:14–23; 12:10). The healing is briefly mentioned as the occasion for the controversy. Jesus has previously healed blind people and mute people, but this is the only time in the Gospels where Jesus heals a person who experiences both maladies. The reaction of the crowds is in stark contrast to that of the Pharisees. They are amazed and begin to wonder whether Jesus is the son of David. The messianic significance of the expression "son of David" is discussed under "Christology" in the introduction to this commentary (cf. Matt. 1:1, 20; 9:27; 12:23; 15:22; 20:30–31; 21:9, 15; 22:41–45; Duling 1978; J. M. Gibbs 1963–64; Loader 1982).

ii. The Accusation (12:24)

12:24   The Pharisees view Jesus not as messianic but as demonic (cf. 9:34; 10:25). They counter the popular interpretation of Jesus's miracle with its polar opposite.[1] Beelzebul probably means "lord of the house" or "lord of the heights" but is a term used to describe evil supernatural powers or the devil himself, as the appositional "ruler of the demons" clearly shows.[2] See the comments on 9:34 and 10:25. The Pharisees do not deny the reality of Jesus's miracles but attribute them to Satan instead of God (cf. Deut. 13:1–5). Later Jewish sources continued to affirm that not only Jesus but also the early church did miracles through sorcery (Keener 1999: 361–63).

iii. Jesus's Response (12:25–37)

(1) Jesus Refutes the Pharisees' Explanation (12:25–27)

12:25–27   Jesus's answer to the Pharisees (cf. Guijarro 1999) contains two rhetorical questions that refute the Pharisees' false interpretation of his

---

1. The phrasing of the Pharisees' charge (οὐκ ἐκβάλλει . . . εἰ μή) is Semitic (cf. 13:57; 14:17; 15:24; 17:8; 21:19; BDF §376; Moulton and Turner 1976: §37; GKC §163; Segal 1927: §506).

2. For similar expressions, see 1QM 15.5–6; Jub. 48.15; T. Dan 5.6; John 14:30; 16:11; Eph. 2:2; b. Pesaḥ. 110a.

exorcism. These are followed by the true interpretation. He first asks whether Satan would work against himself (12:25–26), then asks whether the Pharisees' own exorcists are empowered by Satan (12:27).[3] Finally he states the real power behind his works: the Spirit of God (12:28).[4] The first question is based on parallel commonsense observations about the need for unity in any kingdom or city and household (12:25). The Pharisees' view of Jesus is untenable, since it is illogical and contrary to experience. Jesus's argument is reductio ad absurdum. His second question is ad hominem, based on the fact that Pharisees also practice exorcisms.[5] The Pharisees' view of Jesus is untenable because it is inconsistent—they slander Jesus for doing the same thing they do. Their own exorcists will judge them.

(2) Jesus Provides the Real Explanation (12:28–30)

After showing that the Pharisees' charge of collaboration with demons is nonsensical and false, Jesus affirms the real power behind his miracles. Far from being demonic, it is the Holy Spirit (cf. Twelftree in D. Wenham and Blomberg 1986: 361–400; 1993). The same Spirit of God who was active in Jesus's conception (1:18, 20) has been empowering him for ministry since his baptism in fulfillment of Isa. 42:1 (Matt. 3:16–4:1; 12:18). The only conclusion that can be drawn from the Spirit-empowered miracles of Jesus is that the saving power of God's kingdom has arrived among Jesus's contemporaries (cf. Matt. 3:2; 4:17; 10:7; 24:14).[6] This probably is Matthew's strongest statement of the presence of the kingdom (cf. 3:2; 4:17; 10:7; Berkey 1963).

12:28

Jesus pictures the presence and advance of the kingdom upon Satan's domain as the tying up (cf. Tob. 3:17; 8:3; Jub. 10.7; 1 En. 10.4, 11–13; 13.1; 69.28; T. Levi 18.12) of a strong man and the looting of his house

12:29

---

3. The expression οἱ υἱοὶ ὑμῶν refers to close association, not biological kinship. It may include the notion of inheriting and perpetuating the secrets of the guild, as in the expression בְּנֵי־הַנְּבִיאִים in the Hebrew Bible. See 1 Kings 20:35; 2 Kings 2:3, 5, 7, 15; 4:1, 38; 5:22; 6:1; 9:1; Acts 3:25; BDB 121; BDAG 1024; Shirock 1992.

4. Matthew 12:26–28 provides a helpful exposé of a common error in the understanding of the Greek syntactical construction called the first-class condition (Wallace 1996: 690–94). It is commonly stated that this construction assumes the truth or reality of the "if" clause (protasis), since the indicative mood is used, and that εἰ should be translated "since." But any assumption of reality is only for the sake of argument, and the argument may demonstrate the unreality of the protasis. This is exactly what happens in 12:26–28, where the first two protases are patently false and only the third (12:28) is in fact true. One would not want to translate εἰ in 12:26–27 as "since"!

5. For other texts on Jewish exorcists, see 1 Sam. 16:14–23; Tob. 8:1–3; 1QapGen 20.29; Mark 9:38; Acts 19:13–14; Josephus, Ant. 8.45–49, J.W. 7.185.

6. The phrase here is ἡ βασιλεία τοῦ θεοῦ, not the more usual ἡ βασιλεία τῶν οὐρανῶν. There is no major distinction between the two terms. The form ἡ βασιλεία τοῦ θεοῦ evidently occurs here to parallel πνεύματι θεοῦ. See 19:24; 21:31, 43 and the discussion under "Kingdom of Heaven" in the introduction to this commentary.

(cf. Ps. Sol. 5.3). His preaching, teaching, and miraculous deeds have been encroaching upon Satan's territory (e.g., Matt. 11:1, 5, 21–23; 12:13, 18, 22; cf. 1 John 3:8). Most scholars acknowledge that Matt. 12:28–29 teaches the presence of the kingdom, that God's saving power began to encroach upon the domain of Satan during the life and ministry of Jesus.[7] Generally, this encroachment or binding is linked in some way to the description of the binding of Satan in the abyss in Rev. 20:1–10.

Among evangelicals, theologians who hold to amillennialism generally argue that Satan was bound by the first coming of Christ so that he can no longer deceive the nations (cf. Rev. 20:3). Those who hold to premillennialism, especially dispensational premillennialism, take an opposite view, stressing that the binding of Satan in Rev. 20 will happen at the second coming of Christ to the earth. There is some truth in each of these views. Dispensationalists must make room for the decisive defeat of Satan at Jesus's first coming, and amillennialists must not underestimate the extent to which Satan's limited power can still injure the church. Satan's power was effectively shattered at Christ's first coming, yet he is still a powerful enemy who must be resisted by all the means of grace (Eph. 6:11–17; James 4:7; 1 Pet. 5:8–9). Only in the future will he be totally incapacitated (Rev. 20:1–10). But the future is already present to a degree (Ladd 1974), and Christians can rejoice that the power of Jesus has already overcome the enemy (John 12:31; 16:11; Acts 26:18; Eph. 2:1–6; Col. 1:13) and that God will eventually fully destroy Satan's evil work so that only righteousness will dwell in the new earth (Rev. 20–22; cf. Jub. 23.29; 1 En. 10.4–7; 54.4–6; Testament of Zebulun 9.8).[8]

12:30 The two clauses of this proverbial saying are in synonymous parallelism. The imagery of gathering and scattering is more likely drawn from sheepherding (cf. 25:32; 26:31; John 10:12; Isa. 13:14; 40:11; Jer. 23:2; Ezek. 34:13; Zech. 13:7–9) than from harvesting (cf. Matt. 3:12; 13:28–30; Job 39:12). If the kingdom of God has arrived through the ministry of Jesus, opposition to him (e.g., Matt. 9:3, 14, 34; 10:25; 12:2, 10, 24) is unthinkable and neutrality is impossible, since the one who does not actively support Jesus and the kingdom is in opposition to him. Perhaps these words are intended to warn the wondering crowd more than the Pharisees, whose minds seem to be made up.

(3) Jesus Warns of the Unforgivable Sin (12:31–37)

12:31–32 Here Jesus changes from defense to offense, from explanation to warning (W. Davies and Allison 1991: 344). He tells the Pharisees in no un-

---

7. Adherents of "consistent eschatology" are exceptions. See Hiers 1973; 1981: 62–71; Toussaint 1980: 163–64; J. Weiss 1971: 65–74. On Jesus's eschatology, see Marcus in Chilton and Evans 1999a: 247–77; N. Wright 1996: 451–54.

8. For further study of Jesus's teaching on the kingdom, see Beasley-Murray 1986; Chilton 1984; Strawson 1959: 56–68; J. Thomas 1993.

certain terms that their slanderous charges (cf. 9:34; 10:25; 12:24) are unforgivable.[9] Matthew 12:31 and 12:32 are both antithetical couplets, and the two verses are in synonymous parallelism. Each verse's positive first clause is countered by its negative second clause. The more specific terms of 12:32 explain what is meant by the more general language of 12:31. If the Pharisees had merely spoken against Jesus, their sin might be forgiven. But they have spoken against the Spirit by attributing the work of the Spirit to the prince of the demons. Since the power of the Spirit is behind Jesus's works (12:28), it is really the Spirit who is being slandered, not Jesus (cf. Isa. 63:10; Acts 7:51). The consequences of such sin are eternal: it will not be forgiven in the present or the future world (cf. Matt. 13:22, 39, 40; 24:3).

All readers of Matthew should take the solemn words of 12:31–32 with utmost seriousness. The Hebrew Bible speaks of deliberate rebellion against God as "sinning with a high hand" (Num. 15:30–31; cf. CD 8.8). Certain sins were viewed as unforgivable (Deut. 29:18–20; Jub. 15.34; 1QS 7.15–17, 22–23; Heb. 6:6). In the church there has been much discussion, dating back to ancient times, regarding the precise nature of "the unpardonable sin." Some scholars have taken it to refer to denial of prophetic inspiration in general (Did. 11.7). Many have taken it as postconversion relapse into sin (Origen, *First Principles* 1.3.7). Augustine took the reference to a sin not forgivable in the age to come as implying the existence of purgatory (*City of God* 21.24). Well-meaning but overzealous preachers have utilized this verse to threaten their listeners that lack of response to a gospel invitation amounts to the unpardonable sin (Irenaeus, *Haer.* 3.11.9). One may encounter individuals who sincerely think that there is no hope for them because they have "sinned away their day of grace" (cf. John Bunyan, *Grace Abounding to the Chief of Sinners*). Theologians tend to generalize the unpardonable sin, equating it with unbelief and linking Matt. 12:31–32 to texts such as John 3:18; 16:9; 1 John 5:16 (e.g., Hauerwas 2006: 122). But as serious as lack of belief in Jesus is, those who take this passage as a reference to it are mistaken (cf. Matt. 12:32a). Many who previously rejected Jesus with much vehemence eventually come to believe in him and receive forgiveness.

Matthew 12 centers on the Spirit-empowered miracles of Jesus, which should have been viewed as evidence of his messianic status (12:23) and his authority to forgive sins on earth (9:6). But the Pharisees' response to this goes well beyond mere unbelief. They slander the Spirit's ministry to Jesus by accusing him of collaborating with the very forces he is overpowering (12:29). This is the unforgivable sin. Whether it can be committed today is debatable, but putative current examples must

---

9. Cf. 1 Sam. 3:14; Mekilta on Exod. 20:7; 'Abot R. Nat. 39. On the unpardonable sin, see Boring 1976; 1991: 219–21; O. Evans 1957; A. Fuchs 1994; Lövestam 1968; O'Neill 1983; J. Williams 1965.

recapitulate the essence of the situation narrated in Matt. 12. It would therefore be wise for expositors to exercise caution in broadly applying this text to unbelief in general. Ultimate unbelief in Jesus is unforgivable, but the point of 12:24–32 is not so much to narrate unbelief despite clear evidence that Jesus is the Messiah as it is to stress the slanderous attempt to portray this messianic evidence as demonic evidence. People are always accountable to believe the gospel when they hear it, but this does not warrant the notion that those who do not immediately believe the gospel have entered an unalterable state of unforgivable doom.

12:33–37 Jesus's rejoinder continues with a new metaphor, that of a tree and its fruit (cf. 3:7–10; 7:16–20). Jesus demands that the Pharisees be consistent. They must either view Jesus (the tree) and its fruit (his words and deeds) as worthless or view them as good (12:33). Jesus's good fruit demonstrates that he is good (cf. Gos. Thom. 45), but the Pharisees attribute the good deeds to a demonic source. Conversely, the Pharisees' words are like the worthless fruit of a worthless tree because they speak from an evil heart (Matt. 12:34–35; cf. 15:11, 19; Sir. 27:6). Their slander against Jesus reveals their own inner corruption. Jesus's depiction of the Pharisees as a brood of vipers recalls Matt. 3:7 and anticipates 23:33. The words of the Pharisees (cf. Derrett 1998) are therefore suggestive of their ultimate destiny. Evil words spoken from the treasury of an evil heart portend eschatological doom (12:36). The words spoken against the Spirit will ultimately condemn the Pharisees. On judgment day, good words that manifest a good heart will vindicate good people, but bad words from a bad heart will condemn bad people (12:37).

Sadly, the Pharisees next respond to these scorching words by asking Jesus for a sign that will authenticate his words (12:38). This is ironic, since their slanderous response to previous miraculous signs has led to these words. They are not in need of good evidence but good hearts. What use are further miracles?

Additional Note

12:25. Evidently, the original reading εἰδὼς δέ (ℵ*, B, cop^sa) was supplemented by scribes who added ὁ Ἰησοῦς (C, L, W, f¹, f¹³, *Byz, Lect,* and others) to improve the clarity of the passage.

b. Some Legal Experts and Pharisees Ask for a Sign (12:38–45)

Evidently in response to Jesus's sharp warning about unforgivable sin,[1] certain legal experts and Pharisees ask Jesus for a sign (12:38). His answer does not supply them with a new sign but only reminds them of the old "sign" of Jonah (12:39–41; cf. Jon. 1:17)[2] and the trek of the Queen of the South to hear Solomon's wisdom (Matt. 12:42; cf. 1 Kings 10; 2 Chron. 9). With an enigmatic story about an evil spirit, Jesus concludes his answer by warning the listeners that their unbelief will leave them worse than they were before Jesus came (Matt. 12:43–45).

Matthew 12:38–45 presents two perspectives that stress the gravity of the unbelief of Jesus's contemporaries, described four times as "this evil generation" (12:39, 41–42, 45). The first perspective contrasts the Pharisees' unbelief with surprising cases of belief in the Hebrew Bible (12:38–42). The second perspective portrays this unbelief parabolically, showing that Israel will be worse off after not believing in Jesus than it was before he came. This is probably a cryptic warning against superficial repentance and a veiled prophecy of the eschatological doom of Jesus's contemporaries (cf. Luke 11:24–26). (On this passage, see Linton 1965.)

The outline of this unit is as follows:

   i. The request (12:38)
  ii. The answer (12:39–45)
     (1) The sign of Jonah (12:39–41)
     (2) The queen of the South (12:42)
     (3) The unclean spirit (12:43–45)

Exegesis and Exposition

[38]Then some of the legal experts and Pharisees answered him, "Teacher, we want to see a sign from you." [39]But in response he said to them, "An evil and

---

1. Many scholars do not think of 12:38 as an answer because of the clear Semitic idiom (Moulton and Turner 1963: 155–56) and the pleonastic construction. Yet the juxtaposition of the Pharisees' request with Jesus's warning indicates the narrative connection that Matthew wished to convey.

2. On the sign of Jonah, see R. Edwards 1971; Merrill 1980; Mora 1983; R. Scott 1965; Vögtle 1971: 103–36.

adulterous generation seeks for a sign; yet no sign will be given to it except the sign of Jonah the prophet.[40]For just as 'Jonah was three days and three nights in the belly of the sea monster,' so will the Son of Man be three days and three nights in the heart of the earth. [41]The men of Nineveh will stand up with this generation at the judgment and will condemn it because they repented at the preaching of Jonah and, behold, something greater than Jonah is here. [42]The queen of the South will rise up with this generation at the judgment and will condemn it because she came from the ends of the earth to listen to Solomon's wisdom and, behold, something greater than Solomon is here.

[43]"Now when the unclean spirit goes out of a person, it passes through waterless places seeking rest yet does not find it. [44]Then it says, 'I will return to my house from which I came'; and when it comes, it finds it unoccupied, swept, and put in order. [45]Then it goes and brings along with it seven other spirits more wicked than itself, and they enter and live there; and the last state of that person becomes worse than the first. So it will also be with this evil generation."

i. The Request (12:38)

12:38   Jesus's solemn words about the Pharisees' accountability for the accusation in 12:24 leads them to ask him to prove himself with a sign (16:1, 4; 24:3, 30; cf. Mark 8:11–12; Luke 11:15–26, 29–32; 1 Cor. 1:22; Josephus, *Ant.* 18.85; 20.97, 170). But Jesus has already performed many miracles before the Pharisees, and his last miracle led them to slander the Holy Spirit. So why should he perform an especially significant miracle, a "sign" (cf. John 6:30)? The Pharisees' reference to Jesus as "teacher" appears respectful, but those who address Jesus as teacher in Matthew are not believers in him (cf. Matt. 8:19; 9:11; 17:24; 22:16, 36). Perhaps their tone of voice reveals their insincerity or even sarcasm.

ii. The Answer (12:39–45)

(1) The Sign of Jonah (12:39–41)

12:39   Although there was precedent for Israel's leaders to perform signs (Exod. 4:30–31), Jesus simply answers that this evil and adulterous generation (cf. Matt. 11:16–19; 16:4; 17:17; 23:29–36; 24:34; cf. Deut. 1:35; 32:5; Jub. 23.14; 1QSb 3.7) will see no more signs except that of the prophet Jonah (cf. Matt. 16:4; Liv. Pro. 10.10–11 [Jonah]). Jesus, in describing his contemporaries as adulterous, uses a common biblical metaphor for sin (e.g., Deut. 32:5; Isa. 57:3; 54:5; Jer. 2:2; 3:9–10; Ezek. 16:32; Hos. 1–3; James 4:4). This incident is similar to that in Matt. 16:1–4.

12:40–41   The reference to Jon. 1:17 provides a cryptic prophecy of the death and resurrection of Jesus. The resurrection presents the ultimate validation of Jesus's identity and mission (cf. Acts 2:24, 32, 36; 3:15; 13:37; 17:31). Jonah himself is the sign: his three days and nights in the belly of the sea monster are to be compared to Jesus's upcoming three days and nights in the earth. This language does not require that Jesus be in the grave for seventy-two hours, since in Jewish reckoning any part of a day could count as a day (cf. Gen. 42:17–18; 1 Sam. 30:1, 12–13; 1 Kings 20:29; 2 Chron. 10:5, 12; Esth. 4:16–5:1). This is the first time Matthew portrays Jesus as hinting that he will die (cf. Matt. 16:21; 17:9, 22–23). The allusion to Jonah continues in 12:41 with the unfavorable comparison of Jesus's contemporaries to Jonah's audience. In language reminiscent of 11:21–24, Jesus underlines the severity of the sin of his contemporaries: although the Ninevites repented when Jonah preached (Jon. 3:2), Jesus's contemporaries do not repent when one greater than Jonah preaches (cf. Matt. 12:6).

(2) The Queen of the South (12:42)

The queen of Sheba (literally, "the South") came from a distant land   **12:42** to hear and test Solomon's wisdom (1 Kings 10:1–13; 2 Chron. 9:1–12; Josephus, *Ant.* 8.165–73), but Jesus's contemporaries will not accept the wisdom of one greater than Solomon (cf. the implicit comparison to David in Matt. 12:3; L. Perkins 1998). Therefore on judgment day both the Ninevites and the queen of the South will condemn Jesus's contemporaries.

(3) The Unclean Spirit (12:43–45)

This parabolic passage about the activities of an unclean spirit (cf. 10:1)   **12:43–45** returns to the matter of exorcism, with which Jesus's debate with the Pharisees began (12:22–29). The spirit leaves its human abode for the desert (cf. Isa. 13:21; 34:14) and later returns with seven other spirits to the man, who has become a more attractive abode. Now inhabited by the original spirit and seven others, the man is much worse off than he was before the first spirit left. Evidently, after the first spirit left, nothing good came into the man to fill the vacuum. For various views of this enigmatic passage, see W. Davies and Allison 1991: 359–62. It seems that the overall idea is that although a great multitude of Jews have profited from Jesus's healings and exorcisms, comparatively few have genuinely understood Jesus's message and repented. The nation, like a recently cleaned house, has had its demons removed. Yet it has done nothing to ensure itself against their more rigorous re-entrenchment.

This passage uniquely emphasizes the evils of hardened unbelief. Although the Pharisees have seen Jesus do many miracles, they attribute the miracles to Satan. When they are shown the untenability of that position, they respond with an evidently insincere request for another miracle. Their unbelief despite overwhelming evidence is contrasted with the Ninevites and the queen of the South, who believed despite relatively little evidence. They provide a grim illustration of Matt. 11:25: God has hidden the message of the kingdom from those who are wise in their own estimation and has revealed it to those who are childlike. Further signs will not bring them to faith, not even the resurrection of Jesus from the dead (12:40; cf. 28:11–15; Luke 16:27–31; 1 Cor. 1:22). In any event, Jesus's miracles are deeds of power done with compassion for those in need, not spectacular feats designed to convince skeptics.

This enigmatic parable implies that the absence of evil spirits does not equate with the presence of redemption. The house has been cleaned, but a good tenant has not taken up residence. Relatively few of Jesus's contemporaries genuinely repent. Without national repentance, prospects for the future are bleak (23:36).

c. The True Family of Jesus (12:46–50)

The desire of Jesus's mother and brothers to speak with him (12:46–47) provides an opportunity for Jesus to speak of his true family, those who do the will of his Father in heaven (see Blinzler 1967). Jesus teaches by means of a question (12:48), an answer (12:49), and an explanation (12:50). After the previous two pericopes stressing unbelief, it is refreshing to find Jesus speaking positively about the community of those who follow him (12:50). Yet this positive note has a dark side, as the matter of the kingdom dividing families is revisited (cf. 10:34–39).

This unit can be outlined as follows:

i. The occasion (12:46–47)
ii. Jesus's teaching on family (12:48–50)

Exegesis and Exposition

⁴⁶While he was still speaking to the crowds, here came his mother and brothers and stood outside so that they could speak to him. ⁴⁷ᴿAnd someone said to him, "Behold, your mother and your brothers are standing outside seeking to speak to you."⁻ ⁴⁸But Jesus answered the one who told him, "Who is my mother and who are my brothers?" ⁴⁹And stretching out his hand toward his disciples, he said, "Look at my mother and my brothers! ⁵⁰For whoever does the will of my Father who is in heaven is my brother and sister and mother."

i. The Occasion (12:46–47)

As Jesus continues to speak to the crowd, his mother and brothers (cf. **12:46–47** 1:16, 18; 13:55–56) appear outside and wish to speak with him (cf. Mark 3:31–35; Luke 8:19–21; 11:27–28). The press of the crowd evidently prevents them from getting inside. From Matthew's narrative one might suppose that they are concerned over the intensifying conflict between Jesus and the Pharisees. Mark 3:21, 31 indicates that they were concerned about Jesus's mental stability. The absence of Joseph is often taken to indicate that he had died by this time. Be that as it may, for Matthew's narrative and theological purposes, Jesus has only one Father (Matt. 1:16, 18–25; 3:17; 7:21; 10:32; 11:27; 12:50; 16:17; 18:10, 19; 20:23; 25:34; 26:39, 42, 53), and it would be inappropriate for Joseph to play a role in this scene. Verseput (1986: 284) argues that 12:47 is a later interpolation. (See the additional note at the end of this unit.)

ii. Jesus's Teaching on Family (12:48–50)

12:48–50   Other passages make it clear that Jesus's family was not always in complete sympathy with his messianic mission (Mark 3:21; John 7:1–5). It
is perhaps significant that Jesus's mother and brothers are "outside."
If so, Jesus's disciples, who do the will of his Father in heaven, are
"inside" and are his true family (cf. Matt. 23:8; 28:10; Bruner 1987:
471–72). Yet Fenton (1963: 206) goes too far when he says that Jesus
here disowns his family, which represents the whole of Israel. Jesus
disowns neither his family nor Israel. Rather, he challenges any notion
that ethnic descent or family loyalty defines the people of God. In this
passage, the mention of Jesus's brothers (and sisters in Matt. 13:56)
makes the notion of Mary's perpetual virginity difficult to maintain.
The Roman Catholic author Harrington (1991: 191) acknowledges that
it is doubtful that Matthew was aware of the perpetual-virginity tradition. Yet Calvin was hesitant to attack this tradition (1972: 1.70, 136).
According to Tertullian (*Marc.* 4.19; *The Flesh of Christ* 7), Docetists
in the early third century CE used 12:48 to argue that Jesus was never
born and had no human family. See further the comments on 1:25.

In this passage Jesus's own family serves as a warning against superficial discipleship. Jesus affirms the family in other passages (15:1–9;
19:19; John 19:27), and so the point here is not disrespect for family but
allegiance to those whose lives are ordered by Jesus's values.[1] W. Davies
and Allison (1991: 364) put it well: "The words do not dissolve family
bonds but rather relativize them." Jesus's disciples may have to leave
their families behind (19:29), and they may even face betrayal by the
members of their own families (10:21, 35–37). Everyday family duties
(cf. 4:22; 8:22) cannot take precedence over one's loyalties to the Messiah
and his kingdom. Yet loyalty to the kingdom is carried out in community
with other like-minded followers of Jesus, who constitute the family of
God (cf. Roh 2001). The call to follow Jesus "is not a call to solitary existence" (W. Davies and Allison 1991: 367) but a call to the most profound
experience of authentic community. Innate human needs for identity,
security, and nurture can be met best through the community of those
who follow Jesus. This passage must be pondered and implemented by
every local Christian assembly. (See Barton 1994.)

Matthew 11–12 has gradually made its readers aware of the rising
tide of opposition and rejection. Matthew 12:1–14 makes it clear that
Jesus's approach to Sabbath law is at variance with that of the Pharisees. Matthew has previously alluded briefly to the issue that erupts here
into unforgivable blasphemy and a major rift with the religious leaders (9:34; 12:24–32). Despite the presence of God's saving reign in the

---

1. The priority of ethical-spiritual community over the nuclear family may be implied
in Deut. 33:9; Prov. 18:24 and was certainly practiced by the Qumran community. Cf. 1QS
1–9, esp. 1.1–17; 2.24–3.1; Josephus, *J.W.* 2.120–58.

person of Jesus, they ominously plan to murder (12:14) God's beloved servant (12:17–21), one greater than David, Solomon, Jonah, and sacred institutions such as the temple and the Sabbath (12:3, 6, 8, 41–42). The chapter concludes with an incident showing that even the members of Jesus's own family are not necessarily his real family (12:46–50). As this opposition escalates, Jesus begins to speak more in parables, by which he communicates with the true family of his disciples even as he obscures the truth from the crowds of superficial "followers" and from those who are already plotting to do away with him (Verseput 1986: 294).

Additional Note

12:47. The editors of UBS[4] decided to enclose 12:47 in brackets because it is omitted by ℵ*, B, L, 579, and others. But the omission is likely due to homoeoteleuton (similar ending), since λαλῆσαι ends both 12:46 and 12:47. Matthew 12:47 seems necessary for the flow of the passage and is well supported by ℵ[1], C, D, W, f[1], f[13], *Byz, Lect.*

IV. Growing Opposition to the Kingdom of Heaven (11:2–13:52)
   A. Narrative 3: Three Cycles of Unbelief and Belief (11:2–12:50)
➤ B. Discourse 3: Parables of the Kingdom of Heaven (13:1–52)

B. Discourse 3: Parables of the Kingdom of Heaven (13:1–52)

Structure of the Discourse on Parables

After noting the setting (13:1–2), Matthew narrates Jesus's third major discourse in 13:3–52. If 13:51–52 is correctly interpreted as a parable, the discourse can be seen as having two sections of four parables each. The first is addressed to the crowds (13:3–33) and the second to the disciples (13:36–52). Between the two sections is an editorial comment on the parables as prophetic fulfillment (13:34–35). In both sections Jesus answers a question from the disciples about parables (13:10–17, 36–43). A pair of similar short parables concludes the first section and begins the second section (13:31–33, 44–46). Although some scholars (e.g., Hagner 1993: 362–64) doubt the symmetrical structure of the discourse, at least two proposals have merit.

D. Wenham (1978–79) presents a chiastic structure:

A Parable of the sower: Hearing the word of the kingdom (13:1–9)
　　B Disciples' question and Jesus's answer: Interpretation of the sower (13:10–23)
　　　　C Parable of the weeds: Good and evil (13:24–30)
　　　　　　D Parables of the mustard seed and leaven: Growth (13:31–33)
　　　　　　　　E Explanation of parables and interpretation of the weeds (13:34–43)
　　　　　　D′ Parables of treasure and pearl: Sacrifice (13:44–46)
　　　　　C′ Parable of the net: Good and evil (13:47–50)
　　　B′ Jesus's question and disciples' answer: Understanding parables (13:51)
A′ Parable of the homeowner: Trained for the kingdom (13:52)

Wenham's analysis notes well the two halves of the discourse, its public and private segments. He also is correct in seeing the symmetry of the paired short parables of mustard seed/leaven and treasure/pearl. But his nonsymmetrical placement of Jesus's two interpretations of parables (13:10–17, 34–43) is somewhat problematic.

W. Davies and Allison (1991: 370–71) suggest a tripartite structure. Each part begins with a parable and contains both an interpretation of a parable and discussion of the parables:

I. Parable of the sower (13:1–9)
   Discussion of parables with a scriptural citation (13:10–17)
   Interpretation of the sower (13:18–23)
II. Parables of weeds, mustard seed, and leaven (13:24–33)
   Discussion of parables with a scriptural citation (13:34–35)
   Interpretation of the weeds (13:36–43)
III. Parables of the treasure, pearl, and net (13:44–48)
   Interpretation of the net (13:49–50)
   Discussion of parables (13:51–52)

This approach has some merit and is adopted by Boring (1995: 301), but it tends to break down in section III, where the order of discussion and interpretation is reversed. The outline used in the following commentary is based on Wenham's approach. (On the structure of Matt. 13, see Gerhardsson 1972–73; Marin 1971; Vorster 1977.)

The Interpretation of Parables

Both church history and Christian experience testify to the prevalence of imaginative interpretations of Jesus's parables.[1] Multitudes of such "heavenly meanings" have been superimposed upon the "earthly stories" of the parables. The patristic transformation of the parable of the good Samaritan into the story of Adam's fall and redemption (Kissinger 1979: 2–4, 18, 26–27) may be the most notorious example of this allegorizing approach, which atomizes the parables and tends to ignore their historical and literary contexts. More recently reader-response criticism tends to yield results that have only a tangential relationship to the original context of the parables (Blomberg 1990a: 155–60; Tolbert 1979). More than a hundred years ago, in reaction to the excesses of the allegorizers, Jülicher (1899)—and many others since him—argued that Jesus's parables, unlike allegories, have only one main point. But this narrow approach seems contrary to Jesus's own interpretations of his parables (13:18–23, 37–43), let alone the flexibility, if not polyvalence, of meaning inherent in the use of stories by skilled speakers and authors (Stein in Longenecker 2000: 30–50).

Therefore it seems best to look at each parable in its own context in order to determine the degree to which its earthly details convey a heavenly meaning (Blomberg 1990a: 68–69; Ryken 1984: 145–53, 199–203; 1987: 61–76). Parables are indeed allegories, but they must not be allegorized (cf. Carlston 1981; Klauck 1978; Sider 1985). Their imagery must be

1. Among the voluminous literature on the interpretation of parables, see K. Bailey 1976: 15–75; Blomberg 1990a; W. Davies and Allison 1991: 378–82; Gerhardsson 1988; Hultgren 2000: 1–19; Kingsbury 1971; Kissinger 1979; Payne in France and Wenham 1981: 329–44; Sider 1995; Snodgrass in Longenecker 2000: 3–29; Snodgrass in McKnight and Osborne 2004: 177–90; Tolbert 1979. On parables in Matthew, see Carter and Heil 1998; Gerhardsson 1972–73; I. Jones 1995; Kingsbury 1969; Lambrecht 1992; Luz 2001: 288–98; Overman in Lovering 1995: 425–39.

understood in terms of their own ancient historical and literary conventions, not in terms of extraneous categories superimposed upon them by ancient, medieval, modern, or postmodern allegorizers.[2] The imagery of Jesus's parables is drawn from first-century Palestine (K. Bailey 1976), and so understanding the historical context is crucial. It is also important to note the literary context, since parables are metaphorical narratives embedded in the larger Gospel narrative (Blomberg 1990a: 101–31; Carter in Carter and Heil 1998: 36–63; Gerhardsson 1988, 1991). The preceding context can be crucial, since parabolic imagery is tied to key characters and issues in the narrative. At times a concluding general comment applies the parabolic imagery to a contextual matter. It is also enlightening to compare and contrast Jesus's parables with those of the Jewish rabbis, although the problem of anachronism is difficult to resolve.[3]

The Interpretation of Matthew 13

Matthew 13 indicates that Jesus intended his parables to reveal truths of the kingdom to his disciples and to conceal these truths from others (13:10–16). The primary focus of these parables is the varied responses to the kingdom message (13:19). Thus the primary background for the parables of Matt. 13 is the increasing opposition, narrated in Matt. 11–12, to Jesus and his message. The parables originally helped Jesus's disciples understand the opposition to themselves and later, as narrated by Matthew, similarly enabled his community to grasp its own identity and struggles.

With this in mind, it is apparent that classical dispensationalism is mistaken in its attempt to understand the parables as referring primarily to the future millennium or as teaching the "mystery" of the offered, rejected, and postponed kingdom (Toussaint 1980: 170–76; Walvoord 1974: 96–97). The kingdom is already inaugurated in Matthew (cf. 3:2; 4:17; 10:7; 12:28; and "Theological Emphases: Kingdom of Heaven" in the commentary introduction), and the parables are about its present progress as well as its future glories (13:43). No doubt, application must be drawn from this historical context to modern contexts where the message of the kingdom is proclaimed. The disciples continue the mission of Jesus (24:14; 28:19), and their ministry continues until the end of the age (13:39, 43, 49; 24:14; 28:18–20).[4] (On the kingdom in Matt. 13, see M. Bailey 1999a.)

2. This would certainly include the Hebrew Bible, as is obvious in 21:33, drawn from Isa. 5:1–2. See Westermann 1990.
3. For discussions of Jesus's parables in the light of rabbinic parables, see C. A. Evans in Longenecker 2000: 51–75; Flusser 1981; McArthur and Johnston 1990; Oesterley 1936; Pautrel 1936, 1938; D. Stern 1991: 188–206; Thoma and Wyschogrod 1989; B. Young 1989: esp. 236–81.
4. On the interpretation of Matt. 13, see Dupont 1967; Dupont in Didier 1972: 221–59; Hagner in Longenecker 2000: 102–24; Heil in Carter and Heil 1998: 64–95; I. Jones 1995: 282–358; Kingsbury 1969; Lambrecht 1977b; Luz 2001: 228–32; Phillips 1985; B. Young 1989: 189–235.

1. Parables to the Crowds (13:1–35)

Since the conclusion of the mission discourse (11:1), Matthew has stressed the increasing opposition to Jesus. The disciples have experienced the same trials during their own mission trip (10:18, 24–25). John the Baptist (11:1–6), Jesus's family (12:46–50), and the residents of Nazareth (13:53–58) are not in step with Jesus's mission. The Pharisees' murder plot (12:14) indicates their implacable opposition. Bracketed by the unbelief of Jesus's family and those who watched him grow up (Garland 1993: 143), Matt. 13:3–53 interprets the mixed response to the kingdom message and indicates that such a response will continue until judgment day (13:23, 30, 40–43, 49–50).

Jesus first addresses the crowd (13:1–33) as a mixed multitude representing different responses to the kingdom message. The parable of the sower is the ruling parable of this discourse, since it leads to the disciples' question about the purpose of parables (13:10) and is interpreted in detail by Jesus (13:18–23). It becomes clear that many will not receive the kingdom message (13:3–9, 19–23), and some who seem to receive it will ultimately turn out to be satanic counterfeits (13:24–30, 36–43). The parables conceal the kingdom from such unbelievers (13:10–17), but they also reveal the glorious destiny of those who truly believe the message (13:43).

The unit outline is as follows:

a. The setting (13:1–2)
b. Parable of the sower (13:3–9)
c. Interaction with the disciples (13:10–23)
    i. Reason for parables (13:10–17)
    ii. Jesus explains the parable of the sower (13:18–23)
d. Parable of the weeds (13:24–30)
    i. The enemy's plot (13:24–26)
    ii. The landowner's response (13:27–30)
e. Parable of the mustard seed (13:31–32)
f. Parable of the yeast (13:33)
g. Editorial conclusion: The biblical basis for parables (13:34–35)

Exegesis and Exposition

¹That day Jesus went out of the house and was sitting beside the sea. ²And such large crowds gathered to him that he got into a boat and sat down, and the whole crowd was standing on the shore. ³And he spoke many things to them in parables:

"Behold, a sower went out to sow; ⁴and as he was sowing, some seeds fell beside the path, and the birds came and ate them up.· ⁵Now other seeds fell on the rocky places, where they did not have much soil; and immediately they sprang up because they had no depth of soil. ⁶But when the sun came up, they were scorched; and they withered, since they had no root. ⁷And others fell among thorns, and the thorns grew up and choked them. ⁸But others fell on the good soil and yielded a crop, some a hundredfold, some sixty, and some thirty. ⁹Anyone with ⸢ears⸣, listen!"

¹⁰And the disciples came to him and asked, "Why do you speak to them in parables?" ¹¹Jesus answered them, "Because to you it has been given to know the mysteries of the kingdom of heaven, but to them it has not been given. ¹²For more shall be given to anyone who has, and that person will have a great abundance; but anyone who does not have, even what that person has shall be taken away. ¹³Therefore I speak to them in parables; ⸢because although they see, they do not perceive, and although they hear, they do not listen, nor do they understand.⸣ ¹⁴In their case the prophecy of Isaiah is being fulfilled, which says,

'You will indeed hear, but you will never understand;
You will indeed see, but you will never perceive.
¹⁵For the heart of this people has become dull,
and with their ears they scarcely hear,
and they have closed their eyes,
so that they might not see with their eyes,
and hear with their ears,
and understand with their heart and turn,
And I would heal them.'

¹⁶But blessed are your eyes because they see; and your ears because they hear. ¹⁷For truly I tell you that many prophets and righteous people longed to see what you see, yet did not see it, and to hear what you hear, yet did not hear it.

¹⁸"Hear then the parable of the sower. ¹⁹When anyone hears the word of the kingdom and yet does not understand it, the evil one comes and snatches away what has been sown in that person's heart. This is what was sown beside the path. ²⁰And what was sown on the rocky places, this is the person who hears the word and immediately receives it with joy; ²¹yet this person has no firm root but is only temporary, and when affliction or persecution happens because of the word, this person immediately falls away. ²²And what was sown among the thorns, this is the person who hears the word, and the concern for this world and the deception that comes from wealth choke the word, and it does not yield a crop. ²³And what was sown on the good soil, this is the person who hears the word and understands it, who indeed bears fruit and yields, one a hundredfold, another sixty, and another thirty."

²⁴Jesus put before them another parable: "The kingdom of heaven may be

compared to a man who sowed good seed in his field. ²⁵But while people were sleeping, his enemy came and sowed weeds among the wheat and went away. ²⁶But when the plants sprouted and bore grain, then the weeds also appeared. ²⁷Then the landowner's slaves came and said to him, 'Master, did you not sow good seed in your field? How, then, does it have weeds?' ²⁸And he said to them, 'An enemy did this!' And the slaves said to him, 'Then do you want us to go and pull them up?' ²⁹But he said, 'No; for while you are pulling up the weeds, you may uproot the wheat with them. ³⁰Let both grow together until the harvest; and at harvesttime I will tell the reapers, "First pull up the weeds and tie them in bundles to burn them; but gather the wheat into my barn."'"

³¹He put before them another parable: "The kingdom of heaven is like a mustard seed, which a man took and sowed in his field; ³²This is smaller than all other seeds, but when it is full grown, it is larger than the garden plants and becomes a tree, so that 'the birds of the air' come and 'nest in its branches.'"

³³He told them another parable: "The kingdom of heaven is like leaven, which a woman took and hid in three pecks of flour until it was all leavened."

³⁴All these things Jesus told the crowds in parables, and he did not speak to them without a parable ³⁵in order that what was spoken ⌜through the prophet⌝ might be fulfilled:

> "I will open my mouth in parables;
> I will utter things hidden ⌜since the beginning of the world⌝."

a. The Setting (13:1–2)

The setting of the third discourse is similar to that of the first (cf. 5:1)   **13:1–2**
in that Jesus is again surrounded by crowds (cf. Mark 4:1–2; Luke 8:4). Jesus has been speaking to a crowd, evidently from a house (cf. Matt. 8:14), when his family arrives (12:46; 13:1). He leaves the house for the nearby Sea of Galilee, where he speaks while seated (cf. 5:1; 24:3) in a boat to the crowd standing at the shore (cf. Mark 4:1–9; Luke 8:4–8). As will be seen when it is interpreted (Matt. 13:18–23), this parable is about the crowd—they must grasp its message (13:9). Matthew narrates Jesus's move from the seashore back to the house in 13:36.

b. Parable of the Sower (13:3–9)

Although this parable is usually called the parable of the sower, its interpretation by Jesus indicates that it is really about the soil, which stands for the varying responses to the message of the kingdom (13:19–23). The parable amounts to an explanation of the mixed response to the kingdom mission of Jesus and his disciples (cf. Mark 4:1–9; Luke 8:4–8; Gos. Thom. 9).

Matthew's narrative of Jesus's teaching has already included occasional   **13:3**
parabolic elements (7:24–27; 9:15–17; 11:16–19; 12:29, 33, 43–45), but the

word "parable" (παραβολή, *parabolē*; 13:3, 10, 13, 18, 24, 33–36, 53; 15:15; 21:33, 45; 22:1; 24:32) occurs here for the first time. Παραβολή is the NT equivalent of the word מָשָׁל (*māšāl*; cf., e.g., 1 Sam. 10:12; Num. 23:7, 18; Ezek. 17:2; 21:5; 24:3) in the Hebrew Bible. Both words are used to describe a proverb, an enigma, a riddle, a taunt, a simile, or an allegorical story. In all of these nuances, the common denominator is the use of a concrete analogy to illumine or obscure an abstract thought (Sider 1981).

From Matt. 13:3, we assume that Jesus told many parables (cf. 1 Kings 5:12 LXX [4:32 Eng.]) and that Matthew selects representative stories reflecting the gist of Jesus's teaching, parables that Matthew views as most relevant for his community. The picture is of a farmer scattering seed by hand while walking through a field (cf. Isa. 55:10–11; Ps. 126:5–6; 2 Esd. [4 Ezra] 4:26–32; 8:41; 9:31–37; 1 Cor. 3:6–9).[1] Scholars debate whether the sowing would be preceded or followed by plowing (see Payne 1978), but this seems to have little impact on the interpretation of the parable.[2]

13:4–7 In 13:4–8 (cf. Mark 4:3–9; Luke 8:5–8) Jesus speaks of four types of soil where the scattered seed falls. In the first three cases, the seed does not produce a crop because it falls beside the path (Matt. 12:1; *m. Pe'ah* 2.1) and is eaten by birds, falls on shallow soil, or is choked by thorns (cf. Job 31:40). But in the fourth case, the seed falls on fertile ground and produces various levels of crops. The rocky soil of Matt. 13:5–6 refers to an underlying shelf of bedrock, not multiple rocks in the soil. Such soil warms rapidly and the seed sprouts quickly, but the plant soon wilts as the soil loses moisture (cf. James 1:11).

13:8–9 Scholars debate over the size of the harvest in 13:8. Some think the yield is fantastic, picturing the ultimate success of the kingdom mission despite present adversity (Jeremias 1972: 150), but this is not necessarily so, given other ancient descriptions of yields.[3] Jesus's affirmation in 13:9 (cf. 11:15; 13:43; Mark 4:23; Luke 14:35; Rev. 2:7; 13:9) underlines the importance of the crowd's grasping the meaning of the parable. His interpretation of the parable (Matt. 13:18–23) shows its relevance to the crowd's relationship to the message of the kingdom.

c. Interaction with the Disciples (13:10–23)

i. Reason for Parables (13:10–17)

The disciples' question about why Jesus is speaking in parables implies that there is something unusual happening here. Some scholars take

---

1. The NASB renders ὁ σπείρων as "the sower," but the article is generic (Wallace 1996: 227–31) and the translation "a sower" (NRSV) or "a farmer" (NIV) is preferable.

2. Plowing before sowing is found in Isa. 28:24–26; Jer. 4:3; Ezek. 36:9; Gos. Thom. 20; Pliny, *Nat.* 18.176, 180–81. The opposite order is found in Jub. 11.11, 24; *m. Šabb.* 7.2.

3. See Sib. Or. 3.263–64; Strabo, *Geography* 15.3.11; Pliny, *Nat.* 18.21.94–95; see Luz 2001: 241–42; McIver 1994.

this to mean that the Jews have decisively rejected the kingdom mission and that Jesus will now speak only of a postponed kingdom and only in mysterious language (Toussaint 1980: 168; Walvoord 1974: 96). But Jesus has previously used parabolic imagery (7:24–27; 9:15–17; 11:16–19; 12:29, 33, 43–45), and he continues to speak plainly (without parables) to unbelievers as the narrative proceeds (cf., e.g., 15:3–7; 16:2–4; 19:4–9, 17–22; most of 21–23). Matthew 13 does mark a transition in Jesus's ministry, but it is not abrupt. Opposition has come to a head in Matt. 12, but Matt. 13 is neither a novel method of teaching nor a new teaching about a postponed kingdom. Jesus's parables describe the present response of Israel to the kingdom message. After Jesus's death and resurrection, the parables will just as accurately describe the response of the nations to the preaching of the church until the end of the age. Although Matt. 13 describes something of a turning point, there is no change in the meaning of the kingdom. (On the purpose of the parables, see Van Elderen in Longenecker and Tenney 1974: 180–90.)

As Jesus speaks to the crowd, his disciples ask him why he is speaking in parables (cf. Mark 4:10–12; Luke 8:9–10). Jesus's answer implies that this manner of speaking is due to the rejection of his message by many of his listeners, but it is ultimately due to God's sovereign purpose to reveal the mysteries of the kingdom (cf. Mark 4:11; Luke 8:10) to whom God chooses (cf. Matt. 11:25–27).[4] These mysteries evidently amount to the kingdom truths signified in the parables of this chapter, centering on its present growth. God gives to some the capacity to understand these secrets but does not give this understanding to others.[5] To those who have this understanding, more understanding will be given, but those who do not have it will lose what little they do have (cf. 25:29). These solemn words confront Jesus's disciples with God's sovereign activity in graciously revealing himself to some and in justly withholding that revelation from others (cf. 1QS 5.11–12; 2 Bar. 38.1; 51.4). **13:10–12**

Jesus's language in 13:13 echoes Isa. 6:9–10. In Matt. 13:14–15 he directly cites these verses as a biblical pattern now fulfilled in his own ministry (cf. John 12:39–40; Acts 28:26–27).[6] Isaiah 6 describes a vision **13:13–15**

---

4. This is the only context in which the word μυστήριον appears in the Gospels (cf. Mark 4:11; Luke 8:10). Found more than twenty times in Paul (e.g., Rom. 11:25; Eph. 3:4; 2 Thess. 2:7), it is semantically related to the Aramaic word רָז (Dan. 2:18–19, 27–30, 47; 4:6). See 1 En. 68.5; 103.2; 2 Esd. (4 Ezra) 10:38; 12:36–37; 14:5; 2 Bar. 48.2–3; 81.4; 1QS 9.17; BDAG 661–62; Bornkamm, *TDNT* 4:802–28; R. Brown 1968.

5. Divine agency is expressed here through understated "divine passive" verbs: δέδοται in 13:11 and δοθήσεται, περισσευθήσεται, and ἀρθήσεται in 13:12. See Wallace 1996: 437–38.

6. Matthew 13:14–15 is an almost verbatim citation of Isa. 6:9–10 LXX (lacking only αὐτῶν from Isa. 6:10b in Matt. 13:15b, though some LXX MSS also lack αὐτῶν). The LXX is an accurate and literal rendering of the MT. The chiastic pattern of heart–ears–eyes–eyes–ears–heart from Isa. 6:10 is clear also in Matt. 13:15. On the use of Isa. 6:9–10, see

that occurred during the year of King Uzziah's death. This well-known vision of God in all his holiness leads Isaiah to acknowledge his own and his people's sinfulness. God cleanses Isaiah of his sin and calls him to ministry to sinful Israel. The commission includes the awesome responsibility of confronting the people with their rebellion against God's message. They have had revelation, but they do not understand what they hear or perceive what they see. Because of their hardened hearts, they are unable to respond with believing ears and eyes in turning to God so that God might heal them (cf. Jer. 5:21–23). Similarly, the rebellious response to Jesus's kingdom message leads to judicial hardening through further enigmatic teaching that those on the outside are not able to grasp.[7] God is sovereign over the initial rebellious response as well as the further hardening. Mark 4:11 makes an even stronger statement about the use of parables to conceal truth. (On Isa. 6:9–10 in the NT, see C. A. Evans 1989c.)

13:16–17 By contrast, the disciples are graciously blessed with seeing eyes and hearing ears. This blessedness exceeds that of many prophets and righteous people, who longed to hear and see what the disciples have heard and seen. Jesus's disciples are privileged to experience the eschatological words and deeds of Jesus that inaugurate the kingdom. The biblical luminaries could only anticipate these things (cf. 11:11–13; John 8:56; Heb. 11:13, 39–40; 1 Pet. 1:10–12; Eph. 3:4–5), but Jesus's disciples see and hear them and receive Jesus's private explanations of their significance (Matt. 13:18–23, 36–53).

Finite humans will never fully understand the interplay of God's sovereignty and human responsibility. Matthew 13:11–15, with its citation of Isa. 6:9–10, is one of the strongest biblical affirmations of God's prerogative to reveal himself as he sees fit. This statement is perhaps as striking as Matt. 11:25–27, which speaks even more bluntly of God "hiding" the kingdom message from those who reject it. Matthew 11:27 also goes beyond 13:11–15 in affirming that Jesus shares the divine prerogative of revealing the Father to whomever he wills. One can only respond to these affirmations of divine sovereignty with awe and worship. In the Bible, if not always in Christian theology, the sovereignty of God and the responsibility of God's creatures go hand in hand. This is clear when Matt. 11:25–27 is compared with 11:28–30 and when Peter willingly confesses the identity of Jesus that God has revealed to him (16:15–17). It is also clear that those whom God sovereignly rejects are those who willfully reject God. God does not cast his pearls before swine (7:6). God's sovereign election, adapting F. P. Dunne's famous saying, "comforts those

---

C. A. Evans 1989b; Gnilka 1961. Judging from its use in the NT, Isa. 6:9–10 was important for the early church. See also John 12:40; Acts 28:26–27; Rom. 11:8.

7. The extreme lack of insight and perception is expressed with the double or emphatic negation constructions οὐ μὴ συνῆτε and οὐ μὴ ἴδητε. See Wallace 1996: 468–69.

afflicted by sin and afflicts those comfortable with sin." The preaching of the kingdom message will be attended with God's blessing in bringing people to faith. God will bring his people to himself through gospel proclamation. (See Kagarise 2001.)

ii. Jesus Explains the Parable of the Sower (13:18–23)

Here the disciples obtain more understanding of the kingdom, as Jesus promised in 13:11–12. Jesus begins his explanation of the parable of the sower by telling them to "hear" it (cf. Mark 4:13–20; Luke 8:11–15).[8] Matthew 13:19–23 simply lays out the four types of soil in order and explains their significance in portraying four responses to the kingdom message (cf. 4:23; 9:35; 24:14). The seed beside the path, which was eaten by birds, stands for a superficial hearing of the kingdom message that is thwarted by the evil one, Satan (cf. 13:25, 28, 39; Jub. 11.11–12; Apoc. Abr. 13). The seed that sprouted in shallow soil and withered in the sun stands for a fickle hearing of the message where initial enthusiasm turns to apostasy (Matt. 24:10) due to problems or persecution (cf. 5:11–12; 10:16–25; 23:34–36; 24:9–13). The seed that sprouts and grows but is choked by thorns stands for a promising hearing of the message that ends because of competition from secular concerns, especially greed (cf. 6:19–34). Each of these three types of soil successively represents more growth—from the seed snatched before it sprouts to the wilted sprouts to the choked plants—but none of them yields any fruit.

                                                    13:18–22

Only the fourth soil produces fruit, which signifies genuine discipleship: obedience to God's law as taught by Jesus (cf. 3:8–10; 7:16–20; 12:33; 21:19, 34, 41, 43). It is significant that fruit is borne only when there is understanding of the message. As pointed out in 13:13–15, such understanding and the lack of it are both matters of God's sovereignty and human responsibility.

                                                    13:23

Implications of the Parable of the Sower

Jesus's detailed interpretation of the parable invalidates the popular idea that a parable has only a single point of reference to reality. Although the central point is clearly the reception of the kingdom message, several details add depth and detail to this central point. Jesus himself is the sower, but the parable has immediate application to the disciples' ministry and ultimate application to the later church's proclamation. As W. Davies and Allison (1991: 402–3) point out, the

---

8. The imperative ἀκούσατε means "understand," not merely "hear" (BDAG 38). This answers to the play on words in 13:14 that begins the allusion to Isa. 6:9–10. Those signified by the seed that falls beside the path hear without understanding (13:19). Those represented by the good soil hear and understand the message (13:23).

purpose of the parable of the sower is not to exhort believers but to explain unbelief. Jesus and the disciples have faithfully proclaimed the kingdom message, but relatively few have truly grasped it. This is explained by hardness of heart, persecution, worldliness, and satanic opposition. Thus the purpose of the parable of the sower is similar to that of Rom. 9–11.

The first three types of soil successively lay out three factors that hinder the reception of the kingdom message: Satan, persecution, and greed. Satanic opposition is pictured as effective when the seed falls on the hard ground beside the path, which probably represents hearts hardened by both human sin and divine abandonment (Matt. 13:15; cf. 9:4; 12:34; 15:8, 18, 19; 24:48). Persecution is effective when there is an immediate joyful reception of the message: evidently a solely emotional response, lacking the "root" of intellectual understanding (13:21). Greed and secular concerns are also effective in thwarting the reception of the kingdom message, evidently when the demands of discipleship confront a materialistic lifestyle (13:22; cf. 6:19–34; 16:24–26; 19:23).

In light of this, preachers of the gospel will do well to warn their listeners of the danger of having a heart hardened to God but available to Satan. Similarly, a heart open to superficial, emotional influences but closed to deeper understanding of the kingdom readily turns from God when troubles arise. Finally, a heart that is easily attracted to worldly stature and wealth is a heart that is soon distracted from the kingdom message. These solemn matters are heard all too seldom from Christian pulpits.

Another crucial question here is whether only the good ground (13:23) represents a genuine disciple of the kingdom or whether others who bear no fruit should be viewed as genuine though unproductive disciples. There are those whose belief in "eternal security" leads them to conclude that any profession of receiving the gospel leads to eternal bliss in heaven. But this will not do for Matthew, who teaches consistently that "fruit" is an indispensable test of genuine discipleship (3:8–10; 7:16–20; 12:33; 21:19, 34, 41, 43). On the other hand, there are degrees of fruit-bearing (13:23), which should lead those who stress discipleship to avoid legalism and perfectionism. One must not condemn as unbelievers would-be disciples who do not meet legalistic human standards. Mature discipleship does not happen overnight, since godliness, like fruit-bearing, requires a growing season before there can be a harvest.

In the flow of Matthew's narrative, 13:1–23 explains the rejection experienced by Jesus in Matt. 11–12 (W. Davies and Allison 1991: 402–3). The message has come to many, but relatively few have received it and borne fruit. The very next parable and its interpretation (13:24–33, 36–43) make it clear that such a mixed response to the kingdom will continue until the end of the age. The explanation for this is found in the wickedness of humans but ultimately in God's mysterious and sovereign purpose.[9]

d. Parable of the Weeds (13:24–30)

Jesus's second parable utilizes the comparison formula "The kingdom of heaven is like. . . ."[10] This or a similar formula appears many times in Matthew. The weeds parable, like the first, uses the image of sowing seed and leads to the disciples' request for interpretation (13:36–43). But it introduces new features such as the landowner, his slaves, his enemy (although see 13:19), and the weeds. See also Gos. Thom. 57.

i. The Enemy's Plot (13:24–26)

The second parable begins the same as the first, with a farmer planting   **13:24–26**
seed, but here the seed is called "good." This parable features the nefarious act of an enemy (cf. 22:44) who plants weeds among the wheat one night while everyone is asleep. As the wheat grows, so do the weeds. But the weeds are indistinguishable from the wheat until the point in the growing season when the wheat begins to form heads of grain.[11] This may be a picture of false disciples as opposed to unbelievers in general (Gundry 1994: 261–62), although nothing is made of it in Jesus's later interpretation (W. Davies and Allison 1991: 408–9).

ii. The Landowner's Response (13:27–30)

When the wheat produces heads of grain, the landowner's slaves notice   **13:27–30**
the weeds growing together with the wheat. They inform the landowner of the problem, and he correctly surmises that an enemy is responsible. He tells his slaves not to attempt to root out the weeds at this point, since this would also damage the wheat. Instead the weeds will be gathered and burned at harvesttime, when the wheat is gathered into the barn (cf. 3:12; 6:26). This portrayal of eschatological judgment will be explained in 13:36–43.

This parable is yet to be interpreted (cf. 13:36–43), but attentive readers will already be drawing tentative conclusions about it, since it is similar to the first parable, which Jesus has already interpreted. Similar motifs include sowing, seed, an enemy, and mixed results. As 13:36–43 will show, it would be a mistake to try to identify the realities portrayed

---

9. On the interpretation of the sower, see M. Bailey 1998b; Du Plessis 1987; C. A. Evans 1985; Gerhardsson 1968; Hultgren 2000: 180–202; Kissinger 1979: 379–85; Payne 1980; in France and Wenham 1980: 163–207; Weeden 1979; D. Wenham 1974.

10. The formula is ὡμοιώθη ἡ βασιλεία τῶν οὐρανῶν. See also 13:31, 33, 44, 45, 47, 52; 18:23; 20:1; 22:2; 25:1; cf. 7:24, 26; 11:16; Carson 1985.

11. The word translated "weeds" (ζιζάνιον) does not occur in the LXX and is presumably Semitic in background. Cf. BDAG 429; Apoc. Mos. 16.3; Gos. Thom. 57. On whether this feature of the parable is realistic, see Kerr 1997; Tripp 1999.

by the details of the two parables. And there are new elements, such as the enemy (but see 13:19), the weeds (but see 13:7, 22), the landowner, the slaves, the harvest and harvesters, the fire, and the barn. Jesus will interpret the details of this imagery in 13:36–43, but the developing dualism between landowner and enemy, good seed/wheat and weeds, and barn and fire already offers a glimpse of an ominous battle between the cosmic forces of good and evil.

e. Parable of the Mustard Seed (13:31–32)

13:31–32 The parables of the mustard seed (13:31–32; cf. Mark 4:30–32; Luke 13:18–21; Gos. Thom. 20) and yeast (Matt. 13:33) are much shorter than the previous parables of the sower and the weeds. They do not contain narrative development of the initial image as the first two parables do, but they are called parables just the same. Both are introduced with the formula first noted in Matt. 13:24, and both seem to have a similar point—the growth of the kingdom. Some scholars quibble with the scientific accuracy of Jesus's statement that the mustard seed is the smallest seed (cf. 17:20; m. Nid. 5.2; m. Tohar. 8.8), but it should be taken in its context as affirming only that the mustard seed was the smallest herb seed commonly planted in Palestine (cf. Sproule 1980). This parable emphasizes how the kingdom grows from an insignificant beginning ("the smallest of all seeds"; cf. 17:20) into the largest of garden shrubs, suitable for nesting birds.[12] (On this parable, see M. Bailey 1998a; Hultgren 2000: 393–403.)

f. Parable of the Yeast (13:33)

13:33 The yeast also portrays the subtle though real influence of the kingdom in permeating the world (cf. Luke 13:20–21; Gos. Thom. 96). The Mishnah contains instructions on the use of yeast, which probably refers here to old or sour dough (m. Menah. 5.1–2). The amount of flour leavened by the yeast is literally "three satas" (σάτα τρία, sata tria). This is surprisingly large, since a σάτον (saton) was about thirteen liters. Three measures would amount to almost forty liters, nearly a bushel of flour, enough to feed around 150 people (Josephus, Ant. 9.71, 85; BDAG 917; Hagner 1993: 390). (On this parable, see Hultgren 2000: 403–9.)

Interpreting the Mustard Seed and the Yeast

There is much debate over the meaning of the consecutive short parables of the mustard seed and yeast. Most classical dispensationalists interpret the imagery as portraying the presence of evil within professing

---

12. Matthew 13:32b contains allusions to Ps. 104:12; Ezek. 17:23; 31:6; Dan. 4:10–12, 21. For the image of the large tree with birds nesting in its branches, cf. Judg. 9:7–15; Ps. 80:8–13; Ps. Sol. 14.2–3; 1QH 6.14–16; 8.4–8.

Christendom.[13] This is due primarily to bifurcating the kingdom of God (understood as the future millennium) and the kingdom of heaven (understood as a "mystery" encompassing Christendom, viewed as organized, or nominal, Christianity). Christendom as a whole contains evil elements mixed with the good, and both parables are usually viewed as picturing that evil. The birds nesting in the mustard tree are unbelievers.[14] It is pointed out that since leaven is a symbol of evil (Exod. 12:15–20; 34:25; Lev. 2:11; Matt. 16:6, 11–12; 1 Cor. 5:6–8; Gal. 5:9; but see Lev. 7:13–14; 23:17; Philo, *Spec. Laws* 2.184–85), this parable portrays the growth of evil within Christendom (Walvoord 1974: 103–4; Toussaint 1980: 182). This approach is often taken to oppose postmillennialism, which interprets the images of the growth of the kingdom as indicating the ultimate conversion of the world to Christianity before Christ returns.

The classic dispensational position depends on the dubious understanding of the kingdom of heaven as the mystery of evil within Christendom between the two advents of Jesus. But the kingdom in Matthew is the rule of God, inaugurated through the words and works of Jesus and consummated at his return. It is also very doubtful that straightforward statements that compare the kingdom of God to leaven or to mustard seed should be understood as a portrayal of evil. It is the growth of God's rule, not Satan's, which is being portrayed here. Birds or yeast need not always be viewed as symbols of evil, since a lion may signify Satan in one context and Jesus in another (1 Pet. 5:8; Rev. 5:5). These parables both speak of the deceptively subtle yet dramatically significant growth of God's kingdom.

Followers of Jesus should be encouraged that despite frequent fruitless responses to the kingdom message, it does indeed bear much fruit in many cases (cf. Matt. 13:23). Even John the Baptist may doubt its advance, but it is advancing just the same (11:1–6). The strong man is being bound, and his goods are being plundered (12:29). Although postmillennialists may view the advance of the kingdom overoptimistically, classic dispensationalists view the present age too pessimistically because they do not acknowledge that the kingdom has been inaugurated during the earthly ministry of Jesus. It may presently seem as insignificant as a mustard seed, but it will eventually be the largest tree in the garden. Its growth may be as imperceptible as the influence of yeast in a loaf of bread, but in the end it will be pervasive throughout the earth. The use of humble symbols such as mustard seed and leaven is appropriate for God's humble servant, who does not cry out in the streets (12:19) and who rides into Jerusalem on a donkey, not a stallion (21:1–11).

13. Barbieri in Walvoord and Zuck 1983: 51 wavers between positive and negative interpretations of these parables. Cf. M. Bailey 1998a, 1999c.
14. Gaebelein 1910: 285–86; W. Thomas 1961: 197–98; Walvoord 1974: 101. Toussaint 1980: 181 disagrees, viewing the mustard tree as portraying the kingdom positively.

W. Davies and Allison (1991: 415) are correct that these parables portray a contrast between the present reality and the ultimate destiny of the kingdom. What is humble now will be glorious then. The realization that God is already at work unifies the present with the ultimate and so supplies hope. (For additional resources on the mustard seed and the leaven, see Hultgren 2000: 402–3, 408–9.)

g. Editorial Conclusion: The Biblical Basis for Parables (13:34–35)

13:34–35   These verses transition from the parables spoken by Jesus to the crowd from the boat (13:2–35), to his parables spoken in the house to his disciples (13:36–53). Jesus's move into a more private setting amounts to turning from those who for the most part do not understand to those who do (13:11–12). Matthew's editorial insertion states that Jesus's customary way of speaking to the crowds at this time is through parables, and asserts that Jesus's parabolic speech fulfills what the prophet said in Ps. 78:2 (cf. Mark 4:33–34; John 6:31; Menken in Rutgers et al. 1998: 61–77).[15] In this lengthy psalm, Asaph the seer (1 Chron. 25:2; 2 Chron. 29:30) recounts the history of Israel for the next generation (Ps. 78:4). The psalm stresses Israel's unbelief (Ps. 78:8, 11, 17–22, 32–33, 36–37, 39–42, 56–58), which led to God's discipline (78:21, 31–34, 59–64). In spite of this, God continues to manifest his faithfulness to Israel through powerful acts (78:4–7, 12–16, 23–29, 38–39, 42–55) and by choosing David to shepherd them (78:65–72). In Matthew's view, Jesus is the son of David who fulfills the Davidic role as Israel's ultimate shepherd (Matt. 1:1; 9:36). His parables, like those of Asaph, portray Israel's unbelief and God's discipline, but more important, they stress God's ongoing faithfulness to Israel through Jesus's kingdom mission.

Matthew 13:35 contains the second biblical-fulfillment citation of this discourse. The first demonstrates that the unbelief of many who see his deeds and hear his words is not unprecedented. The pattern of hard hearts and unbelief from Isaiah's days is recurring in the days of Jesus. Israel as a whole did not believe Isaiah's warnings of impending invasion, and neither does it believe Jesus's kingdom message (13:14–15; Isa. 6:9–10). Here Matthew inserts his own commentary on Jesus's discourse, citing Ps. 78:2 as the pattern that Jesus fulfills, which includes God's past faithfulness to Israel despite its sin and discipline. To coming generations (Ps. 78:4), this psalm's recounting of God's mighty acts seemed like secrets hidden since ancient times (78:2), but in reality these matters were known

---

15. Psalm 78 was widely used in the NT: 78:2 is cited here, and 78:24 is cited in John 6:31. Several other portions are plausibly alluded to: Pss. 78:15–16 (in 1 Cor. 10:4); 78:18 (in 1 Cor. 10:9; Rev. 20:9); 78:23 (in Rev. 4:1); 78:24–25 (in 1 Cor. 10:3); 78:31 (in 1 Cor. 10:5); 78:35 (in Acts 7:35); 78:36–37 (in Matt. 15:8); 78:37 (in Acts 8:21); 78:44 (in Rev. 16:4); 78:45 (in Rev. 16:13); 78:70 (in Rom. 1:1); 78:71–72 (in John 21:16). See NA²⁷: 785–86.

by Asaph's generation because they were told them by their ancestors. Asaph in turn passed on these ancient secrets to the next generation. But Ps. 78 unfolds a narrative of God's faithfulness despite his people's rebellion, not a mysterious discourse full of enigmatic sayings.

There are two key questions here. The first concerns why Asaph in 78:2 styles his historical narrative as parabolic and enigmatic. He does this because events well known by his contemporaries would be ancient secrets to the coming generation. There may be a touch of poetic hyperbole here, but the point is clear. Asaph's psalm is also parabolic because his recounting of the past historical events reveals a profound pattern (Carson 1984: 321). Asaph does not merely chronicle Israel's history but also interprets it as the story of God's faithfulness to his people in spite of their sin and deserved discipline. His faithfulness is manifested in powerful redemptive acts (78:4, 7, 11–12, 32, 42–43). Asaph's interpretation of Israel's history revealed to a new generation the profound truth of God's redeeming grace, and Matthew utilizes it for yet another generation.

Another question concerns Matthew's reasons for citing Ps. 78:2. At first glance, despite the clear connection of the word "parable," Matthew appears to take the psalm out of context (so Boring 1995: 310). Granted, Ps. 78 is not a prediction of Jesus, but Matthew's penchant for typology, his finding biblical patterns that are filled with their ultimate significance by Jesus, is well known (cf. esp. Matt. 1–2). Matthew finds in Asaph's words a precedent providing a pattern that Jesus fulfills. Just as Asaph utters profound truths for the next generation, so Jesus reveals the ultimate secrets of the kingdom of heaven to his own generation (Matt. 13:11; cf. 12:39, 41–42). Just as Asaph discerns the pattern of God's faithfulness to his people that overrides their disobedience, so Jesus's parables lay out for his disciples the pattern of kingdom reception and rejection until the day of ultimate judgment and reward (13:19, 39–43). Asaph's reflection on the "old days" brought out truth for a new generation, and Jesus's parables equip his disciples to bring out of their treasure things new and old in their own teaching (13:51–52). What was new for Asaph's audience is now part of what is old in the disciples' treasury, but what they have learned from Jesus will remain new while they teach all nations, as he is with them until the end of the age (28:19–20; cf. Carson 1984: 322–23).

Additional Notes

13:9. The question here is the same as in 11:15, whether to read ὦτα with UBS[4] or ὦτα ἀκούειν (see the discussion there). The evidence is even stronger for the shorter reading here than in 11:15.

13:13. The UBS[4] reading (ὅτι βλέποντες οὐ βλέπουσιν καὶ ἀκούοντες οὐκ ἀκούουσιν οὐδὲ συνίουσιν) is very well supported by ℵ, B*, C, L, W, *Byz, Lect.* Other readings that are relatively poorly supported have ἵνα and subjunctive verbs instead of ὅτι and indicatives, and other minor differences.

13:35. Instead of the UBS⁴ reading διὰ τοῦ προφήτου (א¹, B, C, D, L, W, *Byz, Lect*), the original hand of א (as well as Θ, *f*¹, *f*¹³, 33, and MSS known to Jerome and Eusebius) reads διὰ Ἠσαΐου τοῦ προφήτου. The erroneous attribution of a text from Ps. 78 to Isaiah is the more difficult reading, but the UBS editors prefer the shorter reading on the weight of the external evidence and the plausibility of a scribe inserting the name of a well-known prophet. It is also possible that MSS originally attributing the citation to the obscure Asaph (cf. 2 Chron. 29:30; Jerome cites such MSS but none exist today) were altered to the more famous Isaiah. See Metzger 1994: 27–28.

Another variant in 13:35 occurs at the end of the Ps. 78:2 citation, where one must choose whether to read ἀπὸ καταβολῆς (א¹, B, 1,and others) or ἀπὸ καταβολῆς κόσμου (א*,², C, D, L, W, *Byz, Lect*, most Latin MSS). Because of uncertainty over preferring the shorter reading or the reading with better external support, UBS⁴ chooses to enclose κόσμου in square brackets to indicate some doubt as to its authenticity.

2. Parables to the Disciples (13:36–52)

In the middle of the discourse, Jesus returns to the house (cf. 9:28; 13:1) and at the disciples' request interprets the previous parable of the wheat and weeds (13:36–43). Then he tells the disciples four parables that correspond to the four parables told to the crowd in 13:3–33. He first tells two short parables of sacrifice, those of the treasure and the pearl (13:44–46). These correspond to the two short parables of growth, those of the mustard seed and leaven (13:31–33). Next comes the parable of the net (13:47–50), which is quite similar to the parable of the wheat and weeds (13:24–30). A final parable challenges the disciples to grasp Jesus's teachings so that they may be wise scribes of the kingdom (13:51–52).

The unit can be outlined as follows:

a. Interaction with the disciples (13:36–43)
b. Parable of the hidden treasure (13:44)
c. Parable of the expensive pearl (13:45–46)
d. Parable of the net (13:47–50)
e. Parable of the householder (13:51–52)

Exegesis and Exposition

[36]Then he left the crowds and went into the house. And his disciples came to him and said, "Explain to us the parable of the weeds of the field." [37]And he answered, "The one who sows the good seed is the Son of Man, [38]and the field is the world; and as for the good seed, these are the children of the kingdom; and the weeds are the children of the evil one; [39]and the enemy who sowed them is the devil, and the harvest is the end of the age; and the reapers are angels. [40]Just as the weeds, then, are pulled up and burned with fire, so shall it be at the end of the age. [41]The Son of Man will send his angels, and they will weed out of his kingdom all who cause sin and those who commit lawlessness, [42]and will throw them into the furnace of fire, where there will be weeping and gnashing of teeth. [43]Then 'the righteous will shine like the sun' in the kingdom of their Father. Anyone with ⌜ears⌝, listen!

[44]"The kingdom of heaven is like a treasure hidden in the field, which a man found and hid again; and because of his joy over it, he goes and sells all that he has and buys that field.

[45]"Again, the kingdom of heaven is like a merchant seeking fine pearls, [46]and when he found one very valuable pearl, he went away and sold everything he had and bought it.

[47] "Again, the kingdom of heaven is like a net that was thrown into the sea and gathered every kind of fish. [48]When it was full, they pulled it up on the shore, sat down, and gathered the good fish into baskets, but they threw away the bad. [49]So it will be at the end of the age; the angels will come forth and remove the wicked from among the righteous [50]and will throw them into the furnace of fire, where there will be weeping and gnashing of teeth.

[51] "Have you understood all these things?" They said to him, "Yes." [52]So Jesus said to them, "Therefore every legal expert who has become a disciple of the kingdom of heaven is like a head of a household, who brings out of his storeroom things new and old."

a. Interaction with the Disciples (13:36–43)

Following Matthew's editorial comment on Jesus's parables as fulfillment of Ps. 78:2, the narrative picks up again. After telling the parable of the weeds, Jesus leaves the boat and returns to the house, reversing the movement of Matt. 13:1–2 (13:36a). He is no longer speaking to the crowds, where there would be many to whom the secrets of the kingdom would not be revealed, but to the disciples, to whom these mysteries are revealed (13:10–13). In response to the disciples' question (13:36b), Jesus explains the parable of the weeds (13:37–43a) and warns the disciples to be attentive (13:43b; cf. 11:15; 13:9).

13:36–39 Jesus's earlier explanation of the parable of the sower (13:18–23) came as part of his response to the disciples' question about the purpose of parables. His explanation of this parable is in response to their direct question as to its meaning. Their question styles the parable as that of the weeds, and Jesus's interpretation likewise focuses on the sobering detail of their burning (13:40–42). His explanation of this parable is at least as detailed as that of the previous one, with seven key details featured:

1. The sower (Jesus; cf. 13:24) sows
2. good seed (the children of the kingdom; cf. 8:12) in
3. the field (the world; cf. John 4:35). In contrast,
4. the enemy (the devil) sows
5. weeds (the children of the evil one; cf. Matt. 5:37; 6:13; 23:15; John 8:44; Acts 13:10; 1 John 3:10; 4QFlor 1.8). There will be a
6. harvest (the end of the age; cf. Matt. 3:12; 9:37; Isa. 18:4; 27:12; Jer. 51:33; Hos. 6:11; Joel 3:13; Rev. 14:14–20; 2 Esd. [4 Ezra] 4:26–37; 9:17; 2 Bar. 70.1–2) with
7. reapers (angels; cf. Matt. 24:31; 25:31–33; Rev. 14:15–19; 1 En. 54.6; 63.1).

13:40–43 Having listed seriatim the meaning of seven details of the parable, Jesus now develops the drama of eschatological harvest. At the end of the age (28:20; cf. 1 En. 16.1; 2 Esd. [4 Ezra] 7:113; 2 Bar. 13.3; 19.5; 21.8; 27.15), the angels separate the devil's people from Jesus's people, throwing the former into the fiery furnace of hell (cf. Matt. 3:12; 5:22; 18:8–9; Dan. 3:6; 2 Esd. [4 Ezra] 7:36; Sim 1999a) and gathering the latter into the kingdom (cf. Matt. 3:12). A few of the details are particularly noteworthy. The judgment at the end of the world is portrayed as the removal of sinners from God's kingdom, not the removal of saints from the world that is to be destroyed (13:41). The people of Satan are characterized as lawless ones (cf. 7:23; 23:28; 24:12) who cause people to sin, an allusion to Zeph. 1:3. The pain of their judgment is vividly described (Matt. 13:41–42, 50; cf. 8:12; 22:13; 24:51; 25:30). In an allusion to Dan. 12:3, the glorious bliss of Jesus's disciples, the righteous ones (Matt. 10:41; 13:49; 25:37, 46), is portrayed as the shining of the sun (13:43; cf. 17:2; Judg. 5:31; 2 Sam. 23:3–4; Sir. 50:7; 1 En. 39.7; 104.2). Both of these allusions show how Jesus's parabolic imagery and teaching content are rooted in biblical apocalyptic. The solemn encouragement to listeners underlines the importance of the disciples' understanding Jesus's explanation (Matt. 13:43; cf. 11:15; 13:9).

Jesus's interpretation of his second parable has a more dualistic and eschatological tone than the first one. Instead of describing people (soils) who bear fruit and those who do not, as in the former parable, this second parable vividly stresses the destinies of two groups (cf. 1QS 3.20–26; 1QM 1.1). The contrasting ethical qualities (lawlessness versus righteousness) that lead to these opposite destinies are also brought out (Matt. 13:41–43). There is also a clear contrast of the roles of Jesus (13:37) and the devil (13:38–39; cf. 13:19), the ultimate protagonist and antagonist behind the cosmic struggle portrayed here. The image of Jesus sowing the good seed is a picturesque way of putting what Jesus stated previously—he is the sole revealer of the Father (11:27). But the enemy, Satan, like the wolves who wear sheep's clothing (7:15), also sows seed, and his weeds are difficult to distinguish from Jesus's wheat. Satan is the great imitator.

Matthew's narrative frequently stresses the end of the age and the judgment to follow. John the Baptist's vivid language anticipates Jesus's words in this passage (3:12). Jesus speaks of himself as the eschatological judge in the Sermon on the Mount (7:22–23) and stresses the bliss of the future kingdom on earth as the reward for faithful discipleship (5:3, 5, 10; 6:10; 7:21). Unexpectedly, many Gentiles will share in the eschatological banquet with the patriarchs (8:11–12). Confessing Jesus and aiding his messengers will be rewarded (10:32–33, 41–42). The fate of the towns that did not believe Jesus will be worse than that of notorious biblical towns when the judgment comes (11:22, 24; 12:41). Those who slander the Holy Spirit will never be forgiven (12:32). With this background, the reader of Matthew is not surprised at this parable's vivid portrayal of the end of the age. And much additional teaching on this matter lies ahead (13:49; 16:27; 17:11; 18:8–9; 19:27–30; 22:1–13, 30–32; 24–25; 26:29; 26:64; 28:20).

This parable should not be cited as supporting a less-than-rigorous attitude toward church discipline (Boring 1995: 311; Gundry 1994: 262; C. W. Smith 1963). No doubt there are false disciples in the church (7:21–23; 22:11–14; 24:10–12; cf. Gundry 2000; Luomanen 1998a), but Jesus states that the field is the world, not the church (13:38; W. Davies and Allison 1991: 409–10, 428, 430; Luz 2001: 271–74). This implies the eventual global mission of the church (24:14; 28:19). Other texts in Matthew make it clear that God does not take lightly the sin of professing Christians (e.g., 7:21–23; 18:15–17, 21–35; 22:11–14; 24:10–12). It is not easy to maintain a pure church, but it is a mandatory task for those who take seriously Jesus's call to discipleship.[1]

b. Parable of the Hidden Treasure (13:44)

13:44 The parables of the hidden treasure (13:44; cf. Gos. Thom. 109) and the pearl (Matt. 13:45–46; cf. Gos. Thom. 76) make a similar point on the value of the kingdom. The first parable speaks of a man who sells all that he has so that he may buy a field in which he has discovered a buried treasure (cf. 25:25; Prov. 2:4; Sir. 20:30; 2 Bar. 6.7–9; Josephus, *J.W.* 7.114–15). Evidently, he was not looking for the treasure and has come upon it accidentally. Boring (1995: 313) envisions a man plowing a field. The ethics of the man who finds the treasure and then buys the field are irrelevant to the parable (W. Davies and Allison 1991: 436). This is another picture of the sacrifice entailed in discipleship when kingdom values are taken seriously (cf. 6:19–34). (For additional resources on this parable, see Hultgren 2000: 416.)

c. Parable of the Expensive Pearl (13:45–46)

13:45–46 The parable of the pearl describes a merchant who sells all he has so that he may purchase a pearl of great value (7:6; cf. Job 28:18; Prov. 3:15; 8:11; 1 Tim. 2:9; Rev. 17:4; 18:12, 16). This parable differs from the previous one in that the merchant is actively seeking the pearl (Matt. 13:45). This pair of short parables to the disciples corresponds to the pair of parables told to the crowd: the mustard seed and the yeast (13:31–33). Jesus does not interpret these parables, and this leads to some disagreement among interpreters. (For additional resources on this parable, see Hultgren 2000: 422–23.)

This pair of parables similarly describes the sacrificial pursuit of a singular goal. Although some dispensational interpreters view the parables as pictures of the redemption of Israel and the church by God

---

1. On the parable of the weeds, see M. Bailey 1998c; Catchpole 1978; Doty 1971; de Goedt 1959; Hultgren 2000: 292–303; Marguerat 1978; 1981: 436–47; McIver 1995a; Strelan 1996.

through Jesus (Gaebelein 1910: 298–302; Toussaint 1980: 183–84; Walvoord 1974: 104–6), this approach tends to neglect the context and read Pauline theology into Matthew. Although Matthew does speak of Jesus as a ransom for many (20:28; cf. 26:28), another approach better fits the context. Throughout Matt. 13 Jesus speaks parabolically of the mixed response to the kingdom mission. As to positive responses, in the parable of the sower, the good soil produces fruit (13:8, 23). The secrets of the kingdom are revealed to the disciples (13:11). The parable of the wheat and weeds portrays the glorious future of the righteous as good seed gathered into a barn (13:43), and this is reinforced by the parable of the fishing net (13:47–48). The parables of the mustard seed and yeast speak of the almost imperceptible growth of the kingdom from insignificance to greatness (13:31–33).

This pair of parables fits into the pattern of positive response to the kingdom (Garland 1993: 151–52; Keener 1999: 391–92; Overman 1996: 202–3). The kingdom is portrayed as a hidden treasure and a valuable pearl, pursued by men who sacrifice everything to gain it.[2] This is the picture of discipleship found throughout Matthew. Jesus's first disciples leave their families and fishing gear to follow Jesus (4:20, 22; cf. 9:9). Following Jesus entails the sacrifice of one's life for Jesus (16:25–26). The rich young ruler will not sell all he has to follow Jesus (19:21–22), but all who do make such a sacrifice will be richly rewarded (19:27–29). These parables present both the sacrifice and the resulting joy of those who follow Jesus (13:44; cf. 2:10; 28:8; for temporary joy see 13:20). Despite the lure of wealth and worldly distractions (13:22), millions continue to follow Jesus at great cost in the present life but with greater prospects for the future. "Blessed are the poor in spirit, for theirs is the kingdom of heaven" (5:3).[3]

d. Parable of the Net (13:47–50)

The parable of the net (13:47–48; cf. Gos. Thom. 8) is immediately explained (13:49–50) as a picture of eschatological judgment. It uses the imagery of fishing to similar effect as that of the wheat and the weeds earlier (13:24–30, 36–43).

The net (σαγήνη, *sagēnē*; cf. Isa. 19:8 LXX) is not the small one used by **13:47–48** anglers to land a hooked fish but a large net or seine with weights on the bottom and floats on the top that encircles many fish. Such a net could contain hundreds of fish and require a great deal of effort to haul in (cf. Luke 5:4–9; John 21:6–8, although the word δίκτυον [*diktyon*; cf.

2. The patristic interpretation of the treasure and pearl as Jesus (Acts of Peter 20; Acts of John 109; Irenaeus, *Haer.* 4.26.1; Clement of Alexandria, *Paed.* 2.12; Fenton 1963: 227) stems from pious motives but is untenable (W. Davies and Allison 1991: 439).

3. For further study of 13:44–46, see M. Bailey 1999b; Dehandschutter 1979; Dupont 1968b; J. A. Gibbs 1987; Hultgren 2000: 409–16; von Nagel 1999; Sider 1984.

Matt. 4:18–21] is used in these passages). The parable pictures a large catch being sorted on the beach.

13:49–50 The interpretation of this parable does not identify its individual entities (as in 13:37–39) but simply describes eschatological events. Angels (fishermen) will separate (sort the contents of the net) the wicked people (bad fish) from the righteous people (good fish). They throw the bad fish away (the furnace or hell). There is no mention here (unlike 13:43) of what is done with the good fish in terms of the glory and bliss of the righteous disciples, but the description of the punishment of the wicked is similar (13:49–50). In view of the parabolic formula found in 13:52, this parable should not be viewed as the last in Matt. 13 (contra Hagner 1993: 398).

The similarities of the parable of the net and the parable of the weeds are evident. But among the differences between the two is the presence of "fish of every kind" in this parable, as opposed to only two kinds of plants, wheat and weeds, in the previous parable. Perhaps this is a subtle reminder of the universality of the kingdom mission, which is mandated to "all the nations" (28:19–20). The net does not discriminate as it gathers the fish, and neither should disciples of the kingdom as they fish for people (cf. 4:19; 22:9–10).[4]

e. Parable of the Householder (13:51–52)

13:51–52 The disciples acknowledged a lack of understanding when they previously asked Jesus twice about his parables (13:10, 36), and so it is not surprising that Jesus now asks them whether they have finally grasped his parabolic teaching. Evidently, "all these things" refers to the growth of the kingdom despite the mixed reception of its message. When the disciples affirm their understanding, Jesus responds with what should be viewed as the eighth and final parable of Matt. 13, introduced with the characteristic formula "is like" (ὅμοιός ἐστιν, *homoios estin*; cf. 13:24, 31, 33, 44, 45, 47; Carson 1985). This parable is also about disciples of the kingdom, who are described as legal experts and likened to a homeowner (cf. 20:1; 21:33) who brings both new and old things from his storeroom (cf. 12:35). Jesus calls the disciples he has trained legal experts or scribes of the kingdom because their ministries will entail teaching the kingdom message as they draw upon what Jesus has taught them and teach their own disciples new truths tied to old truths (cf. 23:34; 5:17–48; 9:16–17; 11:11–13).

It is clear from Matt. 11–13 that many in the "crowds" do not understand the kingdom message, and the animosity of the Jewish religious leaders toward Jesus is becoming potentially lethal. Even Jesus's disciples

---

4. For further study of 13:47–50, see Archbald 1987; M. Bailey 1999c; Morrice 1984: 269–73.

are slow to grasp what all this means (13:10, 36). Jesus's parables have taught that the kingdom will have a mixed reception until the end of the age. Kingdom growth will be real, though imperceptible, and its humble beginnings will eventually lead to a substantial entity. Those who abandon everything else to follow Jesus will be greatly rewarded. But all this has been stated parabolically and mysteriously, and even though three of the parables have been interpreted, it is not certain that the disciples have clearly understood. When Jesus asks them if they have understood, however, they answer affirmatively. The parables have evidently been an effective means of communication to those to whom it has been given to understand the secrets of the kingdom (13:11).

Since they affirm that they understand his parabolic teaching (but see 15:15–20), Jesus concludes the third discourse with yet another parable. It is short, more of a simile than a story, and as with the two previous pairs of short parables, Jesus does not interpret it (cf. 13:31–33, 44–46). It is a bit surprising that Jesus speaks of his disciples as legal experts, since the legal experts are consistently among Jesus's enemies in Matthew.[5] But in their teaching capacity, they will function in Matthew's Christian Jewish community like the legal experts in the larger Jewish community (cf. 23:34; Cope 1976b; Orton 1989). Their role is compared to that of a homeowner who draws upon new and old resources in managing his household. Evidently, the new and old things should be understood in light of Jesus's teaching that he has come not to cancel but to fulfill the law and the prophets (5:17–20). Israel's Scriptures are not old in the sense of outdated or obsolete, since they are still part of the resources of the kingdom's legal experts. But the new things, the ultimately definitive teachings of Jesus, are mentioned first as the legal experts' primary resource.

Matthew makes much of the teachings of Jesus, featuring them in five major discourses (Matt. 5–7; 10; 13:1–52; 18; 24–25). This Gospel concludes with Jesus's mandate that all nations be discipled and that disciples be taught all that Jesus has commanded. Kingdom scribes must manage God's household with the resources of Jesus's new definitive teachings about the eschatological inauguration of God's reign, which fulfills the old Scriptures of Israel. Hagner (1993: 402) is correct that Jesus's followers "must represent a Christianity encompassing both Testaments."[6]

Additional Note

13:43. See the additional notes on 11:15 and 13:9, where the same variant occurs.

5. Additional uses of γραμματεύς in Matthew are 2:4; 5:20; 7:29; 8:19; 9:3; 12:38; 15:1; 16:21; 17:10; 20:18; 21:15; 23:2, 13–15, 34; 26:57; 27:41; cf. Ezra 7:11; Jer. 36:26, 32; 1 En. 12.3–4; 15.1; 2 Esd. (4 Ezra) 14:50; 2 En. 64.5; Sir. 39:1–3.
6. For further study of 13:51–52, see M. Bailey 1999b; Hagner 1998b; I. Jones 1995: 189–211; Légasse 1961; Lybaeck 2002; Orton 1989: 137–76.

III. Galilean Ministry Continues (8:1–11:1)
IV. Growing Opposition to the Kingdom of Heaven (11:2–13:52)
➤ V. Opposition to the Kingdom Continues (13:53–19:2)
VI. Opposition Comes to a Head in Judea (19:3–26:2)

V. Opposition to the Kingdom Continues (13:53–19:2)

The fourth narrative-discourse block in Matthew is perhaps the hardest to analyze. The narrative section (13:53–17:27) contains as many as sixteen pericopae, and the discourse (18:1–19:2) is susceptible to at least two plausible analyses. Overall, it appears that Matthew's narrative has two main concerns. First, he reveals that the increasing opposition to Jesus will result in his crucifixion in Jerusalem (16:21; 17:22–23). Second, he portrays Jesus's words and deeds in a way that prepares his disciples for his absence. This second concern is seen especially in Jesus's teaching that the disciples must orient themselves to the cross (16:24–28) and in his discourse on the values of the kingdom, which turns the disciples from an orientation to status and prestige to one of humility, hospitality, and forgiveness.

V. Opposition to the Kingdom Continues (13:53–19:2)
➤ A. Narrative 4: Various Responses to the Son of God (13:53–17:27)
   B. Discourse 4: Values and Relationships in the Kingdom Community (18:1–19:2)

A. Narrative 4: Various Responses to the Son of God (13:53–17:27)

Matthew 13:53–17:27, the narrative block between the third (Matt. 13) and fourth (Matt. 18) discourses, may be the most difficult section of this Gospel to analyze as to structure.[1] The conventional wisdom among scholars who believe that Matthew depended on Mark is that at this point Matthew concludes his distinctive topical arrangement of Jesus traditions and begins to follow the order of Mark (W. Davies and Allison 1991: 451; Hagner 1995a: 410).[2] Although Matthew's structuring of the material in this narrative block may not be as meticulous as up to this point, it is clear that he wishes to convey the increasing polarization of the responses to Jesus. In what is probably the crucial text in this section (16:13–28), the contrast between the false and the true views of Jesus (16:13–16) and of discipleship (16:21–26) is made clear, as is the ultimate fate of Jesus at the hands of the Jerusalem religious leaders (16:21; cf. 17:9, 12, 22–23; 20:17–19; 21:39).

There are approximately sixteen pericopes in the narrative block of Matt. 13:53–17:27. Of these, at least seven emphasize a negative, unbelieving response to Jesus and the kingdom (13:53–58; 14:1–12; 15:1–20; 16:1–4; 16:5–12; 16:21–28; 17:22–23). Five stress a positive, believing response (14:22–33; 15:21–28; 15:29–39; 16:13–20; 17:1–13), and the remainder are ambiguous since they contain no clear affirmation of faith (14:13–21; 14:34–36; 17:14–21; 17:24–27). These ambiguous episodes highlight a miracle or teaching of Jesus but do not clearly portray an ethical response to it.

Another clear theme of this material is the development of the "little faith" of the disciples. This theme occurs in negative (15:12–20; 16:5–12, 22; 17:23), positive (15:23; 17:4–6, 10–13), and ambiguous (14:15, 31; 15:33; 17:16, 19–20, 25) episodes. Jesus takes every opportunity to strengthen his disciples for their future ministries in his absence. Peter is often at the forefront of such episodes. Although deficiencies in the disciples' faith have already been noted (8:26), this theme comes into its own in this narrative block. Therefore, despite the relative absence of triadic patterns and other clear structural devices in this material, Matthew still addresses his central concerns as he narrates the increasingly

---

1. On the structure of 13:53–17:27, see Gooding 1978; Murphy-O'Connor 1975; Van Aarde 1982; Verseput 1992.
2. Cf. the discussion of the synoptic problem and the Markan-priority consensus under "Source Criticism and the Synoptic Problem" in the introduction to this commentary.

polarized responses to Jesus and the kingdom message. The following chart displays this material in terms of the analysis presented above.

The Key Themes of Matthew 13:53–17:27

The sixteen pericopes of the narrative block 13:53–17:27 do not seem to follow as clear a pattern as the previous interdiscourse narrative blocks Matt. 8–9 and 11–12. Two themes, however, are consistently stressed:

1. Intensifying opposition and conflict with the Jewish leaders
2. Words and works done by Jesus to strengthen the disciples' faith

The list below shows that of the sixteen passages, eight concern conflict and eleven concern the disciples' faith. Four passages contain both themes. **Negative** passages are in bold, *positive* in italic, and ambiguous in normal font.

Text	Content	Conflict	Disciples' faith
1. **13:54–58**	Rejection in Nazareth	X	
2. **14:1–12**	Herod the tetrarch and Jesus	X	
3. 14:13–21	Jesus feeds the 5,000		X
4. *14:22–33*	Jesus walks on the water		X
5. **14:34–36**	Jesus heals at Gennesaret		
6. **15:1–20**	Conflict over the elders' tradition	X	
7. *15:21–28*	Faith of the gentile woman		X
8. *15:29–39*	Jesus feeds the 4,000		X
9. **16:1–4**	Second request for a sign	X	
10. 16:5–12	Warning against Jewish leaders		X
11. *16:13–20*	Peter's confession and Jesus's promise	X	X
12. **16:21–28**	Jesus's first passion prediction	X	X
13. *17:1–13*	Jesus's transfiguration	X	X
14. 17:14–21	An epileptic boy healed		X
15. **17:22–23**	Jesus's second passion prediction	X	X
16. 17:24–27	Question about the temple tax		X

1. Rejection in Nazareth (13:53–58)

Jesus's rejection in Nazareth provides a sad yet fitting introduction to the narrative block 13:53–17:27. Jesus has made it clear that the message and messengers of his kingdom will often be rejected (cf. 5:10–12; 10:14–39; 11:12; 12:2). This rejection begins with Jesus himself (cf. 5:11; 8:34; 9:3, 11, 34; 11:19–24; 12:10, 14, 24–45) and includes even his hometown, Nazareth (cf. 2:23; 4:13; 21:11; 26:71; John 1:45; Acts 2:22; 3:6; 4:10; 6:14; 10:38; 22:8; 24:5; 26:9), which he left for Capernaum to begin his ministry (Matt. 4:13). Chiastic analysis of this pericope has merit, since the pericope begins and ends with references to Jesus's hometown (πατρίς, *patris*, 13:54, 57) and focuses in its center on the cynical questions from the Nazarenes (13:54c–56). The following is adapted from W. Davies and Allison 1991: 451–52 (cf. van Segbroeck 1968):

A Overture: Arrival and ministry in Jesus's hometown (13:54a)
B The Nazarenes are astonished (13:54b)
C Five questions from the Nazarenes, bracketed by πόθεν [*pothen*, where] . . . (13:54c–56)
B′ The Nazarenes are offended (13:57a)
A′ Response: Jesus is dishonored and does few miracles in his hometown (13:57b–58)

An outline of the unit is as follows:

a. Narrative transition (13:53)
b. Rejection in Nazareth (13:54–58)
   i. Reaction to Jesus's teaching (13:54–56)
   ii. Jesus's response to rejection (13:57–58)

Exegesis and Exposition

[53]When Jesus finished these parables, he departed from there. [54]And he came to his hometown and began teaching them in their synagogue, so that they were astonished and said, "Where did this man get this wisdom and these powerful deeds? [55]Is not this the builder's son? Is not his mother called Mary, and his brothers, James and ⌜Joseph⌝ and Simon and Judas? [56]And his sisters, are they not all with us? Where, then, did this man get all these things?" [57]And they took offense at him. But Jesus said to them, "A prophet is not without honor except

in his hometown and in his own household." [58]And he did not do many powerful deeds there because of their unbelief.

a. Narrative Transition (13:53)

13:53 With his characteristic transitional statement (13:53a; cf. 7:28; 11:1; 19:1; 26:1), Matthew's story of Jesus moves from the third discourse to another narrative block (13:53b–17:27), which continues the story of mixed response to Jesus that has just been interpreted in the parabolic discourse.

b. Rejection in Nazareth (13:54–58)

i. Reaction to Jesus's Teaching (13:54–56)

13:54–56 Jesus departs from the house (evidently in Capernaum; cf. 9:1, 28; 13:1, 36) and returns to his hometown, Nazareth (4:13; cf. Mark 6:1–6; Luke 4:16–30). Although a naive reader might expect otherwise, his reception there is not warm. His synagogue teaching leads to astonishment and skepticism about the source of his wisdom and power instead of praise to God for its blessings. The wisdom of Jesus's words (see Deutsch 1990) and the power of his deeds both signify the inauguration of the kingdom. But since the people of Nazareth are aware of his humble background, they are perplexed as to how he has become so formidable (Matt. 13:55–56). Perhaps they are referring to Jesus's lack of a rabbinical education (cf. John 7:15). The source of Jesus's power has already been an issue (Matt. 9:34; 10:25; 12:24). The problem is their frame of reference: the extraordinary words and deeds of Jesus are explained away by associating them with his familiar humble past (W. Davies and Allison 1991: 455). Joseph is traditionally viewed as a carpenter, but the word τέκτων (*tektōn*; cf. Mark 6:3) means simply "builder," and in ancient Galilee this would likely entail working with stone (BDAG 995; K. M. Campbell 2005). Jesus's mother and brothers are mentioned in Matt. 12:46–50, but here the brothers are named, and sisters are mentioned. For discussion of how this relates to the tradition of Mary's perpetual virginity, see the comments on 12:46–50.

ii. Jesus's Response to Rejection (13:57–58)

13:57–58 The lack of understanding by Nazareth's residents precipitates a disastrous fall into sin. Their "taking offense" at Jesus describes their settled intention not to believe in him.[1] So they fall into the same sin as did the residents of Chorazin, Bethsaida, and Capernaum (cf. 11:20–24), and

---

1. Ἐσκανδαλίζοντο ἐν αὐτῷ could be translated "They were stumbling because of him," or "They fell into sin because of him" (cf. 11:6; 26:31, 33). The verb σκανδαλίζω occurs rather frequently in Matthew to describe serious sin, unbelief, and apostasy (cf. 5:29, 30; 11:6; 13:21; 15:12; 17:27; 18:6, 8, 9; 24:10; 26:31, 33).

the recent parable of the sower sadly fits yet another situation. Jesus's response to their unbelief is proverbial, reflecting on the common human experience that well-known people are often not highly regarded by those who knew them before they achieved fame. Familiarity should not necessarily breed contempt in such cases, and especially not in this one. In a circumstance where unbelief reigns supreme, Jesus does not do many miracles.

Unbelief is always sad, but here it is especially pathetic. Matthew 12:46–50 and 13:54–58 bracket the parabolic discourse by relativizing familial and social relationships (W. Davies and Allison 1991: 461). Jesus, like most people who return home, arrives with memories and acquaintances. But his fellow residents of Nazareth refuse to accept his kingdom mission because they remember his humble beginnings. Perhaps there is an element of jealousy in their unbelief. But they are not merely quibbling over the anomaly of Jesus's humble roots and his powerful ministry; they are rejecting God's saving rule.

Jesus's lack of miracles in Nazareth should not be viewed as a matter of impotence but as a matter of choice. Jesus's power is not relativized by unbelief, but he will not perform miracles simply to please skeptics or create a sensation (cf. the discussion of 12:15–21, 38–39). The parable of the sower has become a veiled prophecy. Jesus tells this parable and soon he expeiences its wisdom in his own hometown. People before whom and with whom he grew up refuse to grasp his messianic identity and kingdom mission even though they acknowledge his wisdom and power (13:54, 56). Their lack of understanding is probably to be linked with the case of the seed that is sown on the soil beside the path and devoured by birds (Satan) before it can even sprout (13:4, 19). But perhaps even in Nazareth there was some good soil, a few people to whom understanding of the secrets of the kingdom was given (11:25–27; 13:11). Jesus's appeal in 11:28–30 would also be made to the obstinate residents of Nazareth. (For further study of 13:53–58, see Temple 1955; van Segbroeck 1968.)

This pericope on the rejection of the prophet Jesus (13:57) at Nazareth leads into the following pericope on the rejection and murder of the prophet John (14:5). These two prophetic rejection passages prepare the reader for 17:12 and set an ominous tone for what is to come in this narrative block as a whole.

Additional Note

13:55. There are several variants on the name of Jesus's brother Joseph. UBS[4] prefers Ἰωσήφ, supported by א[1], B, C, N, and many Latin MSS. Ἰωσῆς is found in L, W, Δ, f[13], *Byz*, *Lect*[pt] (cf. Mark 6:3), and Ἰωσῆ in 157, 700*, 1006, and others. Some MSS even read Ἰωάννης. Metzger 1994: 28 states that Ἰωσῆς and Ἰωσῆ represent the Galilean pronunciation of the Hebrew name יוֹסֵף.

2. Herod the Tetrarch, Jesus, and the Death of John the Baptist (14:1–12)

The violent history of the Herodian dynasty now intersects Matthew's narrative for a second time. Herod the Great's checkered reign is well chronicled in ancient history (Perowne 1973; Sandmel 1987), and Matt. 2 has portrayed his scheme to murder Jesus (France 1979). Here Antipas (see F. Bruce 1963–65; Hoehner 1972) proves to be his father's son, although his conscience plagues him (14:9). Antipas is a pathetic figure, prompted by his vengeful wife's suggestion to her daughter. Instead of humbly acknowledging the error of his rash promise, he saves face by destroying God's prophet. His palace guests are shown a blatant example of despotic power, and Antipas takes his place in the roster of evil rulers who rejected God's messengers.

In Matthew's narrative, John's execution by Antipas follows upon the rejection of Jesus by the people at Nazareth. At the time of Jesus's rejection in Nazareth, Antipas comes to the superstition that Jesus can do miracles because he is John the Baptist redivivus (14:1–2).[1] The remainder of this pericope (14:3–12) is a flashback of sorts that provides the background for Antipas's bizarre notion. The two episodes in 13:53–14:12 stress unbelief in two different situations, but the unifying theme is the rejection of God's messengers (11:18–19). The rejection of the prophets has been mentioned previously (5:12) and will be greatly stressed in 23:29–37. Israel's rejection of its own prophets was well known from the Scriptures (e.g., 2 Chron. 36:16; Dan. 9:6, 10), but for Matthew, the rejection of the prophets culminates in the rejection of Jesus, the ultimate prophet (Matt. 23:32).[2] Antipas's explanation for Jesus's miraculous powers is erroneous and even bizarre, but it contains an element of truth in terms of Matthew's theology: John and Jesus are inseparably linked in terms of their message and destiny (3:2; 4:17; 11:18–19; 17:12–13).

---

1. Antipas's theory on the source of Jesus's power is just as erroneous but not as sinister as that of the Pharisees (cf. 9:34; 10:25; 12:28).

2. On Matt. 14:1–12, see Aus 1988; Cope 1976a; Derrett 1965; Gnilka in Hoffmann 1973: 78–92; Hoehner 1972: 110–71; Kraemer 2006; La Potterie 1966; Meier 1980a; Schenk 1983; Theissen 1991: 81–97; Trilling 1959; Wink 1968: 27–41. On the structure of Matt. 14–17, see Murphy-O'Connor 1975.

This unit can be outlined as follows:

a. Herod's explanation of Jesus's miracles (14:1–2)
b. Herod's previous execution of John (14:3–12)
   i. John's imprisonment (14:3–5)
   ii. John's execution (14:6–11)
   iii. John's burial (14:12)

Exegesis and Exposition

¹At that time Herod the ⌜tetrarch⌝ heard the news about Jesus, ²and he said to his attendants, "This is John the Baptist; he has risen from the dead, and that is why miraculous powers are at work in him." ³For Herod had arrested John, bound him, and put him in prison because of Herodias, the wife of his brother ⌜Philip⌝. ⁴For John had been telling him, "It is not lawful for you to have her." ⁵And though Herod wanted to execute him, he feared the crowd because they regarded him as a prophet. ⁶But when Herod's birthday came, the daughter of Herodias danced before them and pleased Herod. ⁷Therefore he promised with an oath to give her whatever she asked. ⁸Prompted by her mother, she said, "Give me the head of John the Baptist here on a platter." ⁹And ⌜though he was grieved⌝, the king commanded it to be given ⌜because⌝ of his oaths and because of his dinner guests. ¹⁰He sent and had John beheaded in the prison. ¹¹And his head was brought on a platter and given to the girl, and she brought it to her mother. ¹²Then his disciples came and took away the body and buried ⌜it⌝; and they went and brought a report to Jesus.

a. Herod's Explanation of Jesus's Miracles (14:1–2)

At about the time of Jesus's rejection in Nazareth, his ministry comes to the attention of Herod the tetrarch (cf. Mark 6:14–29; Luke 9:7–10). A tetrarch was originally a ruler of one-fourth of a kingdom, in this case Herod the Great's. But the term had come to be applied to princes who ruled with Rome's permission. Antipas ruled over Galilee and Perea, the area east of the Jordan, from 4 BCE to 39 CE (cf. Mark 8:15; Luke 3:1, 19–20; 8:3; 9:7; 13:31–32; 23:7–12, 15; Acts 4:27; 12:1; Josephus, *Ant.* 17.188; 18.27, 102, 109, 122, 240–56). He was of minor importance compared to his father, Herod the Great (Matt. 2:1; Hoehner 1972: 110–71). Antipas's superstitious explanation for Jesus's miraculous powers (cf. 13:54) evidently stems from a guilty conscience. But his mistaken explanation of Jesus's power serves Matthew's purpose to link John's mission and destiny to that of Jesus (11:18–19; 17:12). With a guilty conscience due to his unjust treatment of John (14:3–12), Antipas must have found it terrifying to think that John had been raised from the dead. Antipas was evidently not the only one to think that Jesus was John the Baptist (16:14).

14:1–2

b. Herod's Previous Execution of John (14:3–12)

i. John's Imprisonment (14:3–5)

14:3–5   Matthew 14:3–12 is a flashback that fills in the grisly details of the death of John the Baptist, mentioned in 14:2. Antipas had divorced his first wife in order to marry Herodias, who was formerly married to his half brother Philip. John had persistently[3] pointed out that this was illegal (Lev. 18:16; 20:21; cf. Josephus, *Ant.* 17.341; 18.116–19, 136–37; *J.W.* 2.116). Although Antipas wanted to execute John,[4] he feared the crowd's response to the execution of a man they believed to be a prophet (cf. Matt. 11:9; 21:26). John's prophetic role and his maltreatment by Antipas link him to Jesus's previous saying about his own rejection at Nazareth (13:57). Further, Antipas's fear of the crowd anticipates the fear experienced by the Jerusalem religious leaders to arrest Jesus (21:46).

ii. John's Execution (14:6–11)

14:6–8   Antipas's concern for political expedience is now evidently trumped by two greater concerns. No doubt he desired harmony with his second wife (14:8) and prestige before his dinner guests. Herodias apparently holds a grudge against John for denouncing her marriage to Antipas, and she found a way to be rid of John when her daughter's dance at Antipas's birthday party led to his rash promise (cf. Esth. 5:3, 6; 7:2). The word describing Herodias's daughter in Matt. 14:11 is the diminutive κοράσιον (*korasion*), which refers to a little girl (cf. 9:24–25; Hoehner 1972: 154–56). The use of this word and the absence of risqué details in the context make it debatable whether the dance that so enthralled Antipas was erotic (contra Keener 1999: 399–401; Schlatter 1963: 460). This unnamed daughter was probably Salome, Herodias's daughter by her former husband, Philip, Antipas's half brother. Herodias prompted her daughter to ask for a grotesque present, John's head on a platter (cf. Mark 6:19). (See Aus 1988 on the similarities of this passage to Esth. 1:11; 2:9; 5:3; 7:2.)

14:9–11   Although he regretted his rash oath,[5] Antipas granted the girl's request because he did not wish to lose face with his palace guests. John was beheaded without a trial, and the macabre scene at the birthday party played out (14:11). Herodias thereby avenged herself on John, but Antipas's guilty conscience led to his fear that Jesus was John brought back

---

3. The imperfect ἔλεγεν should be taken in an iterative or customary sense. John had been repeatedly or continually condemning the marriage. See Wallace 1996: 546–48.

4. The participle θέλων should be viewed as concessive. See Wallace 1996: 634–35.

5. The participle λυπηθείς should probably be viewed as concessive. See Wallace 1996: 634–35. Herod's mental state was conflicted, to say the least (cf. Mark 6:20; Keener 1999: 398). He wanted to execute John but feared the crowd (Matt. 14:5). When he had to execute John because of his rash oath, he was grieved. The similarity of 14:5 to 21:46 is striking.

to life. Although beheading did not carry with it all the horrors of crucifixion, it was nevertheless a shameful way to die, one usually reserved for egregious wrongdoers.[6] John prepares the way for Jesus even in the manner of his execution. (See Hoehner 1972: 124–65.)

iii. John's Burial (14:12)

John's ignominious end was a terrible atrocity, yet his disciples were loyal to the bitter end, caring for his body and properly burying it. Devout Jews were concerned for proper burial of corpses (Tob. 1:16–20; 2:3–9; 4:3–4; 12:12–14; 14:10–12). After the burial, John's disciples informed Jesus of John's horrible demise (cf. Matt. 9:14; 11:2). Jesus's withdrawal in 14:13 is thus linked to the events of 14:1–12. Jesus's ministry began when John was imprisoned (4:12), and so John's death is also significant (17:12).

14:12

Jesus said that there was no greater human than John the Baptist (11:11). John fearlessly and faithfully prepared the way for Jesus. Antipas may have been "king" at his birthday party when he ordered John's execution, but one day he will stand before the King of kings and give account for his atrocious treatment of the King's forerunner (16:27). This section of Matthew stresses how Jesus develops the faith of his disciples, and the action of John's disciples in properly burying him should be read as a lesson for Jesus's disciples. John's death anticipates that of Jesus (17:12), and the action of John's disciples is exemplary for Jesus's disciples (27:57–61). Antipas's reluctance to behead John may anticipate Pilate's reluctance to crucify Jesus (14:9; 27:18–24). The similarities between John and Jesus are almost uncanny, leading W. Davies and Allison (1991: 476) to describe 14:1–12 as a christological parable.

Additional Notes

14:1. The two spellings of the Greek for "tetrarch" involve the presence (τετραάρχης, ℵ, C, Z, and others) or absence (τετράρχης) of hiatus in word formation. See BDF §124; Moulton and Howard 1920: 62–63.

14:3. A variant reading (in D, some old Latin MSS, and others; cf. Luke 3:19) omits Φιλίππου (UBS[4], supported by ℵ, B, C, L, f[1], f[13], Byz, Lect; cf. Mark 6:17), resulting in Herodias's being described simply as Herod's brother's daughter instead of Herod's brother Philip's daughter. The variant is in keeping with Josephus (*Ant.* 18.136–37), who says that Herodias's first husband was named Herod (son of Mariamne II) and that Philip was the husband of Salome, Herodias's daughter. This matter is made all the more difficult by the convoluted family tree of the Herodian dynasty. In support of the historical veracity of the reading, see Hoehner 1972: 131–36, who argues that Herod son of Mariamne II was also named Philip. Cf. Metzger 1994: 28–29.

14:9. The variant reading ἐλυπήθη ὁ βασιλεὺς διὰ δέ (ℵ, C, L[c], W, Byz, Lect) clarifies the ambiguous connection of the prepositional phrase διὰ τοὺς ὅρκους to either the preceding participle, λυπηθείς,

---

6. On beheading, see Gen. 40:19; 2 Sam. 16:9; 2 Kings 6:30–33; 10:6–8; Acts 12:2 (?); Rev. 20:4; Josephus, *Ant.* 14.125; *m. Sanh.* 7.1, 3; Mekilta on Exod. 22:23.

or the following verb, ἐκέλευσεν, in the UBS[4] text (supported by B, D, Θ, *f*[13], and others). The editors of UBS[4] preferred the more difficult reading although external evidence is arguably stronger for the variant.

14:12. The textual tradition, for the most part, supports reading the neuter αὐτό (agreeing with πτῶμα), but ℵ, B, and a few others read the masculine αὐτόν (evidently a *constructio ad sensum*). UBS[4] prints αὐτό[ν] and leaves the question open.

3. Jesus Feeds the Five Thousand (14:13–21)

The feeding of the five thousand is found in all four Gospels (cf. Mark 6:32–44; Luke 9:10–17; John 6:1–13), although the later similar feeding of the four thousand is found only in Matt. 15:32–39 and Mark 8:1–10. As this pericope begins, Jesus has withdrawn, evidently seeking solitude to reflect on John's death. Yet crowds seek him out, and he compassionately heals their sick (Matt. 14:13–14; cf. 15:30–31). His compassion is also manifested in providing the miraculous meal (14:15–21). In contrast to the disciples, Jesus wishes to feed the crowd (14:15–16; cf. 15:32–33). The disciples' provisions are laughably inadequate, but Jesus multiplies them into food sufficient for all, with leftovers (14:17–20; cf. 15:34–37). An editorial comment underlines the power of Jesus by noting that five thousand males were fed, plus women and children (14:21; cf. 15:38).[1]

The outline of this unit is as follows:

a. The setting (14:13–14)
b. The conversation between Jesus and the disciples (14:15–18)
c. The miraculous meal (14:19–21)

Exegesis and Exposition

[13]Now when Jesus had heard, he withdrew from there in a boat to an isolated place by himself; and when the crowds heard of this, they followed him on foot from the towns. [14]When he went ashore, he saw a large crowd and felt compassion for them and healed their sick. [15]When it was evening, the disciples came to him and said, "This place is isolated and the time is already late; so send the crowds away that they may go into the villages and buy food for themselves." [16]But Jesus said to them, "They do not need to go away; you give them something to eat!" [17]They said to him, "We have nothing here except five loaves and two fish." [18]And he said, "Bring them here to me." [19]And he ordered the crowds to recline on the grass. He took the five loaves and the two fish, and looking up toward heaven, he pronounced the blessing and broke the loaves and gave them to the disciples, and the disciples gave them to the crowds. [20]And they all ate

---

1. On Matt. 14:13–21, see R. Fowler 1981; Masuda 1982; A. Richardson 1955; Schenke 1983; van der Loos 1965: 619–37. For similar biblical stories, see 1 Kings 17:8–16; 2 Kings 4:1–7, 42–44.

and were satisfied, and they picked up twelve full baskets of the broken pieces that were left over. ²¹There were about five thousand men who ate, besides women and children.

a. The Setting (14:13–14)

14:13–14 As bizarre as Herod's explanation for Jesus is, it does contain the truth that Jesus is indeed the sequel to John. As John's imprisonment marks the beginning of Jesus's ministry (4:12), so John's death prompts Jesus to withdraw to a remote place. John's demise hints at the demise of Jesus (17:12), and at this strategic time Jesus withdraws by boat, evidently to the more uninhabited region east of the Sea of Galilee (cf. 2:12, 14, 22; 12:15; 15:21). Why Jesus leaves is not stated, but perhaps it is to grieve and pray (14:23), to avoid Antipas's interest and hostility (14:1–2), or to teach the disciples privately. But the press of the needy does not permit private reflection, and so Jesus responds with compassion and heals the sick among the crowd that follows him from the towns. The description of Jesus as a compassionate healer recalls 4:23–24; 9:35–36 and anticipates 15:30–32. It contrasts with the less-concerned, more pragmatic view of the disciples in 14:15; 15:33.

b. The Conversation between Jesus and the Disciples (14:15–18)

14:15–18 In contrast to their compassionate master, the disciples wish to be rid of the needy. Perhaps their request is motivated only by common sense (Keener 1999: 403–4). They ask Jesus to dismiss the crowd so that the people can care for their own needs (14:15). Jesus contradicts the disciples by telling them to feed the crowd (cf. 2 Kings 4:42), but they claim that their food supplies are inadequate (Matt. 14:16–17; cf. Num. 11:13, 21–22; 1 Kings 17:12; 2 Kings 4:2). Bread and fish were staples of the Galilean diet (Matt. 7:9–10; John 21:9–10). There is no good reason to look for symbolic meanings of the five loaves (the five books of the Torah?) or the two fish (the Prophets and the Writings?). The reluctance of the disciples and the paucity of their resources set the scene for the astonishing resolution of the problem.

c. The Miraculous Meal (14:19–21)

14:19–21 Jesus orders the crowds to recline on the grass (cf. Ps. 23:2). Acting as the host of the meal, he takes the five loaves and two fish (evidently dried). Jesus looks up to heaven and blesses the bread (Matt. 26:26; cf. Luke 24:30; 1 Cor. 14:16; Jeremias 1966a: 175).[2] The blessing is praise to God for supplying it. Perhaps it is similar to the traditional Jewish hamotzi,

---

2. For looking up to heaven while praying, see Ps. 123:1; Mark 7:34; Luke 18:13; John 11:41; 17:1; 1 Esd. 4:58; Josephus, *Ant.* 11.162; Philo, *Contempl.* 66.

"Blessed art thou, O Lord our God, King of the world, who brings forth [הַמּוֹצִיא, *hammôṣîʾ*] bread from the earth" (*m. Ber.* 6.1). Jesus then breaks the bread and fish into pieces and distributes the pieces to the disciples, who in turn pass them on to the crowd (Matt. 14:19). Amazingly, the supplies are more than sufficient, since there is much more left over (twelve full baskets; cf. Exod. 29:32; Num. 6:15; 11QT 15.3) than there was to begin with (Matt. 14:20; cf. 15:37; John 6:11–13; 1 Kings 17:16; 2 Kings 4:6–7, 44). Underlining the power of Jesus is the final comment, that about five thousand men were fed, plus the women and children who accompanied them (Matt. 14:21; cf. 15:38; Exod. 12:37).

It is clear that Jesus performs this miracle out of compassion for hungry people (Matt. 14:14; cf. 9:36; 15:32) and to demonstrate kingdom authority so that people will believe in him (9:6). But additional approaches to the interpretation of the miracle have been suggested.[3] Barclay (1975: 2.102–3) suggests that the miracle should be understood as a spontaneous sharing of food brought by many individuals, due to the power of Jesus's example. Jesus begins to distribute the meager stores the disciples have brought, others follow suit, and in the end there is more than enough to go around. Thus the "miracle" is that of generosity overcoming selfishness as everyone follows Jesus's example. Despite the wholesome lesson, this interpretation cannot be sustained exegetically. It is clear from the passage that five loaves and two fish are miraculously multiplied to feed a crowd of perhaps twenty thousand people. There is no mention of others having additional food or of selfishness being turned into generosity. This is a miracle story, not a fable about generosity.

A more credible interpretation stresses the eucharistic overtones in the passage, viewing it as "an allegory of the eucharist" (W. Davies and Allison 1991: 481). Indeed, there are so many clear verbal parallels between Matt. 14:13–21 and 26:20–29 that some connection between the two seems undeniable. Perhaps the several similarities are due to the common features of Jewish meals, but it is at least plausible that Matthew intended the miraculous feeding to foreshadow the Last Supper. The difficulty with this view is its potential to transform a story of a historical miracle into an allegorical symbol (Hagner 1995a: 416–17). It is problematic when the historicity of the miracle is doubted and it is viewed solely in eucharistic terms (Beare 1981: 326–27) rather than as a miracle with eucharistic overtones.

It is more likely that Matthew intends this story to remind his readers of the past miraculous feeding of the Israelites with manna in the wilderness (Exod. 16; Deut. 8:3, 16; Neh. 9:20; Ps. 78:24; John 6:30–59). This connects with the Moses typology found elsewhere in Matthew (Allison

---

3. For a summary of interpretations, see Boring 1995: 325–26; W. Davies and Allison 1991: 483–85; Luz 2001: 312–13.

1993b: 137–270, esp. 238–42). The story is also intended to anticipate the eschatological messianic banquet alluded to in Matt. 8:11 and 26:29 (cf. 22:4; 25:10; Rev. 2:17; 19:9; 1QS 6.4–5; 1QSa 2.11–22; Schweitzer 1968: 376–80). In fact, both Moses's manna and Jesus's multiplied loaves anticipate the ultimate satisfaction of the needs of God's people in the future kingdom (Matt. 26:29; 1 Cor. 11:26).

There are also echoes here of the ministries of Elijah (1 Kings 17:8–16) and Elisha (2 Kings 4:1–7, 42–44). Typologically, as God miraculously met the needs of his people in former days through Moses, Elijah, and Elisha, so God meets their needs ultimately through his beloved Son, the definitive prophet and teacher of Israel, Jesus (Ps. 132:13–18; cf. Pss. 107:9; 147:14). Although the number of loaves (five) and fish (two) seems intended only to show the inadequacy of the disciples' resources (Matt. 16:9–10), the detail that there are twelve baskets of food left over is probably significant (cf. 10:1, 19:28; Rev. 7:4–8; 21:12–14, 16–17; Quesnell 1969: 229, 70–74). The point is that in Jesus the Messiah there is abundant *shalom*, full blessings for Israel.

In this passage Jesus continues to strengthen and develop his disciples by modeling compassion and inspiring faith. The disciples' indifference to the multitudes is challenged by Jesus's compassion. They view resources as inadequate for the need, but Jesus nevertheless commands them to meet the need, and when they obey, the need is more than met. The disciples are learning to model their ministries after Jesus's compassion and to believe in his power to multiply their resources.

4. Jesus Walks on the Water (14:22–33)

Immediately after the miraculous feeding, Jesus miraculously walks on the Sea of Galilee. Again the disciples' faith is tested as they are sent into a storm without Jesus, who is again alone praying (14:22–23; cf. 14:13). Far from land, the disciples encounter not only the storm but also Jesus walking on the water (14:24–25). Initially they think he is a ghost, but he identifies himself and tells them not to be afraid (14:26–27). The pericope centers here on Jesus's self-identification ("It is I") and Peter's response to it ("If it is you . . ."). Peter's abbreviated walk on the water and the lesson on faith he receives are important for all the disciples (14:28–31; cf. 8:26). The pericope concludes with the wind stopping, Jesus entering the boat, and the disciples worshiping him as the Son of God (14:32–33). Overall, the passage is quite similar to 8:23–27, especially in the parallel outcomes that challenge the disciples' little faith (8:26; 14:31) despite their high view of Jesus (8:27; 14:33).[1]

The unit outline is as follows:

a. The setting of the miracle (14:22–23)
b. Jesus meets the disciples on the sea (14:24–27)
c. Jesus and Peter (14:28–31)
d. Conclusion to the miracle (14:32–33)

Exegesis and Exposition

²²Then immediately he urged the disciples to get into the boat and go on ahead of him to the other side while he sent the crowds away. ²³After he had sent the crowds away, he went up the mountain by himself to pray. When it was evening, he was there alone. ²⁴Now the boat was already ⌜a long way from land⌝, battered by the waves; for the wind was against them. ²⁵And during the fourth watch of the night, he came to them, walking on the sea. ²⁶When the disciples saw him walking on the sea, they were terrified and said, "It is a ghost!" And they cried out from fear. ²⁷But immediately Jesus spoke to them, "Take courage, it is I; do not be afraid." ²⁸Peter answered him, "Lord, if it is you, command me to come to you on the water." ²⁹And he said, "Come!" So Peter got out of the boat, started walking on the water, ⌜and came⌝ toward Jesus. ³⁰But seeing the

---

1. On 14:22–33, see Achtemeier 1962; Carlisle 1985; Derrett 1981; Heil 1981; Hill 1988; Lapide 1980; Ritt 1979; Smit Sibinga in Epp and Fee 1981: 15–33.

⌜strong⌝ wind, he became frightened, and when he began to sink, he cried out, "Lord, save me!" [31]And immediately Jesus reached out his hand and took hold of him, and said to him, "You of little faith, why did you doubt?" [32]And when they got into the boat, the wind stopped. [33]And those who were in the boat worshiped him, saying, "Truly you are the Son of God!"

a. The Setting of the Miracle (14:22–23)

14:22–23 After meeting the crowd's need, Jesus sends them away (cf. 14:15) and has the disciples take the boat back to the other side of the lake, evidently retracing the voyage of 14:13 (cf. Mark 6:45–51; John 6:16–21). He remains on the east side of the Sea of Galilee and finds a place on the mountain (cf. Matt. 5:1–2; 17:1–8) for prayer (cf. Luke 6:12; Exod. 24:2; 32:30–34). Matthew portrays Jesus as praying only here, in 11:25–26, and in Gethsemane (26:36–44; but cf. Luke 5:16; 6:12; 9:18, 28–29; 11:1). This was likely Jesus's original goal in Matt. 14:13, but he was hindered by the crowds. Finally alone, he prays on into the night.

b. Jesus Meets the Disciples on the Sea (14:24–27)

14:24–27 The disciples are also alone, struggling against the contrary wind (cf. Acts 27:4) and waves on the lake (cf. Matt. 8:23–27 for a similar story). They are at some distance from land,[2] perhaps a mile or two from the shore. The phrase "fourth watch of the night" reflects the custom of dividing the night from around 6 p.m. to around 6 a.m. into four watches of three hours each (cf. 24:43; Exod. 14:24 LXX). After the disciples have rowed through most of the night under terrifying conditions and when dawn is near, Jesus suddenly appears, miraculously walking on the water. They do not recognize him and cry out that a ghost has appeared to them. It is not clear whether φάντασμα (*phantasma*) refers to the spirit of a dead person, an angel, or a demon (cf. Job 20:8 LXX; Josephus, *Ant.* 1.331–33; 5.213). Matthew likely intends that his readers recall the biblical texts where God is the ruler of the sea (e.g., Ps. 77:19; Job 9:8; Isa. 43:16; 51:9–10; Hab. 3:15; cf. Sir. 24:5–6) and where prayers for deliverance from trials are put in terms of storms on the sea (e.g., Pss. 69:1–3, 13–15; 107:23–32; cf. Exod. 14:10–15:21; Jon. 1:1–16; Wis. 14:2–4; see Heil 1981: 56–57). Jesus then identifies himself and tells the disciples not to fear (cf. Matt. 17:7; 28:5, 10; Isa. 43:1–2, 5; Luke 1:13, 30; 2:10; Rev. 1:17; 1 En. 1.8) but to take courage (cf. Matt. 9:2, 22).[3]

2. The phrase is σταδίους πολλούς (many stadia; cf. Luke 24:13; John 6:19; 11:18; Rev. 14:20; 21:16; Josephus, *Ant.* 15.415; 18.60; *J.W.* 5.192; 7.284). A στάδιον was ca. 192 meters, just more than six hundred feet or just under one-eighth of a mile in length, and the Sea of Galilee is up to five miles wide. See the additional note on 14:24 for discussion of the textual variant here.

3. Jesus's words ἐγώ εἰμι (cf. 22:32) may allude to Exod. 3:14 (אֶהְיֶה אֲשֶׁר אֶהְיֶה) or, more likely, to the revelation formula אֲנִי־הוּא (Deut. 32:39; Isa. 41:4; 43:10, 13; 46:4;

c. Jesus and Peter (14:28–31)

At this point Peter proposes a test: if it is really Jesus, will he command **14:28–31**
Peter to come to him on the water?[4] Jesus agrees and Peter does indeed
walk on the water toward Jesus, but only briefly. He is terrified by the
wind and waves and begins to sink. He cries out for Jesus to rescue him
(cf. 8:25; cf. the cry in Ps. 69:1–3, 14–15). In view of the discipleship
context of the previous storm miracle (Matt. 8:23–27), it is not a mistake
to regard Peter's faith and doubt in the face of danger as exemplary of
the trials of discipleship (Held in Bornkamm, Barth, and Held 1963:
288–91; Overman 1996: 220–22).

d. Conclusion to the Miracle (14:32–33)

Jesus rescues Peter by grasping him with his hand (cf. LXX: Pss. 18:15–16; **14:32–33**
144:7; 2 Sam. 15:5), but his words to Peter are aimed at a higher sort of
deliverance. He notes Peter's weak faith and asks why Peter doubted him
(cf. Matt. 6:30; 8:26; 16:8; 28:17). Peter and Jesus climb into the boat,
and the storm ceases, this time without a command as in 8:26. Here the
presence of Jesus is all that is needed (cf. Job 26:11–12; Pss. 65:7; 89:9–10;
107:29; Jon. 1:15; Sir. 43:23; 4Q381 15.4). When the disciples realize that
Jesus has indeed walked on the storm-tossed sea and stopped the storm,
they worship him (cf. Matt. 28:17) and utter a ringing confession of his
unique divine sonship (cf. 8:27 and 2:15; 3:17; 4:3, 6; 8:29; 12:18; 17:5;
27:54). See further biblical responses to sea rescues in Exod. 14:31; Ps.
107:31–32; Jon. 1:16; 2:2–9.

The rescued disciples' confession that Jesus is God's Son should be
seen in the light of biblical texts that represent the stormy sea as a place
of evil chaos from which only God can deliver (Exod. 14:10–15:21; Ps.
107:23–32; Jon. 1:4–2:10; cf. Wis. 14:2–4; 1QH 6.22–25; Heil 1981: 35).
Thus, in walking on the water and delivering the disciples from the
storm, Jesus exercises divine attributes and accomplishes feats that are
the prerogative of God alone. It is also significant that Jesus can share
his capacity to walk on water with Peter. "If a man walks on the sea,
he does so only by divine authority" (Heil 1981: 61; cf. Job 9:8; 38:16).
But authority to walk on water is relatively inconsequential when it is
compared with authority to extend God's kingdom (Matt. 10:1, 7; 11:27;
28:18–20). Peter's faith (and that of the disciples collectively) may be
weak, but Jesus's presence will continue to empower and rescue as inevitable future trials are encountered.

52:6), which is rendered by ἐγώ εἰμι in the LXX. Isaiah 43:1–13 is particularly interesting
because the statement occurs in a context where God rescues from water and tells Israel
not to fear (43:1–2, 5). See Harner 1970; Zimmermann 1960.
   4. In Matthew, Peter frequently responds after Jesus has spoken to the disciples
collectively. See 15:15; 16:16; 17:4; 18:21; 19:27; 26:33, 35.

Additional Notes

14:24. Several readings slightly alter the meaning of the clause that describes the boat's distance from the land. The most significant variant is μέσον τῆς θαλάσσης ἦν (ℵ, C, L, W, *Byz, Lect*; cf. Mark 6:47). The evidence for this reading is impressive, but the UBS[4] editors consider it an assimilation from Mark 6:47 and prefer the reading σταδίους πολλοὺς ἀπὸ τῆς γῆς ἀπεῖχεν (B, *f* [13]) as the one that best explains the rise of the others.

14:29. The UBS[4] editors prefer the reading καὶ ἦλθεν (B, C*[vid], 700, 1010) instead of the more widely supported purpose infinitive ἐλθεῖν (ℵ[2], C[2], D, L, W, *f* [1], *f* [13], *Byz, Lect*).

14:30. The UBS[4] editors bracket ἰσχυρόν despite its support by B[2], C, D, L, *f* [1], *f* [13], *Byz, Lect*, and most of the Latin tradition, evidently because it is absent from ℵ, B*, 073, 33 and because of the possibility that it was added by later scribes to heighten the drama of the text. See Metzger 1994: 30.

5. Jesus Heals Many at Gennesaret (14:34–36)

Jesus's geographical movements are not clearly explained in Matt. 14. He is in Nazareth as Matt. 13 concludes, but evidently near the north shore of the Sea of Galilee for the feeding of the five thousand. The disciples were on their way in the boat to "the other side" (14:22) when the storm struck. Mark 6:45 specifies their initial destination as Bethsaida, but they eventually disembark at Gennesaret, on the northwest side of the lake between Capernaum and Tiberias (14:34; Josephus. *J.W.* 3.516–21). Perhaps the contrary winds blew the disciples' boat westward.

Matthew 14:34–36 provides the kind of summary that is by now familiar to the reader of Matthew (4:23–24; 8:16; 9:35; 14:14; 15:30–31). Soon after arriving in Gennesaret, Jesus is recognized and begins again to heal all who are brought to him. In Matt. 14 the two summaries of healing (14:14, 35–36) bracket the two miracle stories (14:15–21, 22–33).

Exegesis and Exposition

³⁴And when they had crossed over, they landed at Gennesaret. ³⁵And when the people of that place recognized him, they sent word to the whole region and brought to him all who were sick; ³⁶and they implored him that they might just touch the fringe of his cloak; and as many as touched it were cured.

The storm is over, and presumably, the lesson has been learned. Jesus **14:34–36** and the disciples land at Gennesaret, about three miles southwest of Capernaum on the west shore of the Sea of Galilee (cf. Mark 6:53–56). Jesus is again pressed by crowds of needy people when news of his arrival is spread, and again many are healed (cf. Matt. 14:13–14). People who merely touch the fringe of Jesus's robe are healed, as in a previous miracle (9:20–21).

Christology and Discipleship

Jesus's appearance to the disciples during the storm follows on the heels of the feeding of the five thousand. These two stories both focus on Jesus's messianic powers and provide a contrast to the two previous episodes, which stress unbelief (13:53–58; 14:1–12). Jesus's messianic powers must be seen in the context of the Hebrew Bible. Walking on the sea and calming a storm are prerogatives belonging to God alone (Job 26:11–12; Pss. 65:7; 89:9–10; 107:29; Jon. 1:15; Sir. 43:23). These actions of Jesus demonstrate the status of which Jesus spoke in Matt. 11:25–27: he is the sole revelator of the Father. The worship and testimony of the disciples to Jesus's messianic sonship in 14:33 are the direct results of the divine acts performed by Jesus.

Jesus is "worshiped" in Matthew by the magi, a leper, a synagogue official, a Canaanite woman, the mother of Zebedee's sons, and the disciples (2:2, 8, 11; 8:2; 9:18; 15:25; 20:20; 28:9, 17). The word προσκυνέω (*proskyneō*) sometimes describes only a respectful bow to a superior, not the religious worship of deity (18:26), but in the overall and immediate contexts of Matthew, the translation "worship" is warranted in most cases. In 14:33 the disciples worship Jesus and confess that he is really the Son of God after seeing him feed thousands of people, walk on water, and stop a perilous storm. Their confession of Jesus's divine sonship should also be viewed in the highest sense, given other Matthean texts (e.g., 2:15; 3:17; 4:3, 6; 8:29; 16:16; 17:5; 21:37; 22:2, 45; 26:63; 27:40, 43, 54; 28:19). The confession in 14:33 is especially noteworthy as anticipating 16:16; 26:63; 27:54; 28:19. The one who makes claims such as those in 11:25–27 and who does deeds such as those narrated in 14:13–33 can only be worshiped as the Son of God. See the discussion of Jesus as Son of God under "Christology" in the introduction to this commentary.

The disciples' faith is implicitly challenged in the feeding miracle (14:15, 17) and directly challenged by the storm miracle, which confronts their need for stronger faith and provides the occasion for their stirring confession (14:31–33). W. Davies and Allison (1991: 512–13) state it well: "So often the First Evangelist, while addressing christological themes with his right hand, is at the same time delivering teaching on discipleship with his left." This second storm miracle, just like the first (8:23–27), should be read as a picture of discipleship in the midst of life's trials. Matthew's version of the miracle uniquely portrays Peter as the model disciple (14:28–30). Peter's action leads to the disciples' confession (14:33), which anticipates Peter's confession on their behalf in 16:16. Peter is primus inter pares, first among equals. Blomberg (1992a: 235) correctly notes Matthew's distinctive positioning of Peter in this section (cf. 15:15; 16:17–19; 17:24–27; 18:21). Peter's vacillating faith and failures, as well as his successes, provide important lessons on disciplesship (see D. Turner 1991).

Looking back on Matt. 14, one can conclude that in the midst of growing opposition, the authority of the kingdom is also growing through the miracles and through the weak but genuine and maturing faith of the disciples.

6. Conflict over the Tradition of the Elders (15:1–20)

The flow of Matt. 15:1–20 develops out of the Pharisees' question (15:1–2), answered in 15:3–9 by Jesus, who then addresses the crowd parabolically in the presence of the Pharisees (15:10–11). Next, responding to two questions from the disciples, Jesus first denounces the Pharisees (15:12–14) and then explains the enigmatic saying of 15:11 to the disciples (15:15–20). The focus moves from (1) Jesus's enemies, the Pharisees; to (2) the crowd, which views Jesus in a very superficial manner; to (3) the disciples, whose understanding of Jesus is genuine if flawed. The passage contains an *inclusio*; it begins and ends with the question of eating with unwashed hands (15:2, 20). This is an important factor for the issue of Jesus and the oral and written law (W. Davies and Allison 1991: 516, 37).[1]

The unit can be outlined as follows:

a. Jesus and the Pharisees on ritual purity (15:1–9)
   i. The Pharisees' objection (15:1–2)
   ii. Jesus's answer (15:3–9)
      (1) The Pharisees transgress Torah (15:3–6)
      (2) The Pharisees fulfill prophecy (15:7–9)
b. Jesus teaches the crowds (15:10–11)
c. Jesus teaches the disciples (15:12–20)
   i. The disciples' concern about the Pharisees (15:12–14)
   ii. Peter's question about Jesus's teaching (15:15–20)

Exegesis and Exposition

[1]Then some Pharisees and legal experts came to Jesus from Jerusalem and said, [2]"Why do your disciples break the tradition of the elders? For they do not wash their hands when they eat bread." [3]But he answered them, "And why do you yourselves break the commandment of God for the sake of your tradition? [4]For God ⌜said⌝, 'Honor your father and your mother,' and 'The one who speaks evil of father or mother is to be put to death.' [5]But you say, 'Whoever tells father or mother, "Whatever might have profited you from me has been given to God,"

---

1. On Matt. 15:1–20, see Banks 1975: 132–46; A. Baumgarten 1984; Booth 1986; Carlston 1968; Held in Bornkamm, Barth, and Held 1963: 105–12; Lambrecht 1977a; Zeitlin 1924.

⁶this person must not honor ⌐father or mother⌐.' And by this you have invalidated the ⌐word⌐ of God for the sake of your tradition. ⁷You hypocrites, Isaiah correctly prophesied about you:

⁸'This people honors me with their lips,
But their heart is far from me.
⁹And in vain they worship me,
since they teach human precepts as doctrines.'"

¹⁰Then Jesus called the crowd to himself and said to them, "Hear and understand: ¹¹What goes into the mouth does not make a person impure, but what comes out of the mouth makes a person impure." ¹²Then the disciples came to him and said, "Do you know that the Pharisees took offense when they heard this statement?" ¹³But he answered, "Every plant that my heavenly Father did not plant shall be uprooted. ¹⁴Let them alone; ⌐they are blind guides of the blind⌐. And if a blind person guides a blind person, both will fall into a pit." ¹⁵And Peter replied, "Explain ⌐this⌐ parable to us." ¹⁶Jesus said, "Are you also still lacking in understanding? ¹⁷Do you not understand that everything that goes into the mouth passes into the stomach, and then into the toilet? ¹⁸But the things that come out of the mouth come from the heart, and those make a person impure. ¹⁹For out of the heart come evil thoughts, murders, adulteries, fornications, thefts, false witness, slanders. ²⁰These are the things that make a person impure; but eating with unwashed hands does not make a person impure."

a. Jesus and the Pharisees on Ritual Purity (15:1–9)

i. The Pharisees' Objection (15:1–2)

15:1–2   The Pharisees and legal experts have not been mentioned since 12:38, but they reappear here to accuse Jesus's disciples of not observing traditional teaching about washing hands before a meal (cf. Mark 7:1–23; Luke 11:38; John 2:6?; *m. Yad.* 1.1; *m. Ḥag.* 2.5; Let. Aris. 305–6; Jdt. 12:7?).[2] They have come all the way to Galilee from Jerusalem, which has not been mentioned since Matt. 5:35 (cf. 2:1, 3; 3:5; 4:25; 5:35; 16:21; 20:17–18; 21:1, 10, 18; 23:37). Perhaps this is an official inquiry stemming from earlier conflicts (cf. 4:25; Mark 3:22; John 1:19). It is not clear why they accuse the disciples instead of Jesus, but any fault of the disciples could be attributed to their master. Evidently, the disciples do not practice this tradition because Jesus does not practice it (cf. Luke 11:38). The complaint is not about the direct violation of biblical ritual purity law (Exod.

2. Eating bread (ἄρτον ἐσθίωσιν) simply means eating, since bread would be a main component of a meal. Cf. LXX: Gen. 31:54; Exod. 2:20; 1 Sam. 20:34; 2 Sam. 9:7; 1 Kings 13:15; NT: Mark 3:20; Luke 14:1.

30:17–21; Lev. 15:11; Deut. 21:1–9), since this concerns the priests, not Israel as a whole.[3] But evidently, the Pharisees extrapolated the laws of priestly purity to themselves and theoretically to all Jews (Mark 7:3–4; Neusner 1973: 83; Nolland 2005: 611–15).

Jesus's disciples are accused of breaking the oral "law" that has grown up to protect the written biblical law (*m. 'Abot* 1.1–3; *m. Yad.* [all]; Josephus, *Ant.* 10.51; 13.297, 408; 17.41; Gal. 1:14; Baumgarten 1987).[4] The Pharisees believed that God had revealed to Moses not only the written Torah but also the traditional oral law that explained and applied the written law. This oral law was handed down from generation to generation and could be deduced from the written law if it was properly interpreted. This oral tradition was eventually redacted in written form as the Mishnah by Rabbi Judah ha-Nasi (the Patriarch) around 200 BCE. The extensive rabbinic commentary (Gemara) that grew around the Mishnah for the next three or four centuries became the Babylonian Talmud.[5]

ii. Jesus's Answer (15:3–9)

(1) The Pharisees Transgress Torah (15:3–6)

Jesus's answer bluntly confronts the Pharisees with a parody of their question to him. Jesus brushes aside the specific issue of violation of the tradition on hand washing with the general charge that by such traditions the Pharisees break God's command (cf. 2 Chron. 24:20; CD 4–5; Tob. 4:5; Jub. 23.19–21; 4 Macc. 13:15; 16:24; T. Levi 14.4; T. Ash. 7.5).[6] Specifically, Jesus cites the fifth commandment on the respect due one's parents (Matt. 15:4; cf. 19:19) and asserts that the tradition of the elders on gifts to God (15:5) has invalidated the true intent of the law.[7] In 15:4 Jesus cites Exod. 20:12/Deut. 5:16 and Exod. 21:17/Lev. 20:9, which

15:3–6

---

3. But there is biblical warrant for national Israel's priestly function in such texts as Exod. 19:6; Isa. 61:6; cf. 1 Pet. 2:5, 9. One text pertaining to nonpriests washing their hands is Lev. 15:11, where, evidently, impurity resulting from bodily discharge could be removed by washing one's hands in water.

4. Rabbinic terminology distinguished between oral and written Torah with the terms תורה שבכתב (Torah in writing) and תורה שבעל פה (Torah by word of mouth). See, e.g., *b. Git.* 60b; Midr. Tanḥuma, *Ki Tassa* §17; Song Rab. 1.10.1; Seder Eliyahu Zuta 2.

5. On the development of rabbinic tradition, see Helyer 2002; Mielziner 1968: 4–114; S. Safrai 1987; Strack and Stemberger 1992.

6. Jesus and his followers were not the only Second Temple Jews who did not accept certain Pharisaic traditions. The Sadducees rejected these traditions (Josephus, *Ant.* 13.297; 'Abot R. Nat. 5), as did the Qumran community, which was most likely composed of Essenes (1QH 4.14–15; 4QMMT).

7. On the fifth commandment in the Bible, see Exod. 20:12; 21:17; Lev. 20:9; Deut. 5:16; 27:16; Prov. 6:20; 23:22; 28:24; Ezek. 22:7; Rom. 1:30; Eph. 6:1–3; Col. 3:20; 1 Tim. 5:1–4; 2 Tim. 3:2. Cf. Sir. 3:7–8, 12–15; Jub. 7.20; 29.14–20; 35.1–6, 11–13; Let. Aris. 228, 238; Josephus, *Ag. Ap.* 2.206; *Life* 204; Philo, *Drunkenness* 17; *Spec. Laws* 2.234–36; *Good Person* 87.

amount to positive (honor is due) and negative (slander is forbidden) statements about the duty of children to their parents.[8]

In 15:5 Jesus makes reference to the practice of קָרְבָּן (qorbān). In the Hebrew Bible, this word describes all kinds of offerings (BDB 898; Lev. 1:2, 3, 10; 2:1, 5; Num. 6:14; 31:50), but it had come to refer to items removed from common use and dedicated to God, including funds pledged to the temple (Matt. 27:6; Mark 7:11; CD 16.14–15; Josephus, *Ant.* 4.72–73; *Ag. Ap.* 1.166–67; *m. Maʿaś. Š.* 4.10–11; *m. Ned.* 1.2–4; 3.11; 5.6; 9.1, 7). Evidently, such funds were not transferable to others, such as one's parents, but were still available to the one who pledged them. One could claim inability to meet a charitable obligation because one's resources had already been pledged to God, when in fact no money had yet changed hands.[9] In Matt. 15:4–5 Jesus juxtaposes God's word and human traditions and concludes in 15:6 that the human traditions have cancelled or rendered void God's word. Jesus twice refers to the tradition as "your" tradition (15:3, 6). He does not view these traditions as having authority on a par with the written Torah.

(2) The Pharisees Fulfill Prophecy (15:7–9)

15:7–9   Jesus's accusation transcends behavioral violation of the law to a matter of the heart: these Pharisees and legal experts are hypocrites (cf. 23:13–15, 23, 25, 27, 29) whose external obedience to the law is pretense masking internal disobedience (cf. 6:1–2, 5, 16; 23:13–30). Isaiah critiques a similarly hypocritical situation in his day (Isa. 29:13; cf. Ps. 78:36–37), yet Jesus tells the Pharisees that "Isaiah prophesied concerning *you*."[10] Both Isaiah and Jesus denounce empty worship stemming

8. The text of these citations is close to the LXX. Matthew has no possessive pronouns with πατέρα and μητέρα, as MT and LXX have in both texts. Exodus 21:16 LXX has the future indicative τελευτήσει θανάτῳ whereas Lev. 20:9 LXX has the present middle imperative θανάτῳ θανατούσθω. Matthew 15:4 has the present active imperative θανάτῳ τελευτάτω. All three expressions render the Hebrew closely.

9. Whether one could renege on a קָרְבָּן vow is debatable. Biblical texts seem to say otherwise (Num. 30:1–5; Deut. 23:21–23). Mistaken vows are discussed in the Mishnah (*m. Ned.* 4.7–8; 9.1), but one cannot assume that the written halakah of 200 CE was already operating as oral tradition in the days of Jesus. On קָרְבָּן, see A. Baumgarten 1984; Belkin 1936; Berger 1972: 1.272–77, 461–507; Booth 1986; Derrett 1970a; Fitzmyer 1959.

10. The citation of Isa. 29:13 omits the predicate of the first clause of the passage. The next two clauses are rendered closely except for Matthew's omission of "their" with "lips," which is found in both MT and LXX. Matthew evidently takes "people" as a collective noun and uses τιμᾷ instead of the LXX's τιμῶσιν. The last clause of Isa. 29:13 MT is rendered more loosely by the LXX and Matthew. A literal translation of the MT would be, "Their fear of me is commandments of men, learned by rote." Matthew follows the LXX with μάτην δὲ σέβονταί με but changes the LXX word order διδάσκοντες ἐντάλματα ἀνθρώπων καὶ διδασκαλίας to διδάσκοντες διδασκαλίας ἐντάλματα ἀνθρώπων. Key to the use of the passage is the LXX's interpretive addition μάτην, which highlights the emptiness of religious observance based on human tradition, and the change in the word order of the last clause.

from human tradition that sets aside the authority of God's word. For Jesus, קָרְבָּן is false piety cloaking the deeper impiety of neglecting parents. Human traditions engage the lips, but only God's word can engage the heart (cf. Col. 2:22; Titus 1:14). A similar point is made in Matt. 9:13; 12:7 (cf. Hos. 6:6). See Hatina 2006 for a discussion of the historicity of Jesus's use of Isa. 29:13 in light of targumic traditions about purity.

b. Jesus Teaches the Crowds (15:10–11)

The conflict provides an opportunity to teach the crowd (15:10–11) and then the disciples (15:12–20). Jesus summons the crowd and teaches them that true purity is not participation in a ritual that protects one from what may enter one's mouth from outside. Rather, true purity is a matter of how the heart influences what comes out of one's mouth. Jesus changes the subject from a specific tradition about ritual hand washing to a general maxim about ethical purity. It is clear from 15:15 that the teaching of Jesus to the crowd in 15:11 was viewed as difficult or enigmatic. But what is confusing to the crowd is explained more fully to the disciples, in keeping with the principle Jesus has enunciated in 13:10–23. Public parabolic teaching is augmented by private explanation to the disciples. Jesus's stress on inner purity is not novel but is consistent with the Hebrew Bible and later Jewish literature (Exod. 20:17; 2 Chron. 30:18–20; Pss. 24:3–4; 51:2–3, 6, 10, 16–17; 78:37; 1QS 3.6–9; 5.13–14; Josephus, *Ant.* 18.117; *m. 'Abot* 2.9).

15:10–11

c. Jesus Teaches the Disciples (15:12–20)

i. The Disciples' Concern about the Pharisees (15:12–14)

Perhaps the disciples are concerned that the opposition of the Pharisees will be exacerbated by Jesus's scathing words. Or if Josephus can be trusted (*J.W.* 1.110–12; *Ant.* 13.399–404), perhaps they are nervous about Jesus's directly confronting the most popular interpreters of the law. In any event, Jesus does not share their concern that the Pharisees are offended (cf. 11:6; 13:57). His description of the Pharisees in 15:13 as uprooted plants alludes to Isa. 60:21 and 61:3, which speak positively of plants God has planted.[11] The Pharisees have not been planted by God, and so they will be uprooted by eschatological judgment (cf. Matt. 3:10; Gos. Thom. 40; Ps. 28:5; Jer. 1:10; 11:17; 18:7; 24:6; 31:4, 28; 42:10; 45:4; T. Ash. 1.7). This contrasts with the Mishnah's assumption that all Israelites are God's "planting" and will have a part in the world to come (*m. Sanh.* 10.1, which alludes to Isa. 60:21). Jesus's

15:12–14

---

11. For additional texts that speak of God's election of Israel under the metaphor of planting, see 13:24–30, 37–43; Jer. 32:41; 1 En. 10.16; 84.6; 93.2, 5, 10; Jub. 1.16; 7.34; 1QS 8.5; 11.8; CD 1.7; 1QH 6.15; Ps. Sol. 14.2–3; Mart. Ascen. Isa. 4.3; M. Elliott 2000: 329–44.

command that the disciples leave the Pharisees alone (ἄφετε αὐτούς, *aphete autous*) echoes the command of the farmer about permitting the weeds to grow in the wheat until the harvest (Matt. 13:30). The bitingly sarcastic language about blind guides (15:14) anticipates 23:16, 24 (cf. Isa. 3:12, 14; 6:10; 9:16; CD 1.9–11; Luke 6:39; Rom. 2:19). The mention of falling into a ditch or pit reminds the reader of Matt. 12:11 (cf. Ps. 7:15; Prov. 26:27; Isa. 24:18; Jer. 48:44). Jesus counsels the disciples to ignore the Pharisees or leave them alone. Evidently, he regards their hardened opposition as irremediable (cf. Matt. 7:6), or he is subtly alluding to the parable of the weeds, in which the weeds are to be left alone until harvest.

ii. Peter's Question about Jesus's Teaching (15:15–20)

15:15–20 The disciples are not only concerned about the opposition of the Pharisees; they are also confused by Jesus's teaching about purity in 15:11. Peter characteristically speaks for the group (cf. 16:16) and asks what Jesus means. One might think that Peter's question in 15:15 refers to what has just been said by Jesus in 15:12–14 (as does Schweizer 1975: 326), but Jesus's response in 15:16–20 addresses 15:11. Again the pattern of 13:10–23 is repeated: outsiders hear enigmatic words, and insiders hear the explanation. Jesus's question "Are you also still lacking in understanding?" casts the disciples' degree of understanding in a negative light (cf. 13:13–15, 51; 15:10). The question implies a rebuke: by now they should have understood. Jesus states that whatever goes into the mouth, whether "clean" or "unclean, " passes from the body as waste and is eliminated (15:17). But whatever comes out of the mouth originates in the heart, the source of ethical impurity (15:18). The list of seven sins that come from the heart in 15:19 begins with a general statement about internal thoughts and goes on to list external acts that, for the most part, are prohibited by the second table of the Ten Commandments (Exod. 20:13–17; Deut. 5:17–21).[12] The last sin mentioned is slander, which could be aimed at the Pharisees' efforts to defame Jesus (Schnackenburg 2002: 149). Jesus's ethic stresses internal intention (cf. Matt. 5:21–22, 27–28), perhaps focusing on the tenth commandment (Exod. 20:17; Deut. 5:21). This clashes not with the law of Moses but with the Pharisees' oral tradition, which stresses external behavior. (See Carlston 1968.)

---

12. For similar vice lists, see Wis. 14:25–26; 1QS 4.9–11; Philo, *Sacrifices* 32; *Posterity* 52; T. Reu. 3.3–6; T. Levi 17.11; As. Mos. 7.3–10; Rom. 1:29–31; 1 Cor. 6:9–10; 2 Cor. 12:20; Gal. 5:19–21; Eph. 5:3–5; Col. 3:5, 8; 1 Tim. 1:9–10; 2 Tim. 3:2–8; Titus 3:3; 1 Pet. 4:3; Rev. 9:20–21; 21:8; Did. 5.1. On the sins listed, cf., on evil thoughts, Matt. 9:4; on murder, 2:16; 5:21–26; 14:10; 23:34–35; 27:24–25; on adultery and fornication, 5:27–32; 12:39; 14:3–6; 19:9; 21:31; on theft, 27:64; on false witness, 2:8, 16; 26:59–61; and on slander, 12:31–32. Cf. W. Davies and Allison 1991: 535–37.

Jesus on the Oral and Written Torah

This passage is crucial for understanding the relationship of Jesus's teaching to the traditions of the Pharisees and the law of Moses. Jesus sets aside the tradition of ritual hand washing because it is at cross-purposes with God's word (15:3–6), but does he do the same with the biblical dietary laws (Lev. 11; Deut. 14)? Those who answer affirmatively (e.g., Beare 1981: 338; Blomberg 1992a: 239; Meier 1978: 100–104) stress Matt. 15:11, 17 to prove that Jesus denies that food can defile a person. They also note that any lack of clarity in Matthew is removed by Mark's editorial comment "He declared all foods clean" (Mark 7:19b). But Matt. 5:17–48 indicates that it is simplistic at best to think that Matthew would present Jesus as dismissing a key biblical law in such an abrupt and facile manner.

Others argue that Matthew does not present Jesus as annulling the biblical dietary laws (e.g., Boring 1995: 333; W. Davies and Allison 1991: 528–31; Hagner 1995a: 437; Hare 1993: 173; Harrington 1991: 232–34; Overman 1996: 226–27). Such scholars, assuming Matthew's use of Mark, argue that Matthew has toned down Mark's version of this incident, mainly by omitting Mark 7:19b. Another argument is that Matt. 15:11 is hortatory and that its antithesis is a rhetorical strategy, not a prosaic proposition. It is also pointed out that Matthew's stress is on Jesus's disagreement with the Pharisees, not with the law itself, as is shown by the *inclusio* of 15:2, 20, which focuses on the validity of the Pharisaic tradition on washing hands, not the dietary laws. Additionally, Jesus does not interpret the enigmatic saying of 15:11 in terms of dietary law but in terms of the Pharisaic traditions. Jesus does indeed say that whatever the food (clean or unclean) that enters the mouth, it is eliminated and that what comes out of the mouth is the real problem. But his final comment contrasts the sins that defile not with eating unclean food but with eating with unwashed hands (15:20). Accordingly, Matthew does not intend for his readers to conclude that Jesus is annulling the dietary laws.

Carson (1984: 352) correctly points to 5:17–48 as the key to the interpretation of 15:1–20. Jesus does not annul but fulfills the law and the prophets. His definitive teaching accomplishes the law's purpose. Jesus fulfills the biblical dietary laws by showing that defilement is ultimately a matter of the heart. It is helpful to frame the issue here in terms of the six contrasting structures found in 5:21–48 (W. Davies and Allison 1991: 530). If one compares 15:11 to Matt. 5:27–28 on adultery, Jesus is not permitting adultery or eating unclean food (5:27; 15:17) so much as he is forbidding lust and evil thoughts (5:28; 15:19). A perhaps closer analogy would compare 15:11 to 5:33–34 on vows or 5:38–39 on vengeance. If Jesus's teaching on vows is analogous, Jesus would be saying that vows and dietary restrictions (5:33–34; 15:17) are unnecessary when one's priority is integrity and the heart (5:37; 15:19). In this case, the continuing role of vows or dietary laws might be a cultural preference, not a normative duty. Or perhaps dietary laws might be analogous to tithing garden herbs—as lighter matters that should be obeyed but that should not eclipse the weightier matters of the law (23:23).

Eventually the implications of 15:11 for the biblical dietary laws will be recognized by the apostolic church (cf. Acts 10:10–16, 28; 11:3–18; 15:5, 19–29; 21:20–26; Rom. 14:2–3, 6, 14–15; Col. 2:16). But Matthew narrates the teaching of Jesus for his Christian Jewish community in an implicit, even cryptic manner. It is clear that the priority is internal ethical matters rather than Pharisaic hand-washing traditions. Yet Matthew's community evidently continued practicing the biblical dietary laws as reminders of the deeper ethical concerns voiced by Jesus, the ultimate teacher of Torah.

Christians today are usually not concerned with whether Jesus annulled the biblical dietary laws, but the larger issue raised by this passage is the relationship of subsequent ecclesiastical traditions to the teaching of the original canonical Scriptures. The root problem is identified by Jesus in terms of Isa. 29:13—"teaching as doctrines human precepts" (Matt. 15:9). Protestants tend to think of this as a problem for only Roman Catholic and Eastern Orthodox Christianity, but they too are prone to elevating their various denominational traditions to a position of functional authority over Scripture. Such traditions are not wrong in themselves, since tradition inevitably results from applying Scripture to new situations that the church encounters in mission (28:19–20). The church must contemporize biblical teaching and draw specific concrete conclusions from general biblical principles, but it also must remember that only the Scriptures possess magisterial authority over all the ideas and practices developed by the church. The church is mandated to teach disciples to obey all that Jesus commanded (28:19), not all of its own traditions, even though such traditions are purportedly developed from scriptural inferences (see Hare 1993: 175–76).

Additional Notes

15:4. Instead of the UBS[4] reading εἶπεν (א[1], B, D, f[13], most early versions; cf. Mark 7:10), other MSS (א*,[2], C, L, W, Byz, Lect) have ἐνετείλατο λέγων. The UBS[4] editors conclude that their reading explains the other reading better than vice versa and theorize that the variant ἐνετείλατο arose due to the cognate ἐντολήν in 15:3. Cf. Metzger 1994: 31.

15:6. The shorter reading τὸν πατέρα αὐτοῦ (א, B, D) is favored by UBS[4], whose editors cite superior external evidence (Metzger 1994: 31). Three other readings add μητέρα with different phrasings. Transcriptional probability can be argued either way in light of the phrase τῷ πατρὶ ἤ τῇ μητρί in 15:5.

Another difficulty in 15:6 concerns τὸν λόγον (א[1], B, D; cf. Mark 7:13). Two other readings are found, τὸν νόμον (א*,[2], C, 073, f[13]) and τὴν ἐντολήν (L, W, f[1], Byz, Lect; cf. 15:3). UBS[4] editors discount τὴν ἐντολήν as accommodation to 15:3 and take the external evidence for τὸν λόγον as outweighing the possibility that this reading replaced τὸν νόμον because of harmonization with Mark 7:13. Cf. Metzger 1994: 31.

15:14. The UBS⁴ reading τυφλοί εἰσιν ὁδηγοὶ τυφλῶν is found in ℵ¹, L, Z, *f*¹, *f*¹³. Τυφλῶν is bracketed in UBS⁴ because it is absent from ℵ*, 2 (which also transposes the word order), B, D. Other MSS, such as C, W, *Byz*, and *Lect* have ὁδηγοί εἰσιν τυφλοὶ τυφλῶν. Metzger 1994: 31–32 indicates that the UBS⁴ reading best explains the emergence of the other readings.

15:15. The UBS⁴ reading τὴν παραβολὴν ταύτην is found in C, D, L, W, *Byz*, *Lect*. Ταύτην is bracketed in UBS⁴ because it is absent from ℵ, B, Zᵛⁱᵈ, *f*¹, although the absence is likely because the cited parable does not immediately precede 15:15. Cf. Metzger 1994: 32.

7. Exorcism of the Canaanite Woman's Daughter (15:21–28)

This passage contains a dialogue in which Jesus responds three times to the pleas of the Canaanite woman and once to his disciples (cf. Mark 7:24–30).[1] The disciples' request comes after Jesus first ignores the woman (Matt. 15:22–23). His response to their request seems also to be directed to the woman: he denies that his mission concerns her (15:24). His third response to the woman, whose pleas this time are underlined by her bowing before him, bluntly compares the woman to a dog that cannot have the children's bread (15:25–26). The woman's final plea is amazing in both humility and insight, asking Jesus to permit her a scrap from the children's bread. His response commends her great faith and grants her request (15:27–28). The drama of repeated requests and responses heightens the reader's anticipation as Jesus places obstacle after obstacle in front of the woman. The inclusion of Ruth and Tamar in Jesus's genealogy (1:3, 5) prepares the attentive reader for this episode.[2]

The unit outline is as follows:

a. The setting (15:21)
b. The first request/response (15:22–23a)
c. The second request/response (15:23b–24)
d. The third request/response (15:25–26)
e. The fourth request/response (15:27–28)

Exegesis and Exposition

[21]Jesus went away from there and withdrew to the region of Tyre and Sidon. [22]And suddenly a Canaanite woman from the vicinity came and began to cry out, "Have mercy on me, Lord, son of David; my daughter is severely demon-possessed." [23]But he did not answer her a word. And his disciples came and

---

1. Jesus's four responses all use a form of ἀποκρίνομαι. In 15:23a Jesus does not respond verbally (ὁ δὲ οὐκ ἀπεκρίθη αὐτῇ λόγον). In 15:24, 26 Jesus's response is introduced by ὁ δὲ ἀποκριθεὶς εἶπεν. In 15:28 the response begins with τότε ἀποκριθεὶς ... εἶπεν. Matthew 15:21–28 is therefore a developing dialogue in four steps.

2. On 15:21–28, see Burkill 1967; Dermience 1982; Harrisville 1966; G. Jackson 2002; Jeremias 1966b: 25–39; Légasse 1972b; A. Levine in Aune 2001: 22–41; Russell in Livingstone 1980: 163–200; Woschitz 1985.

started asking him, "Send her away, because she keeps shouting at us." ²⁴But he answered, "I was sent only to the lost sheep of the house of Israel." ²⁵But she came and began to bow down before him and say, "Lord, help me!" ²⁶But he answered, "It is not good to take the children's bread and throw it to the dogs." ²⁷So she said, "Yes, Lord; but even the dogs eat the crumbs that fall from their masters' table." ²⁸Then Jesus answered her, "O woman, your faith is great; let it be done for you as you wish." And her daughter was healed from then on.

a. The Setting (15:21)

Blomberg's view (1991: 242) that Jesus withdraws from Israel ideologically in 15:1–20 and geographically in 15:21–28 is debatable. Certainly, Jesus has withdrawn from Pharisaic traditionalism, but one could argue that it is the Pharisees, not Jesus, who have withdrawn from Israel. This is Jesus's fourth strategic withdrawal from conflict (cf. 2:12–14, 22; 4:12; 12:15; 14:13). He leaves Galilee for the region of Tyre and Sidon (cf. 11:22; Isa. 23:1–4; Jer. 25:22), a journey less than fifty miles to the north (cf. Mark 7:24–30).³ Jesus's previous statements about true purity (Matt. 15:10–20) are immediately put into practice in ministry to unclean Gentiles.

15:21

b. The First Request/Response (15:22–23a)

At first Jesus uncharacteristically ignores the gentile (literally, "Canaanite") woman's request that he have mercy on her and help her demon-possessed daughter (cf. 4:24; 9:32; 12:22). He is evidently testing her faith. Her surprising reference to him as "Lord" (e.g., 3:3; 4:7, 10; 7:21–22; 8:2, 6, 8, 25; 9:28; 10:24–25; 12:8; 14:28, 30) and "son of David" (1:1, 20; 9:27; 12:23; 20:30–31; 21:9, 15; 22:42) shows that she has genuine insight into his identity and mission.

15:22–23a

c. The Second Request/Response (15:23b–24)

The disciples urge Jesus to send the woman away, again showing insensitivity toward needy people (cf. 14:15; 15:32–33). But Jesus tells the woman that the lost sheep of Israel are his sole mission priority (cf. 9:36; 10:6; cf. 18:12; Isa. 53:6; Jer. 50:6; Ezek. 34:15). It is possible that Matt. 15:23–24 should be understood a bit differently, with the disciples asking Jesus to heal the woman in 15:23 and with Jesus answering them, not her, in 15:24 (Légasse 1972b: 28). But it is unlikely that ἀπόλυσον (apolyson) means "set free" (by healing her daughter) rather than "dismiss" (cf. BDAG 117–18).

15:23b–24

3. Jeremias 1966b: 36 argues that the territory of Tyre and Sidon extended inland as far as Caesarea Philippi and even Damascus and that this area was likely populated mainly by Jews.

d. The Third Request/Response (15:25–26)

15:25–26   Undaunted (cf. Luke 18:1–8), the woman persists, this time bowing before Jesus and calling him Lord for the third time.[4] Matthew likely intends the reader to view this as worship in the strongest sense of the word (cf. Matt. 14:33). Jesus's reply uses terms that metaphorically reflect the Jews' special covenant relationship with God (the children's food) and the Gentiles' lack of such a relationship (dogs under the master's table; see Keener 1999: 416–17; Luz 2001: 340–41 for ancient texts about dogs). The "children" of 15:26 (cf. 3:9) are God's "lost sheep," the people of Israel, in 15:24. The language describing Gentiles is offensive to modern sensibilities even if the word Jesus uses (κυνάριον, *kynarion*) is pressed as a diminutive (BDF §111.3; Moulton and Howard 1920: §139; D. Swanson 1958), implying the affection one might have for a house pet, instead of κύων (*kyōn*), which often describes wild scavengers (cf. 7:6; Luke 16:21; Phil. 3:2; 2 Pet. 2:22; Rev. 22:15; Did. 9.5; BDAG 579).[5] The point here is the redemptive-historical priority of Israel (Calvin 1972: 2.169–70; Carson 1984: 355–56). Jews come first in Jesus's ministry, yet he can also be compassionate to Gentiles once the "children" have been fed. Ancient negative stereotypes resulted in frequent epithets like this being hurled by Gentiles at Jews and by Jews at Gentiles, but Jesus's speech is motivated by pastoral concerns. His blunt language reflects his culture, yet his commendation of the woman's faith and his upcoming gentile mission transcend that culture.

e. The Fourth Request/Response (15:27–28)

15:27–28   Despite the pejorative nature of Jesus's words, the woman doggedly persists in yet a third plea for her daughter. She even adapts Jesus's metaphor and extends it, requesting Jesus's mercy as a dog might beg for table scraps (15:27). Jesus commends the woman's great faith (cf. 9:22, 29) and immediately heals her daughter.[6] She has persisted through three

---

4. The imperfect verb προσεκύνει could be understood as inceptive (she began to bow down) or as iterative (she bowed repeatedly). See Wallace 1996: 544–47.

5. Luz 2001: 340–41. Boring's appeal (1995: 336) to Jesus's Aramaic ipsissima verba is somewhat beside the point, since exegesis pertains primarily to Matthew's Greek text, not a hypothetical Aramaic reconstruction. Attempts to make Jesus's words seem more politically correct by resorting to his supposed facial expression, humor, or the twinkle in his eye (as in, e.g., Barclay 1975: 2.122; France 1985: 247; McNeile 1915: 231; Schnackenburg 2002: 150–51) are understandable but probably misguided. At the other extreme is A. Levine's blunt comment in Aune 2001: 32: "Being called 'little bitch' is no improvement to being called 'bitch.'" Cf. Beare 1981: 342–44, who views these words as atrocious and the worst sort of chauvinism, albeit not of Jesus but of the early church, which has retrojected its own controversies into this fictional account that supports mission to Gentiles.

6. The interjection ὦ with the vocative γύναι here indicates that Jesus is deeply moved by the woman's faith. This expression, which conveys exclamation, unusual emotion, or other emphasis, occurs only eight times in the NT: Matt. 15:28; Acts 1:1; Rom. 2:1, 3; 9:20; 1 Tim. 6:11, 20; James 2:20; cf. 4 Macc. 15:17; Josephus, *Ant.* 1.252; 6.305; 17.74.

rebuffs from Jesus, and her requests show her amazing understanding of Jesus's identity, power, and mission. She takes her place along with other notable Gentiles in Matthew, including the magi (2:1–12), the centurion at Capernaum (8:5–13; cf. W. Davies and Allison 1991: 558–59), and the Roman soldiers at Jesus's crucifixion (27:54). (See Burkill 1967; Dermience 1982; Harrisville 1966.)

Jesus and the Gentiles

Matthew has already made it clear that Jesus and his disciples minister only to the lost sheep of Israel (9:35–36; 10:5–6). The previous exception to this rule, the healing of the Roman officer's servant (8:5–13), and the present case of ministry to Gentiles both revolve around exceptional faith (8:10; 15:28). Both instances also contain requests for another person, the officer's servant and the woman's daughter (8:6, 8; 15:22). Further, both cases speak metaphorically of messianic blessing as table fellowship (8:11; 15:26–27), described in terms of the primacy of Israel. The official may look forward to sitting down at table with the Jewish patriarchs, and the woman may have scraps of the children's bread. The table language is clearly eschatological in 8:11 and is implicitly so in 15:26–27, since the healing of the woman's daughter flows from the presence of the kingdom (12:28). The table language also reminds the reader of the miracle meal previously narrated (14:14–21) and anticipates another miracle meal that comes next in the story (15:32–39). These meals also anticipate the *shalom* that will one day come to the disciples of Jesus from Israel and all the nations. The language of Jesus at the Last Supper also has an eschatological context (26:29). Every time Christians enjoy table fellowship and, even more so, every time they participate in the Eucharist, they anticipate the eschatological feast with Jesus (cf. 1 Cor. 11:26). "Blessed is everyone who eats bread in the kingdom of God" (Luke 14:15).

W. Davies and Allison (1991: 557) correctly point out that Jesus's response to the Canaanite woman's request "makes it abundantly plain that the biblical doctrine of Israel's election must be taken seriously." As Jesus said to the Samaritan woman, "Salvation is from the Jews" (John 4:22). The universal mission of the church (Matt. 24:14; 28:18–20; cf. Dan. 7:13–14) does not replace the earlier mission to Israel but expands it. Matthew would agree with Paul that, through Jesus, Gentiles have been brought near to Israel's covenant promises (Eph. 2:11–22; Rom. 11:17; 15:7–12). Ultimately both Matthew's and Paul's views arise from Gen. 12:3—"In you [Abraham] shall all the families of the earth be blessed" (Matt. 1:1; Rom. 4). (See the comments on 10:5–6; A.-J. Levine 1988; Schnabel 2004; J. J. Scott 1990.)

See BDAG 1101; BDF §146.1b; Moulton and Turner 1963: 33; Wallace 1996: 68–69; Winer 1882: 228–29; Zerwick 1963 §35.

8. Another Miracle Meal (15:29–39)

The structure of this passage (cf. Mark 7:31–8:10) is the same as the previous account of the feeding of the five thousand (Matt. 14:13–21). After the setting (14:13–14; 15:29–31), Jesus discusses the crowd's needs with the disciples (14:15–18; 15:32–34) and then performs the miracle (14:19–20a; 15:35–37a). The miracle is amplified by the mention of leftover food and the size of the crowd (14:20b–21; 15:37b–38). In both accounts:

1. Jesus withdraws and is alone (14:13a; 15:21, 29).
2. Crowds approach Jesus (14:13b; 15:30a).
3. Jesus compassionately heals (14:14; 15:30b–31).
4. Jesus desires to feed the crowd (14:16; 15:32).[1]
5. The disciples state that their food resources are inadequate (14:17; 15:33).
6. Jesus takes the disciples' food (14:18; 15:36).
7. Jesus orders the crowd to recline (14:19; 15:35).[2]
8. Jesus blesses the food and distributes it to the disciples, who distribute it to the crowd (14:19; 15:36).
9. The crowd's hunger is fully satisfied, and there is food left over (14:20; 15:37).
10. The number of the crowd is delineated (14:21; 15:38).

(On 15:29–39, see T. Donaldson 1985: 122–35; Ryan 1978; Trilling 1964: 99–105; the sources listed previously for 14:13–21.)
   The outline for this unit is as follows:

a. The setting (15:29–31)
b. Discussion with the disciples (15:32–34)
c. The miracle (15:35–36)
d. The aftermath (15:37–38)
e. Departure to Magadan (15:39)

---

1. In 14:15–17 the disciples bring up the subject of dismissing the people so that they can find food for themselves. When Jesus tells them to feed the crowd, they protest that their supplies are inadequate. In 15:32–33 Jesus brings up the subject of feeding the crowd, and then the disciples mention their inadequate resources.
2. In 14:18–19 Jesus takes the disciples' food before ordering the crowd to recline. In 15:35–36 he orders the crowd to recline before he takes the food from the disciples.

Exegesis and Exposition

²⁹After he left there, Jesus passed along the Sea of Galilee, and he went up on the mountain and was sitting there. ³⁰And large crowds came to him, bringing with them the lame, the blind, the crippled, the mute, and many others. They laid them down at his feet, and he healed them, ³¹so that the crowd was amazed to see the mute ⌜speaking, the crippled made well,⌝ and the lame walking, and the blind seeing; and they praised the God of Israel.

³²And Jesus called his disciples to him and said, "I feel compassion for the crowd because they have already been with me for three days and they have nothing to eat. I do not want to send them away hungry, for they will become exhausted on the way." ³³But the disciples said to him, "Where are we to get enough loaves in this remote place to feed such a crowd?" ³⁴And Jesus said to them, "How many loaves do you have?" And they said, "Seven, and a few small fish." ³⁵Then he ordered the crowd to recline on the ground, ³⁶and he took the seven loaves and the fish; and after he blessed them, he broke them and started giving them to the disciples, and the disciples gave them to the crowds. ³⁷And they all ate and were satisfied, and then they picked up seven baskets full of what was left over of the broken pieces. ³⁸And there were four thousand men who ate, besides women and children. ³⁹And after sending away the crowds, Jesus got into the boat and went to the region of ⌜Magadan⌝.

a. The Setting (15:29–31)

Jesus withdraws from Tyre and Sidon to a mountain (cf. 5:1; 14:23; **15:29–31** 17:1; T. Donaldson 1985) overlooking the Sea of Galilee (cf. Mark 7:31–37). It is impossible to track Jesus's movements closely, since there are no details. Perhaps the journey of Matt. 15:21 was reversed. Magadan (15:39) is an obscure reference and cannot be located with certainty. Nevertheless, many expositors (e.g., Blomberg 1992a: 245; Carson 1984: 356–57; Gundry 1994: 317–22) believe it is likely that Jesus traveled into gentile territory northeast of the Sea of Galilee (Mark 7:31; cf. Matt. 8:28–34). It is argued that viewing the feeding of the four thousand as a miracle meal for Gentiles fits the parallel passage in Mark 7 and best explains the praise of "the God of Israel" (but see Hagner 1995a: 446; Luz 2001: 344–45) and the "wilderness" place (Matt. 15:31, 33).

The general statement about many miracles in 15:30–31 is similar to those found elsewhere in Matthew (4:23–24; 8:16; 9:35; 14:14, 34–36; 19:2). Jesus heals all who are afflicted with diseases. If this occurs in a gentile region, the receptivity of the Canaanite woman and these Gentiles to Jesus's works contrasts with his rejection by the residents of Nazareth and the Pharisees (13:54–58; 15:1–14). But this view is debatable, as will be seen below.

b. Discussion with the Disciples (15:32–34)

15:32–34 The resemblance of this second miracle meal to the first (14:13–21) leads some scholars to view it as an unhistorical doublet, or a second version of one event (Hagner 1995a: 449–50; Schnackenburg 2002: 152; but see Blomberg 1987b: 146–48 for a rebuttal). Jesus tells the disciples that he feels compassion for the hungry crowd that has been with him for three days (cf. 9:36; 14:14; 20:34). The disciples respond with an incredulous question indicating that they believe their resources are inadequate (15:33). Evidently, their memories are also inadequate or they would recall Jesus's ability to multiply their supplies.

c. The Miracle (15:35–36)

15:35–36 Again Jesus uses the disciples' meager resources, seven loaves and a few small fish. The miracle probably occurs in Jesus's hands after he prays, as he distributes the food to the disciples rather than as they in turn hand it out to the crowd. It is doubtful that the seven loaves here or the seven baskets of leftovers in 15:37 symbolize the Gentiles.

d. The Aftermath (15:37–38)

15:37–38 The crowd eats until it is satisfied. There are seven baskets of food left over after the four thousand men plus women and children have eaten. If this miracle is understood as occurring in gentile territory, Matthew's purpose in including a second miracle meal story is evidently to demonstrate Jesus's concern for the Gentiles and to underline the theme of gentile world mission, with which this Gospel concludes.

e. Departure to Magadan (15:39)

15:39 After the miracle, Jesus crosses over the sea in a boat and arrives at Magadan. This is an obscure town, like Mark's Dalmanutha (Mark 8:10). Both are mentioned only in the Gospels. Perhaps Magadan should be identified with Magdala on the west side of the Sea of Galilee. See the additional note on 15:39. At any rate, Jesus is clearly now in Jewish territory and back in touch with the Pharisees' opposition (Matt. 16:1).

Why Another Miracle Meal?

W. Davies and Allison (1991: 563–64) lay out a convenient summary of the reasons many scholars view the feeding of the four thousand as a miracle meal for Gentiles, which balances the previous feeding of five thousand Jews. This is consistent with Matthew's theological purposes but cannot be proved. The geographical language is vague and the location of Magadan/Magdala is too obscure to prove that Jesus was in gentile territory. The statement that the crowd witnessing the healing "glorified the God of Israel" (15:31) is fitting in the mouths of Gentiles, but it also is a common biblical phrase for Israel's worship (e.g., Exod. 5:1; 1 Kings 1:48; 1 Chron. 16:36; Pss. 41:13; 59:5; 68:35; 69:6; 72:18; 106:48; Isa. 24:15; 29:23; 37:16; Luke 1:68).

If neither the geography nor this key phrase proves that the meal was for Gentiles, one must make the case from the context in which the meal occurs. Jesus has just gone to an area bordering Israel and has healed a Canaanite woman's daughter, so the healings and miracle meal in Matt. 15:32–39 could plausibly be understood as additional ministry to Gentiles. One might even view the four thousand people as symbolic of Gentiles from the four corners of the earth, and the seven baskets of leftover food as symbolic of the completeness of Jesus's kingdom mission, but this would be speculation to support a preconceived theory. Actually, the previous context probably speaks against the view that four thousand Gentiles were fed, since it stresses the exceptional nature of Jesus's ministry to the Canaanite woman (15:24; Hagner 1995a: 446). To this point in Matthew, the Gentiles to whom Jesus ministers exercise unusually great faith, but there is no indication that such exceptional faith is exercised by the four thousand. Thus there is considerable doubt that this was a miracle for Gentiles.

If the feeding of the four thousand is not a miracle for Gentiles, why did Matthew include it? For one thing, if Matthew was following Mark, this story is also found there (Mark 8:1–10). But Matthew has a theological motive, not just a historical one. T. Donaldson (1985: 122–35) argues that the passage contains "Zion eschatology," portraying the gathering of scattered Israel to Mount Zion for healing, a great feast, and many additional blessings (cf. Isa. 35:5–6). In this view, Matthew crafted the narrative of this miracle in conjunction with prophetic images of God's eschatological blessing upon his people. Allison (1993b: 238–42) adds to this imagery the likelihood of linkage with Moses, finding in the mountain and the miraculous meal echoes of Sinai and manna from heaven.

Matthew's second miraculous meal story reminds those familiar with the Scriptures of God's past and future blessing of his people, as would be expected in a Gospel stressing the role of Jesus as the ultimate fulfillment of the law and the prophets. Moses was associated with two feeding miracles (Exod. 16; Num. 11), as was Elisha (2 Kings 4:1–7, 38–44; cf. Elijah in 1 Kings 17:8–16). Also, within the narrative of Matthew itself, the second miracle meal emphasizes such lessons as the compassion of Jesus, his power to do great things with meager resources, and the foreshadowing of the eschatological feast with Jesus. On the basis of these two miracle stories, another lesson will be taught in Matt. 16:5–11, where the disciples' "little faith" will once again be confronted with their preoccupation with physical needs instead of kingdom truth and priorities.

In each of the main sections of Matt. 15, Jesus addresses the genuine but flawed faith of the disciples. The controversy over purity (15:1–20) portrays the disciples as slow to perceive the irreversible rift between Jesus and the Jewish leaders. They are overly concerned that the Pharisees were offended by Jesus's teaching (15:12–14). The disciples are also slow in grasping Jesus's teaching that genuine purity comes from within. Jesus's reply to their question makes it clear that the disciples should have understood what he meant (14:15–16). This passage shows that the disciples' assertion of 13:51 cannot be taken at face value. They doubtlessly thought they understood the kingdom well, but their genuine knowledge needed considerable deepening. In the other two sections of Matt. 15, the disciples appear to be impatient with the needs of people. They ask Jesus to dismiss the Canaanite woman, whose repeated pleas irritate them (15:23). They are incredulous that Jesus wants to feed the four thousand, because they have inadequate provisions (15:33). They have evidently forgotten Jesus's gracious response to another amazing Gentile (8:5–13) and Jesus's ability to feed a crowd even larger than this one (14:13–21). From the disciples' lack of compassion and short memories, Matthew's readers learn that they must care for the needy and trust Jesus to use their inadequate resources to meet the needs of others. In the very next section of Matthew, the "little faith" of the disciples is once again exposed (16:8), and Matthew's readers are once again reminded of the power of the kingdom.

Summary of Matthew 15

The events of 13:53–14:36 illustrate the mixed response to the gospel that Jesus stressed in the parables of 13:1–52. Opposition in this section (13:57; 14:12) does not come from the Pharisees, whose ultimate slander was stressed in 12:1–45. Even though the murder of John anticipates that of Jesus (12:14; 14:10; 17:12), the absence of the Pharisees from Matt. 13–14 reduces the tension from the level it reached in Matt. 12. But the Pharisees return (15:1) to criticize Jesus's disciples for not obeying the "traditions of the elders." Jesus answers the criticism (15:1–20) and then withdraws to gentile territory and heals the daughter of a remarkable Canaanite woman (15:21–28). Then he moves into territory near the Sea of Galilee for additional miracles of healing (15:29–31) and another miraculous feeding (15:32–39).

The three sections of Matt. 15 (1–20, 21–28, 29–39) all involve bread (Garland 1993: 159). The Pharisees complain that Jesus's disciples eat it without washing their hands (15:2), the Canaanite woman asks for bread crumbs (15:26–27), and Jesus multiplies the disciples' seven loaves and feeds the four thousand (15:36).

The events of this chapter not only portray the continuing obduracy of the Pharisees but also further the reader's understanding of Jesus as the fulfiller of the law (cf. 5:17–48). As he confronts the Pharisees (15:1–9), teaches the multitudes (15:10–11), and explains the teaching to the disciples (15:12–20), Jesus in effect repeats the formula of 5:21–48 and emphasizes a righteousness that exceeds that of the legal experts and Pharisees. This righteousness is not appreciated by the Pharisees, but it is received by the Canaanite woman, who eagerly takes the crumbs from the meal the Pharisees refuse to eat. Her great faith (15:28) reminds the reader of the centurion who would participate in the eschatological meal (8:10–12). The ensuing miracles and meal continue the portrayal of Jesus as compassionate miracle worker and patient teacher. But the controversy continues.

Additional Notes

15:31. Several variant readings alter the words and word order of this verse. The UBS[4] reading λαλοῦντας, κυλλοὺς ὑγιεῖς is supported by a wide variety of MSS (C, L, W, Δ, 0233, *Byz*, *Lect*).

15:39. UBS[4] prefers the obscure place name Μαγαδάν (supported by ℵ*, B, D). Three other readings exist: Μαγεδάν (in ℵ[2], most Latin MSS), Μαγδαλάν (in C, N, O, W), and Μαγδαλά (in L, Δ, Θ, *f*[1], *f*[13], *Byz*, *Lect*). The parallel passage, Mark 8:10, has "the districts of Dalmanutha."

9. The Second Request for a Sign (16:1–4)

Earlier in Matthew, confrontations with the Pharisees (and other religious leaders) occur as they respond to the words and works of Jesus (3:7; 9:3, 11, 34; 12:2, 10, 14, 24, 38). As things proceed, however, the Pharisees begin to seek Jesus out in order to initiate confrontation (15:1; 16:1; 19:3; 21:23; 22:23, 34). Their second request for a sign (16:1–4; cf. 12:38) necessitates Jesus's warning about their teaching (16:5–12). This leads to what is perhaps the most crucial christological pericope in this Gospel, where Jesus receives Peter's representative confession of his messiahship and promises to build and empower his church (16:13–20). At this crucial juncture, Jesus clearly announces his death and resurrection for the first time and then points his disciples to a self-denying lifestyle that will be rewarded when he comes again (16:21–28).

Matthew 16:1–4 (cf. Mark 8:11–13; Luke 12:54–56) reprises Matt. 12:38–40 and prepares the reader for the cryptic warning of 16:6 and the later "test" put to Jesus on divorce in 19:3 (cf. 22:15). The passage consists of the Pharisees' request (16:1), Jesus's answer (16:2–4a), and his departure from their presence (16:4b; cf. 15:14a).

This unit can be outlined as follows:

a. The request of the Pharisees (16:1)
b. The answer of Jesus (16:2–4)

Exegesis and Exposition

¹Then the Pharisees and Sadducees came to test Jesus, and they asked him to show them a sign from heaven. ²But he answered them, ⌜"When it is evening, you say, 'It will be fair weather, for the sky is red.' ³And in the morning, 'There will be a storm today, for the sky is red and gloomy.' You know how to interpret the appearance of the sky, but you cannot interpret the signs of the times.⌝ ⁴An evil and adulterous generation wants a sign; but a sign will not be given to it except the sign of Jonah." And he left them and went away.

a. The Request of the Pharisees (16:1)

16:1 Again the Jewish leaders ask Jesus for a sign (cf. 12:38; 1 Cor. 1:22), and this time their motive is exposed: they wish to test him (cf. Matt. 4:1, 3, 7; 19:3; Exod. 17:2, 7; Deut. 6:16; Ps. 78:41, 56; Jer. 10:2; 1 Cor.

10:9).[1] Although some scholars doubt the likelihood of the Pharisees' association with the Sadducees here and in other places in Matthew, it is historically plausible that these normally disparate groups would share a common cause in opposing Jesus (cf. Matt. 3:7; 16:1, 6, 11, 12). A "sign from heaven" would evidently be something so spectacular and undeniable that it would be clear that it had come from heaven (cf. Jer. 10:2; John 6:26; Let. Jer. 66–67 = Bar. 6:66–67). In this understanding, "heaven" is probably metonymy for God. Or perhaps the desired sign would be in the heavens, as in Matt. 24:27, 30; Rev. 12:1, 3; 2 Esd. (4 Ezra) 5:4; 7:39–40. But Jesus has just now fed perhaps ten thousand people with seven loaves of bread and a few small fish (Matt. 15:32–39). Could another sign be more convincing? In any event, Jesus performs signs out of compassion for those in need, not in response to what amounts to a dare from his opponents. This juxtaposition of the miracle meal and the request for a sign proves that seeing is not always believing (cf. Luke 16:31; W. Davies and Allison 1991: 583–84).

b. The Answer of Jesus (16:2–4)

Jesus's answer in 16:2–4 has two parts. The first part (16:2–3) contrasts the religious leaders' competence in basic meteorology with their incompetence in discerning prophetically significant times.[2] The second part of the answer (16:4) gets to the root of their question. They are culpable for not discerning that Jesus's miracles demonstrate the messianic significance of his ministry (cf. 9:6–8; 12:28). But 16:2–3 is not found in many early MSS (cf. Luke 12:54–56; Metzger 1994: 33; the additional note on 16:2–3). This second request for a sign is met with the same enigmatic answer as the first request, "the sign of the prophet Jonah" (cf. 12:39–40; R. Edwards 1971). Jesus's answer here does not continue with the explanation of 12:40–41, to the effect that Jonah's experience in the belly of the great fish typifies Jesus's entombment. Jesus's resurrection will be the ultimate sign from heaven, yet this generation will still not believe Jesus's message as the Ninevites believed Jonah's message. At this point Jesus walks away from the Pharisees and Sadducees. This physical act demonstrates the total incompatibility of Jesus and the religious leaders (cf. 15:14a; 24:1a).

16:2–4

Additional Note

16:2–3. Jesus's answer in 16:2–3 (ὀψίας … δύνασθε) is omitted by several sources, including ℵ, B, X, f¹³, 157, 579, Origen, and MSS according to Jerome. It is possible that it has been interpolated

1. The participle πειράζοντες is telic. Cf. the participles in 19:3; 22:35; the infinitive in 4:1; Wallace 1996: 635–37.
2. For eschatologically significant καιροί, see 21:41; Ezek. 12:27 LXX; Dan. 7:25; 9:27; 11:14 LXX; Tob. 14:5; Luke 21:24; Acts 1:7; 3:20; Eph. 1:10; 1 Thess. 5:1–2; 1 Tim. 4:1; 6:14–15; Rev. 12:14; Barn. 4.3; 2 Esd. (4 Ezra) 4:37.

from Luke 12:54–56 or a common source. Yet it is included in C, D, L, W, f^1, *Byz*, *Lect*, and many more. The ambiguity of the evidence leads the UBS[4] editors to include the passage, but in square brackets. See W. Davies and Allison 1991: 580–81n12; Hirunuma in Epp and Fee 1981: 35–45; Metzger 1994: 33.

Another matter is the punctuation of the last two clauses of 16:3, which may be taken as a statement of fact (NIV, NRSV) or as a rhetorical question (NA[27], UBS[4], KJV, NASB).

10. Warning against the Pharisees and Sadducees (16:5–12)

In 16:5–12 Jesus uses the disciples' forgetfulness (16:5) to warn them about the teaching of the religious leaders (16:12). The leaders' unbelief is underlined by their request for a sign in the previous pericope (16:1–4). Jesus now speaks of their error with the metaphor of leaven, since the disciples are preoccupied with food, not with the spiritual gravity of the situation. After mentioning the occasion (16:5), Matthew narrates a conversation between Jesus and the disciples (16:6–11) in which their initial lack of understanding (16:6–7) is criticized by Jesus, who reminds them of the obvious: he can supply their lack of bread (16:8–11). An editorial conclusion that interprets the metaphor of leaven as teaching (16:12) is appended to the *inclusio* formed by Jesus's two identical warnings against the religious leaders (16:6, 11b).

The unit may be outlined as follows:

a. The occasion (16:5)
b. The conversation (16:6–11)
    i. The disciples' lack of understanding (16:6–7)
    ii. Jesus's criticism of the disciples (16:8–11)
c. The result (16:12)

Exegesis and Exposition

⁵And when the disciples came to the other side of the sea, they had forgotten to bring any bread. ⁶And Jesus said to them, "Pay attention and beware of the leaven of the Pharisees and Sadducees." ⁷They began to discuss this among themselves, saying, "He said that because we did not bring any bread." ⁸But when Jesus became aware of this, he said, "You of little faith, why are you discussing among yourselves that you have no bread? ⁹Do you not yet understand or remember the five loaves of the five thousand, and how many baskets you gathered? ¹⁰Or the seven loaves of the four thousand, and how many baskets you gathered? ¹¹How could you not understand that I did not speak to you about bread? But beware of the leaven of the Pharisees and Sadducees." ¹²Then they understood that he did not say to beware of the leaven ⌜of bread⌝ but of the teaching of the Pharisees and Sadducees.

a. The Occasion (16:5)

16:5 It is difficult to follow the movements of Jesus and the disciples in this passage (cf. Mark 8:13–21). If Matt. 15:39 implies that Jesus left the disciples behind when he took the boat trip to Magadan, then the disciples evidently rejoin him at 16:5, as implied by the NASB and the NLT (cf. Hagner 1995a: 454–55, 458–59). Another viewpoint takes 15:39 as indicating a trip of Jesus and the disciples to Magadan and 16:5 as a return trip, as implied by the NIV (cf. Blomberg 1992a: 248).

b. The Conversation (16:6–11)

i. The Disciples' Lack of Understanding (16:6–7)

16:6–7 The disciples' forgetting to bring bread serves as a springboard for Jesus's cryptic warning about the "yeast of the Pharisees and Sadducees."[1] In light of 16:8–12, verses 6–7 evidently indicate that the disciples think Jesus is angry with them because they have forgotten to bring bread or, less likely, that he is warning them not to buy bread from Pharisees and Sadducees. Bread has been mentioned several times in the narrative, and there has been ample teaching on the necessity of faith in God's provision, with two examples of Jesus's miraculous ability to supply it (4:3–4; 6:11, 25, 31; 7:9; 12:4; 14:17, 19; 15:2, 26, 33–34, 36; 16:5–12; 26:26; cf. Deut. 8:3, 16; Exod. 16).

This is not one of the disciples' better moments. Their previous claim to have understood Jesus's parabolic teaching about the kingdom (13:51–52) is contradicted by their response to him here. They forget Jesus's recent warning about the blindness of the Pharisees (15:13–14), not to mention two astounding examples of his ability to provide food in a miraculous fashion (14:13–21; 15:32–38). This memory lapse renders them imperceptive to the danger posed by the Pharisees and Sadducees and to Jesus's cryptic warning. Unaware of the seriousness of the spiritual conflict between Jesus and the religious leaders, they are preoccupied with temporal matters. They associate Jesus's yeast metaphor (cf. 13:33; Mitton 1973) with their hunger rather than with the escalating controversy with the religious leaders (cf. 15:1–14) and the mortal danger it poses to Jesus (12:14; 16:21).

ii. Jesus's Criticism of the Disciples (16:8–11)

16:8–11 The disciples lack not only perception but also faith in Jesus's ability to provide bread for their needs. Their "little faith" (cf. 6:30; 8:26; 14:31; 17:20) is amazing in view of the two miraculous feedings in which they have recently participated (14:13–21; 15:29–39). Five loaves fed more

---

1. It is unclear in 16:7 whether the ὅτι is causal or recitative (Wallace 1996: 454–55, 460–61). If the former, the disciples conclude that Jesus warned them *because* they did not bring bread. If the latter, they are simply discussing the fact *that* they did not bring bread.

than five thousand people, and seven loaves fed more than four thousand, with more food left over than was available to begin with. But somehow the disciples obtusely conclude that Jesus has a problem with their lack of food. Jesus asks them how they could have possibly concluded that he has a problem with a lack of bread, and then he repeats the warning of 16:6, completing the *inclusio*.

c. The Result (16:12)

This editorial comment indicates that the disciples finally do grasp that Jesus's concern is the false teaching of the Pharisees and Sadducees.[2] These two groups had obvious differences on such matters as the validity of the oral law and the existence of an afterlife (cf. 15:1–2; 22:23–33), and so their association here can only come from their common opposition to Jesus (cf. 3:7–8). His miracles (9:1–6, 34; 12:24, 38; 16:1) and his definitive teaching of the Torah (5:17–48; cf. 12:2, 14; 15:2, 12; 19:3; 21:15, 23; 22:15–16, 23, 34–35, 41) have been immensely problematic for their power and prestige among the people. All this comes to a head in several heated exchanges between Jesus and various religious leaders after he enters Jerusalem (21:12–22:46). Properly understood (contra Luz 2001: 351–52), the warnings of 16:6, 11 do not contradict Jesus's remarks in 23:2–33, which give qualified support to the Pharisees' teaching (cf. Luke 12:1; W. Davies and Allison 1991: 593; Rabbinowitz 2003).

16:12

In this passage Jesus patiently yet firmly deals again with the "little faith" of the disciples. He improves their spiritual perception by prodding their memory. If they recall the previous miracle meals, they will realize that food is not the problem and that they must deal with the increasing opposition to Jesus. If they watch out for the teaching of the Jewish leaders, Jesus will care for their food problems. This rebuke of the forgetful disciples should sharpen the mental and spiritual focus of God's people today. Preoccupation with temporal and material concerns continues to render disciples dull and forgetful of the values of the kingdom and of false teaching that endangers it.

Additional Note

16:12. Several plausible readings are found for the genitive words modifying τῆς ζύμης. UBS[4] reads the plural τῶν ἄρτων (ℵ[2], B, L, 157, 892), but the singular τοῦ ἄρτου is also found (C, W, Δ, 13, 28, *Byz, Lect*). ℵ*, 579 have τῶν Φαρισαίων καὶ Σαδδουκαίων, which makes an exact parallel with the last phrase of the verse. MS 33 has only τῶν Φαρισαίων, and several MSS (D, Θ, *f*[13], 565) have no genitive modifier at all. It is possible to prefer this last reading, since it is the shortest and could have given rise to the others, but its external evidence is not convincing. See Metzger 1994: 33.

---

2. See *y. Ḥag.* 2.76c for a similar metaphor of Torah as leaven.

11. Peter's Confession and Jesus's Promise (16:13–20)

Matthew 16:13–20 (cf. Mark 8:27–30; Luke 9:18–21) takes its place with such texts as Matt. 3:17; 11:25–27; and 17:5 as a christological high point of this Gospel. The passage uses Peter's confession and Jesus's response to tie together the implications of many aspects of the words and deeds of Jesus narrated thus far: Jesus is none other than the Messiah, Son of the living God. He will equip his new community with the authority to become the center of God's redemptive activity in the world.

Structurally, the passage is a conversation between Jesus and the disciples (16:13b–19), clearly framed by a narrative introduction (16:13a) and conclusion (16:20). The conversation is structured in three levels of triplets (W. Davies and Allison 1991: 602). Jesus speaks three times, asking questions in 16:13, 15 and responding to Peter's confession (16:16) in 16:17–19. This response consists of three statements, the first pronouncing the confessing Simon blessed (16:17), the second promising to build the church on Peter the confessor, and the third granting to Peter victorious authority over entrance to the kingdom (16:17–19). Each of these three response statements has three elements: an initial proposition that is developed by two antithetical statements.[1]

The outline of this unit is as follows:

    a. The setting (16:13a)
    b. The first question and answer (16:13b–14)
    c. The second question and answer (16:15–16)
    d. Jesus's response to Peter (16:17–19)
    e. Jesus warns that his messianic identity must be kept secret (16:20)

Exegesis and Exposition

[13]When Jesus came into the district of Caesarea Philippi, he was asking his disciples, "⌜Who do people say that the Son of Man is⌝?" [14]And they said, "Some say John the Baptist; but others, Elijah; and yet others, Jeremiah, or one of the

---

1. The literature on the many exegetical and theological facets of this pericope is enormous. For bibliographies, see W. Davies and Allison 1991: 643–47; Hagner 1995a: 461–62; Luz 2001: 353–54; Nolland 2005: 655–57.

prophets." ¹⁵He said to them, "But who do you say that I am?" ¹⁶And Simon Peter answered, "You are the Messiah, the Son of the living God." ¹⁷And Jesus answered him, "Blessed are you, Simon son of Jonah, because flesh and blood has not revealed this to you, but my Father who is in heaven. ¹⁸And I also tell you that you are Peter, and upon this rock I will build my church; and the gates of hades will not overpower it. ¹⁹I will give you the keys of the kingdom of heaven; and whatever you bind on earth shall be bound in heaven, and whatever you loose on earth shall be loosed in heaven." ²⁰Then he ordered the disciples not to tell anyone that he was ⌜the Messiah⌝.

a. The Setting (16:13a)

Jesus travels to Caesarea Philippi (Josephus, *Ant.* 15.363–64; *J.W.* 1.404–6; 2.168; 3.509–15), which was located near the source of the Jordan River about twenty-five miles north of the Sea of Galilee. It is unclear where this trip began (cf. the comments on 15:39; 16:5). Caesarea Philippi was a gentile town at the southern edge of Mount Hermon. Its Greek name honored the god Pan, and a cave there was turned into a shrine to this god. It is possible that certain geographical features of this city are alluded to in 16:17–19. On this point, see Burgess 1976; Immisch 1916; Kutsko, *ABD* 1:803; Nickelsburg 1981.

16:13a

b. The First Question and Answer (16:13b–14)

Jesus's first question concerns the popular consensus on his identity. The disciples' answer indicates something of the messianic speculation of those times. Herod Antipas has already identified Jesus as John the Baptist redivivus (14:2). The view that Jesus is Elijah evidently comes from Mal. 4:5, which speaks of God sending Elijah before the day of the Lord (cf. Matt. 11:10; 17:10–13; 27:45–49). Perhaps Jesus's miracles remind the people of the biblical accounts of Elijah's miracles. It is harder to explain the speculation that Jesus is Jeremiah or another of the prophets (cf. 21:11). Perhaps this association is due to Jeremiah's judgment oracles and opposition to the temple leaders of his day.² Additionally, Deut. 18:15–18 was understood messianically by some Jews in Jesus's day (cf. John 1:21, 25; 6:14–15; 7:40). All these popular views of Jesus are positive, but they are inadequate. Although the crowd views Jesus as a prophet (Matt. 21:11, 26), their understanding proves to be superficial and fickle (27:15–26).

16:13b–14

c. The Second Question and Answer (16:15–16)

Jesus's second question probes the disciples' understanding of his identity. Peter answers for the group in 16:16, and this implies that Jesus

16:15–16

---

2. See 2 Esd. (4 Ezra) 2:16–18; 2 Macc. 15:12–16; Dahlberg 1975; Knowles 1993: 81–95; Menken 1984; Whitters 2006; Winkle 1986; Zucker 1990.

speaks to Peter as spokesman for the group in 16:17–19 (cf. 15:15; 19:27). Peter's remarkable answer links Jesus's identity as Messiah (1:1, 16–18; 2:4; 11:2; 16:16, 20; 22:42; 23:8, 10; 24:5, 23; 26:63, 68; 27:17, 22) to his divine sonship (2:15; 3:17; 4:3, 6; 8:29; 11:27; 14:33; 16:16; 26:63; 27:40, 43, 54; 28:19; cf. Mark 14:61; Luke 22:67, 70; John 1:49; 6:69; 11:27; Verseput 1987). The probable biblical background for the linking of the terms "Messiah" and "Son of God" is found in 2 Sam. 7:14; 1 Chron. 17:13; Pss. 2:6–8, 12; 89:27–29. Ironically, the high priest's demand that Jesus identify himself (Matt. 26:63) reiterates the main themes of Peter's confession. If Peter's faithful confession is the christological high point of the Gospel, the high priest's angry question is certainly the low point. The expression "the living God" implicitly distinguishes between the true God of Israel and the false pagan gods.[3]

d. Jesus's Response to Peter (16:17–19)

16:17–18 Jesus first responds to Peter with a beatitude (16:17; cf. 5:3–12). Peter's awareness of Jesus's true identity amid popular confusion (16:14) is not due to human brilliance but to divine revelation (cf. 11:25–27; 13:10–17; cf. John 6:63, 65). Jesus continues with a pronouncement of Peter's foundational authority in the church that Jesus will build (Matt. 16:18). The word ἐκκλησία (*ekklēsia*) occurs only here and in 18:17 in the Gospels.[4] It has a more global sense here (cf. Acts 20:28; 1 Cor. 12:28; Eph. 1:22; 5:25; Heb. 12:23) and a more local sense in Matt. 18:17 (cf. Acts 8:1; 14:23; 1 Cor. 1:2; Rev. 1:4). Jesus's use of this word for his future community of disciples evokes the rich heritage of Israel as God's assembled covenant community (cf. 1 Cor. 10:1–11; Heb. 12:18–24; 1QM 4.10; 1QSa 2.4; CD 7.17; 11.22; 12.6).

Although some Protestants disagree (see esp. Caragounis 1989), Jesus plays on the nickname Peter in speaking of him (as spokesman for the disciples) as the foundation of the nascent church (cf. Eph. 2:20; Rev. 21:14).[5] This more natural understanding of Jesus's words is preferable to

---

3. See Deut. 5:26; 1 Sam. 17:26; 2 Kings 19:4; Pss. 42:2; 84:2; cf. Acts 14:15; Rom. 9:26; 2 Cor. 3:3; 6:16; 1 Thess. 1:9; 1 Tim. 3:15; 4:10; Heb. 3:12; 9:14; 10:31; 12:22; 1 Pet. 1:23; Rev. 7:2; 15:7.

4. Ἐκκλησία occurs ca. a hundred times in the LXX. It translates קָהָל, which refers to the assembly, convocation, or congregation of Israel (e.g., Deut. 4:10; 18:16; 31:30; 1 Chron. 28:2, 8; Neh. 8:2; 1 Macc. 4:59; Pss. 21:23 [22:22 Eng.]; 34:18 [35:18 Eng.]; cf. BDB 874; Acts 7:38; Heb. 2:12). The idea of assembled community rather than the etymologically derived "the ones called out" is at the heart of the meaning of ἐκκλησία. See Berger 1976; J. Campbell 1948; Dahl 1963; Marshall 1973; Schrage 1963; Schmidt, *TDNT* 1:501–36, esp. 518–26.

5. Cf. the giving of a second name to Abram (Gen. 17:1–8), Sarah (17:15), and Jacob (32:22–32). Abraham is described as a rock in Isa. 51:1–2 (cf. *L.A.B.* 23.4; Matt. 3:9). On when Jesus first gave Simon the name Peter, see W. Davies and Allison 1991: 625. The prophetic use of symbolic names (Isa. 7:3; 8:3–4; 9:6; Jer. 20:1–6; 23:6; Hos. 1:4–9; Zech. 6:12) is also noteworthy.

other views that take the rock to be Jesus or Peter's confession of Jesus. The "gates of hades" probably alludes to biblical "sheol" as the domain of Satan and death (cf. Isa. 28:15–19; 38:9–10; Wis. 16:13; 3 Macc. 5:51; Ps. Sol. 16.2; "the gates of death" in Job 38:17; Pss. 9:13; 107:18; 1QH 14.24; 4Q184 frg. 1.10). Jesus promises that the evil powers arrayed against it will not destroy the church that he will build[6] on the foundation of Peter and the apostles.[7] See further discussion below.

The third statement in Jesus's response to Peter links the church to the kingdom by giving the kingdom's keys to Peter, the church's foundational apostle. This indicates that the church is the agency of kingdom authority on the earth. Keys may symbolize authority (cf. Isa. 22:22; Luke 11:52; Rev. 1:18; 3:7; 2 Bar. 10.18; 3 Bar. 11.2; 4 Bar. 4.4; 9.5; 3 En. 18.18), and the authority includes forbidding and permitting (literally, "binding" and "loosing")—a controversial subject. This authority has been taken to refer to exorcism, eternal destiny, exegetical and doctrinal pronouncements, or church discipline.

16:19

Another difficulty is the interpretation of the two future perfect periphrastic verbal constructions.[8] If the constructions are translated, "will be bound . . . will be loosed," Jesus promises that the apostles' decisions on earth will be ratified in heaven (Matt. 18:18; Cadbury 1939). If they are translated, "will have been bound . . . will have been loosed," the implication is that heaven's prior decisions are ratified on earth by the apostles (cf. 18:18; John 20:23).[9] The former translation subtly emphasizes the apostles' authority more than the former, and it clearly fits better with the order in Matt. 18:18. Ultimately, in any case, Peter binds (forbids) or looses (permits) as he, with the other disciples, proves true to the confession of 16:16.[10] See "The Rock of the Church" below for additional discussion of the exegetical and theological difficulties of 16:18–20.

---

6. Many biblical texts speak of the "building" of the people ("house") of God (e.g., Jer. 12:16; 18:9; 31:4; 33:7; 42:10; Amos 9:11; 1 Cor. 3:9–15; 14:4–5, 12; Eph. 2:19–20; 1 Tim. 3:15; Heb. 3:1–6; 1 Pet. 2:5; 4:17; cf. 1QS 5.5–7; 8.4–10; 9.3–6; CD 3.18–4.10; 1QpHab 12.3; 4Q164).

7. On the various views of the "gates of hades," see C. Brown 1987; W. Davies and Allison 1991: 630–34; Luz 2001: 363–64.

8. These rare constructions (ἔσται δεδεμένον . . . ἔσται λελυμένον; cf. 18:18; Luke 12:52; Heb. 2:13; LXX: 2 Sam. 22:3; Isa. 8:17) use the future indicative of εἰμί with the perfect passive participle. See H. Smyth 1956: §§1955–58 for a summary of the future passive tense in classical Greek.

9. Mantey 1939, 1973, 1981 seems to have advocated this view out of theological concerns about sacerdotalism. Moulton and Turner 1963: 82; N. Turner 1965: 80–82 seem to agree with Mantey, as does Morris 1992: 426. Elbert 1974 follows Mantey in positing a charismatic endowment whereby disciples are made aware of heaven's prior decrees in matters of binding and loosing. S. Porter 1988 critiques Mantey's syntactical arguments.

10. Dayton 1945 handles this matter in depth with helpful citations from extrabiblical Greek literature. Although there is little help with 16:19, the periphrastic participle is discussed in BDF §§352–54; Moule 1959: 16–19; Moulton 1906: 225–27; Moulton and

e. Jesus Warns That His Messianic Identity Must Be Kept Secret (16:20)

16:20   After the remarkable revelatory moment of 16:16–17, it is shocking that Jesus warns the disciples against making him known as the Messiah (cf. 8:4; 9:30; 12:16; 17:9). Jesus probably does this to lessen the excitement of the crowd, which tends to view the Messiah as a merely political figure. His warning may also be due to the increasing opposition of the Jewish leaders. It also reflects the principle of God's sovereignty in election (7:6; 11:25–27; 13:10–17).

The Rock of the Church

Since the Reformation, 16:18 has loomed large in discussions between Protestants and Roman Catholics. In response to Roman Catholic teaching about Peter as the first pope and about apostolic succession, many Protestants have argued that Jesus did not mean that Peter was the rock.[11] It has been suggested that Jesus was speaking of himself (Lenski 1961: 626; Walvoord 1974: 123; Wilcox 1975) or of Peter's confession (most credibly argued by Caragounis 1989; cf. Calvin 1972: 2.188; McNeile 1915: 241; Toussaint 1980: 201–2) as the foundation of the church. Gundry (1994: 334–35) argues that 16:18 alludes to 7:24 and that Jesus means that he will build his church on his own words. But the distance of 7:24 from 16:18 renders such an allusion extremely subtle at best. It is also argued that Peter cannot be the rock, since the name Peter (Πέτρος, *Petros*) is masculine and the word rock (πέτρα, *petra*) is feminine. But grammatical precision is not required in metaphors such as this. Another argument is that Peter is not the foundation of the church because πέτρα means bedrock and Πέτρος means an individual stone. But this extremely subtle distinction would make metaphorical speech impossible. Jesus is speaking of Peter in 16:18 just as clearly as Peter is speaking of Jesus in 16:16 (France 1985: 254).[12]

In the NT, the "foundation" metaphor refers to Jesus's teaching (7:24), Jesus himself (1 Cor. 3:10), Jesus's apostles (Eph. 2:20; Rev. 21:14), and repentance (Heb. 6:1). The context of a metaphor determines the entity to which it points. Here Jesus's response to Peter's confession is a pun, or paronomasia, on the nickname he has evidently just given Peter (Matt. 4:18; 10:2). The pun concerns Peter's unique role as the model disciple in Matthew. Peter's future role as preacher to Jews and Gentiles (Acts 2, 10)

Howard 1920; Moulton and Turner 1963: 87–89; Wallace 1996: 647–50; Winer 1882: 437–40; R. Young 1994: 161–62; Zerwick 1963 §360–62.

11. Exceptions include Boring 1995: 345; Hare 1993: 189–90; Overman 1996: 240–41, 246–50; Plummer 1915: 228–29; Schweizer 1975: 341.

12. On the complicating matter of the likely Aramaic original כֵּיפָא (Cephas), see John 1:42; 1 Cor. 1:12; Gal. 1:18; J. K. Elliott 1972; Fitzmyer in E. Best and Wilson 1979: 121–31.

is also projected here. Jesus is not speaking of himself as the foundation of the church, since he describes himself as the builder. Neither is Peter's apostolic confession the foundation of the church—he, as the confessing apostle, is that foundation. And it is not Peter alone but as first among equals, since the context makes it clear that Peter is speaking for the apostles as a whole in Matt. 16:16 (D. Turner 1991; Viviano 1990b: 660). This best fits the Matthean context, and it also coheres with other NT texts that speak of an apostolic foundation for the church (Eph. 2:20; Rev. 21:14). The Baptist scholar J. Broadus (1886: 355–58) recognized this 120 years ago, and most of the recent evangelical commentators on Matthew concur.[13]

The real difficulty Protestants have with the Roman Catholic teaching concerning Peter is the notion of sole apostolic succession emanating from Peter as the first bishop of Rome (Calvin 1972: 2.189–90; Morris 1992: 424). This dogma is anachronistic for Matthew, who knows nothing about Peter being the first pope or of the primacy of Rome over other Christian churches. Matthew would not have endorsed the idea of Peter's infallibility or sole authority in the church, since Peter speaks as a representative of the other apostles and often makes mistakes (15:15; 16:16; 17:4, 25; 18:21; 19:27; 26:33–35; cf. Acts 11:1–18; Gal. 2:11–14). In 18:18, binding and loosing is a function of the church, not Peter. Peter is later sent by the church and is accountable to the church (Acts 8:14; 11:1–18). James presides over Peter, and Paul rebukes Peter (Acts 15; Gal. 2:11–14). Peter himself speaks of Jesus as the chief shepherd, senior pastor, or *pontifex maximus* of the church (1 Pet. 5:4).[14]

The Keys and Binding and Loosing

Jesus also speaks of Peter as custodian of the keys of the kingdom. The linking of the "foundation" and "key" metaphors indicates that one cannot divorce the church and the kingdom (as do W. Allen 1912: 177; Toussaint 1980: 204–5) and that the church is the agency that extends the kingdom on earth. Peter and the other apostles (Kingsbury 1979: 73) carry out their foundational ecclesiastical role through handling the keys or exercising kingdom authority (cf. Isa. 22:15, 22; Rev. 1:18; 3:7; 9:1–6; 20:1–3). This authority is exercised through binding and loosing.[15] Some scholars stress the idea that keys are a metaphor of authority in exorcism

13. E.g., Blomberg 1992a: 251–53; Bruner 1990: 573–74; Carson 1984: 368; France 1985: 254–56; Hagner 1995a: 469–71; Hendriksen 1973: 645–49; Keener 1999: 426–27; Morris 1992: 422–24; Ridderbos 1987: 303–4.
14. On Peter, see Allison 1992c; R. Brown et al. 1973; Bruner 1990: 579–82; Cullmann 1962b; W. Davies and Allison 1991: 647–52; Hauerwas 2006: 149–53; Hoffmann in Lange 1980: 415–40; Kingsbury 1979; Luz 2001: 366–77; Nau 1992; D. Turner 1991; Witherington 2006: 311–15.
15. On binding and loosing, see Basser 1985; Bornkamm 1970; Derrett 1983a; Duling 1987; Emerton 1962; Hiers 1985; Marcus 1988b.

(T. Levi 18.12; T. Sol. 1.14; Hiers 1985). Others understand authority over entrance to be in view: the apostles, through their confession of Jesus, control who may enter the church and have their sins forgiven (cf. Matt. 10:7; 13:19–23; 24:24; 28:18–20; Calvin 1972: 2.187–88; Falk 1974; Schweitzer 1968: 371n1). Others compare 16:19 to 18:18 and conclude that binding and loosing describe church discipline. This is supported by references to rabbinic texts[16] where the motif of binding and loosing refers to halakic interpretation of biblical law resulting in specific behaviors being permitted or forbidden (Beare 1981: 335; W. Davies and Allison 1991: 638–39; Overman 1996: 245–46; B. Robinson 1984; Acts 15:10?).

It is difficult to judge among the above interpretations. Perhaps it is best (with Barclay 1975: 2.144–46) to combine the ideas of entry into the kingdom (Matt. 16:19a, the "keys") and maintenance of acceptable life within the community (16:19b–c, "binding" and "loosing"). If so, the "doctrine" and "discipline" are really one (Bruner 1990: 577), and "through preaching the will of God, . . . the authorized agent opens the door to the Reign of God or shuts it off" (Schnackenburg 2002: 160).

But interpreting 16:19 in terms of 18:18 may be problematic. It appears that people, not behaviors, are bound or loosed in 16:19 (cf. 23:13; Luke 11:52; Carson 1984: 372–74). It is somewhat anachronistic to read the rabbinic usage of binding and loosing back into Matthew. In context, the imagery of Matt. 16:16–19 concerns the building of the church by the entrance of those who echo the apostolic confession of Jesus as Messiah, Son of God. As the foundational leaders of the church, the agency that extends the kingdom on earth, Peter and the apostles are the gatekeepers of the kingdom. They guide the ongoing authoritative proclamation of the truth of 16:16, and in doing so, they permit entrance to the kingdom through the church for those who confess Jesus. Those who do not confess Jesus are forbidden entrance. (See W. Davies and Allison 1991: 635–39; Hagner 1995a: 472–74; Hiers 1985 for further discussion of the possibilities.)

Additional Notes

16:13. The major variants of this verse exhibit changes in word order and the addition of με. UBS[4] reads τίνα λέγουσιν οἱ ἄνθρωποι εἶναι, supported by B and certain early versions. ℵ* varies the word order to τίνα οἱ ἄνθρωποι εἶναι λέγουσιν. Two other variants add με, either before (L, Δ, Θ, f[13], Byz, Lect; cf. Mark 8:27; Luke 9:18) or after (C, W) λέγουσιν.

16:20. The shorter reading ὁ χριστός is well attested (ℵ*, B, L, Δ, Θ, f[1], f[13], and others). The longer readings Ἰησοῦς ὁ χριστός (ℵ[2], C, W, Byz, Lect) and ὁ χριστὸς Ἰησοῦς (D) seem to be tautologous.

---

16. E.g., b. Ḥag. 3b; cf. CD 13.9–10; Josephus, J.W. 1.111; Overman 1990b: 104–6.

12. Jesus's Suffering and a Model of Discipleship (16:21–28)

In this passage (cf. Mark 8:31–9:1; Luke 9:22–27) Jesus's crucial first passion prediction (Matt. 16:21; cf. 17:22–23; 20:18–19; M. Black 1969; Feuillet 1967–68) is contested by Peter (16:21–23) and becomes an occasion for teaching all the disciples about the essence of following Jesus (16:24–28). Peter's astonishingly rapid change from the foundation of the church to a stumbling stone in Jesus's path to the cross (16:18, 23) teaches all disciples that to be Christ-centered is to be cross-centered (Bruner 1990: 587–88). The prospect of persecution and martyrdom for God's messengers is firmly entrenched in the Bible and in this Gospel (5:11–12; 10:16–39; 21:33–46; 23:29–39; cf. 2 Chron. 24:19–21; 36:15–16).

The unit outline is as follows:

a. Jesus's first passion prediction (16:21)
b. The exchange between Jesus and Peter (16:22–23)
c. The teaching about discipleship (16:24–28)
   i. The essence of discipleship (16:24)
   ii. Three explanations of the necessity of discipleship (16:25–28)

Exegesis and Exposition

²¹From that time Jesus began to make known to his disciples that he must go to Jerusalem, and suffer many things from the elders and chief priests and legal experts, and be killed, and be raised up on the third day. ²²And Peter took him aside and began to rebuke him, "God forbid it, Lord! This shall never happen to you." ²³But he turned and said to Peter, "Get behind me, Satan! You are a stumbling block to me; for you are not setting your mind on God's interests but on human interests."

²⁴Then Jesus told his disciples, "If any one wishes to come after me, that person must practice self-denial and take up the cross and follow me. ²⁵For the one who wishes to save one's life will lose it; but the one who loses one's life for my sake will find it. ²⁶For what will it profit one to gain the whole world and forfeit one's soul? Or what will one give in exchange for one's soul? ²⁷For the Son of Man is going to come in the glory of his Father with his angels, and then he will repay each person according to ⌜what that person has done⌝. ²⁸Truly I tell

you, there are some of those standing here who will not taste death until they see the Son of Man coming in his kingdom."

a. Jesus's First Passion Prediction (16:21)

16:21 At a second crucial point in the narrative (cf. 4:17), Jesus begins a new activity. According to one view of the structure of Matthew, the phrase "from then on" begins the third major section of the narrative (cf. 4:17; Bauer 1988; Kingsbury 1989: 89). This threefold view of Matthew's structure has not been followed here (see the introduction to this commentary and Neirynck 1988), but nonetheless 16:21 remains the first of four times in Matthew where Jesus unambiguously announces his death and resurrection to his disciples (cf. 17:22–23; 20:17–19; 26:1–2). The rest of the narrative in Matt. 16–28 is encapsulated in this single verse.

Jesus must suffer, be killed, and be raised up (cf. 17:9, 22–23; 20:17–19, 28; 26:2, 12, 20–32).[1] Until now this has only been implied (cf. 1:21; 10:21, 28, 38; 12:14, 40; 14:12–13; 16:4), but now it is revealed as a divine necessity that will fulfill Scripture (17:10; 24:6; 26:54; cf. Luke 24:26–27). The Pharisees and the Sadducees are not mentioned here, but the chief priests were mostly Sadducees, and the legal experts were often associated with the Pharisees. The "elders" here, unlike those in 15:2, to whom traditions were traced, are venerable present leaders, perhaps members of the Sanhedrin, or supreme court (cf. Matt. 21:23; 26:3, 47, 57; 27:1, 3, 12, 20, 41; 28:12; Josephus, *Ant.* 11.83; 12.406; Bornkamm, *TDNT* 6:651–61; Jeremias 1962: 222–32; Klijn 1959). Matthew presents the current leaders of Israel, not the Jewish people as a whole, as united in opposition to Jesus. Even in 27:24–26, the crowd that demands Jesus be crucified is manipulated by the leaders (27:20; cf. 21:45).

b. The Exchange between Jesus and Peter (16:22–23)

16:22 In 16:22 Peter exposes a fundamental misunderstanding of Jesus's mission (cf. Mark 8:31–9:1; Luke 9:22–27). His words strongly protest against what Jesus has just said about his death and resurrection.[2] Jesus's death is incompatible with Peter's notion of God's plan for the Messiah. Peter's Messiah is evidently the glorious Messiah who judges the world and reigns over it (Matt. 16:27–28), not one who suffers. Peter grievously errs here, but even the biblical prophets had difficulty reconciling the

---

1. Jesus's destiny is expressed by δεῖ as a divine necessity (17:10; 24:6; 26:54; cf. Acts 27:26; Rev. 1:1; 22:6; T. Naph. 7.1). See W. Bennett 1975; Fascher 1954; Grundmann, *TDNT* 2:21–25. The implied prophetic basis for this necessary course of action (Matt. 26:56) would be texts such as Pss. 22; 34:19–22; 89:38–45; 118:10–25; Isa. 52–53; Dan. 7; Zech. 13:7–9.

2. On ἵλεώς σοι, see the LXX: Gen. 43:23; 2 Sam. 20:20; 23:17; 1 Chron. 11:19; Isa. 54:10; 1 Macc. 2:21; see also Jos. Asen. 6.4. Literally, it reads, "[May God be] merciful to you!" but in the LXX it can render חָלִילָה, which means "far be it" (1 Sam. 14:45; 2 Sam. 20:20; 1 Chron. 11:19; BDB 321). חָלִילָה is rendered by μὴ γένοιτο in Gen. 44:7, 17; Josh. 24:16. BDF §128.5 argues for "Far be it from you, Lord!" (cf. KJV and Vulgate).

sufferings and glory of the Messiah (1 Pet. 1:10–12). Peter's disillusionment with the prospect of Jesus's suffering is not unlike John's doubt while in prison (cf. Matt. 11:1–6).

Jesus's rebuke of Peter echoes the words he used at his temptation to confront Satan (4:10).³ It is striking that in so short a time Peter has gone from being the rock-solid foundation on which Jesus will build the church (16:18) to being a dangerous trap or a stone over which Jesus may trip (cf. 18:7; Isa. 8:14; Wis. 14:11; 1 Macc. 5:4; Ps. Sol. 4.23; Humbert 1954; Stählin, *TDNT* 7:338–58). This is due to Peter's mental fixation on human priorities, not divine revelation. Matthew 16:23 is the polar opposite of 16:17: Peter confesses Jesus as Messiah because of divine revelation, but he opposes Jesus's passion prediction because he thinks in line with human interests, not God's. Jesus's sharp rebuke does not mean that Jesus identifies Peter with the devil but that Peter's opposition to the cross makes him Jesus's adversary. Peter's attempt to keep Jesus from doing the Father's will is similar to Satan's (4:8–10), but it is crucial to note that despite his misunderstanding, Peter still calls Jesus "Lord."

16:23

Peter's swift shift from blessed confessor to rebuked adversary speaks loudly to every disciple of Jesus—"Peter's pre-eminence makes his misunderstanding in effect universal" (W. Davies and Allison 1991: 665). Peter's mind-set becomes momentarily satanic, since he seeks to dissuade Jesus from following the Father's will to the cross (cf. 4:8–9). Peter seems to hear only that Jesus will be killed; the words about resurrection do not register. Disciples today likewise often do not grasp that their present sufferings are not worthy to be compared to future glory (16:27; cf. Rom. 8:18; 2 Tim. 2:11–13). Those who seek to follow Jesus still need periodic reorientation to kingdom values (cf. Matt. 20:20–28). Glory and rewards await faithful disciples (19:27–29), but these come only after a life of self-denying service that follows in the steps of Jesus to the cross, as 16:24–28 shows.

c. The Teaching about Discipleship (16:24–28)

i. The Essence of Discipleship (16:24)

Jesus's stinging rebuke of Peter (compare 16:23 with 4:10) becomes an opportunity for Jesus to explain that the cross defines not only his own future but also the disciples' future (cf. 10:38). Jesus turns from the model disciple, Peter, to the disciples as a whole with the message of cross before crown, suffering before glory, service before reign. The

16:24

3. Here Jesus says ὕπαγε ὀπίσω μου, σατανᾶ whereas 4:10 has simply ὕπαγε, σατανᾶ. In 16:24 Jesus describes discipleship as "coming after him" (ὀπίσω μου ἐλθεῖν). In light of this, the rebuke of 16:23 may not be "Get away from me" but "Get back behind me" (as a genuine follower). Current slang might be "Back me up."

self-denial required in following Jesus entails nothing less than death. The imagery is probably taken from the Roman custom of having the condemned person take up the horizontal beam of the cross (*patibulum*) and carry it to the place of execution, where the vertical post has already been erected (Fitzmyer 1978). Peter has voiced a way of thinking that is evidently pervasive among the disciples, and so all of them must be shown their fundamental error. The way of the cross is for the present; glory and reward will come only in the future, when Jesus comes again to reign. Discipleship means certain death.

ii. Three Explanations of the Necessity of Discipleship (16:25–28)

16:25–27   As 16:24 reiterates 10:38, so 16:25–27 expounds 10:39. Three reasons support the point in 16:24 about Christlike self-denial.[4] All three focus on the prospect of final judgment, although the first two do so implicitly.

The first is a parallel oxymoron stating that self-preservation in the present life leads to ultimate self-destruction, and self-denial leads to ultimate self-fulfillment (16:25; cf. 10:39). Those who think they may avoid the cross and save their lives will in the end lose their lives, but those who accept the cross will find their lives after all.

The second reason for self-denial speaks of the folly of gaining material wealth in the present life and ultimately losing one's own soul (16:26; cf. 4:8; 6:19–24; Ps. 49:7–9; Eccles. 1:3; Luke 12:13–21; 1 Tim. 6:6–19; Rev. 3:17–18; *m. 'Abot* 4.17; 2 Bar. 51.15; Sir. 11:18–19; 1 En. 108.10). The implication is that one does not experience true humanness in the present life or find ultimate acceptance with God by acquiring goods but by sacrificing one's own interests while serving others. The stress on self-denial here should be contrasted with its polar opposite, the denial of Jesus, in Matt. 10:33; 26:34–35, 70–75.

The third reason for taking up one's cross is the near prospect of future reward at the glorious return of Jesus with his angels (13:40–41; 24:30–31; 25:31; 26:64; cf. Zech. 14:5).[5] The language of Matt. 16:27b echoes several OT passages, including Pss. 28:4; 62:12; Prov. 24:12 (cf. Rom. 2:6; 14:12; 1 Cor. 3:10–15; 2 Cor. 5:10; 11:15; 2 Tim. 4:14; 1 Pet. 1:17; Rev. 20:12; 22:12; Sir. 35:24; Ps. Sol. 2.16; 17.8–10; T. Job 17.3; *L.A.B.* 3.10).

16:28   In 16:27 Jesus promises his disciples that their lives of self-denial will be rewarded when he returns in his Father's glory (19:28; 25:31; Luke

---

4. In these three verses, the conjunction γάρ introduces explanatory clauses supporting the idea of 16:24. "The logic is relentless" (Carson 1984: 379). The passage is also tied together with catchwords: θέλει/θέλῃ (vv. 24–25); δώσει/ἀποδώσει (vv. 26–27); and ὁ υἱός/τὸν υἱὸν τοῦ ἀνθρώπου (vv. 27–28). Perhaps Paul was reflecting on these dominical traditions when he wrote texts such as Rom. 6:2–11; Gal. 2:20; Col. 3:3.

5. In view of its use in 2:13; 17:12, 22; 24:6 and the upshot of 16:28, μέλλει implies that the coming of Jesus will occur sooner rather than later.

9:32; 1 En. 45.3; 55.4; 61.8; 62.2; 69.29) with his angels. This clearly refers to the coming of Jesus to the earth and the final judgment (cf. Matt. 13:40–41; 24:30–31; 25:31; 26:64). But 16:28 is perplexing because it stresses the certainty of this future coming by stating that some of Jesus's contemporaries will live to see "the Son of Man coming in his kingdom."[6] All of Jesus's disciples died long ago, and so either Matthew was wrong (W. Allen 1907: 183; Beare 1981: 360, 472–73; Boring 1995: 351; Hare 1993: 197–98; Plummer 1915: 236–37) or the "coming" spoken of here is not the event that ushers in the final judgment. Those who take the latter option suggest that Jesus is speaking of his transfiguration (Blomberg 1992a: 261; Keener 1999: 436; Schnackenburg 2002: 164; Toussaint 1980: 209; many patristic sources and possibly 2 Pet. 1:16–18), his resurrection (W. Davies and Allison 1991: 679; Meier 1979: 26–41, 120–21; 1980b: 188), his sending the Spirit at Pentecost (McNeile 1915: 248), or the judgment of Jerusalem in 70 CE (Alford 1968: 1.177; Hagner 1995a: 486–87). Many attempt to see Matt. 16:28 as a generic prediction of Christ's future glory up to his return to earth, encompassing the resurrection, ascension, Pentecost, and present heavenly session.[7]

Although the last view mentioned above has merit, the first seems most likely. Viewed from the perspective of 16:28, the transfiguration, which occurs only six days later (17:1), is a foreshadowing of the future glorious coming. "Probably the transfiguration proleptically introduces the whole eschatological sphere" (Keener 1999: 436). The transfiguration will be a glorious experience (17:2, 5), but it will be only a temporary preview of what will come with permanence when Jesus returns to the earth. Some of those who hear Jesus make the prediction in 16:28 (i.e., Peter and James and John) will witness the transfiguration (17:1–2). In 2 Pet. 1:16–18, Peter seems to reflect on his participation in the temporary glory of the transfiguration as a confirming anticipation of Christ's powerful return. (For further discussion, see Beasley-Murray 1986: 187–93 and the comments on 10:23.)

Matthew 16 continues to underline the theme of opposition from the Pharisees, but now for the first time Jesus clearly tells the disciples that the opposition will lead to his death (16:1–12, 21). Once again the "little faith" of the disciples is confronted as Jesus prepares them to carry on the kingdom mission in his absence (16:8). In spite of their weakness, they have received the Father's revelation that Jesus is the Messiah, and they will become the foundation of the messianic community that Jesus will build (16:16–18). Their future will be tied to that of Jesus;

---

6. On the expression οἵτινες οὐ μὴ γεύσωνται θανάτου, see John 8:52; Heb. 2:9; 2 Esd. (4 Ezra) 6:26; *b. Yoma* 78b; Chilton in Livingstone 1980: 29–36.

7. Barclay 1975: 2.156; Carson 1984: 380–82; France 1985: 261; Hendriksen 1973: 659–60; Morris 1992: 434–35; Ridderbos 1987: 314–15. Calvin 1972: 2.196 is often cited as an advocate of the resurrection view, but he clearly speaks not only of the resurrection but also of subsequent glorious events as fulfilling Jesus's prediction.

they will likewise bear a cross on their way to future glorious reward (16:24–28).

Additional Note

16:27. UBS⁴ reads the collective singular τὴν πρᾶξιν (with the strong support of ℵ², B, C, D, L, W, *Byz, Lect*), but the more usual plural expression τὰ ἔργα occurs in ℵ*, F, 1, and many early versions (cf. Ps. 62:13). The UBS⁴ reading seems to have the better external support and is the more difficult reading.

13. The Transfiguration and Its Aftermath (17:1–13)

This passage (cf. Mark 9:2–13; Luke 9:28–36) contains a brief account of the transfiguration of Jesus (Matt. 17:1–3), a lesson on the preeminence of Jesus (17:4–8), and a lesson on the continuity of John the Baptist with Elijah and with Jesus himself (17:9–13). After the brief transfiguration account, Peter's reaction to Jesus's glory is countered by the heavenly voice heard already at Jesus's baptism (17:4–8; cf. 3:17). Second, Jesus again forbids the disciples to make him known (cf. 16:20), which leads to their question about the coming of Elijah (17:9–13). Jesus answers the question somewhat cryptically, speaking of a past and a future coming of "Elijah." When he compares his own approaching suffering to what has already happened to this "Elijah," the disciples finally grasp that he is speaking of John the Baptist.[1] The unit outline is as follows:

a. The transfiguration (17:1–3)
    i. The setting (17:1)
    ii. Jesus is transfigured (17:2)
    iii. The appearance of Moses and Elijah (17:3)
b. The voice from heaven (17:4–8)
    i. Peter's suggestion (17:4)
    ii. The divine message (17:5)
    iii. The aftermath (17:6–8)
c. Jesus, John, and Elijah (17:9–13)
    i. Jesus's command (17:9)
    ii. The disciples' question (17:10)
    iii. Jesus's answer (17:11–12)
    iv. The disciples' understanding (17:13)

Exegesis and Exposition

[1]Six days later Jesus took with him Peter and James and John his brother and led them up on a high mountain by themselves. [2]And he was transfigured

---

1. On the transfiguration, see Chilton 1980; Danker 1990; T. Donaldson 1985: 136–56; Feuillet 1958; Frieling 1969; Liefeld in Longenecker and Tenney 1974: 162–79; Liefeld in J. Green and McKnight 1992: 834–41; McGuckin 1986; Moses 1996; Murphy-O'Connor 1987; Pedersen 1975; Ramsay 1946; Refoulé 1993; M. Smith 1980; Trites 1979. For additional bibliography, see T. Best 1981; W. Davies and Allison 1991: 708–9.

before them; and his face shone like the sun, and his garments became as white as ⌐light⌐. ³And behold, Moses and Elijah appeared to them, talking with him. ⁴Peter said to Jesus, "Lord, it is good for us to be here; if you wish, ⌐I will make⌐ three shelters here, one for you and one for Moses and one for Elijah." ⁵While he was still speaking, a bright cloud suddenly covered them, and behold, a voice from the cloud said, "This is my beloved Son, with whom I am well pleased; listen to him!" ⁶And when the disciples heard this, they fell face down and were terrified. ⁷And Jesus came to them and touched them and said, "Get up and do not be afraid." ⁸And when they looked up, they saw no one except Jesus himself alone.

⁹And as they were coming down from the mountain, Jesus ordered them, "Tell the vision to no one until the Son of Man has been raised from the dead." ¹⁰And his disciples asked him, "Why, then, do the legal experts say that Elijah must come first?" ¹¹And he answered, "Elijah is indeed coming and he will restore all things; ¹²but I tell you that Elijah has already come, and they did not acknowledge him but did to him whatever they pleased. So also the Son of Man is going to suffer at their hands." ¹³Then the disciples understood that he had spoken to them about John the Baptist.

a. The Transfiguration (17:1–3)

i. The Setting (17:1)

17:1 If one assumes the view of 16:28 suggested above, Jesus's promise that some of his disciples would see a royal "coming" before they died is fulfilled only six days later. Peter, James, and John (three of the first four disciples Jesus called; 4:18–22) observe the miracle (cf. 26:37). Those who accompany Jesus may remind the reader of Moses's companions Aaron, Nadab, and Abihu (Exod. 24:1). The unnamed high mountain may remind the reader of the giving of the law to Moses from Sinai (cf. Matt. 5:1; 15:29; Exod. 24:12–18; 31:18; 33:7–11; 34:29–35). On the typology of the transfiguration, see "The Transfiguration and Theology" following the comments on 17:6–8.

ii. Jesus is Transfigured (17:2)

17:2 The traditional yet ambiguous term "transfiguration" illustrates the difficulty in describing the transformation of Jesus. Jesus's metamorphosis (μετεμορφώθη, *metemorphōthē*; cf. Rom. 12:2; 2 Cor. 3:18; Philo, *Moses* 1.57) was evidently more than the mere reflection of an external radiance. Matthew describes this glorious event with two dazzling similes: Jesus's face, like that of Moses (Exod. 34:29–35; Philo, *Moses* 1.70; *L.A.B.* 12.1), shines like the sun (cf. Rev. 1:16; 10:1; T. Levi 18.40); and his clothes become white as light (cf. Ps. 104:2; Rev. 3:4–5; 7:9; 1 En. 63.15–16). For similarly radiant angelic beings, see Matt. 28:3; Dan. 10:6; 1 En. 71.1. Perhaps Jesus's transfiguration is intended to anticipate the eschatological radiance of God's people (cf. Matt. 13:43; Rev. 3:4–5; 7:9; Dan. 12:3; 1 En. 38.4; 104.2; 2 Bar. 51.1–3, 10, 12; 2 Esd. [4 Ezra] 7:97).

iii. The Appearance of Moses and Elijah (17:3)

Given other Matthean allusions, the appearance of Moses (cf. 5:17; Deut. 18:15–19) and Elijah (Matt. 11:14; 17:10–13; Mal. 4:5–6) to converse with Jesus is noteworthy although tantalizingly brief. Some scholars argue that Moses and Elijah represent respectively the OT law and the prophets (Hagner 1995a: 493; cf. Matt. 5:17; 7:12). Elijah's zeal for the law is noted in 1 Macc. 2:58 as the reason for his translation to heaven (2 Kings 2:11). Others point out that both had mountaintop experiences with God (Gundry 1994: 343), Moses at Sinai (Exod. 19:20) and Elijah at Horeb (1 Kings 19:8–14). In later Jewish reflection on Deut. 18:15–19, Moses was to accompany Elijah's return (Deut. Rab. 3.17). (See Thrall 1970.) In any event, Moses and Elijah were both key prophetic figures, and so their conversation with Jesus is fitting. If their presence is understood typologically, Jesus is the "prophet like Moses" spoken of in Deut. 18:15 (Allison 1993b: 243–48), and John is Elijah (Matt. 17:10–13). Luke 9:31 indicates ominously that the conversation concerned Jesus's upcoming departure from the world, a departure that would be fulfilled in Jerusalem.

17:3

b. The Voice from Heaven (17:4–8)

i. Peter's Suggestion (17:4)

Peter's spontaneous reaction to this glorious manifestation perhaps implies a reenactment of the Feast of Tabernacles (סֻכּוֹת, sukkôt, booths; cf. Lev. 23:42–43; Zech. 14:16–21; Boobyer 1942; Riesenfeld 1947). This festival centered on the harvest, which can be a metaphor for eschatological judgment (Matt. 3:12; 13:39; Carson 1984: 386). In this view, Peter would be thinking of the imminent fulfillment of Jesus's words in 16:27. The alternative suggestion that Peter is thinking in terms of memorializing the "tent of meeting" where God spoke with Moses outside the camp (Exod. 33:7–11; Num. 12:5–9; Hagner 1995a: 493) does not account for *three* dwellings. It is possible that Peter simply wishes to be hospitable.

17:4

ii. The Divine Message (17:5)

Peter's well-intentioned suggestion does acknowledge Jesus's lordship and prerogatives, yet his plan would blur the uniqueness of Jesus as God's Son. He is interrupted by the heavenly voice, which reiterates the words of endorsement heard at Jesus's baptism (Matt. 3:17; cf. Ps.

17:5

2:7; Isa. 42:1) with a significant addition, "Listen to him."[2] This command quashes Peter's idea in language that alludes to Deut. 6:4; 18:15, 18–19. As the eschatological prophet like Moses, Jesus alone must be obeyed.[3] It is significant that this endorsement occurs soon after Jesus's clear announcement of his upcoming suffering in Jerusalem and Peter's negative response to it (Matt. 16:21–22).[4] The disciples are evidently still somewhat perplexed by the prospect of a suffering Messiah, and this renewed divine endorsement of Jesus is necessary. The coming of the voice from the bright cloud is similar to revelations to Israel from clouds in Moses's day (Exod. 34:29–35; 40:34–38; cf. 2 Macc. 2:8; 2 Cor. 3:7–18). The cloud's brightness seems oxymoronic, but it suggests the Shechinah, or visible manifestation of God's glory (Exod. 24:16–17; cf. Ezek. 1:4; 10:4). It also anticipates the accompanying clouds at Jesus's return (Matt. 16:27; 24:30; 26:64).

Setting up tents for Moses, Elijah, and Jesus would have two detrimental results: the damning of Jesus with faint praise and the arrogation of messianic status to Moses and Elijah. As great as God's servants Moses and Elijah were, they were not God's beloved Son (3:17). Moses was the prototypical prophet who spoke of Jesus as the definitive eschatological prophet whose words must be obeyed (Deut. 18:15–19). Elijah courageously stood for the law of Moses, but Jesus, the definitive teacher of the law, brings it to its ultimate goal (Matt. 5:17–48). However well meaning Peter's proposal is, it suggests the unthinkable: that Moses and Elijah are on the same level as Jesus. But Jesus alone is the beloved Son who pleases the Father, and Jesus alone must be obeyed. Other scriptural sources suggest that Peter learned this lesson on Jesus's preeminence (cf. Acts 3:22–23; 2 Pet. 1:16–19).

iii. The Aftermath (17:6–8)

17:6–8 Peter's enthusiasm rapidly changes to terror at the heavenly voice from the cloud (cf. Josephus, *Ant.* 4.326). He and the other disciples fall on

---

2. The genitive absolute ἔτι αὐτοῦ λαλοῦντος indicates that Peter still had more to say, perhaps to support his suggestion. Genitive absolutes are used at several transitional points in the Matt. 17 narrative: 17:5, 9, 14, 22, 24, 26. In 17:14, 26 the genitive participle is not accompanied by a genitive substantive (cf. BDF §423.6). Cf. 8:1, 5, 16, 28; 9:32, 33; 18:24, 25; 20:29; 21:10, 23; 22:41; 24:3; Wallace 1996: 654–55.

3. Although hearing is not necessarily obeying (7:24, 26; 13:13–15), the command ἀκούετε αὐτοῦ enjoins obedient action, not merely passive reception of Jesus's teaching. Cf. 10:14; 11:15; 13:9; 18:15–16; and שׁמע in texts such as Exod. 6:12; Deut. 6:4; 18:15, 18–19; 2 Chron. 28:11. W. Davies and Allison (1991: 684) present a plausible chiastic analysis of Matt. 17:1–8 that places the heavenly voice at the structural center of the pericope. Be that as it may, the message of the heavenly voice is, without question, the theological center of the pericope.

4. On the possible nuances of the aorist verb εὐδόκησα, see the discussion on 3:17. It seems most likely that the aorist here, as in 3:17, is ingressive, not gnomic. Jesus's baptism at the outset of his ministry brought pleasure to the Father, as did Jesus's recent statement of commitment to the Father's plan that he go to Jerusalem (16:21).

their faces until Jesus comes, touches them, and tells them to get up and stop being afraid.[5] When they look around, Moses and Elijah are gone and only Jesus is with them, which underlines the word from heaven that Jesus alone is to be obeyed.[6] Boring (1995: 364) plausibly argues that the sole presence of Jesus at the end of this pericope contrasts with Peter's previous idea to build three tabernacles and teaches that Jesus is now the locus of God's presence with his disciples (1:23; 28:20). (Whether there is a theological parallel between 17:7 and 28:18 is discussed in Stein 1976.) As Jesus travels ominously closer to Jerusalem, the disciples must not lose their focus on him.

The Transfiguration and Theology

The obvious biblical background for understanding the transfiguration is Moses's reflection of God's glorious presence on Sinai at the giving of the law (Allison 1993b: 243–48; T. Donaldson 1985: 136–56). Common details include:

1. The six-day interval (17:1; Exod. 24:16)
2. The presence of three witnesses (17:1; Exod. 24:1)
3. The high mountain (17:1; Exod. 24:12)
4. The glorious appearance of the central figure (17:2; Exod. 34:29–30, 35; cf. 2 Cor. 3:12–18)
5. The overshadowing cloud (17:5; Exod. 24:15–18)
6. The voice from the cloud (17:5; Exod. 24:16)
7. The fear of those who witnessed the glory (17:6; Exod. 34:29–30)

But in terms of NT biblical theology, the transfiguration should be viewed not as the external illumination of the man Jesus but as the temporary uncovering of the Son of God's intrinsic glory, which has been temporarily veiled and is to be reassumed at the resurrection and the ascension (John 17:4–5, 24; Phil. 2:5–11; Col. 1:16–19; 2:9; Heb. 1:1–4; Rev. 5:6–14). There is also the implication that Jesus's followers will be transformed by his glory at his return.[7] The glory of Jesus as Immanuel (Matt. 1:23) was not borrowed or reflected (Eusebius, *Demonstration of the Gospel* 3.2; Ramsay 1946: 120). As great as Moses was, the law that was initially mediated by him was definitively fulfilled and ultimately interpreted by Jesus. Moses's typological glory pales in comparison with

5. Cf. 8:25–26; 14:26–27; 28:4, 8; cf. Gen. 15:12; 28:17; Exod. 34:30; Deut. 4:33; Dan. 8:17–18; 10:8–12; Ezek. 1:28–2:2; Rev. 1:17; Tob. 12:17; 1 En. 14.13–14; 60.3–4; 71.2–3; 2 En. 1.8; 20.2; 21.2–3; 22.4–5; 3 En. 1.7–9; 4 Macc. 4:11; 2 Esd. (4 Ezra) 4:11; 5:14–15; 10:30; 2 Bar. 13.1–2.
6. The uniqueness of Jesus as sole revelator is emphasized in 17:8 by the use of αὐτός in the phrase αὐτὸν Ἰησοῦν μόνον.
7. Cf. the texts cited in the comments above on 17:2, as well as Exod. 33:18–34:9; Matt. 25:21, 23, 31, 34, 46; 2 Cor. 3:18; W. Davies and Allison 1991: 704–5; Luz 2001: 400–404.

the glory of the antitype, Jesus. Although Jesus appears in the company of Moses, at the end he alone must be obeyed (17:5).

But the manner of Jesus's transfiguration remains as mysterious as the manner of his incarnation as God-with-us (1:23; Luke 1:35; John 1:14, 18). Systematic theologians are challenged by the transfiguration to attempt an explanation of what must ultimately be inexplicable to mere humans. Precisely how the eternal Son of God came to earth as a truly human child and how the divine and human natures of Jesus were implicated in his transfiguration are known to God alone.

The amazing transfiguration of Jesus should not be totally unexpected by Matthew's readers. Jesus was born miraculously and his ministry began with the Father's endorsement. Jesus has performed compassionate works and has definitively and authoritatively taught the Torah. He has supernaturally calmed storms and fed thousands of people with a few loaves of bread. He has promised to return in glory, to judge all humankind, and to reign righteously on the earth. After his resurrection he will receive universal authority, and his presence will accompany his disciples as they disciple all nations until the end of the present age (Matt. 28:18–20). Thus, from the standpoint of Matthew as a whole, the transfiguration fits Jesus's status as the Son of God, his fulfillment of biblical patterns and predictions, and his promise of a future kingdom. The transfiguration is an integral part of Matthew's Son of God Christology and his apocalyptic eschatology. It authenticates Jesus's identity and anticipates his future rule over the world. In the transfiguration the disciples glimpse who Jesus is and what he will do. The worthies Moses and Elijah are only supporting actors in the drama of redemption. As the curtain falls, they have exited and Jesus alone stands at the center of the stage. The heavenly voice's "listen to him" prepares the disciples to hear Jesus "teaching them to observe all things I have commanded you."

c. Jesus, John, and Elijah (17:9–13)

i. Jesus's Command (17:9)

17:9   As they descend the mountain, Jesus commands the disciples not to tell others of his transfiguration until he has risen from the dead. This is the last time Jesus enjoins silence concerning miraculous events (cf. 16:20). Such commands are evidently to avoid "superficial political messianism" (Carson 1984: 388) that would not only confuse the nature of his mission but also exacerbate the enmity of the Jewish leaders. After Jesus has been vindicated by resurrection, the nature of his ministry will be clearer, and the story of his miracles can be told in their proper context (9:6).

ii. The Disciples' Question (17:10)

17:10   The disciples' question shows that despite Jesus's previous words in 11:10–14, they still do not understand how Jesus's death and resurrection relate to the coming of Elijah. The appearance of Elijah with Jesus evidently brings to their minds the current scribal interpretation of Mal. 4:5–6 on the coming of Elijah as a herald of messianic times and the day of the Lord (cf. Sir. 48:10; *m. B. Meṣiʿa* 1.8; 2.8; 3.4–5; *m. ʿEd.* 8.7; *m. Šeqal.* 2.5; *b. Sanh.* 118a; *b. ʿErub.* 43b). Since Elijah had just appeared,[8] they evidently wonder why Jesus still must suffer in Jerusalem and why the restoration spoken of by Malachi must be delayed.

iii. Jesus's Answer (17:11–12)

Jesus's complex answer has three elements. First, he alludes to a yet-future coming of Elijah, who will restore all things (17:11; cf. 11:14; 19:28; Acts 1:6; 3:21; Mal. 3:22–23 LXX [4:5–6 Eng.]).[9] It is not completely clear whether Jesus is simply acknowledging the scribal teaching before he corrects it in Matt. 17:12[10] or whether he affirms a past coming of Elijah as John as well as a future glorious coming of Elijah (Gundry 1994: 347). See the comments on 17:13. Second, Jesus reiterates (cf. 11:14) the difficult linkage between John the Baptist and Elijah (17:12a). Third, he connects the maltreatment of John with his own coming suffering in Jerusalem (17:12b). The gist of this is that the disciples should focus on John's past Elijah-like ministry, not the recent appearance of Elijah at Jesus's transfiguration. If they do this, they will understand that John's death foreshadowed the death of Jesus.   **17:11–12**

iv. The Disciples' Understanding (17:13)

In contrast with those who did not recognize John but rejected and executed him, the disciples now understand (cf. 16:12) Jesus's teaching that John's ministry fulfilled Malachi's prophecy and that John's suffering and death anticipated what would happen to Jesus. The understanding of Jesus's disciples or their lack of understanding is a key part of Matthew's story of Jesus's approaching Jerusalem (13:51; 16:9, 12). The ministries of Elijah, John, and Jesus are intricately interwoven. In his own right, John was not Elijah but came to minister in the spirit of Elijah (John 1:21; Luke 1:17). John's ministry as the forerunner of Jesus was in the mold of the one, spoken of by Isaiah, who would prepare the Lord's way (Matt. 3:3; Isa. 40:3; 2 Esd. [4 Ezra] 6:26; Sir. 48:10).   **17:13**

---

8. The conjunction οὖν indicates that the premise of their question is Elijah's appearance with Jesus and Jesus's mention of his resurrection.
9. The combination of the futuristic present ἔρχεται and the future ἀποκαταστήσει can be understood in at least four different ways. See Boring 1995: 364–65 and the comments on 17:13.
10. This seems to be the majority view of the passage. See, e.g., Blomberg 1992a: 266; Carson 1984: 389; Hagner 1995a: 499; McNeile 1915: 253; Ridderbos 1987: 322.

Matthew 17:11 remains perplexing, since it leaves room for a yet-future coming of Elijah.[11] The previous reference to John and Elijah in Matt. 11:14 can also be understood to teach a future coming of Elijah.[12] Revelation 11:3–6, itself perplexing, speaks of the coming of two "witnesses" whose ministry resembles that of Elijah. Whether all of this points to a future return of Elijah himself (John Chrysostom, *Hom. Matt.* 57.1; Gundry 1994: 347) or the coming of one whose office and ministry is Elijah-like (Kaiser 1982; cf. Luke 1:17) is debatable. In this view, Matthew's Elijah-John-Jesus typology includes a humble first coming and glorious second coming for both Elijah/John and Jesus. Boring (1995: 365) insightfully remarks that the understanding of Elijah as the rejected and executed John is just as scandalous as the identification of the Messiah as Jesus, who has announced his own suffering and death. But for this typology to be complete, a future restoring Elijah (Matt. 11:14; 17:11) is just as necessary as a future glorious reigning Jesus (7:21; 13:41; 16:27; 19:28; 24:30; 25:31).[13]

Additional Notes

17:2. Instead of τὸ φῶς, which is supported by strong witnesses from each text type, some Western witnesses (e.g., D and some Latin MSS) have χιών (snow), which is also the less difficult reading.

17:4. Instead of the UBS[4] singular indicative ποιήσω ὧδε (ℵ, B, C, 700*), other readings include the plural indicative (ποιήσομεν ὧδε) and the hortatory subjunctives ποιήσωμεν (579; Mark 9:5; Luke 9:33) and ποιήσωμεν ὧδε (D, L, W, f[13], Byz, Lect). The UBS[4] reading has Peter volunteer, perhaps characteristically, to build the shelters himself; the plural readings involve the other disciples in the proposed project.

11. An important question here is the semantic relationship of the clauses in 17:11–12a introduced by μέν and δέ. In the more common view of the passage, μέν (cf. 3:11; 9:37; 10:13; 13:4, 8, 23, 32; 16:3, 14; 17:11; 20:23; 21:35; 22:5, 8; 23:27, 28; 25:15, 33; 26:41) is understood as "indeed" and merely introduces the common scribal view, which Jesus shows in the δέ clause to be inadequate at best. In this view, the two clauses are taken as antithetical, the first merely conceding the existence of the scribal view and the second correcting it. But on syntactic grounds, the clauses may be complementary, with the first clause conceding the essential correctness of the scribal view and the second clause stating a more important complementary matter, as in 3:11; 9:37; 16:3; 20:23; 22:8; 23:27, 28; 25:33; 26:41.

12. The phrase ὁ μέλλων ἔρχεσθαι in 11:14 probably also speaks of a future coming of Elijah. Similar language is used elsewhere as a messianic title, "the coming one" (3:11; 11:3; 21:9; cf. Ps. 118:26; John 6:14; 11:27; Heb. 10:37), but ὁ μέλλων ἔρχεσθαι implies a futuristic view of Mal. 4:5–6.

13. On Matt. 17:9–13 and related questions, see Allison 1984; Blomberg 1987a; Faierstein 1981; Fitzmyer 1985: 295–96; Kaiser 1982; J. A. Robinson 1958; J. Taylor 1991; Wink 1968: 13–17, 30–33.

14. An Epileptic Boy Healed (17:14–21)

The story of the exorcism of an epileptic boy (cf. Mark 9:14–29; Luke 9:37–43) has two main parts, the healing itself (Matt. 17:14–18) and the subsequent question from the disciples (17:19–21). Both parts contain a request (17:14–16, 19) and a response from Jesus (17:17–18, 20–21). In both parts the disciples' inability (17:16, 19) is contrasted with Jesus's power (17:18, 20). The problem throughout is the lack of faith, both of Jesus's contemporaries (17:17; cf. 3:7; 8:10; 11:16–24; 12:39–42; 13:19–22, 58; 21:32; 23:33, 36; 24:34) and even of his own disciples (17:20; cf. 6:30; 8:26; 14:31; 16:8). This lack of faith is striking when it is contrasted with the glory of Jesus's transfiguration, and it receives Jesus's rebuke in 17:17. Garland (1993: 184) correctly observes that this pericope is not so much about what Jesus is able to do, since this has already been established. Rather, it is about what the disciples will be able to do in Jesus's absence. The exorcism furnishes the occasion for the important pronouncement in 17:20.[1]

This unit can be outlined as follows:

a. The exorcism (17:14–18)
   i. The father's request (17:14–16)
   ii. Jesus's response (17:17–18)
b. A lesson on faith (17:19–21)
   i. The disciples' question (17:19)
   ii. Jesus's answer (17:20–21)

Exegesis and Exposition

[14]When they came to the crowd, a man came up to him, kneeling down before him [15]and saying, "Lord, have mercy on my son, for he has seizures and suffers horribly; for he often falls into the fire and into the water. [16]I brought him to your disciples, but they were not able to cure him." [17]And Jesus answered, "O unbelieving and perverse generation, how long will I be with you? How long will I put up with you? Bring him here to me." [18]And Jesus rebuked the demon, and it came out of him, and the boy was healed from that moment.

[19]Then the disciples came to Jesus privately and said, "Why were we unable to cast it out?" [20]And he said to them, "Because of your ⌜little faith⌝; for truly I tell you, if you have faith the size of a mustard seed, you will say to this mountain, 'Move from here to there,' and it will move; and nothing will be impossible for you. [21]⌜But this kind does not go out except by prayer and fasting.⌝"

---

1. On this pericope, see Derrett 1988b; Duplacy in Jourjon et al. 1961: 272–87; Hahn 1985; Held in Bornkamm, Barth, and Held 1963: 187–92; Schenk 1972; Sterling 1993; Twelftree 1993: 91–97; van der Loos 1965: 397–405; Wilkinson 1967.

a. The Exorcism (17:14–18)

i. The Father's Request (17:14–16)

17:14–16   The father's intercession for his son is in keeping with other episodes in Matthew (8:5–13; 9:18–26; 15:21–28). The boy's epileptic seizures (cf. 4:24; Ross 1978) are life-threatening because they occur when he is near bodies of water or fires for cooking and heating. This is not accidental but sinister: he is demon-possessed (17:18). Jesus's disciples' inability to heal the boy (cf. 2 Kings 4:18–37) is puzzling in view of their commission in Matt. 10:8, but it is explained by a familiar theme in 17:20 (cf. the disciples' failures and misunderstandings in 14:16–21, 26–27, 28–31; 15:16, 23, 33; 16:5, 22; 17:4, 10–11).

ii. Jesus's Response (17:17–18)

17:17–18   Jesus speaks of his contemporaries in very negative terms: they are not only faithless but also morally crooked or depraved (cf. 11:16; 12:39, 45; Deut. 32:5, 20). It is unclear whether Jesus directs this rebuke only to the crowd, including the man whose epileptic son is demon-possessed, or to the crowd and his disciples. Although some conclude that Jesus includes the disciples with the crowd (Blomberg 1992a: 267; W. Davies and Allison 1991: 724), the disciples' "little faith" hardly characterizes them as a faithless and perverse generation. Their problem is addressed in 17:20, and so it is better to take 17:17 as Jesus's exasperation with the crowd, which expects miracles from him but does not grasp his identity and mission (16:13–14). Jesus's repeated rhetorical questions ("how long . . . how long . . .") are striking, since his compassion for the crowd has been frequently stressed (cf. 15:29–32; Isa. 46:4). The questions seem to echo God's complaint against Israel (Num. 14:27) and Isaiah's question (Isa. 6:11; cf. John 14:9). Yet compassion is not lacking here, since Jesus does cast out the demon. On balance, Jesus's "prophetic exasperation" (Hill 1972: 270) is becoming more intense as the shadow of the cross looms larger.

b. A Lesson on Faith (17:19–21)

i. The Disciples' Question (17:19)

17:19   After the instantly efficacious healing, the disciples privately come to Jesus and ask why they were unable to exorcise the demon (cf. 17:16). The pattern here is similar to previous private questions (13:36; 15:12).

ii. Jesus's Answer (17:20–21)

17:20–21   Jesus prefaces his answer with the phrase "Truly I tell you," which stresses the importance and authority of the answer. This phrase occurs on the lips of Jesus more than thirty times in Matthew (cf., e.g., 5:18). The disciples' problem is all too familiar—their "little faith" (cf. 6:30; 8:26;

14:31; 16:8). Their weaknesses have been repeatedly mentioned in the narrative section 13:53–17:27 (e.g., 14:16–21, 26–31; 15:16, 23, 33; 16:5, 22; 17:4, 10–11). Their commission to do miraculous works (10:8) was evidently conditioned upon their faith. Jesus challenges them with hyperboles for both the minuscule size (mustard seed; cf. 13:31) and the huge potential (moving mountains; 17:1, 9; 21:21; 1 Cor. 13:2; cf. Isa. 54:10; Josephus, *Ant.* 2.333; T. Sol. 23.1; *b. Sanh.* 4a; *b. Ber.* 64a; *b. B. Bat.* 3b; *b. Soṭah* 9b) of their faith. When Jesus says, "Nothing will be impossible," he has in mind his commission for them to preach the kingdom and do miraculous works of compassion, not literally to move mountains (Matt. 10:7–8). It is doubtful that the "mountain" metaphor has eschatological overtones here, despite such texts as Isa. 40:3–5; 49:11; Zech. 14:10. See the additional note on the textual problems of 17:21 (cf. Mark 9:29). The idea of this disputed verse is that true faith will manifest itself in prayer and fasting (Matt. 6:16–18) in difficult situations.

Disciples of Jesus are susceptible to the moral and spiritual values of their contemporaries. Jesus's disciples lived among a faithless generation, and they themselves had "little faith." Even those, such as the man with the epileptic son, who believed that Jesus could heal their illnesses had a "faith" that did not recognize that his miracles signified his identity as the Messiah, the Son of the living God, who has authority on earth to forgive sins (9:6). Rather, he was viewed only as a prophet (16:14; 21:11). In contrast, Jesus's disciples have "little," yet genuine, faith, which recognizes and confesses the true identity of their Lord (14:33; 16:16). The issue here is not the intensity or amount of faith but the extent of their ability to perceive the object of faith. The power of faith is in the person to whom it is directed. Jesus's disciples were unable to heal the epileptic boy because they had taken their eyes off Jesus and looked at the obstacles, just as Peter did during the storm when he began to sink (14:30). Faith is not believing that God will do whatever disciples demand but whatever is best for them. God will not perform the disciples' selfish bidding but will empower them to extend his kingdom through word and deed.

Additional Notes

17:20. The UBS[4] reading ὀλιγοπιστίαν (ℵ, B, Θ, *f*[1], *f*[13], 33, 579) is more likely than ἀπιστίαν (C, D, L, W, *Byz, Lect*; cf. ἄπιστος in 17:17), since it better fits the ὀλιγόπιστος theme in Matthew (6:30; 8:26; 14:31; 16:8).

17:21. It is difficult to understand why this verse (τοῦτο δὲ τὸ γένος οὐκ ἐκπορεύεται εἰ μὴ ἐν προσευχῇ καὶ νηστείᾳ) would be omitted by ℵ*, B, Θ, 33, 579 if it were original. Its occurrence in C, D, L, W, *f*[1], *f*[13], *Byz, Lect* may be due to assimilation to Mark 9:29.

15. The Second Passion Prediction (17:22–23)

Jesus evidently moves south from Caesarea Philippi (16:13) back into Galilee here (cf. Mark 9:30–32; Luke 9:43–45). Some versions imply that Jesus spoke these words after the trip (NIV), but it is more likely that he spoke as they traveled (NASB, NRSV).[1] This is the second of four clear passion predictions (cf. 16:21; 20:18–19; 26:1–2), although there have been previous hints (9:15; 10:38; 12:40; 16:4; 17:12). This short section contains a narrative setting (17:22a), the prediction proper (17:22b–23b), and its result (17:23c). (On 17:22–23, see Brodie 1992; W. Thompson 1970: 16–49.)

Exegesis and Exposition

22And as they ⌜were gathering⌝ in Galilee, Jesus said to them, "The Son of Man is going to be handed over into the hands of men; 23and they will kill him, and he will be raised on the third day." And they were deeply grieved.

17:22–23   This second prediction adds the detail that Jesus will be handed over, hinting at Judas's sordid role.[2] Jesus speaks of himself here as the Son of Man and of his enemies with the generic phrase "into the hands of men," which replaces the previous terminology for the religious leaders.[3] Another new feature is the mention of the disciples' deep grief, which anticipates their grief at the Last Supper and Jesus's grief at Gethsemane (26:22, 37).[4] They are finally accepting the stark reality of the impending events in Jerusalem, and they do not seek to dissuade Jesus as Peter did in 16:22. But this deep grief implies that they have not yet grasped the full significance of Jesus's resurrection (Hill 1972: 271).

---

1. The genitive absolute construction συστρεφομένων δὲ αὐτῶν uses the present participle, which normally portrays action simultaneous with the main verb. Cf. BDF §§339, 423.

2. For additional texts that use παραδίδωμι for the betrayal or arrest of John, Jesus, or the disciples, see 4:12; 10:4, 17, 19, 21; 18:34; 20:18–19; 24:9–10; 26:2, 15–16, 21, 23–25, 45–46, 48; 27:2–4, 18, 26; cf. Acts 3:13; Rom. 4:25; 8:32; 1 Cor. 11:23. The passive voice in such texts implies a divine agency that does not violate the moral responsibility of the human betrayers (cf. Acts 2:23).

3. Cf. similar language in texts such as Deut. 1:27; Josh. 2:24; Judg. 2:14; 1 Sam. 30:15; 2 Kings 21:14; Ps. 106:41; Dan. 11:11; 1 Macc. 4:30; Josephus, Ant. 2.20.

4. The verb ἐλυπήθησαν probably should be viewed as ingressive (Wallace 1996: 558–59), indicating that at this point the disciples begin to grieve in earnest as Jesus's repeated passion predictions become all the more real to them.

Additional Note

17:22. UBS⁴ has the unusual συστρεφομένων, found in ℵ, B, *f*¹, 892. The more familiar ἀναστρεφομένων is found in C, L, W, Δ, *f*¹³, *Byz, Lect.* The former is the more difficult reading, implying that the disciples were gathering or pressing around Jesus rather than merely staying with him.

16. The Question about the Temple Tax (17:24–27)

This narrative has Peter answering two questions, the first from the tax collectors (17:24–25a) and the second from Jesus (17:25b–26a). The rest of the passage (17:26b–27) contains Jesus's teaching on the matter, both in principle (17:26b) and in practice (17:27). Peter answers the tax collectors' question wrongly and Jesus's question correctly. There is a striking blend of humility and power in this passage as Jesus works a miracle in order to submit to the tax collectors and avoid causing them offense. And Peter learns another lesson about the danger of speaking too quickly. Many scholars find this account to be nonhistorical folklore (e.g., W. Davies and Allison 1991: 741–42). Bauckham (in D. Wenham and Blomberg 1986: 242–43) points out that the folkish content of the story is not incompatible with historicity.[1]

Here is an outline of this unit:

a. Peter questioned by the tax collectors (17:24–25a)
b. Peter questioned by Jesus (17:25b–26)
c. Peter instructed to pay the tax (17:27)

Exegesis and Exposition

[24]After they had come to Capernaum, those who collected the two-drachma tax came to Peter and said, "Does your teacher not pay the two-drachma tax?" [25]He said, "Yes." And when he came into the house, Jesus spoke to him first, "What do you think, Simon? From whom do the kings of the earth collect customs or tax, from their children or from strangers?" [26]˹When Peter said˺, "From strangers," Jesus said to him, "Then the children are exempt. [27]However, so that we do not offend them, go to the sea, throw in a hook, and take the first fish that comes up; and when you open its mouth, you will find a stater coin. Take that and give it to them for you and me."

---

1. Much has been written on this remarkable passage, including Banks 1973; Bauckham in D. Wenham and Blomberg 1986: 219–52; Cassidy 1979; Daube 1987: 39–58; Dautzenberg in Oberlinner and Fiedler 1991: 223–38; Derrett 1970b: 247–65; Flusser 1961–62; Garland in Bauer and Powell 1996: 69–98; Horbury in Bammel and Moule 1984: 265–86; Légasse 1972a; Liver 1963; Mandell 1984; McEleney 1976; H. Montefiore 1963–64; Schwarz 1992a; Van Aarde 1989.

a. Peter Questioned by the Tax Collectors (17:24–25a)

Again Peter's spontaneous reaction requires correction (cf. 17:4–5). After   **17:24–25a**
arriving in Capernaum, tax collectors ask Peter whether Jesus pays the
annual temple tax of two drachmas (Exod. 30:11–16; 38:25–26; Neh.
10:32–33; 4QOrdinances [4Q159] frg. 1.2.6–7; Josephus, *Ant.* 16.172;
18.312; *J. W.* 5.210; 7.218; Philo, *Spec. Laws* 1.76–77; *m. Šeqal.* 1–2).² Jesus
is described as a teacher here and in Matt. 8:19; 9:11; 23:8. A drachma
was roughly equivalent to a denarius, a day's wage for a laborer (20:2,
9, 10, 13). Perhaps Peter is approached because he is perceived as the
leader of the disciples. The question is phrased in a manner that expects
an affirmative answer, and Peter so replies without bothering to check
with Jesus.³

b. Peter Questioned by Jesus (17:25b–26)

Peter then goes into the house (cf. 9:10; 13:1, 36), and Jesus speaks first,   **17:25b–26**
displaying supernatural knowledge (cf. 9:4; 12:25; 26:10, 25). He asks
Peter a quasi-parabolic question about whom the kings of the earth tax.⁴
The terms τέλη (*telē*, customs; cf. Rom. 13:7; 1 Macc. 10:31; 11:35; Josephus, *Ant.* 12.141) and κῆνσον (*kēnson*, tax; cf. Matt. 22:17, 19) summarize
every kind of tax. The answer is clear: kings do not tax their children (υἱοί,
huioi, sons) but their subjects. Accordingly, Jesus, as the unique Son of
God, is greater than the temple and is exempt from paying this tax to his
Father's house (cf. 12:6; 21:12–13). The plural υἱοί includes the disciples
(5:9, 45; 6:9, 26) and probably all Israelites (Bauckham in D. Wenham
and Blomberg 1986: 223; Horbury in Bammel and Moule 1984: 282–84).
If so, Jesus teaches that God's temple should not be maintained by com-
pulsory taxes but by voluntary offerings (Luz 2001: 414–18).

c. Peter Instructed to Pay the Tax (17:27)

Despite being exempt, Jesus decides to pay the temple tax to avoid offense   **17:27**
(cf. 12:19; 22:15–22). The money will be provided in an amazing, even
bizarre fashion (17:27), prompting Blomberg's remark (1992a: 271) "This
verse is perhaps the strangest in Matthew's Gospel." The stater coin that

---

2. See W. Davies and Allison 1991: 738–41 for a discussion and dismissal of Cassidy
1979 and others who argue that a Roman civil tax is in view here. According to Josephus
(*J. W.* 7.218–29), the Romans diverted the temple tax to the temple of Jupiter in Rome after
the destruction of the Jerusalem temple in 70 CE. Overman 1996: 254–60 argues that the
originally Jewish context of this tax would have been conflated with the evils of Roman
imperial rule in colonial Judea.
3. The use of οὐ implies a question such as, "Your teacher pays the temple tax,
doesn't he?" and an answer such as, "Certainly!" Cf. BDF §§427, 440; Moulton and Turner
1963: 282–83.
4. "Kings of the earth," a common phrase, often has pejorative connotations. Cf.
Josh. 12:1; Ezra 9:7; Ps. 76:12; Lam. 4:12; Ezek. 27:33; Rev. 1:5; 6:15; 1 En. 48.4; 2 Esd.
(4 Ezra) 15:20.

Peter will find in the fish's mouth is worth four drachmas and would pay the tax for both Peter and Jesus (BDAG 940; Josephus, *Ant.* 7.379).[5] Jesus commands Peter to fish with a hook, not a net, evidently since this time only one fish would be needed (cf. 4:18, 20, 21; 13:47). Perhaps the use of this windfall coin rather than the common funds of the disciples (cf. John 12:6; 13:29) implies that although Jesus pays this tax, he denies its legitimacy (Horbury in Bammel and Moule 1984: 274).

Jesus did not mind offending the Pharisees on the matter of ritual hand washing (Matt. 15:12), but in the spirit of 12:19 (cf. Isa. 42:2) he does not protest the temple tax. He has had cordial relations with the tax collectors at Capernaum, yet this only exacerbated his tension with the Pharisees (Matt. 9:9–11). Jesus generally treated sinners gently (yet cf. 15:21–28) and religious hypocrites more harshly, but his followers today tend to get this backward, treating religious hypocrites with much deference and protesting loudly against known sinners. Foregoing one's liberties in order to avoid offense and further the kingdom's testimony is also a Pauline teaching (Rom. 14:13–23; 1 Cor. 8:9–9:1; 9:19–23). For similar teaching on paying taxes, see Matt. 22:15–22; Rom. 13:1–7; 1 Pet. 2:13–17. Matthew's inclusion of this pericope in his Gospel implies that his putative Christian Jewish audience is still aligned with Judaism. On the implications of this pericope for the responsible use of Christian freedom, see W. Davies and Allison (1991: 749): "Freedom is a task."

With several themes that are prevalent throughout this section, Matt. 17 concludes the narrative block that began in 13:53. Jesus has done many miracles, but many of his evil contemporaries do not believe in him. The conflict with the religious leaders is worsening. Despite this, Jesus faithfully teaches his disciples, and their little faith is growing. They have sadly accepted his clear prediction that he will suffer, die, and rise again in Jerusalem. But they are still preoccupied with selfish concerns, such as who is and will be the greatest (18:1; cf. 16:23; 20:21). There is still much for them to learn about authentic kingdom community before they make the fateful trip to Jerusalem with Jesus.

Additional Note

17:26. The UBS[4] reading εἰπόντος δέ (B, Θ, 1, 700, 892*) is a genitive absolute without a substantive. This is the more difficult reading, which explains the origin of several others, including λέγει αὐτῷ ὁ Πέτρος (W, Δ, *f*[13], *Byz*, *Lect*).

---

5. The use of the preposition ἀντί implies the same sort of substitution found in 20:28. See Wallace 1996: 365–67.

V. Opposition to the Kingdom Continues (13:53–19:2)
    A. Narrative 4: Various Responses to the Son of God (13:53–17:27)
➤ B. Discourse 4: Values and Relationships in the Kingdom Community (18:1–19:2)

B. Discourse 4: Values and Relationships in the Kingdom Community (18:1–19:2)

The common view of Matt. 18 as a church discipline passage is rather superficial and simplistic. Attempted comparisons of this passage to the Rule of the Community at Qumran (esp. 1QS 5.25–6.1; cf. CD 9.2–8; 14.21) can only point to limited connections (Carson 1984: 396; W. Davies 1964: 220–28; Ito 1992; Wansbrough 2000). A more accurate understanding approaches Jesus's fourth discourse as a sermon on the values of the kingdom and how these guide the community in handling interpersonal relationships. Jesus continues here what he began in earnest in Matt. 13:54—the preparation of his disciples to function as his community in his absence. As in the first three, this discourse has a narrative setting (18:1) and is concluded with the characteristic "when Jesus had finished" (19:1). The setting is somewhat vague in that "At that time" refers to the general period when Jesus had begun to tell his disciples about his death and resurrection.[1] The disciples first rejected (16:22) and then grievingly accepted this announcement (17:23). Yet their grief sadly turned to speculation, evidently based on 16:27–28; 17:11, over who is or would be the greatest in the kingdom of heaven (18:1; cf. 20:20–28). In this fourth discourse, Jesus answers this question and another one by Peter about forgiveness (18:21). A unique feature is Jesus's use of a child as a visual aid (18:2) to his verbal response to the question.

The fourth discourse concerns genuine spiritual greatness and its basis in kingdom community values. Jesus uses a child to illustrate humility and the duty of hospitality (18:1–5). Then he vividly warns against the opposite of hospitality, offending a disciple by causing him or her to sin (18:6–14). Instructions follow on handling fellow disciples who sin (18:15–20). Peter's question about long-suffering in forgiveness flows from these instructions, and Jesus answers it with a statement followed by a parable (18:21–35). The coherence of the discourse flows from Jesus's concern for the "little ones" who believe. Their humble status renders them vulnerable, but they are guarded by their heavenly Father; woe to those who cause the little ones to sin (18:6–7). Even the promptness and solemnity with which sin in the community must be handled underline the Father's concern for his children (18:15–20). Peter's question with

---

1. It is not clear that 17:24–27 should be viewed as the first section of the discourse, providing its setting (contra Garland 1993: 186–87; W. Thompson 1970: 16).

Jesus's answer emphasizes the overriding necessity that forgiveness must rule in the community of Jesus's disciples (18:35).

Some scholars doubt the presence of a clearly discernible structure to the discourse (e.g., Hagner 1995a: 514–15). Hare (1993: 208–19) divides it into three sections, 18:1–14, 15–20, 21–35. It could be divided into two parts, each beginning with a question (18:1–20, 21–35; Luz 2001: 422, following W. Thompson 1970: 239–40, 244). This last approach takes Peter's question in 18:21 as a pivotal narrative insertion that divides between the previous general focus on the disciples and the following specific focus on Peter. A better and more-common approach recognizes two sections, each ending in a parable (18:1–14; 18:15–35).[2] The section on discipline, 18:15–20, is the hinge or pivotal point. It can be plausibly viewed as concluding the section 18:1–20 or as introducing the section 18:15–35. But the clear linkage of 18:14 to 18:35 renders the second option the better one.[3]

The discourse holds together through its use of key terms for the disciples: "children" (18:2–5), "little ones" (18:6, 10, 14), "brothers" (18:15, 21, 35), and "fellow slaves" (18:29, 31, 33). This use of family and household imagery for the community of disciples is the most prominent motif of the discourse. Disciples are children, and even those who sin against them are their brothers (18:15), fellow children and slaves of the heavenly Father (18:10, 14, 19, 29, 31, 33, 35). The language of 18:8–9 exhibits a symmetrical parallelism. The repetition of "little ones" and "Father in heaven" renders 18:10–14 an *inclusio* that frames the brief parable in 18:12–13. The repetition of conditional clauses links 18:15–17. The use of "two or three" links 18:15–17 with 18:18–20. The juxtaposition of heaven and earth provides the basic framework of 18:18–20. The forgiveness of the sinning brother forms an *inclusio* in 18:21–35.[4]

2. Supporters include Beare 1981: 373; Boring 1995: 372; W. Davies and Allison 1991: 750–51; Garland 1993: 188; Gnilka 1986–88: 2.119–20; Harrington 1991: 265; Meier 1980b: 199; Patte 1987: 247, 252; W. Pesch 1966: 15–50; Schweizer 1975: 359.

3. Matthew 18:14 and 18:35 are both conclusions to parables. Both are introduced by οὕτως, and both emphasize the concern of the Father in heaven for his little ones who err.

4. On the structure of 18:1–35, see Bonnard 1980: 111–20; Genuyt 1996; Hermant 1996; Vaganay 1953; Van Zyl 1982. On the discourse in general, see Maisch in Oberlinner and Fiedler 1991: 239–66; Martinez 1961; W. Pesch 1963; W. Thompson 1970.

1. Humility and the Value of the Little Ones (18:1–14)

Matthew 18:1–14 contrasts the concerns of the disciples with those of Jesus. They are preoccupied with status, and he redirects their thoughts toward humility (18:4), hospitality (18:5), and restoration of an erring brother or sister (18:12). Those preoccupied with status easily fall prey to hubris, and Jesus warns against this in the strongest terms (18:6–10). Metaphorical language characterizes this section, including the child (18:2), the millstone and the sea (18:6), the stumbling block (18:7), amputation (18:8), and the lost sheep (18:12). Overall, Jesus reorients the disciples from themselves and status to others and service.

a. Authentic Spiritual Greatness (18:1–5)

The total dependence on God exemplified by a child's dependence on parents cuts against the grain of the disciples' self-interested question about greatness. A child as an example of greatness! Jesus's welcoming a child into the disciples' midst is an acted parable that illustrates the humility and hospitality required for authentic greatness. Matthew's readers have not been challenged with such a seeming contradiction since the beatitude on the gentle inheriting the earth (5:5).

The outline of this unit is as follows:

i. The disciples' question (18:1)
ii. Jesus's answer (18:2–5)

Exegesis and Exposition

[1]At that time the disciples came to Jesus and said, "Who, then, is greatest in the kingdom of heaven?" [2]And he called a child and had him stand among them, [3]and said, "Truly I tell you, unless you change and become like children, you will never enter the kingdom of heaven. [4]Whoever, then, humbles himself like this child is the greatest in the kingdom of heaven. [5]And whoever welcomes one such child in my name welcomes me."

i. The Disciples' Question (18:1)

18:1   Perhaps while Jesus is still at Capernaum (17:24), the disciples come to him with a question (cf. Mark 9:33–37; Luke 9:46–48; cf. similar questions in Matt. 13:10; 15:12; 17:19; 21:20; 24:3). What led to this question about greatness (cf. 5:19; 11:11) is unclear.[1] Perhaps the disciples' minds are on future glory because of recent teaching by Jesus (16:27–28; 17:11). Or perhaps they are concerned about the prominence of Peter (Origen, *Commentary on Matthew* 13.14; Hendriksen 1973: 684–85), James, and John (16:17–19; 17:1, 24). In any event, their desire for greatness (cf. 20:25; Esth. 10:2; 1 Macc. 7:8) contradicts what Jesus taught in Matt. 16:21–28. It is unclear whether they are concerned about greatness in the present or in the future manifestation of the kingdom, but if this story should be understood in light of 20:20–28, the future kingdom is in view.

---

1. The disciples' question uses the comparative adjective μείζων with superlative meaning. Cf. BDF §§60–61; Moulton and Turner 1963: 29–30; Wallace 1996: 299–300.

It is clear that the disciples still have many lessons to learn. Jesus has made it clear that his destiny is suffering, death, and resurrection and that his disciples must share in this destiny. Suffering comes before reward (16:21–28). Thus it is highly ironic that the disciples are preoccupied with greatness so soon after Jesus's clear teaching on his destiny and theirs (Hagner 1995a: 517). This preoccupation does not go away (20:20–28). The disciples of Jesus must constantly remind themselves that their Lord's experience must be the paradigm of their own (10:38; 11:29; 16:24; 20:28; Phil. 2:5–11; Col. 1:24; Heb. 10:32–38; 1 Pet. 2:21–25; Rev. 1:9).

ii. Jesus's Answer (18:2–5)

Jesus answers the question visually by having a child stand before the disciples as a sort of acted parable before he verbally explains greatness (18:2–4).[2] It is difficult to know the exact age of the child, since the word παιδίον (*paidion*) can refer to a child of any age from infancy to puberty (BDAG 749; cf. Matt. 2:8–21; 11:16; 14:21; 15:38; 19:13–14). The child is old enough to respond to Jesus's calling him or her into the midst of the disciples.[3]

18:2

Jesus's countercultural answer continues with the solemn words "I tell you the truth" (cf. 17:20). He says that no one will enter the kingdom (5:20; 7:21; 19:23–24; 23:13; cf. 19:17; 25:21, 23) unless one turns from sin and becomes like a child (cf. Gos. Thom. 22, 46).[4] Jesus does not choose a child out of a sentimental notion of the innocence or subjective humility of children, since children may already exhibit in seed form the traits that Jesus speaks against here. The childlike character trait that is foremost in the simile of becoming like a child is humility.[5] In this sense, conversion entails a radical change (Dupont in E. Ellis and Wilcox 1969: 50–60) amounting to the renunciation of all one's human prestige and the acceptance of kingdom values. Children are not innocent or selfless, nor do they consistently model humility. Rather, children have no status

18:3–4

2. Although W. Davies and Allison (1991: 754, 761) opine that 18:1–5 is about literal children, it seems clear that, immediately after being introduced, the child becomes a simile for humility, the foundational characteristic of spiritual greatness. The words ὡς τὰ παιδία (18:3), ὡς τὸ παιδίον τοῦτο (18:4), and ἓν παιδίον τοιοῦτο (18:5) underscore this.
3. Could the imagery of this passage (παιδίον in 18:2–5 and μικρῶν in 18:6, 10, 14) be an allusion to Isa. 11:6 LXX (παιδίον μικρὸν ἄξει αὐτούς)?
4. The absolute impossibility of entering the kingdom without radical change to childlike humility is expressed with the double, or emphatic, negation οὐ μὴ εἰσέλθητε. Cf. Wallace 1996: 468–69.
5. For Jewish texts that may imply a low view of children, see *m. 'Abot* 3.11; *m. B. Qam.* 4.4; 6.2, 4; *m. 'Erub.* 3.2; *m. Šeqal.* 1.3; *m. Sukkah* 2.8; 3.10. On various interpretations of the meaning of the child here, see R. Brown 1982; Crossan 1983; Dupont in E. Ellis and Wilcox 1969: 50–60; Légasse 1969; Luz 2001: 427–29; P. Müller 1992; Oepke, *TDNT* 5:636–53, esp. 649; Patte 1983; Robbins 1983; Schnackenburg in Schenke 1988: 269–82; D. Wenham 1982.

in society; they are at the mercy of adults. Similarly, repentant disciples admit that they have no status before God and that they depend solely on the love of the heavenly Father. Although the prophets stressed the characteristic of humility (e.g., Isa. 57:15; 66:2; Mic. 6:8; cf. Josephus, *Ant.* 3.212; *m. 'Abot* 3.1, 12; 4.4, 10; 6.1), the view of greatness inculcated here and based on the model of the child is evidently antithetical to the emphasis on hierarchical rank in the Qumran community (CD 15.15–17; cf. 12.3–6; 14.3–6; 1QS 2.19–25; 5.23; 6.4, 8–13, 22; 9.2, 16). Similarly, *m. 'Abot* 3.12 speaks disparagingly of children's talk, linking it with drinking wine in the middle of the day and associating with ignorant people as activities in which God finds no pleasure (but cf. *b. Yebam.* 48b). (On the possible relationship of this passage to John 3:3–5, see W. Davies and Allison 1991: 758; Pryor 1991b.)

18:5   Disciples demonstrate their humility by welcoming other disciples, not causing them to sin. Since those who exercise childlike faith exhibit the essence of the kingdom (cf. 21:15–16), they must be welcomed, not caused to sin (18:6–10). Here the use of the metaphor shifts from a child as the model of humility (18:1–4) to a child as the object of godly or sinful behavior. Hospitable welcoming of Jesus's little ones (18:5; cf. 10:11–14, 40–42; 25:35–40; John 13:20; 2 John 10–11; 3 John 5–10) is contrasted with causing them to sin in the next section (Matt. 18:6–10). Giving such a welcoming reception to Jesus's disciples is itself an act of humility, since one's status in the world is not enhanced by it. Jesus himself soon models this principle again in 19:13–15.

b. Warnings against Causing Believers to Sin (18:6–9)

As 18:1–5 commands the proper value to be placed on childlike believers, so 18:6–9 warns against devaluing the little ones by causing them to sin. Matthew 18:6 is a transitional verse that can be taken either as the concluding antithesis of 18:4–6 or as the introduction to 18:6–9. Similarly, 18:10 can be taken either as the conclusion to the warning against causing believers to sin, which began in 18:6, or as the introduction to the parable of the lost sheep in 18:12–14.

Exegesis and Exposition

[6]"But whoever causes one of these little ones who believe in me to sin, it would be better for a heavy millstone to be hung around that person's neck and for that person to be drowned in the depth of the sea. [7]Woe to the world because of things that cause sin! For things that cause sin must come; but woe to that person through whom they come! [8]If your hand or your foot causes you to sin, cut it off and throw it away from you; it is better for you to enter life maimed or crippled than to have two hands or two feet and be thrown into the eternal fire. [9]If your eye causes you to sin, gouge it out and throw it away from you. It is better for you to enter life with one eye than to have two eyes and be thrown into the hell of fire."

A transition in metaphors from a child (18:2–5) to the little ones (18:6, 10, 14; cf. 10:42; 11:11; 13:32; 25:40, 45) occurs here. If receiving Jesus's little ones hospitably is tantamount to receiving Jesus (10:40–41; John 13:20), causing them to sin is tantamount to rejecting Jesus (cf. Mark 9:42–47; Luke 17:1–2). This brings the most ominous consequences. The "heavy millstone" is literally a millstone (cf. Rev. 18:21; Jer. 51:63–64) turned by a donkey (μύλος ὀνικός, *mylos onikos*). The depth of the sea also vividly portrays the horrible consequences of causing a believer to sin. To cause someone to sin is metaphorically to entrap or cause a person to trip and fall. It is to entice and corrupt the person morally and to render that one liable to eternal punishment (18:7–9; cf. 5:29–30; 17:27).[1]

18:6

---

1. For background, see Lev. 19:14; Ezek. 14:3, 7; 18:30; cf. Jub. 1.9; Sir. 9:5; 25:21; 34:7; 1QS 2.12; 3.24; 1QpHab 11.7–8. In the NT the language of offense includes both the verb σκανδαλίζω (Matt. 5:29–30; 11:6/Luke 7:23; Matt. 13:21/Mark 4:17; Matt. 13:57/Mark 6:3; Matt. 15:12; 17:27; 18:6, 8, 9/Mark 9:42–47/Luke 17:2; Matt. 24:10; 26:31, 33/Mark 14:27, 29; cf. John 6:61; 16:1; 1 Cor. 8:13; 2 Cor. 11:29) and the noun σκάνδαλον (Matt. 13:41;

18:7   Jesus's dual pronouncement of woe upon those who cause his disciples to fall into sin recalls 11:21 and anticipates 23:13–16, 23–29; 24:19; 26:24 (D. Turner 2004). It is not surprising that offense may come from outsiders, but this text warns that it may come even from inside the community. The two pronouncements of woe (18:7a, 7c) are first generic and then specific. These surround a statement about the inevitability of offenses (18:7b), demonstrating that instances of causing sin are inevitable (24:10–11) yet culpable (13:41; cf. 26:24).[2] God's sovereignty and human responsibility are juxtaposed as complementary truths. The offense spoken of here is different from that in 17:27, which speaks of hindering those who do not believe.

18:8–9   The repeated pronouncement of woe in 18:7 requires that any potential offense be dealt with promptly and decisively. The dual woe of 18:7 is matched by dual hyperbolic commands in 18:8–9. Their symmetrical structure is clear:

> **18:8**   Potential offense: Hand or foot causes sin.
>   Radical response: Cut it off and throw it away.
>   Reason: Better to enter life maimed than to go to hell whole.
> **18:9**   Potential offense: Eye causes sin.
>   Radical response: Gouge it out and throw it away.
>   Reason: Better to enter life maimed than to go to hell whole.

Failure to deal radically with sinful proclivities indicates that one is in danger of punishment in hellfire (cf. 3:10–12; 5:22; 25:41). As grotesque as these images of amputation and gouging are, the prospect of eternal punishment is far worse. This language is hypothetical[3] as well as hyperbolic (cf. 5:29–30). Ridding oneself of one's hands, feet, and eyes would not reach the root of sin, the heart (15:18–20). The point is, rather, that one must deal radically with one's sinful tendencies (cf. Prov. 4:23–27; Rom. 13:11–14). This is necessary before one attempts to correct another member of the community (Matt. 18:15; cf. 7:3–5; Gal. 6:1).

16:23; 18:7/Luke 17:1; cf. Rom. 9:33; 11:9; 14:13; 16:17; 1 Cor. 1:23; Gal. 5:11; 1 Pet. 2:8; 1 John 2:10; Rev. 2:14). Cf. Stählin, *TDNT* 7:339–58.

2. The agency of offense is expressed in 18:7a by ἀπό (BDAG 106; BDF §§176, 210) and in 18:7c by διά (BDAG 225; BDF §223).

3. The language of the conditional clause (εἰ . . . σκανδαλίζει) does not necessarily imply the existence of offenses in the Matthean community (Morris 1992: 463n22; contra W. Thompson 1970: 112). The first-class condition (εἰ with indicative mood) assumes the reality of the situation expressed in the protasis only for the sake of argument (cf. 12:28; BDF §372; Wallace 1996: 690–94, 711). Other historical and literary considerations must be taken into account.

c. Parable of the Lost Sheep (18:10–14)

Far from disdaining their fellows (18:10), Jesus's disciples must mimic the action of a shepherd seeking a lost sheep (18:12–13), since this enacts the heavenly Father's compassion (18:14). The authenticity of 18:11 is doubtful. It probably has been interpolated from Luke 19:10. (See additional note on 18:11 and Metzger 1994: 36.) W. Davies and Allison (1991: 768) point out the *inclusio* of the heavenly Father and the little ones in 18:10, 14. Gaechter (1967: 50–52) demonstrates a plausible chiasmus in 18:10–14.

The unit can be outlined as follows:

i. Warning against despising the little ones (18:10–11)
ii. The parable stated (18:12–13)
iii. The parable applied (18:14)

Exegesis and Exposition

[10]"See that you do not despise one of these little ones, for I tell you that their angels in heaven continually see the face of my Father who is in heaven. [11r]For the Son of Man has come to save what was lost.⌉ [12]What do you think? If a man has a hundred sheep and one of them has gone astray, does he not leave the ninety-nine on the mountains and go and search for the one that is straying? [13]And if it happens that he finds it, I tell you truly, he rejoices over it more than over the ninety-nine that did not stray. [14]Likewise it is not the will of ⌈your⌉ Father who is in heaven that one of these little ones perish."

i. Warning against Despising the Little Ones (18:10–11)

In addition to dealing decisively with sin in their own lives, disciples must also avoid contempt for fellow members of the community (cf. Rom. 14:3, 10, 15; 1 Cor. 11:22; 1 Tim. 4:12), described here, as in 18:6, as "little ones." These must not be despised, because angels represent them before God (cf. Heb. 1:14). Such angelic ministry to believers is real, albeit mysterious.[1] All in all, the flow of Matt. 18:1–10 alternates between warnings of eschatological judgment (18:3, 6–10) and promises

18:10–11

---

1. The ministry of angels must not be pressed unduly (W. Davies and Allison 1991: 772), since it cannot eclipse the presence of Jesus with believers (18:20; 28:20). Nevertheless, many Scriptures speak of angelic ministry to God's people (cf. Josh. 5:13–15?; Job 33:23?; Pss. 34:7; 91:11–12; Ezek. 40:3; Dan. 10:10–14; 12:1; Luke 1:19; Acts 12:15; Rev. 2:1, 8, 12, 18; 3:1, 7, 14; 8:2; cf. 1QH 6.13; 4Q400 1.1.4; 1QSb 4.25–26; Jub. 2.2, 18; 31.14; Sir.

of eschatological blessing (18:4–5), depending on the course of action chosen.

ii. The Parable Stated (18:12–13)

18:12-13 The question "What do you think?" (cf. 17:25; 21:28; 22:17, 42; 26:66) introduces a brief parable about a lost sheep (cf. Luke 15:3–7; Gos. Thom. 107). For the image of a lost sheep, see Ps. 119:176; Isa. 53:6; Jer. 50:6; Ezek. 34:15–16; 1 Pet. 2:25. The parable is structured around a shepherd's response to two contingencies.[2] The first is about the certainty of the shepherd searching if one of his sheep becomes lost (Matt. 18:12).[3] The second is about the shepherd's greater joy over finding the one lost sheep than over the rest of the flock that is safe (cf. Mekilta on Exod. 19:21). Although it is not stated, one tends to assume that the shepherd would not jeopardize the entire flock in order to seek the single lost sheep (contra Huffman 1978: 211). The phrasing of the parable may allude to Ezek. 34:10–12, 16. The image of a straying sheep portrays the danger of apostasy, not apostasy itself (Gundry 1994: 367). Pastoral intervention may prevent backsliding from resulting in lostness (W. Thompson 1970: 157).

iii. The Parable Applied (18:14)

18:14 By analogy (οὕτως, *houtōs*), the Father does not wish that any of his little ones (disciples) perish (cf. 5:29–30; 10:28).[4] The metaphor of believers as sheep is common in Matthew (9:36; 10:6, 16; 12:11–12; 15:24; 18:12; 25:32–33; 26:31) and is thoroughly biblical (e.g., Ps. 23; Ezek. 34; Jer. 23; Mic. 2; John 10; cf. Keener 1999: 450–52). In the Scriptures, God is the shepherd who pastures his people Israel through theocratic leaders such as kings and priests. The imagery has eschatological overtones in 2 Sam. 7:7–8; Isa. 40:11; Jer. 23:4–5; 31:10; Ezek. 34:11–16, 23. In Matthew, Israel's leaders are not faithful shepherds, and Jesus compassionately rescues the lost sheep of Israel (Matt. 9:36; 10:6; 15:24, 32; 26:31). By implication, Jesus's disciples must model their lives and ministries after the concern of the Father as exemplified in Jesus and expressed by the parable. Jesus calls on his followers to serve one another as he has

---

17:17; Tob. 12:15; 2 Macc. 11:6; 3 Macc. 6:18–19; 1 En. 14.21; 20.5; 40.6, 9; 104.1; T. Levi 3.5; 5.6; *L.A.B.* 15.5; Life of Adam and Eve 33.1).

2. The words ἐὰν γένηται introduce the parallel protases of conditional clauses in 18:12 and 18:13.

3. The shepherd's ownership of the sheep is expressed by the dative of possession, τινι ἀνθρώπῳ. Cf. Wallace 1996: 149–51.

4. "Of the Father" translates ἔμπροσθεν τοῦ πατρός, which is equivalent to a simple genitive (cf. 11:26; Luke 10:21; Acts 10:4). This use of ἔμπροσθεν is Semitic (cf. בְּעֵינֵי יְהֹוָה and לִפְנֵי יְהֹוָה). It may be reverential (BDAG 325) and perhaps occurs to avoid anthropomorphism (Jeremias 1972: 39).

sacrificially served them (20:27–28). Disciples must receive one another, not cause one another to go astray (18:5–9).[5]

Additional Notes

18:11. This verse is likely interpolated from Luke 19:10. It is omitted by ℵ, B, L*, Θ*, *f*[13], 33, and others. A version identical to Luke 19:10 is found in G, 157, *Lect*[pt], and a version similar to Luke 19:10 is found in D, W, Δ, Θ[c], *Byz, Lect*.

18:14. It is very difficult to decide between τοῦ πατρὸς ὑμῶν (ℵ, D[c], L, W, Δ, *f*[1], *Byz*, and others; cf. 5:48; 6:14, 26, 32) and τοῦ πατρός μου (B, F, H, N, O, Θ, Σ, 33, etc.; cf. 15:13; 18:10, 35).

---

5. For further study, see Barton in Longenecker 2000: 199–216; Derrett 1979b; Dupont 1968a; 1989: 331–50; Hultgren 2000: 46–63; I. Jones 1995: 273–80; Petersen 1981; Roloff 1992.

2. Rebuke and Forgiveness in the Community (18:15–35)

Matthew 18:15–35 contains two sections, the first about the procedure and promises involved in confronting a sinning disciple (18:15–20) and the second about the teaching and parabolic illustration of forgiveness in the community (18:21–35). Matthew 18:35, like 18:14, applies the parable that precedes it to the heavenly Father's will for the community.

a. Rebuking a Fellow Disciple Who Sins (18:15–20)

Matthew 18:15–20 contains a three-step procedure for discipline (18:15–17) based on a theological foundation (18:18–20) that includes the authority of the church, the promise of answered prayer, and the presence of Jesus. The procedure spelled out here will be necessary, since Jesus has just taught that offenses are inevitable. The Father's total dedication to his little ones dictates that offenses within the community be dealt with promptly and fairly. (On the social setting of the passage, see White in Balch 1991: 211–47. See Bruner 1990: 645–55 for an exceptionally rich theological exposition.)

The unit may be outlined as follows:

    i. Three stages of community discipline (18:15–17)
    ii. The theological basis of community discipline (18:18–20)

Exegesis and Exposition

[15]"If a fellow disciple ⌜sins against you⌝, go and point it out privately just between the two of you. If that person listens to you, you have regained a fellow disciple. [16]But if that person does not listen, take along one or two others with you, so that 'by the testimony of two or three witnesses every matter may be confirmed.' [17]But if that one refuses to listen to them, tell it to the church; and if that one even refuses to listen to the church, let that one be to you as a Gentile and a tax collector.

[18]"I tell you truly, whatever you bind on earth shall be bound in heaven; and whatever you loose on earth shall be loosed in heaven. [19]Again I tell you ⌜truly⌝ that if two of you agree on earth concerning any matter about which they ask, it shall be done for them by my Father who is in heaven. [20]For where two or three are gathered together in my name, I am there among them."

i. Three Stages of Community Discipline (18:15–17)

The structure of 18:15–17 (see the chart) alternates between conditional clauses (with ἐάν [ean] followed by the aorist subjunctive) and consequences (expressed by imperatives) (W. Thompson 1970: 176). The conditional clauses present hypothetical confrontation situations (18:15a, 16a, 17a, 17c). Each is immediately followed by an imperative that enjoins an appropriate response (18:15, 16b, 17b, 17d). This pattern is broken twice, first in 18:15c–d, which describes a hypothetical positive response and resulting reconciliation. Evidently, this positive response/reconciliation is possible at later confrontation steps and is implicit after 18:16c, 17b, and possibly even 17d. The only other interruption is in 18:16c, where scriptural support for two or three witnesses (cf. 18:19–20) in the second step is adduced. (See Luz 2001: 448.)

The Structure of Matt. 18:15–17

Hypothetical initial offense (v. 15a)
> *First step:* Personal confrontation (v. 15b)
> Hypothetical positive response (v. 15c)
> Reconciliation (v. 15d)

Hypothetical negative response to personal confrontation (v. 16a)
> *Second step:* Peer confrontation (v. 16b)
> Scriptural support (v. 16c)*

Hypothetical negative response to peer confrontation (v. 17a)
> *Third step:* Community confrontation (v. 17b)*

Hypothetical negative response to the third step of confrontation (v. 17c)
> *Fourth step:* Extracommunity confrontation (v. 17d)*

*Evidently, the positive response and reconciliation of 18:15c–d would be possible here as well.

18:15 The warnings against despising a fellow disciple[1] or causing him or her to fall into sin inform the procedure laid out here (18:6, 10; cf. 5:22–24). The first step of confrontation is a conversation between two individuals. This intramural emphasis and Peter's question in 18:21 render the disputed words "against you" in 18:15 plausibly authentic despite their absence in many early MSS (cf. W. Davies and Allison 1991: 782 and the additional note on 18:15). As the shepherd rescued the straying sheep, the offended person must take the initiative to reconcile the offender (18:12, 15). Bitterness and gossip are inappropriate (cf. Prov. 25:9–10). The basic duty of the offended person is expressed by ἔλεγξον (*elenxon*), which refers to rebuke that is based on evidence and attempts to persuade the offender of having sinned and to lead toward reconciliation (cf. Lev. 19:17 LXX; W. Thompson 1970: 178).[2] The three stages of confrontation that begin here involve successively more members of the community. Ideally, the sin of one against another can

---

1. In the translation of 18:15, the word ἀδελφός has been rendered "fellow disciple" because the word refers to another person in the community of Jesus's disciples, whether male or female. Cf. BDAG 18; Matt. 5:22–24; 7:3–5; 12:50; 18:15, 21, 35; 23:8; 25:40; 28:10; Duling 1999.

2. On rebuke in the community, see Lev. 19:15–18; Prov. 3:12; 10:18; 25:9–10; 26:4–5; 27:5–6; Sir. 19:13–20:2; T. Gad 4; 6.3–5; 1QS 5.24–6.1; 9.16–18; CD 7.2–3; 9.2–8, 16–22; 1 Tim. 5:20; 2 Tim. 3:16; 4:2; Carmody in Horgan and Kobelski 1989: 141–58; Kugel 1987.

be reconciled between the two of them (Matt. 18:15; cf. Lev. 19:17–18; Prov. 3:12; 25:9–10; 27:5–6).

A positive response is envisioned in 18:15, but if the offender does not obey the private personal rebuke, the second step is to bring in one or two other disciples to back up the offended person.[3] This is calculated to underline the gravity of the problem and to add their wisdom to its solution (18:16). A similar situation is described in *y. Yoma* 45c except that there the offender takes the initiative to apologize. Deuteronomy 19:15 is cited as supporting this procedure.[4] If this rebuke by a small group of peers cannot resolve the matter, it must be taken before the entire local community, the "church" (cf. Matt. 16:18). — **18:16**

Three increasingly grave rebukes provide to the offender every opportunity to acknowledge error. But if the offender will not heed even the church, there is no higher earthly court of appeal. The only remaining course of action is to withdraw community fellowship and to regard the offender as a Gentile and a tax collector, as an outsider who cannot participate in the community's activities. But Jesus himself treated notorious sinners compassionately (5:46–47; 9:10–13; 10:3), and so absolute shunning or total withdrawal from personal contact is not necessarily commanded here (Garland 1993: 192). — **18:17**

These three stages of confrontation ensure the fair treatment of both offending and offended individuals with as little fanfare as possible. Though church discipline is often taken lightly, it is an ominous matter, an aspect of doing God's will on earth as it is in heaven (6:10).[5] Repeated rejection of the overtures of a fellow disciple, of two or three additional witnesses, and then of the entire community is tantamount to rejection of Jesus and the Father.

ii. The Theological Basis of Community Discipline (18:18–20)

The consequences of the disciplinary process are ominous because the community on earth acts in conjunction with the God of heaven. The binding and loosing mentioned here recalls 16:19 and is tied to the exercise of the keys of the kingdom (cf. John 20:23).[6] The locus of author- — **18:18**

---

3. The positive response to confrontation in 18:15c (ἀκούσῃ) and the negative response in 18:16a (μὴ ἀκούσῃ) both refer to obedient heeding (cf. 10:14; 17:5; Deut. 6:4; 18:15), not merely the use of auditory faculties (Matt. 7:24, 26; 13:19). The negative responses in 18:17a and 18:17c (παρακούσῃ) describe disobedient refusal to pay attention and are semantically equivalent to μὴ ἀκούσῃ (cf. Esth. 3:8 LXX; Tob. 3:4).

4. Cf. 26:60; Num. 35:30; Deut. 17:6; CD 9.17–23; 11QT 61.6–7; 64.8–9; John 8:17; 2 Cor. 13:1; 1 Tim. 5:19; Heb. 6:18; 10:28; Rev. 11:3; Josephus *Ant.* 4.219; *Life* 49, 256; B. Jackson 1975: 153–71; van Vliet 1958.

5. Cf. Gal. 6:1–5; 1 Cor. 5:1–6:11; 2 Cor. 2:5–11; 13:1–2; 2 Thess. 3:6, 14–15; 1 Tim. 5:19–20; 2 Tim. 4:2; Titus 2:15; 3:10; 1 John 5:16; 2 John 10; 3 John 10; Jude 20–23.

6. See the comments on 16:19 for discussion of the exegesis of the future perfect periphrastic constructions.

ity here is the local community, not just Peter or even the apostles as a group. The community is authorized to determine whether a sinning disciple continues with the community or is excluded. This depends on the outcome of the process laid out in Matt. 18:15–17. Repentance leads to loosing, or forgiveness, and continued fellowship. The lack of repentance leads to binding, or retention of sin, and exclusion from the community. In 18:18 the consequences of the process of 18:15–17 are shown to be extremely serious, affecting the eternal destiny of the offending party.

18:19   The authority of the community is clarified here as emanating from the spiritual harmony of its members. The promises in 18:19–20 of answered prayer and God's presence must be seen in the context of the solemn matter of the sinning disciple. It is possible that the two who agree in 18:19 are members of a three-member court that represents the community (*m. Sanh.* 1.1; Hagner 1995a: 533; cf. 5:21–22). During the discipline process, the church on earth may be assured that the heavenly Father will guide and confirm its deliberations and prayers. Derrett (1979c) unconvincingly argues that the two who ask in 18:19–20 are the offending and offended persons of 18:15–17 and that their request is to judicial authorities.

18:20   The promise of Jesus's presence with disciples who gather in his name (cf. von Dobbeler 2002) ameliorates the difficulties of the discipline process. "The community's prayer becomes Jesus's prayer, and his prayer cannot but be answered" (W. Davies and Allison 1991: 789). The idea of Jesus's presence during the discipline process is similar to the rabbinic teaching that God's presence (the Shechinah) is with a group as small as two people who are studying the Torah (*m. 'Abot* 3.2, 3, 6; Mekilta on Exod. 20:24; Sievers in Finkel and Frizzell 1981: 171–82). Jesus's promise that he is with his church speaks of activity that is divine (Ezek. 43:7; Joel 2:27; Zech. 2:10–11; cf. 11QT 46.12). It recalls Matt. 1:23 and anticipates 28:20. The high Christology of Matthew is once again clear. Jesus is also associated with God's glory in John 1:14; Heb. 1:3. The language of 1 Cor. 5:4 also speaks of the presence of Jesus with a community gathered in his name for the purpose of discipline. (See Kupp 1996; Ziesler 1984.)

The process and promises of Matt. 18:15–20 seem mechanical and harsh when these verses are isolated from their setting. But the passage is "embedded in a section filled with kindness" (W. Davies and Allison 1991: 804). Jesus has been speaking tenderly of his disciples as humble children (18:5), little ones (18:6), lost sheep (18:12–13), and brothers (or sisters; 18:15, 21, 35). He has emphasized the necessity of proper care of these little ones (18:6–14). He will go on to stress the necessity of forgiveness (18:21–35). Even the discipline process allows three chances for repentance. Those who are involved in it should view themselves as agents of the Father/Shepherd seeking straying little ones/sheep. The goal is reconciliation and return to the fold, not severance from the flock. The location of the discipline process in a setting of familial tenderness and reconciliation should warn Christian communities that the discipline must be permeated with humility, familial love, and a passion for forgiveness and restoration. (On the difficulties of implementing 18:15–20 in the history of the church, see Luz 2001: 455–57, 463–64.)

Another comment is warranted by the flippant way in which 18:19–20 is often cited to assure small meetings of Christians that God is with them. This is disturbing because it twists a solemn passage into a humorous cliché. Indeed God is present with any legitimate meeting of his people, whatever its size, yet one should not mishandle Scripture to prove this. Taking this solemn passage out of context profanes it and makes light of the sacred duty of the church to maintain harmonious interpersonal relationships (cf. 5:21–26).

Additional Notes

18:15. It is difficult to decide between the shorter and longer readings, ἁμαρτήσῃ (supported by ℵ, B, 579) and ἁμαρτήσῃ εἰς σέ (supported by D, L, Δ, Θ, 078, f¹³, *Byz*, *Lect*ᵖᵗ, and most Latin MSS). The longer reading makes sense and is similar to ἁμαρτήσει εἰς ἐμέ in 18:21. It could be argued that εἰς σέ was deliberately added to 18:15 because of influence from 18:21 or that it was deliberately removed to make the passage applicable to sin in general (Metzger 1994: 36). A complicating factor is that the phrase in question, εἰς σέ, sounds much like the verb ending -ησῃ, which could lead to accidental omission if the text was being dictated to the copyist by a reader. There are two additional readings with the aorist subjunctive ἁμάρτῃ, one without εἰς σέ (weak patristic support; cf. Luke 17:3) and one with εἰς σέ (W, 33, 180, *Lect*ᵖᵗ). UBS⁴ places εἰς σέ in brackets because each is equally possible.

18:19. Πάλιν ἀμὴν λέγω is supported by B, 058, 33, *Byz*, *Lect*, but ἀμήν is omitted by ℵ, D, L. Two additional weakly attested readings also omit ἀμήν, but it is included in the reading ἀμὴν λέγω in f¹³. Discussions of this variant must deal with the presence of ἀμὴν λέγω in 18:18. This is the only occurrence of πάλιν ἀμὴν λέγω in the Gospels. UBS⁴ places ἀμήν in brackets because of these difficulties.

b. The Necessity of Forgiveness (18:21–35)

The impetus of this section is Peter's question about the extent of forgiveness (18:21), which Jesus answers first propositionally (albeit hyperbolically; 18:22) and then parabolically (18:23–35). Matthew 13:36 provides another example of a discourse that contains an interruption by the disciples. Matthew 18:21–35, together with 18:1–14, provides the appropriate context for the disciplinary process of 18:15–20, guarding against an overly rigorous, unfeeling approach to relationships within the community.

The unit can be outlined as follows:

    i. Peter's question answered hyperbolically (18:21–22)
   ii. Peter's question answered parabolically (18:23–35)
      (1) A huge debt is forgiven (18:23–27)
      (2) A paltry debt is not forgiven (18:28–30)
      (3) A reversal of fortune (18:31–34)
      (4) The application (18:35)

Exegesis and Exposition

[21]Then Peter came to him and said, "Lord, how often shall I forgive a fellow disciple of sin against me? Up to seven times?" [22]Jesus said to him, "I do not tell you, up to seven times, but up to seventy-seven times.

[23]"For this reason the kingdom of heaven may be compared to a king who wanted to settle accounts with his slaves. [24]When he began to settle, one who owed him ten thousand talents was brought to him. [25]But since he was unable to repay, the master commanded him to be sold, with his wife and children and all that he had, and repayment to be made. [26]Then the slave fell to the ground and bowed before him, saying, ⌜ ⌝Be patient with me and I will repay you everything.' [27]And the master of that slave felt compassion and released him and forgave him the debt.

[28]"But that slave went out and came upon one of his fellow slaves who owed him a hundred denarii; and he grabbed him and began to choke him, saying, 'Pay back what you owe.' [29]Then his fellow slave fell to the ground ⌜ ⌝ and pleaded with him, 'Be patient with me and I will repay you.' [30]But he refused and went and had him thrown in prison until he repaid the debt.

[31]"Then his fellow slaves saw what had happened, and they were deeply grieved and came and reported to their master all that had happened. [32]Then his master summoned him and said to him, 'You wicked slave, I forgave you all

that debt because you pleaded with me. [33]Should you not also have had mercy on your fellow slave, just as I had mercy on you?' [34]And his master was enraged and handed him over to the merciless jailers until he repaid all the debt. [35]So will my heavenly Father also do to you if each of you does not forgive your fellow disciple from your heart ⌐ ⌐."

i. Peter's Question Answered Hyperbolically (18:21–22)

Peter characteristically speaks up, perhaps for the rest of the disciples (cf. 14:28; 16:16, 22; 17:24; 26:33–35), with a question about forgiveness.[1] Peter has heard Jesus's previous teaching about forgiveness (5:21–26; 6:12, 14–15), but he remains concerned about the extent of the long-suffering to be shown to a repeat offender. The recidivist sin about which Peter is concerned probably relates to the process outlined in 18:15–17, and Peter is asking how many times 18:15 must be repeated. Peter thinks that it is adequate to forgive seven times (cf. Luke 17:4),[2] but Jesus's hyperbolic answer indicates that forgiveness must be unending. The rabbis evidently took a view more rigorous than Peter's (*m. Yoma* 8.9; *t. Yoma* 5.13; *b. Yoma* 86b–87a).

18:21

Ἑβδομηκοντάκις ἑπτά (*hebdomēkontakis hepta*) should probably be translated "seventy-seven times" (NIV, NRSV; BDAG 269; cf. Gen. 4:15, 24; T. Benj. 7.4), not "seventy times seven" (KJV, NASB, NLT, RSV). In any event, the following parable (Matt. 18:23–35) shows that forgiveness must be unending, since disciples have been forgiven by their heavenly Father of much more than they could ever forgive their fellow disciples (cf. 5:21–26, 38–48; 6:12, 14–15; 1 Cor. 13:5). To be forgiven is to be freed and empowered to forgive. "Whoever *counts* has not forgiven at all, but is only biding his or her time" (Boring 1995: 380). The response to offense mandated by Jesus is the opposite of Lamech's boast that he will avenge himself seventy-seven times upon anyone who injures him (Gen. 4:15, 24).

18:22

ii. Peter's Question Answered Parabolically (18:23–35)

The parable of the unforgiving servant is introduced in 18:23a and applied in 18:35. It has three scenes (vv. 23a–27, 28–30, 31–34), presenting respectively the king's compassion, the forgiven servant's lack of compassion for his fellow servant, and the king's anger at the servant's lack of compassion. In the first scene the king forgives, in the second the forgiven servant imprisons his fellow servant, and in the third the king

---

1. Peter's deliberative question is expressed with the future indicative ἁμαρτήσει . . . ἀφήσω rather than the more common aorist subjunctive. See Wallace 1996: 570.

2. Other texts connect the number seven in other ways with sin, vengeance, and forgiveness: Gen. 4:15, 24; Lev. 16:14, 19; 26:18, 21, 24, 28; Prov. 24:16; 2 Sam. 12:6; *L.A.B.* 6.6; 4Q511 2f.35.

in response revokes forgiveness and punishes the unforgiving servant. This parable does not answer Peter's question as directly as 18:22 does, but it is clearly on the mark. The point of 18:22 is the unlimited extent of forgiveness within the community, and the point of 18:23–35 is the motivating factor of the Father's judgment (18:35). Additionally, the parable shows that God has forgiven disciples of offenses far greater than those for which they will need to forgive their fellows.[3]

(1) A Huge Debt Is Forgiven (18:23–27)

18:23 Jesus's answer continues with a parable of the kingdom, introduced by the common formula (cf. 13:24, 31, 33, 45, 47; 20:1; 22:2; 25:1). This leads the reader to connect the parabolic king with God, as in numerous rabbinic parables (Keener 1999: 457n34), and the king's slaves with God's people. The first scene of the story tells the reader that a slave (cf. Glancy 2000) was forgiven a large debt by a king who wished to settle his financial affairs. The king's slaves probably should be understood as his officials, since ordinary slaves might not be entrusted with so much money (BDAG 260; LXX: 1 Sam. 29:3; 2 Kings 5:5–6; Josephus, *Ant.* 2.70).

18:24–27 The servant owes the king an astonishingly large amount of money, "ten thousand talents." A talent was probably worth around six thousand drachmas (17:24) or denarii (20:2, 9, 10, 13; BDAG 988), and a laborer was paid a denarius a day (20:2). Thus a laborer would have to work sixty million days, or roughly 193,000 years (60,000,000 days divided by 310 workdays per year), to earn this much money. But the amount is hyperbolic (cf. 1 Chron. 29:3–7; Josephus, *Ant.* 12.175–76; 17.320); BDAG 661 suggests the English slang "zillions" as a translation. The unimaginably large amount here is intended to contrast with the relatively small amount owed this servant by his fellow in Matt. 18:28. It is evidently legal for the king to sell the servant and his family in order to obtain some satisfaction for the debt.[4] Yet the servant's abject posture and pleas for more time to pay touch the king's heart and change his mind. Instead of merely allowing his servant time to repay the enormous debt, with astonishing mercy he forgives it. The mercy of the king speaks of the compassion of Jesus (9:36; 14:14; 15:32; 20:34).

(2) A Paltry Debt Is Not Forgiven (18:28–30)

18:28–30 The second scene (18:28–30) recapitulates much of the first, but the forgiven servant's activity contrasts sharply with that of the compas-

---

3. On the interpretation of the parable, see further Buckley 1991; de Boer 1988; Derrett 1970b: 32–47; Heil in Carter and Heil 1998: 96–123; Hultgren 2000: 21–33; Hylen 2000; I. Jones 1995: 211–26; Keesmaat in Longenecker 2000: 263–85; B. Scott 1985; B. Weber 1993, 1994.

4. Cf. Exod. 22:3; 1 Sam. 22:2; 2 Kings 4:1; Neh. 5:1–13; Isa. 50:1; Amos 2:6; 8:6; Josephus, *Ant.* 16.3; *m. Soṭah* 3.8.

sionate king. Although the servant has been forgiven an enormous debt by the king, he refuses to forgive his fellow servant a comparatively small debt, literally, "one hundred denarii" (cf. 20:2, 9, 10, 13; 22:19). This would amount to roughly four months' work for a laborer. If one contrasts the huge amount of 18:24 with the paltry amount here, the servant was forgiven 579 times the amount he refuses to forgive. But this is hyperbole, and the point is the monstrous inconsistency between being forgiven "zillions" and refusing to forgive "peanuts." Despite the pleas of his fellow servant, the unforgiving servant chokes him (cf. *m. B. Bat.* 10.8) and has him incarcerated until he can repay (cf. 5:25–26; 24:49). The unforgiving servant does not do for the other what he would like the other to do for him (7:12), let alone do for the other what the king has already done for him. He hypocritically accepts mercy but is not willing to grant it to another.

(3) A Reversal of Fortune (18:31–34)

In the third scene, other servants hear how the forgiven servant treated his fellow. They are horrified at this glaring hypocrisy.[5] This servant should have imitated the mercy he received from the king. He has been forgiven a debt that would take untold lifetimes to repay, yet he refuses to forgive a debt that could be repaid in a few months. So the other servants tell the king, who angrily reverses his compassionate decision and severely punishes the previously forgiven servant. The evil servant (cf. 25:26) is to be tortured until the king is repaid.[6] There is irony here in that the unforgiving servant is treated in the end as he treated his fellow servant (18:30, 34); the *lex talionis* resolves the incongruity between the first and second scenes.

18:31–34

(4) The Application (18:35)

As in 18:14, the application of the story comes at its conclusion: the heavenly Father's actions toward unforgiving disciples will be like that of the unforgiving servant's master. This was made clear when the king asked the evil servant why he did not treat his fellow servant as the king had treated him (18:32). The unforgiving servant's behavior shows that his plea for mercy was a hoax (18:26) and that his forgiveness was ob-

18:35

---

5. Perhaps the expression describes anger more than grief. Cf. LXX: Neh. 5:6; Dan. 6:15; Jon. 4:4, 9; Tob. 3:10; 1 Macc. 10:68; 14:16.

6. The word translated "merciless jailers" is βασανιστής, which occurs only here in the NT (cf. Philo, *Spec. Laws* 4.82; *Good Person* 108; *Flaccus* 96), although its cognates occur elsewhere: βασανίζω (Matt. 8:6, 29; 14:24; Mark 5:7; 6:48; Luke 8:28; Rev. 9:5; 11:10; 12:2; 14:10; 20:10; cf. Sir. 4:17; 2 Macc. 7:13, 17; 4 Macc. 6:5; Josephus, *Ant.* 2.105; 9.101; 12.413; 16.232), βασανισμός (Rev. 9:5; 14:11; 18:10, 15; cf. 4 Macc. 9:6; 11:2), and βάσανος (Matt. 4:24; Luke 16:23; cf. 1 Macc. 9:56; 4 Macc. often; Philo, *Abraham* 96; Josephus. *Ant.* 12.255; 13.241; 16.245; *J.W.* 1.635). The word group describes severe suffering of various kinds, whether from physical torture, disease, or divine judgment.

tained under false pretenses. If the details are pressed, the unforgiving servant will never be able to repay all that he owes to the king, and this perhaps hints at the horror of eternal punishment (cf. 18:6–9; Bruner 1990: 662). The connection of the story with 6:14 is clear. Disciples cannot presume that God will forgive them if they are unwilling to forgive their fellows. Those who have genuinely received forgiveness will be forgiving to others (6:14–15; cf. Luke 6:36; Eph. 4:31–5:2; James 2:13; 1 John 4:11). And this forgiveness must be genuine, from the heart, another important Matthean theme (cf. Matt. 5:8, 28; 6:21; 11:29; 12:34; 13:15, 19; 15:8, 18, 19; 22:37; 24:48).

The Delicate Balance of Discipline and Forgiveness

It may be difficult to reconcile the discipline process in 18:15–20 with the obligation of unlimited forgiveness in 18:21–35. Yet both are consistent with the controlling motif of the chapter: the proper treatment of the little ones, the brothers and sisters, the children of the heavenly Father. Disciples dare not allow this family to be disrupted by offenses, yet they cannot resolve offenses without a forgiving spirit. A straying sheep cannot be left alone in the wilderness, but those who seek it must be willing to receive it back into the flock. If this delicate balance between discipline and forgiveness is faithfully maintained, excommunication is self-imposed exile (W. Davies and Allison 1991: 804).

Summary and Transition

In one key sense, the journey to Jerusalem began with Jesus's announcement of his suffering, death, and resurrection in 16:21, and the disciples must realistically face similar grim prospects. This will be impossible if they have a selfish preoccupation with personal greatness and an accompanying devaluation of others. Instead, disciples must receive each other as they would a child (18:5–10), shepherd each other as they would a lost sheep (18:12–14), deal patiently but decisively with unrepentant sinners in their midst (18:15–20), and genuinely forgive those who sin against them as many times as necessary (18:21–35). These values will strengthen the community's relationships and enable it to withstand the rigors that are ahead in Jerusalem and beyond.

With 19:1 the journey to Jerusalem does indeed begin. Jesus continues to model the values he has inculcated in Matt. 18 (e.g., 19:14), and the disciples continue to struggle with a worldly notion of greatness (e.g., 20:20–28).

Additional Notes

18:26. The editors of UBS[4] prefer the shorter reading λέγων (attested in B, D, Θ, 700, and others) to the longer reading λέγων κύριε (attested in ℵ, L, W, f[1], f[13], *Byz, Lect*) on the theory that κύριε was added to adapt the text to a spiritual interpretation. But they acknowledge that κύριε may have been deleted to conform 18:26 to 18:29 (Metzger 1994: 37).

18:29. After πεσών οὖν ὁ σύνδουλος αὐτοῦ the Majority text (e.g., E, F, H, K, M, and most minuscules) has the prepositional phrase εἰς τοὺς πόδας αὐτοῦ. The shorter text preferred by UBS[4] is supported, e.g., by ℵ, B, C*, D, and most Latin MSS (Metzger 1994: 37).

18:35. At the end of the verse, the Majority text has the phrase τὰ παραπτώματα αὐτῶν, which appears in 6:14. The shorter text, preferred by UBS[4], is supported by, e.g., ℵ, B, D, L, and many Old Latin MSS.

3. Narrative Conclusion (19:1–2)

Following the characteristic formula that concludes each of Jesus's five discourses (cf. 7:28; 11:1; 13:53; 26:1), Matt. 19 begins with the fateful geographical note that Jesus leaves Galilee for the area of Judea east of the Jordan. He will not return to Galilee until after the resurrection (28:7, 16).

Exegesis and Exposition

¹Now when Jesus had finished these words, he left Galilee and went into the region of Judea beyond the Jordan. ²And large crowds followed him, and he healed them there.

19:1–2   From the perspective of Jerusalem, to be beyond or across the Jordan (cf. 4:15, 25) was to be "trans-Jordan," or east of the Jordan River. From Galilee the journey south of more than fifty miles would customarily be made on the east side of the Jordan in order to avoid Samaria (10:5; cf. Luke 9:51–53; John 4:3–4, 9). The reference in Matt. 20:29 to Jericho as the point where the journey back to Jerusalem will begin could mean that Jesus has already crossed the Jordan from east to west at Jericho. Despite the prospect of suffering in Jerusalem, Jesus characteristically continues to heal the sick in the large crowd that follows him (cf. 4:23–25; 9:35; 12:15; 14:14; 15:30–31).

IV. Growing Opposition to the Kingdom of Heaven (11:2–13:52)
V. Opposition to the Kingdom Continues (13:53–19:2)
➤ VI. Opposition Comes to a Head in Judea (19:3–26:2)
VII. Epilogue/Conclusion: Passion, Resurrection, and Commission (26:3–28:20)

VI. Opposition Comes to a Head in Judea (19:3–26:2)

With this section, the reader comes to the final narrative-discourse block in the first Gospel. The opposition to Jesus alluded to early in the story (e.g., 2:13; 4:1–11; 5:10–12; 8:28–34) reaches the point where it becomes potentially lethal (9:34; 11:20–24; 12:14, 24; 16:21). As Jesus moves south from Galilee (19:1), the scene in Jerusalem is already set with the shadow of the cross. As Jesus begins to travel toward Jerusalem (19:3–20:34), he is immediately tested by some Pharisees (19:3). In Jerusalem, he is soon embroiled with the temple hierarchy and has increasingly intense confrontations with various other religious leaders (21:1–23:39). The prospect of Jerusalem's coming judgment leads the disciples to ask Jesus about the future (24:1–3), and his final discourse (24:4–25:31) addresses their chronological concerns (24:4–35) but also, more importantly, his ethical concerns (24:36–25:31). In the face of Jesus's impending death, his disciples must steel themselves for faithful ministry to all the nations (24:14). At the end of this discourse, Matthew notes that Jesus has finished all his words, and Jesus turns the disciples' attention to his crucifixion (26:1–2).

A. Narrative 5: Ministry in Judea (19:3–23:39)

The narrative block between Matthew's fourth (Matt. 18) and fifth (Matt. 24–25) discourses begins with Jesus's journey south from Galilee to Judea east of the Jordan (19:1). After a time he evidently crosses the river at Jericho in the deep rift valley (20:29) and then moves up into the hills toward Jerusalem as far as Bethphage and the Mount of Olives (20:17; 21:1). After arrangements are made, Jesus enters the city (21:10), confronts the temple leaders, and leaves to spend the night in Bethany (21:17). The next morning he returns to the city (21:18) and the temple (21:23) and becomes embroiled in a series of heated disputes with various religious leaders. These disputes culminate in the seven woe oracles of Matt. 23, after which Jesus leaves the temple for the Mount of Olives (24:1–3), the setting for the fifth and final discourse. In all of this, Matthew's story is similar to that found in Mark, with few significant differences (W. Davies and Allison 1997: 1).

Matthew 19–23 continues such basic themes as Jesus's healing and teaching his disciples, the religious leaders' opposition, and preeminently the movement of Jesus ever closer to his predicted suffering in Jerusalem. Such themes are arranged more topically than in the last narrative block. There is less stress on healing (19:2; 20:34; 21:14) and passion predictions (20:17–19; cf. the cryptic language in 21:37–39; 23:32). Much of the material is devoted to Jesus's teaching his disciples (19:10–20:28) and confronting the religious establishment (21:12–23:39). The disciple-oriented sections of Matt. 19–20 continue themes from the discourse in Matt. 18 on kingdom values. In the sections covering Jesus's confrontations with the religious leaders, an already bad situation becomes increasingly worse (Matt. 21–22) and then climaxes (Matt. 23).

W. Davies and Allison (1997: 1–3) helpfully analyze this fourth narrative block as containing four major sections. In the first, Jesus teaches the disciples on family obligations (19:3–20:28). Next, Jesus speaks and acts prophetically in healing, cleansing the temple, and disputing with the chief priests (20:29–21:22). Third, Jesus engages in controversy dialogues with various Jewish leaders (21:23–22:46). Finally, Jesus turns back to the disciples to warn them against Pharisaic practices before he announces seven woes on the Pharisees and laments the fate of Jerusalem (23:1–39).

1. Family Values and Sacrificial Service (19:3–20:34)

Matthew 19:3–20:34 provides the immediate background for Jesus's arrival in Jerusalem (21:1). Jesus is involved in a healing ministry near the Jordan River (19:1–2). There is first a focus on the family (19:3–15) when Jesus's answer to the Pharisees' question on divorce (19:3–9) leads to his answering a related question from the disciples (19:10–12) and blessing children who are brought to him (19:13–15). Next, the focus turns to wealth (19:16–20:16) as Jesus's answer to a question from a rich young man (19:16–22) leads him to teach the disciples on wealth's deceitfulness (19:23–26) and to answer Peter's question about future reward (19:27–20:16). Jesus's third passion prediction (20:17–19; cf. 16:21; 17:22–23) underlines the inappropriateness of the question from Zebedee's sons (20:20–23), but Jesus turns this into a lesson on ministry for all the disciples (20:24–28). Finally, as Jesus leaves Jericho to go up through the Judean wilderness to Jerusalem, he heals two blind men who follow him on his journey (20:29–34).

The section as a whole is bracketed by Jesus's compassionate healings, and it contains his kingdom-oriented teaching on family, wealth, and sacrificial ministry.

a. Marriage and Divorce, Singleness, and Children (19:3–15)

There are three units in 19:3–15 as the debate with the Pharisees on marriage and divorce (19:3–9) leads to Jesus's correcting the disciples' views of marriage (19:10–12) and children (19:13–15). The transition from the first unit occurs when Jesus's strictures against divorce occasion the disciples' jaded remark on the superiority of singleness (19:10). In this pericope Jesus responds four times: twice to the Pharisees (19:3, 7) and twice to the disciples (19:10, 13). Jesus's discussions of singleness and children with his disciples amount to what might be called *Haustafeln* (household codes; Carter 1994a), with similarities to certain Pauline passages (Eph. 5:21–6:9; Col. 3:18–4:1).

The unit outline is as follows:

    i. Jesus answers the Pharisees' question on divorce (19:3–9)
    ii. Jesus responds to the disciples' view of singleness (19:10–12)
    iii. Jesus blesses the children (19:13–15)

Exegesis and Exposition

³Now some Pharisees came to test Jesus and asked him, "Is it lawful for a man to divorce his wife for any and every reason?" ⁴And he answered, "Have you not read that the ⌜Creator⌝ from the beginning 'made them male and female' ⁵and said, 'For this reason a man shall leave his father and mother and be joined to his wife, and the two shall become one flesh'? ⁶So they are no longer two but one flesh. Therefore what God has joined together humans must not separate."

⁷They said to him, "Why, then, did Moses command to 'give her a certificate of divorce and send ⌜her⌝ away'?" ⁸He said to them, "Because of your hardness of heart, Moses permitted you to divorce your wives; but from the beginning it has not been this way. ⁹And I tell you, whoever divorces his wife, ⌜except for sexual infidelity, and marries another woman commits adultery⌝."

¹⁰⌜His⌝ disciples said to him, "If the relationship of a husband with his wife is like this, it is better not to marry." ¹¹But he said to them, "Not everyone can accept ⌜this⌝ word, but only those to whom it is given. ¹²For there are eunuchs who were born so from their mother's womb; and there are eunuchs who were made so by people; and there are eunuchs who made themselves so for the sake of the kingdom of heaven. He who is able to accept this, let him accept it."

¹³Then some children were brought to him so that he might lay his hands

on them and pray, yet the disciples rebuked them. ¹⁴But Jesus said, "Let the children alone, and do not hinder them from coming to me; for the kingdom of heaven belongs to such as these." ¹⁵After laying his hands on them, he went on from there.

i. Jesus Answers the Pharisees' Question on Divorce (19:3–9)

The fourth discourse ends with 18:35/19:1, but emphasis continues on   **19:3–6**
Jesus's teaching until 20:28. Evidently while Jesus is still east of the Jordan, he is engaged by some Pharisees who wish to test his understanding of divorce law (19:3; cf. 5:31–32; 12:2–14; 14:4; 22:17; 27:6; Mark 10:1–12).[1] Their desire to show that Jesus contradicts Moses (Matt. 19:7) reminds the reader of the religious leaders' opposition to Jesus (cf. 12:14, 24, 38; 15:1, 12; 16:1; 22:18, 35). Jesus's response (19:4–6) borders on the incredulous, implying that these Pharisees have not really read the creation account.[2] He cites Gen. 1:27; 2:24 and deduces God's intent that marriage be permanent.[3] Here Jesus was not innovative; the prophet Malachi and the Damascus Document had already made similar arguments.[4]

This passage reprises Jesus's previous teaching in the Sermon on the Mount (Matt. 5:31–32).[5] As the chart below indicates, the two passages are quite similar (important points of connection are highlighted in boldface type). Both allude to the Pharisees' interpretation of Moses (5:31a; 19:7a), both cite Deut. 24:1 (Matt. 5:31b; 19:7b), both present Jesus's teaching in contrast to that of the Pharisees (5:32a; 19:9a), and both teach that divorce amounts to adultery unless it is due to sexual immorality (5:32; 19:9). There are differences between the passages, particularly the inclusion of an explanation for Deut. 24:1 in Matt. 19:8 and the difference in perspectives between 5:32 (the divorced wife is made an adulteress) and 19:9 (the husband who remarries commits adultery).

---

1. The participle πειράζοντες is probably telic in force, as in 16:1; 22:35.

2. Questions with the negative particle οὐκ expect a positive answer. Cf. Moulton and Turner 1963: 282–83.

3. The citation of Gen. 1:27 is identical to the LXX, but Gen. 2:24 differs slightly in a few points. Matthew has ἕνεκα instead of the LXX's ἕνεκεν; the LXX has the possessive αὐτοῦ with "father" and "mother" and uses the compound προσκολληθήσεται instead of κολληθήσεται. Matthew has the dative τῇ γυναικὶ αὐτοῦ instead of the prepositional phrase πρὸς τὴν γυναῖκα αὐτοῦ (Codex Alexandrinus has the dative). Imperatival futures (cf. Matt. 1:21; 4:7, 10; 5:21, 27, 33, 43, 48; 6:5; 19:18; 20:26, 27; 21:3; 22:37, 39; 27:4, 24; Wallace 1996: 569–70) render the commands of Gen. 2:24 in both the LXX and Matthew.

4. Malachi 2:10–16 stresses creation as the basis for justice in domestic situations and implicitly as the reason God hates divorce. CD 4.21 also cites Gen. 1:27 as "the principle of creation" (יסוד הבריאה). CD 4.17–5.6 seems to be denouncing polygamy more than divorce, although it is possible that divorce is also in view. Cf. 11QT 54.4.

5. Garland 1993: 197 points out that several themes from the sermon are taken up again in 19:2–20:16.

Matt. 5:31–32	Matt. 19:7–9
³¹Ἐρρέθη δέ· ὃς ἂν ἀπολύσῃ τὴν γυναῖκα αὐτοῦ, δότω αὐτῇ ἀποστάσιον.	⁷λέγουσιν αὐτῷ· τί οὖν Μωϋσῆς ἐνετείλατο δοῦναι βιβλίον ἀποστασίου καὶ ἀπολῦσαι [αὐτήν]; ⁸λέγει αὐτοῖς ὅτι Μωϋσῆς πρὸς τὴν σκληροκαρδίαν ὑμῶν ἐπέτρεψεν ὑμῖν ἀπολῦσαι τὰς γυναῖκας ὑμῶν, ἀπ' ἀρχῆς δὲ οὐ γέγονεν οὕτως.
³²ἐγὼ δὲ λέγω ὑμῖν ὅτι πᾶς ὁ ἀπολύων τὴν γυναῖκα αὐτοῦ παρεκτὸς λόγου πορνείας ποιεῖ αὐτὴν μοιχευθῆναι, καὶ ὃς ἐὰν ἀπολελυμένην γαμήσῃ, μοιχᾶται.	⁹λέγω δὲ ὑμῖν ὅτι ὃς ἂν ἀπολύσῃ τὴν γυναῖκα αὐτοῦ μὴ ἐπὶ πορνείᾳ καὶ γαμήσῃ ἄλλην μοιχᾶται.
³¹Errethē de: hos an apolysē tēn gynaika autou, dotō autē apostasion.	⁷legousin autō: ti oun Mōüsēs eneteilato dounai biblion apostasiou kai apolysai [autēn]? ⁸legei autois hoti Mōüsēs pros tēn sklērokardian hymōn epestrepsen hymin apolysai tas gynaikas hymōn, ap' archēs de ou gegonen houtōs.
³²egō de legō hymin hoti pas ho apolyōn tēn gynaika autou parektos logou porneias poiei autēn moicheuthēnai, kai hos ean apolelymenēn gamēsē, moichatai.	⁹legō de hymin hoti hos an apolysē tēn gynaika autou mē epi porneia kai gamēsē, allēn moichatai.
³¹"And it was said, 'Whoever divorces his wife must **give** her a **certificate of divorce**.'	⁷They said to him, "Why, then, did Moses command to **give** her a **certificate of divorce** and send her away?" ⁸He said to them, "Because of your hardness of heart, Moses permitted you to divorce your wives, but from the beginning it has not been this way.
³²**And I tell you that** everyone who **divorces his wife**, except for **sexual infidelity**, makes her commit adultery, and whoever **marries** a divorced woman **commits adultery**."	⁹**And I tell you that** whoever **divorces his wife**, except for **sexual infidelity**, and **marries** another woman **commits adultery**."

The rabbinic dispute between Hillel and Shammai (first century BCE) over divorce and Deut. 24:1–4 seems relevant to this passage (*m. Giṭ.* 9.10; cf. *m. Ketub.* 7.6; *b. Giṭ.* 90b; Josephus, *Ant.* 4.244–59; Neudecker 1994). Hillel took a flexible view of the shameful or indecent matter mentioned in Deut. 24:1 and permitted divorce for any reason. But Shammai interpreted Deut. 24:1 strictly as a reference to sexual impropriety. Josephus's practice appears to have cohered with Hillel (*Life* 426; *Ant.* 4.253), but Philo laments divorce based only on a husband's mood (*Spec. Laws* 3.30, 79–82). Jesus does not focus on Deut. 24:1 but on Gen. 1:27; 2:24 (cf. Gen. 5:2; 1 Cor. 6:16; Eph. 5:31), stressing God's original purpose for marriage. The gist of his teaching is that the original divine plan for monogamy is normative, not the subsequent concession to human sinfulness in Deut. 24:1.[6] The "one flesh" relationship in marriage (Gen. 2:24) makes divorce wrong unless there has been illicit sexual union outside marriage. When God has united two people, humans may not split them apart. When two people are married, their identity as their parents' children is altered, and their new identity as husband and wife is permanent unless ruined by human sinfulness.

Jesus's argument for the permanence of marriage evidently concerns the Pharisees because of the prevalence of divorce in the Jewish culture of that time. Their response to Jesus pits a view of Deut. 24:1 similar to that of Hillel against Gen. 1–2. They seem to think that Deut 24:1 commands divorce, but Jesus's citation of Gen. 1–2 places the creation narrative in Genesis over the ad hoc legislation of Deut. 24. God's original purpose for marriage overrides the Mosaic concession for human sin.[7] Moses *permitted* divorce; he did not command it. Sexual infidelity is the only permissible ground for the dissolution of a marriage. Jesus's teaching here is similar to the strict perspective of Shammai, but his appeal to the creation account rather than to Deut. 24 is not found in either Shammai or Hillel. The original divine ordinance of marriage trumps the subsequent human expedient of divorce. This is quite different from the rabbinic view that unfaithful wives had to be divorced by their husbands (*m. Ned.* 11.12; *m. Soṭah* 5.1; *m. Yebam.* 2.8). But divorce is not a matter of course in the Bible (Lev. 21:7; Ezek. 44:22; Mal. 2:16).

19:7–9

Jesus on Divorce and Remarriage

Deuteronomy 24:1–4 prohibits a woman who has been married to and divorced from two different men from remarrying her first husband.[8] It

---

6. Luz 2001: 490–91 views this passage as a major point of departure that bifurcates God's will and Moses's commands. But this view neglects the global purview of Gen. 1–2 and the specific focus of Deut. 24:1. It is doubtful that the Jesus of Matt. 5:17–20 would countenance the sort of point of departure that Luz proposes.

7. Hardness of heart (σκληροκαρδίαν) is a common biblical image of sin (LXX: Deut. 10:16; Jer. 4:4; Prov. 17:20; Ezek. 3:7). Cf. Sir. 16:9–10; 1 En. 16.3; Philo, *Spec. Laws* 1.305; Mark 16:14; and the use of Ps. 95:7–8 in Heb. 3:7–11, 15; 4:7.

8. Deuteronomy 24:1–4 is part of a series of casuistic laws concerning hypothetical situations introduced by כִּי (cf. MT: Deut. 22:27, 28; 23:10, 11, 23, 25; 24:5, 7, 10, 19, 20, 21). The gist is that remarriage of the same pair is forbidden when a sequence of several events ensues: (1) the wife displeases the husband, (2) the husband writes a divorce docu-

is not an apodictic law enjoining universal practice but a specific stipulation for the case of remarriage. Jesus views it as a concession to the hardness of human hearts. He interprets the original "one flesh" implications of marriage (Gen. 2:24) as requiring its permanence.[9] He permits divorce only in the instance of sexual infidelity, which breaks the "one flesh" character of the union. Divorce leads to adultery except in cases of infidelity. Jesus's language assumes, as did the Hebrew Bible, that a man could divorce his wife but a wife could not divorce her husband (Matt. 19:3, 9; cf. 5:31). A wife could only appeal to the community elders for redress of grievances (m. Ketubbot).

The exegetical difficulties of 19:9 (cf. 5:32) are compounded by textual problems (see the additional note). One difficulty is the meaning of πορνεία (porneia), which has been understood variously as marital infidelity (NLT), premarital infidelity (cf. 1:19), or incest (cf. Lev. 18; 1 Cor. 5:1; BDAG 854; Witherington 2006: 363). There seems to be no contextual restriction of the general sense of πορνεία as extramarital sexual activity (Keener 1999: 467–69). Another difficulty is the scope of the "exception clause" μὴ ἐπὶ πορνείᾳ (mē epi porneia). The question is whether this clause excepts both divorce and remarriage or divorce alone from Jesus's strictures against divorce. Most Protestant scholars take the former view (W. Davies and Allison 1997: 17), but there are notable exceptions (e.g., Gundry 1994: 381; Hagner 1995a: 549; Heth and Wenham 1984). Those who take the latter view tend to view 19:11–12 as requiring celibacy for those who have been divorced.

This issue cannot be fully resolved by grammatical arguments alone, but the view that both divorce and remarriage are permitted in the case of infidelity seems more likely. If divorce does not convey freedom to remarry (m. Giṭ. 9.1–3), it is essentially meaningless. Additionally, it is arbitrary to think that divorced people are universally gifted with celibacy. Repentant people who have been divorced because of infidelity should have the freedom to remarry.[10]

Those who participate in Christ's kingdom are a newly created humanity whose identity and relationships have been transformed (cf. 2 Cor. 5:17; Eph. 2:11–22). When Jesus says that divorce was not what God originally intended (Matt. 19:8), he tells his disciples that they are

---

ment and (3) gives it to his wife and (4) sends her away, and (5) she marries another man who (6) subsequently divorces her or (7) dies.

9. "The created order is a guide for the moral order" (W. Davies and Allison 1997: 10). Evidently, the author of Sirach would disagree, since Sir. 25:26 counsels divorce of an evil wife in language that likely alludes to Gen. 2:24: "cut her off from your flesh."

10. For a helpful summary of the scholarly literature on the several exegetical difficulties here, see Carson 1984: 412–18. For helpful, pastorally oriented discussion, see Bruner 1990: 675–87; Witherington 2006: 361, 382–84. Instone-Brewer 2002 provides not only an exegetical treatment of Jesus's teaching (133–88) but also a history of ancient and current Christian views on divorce (238–99) followed by pastoral conclusions (300–314).

to recapitulate the harmonious relationships of humanity before the fall, when hard hearts began to pervert God's original plan. Jesus's disciples anticipate the future renewal of the world (19:28), but until then they long for God's will to be done on earth as it is in heaven (6:10). In this light, marital permanence ought to be the rule in the Christian community as an aspect of righteous life that anticipates the coming of God's kingdom to the earth (Hagner 1995a: 549–51). Moses did not command divorce, and certainly neither did Jesus. Even in the case of marital infidelity, divorce should not be the first option. The deep wounds caused by marital infidelity can be healed by the love of God in Christ. Couples contemplating divorce must contemplate the implications of 18:21–35 and 19:8. When one is sinned against, forgiveness is the primary Christian duty. Forgiveness can lead to restored relationships and is a powerful testimony to the power of Jesus's gospel. If God hated divorce under the old covenant (Mal. 2:14–16), how much more so now that the kingdom has been inaugurated. (For a pastoral perspective, see Molldrem 1991.)

ii. Jesus Responds to the Disciples' View of Singleness (19:10–12)

At this point it becomes clear that the Pharisees are not alone in thinking that Jesus's teaching is overly restrictive. The disciples are also amazed at Jesus's approach and prefer a life of celibacy to marriage under such tight constraints (19:10; cf. Sir. 25:16–26). But Jesus teaches that celibacy is only for divinely gifted people (Matt. 19:11; cf. 1 Cor. 7:1–2, 7–9).[11] The disciples are familiar with eunuchs,[12] those who cannot have children because of congenital defect or castration, but Jesus adds a third category: those who choose singleness and sexual abstinence because of their kingdom commitment (Matt. 19:12).[13] Such "making a eunuch of oneself" is not to be taken literally.[14] Among those who fit this category are probably John the Baptist, Jesus, Paul, and Philip's four daughters (cf. 1 Cor. 7:32–38; 9:5; Acts 21:9).[15] For them, the eschatological urgency of the kingdom takes priority over normal family relationships (cf.

19:10–12

11. The verb δέδοται is a "divine passive," an understated way of expressing divine agency. Cf. Wallace 1996: 437–38. The words τὸν λόγον τοῦτον find their antecedent in the disciples' mistaken conclusion of 19:10 that it is better not to marry at all. Jesus does not refer back to his own teaching in 19:3–9.
12. See Lev. 21:20; 22:24; Deut. 23:1; 2 Kings 9:32; 20:18; Isa. 39:7; 56:3–5; Jer. 29:2; 34:19; 38:7; 41:16; Dan. 1:3; Acts 8:26–40; cf. Wis. 3:14; Philo, *Migr.* 69; Josephus, *Ant.* 4.291; *m. Zabim* 2.1; *m. Yebam.* 8.4; *b. Sanh.* 152a; *b. Yebam.* 80b.
13. The solemn affirmation ὁ δυνάμενος χωρεῖν χωρείτω in 19:12 is similar to ὁ ἔχων ὦτα ἀκουέτω in 11:15; 13:9, 43.
14. But see Philo, *Worse* 176; Eusebius, *Eccl. Hist.* 6.8. Cf. Justin Martyr, *First Apology* 29; canon 1 of the First Council of Nicea.
15. Daniel's chastity led to his being viewed as a eunuch (Josephus, *Ant.* 10.186; Liv. Pro. 4.2; *b. Sanh.* 93b). Similar views were held of Moses (Philo, *Moses* 2.68–9).

Matt. 8:21–22; 12:46–50). On the other hand, rabbinic reflection on Gen. 1:28 concluded that no man is exempt from the duty to have children (*m. Yebam.* 6.6; *b. Yebam.* 61b–64b).

Matthew 19:10–12 should not be read as requiring singleness for all those who have been divorced (contra Gundry 1994: 381–82; Heth and Wenham 1984: 88). This would imply that God has gifted all divorced people with celibacy. It should also be noted that this passage does not teach that celibates are holier than married people or that their lifestyle is morally superior. Only those who are enabled by special gift should choose a celibate lifestyle for the sake of the kingdom. This passage does not promote asceticism as the ideal for human existence.[16]

iii. Jesus Blesses the Children (19:13–15)

19:13   Jesus is asked to bless some children who were brought to him (cf. 4:24; 8:16; 9:2, 32; 12:22; 14:35; 17:16) by laying his hands on them and praying for them (cf. Gen. 48:14–15).[17] This incident recalls and reinforces Matt. 18:1–14 (cf. Mark 10:13–16; Luke 18:15–17). It is fitting here, since Jesus has been discussing divorce, marriage, and singleness, and it fits the general pattern of Paul's household exhortations (Eph. 5:21–6:4; Col. 3:18–21; cf. Philo, *Flight* 1.3; Josephus, *Ag. Ap.* 2.199–204). It is unclear whether the disciples' rebuke (cf. Matt. 20:31) is directed against the children or those who brought them to Jesus. Presumably, the disciples thought Jesus would not want to be bothered with such an unimportant task. Both this rebuke and the disciples' jaded view of marital commitment (19:10) indicate a low view of the nuclear family.

19:14–15   Jesus emphatically turns the rebuke back on the disciples in 19:14 with three statements: a command, a prohibition, and an explanation. They must never keep children from coming to him, because children exemplify the central value of the kingdom. Here as in 18:3–5 children represent the humble ones to whom the kingdom belongs, Jesus's disciples. Jesus welcomes them, lays his hands on them, and evidently prays for them. Then he leaves the area, perhaps to avoid further strife with the Pharisees (cf. 19:3).

Jesus's affirmation of and care for children provide an important model for his disciples. Yet this passage should not be pressed into the

---

16. For further discussion of celibacy, see Heth 1987; Kodell 1978; McArthur 1987; Trautman 1966; Wolff 1988. On Matt. 19:1–12, see Allison 1993a; Blomberg 1990b; Bockmuehl 1989; Derrett 1970b: 363–88; Dupont 1959; Fitzmyer 1976; Harvey in C. A. Evans and Stegner 1994: 55–65; Kampen in Brooke and García Martínez 1994: 149–68; Moloney 1979; Sand 1983; Sigal 1986: 83–118; Stein 1979; Stock 1978.

17. Laying on hands with prayer is common in the Bible on occasions such as ordination, healing, and other blessings. Cf. Gen. 48:14; Num. 27:18–23; Deut. 34:9; Matt. 9:18; Mark 6:5; 7:32; 8:23, 25; Luke 4:40; Acts 6:6; 8:17–19; 9:12, 17; 13:3; 19:6; 28:8; 1 Tim. 4:14; 5:22; 2 Tim. 1:6; Daube 1973: 224–46; Knoch 1983; Parratt 1969.

service of later theological concerns such as infant baptism.[18] Children here stand for Jesus's disciples.[19] The use of little children to illustrate kingdom humility fits Matthew's overall teaching (cf. 10:42; 11:25; 18:14; 19:13–15; 21:15–16; 25:40, 45). Infant baptism is not clearly mentioned in patristic literature until Tertullian (*On Baptism* 18), who opposed it in the late second century CE. (For a well-stated contrary view, see Bruner 1990: 695–98.)[20]

The permanence and normativeness of marriage are the major point of 19:3–15, supported by Jesus's view of Gen. 1–2, his strict view of divorce, and his explanation of celibate singleness as a lifestyle appropriate only for relatively few specially gifted people. Jesus's affirmation of children also implicitly supports marriage. Today, as in Jesus's day, divorce is all too common, and noncelibate singleness is often viewed as the most fulfilling lifestyle. Similarly, children are deprecated as a time-consuming distraction from career goals and personal pleasure. But Jesus advocates marriage as the divine pattern for everyone except those who have been specially gifted, a pattern that may be abandoned by legal divorce only after it has been broken by sexual infidelity. The offspring of this pattern must be affirmed and blessed.

Marriage should be viewed in terms of Jesus's teaching on taking up one's cross and denying oneself (16:24). Divorce, singleness, and childlessness may seem to be the way of success and fulfillment, but in the end the seemingly carefree life will be a lonely, lost life. Being "married with children" may appear to be boring drudgery, but in the end it will prove to be the richest life because it accords with the Creator's pattern. In the present fallen world, the ideals of the creation pattern are not easily attained. Yet the inauguration of God's rule empowers disciples to approximate the created pattern. Despite their best efforts, genuine followers of Jesus can and do fail in these areas, and the church must reach out and restore them to fellowship and obedience. (For a fine pastorally oriented discussion of this passage, see Bruner 1990: 675–87.)

Additional Notes

19:4. Instead of the UBS[4] reading κτίσας (supported by B, Θ, 1, 700), other ancient MSS (including ℵ, C, D, W, Z, *f*[13], *Byz, Lect,* following Gen. 1:27 LXX) have ποιήσας. Κτίσας is closer to the Hebrew אָרָב in Gen. 1:27.

18. As in Cullmann 1950: 71–80; Jeremias 1960; Lindemann 1983. For a contrary view, see Beasley-Murray 1962: 306–59, esp. 320–29; Luz 2001: 504–7. On infant baptism, see Lane 2004; Strobel in Perels 1963: 7–69; D. Wright 2005. On children in Matthew, see Weren 1996.
19. In 19:14 τῶν . . . τοιούτων portrays believers as children, as in 18:5–6.
20. For additional studies of 19:13–15, see R. Brown 1982; Derrett 1983c; Légasse 1969: 36–43; Ringshausen 1986; and the articles on "Kingdom and Children" in *Semeia* 29 (1983).

19:7. UBS⁴ prefers αὐτήν (supported by B, C, W, Δ, *f*¹³, *Byz, Lect*) but places it in brackets because of the plausible shorter reading (supported by ℵ, D, L, Z, Θ, 579) that provides no object for the infinitive ἀπολῦσαι (cf. Mark 10:4). The object τὴν γυναῖκα is weakly attested in a few versions and patristic sources (cf. Matt. 19:9).

19:9. The textual tradition of this verse is complex. There are two major variations, both evidently due to assimilation of 19:9 to 5:32. First, the reading of the "exception clause" and predicate of 19:9 in UBS⁴, μὴ ἐπὶ πορνείᾳ καὶ γαμήσῃ ἄλλην μοιχᾶται, is widely supported by ℵ, C³, L, Z, 078, 28, 157, *Byz, Lect*. It seems likely that the variant παρεκτὸς λόγου πορνείας ποιεῖ αὐτὴν μοιχευθῆναι (supported by B, 0233, 1) arose as an assimilation to 5:32, where the text is firm. Another variant (supported by D, *f*¹³) evidently interpolates just the exception clause παρεκτὸς λόγου πορνείας from 5:32.

Second, UBS⁴ prefers the shorter reading of 19:9, which is supported by ℵ, D, L, Z, 1241. A longer reading of the verse, supported by K, W, Δ, Θ, Π, *f*¹³, adds the clause καὶ ὁ ἀπολελυμένην γαμῶν μοιχᾶται. It is again probable that this reading reflects the influence of 5:32, although it is possible that the shorter reading is due to accidental omission (homoeoteleuton with μοιχᾶται). See Duplacy 1987: 387–412; Holmes 1990; Metzger 1994: 38–39.

19:10. Although οἱ μαθηταὶ αὐτοῦ is read by 𝔓²⁵, C, D, L, W, Z, *f*¹, *f*¹³, *Byz, Lect*, αὐτοῦ is placed in brackets by UBS⁴ because a shorter reading, οἱ μαθηταί, is found in ℵ, B, Θ.

19:11. Although τὸν λόγον τοῦτον is read by ℵ, C, D, L, W, Z, *f*¹³, 28, 33, *Byz, Lect*, as well as by many versions and fathers, τοῦτον is placed in brackets by UBS⁴ because a shorter reading, τὸν λόγον, is found in B, 1, 892*.

b. Wealth and the Kingdom: Three Conversations on Sacrificial Discipleship (19:16–20:16)

This passage addresses the relationship between present sacrifice and future reward three times: first, when the young man refuses to sacrifice his riches to follow Jesus (19:16–22); second, when Jesus interacts with the disciples on the matter (19:23–26); and third, when Peter reminds Jesus of the disciples' sacrifice (19:27–20:16). Each of these three exchanges concludes with Jesus's having the final word. In the third exchange Jesus's response to Peter moves from a brief prose comment (19:27–29) to a lengthier parabolic illustration (19:30–20:16; cf. the same pattern in 18:21–22, 23–35). The interpretation of the concluding parable is notoriously difficult. Overman's presentation (1996: 285–89) of this entire pericope as a discussion of hierarchy and position is unconvincing. Although hierarchy is at the heart of 20:20–28, it is not the overriding concern of 19:16–20:28.

i. The Conversation with the Wealthy Young Man (19:16–22)

A passage reminiscent of Mic. 6:8, Matt. 19:16–22 interweaves a young man's three questions and Jesus's three answers (19:16–17, 18–19, 20–22). The first question concerns how to obtain eternal life, and when Jesus directs the young man to God's commands, the young man's second question asks which command is relevant. When Jesus cites several, the young man affirms he has already kept these and asks for more. When Jesus tells him to divest himself of his resources, the young man departs with sadness. The interchange with this rich young man provides Jesus with an occasion to teach the disciples about the incompatibility of wealth, or at least the love of wealth, and the kingdom (19:23–24). As on two immediately prior occasions, his teaching challenges the disciples' views (19:25–26; cf. 19:10, 14–15). The Markan and Lukan versions of this episode contain important differences from Matthew's account (cf. Mark 10:17–22; Luke 18:18–23; Bock 1996: 1473–84).

Exegesis and Exposition

¹⁶Then a man came to him and said, "⸂Teacher⸃, what good thing should I do in order to obtain eternal life?" ¹⁷And he said to him, "⸂Why do you ask me about what is good? There is only One who is good⸃; but if you wish to enter life, keep the commandments." ¹⁸He said to him, "Which ones?" And Jesus said,

> "You shall not murder;
> You shall not commit adultery;
> You shall not steal;
> You shall not give false testimony;
> ¹⁹Honor your father and your mother; and
> You shall love your neighbor as yourself."

²⁰The young man said to him, "⸂I have kept⸃ all these; what do I still lack?"
²¹Jesus said to him, "If you wish to be complete, go, sell your possessions, and give to the poor, and you will have treasure in heaven. Then come, follow me." ²²But when the young man heard this word, he went away in sorrow; for he had many possessions.

The second section of Matt. 19 begins with a question, as did the first half (19:3).[1] After his teaching on family matters, Jesus is approached by a man who wishes to know what good thing he must do to inherit eternal life (cf. 7:14; 18:8–9; 19:29; 25:46). The young man addresses Jesus as "teacher," which implies an inadequate grasp of Jesus's identity (cf. 8:19; 12:38). Yet the passage does not indicate that the man approaches Jesus with insincere motives. Jesus inquires as to why the man asks him about what is good, since only One is good (perhaps an allusion to Deut. 6:4; cf. Matt. 20:15; Ps. 16:2). This puzzling question may mean that the man should focus not on his own goodness but on God's. Or it may imply that God's goodness ensures that his commandments supply a detailed explanation of goodness (see Cope 1976b: 111–19; U. Luck in Schrage 1986: 282–97; J. Wenham 1982). In either case, Jesus's reply that the man should keep the commandments is not novel but summarizes Lev. 18:5.   **19:16–17**

The man's request that Jesus be more specific is puzzling, since all the Torah is binding (cf. Luke 10:25–29). Perhaps his question is similar to that of the Pharisee who asks Jesus to identify the great commandment in the law (Matt. 22:36). Or perhaps he wants Jesus to assign him one outstanding feat that would assure him of eternal life. Jesus's reply focuses on the second table of the law (cf. 5:21–48), citing five of the ten commandments, the sixth through the ninth, followed by the fifth (cf. Exod. 20:12–16; Deut. 5:16–20). He adds the Golden Rule, Lev. 19:18.[2] Perhaps Matt. 19:17 should be viewed as a summary of the first table of the law. The sixth through ninth commandments prohibit specific social sins whereas the fifth commandment and the Golden Rule enjoin godly behavior toward one's parents and one's neighbors (cf. Philo, *Decalogue* 121). The man baldly affirms that he has kept all these (cf. Phil. 3:6), but acknowledges that he still lacks something.   **19:18–20**

Jesus has reaffirmed the central social tenets of the Torah; now he adds his own definitive directives (cf. 5:17–48). In order to be complete (τέλειος, *teleios*; see Yarnold 1968: 269–73), the man must sell his possessions and give them to the poor (cf. Tob. 4:5–11; Luke 12:33; Acts 2:43–47; 1 Cor. 13:3; *b. B. Bat.* 10a). The word "complete" alludes to a level of spiritual maturity or development that contrasts with the man's admitted inadequacies (Matt. 5:48; BDAG 996; cf. 1 Kings 11:4 LXX). In addition to   **19:21–22**

---

1. In both 19:3 (προσῆλθον) and 19:16 (προσελθών), Jesus is approached by those who question him about his interpretation of the law.

2. For the wide citation of Lev. 19:18 in Second Temple literature, see Neudecker 1992; CD 6.18–20; 1QS 5.25; Sir. 13:15; Jub. 7.20; 20.2; 36.4, 8; T. Reu. 6.9; T. Iss. 5.2; T. Gad 4.2; T. Benj. 3.3–4. In the NT, see Matt. 5:43; 7:12; 22:39 and parallels; Rom. 12:9–10; 13:9; Gal. 5:14; James 2:8. Cf. John 13:34; Did. 1.2. According to Sipra on Lev. 19:18, Rabbi Akiba made Lev. 19:18 the central principle of the Torah. Cf. Philo, *Decalogue* 18–19; *Spec. Laws* 1.1; Sipra on Lev. 19.1–4; Daube 1973: 63–66.

exchanging earthly for heavenly treasure (cf. Matt. 6:19–21; 13:44–46), he must follow Jesus as an itinerant disciple (4:22; 8:22; 9:9). Jesus demands that the young man forsake his wealth (cf. 1QS 1.11–13; 6.19–22; 7.6–7, 24–25; 9.8–9, 22; Malina 1987), since his devotion to it is preventing him from loving God and neighbor.[3] It is striking (but not surprising in light of 5:17–48) that Jesus appends his own commands to those of Moses. Jesus alone determines what is genuine Torah obedience. His demand for total commitment to the kingdom is in reality a gracious gospel offer that calls the man to rely not on wealth but on Jesus and the values of the kingdom (cf. 6:21, 24; 13:22). The young man walks away from Jesus in a very sad frame of mind. Jesus has identified the inadequacy that haunts him, but he is not yet willing to obey Jesus. (For additional study of 19:16–22, see Klijn 1966; R. Thomas 1982.)

Jesus the Evangelist

This episode is frequently viewed as relevant for personal evangelism (cf. John 4:1–42). But it can be misunderstood. Jesus's stress on the second table of the law does not amount to salvation by mechanical observation of the commandments. Nor does his use of the term τέλειος (Matt. 19:21) imply two levels of discipleship (W. Thomas 1961: 292). Jesus answers the man's question by getting to his root problem, covetousness. Jesus begins by shifting the focus from one's own goodness to God's goodness (19:16–17). Perhaps the man is asking Jesus to assign him one outstanding good deed that would bring him eternal life. When Jesus directs him to the commandments, he wonders which are relevant. When Jesus cites the second table, he claims he has kept all those, but wonders if he still lacks something.

At this point Jesus gets to the heart of the problem by commanding the man to give his wealth to the poor and become a disciple. In effect, Jesus asks the man to reprise a role previously scripted in two parables (13:44–46). The man will lose everything, but he will gain Jesus and the kingdom, which he has lacked all along (16:24–26). His sorrowful departure demonstrates he has not loved his neighbor as himself (19:19) and thus he has not kept all the commandments after all. Jesus did not directly cite the tenth commandment, "You must not covet" (Exod. 20:17), but the man's response clearly shows that he has broken it. Finally the man implicitly acknowledges what he lacks. His wealth has become an idol, and he is violating the first commandment (Exod. 20:2–3). His refusal to do a good thing—to divest himself of wealth and follow Jesus—shows that he does not acknowledge God's goodness. He serves money, and so he cannot serve God (Matt. 6:24). "Jesus demands not alms but everything" (W. Davies and Allison 1997: 46; cf. Calvin 1972: 2.256–57). But

---

3. Cf. 6:24; 13:22; cf. Prov. 15:16–17; Sir. 31:5–7; T. Jud. 19.1–2; Luke 19:8; 1 Cor. 1:26–29; 1 Tim. 6:10; Rev. 3:17.

materialism prevents him from seeking the kingdom first (6:33). His sorrow indicates not only that he is not ready to follow Jesus but also that now he knows what he lacks. Perhaps he eventually will follow Jesus's instructions, since "with God everything is possible" (19:26).

Jesus's commands to the rich young man are directed specifically toward his individual need. Yet all of Jesus's disciples must help the poor (e.g., 5:3; 25:34–40; 26:6–13; Acts 4:34–37; Gal. 2:10; 6:10; James 2:1–17; 1 John 2:17). They need not totally divest themselves of wealth to do so (e.g., Matt. 27:57; Luke 8:3; 19:2, 8–9; Acts 5:4; James 1:9–11). Greed bars one from the kingdom (cf. 1 Tim. 6:9–10; Sir. 31:7), but greed is not limited to the rich. There are genuine disciples who by God's providence are rich (1 Cor. 1:26), and they are accountable to use their resources to further God's work (1 Tim. 6:17–19). (See Luz 2001: 518–23 for a helpful discussion of the history of this text's interpretation and application.)

Additional Notes

19:16. The shorter reading διδάσκαλε (supported by ℵ, B, D, L, 1, 892*) is more likely original because ἀγαθέ in the longer reading διδάσκαλε ἀγαθέ (supported by C, W, Δ, Θ, *f*¹³, *Byz, Lect*) was probably interpolated by copyists from Mark 10:17; Luke 18:18. Another interpolation is possible in 19:17.

19:17. UBS⁴ prefers the shorter reading τί με ἐρωτᾷς περὶ τοῦ ἀγαθοῦ; εἷς ἐστιν ὁ ἀγαθός· (supported by ℵ, B² [B* omits εἷς], L, Θ). Some versions and fathers add "God" or "my father" in apposition to ὁ ἀγαθός. The reading τί με λέγεις ἀγαθόν; οὐδεὶς ἀγαθὸς εἰ μὴ εἷς ὁ θεός (supported by C, W, Δ, *f*¹³, 28, 33, *Byz, Lect*) was probably interpolated from Mark 10:18; Luke 18:19 to replace the more difficult previous reading.

19:20. UBS⁴ prefers the shorter reading ἐφύλαξα (supported by ℵ*, B, L, Θ, *f*¹) over the longer reading ἐφυλαξάμην ἐκ νεότητός μου since Matthew identifies the man as young in 19:20, 22 (Metzger 1994: 40). The longer reading (supported by C, W, Δ, *f*¹³, 28, 33, *Byz, Lect*, etc.) may well have been interpolated from Mark 10:20; Luke 18:21.

ii. The Conversation with the Disciples (19:23–26)

Evidently, the disciples have been observing Jesus's conversation with the rich young man. This conversation leads to a teachable moment, and Jesus explains—to the disciples' surprise—that wealth is a barrier to eternal life, one that can be broken only by the power of God.

Exegesis and Exposition

[23]Then Jesus said to his disciples, "Truly I tell you, it is hard for a rich person to enter the kingdom of heaven. [24]Again I tell you, it is easier for a ⌜camel⌝ to go through the eye of a needle than for a rich person to enter the kingdom of God." [25]When the disciples heard, they were totally amazed and said, "Then who can be saved?"
[26]But Jesus looked at them and said, "For humans this is impossible, but for God all things are possible."

19:23–24 The incident with the rich young man provides an occasion for Jesus to teach his disciples about the deceitfulness of riches (cf. Mark 10:23–27; Luke 18:24–27). Wealth can desensitize people to their deepest needs just as poverty can alert them to the kingdom (Matt. 5:3).[1] Matthew 19:24 restates 19:23 with a hyperbolic metaphor that utilizes the largest animal and the smallest opening in the everyday life of the disciples. As it is humanly impossible for a camel to pass through the eye of a needle,[2] so it is impossible, apart from God's power, for a rich person to enter God's kingdom.[3]

In 19:16–30 five different terms are used to describe salvation. In 19:23–24 Jesus speaks of the "kingdom of God" in parallel with the more usual Matthean term "kingdom of heaven" (19:23), this in response to

---

1. The future εἰσελεύσεται in 19:23 is more likely gnomic than predictive. See Wallace 1996: 571.
2. See a similar camel hyperbole in 23:24. Later the Talmud spoke of the impossibility of an elephant passing through the eye of a needle (*b. Ber.* 55b; *b. B. Meṣiʿa* 38b).
3. Despite sermonic lore based on medieval tradition and modern anecdotes, there is no early historical evidence for the existence of a small gate in Jerusalem, supposedly called the Needle's Eye, through which a camel on its knees could barely squeeze. This mistaken understanding weakens Jesus's hyperbole and implies that it is not actually impossible for rich people to enter the kingdom (Broadus 1886: 408–9; Bruner 1990: 713–14; W. Davies and Allison 1997: 51–52). See E. Best 1970; Derrett 1986a; Lindeskog in Kiilunen et al. 1983: 109–22; the additional note on 19:24.

the young man's question about inheriting "eternal life" (19:16, 29). Jesus further describes salvation as being "perfect" (19:21), and the disciples refer to it as being "saved" (19:25; cf. 1:21; 10:22; 16:25; 18:11). This semantic interplay shows that there is no real difference between the kingdom of God and the kingdom of heaven in Matthew, as is also evident from synoptic comparisons.[4] Rather, "kingdom of God" is occasionally used (12:28; 19:24; 21:31, 43) for subtle literary and contextual reasons to describe the same referent as the more common "kingdom of heaven." Although the language about obtaining or entering eternal life (19:16–17, 23–24) and having treasure in heaven (19:21) may imply that the kingdom is future, the language of being "complete" and "saved" (19:21, 25) implies that the kingdom may be experienced genuinely, if only partially, in the present life. Those who do not recognize both present and future aspects truncate scriptural truth.

The disciples' incredulous question may be based on the notion that riches are always proof of God's approval. Perhaps this is based on a misunderstanding of texts such as Deut. 7:12–13; 28:1–14; Prov. 22:4, for other biblical texts warn of coveting and hoarding riches (Prov. 22:16, 22; cf. Sir. 31:7). If such a notion were correct, the rich would be most likely of all people to enter the kingdom. Jesus is not condemning riches but the idolatrous coveting of riches (Matt. 6:24; cf. 27:57; Acts 5:1–4; 1 Tim. 6:10). Only by the sovereign grace of God can such idolatry be overcome. And there is at least the possibility that the young man's riches have been obtained by oppressing others and leaving them in poverty.[5] If so, his sin would involve more than mere covetousness. **19:25–26**

Additional Note

19:24. The reading κάμιλον (rope, cable) is poorly supported (579, 1424, and a few others) and is clearly secondary. It is either a mistake due to itacism for κάμηλον (well supported by ℵ, B, C, D, L, W, *f*¹, *f*¹³, *Byz*, *Lect*) or an attempt to soften Jesus's teaching. Cf. Mark 10:25; Luke 18:25.

---

4. E.g., Matt. 13:31–32//Mark 4:30–32//Luke 13:18–19; and Matt. 19:14//Mark 10:14// Luke 18:16.
5. Cf. Malina 1987 and such texts as Neh. 5:1–13; Prov. 22:22–23; 23:10–11; Isa. 5:8–10; Amos 5:11–12; James 5:1–6; Sir. 13:3–4; 34:20–26; 1 En. 92–105.

iii. The Conversation with Peter (19:27–20:16)

Peter calls Jesus's attention to the disciples' sacrifice, which contrasts with the young man's attachment to his possessions, and asks about their reward (19:27). Jesus answers first with a brief promise of reward (19:28–30) and then with a parable that emphasizes God's sovereignty in reward (20:1–16). Both the prosaic promise and the poetic warning end on the note of eschatological reversal hinted at in the parable (20:8).

The unit outline is as follows:

(1) The promise of reward (19:27–30)
(2) A warning: The parable of the workers (20:1–16)

Exegesis and Exposition

[19:27]Then Peter replied, "Look, we have left everything and followed you; what, then, will there be for us?" [28]And Jesus said to them, "Truly I tell you that you who have followed me, when the world is renewed and the Son of Man sits on his glorious throne, you also shall sit upon twelve thrones, judging the twelve tribes of Israel. [29]And everyone who has left houses or brothers or sisters or ⌜father or mother⌝ or children or farms, for my name's sake, will receive ⌜many times as much⌝ and will inherit eternal life. [30]But many who are first will be last; and the last, first.

[20:1]"For the kingdom of heaven is like a landowner who went out early in the morning to hire laborers for his vineyard. [2]After he had agreed with the laborers to pay them a denarius for the day, he sent them into his vineyard. [3]When he went out about nine a.m., he saw others standing around idle in the marketplace. [4]So he said to them, 'You also go into my vineyard, and I will pay you whatever is right.' [5]And so they went. And he went out again at noon and at 3 p.m. and did the same thing. [6]And at about 5 p.m. he went out and found others standing around, and he asked them, 'Why have you been standing around idle all day long?' [7]They said to him, 'Because no one hired us.' He said to them, 'You also go into my vineyard.'

[8]"When evening came, the owner of the vineyard said to his manager, 'Call the laborers and pay them their wages, beginning from the last group to the first.' [9]When those hired at 5 p.m. came, each one received a denarius. [10]So when those hired first came, they thought that they would receive more; yet ⌜each of

them also received a denarius⌐. [11]As they took it, they started grumbling at the landowner, [12]'These hired last worked one hour, yet you treated them the same way you treated us who have borne the burden of the day and the scorching heat.' [13]But he answered one of them, 'Friend, I am not cheating you; did you not agree with me to work for a denarius? [14]Take your pay and go. But I wish to pay those hired last the same as you. [15]⌐Or⌐ am I not permitted to do what I wish with what is mine? Or are you envious because I am generous?' [16]So the last shall be first, and the first last ⌐ ⌐."

(1) The Promise of Reward (19:27–30)

Evidently speaking for the disciples again (cf. 15:15; 16:16; 17:4), Peter asserts that the disciples have done what the young man would not do (19:21) and inquires about their reward (cf. 10:41–42; 16:27). That Jesus does not rebuke Peter may surprise those who think that the prospect of reward is not a proper motive for serving God. The prospect of a gloriously enthroned Jesus anticipates 25:30–31.[1] The terminology focusing on the twelve tribes of Israel is remarkable (cf. Luke 22:30; Rev. 21:12; J. Baumgarten 1976), as is the description of the eschaton as a time of regeneration.[2] Eschatological renewal of the transitory present world (Matt. 5:18; 24:35) is part of the messianic salvation accomplished by Jesus (1:21; 20:28; 26:26–29; cf. Rom. 8:18–23). Cosmic eschatological renewal is linked to Jesus's previous stress on the priority of the created order in Matt. 19:4, 8. The moral disorder of the present world is contrary not only to God's past creation but also to God's future renewal of that creation. The end will renew the beginning; eschatology restores protology. The judgment of Israel probably implies both sharing in final judgment and ruling in the world to come.[3] The striking teaching that

19:27–28

---

1. The phrase ἐπὶ θρόνου δόξης αὐτοῦ should be translated "on his glorious throne," with δόξης as an adjectival genitive of quality, corresponding to the construct state in Biblical Hebrew. See BDF §165; Moule 1959: 37–38; Moulton and Turner 1963: 212–14; Wallace 1996: 86–88; Zerwick 1963: 14–15.

2. The word παλιγγενεσία also occurs in Titus 3:5 (cf. Josephus, *Ant.* 11.66; Philo, *Moses* 2.65; Büchsel, *TDNT* 1:685–88). For the concept of a renewed world to come, cf. Isa. 65:17; 66:22; Mark 10:30; Acts 3:21 (ἀποκατάστασις πάντων); Rom. 8:18–23; 2 Pet. 3:13; Rev. 21–22; 1QS 4.25; 1QH 13.11–12; Jub. 1.29; 1 En. 45.3–5; 72.1; *L.A.B.* 3.10; 2 Esd. (4 Ezra) 7:75; 2 Bar. 32.1–6; 44.12; 57.2. Elsewhere Matthew speaks of the present world passing away (5:18; 24:35) and of the end of the present age (28:20). See Burnett 1983; Derrett 1984; Dupont 1985a: 2.706–43; Hoch 1995: 268–70.

3. Although some take κρίνοντες in 19:28 to be speaking of the condemnation of unbelieving Jews at the final judgment (John Chrysostom, *Hom. Matt.* 64.2; Dupont 1964: 370–81; Gnilka 1986–88: 171–72; Meier 1979: 141; 1980b: 223; Schnackenburg 2002: 190; Schweizer 1975: 389), it seems more likely that eschatological rule or governing is meant (20:20–21). Although Matthew does not use κρίνω with this nuance elsewhere (cf. 5:40; 7:1–2), its use in the LXX certainly supports this view (contra Luz 2001: 517) in many texts where κρίνω renders טָפַשׁ (e.g., Lev. 19:15; Deut. 1:16–17; 16:18; Judg. 3:10; 4:4–5; Ruth 1:1; 1 Kings 3:9; 2 Chron. 1:10; Pss. 2:10; 57:2; 71:2, 4; Prov. 31:8–9; Zech. 7:9; Isa.

the disciples will share with Jesus the rule of the coming kingdom may be based on Dan. 7:9, 13–14, 18, 22, 27 (cf. Luke 22:30; 1 Cor. 6:2; Rev. 2:26–27; 3:21; 20:6; Wis. 3:8). See the additional note on 19:29 for discussion of the textual problem with the hundredfold reward. The eschatological reward of Jesus's followers will far outweigh their present sacrifice and should motivate them to suffer with Jesus in the present (16:24–28; Rom. 8:18–25).

19:29–30 Jesus speaks of the reward not only for the Twelve but also for all who have sacrificed to follow him (19:29). The enigmatic saying of 19:30 is repeated in 20:16, bracketing the parable of the vineyard in 20:1–15. Jesus speaks to those who, like the rich young man, are currently among the "first" of the world and warns them against leveraging present temporal wealth against future eternal destiny. The disciples can be encouraged that their sacrifice will be rewarded, but they also are warned against presuming on the grace of God. The promise is that although they are presently "last," they will be "first" in the eschaton. The warning is that although their prospect is to be "first," they could yet be "last" if they forget the way of the cross and God's sovereignty in dispensing reward. The unfortunate chapter division at 20:1 obscures the fact that the parable of the landowner in 20:1–16 continues the answer to Peter's question, as did the parable of the unforgiving servant in 18:21–35.

The description of the future kingdom in terms of the twelve tribes of Israel appears to justify belief in the eschatological conversion of the nation of Israel to faith in Jesus as the Messiah. This would be in keeping with Matthew's overall emphasis on the fulfillment of Scripture preeminently through the words and deeds of Jesus the Messiah. The followers of Jesus, the ultimate teacher of the Torah, constitute Israel within Israel, the eschatological remnant (cf. Rom. 9:6). In the end they, not the faithless shepherds who presently lead God's flock (Matt. 9:36; 10:6; 15:24), who will judge or govern the nation as a whole (21:43; Gundry 1994: 393–94; Overman 1996: 285). A different approach views this language as indicating that the gentile church, which is understood to supersede Israel, will rule over the nations as a whole (Blomberg 1992a: 301; France 1982: 65–67; Hendriksen 1973: 730). This understanding anachronistically renders Matthew's Jewish language as symbolic and dissolves Jesus's distinction between the disciples' rule over Israel (19:28) and the reward of all who sacrifice to follow Jesus (19:29). If the church supersedes Israel, this distinction would be meaningless.

1:12, 23; Jer. 5:28; Ezek. 44:24; Dan. 9:12; cf. 1 Esd. 6:21 [6:22 Eng.]; 1 Macc. 9:73; 11:33; 2 Macc. 11:25, 36; 3 Macc. 6:30; Wis. 1:1; 3:8; Sir. 4:9; 42:8; Ps. Sol. 17.28). Cf. 1 Cor. 5:3, 12; 6:2–3; BDAG 569; L&N 1988: 1:478, 555; 2:147. Closely related are Rev. 2:26, 28; 3:21; 20:4, 6; 22:2, 5.

b. Wealth and the Kingdom: Three Conversations on Sacrificial Discipleship

iii. The Conversation with Peter   **Matthew 19:27–20:16**

Summary and Transition

Matthew 19 carries over to 20:16, since the parable of the vineyard workers continues Jesus's answer to Peter's question in 19:27. Significantly, Jesus's third passion prediction, which again stresses proximity to Jerusalem, comes immediately after this answer (20:17–19). After yet another question and answer about rewards (20:20–28), the triumphal entry takes place and the passion week begins. The geographical movement of 19:1 signifies the beginning of the end of Jesus's earthly ministry (Verseput 1994).

Matthew 19 reiterates several prominent themes. Jesus continues to heal multitudes of people (19:2; cf. 20:29). The Pharisees reappear with another trick question (19:3; cf. 21:23; 22:15, 35). The theme of reward, stressed by Jesus after his initial passion prediction (16:27), is amplified in this chapter as well (19:27–20:15; 20:20–28). The disciples express amazement at Jesus's radical teachings on divorce and riches (19:10, 25). Their astonishment shows that Jesus is working with people of little faith, whose understanding is growing still more limited. Related to this is Peter's ongoing role as the model disciple, primus inter pares (first among equals), who raises questions that are on the minds of the other apostles (19:27; cf. 14:28; 16:16, 22; 17:4, 24; 18:21; 26:33–35, 40, 58, 69–75).

(2) A Warning: The Parable of the Workers (20:1–16)

The chapter division at 20:1 is not helpful, since this parable expands the cryptic saying of 19:30 about the reversal of those who are first and those who are last. On the nature of this reversal, see the discussion below following 20:16. The reversal saying of 19:30 is repeated (with its clauses transposed) in 20:16 as the conclusion of the parable, and so it is clear that the parable completes Jesus's answer to Peter's question in 19:27. The first "act" of the parable describes the hiring of the first to the last groups of laborers (20:1–7), and the second "act" describes the payment of the laborers from the last to the first (20:8–15). The structure reinforces and enhances the message of reversal (see chart).

The concept of eschatological reversal is both a warning and a promise. The rich young man is first now but will be last then (19:16–22). The apostles are last now but will be first then (19:23–29). But in the meantime they must not mimic those who are first now. Rather, they must view Jesus's destiny as their own (20:17–19), and they must not mimic the first ones of the present world (20:20–28).

The parable is introduced with the familiar introductory formula "The kingdom of heaven is like . . ."[4] It is about a landowner (10:25; 13:27, 52;   **20:1–2**

---

4. Forms of the adjective ὅμοιος are found here and in 11:16; 13:31, 33, 44, 45, 47; 52; 22:39. The verb ὁμοιόω occurs in 7:24, 26; 11:16; 13:24; 18:23; 22:2; 25:1.

The Structure of Matt. 19:30–20:16

Opening reversal statement (19:30):

πολλοὶ δὲ ἔσονται πρῶτοι ἔσχατοι

But many who are first will be last

καὶ ἔσχατοι πρῶτοι.

and the last first.

Morning: Workers *hired* from first to last (20:1–7)

Parable

Evening: Workers *paid* from last to first (20:8–15)

Closing reversal statement (20:16):

οὕτως ἔσονται οἱ ἔσχατοι πρῶτοι

Thus the last will be first

καὶ οἱ πρῶτοι ἔσχατοι.

and the first last.

21:33; 24:43) who at different times through the day hires five groups of day laborers (9:37, 38; 10:10; 20:1–2, 8; cf. 1 Tim. 5:18; James 5:4) to harvest his vineyard (Matt. 21:28, 33, 39–41). Those hired at dawn are promised a denarius,[5] the normal daily wage (18:28; 22:19; cf. Tob. 5:15). See Y. Hirschfeld in Charlesworth 2006: 384–92 on archaeological data that demonstrate the socioeconomic gulf between wealthy landowners and poor laborers in the days of Jesus.

20:3–5 Four additional groups of workers are hired at the third, sixth, ninth, and eleventh hours (20:3, 5, 6). The various hours count from 6 a.m. and represent 9 a.m., noon, 3 p.m., and 5 p.m. respectively (cf. 27:45–46). If it seems unrealistic that workers would be hired throughout the day, this may be due to the urgency of completing the harvest. The workers are hired in the marketplace (ἀγορά, *agora*), the center of a village's activities (11:16; 23:7). Those hired at 9 a.m., noon, and 3 p.m. are promised just recompense, which would be proportionately less than a denarius.

20:6–7 Those hired last at 5 p.m. could expect only a pittance for working such a short time. In keeping with the contextual stress on first and last, the brief narrative of the hiring of the workers at 9 a.m., noon, and 3 p.m. (20:3–5) contrasts with the more extended descriptions of the hiring of the first and last workers (20:1–2, 6–7). Hagner (1995a: 571) may be correct in interpreting the detail that no one had hired the last group of workers all day long as indicating that no one had considered outcasts

5. The prepositional phrase ἐκ δηναρίου is evidently periphrasis for the genitive of price or value. Cf. 27:7; BDAG 297; BDF §179.

b. Wealth and the Kingdom: Three Conversations on Sacrificial Discipleship

iii. The Conversation with Peter   **Matthew 19:27–20:16**

such as the tax collectors and sinners worthy of the kingdom until Jesus called them to repentance (cf. 9:9–13; 11:19; 21:31–32).

The second "act" of the parable concerns payment of the wages that are   **20:8–12** due at sundown (Lev. 19:13; Deut. 24:15; Josephus, *Ant.* 20.220). The owner of the vineyard instructs his manager (cf. Philo, *Good Person* 35; Josephus, *Ant.* 7.369) to pay the workers and specifies that those hired last are paid first. Those who were hired last are astonished to receive twelve times what they might have expected. Those who were hired first, who toiled all day in the heat, observe this and expect to receive much more.[6] When they are paid the same amount as those who worked only one hour, they begin grumbling to the vineyard owner.[7]

The landowner rather coldly insists that the grumblers were treated   **20:13–15** fairly, since they were paid what they had agreed to (20:2).[8] For reasons known only to himself, the owner of the vineyard wants to be especially generous to the last group of workers. The other workers have no right to complain, since they received a normal wage. The owner concludes with two rhetorical questions (20:15), affirming that he has acted legally and accusing the first workers of being jealous of the last workers, who were treated so generously. The second question is, literally, "Is your eye evil because I am good?" The goodness of the landowner is probably intended to remind the reader of God, who alone is good (19:17). The expression "evil eye" reflects the deep envy of the first workers and perhaps their intent to do harm to the owner of the vineyard (6:23; Mark 7:22; cf. Deut. 15:9; Prov. 23:6; 28:22; Tob. 4:7; Sir. 14:8–10; *m. 'Abot* 2.9, 11). The landowner has been fair to those who worked all day (Matt. 20:13) and generous to those who worked only a short time (20:14), since he wishes to treat all his workers equally (20:16; Blomberg 1990a: 224).

The parable proper has concluded and is here framed with the same   **20:16** cryptic pronouncement that introduced it. But 20:16 reverses the order of 19:30: there the first are mentioned before the last, but here the last are mentioned before the first (cf. 2 Bar. 30.2). The idea of reversal is clear, but the identities of the first and the last are not. The parable immediately follows the promise of reward to the disciples in Matt. 19:28–29. The first reversal pronouncement in 19:30 is more of a promise to the disciples than a warning; the rich young man and the poor disciples will experience role reversal, as it were. The repetition of the pronouncement

---

6. The future tense in the construction ὅτι πλεῖον λήμψονται either is due to retention, in indirect discourse, of the tense in the implied original discourse (Wallace 1996: 457) or is future relative to the verb ἐνόμισαν (BDF §349).

7. The verb ἐγόγγυζον should probably be taken as ingressive (Wallace 1996: 544–45).

8. The term ἑταῖρε refers to an associate without necessarily conveying warmth or intimacy. Cf. 11:16 v.l.; 22:12; 26:50; BDAG 398; Rengstorf, *TDNT* 2:699.

in 20:16 is more of a warning against the simplistic assumption that reward is an automatic entitlement of disciples (cf. 20:20–28).[9]

Interpreting the Parable of the Vineyard Workers

Many interpreters tend to agree that the vineyard stands for Israel and that the vineyard owner represents God (cf. Isa. 5:1–7; Jer. 12:10; Matt. 21:28, 33–41), who sovereignly and graciously bestows rewards upon his servants. The harvest speaks of eschatological judgment (cf. Matt. 3:10; 7:19; 13:39). Beyond this the identification of the first and the last (19:30; 20:8, 16, 27) is more controversial. Perhaps the rich young man is "first" and the disciples last, and they are promised a rich reward for their sacrificial service. Or perhaps Peter and the disciples are first, given Peter's question in 19:27, and they are warned not to presume upon God's grace just because they have sacrificed to serve God's kingdom (cf. 20:20–28). Their rigorous service will be fairly rewarded, but they must not grumble about how God chooses to reward others (20:11–12). God's gracious generosity vastly exceeds human merit-based expectations, and his servants will receive a reward appropriate to their work.[10]

All in all, taking 19:30 as a promise to disciples and 20:16 as a warning anticipating 20:20–28 seems best. Yet there are many specific contextualized approaches to this fecund imagery.[11] The reversal spoken of here has been understood as a warning to many different "in" groups that they should not despise "out" groups. Bruner (1990: 723) gives several potential examples of such interpretations. Three approaches to the reversal described in the crucial bracketing saying (19:30; 20:16) are particularly noteworthy:

1. *Religious* reversal: The tax collectors and sinners who enter the kingdom last are preferred by God to the Jewish religious leaders (Beare 1981: 404; Hagner 1995a: 573; Hare 1993: 230–31; Hill 1972: 285). No doubt this is a key Matthean theme (9:11–13; 11:19; 21:31).
2. *Redemptive-historical* reversal: The workers hired at different times represent successive epochs in history. Gentiles instead of Jews eventually come into prominence (Barclay 1975: 2.224; Gundry 1994: 399). In many places, Matthew indicates that, surprisingly, many

---

9. Among the voluminous literature on this parable, see Busse 1996; Culbertson 1988; Derrett 1974; Doyle 1994; J. H. Elliott 1992; Fortna 1990; Haubeck in Haubeck and Bachmann 1980: 95–107; Hultgren 2000: 33–46; Knowles in Longenecker 2000: 286–305; Lowe 1990; Menahem 1990; Pak 1997; Roloff 1992; Schenke in Schenke 1988: 245–68; Shillington in Shillington 1997: 87–101; Tevel 1992; Carter 1994a: 146–60; Carter and Heil 1998: 124–46.

10. Certain rabbinic parables have varying degrees of similarity to this parable. See, e.g., *m. 'Abot* 2.15–16; Sipra on Lev. 29:6; *y. Ber.* 2.8; Hezser 1990: 193–236.

11. On the various interpretations, see W. Davies and Allison 1997: 67–68; Luz 2001: 526–30, 537–38.

Jews reject the kingdom, and many Gentiles receive it (e.g., 8:10–12; 15:22–28). This may well be the most prominent view throughout the history of the church (Irenaeus, *Haer.* 4.36.7; Augustine, *Homilies on the Gospels* 37; Hauerwas 2006: 176–77).

3. *Ecclesiastical* reversal: Those among the disciples who wish to be prominent will be humbled, but those who are humble will be considered truly great. At least two important texts underline this point (18:1–4; 20:25–28; Barclay 1975: 2.224).

The problem with all the above approaches is that they are not supported by the immediate context, which places the parable's promise and warning in tension: although Peter and the disciples will be rewarded, they must not presume upon God's grace and seek rewards (Schweizer 1975: 395). They are in danger of grumbling against God (cf. Exod. 16:7–12; Num. 14:27; Deut. 1:27) when others who come into the kingdom (Matt. 19:29) are rewarded. They must accept whatever reward God graciously gives them without comparing themselves with others (cf. *m. 'Abot* 1.3, 13; 4.5; Hultgren 2000: 42–43). This parable anticipates the problem of Zebedee's sons—ambitiously seeking the greatest status in the future kingdom (20:20–28).

Additional Notes

19:29. There are two sets of variants in this verse. In the first, UBS[4] prefers the shorter reading πατέρα ἢ μητέρα (supported only by B and a few versions; cf. Mark 10:29) to the longer πατέρα ἢ μητέρα ἢ γυναῖκα (supported more widely by ℵ, C, L, W, Δ, Θ, *f*[13], 28, 33, *Byz*, *Lect*; cf. Luke 18:29). In the second, there is variation concerning the extent of reward. UBS[4] prefers ἑκατονταπλασίονα (supported by ℵ, C, W, Δ, Θ, *f*[1], *f*[13], 28, 33, *Byz*, *Lect*; cf. Mark 10:30). A variant is πολλαπλασίονα (supported by B, L, 579, 1010; cf. Luke 18:30).

20:10. In the phrase τὸ ἀνὰ δηνάριον καὶ αὐτοί the anaphoric article (Wallace 1996: 217–20) τό is placed in brackets by UBS[4] even though it is found in ℵ, L, Z, Θ. The article is also included by certain MSS with the transposed word order καὶ αὐτοὶ τὸ ἀνὰ δηνάριον (C, N, O, Σ). The article is lacking in B and in many MSS with the same transposed word order (D, W, Δ, 0300, *f*[1], *f*[13], 28, 157, *Byz*, *Lect*). A decision is difficult, and in any event, the meaning is not changed. On the distributive use of ἀνά, see BDAG 58; BDF §§204, 266: Moulton and Turner 1963: 14, 187.

20:15. Although many MSS from diverse text types include the particle ἤ (ℵ, C, W, Δ, 085, *f*[1], *f*[13], 28, *Byz*, *Lect*), UBS[4] places the particle ἤ in brackets to indicate serious doubt as to its authenticity. This is due to its absence in B, D, L, Z and to transcriptional considerations (see Metzger 1994: 41).

20:16. At the end of this verse, the words πολλοὶ γάρ εἰσιν κλητοί, ὀλίγοι δὲ ἐκλεκτοί are present in many MSS, including D, W, Δ, 0300, *f*[1], *f*[13], 33, 157, *Byz*, *Lect*, and much of the Latin tradition. But the words are lacking in ℵ, B, L, Z, 085, 892*, 1243* and may have been interpolated from 22:14.

c. The Third Passion Prediction (20:17–19)

The third passion prediction is the most lengthy. New details include the involvement of the Gentiles in mocking, flogging, and crucifying him. Jesus's focus on his coming suffering in this unit is in stark contrast to his two disciples' focus on their future reigning in the next unit.

Exegesis and Exposition

¹⁷Now as Jesus was going up to Jerusalem, he took ⌜the twelve disciples⌝ aside by themselves, and on the way he said to them, ¹⁸"Look, we are going up to Jerusalem; and the Son of Man will be handed over to the chief priests and scribes, and they will condemn him to death ¹⁹and will hand him over to the Gentiles to be mocked and flogged and crucified, and on the third day he will be raised up."

20:17 Matthew's mention that Jesus has begun the ominous journey to Jerusalem (reiterated in the words of Jesus in 20:18) lends drama and urgency to the third passion prediction (cf. Mark 10:32–34//Luke 18:31–34). This private announcement (cf. Matt. 17:1; 26:37) is probably difficult, since crowds constantly follow Jesus (19:2; 20:29). Jesus will make an additional brief announcement of his impending crucifixion in 26:2.

20:18–19 This prediction is more explicit than the first two in stating that the Jewish authorities will condemn Jesus to death (26:66) and that the gentile authorities will carry out the execution (27:2–37; cf. John 18:31). Perhaps this stresses the universality of Jesus's rejection (W. Davies and Allison 1997: 80–81). This is the first mention of crucifixion in the passion predictions (cf. Matt. 10:38; 16:24; 23:34; 26:2; 27:22–23, 26, 31–32, 35, 38, 40, 42; 28:5). Crucifixion was not a Jewish but a Roman means of execution (*m. Sanh.* 7.1–4), but it may have been viewed as an indication of being cursed by God (Deut. 21:23; cf. Gal. 3:13). Jesus's mention of the leading priests and scribes recalls Matt. 2:4. Jesus's detailed description of his sufferings (20:19) anticipates what occurs later: he is mocked (27:29, 31, 41; cf. Ps. 22:7), flogged (27:26), and crucified (27:35). These additional details serve to stress the exactness of Jesus's knowledge of what will happen. All three of the passion predictions conclude with the resurrection of Jesus, which becomes the central focus of the preaching of the early church (26:32; 27:63; 28:6; Acts 2:24–36; 3:15; 4:10; 5:30; 10:40; 13:30, 33–37; 1 Cor. 15:4–28).

Jesus's Passion Predictions in Matthew

As noted previously, 20:17–19 is the third of three (four if 26:2 is counted) explicit predictions of Jesus's sufferings, death, and resurrection in Jerusalem. There are also several implicit references to the passion, which prepare the reader for these explicit predictions (e.g., 10:21, 24–25, 28, 38; 12:14, 38–40; 16:4). The columns below show the similarities and differences and indicates that the third prediction is the most detailed (points of connection are highlighted in boldface type). It stresses the involvement of both Jewish (26:47–68; 27:1–10, 12, 20, 41–43, 62–66; 28:11–15) and Roman authorities (27:2, 11–37, 54, 65–66). There is also a detailed description of the horrible sufferings of Jesus (20:19; cf. 26:67–68; 27:26–31, 35). Only the third prediction mentions that Jesus's death will be by crucifixion (20:19; cf. 26:2; 27:1, 22–26, 31, 35). The second prediction alone omits Jerusalem and includes the disciples' grief. Only the first prediction is narrated indirectly by Matthew instead of being presented as a direct quotation from Jesus. (For a Matthean-priority view of the three passion predictions, see Farmer 1990.)

Jesus's Three Passion Predictions

Matt. 16:21	Matt. 17:22–23	Matt. 20:17–19
²¹Ἀπὸ τότε ἤρξατο ὁ Ἰησοῦς δεικνύειν τοῖς μαθηταῖς αὐτοῦ	²²Συστρεφομένων δὲ αὐτῶν ἐν τῇ Γαλιλαίᾳ εἶπεν αὐτοῖς ὁ Ἰησοῦς·	¹⁷Καὶ ἀναβαίνων ὁ Ἰησοῦς εἰς Ἱεροσόλυμα παρέλαβεν τοὺς δώδεκα [μαθητὰς] κατ᾽ ἰδίαν καὶ ἐν τῇ ὁδῷ εἶπεν αὐτοῖς·
ὅτι δεῖ αὐτὸν εἰς Ἱεροσόλυμα ἀπελθεῖν	μέλλει ὁ υἱὸς τοῦ ἀνθρώπου	¹⁸ἰδοὺ ἀναβαίνομεν εἰς Ἱεροσόλυμα, καὶ ὁ υἱὸς τοῦ ἀνθρώπου
καὶ πολλὰ παθεῖν ἀπὸ τῶν πρεσβυτέρων καὶ ἀρχιερέων καὶ γραμματέων	παραδίδοσθαι εἰς χεῖρας ἀνθρώπων,	παραδοθήσεται τοῖς ἀρχιερεῦσιν καὶ γραμματεῦσιν,
		καὶ κατακρινοῦσιν αὐτὸν θανάτῳ ¹⁹καὶ παραδώσουσιν αὐτὸν τοῖς ἔθνεσιν εἰς τὸ ἐμπαῖξαι
καὶ ἀποκτανθῆναι	²³καὶ ἀποκτενοῦσιν αὐτόν,	καὶ μαστιγῶσαι καὶ σταυρῶσαι,
καὶ τῇ τρίτῃ ἡμέρᾳ ἐγερθῆναι.	καὶ τῇ τρίτῃ ἡμέρᾳ ἐγερθήσεται.	καὶ τῇ τρίτῃ ἡμέρᾳ ἐγερθήσεται.
	καὶ ἐλυπήθησαν σφόδρα.	
²¹Apo tote ērxato ho Iēsous deiknyein tois mathētais autou	²²Sustrephomenōn de autōn en tē Galilaia eipen autois ho Iēsous:	¹⁷Kai anabainōn ho Iēsous eis **Hierosolyma** parelaben tous dōdeka [mathētas] kat' idian kai en tē hodō eipen autois:
hoti dei auton eis **Hierosolyma** apelthein	mellei **ho huios tou anthrōpou**	¹⁸idou anabainomen eis **Hierosolyma**, kai **ho huios tou anthrōpou**

Matt. 16:21	Matt. 17:22–23	Matt. 20:17–19
kai polla pathein apo tōn presbyterōn kai **archiereōn** *kai grammateōn*	**paradidosthai** *eis cheiras anthrōpōn,*	**paradothēsetai** *tois archiereusin kai grammateusin,*
		kai katakrinousin auton thanatō ¹⁹*kai paradōsousin auton tois ethnesin eis to empaixai*
kai **apoktanthēnai**	²³*kai* **apoktenousin** *auton,*	*kai mastigōsai kai staurōsai,*
kai tē tritē hēmera egerthēnai.	*kai tē tritē hēmera egerthēsetai.*	*kai tē tritē hēmera egerthēsetai.*
	kai elypēthēsan sphodra.	
²¹From that time Jesus began to make known to his disciples	²²And as they were gathering in Galilee, Jesus said to them,	¹⁷Now as Jesus was going up to Jerusalem, he took the twelve [disciples] aside by themselves, and on the way he said to them,
that he must go to **Jerusalem,**	**"The Son of Man** is about	¹⁸"Look, we are going up to **Jerusalem,** and **the Son of Man**
and suffer many things from the elders and **chief priests and scribes,**	**to be handed over** into the hands of men;	**will be handed over** to the **chief priests and scribes,**
		and they will condemn him to death ¹⁹and will hand him over to the Gentiles to be mocked
and **be killed,**	²³and **they will kill** him,	and flogged and crucified,
and on the third day be raised.	**and on the third day he will be raised."**	**and on the third day he will be raised."**
	And they were deeply grieved.	

Note: Matthew 26:2b is also a brief passion prediction: ὁ υἱὸς τοῦ ἀνθρώπου παραδίδοται εἰς τὸ σταυρωθῆναι (*ho huios tou anthrōpou paradidotai eis to staurōthēnai*, the Son of Man is being handed over to be crucified). This short prediction has in common with the major predictions its reference to Jesus's being handed over (or betrayed) and to crucifixion. Matthew 26:3 goes on to mention the involvement of the religious authorities. But in contrast to all three major predictions, the resurrection is omitted.

Additional Note

20:17. Although the phrase τοὺς δώδεκα μαθητάς is well supported (B, C, W, Δ, 085, 28*, 33, *Byz*), UBS⁴ puts μαθητάς in brackets because it is omitted in ℵ, D, L, Θ, *f*¹, *f*¹³, 892* (and in the parallels Mark 10:32; Luke 18:31; cf. Matt. 10:5; 26:14, 20, 47). A longer text, τοὺς δώδεκα μαθητὰς αὐτοῦ, is found in 13, 828, *Lect* (cf. Matt. 10:1; 11:1), but the shortest text is probably to be preferred here.

d. A Dispute over Greatness in the Kingdom (20:20–28)

In Matt. 20:20–28 the disciples' pride and desire for glory are shockingly juxtaposed to Jesus's humility and suffering (20:17–19, 28). The structure of this passage includes a dialogue (20:20–23) that turns into an occasion of teaching (20:24–28). Jesus responds to a request from the mother of Zebedee's children (20:20–23). When the rest of the disciples learn of the request, their anger becomes another opportunity for Jesus to teach his disciples about genuine greatness in his kingdom (20:24–28). This teaching puts two parallel statements about worldly greatness (20:25) in antithesis to two parallel statements about kingdom greatness (20:26–27), which entails following the steps of Jesus on the path of sacrificial service (20:28; cf. 10:38–39; 16:24–26; 19:21). The reader is influenced to respond with sympathy for Jesus and antipathy for the disciples. Their ignorance, false confidence, and pride contrast with Jesus's knowledge, resignation to the Father's will, and humility.

The unit can be outlined as follows:

    i. Dialogue: Jesus, a mother, and her two sons (20:20–23)
    ii. Teaching: Greatness in the kingdom (20:24–28)

Exegesis and Exposition

²⁰Then the mother of Zebedee's sons came to Jesus with her sons, bowing down and asking for something from him. ²¹So he said to her, "What do you want?" She said to him, "Command that these two sons of mine may sit, one on your right and the other on your left, in your kingdom." ²²But Jesus answered, "You do not know what you are asking. Are you able to drink the cup that I am about to drink⌜ ⌝?" They said to him, "We are able." ²³He said to them, "My cup you shall drink⌜ ⌝; but to sit on my right and on my left, ⌜this⌝ is not for me to grant, but it is for those for whom it has been prepared by my Father." ²⁴And when the ten heard about this, they became angry with the two brothers. ²⁵But Jesus called them to himself and said, "You know that the rulers of the Gentiles lord it over them, and their great men exercise authority over them. ²⁶It ⌜shall not be⌝ this way among you, but whoever among you wishes to become great shall be your servant, ²⁷and whoever among you wishes to be first shall be your

slave, [28]just as the Son of Man did not come to be served but to serve and to give his life as a ransom for many⌐ ⌐."

i. Dialogue: Jesus, a Mother, and Her Two Sons (20:20–23)

20:20–21 In clear contrast to Jesus's projected sufferings (20:17–19), the mother of Zebedee's sons seeks their future glory (cf. Mark 10:35–45; Luke 22:24–30).[1] Zebedee's sons are James and John (cf. Matt. 4:21; 10:2; 17:1; 26:37; 27:56). The mother's posture of kneeling or prostrating herself may imply worship.[2] Sitting at the right and left hand connotes proximity to the king's prestige and authority in ruling the future kingdom (19:28) rather than simply sitting next to him at the eschatological banquet (8:11) or at the final judgment (25:31). The fact that the mother makes the request for the sons probably reflects negatively on them, not her.[3] The problem is that neither James, John, nor their mother has begun to understand the significance of Jesus's repeated passion predictions or the meaning of such teachings as 5:5; 18:1–4; 19:30; 20:16.

20:22–23 It is not entirely clear whether these verses are addressed to the mother and her sons (Wainwright 1991: 256) or to the sons alone, but the latter is most likely, in view of 20:23. Evidently, the sons have instigated their mother's request. None of them understands the gravity of the request or how grotesquely inappropriate it is at this moment. Drinking the cup is a metaphor for experiencing suffering (26:39; cf. John 18:11; Pss. 11:6; 75:8; Isa. 51:17, 22; Jer. 25:15–17; 51:7; Ezek. 23:31; Hab. 2:16; Zech. 12:2). Although the brothers' answer to Jesus's question is sincere, it is at best brash, since they do not fathom what they are talking about. At the Last Supper, all the disciples similarly promise Jesus that they will not desert him during his sufferings (26:35). Jesus affirms that the disciples will indeed share in drinking the cup of suffering with him, but he cannot promise them the best seats in his future kingdom. Jesus acknowledges his incarnational limitations here much as he will do later in 24:36. James was martyred by Herod Agrippa I, but John was evidently spared such a fate (Acts 12:1–2; John 21:20–23).

ii. Teaching: Greatness in the Kingdom (20:24–28)

20:24–28 Matters get worse when the ambition of James and John angers the remaining disciples, who are probably jealous (20:24). James and John's

---

1. The participles προσκυνοῦσα and αἰτοῦσα should probably be viewed respectively as modal and telic (Wallace 1996: 627–28, 635–37).

2. In Matthew προσκυνέω is directed preeminently toward Jesus (2:2, 8, 11; 8:2; 9:18; 14:33; 15:25; 28:9, 17). At the temptation, Jesus refuses to worship Satan (4:9) and cites Deut. 6:13 that only God should be worshiped (Matt. 4:10). In a parable, a slave "worships" his master (18:26).

3. In the construction εἰπὲ ἵνα, the ἵνα is nonfinal, expressing the content of what Jesus is to say regarding James and John rather than its purpose (cf. 20:33; Wallace 1996: 475).

quest for status is an opportune moment for Jesus to call the disciples together (cf. 10:1; 15:32) and teach them kingdom values. World rulers do not provide a model for Jesus's community. Jesus once again explains the norms of the kingdom for spiritual greatness (18:1–14; cf. 10:39; 16:25; 19:30; 23:11–12). He first contrasts the world's values (20:25) with kingdom values (20:26–27). Then he points to his own life and death as the model for his disciples' aspirations to greatness (20:28). Instead of the ostentatious pomp and circumstance of world rulers who flaunt their power and status,[4] Jesus's humble service and redemptive ransom (cf. 1 Tim. 2:6) are the quintessence of greatness in his kingdom.

Boring (1995: 399) helpfully points out how the three Son of Man sayings in this context illumine its meaning: ultimately the Son of Man will rule the renewed world (Matt. 19:28), but in the near future he will die in Jerusalem and be raised (20:18–19). For the present, he models the sacrificial service his disciples are privileged to continue after his departure (20:28).

Jesus's Passion and the Disciples' Ambition

Matthew 20:20–28 is yet another remarkable study in the definition of authentic greatness. Fallen human cultures define greatness in terms of prestige, power, and status. Jesus mentions this state of affairs and immediately repudiates it in 20:25–26. His definition of greatness as service turns the world's model on its head. His disciples must follow his example of sacrificial servanthood to the point of death. McNeile (1915: 290) capsulizes Jesus's teaching as *Servire est regnare*—"To serve is to reign." Jesus's words from Luke's account of the Last Supper underline this point: "Who is greater, the one who reclines at the table or the one who serves the table? . . . But I am among you as the one who serves" (Luke 22:27). John's account of Jesus's explanation for his washing the disciples' feet also fits here (John 13:12–17). Paul likewise clearly grasped this radically altered definition of greatness (2 Cor. 4:5; 10:1; 12:9–10; Phil. 2:5–11).

In reading this passage, one's emotions are torn between positive feelings for Jesus and negative feelings for Jesus's disciples. Jesus has announced his coming sufferings in Jerusalem three times, but inexplicably and inexcusably his disciples have forgotten their previous grief over this. One would expect the mother of two disciples to have more spiritual insight than a Canaanite woman, but the selfish request of the mother of Zebedee's sons compares quite unfavorably with the Canaanite woman's selfless request for her daughter (Matt. 15:21–28). The disciples are preoccupied with thoughts of their own glory instead of being concerned for their Lord's sufferings. W. Davies and Allison

4. The present-tense verbs κατακυριεύουσιν and κατεξουσιάζουσιν should be viewed a gnomic, expressing a timeless reality of life in Jesus's day (Wallace 1996: 523–25).

(1997: 82) perceptively comment, "The loneliness of the passion narrative begins here." Later Peter and the same two disciples who wish to sit at Jesus's right and left in the kingdom sleep as Jesus agonizes in the garden of Gethsemane (26:36–46). As he has predicted, Jesus does not sit on a throne in Jerusalem but is crucified, not with disciples but with thieves on his right and left (27:38). The disciples' insensitivity to Jesus's priorities is shocking, both then and now. (See Doyle 1996; Duling 1997.)

Jesus as a Ransom for Many

In giving himself (ψυχή, *psychē*, self, life; cf. 2:20; 6:25; BDAG 1098–1100) as a ransom price (λύτρον, *lytron*; cf. Büchsel, *TDNT* 4:341–56) in the place of (ἀντί, *anti*; cf. 2:22; LXX: Gen. 22:13; Isa. 53:12; Josephus, *Ant.* 14.107) many (πολλοί, *polloi*; cf. Rom. 5:15, 19; 1QS 6.1, 7–8; Dan. 11:33–34; 12:10), Jesus frees them from slavery to sin (cf. Mark 10:45; Luke 1:68; 2:38; 1 Tim. 2:6; Titus 2:14; Heb. 9:12; 1 Pet. 1:18; W. Davies and Allison 1997: 94–100; Jeremias 1971: 292–93). The concept of ransom probably draws on such biblical texts as Exod. 30:12; Ps. 49:7–9; and especially Isa. 53:10–12; since Matthew previously presented Jesus as the Suffering Servant in 8:17 (citing Isa. 53:4) and in 12:18–21 (citing Isa. 42:1–4). (See France 1968; Moulder 1977.)

Matthew 20:28 recalls 1:21 and anticipates 26:28.[5] In 1:21 it is stated that Jesus will save his people from their sins. This play on the meaning of the name Jesus indicates that Israel's root problem is not Roman occupation but sin. Matthew 20:28 shows *how* Jesus will deliver his people from their sins: he will pay a ransom that will free them from the bondage of alienation from God. In light of Isa. 53:10–12, the haunting question of Matt. 16:26 ("What will one give in exchange for one's soul?"), and the use of the preposition ἀντί (*anti*, instead of, in behalf of) in 20:28, Matthew teaches vicarious redemption: Jesus substitutes his own life for that of his people (Barrett 1972: 20–26; R. Davies 1970: 71–91; Stuhlmacher 1986: 16–29). Matthew 26:28 shows *when* Jesus will pay this ransom: the wine of the Last Supper is a sacred sign of the blood of Jesus, shed at his crucifixion for the remission of his people's sins (cf. 1 Pet. 1:18–19). The tearing of the temple veil when Jesus dies probably signifies the completion of this redemption (Matt. 27:51). Matthew teaches that Jesus saves his people by shedding his blood as a ransom, which frees them from the bondage of their sins. Although this falls short of a comprehensive "doctrine" of the atonement, W. Davies and Allison (1997: 100) are overly pessimistic when they say that "it is impossible to construct a Matthean theory of the

---

5. On the authenticity of 20:28 as a word of the historical Jesus, see Blomberg 1987b: 243–44; Carson 1984: 432–33; Hagner 1995a: 579–80; Page in France and Wenham 1980: 137–61.

atonement." No doubt there are some unanswered questions, but the general thrust is clear.[6]

Additional Notes

20:22. The main question here is whether to include ἢ τὸ βάπτισμα ὃ ἐγὼ βαπτίζομαι βαπτισθῆναι; after μέλλω πίνειν. These words are found in C, W, Δ, 13, 28, 33, *Byz, Lect* but are omitted in ℵ, D, L, Z, Θ, *f*¹³. The longer reading is arguably interpolated from Mark 10:38 (cf. Luke 12:50).

20:23. The issue of the longer and shorter readings in Jesus's question in 20:22 is largely repeated in Jesus's answer in 20:23. Also, UBS⁴ brackets the word τοῦτο in the phrase οὐκ ἔστιν ἐμὸν τοῦτο δοῦναι because it is omitted in many MSS, including ℵ, B, L, Z, Θ, *f*¹, *f*¹³, 28, 157, *Byz, Lect*. Τοῦτο is found in C, D, W, Δ, 085, 33. The parallel Mark 10:40 does not have τοῦτο.

20:26. The MS tradition diverges between the future ἔσται, read by UBS⁴ (widely supported in ℵ, C, L, W, Δ, Θ, 085, *f*¹, *f*¹³, 28, 157, *Byz, Lect*), and the present ἐστίν (supported in B, D, Z). The same question arises in the parallel Mark 10:43. The future should be read and interpreted as imperatival.

20:28. At the end of this verse, a lengthy expansion occurs in D, Φ, and other Western witnesses to the effect that the disciples should seek humility and sit at less prominent places at banquets (cf. Luke 14:8–10). See the text of the expansion in Metzger 1994: 43.

---

6. On Matt. 20:20–28, see Feuillet 1967; Kynes 1991; Légasse 1974; O'Callaghan 1990; Seeley 1992.

e. Jesus Heals Two Blind Men (20:29–34)

When Jesus and the disciples leave Jericho, Jerusalem is only fifteen miles away, and the ominous events repeatedly predicted by Jesus will occur soon. But Jesus does not focus on his own concerns. He has just told his disciples that true greatness is measured by service, not power. He now compassionately uses his power to serve the blind men in their need. They respond to their healing by following Jesus on the way to Jerusalem. Jesus does not command the blind men to be silent (contrast 8:4; 9:30), since Jesus's hour has come. Their cries to the son of David (20:30–31) will soon be echoed by others on the approach to Jerusalem, but the religious leaders do not join the chorus (21:9, 15–16).[1]

The details of this pericope present several difficulties when compared with the accounts in Mark and Luke (cf. Mark 10:46–52; Luke 18:35–43; Blomberg 1987b: 128–30). Although it is most likely that all three synoptic accounts describe the same event (Calvin 1972: 2.278–79), some scholars argue that two different healing events occurred (G. Maier 1979–80: 2.139–40). The passage is not an anticlimactic second version or doublet of 9:27–31 (contra many, e.g., Hare 1993: 236; Luz 2001: 548–49). Rather, Matthew narrates another of Jesus's many healings because it perfectly illustrates how Jesus models genuine greatness (20:28). The two blind men here may be intended to contrast with the two self-seeking disciples in 20:20–24. This episode is framed as an *inclusio* by the references to following Jesus at its beginning and end (20:29, 34):

A The crowd follows Jesus toward Jerusalem (20:29)
  B The crowd rebuffs two blind men who request healing
    (20:30–31)
  B′ Jesus heals the two blind men (20:32–34c)
A′ The blind men follow Jesus (20:34d)

The unit can be outlined as follows:

  i. The requests of the blind men (20:29–31)
  ii. The response of Jesus (20:32–34)

---

1. On Jesus as son of David, see 1:1, 20; 9:27; 12:23; 15:22; 21:9, 15; 22:41–46; Burger 1970; Duling 1978; J. M. Gibbs 1963–64; Loader 1982; Masson 1982; Rogers 1993; Suhl 1968.

Exegesis and Exposition

[29]And as they were departing from Jericho, a large crowd followed him. [30]And two blind men sitting beside the road heard that Jesus was passing by and suddenly began shouting, "⌐Have mercy on us, Lord⌐, son of David!" [31]And the crowd sternly warned them to be quiet, but they cried out even more loudly, "⌐Have mercy on us, Lord⌐, son of David!" [32]So Jesus stopped and called out to them, "What do you want me to do for you?" [33]They said to him, "Lord, let our eyes be opened." [34]And Jesus was moved with compassion and touched their eyes; and immediately they regained their sight and followed him.

i. The Requests of the Blind Men (20:29–31)

Jesus and the disciples leave Jericho, about ten miles northwest of the   20:29-31
Dead Sea. They will walk about fifteen miles southwest to reach Jerusalem (Wilkinson 1975). This entails an uphill climb of almost thirty-five
hundred feet, since Jericho (846 feet below sea level) is in the Jordan rift
valley, near the lowest spot on earth, the Dead Sea, and Jerusalem (2,625
feet above sea level) is in the central hills of Judea. Matthew has previously included another story of the healing of two blind men (9:27–31),
but this is a different event. Perhaps Matthew intends for the two stories
to provide two witnesses to Jesus's power (Deut. 19:15). As usual, Jesus
and the disciples are followed by a large crowd (cf. esp. Matt. 4:25; 8:1;
13:2; 14:13; 15:30; 19:2; 21:8–9), and two blind men suddenly begin shouting at him.[2] The crowd disdains their first cry for help, but they persist
(Keener 1999: 488–89) and beseech Jesus again. Jesus's reputation has
preceded him, since the blind men call to him as soon as they hear that
he is coming. They call Jesus Lord (e.g., 7:21–22; 8:2–25; 9:28; 10:24–25;
12:8; 14:28; 15:22) and son of David (1:1, 20; 9:27; 12:23; 15:22; 21:9, 15;
22:42). These terms are often associated with healing in Matthew. They
ask him to have mercy on them (cf. 5:7; 9:27; 15:22; 17:15; 18:33). The
crowd tries to silence the blind men, perhaps because they do not want
Jesus to be delayed from his trip to Jerusalem. But the men cry out all
the more when they are opposed.

ii. The Response of Jesus (20:32–34)

Jesus stops to help the blind men, asking them what they want. Their   20:32-34
intention seems obvious, but he probably asks the question to draw out
their faith. In response to their request that Jesus open their eyes, he
touches them and instantly they see (cf. 8:3, 15; 9:29–30). Jesus stands
above the crowd in showing compassion to the blind men (20:34; cf. 9:36;
14:14; 15:32). Significantly, the men join the throng following Jesus on

2. The use of ἰδού and the ingressive aorist (Wallace 1996: 558–59) ἔκραξαν portray the blind men's shouts as an abrupt interruption of Jesus's itinerary.

the way up to Jerusalem (21:8–9). The trip that began in 19:1 is nearly complete. At this point Jesus's entry into Jerusalem may seem triumphal, but any triumph will soon turn to tragedy.

Summary and Transition

Matthew 20 revolves around Jesus's proximity to Jerusalem and his plan to go there (20:17, 18, 29; cf. 2:1, 3; 3:5; 4:25; 5:35; 15:1; 16:21; 21:1, 10; 23:37). His passion prediction is made all the more dramatic by his nearness to Jerusalem. The mother of Zebedee's sons makes her request at a late hour in Jesus's earthly career, and Jesus's response stresses that his humble service to mankind entails his sacrificial death (20:28). The healing of the blind men features their confession that Jesus is the messianic son of David, a confession that is soon echoed in Jerusalem at the "triumphal entry" (20:30–31; 21:9, 15). All these occurrences alert the reader to anticipate the epochal events about to be accomplished in Jerusalem. (See Held in Bornkamm, Barth, and Held 1963: 219–23.)

Additional Notes

20:30. There are several variations on the words of the blind men, ἐλέησον ἡμᾶς, κύριε (supported in 𝔓⁴⁵ᵛⁱᵈ, C, W, Δ, 1, 28, 33, *Byz*, *Lect*; cf. Matt. 20:31). UBS⁴ places the word κύριε in brackets because of several complications. D, 13, 157, among others, read simply ἐλέησον ἡμᾶς (cf. Matt. 9:27). ℵ, Θ, *f*¹³, 700 have Ἰησοῦ instead of κύριε (cf. Mark 10:47; Luke 18:38). N, Σ have the conflation κύριε Ἰησοῦ. B, 085 transpose the word order with the vocative κύριε preceding the imperative. L, 892 place κύριε before the imperative and Ἰησοῦ after it. The external evidence is widely spread, but the UBS⁴ reading has the best of it. See further the next additional note, on 20:31.

20:31. The textual diversity here is similar to that of the preceding verse. Support for the UBS⁴ reading, ἐλέησον ἡμᾶς, κύριε, mainly duplicates that of 20:30. Evidence for κύριε, ἐλέησον ἡμᾶς is stronger (ℵ, B, D, L, Z, 085, *f*¹³, 892). See Metzger 1994: 43–44.

2. Approaching Jerusalem: The Triumphal Entry (21:1–11)

This passage may be analyzed in three parts: the preparations (21:1–5), the entrance (21:6–9), and the result (21:10–11). Scripture punctuates the first and second sections (21:4–5, 9). Matthew sets the scene in 21:1. Jesus instructs the disciples to acquire a donkey and a colt (21:2–3), and Matthew notes the fulfillment of Zech. 9:9 (Matt. 21:4–5). The disciples carry out Jesus's instructions (21:6–7), and Jesus enters the city on a road covered with garments and palm branches, accompanied by the crowd's shouts echoing Ps. 118:25–26 (Matt. 21:8–9). The entry causes quite a stir in the city as Jesus is celebrated as a prophet from Nazareth (21:10–11). The pattern of instructions, scriptural citation, and obedience to instructions in 21:2–6 is also found in 1:20–24 (cf. W. Davies and Allison 1997: 111).[1]

The unit outline is as follows:

    a. Preparations for Jesus's entrance (21:1–5)
    b. Jesus's entrance (21:6–9)
    c. The results (21:10–11)

Exegesis and Exposition

[1]When they had drawn near to Jerusalem and had come to Bethphage, at the Mount of Olives, Jesus sent two disciples, [2]saying to them, "Go into the village ahead of you, and immediately you will find a donkey tied and her colt with her; untie them and bring them to me. [3]And if anyone says anything to you, just say, 'The Lord needs them,' and immediately he will send them." [4]This took place to fulfill what had been spoken through the prophet:

    [5]"Say to the daughter of Zion,
    'Look, your king is coming to you,

---

1. Matthew 21:1–11 is a type-scene in that its content follows a conventional literary structure that is similar to other Jewish texts that narrate the glorious arrival of a ruler or conquering hero with public acclaim and temple activity. Examples include Solomon (1 Kings 1:32–40), Judas Maccabeus (1 Macc. 5:45–54; Josephus, *Ant.* 12.348–49), Simon Maccabeus (1 Macc. 13:49–53), Antiochus (2 Macc. 4:21–22), Alexander the Great (Josephus, *Ant.* 11.325–29, 340–45), Antigonus (Josephus, *Ant.* 13.304–6), Marcus Agrippa (Josephus, *Ant.* 16.12–15), Archelaus (Josephus, *Ant.* 17.193–205). Cf. Catchpole in Bammel and Moule 1984: 319–34; Duff 1992.

humble, and mounted on a donkey,
even on a colt, the foal of a beast of burden.'"

⁶So the disciples went and did just as Jesus had instructed them. ⁷They brought the donkey and the colt and put their coats on them, and he sat on them. ⁸A very large crowd spread their cloaks on the road, and others were cutting branches from the trees and spreading them in the road. ⁹The crowds going ahead of him, and those who followed, were shouting,

"'Hosanna' to the son of David;
'Blessed is he who comes in the name of the Lord';
'Hosanna' in the highest!"

¹⁰When he had entered Jerusalem, the whole city was stirred up and asked, "Who is this?" ¹¹And the crowds were saying, "This is the prophet Jesus from Nazareth in Galilee."

a. Preparations for Jesus's Entrance (21:1–5)

21:1   Jesus finally approaches the ultimate destination of his trip from Galilee, the city where he will be crucified as he has predicted (16:21; 19:1; 20:18–19; cf. Mark 11:1–11; Luke 19:29–44; John 12:12–19). The arduous upward hike from Jericho has covered about fifteen miles and climbed about thirty-five hundred feet. The Mount of Olives is a north-south ridge, about two and a half miles long, lying just east of Jerusalem.² In the Bible, Bethphage is mentioned only here and in the synoptic parallels to this verse (Mark 11:1; Luke 19:29; cf. Jerome, *Epistles* 108.12; *b. Sanh.* 14b; *t. Pesaḥ.* 8.8). It was evidently located on the east slope of the Mount of Olives near Bethany. From the top of the Mount of Olives, the panorama of Jerusalem just across the Kidron valley to the west is magnificent.

21:2–5 For his entrance into Jerusalem, Jesus tells two disciples to acquire a donkey and its colt (cf. Judg. 5:10; 10:4; 12:13–14; 1 Sam. 9:3–5; 10:2; 2 Sam. 13:29; 1 Kings 1:33; *b. Ber.* 56b; *b. Sanh.* 98a) from a village near Bethphage (Bethany? Mark 11:1). If anyone asks about their taking the donkeys, the disciples need only say that the Lord needs them. Jesus's supernatural knowledge and control of this situation are remarkable in light of Matthew's emphasis on his humility. To stress the entry as an acted parable (Hill 1972: 290) of Jesus's humility, Matthew cites Zech. 9:9, conflated with introductory words from Isa. 62:11 (cf. John 12:14–15).³ The term "daughter of Zion" is a common biblical expression

2. Cf. 24:3; 26:30; 2 Sam. 15:30; 1 Kings 11:7; 2 Kings 23:13; Ezek. 11:23; Zech. 14:4; Josephus, *Ant.* 20.169; *J.W.* 2.262; Heard, *ABD* 5:13–15.
3. Matthew's εἴπατε τῇ θυγατρὶ Σιών agrees with Isa. 62:11 LXX. Ἰδοὺ . . . ἐπιβεβηκώς slightly abbreviates Zech. 9:9 LXX, omitting the LXX's δίκαιος καὶ σῴζων αὐτός. This

that refers to Jerusalem and its inhabitants (cf., e.g., 2 Kings 19:21; Ps. 9:14; Isa. 1:8; 16:1; 37:22; Jer. 4:31; 6:2; Lam. 1:6; Mic. 4:8, 10, 13; Zeph. 3:14; Zech. 2:10). Zechariah 9:9 mentions that the coming king will be just, bring salvation, and be humble, but Matthew selects only the last characteristic, humility (cf. Matt. 5:5, 9; 11:29). Humility is commonly mentioned as a characteristic of biblical kings: Saul (1 Sam. 9:21), David (2 Sam. 7:18–19), Ahab (1 Kings 21:29), and Josiah (2 Kings 22:18–20). In Zech. 9:9 the words "donkey" and "donkey's colt" are in synonymous parallelism and do not refer to two animals. On this point, see the comments on 21:7.

The prophecies of Zechariah frequently concern the troubles of Jerusalem and God's concern for it (e.g., Zech. 1:12–17; 2:2–5, 12; 3:2; 8:3–8; 12:2–9; 13:1; 14:2–8). Particularly noteworthy are texts that speak of God's coming to Zion (1:16; 8:3; 9:9; 14:4, 5b), the joining of Gentiles to God's people (2:11; 8:22–23), and eschatological worship of the king (14:9, 16–17). The passion narrative of Matthew cites Zech. 9–14 several times (Allison 1985a: 33–36; F. Bruce 1961; Ham 2005; Moo 1983: 173–224):

Matthew	cites	Zechariah
21:4–9		9:9
21:12–13		14:21
26:15–16		11:12
26:26–29		9:11
26:30–35		13:7
27:3–10		11:12–13
27:51–53		14:4–5

b. Jesus's Entrance (21:6–9)

The disciples do as Jesus has commanded (cf. 1:24; 26:19). In God's providence those in charge of the donkeys permit the disciples to take them (cf. Luke 19:32–34; 1 Kings 1:32–40). The synoptic parallels say that the disciples threw their garments on the colt and that Jesus sat on it (Mark 11:7; Luke 19:35). Matthew 21:7, however, says that the disciples put their garments on both donkeys (ἐπ' αὐτῶν, *ep' autōn*) and that Jesus sits on *them* (ἐπάνω αὐτῶν, *epanō autōn*). The pronoun αὐτῶν in the second phrase may refer either to the donkeys or to the garments thrown on the donkeys.[4] One wonders whether Matthew affirms that Jesus somehow straddles both animals (Gundry 1994: 409–10), although

21:6–9

---

places the emphasis on πραΰς. Ἐπὶ ὄνον καὶ ἐπὶ πῶλον υἱὸν ὑποζυγίου follows the MT rather than the LXX. Cf. Bartnicki 1976; Brandscheidt 1990; Gundry 1967: 120–21; Menken in Denaux 1992: 571–78.

4. Moulton and Turner (1963: 26) argue that αὐτῶν is a generalizing plural (cf. BDF §141; Robertson 1934: 400; Zerwick 1963: 3), but cf. Soarés-Prabhu 1976: 151.

some scholars argue that Matthew does intend this because of a mis-understanding of the Hebrew parallelism in Zech. 9:9 (e.g., Meier 1978: 21–22, 144). Others think that Matthew understands the parallelism but maximizes the details of the correspondence with Zech. 9:9 with a typically rabbinic hermeneutic (cf. Boring 1995: 403; Hagner 1995a: 594; Stendahl 1968: 119). More likely, Matthew means that Jesus rides sitting on the garments spread on the colt (cf. Mark 11:7; Luke 19:35; John 12:14), although the garments have been spread on both mother and colt. Only Matthew mentions two donkeys; Mark and Luke state that Jesus rode a colt that had never been ridden previously. Matthew's mention of the colt's mother stresses its youth and implies that it has not been ridden before (see W. Davies and Allison 1997: 120–23; Soarés-Prabhu 1976: 150–54).

The spreading of garments and palm branches on the road marks the festive acknowledgement of Jesus's kingship (cf. 1 Kings 1:32–40; 2 Kings 9:13; 1 Macc. 5:45–54; 13:51; 2 Macc. 10:7). The crowd's excited shouts echo Ps. 118:26.[5] "'Hosanna' to the son of David" is literally a cry for help ("Save!") but idiomatically expresses jubilant praise.[6] Jesus is frequently called the son of David in Matthew (1:1; 9:27; 12:23; 15:22; 20:30–31; cf. 12:3; 22:41–46; 2 Sam. 7:12–16). Another messianic title is "the one who comes" (Matt. 3:11; 11:3; 23:39). "'Hosanna' in the highest" probably echoes Ps. 148:1 (cf. Luke 2:14; 19:38). Psalms 113–18 were known as the Hallel and may have been sung at Passover, Tabernacles, and Hanukkah during the Second Temple period (b. 'Arak. 10a). Sadly, the excitement of the crowd is only temporary and is not in the end matched by faithful commitment to Jesus (Matt. 27:20). Their belief that Jesus is a prophet is inadequate (21:11).

c. The Results (21:10–11)

21:10–11 Jerusalem is accustomed to crowds of pilgrims during religious festivals, yet Jesus's entrance results in an uproar. Everywhere people ask about the identity of the one who enters the city to such fanfare (cf. 2:3). The crowds' answer here does not echo the messianic language of 21:9. Jesus is described accurately yet inadequately as the prophet from Nazareth in Galilee (2:23; 13:54, 57; 16:14). Hagner's suggestion (1995a: 596) that the crowds in 21:11 are Jerusalem residents, not the pilgrims of 20:29; 21:8, 9, is debatable.

---

5. Matthew 21:9 presents the shouts of the crowd in three lines. The first and third lines begin with ὡσαννά, drawn from נָא הוֹשִׁיעָה, which occurs once in Ps. 118:25a MT. Psalm 117:25a LXX renders הוֹשִׁיעָה נָא as σῶσον δή. The second, or middle, line of 21:9 has εὐλογημένος ὁ ἐρχόμενος ἐν ὀνόματι κυρίου, which is identical to Ps. 117:26a LXX, itself a literal rendering of Ps. 118:26a MT (cf. Matt. 23:39). See Brandscheidt 1990; Gundry 1967: 40–43; J. T. Sanders in C. A. Evans and Stinespring 1987: 177–90.

6. Cf. 2 Sam. 14:4; 2 Kings 6:26; Ps. 118:25; Did. 10.6; Fitzmyer in Hawthorne and Betz 1987: 110–18; Hart 1992; Kennard 1948; Lohse 1963; Pope 1988; Werner 1946.

The scene played out here is familiar: a conquering king parades gloriously into a city. Yet much is strange about this "triumphal" entry. The king is clothed plainly, not in military or royal splendor. He rides a young donkey, not a warhorse. He is meek, not bellicose. This combination of the trappings of power and glory with the imagery of humility sends mixed signals that perplex all Jerusalem. Throughout his ministry Jesus has exemplified humility and downplayed pride (e.g., 5:5; 8:20; 11:25; 12:18–21; 16:24–25; 18:4; 19:14; 20:26–28; 21:5; 23:8–12). His triumphal entry therefore epitomizes the upside-down values of the kingdom. His model of greatness reverses the world's paradigm of powerful rule to humble service. But the picture of Jesus's return in judgment is very different (cf. 7:21–23; 13:41–43; 16:27; 19:28; 21:41–46; 24:29–31; 25:31–46; 26:64; 28:20).

The crowd's shouts, at the same time correct and incorrect, are highly ironic. They correctly describe Jesus with messianic language, but they incorrectly understand this language. They rightly quote messianic texts, but they wrongly model their Messiah after a conquering military hero. This should not be surprising, since even the disciples have not yet fully grasped this (20:26). Jesus's identity as a prophet (21:11) has overtones of persecution and impending death (5:10–12; 23:29–39). As the narrative unfolds, the triumphal entry is shown in reality to be a very tragic entry. Jesus's "exit will not be as his entrance" (W. Davies and Allison 1997: 129).[7]

---

7. On Matt. 21:1–11, see Burger 1970: 81–87; Jacob 1973; S. L. Johnson 1967a; Lohfink in Schenke 1988: 179–200; P. Meyer 1986; Patsch 1971; Trilling in Blinzler et al. 1963: 303–9.

3. Cleansing and Controversy in the Temple (21:12–17)

Jesus's first action in Jerusalem is directed against the financial interests entrenched there (21:12–13). He also continues to heal those in physical need (21:14). These acts and the praises of children arouse the ire of the temple authorities, who call Jesus's attention to the messianic overtones of the children's praise to the son of David (21:15–16a). In reply Jesus cites Ps. 8:2 and leaves the temple to spend the night in Bethany (21:16b-17).

This passage has two sections, the first narrating Jesus's arrival and activities in the temple, with scriptural support for his action against the financial dealings there (21:12–14; Isa. 56:7; Jer. 7:11). In the second section, the temple chief priests and scribes reproach Jesus for allowing the messianic cries of the children, and he answers with scriptural vindication of the children (Matt. 21:15–16; Ps. 8:2) before departing from the temple and the city (Matt. 21:17). The opposition between Jesus and the temple authorities that pervades Matt. 21–23 begins here. It may be displayed as follows:

> Jesus arrives at the temple (21:12a)
> > Jesus protests against the temple financial activities (21:12b) and heals (21:14)
> > *Scriptural Support (21:13; Isa. 56:7; Jer. 7:11)*
> > Temple authorities protest against Jesus's actions (21:15–16a)
> > *Scriptural Support (21:16b; Ps. 8:2)*
> Jesus leaves the temple (21:17)

The unit can be outlined as follows:

> a. Confrontation in the temple (21:12–13)
> b. Healing in the temple (21:14)
> c. Opposition by the religious leaders (21:15–17)

Exegesis and Exposition

[12]And Jesus entered the ⌜temple⌝, and drove out all those who were selling and buying in the temple, and overturned the tables of the money changers and the seats of those who were selling doves. [13]And he said to them, "It is written,

'My house shall be called a house of prayer';
but you are making it a 'den of robbers.'"

[14]And the blind and the lame came to him in the temple, and he healed them. [15]But when the chief priests and the scribes saw the wonderful things he did and the children who were shouting in the temple, "'Hosanna' to the son of David," they became angry [16]and said to him, "Do you hear what these children are saying?" And Jesus said to them, "Yes; have you never read,

'Out of the mouths of infants and nursing babies
you have prepared praise for yourself'?"

[17]And He left them and went out of the city to Bethany and spent the night there.

a. Confrontation in the Temple (21:12–13)

Jesus goes to the temple area and disrupts the financial dealings taking place there (cf. Mark 11:15–18; Luke 19:45–48). The word "temple" (ἱερόν, *hieron*) refers to the entire walled second-temple complex enlarged by Herod the Great (see D. Bahat in Charlesworth 2006: 300–308). It was roughly rectangular, with an area of 172,000 square yards, the size of thirty-five football fields. The outer Court of the Gentiles was probably where Jesus drove out the merchants, healed the blind and lame, and received the children's praise (Matt. 21:12, 14–15). The first inner court was the Court of the Women, where all Jews could enter (Mark 12:41–44; Luke 2:37; John 8:2–3). Only ritually pure Jewish males could go further into the Court of the Israelites, where the sacrificial altar stood (Mark 11:11; Luke 18:10–11; 24:53). Beyond this area was the temple proper, or Court of the Priests, where only priests could go.[1]

    The buying and selling in the temple centered on the sacrifices offered there. There would also be commerce in buying supplies for the temple and in selling items that had been donated to the temple (*m. Šeqal.* 5.6; Bauckham in Lindars 1988: 78).[2] Such activities would require a treasury or bank.[3] Money changers serviced the many pilgrims holding foreign coins who came for major festivals (*m. Šeqal.* 1.6). Evidently, it was of-

21:12–13

---

1. On Herod's temple, see Wise in J. Green and McKnight 1992: 812; Meyers, *ABD* 6:362–68; Ritmeyer and Ritmeyer 1989; E. Sanders 1992: 47–76, 306–14.
2. Zechariah 14:21 may envision a day when traders or merchants (כְּנַעֲנִי) will no longer operate in the temple (BDB 489; NJPS, NRSV). But כְּנַעֲנִי may mean "Canaanites" (LXX, NIV).
3. The temple treasury is mentioned in LXX 1 Kings 7:51; 2 Kings 18:15; 1 Macc. 14:49; 2 Macc. 3:1–6, 24, 28, 40; Neh. 12:14; 13:4–9; 4Q169 frgs. 3–4.1.11; 1QpHab 9.4–5; Josephus, *Ant.* 14.105, 110; 19.294; *J.W.* 5.200; 6.282; *m. Šeqal.* 5.6; 6.5. Γαζοφυλάκιον in John 8:20; Mark 12:41, 43; Luke 21:1 may refer to a receptacle for donations or to a place of storage. Cf. Hamilton 1964.

fensive for the pilgrims to use coins with pagan inscriptions when they paid the half-shekel temple tax (Matt. 17:24–27; Exod. 30:11–16). Doves were a permissible sacrifice for those who could not afford a lamb for a sin offering, a firstborn offering, or an offering for the ritual purity of a recent mother (Luke 2:22–24; Exod. 13:2, 12; Lev. 5:7, 11; 12:6, 8; 14:22; 15:14, 29; *m. Ker.* 1.7). Jesus's disgust is probably not against the financial activities as such, since these are necessitated by duties required by the Torah. The problem is evidently that the transactions are taking place within the temple itself or that the merchants are dealing dishonestly with the pilgrims, either by not changing money equitably or by charging them exorbitant prices for their sacrificial animals (Matt. 21:13; *m. Ker.* 1.7).

Jesus's disruptive acts are based on biblical citations that highlight the incongruity of turning a place of prayer (Luke 2:37; 18:10; Acts 3:1; cf. Ps. 141:2; 2 Macc. 10:26; Sir. 51:14) into a den of thieves (Isa. 56:7; Jer. 7:11; Brandscheidt 1990).[4] "Thieves" may be insurrectionists rather than mere robbers (cf. Matt. 26:55; 27:38, 44; BDAG 594). If so, Jesus is opposing not merely simple dishonesty but revolutionary extremism. His actions should perhaps be viewed as a portent of the Roman destruction of the temple in 70 CE (C. A. Evans 1989a).

b. Healing in the Temple (21:14)

21:14 Jesus also acts on behalf of those who are physically needy. This account of healing the blind and lame is the last healing account in Matthew (cf. 9:27–28; 11:5; 12:22; 15:30–31; 20:30). Evidently, it occurs in the outer Court of the Gentiles, since blind and lame people are to be excluded from the temple (Lev. 21:18–19; 2 Sam. 5:8; *m. Ḥag.* 1.1; cf. CD 15.15–17; 1QSa 2.8–9; 1QM 7.3–4; 4Q394 [MMTª] frg. 2.18–19; but cf. John 9:1; Acts 3:1–2). In any event, Jesus removes the barrier to their full participation in God's house of prayer. His clearing the temple of financial dealings amounts to casting out the insiders; his healing amounts to welcoming the outsiders (Boring 1995: 406; Patte 1987: 290).

c. Opposition by the Religious Leaders (21:15–17)

21:15–17 Jesus's activities in the temple model the values of Hos. 6:6: God prefers mercy over sacrifice (cf. Matt. 9:12–13; 12:7; Blomberg 1992a: 315). The chief priests and scribes were consulted by Herod as to the place of Jesus's birth (2:4), and they appear in two of Jesus's passion predictions

---

4. In 21:13 ὁ οἶκός μου οἶκος προσευχῆς κληθήσεται is identical to Isa. 56:7 LXX (except that the LXX has ὁ γὰρ οἶκος), which is a literal rendering of the MT. Matthew omits πᾶσιν τοῖς ἔθνεσιν at the end of the verse. The rest of 21:13, ὑμεῖς δὲ αὐτὸν ποιεῖτε σπήλαιον λῃστῶν, alludes to Jer. 7:11, which asks whether God's house (ὁ οἶκός μου) has become a den of thieves (σπήλαιον λῃστῶν). This passage occurs in an oracle that threatens the temple's destruction (7:12–14; Knowles 1993: 173–76).

(16:21; 20:18). Given their earlier opposition, their indignation here is not surprising. They are incensed at Jesus's miracles and at the messianic overtones of the children's cries, which echo the citation of Ps. 118:26 in Matt. 21:9 (Brandscheidt 1990). Jesus responds by citing Ps. 8:2 to vindicate the children.[5] His introduction, "Have you never read" stresses their obstinance more than their ignorance. They have read Ps. 8:2 but will not believe that Jesus is the Messiah (cf. Matt. 12:3, 5; 19:4; 21:42). By contrast, the children's messianic praise language recalls Matthew's "little ones" who receive the kingdom (cf. 10:42; 11:25; 18:1–6; 19:14; 25:40, 45). Psalm 8 is understood messianically elsewhere in the NT (1 Cor. 15:27; Eph. 1:22; Phil. 3:21; Heb. 2:6–9; 1 Pet. 3:22). An additional nuance of the use of Ps. 8:2 is that the rest of the verse speaks of how the children's praise causes God's adversaries to cease. After the confrontation with the temple authorities, Jesus leaves the temple and returns to Bethany (Matt. 26:6; cf. Mark 11:1, 11–12; 14:3; Luke 19:29; 24:50; John 11:1, 18; 12:1) to spend the night. Perhaps Jesus's departure from the temple anticipates his later departure after pronouncing it desolate (Matt. 23:38–24:1).[6]

Renewal or Destruction?

This episode reinforces the previous episode's stress on Jesus as the messianic son of David. Jesus's first action upon entering Jerusalem is to deliver it not from the oppressive Roman occupying forces but from its own hypocrisy. His entrance to the city is royal, but his action in the temple is prophetic (W. Davies and Allison 1997: 133–34). Previous "cleansings" of the temple were accomplished by Josiah, Hezekiah, and Judas Maccabeus (2 Kings 22–23; 2 Chron. 29:3–11; 1 Macc. 4; 2 Macc. 10). Instead of directly threatening the political status quo, Jesus confronts the temple, the religious center of Israel, and its established leadership. His major activities in the temple are directed against hypocrisy and on behalf of the needy. As did the prophets before him, Jesus spoke and acted against the corruption of Israel's established worship (cf. Zech. 14:21; Mal. 3:2–4) and for those who were without status. Therefore Jesus's acts in the temple augur the eschatological reversal in which the meek "will

5. The citation agrees verbatim with Ps. 8:3 LXX, which renders the MT יִסַּדְתָּ עֹז ("You have established strength") as κατηρτίσω αἶνον. France 1982: 251–52 argues that in the MT it could be taken as praise for God's strength, as in Pss. 29:1; 59:17; 68:34; 96:7 (cf. Gundry 1967: 121–22; Stendahl 1968: 134). Perhaps Matthew's use of LXX over MT should be linked to Jewish exegesis that linked the praise of God's strength in Exod. 15:2 to Ps. 8:3. עֹז occurs in both Exod. 15:2 and Ps. 8:3, and the tradition arose that children praised God at the exodus (cf. Mekilta on Exod. 15:1; t. Soṭah 6.4; y. Soṭah 5.4; and W. Davies and Allison 1997: 142).

6. On 21:12–17, see Bauckham in Lindars 1988: 72–89, 171–76; Buchanan 1991; Derrett 1977; C. A. Evans 1989a; Kallemeyn 1992; Losie 1984; Paesler 1999; Söding 1992; Watty 1982.

inherit the earth" while the corrupt leaders will be brought low. Jesus's healing in the temple and his cleansing it both demonstrate the truth of Matt. 12:6: "Something greater than the temple is here" (cf. Mal. 3:1). Jesus's citation of Ps. 8:2 in Matt. 21:16 is an implicit claim that he is worthy of the praise and worship that the psalm directs to God.

Jesus's action in the temple has been commonly viewed as an act of correction or purification. But some scholars argue that Jesus was not so much reforming the temple as announcing its doom (R. Horsley 1987; E. Sanders 1985). Jesus did in fact predict the destruction of the temple (24:2; cf. Jer. 26:1–11; Josephus, *J.W.* 6.300–309), but his activities here condemn not the priestly sacrifices or the temple as a divine institution but its parasitic commercial enterprises. Although the biblical prophets commonly denounced the corruption of the temple and its priests, their oracles did not oppose the sacrificial system itself but the abuses of it. Later Jewish texts also critique the corruption of Jerusalem and the temple.[7]

The cleansing of the temple symbolizes both the reformation of its abuses and the judgment that will come if the abuses continue (W. Davies and Allison 1997: 135–37; Keener 1999: 496–501). Protest against present corruption and warning of future destruction are compatible elements of the prophetic message when there is hope of repentance (Matt. 23:39) and the rise of an eschatological temple (Ezek. 40–48). Biblical prophetic ministry confronts Israel's abandonment of covenant obligations, calls Israel to repentance, and promises judgment and hope based on Israel's response. Matthew perhaps saw in Jesus's acts a fulfillment of the Lord coming suddenly into his temple (Mal. 3:1–4). Another possibility is stated by the most likely translation of Zech. 14:21, which envisions a day in which there will be no more merchants in the house of the Lord.

In distinction from the synoptic accounts that Jesus cleared the temple at the end of his ministry, John's Gospel describes a similar scene at the beginning of Jesus's ministry (John 2:14–22). It is possible that John's account adapts the synoptic account for literary purposes, but it is more likely that there were two clearings of the temple by Jesus. (See Herzog in J. Green and McKnight 1992: 817–21.)

Additional Note

21:12. There is strong support for the shorter reading ἱερόν, favored by UBS[4] (including ℵ, B, L, Θ, *f*[13], 33, 700, 892; cf. Mark 11:15; Luke 19:45). The words τοῦ θεοῦ (found in C, D, W, Δ, 0233, *f*[1], 28, *Byz, Lect*) appear to be a later expansion.

---

7. For biblical texts, cf., e.g., 1 Sam. 22:18–19; Isa. 28:7; Jer. 6:13; Ezek. 8–10; Hos. 4:4–6; Mic. 3:11; Zeph. 3:4. For later texts, cf. 4Q390; 1QpHab 8.8–13; 9.3–7; Jub. 23.21; T. Levi 14.1–8; 17.11; Ps. Sol. 1.8; 2.3–5; 8.11–13; T. Mos. 5.3–6.1; 7.8–10; 1 En. 83–90; 2 Esd. (4 Ezra) 3:25–27; 2 Bar. 1.1–5; 10.18; 13.4; Apoc. Abr. 25.1–6; 27.1–7; 4 Bar. 4.3–8; Josephus, *Ant.* 20.179–81, 204–7, 213; *Life* 193–96; *m. Ker.* 1.7; *t. Menaḥ.* 13.18–22; *t. Zebaḥ.* 11.16–17.

4. Cursing the Fig Tree (21:18–22)

In this short section, a provocative action leads to a question that in turn leads to an authoritative pronouncement (W. Davies and Allison 1997: 147). Jesus curses a fruitless fig tree, which withers immediately (21:18–19). This astounds the disciples and leads to an opportunity for Jesus to teach on prayer (21:20–22). Mark's version of the cursing of the fig tree (Mark 11:12–14, 20–24) wraps it around Jesus's activities in the temple (Mark 11:15–19). Matthew's account evidently telescopes into a single narrative events that originally took place over two days. The fig tree incident takes its place with the entry to Jerusalem and the cleansing of the temple as yet another acted parable with important symbolic significance.

The unit outline is as follows:

a. Cursing the fruitless fig tree (21:18–19)
b. Teaching the astonished disciples (21:20–22)

Exegesis and Exposition

[18]Now early in the morning, as he was returning to the city, he became hungry. [19]Seeing a single fig tree by the road, he came to it and found nothing on it except leaves only; and he said to it, "No longer shall there ever be any fruit from you." And at once the fig tree withered. [20]Seeing this, the disciples were amazed and asked, "How did the fig tree wither all at once?" [21]And Jesus answered and said to them, "Truly I tell you, if you have faith and do not doubt, you will not only do what was done to the fig tree, but even if you say to this mountain, 'Be taken up and cast into the sea,' it will happen.

[22]"And all things you ask in prayer, believing, you will receive."

a. Cursing the Fruitless Fig Tree (21:18–19)

When Jesus returns to the temple the next day, he becomes hungry (cf. 4:2) and looks for figs on a roadside tree. The tree, however, has leaves but no fruit.[1] The leaves create an appearance of life that promises fruit

21:18–19

---

1. Why does Jesus look for figs out of season and then destroy the tree? This question, engendered by Mark 11:13 (ὁ γὰρ καιρὸς οὐκ ἦν σύκων; see Cotter 1986), is not properly a part of the exegesis of Matthew, since Matthew omits this detail. Nevertheless, Jesus's use of his power for a seemingly destructive purpose troubles some scholars (e.g., Boring 1995: 407; Patte 1987: 292). But Jesus's act is not a *Strafwunder* (punishment miracle) since vegetation cannot be punished (Schnackenburg 2002: 204). Rather, Jesus's prophetic

(cf. 21:34; Pliny, *Nat.* 16.49; Carson 1984: 445). Jesus curses the tree and it immediately dries up, proof that it will indeed never bear fruit again. The cursing of the fig tree amounts to a prophetic parable in action (cf. Isa. 8:1–4; Jer. 13; 19; 27–28; Ezek. 3:1–3; 4:1–5:17; Hos. 1:2–9). In prophetic texts, fruitless fig trees symbolize judgment (Isa. 34:4; Jer. 8:13; 24:1–10; Hos. 2:12; Joel 1:7). Here the cursed tree symbolizes judgment on Jerusalem and the leaders of Israel, particularly the temple leaders (W. Davies and Allison 1997: 148, 151–52; Harrington 1991: 297–98; Overman 1996: 295–96), not Israel as a whole (Blomberg 1992a: 318; Hagner 1995a: 603–4; Meier 1980b: 237; Schnackenburg 2002: 204–5).

b. Teaching the Astonished Disciples (21:20–22)

21:20–22 The object lesson of the fig tree now receives a new twist. The disciples' amazement at how rapidly the tree withers overrides their perception of why it has withered and what it signifies. Again they do not understand what Jesus is doing, and their question is beside the point of Jesus's action. Yet he uses the occasion to teach them about faith and prayer. If they pray in faith (cf. 6:8; 7:7–11; 18:19), they will see even greater things than a dried-up tree: they will see a mountain thrown into the sea (cf. 17:19–20; Luke 17:6; Rom. 4:20; 1 Cor. 13:2; Eph. 3:20; James 1:6).[2] This emphasis on believing prayer that God will do what is humanly impossible must be correlated with the emphasis in the Lord's Prayer (Matt. 6:9–13) on God's reputation and rule. If "this mountain" refers to the Temple Mount, its being thrown into the sea may picture the temple's destruction. In this view, the cursing of the fig tree portends the Roman destruction of the temple in 70 CE (Telford 1980).[3]

The cursing of the fig tree is Jesus's third symbolic act in this context. He has ridden the colt into the city and cleared its temple of commercial activity. These two acts respectively convey Jesus's kingly and prophetic roles. The prophetic role continues here with the cursing of the fig tree, which by all accounts is one of the strangest things Jesus ever did. But the acted biblical prophetic parables are often strange. The cursing of the fruitless fig tree portrays the fruitless (cf. 3:10, 12; 7:16–20; 13:18–23, 37–43) religious leaders, whose temple was just cleared. They have less appreciation for Jesus than the children do (21:15–16). They respond to Jesus's miracles by questioning his authority instead of praising God for his blessings. Their fruitlessness will be fully and finally denounced in Matt. 23. The fig tree incident also shows that Jesus's disciples still

---

act of power (Overholt 1982) simply uses an inanimate object symbolically to teach the disciples constructive lessons about divine judgment and prayer.

2. The image of a mountain cast into the sea may be an allusion to Zech. 14:4, which concerns the Mount of Olives.

3. On 21:18–22, see Derrett 1988b; Ellul 1992; Hedrick 1990; Oakman 1993; Schwarz 1992b; Telford 1980.

need to develop faith that God will answer prayer. Jesus has previously rebuked their "little faith" (6:30; 8:26; 14:31; 16:8; 17:20). Here their faith is challenged again in a context connected with the temple, which is called "a house of prayer for all nations" (Isa. 56:7; Matt. 21:13). The fruitlessness of the unbelieving religious leaders is contrasted here with the potential fruitfulness of Jesus's believing disciples (Hagner 1995a: 606–7).

5. Increasing Controversy with the Leaders in the Temple (21:23–22:46)

Jesus's final conflict with the Jerusalem religious leaders began when he entered the city and acted prophetically in the temple (21:15–17), but at this point it escalates. The leaders' question about the source of his authority tends to set the tone for the controversy stories found throughout 21:23–22:46. Boring (1995: 409) takes all of 21:24–22:46 as a response to the leaders' question in 21:23. In his view, the two unanswerable questions Jesus puts to the leaders form the poles of a chiasmus:

A Jesus's question (21:24–27)
  B Three parables (21:28–32; 21:33–46; 22:1–14)
  B' Three controversy stories (22:15–22; 22:23–33; 22:34–40)
A' Jesus's question (22:41–46)

Whether or not the chiasm is valid, the ultimate conflict between Jesus and the leaders is indeed over the matter of his authority.

a. Three Questions about Authority (21:23–32)

The question put to Jesus about the source of his authority (cf. Mark 11:27–33; Luke 20:1–8) is not an innocent one (W. Davies and Allison 1997: 159; Shae 1974). In Matthew's narrative, Jesus's powerful words and works have repeatedly made it plain to the Jewish leaders that Jesus's authority is from heaven (9:1–8; 12:6, 8, 28, 38, 41–42; 15:1–12; 16:1).[1] But they are less perceptive than the crowd they presume to lead, since even the crowd regards John and Jesus as prophets. The leaders' question is motivated by animosity and probably by the desire to trap Jesus into saying something that could be construed as blasphemous (9:3, 34; 12:24; 22:15; 26:59–65). But Jesus turns the tables on this line of questioning by asking the leaders a question they dare not answer—the question about the source of John's authority (21:25). Then he asks them to respond to a parable about two sons, and this time their answer condemns them (21:28–31). They not only refuse to do what they promised, like the second son. They also refuse to follow the example of the first son, who stands for the tax collectors and prostitutes and whose repentance ought to have influenced the leaders to repent (21:32). Jesus's actions in the temple demonstrate his authority over it: "Something greater than the temple is here" (12:6).

The unit can be outlined as follows:

i. The leaders' question about Jesus's authority (21:23)
ii. Jesus's question about John's authority (21:24–27)
iii. A parable: Jesus's question about God's authority (21:28–32)

Exegesis and Exposition

²³When he entered the temple, the chief priests and the elders of the people came to him while he was teaching, and said, "By what authority are you doing these things, and who gave you this authority?" ²⁴Jesus said to them, "I will also ask you a question. If you answer me, I will also tell you by what authority I am doing these things. ²⁵The baptism of John was from what source, from heaven or

---

1. Here the juxtaposition of ἐξ οὐρανοῦ and ἐξ ἀνθρώπων makes it clear that heaven is an indirect reference to God. Cf. texts that speak of heaven as God's dwelling (e.g., 1 Kings 8:30; Dan. 2:28; Matt. 5:16; 6:9) and Luke 15:18, 21; John 3:27. The metonymy of "God" and "heaven" is probably the main reason for Matthew's distinctive "kingdom of heaven." See BDAG 738–39; and Traub, *TDNT* 5:520–22.

from humans?" And they began reasoning among themselves, "If we say, 'From heaven,' he will say to us, 'Then why did you not believe him?' ²⁶But if we say, 'From humans,' we fear the people; for they all regard John as a prophet." ²⁷And they answered Jesus, "We do not know." So he also said to them, "Neither will I tell you by what authority I am doing these things.

²⁸"But what do you think? A man had two sons, and he went to the first and said, 'Son, go work in the vineyard today.' ²⁹And he answered, ⌜'I will not'; but later he changed his mind and went. ³⁰The man went to the other son and said the same thing; and he answered, 'I will, sir'; but he did not go. ³¹Which of the two did the will of his father?" They said, "The first."⌝ Jesus said to them, "Truly I tell you, the tax collectors and prostitutes will get into the kingdom of God before you. ³²For John came to you in the way of righteousness and you did not believe him; but the tax collectors and prostitutes believed him. Yet even after you had seen this, you did not change your mind and believe him."

i. The Leaders' Question about Jesus's Authority (21:23)

21:23   When Jesus returns to the temple, the religious leaders' question about his authority renews the controversy begun in 21:12–16. This running controversy grows more and more heated as it leads up to the prophetic woes of Matt. 23. The leading priests and elders (also paired in 26:3, 47; 27:1, 3, 12, 20) are in charge of the temple, and so it is not surprising that they question Jesus's activities, which presume an authority that overrides their own (cf. Acts 4:7). The authority of Jesus's words and deeds is an important Matthean theme (Matt. 7:29; 8:9; 9:6, 8; 10:1; 21:23, 24, 27; 26:64; 28:18; cf. Acts 4:7; 8:19; 26:18).

ii. Jesus's Question about John's Authority (21:24–27)

21:24–27   Instead of directly answering the question, Jesus strikes a sort of bargain with them. He will answer their question only if they answer his counterquestion (cf. 12:3–5, 11, 26; 15:3; 19:4–5; Daube 1973: 151–57) about the source of John's authority (cf. Acts 5:38–39).² This puts them in a quandary: if they answer that John's authority was merely human, they will anger the crowds, who regard John and Jesus as prophets speaking from God (cf. Matt. 14:5; 21:46; Josephus, *Ant.* 18.118).³ But if they recognize John's divine authority (cf. 11:7–15), their unbelief will be exposed. Jesus's response to their question with one of his own is typical in this section of Matthew. His questions repeatedly foil the leaders as they attempt to trip him up (21:27, 31, 41; 22:21, 42, 46).

2. Jesus's phrase "the baptism of John" is synechdochal in that a conspicuous aspect of John's ministry stands for his entire mission.

3. The leaders' fear of the crowd (φοβούμεθα τὸν ὄχλον) is syntactically awkward because of the mixture of direct and indirect speech. Although it is not in the third person, perhaps this statement should be read as an editorial comment. Cf. BDF §470 (3); W. Davies and Allison 1997: 162.

5. Increasing Controversy with the Leaders in the Temple
a. Three Questions about Authority
Matthew 21:23–32

The leaders feign ignorance to avoid the quandary, but their refusal to answer betrays their negative estimate of John. Jesus responds in kind by refusing to answer their question about his authority.[4] In so doing, he subtly affirms John (W. Davies and Allison 1997: 162).

iii. A Parable: Jesus's Question about God's Authority (21:28–32)

The stalemate continues with a parable about two sons who respond **21:28–30** oppositely to their father's request to work in his vineyard (cf. 20:1–15; 21:33–46). This is the first of a set of three parables that rebuke the religious leaders for their unbelief (21:28–32, 33–44; 22:1–14; cf. Olmstead 2003). For the question "What do you think?" (21:28), see 17:25; 18:12; 22:17. The father's two commands and the sons' two responses are structurally parallel but ethically antithetical. The first son initially refuses but eventually does work. The second initially agrees to work but eventually does not. See the additional note for discussion of the considerable textual difficulties of this parable. Certain later rabbinic parables are similar to this one (cf. Exod. Rab. on Exod. 18:1; Deut. Rab. on Deut. 28:1).

Jesus's question applies the parable to the leaders. This time they do **21:31–32** answer, but their answer condemns them (cf. 21:41). Jesus responds with an accusation (21:31b) and an explanation (21:32). Their unbelief in John likens them to the second son, who promised to work but did nothing. In contrast, the tax collectors' and prostitutes' belief in John (cf. 9:10–11; 11:19; Gibson 1981; Keener 1999: 508–9) likens them to the first son, who did work in the vineyard despite his initial refusal. Therefore even the most notorious sinners who repent will enter the kingdom before the leaders,[5] who are still unrepentant even after they see the notorious sinners repent. Their promise of righteousness without performance likens them to the fig tree with leaves but no fruit (21:19). The reference to John's coming in the way of righteousness[6] implicitly affirms that heavenly authority supported John's life and testimony for Jesus.

This passage teaches that discipleship is fundamentally about deeds, not words (cf., e.g., 7:21–27). For good or ill, a disciple's initial words may

4. Jesus's ἐν ποίᾳ ἐξουσίᾳ ταῦτα ποιῶ in 21:27 matches the leaders' ἐν ποίᾳ ἐξουσίᾳ ταῦτα ποιεῖς in 21:23, forming an *inclusio*.
5. Some interpret the precedence (προάγουσιν ὑμᾶς) of tax collectors and prostitutes over the leaders in entering the kingdom exclusively: these repentant sinners will enter and the leaders will not enter (e.g., BDF §245a; W. Davies and Allison 1997: 169–70; Jeremias 1972: 125; Morris 1992: 537). But this is not the usual meaning of προάγω (BDAG 864). It is more likely that the language leaves room for the leaders' eventual repentance (W. Allen 1912: 227; Hultgren 2000: 221–22; McNeile 1915: 306).
6. On ἐν ὁδῷ δικαιοσύνης as an expression connoting life in obedience to God's commands, see Job 24:13; Ps. 23:3; Prov. 2:20; 8:20; 12:28; 16:7, 31; 21:16, 21; 1QS 4.2; CD 1.16; 1QH 7.14; Tob. 1:3; 1 En. 82.4; 92.3; 94.1; 99.10; Jub. 1.20; 23.26; 25.15; 2 Pet. 2:21; Barn. 1.4; Przybylski 1980: 94–96.

be reversed by subsequent deeds. Amazingly, the temple officials do not obey the Father's will despite their knowledge of the law and religious occupation. Even more amazingly, the grace of God can draw notorious sinners in repentance into the kingdom (cf. 9:10–13). The lesson of this passage is that today's disciples must not assume the permanence of either their own supposed righteous standing before God or the unrighteous status of notorious sinners. Disciples are obliged to persevere and sinners are obliged to repent. It is a mistake to be complacent about either one's own supposed righteousness or about the supposed unrighteousness of another. The Father still powerfully calls people into the kingdom, but entrance is promised not to those who merely say, "I will go," but to those who actually do the will of the Father (7:21).[7]

The Parable of the Two Sons and the Question of Israel and the Church

Christian exegetes commonly view the parable of the two sons in terms of salvation history, with the first son, who initially refused but later obeyed, representing the Gentiles and with the second son, who initially promised but later refused, representing Israel (e.g., John Chrysostom, *Hom. Matt.* 67.2; K. Clark 1947: 166–67; Meier 1978: 149–50).[8] But the supersessionist interpretation posits something extraneous to Matthew's context: Gentiles superseding Jews in redemptive history. The context focuses on the Jewish response to John, and so the parties contrasted by this parable are groups within Israel, not Jews and Gentiles. John and Jesus both confront the Jews with eschatological reversal: the unrepentant establishment will be replaced by repentant people of no status. But the recently enfranchised replacements and the disenfranchised former leaders are both Jewish. Today's predominantly gentile church must ponder Paul's warning in Rom. 11:18–23 and not repeat the error of the Jewish establishment. (On this question, see the comments on Matt. 21:43; Martens in Longenecker 2000: 172–75; D. Turner 2002.)

Additional Note

21:29–31. "The textual tradition of the parable of the two sons is very much confused" (Metzger 1994: 44), rendering it "unquestionably among the most difficult problems of New Testament textual criticism" (Aland and Aland 1989: 316). Only a brief summary of the major issue, the order of the two sons in 21:29–30, is possible here. Does the ultimately obedient son (as in ℵ*, C*, K, W, Δ, Π,

7. On 21:23–32, see Daube 1973: 217–23; Derrett 1971: 109–16; Hultgren 2000: 218–25; Langley 1996; Marucci 1986; W. Richards 1978; Shae 1974; van Tilborg 1972b: 47–63; W. Weiss 1989.

8. Matthew 21:28–32 is the first of three parables (cf. 21:33–46, the vineyard workers; 22:1–14, the wedding feast) that are viewed by some as defining the true Israel. See Carter in Carter and Heil 1998: 147–76; Dillon 1966; Martens in Longenecker 2000: 151–76; Ogawa 1979; van Tilborg 1972b: 47–52.

Byz) or the ultimately disobedient son (as in B, Θ, 0233, *f*¹³, 700) come first? Internal considerations seem to favor the latter reading (Metzger 1994: 46), but external support is stronger for the former, which is also the more difficult reading. D and some Old Latin MSS have the rather unlikely scenario that the first son ultimately obeys, the second ultimately disobeys, and the religious leaders answer the question of 21:31 that the second son did the will of the father. See Aland and Aland 1989: 312–16; Metzger 1994: 44–46; Michaels 1968; J. Schmid in Adler 1951: 68–84.

b. Parable of the Tenant Farmers
(21:33–46)

The parable of the wicked tenant farmers (cf. Mark 12:1–12; Luke 20:9–19; Gos. Thom. 65) begins with a landowner building a vineyard (echoing Isa. 5:1–2), leasing it to tenants, and taking a trip (Matt. 21:33).[1] In the rest of the parable, the landowner acts three times to obtain fruit from his vineyard, and each time he is thwarted by the violent responses of his recalcitrant tenants (21:34–35, 36, 37–39). At this point Jesus asks what will happen next, inviting the religious leaders to finish the story. They provide the obvious answer: the landowner will replace the wicked tenants with new tenants who will provide him with fruit (21:40–41). Jesus then confirms the self-incriminating answer of the leaders with scriptural support (21:42–44). The pericope concludes with the leaders' awareness of the implications of the parable and their plan to do away with Jesus (21:45–46).

This parable joins two biblical themes—Israel as God's vineyard and its rejection of the prophets—with two new themes: Jesus as the culmination of God's revelation and his rejection as the culmination of Israel's rebellion (W. Davies and Allison 1997: 176–77). Jesus's answer to the Jewish leaders' question on the source of his authority (21:23) continues here. Jesus's authority comes from the vineyard owner, God, who has been extremely patient with the leaders of his people, who have repeatedly rejected his messengers. Fruit, or life in obedience to the law, has not been produced by these leaders. Now they are about to destroy the vineyard owner's son, Jesus, because they think that this will lead to their ongoing authority over the people. But the owner of the vineyard will have the last word when he replaces these leaders with Jesus's disciples who will produce fruit. Thus the parable of the wicked tenants is a miniature history of redemption. In its own way, it is as much a prediction of Jesus's death and resurrection as Jesus's passion predictions (16:21; 17:22–23; 20:18–19).

An outline of the unit is as follows:

i. The Building of the vineyard (21:33)
ii. The first and second attempts to obtain fruit (21:34–36)

---

1. Similar rabbinic parables are found in Sipre on Deut. 32:9; Exod. Rab. on Exod. 3:1; Lev. Rab. on Lev. 4:2; 18:3. Cf. 1 En. 89; Shepherd of Hermas, *Similitude* 5.2. See C. A. Evans 1995: 390–94; D. Stern in Thoma and Wyschogrod 1989: 42–80.

iii. The third attempt to obtain fruit (21:37–39)
iv. The owner's retribution (21:40–41)
v. The parable applied (21:42–44)
vi. The parable understood (21:45–46)

Exegesis and Exposition

[33]"Listen to another parable. There was a landowner who 'planted a vineyard, put a wall around it, dug a wine press in it, built a watchtower.' Then he leased it to tenant farmers and went away on a journey. [34]When the harvesttime was near, he sent his slaves to the tenant farmers to get his fruit. [35]But the tenants seized his slaves. They beat one, killed another, and stoned a third. [36]Again he sent other slaves, more than the first time, and they treated them similarly. [37]So finally he sent his son to them, saying, 'They will respect my son.' [38]But when the tenants saw the son, they said to each other, 'This is the heir; come, let us kill him so we can have his inheritance.' [39]So they seized him, ⌐threw him out of the vineyard, and killed him⌐.

[40]"Therefore, when the owner of the vineyard comes, what will he do to those tenant farmers?" [41]They said to him, "He will utterly destroy those wicked men and will lease the vineyard to other tenants who will give him his fruit at harvesttime."

[42]Jesus said to them, "Have you never read in the Scriptures,

'The stone that the builders rejected,
this has become the cornerstone.
This came about from the Lord,
and it is amazing in our eyes'?

[43]Therefore, I tell you, the kingdom of God will be taken away from you and given to a people who will produce its fruit. [44]⌐And anyone who falls on this stone will be broken to pieces; but anyone on whom it falls will be scattered like chaff.⌐"

[45]When the chief priests and the Pharisees heard his parables, they understood that he was speaking about them. [46]But although they wanted to seize him, they feared the crowds because they considered him to be a prophet.

i. The Building of the Vineyard (21:33)

This second parable (cf. Mark 12:1–12; Luke 20:9–19) is also based on the familiar biblical image of a vineyard (Matt. 21:28).[2] But here the workers are tenant farmers, not the owner's sons. Isaiah's song of the vineyard (Isa. 5:1–7) is alluded to here, but Matthew adds a crucial new element:

21:33

2. On the vineyard, see Ps. 80:8–13; Isa. 27:2; Jer. 2:21; 12:10; Ezek. 19:10–14; Hos. 10:1; 1 En. 10.16; 84.6; Jub. 1.16; Ps. Sol. 14.3–4; Combet-Galland 1987; M. Elliott 2000: 329–44.

tenant farmers who lease the vineyard while the owner goes on a journey (Matt. 25:14–15; Weren 1998). The vineyard is Israel, the recipient of God's kingdom blessings (21:43; Isa. 5:7); the tenant farmers are Israel's leaders (Matt. 21:43, 45). The crucial tension in the plot of the parable is the owner receiving his share of the fruit, a Matthean metaphor for right living or obedience to God's law (3:8, 10; 7:16–20; 12:33; 13:8, 26; 21:19, 34, 41, 43). Israel's relationship with God covenantally obligated its leaders to righteousness, just as the tenants were contractually obligated to produce fruit for the owner of the vineyard.

Isaiah 5:1–7 poignantly decries Israel's infidelity with the imagery of a well-cultivated vineyard that inexplicably fails to produce good fruit. Isaiah 5:1b–2a describes six steps in the transformation of a fertile hill into a promising vineyard. Matthew 21:33–34 clearly alludes to Isa. 5:1–2, although the steps are not in the same order. Matthew omits mention of digging and removing stones but adds building a wall. Yet there is a crucial difference between Isa. 5:1–7 and Matt. 21:33–46: the tenant farmers, the crucial antagonists in Jesus's parable, are not even mentioned in Isaiah. The problem in Isaiah is the lack of good fruit, but the problem in Matthew is the recalcitrant tenants who will not give the fruit to the owner. The resolution of the problem in Isaiah is the destruction of the vineyard (but see Isa. 27:2–6) whereas in Matthew the problem of the recalcitrant tenants is solved by replacing them with new tenants who will give fruit to the owner.

Matthew's use of Isa. 5 is not unlike its interpretation in the Aramaic Targum.[3]

ii. The First and Second Attempts to Obtain Fruit (21:34–36)

21:34–36 When harvesttime draws near, the vineyard owner expects his share of the fruit (cf. 3:12; 7:16; 13:23, 39), and so he sends three slaves to acquire it. But the tenants beat, kill, and stone them (21:34–35). A second group of slaves is sent to the vineyard, but they are mistreated in the same way (21:36).

iii. The Third Attempt to Obtain Fruit (21:37–39)

21:37–39 The third time, the owner sends his son (10:40; 15:24), whom he unwisely thinks the recalcitrant tenants will respect. But the tenants also kill the

---

3. Targum Isa. 5:1 anticipates Isa. 5:7 MT by likening Israel to a vineyard. The targum speaks of the vineyard as a "heritage" or "inheritance" that coheres with the tenants' desire to acquire the son's inheritance by killing him. The targum interprets the watchtower and wine vat of Isa. 5:2 as the temple sanctuary and altar. The good and bad grapes of Isa. 5:2 MT are interpreted by the targum as good and bad deeds, which is in keeping with the emphasis on fruit found in Matt. 21. See Chilton 1984: 111–14; C. A. Evans 1995: 397–401. Other texts that interpret Isa. 5:1–2 as speaking of the temple include t. Me'ilah 1.16; t. Sukkah 3.15; 1 En. 89.56, 66–67, 73; 4Q500 2–7; Barn. 16.1–5.

son, thinking that they will acquire the vineyard if they remove the heir. The maltreatment of the slaves and son sent by the landowner is meant to portray Israel's ongoing rejection of its prophets.[4] The detail of the son's being thrown out of the vineyard before being killed may implicitly refer to Jesus's being crucified outside Jerusalem's walls.[5] This parable anticipates Jesus's accusation in 23:29–39 that his rejection by Israel's leaders is the culmination of their habitual rejection of God's prophets. At this point in the story, one is impressed not only by the unprovoked violence of the tenants but also by the extreme patience, if not naïveté, of the owner. But the story is not over. How will the owner respond to the atrocity of his son's murder?

iv. The Owner's Retribution (21:40–41)

Jesus draws his listeners into the story by asking them how it will end. **21:40–41** They realize that the owner's remarkable patience has reached its end, and so they say that the owner will bring the tenants to an end befitting their wicked deeds and replace them with new tenants who will give the owner his share of the produce. Here the religious leaders again condemn themselves with their own words (21:31). Jesus in 21:43 provides his own interpretation of the tenants' replacement. The reference to the owner's getting his share of the crop after each harvest may allude to Ps. 1:3 (cf. Matt. 21:34, 43).

v. The Parable Applied (21:42–44)

Jesus's incredulous question in 21:42 reproves the Jewish leaders (cf. **21:42–43** 12:3; 19:4; 21:16). They are again portrayed as ignorant of the Scriptures, specifically Ps. 118:22. Psalm 118:25–26 has already been cited in Matt. 21:9, 15 (cf. Acts 4:11; 1 Pet. 2:7; cf. Isa. 8:14; 28:16). In light of the Targum on Psalms, there may be a play on the words "son" and "stone."[6] The son's murder (Matt. 21:37–39) answers to the stone's rejection (21:42). Also, the Targum on Isaiah interprets the "fertile hill" of Isa. 5:1 as the Temple Mount (C. A. Evans 1995: 397–405; Snodgrass 1983: 95–118). The architectural function of the stone that becomes the cornerstone (literally, "the head of the corner") may be as a typical

---

4. See esp. 5:12; 22:6; 23:29–37; cf. 1 Kings 18:4; 2 Chron. 24:19–21; 30:10; 36:16; Neh. 9:26–30; Jer. 7:25–26; 20:1–2; 25:4; 26:21–23; Amos 7:10–17; Dan. 9:6, 10; Acts 7:52; 1 Thess. 2:15; Heb. 11:32–39; James 5:10; Rev. 11:3.

5. See John 19:17, 20; Acts 7:58; Heb. 13:12; cf. Lev. 24:14, 23; Num. 15:36; Deut. 17:5; 1 Kings 21:10, 13.

6. Targum Ps. 118:22 evidently uses the paronomasia of בֵּן ("son") for אֶבֶן ("stone," Ps. 118:22 MT) when it says that a "boy" [תַּלְיָא] whom the builders abandoned was among the sons of Jesse and is worthy to be appointed king and ruler. This understanding of Ps. 118:22 may account for the association of the psalm text about the rejected stone with the parabolic detail of the murdered son. See C. A. Evans 1995: 402–5; Snodgrass 1983: 95–106, 113–18.

foundational cornerstone, as the keystone of an arch, or as the capstone at the top of a corner.

Another crucial matter concerns Jesus's statement in Matt. 21:43 about the taking away and giving of the kingdom (cf. 1 Sam. 15:28; LXX: Dan. 2:44; 7:27). A common view is that the kingdom is taken away from the Jewish people as a whole and and given to the the predominantly gentile church (Blomberg 1992a: 325; Hendriksen 1973: 786). But a preferable view is that the kingdom is to be taken away from the disobedient religious leaders and given to the twelve disciples who will lead Jesus's church (Matt. 16:18–19; 19:28; Nolland 2005: 879; Overman 1996: 302–4). In several important biblical passages, the word "nation" refers to Israel, not the Gentiles.[7] Matthew does not view the church as a gentile entity that supersedes Israel but as the eschatological Jewish remnant that spreads the kingdom message to all the nations, including Israel. See further below.

21:44 The stone metaphor is continued in 21:44, which echoes Isa. 8:14–15 and Dan. 2:34–35, 44–45. There is doubt over the authenticity of this verse, which may be interpolated from Luke 20:18 (see the additional note). In any event, those who reject the cornerstone are pictured as stumbling over it and falling, and at the same time their judgment will be like the stone falling on them. The temple's destruction in 70 CE was part of the judgment Jesus speaks of here (cf. Matt. 24:2; Luke 21:20).

vi. The Parable Understood (21:45–46)

21:45–46 It is clear that the tenant farmers represent Israel's leaders, not Israel as a whole: the leaders themselves recognize this. The high priests and Pharisees are joined together elsewhere only in 27:62. Tragically, they understand what Jesus is saying but refuse to agree with it. Told that they will be crushed by God's cornerstone if they reject it, undaunted they set out to crush the cornerstone. Their fear of the crowd of festival pilgrims who regard Jesus as a prophet slows their murder plot (cf. 12:14; 21:11, 26; 26:3–5). Their open arrest of Jesus could cause the volatile crowd of pilgrims to riot and bring Roman soldiers down on the temple. But soon Judas will betray Jesus to them. Then they will co-opt the Romans and persuade the fickle crowd to see things their way (26:3–5, 14–16, 21–25, 46–56; 27:2, 20–26).[8]

---

7. See, e.g., Gen. 12:2; Exod. 19:6, cited in 1 Pet. 2:9; 2 Sam. 7:23; Ps. 33:12; Isa. 1:4; 26:2; Jer. 31:36; Ezek. 37:22.

8. Among the voluminous literature on 21:33–46, see esp. Chilton 1984: 111–16; Derrett 1974; Dormandy 1989; C. A. Evans 1989b; 1995: 381–406; 1996; Hengel 1968; Hester 1992; Horne 1998; Hubaut 1976; Huber 1996; Hultgren 2000: 359–82; Kingsbury 1986b; Milavec 1989; Milavec in Thoma and Wyschogrod 1989: 81–117; Moor 1998; Newell and Newell 1972: 226–37; J. C. O'Neill in Shillington 1997: 165–76; J. A. Robinson 1975; Snodgrass 1983, 1998; D. Stern in Thoma and Wyschogrod 1989: 42–80; Trilling 1964: 55–65; Trimaille in Delorme 1989: 247–58; D. Turner 2002; B. Young 1989: 282–316.

The Kingdom Taken and Given

Christian exegesis has often viewed 21:43 as predicting the demise of Israel as the people of God and its replacement by the predominantly gentile church (e.g., Schnackenburg 2002: 212). But what group is represented by the recalcitrant tenants, from whom authority over the vineyard is to be taken? In the parable the vineyard represents Israel and the tenants stand for the leaders of Israel. This is clear in the leaders' response to the parable and its application; they recognize Jesus has been talking about them (21:45). They are the recalcitrant tenants (21:35–39), the builders who reject the stone (21:42), only to be broken to pieces and ground into powder by it (21:44). This view is in keeping with prophetic denunciations in the Hebrew Bible that blame the leaders for causing the people to sin[9] and that stress the sins of Jerusalem,[10] particularly those committed in connection with the temple.[11] It is not that the people as a whole are not accountable for their sins, but the leaders' conduct is even more blameworthy. Not only do they not enter the kingdom themselves, but they also prevent other people from entering it (23:13). The identification of the recalcitrant tenants with the current religious leaders is clear.[12]

But if 21:43 speaks of kingdom authority being taken away from the religious leaders, to whom does the text say kingdom authority will be given? Many scholars take 21:43 as teaching that a new "nation," the church, has replaced the nation of Israel in God's plan.[13] But this view is dubious if the kingdom is taken from the leaders, not from Israel. The parabolic antecedent of the pronoun "you" in 21:43 is the recalcitrant tenants, not the fruitful vineyard. According to 21:45, the Jewish leaders realize that Jesus is talking about them, not Israel as a whole. It is thus a mistake to view 21:43 as indicating the replacement of Israel by the gentile church (Hauerwas 2006: 187).

9. E.g., Isa. 1:23–26; Jer. 23; Lam. 4:13; Ezek. 34; Mic. 3:1–5; Zeph. 3:3–4. The prophets also confronted the people's complicity in their leaders' sins, as in, e.g., Isa. 1:10; Jer. 5:4–5, 30–31; Hos. 4:4–6.
10. E.g., Isa. 1:21; Jer. 4:14; 8:5; Lam. 1–5; Ezek. 9:8–9; 16; 22; Dan. 9:7, 12, 16, 20, 24; Mic. 3:9–10; Zeph. 1:4, 12; 3:1.
11. E.g., Jer. 7:1–11; Ezek. 8; 23:38–39; 44:6–14; Zeph. 1:4; 3:4; Mal. 1:6–2:9.
12. Carson 1984: 454; W. Davies and Allison 1997: 189–90; Harrington 1991: 303–5; Keener 1999: 510–11, 515–16; Overman 1990b: 148–49; 1996: 302–4; Saldarini 1994: 59–63; Sim 1998b: 148–49. Curiously, some scholars who acknowledge that the tenants represent the current religious leaders still affirm that Matthew views the gentile church as taking the place of Israel (e.g., Beare 1981: 430–31; Boring 1995: 415; Kingsbury 1986b: 645–46; Morris 1992: 544). On Matthew and the leaders, see Carter 1996: 229–41; Kingsbury 1987a; Overman 1990b: 19–23, 141–47; Powell 1988; Saldarini 1994: 44–67; D. Turner 2002: 53–56.
13. According to W. Davies and Allison (1997: 189), this is "the dominant interpretation in Christian history." See, e.g., Bruner 1990: 770; France 1985: 310; 1989: 223–32; Hagner 1995a: 623; Hare 1967: 153; 1993: 248–49; Menninger 1994: 33–34, 152–53; Stanton 1992b; Trilling 1964: 55–65.

Nor does Matthew's use of the word "nation" (ἔθνος, *ethnos*, 21:43) clearly support this view (A.-J. Levine 1988: 187–89, 207–11; Saldarini 1994: 58–63, 243–47). If the Gentiles were in view here, one would expect the plural, "nations" (4:15; 6:32; 10:5, 18; 12:18, 21; 20:19, 25; 24:9, 14; 25:32; 28:19). The singular ἔθνος would remind Christian Jews of their nation's lofty role in redemptive history. Although generally the Hebrew Bible uses גּוֹי (*gôy*, nation) or גּוֹיִם (*gôyim*, nations) for Gentiles and עַם (*'am*) for the Jews, many texts use גּוֹי for the nation of Israel, and the LXX usually translates גּוֹי in these texts by the word ἔθνος.[14] In Gen. 12:2 God promises to make Abraham into a great nation;[15] in Exod. 19:6 Israel's vocation as a holy nation is stressed at the giving of the Torah (cf. 1 Pet. 2:9). In 2 Sam. 7:23 (cf. 1 Chron. 17:21) David thanks God for the promise of his dynasty by reflecting on Israel as a unique nation. In Ps. 33:12 the psalmist extols the blessedness of the nation whose God is the Lord. Isaiah 1:4 laments the sinful nation. Isaiah 26:2 envisions a day in which the gates of Jerusalem will be thrown open for a righteous nation. Jeremiah 31:36 affirms that Israel will cease to be a nation only if God's decrees for the sun, moon, and stars cease. Ezekiel 37:22 envisions Israel as one nation.[16] The cumulative weight of some fifty such texts indicates that one should not assume the word ἔθνος refers to Gentiles as opposed to Jews. Matthew's Christian Jewish community would more likely understand ἔθνος as an echo of many biblical texts that call on Israel to fulfill its unique covenantal role (Keener 1999: 515–16). Those who keep covenant (produce fruit) will replace the tenants who refused to do so. Matthew's community, with Jesus as its ultimate Torah teacher (Matt. 5:17–48), will bear such fruit and will replace the current Jerusalem religious establishment as the leaders of Israel. In this view, "the parable offers a sharp prophetic criticism of the temple establishment and a warning that its days of administration were nearing an end" (C. A. Evans 1995: 406).

Israel and the Church

Matthew 21:33–46 is part of Matthew's indictment of the Jerusalem religious establishment. The "nation" of 21:43 is the Matthean community as an eschatological messianic remnant whose leaders will replace the current Jerusalem religious establishment and lead Israel in bearing the fruit of righteousness to God. Thus this parable is about ethics, not ethnicity, and a Jewish remnant, not a gentile replacement. This remnant is

14. Occasionally the LXX translates עַם with ἔθνος, as in Deut. 7:7; Zeph. 2:9, and גּוֹי with λαός, as in Josh. 3:17; 4:1; Isa. 9:2; Jer. 9:8 (9:9 Eng.).

15. Echoes of this "great nation" text include Gen. 46:3; Exod. 32:10; Num. 14:12; Deut. 4:6–8; 26:5.

16. Additional texts include Exod. 33:13; Deut. 4:34; 9:14; 32:28; Josh. 5:6, 8; 10:13; Judg. 2:20; Pss. 43:1; 106:5; 147:20; Prov. 14:34; Isa. 10:6; 26:15; 58:2; 60:22; 65:1; 66:8; Jer. 5:9, 29; 7:28; 31:36; 33:24; Mic. 4:7; Zeph. 2:1; Hag. 2:14; Mal. 3:9.

pictured as a repentant son (21:29), as responsible tenants (21:41), and as responsive guests (22:9–10). None of these parabolic details should be interpreted in ethnic terms (A.-J. Levine 1988: 193–239). To read this passage as Israel's rejection and replacement by the gentile church is to read into it a later theology of supersession (Hultgren 2000: 372–74; Saldarini in Aune 2001: 170–73). This view has contributed, unwittingly in some cases, to anti-Semitism. Supersessionism may not lead inexorably to the practice of anti-Semitism, but there are all too many cases when it did so in church history. An exegesis supporting a theology that is often complicit in the practice of anti-Semitism must be reconsidered (Farmer 1999: 30–31, 40, 48).

Matthew 21:33–46 should, rather, be interpreted as an intramural transfer of leadership from the fruitless Jerusalem religious establishment to the fruitful Matthean Christian Jewish community, led by the apostles of Jesus.[17] This community should be viewed as the eschatological remnant of Israel[18] that continues its mission to Israel while expanding its horizons to all the nations. This Jewish remnant becomes the nucleus of the nascent church. Although the church expands primarily by winning Gentiles to faith in Jesus, its roots in the promises of God to the seed of Abraham must not be forgotten (cf. John 4:22; 10:16; Acts 24:14; 28:20; Rom. 11:16–24; 15:7–13; Eph. 2:11–22; Rev. 21:12).

Summary and Transition

After earlier predictions of his death in Jerusalem (16:21; 17:22–23; 20:18) and after Matthew has set the scene geographically (19:1; 20:17, 29), the "triumphal entry" occurs (21:1–11). Matthew next describes Jesus's temple activities, including casting out the money changers, healing the blind and the lame, and confronting the chief priests and scribes (21:12–17). The next day the ominous cursing of the fig tree becomes an object lesson for prayer (21:18–22). Reentering the temple, Jesus answers the chief priests' and elders' question regarding his authority (21:23–44) by (1) posing a question to the religious leaders that they refuse to answer (21:24–27), (2) telling a brief story about a man who had two sons (21:28–32), and (3) telling another story about a landowner and his vineyard (21:33–44). The chapter concludes by noting that the Pharisees understand that Jesus's stories condemn them and by observing that they want to seize him although they fear the crowds (21:45–46). Matthew 22 continues in the same vein, with

---

17. Matthew presents the future of the community as a time of sacrificial service, worldwide mission, severe persecution, eventual reward, and ultimate rule. See, e.g., 10:1–8; 13:43; 16:15–19; 18:15–20; 19:28; 20:20–28; 23:9–12, 34; 24:14; 26:29, 32; 28:7, 16–20.

18. See M. Elliott 2000: 639–64 for a discussion of the implications of remnant theology for the NT. Elliott's discussion of "destruction-preservation soteriology" (2000: 621–34) is also helpful.

Jesus telling additional parables to the Pharisees, who escalate their plot against him (22:1, 15). The "judgmental tone" of Matt. 21–22, seen especially in the parables, sets the scene for the prophetic oracles of woe found in Matt. 23 (Garland 1979: 82–84).

Additional Notes

21:39. UBS⁴ prefers the well-supported reading ἐξέβαλον ἔξω τοῦ ἀμπελῶνος καὶ ἀπέκτειναν (supported by ℵ [ἔβαλον], B, C, L, W, Z, Δ, 0102, 0233, f^1, f^{13}, *Byz, Lect*; cf. Luke 20:15; see also John 19:17, 20; Heb. 13:12; Metzger 1994: 47). Western MSS (D, Θ, several Old Latin) have ἀπέκτειναν καὶ ἐξέβαλον ἔξω τοῦ ἀμπελῶνος, probably because of assimilation to Mark 12:8.

21:44. UBS⁴ doubts the authenticity of this verse (omitted in D, 33, several Old Latin MSS) and places it in brackets despite its considerable ancient support (ℵ, B, C, L, W, Z, Δ, Θ, 0102, 0233, f^1, f^{13}, 28, 157, *Byz, Lect*; cf. Luke 20:18).

c. Parable of the Wedding Feast (22:1–14)

Matthew 22:1–14 consists of a narrative introduction (22:1), the parable proper (22:2–13), and a generalizing conclusion (22:14). The two parts of the parable, both ending in judgment (22:7, 13), chronicle five cycles of activity initiated by a king. In the first part, there are two cycles of invitation and rejection (22:2–3, 4–6), followed by punishment (22:7). In the second part, yet another invitation is accepted (22:8–10), but an improperly attired man is punished (22:11–13). Finally a conclusion supplies the lesson conveyed by the parable (22:14).

This parable is the third in a set of three parables that share several themes. Most prominently, these parables portray the failure of the religious leaders to respond to God's call through the second son (21:30), the wicked tenants (21:35–39), and those originally invited to the wedding feast (22:3–7). But the man without wedding clothes in this parable warns those within Matthew's community that they must focus on their own fidelity, not on the errors of the outsiders, the religious leaders (22:10–13; W. Davies and Allison 1997: 188–89, 207–8). There is a sort of historical progression in the three parables (Boring 1995: 417; Gundry 1994: 432) in that the first focuses on John (21:32), the second on Jesus (21:37, 42), and the third on the church (22:10–14). (On this parabolic trilogy, see Olmstead 2003.)

The parable of the great banquet in Luke 14:15–24 (cf. Gos. Thom. 64) is very similar to this parable (Hultgren 2000: 333–36). Those who affirm Q and Markan priority assign this parable either to Matthew's unique source, M (W. Davies and Allison 1997: 194), or to the common source, Q (Hagner 1995a: 627), depending on their view of the similarities (ostensibly traceable to Q) and differences (due to Matthew's sole dependence on Q). In any event, the respective settings of the two parables differ greatly, with Luke's parable occurring in a Pharisee's house on the way to Jerusalem and with Matthew's occurring later in Jerusalem. The historicity of such details should be accepted; the parables were originally uttered on two different occasions during the life of Jesus.

The outline for this unit is as follows:

    i. The first cycle of invitation and rejection (22:1–3)
   ii. The second cycle of invitation and rejection (22:4–6)
  iii. The king's response: Punishment of the rejecters (22:7)
   iv. The third cycle: Invitation and acceptance (22:8–10)

v. The king's response: Punishment of an improperly dressed man (22:11–13)
vi. The lesson of the parable (22:14)

Exegesis and Exposition

[1]And Jesus answered them again in parables, saying, [2]"The kingdom of heaven may be compared to a king who prepared a wedding feast for his son. [3]He sent out his slaves to call those who had been invited to the wedding feast, but they were not willing to come. [4]Again he sent out other slaves, saying, 'Tell those who have been invited, "Look, I have prepared my dinner; my oxen and my fattened cattle are butchered and everything is ready; come to the wedding feast."' [5]But they paid no attention and went their way, one to his own farm, another to his business. [6]And the rest seized his slaves and mistreated them and killed them. [7]Then the king was enraged, and he sent his troops and destroyed those murderers and burned their city.

[8]"Then he said to his slaves, 'The wedding feast is ready, but those who were called were not worthy. [9]Go therefore to the main streets, and call whomever you find to the wedding feast.' [10]So those slaves went out into the streets and gathered together everyone they found, both evil and good; and the ⌜wedding hall⌝ was filled with guests.

[11]"But when the king came in to see the guests, he noticed a man there who was not wearing a wedding robe, [12]so he said to him, 'Friend, how did you get in here without a wedding robe?' And he was speechless. [13]Then the king said to the attendants, 'Tie him up hand and foot, and throw him into the darkness outside, where there will be weeping and gnashing of teeth.' [14]For many are called, but few are chosen."

i. The First Cycle of Invitation and Rejection (22:1–3)

22:1–3 Jesus utters the third in a set of three parables that portray an authority figure's problems with his subordinates (cf. 21:28, 33). This parable begins exactly like that of the unforgiving slave (18:23) and many rabbinic parables (Exod. Rab. on Exod. 12:19). The standard comparison formula "The kingdom of heaven may be compared to" (22:2; cf., e.g., 13:24, 31, 33, 44, 45, 52; 18:23) introduces this parable. The previous two parables speak of a vineyard owner who deals respectively with his sons and tenant farmers. Here a king sends his slaves to summon those he has already invited to his son's wedding feast (cf. 25:1–10), but amazingly they are not willing to come (cf. 23:37). In this context, there can be little doubt that this portrays the religious leaders, who do not believe God's prophets and who ultimately reject God's Son, Jesus, and his kingdom, which is spoken of elsewhere as a great eschatological feast (8:10–12; 9:15; 15:26–27; 26:26–29; cf. Luke 13:29; Rev. 19:9).

ii. The Second Cycle of Invitation and Rejection (22:4–6)

The king patiently sends out a second group of slaves (cf. 21:36) to reaffirm the invitation. This time the slaves are instructed to point out in detail the nature and readiness of the preparations that have been made. Surely this should entice the invited guests to come, but they pay no heed. Some are merely disloyal—they are too busy with everyday concerns (cf. 8:21; Luke 9:57–62). Others are subversive and revolt against the king by apprehending his slaves, mocking them, and killing them (cf. 2 Sam. 10:4; Josephus, *Ant.* 9.263–66). Perhaps this distinction between indifference and violent hostility is intended to portray the varying responses of Israel to Jesus. This horrible turn of events could not have been anticipated. The slaves' repeated announcement that the feast is prepared refers to the nearness of the kingdom (cf. 3:2; 4:17; 10:7; 12:28). The religious leaders' recalcitrance is habitual; they have regularly rejected and even killed God's messengers (cf. 5:12; 21:35, 39; 23:29–36).

22:4–6

iii. The King's Response: Punishment of the Rejecters (22:7)

The king's patience now gives way to fury (cf. 18:34) as he sends troops to destroy the murderers of his slaves and to put their city to the torch (cf. Luke 21:20; Judg. 1:8; Isa. 5:24–25; 1 Macc. 5:28; 2 Bar. 7.1; 80.3; Josephus, *J.W.* 6.353–55, 363, 406–8). The king's angry treatment of his treacherous subjects represents the judgment of the Jerusalem establishment (cf. Matt. 21:41–45; 24:2, 15). The destruction of Jerusalem and the burning of the temple in 70 CE by the Romans are at least a partial fulfillment of this veiled prophecy (cf. 24:15–16; Luke 21:20; Blomberg 1992a: 328). God's use of the Romans as instruments of judgment is not unlike the previous roles of Assyria, Babylon, and Persia (2 Chron. 36:22; Isa. 10:5–11; 44:28; 45:1; Dan. 1:2; 2:37; Hab. 1:6; 2 Esd. [4 Ezra] 5:21–40).

22:7

iv. The Third Cycle: Invitation and Acceptance (22:8–10)

The king tells his slaves for the third time that the feast is ready and that those previously invited were not worthy (3:8; 10:10–11, 13, 37–38). He sends the slaves out to invite anyone they can find. The "main streets" more likely refers to the places where the streets leave town and go into the surrounding countryside (BDAG 244). The slaves do as they were told, and the banquet hall is filled with guests.[1] The presence of both good and bad people at the feast is similar to other parabolic portrayals of mixed response to the kingdom message (7:15–27; 13:20–23, 25–26, 41–42, 49–50).

22:8–10

1. Boring's suggestion (1995: 418) that συνήγαγον is an obvious pun contrasting Jewish synagogues with Matthew's true church is overstated to say the least.

v. The King's Response: Punishment of an Improperly Dressed Man (22:11–13)

22:11–13   As the king greets the guests, he discovers one who is not wearing proper wedding clothes (see Sim 1990). Addressing him ominously as "friend" (cf. 20:13; 26:50), the king asks how he has come to the feast in inappropriate attire. It may have been the custom in that day for kings to provide suitable clothing for such feasts,[2] but the evidence cited for the custom is weak (Carson 1984: 457; Hagner 1995a: 631). Perhaps the man is wearing dirty clothing. In any event, the man's attire insults the king. He cannot explain his inappropriate attire, and so he is arrested and severely punished (8:11–12; 13:40–42; 24:51; 25:30; 1 En. 10.4–5; Sim 1992).[3]

vi. The Lesson of the Parable (22:14)

22:14   The parable prepares the listeners for the conclusion: "Many are called, but few are chosen." The point of this imagery is, to some extent, similar to that of the parable of the two sons. The established leaders of Israel have rejected Jesus and the kingdom, but some from the dregs of society have repented (9:10–13; 21:31–32). But even among these who overtly respond to the kingdom message, there are both good and bad (22:10; cf. 5:45; 7:21–23; 13:19–23, 38, 48). God calls many, good and bad alike, into his kingdom, but not all of them are truly obedient to the call (7:13–14; cf. 2 Esd. [4 Ezra] 8:1, 3, 55; 9:15; 2 Bar. 44.15; B. Meyer 1990).[4] See 11:27; 24:22, 24, 31 for Matthew's view of divine election.

Interpretation and Theology

According to a common view of this parable, the king (God; 5:35) sends his servants (prophets) to invite his subjects (Israel) to a wedding feast for his son (Jesus; cf. 8:11; 9:15; 25:1; 2 Cor. 11:2; Rev. 19:7, 9; Hos. 2:16; 3:1; Isa. 54:5–8; 62:4–5; Ezek. 16:7–8). The subjects, refusing to come, kill the king's servants. The king sends his armies (Rome) and destroys the city (Jerusalem). Then the guests are secured from the main highways (Gentiles). A wedding guest without a wedding garment (hypocrite) is punished. There is some truth to this view, but it is doubtful that the parable is intended to portray a redemptive-historical transition from Jews to Gentiles (as, e.g., Hagner 1995: 632; Manns 1988). As in the previous parable of the wicked tenants, those who seized, mocked, and killed God's messengers are not Israel as a whole but the leaders of Israel

---

2. Cf. Gen. 45:22; Judg. 14:12; 2 Kings 25:29; Esth. 6:8–9; Zech. 3:3–5; Luke 15:22; Rev. 19:8; Josephus, *J.W.* 2.129, 131; Gundry 1994: 439.

3. On τὸ σκότος τὸ ἐξώτερον, see Gk. Apoc. Ezra 4.38; Ques. Ezra, Recension A, 3. Cf. 2 Pet. 2:17; Jude 13; Wis. 17:20 LXX; Ps. Sol. 14.9.

4. For further study of 22:1–14, see Ballard 1972; Derrett 1970b: 126–55; Hasler 1962; Manns 1988; Martens in Longenecker 2000: 162–66; Swaeles 1960, 1963; Via 1971; Wainwright 1988; Wrembek 1991.

(Overman 1996: 300–302). "The exegete must be careful not to assume that the allegorical destruction of Jerusalem terminates Israel's role in God's story" (W. Davies and Allison 1997: 202; cf. 207n76).

The conclusion of the parable is that "many are called, but few are chosen." This is the point of the whole parable, not just Matt. 22:11–13. The parable stresses the contempt with which the religious leaders have treated both the prophets and Jesus the Messiah. Some have merely been indifferent (22:5), but others are extremely hostile (22:6). The invitation has gone out to many, but only relatively few have responded. Yet this surprising turn of events does not catch God unawares, since God's plan will be accomplished and his Scriptures fulfilled (cf. 11:25–27; 24:22, 24, 31; 26:24, 31, 42, 54, 56). The biblical concept implied by 22:14 is that of the remnant (Boring 1995: 418; Gundry 1994: 441),[5] a concept that appears to be in tension with *m. Sanh.* 10.1, "All Israel has a place in the world to come."

The disastrous end of the improperly attired man adds a dimension not found in the previous two parables. This man has responded to the king's invitation and has assembled in the wedding hall, yet his garment shows he does not truly belong there.[6] His fate reminds the reader of the false prophets in 7:15–23 and of the lawless ones in 13:41–42. The unique contribution of this parable is Jesus's warning that his disciples' troubles will not come merely from outsiders. They cannot become complacent and forget the necessity of obedience to all that Jesus has commanded. Soon Jesus's betrayal will make this point crystal clear: Judas Iscariot was called but not chosen. In the future, outsiders will bring many troubles to the disciples (24:9–11), but defectors from within the church will also be problematic, and only those who endure to the end will be saved (24:12–13; Garland 1993: 221–23; Gundry 2000; Schnackenburg 2002: 215). The fate of the improperly attired man vividly portrays the horrific end of anyone who finally rejects Jesus's kingdom. Matthew 22:11–13 parabolically portrays final judgment.

Additional Note

22:10. UBS[4] reads ὁ γάμος, supported by B[1], D, W, Δ, Θ, 085, 0233, *f* [1], *f* [13], Byz, Lect. Perhaps the unusual usage of this word here (BDAG 188–89; Metzger 1994: 47) led to the reading ὁ νυμφών, supported by ℵ, B*, L, 0102, 892. The clearly inappropriate ὁ ἄγαμος, supported by C, is probably due to an error of the ear during transcription.

5. E.g., Isa. 1:9; 10:20–22; Rom. 9:6, 29–31; 11:1–5; cf. Wis. 3:9; 4:15; 1 En. 5.1–9; Apoc. Abr. 29; M. Elliott 2000.

6. The symbolism of the garment is not clear, although most scholars tend to think of it in terms of personal righteousness. Cf. Isa. 61:10; 64:6; Rev. 3:4–5, 18; 19:8; 22:14; 1 En. 62.15–16; *m. Ta'an.* 4.8; Gundry 1994: 439; Hultgren 2000: 347–48. See W. Davies and Allison (1997: 203–6), who view it as the glorious resurrection body or garment, in contrast to the utter darkness experienced by the improperly attired man in Matt. 22:13.

d. The Pharisees' Question: Paying Taxes to Caesar (22:15–22)

After narrating Jesus's three parables that address the question about the source of his authority (21:23–22:14), Matthew now presents three further questions from the religious leaders (22:15–22, 23–33, 34–40), who attempt to challenge Jesus's wisdom and insight into the Torah. But Jesus's teaching surpasses that of the Pharisees (22:15, 34), Sadducees (22:23), and Herodians (22:16). All questions come to an end when the Pharisees are unable to answer Jesus's questions about the Messiah's identity in light of Ps. 110:1 (Matt. 22:41–46). He answers all their questions, but they cannot answer one of his.

The first question (cf. Mark 12:13–17; Luke 20:20–26; Gos. Thom. 100) comes from some Pharisees who, with some Herodians, plan to entrap Jesus (Matt. 22:15) on the matter of paying taxes to the emperor. The Herodians were loyalists and would evidently support the propriety of taxation. The passage is framed by the plot and approach of Jesus's interlocutors at its beginning (22:15–16) and by their astonished departure at its end (22:22). The interview itself contains three interchanges, concluded by Jesus's directive on taxes (22:21b). The leaders initiate the first interchange (22:17–18), but then Jesus takes charge and initiates the second (22:19) and third (22:20–21a) interchanges. The pericope begins with the implication of the intellectual prowess of the Pharisees (22:15–17), but it ends with their befuddlement (22:18–22).

The unit outline is as follows:

   i. The attempt to trap Jesus (22:15–17)
   ii. Jesus's response to the trap (22:18–22)

Exegesis and Exposition

[15]Then the Pharisees went and planned together how they might trap him in what he said. [16]So they sent their disciples to him, along with the Herodians, saying, "Teacher, we know that you are honest and teach the way of God in truth, and you do not defer to anyone; for you are partial to no one. [17]Tell us, then, what do you think? Is it lawful to pay taxes to Caesar, or not?"

[18]But Jesus perceived their malice and said, "Why are you testing me, you hypocrites? [19]Show me the coin used for the tax." And they brought him a denarius.

²⁰So he asked them, "Whose likeness is this, and whose inscription?" ²¹They said to him, "Caesar's." Then he said to them, "Therefore give what is Caesar's to Caesar and what is God's to God." ²²When they heard this, they were amazed, and they left him and went away.

i. The Attempt to Trap Jesus (22:15–17)

The Pharisees (cf. 21:45) regroup and confer on how to trap Jesus in his speech.[1] Their desire to test and destroy Jesus is not a new development (cf. 12:14; 16:1; 19:3; 22:35). It would probably be unusual for the Herodians (cf. Mark 3:6) to join in common cause with the Pharisees, who did not support either the pro-Roman Herodian dynasty or a tax that was not based on the Torah. Little is known about the Herodians, who were evidently a small but well-positioned group that profited from the status quo. (On the possibility that the Herodians were Essenes, see Braun 1989.)   **22:15–16a**

This mixed group speaks flattering words to Jesus in order to set their trap (22:16). If they really believed that Jesus teaches truth without partiality, they would not attempt to flatter him. Their question about paying taxes to the Roman emperor is evidently about the "head tax" (*tributum capitis*), which was based on a census of Israel's population by the Romans (Luke 2:1–5; Josephus, *J.W.* 1.154; 2.118, 403–5, 433; Tacitus, *Ann.* 2.42; Schürer 1973: 1.399–427). This is different from the biblically mandated tax to support the temple, which Jesus did pay (17:24–27). The Jewish leaders evidently wish to catch Jesus in a dilemma. If he supports the tax, he will alienate the Pharisees, and if he rejects the tax, he will alienate the Herodians and be treasonous to Rome (cf. John 19:12; Gundry 1994: 442). The question could be translated, "Is it right . . . ?" (ἔξεστιν, *exestin*; BDAG 348), but more likely it should be rendered, "Is it lawful . . . ?" since Jesus is being asked to provide halakah ostensibly based on Torah (cf. Matt. 12:2, 4, 10; 14:4; 19:3; 27:6).   **22:16b–17**

ii. Jesus's Response to the Trap (22:18–22)

"Jesus recognizes the daggers in the men's smiles" (W. Davies and Allison 1997: 215). He sees the evil motive behind the flattery and asks his questioners why they are putting him to the test. Satan is the first to   **22:18**

---

1. This is the only time in Matthew where the disciples of the Pharisees are mentioned (cf. Mark 2:18). With Jesus's activities centering on the temple, it is not surprising that the chief priests are featured as opposing him (Matt. 16:21; 20:18; 21:15, 23, 45; 26:3, 14, 47, 51, 57–65; 27:1–7, 12, 20, 41, 62; 28:11). The Sadducees are not as prominent (16:1, 6, 11–12; 22:23, 34; cf. Acts 4:1–2; 5:17–18; 23:6–10). Jesus's strongest invective is directed toward the Pharisees (esp. Matt. 5:20; 9:11, 34; 12:2, 14, 24, 38; 15:1, 12; 16:1, 6, 11–12; 19:3; 21:45; 22:15, 34, 41; 23:2, 13, 15, 23, 25, 26, 27, 29; 27:62). Presumably, the elders (πρεσβύτεροι), who are often associated with the high priests (15:2; 16:21; 21:23; 26:3, 47, 57; 27:1, 3, 12, 20, 41; 28:12), would have represented both Sadducees and Pharisees.

test Jesus (4:1–11; cf. 1 Cor. 7:5; 1 Thess. 3:5; Heb. 4:15; Rev. 2:10), and others follow (Matt. 16:1; 19:3; 22:18, 35). Their testing of Jesus bears similarities to incidents in the Hebrew Scriptures.[2] Jesus's opponents are often described as hypocrites in Matthew (cf. 6:2, 5, 16; 7:5; 15:7; 23:13, 15, 23, 25, 27, 29; 24:51). His severe language unmasks their insincerity and prepares the reader for the extended diatribe in Matt. 23.

22:19–22 Jesus tells his interrogators to produce the coin used for the tax, a denarius (18:28; 20:2, 9–10, 13). With this visual aid, he answers their question with one of his own, asking them whose image and inscription is on the coin.[3] When they reply that it is Caesar's, he tells them to give Caesar what belongs to him and to give God what belongs to God. This answer assumes God's control over the temporal powers (Dan. 1:1–2; 2:21, 37–38), and on the surface it seems to support the Herodians. The image of the emperor on the coin would indicate that it is appropriate to pay it back to him. A Jew who was obedient to the second commandment (Exod. 20:4; Deut. 5:8; Josephus, *Ag. Ap.* 2.76–77), however, might not be comfortable with the coin anyway. The inscription on the denarius referred to Tiberius Caesar as divine and as high priest, and this would also tend to be offensive to Jews. Jesus's distinction between duty to state and duty to God subtly indicates that Tiberius is neither divine nor high priest. Giving God what is God's may be intended to recall the fruit not given to the landowner in Matt. 21:33–46. Jesus's reply stuns his interrogators (cf. 8:27; 9:33; 15:31; 21:20), who leave without a word. The would-be trappers have been trapped.

Jesus's response confounds both the Herodians and the Pharisees. Since Jesus befriended tax collectors, his interrogators might have expected him to answer their question affirmatively. Such an answer would have alienated the Pharisees and others who are even more nationalistic.[4] Since Jesus has recently accepted messianic praise (21:1–11), a simple negative answer might have been expected. But this would have left Jesus open to the charge of sedition (W. Davies and Allison 1997: 212). Perhaps the Herodians expected a positive answer and the Phari-

2. Cf. Exod. 17:2, 7; Num. 14:22; Deut. 6:16 (cited in Matt. 4:7); Pss. 78:18, 41, 56; 95:9 (cited in Heb. 3:9); 106:14; cf. also Acts 5:9; 15:10; 1 Cor. 10:9.

3. It is likely that the coin was the silver imperial denarius, found in excavations of this period in Judea. On one side, the head of Tiberius appeared with the Latin inscription TI CAESAR DIVI AUG F AVGVSTVS, "Augustus Tiberius Caesar, son of the divine Augustus." The other side of the coin pictured a seated woman (perhaps the goddess Roma or empress Livia, symbolizing the pax Romana) with the inscription PONTIF MAXIM, identifying Tiberius as the high priest of Roman religion. See Ferguson 1993: 86–87; Hart in Bammel and Moule 1984: 241–48.

4. It is unclear whether the "Zealots" were a recognized sect with anti-Roman views (cf. Luke 6:15; Acts 1:13; 21:20, 38; Rhoads, *ABD* 6:1043–54). According to Josephus, Judas the Galilean and his descendants who adhered to the "fourth philosophy" opposed Roman census taking and taxation (Josephus, *J.W.* 2.118, 433; 7.253–57; *Ant.* 18.4–10, 23–25, 102). Later, the Talmud enjoined Jews to pay taxes (*b. Pesaḥ.* 112b; *b. B. Qam.* 113a).

sees a negative answer, but both are astounded by what they hear. The anti-Herod Pharisees are told to pay taxes to the Roman government, evidently because the providence of God has placed the Romans over the Jews (cf. Rom. 13:1–7; 1 Pet. 2:13–17; Abel 1969). The Herodians are reminded that their allegiance to God supersedes allegiance to the emperor. Both should recognize that the inscription on the emperor's coin is wrong—he is neither God nor high priest—and his blasphemous coin does not belong in God's temple (W. Davies and Allison 1997: 215). Jesus does not support the Pharisees by opposing Caesar's tax, but neither does he support the Herodians by affirming total loyalty to Rome. Ironically, Jesus has truly taught the way of God despite the insincere flattery of his questioners (Matt. 22:16).[5]

W. Davies and Allison (1997: 218) correctly say that there is "no precise theory of governmental authority" in the aphorism of 22:21. Yet this passage is one of many biblical texts teaching that God's providence places governments in authority and that believers ought to obey government as long as such obedience is not disobedient to God.[6]

---

5. For further study of Matt. 22:15–22, see F. F. Bruce in Bammel and Moule 1984: 249–63; Daube 1973: 158–63; Derrett 1970b: 313–38; Finney 1993; Giblin 1971; Hart in Bammel and Moule 1984: 241–48; Kennard 1950; Klemm 1982; Loewe 1940; Oster 1985; Owen-Ball 1993; Stenger 1988.

6. Cf. Prov. 8:15; Jer. 27:5–11; Dan. 1:2; 2:21, 37–38; John 19:11; Rom. 13:1–7; 1 Tim. 2:1–2; 1 Pet. 2:13–17; Josephus, *J.W.* 2.409–10; *b. 'Abodah Zarah* 18a. On the necessity of disobeying government at times, cf. Exod. 1:17; Dan. 3:16–18; 6:6–10; Matt. 10:17–18, 28–33; Acts 4:19–20; 5:29. See Barrett 1972: 1–19; John Chrysostom, *Hom. Matt.* 70.2; Cranfield 1962.

e. The Sadducees' Question: Marriage in the Resurrection (22:23–33)

Within its narrative setting (22:23, 33), this passage contains a question from certain Sadducees (22:24–28), followed by Jesus's answer (22:29–32). The Sadducees cite the Torah on levirate marriage (22:24; cf. Deut. 25:5) and then tell a story (Matt. 22:25–27) to set up their question (22:28). Jesus in reply affirms that the Sadducees have erred (22:29), explains the nature of life in the resurrection (22:30), and then proves the fact of resurrection by citing another Torah text, Exod. 3:6 (Matt. 22:31–32).

The unit may be outlined as follows:

  i. The Sadducees' question (22:23–28)
  ii. Jesus's answer (22:29–33)

Exegesis and Exposition

²³On that day some Sadducees, ⌜who say⌝ there is no resurrection, came to Jesus and questioned him, ²⁴asking, "Teacher, Moses said, 'If a man dies without children, his brother as next of kin shall marry his wife, and raise up descendants for his brother.' ²⁵Now there were seven brothers among us; and the first married, died without children, and left his wife to his brother; ²⁶so also the second, and the third, until the seventh. ²⁷Last of all, the woman died. ²⁸In the resurrection, then, whose wife of the seven will she be? For all of them had married her."

²⁹But Jesus answered them, "You are mistaken, since you do not know the Scriptures or the power of God. ³⁰For in the resurrection they neither marry nor are given in marriage, but are like ⌜angels⌝ in heaven. ³¹But concerning the resurrection of the dead, have you not read what was said to you by God: ³²'I am the God of Abraham, and the God of Isaac, and the God of Jacob'? ⌜He is⌝ the God not of the dead but of the living." ³³And when the crowds heard this, they were astonished at his teaching.

i. The Sadducees' Question (22:23–28)

22:23   Jesus has been telling parables, and now the Sadducees approach him with a sort of riddle-parable of their own (cf. Mark 12:18–27; Luke 20:27–40). The Sadducees, in their denial of an afterlife, disagreed with the Pharisees (Acts 23:8; Josephus, *Ant.* 18.12–17; *J.W.* 2.162–66). This was evidently due to their rejection of the Pharisees' oral tradition and their emphasizing the five books of Moses over the rest of the canon. Like others who are not Jesus's disciples in Matthew, they address Jesus as "teacher" (cf. Matt. 8:19; 9:11; 12:38; 17:24; 19:16; 22:16, 36). On the different views on resurrection faith in Second Temple Judaism, see E. Puech in Charlesworth 2006: 639–59.

The Sadducees present a hypothetical case based upon Deut. 25:5–10, the law of levirate marriage, in which a brother is responsible for having a child with his childless deceased brother's widow so that the deceased brother may have an heir (cf. Gen. 38:6–30; Ruth 3–4; Matt. 1:3, 5; Josephus, *Ant.* 4.254–56; *m. Yebam.*; Belkin 1970; Burrows 1940; Manor 1982). The biblical citation gives the gist of Deut. 25:5–6 and probably comes from memory instead of being the citation of a specific text-type.[1] The Sadducees are not sincerely inquiring about religious truth but are seeking to trap Jesus and discredit his teaching.

22:24

The caricaturized circumstances of the Sadducees' story show that it is meant to ridicule the idea of life after death, an issue on which Jesus agrees with the Pharisees (cf. Dan. 12:2; Job 19:25–27; Isa. 26:19; 2 Macc. 7:9–11; Jub. 23.11–31; Nickelsburg 1972). Their unlikely scenario posits a woman who is successively married to seven brothers (cf. Tob. 3:7–8; 4 Macc. 8–18), each of whom dies childless. In the end, the woman dies. This raises a question: to which of the brothers will she be married in the resurrection?[2] The Sadducees believe the question is unanswerable and that it will discredit Jesus.

22:25–28

ii. Jesus's Answer (22:29–33)

Again Jesus does not directly answer his interlocutors. Instead he strongly rebukes them, telling them that their ignorance of Scripture and of God's power has led to error (22:29). He first responds to their argument from Deut. 25:5 by affirming that people, like angels, do not live as married couples in the afterlife (Matt. 22:30). The Sadducees evidently err in assuming that the afterlife will be just like the present life, extrapolating

22:29–30

---

1. The LXX form of this verse is an accurate translation of the MT, and Matthew's rendering is abbreviated. Matthew's ἐάν τις ἀποθάνῃ μὴ ἔχων τέκνα summarizes the protasis of Deut. 25:5, which amounts to seventeen words in the LXX. Matthew's τέκνα renders the MT's בֵּן (σπέρμα in the LXX). Matthew omits the apodosis clause forbidding the widow's marriage to a stranger in Deut. 25:5b. Deuteronomy 25:5b–6 in MT and LXX uses several verbs to describe the brother-in-law's duty, but Matthew's ἐπιγαμβρεύσει [a hapax; cf. Gen. 38:8 LXX v.l.; Deut. 25:5 (Aquila); T. Jud. 10.4; וְיַבְּמָהּ (MT)] . . . καὶ ἀναστήσει σπέρμα τῷ ἀδελφῷ αὐτοῦ summarizes Deut. 25:5b–6 by adapting the wording of Gen. 38:8 LXX.

2. For ἀνάστασις as the beginning of the afterlife, see Mark 12:23; Luke 14:14; 20:33, 35; John 5:29; 11:24–25; Acts 17:32; 23:6; 24:15, 21; 1 Cor. 15:12–13, 42; Phil. 3:11; 2 Tim. 2:18; Heb. 6:2; 11:35; Rev. 20:5–6. Cf. παλιγγενεσία in Matt. 19:28.

from the present to the future (Hagner 1995a: 641). They also err in not accounting for the power of God to transform human existence.[3]

22:31–33   Second, Jesus proves the resurrection from the Scriptures, specifically from the Torah, which the Sadducees favor (22:31–32). He cites Exod. 3:6, where God speaks from the burning bush, identifying himself as the God of the patriarchs. Jesus evidently reasons from the present tense "I *am* [εἰμι, *eimi*] the God of Abraham" that God's covenantal loyalty to the patriarchs did not end at their death. Hundreds of years after they died, God is still their God (cf. Luke 16:19–31; *L.A.B.* 4.11; 4 Macc. 7:19; 13:17; 16:25). God's ongoing covenantal relationship with the patriarchs implies their eventual resurrection. God's being the God of the patriarchs during the "intermediate state" between their death and resurrection is tantamount to and guarantees his relationship with them in their final resurrected state (cf. 1 En. 20.8; 22.1–14; 60.8; 62.15; 2 Macc. 7:9, 36; 2 Esd. [4 Ezra] 7; Josephus, *J.W.* 3.374). The Sadducees have no rejoinder to this argument (Matt. 22:34), and the watching crowd is amazed (cf. 7:28; 13:54; 19:25). Jesus's reference to angels in 22:30 may be intended to irritate the Sadducees, who do not believe in angels (Acts 23:8; Blomberg 1992a: 333; but see W. Davies and Allison 1997: 227 for a contrary view).

In both this encounter with the Sadducees and the previous one with the Pharisees, Jesus is asked a difficult question that is intended to discredit him. But both times Jesus discredits and amazes his interlocutors. Here the question concerns not a hot political issue, taxation, but theology and the interpretation of Scripture. The Sadducees evidently believe that Torah-based levirate marriage cannot be squared with the Pharisees' notion of an afterlife. Perhaps they want Jesus to align with them against the Pharisees (Hagner 1995a: 640). Whatever their agenda, Jesus says that their denial of the resurrection is an error caused by ignorance. They think of resurrection and the afterlife as mere reanimation to life as before. They are ignorant that God's transforming power means that people after resurrection are no longer sexually active (cf. 1 Cor. 15:35–39). Sexuality is part of the goodness of creation, but life in the resurrection will transcend this aspect of creation. This renders the levirate law moot. Jesus's argument from Exod. 3:6 shows that the Sadducees are also ignorant of the scriptural inference that God's covenantal loyalty to the patriarchs proves their eventual resurrection, along with that of all God's people.[4]

---

3. In many ancient texts, humans and angels are described similarly or compared to one another. Cf. 1 Sam. 29:9; 2 Sam. 14:17; 19:27; Luke 24:4; Acts 12:15; 1 En. 104.1–6; 2 Bar. 51.5, 10; 1QH 3.21–23; 6.13; 1QS 11.7–8; 1QSb 4.25; 4Q511 frg. 35; Wis. 5:5; W. Davies and Allison 1997: 227–30.

4. Arguments against denials of the afterlife are also found in Wis. 2:1–5; 1 En. 102.6–11; *m. Sanh.* 10.1; *b. Sanh.* 90b.

Modern philosophical naturalists (cf. P. Johnson 1995) also deny God's miraculous power to resurrect and transform humanity. Matthew's narration of Jesus's repeated prediction of the resurrection as well as the narration of the event itself confront this skepticism. Postmodern relativists also have a way of denying the resurrection. They do not necessarily deny the fact of the resurrection but deny its universal significance (Craig in Wilkins and Moreland 1995: 141–76). For Paul, the resurrection of Jesus guarantees that the followers of Jesus will also be raised (Rom. 8:11; 1 Cor. 15:51–58). Belief in the resurrection and the coming judgment is strong motivation for faithful discipleship.[5]

Additional Notes

22:23. The main textual question here is whether an article should appear before λέγοντες. UBS[4] prefers Σαδδουκαῖοι, λέγοντες, supported by א*, B, D, W, 0102, f[1], 33, Lect[pt]. This reading has the Sadducees preface their comments to Jesus with a denial of the resurrection (NRSV). The other reading, Σαδδουκαῖοι, οἱ λέγοντες, is supported by א[2], L, 0107, Byz. It makes the Sadducees' denial of the resurrection a matter of the narrator's explanation rather than their own affirmation (NIV).

22:30. UBS[4] prefers the shorter reading ἄγγελοι (supported by B, D, 0233, 205, 700; cf. Mark 12:25). Another reading is οἱ ἄγγελοι (supported by Θ, f[1]). Other MSS have the longer readings ἄγγελοι θεοῦ (supported by א, L, Σ, f[13], 28, 33, Lect[pt]) or ἄγγελοι τοῦ θεοῦ (supported by W, Δ, 0102, 0161, Byz, Lect[pt]). It seems more likely that the longer readings arose to clarify the shorter than that the shorter reading arose by omission of θεοῦ, either accidentally or intentionally.

22:32. UBS[4] prefers the reading ἔστιν ὁ θεός (supported by B, L, Δ, f[1], 33, 157*). The same reading minus the article is found in א, D, W, 28; hence [ὁ] in UBS[4]. The other major reading, ἔστιν ὁ θεὸς θεός (supported by 0102, 0233, 180, 565, Byz, Lect), makes the meaning more precise (cf. Mark 12:27).

---

5. Cf. Matt. 5:3–12; 8:11; 13:40–43; 16:27; 19:28; 24:13, 29–31, 33, 42, 44–47; 25:13, 29, 34, 46; 26:29; 28:20; John 5:28–29; Acts 17:30–31; Heb. 11:35; 2 Pet. 3:11–14.

f. The Pharisee Lawyer's Question: The Greatest Commandment (22:34–40)

This third story of Jesus's debates with the religious leaders is the least controversial (cf. Mark 12:28–34; Luke 10:25–28). In this exchange Jesus succinctly synthesizes the ethical teaching of the Scriptures (cf. Matt. 7:12). The structure of the passage is straightforward: it contains a narrative introduction (22:34), the Pharisee lawyer's question (22:35–36), and Jesus's answer (22:37–40). His answer intersperses Torah quotations and his own comments:

> First scriptural citation: Deut. 6:5 (Matt. 22:37)
> First comment: This is the foremost commandment (22:38)
> Second comment: Another commandment is like the first (22:39a)
> Second scriptural citation: Lev. 19:18 (Matt. 22:39b)
> Third comment: The entire Torah depends on these two commandments (22:40)

The absence of a rejoinder from the lawyer may indicate that Jesus's view of the greatest commandment is not contrary to that of his contemporaries (Hagner 1995a: 644).[1]

Jesus's relationship to, and interpretation of, the law have been prominent in his teaching (5:17–48; 12:1–14; 15:1–20; 19:1–22). For Jesus, the heart of Torah observance is love for God and for those created in God's image. If one truly loves God, one will love his imagers (cf. James 3:9–10; 1 John 3:13–17; 4:19–21). When one loves human beings, one expresses love to their Creator. This principle is the basis of the specific stipulations of the Torah, and of the message of the prophets who called Israel to obey Moses (9:13; 12:7; 23:23). Other NT texts echo this in affirming love as the root obligation of the law (Rom. 13:9–10; Gal. 5:14; Col. 3:14; James 2:8; cf. Furnish 1972).

The unit may be outlined as follows:

---

1. Similar statements of a "double commandment" that states the quintessence of the Torah are found in Jewish literature: cf. T. Iss. 5.2; 7.6; T. Dan 5.3; Let. Aris. 229; Philo, *Virtues* 51; *Spec. Laws* 2.63; *Abraham* 208; *Good Person* 83; Josephus *Ant.* 3.213. Philo viewed the two tables of the law as respectively inculcating piety toward God and uprightness toward people (*Decalogue* 50–51, 106, 108–10, 121) and believed that the two tables summarized the entire Torah (*Decalogue* 20, 154). See R. Pesch in Merklein 1989: 99–109.

i. The setting (22:34)
ii. The Pharisee lawyer's question (22:35–36)
iii. Jesus's answer (22:37–40)

Exegesis and Exposition

[34]Now when the Pharisees heard that Jesus had silenced the Sadducees, they gathered together. [35]And one of them, ⌜a lawyer,⌝ asked him a question to test him: [36]"Teacher, which is the great commandment in the law?" [37]And he said to him, "'You shall love the Lord your God with all your heart, and with all your soul, and with all your mind.' [38]This is the greatest and foremost commandment. [39]The second is like it: 'You shall love your neighbor as yourself.' [40]All the law and the prophets hang on these two commandments."

i. The Setting (22:34)

When the Pharisees learn that Jesus has silenced the Sadducees,[2] they come together for yet another attempt to trap him (cf. Mark 12:28–34). It will be their last. This language may allude to the gathering of the nations against the Lord's anointed in Ps. 2:2 (cf. Acts 4:26).[3] Ironically, the Pharisees would have agreed with Jesus's response to the Sadducees, but this is a small matter in comparison to their many problems with Jesus (cf. Matt. 16:1–2, 6, 11–12; 27:62).

22:34

ii. The Pharisee Lawyer's Question (22:35–36)

A Pharisaic legal expert (cf. Luke 10:25; 11:45, 52; 14:3) would evidently be a more formidable interlocutor than the Pharisaic disciples who confronted Jesus previously (22:16). His request that Jesus identify the greatest[4] commandment in the law may reflect a debate within Judaism at that time (Blomberg 1992a: 334), but his purpose is to trap Jesus, not to gain insight into the exegesis of Torah (cf. 16:1; 19:3; 22:15, 18). The Scriptures themselves present summaries of the crucial demands of the law (e.g., Mic. 6:8). The Mishnah offers a different perspective when it states that the more commandments, the more potential for merit for Israel (*m. Mak.* 3.16; *m. 'Abot* 6.11). Yet Montefiore and Loewe (1974: 199–201) cite several rabbinic passages that prioritize certain key commandments. Of these, *b. Mak.* 23b–24a may be the most noteworthy,

22:35–36

---

2. The word ἐφίμωσεν can refer to muzzling an animal and implies inability to speak, not merely the absence of speech. Cf. 22:12; BDAG 1060.
3. Matthew's phrase συνήχθησαν ἐπὶ τὸ αὐτό is also found in the LXX: Neh. 4:2; 6:2; Pss. 2:2; 101:23. Cf. Acts 4:26. It evidently refers to a gathering at the same place or for a common purpose (BDAG 153).
4. The positive-degree adjective μεγάλη functions as a superlative, evidently under Semitic influence; cf. 5:19; BDF 245; Moulton and Turner 1963: 31; Wallace 1996: 298.

since it progressively reduces the 613 commandments of the Torah (365 negative and 248 positive) to a single commandment, Hab. 2:4.

iii. Jesus's Answer (22:37–40)

22:37–38 This is the most straightforward of all Jesus's answers to questions in this section of Matthew. Without hesitation Jesus cites Deut. 6:5 as the greatest commandment. The former text enjoins love for God with one's entire being, and the latter, love for one's neighbor (cf. Matt. 5:43; 19:19; Josh. 22:5). The command to love God with all one's heart, soul, and mind means that one must love God with one's entire being (cf. Jub. 1.15–16; 16.25; 19.31; 36.24), not that one is responsible to love God with some of one's faculties and not with the others.[5] Jesus's description of Deut. 6:5 as the greatest and first commandment (cf. Josephus, *Ag. Ap.* 2.190) is similar to the phrase "the weightier provisions of the law" in 23:23.

22:39–40 Jesus appends Lev. 19:18 as a text of similar import to Deut. 6:5 (cf. Matt. 5:43; 19:19).[6] This second text (cf. *Did.* 1.2) strikingly echoes the obligation of love from the first text (probably *gezerah shawah*; cf. Gerhardsson in Hamerton-Kelly and Scroggs 1976: 138) but changes the object of love from God the Creator to God's human creatures. The context of Lev. 19 stresses love for strangers as well as fellow Jews (cf. Lev. 19:33–34; contra Boring 1995: 426). Both of these passages were central in the Judaism of Jesus's day. Pious Jews recited the Shema, a prayer named for the first word of Deut. 6:4 ("Hear!"), twice daily (*m. Ber.* 1.1–2). Rabbinic sources allude to Lev. 19:18 as the fundamental principle of the law (*m. 'Abot* 1.12; Sipre on Lev. 19:18, citing Akiba; *b. Šabb.* 31a; cf. CD 6.20–21; Philo, *Spec. Laws* 2.15, 63; Josephus, *J.W.* 2.119).

After citing these two texts, Jesus states that all of the law and the prophets depend (κρέμαται, *krematai*; literally, "hang"; cf. 18:6) on them. In other words, all Scripture is an exposition of the ideals expressed in Deut. 6:5 and Lev. 19:18. The thought is similar to that of Matt. 7:12. These two texts are the "encompassing principle" of the Torah (cf. Sipra on Lev. 19:18).[7] There is no mention here of the lawyer's response or of

---

5. Matthew's quotation differs from the LXX in some particulars. The LXX renders the threefold בְּכָל־ of the MT with ἐξ ὅλης, but Matthew has the more literal ἐν ὅλῃ. Also, the LXX renders the MT מְאֹדֶךָ with δύναμίς σου, but Matthew has διάνοιά σου as in Mark 12:30; Luke 10:27. See further discussion of the textual differences in W. Davies and Allison 1997: 240–43; Gundry 1967: 22–24. Cf. the similar terminology in Deut. 10:12; 30:10; 2 Kings 23:25; 4Q398 14–17; 2 Bar. 66.1.

6. Matthew's wording is identical to the LXX, which literally renders the MT. On Jewish interpretation of Lev. 19:18, see Neudecker 1992.

7. A story attributed to Hillel in *b. Šabb.* 31a is also relevant. Hillel teaches the entire Torah "while standing on one foot" with the words "What is hateful to you, do not do to your neighbor. This is the whole law. The rest is commentary." Cf. *b. Ber.* 63a, which posits Prov. 3:6 as a text on which all basic Torah principles depend; Exod. Rab. on Exod. 21:1, which affirms that the Torah "hangs" on justice.

his departure. In contrast to preceding interchanges, the lawyer evidently finds no fault with Jesus and has no rejoinder to him. If so, 22:46 could describe this interchange as well as that of 22:41–45 (cf. 22:22, 33). The absence of a rejoinder or a narrative conclusion makes the episode close with the words of Jesus still ringing in the reader's ears.[8]

The Quintessence of Torah: Deut. 6:4 and Lev. 19:18

Jesus's placement of Lev. 19:18 alongside Deut. 6:5 as being "similar" (ὁμοία, *homoia*) to it surprisingly affirms that loving God's creatures is of the same nature as, and accordingly just as important as, loving their Creator (cf. BDAG 706). "Their equality reflects their unity" (W. Davies and Allison 1997: 243). Yet loving humans derives from loving their Creator, since Jesus's labeling of Deut. 6:5 as the "greatest and foremost commandment" indicates that it must be viewed as foundational for Lev. 19:18. Fallen humans cannot love their neighbors as themselves if they have not first acknowledged their obligation to love the only true God. God's initiating love to humans enables them to respond lovingly to God and to their fellow humans. The appearance of the statement "I am the Lord your God" at the beginning of the Ten Commandments shows that the theocentric vertical obligation is the basis of the anthropocentric horizontal obligation (Exod. 20:2; Deut. 5:6). Although Lev. 19:18 has an ethical importance equal to Deut. 6:5, it stands on the gracious covenantal foundation of Deut. 6:4. Yet without Lev. 19:18 one cannot practice Deut. 6:5, since one expresses love to God by obeying his commandments, many of which concern human relationships. Hagner (1995a: 648) notes that loving God entails reverence and obedience whereas loving humans entails serving them and seeking their well-being. This is exemplified in Matt. 25:31–46. (See W. Davies and Allison 1997: 244.)

    Leviticus 19:18 and its NT echoes (John 13:34–35; Rom. 13:8–10; Gal. 5:14; James 2:8; 1 John 4:19–21) assume that one will instinctively love oneself. Psychological jargon about the necessity of loving oneself as a prerequisite for loving God and one's neighbor turns the biblical pattern on its head (Eph. 5:28–29; despite Augustine, *City of God* 19.14). A proper biblical view of oneself as a flawed yet redeemed individual hardly amounts to uncritical self-affirmation. For Paul, viewing oneself as a new creation "in Christ" (e.g., Rom. 6:1–23; 2 Cor. 5:17; Eph. 4:17–24; Col. 3:1–4) is crucial. But this assumes self-crucifixion with Christ, which is not far from the counsel of Jesus to take up one's cross (Matt. 16:24–26; cf. Gal. 2:20; 6:14). For Jesus, self-love is death, and self-denial is life (Matt. 10:38–39; 16:24–25; 20:26–28).

8. On 22:34–40, see Banks 1975: 164–73; T. Donaldson in Lull 1990: 14–30; Furnish 1972; Gerhardsson in Hamerton-Kelly and Scroggs 1976: 129–50; Hultgren 1974; Kiilunen 1989; P. Perkins 1982; R. Pesch in Merklein 1989: 99–109; J. Stern 1966; Strecker in Hawthorne and Betz 1987: 53–67.

Additional Note

22:35. The word νομικός is well supported by ℵ, B, D, L, W, Δ, Θ, 0102, 0161, f^{13}, 28, 33, *Byz*, *Lect*$^{1/2}$, but it is bracketed in UBS^4 because it is absent from f^1 and versional witnesses that are widely scattered geographically (including some Old Latin, Syriac, Armenian, and Georgian MSS and Origen) and is a hapax legomenon in Matthew, and interpolation from Luke 10:25 is suspected (Metzger 1994: 49).

g. Jesus Questions the Pharisees: David's Son Is David's Lord (22:41–46)

Jesus has responded wisely to three questions from his opponents and has silenced them. Now he takes the initiative and reciprocates with his own questions (cf. Mark 12:35–37; Luke 20:41–44). Framed by a narrative introduction and conclusion (Matt. 22:41, 46),[1] this passage contains two pairs of questions put by Jesus to the Pharisees (22:42a–b, 43–45). They answer the first questions but are unable to answer the second pair, which are based on Ps. 110:1. The passage may be displayed as follows:

> Narrative introduction: Jesus questions the gathered Pharisees (Matt. 22:41)
> The first pair of questions: Whose son is the Messiah? (22:42a–b)
> The answer: The Messiah is David's son (22:42c)
> The second pair of questions: In view of Ps. 110:1, how can David's son be David's Lord? (Matt. 22:43–45)
> Narrative conclusion: The Pharisees cannot answer and dare not question Jesus further (22:46)

In this passage Jesus turns the tables and questions the Pharisees, not to trap them or even to win a debate but to win their hearts (cf. 23:37). This is not a mere counterattack (contra Schnackenburg 2002: 224). The paramount considerations at this decisive point in Israel's history are Jesus's identity and the source of his authority (21:23). His relationship to King David is worthy of their consideration. The Jewish leaders and Jesus agree that the Messiah is David's son (22:42), but the real question is what it means to be David's son in light of Ps. 110:1 (Matt. 22:43–45).

The unit outline is as follows:

i. The first pair of questions answered (22:41–42)
ii. The second pair of questions unanswered (22:43–46)

---

1. The passage is an *inclusio*. Jesus questions (ἐπηρώτησεν, 22:41) the Pharisees, but they cannot answer him and dare not question (ἐπερωτῆσαι, 22:46) him further.

Exegesis and Exposition

[41]Now while the Pharisees were gathered together, Jesus questioned them: [42]"What do you think about the Messiah? Whose son is he?" They said to him, "The son of David." [43]He said to them, "Then how does David in the Spirit call Him 'Lord,' saying,

[44]'The Lord said to my Lord,
"Sit at my right hand,
Until I put your enemies under your feet"'?

[45]If, then, David calls him 'Lord,' how is he his son?" [46]But no one could answer him even a word, nor did anyone dare to question him from that day on.

i. The First Pair of Questions Answered (22:41–42)

22:41–42   Jesus's first question regarding the sonship of the Messiah is answered easily and correctly by the Pharisees. The Messiah is indeed David's son, but the Pharisees evidently view the Messiah's Davidic roots in a nationalistic and militaristic fashion.[2] Since they look for a powerful leader to liberate them from Roman oppression, they look past Jesus, who promises no such thing (e.g., 5:3–12, 39, 44; 10:17–22, 34–39; 11:29; 12:18–21; 21:5). But this is not the whole truth of the matter, as the next pair of questions shows.

ii. The Second Pair of Questions Unanswered (22:43–46)

22:43–44   Jesus's second pair of questions centers on his exegesis of Ps. 110:1 and clarifies the Messiah's relationship to David.[3] Jesus understands Ps. 110:1 to say that David refers to his son the Messiah as his Lord. Sons customarily speak in such lofty terms of their fathers, not fathers of their sons. How could David's son be David's Lord, one who possesses higher authority than the vaunted king of Israel? This citation of Ps. 110 assumes the Spirit's moving David to write it (cf. Acts 1:16; 2:30;

2. Many texts affirm the Davidic sonship of the Messiah (e.g., 2 Sam. 7:12–14; 1 Chron. 17:11–14; Ps. 89; Isa. 11:1, 10; Jer. 23:5–6; 33:15; Ezek. 34:23–24; 37:24; Ps. Sol. 17.21–43; 18.7–9; 4QFlor [4Q174] 1.10–14; Matt. 1:1; 9:27–28; 20:30; 21:9, 15; John 7:42; Rom. 1:3; 15:12; Rev. 5:5; 22:16).
3. Psalm 109:1 LXX closely renders Ps. 110:1 MT. Matthew's version follows the LXX closely except for omitting ὁ before κύριος and using the preposition ὑποκάτω instead of the LXX's more literal ὑποπόδιον in the last phrase. Psalm 110 is perhaps the most cited psalm in the NT; Boring (1995: 427) counts 37 NT echoes. Psalm 110:1 is cited in Matt. 26:64; Mark 12:36; 14:62; Luke 20:42–43; 22:69; Acts 2:34–35; Heb. 1:13. Psalm 110:4 is cited in Heb. 5:6; 7:17–21. Additional possible allusions to Ps. 110:1 occur in Mark 16:19; Rom. 8:34; 1 Cor. 15:25; Eph. 1:20; Col. 3:1; Heb. 1:3; 8:1; 10:12–13; 12:2; Rev. 3:21. Additional possible allusions to Ps. 110:4 occur in John 12:34; Rom. 11:29; Heb. 5:10; 6:20; 7:3, 11, 15. Romans 2:5 may allude to Ps. 110:5.

4:25; Josephus *Ant.* 6.166). Jesus understands David to be the speaker in Ps. 110:1. If David is not the speaker, a third party, such as a prophet, is speaking about what God said to David or another Israelite king, who is described as "my Lord." In this understanding, the psalm does not speak of the Messiah. There are two different Hebrew words in Ps. 110:1—"The Lord [יְהֹוָה, Yahweh] said to my Lord [לַאדֹנִי, *la'dōnî*]." The reference to David's אֲדֹנָי (*'ădōnāy*, Lord) sitting at the right hand of יְהֹוָה (Yahweh) describes messianic authority in terms similar to Ps. 2:9 and Dan. 7:13–14. This reference is ominous in view of Matt. 26:64, where Jesus's application of Dan. 7:13–14 to himself is taken by the high priest as blasphemous. The reference to Jesus's coming exaltation (Matt. 28:18) and eventual triumph over his enemies (7:22–23; 13:41; 16:27; 22:7; 24:30; 25:31) is clear.[4]

After citing Ps. 110:1, Jesus builds on the previous question about how David can call his son his Lord. Now he asks conversely how David's Lord can be his son. The answer to the enigma is based on the Matthean teaching of Jesus's dual "paternity." Jesus is David's son because he is humanly descended from David, and yet more profoundly he is also David's Lord because he is God's Son. Jesus's transcendent sonship is prominently featured in Matthew.[5] Matthew's understanding of the Messiah's sonship is ostensibly based on additional biblical texts that describe one who transcends human limitations (e.g., Ps. 45:6–7; Isa. 9:6; Jer. 23:5–6; 33:15–16; Zech. 12:10; 13:7). Isaiah 11:1, 10, where the Messiah is both David's offshoot and David's root, is especially significant.

    22:45

The two questions encompassing Ps. 110:1 address the same issue from opposite directions. The initial question in Matt. 22:43 seems to assume the humanity of the Messiah as David's descendant. If the Messiah is the human descendant of David, how does David call him Lord in Ps. 110:1? The follow-up question in Matt. 22:45 puts it the opposite way: if the Messiah is David's Lord, how can he be David's descendant? In Matthew's narrative Jesus's humble Davidic roots (1:1, 16–17, 20; cf. Luke 1:27, 32, 69; 2:4, 11) are not the whole story. Jesus is also the miraculously born, divinely attested Son of God (Matt. 1:23; 3:17; 16:16; 17:5; 21:37; 22:2; 26:63–64). That Jesus is greater than David is already clear (12:1–4; cf. 12:6, 8, 41), but now Matthew explains why: the Messiah is the son of David and the Son of God. But the Pharisees will not accept a Messiah who, as David's Lord, is greater than David. On this extremely sad note ends Matthew's story of Jesus's conflict with the religious leaders in Jerusalem. Nothing more can be said, and unfortunately, the conflict remains a theological watershed

---

4. For further discussion of the messianic interpretation of Ps. 110, see Fitzmyer 1997: 113–26; Hay 1973.

5. See esp. 1:23; 2:15; 3:17; 4:3, 6; 7:21; 8:29; 11:25–27; 16:16; 17:26; 21:37–39; 22:2; 24:36; 26:29, 39, 42, 53, 63; 27:40, 43, 46, 54; 28:19.

today as Judaism expects a human Messiah and Christianity worships a divine one.

22:46 The silence of the religious leaders does not mean that they have come to agree with Jesus but that they have abandoned hope of publicly refuting him. This pericope begins with Jesus speaking to the Pharisees (22:41), but it ends more broadly. In 22:46 no one (οὐδείς, *oudeis*) is able to answer Jesus, nor does anyone (τις, *tis*) dare to question him further. Thus 22:46 summarizes the result of Jesus's debates with all the religious leaders, going back as far as 21:15. The leaders have been vanquished by Jesus's biblical and rhetorical prowess, yet they are unwilling to believe in him. Their plot to execute him will resurface in 26:3–5, 14–16, 47–56. Jesus has been temporarily vindicated, but his repeated predictions of what is about to happen indicate that this is not a moment of celebration. Jesus will be questioned again—by the high priests and Pilate (26:62–63; 27:11, 13).

Summary and Transition

Matthew 22 continues the description of escalating controversies between Jesus and the religious leaders that began soon after the triumphal entry. Following the triple-parable sequence (21:23–22:14), there is a triple-controversy story sequence (22:15–40) before Jesus asks a final unanswerable question (22:41–46). Matthew 22 takes the verbal hostilities between Jesus and the Jewish leaders to its sorry end. Jesus's parables magnify the unbelief of Israel's leaders, their guilt in not submitting to God's rule, and their liability to judgment. The questions of the religious leaders attempt to trap Jesus and to discredit his teaching. All hope of rapprochement between Jesus and the religious leaders is dashed. His final question to them is unanswerable; the only way that David can call his messianic son "Lord" is if his son is divine. The Pharisees who wished to trap Jesus are now trapped by Jesus. But all dialogue has ceased, with ominous implications. This final confrontation leaves Jesus and the Jewish leaders at a hopeless impasse and leads inevitably to the woes of Matt. 23.

6. Warnings to the Disciples and Woes to the Pharisees (23:1–39)

Matthew 23 and the Argument of Matthew

The place of Matt. 23 in the argument of the book has been understood in two ways. We can connect Matt. 23, as discourse, with Matt. 24–25.[1] In this view, Matt. 23–25 follows the pattern of Matt. 13 (cf. 13:34–36), with public teaching (Matt. 23) followed by private instruction (Matt. 24–25). But the public and private portions of Matt. 13 have a common theme, genre, and literary structure, and there are differences between Matt. 23 and Matt. 24–25 in terms of audience (compare 23:1, 13 with 24:1–3), tone, content, and setting. Therefore it is probably better to take the second approach and view Matt. 23 as the culmination of Jesus's confrontations with Jerusalem's religious leaders that began in 21:15 (Hagner 1995a: 654; Hill 1972: 308). At the same time, there are clear connections between Matt. 23 and Matt. 24–25: the persecution of Jesus's disciples (23:29–36; cf. 24:9–13, 21–22; 25:34–40), the desolation of the temple (23:38; cf. 24:1–3, 15), and the return of Jesus (23:39; cf. 24:3, 30, 37, 39, 42, 44; 25:6, 13, 19, 31). On balance, Matt. 23 functions as a bridge or hinge that concludes the preceding conflict narrative and prepares the reader for the following eschatological discourse (Meier 1979: 159–60; see Garland 1979: 23–32).[2]

Many scholars agree that Matt. 23 has three major sections: verses 1–12, 13–36, and 37–39.[3] First Jesus warns the crowds and his disciples against the errors of the scribes and Pharisees (23:1–12). Then he denounces the religious leaders with prophetic woes and oracles that tie their rebellion to that of their ancestors (23:13–36). Finally he poignantly laments rebellious Jerusalem with words that depict his longing for them as well as their deserved judgment (23:37–39).

---

1. Scholars who view Matt. 23 as the first part of the eschatological discourse include Blomberg 1992a: 25, 49, 339; Boring 1995: 428–29; Gundry 1994: 453; Keener 1999: 535; Scaer 2004: 343, 374.

2. Witherington (2006: 15–16, 421) suggests taking Matt. 23 as a sixth discourse. He is correct that the Moses typology in Matthew does not require five discourses, but his view is weakened considerably by the lack of a narrative section between Matt. 23 and Matt. 24–25 as well as by the absence of the characteristic transitional formula (e.g., 7:28) at the end of Matt. 23.

3. Hagner's view (1995a: 673) that 23:34–36 is a distinct prophetic appendix to 23:13–33 yields four sections. W. Davies and Allison (1997: 311) begin the lament at 23:34 instead of 23:37. Harrington (1991: 329–30) takes 23:32–39 as a final warning. Garland (1979: 32–33) proposes vv. 1–12, 13–28, and 29–39 as the main sections of Matt. 23.

Matthew 23 culminates the running dispute of Jesus with the leaders of the Jerusalem religious establishment that has been narrated since 21:12. Jesus has successively confronted

1. The chief priests and scribes (21:12–17)
2. The chief priests and elders of the people (21:23–22:14; according to 21:45, this included Pharisees)
3. The disciples of certain Pharisees (22:15–22)
4. Certain Sadducees (22:23–33)
5. A Pharisaic lawyer (22:34–46)

These confrontations typically include questions by the leaders (21:16, 23; 22:17, 28, 36) and responses by Jesus that include scriptural quotations (21:16, 33, 42; 22:32, 37, 39, 44), parables (21:28–30, 33–39; 22:1–14), and counterquestions (21:16, 25, 28, 31, 40, 42; 22:18, 20, 42, 43, 45). When these confrontations come to the point where no further dialogue is possible, the indictments of Matt. 23 ensue.

Matthew 23 also introduces the eschatological discourse of Matt. 24–25. After the impasse between Jesus and the religious leaders (22:46), Jesus warns his followers against mimicking these leaders (23:1–12). He pronounces woes upon them (23:13–36) and laments Jerusalem's fate (23:37–39). Yet he holds out hope for the future if Jerusalem will sincerely call upon him (23:39; Ps. 118:26; cf. Matt. 21:9). When his disciples nervously point out to him the glorious architecture of the temple as he departs (24:1), he speaks bluntly about its coming destruction. With this the disciples ask the double question that gives rise to the discourse: "When will these things happen, and what will be the sign of your coming and of the end of the age?" (24:2–3). In this way the judgment of Jerusalem is justified in Matt. 23 before it is predicted in Matt. 24–25.[4]

---

4. For further study of Matt. 23, see esp. Garland 1979; Newport 1995.

a. Warning the Disciples (23:1–12)

Jesus's warning (cf. Mark 12:38–39; Luke 20:45–46) first points out the inconsistencies of the religious leaders (Matt. 23:2–7) and then enjoins his own community to be different (23:8–12). The disciples should do what the leaders say because they are Moses's proxies (23:2–3a), but the disciples should not follow the leaders' example (23:3b) because (1) they do not practice what they preach (23:3c), (2) they do not serve the people they have burdened (23:4), and (3) they perform their deeds to be applauded by people (23:5–7). The disciples' countercultural community must eschew vain prestigious titles (23:8–10) and instead seek to serve others, mindful of the reckoning and reward to come (23:11–12).

The unit can be outlined as follows:

    i. A general warning against Pharisaic practices (23:1–3)
    ii. Specific Pharisaic inconsistencies (23:4–7)
    iii. Contrasting practices of Jesus's disciples (23:8–12)

Exegesis and Exposition

¹Then Jesus spoke to the crowds and to his disciples, ²"The scribes and the Pharisees sit in the chair of Moses; ³therefore do and observe whatever they tell you, but do not do according to their works; for they talk but they do not act. ⁴They tie up ⌜heavy burdens that are hard to carry⌝ and lay them on people's shoulders, but they themselves are not willing to lift a finger to move them. ⁵And they do all their works to be noticed by people; for they make their phylacteries wide and the tassels of their garments long. ⁶They love the place of honor at banquets and the chief seats in the synagogues, ⁷and being greeted in the markets, and being called Rabbi by people.

⁸"But you must not be called Rabbi; for one is your teacher and you are all brothers. ⁹And do not call anyone on earth ⌜your⌝ father, for one is your Father, he who is in heaven. ¹⁰Neither should you be called teachers; for one is your teacher, the Messiah. ¹¹But the greatest among you will be your servant. ¹²All who exalt themselves will be humbled; and all who humble themselves will be exalted."

i. A General Warning against Pharisaic Practices (23:1–3)

The various religious leaders with whom Jesus has been in conflict since 21:12 are now absent, evidently because they are incorrigible (cf. Mark

23:1–2

12:38–40; Luke 20:45–47). Jesus speaks to the crowds and to his disciples with surprising words that seem to authenticate the role of his opponents, the scribes and Pharisees (cf. Matt. 5:20; 12:38; 15:1). In Matt. 23 they receive the brunt of Jesus's denunciation (23:2, 13–15, 23, 25, 27, 29), but here Jesus acknowledges their capacity as official Torah interpreters.[1] The chair or seat of Moses may be a metaphor or may refer to such a seat in synagogues where authoritative teaching occurred, although the evidence for an actual seat comes from later times.[2] In any event, occupying this "chair" signified the ongoing exercise of the quasi-Mosaic authority that came from Sinai (*m. 'Abot* 1.1, 3–4, 6, 8, 10, 12; 2.8).

23:3   Jesus's surprising counsel that his disciples obey the teachings of those with whom he has had so many conflicts echoes Deut. 17:10 (cf. Matt. 23:23), but many interpreters downplay this command. France (1985: 324) views this language as tongue in cheek. Carson (1984: 473–74; cf. Jeremias 1971: 210) views 23:2–3a as irony or sarcasm, followed by Jesus's true intent in 23:3b–4. Yet Jesus enjoins obedience to the leaders' teachings despite their hypocritical example. Their teaching should be followed in principle because of their authoritative position, but their example is inconsistent with this teaching and must not be imitated (cf. Rom. 2:21–24; Rabbinowitz 2003: 443–47).

ii. Specific Pharisaic Inconsistencies (23:4–7)

23:4   Jesus's imagery of heavy burdens being loaded on people's shoulders (cf. Luke 11:46) speaks of the Pharisaic traditions (Matt. 15:3–9). The heavy burden of the Pharisaic system contrasts with the light load of Jesus in 11:30 (cf. Acts 15:10, 28; 1 John 5:3; CD 1.18–19). In view of Matt. 5:20, the point of the metaphor is not to contrast the hardness of the Pharisees' rules with the easiness of Jesus's teachings (Calvin 1972: 3.48), or even Pharisaic multiplicity with Jesus's simplicity (contra Schweizer 1975: 438). Rather, Jesus contrasts the Pharisees' preoccupation about relatively trivial matters with their neglect of the central internal virtues that enable and animate obedience to Torah (23:23; cf. 5:21–22, 27–28; 9:13; 12:7; 15:1–20). In addition, the Pharisees refuse to help people keep their rules.

    1. The aorist verb ἐκάθισαν may be understood as gnomic, a timeless reference to a generic state of affairs (Robertson 1934: 836–37, 866; Wallace 1996: 562; Zerwick 1963: §256 is dubious), or ingressive, connoting a past entrance into present religious authority (Moulton and Howard 1920: 458; Wallace 1996: 558–59). Moulton and Turner (1963: 72) similarly view it as perfective, connoting the result of past action (cf. BDF §342.1; Burton 1898: §55; Moule 1959: 11 disagrees). W. Allen's suggestion (1912: 244) that the reference is to past authority formerly wielded by the Pharisees does not fit the context.

    2. On the chair of Moses, see W. Davies and Allison 1997: 268; Newport 1990; Powell 1995a; Rabbinowitz 2003: 423–27; Rahmni 1990; Roth 1949; Sukenik 1930; 1934: 57–69.

Here Jesus exposes the Pharisees' goal of garnering human applause by **23:5–7**
ostentatious means. The disciples must not imitate the motives of the
religious leaders any more than their example (cf. 6:1–18). The general
statement of 23:5a is illustrated in 23:5b–7 by six examples, arranged
in three pairs. Phylacteries and tassels were ways of publicly displaying
one's piety. Phylacteries, or tefillin (תְּפִלִּין; Jastrow 1971: 1687), are small
leather boxes containing Torah portions that men wore on the arm and
the forehead on the basis of a literal understanding of Exod. 13:9, 16;
Deut. 6:8; 11:18.[3] Tassels (צִיצִית, ṣîṣît; Jastrow 1971: 1280) were fringes
on robes or prayer shawls (טַלִּית, ṭallît; Matt. 9:20; 14:36; Num. 15:37–39;
Deut. 22:12). Seeking prominent places at public functions is the second
example of these leaders' concern for prestige (Matt. 23:6; cf. Luke 11:43;
14:7–11; 20:46; James 2:1–4). The third illustration concerns preoccupation with public greetings (Matt. 26:49) that stress honorific titles.
In Jesus's time, "Rabbi" was a respectful greeting that literally meant
"my master" (26:25, 49; Mark 9:5; 11:21; 14:45; John 1:38, 49; 3:2, 26;
4:31; 6:25; 9:2). After the events of 70 CE, the word came to be used to
describe someone who occupied an ordained position of religious and
civil leadership (J. Donaldson 1972–73; Shanks 1974).

iii. Contrasting Practices of Jesus's Disciples (23:8–12)

Now Jesus turns from denouncing the leaders' false piety to commanding **23:8–10**
true piety for his disciples. Jesus forbids them from using the ostentatious
greetings of 23:7. In 23:8–10 are three prohibitions, each followed by a
reason. The disciples are forbidden the ostentatious use of honorific titles
such as "rabbi," "father" (2 Kings 2:12; 5:13; 6:21; 13:14; Sir. 44; Acts 7:2;
22:1), and "teacher" (or "tutor;" cf. Byrskog 1994; Winter 1991) because
no human being is worthy of such honor. Rather, such titles should be
reserved for the heavenly Father and Jesus the Messiah (Derrett 1981).
Jesus's disciples form an egalitarian family whose members view one
another simply as brothers and sisters (Hoet 1982).

The Egalitarianism of Jesus

North American evangelicals are engaged in what, with only slight exaggeration, has been called a "gender war." "Complementarians" argue from
Scripture to support traditional roles for men and women in the home
and in the church, but "egalitarians" work with the same scriptural texts
in order to press for equal opportunity.[4] Both groups need to beware

---

3. See Josephus, *Ant.* 4.212–13; Let. Aris. 159; *m. Šebu.* 3.8, 11; *m. Ber.* 3.3; *m. Sanh.*
11.3; *b. Menaḥ.* 35a; *b. Šabb.* 8b; Bowman in Aland 1959: 523–38; Fagen, *ABD* 5:368–70;
Tigay 1979.
4. For presentations and interactive discussions of various views, see Beck and
Blomberg 2001; Clouse and Clouse 1989. For a helpful categorized bibliography, see
W. Webb 2001: 281–85.

of the danger of using Scripture to retain or acquire status and power. Jesus's egalitarianism is of another sort entirely. He does not intend to "liberate" any social, ethnic, or gender-based entity so that it can turn the tables and rule over the entity that formerly oppressed it. Instead his egalitarianism frees his disciples to live in a community where humble reciprocal service rules (18:1–5; 20:25–28). Social, ethnic, and gender differences are relativized in Jesus's family, which devalues status and prizes submission to his teachings.[5] On balance with Jesus's teaching elsewhere (e.g., 10:1–4; 19:28; 23:34; 28:19), such egalitarianism is not inconsistent with the presence of specially gifted and commissioned leaders in the community (cf. Eph. 4:11–16; 1 Thess. 5:12–13; 1 Tim. 5:17; Heb. 13:17) or even with what W. Webb (2001: 26–27) calls "soft patriarchy." Jesus did not find male apostolic leadership to be contrary to this ideal, and evidently neither did Paul (1 Tim. 3:2; Titus 1:6). But gifted individuals who exercise office in the church, whether male or female, must do so with humble service as their ideal and with Jesus's family imagery as their model. Roman Catholic (Meier 1980b: 265) and Protestant (Bruner 1990: 816–18; Keener 1999: 545–46) scholars alike have noted the need for reforming and revisioning hierarchical ecclesiastical structures in light of Jesus's teaching.

23:11–12 Here the kingdom's contrasting norms are explained in words that remind the reader of 20:25–28 (cf. 18:4). True greatness pertains to service, not to title. Those, like the leaders, who seek to exalt themselves will be humbled, but Jesus's disciples who seek to serve others will be exalted. This language envisions eschatological reversal: Jesus's disciples have humbled themselves and will be exalted. The leaders' vain attempt to exalt themselves over God's Messiah will result in their being humbled.

Matthew 23:1–12 is spoken to the crowds and disciples, not to the religious leaders. But the leaders are still very much in the picture as a foil to Jesus's disciples, who must not imitate their hypocrisy (23:3b), oppressive demands (23:4), and love of prestige and status (23:5–7). Jesus's disciples are to revere only the Father and the Messiah (23:8–10). The egalitarian family model must permeate and constrain whatever hierarchical structures the community enacts in order to acknowledge specially gifted servant-leaders and govern itself (cf. 20:25; Gal. 6:1–6; 1 Tim. 5:1–2). That Jesus himself humbly practices what he preaches is clear from Matt. 20:28.

But the Jewish leaders do not practice what they preach, and so Jesus warns his disciples against their errors. He does not attack the formal legitimacy of their authority but tells his disciples to follow their exposition of the Torah and the halakah (23:3a, 23). The difficulty of many scholars with this point is due to their assumption that Matthew's com-

---

5. Matt. 12:50; cf. James 1:9–11; Paul's *Haustafeln*, where being "in Christ" transforms every human relationship: Eph. 5:21–6:9; Col. 3:18–4:1.

6. Warnings to the Disciples and Woes to the Pharisees
a. Warning the Disciples
Matthew 23:1–12

munity has already broken from Judaism. But 23:3a makes good sense if Matthew's community is still engaged in an intramural dispute with the leaders of formative Judaism.[6] The explicit contrast of Jesus's norms for his disciples with the ostentatious practices of the leaders in 23:2–12 provides a key for interpreting the seven woes of 23:13–36. These rebukes not only are directed to the leaders but also are meant to prevent Jesus's disciples from similar errors (Beare 1981: 461; Garland 1979: 62–63).

Additional Notes

23:4. The editors of UBS[4] place the words καὶ δυσβάστακτα (supported by B, D[2], W, Δ, Θ, 0102, 0107, f[13], 28, 33, *Byz, Lect*) in brackets because they suspect interpolation from Luke 11:46. But the evidence for the shorter reading, βαρέα (L, f[1], 205, 892; ℵ has μεγάλα βαρέα), is not impressive (contra Metzger 1994: 49).

23:9. The first ὑμῶν (supported by ℵ, B, L, W, f[1], f[13], 28, *Byz, Lect*) is omitted by a few MSS (1241, 1424), and others have ὑμῖν instead (D, Θ).

6. For further study of 23:1–12, see Becker 1990; Rabbinowitz 2003; Viviano 1990c.

b. Denouncing the Pharisees (23:13–36)

Prophetic Woe Oracles

Jesus's denunciation of the religious leaders must be viewed against the background of the biblical prophets, who frequently cried woe against Israel's sins.[1] These oracles blend anger, grief, and alarm about the excruciating consequences that will come upon Israel due to its sin. The form of such oracles includes an initial pronouncement of woe followed by a description of the persons upon whom the woe will come. This description amounts to the reason the woe is merited. Thus a woe oracle states the conclusion and then the premises on which it is based. Woe oracles may have developed from covenant curses (Deut. 27:15) or even from funeral lamentations (Jer. 22:18). (See Clements, *ABD* 6:945–46; Westermann 1967: 192–95.)[2]

In oracles of woe, the prophet's attitude is anger tempered at times by grief and alarm at the horrible price Israel will pay for its sin. Prophets are angry because they are speaking for God against sin. But prophets are also stricken with grief because this anger is directed toward their own people. The palpable pathos of woe oracles is due to the prophet's dual solidarities. The prophets must speak for God, but in announcing oracles of judgment, the prophets know that they are announcing the doom of their own people.

In light of this biblical background, Jesus's pronouncements of woe upon the religious leaders were not innovative. His severe language must have had a familiar ring in the leaders' ears. In light of the woe oracles in Second Temple literature, Jesus's woes would have sounded rather contemporary. His woe oracles were not merely an exercise of

---

1. E.g., see Isa. 5:8, 11, 18, 20, 21, 22 (a series of six woes); Amos 5:18; 6:1, 4; Hab. 2:6, 9, 12, 15, 19 (a series of five woes); Zech. 11:17. The NT records additional woe oracles in Matt. 11:21; 18:7; 24:19; 26:24 and synoptic parallels; cf. Luke 6:24–26; 1 Cor. 9:16; Jude 11; Rev. 8:13; 9:12; 11:14; 12:12; 18:10, 16, 19. In Second Temple literature, see Jdt. 16:17; Sir. 2:12–14; 41:8; 2 Esd. (4 Ezra) 13:16, 19; 1 Macc. 2:7; Gk. Apoc. Ezra 1.9, 24; 4Q169 frgs. 3–4.2.1–11; 4Q179 frg. 1.1.4; 1.2.1; 4Q185 frgs. 1–2.1.9; 4Q286 frg. 7.2.2–12; 4Q511 frgs. 63–64.3.5; 1QpHab 10.5–6 (on Hab. 2:12–13); 11.2 (on Hab. 2:15); 12.5 (on Hab. 2:17), 14–15 (on Hab. 2:19–20); 1QS 2.5–9; 1 En. 94.6–95.7; 96.4–8; 98.9–99.2; 100.7–9; 2 En. 13.64–70; Josephus, *J.W.* 6.301–11.

2. Although the content of a woe oracle is semantically the opposite of a beatitude, the form is the same. Perhaps the woe oracles of Matt. 23 form a sort of rough *inclusio* with the Beatitudes of the Sermon on the Mount (5:3–12; Meier 1979: 163).

spite against his opponents; as is clear in Matt. 23:37, his words come at least as much from grief as from anger.

The Structure of Matthew 23:13–36

The seven[3] woes of Matt. 23:13–36 are best understood as three pairs followed by a climactic concluding woe (Blomberg 1992a: 343; Garland 1993: 231; Sabourin 1978: 294–95). Each woe—except the third, which addresses "blind guides" (23:16)—is spoken to the "scribes and Pharisees, hypocrites." The first two woes follow the simple format of a pronouncement followed by the reason, but the others develop the reason in various ways. The third woe contains a refutation of the religious leaders' casuistic approach to oaths (23:17–22; cf. 5:33–37). The fourth woe castigates the leaders for not emphasizing the weightier matters (23:23c) and concludes with a second denunciation of the leaders as "blind guides" (23:24; cf. 23:16). The fifth woe adds a command that the leaders clean the inside of the cup first (23:26). The sixth woe develops the reason by explaining the metaphor of whitewashed tombs as portraying external righteousness that hides internal sin (23:28). The seventh and final woe develops the reason most fully by portraying the leaders' violent treatment of Jesus and his disciples as the culmination of Israel's history of rejecting its own prophets (23:31–36). The woes can be displayed as follows:

The Seven Woes of Matt. 23:13–36

The first pair: Entering the kingdom
1. The leaders prevent access to God (23:13).[4]
2. The leaders make proselytes for Gehenna (23:15).

The second pair: Halakic matters
3. The leaders mislead the people concerning oaths (23:16–22).
4. The leaders neglect the weightier matters of the Torah (23:23–24).

The third pair: Internal versus external matters
5. The leaders clean only the outside of the cup (23:25–26).
6. The leaders are like whitewashed tombs (23:27–28).

The climactic conclusion
7. The leaders culminate a history of rejecting the prophets (23:29–36).

---

3. There are eight woes if 23:14 is authentic, but it is unlikely that this verse was a part of the original text of Matthew. See the additional note on 23:14.

4. As stated, the textual authenticity of 23:14 is doubtful. Whatever its authenticity, 23:14 resonates with the prevalent prophetic theme of justice for widows (cf., e.g., Deut. 10:18; 14:29; 27:19; Prov. 15:25; Isa. 1:23; 5:8; James 1:27).

The unit outline is as follows:

i. The first pair of woes: Entering the kingdom (23:13, 15)
  (1) The first woe (23:13)
  (2) The second woe (23:15)
ii. The second pair of woes: Halakic matters (23:16–24)
  (1) The third woe (23:16–22)
  (2) The fourth woe (23:23–24)
iii. The third pair of woes: Internal versus external matters (23:25–28)
  (1) The fifth woe (23:25–26)
  (2) The sixth woe (23:27–28)
iv. The climactic seventh woe: Rejecting the prophets (23:29–36)
  (1) The woe proper (23:29–30)
  (2) Jesus as the ultimate rejected prophet (23:31–33)
  (3) Jesus promises judgment (23:34–36)

Exegesis and Exposition

[13]"But woe to you, scribes and Pharisees, hypocrites, because you shut off the kingdom of heaven from people; for you do not enter yourselves, and you do not permit those who are trying to enter to get in.

[14]⌜"Woe to you, scribes and Pharisees, hypocrites, because you devour widows' properties, and you make long prayers for a pretext; therefore you will receive more severe condemnation.⌝

[15]"Woe to you, scribes and Pharisees, hypocrites, because you travel over sea and land to make one proselyte; yet you make the proselyte twice as much a child of hell as yourselves.

[16]"Woe to you, blind guides, who say, 'Whoever swears by the temple is not obligated; but whoever swears by the gold of the temple is obligated.' [17]You fools and blind men! Which is more important, the gold or the temple that sanctifies the gold?

[18]"And, 'Whoever swears by the altar is not obligated, but whoever swears by the offering on it is obligated.' [19]⌜You blind men⌝, which is more important, the offering or the altar that sanctifies the offering? [20]Therefore whoever swears by the altar swears by it and by everything on it. [21]And whoever swears by the temple swears both by the temple and by him who dwells in it. [22]And whoever swears by heaven swears by the throne of God and by him who sits upon it.

[23]"Woe to you, scribes and Pharisees, hypocrites! For you tithe mint and dill and cummin, yet you have neglected the weightier matters of the law: justice and mercy and faithfulness. These you should have done without ⌜neglecting⌝ the others. [24]You blind guides, who strain out a gnat and swallow a camel!

[25]"Woe to you, scribes and Pharisees, hypocrites! For you clean the outside of the cup and of the dish, but inside they are full of greed and ⌜self-indulgence⌝.

²⁶You blind Pharisee, first clean the inside ⌜of the cup and of the dish, so that the outside of it may also become⌝ clean.

²⁷"Woe to you, scribes and Pharisees, hypocrites! For you are like whitewashed tombs that look beautiful on the outside, but inside they are full of the bones of the dead and all uncleanness. ²⁸So you, too, look righteous on the outside to people, but inside you are full of hypocrisy and lawlessness.

²⁹"Woe to you, scribes and Pharisees, hypocrites! For you build the tombs of the prophets and adorn the graves of the righteous. ³⁰And you say, 'If we had been living in the days of our ancestors, we would not have taken part with them in shedding the blood of the prophets.' ³¹So you testify against yourselves that you are descendants of those who murdered the prophets. ³²So fill up the measure of your fathers! ³³You snakes, you offspring of vipers, how will you escape from the judgment of hell?

³⁴"Therefore, behold, I am sending you prophets and wise men and scribes. Some of them you will kill and crucify, and others you will flog in your synagogues and persecute from town to town, ³⁵so that upon you may come all the righteous blood shed on earth, from the blood of righteous Abel to the blood of Zechariah, the son of Berechiah, whom you murdered between the temple and the altar. ³⁶Truly I tell you, all these things will come upon this generation."

i. The First Pair of Woes: Entering the Kingdom (23:13, 15)

(1) The First Woe (23:13)

Here seven prophetic denunciations of the Pharisees begin (23:13, 15, 16, 23, 25, 27, 29; cf. 11:21; 18:7; 24:19; 26:24). The first two woes contain the charge that the scribes and Pharisees, who claim to open the door to God, in fact keep people out of the kingdom. Ironically, they "are not leaders but misleaders" (W. Davies and Allison 1997: 285). It is not only that they do not enter the kingdom; they also prevent others from doing so.[5] This amounts to rank hypocrisy. The description here is similar to that of Jer. 23:2 and Ezek. 34:2–8, which compare the leaders of Israel to shepherds who feed themselves and scatter the flock.

23:13

The Charge of Hypocrisy

Hypocrisy is mentioned fourteen times in Matthew (6:2, 5, 16; 7:5; 15:7; 22:18; 23:13, 14, 15, 23, 25, 27, 29; 24:51). The various Greek words in the "hypocrite" group come not from the Hebrew Bible but from the Greco-Roman world, describing someone who gives an answer, interprets an oracle, mimics another person, or acts a part in a drama. At times the idea of pretending in order to deceive is present, but the word itself

---

5. Τοὺς εἰσερχομένους should probably be taken as conative, implying that the Pharisees prevent those who are *attempting* to enter from entering the kingdom (Wallace 1996: 534–35).

does not have a negative connotation (BDAG 1038; Wilckens, *TDNT* 8:559–71). In Matthew hypocrites are those who live for fleeting human applause rather than for eternal divine approval (Matt. 6:2, 5, 16). Hypocrites honor God outwardly, but their hearts are far from God (15:7–8). Hypocrites feign sincerity when questioning Jesus with evil intent (22:18). They say one thing but do another (23:3; cf. Rom. 2:21–24). In Matthew hypocrisy entails religious fraud, a basic discrepancy between outwardly righteous behavior and evil thoughts or motives (R. H. Smith in J. Green and McKnight 1992: 352).

For Matthew, Isa. 29:13 is the most important prophetic text on hypocrisy. This passage concerns the religious leaders (Isa. 29:1, 10, 14, 20–21) of Jerusalem ("Ariel"; 29:1, 2, 7). The fraud perpetrated here concerns apparently pious words and traditional rulings that in reality disguise hearts that are far from God and plans that are thought to be hidden from God's sight (29:15). Israel's charismatic leaders, the prophets, are mute (29:10–12) and its judges are corrupt (29:20–21). In spite of this, Israel's outward religious observances go on (29:1). In Matt. 15:7–9 Jesus applies this passage to certain Pharisees and scribes who insist on the ritual washing of hands before meals but dishonor their parents by the fraudulent corban claim that what might have been given to the parents had already been promised to God (15:5). For Jesus, this traditional practice sets aside God's law (15:6). Additionally, the practice of ritual washing of hands fundamentally errs, viewing defilement as coming from external sources rather than from an evil heart (15:11–20). Jesus's rebuke of hypocrisy is deeply rooted in the Scriptures and is similar to rebukes found in Second Temple literature.[6] (See Garland 1979: 91–123.)

23:14 See additional note.

(2) The Second Woe (23:15)

23:15 The second woe builds on the theme of the first. The leaders' efforts to convert others (cf. Acts 2:11; 6:5; 13:43) are tragically ironic. It is not clear whether this should be understood as a project to convert Gentiles to Judaism or to convert fellow Jews to Pharisaism, or even as including both projects. McKnight (1991: 106–8) concludes that the Pharisees did not actively pursue gentile converts but urged "God-fearing" Gentiles (cf. Acts 10:2, 22, 35; 13:16, 26, 43, 50; 16:14; 17:4, 17; 18:7) to become full converts to Judaism and observe the Pharisaic traditions. The descrip-

---

6. Isa. 48:1–2; 58:1–5; Jer. 3:10; 7:4–11; 12:2; Ezek. 33:30–33; Mic. 3:11; Mal. 1:6–14; Pss. 50:16–23; 78:36–37. Cf. Ps. Sol. 4.19–20; As. Mos. 7; 1QS 4.10. Later talmudic discussions of seven types of Pharisees, of whom only the one who acted out of love was approved, are also illuminating. See *y. Ber.* 14b; *y. Soṭah* 20c; *b. Soṭah* 22b, 41b–42a; Mason 1990. Later rabbinic literature also condemns hypocrisy (e.g., *t. Yoma* 5.12; *b. Soṭah* 41b–42a; *b. Pesaḥ.* 113b; Esth. Rab. 1.17).

tion of the extent of their efforts ("sea and land") recalls Jon. 1:9; Hag. 2:6, 21 ("the heavens and the earth").[7] Since the leaders themselves are not entering the kingdom, their efforts result only in preventing others from entering it. Their converts do not become children of the kingdom (Matt. 8:12; 18:3) but of gehenna (5:22, 29–30; 10:28; 18:9; 23:33). The leaders do more harm than good (Keener 1999: 547).

ii. The Second Pair of Woes: Halakic Matters (23:16–24)

(1) The Third Woe (23:16–22)

The first two woes deal with the general matter of preventing access to the kingdom, but the next two speak of specific legal rulings, or hala-koth. This third woe regarding oaths is the most extensively developed of the seven oracles (cf. 5:33–37). It contains (1) a pronouncement of woe (23:16a); (2) the reason for the woe, two false Pharisaic distinctions in oaths (23:16b, 18); (3) two rhetorical questions that expose the respective distinctions (23:17, 19); and (4) three concluding positive statements on oaths (23:20–22). The rather intricate chiastic symmetry that occurs here is partially displayed by W. Davies and Allison (1997: 289).

The bitingly sarcastic expression "blind guides" is repeated in 23:24 (cf. 15:14). Jesus condemns the casuistry of these oaths as an evasion of duty before God (cf. 15:4–6). Two different loopholes based on empty distinctions are exposed, one in 23:16–17 concerning the temple and the gold (Josephus, *Ant.* 14.34–36, 72, 106, 110; 15.395; *J.W.* 5.201–10, 222; *Ag. Ap.* 2.84) within it and another in 23:18–19 concerning the altar and what is offered on it. Although the leaders view some oaths as binding and others as nonbinding, Jesus rejects this as empty casuistry and teaches that all oaths are valid (23:20–22). Previously Jesus has flatly denied the need for any oaths (5:33–37), even though oaths and vows were very important in Second Temple Judaism (*m. Ned.*; CD 15; 16.6–12).

23:16–19

Three conclusions are drawn here from the preceding two examples. In oaths there is no valid distinction between the altar and what is offered on it (23:20, against 23:18). Neither is there a difference between the temple and the One who dwells in it (23:21; against 23:16). Finally, there is no difference between heaven, the throne of God, and God who sits on it (23:22; cf. 5:34). One may not lessen one's obligation to be true to one's word by such facile distinctions. These profane God's name, since their surrogates for God nevertheless represent God (Keener 1999: 549). Integrity demands that one does what one says one will do.

23:20–22

7. On Jewish proselytism, see *m. 'Abot* 1.1, 12; Josephus, *Ant.* 20.17, 34–48; *Ag. Ap.* 2.210; Jos. Asen. 8–11; *b. Šabb.* 31a; Tacitus, *Hist.* 5.5; Dio Cassius, *Roman History* 57.18.5; Horace, *Satires* 1.4.141–44; Braude 1940; Cohen 1983; Feldman 2003; A.-J. Levine and Pervo 1998; Porton 1994.

(2) The Fourth Woe (23:23–24)

23:23–24 The Pharisees are condemned here not for tithing herbs (viewed as a crop; Lev. 27:30; Deut. 14:22–23; cf. *m. Šeb.* 9.1; Keener 1999: 550) but for tithing herbs without attending to the law's weightier matters (cf. Luke 11:42). It is not that tithing herbs is unimportant but that justice, mercy, and faithfulness are *more* important. This is not a hierarchical ethic but an incisive teaching that prioritizes the central values supporting the specific legal obligation (cf. Hos. 6:6; Matt. 9:13; 12:7; Mic. 6:8; Zech. 7:9–10). In terms of the hyperbolic metaphor of 23:24, the Pharisees scrupulously strain out gnats (tithing herbs) but should be more concerned to avoid swallowing camels (omitting the weightier matters). Perhaps this involves a pun, since one of the Aramaic words for "gnat" (קַלְמָא, *qalmāʾ*) sounds much like the Aramaic word for "camel" (גַּמְלָא, *gamlāʾ*; M. Black 1967: 175–76). This may also imply the leaders' inconsistency, since both gnats and camels are unclean and not to be eaten (Lev. 11:4, 23, 41).

iii. The Third Pair of Woes: Internal versus External Matters (23:25–28)

(1) The Fifth Woe (23:25–26)

23:25–26 The fifth and sixth woes together address the matter of the Pharisaic neglect of internal matters. Here the leaders are described as those who clean the outside of tableware but neglect the inside (cf. Luke 11:39–41; Gos. Thom. 89; Maccoby 1982; Neusner 1976). Despite their zeal for the Torah and their traditions, they are characterized by greed and self-indulgence (cf. As. Mos. 7.5–10; Ps. Sol. 4.1–5). W. Davies and Allison (1997: 296–99) are probably correct (contra Garland 1979: 141–50; Neusner 1976) that Jesus is not disputing existing Pharisaic tradition here (cf. *m. Kelim* 25.1–9) but is simply using the washing of tableware metaphorically (cf. Blomberg 1992a: 347; Keener 1999: 552). Pharisaic fastidiousness about such matters renders the metaphor fitting, but Jesus is not critiquing fastidiousness per se. Jesus's critique of those whose external focus causes them to neglect internal matters agrees with certain talmudic insights (*b. Ber.* 28a; *b. Yoma* 72b).

(2) The Sixth Woe (23:27–28)

23:27–28 The sixth woe continues the theme of heart piety as opposed to mere outward piety. Jesus turns from the tableware metaphor to the macabre simile of tombs (cf. Luke 11:44; Acts 23:3). Tombs are beautifully adorned on the outside, but inside are bones and decaying corpses, which ritually defile according to Pharisaic tradition.[8] Similarly, the scribes and Pharisees appear to men as righteous, but their hearts are full of hypocrisy and lawlessness. For Jesus, obedience to the law must emanate from the heart. Outwardly lawful behavior may conceal a lawless heart (Matt. 5:8, 20, 22, 28; 6:1; 7:22–23; 12:34; 13:41; 15:7–9, 19; 18:35; 22:37; 24:12, 48). It is not clear whether the whitewash on the tombs is intended to further beautify their architecture or to indicate that the bones inside are a cause of ritual impurity (W. Davies and Allison 1997: 300–302; Derrett 1986b; Garland 1979: 152–57; Jeremias 1958; Lachs 1975b).

iv. The Climactic Seventh Woe: Rejecting the Prophets (23:29–36)

(1) The Woe Proper (23:29–30)

The simile of tombs (23:27) links the sixth woe to the seventh. But these tombs belong to the prophets murdered by the leaders' ancestors.[9] The leaders beautify the tombs and claim that they would have had no part with their ancestors in killing those who now occupy the tombs (see Derrett in Cross 1968: 187–93). This seventh woe is climactic in that it addresses the root of the problems already addressed. If Israel had listened to the prophets, it would not have had to face the consequences announced by the prophets.

23:29–30

(2) Jesus as the Ultimate Rejected Prophet (23:31–33)

Jesus points out that the leaders' denial of complicity in the murder of the prophets unwittingly implicates them in the guilt of their ancestors (cf. Luke 11:47–48). Their admission that they are the descendants (υἱοί, huioi) of murderers implies inherited character traits, not just physical descent.[10] Modern sayings about a "chip off the old block" or "An apple does not fall far from the tree" speak to the same point. Jesus's ironic imperative,[11] "Fill up the measure of your fathers!" should be understood

23:31–33

---

8. On corpse impurity, see Num. 6:6–8; 19:11–12; *m. Kelim* 1.4; *m. ʾOhol.* 17.1–18.6; *m. Šeqal.* 1.1; *m. Moʿed Qaṭ.* 1.2; *m. Maʿaś. Š.* 5.1; 4Q274 frg. 1.1.9; 4Q397–99 2.80–82; Josephus, *Ag. Ap.* 2.205.

9. For references to well-known tombs, see Acts 2:29; 1 Macc. 13:27–30; Josephus, *Ant.* 7.390–92; 13.249; 18.108; 20.95; *J.W.* 4.531–32.

10. This metaphorical use of υἱός (cf. 8:12; 9:15; 12:27; 13:38; 23:15; Mark 3:17, 28; Luke 16:8; 20:34, 36; John 12:36; 17:12; Acts 4:36; 13:10; Eph. 2:2–3; Col. 3:6; 1 Thess. 5:5; 2 Thess. 2:3) is a Hebraism (cf. בֵּן in, e.g., Num. 17:25; 24:17; Deut. 25:2; 1 Sam. 14:52; 26:16; 2 Sam. 3:34; 1 Kings 20:35; Pss. 79:11; 89:23; 102:21; Prov. 31:5; Isa. 5:1; Amos 7:14; Zech. 4:14). Cf. CD 6.15; 1QM 1.1; Ps. Sol. 17.15; Fohrer, *TDNT* 8:345–47.

11. Such imperatives are ironic because they challenge hearers to do wrong and amount to a threat of consequences if the command is obeyed. Cf. 1 Kings 2:22; 18:27; 22:15; Judg. 10:14; Job 38:3; 40:10; Isa. 6:9; 8:9–10; 29:9; 47:12; Jer. 7:21; 23:28; 44:25; Lam. 4:21; Ezek. 3:27; 20:39; Amos 4:4–5; 5:5; Nah. 3:14–15; Rev. 22:11; GKC §110; Robertson 1934: 948, 1198; Waltke and O'Connor 1990 §34.4b; Winer 1882: 391.

as an aspect of Matthew's characteristic motif of biblical fulfillment. Jesus's words are tantamount to a command to kill him, but their point is to underline the certainty of impending judgment. He speaks of his impending crucifixion as the culmination of Israel's historical pattern of rejecting its own prophets.[12] Jesus's epithets in Matt. 23:33 recall 3:7; 12:34. The sobering "judgment of hell" recalls 5:22, 29, 30; 10:28; 18:9; 23:15.

(3) Jesus Promises Judgment (23:34–36)

23:34 This section takes the rejection of God's messengers further to the persecution of Jesus's disciples after his death. This completes the seventh woe but also provides a conclusion for all seven woes. As the murder of the prophets anticipated Jesus's crucifixion, so the murder of Jesus augurs the persecution of his followers (cf. 10:16–33; 20:23; Acts 7:52; 12:1–3; cf. Hawthorne in Hawthorne and Betz 1987: 119–33). The murder of Jesus will bring horrible judgment because it is the ultimate atrocity in an atrocious sequence that began when Cain murdered his brother Abel (Gen. 4:8–16). Jesus solemnly reaffirms that the wicked generation that rejected him (Matt. 11:16; 12:39, 41, 42, 45; 16:4; 17:17; 24:34) will bear the brunt of the woes he has just uttered.

23:35–36 This generation's leaders are in solidarity with those who murdered Zechariah, and so it is as if they did it themselves. The final woe and its allusion to Zechariah (23:35; cf. 2 Chron. 24:21) assume that Jesus is the climactic prophet of God. Abel (Gen. 4:8–10; Heb. 11:4; 1 John 3:12; Josephus, *Ant.* 1.53; *L.A.B.* 16.2; Jub. 4.3; 1 En. 22.6–7) and Zechariah were the first and last martyrs of the Hebrew Bible, which ends not with Malachi but with 2 Chronicles. The mention of the martyrdom of Zechariah the son of Berechiah (Zech. 1:1) causes some problems in identification, but clearly Matthew has in mind the murder of Zechariah the son of Jehoida in 2 Chron. 24:21.[13]

---

12. See the discussion under "Fulfillment" in the introduction to this commentary. The motif of sin coming to its full measure is found elsewhere. Cf. Gen. 15:16; 2 Kings 21:10–15; Dan. 8:23; 9:24; 4Q387 frg. 3.2.13–14; 11QT 59.8–9; *L.A.B.* 26.13; 2 Macc. 6:14; Jub. 14.16; Acts 7:52; 1 Thess. 2:14–16; Heb. 11:32–38; Rev. 6:10–11.

13. Gundry 1994: 471 suggests that Matthew's literary-theological purpose leads him to conflate the postexilic prophet Zechariah (Zech. 1:1; cf. 11:12–13, cited in Matt. 27:9–10) and the preexilic martyr Zechariah (2 Chron. 24:20). Yet another prominent Zechariah, the son of Baris, was murdered in the temple by Zealots during the first Jewish War (Josephus, *J.W.* 4.334–44). Harrington 1991: 328 and Overman 1996: 323 favor this third Zechariah. Some in the early church mistakenly held that Matt. 23:35 referred to the purported martyrdom, in the temple, of Zecharias the father of John the Baptist (Prot. Jas. 23–24). See Blomberg 1987b: 193–95; W. Davies and Allison 1997: 318–19; Gundry 1967: 86–88; Hagner 1995a: 676–77; Ross 1987. On the death of Zechariah in rabbinic sources, see Blank 1937–38.

The Charge of Rejecting the Prophets

Jesus's charge that Israel has rejected its own prophets (23:29–31) is the most serious accusation found in Matt. 23, since it addresses the root cause of the other problems. This is not the first time Matthew points out that Israel has rejected its prophets. The genealogy of Jesus stresses the exile to Babylon, which was due to rejection of the prophets (1:11–12, 17). The ministry of John the Baptist is presented in terms of prophetic rebuke (3:7–12), and Israel's rejection of John is the rejection of an Elijah-like figure who is more than a prophet (11:7–18; 17:12; 21:32). Jesus's disciples, when persecuted, are to be encouraged because the prophets were similarly persecuted (5:12). Response to Jesus's disciples is described as response to a prophet (10:41–42; 25:35–45). Jesus repeatedly cites the prophets, at times with an introduction stressing his incredulity at the Jewish leaders' ignorance (9:13; 12:7; 13:14–15; 15:7–9; 21:13, 16, 33, 42). All these factors combine to build the case that Israel has rejected its prophets.

This charge that Israel has rejected its prophets echoes many similar biblical statements.[14] Israel disobeyed the law and rejected the prophets whom God sent to remind the people of their obligations (Deut. 28:15–46; 1 Kings 8:46–53). Notable individuals who rejected the prophets include Ahab and Jezebel (1 Kings 18–19; 22), Amaziah (Amos 7:10–17), Pashhur (Jer. 20), Jehoiakim (Jer. 26:20–23), and Zedekiah (Jer. 37–38). The rejection of the prophets is also regularly mentioned in Second Temple literature.[15] Materials from Qumran also refer to Israel's rejection of the prophets.[16] The martyrdom of Zechariah the son of Berechiah (23:35) is also recounted in later rabbinic literature.[17] Matthew's use of this story is not unlike that of the rabbinic materials in that the murder of Zechariah is a particularly egregious sin, one for which the victim implored God's retribution. For Matthew as well as for the rabbis, this retribution is put into the context of lament over the destruction of Jerusalem.[18]

Additional Notes

23:14. It is likely that 23:14 is an interpolation from Mark 12:40; Luke 20:47. It is omitted by א, B, D, L, Θ, *f*[1], 33, 205, 892*. Certain MSS include 23:14 after 23:13 (0233, *f*[13]), but others reverse the order (W, Δ, 0102, 0107, 28, *Byz, Lect*).

14. See, e.g., 2 Chron. 24:17–22; 25:16; 36:15–16; Dan. 9:6, 10; Isa. 30:10; Jer. 7:25–26; 25:4; 26:5; Amos 2:12; 7:12–13; Neh. 9:26, 30.
15. See, e.g., Jub. 1.12–14; 4 Bar. 1.1–8; 9.19–31; Liv. Pro. 1–3; 6–7; 15; 23; Martyrdom and Ascension of Isaiah; Tob. 14:3–7; Josephus, *Ant.* 14.22–24.
16. See, e.g., CD 7.17–18; 4Q166 frg. 1.2.1–6 (on Hos. 2:10); 4Q266 frg. 3.2.18–19; 4Q390 frg. 2.1.5.
17. Lam. Rab. (proem 5, 23; cf. 1.16.51; 2.2.4; 2.20.23; 4.13.16); Midr. Tanḥuma on Lev. 4:1; Eccles. Rab. 3.16; 10.4; Targum Lam. 2:20; *y. Ta'an.* 69a; *b. Giṭ.* 57b; *b. Sanh.* 96b.
18. On the rejection of the prophets, see Amaru 1983; Knowles 1993; Miller 1988; O. Steck 1967; van Tilborg 1972b: 46–72.

23:19. The short reading τυφλοί (supported by ℵ, D, L, Z, Θ, *f*¹, 205, 892) may be preferable to the long reading μωροὶ καὶ τυφλοί (supported by B, C, W, Δ, 0102, 0233, *f*¹³, 28, 33, *Byz, Lect*), which could be based on 23:17.

23:23. The present infinitive ἀφιέναι (C, D, W, Δ, Θ, 0102, *f*¹, *f*¹³, 28, 33, *Byz, Lect*) is more widely supported than the aorist infinitive ἀφεῖναι (ℵ, B, L, 892). It is not clear whether the change was intentional or accidental.

23:25. The UBS⁴ reading ἀκρασίας is strongly supported by ℵ, B, D, L, Δ, Θ, 0102, *f*¹, *f*¹³, 33, 205. The best of the other readings is ἀδικίας, supported by C, 28, *Byz, Lect*.

23:26. The D rating in UBS⁴ indicates the extreme difficulty of arriving at the correct text of this verse. The UBS⁴ editors slightly favor the shorter text, τοῦ ποτηρίου, ἵνα γένηται καὶ τὸ ἐκτὸς αὐτοῦ, supported by Θ, *f*¹, 205, 700 (D has ἔξωθεν instead of ἐκτός). The evidence for the longer reading, τοῦ ποτηρίου καὶ τῆς παροψίδος, ἵνα γένηται καὶ τὸ ἐκτὸς αὐτοῦ, is more impressive (B*, E*, G, *f*¹³, 28, 157; ℵ², B², C, L, W, 0102, 33, 180, *Byz, Lect* have αὐτῶν instead of αὐτοῦ). The additional words of the longer reading (καὶ τῆς παροψίδος) may have been inserted from 23:25, but the external evidence for the longer reading outweighs this possibility.

c. Conclusion: Jesus's Lament over Jerusalem (23:37–39)

Jesus's lament over Jerusalem contains four parts: (1) a touching address (23:37a; cf. Jer. 13:27); (2) a striking exclamation describing the clash of his will with that of Jerusalem's children (Matt. 23:37b–c); (3) an awful warning of divine abandonment (23:38); and (4) a bittersweet promise that the abandonment will cease only when Jerusalem genuinely understands Ps. 118:26, the text shouted by the crowd at the triumphal entry (Matt. 23:39; cf. 21:9).

This tender lament is a remarkable and surprising conclusion to the sustained intense denunciation of the religious leaders. Jesus's compassion is palpable (cf. 9:36; 11:28; 14:14; 15:32; 18:27, 33; 20:34). Other touching biblical laments (e.g., 2 Sam. 1:17–27; 18:33; 19:4; Rom. 9:1–5; Rev. 18:10, 16, 18–19) pale in comparison with this one. Jesus is deeply moved for his people and for his city despite the ongoing opposition of its leaders and the horrible sufferings that are still ahead. Christians today must ponder Jesus's compassion for his people and reflect on their own level of concern for Jews. An arrogant attitude toward non-Christians is always inappropriate, but it is especially despicable when it concerns the Jewish people (cf. Rom. 10:1; 11:16–24).

Exegesis and Exposition

[37]"Jerusalem, Jerusalem, that kills the prophets and stones those who are sent to it! How often I wanted to gather your children together as a hen gathers her chicks under her wings, but you were not willing. [38]Behold, your house is left to you, ⌜abandoned⌝! [39]For I tell you, you will never see me again until you say, 'Blessed is he who comes in the name of the Lord!'"

This is "the climax of Jesus's public ministry to Israel" (Garland 1993: 232). Although 23:37–39 changes the tone from accusation to lament, the element of lament is not entirely lacking in 23:13–36. These final public words of Jesus to his contemporaries articulate unspeakable sadness at their refusal to respond to his words and deeds (cf. Luke 13:34–35). The feminine image of the hen and chicks strikingly portrays divine protection (cf. Exod. 19:4; Deut. 32:10–11; Ruth 2:12; Pss. 17:8; 36:7; 57:1; 61:4; 63:7; 91:1–4; Isa. 31:5; 1 En. 39.7; 2 Bar. 41.4).

23:37

23:38–39 The desolation of "your house" in 23:38 probably refers to the temple (21:13; 24:1–3, 15; cf. 1 Kings 9:7–8; Isa. 64:10–11; Jer. 26:6; 2 Bar. 8.2; Jdt. 9:13), although it may be a metaphor for Jerusalem or the nation itself (Matt. 22:7; Jer. 12:7; 1 En. 89.56). The temple, along with the city, represents the life and destiny of the entire nation (Garland 1979: 98–100). Some scholars take Matt. 23:39 as stressing only the certainty of judgment (e.g., Garland 1979: 204–9; Meier 1980b: 274–75), but the image of the hen gathering her chicks (23:37) speaks of compassion, not rejection (W. Davies and Allison 1997: 323–24; Garland 1993: 232–33). There is a glimmer of hope for salvation if only Israel will acknowledge Jesus to be its Messiah. Israel has sinned in rejecting Jesus, and there will be punishment for that sin. But here as throughout biblical history, repentance after sin and judgment brings grace and redemption (cf. Rom. 11:1–2, 11–12, 15, 23–27). Jesus will return only when Israel in true repentance utters the words that were uttered without adequate understanding in Matt. 21:9. (See Allison 1983; Bruner 1990: 835–37.)

This passage illustrates the mysterious relationship between divine sovereignty and human responsibility. Jesus wished (ἠθέλησα, *ēthelēsa*) to gather the people of Jerusalem, but they did not wish (οὐκ ἠθελήσατε, *ouk ēthelēsate*) to be gathered (cf. 22:3; Acts 7:51). Yet in Matt. 11:27 Jesus accomplishes his purpose in revealing the Father to whomever he wills (cf. 16:17). Despite the judgment announced in 23:38, the tension continues into the future according to the conditional prophecy in 23:39 (Allison 1983). Until the people of Jerusalem utter the words of Ps. 118:26 in faith, they will not see Jesus again. But when they do bless the one who comes in the name of the Lord, they will receive the eschatological blessings they have previously rejected.[1]

Matthew 23, Anti-Semitism, and Jewish-Christian Relations

Matthew 23 has been called "a unique, unparalleled specimen of invective" (Sandmel 1978: 68), and "a mass of vituperation" that Christians are not obligated to defend (Beare 1981: 461). Jesus's disputes with the religious leaders are presented boldly throughout Matthew, and these disputes now come to a head in Matt. 23. These strident denunciations are admittedly disturbing. But heated rhetoric in the service of religious disputes was the norm in ancient times (L. Johnson 1989; Saldarini

---

1. Scholars who see a significant future Jewish turning to Jesus in 23:37–39 include Bruner 1990: 835–37; Garland 1992: 232–33; Keener 1999: 558–59; Nolland 2005: 952–53. Others take Jerusalem's desolation as irreversibly final: Calvin 1972: 3.71; Hare 1993: 272; Meier 1980b: 275; Senior 1975: 208. Stanton 1992b: 247–55 argues that 23:39 does teach the prospect of Israel's future faith in Jesus, and views this teaching as similar to the Deuteronomistic pattern of sin, exile, and return found in the Bible and Second Temple literature. Cf. Ezek. 36:33; Amos 9:8–12; Tob. 13:6; Jub. 1.15–18. See the discussion of Second Temple models of Israel's restoration and "destruction of the nation–preservation of the remnant" soteriology in M. Elliott 2000: 515–637.

1992a). Such rhetoric had been used in Jewish circles from the days of the biblical prophets. It continued in the Second Temple period as various Jewish groups critiqued the religious establishment in Jerusalem. The introduction to this commentary argues that Matthew writes before the final tragic "parting of the ways" between the church and Judaism. Christianity, viewed today as a separate religion from Judaism, was still a sect of the diverse Judaism(s) of the period before the destruction of the temple in 70 CE. Therefore Matthew must not be viewed anachronistically as a Christian outsider rebuking the Jews but as a Christian Jew engaged in a vigorous intramural dispute with other Jews over the identity of the Jewish prophet Jesus.[2]

In this view, Matthew is not attacking Jews or Judaism like a Gentile who claims that his new religion has superseded the outdated religion of the Jews. This mistaken approach may be traced to the polemical writings of certain patristic authors, but it is anachronistic to find it in Matthew on the lips of Jesus. Rather, Matthew presents Jesus's dispute with the religious leaders as a thoroughly *Jewish* prophetic critique calling for a return to biblical values. This is in no way an attack on the Jews as a people at that time, let alone for all time. Jesus's stringent critique is directed against certain scribes and Pharisees who were prominent at that time in the Jerusalem religious establishment. No doubt the polemic critique is ferocious, but as W. Davies and Allison (1997: 261) put it, Matt. 23 is "no more 'anti-Semitic' than the Dead Sea Scrolls." (Cf. S. Motyer 1997 for a similar discussion of the polemic of John's Gospel.)

The theological position outlined above must be conveyed with a sensitive spirit. Christians must care for Jewish people and grieve for the poor state of Jewish-Christian relations (23:37; Rom. 9:1–3). The sad history of Jewish-Christian relations gives Christians much to live down. Matthew 23, especially 23:8–12, is the best place to start a much-needed Christian character check. Matthew 23 must be read not only as a critique of Jerusalem's ancient leaders but also as a warning clearly intended for Jesus's disciples. "All of the vices here attributed to the scribes and Pharisees have attached themselves to Christians, and that in abundance" (W. Davies and Allison 1997: 262). But Christians of integrity who model themselves after their Jewish Messiah can begin to alleviate the damage done by the attitudes and atrocities that mar Jewish-Christian relations yet today.

Summary and Transition

At Jesus's entry into Jerusalem, the crowds shouted Ps. 118:25–26: "Blessed is he who comes in the name of the Lord" (Matt. 21:9) as the leaders looked on angrily. In 23:39 Jesus pronounces judgment upon

---

2. In support, see W. Davies and Allison 1997: 260–61; Harrington 1991: 303–5; Overman 1990b; 1996: 302–4; Saldarini 1994: 59–63; Sim 1998b: 148–49.

these same leaders and uses the same words that the crowds shouted a few days earlier. The sin of the leaders outlined in Matt. 23 is made all the more egregious by their official capacity: they "sit in Moses's seat." This is the context in which Jesus will speak his final discourse. The impressive temple precinct where the bankrupt leadership officiates will be totally destroyed by a desolating sacrilege before Jesus comes again and the nation genuinely turns to him with the words "Blessed is he who comes in the name of the Lord."

Additional Note

23:38. The longer reading, which ends the verse with ἔρημος, appears to cite Jer. 22:5. It is impressively supported by ℵ, C, D, W, Δ, Θ, 0102, *f*¹, *f*¹³, 33, *Byz, Lect.* The shorter reading, without ἔρημος, conforms to the UBS⁴ text of Luke 13:35 but is not as well supported (B, L).

VI. Opposition Comes to a Head in Judea (19:3–26:2)
    A. Narrative 5: Ministry in Judea (19:3–23:39)
➤ B. Discourse 5: Judgment of Jerusalem and the Coming of Christ (24:1–26:2)

B. Discourse 5: Judgment of Jerusalem and the Coming of Christ (24:1–26:2)

Structure of the Olivet Discourse

Jesus's final discourse answers the disciples' questions (24:1–3) with an initial didactic section (24:4–35) followed by exhortations (24:36–25:46) on alertness (24:36–25:13), trustworthiness (25:14–30), and compassion (25:31–46). Jesus first warns his disciples that they will face traumatic yet not terminal circumstances (24:4–14). These will include messianic pretenders (24:4–5), warfare (24:6–7a), famines and earthquakes (24:7b), persecution (24:9), apostasy (24:10), and false prophets (24:11). Their responsibility is not to be misled (24:4), to realize that the end is not yet (24:6), and to persevere in discipleship and mission (24:13–14). These, "the beginning of birth pains" (24:8), will evidently characterize the entire period between the comings of Jesus (Blomberg 1992a: 353–54; Carson 1984: 495; Hagner 1995a: 684–85).

In 24:15 the language turns from ominous to grave with the allusion to Daniel's "desolating sacrilege" (Dan. 9:27; 11:31; 12:11). This time of great tribulation is unprecedented and will never be equaled (Matt. 24:21, 29; cf. Dan. 12:1; Joel 2:2; Rev. 7:14). It is best to take this section (Matt. 24:15–28), with its emphasis on Judea (24:16), as envisioning the destruction of the temple in 70 CE, which anticipates the ultimate judgment that ends the present world.

The coming of Jesus to judge humanity after this tribulation is described with standard biblical apocalyptic imagery in 24:29–31. Jesus uses the fig tree as a parabolic image to stress the urgency and certainty of his coming (24:32–35). At 24:36 the tone becomes more paraenetic with the stress shifting from "What will happen?" to "So what?" *That* Jesus will come is certain although *when* he will come is unknowable. Thus Jesus emphasizes alertness in the allusion to Noah's time (24:36–42) and in three parabolic images: (1) a thief in the night (24:43–44), (2) faithful and evil slaves (24:45–51), and (3) wise and foolish bridesmaids (25:1–13). A further parable emphasizes faithful use of God's gifts (25:14–30). The discourse ends with a vivid portrayal of the last judgment (25:31–46), which indicates that Jesus is still concerned for the "little ones."

The Olivet Discourse makes it clear that biblical prophecy is more than mere prediction. The knowledge of what God will do in the future (24:1–35) must have a profound effect upon God's people in the present (24:36–25:46). A genuine grasp of this prophetic Scripture will not lead to date setting but to alertness, faithfulness, fruitfulness, and service to Jesus's most needy disciples. As W. Davies and Allison (1997: 337) put it, "The question 'when' does not elicit a date but helps to maintain the disciples' faith" (cf. Keener 1999: 566–67; Ladd 1974: 326–28).[1]

Major Views of the Discourse

A crucial interpretive question concerns the relationship of the destruction of the temple in 70 CE to the ultimate eschatological judgment of God. There are three basic views, with shades of difference within each of them. The *preterist* (past) view holds that most or all of the predictions in the discourse were fulfilled in 70 CE, when the Romans quashed the Jewish revolt by besieging Jerusalem and destroying the temple (France 1985: 333–34; Kik 1948; R. Sproul 1998; Tasker 1961: 223–24). Partial preterists take 24:1–35 as describing the destruction of Jerusalem in 70 CE, and 24:36–25:46 as referring to the coming of Jesus. Full or comprehensive preterists attempt to explain the entire discourse as fulfilled in 70 CE. The opposite, *futurist* approach understands the discourse to speak primarily, if not solely, of events just before the second coming of Jesus to the earth (Barbieri in Walvoord and Zuck 1983: 76–77; Toussaint 1980: 266–72; Walvoord 1974: 179–82). In Walvoord's view (1974: 182), Christ does not answer the first part of the disciples' question in 24:3, concerning the destruction of the temple. The preterist and futurist views are both reductionistic and cannot handle the complexities of the passage that stem from the disciples' dual question about the destruction of Jerusalem and the end of the world. A valid approach to the passage must handle both of these matters.

The *preterist-futurist* view understands the discourse as addressing both the historical destruction of Jerusalem and the yet-future coming of Jesus. Some advocates of this view interpret certain portions of the discourse as concerning 70 CE and other portions as concerning the end times. Others interpret the events of 70 CE as an anticipatory fulfillment of events that are consummated at Christ's coming (Barnes 1868: 251; Blomberg 1992a: 352; Carson 1984: 495; Hagner 1995a: 685). This viewpoint accepts the concept of prophetic perspective or foreshortening, in which more than one event fits the typology of the prophetic prediction. At times this has been called generic, double, multiple, or near-and-far fulfillment (Blomberg 2002; Broadus 1886: 479–80; Hendriksen 1973: 846–48; Ladd 1974: 310–11; D. Turner 1989).[2] The present commentary

---

1. On the structure of the discourse, see Agbanou 1983: 37–44; W. Davies and Allison 1997: 326–27, 374, 416–17; Lambrecht in Didier 1972: 309–42; Smit Sibinga 1975.

2. Kaiser (1982, 1988; Kaiser and Silva 1994: 143–45, 156–58) has argued that double-fulfillment language is tantamount to illegitimate double meanings. Kaiser prefers to speak of the prophet's intended meaning as fulfilled by successive yet generically related events. See D. Turner 1989: 13–17.

advocates this approach. Jesus answers both parts of the disciples' question. His prediction of the fall of the temple provides the reader with a picture that anticipates the eventual end of the world. (See W. Davies and Allison 1997: 328–33.)

The Discourse in Synoptic Perspective

As the table shows, Matthew's version of the discourse is much longer than that of Mark and Luke. The three synoptic treatments of the setting (item 1 in the table) and the beginning of birth pains (item 2) are similar. Matthew's version of the abomination of desolation (item 3) is slightly longer than Mark's, and Luke's section on armies around Jerusalem (21:20–24) is much shorter than either Matthew or Mark. Matthew's treatment of the coming of the Son of Man (item 4) is slightly longer than Mark's or Luke's. The three versions of the lesson of the fig tree (item 5) are similar, but Matthew has additional material on the days of Noah. The three versions of the necessity of alertness (item 6) are rather different, although of similar length. Matthew 24:45–25:46 (items 7–10), amounting to around half the discourse, has no parallel in Mark 13 or Luke 21.[3]

Brief Synopsis of the Olivet Discourse

Content	Matthew	Mark	Luke
1. Setting	24:1–3	13:1–4	21:5–7
2. Beginning of birth pains	24:4–14	13:5–13	21:8–19
3. Abomination of desolation	24:15–28	13:14–23	21:20–24
4. Coming of the Son of Man	24:29–31	13:24–27	21:25–27
5. Lesson of the fig tree	24:32–41	13:28–32	21:28–33
6. Necessity of alertness	24:42–44	13:33–37	21:34–36
7. Parable of the servant	24:45–51		
8. Parable of ten virgins	25:1–13		
9. Parable of the talents	25:14–30		
10. Judgment of the nations	25:31–46		

---

3. Among the numerous studies of the discourse, see esp. Agbanou 1983; Beasley-Murray 1993; Broer 1993b; S. Brown 1979; Burnett 1981; Carson 1984: 488–95; Dupont 1985b; Gaston 1970; Hahn in Schenke 1988: 107–26; Hartman 1966; Kümmel 1957; Marguerat 1981: 479–561; Monsarrat 1977; Reiser 1997; Scaer 2004: 343–93; W. Thompson 1974; D. Turner 1989; D. Wenham 1984.

1. Narrative Introduction: A Question While Leaving the Temple (24:1–3)

In 24:1 Jesus leaves the temple after repeated conflicts with various religious leaders (cf. 21:17). These confrontations demonstrate his authority and their unbelief (23:37). The disciples' preoccupation with the temple's grandeur is grossly out of place, given Jesus's recent words of judgment. They focus on the temple's glorious architecture, but Jesus speaks of its demolition (24:2). Jesus's answer to the disciples' question about the time of this destruction and his coming (24:3) is the Olivet Discourse, also called the eschatological discourse (24:4–25:46).

Exegesis and Exposition

[1]When Jesus had come out of the temple and was going away, his disciples came to point out the temple buildings to him. [2]So he asked them, "Do you not see all these things? I tell you truly, not even one stone here will be left upon another that will not be torn down." [3]And while he was sitting on the Mount of Olives, the disciples came to him privately and said, "Tell us, when will these things happen, and what will be the sign of your coming and of the end of the age?"

24:1–2   Jesus leaves the temple after summarily denouncing the scribes and Pharisees (cf. Mark 13:1–4; Luke 21:5–7). He has just announced the desolation of the temple, and so his departure has overtones of divine abandonment (cf. 1 Sam. 4:21–22; Jer. 12:7; Ezek. 8:12; 9:9; 11:23; 2 Bar. 8.1–2; 64.6; *L.A.B.* 19.2; against Nolland 2005: 958). As they walk east across the Kidron valley toward the Mount of Olives, the disciples surprisingly draw Jesus's attention to the impressive temple buildings.[1] Perhaps they wish to break the tension, or they find his prediction of judgment incredible (W. Davies and Allison 1997: 334). But Jesus's graphic statement in Matt. 24:2b that not one stone will be left standing removes any doubts as to the temple's future (cf. 26:61; 27:40; Acts 6:14; Josephus, *J.W.* 6.288–322; 7.1–4).[2]

---

1. Herod had extensively renovated and beautified the temple (Mark 13:1; John 2:20). Ancient testimony to its beauty includes Josephus, *J.W.* 5.184–226; *Ant.* 15.391–402; Tacitus, *Hist.* 5.8; *b. Sukkah* 51b.

2. Jesus's words are expressed with the double negative (οὐ μή) of emphatic negation (Wallace 1996: 468–69), which adds to their force (cf. 5:18, 20, 26; 10:23, 42; 13:14; 15:6; 16:22, 28; 18:3; 23:39; 24:21, 34, 35; 25:9; 26:29, 35). On the destruction of Jerusalem

Jesus sits down on the Mount of Olives (cf. 5:1; 13:1; 15:29; 19:28; 22:44;   **24:3**
23:2; 25:31; cf. Zech. 14:4), from which he can evidently look west at
the entrance to the temple's holiest place (*m. Ber.* 9.5; *m. Mid.* 2.4). The
disciples approach Jesus privately (cf. 17:19) and ask him what is best
understood as a two-part question (not three parts as in Walvoord 1974:
182) concerning the destruction of Jerusalem and his coming to end
the age.[3] In the disciples' thinking, the end of the temple would augur
the end of the present world (cf. 13:39–40, 49; 28:20; Hagner 1995a:
688). Those who read Matthew today should not superimpose their
chronological hindsight here. This hindsight of the historical distance
between the past destruction of the temple in 70 CE and the yet-future
coming of Jesus may obscure the conceptual link between the two events
(D. Turner 1989: 13–17). Jesus's answer to this two-part question does
not stress chronology (24:36–44) but ethics (24:45–25:46). The signs are
imprecise and cannot be used to determine the date, and so disciples
must always be alert.

It is uncertain whether the disciples' question reflects a clear grasp
of Jesus's departure and return. Their grasp of certain matters has been
weak at best (14:17, 31; 15:15, 33; 16:5–12, 22; 17:10; 18:21; 19:10, 13, 25;
20:24), but by now they realize that Jesus is about to go. Their comprehension of his passion predictions (16:21; 17:22–23; 20:18–19; cf. 26:2, 12)
has been indicated by their indignation (16:22) and grief (17:23). They
have also heard Jesus's parabolic teaching on his rejection and subsequent exaltation (21:38–44; 22:2). Jesus has made it clear that he is the
eschatological judge of humanity (7:21–23; 13:40–43; 16:27; cf. 10:23).
The awesome words of 23:39 (Ps. 118:26) regarding the one coming in
the name of the Lord are still ringing in their ears. So, whatever their
subjective lack of perception at various points, Matthew has shown that
they know enough to ask this question. It is not anachronistic (contra
Nolland 2005: 961).

---

and the temple, see Jer. 7:8–15; 9:10–11; 26:6, 18; Mic. 3:12; 2 Macc. 14:33; T. Levi 16.4;
Josephus, *J.W.* 6.300–309; C. A. Evans 1992; 1995: 367–80; Schlosser 1990.

3. The phrase τὸ σημεῖον τῆς σῆς παρουσίας καὶ συντελείας τοῦ αἰῶνος uses only one
article with two nouns connected by καί. If the article had been repeated before συντελείας,
there would be more reason to view the disciples' question as threefold. The single article
indicates not that the two nouns are identical but that they are closely interrelated in the
disciples' thinking: Jesus's appearance would end the age. See Boring 1995: 439; Wallace
1995: 167–84; 1996: 270–90.

2. The Discourse Proper (24:4–25:46)

Jesus gives a two-part answer to the disciples' two-part question, albeit the two parts of their question and his answer do not match. The disciples are concerned with the impending destruction of the temple and Jesus's age-ending coming. Jesus is concerned not so much with the "when?" and the "what?" of these events as he is with the "so what?" Although 24:4–35 speaks to some extent about the when and what, it does so with relative brevity and imprecision. Jesus speaks at more length and detail in 24:36–25:46 about the alertness, trustworthiness, and compassion that will be required of his disciples until he comes. In a word, they are concerned about when he will renew his presence with them, and he is concerned about how they will live in his absence.

a. Exposition: What Will Happen (24:4–35)

In Matt. 24:4–35, Jesus responds to the disciples' questions (24:3). He first speaks in general terms about events that will likely characterize the entire period before his coming (24:4–14). Then he describes an unprecedented season of intense tribulation that will immediately precede his coming (24:15–28), which is briefly described in vivid biblical apocalyptic imagery (24:29–31). A final section speaks parabolically about these matters to reaffirm the trustworthiness and authority of his teaching (24:32–35).

i. The Beginning of Birth Pains (24:4–14)

Jesus's blunt prediction of the destruction of the temple (24:2) leads the disciples to ask him when it will happen (24:3). They link the destruction of the temple with Jesus's coming at the end of the age, and so they wish to know the sign that will indicate that these things are imminent. Their question is about timing: they want to know the notable sign that augurs Jesus's coming. But Jesus does not answer in a precise way (24:4–14). He mentions several matters—false messiahs and prophets, wars, famines, earthquakes, persecution, apostasy, betrayal, and lawlessness—but all these are so general as to be of no help in calculating when the temple's destruction will occur. Jesus also warns them against equating such turmoil with an imminent end of the age (24:6). These "signs" are likened to the first pains of childbirth, which hints at an extended time of "labor" before the end (24:8; cf. 25:5). There will be enough time before the end for the kingdom message to be preached throughout the world (24:14). Therefore the disciples must not ponder the chronology of the end times but their own ethical responsibility to persevere in discipleship and mission (24:13–14; cf. Acts 1:6–8). Jesus has given them the right answer to their wrong question. Paul also warns against thinking that the church's present woes indicate the imminent end of the world (2 Thess. 2:2–3).

The unit can be outlined as follows:

(1) Deceptive, false messiahs (24:4–5)
(2) War, famine, and earthquakes (24:6–8)
(3) Persecution, deception, and apostasy (24:9–12)
(4) Perseverance and mission (24:13–14)

Exegesis and Exposition

⁴So Jesus answered them, "See to it that that no one deceives you. ⁵For many will come in my name, saying, 'I am the Messiah,' and will deceive many. ⁶And you will hear of wars and rumors of wars—see that you are not alarmed, for ⌜this must happen,⌝ but the end is not yet. ⁷For nation will rise up against nation, and kingdom against kingdom, and there will be ⌜famines and earthquakes⌝ in various places. ⁸But all these things are just the beginning of birth pains.

⁹"Then they will hand you over to tribulation, and they will kill you, and you will be hated by all nations because of my name. ¹⁰And then many will fall away and will betray one another and hate one another. ¹¹And many false prophets will rise up and deceive many. ¹²And because lawlessness will be increased,

the love of many will grow cold. [13]But the one who endures to the end will be saved. [14]And this gospel of the kingdom will be preached in the whole world as a testimony to all the nations, and then the end will come."

(1) Deceptive, False Messiahs (24:4–5)

Jesus's prophetic words in 24:4–14 (cf. Mark 13:5–13; Luke 21:8–19) build on what he has already said about the future.[1] His answer to the disciples' question begins with a warning against deception by false messiahs (cf. 2 Thess. 2:3; 1 John 2:26; 2 John 7). This warning is repeated and expanded in Matt. 24:23–27. The deceivers who will come in Jesus's name probably do not claim to be Jesus himself but to be the Messiah. The many false messiahs will deceive many people.[2] The messianic pretender Bar Kokhba led a second Jewish revolt against Rome that ended in 135 CE with the total banishing of all Jews from Jerusalem.[3] False messiahs continue to arise in more recent times.

24:4–5

(2) War, Famine, and Earthquakes (24:6–8)

International aggression and geological disturbances will coincide with religious error. Such events are necessary because God has planned them (cf. 26:54; Dan. 2:28–29, 45; Rev. 1:1; 4:1). But real and rumored warfare (cf. Isa. 19:2; Jer. 51:46; Dan. 7:21; 9:26; 11:44; Zech. 14:3), earthquakes (cf. Joel 2:10; Hag. 2:6; Zech. 14:5; 1QH 3.12–13; Hartman 1966: 71–76), and famine (2 Esd. [4 Ezra] 6:22; 2 Bar. 27.6; 70.8; L.A.B. 3.9; Rev. 6:8; 18:8) should not frighten the disciples because these things do not signify the end (cf. Cuvillier 1996). Rather, these are merely the first stages of the messianic woes to come upon the world. The Jewish revolt against Rome in 66–70 CE is part of the fulfillment of Jesus's words.

24:6–7

The pains of a woman in labor are used as a metaphor for eschatological troubles elsewhere in Jewish literature and the NT.[4] Famine is an inevitable result of warfare, especially in ancient times (Acts 11:27–30; Rev. 6:8; 18:8; 1 Macc. 6:54; Josephus, *J.W.* 3.320; *Ant.* 14.471; 15.7). Earthquakes are especially ominous as chaos extends to nature itself.[5]

24:8

---

1. Cf. 5:3–12; 7:21–27; 8:11–12; 10:23; 11:22–24; 13:36–43, 47–50; 16:27–28; 19:28–30; 22:29–32; 23:39; cf. 26:13, 21, 29, 64.
2. On deception by false messiahs, see 24:24; CD 5.20; 7.21; T. Mos. 7.4; T. Levi 10.2; 2 Bar. 48.34; 2 Thess. 2:8–12; 1 John 2:18, 22; 4:3; 2 John 7; Rev. 2:20; 12:9; 13:4, 8, 14; 19:20; 20:3, 8, 10; Josephus, *J.W.* 6.288.
3. Cf. Theudas and Judas the Galilean, Acts 5:36–37; "that Egyptian," Acts 21:38; cf. Josephus, *Ant.* 17.271–85; 20.97–99, 160–72, 188; R. Horsley and Hanson 1985.
4. Cf. Isa. 13:8; 26:17; 66:7–8; Jer. 4:31; 6:24; 22:23; 30:5–6; 48:41; Hos. 13:13; Mic. 4:9–10; 5:3; 1QH 3.7–10; 1 En. 62.4; 2 Esd. (4 Ezra) 4:42; Targum Ps. 18:14; Mark 13:8; John 16:20–22; 1 Thess. 5:3; Rev. 12:2; cf. Gal. 4:19, 27.
5. Cf. 8:24; 27:54; 28:2; Acts 16:26; Rev. 6:12; 8:5; 11:13, 19; 16:18; Joel 2:10; Hag. 2:6; Zech. 14:4–5; 1 En. 1.6–7; 102.2; 1QH 3.12–13; 2 Esd. (4 Ezra) 6:13–16; 9:3; Josephus, *J.W.* 1.370; 4.286; Hartman 1966: 71–76.

(3) Persecution, Deception, and Apostasy (24:9–12)

24:9–10 Deceptive messiahs, violent wars, and geological upheavals will be accompanied by persecution (cf. 10:17–23; 13:21; 23:34).[6] The disciples will be universally hated because of their identification with Jesus (cf. 5:11; 10:18, 22, 25, 32–33, 38). This hatred and persecution will even result in murder (cf. 10:28; 21:35; 22:6). An example is the martyrdom of James, described by Josephus, *Ant.* 20.200–201 (cf. Tacitus, *Ann.* 15.44). This external pressure will have devastating consequences within the community of the disciples. Some disciples will fall away from their commitment to Jesus and will hate and betray their fellows.[7]

24:11–12 False prophets will promote the coming false messiahs (cf. 24:5, 23–26).[8] This false religious teaching causes lawlessness (7:23; 13:41; 23:28; cf. 2 Thess. 2:8) to increase, with a corresponding decline in the central virtue of discipleship, love (cf. 2 Thess. 2:10; 2 Tim. 3:4; Rev. 2:4; Légasse 1983; J. Taylor 1989; D. Wenham 1980). Loving God and neighbor is the quintessence of the law and the prophets (Matt. 22:34–40), and so its decline amounts to lawlessness that devastates God's people.

(4) Perseverance and Mission (24:13–14)

24:13–14 The response of authentic disciples to all these horrifying circumstances is fidelity. Perseverance in obeying Jesus contrasts with lawlessness as the mark of discipleship. The salvation promised to those who endure is not merely relief from persecution (contra Walvoord 1974: 184, but see 24:22) but future salvific reward for obedience (cf. 1 Thess. 5:9; 2 Tim. 2:10; Heb. 1:14; 9:28; 1 Pet. 1:5, 9; 2 Pet. 1:10–11). This contrasts with those in Matt. 24:10–12 who fall away or promote false teaching (Blomberg 1992a: 356; Carson 1984: 498–99). Matthew 24:13 is a verbatim echo of 10:22.[9] This perseverance will result in the kingdom message (3:2; 4:17, 23; 9:35; 10:7; 13:19; 26:13) being preached to all the nations before the

---

6. Like John the Baptist and Jesus, the disciples will be handed over (παραδίδωμι; 4:12; 5:25; 10:4, 17, 19, 21; 17:22; 20:18–19; 24:10; 26:2, 15, 16, 21, 23–25, 45–46, 48; 27:2–4, 18; Acts 22:4; 1 Cor. 11:23) for persecution or tribulation (θλῖψις; Matt. 13:21; 24:9, 21, 29). As in 24:9, this word sometimes describes the generic troubles that Christians have typically faced (cf. 13:21; John 16:33; Acts 11:19; 14:22; 20:23; Rom. 8:35; 12:12; 2 Cor. 1:4, 6, 8; 2 Thess. 1:4; Rev. 2:9–10, 22), but other times it describes severe, unparalleled eschatological troubles (e.g., Matt. 24:21, 29; Rom. 2:9; 2 Thess. 1:6–9; Rev. 7:14; cf. Dan. 12:1; Joel 2:2; Hab. 3:16; Zeph. 1:15). See Allison 1985a: 5–25.

7. On apostasy, see 5:29–30; 13:21; 18:6, 8–9; 1 Tim. 4:1–5; 2 Tim. 3:1–13; Jude 17–19; Rev. 13:11–18; 1QpHab 2.1–10; 1 En. 90.22–27; 91.7; 93.9; Jub. 23.14–17; 2 Bar. 41.3; 48.38; 2 Esd. (4 Ezra) 5:1–2; *m. Soṭah* 9.15.

8. Cf. 7:15; 24:24; Acts 13:6; 20:29–30; 2 Pet. 2:1; 1 John 4:1; Rev. 16:13; 19:20; 20:10; cf. Deut. 13:1–2; 18:9–22; Josephus, *J.W.* 6.285–87; 7.438.

9. On perseverance, see 3:8; 7:20–27; 10:32–33; 12:33–37; 13:20–23, 41–43; Rom. 12:12; 2 Tim. 2:3, 10, 12; James 1:12; 5:11; 1 Pet. 2:20; Rev. 1:9; 3:10; 13:10; 14:12; Did. 16.5; 2 Esd. (4 Ezra) 6:25; 7:27; 9:7–8; 2 Bar. 70.9.

end comes (cf. 10:22–23; 28:18–20).[10] The affirming statement about the arrival of the end in 24:14 contrasts with the cautions about the delay of the end in 24:6, 8.

Matthew 24:4–14 summarizes the difficulties the church will face in the early days before 70 CE and throughout its existence (Blomberg 1992a: 356–57; Hagner 1995a: 693–94). The similarities between the events described here and those found in Rev. 6:1–11 are noteworthy, and it is most likely that Rev. 6:1–11 also describes the church's present experience in the world, not the final eschatological tribulation.

Additional Notes

24:6. UBS[4] prefers the short reading γενέσθαι (found in ℵ, B, D, L, Θ, *f*[1], 33; cf. Mark 13:7) because it is supported by early MSS and it explains the rise of the other readings better than vice versa (Metzger 1994: 51). Several longer readings exist, including πάντα γενέσθαι (supported by C, W, Δ, 0102, *f*[13], 28, *Byz, Lect*) and ταῦτα γενέσθαι (supported by 565, several old Latin MSS; cf. Luke 21:9).

24:7. UBS[4] prefers the shorter reading λιμοὶ καὶ σεισμοί (supported by ℵ [word order reversed], B, D, E*, 892) rather than λιμοὶ καὶ λοιμοὶ καὶ σεισμοί (supported by C, Δ, Θ, 0102, *f*[1], *f*[13], 28, 157, *Byz, Lect*). The longer reading could have been influenced by Luke 21:11, but the shorter reading may have mistakenly omitted λοιμοί because of its similarity to λιμοί.

---

10. On the conversion of the Gentiles, see Isa. 2:2–4; 45:20–22; 49:6; 55:5; 56:6–8; Mic. 4:1–3; 1 En. 48.4–5; T. Levi 18.5–9; LaGrand 1995.

ii. The Abomination of Desolation (24:15–28)

Matthew 24:15–28 (cf. Mark 13:14–23; Luke 21:20–24) warns of severe, unparalleled persecution and false prophecy, signaled by the desecration of the Jerusalem temple (24:15). This warning includes instructions for flight (24:16–20), a promise that God will shorten those days for the sake of his elect (24:21–22), and a renewed warning against false messiahs and false prophets (24:23–28). This warning primarily relates to the destruction of the temple in 70 CE, but it should be viewed as ultimately intended for God's people in the end times (cf. 24:21–22), who will face the ultimate antichrist. Jesus's disciples have throughout history realized the relevance of his warning against false prophets and messiahs. Persecution inevitably causes disciples to long for the Messiah's appearance, but this longing must not render them vulnerable to deception by messianic pretenders.

The most profound question in this passage is not chronological but existential. The various preterist and futurist views plausibly address the historical referents of the prophecy. But disciples need wisdom as they ponder a divine providence that allows the elect to suffer but limits their suffering so that they are not spiritually ruined. Suffering is a way of life for Jesus's disciples during the present age (5:10; 10:16–42; John 16:33; Acts 14:22; 2 Tim. 3:12), and it will evidently intensify as this age ends. Yet in God's wisdom such suffering accomplishes God's goals, not the persecutors' goals (cf. Gen. 50:20; Acts 4:27–28; Rom. 8:28–39). Although Jesus's disciples may never fully grasp why their suffering is necessary, the example of Jesus assures them that God will enable them to endure it and eventually to reign with Jesus (Matt. 4:1–11; 10:24–33; 19:28–29; Rom. 8:18; 1 Cor. 10:13; 2 Tim. 2:12; 2 Pet. 2:9; Rev. 2:26–28; 3:21–22; 5:10; 20:4).

The unit outline is as follows:

(1) An ominous echo from Daniel (24:15)
(2) Instructions for flight (24:16–20)
(3) God's care during unique tribulation (24:21–22)
(4) False messiahs and false prophets (24:23–28)

Exegesis and Exposition

[15]"So whenever you see the 'desolating sacrilege,' spoken of by Daniel the prophet, standing in the holy place (let the reader understand), [16]then those in

Judea must flee to the mountains. [17]The one who is on the housetop must not go down to get things out of the house. [18]The one in the field must not return to get a cloak. [19]Woe to those who are pregnant and to those who are nursing babies during those days! [20]And pray that your flight will not be during the winter or on a Sabbath. [21]For then there will be a great tribulation such as has not happened since the beginning of the world until now and never will happen again. [22]And unless those days were cut short, no one would be saved; but for the sake of the elect, those days will be cut short. [23]Then, if anyone says to you, 'Behold, here is the Messiah,' or, 'There he is,' do not believe it. [24]For false messiahs and false prophets will rise up and do great signs and wonders to deceive, if possible, even the elect. [25]See, I have told you ahead of time. [26]So, if they say to you, 'Look, he is in the wilderness,' do not go out, or, 'Look, he is in one of the inner rooms,' do not believe it. [27]For just as the lightning comes from the east and is visible as far as the west, so will be the coming of the Son of Man. [28]Where the corpse is, there the vultures will gather."

(1) An Ominous Echo from Daniel (24:15)

This is Jesus's most direct response to the disciples' question about the temple's destruction (24:3; cf. Mark 13:14–23; Luke 21:20–24). The "desolating sacrilege" alludes to Dan. 8:13; 9:27; 11:31; 12:11 (cf. T. Levi 15.1; Apoc. El. 2.41; 4.21). Matthew 23:38 hints at this. Daniel's prophecy of the desecration of the temple is often linked to Antiochus IV (Epiphanes) setting up a pagan altar in the holy place in 167 BCE (1 Macc. 1:54, 59; 6:7; 2 Macc. 6:1–5).[1] But the temple had been previously desecrated in 597 BCE when Nebuchadnezzar conquered Jerusalem, destroyed the first temple, and carried off its treasures (Dan. 1:1–2; 5:2–4, 22–23; cf. 2 Kings 24:10–15). Jesus envisions a future desecration here (cf. 2 Thess. 2:4). The words "Let the reader understand" may mean that Jesus encourages his hearers to read Daniel or that Matthew editorially encourages his own readers to ponder this matter. Either way, these words stress the desecration of the holy place as a key sign of the horrors to come. (See Cuvillier 1997.)

24:15

(2) Instructions for Flight (24:16–20)

When the temple is desecrated, Jesus's disciples must flee to the Judean hill country (24:16, 20, cf. Heb. 11:38; 1 Macc. 2:28, 31; 2 Macc. 6:11; 10:6). Evidently, a siege of Jerusalem is envisioned (Luke 21:20–24; cf. Deut. 28:53–57). The general command in Matt. 24:16 is reinforced by the specific commands of 24:17–18 (cf. Luke 17:31), the woe pronouncement of Matt. 24:19, and the command to pray in 24:20. The urgency of

24:16–20

---

1. Daniel is described as a prophet even though his book is contained in the Writings, or Ketubim, of the Hebrew Bible. The LXX and Christian Bibles put Daniel with the Prophets. Cf. similarly 4QFlor 4.3–4, citing Dan. 12:10; Josephus, *Ant.* 10.249.

the hour precludes packing or even obtaining a coat. Whether one is on a flat clay rooftop (Mark 2:4; Josh. 2:6; 1 Sam. 9:25; 2 Sam. 11:2; Acts 10:9, 20) or in a field, there is no time to go into a house for supplies (cf. 1 Macc. 2:28). Flight will be especially rigorous for pregnant or nursing mothers (cf. Luke 23:28–31; 1 Cor. 7:26; 2 Bar. 10.13–14) or if it is necessary on the Sabbath. Winter would mean colder weather and the rainy season, with muddy roads and slow, laborious travel. It is unclear why flight on the Sabbath would be especially difficult unless Matthew's Christian Jewish community had scruples against breaking the Sabbath travel restrictions (cf. Exod. 16:29; Acts 1:12; *m. ʿErub.*; Stanton 1989; Wong 1991). Perhaps it would be difficult to obtain supplies or to leave a walled city on the Sabbath. Movement on the Sabbath would be more noticeable than on other days. According to Eusebius (*Eccl. Hist.* 3.5.3; cf. Koester 1989; Wehnert 1991), before Jerusalem was destroyed in 70 CE, the Jerusalem Christians fled to Pella, east of the Jordan River and about sixty-five miles northeast of Jerusalem.

(3) God's Care during Unique Tribulation (24:21–22)

24:21–22   The unprecedented severity of these times is the reason for the urgent warnings of the preceding verses. Unlike previous generic troubles that do not augur the end (24:6), anguish like this has never been seen before and will never be seen again.[2] God's concern to deliver his elect (22:14; 24:24, 31; cf. 11:27; 13:38) will result in this most horrible of times being curtailed (Dan. 12:1; 4Q385 frg. 3.2–5; 2 Bar. 20.1–2; 54.1; 83.1; Barn. 4.3). The unique severity of these events is difficult to reconcile with the preterist view that this passage refers solely to the events of 70 CE (Nolland 2005: 975–76). Hagner (1995a: 702–3) is correct that the language is hyperbolic in reference to the catastrophe of 70 CE but literally true of the eschatological horrors.

(4) False Messiahs and False Prophets (24:23–28)

24:23–25   Although false messiahs and prophets will appear throughout history (24:4–5, 11), their activity will be especially intense near the end. Their miraculous works could deceive God's elect if that were possible (cf. Exod. 7:11; Deut. 13:1–5; 2 Thess. 2:9; 2 Pet. 2:1; 1 John 2:18; 4:1; Rev. 13:3; 19:20; Did. 16.4). Jesus's reticence to use miracles to gain a following (4:1–11; 12:15–21, 39; 16:1–4; 27:40) contrasts with the false messiahs' practice. Jesus warns about this danger ahead of time to preserve God's elect.

24:26–28   Matthew 24:26 repeats the gist of 24:23 and reiterates the warning against believing the false prophets. The disciples must not believe claims that

---

2. Cf. 24:29; Dan. 12:1; Joel 2:2; Rev. 7:14; 16:18; 1QM 1.9–14; 1 Macc. 9:27; T. Mos. 8.1; Josephus, *J.W.* 1.12.

the Messiah is in some obscure place, such as the desert or an inner room of a building (cf. 6:6; Luke 17:23–24).[3] In contrast, Jesus's appearance (cf. 1 Cor. 15:23; 1 Thess. 2:19; 3:13; 4:15; James 5:7; 2 Pet. 3:4; 1 John 2:28) will be as unmistakably clear as lightning that flashes across the sky from east to west (cf. Exod. 19:16; Isa. 62:1; Zech. 9:14). This will leave no doubt as to the identity of the Messiah. The meaning of the proverb about the vultures (evidently not eagles; BDAG 23) and the carcass in Matt. 24:28 is difficult (cf. Luke 17:37). In the most common view, the corpse stands for signs and the vulture stands for Jesus's appearance as judge. The former lead to the latter (France 1985: 343). It is very unlikely that the corpse and vulture represent moral corruption (Hendriksen 1973: 861; Walvoord 1974: 190) or the consumption of lifeless Israel by false prophets (Lenski 1961: 946; Toussaint 1980: 276). Perhaps the grisly picture of vultures hovering over the bodies of those who rebel against God speaks of a final eschatological battle (Rev. 19:17–18). (See W. Davies and Allison 1997: 356–57; H. Guenther 1989.)

Interpreting the Abomination of Desolation

The sacrilegious desecration of the temple (24:15) is part of a complex typology of prophecy and fulfillment stretching all the way from Nebuchadnezzar to the eschatological antichrist. Several events form a continuum of fulfillment, including

1. Nebuchadnezzar's conquest in 605 BCE (Dan. 1:1–2; 5:1–4, 22–23)
2. Antiochus IV Epiphanes' sacrilege, which led to the Hasmonean revolt in 167 BCE
3. The Roman conquest of the Hasmonean kingdom in 63 BCE
4. The unfulfilled plan to set up a bust of Caligula in the temple (40–41 CE)
5. The Zealots' misuse of the temple grounds before the Roman destruction of Jerusalem
6. The Roman destruction in 70 CE
7. The further desolation of Jerusalem by the Romans in 135 CE in response to the second Jewish revolt led by Bar Kokhba (Dio Cassius, *Roman History* 69.12.1–2)
8. The ultimate sacrilege of the antichrist (Matt. 24:15; 2 Thess. 2:3–4; 1 John 2:18, 22; 4:3; 2 John 7; Rev. 13:8; 2 Bar. 40.1–3; 2 Esd. [4 Ezra] 5:6; T. Mos. 8.1–5; Did. 16)

In light of all this, there is no warrant for supposing that the predicted desecration of Matt. 24:15 will be fulfilled solely by either the past 70 CE

---

3. Would-be messiahs hid out in the desert, away from the threat of Roman soldiers (Acts 21:38; Josephus, *J.W.* 2.258–63; *Ant.* 20.97–99, 167–72, 188).

destruction of Jerusalem or by the future antichrist (Blomberg 2002). There is good reason to view the various historical desolations of Jerusalem and the temple as a sequence of anticipatory fulfillments that lead up to the ultimate eschatological desolation. This scenario could include the controversial and seemingly implausible future rebuilding of the temple, but this was envisioned in ancient sources.[4] A rebuilding of the temple is a plausible implication of 2 Thess. 2:4 and Rev. 11:1–2.[5]

4. Jewish sources include Tob. 13:16–18; 14:5; 1 En. 90.28–29; Jub. 1.27; 11QT 29.8–10; 4QFlor 1.1–3; 2 Esd. (4 Ezra) 10:25–59; *m. Pesaḥ.* 10.6; *b. Sukkah* 41a; *b. Šabb.* 12b. Christian texts include Barn. 16.3–4; Irenaeus, *Haer.* 5.30.4; Apoc. El. 4.1–6.
   5. On the abomination of desolation, see W. Davies and Allison 1997: 345–46; Ford 1979; Jenks 1991; Keener 1999: 573–75; Peerbolte 1996; Rigaux 1959.

iii. The Coming of the Son of Man (24:29–31)

Most scholars understand 24:15–28 to be speaking of events accompanying the destruction of Jerusalem in 70 CE. Some scholars and the present commentary see an additional eschatological fulfillment. There is a similar debate over the prevalent apocalyptic imagery in 24:29–31. Preterists take it as already fulfilled, and futurists as yet to be fulfilled. Preterist scholars interpret this language as speaking of Jesus's enthronement in heaven and/or the destruction of Jerusalem on earth, but their arguments do not convince futurists, who insist that 24:31 describes the coming of Jesus to judge the earth (W. Davies and Allison 1997: 329). Hagner (1995a: 711–13) understands 24:29–31 as a reference to the events of 70 CE and concludes that Matthew believed that Jesus would come then. But this is unnecessary if 24:15–28 describes both the destruction of Jerusalem in 70 CE and the ultimate eschatological persecution of God's people.

It is argued here that 24:29–31 describes the climactic signs in heaven that immediately precede Jesus's future coming (24:29), that glorious coming itself (24:30), and the purpose of his coming: to gather God's elect for their reward (24:31). Jesus's appearance effects a reversal of business as usual. Since his death and resurrection, the disciples have mourned over their many persecutions (5:10–12; 9:15; 10:23), but when Jesus appears, their persecutors mourn (cf. 13:41–42), and the disciples with joy begin to experience the ultimate reward of their master (25:21, 23).

Biblical Allusions

Biblical imagery permeates Matt. 24:29–31. The table presents the most significant citations and allusions. The crucial text is Dan. 7, where God is pictured as an awesome judge, "the Ancient of Days" (Dan. 7:9), who passes sentence in favor of the son of man, giving universal dominion to him and his people (7:14, 22, 27). The context is eschatological reversal, in which the "little horn" (7:8, 20, 24–25), the archenemy of God and Israel, is judged and defeated. In both Dan. 7 and Matt. 24, the coming of the Son of Man ends the persecution of God's saints and begins their glorious rule with Jesus.

Biblical Allusions in Matt. 24:29–31		
Matthew	Topic	Hebrew Bible
24:29a	Tribulation	Dan. 12:1
24:29b	Sun and moon darkened	Isa. 13:10; 24:23; Ezek. 32:7; Joel 2:10, 31; 3:15; Amos 5:20; 8:9; Zeph. 1:15
24:29c	Stars fallen, shaken	Isa. 34:4; Hag. 2:6
24:30a, 30c	Son of Man coming on the clouds in glory and power	Jer. 4:13; Dan. 7:13–14
24:30b	Tribes mourn	Zech. 12:10, 12
24:31a	Trumpet	Isa. 27:13
24:31b	Elect gathered	Deut. 30:4
24:31b	Four winds	Dan. 7:2; Zech. 2:6
24:31b	Ends of the sky	Deut. 4:32

Exegesis and Exposition

[29]"But immediately after the tribulation of those days, 'the sun will be darkened and the moon will not give its light, and the stars will fall' from the sky, and the powers of the heavens will be shaken. [30]And then the sign of the Son of Man will appear in the sky, and then all the tribes of the earth will mourn, and they will see the 'the Son of Man coming on the clouds of the sky' with power and great glory. [31]And he will send forth his angels with ''a great trumpet'' and they will gather together his elect from the four winds, from one end of the sky to the other.''

24:29 Immediately after the period of unparalleled anguish described in 24:15–28 (cf. Dan. 12:1), heavenly disturbances expressed through apocalyptic imagery augur the appearance of Jesus (cf. Mark 13:24–27; Luke 21:25–27). The cosmic upheaval delineated here develops the lightning imagery of Matt. 24:27. The sun and moon will be darkened, and the stars will fall from the sky (cf. Acts 2:20; Rev. 6:12–13; 8:12; 1 En. 80.4; 2 Esd. [4 Ezra] 5:4–5; T. Mos. 10.5). See the table for the biblical background of these phenomena. The cosmic chaos portrayed here hints at the need for cosmic renewal (Matt. 19:28–29).

24:30 The coming of Jesus is the event to which all the signs point. This verse is a conflation of Jer. 4:13; Dan. 7:13–14; Zech. 12:10, 12. The "sign of the Son of Man" may mean that the coming itself is the sign or that a noteworthy entity will indicate the coming of the Son of Man.[1] Taken with the sounding trumpet in Matt. 24:31, the sign may refer to a military

---

1. Τὸ σημεῖον τοῦ υἱοῦ τοῦ ἀνθρώπου may be understood as an appositional or epexegetical genitive (cf. Wallace 1996: 95–100) and paraphrased, "the sign that is the Son of Man coming" (cf. 12:39; Boring 1995: 444; Zerwick 1963: §46). Or the phrase could be understood as an objective genitive (Wallace 1996: 116–19) and paraphrased, "that which signifies the Son of Man coming."

a. Exposition: What Will Happen
iii. The Coming of the Son of Man

Matthew 24:29–31

ensign, possibly the cross, which musters troops for the eschatological battle.[2] In any event, the sign probably refers back to the disciples' question in 24:3, although the question spoke of "signs," not "the sign." The sign's appearance in heaven is in keeping with the previous heavenly disturbances. It is not clear whether the mourning of the nations (Zech. 12:10; cf. John 19:37; Rev. 1:7) indicates repentance or despair at the prospect of meeting Jesus as judge. His glorious coming on the clouds (Dan. 7:13; cf. Jer. 4:13) may allude to the presence of God in terms of the biblical cloud theophany (Matt. 16:27; 25:31; Acts 1:9–11; Rev. 1:7; cf. Exod. 13:21–22; 40:35–38; Sabourin 1974).

The Son of Man comes to gather his elect, whom he has preserved **24:31** through severe anguish (24:22, 24). Jesus, as Son of Man, exercises a divine prerogative in sending *his* angels (cf. Dan. 7:10) for *his* elect. Biblically, a trumpet was sounded for religious or military purposes.[3] That God's elect are from all the nations is emphasized by their description as coming "from the four winds" (cf. Isa. 43:6; Dan. 7:2; Zech. 2:6 LXX; Rev. 7:1) and "from one end of the sky to the other." The gathering of the elect reminds the reader of John's expression in Matt. 3:12 and may imply a sort of "rapture," as in 1 Thess. 4:17. It is different from Jesus's parabolic language about wicked people being gathered out of his kingdom for judgment (Matt. 13:40–42, 48–50; cf. 25:46). The description of one being taken and another left is similar (24:41–42). Whatever the difference in details, the point of all these passages is the separation of humanity that will be effected when Jesus appears as judge.

Interpreting the Coming of Jesus

In a futurist understanding, the glorious coming of Jesus, already mentioned repeatedly, is here placed most clearly in eschatological context (cf. 10:23; 16:27–28; 23:39; 24:3, 27, 37, 39, 42, 44, 46, 48, 50; 25:6, 13, 19, 31; 26:64). The date of this coming is unknowable (24:36, 42–44; 25:13; cf. Acts 1:6–7), but Jesus's disciples dare not assume that it is in the distant future (24:39, 48). Rather, they must alertly expect Jesus and serve him faithfully until they see him. This coming is placed after the tribulation (24:29), which may give advocates of the pretribulational-rapture theory some pause (see comments on 24:40–41). The coming reverses business as usual, resulting in mourning for all the nations whose persecution previously caused the disciples to mourn, but joy for all the formerly mourning disciples (cf. 2 Thess. 1:6–10). At this time the reign of heaven comes to earth more fully (Matt. 6:9–10; 25:34) with the

2. See Isa. 11:10–12; 18:2; 62:10; Jer. 4:21; 51:27; 1QH 2.13–14; 6.34–35; 1QM 3.13–14; W. Davies and Allison 1997: 359–60; Draper 1993.

3. This passage seems to allude to Isa. 27:13. Cf. Exod. 19:16 (Heb. 12:19); Josh. 6:5; Ps. 81:3; Ezek. 33:3–6; Joel 2:1; Zeph. 1:16; 1QM 2.16–3.11; 1 Cor. 15:52; 1 Thess. 4:16; Rev. 1:10; 4:1; 8:2, 6–13; 9:1, 13–14; 10:7; 11:15; Did. 16.6; Shemoneh Esreh, benediction 10.

judgment of all the nations and the reward of Jesus's disciples (5:4–9, esp. 5:5; 13:40–43; 16:27–28; 19:27–30; 25:46).

A very different scenario is presented by the preterists, who interpret 24:29–31 as symbolizing the theological significance of the temple's destruction (France 1985: 345; cf. Lightfoot 1997: 2.319–20; Tasker 1961: 225–28). The coming of Jesus is viewed as his triumphal arrival in heaven after his resurrection (Dan. 7:13–14). Jesus's exaltation results in Israel's judgment, demonstrated by the destruction of the temple by the Romans in 70 CE. The tribulation mentioned here is viewed as the horrific conditions experienced by the Jerusalem Zealots just before the Roman attack. The heavenly disturbances are understood to be the strange phenomena observed during those days. The sending of the angels to gather the elect is viewed as the church's mission to disciple all the nations (Matt. 24:14; 28:19).

Preterists are motivated by their understanding of 24:34 as Jesus's promise that his words will be accomplished during the lives of his contemporaries. Since he did not literally come during their lifetimes, 24:1–31 is viewed as a prediction of the destruction of the temple in 70 CE. See the comments on 24:34 for a different view of this difficult text. One difficulty with preterism is its truncation of Jesus's eschatology, which brings the reign of heaven to earth (6:10) and renews the world (19:28). If all this has already occurred, one wonders at the underwhelming denouement of the glorious future promised by the biblical prophets, John, and Jesus himself. It is very doubtful that the global language of Matt. 24 (e.g., 24:3, 7, 14, 21–22, 27, 30–31, 40–41; see also 25:31–32) can be satisfactorily explained by a local event in 70 CE, as significant as that event was (Blomberg 1992a: 363; D. Turner 1989: 17–19).

Additional Note

24:31. UBS[4] prefers the shorter reading σάλπιγγος (supported by א, L, W, Δ, Θ, f^1) rather than σάλπιγγος φωνῆς (supported by B, f^{13}, 28, 33, 157, *Byz*, *Lect*). The longer reading could have been influenced by Exod. 19:16. The shorter reading is the only time the expression σάλπιγξ μεγάλη occurs in the NT.

iv. Parable of the Fig Tree (24:32–35)

This passage parabolically expresses the nearness of Jesus's coming (24:32–33) and solemnly affirms its certainty (24:34–35). Jesus's contemporaries are familiar with the fig tree's budding and blossoming in the spring and in the summer bearing fruit (24:32), and so he compares his coming to this process (24:33). In terms of the disciples' question in 24:3, the "sign" is the tree's spring budding and blossoming, and Jesus's "coming" is the summer bearing of fruit. When the disciples see the spring signs, they know that summer's coming is near. The affirmation of 24:34 depends on the eternal trustworthiness of Jesus's words (24:35).

Exegesis and Exposition

³²"Now learn this parable from the fig tree. When its branch already becomes tender and puts forth its leaves, you recognize that summer is near; ³³so also you, when you see all these things, recognize that he is near, right at the door. ³⁴Truly I tell you, this generation will certainly not pass away until all these things happen. ³⁵Heaven and earth will pass away, but my words will not pass away."

The parable of the fig tree (Derrett 1973) resembles the short parables in 13:31–33, 44–46 more than the longer narrative parables in that chapter (cf. Mark 13:28–31; Luke 21:29–33). The parable is stated in Matt. 24:32 and applied in 24:33. As the fig tree's spring buds are a sure sign of the nearness of summer, so "all these things" are reliable indicators that he is near (cf. Isa. 13:6; Ezek. 30:3; Joel 1:15; 2:1; Zeph. 1:7, 14; James 5:8), ready to walk through the door (cf. James 5:9; Rev. 3:20). In the discussion below, it is argued that the crucial expression "all these things" refers to the signs about which the disciples asked and of which Jesus has spoken in Matt. 24:4–28.

24:32–33

These verses contain two statements that affirm that Jesus's parabolic promise of his coming (24:32–33) is reliable. The promise is so reliable that Jesus's contemporaries ("this generation") will live to see its fulfillment. Heaven and earth itself will pass away, but Jesus's promise will not. Jesus's previous statement on the permanence of the Torah is similar to this one, and as the ultimate teacher of Torah, his words are on a par with the Torah itself (cf. 5:18). Jesus's words are equivalent to the words of God, as eternal and authoritative as God himself (Isa. 40:8; Ps. 119:89).

24:34–35

There are two major issues in the interpretation of Matt. 24:34—the meanings of "this generation" and of "all these things." As argued more fully below, Jesus promises his contemporaries that they will still be living when the signs he has mentioned, including the destruction of the temple, occur (D. Turner 1989; Blomberg 1992a: 364). Jesus did not mistakenly predict his coming during his lifetime (McNeile 1915: 355), nor is this a piece of mistaken early church tradition (Beare 1981: 473; W. Davies and Allison 1997: 367–68).

Interpreting the Parable of the Fig Tree

Two crucial terms in 24:34 must be explained. First, what is the meaning of "all these things"? This expression refers to the preliminary signs that anticipate Jesus's coming, not the coming itself. This is clear from the parabolic imagery used by Jesus. If "all these things" (parabolically the fig tree's spring buds) included the coming of Jesus (parabolically the summer), 24:33 would be saying, "When you see the coming of Jesus, you will know that he is near." This tautology goes without saying. But if "all these things" refers only to the preliminary signs, the statement makes sense, since seeing the signs confirms that the coming is near.

The second crucial term is "this generation." Although some futurists argue that the word refers either to the nation of Israel or to the eschatological generation that is alive at Jesus's coming (e.g., Toussaint 1980: 279–80; Walvoord 1974: 192–93), the use of the term clearly shows that Jesus is talking about his contemporaries (cf. 11:16; 12:39, 41–42, 45; 16:4; 17:17; 23:36). Scholars who argue for an understanding of "this generation" that is contrary to Matthew's clear usage wish to protect Jesus from affirming that his coming will occur during the lives of his contemporaries. But if Jesus is speaking only of the signs that augur his coming, he does not err. Jesus simply predicts that his contemporaries will see those signs, including the destruction of the temple by the Romans in 70 CE. (See W. Davies and Allison 1997: 367; Kidder 1983; Lövestam 1995; D. Turner 1989: 22–25; D. Wenham in Rowdon 1982: 127–50.)

This exegetical debate aside, during times of relative peace and prosperity, it is difficult to take Jesus's words to heart. Occupation with everyday life and its pleasures may lead one to forget that it will all end abruptly (24:36–42). But Jesus's disciples cannot become comfortable with the status quo because it will certainly, even if not speedily, bow before the reign of heaven on earth.

b. An Exhortation to Alertness (24:36–25:46)

At this point Jesus moves from speaking predictively to speaking paraenetically. From now on, his goal is not to provide additional information to answer the disciples' question (24:3) but to exhort them on the proper response to that information. This may not be what the disciples want to know, but it is what they need to know. This material is mainly parabolic. The first (24:36–42) and last (25:31–46) sections are not parables, but both utilize quasi-parabolic comparisons (24:37–39; 25:32). W. Davies and Allison (1997: 374) point out that 24:36 sets the tone for the rest of the discourse: ignorance of the time of Jesus's coming should result in constant alertness.

Jesus begins by drawing a lesson on alertness from history (24:36–42). The next three segments underline the lesson on alertness by drawing from scenes from everyday life: (1) an owner of a house and a thief (24:43–44), (2) a faithful and an evil slave (24:45–51), and (3) thoughtful and foolish bridesmaids (25:1–13). Constant alertness (24:42–44, 46, 50; 25:13) is mandatory, since the time of Jesus's coming is unknowable. Alertness must be accompanied by dependable stewardship (25:14–30) and compassion toward needy disciples (25:31–46).

i. Comparison to the Days of Noah (24:36–42)

Jesus alludes to the protological days of Noah (Gen. 5:28–10:32, esp. 6:5–8:22; cf. 1 Pet. 3:20; 2 Pet. 2:5; 3:5–7) as a model of eschatological days. People are oblivious to their impending doom in both settings. This section begins with an affirmation that the day of Jesus's coming is unknowable (24:36). After an introductory general statement comparing Noah's times to eschatological times (24:37), specifics from Noah's times (24:38–39a) are compared to specifics from eschatological times (24:39b–41). An *inclusio* is formed by a second statement that the day of Jesus's coming is unknowable (24:42).

Exegesis and Exposition

³⁶"But of that day and hour no one knows, not even the angels of heaven ⌜or the Son⌝, but the Father alone. ³⁷For as the days of Noah were, so the coming of the Son of Man will be. ³⁸For as in ⌜those⌝ days before the flood, people were eating and drinking, marrying and giving in marriage, until the day that Noah entered the ark, ³⁹and they did not understand until the flood came and took them all away, so will the coming of the Son of Man be. ⁴⁰Then two people will be in the field; one will be taken and one will be left. ⁴¹Two women will be grinding with a hand mill; one will be taken and one will be left. ⁴²Therefore be alert because you do not know on what ⌜day⌝ your Lord is coming."

24:36–37   Jesus has just stressed the nearness of his coming, but now he emphasizes that its timing is unknowable (cf. Mark 13:32). The expression "that day and hour" is a general time indicator, not a precise expression implying a specific time of day (cf. 7:22; 10:19; 24:42, 44, 50; 25:13; 26:45). The word "day" may imply the eschatological significance of the biblical "day of the Lord."[1] This "declaration of eschatological ignorance" (W. Davies and Allison 1997: 374) produces intellectual difficulty and existential tension as one ponders how the time can be near and yet unknowable. In stating that no one knows the time of his coming, Jesus goes so far as to state that not even the angels or even he himself has this information. Only the Father knows, and he alone controls the vicissitudes of

---

1. Cf., e.g., Isa. 2:11–12; 61:2; Jer. 30:7–8; 46:10; Ezek. 7:10–19; 30:3; Joel 1:15; 2:1–2; 3:14; Amos 5:18–20; Zeph. 1:7, 14; Zech. 14:1; Mal. 3:2; 2 Thess. 2:2; 2 Pet. 3:10.

human life.[2] He alone can cut the days of eschatological anguish short (24:22), and he will bring Jesus back to earth at the time indicated by his wisdom. People living in the days preceding Jesus's coming will be as unaware of it as Noah's contemporaries were of the flood (Gen. 6:5–7:24; Isa. 54:9; cf. 2 Pet. 2:5; 3:6). In both instances, God's judgment is totally unanticipated.

The Ignorance of Jesus in Matt. 24:36

Those who hold the classic orthodox doctrine of the Trinity may be concerned with Jesus's claim in 24:36 that he does not know the time of his coming to earth. In ancient times this concern may have led to textual emendation (see the additional note on 24:36). This text (cf. Mark 13:32; Acts 1:7) stresses that the Father alone keeps the timing of Jesus's coming in his own inscrutable counsel. In light of such trinitarian implications as the preexistence and deity of Jesus, this is not easily explained. It is clear, however, that the incarnation of Jesus entailed limitation of the use of his divine attributes (Phil. 2:6–8; Gundry 1994: 492). As a human being, Jesus became hungry, thirsty, and tired (cf. Matt. 4:2; 21:18; John 4:6; 19:28). He was empowered by the Spirit of God for his ministry and his miracles (Matt. 3:16; 4:1; 12:18, 28; cf. Luke 3:22; 4:1, 14, 18; Acts 10:38; John 1:32; 3:34). After the temptation he needed ministry from angels (Matt. 4:11; cf. Luke 22:43). His postresurrection exaltation included the restoration of his glorious preincarnate prerogatives (John 3:13; 17:1–5). Those who are concerned about Matt. 24:36 should focus on its implications for Jesus's genuine humanity (cf. 1 Tim. 2:5). (For a helpful study of the ministry of the Holy Spirit in the life of Jesus, see Hawthorne 1991.)

In Noah's day people were going about their business (cf. Luke 17:26–30), caring for daily needs and making future plans. Despite the preaching of Noah (2 Pet. 2:5), they were oblivious to the threat of impending judgment, and they were surprised by the flood. At that point concern for such matters as food and marriage became pathetically superfluous. The last clause of Matt. 24:38 cites Gen. 7:7. Second Temple literature portrays Noah's generation as notorious sinners (Sir. 16:7; Jub. 20.5–6; 1 En. 67.10; 3 Macc. 2:4; Josephus, *Ant.* 1.72–76).

24:38–39

The connection between Noah's day and the day of Jesus's coming is made clear by two parallel scenes of separation (Matt. 24:40–41; cf. Luke 17:34–35). Two people in the field cultivating crops will be overtaken by Jesus's coming, which takes one and leaves the other. The same separation occurs with two women grinding grain at home. The prospect of such a swift, unexpected separation demonstrates the absolute necessity of

24:40–42

---

2. On eschatological ignorance, see 1 Pet. 1:12; Mekilta on Exod. 16:32; Ps. Sol. 17.21; 2 Bar. 21.8; 48.3; 54.1; 2 Esd. (4 Ezra) 4:52.

alertly expecting Jesus's coming (cf. 1 Cor. 16:13; 1 Thess. 5:6; 1 Pet. 5:8; Rev. 3:2–3; 16:15). Ignorance of the timing must not result in ambivalence concerning the fact of his coming and the abrupt separation of those who expect it from those who do not (cf. Matt. 25:31–46).

Eschatological Separation in Matthew 24:40–42

The language of separation found in 24:40–42 has received extensive discussion among evangelicals who adopt the futurist interpretation. Those who hold the theory of a pretribulational rapture of the church, distinct from Jesus's coming after the unparalleled tribulation of 24:29, debate whether 24:40–42 speaks of the rapture taking believers from the earth and leaving unbelievers (Walvoord 1985). There are two major difficulties. First, Jesus's language does not approximate a distinction between a pretribulational rapture and a posttribulational coming of Jesus to the earth, as Paul arguably does (cf. 1 Thess. 4:13–18; 2 Thess. 1:6–10). Second, the language of one being taken and another being left is ambiguous. During Noah's flood those taken were swept away by the water, and those who were left were protected by the ark (Matt. 24:38–39). This is consistent with Jesus's interpretation of the gathering and burning of the tares in 13:41–42. But 24:31 describes the gathering of God's elect, not those about to be condemned. This is consistent with John's imagery of the wheat gathered into the barn in Matt. 3:12.

One must conclude that there is no pattern in Matthew's use of this language. Further, preoccupation with this question is a diversion from the point of the passage: alert expectation of Jesus's coming (Carson 1984: 509). In cases such as this, exegesis may degenerate into a pedantry that ironically distracts disciples from the teaching of the passage. Exegetical debate must not distract from obedience.

Additional Notes

24:36. UBS⁴ prefers the longer reading, which includes the words οὐδὲ ὁ υἱός (supported by ℵ*, B, D, Θ, f¹³, 28, several old Latin MSS; cf. Mark 13:32). The words are omitted in certain MSS (including ℵ¹, L, W, Δ, f¹, 33, 157, *Byz, Lect*), perhaps out of theological concern. It is much less likely that the words were assimilated here from Mark 13:32 (Metzger 1994: 51–52). The statement that the Father *alone* (μόνος) knows the hour supports the longer reading. See further W. Davies and Allison 1997: 379.

24:38. The word ἐκείναις is omitted by many MSS, including ℵ, L, W, Δ, Θ, 067, 28, 33, f¹, f¹³, *Byz, Lect.* But UBS⁴ includes it in brackets because it is found in other MSS, including B, D, 579.

24:42. UBS⁴ favors the reading ἡμέρα (supported by ℵ, B, C, D, W, Δ, Θ, Σ, 067, f¹³, 1, 33). The Majority text (L, 28, *Byz, Lect*) has ὥρα instead of ἡμέρα, perhaps because of assimilation from 24:44.

ii. Parable of the Thief (24:43–44)

Be ready! In this brief parabolic section, a person whose home is not secured against a burglar provides a negative illustration of the necessity of alertness. The unsuspecting victims of Noah's flood have already illustrated this point (24:36–42). Two further illustrations (24:45–51; 25:1–13) will make this point unmistakably clear.

Exegesis and Exposition

[43]"But understand this, that if the owner of the house had known at what part of the night the thief was coming, he would have been alert and would not have allowed his house to be broken into. [44]Because of this, you also must be ready; for the Son of Man is coming at an hour when you do not think he will."

The necessity of alertness is further illustrated with a story (24:43) and its application (24:44). The story of a thief unexpectedly robbing a house is not unique (cf. 6:19–20; 12:29; 1 Thess. 5:2; 2 Pet. 3:10; Rev. 3:3; 16:15). The owner of the house (Matt. 10:25; 13:27, 52; 20:1, 11; 21:33) has not been warned as to the time of the burglary, and cannot prevent it (cf. Luke 12:39–40). Jesus's disciples do not know *when* Jesus will come but they do know *that* he will come, and so they must be ready to meet him at an unexpected time.

24:43–44

iii. The Faithful and the Evil Slave (24:45–51)

This parable (cf. Luke 12:42–46) symmetrically presents the deeds of a good and an evil slave and the respective consequences. The first slave is found faithfully serving his master when the master returns, and he is rewarded (24:45–47), but the second assumes a delay in the master's return, lives selfishly, and is severely punished (24:48–51). The duality of the parable is reminiscent of 24:40–41 and anticipates the subsequent parables in 25:1–13 and 25:14–30. This parable should probably be taken as a warning to those in authority. Until Jesus comes, those who lead his disciples must use their authority to serve others rather than to aggrandize themselves (Boring 1995: 448). (See further on this parable Harrington 1991; Hultgren 2000: 157–68.)

Exegesis and Exposition

[45]"Who, then, is the faithful and thoughtful slave whom his master put in charge of his household slaves to give them their food at the proper time? [46]Blessed is that slave whom his master finds doing this when he comes. [47]Truly I tell you, he will put him in charge of all his possessions. [48]But if that evil slave says in his heart, 'My master delays,' [49]and begins to beat his fellow slaves and eats and drinks with drunkards, [50]the master of that slave will come on a day when he does not expect him and at an hour that he does not know, [51]and will cut him in pieces and assign him a place with the hypocrites, where there will be weeping and gnashing of teeth."

24:45–47 The parable begins with a rhetorical question, as do others in Matthew (cf. 12:11; 18:12; 21:28). Another household illustration stresses alertness with the contrasting examples of a faithful slave (24:45–47) and an evil slave (24:48–51). Here the unexpected event is the return of a master who has put his slave in charge of feeding his household while he is gone (cf. Luke 12:42–48). Jesus blesses (cf. Matt. 5:3–11; 11:6; 13:16; 16:17; Luke 12:38) the faithful and thoughtful slave (cf. 7:24; 10:16; 25:21, 23; 1 Cor. 4:2), who is promoted to overseeing all his master's possessions. This speaks of eschatological blessings that will be given to faithful disciples (cf. 13:43; 16:27; 19:28–29; 25:21, 23, 29, 34).

24:48–51 In the contrasting scenario, the slave put in charge of the household assumes that his master's return is a long way off (cf. 25:5). This represents the problem of delay in Jesus's promised coming (cf. Ezek. 12:22; Hab. 2:3; 1QpHab 7.1–14; 2 Pet. 3:4). Instead of faithfully performing his assigned duties, the evil slave beats his fellow slaves (cf. Matt. 18:28–33) and overindulges in food and drink with drunkards (cf. 1 Thess. 5:7; Josephus, *Ant.* 15.205–7, 228–29; *J.W.* 2.481–83). But the master's sudden, unexpected arrival catches the partying slave, who is punished by dismemberment (cf. Luke 12:46; Ahiqar 8.38; BDAG 253; O. Betz 1964; K. Weber 1995). Banishment with the hypocrites alludes to the most heinous sin in Matthew (cf. Matt. 6:2, 5, 16; 7:5; 15:7; 22:18; 23:13, 23, 25, 27, 29). Wailing and gnashing of teeth graphically portray the horror of eschatological doom (cf. 8:12; 13:42, 50; 21:41; 22:13; 25:30, 41, 46). Disciples who alertly expect Jesus's coming will avoid this terrifying fate (24:36, 39, 42, 44; 25:13; cf. Luke 21:34–36).

Eschatology and Ethics

The vivid imagery in 24:36–51 warns against such a preoccupation with the tasks and pleasures of daily life that it does not take into account the possibility of imminent divine judgment. Jesus's disciples must be constantly aware that life as they know it could suddenly be terminated by Jesus's coming. They must be like the dependable slave, not like Noah's oblivious generation, the homeowner who does not expect a burglar, or the wicked slave. Disciples must not take up a nonchalant lifestyle that is inconsistent with Jesus's unexpected coming. Matthew 25 will continue with this parabolic and paraenetic emphasis.

Jesus's teaching that his coming will be unexpected exposes the folly of those who link eschatological alertness to the latest news. There are dispensensationalists who constantly scrutinize world events, especially the latest news from the Middle East, searching for prophetic fulfillments that signal the end. Those of this ilk must think that thieves notify homeowners of coming burglaries. Such voices wax and wane in direct proportion to recent news from Israel. But moments of increased tension may be less likely to portend Jesus's coming than days of prosperity and tranquility (cf. 1 Thess. 5:1–3). In any event and whatever world events arise, Jesus's disciples must constantly be about their master's business, vigilantly awaiting his coming. Eschatological correctness is ultimately a matter of ethics, not speculation (Boring 1995: 448).

iv. Parable of the Wise and the Foolish Virgins (25:1–13)

This parable stresses, for the last time in the discourse, that the time of Jesus's coming (24:3) is unknowable. This point has been stated (24:36) and then illustrated both historically from Noah's time (24:37–42) and parabolically from a burglary (24:43) and from good and wicked slaves (24:45–51). The present parable illustrates the point from another familiar scene, a wedding. Five foolish virgins do not prepare for nightfall by bringing extra oil for their lamps, because they expect the bridegroom to arrive immediately. But five others wisely prepare for a delay. The foolish virgins miss the bridegroom and are banned from the wedding feast, but the wise virgins share in the joy of the wedding (cf. 9:15).

Allegorizing interpreters have unnecessarily complicated the exegesis of this parable. Wedding feasts and lamps are used as metaphors elsewhere (e.g., 5:15; 6:22; 9:15; 22:1–14; cf. Ps. 119:105; Prov. 20:27; Rev. 1:12–13; 19:7, 9), and Jesus indicates elsewhere that parabolic details may correspond with reality (Matt. 13:18–23, 37–43, 49–50). But Jesus supplies only a generalizing conclusion for this parable; it is about alertness (25:13). It seems clear enough that Jesus is the bridegroom (9:15; cf. John 3:29; Eph. 5:27) whose arrival is delayed and that the wise and the foolish virgins are alert and lackadaisical disciples. From this one should draw conclusions about spiritual preparedness for final judgment (Blomberg 1990a: 195; Hagner 1995a: 728; Jeremias 1972: 51). Tasker's suggestion (1961: 234) that salvation is not transferable from one person to another is beside the point. One need not be concerned with whether the rapture of believers or the return of Jesus to the earth is in view (contra Walvoord 1974: 196–97). Neither should one identify the oil in the parable with the Holy Spirit (contra M. Green 1988: 240; Hendriksen 1973: 879) or with good works (contra Donfried 1974; Garland 1993: 240–41; cf. Ps. 119). Suggestions such as these only divert attention from the alertness mandated by the context and by the crucial imperative in Matt. 25:13 (cf. Hare 1993: 284–86). Ironically, preoccupation with such interpretive niceties may have the same result as the activities that diverted Noah's generation from awareness of imminent judgment (cf. 24:38–39).[1]

---

1. On this parable, see Donfried 1974, 1975; France in Longenecker 2000: 177–83; Légasse in Delorme 1989: 349–60; Puig i Tàrrech 1983; Sherriff in Livingstone 1980: 301–5; Weder 1978: 239–49; D. Wenham 1984: 77–95.

The unit can be outlined as follows:

(1) The bridegroom delays (25:1–5)
(2) The bridegroom arrives (25:6–10a)
(3) The wedding feast (25:10b–12)
(4) The lesson (25:13)

Exegesis and Exposition

[1]"Then the kingdom of heaven will be like ten virgins who took their lamps and went out to meet ⌜the bridegroom⌝. [2]Five of them were foolish, and five were wise. [3]For when the foolish took their lamps, they did not take oil with them, [4]but the wise took oil in flasks along with their lamps. [5]While the bridegroom was delaying, they all became drowsy and went to sleep. [6]But at midnight a shout was heard, 'Look, the bridegroom! Come out to meet him.' [7]Then all those virgins got up and trimmed their lamps. [8]The foolish said to the wise, 'Give us some of your oil, for our lamps are going out.' [9]But the wise answered, 'No, there will not be enough for both you and us; instead, go to the sellers and buy some for yourselves.' [10]And while they were gone to buy it, the bridegroom came, and those who were ready went in with him to the wedding feast, and the door was shut. [11]Later the other virgins also came and said, 'Lord, lord, open up for us.' [12]But he answered, 'Truly I tell you, I do not know you.' [13]Therefore be alert because you do not know the day or the hour ⌜ ⌝."

(1) The Bridegroom Delays (25:1–5)

This parable begins with the familiar comparison formula (cf. 13:24, 31, 33, 44, 45, 47, 52; 18:23; 20:1; Carson 1985). The wedding setting reminds the reader of the same activity in the days of Noah (24:38). The virgins or maidens are young unmarried women who attend the bride, although one should not read modern customs into this text (cf. Jos. Asen. 2.6). The number ten is significant in Scripture, often indicating a full complement.[2] Whether they wait with the bride at her father's house or wait at the groom's house for the groom to bring the bride for the wedding feast is not clear (cf. Song 3:11; 1 Macc. 9:37–42; Josephus, *Ant.* 13.20). The betrothal contract, or *ketubah*, would already have been executed, and so it remains for the virgins to meet the groom when he takes the bride to the wedding celebration that begins their life together (cf. Song 3:11; 1 Macc. 9:37–42; Jeremias 1972: 171–74).[3]

25:1

---

2. E.g., Gen. 18:32; 45:23; Exod. 34:28; Num. 14:22; Deut. 4:13; 10:4; Ruth 4:2; 1 Sam. 1:8; Job 19:3; Ps. 91:7; Eccles. 7:19; Dan. 1:12; Zech. 8:23; Rev. 2:10; cf. Jub. 19.8; Philo, *Moses* 1.96; Josephus, *J.W.* 6.423; 2 Esd. (4 Ezra) 5:46; *m. 'Abot* 5.1–6; *b. Ketub.* 7b.
3. On marriage customs, see the comments on 1:18 and Argyle 1975; Batey 1971; Keener in C. A. Evans and Porter 2000: 683–87; S. Safrai in Safrai and Stern 1976: 2.748–60. Believers are also likened to virgins in 2 Cor. 11:2; Rev. 14:4.

25:2–5   The foolish (μωραί, *mōrai*, 5:22; 7:26; 23:17) maidens expect the groom to arrive soon, but the wise (φρόνιμοι, *phronimoi*, 7:24; 10:16; 24:45) are prepared for a delay. This duality corresponds to the faithful and the evil servants of the previous parable (24:45, 48), but with a key difference: there the evil servant expected a delay and was not prepared for the master to come soon. The "lamps" (singular, λαμπάς, *lampas*) may be torches, sticks with oil-soaked rags wrapped around one end.[4] The bridegroom's delay (25:5; cf. 24:48) causes all the virgins to grow drowsy and fall asleep (8:24; 9:24; 13:25; 26:38–46; cf. Mark 13:36; 1 Thess. 5:6).[5] The marital imagery of this parable portrays Jesus's relationship with his disciples in a manner equivalent to God's relationship with Israel (e.g., Isa. 54:4–6; 62:5; Jer. 31:32; Ezek. 16:7–22; Hos. 2:16, 19).

(2) The Bridegroom Arrives (25:6–10a)

25:6–10a   At precisely midnight or more likely at some point in the middle of the night (24:43; cf. Exod. 12:29–30 LXX; Mark 13:35–36; Acts 27:27), a shout announces the bridegroom's arrival (cf. the trumpet in Matt. 24:31). The virgins are summoned to meet him. If they are at the bride's house, which seems more likely, they will join the procession to the groom's house for the feast (22:2–14). They may already be at the groom's house when he arrives with the bride. They prepare their lamps (by trimming the wicks and adding oil) or torches (by removing the soot and soaking the rags with oil). But the foolish virgins' lamps are already running out of oil and going out (cf. Prov. 13:9; Job 18:5).[6] The wise virgins refuse to give them oil from their limited supply, and so they must leave to buy more. While they are away, the bridegroom arrives.

(3) The Wedding Feast (25:10b–12)

25:10b–12   The wedding feast (8:11; 22:1–14; Rev. 19:7–10) begins, probably after a procession to the groom's house. The door is locked (Matt. 24:33; cf. Gen. 7:16; Isa. 22:22; Luke 13:25; Rev. 3:7), blocking the admission of the foolish virgins. Their appeal to the groom and his refusal to permit their entry ominously recalls the judgment scene of Matt. 7:21–23 (cf. Luke 13:25; Ps. 1:6). This exclusionary treatment is similar to that experienced by the man without wedding clothes in Matt. 22:11–14.

---

4. So Jeremias in J. Richards 1968: 83–87; John 18:3; Rev. 4:5; 8:10; but see Acts 20:8; Jdt. 10:22; BDAG 585; D. Wenham 1984: 80–81. Hagner (1995a: 729) posits oil lamps tied to poles.

5. The aorist verbs ἐνύσταξαν and ἐκάθευδον are ingressive. Cf. Wallace 1996: 558–59.

6. Wallace (1996: 518–19) takes the verb σβέννυνται as a "narrow band" progressive present depicting the lamps as going out at that very moment, but he notes (1996: 534–35) that a conative nuance is possible, in which case the lamps would be about to go out.

(4) The Lesson (25:13)

Jesus's generalizing conclusion underlines the lesson of the story: constant alertness is necessary because the time of the bridegroom's coming is unknowable (24:3, 36, 39, 42–44, 50; Acts 1:6–7; 1 Thess. 5:2–6). The problem is not so much that the virgins slept when the groom's arrival was delayed but that the foolish virgins were not ready when he eventually did come. They expected the bridegroom to come on their schedule, not his (Weder 1978: 244–47).

The lesson of this parable coheres with Jesus's parabolic teaching elsewhere in Matthew. It is a warning to the church, which is realistically portrayed in its mixed nature (cf. Matt. 22:11–14; 24:10–14; Overman 1996: 342). The foolish virgins' lack of insight is similar to that of the man whose lack of obedience to Jesus is pictured as building a house on the sand (7:24–27). Comparing 25:5 to 24:48 links the lesson of this parable to that of the evil slave. In both cases there is delay in the return of Jesus. But the two reactions to this delay are opposites, and these opposite reactions teach a crucial lesson. The evil slave is irresponsible because he overestimates the delay of the master's return. He is unpleasantly surprised by the master's seemingly early arrival. On the other hand, the foolish virgins are careless and underestimate the delay in the groom's arrival. The evil slave's lackadaisical approach to the master's return is similar to the generation of Noah and the homeowner, neither of whom expected an imminent event (24:36–44). But the foolish virgins took readiness to the extreme and did not plan for any delay. From these opposite errors, the church learns that it cannot know the time of Jesus's coming. It can assume neither an immediate nor an eventual return. Christians must constantly expect Jesus while they persevere in obedience and mission (cf. 10:22; 13:20–21; 24:13). The duties of constant readiness and future preparedness must be held in dynamic tension if the church is to be faithful to the teaching of its master (cf. Luke 12:35–40; Meier 1980b: 294–95). Those who do not exhibit constant alertness jeopardize not only their present opportunities for effective service to Jesus but also their eternal destiny.

Additional Notes

25:1. The UBS[4] reading τοῦ νυμφίου is well supported by ℵ, B, L, W, Z, Δ, 0249, *f*[13], 28, 33, *Byz, Lect.* The reading τοῦ νυμφίου καὶ τῆς νύμφης (supported by D, Θ, Σ, 1, and many Old Latin MSS) may reflect ancient marriage customs but does not fit the common allegorical interpretation of the parable (Metzger 1994: 52–53). There are also two minor readings, τῷ νυμφίῳ (supported by C, 157) and τῶν νυμφίων (supported by 892).

25:13. The shorter reading (supported by 𝔓[35], ℵ, A, B, C*, D, L, W, Δ, Θ, Σ, *f*[1], 33) ends the verse with ὥραν. The longer reading adds the relative clause ἐν ᾗ ὁ υἱὸς τοῦ ἀνθρώπου ἔρχεται (supported by C[3], *f*[13], 1[c], 28, *Byz, Lect*), probably an attempted scribal clarification that (over?)stresses what is already clear from the context (24:36, 42, 44, 50).

v. Parable of the Talents (25:14–30)

The preceding parables have stressed alertness, and this one is about the result of alertness, faithful stewardship. This parable is quite similar to Luke's parable of the pounds (Luke 19:12–27).[1] The issue here is not whether the slaves will be surprised by the master's return but whether they will be dependable in using his resources. His gifts define their tasks. The master entrusts his resources to his slaves according to their individual abilities (Matt. 25:15). The third slave receives just one talent, showing the master's realization of his limited abilities. Yet he ought to have earned something with the single talent entrusted to him.

It seems clear that Jesus is the master whose departure and return frame the events of the parable. The three servants stand for the church, which is once again portrayed as a mixed community (13:23; 22:10–14; 24:10–12; 25:11–12; Keener 1999: 601–2; Overman 1996: 345).[2] Blomberg (1992a: 371) points out that whereas the foolish virgins thought their task was easier than it turned out to be, the lazy slave thought his task was harder than it turned out to be. This shows that faithfulness to Jesus during his absence leads to good stewardship of one's opportunities and abilities (cf. Luke 12:42; Rom. 12:6–8; 1 Cor. 4:1–2; 7:7; 12:4–7; Eph. 4:7–8; Titus 1:7; 1 Pet. 4:10). To be alert is to actively exercise one's gifts and opportunities for service to Jesus and his kingdom. A familiar saying is appropriate here: "Attempt great things for God, expect great things from God."[3] Disciples must not make shaky investments with their Lord's resources, but they cannot excuse their laziness by claiming that they have incurred no losses. "When Christ returns, he will not ask if one had the date right but 'What have you been doing?'" (Garland 1993: 241).

The following layout shows that the structure of this parable is symmetrical, with each of the three scenes dealing with the three

---

1. For introductory discussions of the similarities and differences between the two parables and hypotheses on literary relationships (cf. Mark 13:34), see Bock 1996: 1526–29; Hultgren 2000: 272–74, 283–84.

2. Harrington (1991: 354–55) argues that the third slave represents not the church but post-70 CE proto-rabbinic Judaism. This is overly subtle and injects a foreign polemical element into a hortatory passage.

3. Evidently, some form of this saying originated with William Carey in a sermon at a Baptist association meeting in Northampton, England, on May 30, 1792. Cf. Center for Study of the Life and Work of William Carey, DD (1761–1834), "Expect Great Things; Attempt Great Things," www.wmcarey.edu/carey/expect/expect.htm.

slaves in the same order. Each of the successive three scenes is longer than the preceding one, with the most stress placed at the end on the punishment of the wicked slave. Thus the parable, despite its positive elements in 25:21, 23, is primarily a warning against irresponsibility among professed disciples rather than an encouragement to faithfulness (Hare 1993: 287).[4]

The Structure of the Parable of the Talents (Matt. 25:14–30)[5]

Distribution of resources (25:15)
   Five talents entrusted (25:15)
   Two talents entrusted (25:15)
   One talent entrusted (25:15)
Stewardship of resources (25:16–18)
   Five talents invested and five more earned (25:16)
   Two talents invested and two more earned (25:17)
   One talent hidden and nothing earned (25:18)
Reward for stewardship (25:19–30)
   Good and faithful slave rewarded (25:20–21)
   Good and faithful slave rewarded (25:22–23)
   Wicked and lazy servant punished (25:24–30)

The unit outline is as follows:

(1) The master distributes his resources (25:14–15)
(2) The slaves do business for the master (25:16–18)
(3) The slaves give account to the master (25:19–30)
   (a) The faithful slaves are rewarded (25:19–23)
   (b) The lazy slave is punished (25:24–30)

Exegesis and Exposition

[14]"For it is like a man going on a journey, who called his own slaves and entrusted his possessions to them. [15]To one he gave five talents, to another, two, and to another, one, to each according to his own ability; and he went on his journey. [16] [Immediately][7] the one who had received the five talents went and did business with them, and made five more talents. [17]In the same way the one who had received the two talents made two more. [18]But the one who

---

4. Among the extensive literature on this parable, see Derrett 1970b: 17–31; Dietzfelbinger 1989; Fortna 1992; France in Longenecker 2000: 183–89; Hultgren 2000: 271–81; Manns 1991; F. Martin 1996; Rohrbaugh 1993; Wohlgemut in Shillington 1997: 103–20.

5. See W. Davies and Allison 1997: 401–2; Gnilka 1986–88: 2.356; Puig i Tàrrech 1983: 168. For stories that share certain motifs with this parable, see 3 Bar. 12–16; Mekilta on Exod. 20:2; 'Abot R. Nat. 14a; b. Šabb. 152b; Song Rab. 7.14.1.

received the one talent went away and dug a hole in the ground and hid his master's money.

[19]"Now after a long time the master of those slaves came and settled accounts with them. [20]The one who had received the five talents came forward and brought the other five talents, saying, 'Master, you entrusted five talents to me. Look, I have made five more talents.' [21]His master said to him, 'Well done, good and faithful slave. You were faithful over a few things, I will put you in charge of many things; enter into your master's joy.'

[22]"The one who had received the two talents also came forward and said, 'Master, you entrusted two talents to me. Look, I have made two more talents.' [23]His master said to him, 'Well done, good and faithful slave. You were faithful over a few things, I will put you in charge of many things; enter into your master's joy.'

[24]"The one also who had received the one talent also came up and said, 'Master, I knew you, that you are a cruel man, reaping where you did not sow and gathering where you did not scatter seed. [25]So I was afraid, and I went away and hid your talent in the ground. Look, you have what is yours.' [26]But his master answered him, 'You wicked, lazy slave, so you knew that I reap where I did not sow and gather where I have not scattered seed, did you? [27]Then you should have deposited my money with the bankers, and when I came I would have received my money back with interest. [28]Therefore take away the talent from him, and give it to the one who has the ten talents.' [29]For to everyone who has, more will be given, and he will have an abundance; but from the one who does not have, even what he does have will be taken away. [30]And throw out the worthless slave into the outer darkness, where there will be weeping and gnashing of teeth."

(1) The Master Distributes His Resources (25:14–15)

25:14–15   This parable is introduced only by the words "it is like" (ὥσπερ, *hōsper*; cf. 6:2, 7; 12:40; 13:40; 18:17; 20:28; 24:27, 37; 25:32). It is about an absentee master (cf. 21:33; 24:45–51). As the scene is set, three slaves are entrusted with the master's resources, according to their individual abilities (cf. Josephus, *Ant.* 3.108), respectively with five, two, and one talents (cf. 18:24). A talent was originally a measure of weight and is variously estimated at fifty to seventy-five pounds. As a monetary term, its value also varied, but it always connoted a very large sum, evidently around six thousand silver denarii (BDAG 988). A day laborer would have to work more than nineteen years to earn one talent. Five talents is a huge fortune, perhaps unrealistically so (cf. 18:28), which may "imply the greatness of God's gifts to his people" (W. Davies and Allison 1997: 405). Unlike in Luke 19:13, the slaves are not given specific instructions about what to do with the talents.

(2) The Slaves Do Business for the Master (25:16–18)

See the additional note for discussion of the textual problem concerning whether the adverb εὐθέως (*eutheōs*, immediately) describes the action of the master or the first slave. The translation above takes it as the slave's immediate response to the master. Each slave's stewardship of what was entrusted to him is mentioned here. The first two slaves do business with their talents and gain a 100 percent profit, but the third slave digs a hole in the ground to hide his master's talent (cf. 13:44; Luke 19:20; Sir. 29:10; 2 En. 51.1–2 [J text]; *b. B. Meṣiʿa* 42a; *b. Šabb.* 102b). Just as there were no instructions in Matt. 25:15, there is no mention here of what business enterprise yielded the first two slaves their respective profits.

25:16–18

(3) The Slaves Give Account to the Master (25:19–30)

(a) The Faithful Slaves Are Rewarded (25:19–23)

The matter of delay in the master's return occurs for the third time in the context (cf. 24:48; 25:5). When he arrives after a long absence, the slaves are called to account for his resources (cf. 18:23). This evidently portrays the final judgment. Each of the first two slaves demonstrates his 100 percent profit and is described by the master as "good and faithful" (cf. 24:45). The master heartily rewards their faithfulness with relatively little by assigning them much more (cf. 24:47; 25:28–29; Luke 16:10; 19:17; *m. ʾAbot* 4.2; *b. Ber.* 11b). Entrance into the master's joy probably portrays entrance (Matt. 18:3) into the eschatological feast (8:11; 22:2; 25:10; 26:29) that inaugurates the reign of Jesus on earth. The greatest joy of a follower of Jesus is to share in the joy of Jesus (cf. Heb. 12:2; Rev. 19:7). Both servants receive the same reward even though the first accomplished quantitatively more than the second. This shows that the characteristic of fidelity is rewarded, not merely numerical success.

25:19–23

(b) The Lazy Slave Is Punished (25:24–30)

As one might anticipate from 25:18, the third slave is treated differently. He states that he has preserved the master's talent by hiding it in the ground (cf. 13:44) because he fears his master's harshness. In that culture, the repeated double statement describing the master's harshness (25:24b, 26b) is perhaps proverbial and not necessarily metaphorical (contra W. Davies and Allison 1997: 409). The slave attempts to persuade the master that his caution is commendable. Despite calling his master "Master" (cf. 7:21–23; 25:11), he has earned nothing. His estimate of the master's harshness ironically proves to be correct. The master is angry that this slave, whom he describes as wicked (7:11; 13:49; 22:10) and lazy (ὀκνηρός, *oknēros*; cf. Prov. 6:6, 9 LXX; Rom. 12:11), has not even deposited the money with bankers (cf. Let. Aris. 26; Josephus, *Ant.* 12.32), where it could have earned some interest. Hiding the master's resources

25:24–27

in the ground is as senseless and useless as hiding one's lamp under a basket (Matt. 5:15). Inaction is not prudence but sloth.

25:28–30 After his dialogue with the third slave (25:24–27), the master now gives orders concerning him. The single talent will be taken from him and given to the first servant, who will have eleven talents (cf. Gos. Thom. 41; b. Ber. 55a). The third slave is useless; he has earned nothing for the master, and his severe punishment is just, since he freely admitted that he knew the master's disposition (cf. 8:12; 13:42, 50; 22:13; 24:51). The master's action may seem harsh, but it is balanced by the generosity of the abundant reward given to the first two slaves (13:12; cf. Prov. 9:9; Luke 12:48; 19:26).[6]

From the first two slaves, one deduces that trustworthiness leads to even greater blessing, but the third slave demonstrates a lack of trustworthiness that leads to removal of the original blessing. There is no excuse for inactivity, since it arises out of fear and sloth (Prov. 6:6–9), neither of which is compatible with discipleship. Followers of Jesus have been equipped to serve him and are obligated to use their gifts to extend God's reign (cf. Luke 19:13; Rom. 12:6; 1 Cor. 12:7; Eph. 4:7; 1 Pet. 4:10). God will call disciples to account for the stewardship of their individual abilities (Matt. 25:15), nothing more and nothing less. A previous parable implies that fearful inaction is unwarranted because God will forgive unwise action with his resources (18:23–25). Perhaps the apathy of this third slave should be viewed as the opposite of the enthusiasm of the foolish virgins (25:3, 10–12).

Additional Note

25:15–16. The textual question here concerns whether εὐθέως describes the departure of the man or the obedience of his slave. The ambiguity of the asyndetic UBS[4] reading ἀπεδήμησεν εὐθέως πορευθείς (supported only by ℵ*, B, and limited versional and patristic evidence) is removed by the modern editors' insertion of a period after ἀπεδήμησεν, which understands εὐθέως as describing the immediacy of the slave's response. The placement of δέ in the reading ἀπεδήμησεν εὐθέως δὲ πορευθείς (supported by Θ, f¹, 205, and some early versions) yields the same interpretation, one that is supported by the use of εὐθέως elsewhere in Matthew (cf. 4:20, 22; 8:3; 13:5; 14:22, 31; 20:34; 21:2; 24:29; 26:49, 74; 27:48; Metzger 1994: 53). The reading ἀπεδήμησεν εὐθέως πορευθείς δέ (supported widely by ℵ², A, C, D, L, W, f¹³, 28, 33, Byz, Lect) takes εὐθέως as describing the immediacy of the man's departure, which seems to be beside the point.

---

6. Boring (1995: 453n536) takes 25:28–29 as speaking of an outright gift, not an opportunity for additional stewardship. This view attractively stresses the gracious generosity of the master, but it does so at the expense of the central concept of the parable, the disciples' stewardship of God's resources. In any event, the giving (δοθήσεται) and the taking away (ἀρθήσεται) of 25:29 are divine passives (Wallace 1996: 437–38) that describe God's actions at the final judgment.

vi. The Final Judgment (25:31–46)

Hagner (1995a: 740) cogently observes that "the final section of the eschatological discourse ends fittingly in a great judgment scene." This discourse, which began with the disciples' question about Jesus's coming (24:3), ends with his coming to judge all the nations. But the disciples' question was primarily chronological, and this passage deals with the significance of Jesus's coming, not its timing. It amounts to an exposition of 10:40–42 and 24:29–31. The following simple analysis shows the chiastic structure of this pericope:

The Structure of the Last Judgment Passage (Matt. 25:31–46)

Setting: Glorious return of the Son of Man expressed
    metaphorically: Sheep on the right and goats on the
    left (25:31–33)
Judgment of the sheep (25:34–40)
    Judgment of the goats (25:41–45)
    Destiny of goats: Eternal punishment (25:46a)
Destiny of sheep: Eternal life (25:46b)

The following more detailed analysis displays the symmetry between the two halves of the passage (see also W. Davies and Allison 1997: 416–17; Hagner 1995a: 740–41):

Setting: Glorious return of the Son of Man expressed
    metaphorically: Sheep on the right and goats on the
    left (25:31–33)
Judge's verdict for the sheep: Reward for caring for the judge
    (25:34–36)
    Sheep's surprise: When did they do this? (25:37–39)
    Judge's response: When they cared for the judge's
    siblings (25:40)
Judge's verdict for the goats: Punishment for not caring for
    the judge (25:41–43)
    Goats' surprise: When did they not do this? (25:44)
    Judge's response: When they did not care for the judge's
    siblings (25:45)
Conclusion: Destinies of the two groups (25:46)
    Goats: Eternal punishment (25:46a)
    Sheep: Eternal life (25:46b)

Although some scholars call 25:31–46 a parable (e.g., T. Robinson 1928: 208–9; sources cited in Hultgren 2000: 310n2), its metaphorical elements (25:32b-33) do not extend throughout the discourse. It begins and concludes as a prose narrative of the judgment of the nations. The narrative has four parts: the setting of the judgment (25:31–33), the invitation to the righteous to enter the kingdom (25:34–40), the banishment of the wicked to eternal fire (25:41–45), and the chiastic conclusion (25:46). This final section of the Olivet Discourse adds the lesson of compassion to the lessons of alertness (24:32–25:13) and faithfulness (25:14–30) that have been inculcated as the proper ethical response to Jesus's coming.

Interpreting Matthew 25:31–46

The interpretation of this passage is earnestly debated in an extensive body of literature containing painstaking discussions of each exegetical detail, especially the identity of "all the nations" in 25:32 and of Jesus's siblings in 25:40, 45. This passage requires theologians to probe the depths of the relationship between faith and works (Mitton 1956–57). Its implications for Christian ethics are also undeniable (Donahue 1986; Via 1987). This is perhaps the most profoundly difficult text in Matthew. Gray (1989) notes thirty-two different interpretations of the passage, but three are most commonly encountered (Ladd in Longenecker and Tenney 1974: 191–99).

Most scholars today take the parable as a description of the final judgment, which will be based only on our treatment of our needy fellows.[1] This view stresses social consciousness and Jesus's love command. It takes Jesus's "least of these" as anyone in need and makes salvation depend on one's efforts to help such. Some who hold the view are sensitive that it is not distinctively Christian and attempt to place it in a Christian context (e.g., Boring 1995: 456; Bruner 1990: 912–14, 921–25), but others have no qualms that it makes salvation depend on good works alone (e.g., Beare 1981: 496–97). The strength of the view is its ability to handle the sheep's surprise when they learn they have been helping Jesus, but the identification of Jesus's "brothers" (and sisters) as everyone in need is not tenable in light of Matthew's use of this word elsewhere (see below). Keener (1999: 604–5) is right: the view is not "exegetically compelling," although it "would on other grounds be entirely consonant with the Jesus tradition." In other words, there is no doubt that Jesus modeled and elsewhere taught the necessity of helping all who were needy, but this particular passage is not part

---

1. Barclay 1975: 2.325–26; Beare 1981: 495; Boring 1995: 456; Catchpole 1979; Christian 1975; Cranfield 1994; W. Davies and Allison 1997: 428–29; Friedrich 1977; Hill 1972: 331; Meier 1980b: 304; Schnackenburg 2002: 258–59.

b. An Exhortation to Alertness
vi. The Final Judgment

Matthew 25:31–46

of that teaching. Further, outreach to the needy is the activity of the community of faithful disciples.

A second common view is that of classic dispensationalism, which sets the passage in a specific eschatological niche: the judgment of the nations that survive the future eschatological tribulation. Participation in the future earthly millennium hangs in the balance, and the basis of judgment is how the nations have treated the Jews during their persecution by the antichrist.[2] The strength of this view is its grasp of the necessary connection, in Matthew and elsewhere in the NT, between faith and works. The preceding view cannot handle this crucial point. Matthew, however, does not teach the developed dispensational system of a series of judgments of different groups in the end times.[3] Neither does Matthew's use of the term "brother" permit the identification of Jesus's "least of these" as Jews per se.

The third view is the one most widely held throughout the church's history, and it is accepted in this commentary. As does the first view, it takes the passage as depicting the final judgment of all humanity, but it disagrees on the identity of the needy in the parable, taking them either as Christians in general[4] or Christian missionaries in particular (Michaels 1965; Suh 2006). In this view, the faith of individual humans is tested by their treatment of the community that embodies and extends the message of Jesus. The sheep are those whose faith is demonstrated by works that help needy fellow believers; the goats are those whose lack of such helpful works demonstrates they are not true followers of Jesus, whether they profess to be so or not. The strength of this view is its understanding of Jesus's needy disciples in the Matthean context rather than in a modern context that emphasizes the brotherhood of all humans. One supposed weakness of the view is that it does not account for the surprise of the sheep at their inheritance of the kingdom, but the sheep are not so much surprised that they enter the kingdom as they are surprised that their service to destitute strugglers was actually service to Jesus himself (Blomberg 1992a: 377).

The identity of "the least of my brothers and sisters" is the watershed of the entire discussion. In Matthew a brother (ἀδελφός, *adelphos*) is a sibling, either biologically (1:2, 11; 4:18, 21; 10:2, 21; 12:46–47; 13:55;

2. Barbieri in Walvoord and Zuck 1983: 80–81; Toussaint 1980: 288–89; Walvoord 1974: 202. Cf. 2 Bar. 72.1–6, where the nations are judged on the basis of their treatment of Israel.

3. The separate judgment of Jews and Gentiles entailed in Harrington's view (1991: 358–60; cf. Hare 1993: 289–91) of "all the nations" in 25:32, however, has some affinities with the classical dispensational view.

4. Blomberg 1992a: 377–78; Carson 1984: 518–20; Friedrich 1977; France 1985: 355–56; Garland 1993: 243–45; Gundry 1994: 514–15; Hagner 1995a: 744–45; Keener 1999: 604–6; Overman 1996: 348–52; Stanton 1992b: 214–21.

14:3; 17:1; 19:29; 20:24; 22:24–25) or spiritually. Spiritual brothers (and sisters) are fellow disciples, siblings in the community/family of those who follow Jesus (5:22–24, 47; 7:3–5; 12:48–50; 18:15, 21, 35; 23:8; 25:40; 28:10; Hagner 1995a: 744–45).[5] A related term in Matthew is "the little ones" (οἱ μικροί, *hoi mikroi*, 10:42; 18:6, 10, 14; cf. 11:11), whose repentance renders them humble disciples who no longer seek worldly power and status. One dare not cause the spiritual ruin of these little ones (18:6), and genuine forgiveness must occur if one of them sins against the other (18:21, 35). In Jesus's radically egalitarian community, status and prestige are out of place, since all his disciples are siblings in the same family (20:20–28; 23:8–10).[6] When this community/family goes out in mission, it will encounter the most severe difficulties and will need help to endure its hardships. This help will come from those who are receptive to the message embodied and proclaimed by the community, who will be rewarded (10:40–42).

Matthew 25:31–46 portrays the occasion of this reward: at the final judgment, helping "the least of my brothers and sisters" is tantamount to helping Jesus himself (25:40, 45; cf. 10:40; 18:5; Prov. 19:17; Luke 10:16; John 13:20; Gal. 4:14; 3 John 6; Midr. Taṇḥuma on Deut. 15:9). The word "least" (ἐλάχιστος, *elachistos*) was used as the superlative of μικρός (BDAG 314), and in Matt. 25:40, 45 it repeats and intensifies the parallel expression in 10:42, which uses μικρός. The usage of ἐλάχιστος elsewhere in Matthew illumines the teaching that Jesus's disciples are those of little earthly significance but great heavenly significance. Bethlehem is not really "least" among Judean villages when its significance in God's plan is considered (2:6). Even the least of God's commandments has eternal significance (5:19).[7] Similarly, the real significance of Jesus's disciples may now be masked by their lack of the basic human necessities, but final judgment will reveal that their troubles are in reality the troubles of Jesus. Their identification with him and mission for him have put them in such dire straits,[8] and his reward will unveil their true status as they inherit the kingdom of God.

Itinerant preachers especially need the kind of support described in 25:35–36 (cf. 10:40; 3 John 5–8; Mánek in Lindars and Smalley 1973:

---

5. BDAG 19 seems mistaken in viewing ἀδελφός in 5:22–24; 7:3–5; 18:15, 21, 35 merely as a neighbor with no implications of common faith.

6. Further insight into the humble status of Jesus's community/family is gained by looking into Matthew's use of the words παιδίον (child, 18:2–5; cf. 19:13–14), παῖς (child, 2:16; 21:15), and νήπιος (infant, 11:25; 21:16). One wonders whether the imagery of 18:2–5 is an allusion to Isa. 11:6 LXX—παιδίον μικρὸν ἄξει αὐτούς.

7. Perhaps Paul's use of ἐλάχιστος to describe himself in 1 Cor. 15:9 (cf. 2 Cor. 12:11; 1 Tim. 1:15) is drawn from this dominical tradition. Cf. Paul's unique "comparative-superlative" (Wallace 1996: 302) ἐλαχιστότερος in Eph. 3:8.

8. Cf. Mark 13:13; John 15:18, 20–21; 17:14, 18; Acts 9:4; 22:7; 26:14; 1 Cor. 8:12; 12:26–27; Heb. 2:17–18.

b. An Exhortation to Alertness
vi. The Final Judgment

Matthew 25:31–46

15–25; Michaels 1965), but it is doubtful that they alone are in view here. All of Jesus's disciples are identified with him and persecuted because of their connection with him (5:11; 10:18, 22, 25; 23:34). The privation of Jesus's little brothers and sisters in 25:35–36 is due to their testimony for him. When one shows mercy to a follower of Jesus, in a profound sense one is showing mercy to Jesus himself.

This argument for a restrictive meaning of Jesus's little siblings in 25:40, 45 must be balanced by the fact that in Matthew Jesus models and teaches his disciples to love and help all people, even their enemies (5:47; cf., e.g., 4:23–24; 5:7; 9:13; 12:7; 14:14–21). But there is a special love for one's fellow disciples, and a particular responsibility to meet their needs (cf. Gal. 6:10).[9]

The unit can be outlined as follows:

(1) The setting (25:31–33)
(2) The king and the sheep (25:34–40)
(3) The king and the goats (25:41–45)
(4) Conclusion (25:46)

Exegesis and Exposition

[31]"And when the Son of Man comes in his glory, and all the angels with him, then he will sit on his glorious throne. [32]And all the nations will be gathered before him; and he will separate them from one another, as the shepherd separates the sheep from the goats; [33]and he will put the sheep on his right, and the goats on his left.

[34]"Then the king will say to those on his right, 'Come, you who are blessed by my Father, inherit the kingdom prepared for you from the foundation of the world. [35]For I was hungry, and you gave me something to eat; I was thirsty, and you gave me something to drink; I was a stranger, and you welcomed me; [36]I was naked, and you clothed me; I was sick, and you looked after me; I was in prison, and you visited me.'

[37]"Then the righteous will answer him, 'Lord, when did we see you hungry and give you something to eat, or thirsty and give you something to drink? [38]And when did we see you a stranger and welcome you, or naked and clothe you? [39]When did we see you sick, or in prison, and visit you?' [40]The king will answer them, 'Truly I tell you, whatever you did for one of the least of my brothers and sisters, you did for me.'

[41]"Then he will also say to those on his left, 'Depart from me, accursed ones, into the eternal fire prepared for the devil and his angels; [42]for I was hungry and

9. Among the extensive literature on this passage, see esp. Brandenburger 1980; S. Brown 1990; Catchpole 1979; Christian 1975; France in Longenecker 2000: 189–94; Friedrich 1977; Gray 1989; Heil 1998; Hultgren 2000: 309–30; Luz in Bauer and Powell 1996: 271–310; Panier 1993; Stanton 1992b: 207–31; Via 1987; Watson 1993: 57–84; K. Weber 1997; Weren 1979.

you gave me nothing to eat; I was thirsty and you gave me nothing to drink; [43]I was a stranger and you did not welcome me; naked and you did not clothe me; sick and in prison and you did not visit me.'

[44]"Then they also will answer, 'Lord, when did we see you hungry, or thirsty, or a stranger, or naked, or sick, or in prison and did not help you?' [45]Then he will answer them, 'Truly I tell you, whatever you did not do for one of the least of these, you did not do for me.' [46]And these will depart into eternal punishment, but the righteous into eternal life."

(1) The Setting (25:31–33)

25:31-33 The grim picture of the judgment of the lazy slave (25:30) sets the scene for this account of Jesus's coming with his angels (Zech. 14:5 LXX; cf. Matt. 13:41, 49; 16:27; 24:31) as the glorious Son of Man to judge the nations.[10] An added detail is the mention of his sitting on his glorious throne (Matt. 19:28; cf. 5:34; 23:22; Luke 1:32; Rev. 3:21).[11] This judgment is universal: all nations are gathered[12] on his right and left, just as a shepherd[13] separates sheep from goats (Matt. 13:41, 49; Ezek. 34:17–22). In this context (unlike Matt. 20:23), the right hand is the place of honor (22:44; 26:64; cf. 1 Kings 2:19), and the left hand is the place of shame (cf. 6:3; 27:38; 1 Kings 22:19). This "judgment" is not like a trial, containing suspense about the verdict, but is like a posttrial hearing where the sentence is pronounced (cf. John 5:22, 27; 2 Cor. 5:10). In view of other passages, it is fitting for sheep to stand for genuine followers of Jesus.[14] Sheep were probably more valuable to peasants than goats because of their wool. This passage differs from other judgment scenes because it evidently assumes, rather than men-

10. Cf. 13:41; 16:27–28; 24:31; 26:64; Dan. 7:13–14; Zech. 14:5; John 5:27; 2 Thess. 1:7; 1 En. 1.9; 61.8; 62.1–5; 69.27–29; 90.20–36.

11. The expression ἐπὶ θρόνου δόξης αὐτοῦ is an instance of the attributive genitive, analogous to the construct state in Biblical Hebrew (Waltke and O'Connor 1990: 138–43). Δόξης functions adjectivally with the head noun θρόνου (cf. BDF §165; Wallace 1996: 86–88; Zerwick 1963: 14–15).

12. On the gathering of the nations, see 13:47; cf. Luke 21:35; Isa. 66:18 LXX; Joel 3:2, 11–12; Zeph. 3:8; Zech. 14:2; 2 Esd. (4 Ezra) 7:37; 2 Bar. 72.2; T. Benj. 9.2. Harrington (1991: 358–60) argues that "all the nations" means all the gentile nations, excluding the Jews, but the notion of separate judgments for Jews and Gentiles is doubtful (cf. 24:9, 14; W. Davies and Allison 1997: 422–23; Hagner 1995a: 742). Garland (1993: 243) argues that πάντα τὰ ἔθνη does not include Jesus's disciples, who are not being judged here but stand with Jesus. But it seems that the helpful action of the sheep/righteous in the passage demonstrates that they are Jesus's disciples. It is best to give πάντα τὰ ἔθνη an unrestricted meaning.

13. The Greek ὁ ποιμήν is an instance of the generic article, which describes shepherds as a class rather than an individual shepherd. Cf. Wallace 1996: 227–31.

14. Cf. 9:36; 10:6, 16; 15:24; 18:12; 26:31; cf. 2 Sam. 24:17; Jer. 23:3–4; Ezek. 34:6; John 10; 1 En. 90.6, 30, 32.

tions, a resurrection (cf. Acts 17:31; Rom. 14:10–12; 1 Cor. 15:51–57; 2 Cor. 5:10; Rev. 20:11–15).

(2) The King and the Sheep (25:34–40)

Jesus has been described as the Son of Man, who judges the nations as   25:34–40
a shepherd separates a flock. But when he begins to speak here, he is
identified as a king (2:2; 21:5; 27:11, 29, 37, 42) who determines who
will enter his kingdom. Jesus first tells the sheep on his right hand that
they whom the Father has blessed (5:3–12) will inherit (5:5; 19:29) the
kingdom[15] because they helped him when he was hungry (14:16; 15:32),
thirsty (10:42), away from home (Gen. 18:1–8; Job 31:32; Heb. 13:2;
1 Tim. 5:10), naked (Rom. 8:35; 1 Cor. 4:11; 2 Cor. 11:27), sick (Sir. 7:35;
Josephus, *Ant.* 9.178), and imprisoned (Matt. 10:18–19; Ps. 69:33; Heb.
10:34; 13:3). When the righteous (10:41; 13:43, 49) profess ignorance of
this merciful ministry (cf. Job 22:6–7; 2 Esd. [4 Ezra] 2:20–23), he tells
them that they did it for him when they did it for one of his little brothers and sisters (cf. Cuvillier 2001). The righteous are amazed because
they did not realize that these six acts of ministry to Jesus's suffering
people would be regarded as ministry to him (10:40; cf. 1 Cor. 4:8–13;
2 Cor. 6:1–10). This is the central basis of judgment in this passage (cf.
Prov. 19:17). God's preparation of the kingdom for the blessed ones here
contrasts with the preparation of eternal fire for the devil and his angels
in Matt. 25:41 (cf. 20:23; 22:4; Rom. 9:23; 1 En. 22.3; 54.1–2; 2 Esd.
[4 Ezra] 8:60; 2 Bar. 21.17; 2 En. 9.1).

(3) The King and the Goats (25:41–45)

These verses are symmetrically repetitive of 25:34–40 except that those   25:41–45
on the king's left must depart into eternal fire (7:23; 18:8; cf. Ps. 6:8; Isa.
30:33; Rev. 19:20; 20:10; 1 En. 10.13; 67.13; 2 En. 10.4–6) because they
did not help Jesus when he was in need (cf. Luke 16:19–31). They too
are amazed at the basis of the judgment. Theirs is a catastrophic sin of
omission. The horrifying words "Depart from me" (πορεύεσθε ἀπ᾽ ἐμοῦ,
poreuesthe ap᾽ emou) are similar to the strong statements in 4:10 and
16:23. It is noteworthy, against a fatalistic view of eternal punishment,
that the eternal fire (3:12; 13:42, 50; 18:8–9) is not prepared for those
on the king's left but for the devil and his angels, who are evidently the
demons.[16] Also unlike the kingdom in 25:34, the place of eternal fire is
not said to be prepared from the creation of the world.

---

15. God's preparation of the kingdom ἀπὸ καταβολῆς κόσμου echoes a familiar biblical
phrase. Cf. Luke 11:50; John 17:24; Eph. 1:4; Heb. 4:3; 9:26; 1 Pet. 1:20; Rev. 13:8; 17:8;
As. Mos. 1.14; 2 Esd. (4 Ezra) 6:1; Barn. 5.5.
16. See 4:24; 8:16, 28–34; 9:32–34; 12:22–29, 43–45; 15:22; cf. 2 Cor. 12:7; Jude 6; Rev.
12:7, 9; T. Ash. 6.4; 2 En. 29.4–5.

(4) Conclusion (25:46)

25:46 This summary recapitulates the judgment of those on the right and on the left. The order of the previous narrative (right then left) is inverted here. Those on the left go to eternal punishment (25:41; cf. 1QS 2.15; 5.13; 1QM 1.5; 9.5–6; 4Q510 1.7), and those on the right to eternal life (25:34; cf. 19:16, 29; cf. Dan. 12:2; John 5:28–29; 2 Bar. 51.6). The unique gravity of this judgment is stressed by the repetition of the word "eternal," and the inversion of the narrative order results in stressing the bliss of those who in faith have obeyed the Golden Rule (Matt. 7:12; 19:19; 22:39; cf. Lev. 19:18).

This passage speaks clearly on the most awesome matter, humanity's eternal destiny. The juxtaposition of eternal life and eternal punishment in Matt. 25:46 renders the notion of the annihilation of the lost, sometimes called conditional immortality, as theological wishful thinking (Yarbrough in C. Morgan and Peterson 2004: 67–90, esp. 76, 81–82). The blessed will experience unspeakable joy in God's presence forever, and the cursed will experience unspeakable horror in separation from God. Matthew's descriptions of the destiny of the lost utilize two metaphors, fire (3:12; 13:40, 50; 18:8–9; 25:41, 46; cf. 2 Thess. 1:8; 2 Pet. 3:7; Jude 7; Rev. 14:10; 19:20; 20:10, 14–15; 21:8) and deep darkness (Matt. 8:12; 22:13; 25:30; cf. 2 Pet. 2:4; Jude 6, 13). The eternally excruciating experience of hell is unspeakably worse than these two metaphors portraying it.

The implications of this passage for Christology are similarly awesome. Matthew 25:31–46 is a commentary on the realization of Dan. 7:13–27. Jesus has angels at his disposal (Matt. 26:53; 28:2). He is the ultimate judge of humanity and king of the world. Yet he is about to allow himself to be handed over for crucifixion. In this light, the entire narrative of Jesus's arrest, hearings, and crucifixion is one great irony.

Summary and Transition

The interpretive difficulties in Matt. 24–25 remind Christians of their limitations. When teachers of equal scholarship and devotion do not agree on the particulars of a passage, one should avoid dogmatism and seek further insight. Part of the problem may be the asking of questions that the discourse was never intended to answer. Matthew 24–25 shows that prophecy is not mere prognostication. Only 24:4–35 directly responds to the disciples' question in 24:3 about future details and their timing. Even this section of the discourse stresses the need for an appropriate ethical response (24:4, 13–14, 23, 26). The remainder of the discourse (24:36–25:46) is paraenetic, stressing parabolically how one should live in light of the future. In this second part, future events are mentioned (24:33, 36–37, 39–42, 44; 25:13, 31, 46), but this only supports the exhortation for alertness (24:32–25:13), faithfulness (25:14–30), and compassion (25:31–46). Jesus never speaks of the future

b. An Exhortation to Alertness
vi. The Final Judgment

Matthew 25:31–46

to satisfy curiosity or to provoke speculation. Instead he explains the future for the sake of his hearers' obedience to God's will.

Eschatology appears in each of Jesus's first four discourses, especially at or near their conclusions (7:22; 10:32, 39–42; 13:49; 18:35), and so it is not surprising that Jesus ends *all* his teaching (26:1) in Matthew with eschatology. His teaching equips disciples with ethics befitting his reign (Matt. 5–7), with warnings about the opposition to ministry (Matt. 10), with awareness of the mixed response to the kingdom message (Matt. 13), with values for the kingdom community (Matt. 18), and with a perspective on the future that handles both the unknowable date and the prospect of delay in Jesus's coming (Matt. 24–25). This vigilant perspective does not veer off into frivolous enthusiasm, on one side, or into cold apathy, on the other (24:31–25:13). Rather, its hallmark is faithful stewardship (25:14–30) exercised in helping those in need, especially one's fellow believers (25:31–46).

When Jesus concludes all his words (26:1), the teaching that he commands his disciples to perpetuate and inculcate in his future followers from all the nations of the earth (28:19–20) is complete. With his teaching concluded, his disciples are equipped. Now events will quickly move toward his being handed over to be crucified (26:2). Soon he will give his life as a ransom for many, to save his people from their sins and to inaugurate the new covenant in his blood (1:21; 20:28; 26:28).

3. Narrative Conclusion and the Fourth Passion Prediction (26:1–2)

This short section is transitional. For the fifth and final time (cf. 7:28; 11:1; 13:53; 19:1), Matthew ends a discourse of Jesus with the usual formula. But this time Jesus is portrayed as finishing *all* his teaching (28:20). The keynote of the next two chapters is sounded with 26:2.

Exegesis and Exposition

¹And it came about that when Jesus had finished all these words, he said to his disciples, ²"You know that after two days the Passover is coming, and the Son of Man is to be delivered up for crucifixion."

26:1 Matthew presents 26:1 not simply as the end of a discourse but as the end of all that Jesus has taught in this Gospel (28:20; cf. Deut. 32:44–45; Allison 1993b: 192–94; Boring 1995: 463; Garland 1993: 246). His teaching about the rule of God, begun in Matt. 4:17, is now completed, and the passion narrative begins.

26:2 "The passion commences with a word from Jesus" (W. Davies and Allison 1997: 437). Although the ongoing plot to do away with Jesus continues and Judas will soon defect, Jesus himself sets in motion the narrative of his own suffering and death (Calvin 1972: 3.119–20). The Passover feast begins in two days (cf. John 11:55; 13:1), and Jesus anticipates being handed over to be crucified (cf. Mark 14:1–2; Luke 21:37–22:2). Evidently, Passover day, when the lambs were killed, fell on Nisan 14/ Thursday that year, and the following Feast of Unleavened Bread ran from Nisan 15 to 21 (Lev. 23:5–6; Num. 28:16–17). If so, the meal would have been held just after sundown on Thursday (Blomberg 1992a: 388; W. Davies and Allison 1997: 437), although Hagner (1995a: 754) opts for Friday evening (but cf. pp. 763, 767). In 26:2 Jesus is evidently speaking on Tuesday. His words remind the disciples of all the previous passion predictions (16:21; 17:22–23; 20:18–19). This is the first prediction that connects Jesus's death to the Passover (cf. 1 Cor. 5:7). These words also show that Jesus is not going to be surprised by the nefarious events that transpire in this chapter (Matt. 26:21, 31, 45–46, 50, 54, 56). (For discussion of the historical and synoptic questions, including whether Jesus was crucified in 30 or 33 CE, see Blomberg 1987b: 175–80; Carson 1984: 528–32; Hoehner 1977: 65–114; Keener 1999: 607–11.)

IV. Growing Opposition to the Kingdom of Heaven (11:2–13:52)
V. Opposition to the Kingdom Continues (13:53–19:2)
VI. Opposition Comes to a Head in Judea (19:3–26:2)
➤VII. Epilogue/Conclusion: Passion, Resurrection, and Commission (26:3–28:20)

VII. Epilogue/Conclusion: Passion, Resurrection, and Commission (26:3–28:20)

The climactic events that have been repeatedly predicted since the Galilean ministry are now unfolding (12:38–40; 16:4, 21; 17:12, 22–23; 20:17–19; 21:38–39; 23:32). Jesus is not unaware of the powers arrayed against him (26:2), yet he relishes doing the will of the Father despite the suffering involved (26:36–46). Ironically, the very religious leaders who seek to destroy Jesus become unwitting instruments used by God to fulfill his plan to exalt Jesus (Hagner 1995a: 755).

Jesus's last week is given extended treatment in all four Gospels. This shows that the Gospels are not mere historical chronicles or biographies but theologically motivated literary works. The narrative of events from Palm Sunday on is found in Matt. 21–28; Mark 11–16; Luke 19–24; and John 12–21. The last week of Jesus's life occupies roughly one-third of the content of the four Gospels. It has been said that the Gospels are passion narratives with extended introductions, and this is only a slight exaggeration.

Matthew's narrative of Jesus's suffering is prefaced with the stories of the temple conflicts with the Jewish leaders (Matt. 21–23) and the Olivet Discourse (Matt. 24–25). In both of these sections, Matthew's material is more extensive than either Mark's or Luke's. When it comes to the passion narrative proper (Matt. 26–28), Matthew and Mark are for the most part parallel, with Luke and, more so, John contributing unique material. The general flow of Matthew's material is as follows:

1. Preparation of the disciples (26:1–46)
2. Arrest at Gethsemane (26:47–56)
3. Trial before Caiaphas (26:57–68)
4. Peter's three denials (26:69–75)
5. Trial before Pilate (27:1–2; 11–26) with the interwoven account of Judas's suicide (27:3–10)
6. Jesus mocked and crucified (27:27–56)
7. Jesus buried by Joseph of Arimathea (27:57–61)
8. Jesus's resurrection and its denial (27:62–28:15)
9. The Great Commission (28:16–20)

Although the passion and resurrection consummate Matthew's narrative of Jesus, they do so in a less prominent fashion than in Mark (Allison 2005b: 217). Matthew has stressed teachings of Jesus that do not directly bear on his death and resurrection. Mark contains much less of Jesus's teachings and devotes proportionately more space to Jesus's death and resurrection (three chapters of sixteen in Mark versus three of twenty-eight in Matthew). Yet, several portions of Matthew's passion narrative are unique to his Gospel and presumably indicate his special literary and theological emphases:

1. Jesus reminds the disciples of his impending death (26:1–2). This shows that he is not caught up in random events beyond the Father's control.
2. The amount of money paid Judas is specified as thirty pieces of silver (26:15). This provides two biblical allusions (Exod. 21:32; Zech. 11:12).
3. Judas asks Jesus if he is the betrayer (26:25). This heightens the drama and probes the depths of Judas's psyche.
4. Jesus's blood is poured out for the forgiveness of sins (26:28). This interprets the goal of Jesus's death, in keeping with 1:21; 20:28.
5. The second prayer in Gethsemane is presented as a direct quotation (26:42).
6. Jesus's words to Judas after the kiss are given (26:50).
7. After the high priest's servant's ear is cut off, Jesus comments about violence, the availability of angelic help, and scriptural fulfillment (26:52–54).
8. The high priest demands before God that Jesus speak (26:63).
9. A sarcastic reference is made to Jesus as Messiah (26:68).
10. Jesus is described as a Galilean (26:69).
11. Peter's second denial includes an oath (26:72).
12. The Jewish leaders' morning consultation is for the purpose of executing Jesus (27:1).
13. Pilate describes Jesus as the one who is called the Messiah (27:17, 22).
14. Pilate's wife dreams and calls Jesus righteous (27:19).
15. Pilate washes his hands and the crowd admits responsibility for Jesus's death (27:24–25).
16. The sign on the cross specifies the name of Jesus (27:37).
17. Jesus as the Son of God is emphasized (27:40, 43).
18. An allusion is made to Ps. 22:8 (Matt. 27:43).
19. An account of the earthquake and the opening of the tombs is provided (27:51–53).
20. Joseph of Arimathea is called a disciple (27:57).
21. The Jewish leaders persuade Pilate to guard Jesus's tomb (27:62–66).

22. Jesus meets the women after the resurrection (28:9–10).
23. The conspiracy to deny the resurrection is reported (28:11–15).
24. Jesus meets the disciples in Galilee and states that he has all authority, that all nations are to be discipled, and that disciples are to be taught to obey all that Jesus commanded; he promises to be with the disciples until the end of the age; the trinitarian baptismal formula is used (28:16–20).[1]

Matthew's Passion Narrative answers questions that may have been on the minds of careful readers since earlier stages of the story. For example, now readers can better understand how Jesus will save his people from their sins (compare 26:26–18 with 1:25; 9:6; 20:28). They can view Herod's unsuccessful attempt to kill Jesus (2:16–18) as anticipating Jesus's execution at the order of Pilate. Implicit references to (Matt. 12:14, 39–40; 16:4; 21:37–39; 22:7; 23:32) and explicit predictions of (Matt. 16:21; 17:22–23; 20:17–18, 28; 26:12) Jesus's death are now fulfilled. John's sad demise (11:1–20; 14:1–13; esp.17:9–13) anticipates the suffering and death of Jesus. Jesus's response to shameful treatment during the Passion Narrative provides a concrete example of how his instructions on responding to persecution should be obeyed (compare Matt. 26:67; 27:28–31, 35, 39, 41, 44 with 5:10–12, 38–42; 10:16–39). See further Allison 2005b: 217–35.

1. On Matthew's passion narrative, see Broer in Schenke 1988: 25–46; R. Brown 1994; Dahl 1976: 37–51; Descamps in Didier 1972: 359–415; Garland 1990; Heil 1991b; Lodge 1986; F. Martin 1989; F. Martin and Panier 1987; Matera 1986; Moo 1983; Rieckert 1982; Senior 1975, 1985, 1987; in Didier 1972: 343–57.

VII. Epilogue/Conclusion: Passion, Resurrection, and Commission (26:3–28:20)
➤ A. Preliminary Events and Preparation of the Disciples (26:3–46)
   B. Arrest and Trial (26:47–27:26)
   C. Crucifixion (27:27–56)

A. Preliminary Events and Preparation of the Disciples (26:3–46)

Matthew's narrative of events leading up to the passion alternates between episodes that feature Jesus's actions (26:1–2, 6–13, 17–19, 26–46) and episodes that feature his enemies' actions (26:3–5, 14–16, 20–25). Jesus's actions show that despite appearances to the contrary, he is in control of what is about to transpire. As the plot against him develops, Jesus prepares the disciples for his passion and their failures.

1. The Plot to Kill Jesus (26:3–5)

The conflicts between Jesus and the religious leaders in the temple have intensified their desire to be rid of him, and so they make plans to arrest him after the Passover festival.

Exegesis and Exposition

³Then the chief priests and the elders of the people gathered in the court of the high priest, named Caiaphas, ⁴and they conspired to arrest Jesus by stealth and kill him. ⁵But they were saying, "Not during the festival, or there will be a riot among the people."

The mention of the leaders' plot in 26:3 (cf. Mark 14:1–2; Luke 21:37–22:2; John 11:45–53) immediately confirms Jesus's words in Matt. 26:2. The ongoing plot against Jesus (cf. 12:14; 22:15) is evidently escalated by the recent temple conflicts. The chief priests and elders meet with the high priest Caiaphas (cf. John 11:49; 18:13–14, 24, 28; Josephus, *Ant.* 18.35) to plan their apprehension and execution of Jesus. In Second Temple times, the high priesthood had become a political appointment by Rome. Caiaphas was high priest from 18 to 36 CE. See further C. A. Evans in Charlesworth 2006: 323–29.

26:3–4

Secrecy is necessary, since Jesus is popular with the crowds of pilgrims who have arrived in Jerusalem for the Passover festival (21:26; 27:24). The leaders fear that a public arrest would provoke a riot, so they plan to wait until after the Passover. Judas's upcoming offer to betray Jesus will allow them to accomplish their goal sooner rather than later (26:14–16, 47–56).

26:5

2. Anointing at Bethany (26:6–13)

In this passage (cf. Mark 14:3–9; John 12:1–11) it is striking that an obscure, unnamed woman has greater perception than the disciples of the shortness of Jesus's remaining time on earth. The disciples do have a legitimate point: one should care for the needy. But their sense of timing is all wrong. Despite being at Jesus's side and hearing his repeated passion predictions, they act as if this is a time for business as usual. As the story continues, this woman is portrayed sympathetically whereas the disciples continue to misunderstand and be corrected. The disciples' role in the narrative is between that of the woman and that of her foil, Judas:

Protagonist				Antagonists
Jesus	Unnamed woman	Disciples	Judas	Religious leaders
	(Serves)	(Misunderstand)	(Betrays)	

The unit outline is as follows:

a. The anointing (26:6–7)
b. The disciples' complaint (26:8–9)
c. Jesus's response (26:10–13)

Exegesis and Exposition

⁶While Jesus was in Bethany, at the house of Simon the leper, ⁷a woman came to him with an alabaster vial of very costly ointment, and she poured it upon his head as he was reclining at the table. ⁸But when they saw this, the disciples became indignant and said, "Why this waste? ⁹For this ointment could have been sold for a high price and the money given to the poor." ¹⁰But Jesus, aware of this, said to them, "Why are you causing trouble for this woman? For she did a good work to me. ¹¹For you will always have the poor with you; but you will not always have me. ¹²For when she poured this ointment upon my body, she did it to prepare me for burial. ¹³Truly I tell you, wherever this gospel is preached in the whole world, what this woman has done will also be told in remembrance of her."

a. The Anointing (26:6–7)

The narrative of Jesus's anointing is located between two sections of the   **26:6–7**
betrayal story (cf. Mark 14:3–9; John 12:1–11). Bethany was a village on
the Mount of Olives, less than two miles east of Jerusalem (Matt. 21:17;
John 11:1, 18). Spending time in the home of Simon the leper, who is
mentioned only here in the NT, would render Jesus ritually impure just
before Passover (cf. Matt. 8:2), and so some scholars speculate that Simon
has already been healed by Jesus. Simon is a common name in Matthew
(4:18; 10:2, 4; 13:55; 16:16–17; 17:25; 27:32). The unnamed woman (but
see John 12:3) surprisingly anoints Jesus's head with expensive ointment
(cf. Ps. 132:2 LXX [133:2 Eng.]; Josephus, *Ant.* 19.239) from an alabaster
vial while he is eating.

b. The Disciples' Complaint (26:8–9)

The disciples are indignant at the woman's extravagance (20:24; 21:15).   **26:8–9**
They protest that the expensive perfume could have been sold and the
proceeds given to the poor (cf. 11:5; 19:21; cf. Luke 4:18; 21:1–4). But it
soon becomes clear that their apparent piety masks their lack of spiritual
perception. They are inexplicably oblivious to the exceptional nature of
these epochal days in Jerusalem.

c. Jesus's Response (26:10–13)

Jesus finds fault with the disciples' criticism of the woman. Her action shows   **26:10–13**
her devotion to him and, to some extent, her understanding of the unique-
ness of the hour. Jesus states that poor people will always be around (an
allusion to Deut. 15:11) but his own time on earth is short (Matt. 26:2–3).
In other words, there will always be opportunities to help the poor, but
time to honor him is short. How much the woman realizes about Jesus's
imminent betrayal and death is not clear, but Jesus interprets her action
as a prophetic preparation for his burial (W. Davies and Allison 1997: 447).
Hagner (1995a: 758) goes too far in saying that the woman certainly does
not intend to anoint Jesus for burial. She will be remembered and her deed
rehearsed wherever the gospel is preached throughout the world (24:14;
28:19). The record of this story in Matthew, Mark, and John has ensured
that her act would be remembered. Matthew's narrative of Jesus's burial
does not mention that his body was anointed before being placed in the
tomb (27:59; but cf. Mark 16:1; Luke 24:1; John 19:38–40).[1]

Jesus and the Poor

Jesus's comment (26:11a) on the poor should not be misused to support
a callous attitude about their needs. He alludes to Deut. 15:11, which

---

1. On 26:6–13, see Daube 1973: 310–24; Derrett 1970b: 266–85; Feuillet 1975; Holst
1976; Schedl 1981; Thiemann 1987.

speaks realistically about needy people during the sabbatical year of remission, when debts were to be forgiven (Deut. 15:1–2). God commands that loans not be withheld because the sabbatical year is near and the loan would have to be forgiven before it could be completely repaid (15:7–10). God promises a blessing that will make up for the loan not being repaid (15:4, 6, 10, 14, 18). Deuteronomy 15 enjoins helping the needy so that there will be no poor people in the land (15:4), and so Jesus's allusion to 15:11 in Matt. 26:11 is a reminder of an ongoing responsibility, not a stoic comment about an inevitable situation. But the ongoing responsibility of caring for the poor pales in comparison with the urgency of caring for Jesus during his last few days on earth (cf. the similar teaching in Matt. 9:15).

3. Judas Agrees to Betray Jesus (26:14–16)

Judas's offer to give Jesus up to the leaders fulfills Jesus's recent prophecy (26:20–25) and enables the leaders to remove Jesus before the Passover festival has concluded (26:5).

Exegesis and Exposition

¹⁴Then one of the Twelve, who was named Judas Iscariot, went to the chief priests, ¹⁵and said, "What are you willing to give me to hand him over to you?" And they weighed out to him thirty pieces of silver. ¹⁶And from then on he began looking for an opportunity to give him up.

This passage is a brief return to the betrayal narrative of 26:1–5 (cf. Mark 14:10–11; Luke 22:3–6). It supplies the crucial detail that enables the leaders to act immediately and not wait until after the Passover festival to arrest Jesus (Matt. 26:47–56). With Judas's aid they can apprehend Jesus privately without inciting a riot. Judas has been mentioned previously only in 10:4, where his name occurs last in the list of disciples with the qualifier "the one who betrayed him." Judas clearly initiates the betrayal by seeking money from the chief priests. They pay him thirty silver shekels. In Exod. 21:32 this is the price to be paid to the owner of a slave gored by an ox. Zechariah 11:12–13 speaks sarcastically of this amount of money. Joseph was sold by his brothers to the Midianites for only twenty shekels (Gen. 37:28). A shekel was evidently worth four denarii, and so thirty shekels would be around four months' wages for a day laborer. This sum is not insignificant but is paltry when compared with the value of the ointment the woman used to anoint Jesus.

In Matt. 26:15, the subtle allusion to Zech. 11:12–13 connects Judas's betrayal to biblical prophecy, supporting the theme of Matt. 26 that God is in control even of Jesus's betrayal (26:18, 31, 54, 56). The profound intellectual and existential implications of this matter deserve reflection. The interplay of God's sovereignty and Judas's responsibility boggles the mind, but the two are ultimately complementary (cf. Acts 2:23; 4:27–28). Further, every follower of Jesus should reflect on his or her capacity to imitate the monstrous treachery of Judas and ask, "Surely not I, Lord?" (Matt. 26:22). It should grieve all followers of Jesus that one of the Twelve could betray the Lord.

Judas is pathetically and enigmatically evil (26:24; John 17:12), and his motivation in betraying Jesus is inscrutable (W. Davies and Allison

1997: 451–52). He may have taken this action out of greed, since he asks how much the leaders will pay him (cf. Matt. 6:19–21, 24). John 12:4–6 stresses his disgust at the waste of money when Jesus was anointed with the expensive perfume by the woman at Bethany. Judas may have been looking for a military-political Messiah and become disillusioned when Jesus's message of repentance was not widely received, especially by the religious leaders. Perhaps greed drove Judas to betray Jesus when he realized that Jesus was not a military-political Messiah. Luke 22:3 and John 6:70; 13:2 attribute Judas's action to satanic influence. Blomberg's suggestion (1992: 387) that Judas perhaps committed the unpardonable sin (Matt. 12:32) is doubtful, since there is no reason to suppose Judas attributed Jesus's miracles to the power of the devil. In any event, after he sells out Jesus, Judas later regrets it and commits suicide (27:3–10).[1]

---

1. On Judas, see Gärtner 1971; Klassen 1996; Klauck 1987; Levin-Goldschmidt and Limbeck 1976; Roquefort 1983; Vogler 1983; H. Wagner 1985.

4. The Last/Lord's Supper (26:17–30)

The narrative now returns to Jesus's last hours with his disciples (cf. Mark 14:12–26; Luke 22:7–20; John 13:21–30). He is about to go from Bethany (Matt. 26:6) to Jerusalem (26:18). The mysterious instructions that Jesus gives the disciples for obtaining the room for the Passover meal are similar to the instructions he gave them for obtaining the donkey for his triumphal entry (26:17–19; cf. 21:1–6).

The Passover (Exod. 12:11, 13, 21, 27, 43; Deut. 16:1–2) was the prelude to the weeklong spring Feast of Unleavened Bread (Exod. 12:15; 23:15; 34:18; Deut. 16:3–8, 16; 2 Kings 23:9). By the first century CE, the entire eight-day period could be called Passover (Josephus, *Ant.* 2.317; 17.213; 20.106; *J.W.* 5.99; but see *J.W.* 2.280; 6.423–24). The Mishnah (redacted from oral tradition ca. 200 CE) describes preparations for the entire period in the tractate *Pesaḥim*. The Passover meal liturgy is described in *m. Pesaḥ.* 10, but it is not clear that this liturgy is the same as that practiced by Jesus and the disciples. Neither is it clear at what point in the Passover meal Jesus predicts the betrayal and institutes his supper. Matthew associates these events with a historical Passover meal but does not provide details extraneous to his literary and theological purposes. (For discussion of the historical issues, see Arnott 1984; Hoehner 1977: 76–90; Jaubert 1965.)

The unit can be outlined as follows:

a. Preparing for the Passover (26:17–19)
b. Jesus predicts the betrayal (26:20–25)
c. Jesus institutes the Lord's Supper (26:26–29)
d. Departing to the Mount of Olives (26:30)

Exegesis and Exposition

[17]Now on the first day of Unleavened Bread, the disciples came to Jesus and asked, "Where do you want us to prepare for you to eat the Passover?" [18]And he answered, "Go into the city to a certain man and say to him, 'The teacher says, "My time is near; I will keep the Passover at your house with my disciples."'" [19]So the disciples did as Jesus had directed them; and they prepared the Passover.

[20]And when evening had come, he was reclining at the table with ⌜the Twelve⌝. [21]And while they were eating, he said, "Truly I tell you, one of you will betray me." [22]And being deeply grieved, each one began saying to him, "Surely not I, Lord?"

²³And he answered, "One who dipped his hand with me in the bowl will betray me. ²⁴The Son of Man will go, just as it is written concerning him; but woe to that man by whom the Son of Man is betrayed! It would have been better for that man if he had not been born." ²⁵And Judas who was betraying him answered, "Surely it is not I, Rabbi?" He said to him, "You said it."

²⁶And while they were eating, Jesus took a loaf of bread and thanked God for it. Then he broke it, gave it to the disciples, and said, "Take it and eat; this is my body." ²⁷Then he took ⌜a⌝ cup and thanked God for it. He gave it to them, saying, "Drink from it, all of you; ²⁸for this is my blood ⌜of the covenant⌝, which is poured out for many for the forgiveness of sins. ²⁹And I tell you, I will never drink of this fruit of the vine from now until that day when I drink it new with you in my Father's kingdom." ³⁰And when they had sung a hymn, they went out to the Mount of Olives.

a. Preparing for the Passover (26:17–19)

26:17–19   Since all leaven had to be removed from Jewish homes, Passover was known as the Feast of Unleavened Bread (Exod. 12:1–20; Lev. 23:4–8; Num. 9:1–14; 28:17; Deut. 16:1–8; *m. Pesaḥ.*). On the first day of the eight-day feast, evidently Thursday (Exod. 12:18–20; Gundry 1994: 524), the disciples ask where Jesus will eat the Passover meal. He secures a room for the meal in a way similar to the way he secured a donkey for his entry into Jerusalem (cf. 21:2–3). Again circumstances are providentially ordered (26:18). The statement "My time is near" is a cryptic reference to the impending arrest and crucifixion. It is quite difficult to reconcile the chronology implicit in this narrative with that of John 18:28 (Ruckstuhl 1965).

b. Jesus Predicts the Betrayal (26:20–25)

26:20–22   After sundown on Thursday, Jesus reclines at the table with the twelve disciples, who correspond to the twelve tribes of Israel (Exod. 24:4), to eat the Passover meal. The triclinium custom of eating a formal meal on that day entailed reclining on cushions in a U-shaped pattern around a low table in the middle (Matt. 9:10; 22:11; 26:7; BDAG 65). The Passover meal was normally led by the head of the family and eaten at home. Jesus evidently serves as the head of the disciples' family, as he leads the meal, and so this passage illustrates 12:46–50: those who do the Father's will are Jesus's family (W. Davies and Allison 1997: 458). At some point in the meal, perhaps near the beginning, Jesus announces that he will be betrayed by one of the Twelve. At this point the startled disciples begin to learn what Matthew's readers already know from 26:14–16. Jesus previously implied an act of betrayal (20:18; 26:2), but he is painfully explicit here. He has known perhaps for some time that his betrayal will be accomplished by Judas even though Judas has only just now agreed to do it. The disciples have no inkling of the betrayer's identity as each sorrowfully begins to ask Jesus whether he himself is the betrayer of whom Jesus speaks.

Jesus responds by saying only that the betrayer is someone "who dipped   **26:23–25** his hand with me in the bowl." This probably alludes to the custom of dipping food into haroseth, a sweet sauce or relish (John 13:26; *m. Pesaḥ.* 10.3). The betrayal of Jesus is certain because it has been predicted in Scripture. Yet Jesus's chilling comment on how terrible it will be for the betrayer indicates that the betrayer is accountable (cf. John 18:7; 1 En. 38.2).[1] Again the themes of divine sovereignty and human responsibility appear together in Matthew's narrative (cf. 11:25–30). After Jesus's pronouncement of woe, Judas hypocritically asks if he could be the betrayer. Jesus's response is a somewhat ambiguous affirmation (cf. 26:64; 27:11), similar to the English idiom "You said it." Without alerting the other disciples, this hints to Judas that Jesus is aware of his plot. Judas's waiting until the end to speak may indicate his reluctance (W. Davies and Allison 1997: 464; cf. Hein 1970–71; Schwarz 1988).

c. Jesus Institutes the Lord's Supper (26:26–29)

After the shocking announcement that the betrayer is present, the meal   **23:26–29** evidently proceeds. Jesus invests the unleavened bread and the wine (described as the cup in keeping with 20:22–23; 26:39) with special significance. The elements of the Passover meal were already viewed as symbolic (*m. Pesaḥ.* 10.4–5); Jesus innovates only the referents of the symbolism. Although an explicit word of institution (as in Luke 22:19; 1 Cor. 11:24–25) is lacking here, Christians have universally viewed this event as establishing a practice that is to be repeated, now called the Eucharist, or Lord's Supper (cf. 1 Cor. 11:23–26). The broken bread (Matt. 14:19; 15:36) represents Jesus's body and the cup his blood, shed (or "poured out;" cf. Lev. 4:7–35) for the forgiveness of the sins of many people (Matt. 1:21; 20:28; cf. Exod. 12:21–27; Isa. 53:4, 10, 12; Heil 1991a). The phrase "my blood of the covenant" alludes to Exod. 24:8 (cf. Zech. 9:11; Heb. 9:19–22; 10:29; 13:20). Some MSS read "blood of the *new* covenant," but "new" may be an interpolation from Luke 22:20 (cf. 1 Cor. 11:25; the additional note on Matt. 26:28). At any rate, in Matt. 26:29 Jesus does speak prophetically of drinking *new* wine with his disciples in the future kingdom. The institution of the Lord's Supper is closely tied to the Passover as well as the new covenant (Jer. 31:31–34). It also anticipates the ultimate eschatological feast that inaugurates the future kingdom (Matt. 26:29; cf. 8:11; 22:2; 25:10; Rev. 19:7–9).

---

1. It is likely that the positive adjective καλόν in 26:24 should be understood as a comparative. Cf. 18:8; Moulton and Turner 1963: 31–32; Wallace 1996: 297.

d. Departing to the Mount of Olives (26:30)

26:30   Matthew 26:30 is a hinge verse that connects the private Last Supper to
the ongoing public story that develops on the Mount of Olives. At the
end of the meal, they sing (probably the Hallel, Pss. 115–18; cf. *m. Pesaḥ.*
10.6–7), and once again Jesus leaves the city for the Mount of Olives
(cf. 21:17; 24:1–3). R. Brown's magisterial study of the Gospel passion
narratives begins at this point, although Brown's reasons for doing so
are pragmatic as well as exegetical (1994: 38–39).

The Passover and Theology

This Passover meal is both a beginning and an end. It is Jesus's last meal
with his disciples before his arrest, trials, and crucifixion, and it is also the
first supper, the inaugural remembrance of Jesus by his new community.
As the fulfillment of biblical pattern and prediction, Jesus is bringing from
his treasure things new and old (13:52). Viewed from this perspective, the
Lord's Supper is not the Passover but is founded on the Passover (Stein
in J. Green and McKnight 1992: 446–47). When the disciples reenact
the Last Supper, as they eat the bread and drink the wine, they will remember that Jesus did indeed shed his blood for the forgiveness of their
sins. And they will remember his promise to share the table with them
in the future kingdom. As Paul put it, every time they eat the bread and
drink the cup, they will be announcing the Lord's death until he comes
(1 Cor. 11:26). The Lord's Supper is divinely ordained to remind Jesus's
followers of the past and of the future, what Jesus has done and what
Jesus will do. Their present identity and existence is definitively framed
by his past first coming to redeem them and by his future second coming
to reign over the earth. These truths are powerfully sealed in the hearts
of his people when they participate in faith at the table.

The sacrament of the Lord's Supper is not an impotent memorial, an
empty sign, or an automatic source of saving grace. When it is received
in faith, it dynamically strengthens Jesus's community by proclaiming
the central truth of the gospel (Calvin 1960: 2.1276–1303 [*Institutes*
4.14]; 1972: 3.135–36). The early Christians probably observed the Lord's
Supper as part of a regular fellowship meal or "love feast" (Acts 2:42;
20:7–12; 1 Cor. 11:20–22; Jude 12; 2 Pet. 2:13 v.l.; Did. 9–10; 14.1).

Despite the current popularity of "Passover seder" celebrations in
Christian churches at Easter, the order and customs of the meal in Jesus's time are not certainly known. Reading later Jewish Passover liturgy
(haggadah) back into the NT and investing it with Christian typological significance may be edifying, but the historical foundation is weak.
The earliest source for the seder liturgy is evidently *m. Pesaḥ.* 10, but the
Mishnah was not redacted and written until around 200 CE. Christians
tend to identify the bread of the Lord's Supper with *m. Pesaḥ.* 10.3 and the
cup with the third cup, over which a benediction was said (*m. Pesaḥ.* 10.7;

m. Ber. 6.1). But the NT does not mention the roasted lamb, the four cups of wine, or the traditional Jewish interpretation of these things. And it is not certain that the Mishnah's liturgy is the same as that practiced by Jesus more than 150 years earlier (W. Davies and Allison 1997: 469). It is clear that Jesus used the Passover meal as the foundation of his own Last Supper, and one can say that, for Matthew (cf. 1 Cor. 5:7; 1 Pet. 1:19), the Lord's Supper fulfilled the Passover, but the precise details of the correspondence are not clear.[2]

Additional Notes

26:20. UBS[4] prefers the shorter reading μετὰ τῶν δώδεκα (widely supported by $\mathfrak{P}^{37vid}$, $\mathfrak{P}^{45vid}$, B, D, *f*[1], *f*[13], 28, *Byz*, *Lect*; cf. Mark 14:17). The longer reading adds μαθητῶν (supported by ℵ, A, L, W, Δ, Θ, Σ, 33, 157). The C rating in UBS[4] indicates the editors' considerable doubt, evidently due to the early evidence for the longer reading.

26:27. The question here is whether ποτήριον should have an article. The anarthrous reading favored in UBS[4] is supported by ℵ, B, L, W, Z, Δ, Θ, 0298, *f*[1], *Byz*[pt], *Lect*[pt] (cf. Mark 14:23). The article τό is found in $\mathfrak{P}^{37vid}$, $\mathfrak{P}^{45}$, A, C, D, *f*[13], 157, *Byz*[pt], *Lect*[pt].

26:28. UBS[4] prefers the shorter reading τῆς διαθήκης (supported by $\mathfrak{P}^{37}$, ℵ, B, L, Z, Θ, 33; cf. Mark 14:24). Yet there is also strong support for the longer reading τῆς καινῆς διαθήκης (A, C, D, W, Δ, *f*[1], *f*[13], 28, 157, *Byz*, *Lect*; cf. Luke 22:20; 1 Cor. 11:25), and the idea of newness is present in 26:29. There is no reason καινῆς would have been deleted (Metzger 1994: 54), unless by accident.

2. On the Lord's Supper and Passover, see Bahr 1970; Bokser 1987; Carmichael 1991; Daube 1973: 163–69, 186–95, 278–85, 330–31; Jeremias 1966a; Kodell 1988: 93–104; Marshall 1980; Saldarini 1984; Senn 1986; Stein in Green and McKnight 1992: 444–50.

5. The Disciples' Denial Predicted (26:31–35)

Again (cf. 16:22) Peter denies Jesus's word. In this passage Jesus twice predicts Peter's future behavior (26:31, 34), and twice Peter strongly demurs (26:33, 35). When he is told that the disciples will scatter and later meet Jesus in Galilee, Peter affirms he will never desert Jesus even if everyone else does. When he is told that he will do even worse than desert Jesus, that he will deny him three times, Peter affirms that he will die before he does that. The ensuing narrative shows how wrong Peter is on both counts. He has been wrong before (16:22), but Jesus's resurrection will turn grief into joy, defeat into victory, and desertion into renewed allegiance (26:32; 28:7, 10, 16–20). Peter does not know himself well enough to admit his propensity to desert and deny Jesus, but he will learn this bitter lesson (26:75) and be restored to fellowship with Jesus and ministry (cf. John 21:15–19). According to tradition, eventually he does choose to die rather than deny Jesus.

The unit can be outlined as follows:

a. The first cycle of prediction and denial (26:31–33)
b. The second cycle of prediction and denial (26:34–35)

Exegesis and Exposition

³¹Then Jesus said to them, "You will all fall away because of me this very night, for it is written, 'I will strike the shepherd, and the sheep of the flock shall be scattered.' ³²But after I have been raised, I will go on ahead of you to Galilee." ³³But Peter answered him, "Even if all may fall away because of you, I will never fall away." ³⁴Jesus said to him, "Truly I tell you that this very night, before a cock crows, you will deny me three times." ³⁵Peter said to him, "Even if I must die with you, I will never deny you." And so said all the disciples.

a. The First Cycle of Prediction and Denial (26:31–33)

26:31–32 Judas probably leaves Jesus and the disciples when they go out to the Mount of Olives after the Passover meal. He will return with the arrest party in 26:47. The mood turns even more somber here as Jesus tells the disciples that they will all desert him and scatter this very night (cf. Mark 14:27–31; Luke 22:40; John 13:31–38). Their desertion is a serious fall into sin (σκανδαλίζω, *skandalizō*; Matt. 5:29; 11:6; 13:21, 57; 15:12;

18:6, 8; 24:10; cf. BDAG 926). The disciples will stumble in their faith, perhaps abandoning it altogether, but only temporarily. Jesus supports this dire prediction with Zech. 13:7, which describes the scattering of sheep caused by the shepherd being struck (cf. Matt. 9:36). This desertion will be serious yet not final, since Jesus promises to meet the disciples in Galilee after he is raised (cf. 28:7, 10, 16). Perhaps his going ahead of the disciples to Galilee is intended to cause readers to picture a shepherd going ahead of his flock (cf. John 10:4). The resurrection of Jesus has already been stressed (Matt. 12:40; 16:21; 17:23; 20:19; 27:63–64; 28:6), and it will be the turning point that brings the straying disciples back into the fold.

Peter has not been heard of for some time (19:27), but at this point he speaks up and becomes prominent through the rest of the chapter. Again Peter serves as spokesman for the disciples when he denies that he will deny the Lord (26:35; cf. 26:75). Peter puts this very strongly, since he believes he would be the last person to sin by deserting Jesus. Even in the unthinkable event that all the other disciples fall away, Peter affirms he will remain faithful.   **26:33**

b. The Second Cycle of Prediction and Denial (26:34–35)

When Jesus tells Peter that he will deny Jesus not once but three times, Peter adamantly reaffirms what he has said and adds that he would die before denying Jesus. The mention of a strutting, crowing rooster creates an image that fits Peter's rebuttal of Jesus (W. Davies and Allison 1997: 487). Peter's impetuous personality is highlighted here (as in 14:28–31; 16:21–23), but all the disciples are saying the same thing Peter says (26:35b).   **26:34–35**

6. Deep Distress in Gethsemane (26:36–46)

The narrative of Jesus's agony in Gethsemane (cf. Mark 14:32–42; Luke 22:40–46) underlines the themes of Jesus's dedication to the Father's will and the disciples' inability to grasp the gravity of the hour. Upon arrival in Gethsemane, Jesus tells his disciples that he will go aside to pray (Matt. 26:36). This distance between Jesus and the disciples, both the larger group and the three who fail to stay alert with him, is significant. The narrative presents three cycles that contrast Jesus's prayerful obedience to the disciples' drowsy oblivion:

The Structure of Matt. 26:36–46

Setting: Arrival in Gethsemane (26:36a)
    Jesus withdraws from most of the disciples to *pray* (26:36b)
        Jesus *instructs* Peter and Zebedee's sons (26:37–38)
First cycle: Jesus *prays* alone (26:39)
    Disciples *sleep* (26:40a)
    Jesus *instructs* Peter and Zebedee's sons (26:40b–41)
Second cycle: Jesus *prays* alone (26:42)
    Disciples sleep (26:43)
Third cycle: Jesus *prays* alone (26:44)
    Disciples *sleep* (26:45a)
    Jesus *instructs* Peter and Zebedee's sons (26:45b)
Departure from Gethsemane (26:46)

The outline for this unit is as follows:

a. Arrival in Gethsemane (26:36)
b. The first cycle: Jesus prays and disciples sleep (26:37–41)
c. The second cycle: Jesus prays and disciples sleep (26:42–43)
d. The third cycle: Jesus prays and disciples sleep (26:44–46)

Exegesis and Exposition

[36]Then Jesus went with them to a place called Gethsemane and said to the disciples, "Sit here while I go over there to pray." [37]And he took with him Peter and the two sons of Zebedee and began to be grieved and troubled. [38]Then he said to them, "My soul is deeply grieved, to the point of death; stay here and keep watch with me."

[39]And he went a little farther and fell on his face and prayed, "My Father, if it

is possible, let this cup pass from me; yet not as I will, but as you will." [40]Then he went to the disciples and found them sleeping, and said to Peter, "So, could you not keep watch with me for one hour? [41]Watch and pray so that you may not enter into temptation; the spirit is willing, but the flesh is weak." [42]Again he went away a second time and prayed, "My Father, if this cannot pass from me unless I drink it, let your will be done." [43]And again he went and found them sleeping, for their eyes were heavy. [44]And he left them again, and went away and prayed a third time, saying the same words again. [45]Then he went to the disciples and said to them, "Are you still sleeping and resting? Look, the hour is at hand and the Son of Man is being betrayed into the hands of sinners. [46]Get up, let us go; look, the one who betrays me is near!"

a. Arrival in Gethsemane (26:36)

This is one of the saddest stories in all of Scripture. Jesus and the disciples come to a place called Gethsemane, which is evidently derived from two Hebrew words meaning "oil press." He asks the disciples to stay in one place while he goes aside to pray. This is the first hint in this passage (cf. 26:8–9, 35) of the profound distance between Jesus and his disciples.

26:36

b. The First Cycle: Jesus Prays and Disciples Sleep (26:37–41)

Jesus takes Peter and Zebedee's two sons (17:1; 20:22) with him. He tells the three inner circle disciples (cf. 17:1) that he is crushed by grief to the point of death. He asks them to stay alert with him and leaves them behind so he can pray alone. There may be an intentional echo of Gen. 22:5 here. Perhaps the stress on watchfulness is meant to reenact the vigil of Passover night (Exod. 12:42). Jesus's profound inner agony is like that expressed in, for example, Pss. 3, 6, 31, 42. He is alone, having left behind both the larger group and the inner circle of disciples.

26:37–38

The pathetic cycle occurs three times: Jesus prays alone (26:39, 42, 44; cf. 14:13, 23) but then finds the disciples sleeping instead of staying alert (26:40, 43, 45). As he faces death, his anguish contrasts with their lack of awareness and concern for their master. His prayer in 26:39 (cf. 26:42, 44) expresses his wish to avoid the agonies of the cross, yet he realizes that the Father's plan takes priority over his wishes; the Father's will must be done (6:10; 26:53–54). Jesus portrays his suffering as a cup that must be drunk.[1] His prone posture is in keeping with his submission to the Father (17:6).[2] After praying, he finds the three disciples sleeping. His

26:39–41

---

1. See this metaphor also in 20:22–23 and, e.g., Pss. 11:6; 75:8; Isa. 51:17, 22; Jer. 16:7; 25:15; 49:12; Rev. 14:10; 16:19; 17:4; 18:6.
2. Falling on one's face is a posture of awe, fear, and worship. Cf. Gen. 17:3, 17; Num. 14:5; 2 Sam. 9:6; 1 Kings 18:39; Ruth 2:10; Luke 5:12; 17:16; 1 Cor. 14:25; Rev. 7:11; 11:16; Josephus, *Ant.* 10.11; Jos. Asen. 14.4; Apocalypse of Sedrach 14.2.

response includes a rhetorical question about their insensitivity (26:40b) and an exhortation to alertness (26:41; cf. 24:42–43; 25:13). The words "one hour" in 26:40 may hint that his prayer and their nap have been that long. Their protests in 26:35b indicate their willingness of spirit (cf. Ps. 51:12), but their inability to remain alert with their master during his final and most difficult hours on earth reveals their weakness of flesh (Rom. 6:19; cf. 8:4–17; Gal. 5:16–24). Peter is specifically addressed in Matt. 26:40 because he has protested loudly (26:33–35) and will deny the Lord (26:69–75). But spiritual alertness may overcome human weakness (cf. Rom. 13:11–14).

c. The Second Cycle: Jesus Prays and Disciples Sleep (26:42–43)

26:42–43 Jesus's second prayer implies a deeper resignation to the Father's will (6:10). There is no request for the cup to pass away (26:39), only agreement with the Father that the cup can pass away only if Jesus drinks it. After praying again, Jesus discovers the disciples sleeping again. There is no question or exhortation as in 26:40–41, only the narrative detail that their eyes are heavy.

d. The Third Cycle: Jesus Prays and Disciples Sleep (26:44–46)

26:44–46 Jesus leaves them to pray a third time (cf. 2 Cor. 12:8), as he had previously. When he returns, the disciples are still asleep. This cycle of three lost opportunities to stay alert anticipates the cycle of Peter's three lost opportunities to confess Jesus in Matt. 26:69–75. Since it would be strange for Jesus to tell them to sleep one moment and rouse them the next, 26:45 is most likely a question ("Are you still sleeping and resting?") and not a statement ("Keep on sleeping and resting").[3] In any event, Jesus announces that the time of his betrayal and the betrayer himself are at hand. His agony does not prevent him from recognizing the moment of his betrayal.

The three cycles of Jesus's praying while his disciples sleep make certain points unmistakably clear. Jesus's solitary prayers put the Father's will above his own. Although he anticipates the suffering ahead of him (cf. 27:46) and wishes he could avoid it, he is resigned to obey the Father's plan. This models what he taught his disciples about prayer (6:10). The prayers also model Jesus's exhortation to alertness and his recognition of the weakness of the flesh (26:41). Jesus's prayers reenact the God-centered mind-set he showed at his temptation (4:1–11). He will live by God's word whether or not he has bread. He will not test God but

---

3. Καθεύδετε and ἀναπαύεσθε may be parsed as either indicatives or imperatives, depending on the context.

will worship God alone. He will desire and do the will of God even if it leads to suffering and death. The book of Hebrews stresses how Jesus's sufferings enabled him to be a sympathetic high priest for his followers (Heb. 2:14–18; 4:14–16; 5:7–10). Historic Christian teaching on the Trinity and Jesus's deity should not deter Christians from fully appreciating the intensity of Jesus's distress in the garden (Matt. 26:37–39, 42, 44). Jesus is truly divine and truly human.

Gethsemane also reminds disciples of their weakness (cf., e.g., 6:30; 8:26; 14:31; 16:8, 22; 17:20; 18:21; 19:13). Their lack of perception at Jesus's anointing in Bethany (26:10) has already shown that they were not focused on his reminder that his death was near (26:2). Their unanimous denial that they would desert Jesus when he predicted they would shows their unbelief and sinful self-confidence (26:31–35). Such apparently brave disciples should be able to watch with Jesus through the night, but even their inner circle fails him at the moment of deepest need. Zebedee's sons wanted the highest honors in the kingdom and promised they could drink his cup (20:22), but now they do not even stay awake to share Jesus's burden over the cup he alone will drink. After their performance in Gethsemane, the disciples' desertion when Jesus is arrested (26:56) does not surprise. Their sleep reminds disciples of the necessity of spiritual alertness during moral testing (cf. 1 Cor. 16:13; Eph. 5:14; Col. 4:2; 1 Thess. 5:6–8; 1 Pet. 5:8). Jesus's promises can sustain alert disciples (e.g., Matt. 16:18; 19:28–29; 28:18, 20).[4]

4. On Jesus in Gethsemane, see Blaising 1979; Daube 1973: 330–35; Feldmeier 1987; Feuillet 1977; S. L. Johnson 1967b; Kayalaparampil 1990; Senior 1975: 100–119; Stanley 1980: 155–87.

VII. Epilogue/Conclusion: Passion, Resurrection, and Commission (26:3–28:20)
    A. Preliminary Events and Preparation of the Disciples (26:3–46)
➤ B. Arrest and Trial (26:47–27:26)
    C. Crucifixion (27:27–56)

B. Arrest and Trial (26:47–27:26)

With 26:47 "the preliminaries are over" (Hagner 1995a: 787). Jesus has finished preparing his disciples for his suffering and death and their own failings. During the night he is arrested and his disciples flee. He is then subjected to unjust legal proceedings. In the morning he will appear before Pilate and then be handed over for crucifixion. He will die before three in the afternoon. But through all of this, the unmistakable impression is that Jesus, or rather his Father in heaven, is in charge (cf. John 10:18; W. Davies and Allison 1997: 511).

1. The Arrest of Jesus (26:47–56)

This passage (cf. Mark 14:43–52; Luke 22:47–53; John 18:2–12) shows that Jesus and his disciples are not subversives or "Zealots," despite the false charges soon to be brought against Jesus (Matt. 26:61). Jesus is resigned to drinking the cup the Father has placed before him. He teaches his disciples that violence leads only to more violence. Despite their previous boasts (26:35), the disciples offer only token resistance to Jesus's arrest and then run away. The group sent to arrest Jesus is apparently composed of temple guards commanded by the high priest. This large armed group apprehends Jesus in an obscure place under cover of darkness. The bravery of Jesus, the treachery of Judas, the cowardice of the disciples, and the aggression of the arrest party are all in character with the respective figures. Yet the strong emphasis on God's predetermined plan balances these sinful human acts (26:2, 18, 24, 31, 39, 42, 54, 56) and provides yet another example of the scriptural pattern of the compatibility of divine sovereignty and human responsibility.

The unit may be outlined as follows:

a. Jesus's arrest (26:47–50)
b. Jesus's response to the resisting disciple (26:51–54)
c. Jesus's response to the arrest party (26:55–56)

Exegesis and Exposition

[47]And while he was still speaking, behold, Judas, one of the Twelve, came up, and with him was a large crowd with swords and clubs, from the chief priests and elders of the people. [48]Now his betrayer had given them a sign, saying, "Whomever I kiss, he is the one; arrest him." [49]And immediately he went to Jesus and said, "Hello, Rabbi!" and kissed him. [50]And Jesus said to him, "Friend, why are you here?" Then they came and seized Jesus and arrested him. [51]Suddenly one of those who were with Jesus reached out his hand, drew his sword, and struck the slave of the high priest, cutting off his ear. [52]Then Jesus said to him, "Put your sword back into its place; for all who draw the sword will die by the sword. [53]Or do you think that I cannot call upon my Father, and he will immediately provide me with more than twelve legions of angels? [54]How, then, would the Scriptures be fulfilled, which say it must happen this way?" [55]At that time Jesus said to the crowds, "Have you come out with swords and clubs to arrest me as you would against a rebel? Every day I used to sit in the temple teaching, and yet you did

not arrest me. [56]But all this has happened so that the Scriptures of the prophets may be fulfilled." Then all the disciples deserted him and fled.

a. Jesus's Arrest (26:47–50)

26:47–50 As Jesus urges the disciples to rise, Judas and a large armed group (cf. John 18:12) sent by the leaders arrives to arrest him. The treachery of Judas is emphasized by the detail that he is one of the Twelve (Matt. 26:14, 21; cf. John 13:18; Ps. 41:9). Judas approaches Jesus and greets him with a respectful title ("Rabbi") and a friendly gesture (a kiss). This has been arranged to identify Jesus to the arrest party. Jesus may not be known personally to them, and it is dark. Only Judas addresses Jesus as "Rabbi" in Matthew (26:25, 49; cf. 23:7–8), and his kiss perverts an action that customarily expresses brotherhood, affirmation, and honor (cf. Luke 7:45; Rom. 16:16; 1 Pet. 5:14). Jesus's response to Judas can be understood either as a command telling Judas to do what he has come to do (cf. John 13:27) or as a question asking him what he is doing.[1] The reference to Judas as "friend" seems ironic, but the word ἑταῖρε (*hetaire*; cf. Matt. 11:16 v.l.; 20:13; 22:12; Josephus, *Ant.* 12.302; BDAG 398) refers only to an acquaintance and does not imply a close relationship (Eltester 1962: 70–91).

b. Jesus's Response to the Resisting Disciple (26:51–54)

26:51–52 One of the disciples clumsily wields his sword to resist the arrest but manages only to cut off the ear of the high priest's slave (Luke 22:50–51; John 18:10; Viviano 1989). Jesus's command for him to put his sword away models what Jesus has taught in Matt. 5:38–42. The command has been used to support various stripes of the view known as Christian pacifism or nonresistance (cf. 5:9, 38–42; Gardner 1991: 381–82). In context, however, Jesus is only speaking realistically and proverbially about the way violence reproduces itself in a fallen world.[2] Since the focus is on Jesus, there is no mention of the arrest of the sword-bearer.

26:53–54 Jesus gives a more important reason for forbidding the attempt to resist arrest. He could call upon his Father for the capacity to summon multitudes of angels (cf. 4:6, 11; 13:41; 16:27; 25:31), but he will do the Father's will in fulfillment of the Hebrew Scriptures (26:24, 39, 42, 56). In the Roman military structure, a legion numbered around six thousand soldiers (BDAG 588), and so, on this model, twelve legions of angels would

---

1. The clause ἐφ' ὃ πάρει is ambiguous. R. Brown (1994: 385–88) discusses several views, none of which is convincing. The common view that one must supply an understood imperative ("Do what you came for") seems unlikely. More likely one should take the words as a question (as in the translation above) or as a comment reflecting the irony of the moment (so R. Brown).

2. Cf. Gen. 9:6; Jer. 15:2; Rev. 13:10; *m. 'Abot* 2.7; Sir. 27:25–27; Targum Isa. 50:11; Bruner 1990: 998–99; Calvin 1972: 3.159–60.

be around seventy-two thousand of them. The number twelve has obvious implications (10:1; 19:28; cf. Rev. 21:12–14). Scriptural fulfillment is a key motif in Matthew's theology (cf., e.g., Matt. 1:22–23 and the discussion under "Fulfillment" in the introduction to this commentary). Jesus will not instruct his disciples again until after his resurrection.

c. Jesus's Response to the Arrest Party (26:55–56)

Jesus now turns his rebuke upon the "crowds," which in this context probably means the group that arrested him (26:47). With a touch of sarcasm, he points out that stealth and force are unnecessary, since he has been teaching publicly in the temple every day (21:23) and is not a λῃστής (lēstēs). The latter word has been understood in terms of political subversion or revolution (NIV, NLT) or mere theft (KJV, NRSV). Given the context, the former seems more likely (cf. 27:11, 29, 37–38, 42; BDAG 594).[3] The religious leaders could not arrest Jesus publicly because of his popularity with the crowd, now bolstered by the throngs of pilgrims in Jerusalem for Passover (21:9–11, 15, 26; 26:5). Yet the stealth of the leaders mysteriously fulfills the divinely ordained plan revealed in the prophetic Scriptures (cf. Acts 2:23; 3:13–18). Jesus's words are immediately confirmed by the flight of his disciples, which he had foretold as a fulfillment of Zechariah (Matt. 26:31; Zech. 13:7).[4]

26:55–56

3. The two meanings are related in that rebels often use banditry to foment revolt by disrupting entrenched infrastructure. Cf. 21:13; 27:38, 44; Josephus, *J.W.* 2.253–54; 4.504; *Ant.* 14.159–62; 20.160–67; R. Horsley 1979, 1987; R. Horsley and Hanson 1985.

4. On 26:47–56, see M. Black in Higgins 1959: 19–33; R. Brown 1994: 237–93; Corley in J. Green and McKnight 1992: 841–54; Légasse 1993; Senior 1975: 120–56.

2. Jesus Appears before the Sanhedrin (26:57–68)

This passage (cf. Mark 14:53–65; Luke 22:54–55, 63–71; John 18:13–14, 19–24) presents the first of Jesus's two "trials," although the term "hearing" is preferable. The narrative of Jesus's appearance before the high priest, Caiaphas, exposes the sordid nature of the whole process (Matt. 26:59–61). More important, Jesus's claim to be Israel's Messiah is climactically pressed before the religious leaders. Jesus's clear allusion to Dan. 7:13 portrays him as the messianic Son of Man who will return to judge his false accusers (Matt. 26:64). Yet the leaders reject Jesus's testimony, accuse him of blasphemy, and treat him with sarcasm and contempt (26:65–68). They are infuriated at the prospect of eschatological reversal in Jesus's claim that he will return as the glorious Son of Man to judge his judges. The contrasting confession of the Roman soldiers in 27:54 is in keeping with Matthew's stress on mission to the Gentiles. The religious leaders despise Jesus and crucify him, but the Roman soldiers acknowledge his unique status. This and other features of the story show that irony is its chief literary feature.[1]

The unit outline is as follows:

a. Jesus and Peter arrive at Caiaphas's residence (26:57–58)
b. The false testimony against Jesus (26:59–61)
c. The high priest questions Jesus (26:62–64)
d. The leaders' decision (26:65–68)

Exegesis and Exposition

[57]Then those who had arrested Jesus led him away to Caiaphas, the high priest, where the scribes and the elders had gathered together. [58]And Peter was following him at a distance as far as the courtyard of the high priest. He entered and sat down with the attendants to see how it would end. [59]Now the chief priests and the whole Sanhedrin were seeking false testimony against Jesus in order that they might execute him; [60]but they did not find it although many false

---

1. The literature on Jesus before Caiaphas is voluminous. Only a sampling follows: Bammel et al. 1970; Benoit 1962: 92–110; Brandon 1968; Catchpole 1971b; Cohn 1977; Gerhardsson 1981; Kertelge 1988; Légasse 1994; Matera 1991; R. Pesch 1988; Rivkin 1984; Sandmel 1971; Sloyan 2006; Zeitlin 1942.

witnesses came forward. Finally two came forward [61]and said, "This man said, 'I can destroy the temple of God and rebuild it in three days.'"

[62]Then the high priest stood up and said to Jesus, "Don't you have an answer to what these men are testifying against you?" [63]But Jesus was silent, so the high priest said to him, "I put you under oath by the living God, tell us if you are the Messiah, the Son of God." [64]Jesus said to him, "You said it; nevertheless I tell you, from now on you shall see 'the Son of Man sitting at the right hand of Power' and 'coming on the clouds of heaven.'"

[65]Then the high priest tore his clothes and said, "He has blasphemed! What further need do we have of witnesses? Look, you have now heard his blasphemy; [66]what do you think?" They answered, "He deserves to die!" [67]Then they spit in his face and struck him with their fists, and others slapped him [68]and said, "Prophesy to us, Messiah; who is the one who hit you?"

a. Jesus and Peter Arrive at Caiaphas's Residence (26:57–58)

The disciples flee as Jesus is led away to the residence of the high priest,   **26:57–58**
Caiaphas, where some scribes and elders have gathered. Peter follows at a distance and sits in the courtyard to see what will happen. This sets the scene for the story of Peter's three denials in 26:69–75.

b. The False Testimony against Jesus (26:59–61)

This hearing exhibits anything but the impartiality and fairness mandated   **26:59–61**
by Scripture and Jewish law. Although the chief priests and the Sanhedrin (5:22; 10:17) are trying to obtain false testimony against Jesus (9:3; 12:10, 24, 38; 16:1; 19:3) and many are willing to offer such testimony, nothing admissible is found at first. Eventually two men (18:16; cf. Deut. 17:6; 19:15) come forward to testify that Jesus claimed to be able to destroy the temple and rebuild it in three days. There is no clear record of this in the Synoptic Gospels (cf. Matt. 24:2; 27:40), but the allegation may have come from Jesus's teaching narrated in John 2:18–22 (cf. Acts 6:13–14). Action against the temple would be treason in Jewish eyes and seditious from the Roman viewpoint. Jesus's activities against the temple money changers and merchants (Matt. 21:12–13) are public knowledge and perhaps are taken as corroborating the false testimony.

c. The High Priest Questions Jesus (26:62–64)

Jesus is silent when Caiaphas first presses him to respond to the allega-   **26:62–64**
tions (cf. 27:14; Isa. 53:7; Acts 8:32). Then the high priest adjures Jesus in God's name to declare whether he is the Messiah, the Son of God (Matt. 3:17; 16:16). The word ἐξορκίζω (*exorkizō*; cf. Josephus, *Ant.* 2.200; 11.145) has the force of putting Jesus under oath (BDAG 351; cf. *m. Šeb.*). The apposition of "Son of God" to "Messiah" indicates that the former title was interpreted messianically (cf. 2 Sam. 7:14; Pss. 2:7; 89:26–27).

This question and Jesus's answer raise the key Matthean motif of Jesus's divine sonship (Matt. 1:1, 23; 2:15; 3:17; 4:3, 6; 17:5; 28:19). Jesus first ambiguously affirms the high priest's words ("You said it"; cf. 26:25). He continues[2] with an unambiguous biblical citation that combines Ps. 110:1 and Dan. 7:13 to the effect that he is indeed the glorious Son of Man who will come from the right hand of Power (cf. Matt. 19:28; 24:30; 25:31; John 1:51; 1 En. 62.5). "Power" is an attribute uniquely associated with God, and it stands for God by metonymy. Blomberg (1992a: 403) points out that Matt. 26:64 is "the Christological climax of the Gospel thus far."

Christology

The terse exchange between Jesus and Caiaphas in 26:62–64 contains one of the strongest affirmations of Jesus's identity in this Gospel. Jesus's citation of Dan. 7:13 with Ps. 110:1 shows that he understands his identity and future mission in terms of the glorious, exalted Son of Man. "Nowhere does Jesus reveal himself more than here" (Hagner 1995a: 799).

The time frame implied in Matt. 26:64 is rather broad. Caiaphas himself will see the exaltation of Jesus when he is confronted with the reality of Jesus's resurrection, which installs him as the glorious Son of Man. But Caiaphas will not acknowledge that the person he is unjustly judging will someday justly judge him (cf. 28:11–15). Jesus speaks as the exalted Son of Man when he prefaces his commission to the disciples with the words "All authority in heaven and on earth has been given to me" (28:18). But the resurrection only inaugurates the glorious reign of Jesus (cf. John 7:39; 12:23, 32–33; 17:4–5; Acts 2:32–33; 13:33–37; Phil. 2:9–11; Rev. 5:5–10). This reign will be consummated by his coming to judge and rule the earth.[3] The resurrection vindicates Jesus and defeats his enemies, at least in principle. His coming to earth realizes the final judgment, where all humans stand before the Son of Man. Unbelievers will be condemned, believers will be rewarded, and Jesus will gloriously reign over his people in a new world (19:28).

d. The Leaders' Decision (26:65–68)

26:65–68   The high priest is outraged by Jesus's connecting himself with Daniel's Son of Man. His charge of blasphemy implies that Jesus has arrogated divine prerogatives to himself.[4] He shows his disgust by tearing his robes,

---

2. The continuation of Jesus's answer begins with πλήν, which is generally used to add contrasting information that must be considered. Cf. 11:22, 24; 18:7; 26:39; BDAG 826.

3. Matt. 6:10; 7:22–23; 13:41–43; 16:27; 19:28; 24:30; 25:31; cf. 2 Sam. 7:12–16; Ps. 2; Luke 1:32–33; Acts 17:30–31; 1 Cor. 15:20–28; Rev. 1:7; 2:26–27; 11:15; 19:11–16; 20:4–6.

4. Bock in J. Green and Turner 1994: 181–91 argues that Jesus's words are taken as blasphemous because they concern violation of God's sacred presence, mediated on earth by the holy of holies in the temple and accessible only to the high priest on the Day of Atonement.

an action that signifies extreme sorrow or anger.[5] He asks why any further testimony is necessary, since Jesus's "blasphemy" merits punishment. The assembled leaders evidently agree with his assessment that Jesus deserves to die (cf. Lev. 24:16). They begin to spit on Jesus (Isa. 50:6) and to beat him. The word ἐράπισαν (*erapisan*) may indicate that some use whips or clubs (BDAG 903). They also taunt Jesus by insincerely addressing him as the Messiah and asking him to prophecy to them about who is striking him. Jesus's response exemplifies his teaching in Matt. 5:38–42 (cf. Isa. 50:4–9).

Is Matthew's Presentation of the Trial Anti-Semitic?

It is clear that this trial was not carried out according to the just legal procedures that are found in the Mishnah (*m. Sanh.* 4–7; R. Brown 1994: 357–63), which specifies that trials were not to be held at night and that capital cases could not be decided in one day. Additional details in Matthew's narrative conflict with mishnaic laws for trials. One explanation for this conflict downplays the mishnaic traditions as idealistic and theoretical, written down more than 150 years after the trial of Jesus. But the Mishnah purports to record oral tradition from earlier times. Another explanation is that Matthew created the story as propaganda (Beare 1981: 519–20) to blame the Jews and exonerate the Romans in order to gain Rome's favor for Christians. But this argument breaks down if Matthew and his community still identified themselves as Jews. A better view is that Matthew's narrative presents accurate historical information to show that the religious leaders do not follow Judaism's just standards in dealing with Jesus (cf. Acts 6:11–14; 7:57–58). It is expedient to ignore these rules in order to be rid of Jesus before the crowds become aware of what is happening. Matthew does not blame his Jewish contemporaries for this injustice, let alone the Jews who have lived since then. Rather, the trial narrative continues Matthew's bluntly negative portrayal of the Jerusalem establishment as corrupt shepherds who scatter the lost sheep of Israel (Matt. 9:36). Their interpretation of the law does not focus on the weightier matters (23:23). They follow human traditions that obscure the law's righteousness (15:1–14). When Matthew's narrative highlights the corruption of the Jerusalem establishment, it is not anti-Semitic but prophetic.

From Matthew's theological standpoint, it is not ultimately the corrupt Jewish leaders or the weak Roman governor who are responsible for killing Jesus. Rather, it is God's plan being accomplished through the sinful deeds of Jews and Gentiles alike, so that sinners from every people group might believe in Jesus the Messiah and be forgiven by the shedding of his blood (1:21; 20:28; 26:28).

5. E.g., Gen. 37:29; 1 Sam. 15:27–28; 2 Kings 18:37–19:1; Job 1:20; Acts 14:14; *m. Sanh.* 7.5; Jdt. 14:19; 1 Macc. 11:71; Josephus, *J.W.* 2.316. But cf. Joel 2:13.

3. Peter's Three Denials (26:69–75)

After the account of the hearing before Caiaphas, the story returns to Peter in the courtyard (26:58). The pattern of the narrative presents Peter's "trial" as a foil to Jesus's trial. Jesus confesses, but Peter denies, fulfilling Jesus's prophetic words (26:31–35), which the leaders have just mocked (26:68). This passage contains three accusations that Peter is a follower of Jesus and three increasingly intense denials by Peter. A mere servant girl cows Peter, whose denials are increasingly punctuated with oaths and expletives as he moves farther from Jesus, from the courtyard (26:69–70) to the gateway (26:71–72) to his departure (26:75). With this, all the disciples have deserted Jesus. Peter, who was called first, leaves last. One could sympathize with Peter's denying the Lord once, but his triple, increasingly vehement denial cannot be condoned. Many questions arise when one compares the details here with the other Gospels' accounts (cf. Mark 14:66–72; Luke 22:55–62; John 18:25–27). (On the difficulties of harmonizing the synoptic accounts, see McEleney 1990; J. Wenham 1978–79.)

The outline for this unit is as follows:

a. Peter's first denial (26:69–70)
b. Peter's second denial (26:71–72)
c. Peter's third denial (26:73–74)
d. Peter remembers (26:75)

Exegesis and Exposition

[69]Now Peter was sitting outside in the courtyard, and a servant girl came to him and said, "You also were with Jesus the Galilean." [70]But he denied it before all of them, saying, "I do not know what you are talking about." [71]And when he had gone out to the entrance, another servant girl saw him and said to those who were there, "⌜This⌝ man was with Jesus the Nazarene." [72]And again he denied it with an oath, "I do not know the man." [73]After a little while, those who were standing there came up and said to Peter, "Surely you also are one of them; for your way of speaking makes it clear." [74]Then he began to curse and swear, "I do not know the man!" And immediately a cock crowed. [75]And Peter remembered the word that Jesus had spoken, "Before a cock crows, you will deny me three times." And he went out and wept bitterly.

a. Peter's First Denial (26:69–70)

Outside the high priest's residence, a servant girl[1] accuses Peter of being   **26:69–70**
with Jesus the Galilean (cf. Mark 14:70; Luke 13:1–2; 22:59; 23:6; John
4:45; 7:52; Acts 1:11; 2:7; 5:37), but he denies it before the people in the
courtyard.

b. Peter's Second Denial (26:71–72)

As Peter is leaving, while he is at the gate of the courtyard, another servant   **26:71–72**
girl tells the bystanders that he was with Jesus the Nazarene (cf. 2:23;
Luke 18:37; John 18:5, 7; 19:19; Acts 2:22; 3:6; 4:10; 6:14; 22:8; 24:5; 26:9;
BDAG 664–65). Peter denies it emphatically with an oath, which would
falsely invoke God (Matt. 5:33–37; 14:7, 9; 23:16–22). Jesus's followers
will also soon be called Nazarenes (Acts 24:5).

c. Peter's Third Denial (26:73–74)

A bystander, probably a more formidable accuser than servant girls,   **26:73–74**
notes Peter's Galilean accent (cf. Acts 4:13) and charges him with being
Jesus's companion. Now Peter is desperate, and he punctuates his denial
with vehement curses and oaths, perhaps calling on God to smite him
if he is lying or perhaps even cursing Jesus (W. Davies and Allison 1997:
548–49; Merkel in Bammel et al. 1970: 66–71).

d. Peter Remembers (26:75)

The rooster's crow (Derrett 1983b) after this third denial immediately and   **26:75**
excruciatingly reminds Peter of Jesus's prediction (26:34). Peter boasted
he would die before he denied Jesus, but he does not even respond truth-
fully to a query from a powerless servant girl. His bitter weeping as he
departs may reflect not only his sorrow but also his belief that his curses
will come upon him. (See Lampe 1972–73.)

Peter's Failure

In many cases Scripture presents the weaker moments of its heroes (e.g.,
Noah, Abraham, Moses, David, Solomon). Likewise, Matthew's narrative
does not omit the inconsistencies and failures of Jesus's disciples. Jesus's
subsequent rehabilitation of Peter (cf. John 21:15–22) is not narrated by
Matthew, and so the reader is left with yet another blunt testimony to
the weakness of the disciples. This is tempered somewhat by the teaching on God's forgiveness (Matt. 12:32) and the promise that Jesus will
later meet the disciples in Galilee (26:32; 28:7, 10, 16). Peter's denial
typifies the weakness of all the disciples (26:35), yet their mission will

---

1. The use of μία with παιδίσκη is equivalent to the indefinite pronoun or indefinite
article. Cf. 8:19; 9:18; 21:19; 27:15; BDAG 292; BDF §247 (2).

go on if they are true to the resurrected Messiah and live by his power and presence (28:18–20).

It is instructive to compare Peter and Jesus. Jesus confesses his messianic identity before the supreme leader of Israel, but Peter denies any knowledge of Jesus before a servant girl (cf. 10:32–33; 1 Tim. 6:13). Peter immediately is grief-stricken over his sin, but so was Judas (Matt. 27:3), and so it is also instructive to compare Peter and Judas. As Jesus predicted, Judas betrays the Lord. Afterward he feels remorse, is rebuffed by the Jewish leaders, and commits suicide (27:1–10). As Jesus predicted, Peter also denies the Lord. Afterward he feels remorse, is restored by Jesus, and resumes his role as the leader of the disciples (26:32; 28:10, 18–20). Starkly opposite results come from very similar actions. Peter's human weakness leads to momentary failure, but the pattern of Peter's life is discipleship. In fairness to Peter, in Matthew's narrative he is the only disciple to follow Jesus to the high priest's courtyard (but cf. John 18:15–16). Although he fails miserably there, the other disciples do not even go there. On the other hand, Judas's remorse is not accompanied by deeds indicating genuine repentance (Matt. 26:24–25; cf. John 17:12; Acts 1:16–20; R. Brown 1994: 1394–1418; Schwarz 1988).

In Matthew, Peter is primus inter pares, first among the disciples of Jesus. Throughout the narrative, he is presented as the representative disciple and often speaks for the group (D. Turner 1989). His miserable failure in denying Jesus is a sharp warning to all followers of Jesus. If Peter, of all people, is susceptible to such a fall, no disciple is invulnerable. And yet if Peter, of all people, is restored after such an egregious lapse, no disciple is hopeless. Jesus's followers should be horrified by Peter's denials and thrilled by his restoration. Peter is the representative disciple both then and now (Calvin 1972: 3.169–70).

Summary and Transition

Matthew's narrative presents two alternating stories. As the plot to execute Jesus progresses (26:3–5, 14–16, 47–56), Jesus prepares his disciples for the end of his earthly ministry (26:6–13, 17–29). In the touching Gethsemane scene, the inner circle of disciples cannot even stay awake with Jesus during his agonizing struggle (26:31–46). Judas then betrays the Lord to the religious leaders (26:47–56), who lead Jesus away to Caiaphas (26:57–68). As Jesus affirms his messianic identity (26:64), Peter denies the Lord three times, as Jesus predicted (26:69–75, cf. 33–35).

In Matt. 26, the death of Jesus looms large. Jesus prepares his disciples for it and the Pharisees scheme to cause it. Jesus's predictions of his death (26:2, 12, 21, 23–24, 28, 32, 45, 54) and of his disciples' desertion (26:31–35) show that he remains in control despite the grim circumstances. Even his Gethsemane struggles do not detract from the theme of his control, since he always obeys the Father (26:39, 42, 44). Another clear theme is God's sovereignty, especially in relation to biblical fulfillment (26:24, 31, 54, 56, 64). In this light, the treachery of Judas and the plot of the religious leaders are at the same time both culpable acts (26:24, 64) and divine necessities that lead up to Jesus's crucifixion for the forgiveness of sins (26:28; cf. 1:21; 3:6; 20:28). Matthew 26 is a profound testimony that the sovereignty of God and the responsible agency of people are compatible biblical truths, even though the interplay of these truths is not yet fully grasped.

Additional Note

26:71. UBS[4] prefers the shorter reading οὗτος, well supported by ℵ, B, D (cf. Mark 14:69). In the longer reading, καί appears before οὗτος. This may be an interpolation from Luke 22:59, but it has wide support (A, C, L, W, Δ, Θ, f[1], f[13], 33, 157, *Byz, Lect*).

4. The Sanhedrin's Formal Decision (27:1–2)

By the time morning had arrived, the decision had been made to hand Jesus over to Pilate for execution. Matthew 27:1–2 provides a transition from the subplot of Peter's denials (26:69–75) back to the main story of Jesus's trials and crucifixion.

Exegesis and Exposition

[1]Now when morning had come, all the chief priests and the elders of the people formed a plan against Jesus to put him to death. [2]After they bound him, they led him away and handed him over to ⌜Pilate⌝ the governor.

27:1–2 Jesus's prediction that the religious leaders would hand him over to the Gentiles (20:18–19) is now fulfilled. After the night hearing, in the morning (cf. 26:20) the leaders plan (cf. 12:14; 22:15; 27:7; 28:12) to have Jesus executed.[1] They restrain him (12:29; 14:3; 22:13) and transfer him to Pilate's jurisdiction (cf. Mark 15:1; Luke 22:66–23:1; John 18:28). Evidently, only the Roman governor had authority to order executions (John 18:31; R. Brown 1994: 363–72). Perhaps the reference to the morning decision should be viewed in light of *m. Sanh.* 4.1, which says that capital-case decisions must be reached in the daytime (cf. Blomberg 1987b: 136–38). Pilate served from 26 to 36 CE as one of a series of Roman governors (technically procurators or prefects) of Judea (cf. Luke 3:1; 13:1; Acts 4:27; 1 Tim. 6:13; Josephus, *Ant.* 18.2). Extrabiblical sources portray him as insecure, insensitive to the Jews, and harsh in administering justice (Josephus, *Ant.* 18.35, 55–62, 85–89; *J.W.* 2.169–77; Philo, *Embassy* 299–305; Tacitus, *Ann.* 15.44). An inscription mentioning Pilate as prefect was discovered at Caesarea Maritima in 1961 (C. A. Evans in C. A. Evans and Porter 2000: 804; McGing 1991). See the summary of the literary and archaeological evidence on Pilate by C. A. Evans in Charlesworth 2006: 330–38.

---

1. Matthew's συμβούλιον ἔλαβον may be a Latinism deriving from *consilium capere.* Cf. 12:14; 22:15; 27:1, 7; 28:12; Josephus, *Ant.* 6.38; BDAG 957; BDF §5, 3b.

Additional Note

27:2. The shorter reading Πιλάτῳ found in UBS⁴ is supported by ℵ, B, L, Σ, 33, along with some early versions and patristic sources (cf. Mark 15:1; Luke 23:1; John 18:29). The longer reading Ποντίῳ Πιλάτῳ is found in A, C, W, Δ, Θ, 0250, *f*¹, *f*¹³, *Byz, Lect* (cf. Luke 3:1; Acts 4:27; 1 Tim. 6:13). It is difficult to understand why Ποντίῳ would have been deleted if it had been in the original text.

5. The Remorse and Suicide of Judas
(27:3–10)

Matthew 27:1–2 continues the trial story of 26:57–68, suspended by the narrative of Peter's denials (26:69–75). Next is the account of Judas's suicide (Matt. 27:3–8; cf. Acts 1:18–19), which Matthew views as a fulfillment of prophecy (27:9–10; cf. Zech. 11:12–13; Jer. 32:6–9). Matthew's passion narrative plot pattern weaves stories about supporting characters and issues (Matt. 26:6–13, 20–35; 27:3–10) into the main story of Jesus's suffering.

The unit can be outlined as follows:

a. Judas's regret and suicide (27:3–5)
b. The leaders' use of the blood money (27:6–8)
c. The fulfillment of Scripture (27:9–10)

Exegesis and Exposition

³Then when Judas, who had betrayed him, saw that Jesus had been condemned, he regretted his action and returned the thirty silver coins to the chief priests and elders, ⁴saying, "I have sinned by betraying ⌜innocent⌝ blood." But they said, "What is that to us? You deal with that!" ⁵So he threw the silver into the temple and departed. Then he went away and hanged himself. ⁶And the chief priests took the silver coins and said, "It is not lawful to put them into the treasury, since this is blood money." ⁷And they formed a plan and used the coins to buy the potter's field as a burial place for strangers. ⁸For this reason, that field has been called the Field of Blood to this day. ⁹Then what was spoken through ⌜Jeremiah⌝ the prophet was fulfilled, "And they took the thirty silver coins, the price of the one whose price had been set by the people of Israel; ¹⁰and ⌜they gave⌝ them for the potter's field, as the Lord directed me."

a. Judas's Regret and Suicide (27:3–5)

27:3–5 Matthew inserts his unique narrative of Judas's suicide (cf. Acts 1:16–20; 2 Sam. 17:23) between the Jewish (Matt. 26:57–68; 27:1–2) and Roman (27:11–26) hearings. Although the placement of this passage leads the reader to think that Judas's actions result from the Sanhedrin's in 27:1–2, the chronological relationship of Judas's suicide to the rest of this chapter's events is difficult to ascertain. Judas's regret that Jesus is condemned may refer to Pilate's later decision. Judas may have learned in Caiaphas's courtyard that the Sanhedrin had condemned Jesus. Additional plausible scenarios could be constructed. In any event, the religious leaders in 27:3–5 are free to receive Judas, which may mean they are no longer lobbying Pilate (27:12, 20). It is difficult to understand Judas's regret over Jesus's condemnation, since this was the inevitable outcome of his betrayal.[1] The word used to express Judas's remorse is μεταμέλομαι (*metamelomai*; cf. 21:29, 32; 2 Cor. 7:8; Heb. 7:21), not μετανοέω (*metanoeō*; cf. Matt. 3:2, 8, 11; 4:17; 11:20–21; 12:41; Acts 2:38; 17:30; 26:20), the word most often used for genuine repentance (Calvin 1972: 3.175). Judas returns the thirty silver coins to the Jewish leaders and acknowledges his sin to them (cf. Deut. 27:25), but they coldly rebuff him, telling him that his sin is his own problem (cf. Matt. 27:24). The act of throwing the money down in the temple demonstrates Judas's regrets, but now it is too late to help Jesus. Judas gains no peace of mind from conversing with the religious leaders, and so he deals with his guilt by hanging himself (cf. 2 Sam. 17:23; *m. Sanh.* 10.2; Josephus, *J.W.* 3.369; Tob. 3:10).[2]

b. The Leaders' Use of the Blood Money (27:6–8)

The leaders' scruples regarding the use of Judas's money (cf. Deut. 23:18) is amazing in light of their indifference to Judas's anguish, not to mention their seeking false witnesses against Jesus. Their concern about ritual purity starkly contrasts with their blatant disregard for fundamental Torah values and illustrates Jesus's complaint in Matt. 23:23. Judas's silver coins were "the price of blood," and so the field purchased by the priests with the coins was still "called the Field of Blood" when Matthew later wrote (cf. Acts 1:19). The "strangers" for whom the field was purchased were probably Jews who died in Jerusalem while attending religious festivals there.

27:6–8

c. The Fulfillment of Scripture (27:9–10)

Matthew views Judas's suicide and the purchase of the burial field as a fulfillment of Scripture, primarily Zech. 11:12–13. This is the final fulfillment formula citation in Matthew. Additional allusions to Jer. 19:1–13 (and possibly 18:2; 32:6–9) evidently lead Matthew to refer the prophecy to Jeremiah (Blomberg 1992a: 409; Gundry 1994: 557–58). It is not unusual for biblical citations to combine two or more texts (W. Davies and Allison 1997: 568–69).

27:9–10

---

1. The use of the present participle (παραδιδούς, *paradidous*, betraying) to describe Judas is perhaps to be understood as perfective, emphasizing the ongoing results of a past action. See BDF §322; Wallace 1996: 532–33.

2. On Judas's death, see Benoit 1973: 1.189–207; O. Betz 1964; Conard 1991; Desautels 1986; Moo in France and Wenham 1980: 157–75; van Tilborg in Draisma 1989: 159–74; van Unnik 1974: 44–57.

It may be a bit of a stretch to view this passage as signifying the extension of salvation to the Gentiles (as does Bruner 1990: 1023), since the blood money goes for the burial of strangers or foreigners (cf. Matt. 25:35). Others (e.g., Beare 1981: 525–26) think that Matthew composes a fictional story in 27:3–10 as a midrash on Zech. 11:12–13. But in that case one would expect a closer correspondence between the story and Zechariah. Rather, Matthew notices the similarities between his historical tradition and Zech. 11 (Hagner 1995a: 811) and views Zech. 11 typologically. Zechariah 11 and Jer. 19 combine to form "a pattern of apostasy and rejection that must find its ultimate fulfillment in the rejection of Jesus" (Carson 1984: 566). Matthew sees correspondence between the shepherd doomed to slaughter (Zech. 11:7) and Jesus. The thirty silver coins thrown to the potter in the Lord's house (Zech. 11:13) correspond to Judas's coins thrown into the temple and used to buy the potter's field. Matthew does not make up a story to fit Zechariah but reads Zechariah in light of his conviction that Jesus's passion is anticipated in biblical pattern and prediction. This concept of typological fulfillment is based on a providential view of history.

Judas's Betrayal and Peter's Denial

It is interesting to compare and contrast Judas's regret and suicide after his treachery with the remorse of Peter after his own temporary lapse (see the comments on 26:75). Both acts were despicable, but Peter's pales in comparison with Judas's. Peter returns to following Jesus and is restored to his special office (28:18–20; John 21:15–17). His prominent ministry in the early church is well known.[3] But the regret of Judas does not approach genuine repentance. This is clear not so much from the use of μεταμέλομαι in Matt. 27:3 as from the ensuing events. Although Judas acknowledges his sin and returns his blood money, he never seeks Jesus's forgiveness or rejoins the disciples. His suicide indicates hopeless despair, not repentance (contra W. Davies and Allison 1997: 562, 565, 571; cf. Klassen 1996). Repentance is shown by works, portrayed as fruit (3:8–10; 7:16–20; 13:38–40). Judas's suicide violates the sixth commandment (Exod. 20:13). In light of Matt. 26:24 and John 6:70; 17:12, one should not hope that he was saved but be warned because he was lost. For a different view, see W. Klassen in Charlesworth 2006: 503–20.

Judas and Anti-Semitism?

Just as the corrupt religious leaders do not represent the Jewish people as a whole in Jesus's times or in any subsequent time, neither does Judas. He must not be viewed as typical of the Jewish people then or

---

3. On Peter, cf. Acts 1:15–22; 2:14–39; 3:1–26; 4:8–12, 19–20; 5:1–11, 29–32; 8:14–24; 10:1–11:18; 12:3–17; 15:7–11; 1 Cor. 1:12; 3:22; 9:5; 15:5; Gal. 1:18; 2:7–15; 1 Peter; 2 Peter.

now (Maccoby 1992). Jesus called twelve Jewish disciples, and only one of them betrayed him. The Eleven were restored to ministry for their Messiah and became the church's foundation. The rapid transition to gentile prominence in the church is a mystery of divine wisdom (Rom. 9–11), but gentile believers must never forget the Jewish roots of their faith (M. Wilson 1989).

Additional Notes

27:4. UBS⁴ prefers the less common word ἀθῷον, well supported by ℵ, A, B*, C, W, Δ, *f*¹, *f*¹³, 33, *Byz*, *Lect*. The more common word δίκαιον is found in B¹, L, Θ, and several ancient versions and patristic sources. The expression αἷμα ἀθῷον is relatively common in the LXX, and external evidence strongly favors the UBS⁴ text.

27:9. UBS⁴ prefers the reading Ἰερεμίου, strongly supported by B, L, Δ, Θ, *f*¹, *f*¹³, *Byz*, *Lect* (Metzger 1994: 55). Additional MSS support Jeremiah but with different spellings (e.g., ℵ, A, C*, W, 205, 1292, and several early versions). Because of the difficulty in attributing a text from Zech. 11:12–13 to Jeremiah (see the comments on 27:9–10), a few sources have Ζαχαρίου (22, Syrian and Armenian MSS). Others omit any source for the quotation (Φ, 33, 157, 1579, and a few early versions).

27:10. Among the possibilities, the UBS⁴ reading ἔδωκαν is best supported by both external (Aᶜ, B*, C, L, Δ, Θ, *f*¹, *f*¹³, 33, 157, *Byz*, *Lect*) and internal considerations. Two other readings are less likely on both counts: ἔδωκεν (A*ᵛⁱᵈ) and ἔδωκα (ℵ, B²ᵛⁱᵈ, W).

6. Jesus Appears before Pilate (27:11–26)

Jesus's hearing before Pilate (cf. Mark 15:1–15; Luke 23:1–25; John 18:28–19:16) includes two cycles of Pilate questioning Jesus (27:11; 27:12–14), followed by an explanation of the custom of releasing a prisoner at Passover and a note on the availability of Barabbas (27:15–16). Then there are two cycles of Pilate asking the crowd whom they prefer to be released (27:17–20, 21). After this, Pilate twice protests Jesus's innocence (27:23, 24–25) before handing him over for crucifixion (27:26). Besides Pilate and the crowd, two other characters appear. Pilate's wife is for Jesus (27:19), and the religious leaders are against Jesus (27:12). Sadly, the crowd and Pilate are influenced by the leaders, not Pilate's wife.

The unit can be outlined as follows:

a. Jesus's silence under accusation (27:11–14)
   i. Jesus answers Pilate (27:11)
   ii. Jesus will not answer the leaders' accusations (27:12–14)
b. An opportunity for release: Jesus or Barabbas? (27:15–26)

Exegesis and Exposition

[11]Now Jesus stood before the governor, and the governor asked him, "Are you the king of the Jews?" And Jesus said to him, "You say so." [12]And while he was being accused by the chief priests and elders, he answered nothing. [13]Then Pilate said to him, "Do you not hear how many things they are testifying against you?" [14]Yet he did not answer even a single charge, so that the governor was greatly amazed. [15]Now at the feast the governor was accustomed to release to the crowd a prisoner whom they wanted. [16]At that time they had a notorious prisoner named ⌜Jesus⌝ Barabbas. [17]So when they were gathered together, Pilate said to them, "Whom do you want me to release to you? ⌜Jesus Barabbas⌝ or Jesus who is called Messiah?" [18]For he knew that they had handed Jesus over because of envy. [19]And while he was sitting on the judgment seat, his wife sent a message to him, "Have nothing to do with that innocent man; for I have suffered greatly in a dream today because of him." [20]Now the chief priests and the elders had persuaded the crowds to ask for Barabbas and to have Jesus executed. [21]But the governor answered them, "Which of the two do you want me to release to you?" And they said, "Barabbas." [22]Pilate said to them, "Then what will I do with Jesus who is called Messiah?" They all said, "Crucify him!"

²³And he said, "Why? What evil has he done?" But they kept shouting even more loudly, "Crucify him!"

²⁴And when Pilate saw that he was accomplishing nothing but instead an uproar was beginning, he took water and washed his hands in front of the crowd, saying, "I am innocent of ⌜this man's⌝ blood; you deal with it." ²⁵And all the people answered, "Let his blood be on us and on our children!" ²⁶Then he released Barabbas to them; but he had Jesus flogged and handed him over to be crucified.

a. Jesus's Silence under Accusation (27:11–14)

i. Jesus Answers Pilate (27:11)

Now the narrative of Jesus's trial resumes, picking up from 27:2. Pilate's examination of Jesus begins with an understandable concern about Jesus's kingship. Loyalty to Caesar would lead Pilate to investigate any potential rivals (cf. John 18:36–37). The Roman soldiers would soon taunt Jesus with mocking references to his kingship (Matt. 27:28–29; cf. 37, 42). There is palpable irony here. Jesus responds for the third time in the passion narrative (cf. 26:25, 64) with the mild, semi-enigmatic affirmation "You say so."

27:11

ii. Jesus Will Not Answer the Leaders' Accusations (27:12–14)

To the amazement of Pilate, who expects him to defend himself, Jesus says nothing in response to the leaders' accusations (cf. 26:62). Although Jesus says nothing (cf. Isa. 53:7), Pilate realizes that Jesus poses no threat to Rome (cf. Matt. 27:17–18). Yet the leaders persist by inciting the crowd to pressure Pilate to execute Jesus (27:20).

27:12–14

b. An Opportunity for Release: Jesus or Barabbas? (27:15–26)

An aside notes the Roman custom of releasing a Jewish prisoner at Passover as a goodwill gesture and adds that the Romans are holding the notorious Barabbas. When Pilate offers the crowd their choice of Barabbas or Jesus, he probably thinks they will prefer Jesus. Pilate perceives that there is no substantial charge against Jesus and that envy motivates the leaders.[1] Another testimony to Jesus's innocence enters the narrative when Pilate learns of his wife's bad dream. Dreams were often viewed as significant and even prophetic in the ancient world, and the Bible contains many divine revelations in the form of dreams (1:20; 2:12, 13, 19). His wife's description of Jesus as innocent confirms Pilate's own conclusion. Many ancient MSS have Barabbas's full name

27:15–19

1. See J. Welch in Charlesworth 2006: 349–83 for an argument that the religious leaders sought to execute Jesus because of their fear of his association with the supernatural demonstrated by his miracles.

as Jesus Barabbas. This makes an explicit contrast between Jesus Barabbas (which may mean "son of the father" or "son of the teacher") and Jesus who is called the Messiah. (See the additional note on 27:16–17 and Metzger 1994: 56.)

27:20–23   Another aside notes the nefarious influence of the leaders on the crowd. Pilate's second question about which prisoner should be released is surprisingly answered with a call for Barabbas. His question about Jesus's fate is answered with a demand for his crucifixion. Pilate's feeble protest that Jesus is innocent only incites the crowd to shout more loudly for Jesus to be crucified. Jesus's popularity with the crowd has evaporated (21:9, 11, 26; 26:5), probably because the crowd's hope that Jesus was a political-military Messiah was dashed by his arrest. Jesus's messianic credentials have now been discredited. This crowd may be composed of Jerusalem residents instead of the Passover pilgrims who had praised Jesus when he entered Jerusalem (Blomberg 1992a: 412).

27:24–26   Pilate sees that a riot is imminent, and so he accedes to the crowd. He mildly protests the crowd's choice of Barabbas by washing his hands (Exod. 30:19, 21; 40:31; Deut. 21:1–9; Pss. 26:6; 73:13) to signify his nonparticipation in the decision to crucify Jesus. Pilate affirms that he is not responsible for Jesus's blood (cf. Heil 1991a), and the crowd accepts this responsibility for themselves and their children. The expression "His blood be on us" is not unusual.[2] The statement that their children will also be responsible for Jesus's death assumes the solidarity of the family (Josh. 7:24; 2 Kings 24:3–4; Jer. 31:29; Lam. 5:7; Ezek. 18:2, 19–32). These incriminating words recall Jesus's prediction that the blood of all the righteous since Abel would come upon his contemporaries (Matt. 23:35–36). The destruction of the temple in 70 CE was probably in part God's judgment upon the crowd and its children (W. Davies and Allison 1997: 591–92). The view that this verse constitutes a blood libel for all Jews of all time is patently false (see below). The release of the notorious criminal Barabbas is antithetical to the flogging (20:19) and crucifixion of the humble Messiah, Jesus.

Flogging (*flagellatio*) was a horrible, flesh-ripping experience that hastened the death of those about to be crucified.[3] The victim was tied to a post or forced to the ground. The scourge (*flagrum*) was a short whip that had several leather thongs with lead balls and sharp pieces of bone or metal attached to them. In some cases flogging continued on the way to the place of crucifixion (Dionysius of Halicarnassus, *Roman Antiqui-*

2. Cf. Lev. 20:9; Deut. 19:10; Josh. 2:19; 2 Sam. 1:16; Jer. 26:15; 51:35; Ezek. 18:13; 33:4; Acts 5:28; 18:6; 20:26.
3. Ancient sources include Josephus, *J.W.* 2.306, 308; 5.449; 6.304; 7.200–202; Philo, *Flaccus* 10.75; T. Benj. 2.2–4; cf. Luke 18:33; Acts 22:24–25. Less severe punishments with a whip are described in Luke 23:16; John 2:15.

ties 7.69). Such horrendous punishment would cause deep lacerations of the back, severe pain, and loss of blood.

Anti-Semitism and the "Blood Libel"

Matthew 27:20–25 is often cited as a blatantly anti-Semitic text (e.g., Sandmel 1978: 66). Some scholars think that Matthew portrays Pilate positively in order to exonerate the Romans and indict the Jews (e.g., Beare 1981: 530–31; Hill 1972: 351). But Matthew's picture of Pilate is not all that positive; it is consistent with other ancient sources that present Pilate as insecure and unjust (see the comments on 27:1–2; W. Davies and Allison 1997: 579). Pilate does not intervene to stop the egregious miscarriage of justice; rather, he orders it. He gives in to the crowd's demand because it is expedient to do so (cf. John 19:12–16). The symbolic hand washing is a pathetic, hypocritical gesture. Pilate portrays himself as consenting to the crowd's wish, but why does he permit the crowd to rule? If he does not consent, he should not permit. Pilate is a cowardly ruler who abdicates his responsibility. He lacks the fortitude even to take his wife's advice to leave Jesus alone. "Pilate's title is ironic: the governor leaves the governing to others" (W. Davies and Allison 1997: 583). Pilate must share the guilt for Jesus's crucifixion.

But is Matthew's famous "blood libel" text (27:25) intended to inculpate the Jews as a nation forever? Pilate's washed hands portray denial of responsibility for Jesus's death, and the crowd's members eagerly accept this responsibility for themselves and their descendants. During the church's history, this passage has been frequently understood as teaching that the Jews as a nation are to be viewed as despicable Christ killers. This interpretation is patently false on its surface, since all the founders of the church were Jewish and many Jews have believed in Jesus throughout the church's history. Matthew is a Jew writing to Christian Jews in conflict with non-Christian Jews over the identity of Jesus the Jewish Messiah.

One way Christians have disavowed the blood libel view is to regard 27:25 as fiction (Beare 1981: 531). But this adds a mistake about the historicity of the passage to the mistake about its meaning. On its surface the text is limited to those present before Pilate and their children, not the Jews as a nation at that time or at any other time (Saldarini 1994: 32–33).[4] The comment is made in the heat of the moment, not as a carefully reasoned theological proposition. The gracious God of Moses and Jesus would not hold the crowd to its rash statement any more than the twelve disciples would be held unforgivable for deserting Jesus,

---

4. The phrase πᾶς ὁ λαός (27:25) is often taken as inculpating all Jews of all time (e.g., Schnackenburg 2002: 285). It is true that λαός often refers to Israel as a whole, but here πᾶς ὁ λαός is interchangeable with ὄχλος (27:15, 20), the multitudes who are misled by the leaders (27:20).

and Peter for denying Jesus three times. And there is no guarantee that the just God of Holy Scripture will pardon Pilate for his diffidence and hypocrisy in the empty washing of his hands.

In Matthew's Gospel it is abundantly clear that Jesus came to call sinners—exemplified by notorious tax collectors and prostitutes (9:13; 21:31). Sinners such as these may have been in the manipulated crowd that took responsibility for Jesus's blood, and Matthew's theology makes room for the forgiveness of such sinners upon repentance.

In Matthew's Gospel, Jesus's most severe criticisms are reserved for the religious leaders. This is an important part of the response to the blood libel view of 27:25. In 27:20 the leading priests and elders persuade the crowd to ask for Barabbas. Jesus's Jewish contemporaries were a wicked generation (12:45; 23:36), yet to a significant degree, they were the product of especially wicked leaders who left them as sheep without a shepherd (9:36). These corrupt leaders bear the brunt of the blame for the crowd's unfortunate statement in 27:25 and for Pilate's unprincipled acquiescence to the crowd's inflamed request (W. Davies and Allison 1997: 593).

Thus the blood libel should be viewed in the light of the Matthean theme of Jesus's conflicts with the religious leaders. These leaders are primarily responsible for the death of Jesus, but from the perspective of God's sovereign providence, a deeper level of responsibility can be discerned. In the most profound sense, all humans, Jews and Gentiles alike, are responsible for Jesus's voluntarily pouring out his blood to forgive humanity's sins and inaugurate the new covenant. This was the heavenly Father's plan, and Jesus drank the cup the Father gave him. Ultimately, only those who do not believe in Jesus, Jews and Gentiles alike, will be held responsible for the blood of Jesus (Hagner 1995a: 828).[5]

Additional Notes

27:16–17. Despite weak external evidence, UBS[4] favors the inclusion of Ἰησοῦν in 27:16–17 and resolves the issue by putting the name in brackets. The omission of Ἰησοῦν is well supported in both verses by א, A, B, D, L, W, Δ, f[13], 33, 157, Byz, Lect. The inclusion of Ἰησοῦν in 27:16 is supported by Θ, 700, f[1], a few ancient versions, and additional MSS according to Origen and a note in Codex S attributed to Anastasius of Antioch. In 27:17, Ἰησοῦν Βαραββᾶν is found in Θ, 700, and Ἰησοῦν τὸν Βαραββᾶν in f[1], a few early versions, and MSS according to Origen. See Metzger 1994: 56 for the view that Ἰησοῦν was deliberately deleted in these verses because copyists thought it irreverent to connect the name with Barabbas.

27:24. The short reading τούτου (supported by B, D, Θ) is favored by UBS[4]. The bulk of the external evidence (including א, L, W, f[1], f[13], 33, 157, Byz, Lect, and several ancient versions and patristic sources) has τοῦ δικαίου τούτου. The reading τούτου τοῦ δικαίου is found in A, Δ. This external evidence together with the similarity of the long reading to 27:19 makes it likely to be original.

5. See Buck in P. Richardson and Granskou 1986: 165–80; Overman 1996: 383–91.

VII. Epilogue/Conclusion: Passion, Resurrection, and Commission (26:3–28:20)
    B. Arrest and Trial (26:47–27:26)
➤ C. Crucifixion (27:27–56)
    D. Burial of Jesus (27:57–66)

C. Crucifixion (27:27–56)

The narrative of the crucifixion (cf. Mark 15:16–41; Luke 23:26–49; John 19:17–37) proceeds sequentially through each stage of the gruesome process. The Roman soldiers mock Jesus (Matt. 27:27–31), conscript Simon to carry the cross (27:32), and arrive at Golgotha (27:33). There they offer wine to Jesus (27:34), crucify him (27:35a), gamble for his garments (27:35), observe him (27:36), and put up the sign describing the charge against him (27:37). The next section is an *inclusio* framed by references to the revolutionaries crucified on both sides of Jesus (27:38–44). The mockery by the bystanders (27:39–40), the Jewish leaders (27:41–43), and the revolutionaries (27:44) permeates this section. The death of Jesus (27:45–56) occurs just after his desolate cry that echoes Ps. 22:1. At his death, the tombs are opened, and the Roman centurion is moved to affirm that Jesus is the son of God.

1. Jesus Is Mocked and Led Away to Golgotha (27:27–32)

After Pilate condemns Jesus, the Roman soldiers have their way with him. As a condemned criminal, he is treated with the utmost cruelty, both physical and mental. The soldiers conscript Simon from Cyrene to carry Jesus's cross.

Exegesis and Exposition

²⁷Then the governor's soldiers took Jesus into the governor's residence and gathered the whole cohort around him. ²⁸They ⸢stripped him⸣ and put a scarlet robe on him. ²⁹After weaving a crown from some thorns, they put it on his head. They put a reed in his right hand and knelt in front of him and ⸢mocked⸣ him, saying, "Hail, King of the Jews!" ³⁰They spat on him and took the reed and began striking him on the head. ³¹And after they had mocked him, they took the robe off him and put his garments back on him and led him away to crucify him. ³²And as they were going out, they met a man from Cyrene named Simon, and they pressed him into service to carry Jesus's cross.

27:27   The narrative now leads relentlessly to the cross, with 27:27–37 describing the actions of the soldiers ordered to crucify Jesus. W. Davies and Allison (1997: 597) show that 27:27–31 has a chiastic structure centering on the mocking words "Hail, king of the Jews."

Before taking Jesus to Golgotha (27:31–32), they mock him before the entire cohort in the praetorium, or governor's residence (BDAG 859). This is either at Herod's palace just south of the present Jaffa Gate on the west side the old city or at the Antonia fortress near the northwest corner of the temple enclosure. A cohort was a regiment of soldiers, one-tenth of a legion or six hundred men (BDAG 936).

27:28–31   The Roman soldiers' mockery at Pilate's residence fulfills Jesus's prophecy (20:19; cf. Ps. 22:7; Isa. 50:6). The religious leaders have already mocked Jesus (Matt. 26:67–68), and worse taunting is to come (26:68; 27:39–44). The scarlet robe, crown of thorns, and reed (Pss. 2:9; 110:2; Jer. 48:17) are intended as a cruel parody of royalty. The Romans' derision is probably fueled by the fact that Jesus is purported to be king of a people conquered and ruled by Rome. The profound irony is that one day these soldiers will join all humanity, including the Jews, in homage to the conquering Son of Man (Dan. 7:13–14; Phil. 2:9–11). Those of the cohort who crucify Jesus will soon rethink their mockery (Matt. 27:54). After the mocking charade, Jesus is led away to be crucified.

The conscription of Simon (cf. 5:41) to carry Jesus's cross may indicate   **27:32** that Jesus is unable to do so as a result of the flogging he has already undergone.[1] Normally a condemned criminal is forced to carry his own cross (10:38; 16:24).[2] The passing mention of Simon of Cyrene is a striking historical allusion, perhaps implying that Simon is now or later becomes a disciple of Jesus (cf. 16:24; Blount 1993; Acts 13:1). Cyrene was the capital of the Roman province of Cyrenaica (roughly equivalent to modern Libya) in North Africa on the Mediterranean Sea (cf. Acts 2:10; 6:9; 11:20; 13:1; Josephus, *Ag. Ap.* 2.44; *Ant.* 14.114–18; 16.160). Simon may be in Jerusalem for the feast (Acts 2:10) or may reside there (Acts 6:9). His conscription reminds the reader of Jesus's teaching that one should go two miles if forced (evidently by a soldier) to go one mile (Matt. 5:41). See the summary of the literary and archaeological evidence of Simon of Cyene by C. A. Evans in Charlesworth 2006: 338–40.

Additional Notes

27:28. UBS[4] prefers the reading ἐκδύσαντες αὐτόν (supported by ℵ*,2, A, L, W, Δ, Θ, 0233, *f*[1], *f*[13], *Byz, Lect*). The reading ἐνδύσαντες αὐτόν (supported by ℵ[1], B, 1424; cf. Mark 15:17; John 19:2) may be based on the assumption that Jesus was already stripped for flogging in 27:27.

27:29. UBS[4] prefers the aorist ἐνέπαιξαν (supported by ℵ, B, D, L, 33, 892). The imperfect ἐνέπαιζον is more widely supported by A, W, Δ, Θ, 0233, 0250, *f*[1], *f*[13], *Byz, Lect.*

---

    1. Although practices varied, carrying the cross (σταυρός) normally involved only the horizontal crossbar (*patibulum*). The vertical stake (*stipes* or *staticulum*) was already erected at the site of execution. See "The Crucifixion and History" after the comments on 27:38–44.

    2. Ancient sources attesting this practice include Plautus, *Miles gloriosus* 2.359–60; Plutarch, *De sera numinis vindicta* 9; Artemidorus Daldianus, *Onirocritica* 2.56.

2. Jesus Is Crucified (27:33–37)

The crucifixion detail arrives at Golgotha. Jesus refuses to drink the wine mixed with gall before he is affixed to the cross. The soldiers gamble for Jesus's garments and place above his head a sign with the charge made against him.

Exegesis and Exposition

³³And when they had come to a place called Golgotha, which means "place of a skull," ³⁴they gave him wine mixed with gall to drink; but after he tasted it, he would not drink it. ³⁵And when they had crucified him, they divided up his garments among themselves by casting lots ⌐ ⌐; ³⁶then they sat down and began to keep watch there. ³⁷And they put up above his head the charge that had been written against him: "This is Jesus, the King of the Jews."

27:33   Matthew supplies few details of the crucifixion beyond the actions of the people and the fulfillment of prophecy. Ancient tradition identifies the site of Golgotha with the present-day Church of the Holy Sepulchre. In Hebrew (גּוּלְגֹּלֶת, *Gûlgôlet*) and Aramaic (גֻּלְגַּלְתָּא, *Gûlgaltāʾ*) Golgotha means "skull" (Jastrow 1971: 221). Perhaps a skull-like rock formation there gave rise to this name, but there is no historical evidence that links the present "Gordon's Calvary" and "Garden Tomb" tourist sites to Jesus (Barkay 1986). The Latin word for "skull" is *calvaria*, from which the English word "Calvary" is derived. Occupying forces crucified enemies and subversives as a humiliating public spectacle that would quell resistance, and so Golgotha was probably near a well-traveled street filled with many potential observers (cf. 27:39; 3 Macc. 5:21–24).

27:34–36   Jesus refuses to drink the wine mixed with gall that the soldiers offer him (but cf. 27:48; Ps. 69:21; Prov. 31:6). Probably such mixed wine was customarily offered as a sedative to those about to be crucified (*b. Sanh.* 43a). Or the wine may have been a gesture of mockery, since gall would have made it very bitter (W. Davies and Allison 1997: 612–13). Perhaps this would have furthered Jesus's suffering by making him more thirsty (Koskenniemi et al. 2005). The meager belongings of a crucified person would go to the execution detail, whose members here determine, by casting lots, who obtains Jesus's clothes. In the shorter text that is read here, the allusion to Ps. 22:18 is implicit. See the additional note for the longer reading that cites the psalm (cf. John 19:24).

The placard on which the charge against the crucified person was written **27:37** was called the *titulus*. The phrase "above his head" shows that the cross on which Jesus is crucified is in the traditional † shape (*crux immissa*). It is not a mere stake (*crux simplex*) or a cross whose horizontal beam rests on the top of its vertical beam (*crux commissa*). The charge (cf. Acts 13:28; 23:28; 28:18) against Jesus is profoundly ironic. The religious leaders reject Jesus's kingship, influence the crowd to demand his crucifixion, and mock his kingship (Matt. 27:42). The Romans also mock such a king as Jesus (27:29) and carry out the crucifixion. Yet his crucifixion is the quintessence of his royal power to save his people from their sins, and his resurrection, ascension, and return progressively vindicate his crucifixion (cf. John 19:19–22; 1 Cor. 1:18, 23–25).

Additional Note

27:35. UBS⁴ prefers the short reading of this verse (widely supported by ℵ, A, B, D, L, W, Γ, Π, 33, 71, *Byz*, *Lect*), which mentions the soldiers' casting lots for Jesus's garment but does not cite of Ps. 22:18. A longer form of the text (weakly supported by Δ, Θ, 0233) adds Matthew's characteristic fulfillment formula introduction and Ps. 22:18. This may reflect assimilation from John 19:24.

3. Mockery by Observers (27:38–44)

The focus turns from the soldiers' actions (27:27–37) to the mockery by other observers of the crucifixion. This section is an *inclusio* framed by references to the two revolutionaries crucified with Jesus (27:38, 44). Jesus is successively mocked by people passing by (27:39–40), by the religious leaders (27:41–43), and by the two revolutionaries (27:44). The taunting drips with sarcasm that leverages the incongruity between Jesus's present plight and his lofty claims into a satirical slander of Jesus that emphatically denies his claims. A paraphrase would go something like this: "Surely someone who could destroy and rebuild the temple, someone who was the Son of God, could come down from the cross and save himself! How sad the one who would save others cannot save himself! If only he would come down from the cross, we would believe in him! Wouldn't God come down now and and save his own Son who trusts in him?"

Exegesis and Exposition

³⁸Then two revolutionaries were crucified with him, one on his right and one on his left. ³⁹And those who passed by kept on taunting him, shaking their heads ⁴⁰and saying, "You who would tear down the temple and rebuild it in three days, save yourself! If you are the Son of God, ⌜ ⌝ come down from the cross." ⁴¹In the same way the chief priests also, along with the scribes and elders, were mocking him and saying, ⁴²"He saved others; he cannot save himself. ⌜ ⌝ He is the King of Israel; let him come down from the cross now, and we will believe in him. ⁴³He trusts in God; let him deliver him now if he wants; for he said, 'I am the Son of God.'" ⁴⁴And the revolutionaries also who had been crucified with him were insulting him in the same way.

27:38–40 The two revolutionaries (26:55; 27:44; cf. Isa. 53:12) crucified on Jesus's right and left remind the reader of the two disciples who wanted to reign on Jesus's right and left (20:23). Jesus's alleged plans to destroy the temple come up again here (cf. 26:61) as the passersby shake their heads (cf. Pss. 22:7; 109:25; Jer. 18:16; Lam. 2:15) and mock Jesus. The taunts emphasize the incompatibility between Jesus's purported power and his actual weakness (cf. Matt. 4:3, 6). Someone of his supposed stature could surely save his own life. The taunt to demonstrate divine sonship by coming down from the cross (27:40, 42, 44) is especially perverse, since Jesus endures the cross as the obedient Son of God (cf. 26:39, 42,

44). If Jesus comes down from the cross to save himself, he will not save his people from their sins (1:21; 10:38–39; 16:24–26; 20:28; 26:28). See Moffitt 2006 on the likely allusion to Lam. 2:15 in Matt. 27:39 and its several implications.

The leading priests and elders have followed Jesus from Pilate's residence   **27:41–44** to Golgotha (cf. 27:12). With them are the scribes, last seen at the hearing at Caiaphas's residence (26:57). Their cruel taunts use the third person to speak of Jesus rather than address him directly as the passersby do (27:39–40). They scoff at the notion that Jesus could save others, since he cannot save himself. They offer to believe in him if he will validate his claims by coming down from the cross. They think that God would rescue Jesus if he really were God's trusting Son in whom God took pleasure (Ps. 22:8–9; Wis. 2:18–20; cf. Matt. 3:17; 17:5; 26:63). But God wills that Jesus drink the cup of crucifixion, pour out his blood, and inaugurate the new covenant. Even the doomed revolutionaries crucified with Jesus add their mockery to the cacophany (but cf. Luke 23:39–43).

Biblical Allusions in the Crucifixion Narrative

Biblical citations and allusions permeate the crucifixion narrative. The most prominent follow:

Matthew	Allusion	Hebrew Bible
27:34	Wine mixed with gall (mercy or mockery?)	Ps. 69:21
27:35	Garments divided by casting lots	Ps. 22:18
27:36	Soldiers watch Jesus	Ps. 22:17
27:38	Numbered with transgressors	Isa. 53:12
27:39	Shaking heads in derision	Ps. 22:7
27:43	God will deliver Jesus if he trusts in him	Ps. 22:8
27:45	Darkness at noon	Amos 8:9
27:46	"Why have you forsaken me?"	Ps. 22:1
27:57, 60	Jesus's grave with a rich man	Isa. 53:9

Mockery and Irony

The atmosphere of this section is thick with mockery, whether by the bystanders (27:39–40), the Jewish leaders (27:41–43), or the revolutionaries (27:44). As Jesus was tempted three times (4:1–11), so he is mocked three times. Both the devil and the mockers focus on his identity and mission as God's Son. Both present Jesus with the alternative of ruling without suffering. And both times Jesus will have none of it.

The mockery of the passage is palpably ironic,[1] since Jesus really is the Son of God. The temple will indeed be destroyed within a genera-

---

1. Irony resists precise definition but generally entails the narrative juxtaposition of two opposing layers of meaning, with unawareness, misunderstanding, or innocence

tion. Jesus does in fact save others. He is the King of Israel who trusts in God, and God is well pleased with him. He does not come down from the cross, but he does overcome death by pouring out his own blood of the new covenant. Since every detail of the ridicule is eventually shown to be true, the mockers are unwitting evangelists. The irony is most pronounced in the soldiers' actions. They dress Jesus as a king and offer pretended homage to him (27:27–31), yet their cruel jest unintentionally predicts what will in fact happen one day. The resurrection will exalt Jesus as the glorious Son of Man and invest him with all authority (28:18). His message of God's rule will win disciples from all the peoples of the earth. He will return in glory as the King and sit on his glorious throne to judge humanity at the end of the age (25:31–32). The irony of the mockery is not just that things are not always as they seem but that sometimes they are exactly the opposite of what they seem.

It is also significant that the most vicious mockers of Jesus in the crucifixion narrative are the gentile Roman soldiers (27:27–31). This calls into question the Christian tendency to link Jews with rejection, and Gentiles with reception, of Jesus. France (1985: 397) goes too far when commenting on 27:44 that "the totality of Jesus's rejection by his people is complete." The mockers in the crucifixion narrative are not all Jews (27:27–31), and not all the Jews are mockers (27:55–57). Matthew does not present either a totally negative view of the Jews or a totally positive view of the Gentiles, although such views are unfortunately found in later church history.

The Crucifixion and History

Crucifixion epitomized cruel and unusual punishment.[2] It was practiced long before the Romans, sometimes as a grisly display of enemies who died in battle. The Romans used it in the case of slaves (*servile supplicium*), notorious criminals, and insurrectionists to make a political statement. Crucifixion asserted the dominion of Rome over conquered peoples by making a gruesome example of anyone who dared to upset the pax Romana. According to Josephus (*J.W.* 5.449–51), it was regularly practiced during the siege of Jerusalem in 70 CE. Although practices varied somewhat (Hengel 1977: 22–32; R. Brown 1994: 945–52), crucifix-

---

concerning the real meaning behind the ostensible meaning (Duke 1985: 7–42, esp. 13–18, 23–26). Here the dramatic irony is that the various mockers are unaware that their cruel taunts in fact correspond with ultimate reality.

2. Ancient Roman sources on crucifixion include Cicero, *In Verrem* 2.5.63, 66, 163–70; *Pro Rabirio Perduellionis Reo* 16; Herodotus, *History* 1.126; 3.132, 159; Seneca, *Ad Marciam de consolatione* 20.3; Tacitus, *Hist.* 2.72.1–2. Jewish sources include 11QT 64.6–13; Josephus, *J.W.* 1.97–98; 5.449–51; 7.203; *Ant.* 13.379–83; 18.63–64; Philo. *Posterity* 17.61; *Flaccus* 72.84–85; *m. Šabb.* 6.10. Among recent discussions, see R. Brown 1994: 945–52; W. Edwards et al. 1986; Fitzmyer 1978; J. Green in J. Green and McKnight 1992: 146–54; Hengel 1977; Kuhn 1982; O'Collins, *ABD* 1:1207–10; Tzaferis 1985; Zias and Sekeles 1985.

ion was often preceded by flogging. Long nails (Luke 24:39; John 20:25; Col. 2:14) were frequently driven through the victim's ankles into the vertical post (*stipes* or *staticulum*) of the cross and through the victim's outstretched hands or wrists into the horizontal beam (*patibulum*). Ropes were sometimes used instead of nails to affix the hapless victim to the cross. Once the victim was on the crossbar, it was raised and fastened to the vertical post (Matt. 27:37; R. Brown 1994: 947–49). The victim in some cases would straddle a peg or small shelf (*sedile*) on the stake.

The medical cause(s) of death by crucifixion would be asphyxia, loss of blood, dehydration, and/or shock (R. Brown 1994: 1088–92; W. Edwards et al. 1986). Victims would suffer an agonizingly slow death, since no vital organs were directly injured. Eventually they would have difficulty supporting their own weight with their legs. Breathing would become increasingly difficult from hanging by the arms. The gruesome process could take days. At times the executors would break the legs (an action called *crurifragium*) of the victims to hasten the process, but this is not necessary for Jesus (John 19:31–33; Koskenniemi et al. 2005).

The Crucifixion and Biblical Theology

The crucifixion narrative in Matthew is the culmination of the story of Jesus's rejection. It stresses the taunting of the bystanders, the Jewish leaders, and the revolutionaries crucified with Jesus. They think the crucifixion unmasks Jesus as an impotent messianic pretender. But Jesus never claimed to be a military Messiah who would remove the yoke of Roman oppression. John and Jesus did not foment rebellion against Rome but urged Jews to repent (3:2; 4:17). Jesus's messianic model is capsulized in 12:14–21. The Pharisees plan to kill Jesus because they think his Sabbath healing is work. Jesus withdraws from this conflict and counsels silence on the healing. This fulfills Isa. 42:1–4, which describes the servant who pleases the Father, who is endowed with the Spirit, and who proclaims justice to the Gentiles instead of promoting insurrection in the streets. Jesus's kingdom is not built by the sword (Matt. 26:52) but by healed and repentant disciples who take up their own crosses and follow Jesus. Their lives are kingdom-centered and service-oriented (10:38–39; 16:24–26; 20:23, 26–28). This messianic model achieves justice not by military might but by a transforming message that liberates from sin and empowers humble service to others. Sadly, most of Jesus's contemporaries do not respond positively to a Messiah whose ministry culminates in suffering on a Roman cross.

The crucifixion not only models kingdom values; it accomplishes the redemption that empowers the practice of these values. Jesus saves his people from their sins (1:21) by giving his life as a ransom (20:28) that entails the sacrificial pouring out of his blood to forgive their sins (26:28). Jesus is abandoned by the Father, whose very will he is doing (27:46;

cf. Ps. 22:1). The Torah pronounces a curse on anyone who is hung on a tree (Deut. 21:22–23; cf. Isa. 53:3–6). The NT develops this in terms of substitution: on the cross Jesus bore the curse and paid the penalty for his people's sins so that they would not bear that curse themselves. There are several references to Deut. 21:22–23 (Acts 5:30; 10:39; 13:29; Gal. 3:13; 1 Pet. 2:24) to the effect that Jesus, by taking on himself the sin of his people, accomplished their forgiveness and redemption.[3] Paul develops the theology of crucifixion beyond Matt. 10:38–39; 16:24–25 by teaching that Christians are vitally identified with Jesus in dying to sin in solidarity with Adam and rising to righteousness in solidarity with Jesus (Rom. 5:12–6:11; 1 Cor. 15:20–22; Gal. 2:20; 6:14; Eph. 2:1–6; 4:22–24; Col. 2:8–15; 3:1–4). Paul also develops Matthew's stress on the church's mission to all the nations, since the Messiah's body encompasses Jews and Gentiles alike (Rom. 11:11–24; 15:7–12; 1 Cor. 12:13; Eph. 2:11–22; Col. 3:9–11).[4]

Additional Notes

27:40. Relatively few MSS (including ℵ*, A, D) begin the last clause of 27:40 with καί. This reading requires taking the previous conditional clause (εἰ υἱὸς εἶ τοῦ θεοῦ) with what precedes it. But the MS evidence for omitting καί is arguably stronger (ℵ², B, L, W, 0250, Δ, Θ, f^1, f^{13}, 33, *Byz, Lect*), and the previous conditional clause makes good sense in light of what follows.

27:42. Although many MSS have εἰ βασιλεύς (including A, W, Δ, Θ, f^1, f^{13}, 157, *Byz, Lect*), UBS⁴ prefers βασιλεύς (supported by ℵ, B, D, L, 33, 892) because the editors take the clause as one of a series of ironic statements in the context (Metzger 1994: 58).

---

3. Cf. Rom. 3:24–26; 1 Cor. 1:23–24; 2 Cor. 5:21; 1 Tim. 2:6; Heb. 2:9, 14–15; 7:26–27; 9:11–12, 28; 10:12; 1 Pet. 3:18; Rev. 5:9–10.
4. On the biblical theology of Jesus's death, see Bauckham 1998; J. Green 1988; in J. Green and McKnight 1992: 146–63; Matera 1986; Senior 1975, 1985, 1987; H.-R. Weber 1979.

4. The Death of Jesus (27:45–56)

All of Matthew's narrative points toward the death of Jesus (cf. Mark 15:33–41; Luke 23:44–49; John 19:28–37). In a sense, all of Matt. 1–25 introduces the passion narrative of Matt. 26–28, and the death of Jesus is the center of the passion narrative. Matthew narrates Jesus's death much as he did the crucifixion. There are few details of the event itself but much about the actions of others and accompanying epochal events. The narrative can be analyzed as containing two similar cycles that bracket Jesus's death:

> Cosmic sign: Darkness at noon (27:45; cf. Amos 8:9)
> Jesus's cry of abandonment (27:46; cf. Ps. 22:1)
> Observers (27:47–49)
> Jesus dies (27:50)
> Cosmic signs (27:51–53; cf. Ezek. 37:12)
> Soldiers' cry of amazement (27:54)
> Observers (27:55–56)

Jesus's death is bracketed by darkness (27:45) and an earthquake (27:51), showing that nature itself testifies to the epochal significance of the event. The taunting of Jesus ceases at 27:44. Jesus's desolate cry (27:46) contains what may well be the most amazing words in all of Scripture. The observers misunderstand Jesus's cry (27:47–49), interpreting it as a call for Elijah. Some of those who have been mocking Jesus now seem to wonder seriously whether Elijah will miraculously come and rescue Jesus. But Jesus performs miracles to help needy people, not to excite jaded observers. Since these observers do not comprehend the significance of Jesus's suffering, their speculation about Elijah amounts to a subtle form of mockery.

The earthquake at Jesus's death (27:51–53) splits the temple veil and the bedrock, resulting in opened tombs and resurrected people. The torn veil vindicates Jesus's saying that he was one greater than the temple (12:6). The split rocks and opened tombs foreshadow the ultimate resurrection of humanity, and Jesus's own impending resurrection guarantees it (cf. 1 Cor. 15:20, 23; Rev. 1:5).

Despite Jesus's rejection by Israel's leaders and the temporary desertion of his own disciples, some witnesses to his death are sympathetic. The soldiers who crucify Jesus become believers of a sort when they witness Jesus's death and its results (27:54). Another unsung group, the women (27:55–56), watch in horror as Jesus endures pain and taunting on the cross and are in awe over the earthquake and opened tombs. They will be the first to discover Jesus's resurrection, to meet the resurrected Jesus himself, and to tell the disciples about it.

The unit outline is as follows:

a. Darkness at noon (27:45)
b. Jesus's cry of abandonment (27:46–49)
c. Jesus's death (27:50)
d. The earthquake and its results (27:51–53)
e. The soldiers' confession (27:54)
f. The women who observe from a distance (27:55–56)

Exegesis and Exposition

[45]Now from the sixth hour darkness came over the whole earth until the ninth hour. [46]About the ninth hour Jesus cried out with a loud voice, "Eli, Eli, lema sabachthani?" that is, "My God, my God, why have you forsaken me?" [47]When some of those who were standing there heard, they began saying, "This man is calling for Elijah." [48]And immediately one of them ran and took a sponge, filled it with sour wine, put it on a reed, and gave it to him to drink. [49]But the rest said, "Wait, let us see whether Elijah will come to save him." ⌐ ¬ [50]But Jesus cried out again with a loud voice and gave up his spirit.

[51]And suddenly the veil of the temple was torn in two from top to bottom, and the earth was shaken, and the rocks were split. [52]Then the tombs were opened, and many bodies of the saints who had fallen asleep were raised. [53]Having come out of the tombs, after his resurrection they entered the holy city and appeared to many. [54]Now when the centurion and those who were guarding Jesus with him saw the earthquake and what had happened, they became extremely frightened and said, "Truly this man was the Son of God!"

[55]And many women were there, observing from a distance. They had followed Jesus from Galilee to care for him, [56]among whom was Mary Magdalene, and Mary the mother of James and Joseph, and the mother of the sons of Zebedee.

a. Darkness at Noon (27:45)

27:45   Evidently, Jesus was crucified around midmorning. He dies at the end of a providential darkness during what is typically the brightest part of the day, from noon to 3 p.m.[1] This darkness is appropriate during Jesus's unspeakable suffering and divine abandonment (27:46; cf. 24:29; Exod.

---

1. The three hours of darkness occurred "from the sixth hour . . . until the ninth hour" (ἀπὸ δὲ ἕκτης ὥρας . . . ἕως ὥρας ἐνάτης). This way of reckoning time counts hours from dawn, roughly 6 a.m. Cf. 20:3, 5; John 1:39; 4:6, 52; Acts 2:15; 3:1; 10:9, 30; 23:23; BDAG 1102–3.

10:22; Deut. 28:29; Joel 2:2, 31; Amos 8:9). Allison (2005b: 79–105) examines intertextual and other dimensions of this remarkable darkness.

b. Jesus's Cry of Abandonment (27:46–49)

Jesus has not spoken since responding to Pilate in 27:11, and he speaks   27:46–49
now not to answer his mockers but to express lament to God. Jesus's
lament at about 3 p.m., "Why have you forsaken me?" echoes Ps. 22:1 to
express his profound anguish over loss of communion with the Father.
In Hebrew "my God" (אֵלִי, 'Ēlî) sounds like the first two syllables of the
name Elijah in Hebrew (אֵלִיָּהוּ, 'Ēlîyāhû) and Greek (Ἠλίας, Ēlias). Some
bystanders confuse Jesus's echo of Ps. 22:1 with a cry to Elijah, who became prominent in eschatological speculation on Mal. 4:5–6.[2] Evidently,
the offer of wine vinegar (Ps. 69:21; cf. Num. 6:3; Ruth 2:14) was an act
of kindness not appreciated by those who wished to see whether Elijah
would come to rescue Jesus.[3] Why the offer of wine is made after the
misinterpreted cry of Jesus is not clear.

How could Jesus, whose unique identity, mission, and relationship
to God as the Son have been so featured (Matt. 1:23; 3:17; 11:27; 16:16;
17:5), be forsaken by God? This is "one of the most impenetrable mysteries of the entire Gospel narrative" (Hagner 1995a: 845). With the cry of
abandonment, Jesus does not lose faith but expresses the depths of his
unimaginable pain at being abandoned by his Father. He must drink the
cup of suffering that the Father has given him, leading to the unfathomable agony of being abandoned by the Father (27:46; cf. 2 Cor. 5:21). He
must die in order to pour out his blood as a ransom so as to save his
people from their sins (Matt. 1:21; 20:28; 26:28). Yet his abandonment
is only temporary, and his vindication will come soon.

c. Jesus's Death (27:50)

It is surprising that Jesus would be able to muster a loud shout after he   27:50
has experienced such agonies. Jesus's "giving up" his spirit is sometimes
understood to mean that he decided when he would die (W. Davies and
Allison 1997: 628; Hendriksen 1973: 973), but this may be only an idiomatic expression for death (cf. Gen. 35:18; 1 Esd. 4:21; Josephus, Ant.
1.218; 5.147; 12.430; 14.369).

2. On the linguistic and textual complexities of the echo of Ps. 22:1 in 27:46, see Metzger
1994: 58–59. On Elijah, see 11:14; 16:14; 17:3, 10–13; Luke 4:25–26; 9:8; John 1:21, 25;
Rom. 11:2; James 5:17; Rev. 11:3–6.

3. The words ἄφες ἴδωμεν are difficult to translate. Evidently ἄφες (translated "wait"
above) connotes the idea of letting things be or not interfering with the status quo. On the
imperative-with-hortatory-subjunctive construction, cf. BDAG 157; BDF §364; Robertson
1934: 931–32.

d. The Earthquake and Its Results (27:51–53)

27:51 The earthquake at Jesus's death causes two extraordinary phenomena. Like the providentially darkened sun, this epochal event signifies God's eschatological redemption.[4] The torn temple curtain was probably not between the Court of Israel and the Court of the Gentiles (Blomberg 1992a: 421) but was either the inner veil separating the holy of holies from the holy place (Exod. 26:31–35; Lev. 16:2; 2 Chron. 3:14) or the outer one in front of the holy place (Exod. 26:37; 38:18; Num. 3:26). Some scholars view the tearing of the curtain as a foreshadowing of God's judgment on the temple and of its becoming obsolete.[5] But one wonders whether the destruction of the temple in 70 CE necessitates its final obsolescence. Others take the torn curtain as vindicating Jesus as one who is greater than the temple and its corrupt leaders (12:6; Gundry 1994: 575). W. Davies and Allison (1997: 632) point out that any judgment on the temple is, first of all, judgment on the priests who are the temple's custodians. For Matthew and his Christian Jewish community, Jesus came not to destroy but to fulfill the Torah (5:17–48), and so it is debatable that Matthew is thinking in terms of an absolute end of the temple (but cf. 24:2). (On the veil in history and legend, see Gurtner 2006.)

27:52–53 The opening of the tombs (Ezek. 37:13) is associated with Jesus's death, but the appearance of the saints (Zech. 14:5; Ezek. 37:1–14) in the holy city apparently will not occur until after Jesus's resurrection (27:53).[6] The dead saints are euphemistically described as sleeping.[7] There are many difficulties concerning the nature and sequence of events in this extremely unusual pericope (Hagner 1995a: 849–52), but it is not helpful to take it as a nonhistorical literary-theological creation. If this resurrection is intended to preview the ultimate resurrection of humanity (Gundry 1994: 577), it is important that it be as genuine as that of Jesus. Only a historical resurrection can be an effect of Jesus's resurrection and an omen of the final resurrection (cf. 1 Cor. 15:20–28). For Matthew, the association of the saints' resurrection with that of Jesus marks the decisive turning of the ages. Jesus's resurrection means that the gates of hades cannot prevail against Jesus's church (Matt. 16:18) and that his enemies will answer to his authority (26:64).

---

4. On earthquakes as harbingers of the eschaton, see 24:7; 28:2; cf. Isa. 24:19; 29:6; Jer. 10:10; Joel 2:10; Amos 8:8; Nah. 1:5; Hag. 2:6; Zech. 14:4–5; Rev. 6:12; 8:5; 11:13, 19; 16:18; 1 En. 1.3–9; As. Mos. 10.4; 2 Esd. (4 Ezra) 6:13–16; 9:3; 2 Bar. 70.8; Allison 1985a: 40–46.

5. E.g., Blomberg 1992a: 421; Hagner 1995a: 849, who may be reading too much from Hebrews into Matthew.

6. The syntax of 27:53 (ἐξελθόντες ἐκ τῶν μνημείων μετὰ τὴν ἔγερσιν αὐτοῦ εἰσῆλθον) is ambiguous in that the prepositional phrase μετὰ τὴν ἔγερσιν αὐτοῦ can be taken with either ἐξελθόντες (NRSV) or εἰσῆλθον (NIV).

7. Cf. John 11:11; Acts 7:60; 13:36; 1 Cor. 7:39; 11:30; 15:6, 18, 51; 1 Thess. 4:13–14; 2 Pet. 3:4; 2 Macc. 12:45; Sir. 46:19; 48:13.

Matthew does not mention the ultimate end of those raised. One wonders whether their "resurrection" is merely resuscitation to physical life,
after which they will die. If so, this "resurrection" would be like that of
Lazarus (John 11). If the resurrection is a transformation of the body (cf.
Matt. 19:28; 1 Cor. 15:50–55), like that of Jesus, apparently these saints
will ascend with Jesus to heaven (cf. Acts 1:9–11). But Matthew does not
answer such questions, and this leads many to view Matt. 27:52–53 as a
symbolic theological tale rather than a historical narrative.

e. The Soldiers' Confession (27:54)

The confession of the centurion (cf. 8:5, 8, 13) and the other soldiers is   **27:54**
significant as a foil to the invective hurled at Jesus since 27:27. It also
reminds readers of Matthew's theme of mission to the Gentiles (1:3, 5–6;
8:10–12; 10:18; 15:21–28; 24:14) and anticipates 28:18–20. The soldiers
acknowledge what most of the others refuse to see when they echo the
crucial Matthean theme that Jesus is the Son of God. What they mean
by "Son of God" does not entail all of Matthew's Christology, but they are
at least open to Jesus's true identity (see Verseput 1987: 547–49). Terrified by the midday darkness and the earthquake accompanying Jesus's
death, they come to the conclusion that Jesus is a supernatural being.
Although they do not grasp all that "Son of God" means in Matthew,
their positive response to Jesus implies openness to further Christian
witness. Perhaps some of them will become disciples.

f. The Women Who Observe from a Distance (27:55–56)

A group of many women powerlessly observe the crucifixion from   **27:55–56**
a distance. These women have followed and served Jesus since the
days of the Galilean ministry. Three of the women are named. Mary
Magdalene is evidently from the village of Magdala on the Sea of Galilee and is mentioned in the passion narratives of all four Gospels (cf.
Luke 8:2–3). Mary the mother of James and Joseph may be the wife
of Clopas (John 19:25; cf. Bauckham 2002: 203–23) or even Mary the
mother of Jesus (cf. 13:55). The mother of Zebedee's sons previously
envisioned her sons sitting on both sides of Jesus's throne (20:20–21),
but now she watches Jesus's cross with revolutionaries crucified on
both sides of him. Since the two Marys mentioned here appear again
(27:61; 28:1–10), they become a literary hinge between the burial and
resurrection of Jesus (see Heil 1991c). The prominence of these faithful women in the account of Jesus's death contrasts with the shameful
absence of the disciples and is a powerful warning against chauvinism
in the community of Jesus's disciples (cf. 23:8–12; Gal. 3:28; Kopas
1990; Witherington 1984).

Additional Note

27:49. UBS[4] doubts the originality of the account (appended to the end of 27:49) of blood and water coming out of Jesus's side after it was pierced by a spear (ἄλλος δὲ λαβὼν λόγχην ἔνυξεν αὐτοῦ τὴν πλευράν, καὶ ἐξῆλθεν ὕδωρ καὶ αἷμα; cf. John 19:34). Although this account is found in a few impressive MSS (ℵ, B, C, L, 1010), it is omitted by many others, including A, D, W, Δ, Θ, f[1], f[13], 28, 33, 157, *Byz, Lect*, and most old Latin MSS. Metzger 1994: 59 theorizes that the Johannine account was written in the margin of Matthew from memory and that later it was awkwardly interpolated into the text of 27:49.

VII. Epilogue/Conclusion: Passion, Resurrection, and Commission (26:3–28:20)
   C. Crucifixion (27:27–56)
➤ D. Burial of Jesus (27:57–66)
   E. Resurrection of Jesus (28:1–15)

D. Burial of Jesus (27:57–66)

This account contains two parts, the first describing Jesus's burial (27:57–61; cf. Mark 15:42–47; Luke 23:50–56; John 19:31–42) and the second the action of the religious leaders to prevent the disciples from stealing Jesus's body and claiming a resurrection had occurred (27:62–66). This second part is unique to Matthew (but see Gos. Pet. 28–34). Both sections relate Pilate's granting of requests. This account anticipates Matt. 28 in that Jesus's burial and the securing of his tomb are reversed by the resurrection and the flight of the guards to the chief priests (see France 1989: 133; Giblin 1975; Heil 1991d). "The laughter of God roars through the pericope" (Gnilka 1986–88: 2.489). The resurrection is the religious leaders' worst nightmare. The following display indicates the stunning reversal:

A The crucified Jesus is buried (27:57–61)
  B The religious leaders post the guards (27:62–66)
    C The empty tomb, the angel, and the risen Jesus (28:1–10)
  B′ The guards report to the religious leaders (28:11–15)
A′ The exalted Jesus commissions the disciples (28:16–20)

1. Joseph of Arimathea Buries Jesus (27:57–61)

In the absence of the Twelve (26:31), Jesus is buried by Joseph of Arimathea in his own new tomb. The two Marys witness Jesus's burial as well as his resurrection (28:1).

Exegesis and Exposition

[57]Now when it was evening, a rich man from Arimathea named Joseph came. He himself had also become a disciple of Jesus. [58]This man went to Pilate and asked for the body of Jesus. Then Pilate ordered it to be turned over to him. [59]So Joseph took the body, wrapped it in a clean linen cloth, [60]and laid it in his own new tomb, which he had cut in the rock. He rolled a large stone against the entrance of the tomb and went away. [61]Now Mary Magdalene was there, with the other Mary, sitting opposite the tomb.

27:57   Friday afternoon has turned to evening when Jesus's burial occurs. Joseph of Arimathea's arrival is unexpected. Very little is known about his obscure birthplace (cf. 1 Macc. 11:34; Josephus, *Ant.* 5.342; 13.127). As a rich disciple (cf. Mark 15:43; John 19:38), Joseph is a unique example of God's power to do what is otherwise impossible (Matt. 19:23–26; cf. 1 Cor. 1:26–29; 1 Tim. 6:17–19; James 1:9–11). Unlike the rich young man (19:21–22), Joseph uses his wealth to help the poor: his expensive tomb is given to Jesus. The mention of his riches may allude to Isa. 53:9.

27:58–60   Joseph obtains permission from Pilate, wraps the body in linen, and buries it in his own new tomb, which has been carved out of a rocky escarpment (cf. John 19:38–42). His reverential treatment of Jesus's body remarkably demonstrates his faith. The tomb is closed with a large stone, probably carved into a disklike shape. The stone would roll in a channel carved into the front of the tomb. Visitors to Israel can still see such ancient tombs. Bodies were to be buried before sunset (Deut. 21:22–23), and the burial of corpses was regarded as a righteous work (Acts 5:6, 10; 8:2; Josephus, *J.W.* 4.317; Tob. 1:17–20; 2:3–8; 4:3–4; 6:14; 8:9; 12:13; 14:11–13; M. Davis 2006). On the eve of the Sabbath, this would be even more important. Victims of crucifixion were often left on their crosses after death as an object lesson on the futility of rebelling against Rome. Such victims would commonly be disposed of by being thrown on a trash heap.

The two Marys (27:56) arrive at the tomb at some point and are still   **27:61**
keeping watch over the body of Jesus when Joseph leaves. They return
late on the Sabbath as the first day of the week dawns and are the first
to learn of the resurrection. They are the last to leave the tomb and the
first to discover it empty. They will be the first to announce the resurrection to others (28:1–10).

2. Jewish and Roman Leaders
Secure the Tomb (27:62–66)

Somehow the religious leaders have become aware of Jesus's promise to rise from the dead. They do not believe it but are concerned that Jesus's disciples will steal his body and perpetrate a resurrection hoax. So they take measures with Pilate to avoid the feared hoax, but soon they will need to concoct a hoax of their own (28:11–15).

Exegesis and Exposition

⁶²Now on the next day, which is after the day of preparation, the chief priests and the Pharisees gathered together before Pilate ⁶³and said, "Sir, we remember that when he was still alive, that impostor said, 'After three days I will be raised again.' ⁶⁴Therefore order the grave to be secured until the third day, or his disciples will come and steal him away and tell the people, 'He has been raised from the dead,' and the last deception will be worse than the first." ⁶⁵Pilate said to them, "You can have a guard; go, make it as secure as you know how." ⁶⁶So they went and secured the grave by sealing the stone and stationing the guard.

27:62–64   On the Sabbath, the religious leaders continue to pursue Jesus even after his death. The Pharisees, absent from the narrative since 23:29, join the leading priests in asking Pilate to seal and guard the tomb. These two groups are normally in tension with each other, yet they unite here to accomplish a common goal (cf. 21:45). They fear the highly implausible event that Jesus's disciples will continue his deception (cf. Luke 23:14; John 7:12, 47) by stealing his body and claiming he was raised from the dead. Somehow the chief priests and Pharisees became aware that Jesus predicted his resurrection. These predictions were made to his disciples, not to the religious leaders (16:21; 17:22–23; 20:17–19). Perhaps the veiled prediction in terms of the sign of Jonah was understood by the Pharisees and Sadducees who heard it (12:38–40; 16:4). Or perhaps the disciples told others about Jesus's prediction, and the word eventually made its way to the Pharisees. The Sadducees evidently dismissed the notion of resurrection (22:23–33; cf. Josephus, *J.W.* 2.165; *Ant.* 18.16), but the Pharisees believed in a general resurrection at the end of the age (cf. Acts 23:6–9; Josephus, *J.W.* 2.163; *Ant.* 18.14).

It is unclear whether Pilate's response is a statement that the religious　27:65–66
leaders have at their disposal a temple police force (Carson 1984: 586;
NRSV) or is a permission for the Jewish leaders to take a guard composed of Roman soldiers (W. Davies and Allison 1997: 655; NIV, NLT).[1]
These guards are called soldiers (28:12–13; cf. 27:27; Acts 12:4) and are
ultimately accountable to Pilate (28:14), and so the second view is more
likely. If so, these soldiers and the sealed stone constitute imperial authority over the tomb.[2] The seal would be clay or wax pressed into the
crack between the rolling stone and the tomb's entrance. The imperial
seal stamped on the clay or wax signified Rome's authority (cf. Dan.
6:17; Josephus, *Ant.* 10.258), but a higher power would arrive on the
scene when dawn came.[3]

After all the abusive treatment endured by Jesus, the manner of his
burial is surprising. The ignominy of having his body hang on the cross
after sundown on Sabbath eve during the Feast of Unleavened Bread
is avoided by the action of Joseph, who brings the story of Jesus's horrible death to an end by giving him a decent burial. This kind treatment
answers to that of the unnamed woman who anointed Jesus for burial
(Matt. 26:6–13).

The fear of the religious leaders that the disciples will steal Jesus's body
and deceive people with false resurrection claims seems to be irrational.
They overestimate the scattered, terrified disciples, yet their worse mistake is to underestimate Jesus. They rule out any possibility that God
would make good on Jesus's repeated promises of resurrection. Their
stolen-body explanation is refuted by Jesus's postresurrection appearances (28:9, 17; cf. Acts 1:3–11; 1 Cor. 15:5–8). Their ongoing conspiracy
shows the lengths to which unbelief will go (cf. Matt. 28:11–15; Luke
16:31; John 11:45–53; 12:9–11). The book of Acts recounts the confirmation of the leaders' worst fears. Jesus's followers begin to take the resurrection message to all the nations (Acts 2:24; 3:15; 10:40; 13:30; 17:31;
23:6–10; 24:15, 21; 25:19; 26:8, 23). Paul will eventually arrive in Rome
and proclaim the resurrection in the capital of the empire whose agent
sealed Jesus's tomb (Acts 28:14–31). The tomb's seal is only temporary,
and ironically, the last "deception" does turn out to be "worse" than the
first from the standpoint of the leaders' convictions (Matt. 27:64; cf. Acts
2:41–47; 6:7; 9:31; 21:20).

1. Depending on context, ἔχετε can be an indicative or an imperative. BDAG's suggestion (422) "You can have a guard" takes ἔχετε as an imperative of permission (Wallace
1996: 488–89).
2. It is not easy to determine the meaning of μετὰ τῆς κουστωδίας. Either (1) the soldiers
went with the leaders (NRSV), (2) posting the soldiers along with the seal constituted the
securing of the tomb (NIV), or (3) the soldiers sealed the tomb. Cf. BDAG 637.
3. Although most versions seem to take ἀσφαλίσασθε ὡς οἴδατε in a correlative sense
("Make it *as* secure as you know how"), the meaning could simply be "Secure it, as you
know how to do."

Summary and Transition

Matthew 27 carries the drama of Jesus's arrest and trial before the Jewish leaders to its awful denouement: Jesus is condemned by Pilate, crucified, and buried. The religious leaders try to prevent any further problems by arranging for the tomb to be sealed and guarded. This is the low point of Matthew's Gospel for Jesus's followers, but the victory of Jesus's enemies is only apparent and temporary.

Two contrasting themes are developed in parallel fashion in this chapter. One is the religious leaders' cruel treatment of Jesus, culminating in his crucifixion and burial (27:1, 3–4, 20, 41–43, 62). Their obstinance continues in Matt. 28. The other is Jesus's vindication by both Jews and Gentiles. Judas admits that Jesus is innocent, and the leaders do not even attempt to persuade him otherwise (27:4). Pilate recognizes the leaders' ulterior motives and with his wife regards Jesus as innocent (27:18–19, 23–24). Divine providence brings cosmic phenomena befitting Jesus's atrocious treatment and providing vindication of a sort (27:51–53). Roman soldiers perceive these phenomena as demonstrating that Jesus is the Son of God (27:54). Although they understand relatively little about Jesus's divine sonship, their confession starkly contrasts with the repeated taunts of multitudes and the leaders (27:40, 43). This confession anticipates Jesus's sending his followers to make disciples from all the nations, who likewise confess in baptism the name of the Father, Son, and Holy Spirit (28:19).

VII. Epilogue/Conclusion: Passion, Resurrection, and Commission (26:3–28:20)
    D. Burial of Jesus (27:57–66)
➤ E. Resurrection of Jesus (28:1–15)
    F. Commission by the Risen Lord (28:16–20)

E. Resurrection of Jesus (28:1–15)

Matthew's Gospel concludes with the story of Jesus's resurrection (28:1–10) and its two contrasting results, the coverup perpetrated by the religious leaders (28:11–15) and Jesus's mandate for discipling all the nations (28:16–20). Both of these themes, the opposition of the leaders and the outreach to the Gentiles, are by now familiar to Matthew's readers.

Jesus's resurrection is announced, not explained. The focus of 28:1–10 is the empty tomb, announced by the angel whose rolling away of the stone evidently caused or at least accompanied an earthquake. The glorious angel and the empty tomb so overwhelm the guards that they faint. The angel shows the women that Jesus is no longer where they saw him entombed on Friday evening (27:61). This signifies to the women that Jesus is indeed the Messiah and that they need to stop mourning and tell his disciples that he is risen.

There are multiple witnesses to the resurrection in this passage. The Father is the ultimate witness because his power is the presupposition of everything that happens here. The Father's agency is implied by all the passive verbs that describe Jesus's resurrection and exaltation (28:6–7, 18; cf. 16:21; 17:2, 9, 23; 20:19; 26:32). The glorious angel announces the resurrection as the Father's agent (28:6a). The empty tomb itself says nothing but signifies everything about the resurrection (28:6b). The faithful women hurry to announce the resurrection to the disciples (28:8). Jesus himself meets the women on their way and reiterates that he will meet the disciples in Galilee (28:9–10). Even the guards are unintentional evangelists; their announcement to the leading priests confirms their worst fears (28:11). Beyond these direct witnesses to the resurrection, there are two additional factors. The earthquake that rolls away the stone is a portent of an epochal event (28:2). Even the religious leaders' conspiracy to deny the resurrection bears indirect and ironic witness that it is true (28:11–15).[1]

---

1. On Matt. 28, see Reeves 1993; K. Smyth 1975. Studies of the resurrection are numerous. For a conservative attempt to answer the questions that arise when the four Gospel accounts are compared, see J. Wenham 1984. For the unique emphases of each Gospel, see G. Osborne 1984. Blomberg 1987b: 100–110 discusses historical matters. For apologetic approaches, see Copan and Tacelli 2000; Craig in Wilkins and Moreland 1995: 142–76; Habermas and Licona 2004; Stewart 2006. Allison 2005a: 200–351 examines the historicity of the resurrection from a deistic viewpoint.

1. Mary Magdalene and Another Mary Encounter the Angel (28:1–7)

The comparison of Matthew's resurrection narrative with that of the other Gospels raises a number of questions regarding chronology and harmonization (cf. Mark 16:1–7; Luke 24:1–8; John 20:1). The unit outline is as follows:

a. The women arrive at the tomb (28:1)
b. The angel rolls away the stone (28:2–3)
c. The guards faint (28:4)
d. The angel announces the resurrection (28:5–7)

Exegesis and Exposition

¹And after the Sabbath, as the first day of the week was dawning, Mary Magdalene and the other Mary came to view the tomb. ²Suddenly a severe earthquake occurred, for an angel of the Lord had descended from heaven. He came and rolled away the stone and sat on it. ³Now his appearance was like lightning, and his clothing was as white as snow; ⁴and the guards shook from fear of him and became like dead men. ⁵Then the angel answered and said to the women, "Do not be afraid; for I know that you are looking for Jesus who was crucified. ⁶He is not here, for he was raised, just as he said. Come, see the place where ⌜he was laid⌝. ⁷Then go quickly and tell his disciples: 'He was raised from the dead, and see, he is going before you into Galilee; there you will see him.' See, I have told you."

a. The Women Arrive at the Tomb (28:1)

28:1   The women arrive just as daylight dawns on Sunday. Their purpose is explained more clearly in Mark 16:1. Significantly, once again women are closest to Jesus at a crucial point in the passion story (Matt. 28:1; cf. 26:7; 27:56, 61). The disciples, who promised undying loyalty, are still scattered (26:31–35).

b. The Angel Rolls Away the Stone (28:2–3)

28:2–3   This earthquake reminds the reader of the earthquake that marked Jesus's death on Friday afternoon (27:51–53). Perhaps it is an aftershock of the previous earthquake (Blomberg 1992a: 427) and of the accompanying epochal events that lead up to the resurrection of Jesus. The chronological sequence in 28:1–2 is unclear. The earthquake evidently happens just before the women arrive, or possibly as they view the tomb. It is not clear whether the women witness the angel rolling away the stone, which coincides with or perhaps causes the earthquake. In any event, the stone is rolled aside not to let Jesus out but to show the women that the resurrection has left the tomb empty. The awesome appearance of the angel is similar to other biblical accounts (Dan. 7:9; 10:6; Acts 1:10; Rev. 10:1; 15:6). Matthew begins and ends with angels; they announce both the birth and the resurrection of Jesus (Matt. 1:20; 2:19; cf. Luke 1:11, 26; 2:9).

c. The Guards Faint (28:4)

The detachment of guards and the imperial seal (27:65–66) cannot pre-   **28:4**
vent the removal of Jesus's body because it is not stolen by the disciples but raised by the Father. The glorious angel so astonishes the guards that they faint away as if they, not Jesus, were dead (cf. Dan. 8:17–18; 10:8–9, 15; Rev. 1:17).

d. The Angel Announces the Resurrection (28:5–7)

Unlike the guards, the women endure the glorious angel and receive   **28:5–7**
his message that Jesus has been raised and will meet the disciples in Galilee. The angel's glorious appearance caused the guards to shake with fear and faint, and certainly the women are also frightened. After telling the women not to fear (cf. Luke 1:13, 30; 2:10), the angel announces the resurrection and invites the women to look into the tomb and see for themselves. The words "just as he said" remind the women that Jesus repeatedly predicted his resurrection (cf. Matt. 12:40; 16:21; 17:9, 23; 20:19; 26:32). The angel reiterates Jesus's earlier promise to meet the disciples in Galilee (26:32; cf. 28:10). This promise had been originally made in connection with Jesus's prediction that the disciples would desert him (26:31). The power of the resurrection will transform the deserters back into disciples (28:16). The fact that women are the first witnesses of the resurrection is unusual and adds a ring of truth. Blomberg (1992a: 426) plausibly points out that a fabricated story would likely have male witnesses.

Additional Note

28:6. UBS⁴ prefers the shorter reading (supported by ℵ, B, Θ, 33, 892*), which does not have a subject for ἔκειτο. The longer reading ἔκειτο ὁ κύριος is widely supported (A, C, D, L, W, Δ, 0148, f^1, f^{13}, Byz, Lect), but Metzger counters this external evidence with an argument from internal evidence: "the word κύριος is never applied to Jesus except in his reported sayings" (1994: 59). However, Metzger is evidently speaking only of the nominative form of κύριος. His point is weakened by the fact that the vocative form (κύριε) is used repeatedly in addressing Jesus in this Gospel (8:2, 6, 8, 21, 25; 9:28; 14:28, 30; 15:22, 25, 27; 16:22; 17:4, 15; 18:21; 20:30, 31, 33; 26:22). The longer reading has more merit than is implied by the A rating assigned the shorter reading in UBS⁴.

2. Jesus Appears to the Women (28:8–10)

As they rush to report Jesus's resurrection to his disciples, the two Marys are met by Jesus himself (cf. Mark 16:8–11; Luke 24:9–12; John 20:2–18). As they worship him, he reiterates the message of the angel that he will meet them in Galilee (cf. 26:32; 28:7).

Exegesis and Exposition

⁸So they quickly ⌜departed⌝ from the tomb with fear and great joy and ran to report to his disciples. ⁹⌜And suddenly⌝ Jesus met them and said, "Hello!" They went to him and took hold of his feet and worshiped him. ¹⁰Then Jesus said to them, "Do not be afraid; go and report to my brothers that they should leave for Galilee; there they will see me."

28:8–9 The women's awe is now accompanied by joy that Jesus has been raised. They hurry away to report the news to the absentee apostles as the angel directed them. Suddenly Jesus himself appears and greets them. Their worshipful response to Jesus reminds the reader of similar actions by the magi and others (2:2, 11; 8:2; 9:18; 14:33; 15:25; 18:26; 20:20; 28:9, 17). Jesus reminded Satan that only God is to be worshiped (4:9–10), and so the women's response is indicative of Matthew's high Christology. Allison (2005b: 107–16) explores several interpretations of the women's touching Jesus's feet.

28:10 Jesus's initial postresurrection appearance sets the tone for the proper worshipful response to him for the future. The women are evidently prostrated before Jesus with their faces to the ground and arms outstretched with hands grasping Jesus's feet. Jesus reaffirms his promise (26:32) just repeated by the angel (28:7) and calls the disciples his brothers (12:49–50; 23:8; 25:40; cf. Rom. 8:29; Heb. 2:11). The "family" metaphor shows much love and patience, since the disciples have just run away from home, as it were, when they deserted Jesus. But Jesus welcomes the prodigals back. See Bauckham 2002: 257–310, especially 277–79, on the witness of the women to the resurrection.

The Resurrection and Biblical Theology

Although it is sometimes relegated to Easter Sunday, the resurrection of Jesus is at the heart of the Christian gospel. Without the resurrection, Jesus's ministry ends in defeat. But everything changes if "he is not here, for he was raised, just as he said" (28:6). The resurrection not only culminates the passion narrative but also is at the center of redemption itself. Without it one can only pity Jesus as a martyr whose lofty ideals were sadly misunderstood. With it one must stand in awe of the Messiah, the Son of the living God, who gave his life as a ransom for many and who will one day return in glory to judge humanity.[1]

The resurrection of Jesus is the sine qua non of several themes in Matthew's theology.

> Without the resurrection, Jesus's crucial and climactic redemptive act of dying for sinners would go without divine endorsement. The resurrection amounts to the Father's signaling that Jesus's death was victorious and affirming that Jesus's blood of the new covenant will effectively save his people from their sins (cf. Rom. 4:25).

> If Jesus did not rise from the dead after promising several times that he would do so (12:40; 16:21; 17:9, 23; 20:19; 26:32), he would be pitied or scorned, not believed and obeyed (cf. 1 Cor. 15:16–19). As is commonly said, he would have been a lunatic or a liar, not the Lord of heaven and earth (Rom. 1:4).

> Without the resurrection, Jesus's people could not be saved from their sins (1:21) because his mission would have ended with the ignominy of a cursed person who hung upon a tree (Deut. 21:22–23; Gal. 3:13).

> Without the resurrection, Jesus would never drink the new wine, representing the blood of the new covenant, in his Father's kingdom with his disciples (26:27–29).

> Without the resurrection, there would be no apostolic foundation for the church (16:18), since Jesus's resurrection turned the deserters back into disciples (26:31–32). Nothing but the astonishing yet true resurrection message delivered to them by the two women and then by Jesus himself could have brought the scattered disciples back into the fold (28:7, 10, 16–20).

> Without the resurrection of Jesus, there would be no complete model of sacrificial living. Jesus taught the oxymoron of the crucified life, that genuinely abundant living occurs only when one dies to self-interest and that the self-oriented life is misery. But the model is truncated if Jesus's suffering does not lead to ultimate exaltation, if the crown never replaces the cross (10:38–39; 16:24–26; 20:26–28; 23:12; cf. Rom. 6:1–11).

> Without the resurrection of Jesus, there would be no eschatological *shalom* to rectify all earthly wrongs and renew the world (19:28). The martyrs whose blood cries out from the ground would not

1. On the biblical theology of the resurrection, see Harris 1985, 1990; Luedemann 1995; G. Osborne 1984; in J. Green and McKnight 1992: 673–88; N. Wright 2003.

be vindicated (23:35; Rev. 6:9–11). Those who do violence to their fellow humans would not be held accountable. There would be no ultimate reckoning (Matt. 13:37–42; cf. Dan. 12:2). Satan would win the cosmic battle. But the resurrection guarantees the final judgment of all humanity (Matt. 13:37–42; 16:27; 25:31; cf. Dan. 12:2; Acts 17:31).

Without the resurrection of Jesus, his people could not hope for their own resurrection and reward (13:43; 16:27; 25:31–40; 27:51–53). Jesus's ethical teaching includes the prospect of judgment and reward in the coming kingdom (4:17; 5:12; 6:4; 7:1–2, 21). The disciples' hope and values focus on the kingdom (6:10, 33), but the kingdom could never come to earth if the king had remained in the grave. With Jesus's throne unoccupied, what would become of the twelve thrones of his apostles, and of the rewards Jesus promised to all his disciples (6:19–21; 13:43; 19:27–29; cf. Dan. 12:3; Rev. 2:26–27; 3:21)?

Without the resurrection, Jesus's climactic saving act of dying for sinners by crucifixion would lack interpretation and proof of divine acceptance. Granted, the apostolic proclamation centered on the cross (Gal. 6:14; 1 Cor. 1:18–25; 1 Pet. 1:19; Heb. 2:9, 14; 9:12–14; Rev. 5:6, 9). But the significance of the cross would be unclear apart from the resurrection. Therefore any presentation of the good news of Jesus the Messiah must stress his resurrection as the essential explanation of the meaning of his death. The gospel must be communicated with culturally appropriate methods and language, but the methods and language must expound the resurrection as proof of the saving power of the crucifixion. Any "gospel" that does not place Jesus's resurrection alongside Jesus's death is not the authentic message of Jesus and the apostles.[2]

Additional Notes

28:8. UBS⁴ prefers ἀπελθοῦσαι (supported by ℵ, B, C, L, Θ, f¹³, 33) to its synonym ἐξελθοῦσαι (supported by A, D, W, Δ, 0148, f¹, Byz, Lect) because the editors believe the latter was assimilated from Mark 16:8.

28:9. UBS⁴ prefers the shorter reading καὶ ἰδού, supported by ℵ, B, D, W, Θ, f¹³, 33, Lectᵖᵗ. The much longer reading ὡς δὲ ἐπορεύοντο ἀπαγγεῖλαι τοῖς μαθηταῖς αὐτοῦ καὶ ἰδού is supported by A, C, L, Δ, 28, f¹, Byz, Lectᵖᵗ. It seems that either the longer reading was omitted because of homoeoteleuton (similar ending) or the longer reading originated as an expansion of 28:8.

---

2. On the resurrection, see Acts 2:32; 3:15, 26; 4:2, 10, 33; 5:30; 10:40; 13:30–37; 17:18, 31; 23:6; 24:21; 25:19; 26:8, 23; Rom. 1:4; 4:25; 6:4–5; 8:11; 10:9; 1 Cor. 15; 2 Cor. 4:10, 14; 13:4; Gal. 1:1; Eph. 1:20; 2:5; 4:10; Phil. 2:8–9; Col. 2:12; 3:1–4; 1 Thess. 4:14; 1 Tim. 3:16; Heb. 1:3; 10:12; 12:1; 1 Pet. 1:21; 3:18–22; Rev. 1:5, 18; 2:8; 5:6–10.

3. The "Cover-Up" (28:11–15)

Those who were guarding Jesus's tomb now become evangelists. The leaders had requested guards to avoid a resurrection hoax, but the guards report that a genuine resurrection has occurred. The leaders have outsmarted themselves. Now they are the ones who concoct the hoax, and money changes hands to ensure that everyone sticks to the story. They accused Jesus of deceiving people (27:63–64), but now they deceive people about Jesus. They refused to believe Jesus as the ultimate interpreter of Moses and the prophets, and now they will not be persuaded when someone is raised from the dead (Luke 16:31). Yet the resurrection story is powerful to change lives: Acts speaks of thousands of converts in Jerusalem (Matt. 2:41; 4:4), many of whom were priests (6:7).

Exegesis and Exposition

¹¹Now while they were going, look, some of the guard went into the city and ⌜reported⌝ to the chief priests everything that had happened. ¹²After they had assembled with the elders and formed a plan, they gave a large sum of money to the soldiers, ¹³saying, "You are to say, 'His disciples came by night and stole him away while we were sleeping.' ¹⁴And if this is reported to the governor, we will pacify him and keep you out of trouble." ¹⁵And they took the money and did as they were instructed; and this story has been widely spread among the Jews up to ⌜this day⌝.

The women have left to tell the disciples that Jesus has been raised, and **28:11–12** the narrative returns to the guards, who must also report the resurrection. They are most likely Roman soldiers under Pilate's authority (27:65). How much the guards saw and comprehended is not clear. The angel's appearance caused them to faint (28:4), and they regained consciousness to discover the empty tomb. Their report leads to the priests' conspiracy with the elders to explain away the resurrection and bribe the guards. Ironically, the same guards who were to be an asset in preventing a resurrection hoax become a liability necessitating a hoax. The bribery of Judas to betray Jesus is near the beginning of the passion narrative, and the bribery of the guards to lie about the resurrection is near the end of the passion narrative.

The guards are to tell the same story that the leaders originally used to **28:13–15** secure Pilate's permission to post them at the tomb: the disciples stole the body (cf. John 20:1–2). But they were stationed at the tomb to prevent this very event. So they are told to lie and say that they were asleep when Jesus's body was stolen. The Jewish leaders promise to protect them in case Pilate hears of their dereliction of duty. The leaders have already bribed Judas; now they bribe the guards, and they may need to bribe Pilate too. But the story is patently false: if the guards were asleep, they could not know what became of Jesus's body. Yet they take the money and spawn a hoax that continues until Matthew's Gospel is written. Such stories were still circulating in the days of Justin Martyr (ca. 150 CE; *Dialogue with Trypho* 108.2).

None of the alternative explanations of the resurrection satisfactorily explains what is recorded here. The notion that the disciples stole the body is patently false, and other theories fare no better. One such theory has the women visiting the wrong tomb. Another posits Jesus merely swooning on the cross and later reviving. Perhaps the most fanciful is that the disciples' wishful thinking led to a collective hallucination of seeing the risen Jesus. The resurrection of Jesus can be dismissed only by a priori worldview considerations that rule out supernatural events. The resurrection of Jesus makes far better sense than any of the theories that attempt to explain it away. (On the historicity of the resurrection, see Craig 1989; in Wilkins and Moreland 1995: 142–76.)

Additional Notes

28:11. UBS⁴ prefers the external evidence for ἀπήγγειλαν (A, B, C, L, W, Δ, f¹, f¹³, 28, 33, *Byz, Lect*) to that for ἀνήγγειλαν (ℵ, D, Θ, 565). Ἀναγγέλλω occurs nowhere else in Matthew.

28:15. The originality of ἡμέρας is debatable. It is found in B, D, L, Θ, and most old Latin MSS but not in ℵ, A, W, Δ, f¹, f¹³, 28, 33, *Byz, Lect.* In 11:23 and 27:8, Matthew does not use ἡμέρα with σήμερον. UBS⁴ places ἡμέρας in brackets.

VII. Epilogue/Conclusion: Passion, Resurrection, and Commission (26:3–28:20)
    D. Burial of Jesus (27:57–66)
    E. Resurrection of Jesus (28:1–15)
➤ F. Commission by the Risen Lord (28:16–20)

F. Commission by the Risen Lord (28:16–20)

According to Luke and John, after the resurrection Jesus appeared to the disciples in Jerusalem (Luke 24:13–53; Acts 1:1–11; John 20:19–21:23). Matthew and Mark 16:15–18 narrate a meeting in Galilee to charge the disciples with a mission that will endure throughout the age. They worship him when they meet him there, although some still doubt (cf. Matt. 14:31). The remedy for this doubt will be their growing realization of Jesus's power and presence, truths that bracket the responsibilities of the mission mandate.

One is immediately struck with the repetition of the word "all" in this passage:

1. Jesus has been given *all* authority (28:18).
2. Disciples are to be made of *all* nations (28:19).
3. Such disciples are to be taught to obey *all* that Jesus commanded (28:20).
4. Jesus will be with his disciples *all* the days until the end of the age (28:20).

The Great Commission (cf. Mark 16:15–18; Luke 24:46–49; John 20:21–23; Acts 1:8) culminates Matthew's Gospel. The mandate to make disciples (Matt. 28:19–20a) is bracketed by two christological assertions that have already been anticipated by Matthew: Jesus has been given all authority (28:18), and Jesus will be with the disciples as they obey his mandate (28:20b). Jesus's universal power and perpetual presence provide the dynamic for Jesus's universal discipleship mandate. The Eleven will be able to disciple all the nations only as they recognize that Jesus has been given all authority and that he will be with them all the days until the very end. They can accomplish their present responsibilities only if they reflect on the past empowerment and future presence of their Lord. Jesus's program is daunting, but it can be accomplished because of his power and presence.[1]

This unit can be outlined as follows:

---

1. On 28:16–20, see Hill 1986; Kingsbury 1974; Legrand 1987; Michel in Stanton (ed.) 1995: 30–41; Scaer 1991; Schnabel 2004: 1.348–67; Sparks 2006; von Dobbeler 2000. Studies from a missiological viewpoint include Hennig 2001; Hertig 2001; Hiebert 1992; Krentz 2006.

1. The doubt of the disciples (28:16–17)
2. The power of Jesus (28:18)
3. The program of Jesus (28:19)
4. The presence of Jesus (28:20)

Exegesis and Exposition

[16]But the eleven disciples proceeded to Galilee, to the mountain that Jesus had appointed. [17]And when they saw him, they worshiped him; but some doubted.

[18]And Jesus came to them and said, "All authority in heaven and on earth has been given to me. [19]Therefore go and make disciples of all the nations, baptizing them in the name of the Father and of the Son and of the Holy Spirit, [20]teaching them to obey everything that I have commanded you; and remember, I am with you all the days, even to the end of the age ⌐ ⌐."

1. The Doubt of the Disciples (28:16–17)

28:16 The scene for Jesus's mission mandate is set in 28:16–17. The meeting in Galilee is fitting, since the disciples are Galileans and would normally return home after the pilgrimage to Jerusalem for Passover and the Feast of Unleavened Bread. Galilee has been previously associated with Gentiles (4:14–16; cf. Isa. 9:1–2), and so it is fitting that the mandate for mission to all the nations is given here. The eleven remaining disciples obey Jesus's instructions (Matt. 26:32; 28:10) and travel to an unnamed mountain that Jesus previously designated (28:10). Jesus's meeting them on a mountain echoes the giving of the Torah from Mount Sinai as well as previous mountain experiences in Matthew (4:8; 5:1; 14:23; 15:29; 17:1; 24:3; 26:30; T. Donaldson 1985: 170–90; Allison 1993b: 262–66).

28:17 As did the women (28:9), the disciples worship Jesus when they first see him. Yet some of them "doubted" (ἐδίστασαν, edistasan). The Greek word occurred in 14:31 to describe Peter's wavering faith as he walked on the water and saw the wind. It connotes uncertainty or hesitation (BDAG 252). No doubt some of the disciples are less confident than the others, but probably all of them, to some extent, doubt Jesus or hesitate to worship him (Hagner 1995a: 884–85; cf. Reeves 1998). Blomberg (1992a: 430) argues that the problem is not unbelief so much as a lack of spontaneous worship. But this may understate the problem, since ἐδίστασας in 14:31 is closely related to the familiar theme of "little faith" (cf. 6:30; 8:26; 16:8; 17:20). Whether one thinks of the disciples' response as mere hesitation or actual doubt, it is surprising in light of all Jesus's resurrection promises and the confirming testimony of the two women. The controverted long ending of Mark is even more critical of the disciples' response to the resurrected Jesus (Mark 16:8, 11, 13–14).

2. The Power of Jesus (28:18)

God's bestowal of universal authority or power upon Jesus echoes Dan. 7:13–14, 18, 22, 27 (cf. Matt. 11:27; 26:64; Eph. 1:20–23; Phil. 2:6–11; Col. 1:15–20; 1 Pet. 3:18–22; Rev. 5:1–14).[2] In Dan. 7 and Matthew alike, the Son of Man's authority passes to his community (W. Davies and Allison 1997: 683). Matthew has stressed that Jesus has authority to forgive sins and to save his people (Matt. 1:1, 17, 21; 2:2; 7:29; 8:9; 9:6–8; 10:1; 11:27; 21:23). Jesus demonstrates his authority by word and deed. Hagner (1995a: 886) helpfully points out that the resurrection and exaltation of Jesus amount to a permanent transfiguration of sorts (17:1–8). The glory seen by the disciples at the transfiguration has become the permanent mode of Jesus's life as the exalted Son of Man.

28:18

3. The Program of Jesus (28:19)

"Universal Lordship means universal mission" (W. Davies and Allison 1997: 684). The conjunction οὖν (oun, therefore) is crucial. Having been exalted, Jesus is now in a position to send out his disciples in mission. Mission is possible because Jesus is potent. Jesus previously commissioned the disciples to proclaim the kingdom to Israel alone (10:5–6; cf. 15:24–27), but now he commands them to disciple all the nations (cf. Gen. 12:3; LaGrand 1995; Sim 1995; von Dobbeler 2000). Some scholars (e.g., Hare and Harrington 1975) translate "all the Gentiles" and exclude Jews from the Christian mission, but this is doubtful. Granted, the priority here is the Gentiles, but the mission to them is a supplement to the mission to Israel, not a substitute for it. An ongoing mission to Israel is assumed by Matt. 10:23 (A.-J. Levine 1988). It is clear from the book of Acts that the apostolic church continued the mission to the Jews.

28:19

The disciples' central responsibility is to reproduce themselves. The other tasks (going, baptizing, teaching) describe how disciples are made.[3] A disciple is literally one who follows an itinerant master, as have Jesus's disciples. But Jesus will soon depart from this world, and discipleship

---

2. The universality of the authority is underlined by the expression "in heaven and on earth" (cf. 5:18, 34–35; 6:10, 19–20; 11:25; 16:19; 18:18–19; 23:9; 24:35; Schneider in Schenke 1988: 283–97). Echoes of Dan. 7:13–14 in Matt. 28:18–20 are clearest from the LXX and include ἐδόθη, ἐξουσία, πάντα τὰ ἔθνη, γῆς, οὐρανός, and αἰῶνος. The mention of the oppressed yet ultimately vindicated saints in Dan. 7:22, 25–27 well fits Jesus's teaching on discipleship (cf. Matt. 5:11–12; 10:17–42; 16:24–28; 23:34; 24:9–31). See W. Davies and Allison 1992; Hauerwas 2006: 248–49.

3. One sometimes hears preaching that stresses that the imperative μαθητεύσατε is the only command in the passage. But surely the activities described by the three participles, though not grammatically imperatives, are not optional. The participles may be taken as expressing attendant circumstances (Wallace 1996: 640–45, esp. 645) and translated as imperatives or as modal, explaining how disciples are made (Wallace 1996: 628–29). Wallace takes πορευθέντες as indicating attendant circumstances and βαπτίζοντες and διδάσκοντες as modal.

will take on a more metaphorical meaning. Following Jesus will entail understanding and obeying his teaching. Making disciples from all the nations obviously requires going to them. Baptism will be the key first step that initiates new disciples into the church. This baptism is a single act, distinct from repeated Jewish ritual washings. It is done with the trinitarian formula invoking the Father, Son, and Holy Spirit (Did. 7.1; cf. Schaberg 1982), and so it also differs from John's baptism (see Hartman 1997; Nolland in S. Porter and Cross 1999: 63–80). Those who are baptized are to be taught not only to know all of Jesus's commands but also to obey all of them (28:20). Thus in discipleship the intellectual component is secondary, the means to the end, which is spiritual formation (cf. John 13:17). All this implies the central role of the church as God's primary agency for mission. Only in the community/family that is the church can disciples be baptized and taught to observe all that Jesus has commanded (cf. Matt. 16:18–19; 18:17–20). (On discipleship in Matthew, see Wilkins 1988.)

4. The Presence of Jesus (28:20)

28:20   The mission mandate also requires teaching new disciples to obey all that Jesus commanded. The major discourses of Jesus in Matthew form the core of this teaching. Walvoord (1974: 242) certainly errs by excluding Jesus's interpretation of the law of Moses from what is to be taught and by restricting the word "command" to the new commandment of John 13. Since Jesus is the ultimate and definitive teacher of the Torah (Matt. 4:23; 5:2, 17–48; 7:29; 9:35; 11:1; 13:34; 21:23; 26:55), it is not surprising that his disciples are to continue in this vein. This teaching is not about information so much as ethics. Its goal is not so much knowledge as obedience. Righteous behavior is the mark of Jesus's disciples (5:17–20; 7:21–27).

    This commission began with Jesus announcing his reception of all authority, and now it concludes with Jesus promising to be with his disciples all the days until the end of the age. Although their responsibilities are daunting, their resources in Jesus's power and presence are more than adequate for the task. Jesus has already been called Immanuel, God's presence on earth (1:23; cf. Isa. 7:14). His ministry as the Spirit-enabled servant (12:17–21; cf. Isa. 42:1–4) demonstrated God's saving presence. From now on, although he is physically absent, the disciples will experience his presence in a new way, through the same Spirit that empowered Jesus while he was on earth (Matt. 3:16–17). Even during times of dispute and discipline, Jesus's presence will guide and confirm their decisions (18:18–20). (On Jesus as divine presence, see Kupp 1996.)

    Jesus's presence will last until "the end of the age." This expression (13:39–40, 49; 24:3) clearly refers to the time of eschatological judgment and renewal at the conclusion of the present order (cf. Cuvillier 1999a).

This makes clear that the commission is not only for the original eleven disciples but also for their disciples and their disciples' disciples in perpetuity until Jesus returns. Through all these days, there will never be a single day when Jesus will not be with his disciples as they are busy about his business.

Theology

The theology of Matthew may be summarized by following the trajectories of the themes found in the Great Commission.

When the restored disciples meet Jesus in Galilee (28:16–17), they worship him. Yet there is some hesitation. This is not surprising, since Matthew has already presented the disciples' weaknesses and foibles, especially in the passion narrative.[4] Nevertheless, Jesus promises to build his church on these foundational apostles, and commissions them to reach all the nations because God's empowering presence can overcome their weakness.

Jesus's commission itself is based in Christology. Jesus describes his authority in language that alludes to Dan. 7:13–14, 18, 22, 27. Matthew's theology of the kingdom is found *in nuce* here. The resurrection has already installed Jesus as the glorious Son of Man. His authority is already present on earth through the church's instrumentality. Yet the church longs and prays for fuller manifestation of Jesus's rule in this age and in the age to come (Matt. 6:10).

The goal of Jesus's commission is disciples who obey his teaching, not just casual hangers-on who listen to his teaching but do not practice it (7:26–27). These disciples are to come not only from Israel (10:23) but also from all the nations. Matthew's narrative has elements that have already prepared his Christian Jewish community for gentile converts (cf., e.g., 1:3, 5, 6; 8:5–13; 15:21–28; 24:14).

This universal mission also has cosmic implications. When people from all nations are discipled, a new obedient humanity begins to be formed. Thus obedience to the mission mandate turns out to fulfill, as a by-product, the original creation mandate that God gave to humanity's first parents in the garden of Eden. Adam failed the test, but Jesus successfully resisted the devil (4:1–11). The renewal of the world (19:28) has begun.

The disciples will experience the presence of Jesus every day as they make more disciples from all the nations. The presence of Jesus is the

---

4. See, e.g., the "little faith" texts (6:30; 8:26; 14:31; 16:8), the disciples' lack of compassion for the needy (14:13–15; 15:23, 32–33), misunderstandings of Jesus's teaching (16:5–12, 22–23; 17:4; 18:21), inability to perform exorcism (17:14–20), preoccupation with greatness (18:1; 19:27; 20:20–28; 23:8–12), complaints when Jesus is anointed (26:6–13), denial of their own weaknesses (26:25, 33–35), inability to watch with Jesus (26:40, 43, 45), and desertion and denial of Jesus (26:56, 69–75). Peter is often prominent in such passages.

presence of God, since Jesus is Immanuel (1:23). Through the Spirit, Jesus will tell them what to say when they are under duress from outsiders (10:16–20), and he will be in their midst when they ask for wisdom in dealing with internal problems (18:20).

This special presence of Jesus will end only when his return ends the age. Then the disciples' enemies will be judged and their sacrificial service rewarded (13:37–43; 16:27; 25:31–46). This will lead to nothing less than universal cosmic renewal (19:28), and obedience to Jesus the exalted Messiah will no longer be merely partial. Then God's will shall indeed be done on earth as it is in heaven (6:10). So be it!

Additional Note

28:20. Many MSS, including A², Δ, Θ, *f*¹³, 28, 157, *Byz, Lect,* conclude this verse with ἀμήν, but it is likely that this reading reflects liturgical use. Otherwise it is difficult to understand why ἀμήν would be omitted by MSS such as ℵ, A*, B, D, W, 1, 33 (Metzger 1994: 61).

Works Cited

Abadie, P.
1999 "Les généalogies de Jésus en Matthieu et Luc." *Lumière et vie* 48:47–60.
ABD *The Anchor Bible Dictionary.* Edited by D. N. Freedman et al. 6 vols. New York: Doubleday, 1992.
Abel, E. L.
1969 "Jesus and the Cause of Jewish National Independence." *Revue des études juives* 128:247–52.
1971 "Who Wrote Matthew?" *New Testament Studies* 17:138–52.
1973–74 "The Genealogies of Jesus O XPICTOC." *New Testament Studies* 20:203–10.
Abrahams, I.
1967 *Studies in Pharisaism and the Gospels.* Edited by M. Enslin. 2 vols. New York: Ktav.
Achtemeier, P.
1962 "Person and Deed: Jesus and the Storm-Tossed Sea." *Interpretation* 16:169–76.
Adler, N. (ed.)
1951 *Vom Wort des Lebens: Festschrift für Max Meinertz.* Münster: Aschendorff.
Adna, J.
1992–93 "The Attitude of Jesus to the Temple: A Critical Examination of How Jesus' Relationship to the Temple Is Evaluated within Israeli Scholarship, with Particular Regard to the Jerusalem School." *Mishkan* 17–18:65–80.
Agbanou, V.
1983 *Le discours eschatologique de Matthieu 24–25: Tradition et rédaction.* Paris: Gabalda.

Agnew, F. H.
1995 "Almsgiving, Prayer, and Fasting." *Theologische Bibliothek Töpelmann* 33:239–44.
Agourides, S.
1984 "Little Ones in Matthew." *Bible Translator* 35:329–34.
1992 "The Birth of Jesus and the Herodian Dynasty in Matthew 2." *Greek Orthodox Theological Review* 37:135–46.
Aicher, G.
1908 *Kamel und Nadelöhr: Eine kritisch-exegetische Studie über Mt 19:24 und Parallelen.* Münster: Aschendorff.
Aitken, W.
1912 "Beelzebul." *Journal of Biblical Literature* 31:34–53.
Aland, K. (ed.)
1959 *Studia Evangelica*, vol. 1: *Papers Presented to the International Congress on "The Four Gospels in 1957" Held at Christ Church, Oxford.* Berlin: Akademie.
Aland, K., and B. Aland
1989 *The Text of the New Testament.* Translated by E. Rhodes. 2nd ed. Grand Rapids: Eerdmans/ Leiden: Brill.
Albright, W., and C. Mann
1971 *Matthew.* Anchor Bible. New York: Doubleday.
Alford, H.
1968 *The Greek New Testament.* 2 vols. Reprinted Chicago: Moody.
Allen, L.
1992 "The Sermon on the Mount in the History of the Church." *Review and Expositor* 89:245–62.

Allen, W. C.

1907   *A Critical and Exegetical Commentary on the Gospel according to S. Matthew.* International Critical Commentary. New York: Scribner.

1912   *A Critical and Exegetical Commentary on the Gospel according to S. Matthew.* 3rd ed. International Critical Commentary. Edinburgh: T&T Clark.

Allison, D. C.

1983   "Matt. 23:39 = Luke 13:35b as a Conditional Prophecy." *Journal for the Study of the New Testament* 18:75–84.

1984   "Elijah Must Come First." *Journal of Biblical Literature* 103:256–58.

1985a   *The End of the Ages Has Come.* Philadelphia: Fortress.

1985b   "A Millennial Kingdom in the Teaching of Jesus?" *Irish Biblical Studies* 7:46–52.

1987a   "The Eye Is the Lamp of the Body (Matthew 6:22–23 = Luke 11:34–36)." *New Testament Studies* 33:61–83.

1987b   "Jesus and Moses (Mt 5:1–2)." *Expository Times* 98:203–5.

1987c   "The Structure of the Sermon on the Mount." *Journal of Biblical Literature* 106:423–45.

1988a   "Matthew 10:26–31 and the Problem of Evil." *St. Vladimir's Theological Quarterly* 32:293–308.

1988b   "Two Notes on a Key Text: Matthew 11:25–30." *Journal of Theological Studies* 39:477–85.

1989   "Who Will Come from East and West? Observations on Matt 8:11–12 = Luke 13:28–29." *Irish Biblical Studies* 11:158–70.

1990   "The Hairs of Your Head Are Numbered." *Expository Times* 101:334–36.

1992a   "The Baptism of Jesus and a New Dead Sea Scroll." *Biblical Archaeology Review* 18/2:58–60.

1992b   "Matthew: Structure, Biographical Impulse, and the *Imitatio Christi.*" Pp. 1203–21 in *The Four Gospels, 1992: Festschrift Frans Neirynck.* Edited by F. van Segbroeck et al. Louvain: Louvain University Press.

1992c   "Peter and Cephas: One and the Same." *Journal of Biblical Literature* 111:489–95.

1993a   "Divorce, Celibacy, and Joseph (Matthew 1:18–25 and 19:1–12)." *Journal for the Study of the New Testament* 49:3–10.

1993b   *The New Moses: A Matthean Typology.* Minneapolis: Fortress.

1993c   "What Was the Star That Guided the Magi?" *Bible Review* 9:20–24, 63.

1999   *The Sermon on the Mount: Inspiring the Moral Imagination.* New York: Crossroad.

2005a   *Resurrecting Jesus: The Earliest Christian Tradition and Its Interpreters.* Edinburgh: T&T Clark.

2005b   *Studies in Matthew.* Grand Rapids: Baker Academic.

Alter, R.

1981   *The Art of Biblical Narrative.* New York: Basic Books.

Amaru, B.

1983   "The Killing of the Prophets: Unraveling a Midrash." *Hebrew Union College Annual* 54:153–80.

Anderson, E. E.

1909   *The Gospel according to Matthew.* Edinburgh: T&T Clark.

Anderson, J. C.

1994   *Matthew's Narrative Web: Over, Over, and Over Again.* Journal for the Study of the New Testament: Supplement Series 91. Sheffield: JSOT.

Anderson, J. G.

1980   "Leprosy in Translations of the Bible." *Bible Translator* 31:107–12.

Anno, Y.

1984   "The Mission to Israel in Matthew: The Intention of Matthew 10:5b–6 Considered in Light of the Religio-Political Background." PhD diss., University of Chicago.

Archbald, P.

1987   "Interpretation of the Parable of the Dragnet (Matthew 13:47–50)." *Vox reformata* 48:3–14.

Argyle, A. W.

1963   *The Gospel according to Matthew.* Cambridge Bible Commentary. Cambridge: Cambridge University Press.

1975   "Wedding Customs at the Time of Jesus." *Expository Times* 86:214–15.

Arnott, A.

1984   "'The First Day of Unleavened . . .': Mt 26.17, Mk 14.12, Lk 22.7." *Bible Translator* 35:235–38.

Augsburger, M. S.

1982   *Matthew.* Communicator's Commentary Series. Waco: Word.

Aune, D. E.
1983   *Prophecy in Early Christianity and the Ancient Mediterranean World.* Grand Rapids: Eerdmans.

Aune, D. E. (ed.)
1972   *Studies in New Testament and Early Christian Literature: Essays in Honor of Allen P. Wikgren.* Leiden: Brill.
2001   *The Gospel of Matthew in Current Study: Studies in Memory of William G. Thompson, SJ.* Grand Rapids: Eerdmans.

Aurelius, E.
2001   "Gottesvolk und Aussenseiter: Eine geheime Beziehung Lukas-Matthäus." *New Testament Studies* 47:428–41.

Aus, R.
1988   *Water into Wine and the Beheading of John the Baptist: Early Jewish-Christian Interpretation of Esther in John 2:1–11 and Mark 6:17–29.* Atlanta: Scholars.
2000   *The Stilling of the Storm: Studies in Early Palestinian Judaic Traditions.* Binghamton, NY: Global.

Aveni, A. F.
1998   "The Star of Bethlehem." *Archaeology* 51:34–38.

Bacchiocchi, S.
1984   "Matthew 11:28–30: Jesus's Rest and the Sabbath." *Andrews University Seminary Studies* 22:289–316.

Bacon, B. W.
1918   "The 'Five Books' of Matthew against the Jews." *Expositor* 15:56–66.
1928   "Jesus and the Law: A Study of the First 'Book' of Matthew (Mt. 3–7)." *Journal of Biblical Literature* 47:203–31.
1930   *Studies in Matthew.* New York: Holt.

Badia, L. F.
1980   *The Qumran Baptism and John the Baptist's Baptism.* Lanham, MD: University Press of America.

Bahr, G.
1965   "The Use of the Lord's Prayer in the Primitive Church." *Journal of Biblical Literature* 84:153–59.
1970   "The Seder of Passover and the Eucharistic Words." *Novum Testamentum* 12:181–202.

Bailey, K. E.
1976   *Poet and Peasant: A Literary-Cultural Approach to the Parables in Luke.* Grand Rapids: Eerdmans.

Bailey, M. L.
1998a   "The Parable of the Mustard Seed." *Bibliotheca sacra* 155:449–59.
1998b   "The Parable of the Sower and the Soils." *Bibliotheca sacra* 155:172–88.
1998c   "The Parable of the Tares." *Bibliotheca sacra* 155:266–79.
1999a   "The Doctrine of the Kingdom in Matthew 13." *Bibliotheca sacra* 156:443–51.
1999b   "The Parables of the Dragnet and of the Householder." *Bibliotheca sacra* 156:282–96.
1999c   "The Parables of the Hidden Treasure and of the Pearl Merchant." *Bibliotheca sacra* 156:175–89.
1999d   "The Parable of the Leavening Process." *Bibliotheca sacra* 156:61–71.

Balch, D. (ed.)
1991   *The Social History of the Matthean Community.* Minneapolis: Fortress.

Balla, P.
2005   *The Child-Parent Relationship in the New Testament and Its Environment.* Peabody, MA: Hendrickson.

Ballard, P.
1972   "Reasons for Refusing the Great Supper." *Journal for Theological Studies* 23:341–50.

Bammel, E.
1961   "Matthäus 10,23." *Studia theologica* 15:79–92.
1971   "The Baptist in Early Christian Thought." *New Testament Studies* 18:95–128.

Bammel, E., and C. F. D. Moule (eds.)
1984   *Jesus and the Politics of His Day.* Cambridge: Cambridge University Press.

Bammel, E., et al. (eds.)
1970   *The Trial of Jesus.* London: SCM.
1978   *Donum gentilicium.* Oxford: Clarendon.

Bandstra, A. J.
1981   "The Original Form of the Lord's Prayer." *Calvin Theological Journal* 16:15–37.
1982   "The Lord's Prayer and Textual Criticism: A Response." *Calvin Theological Journal* 17:88–97.

Banks, R.
1973   "Jesus and Custom." *Expository Times* 84:264–69.
1974   "Matthew's Understanding of the Law: Authenticity and Interpretation

in Matthew." *Journal of Biblical Literature* 93:226–42.

1975   *Jesus and the Law in the Synoptic Tradition*. Society for New Testament Studies Monograph Series 28. Cambridge: Cambridge University Press.

Barclay, W.
1975   *The Gospel of Matthew*. Rev. ed. 2 vols. Daily Study Bible. Philadelphia: Westminster.

Barkay. G.
1986   "The Garden Tomb: Was Jesus Buried There?" *Biblical Archaeology Review* 12/2:40–53, 56–57.

Barnes, A.
1868   *Matthew and Mark*. Vol. 1 of *Notes on the New Testament*. Rev. ed. London: Blackie.

Barnett, P.
1977   "Who Were the *Biastai* (Mt 11:12–13)?" *Reformed Theological Review* 36:65–70.

Barr, D. L.
1976   "The Drama of Matthew's Gospel: A Reconsideration of Its Structure and Purpose." *Theology Digest* 24:349–59.

Barr, J.
1988   "'Abba' Isn't 'Daddy.'" *Journal of Theological Studies* 39:28–47.

Barrett, C. K.
1972   *New Testament Essays*. London: SPCK.

Barrick, W. B.
1977   "The Rich Man from Arimathea (Matt 27:57–60) and 1QIsaᵃ." *Journal of Biblical Literature* 96:235–39.

Barta, K. A.
1979   "Mission and Discipleship in Matthew: A Redaction-Critical Study of Mt 10,34." PhD diss., Marquette University.

1988   "Mission in Matthew: The Second Discourse as Narrative." In *Society of Biblical Literature 1988 Seminar Papers*. Atlanta: Scholars.

Bartnicki, R.
1976   "Das Zitat von Zach 9:9–10 und die Tiere im Bericht vom Matthäus über dem Einzug Jesu in Jerusalem (Mt 21:1–11)." *Novum Testamentum* 18:161–66.

1987   "Das Trostwort an die Jünger in Mt 10,23." *Theologische Zeitschrift* 43:311–19.

Barton, S. C.
1994   *Discipleship and Family Ties in Mark and Matthew*. Cambridge: Cambridge University Press.

Basser, H.
1985   "Derrett's 'Binding' Reopened." *Journal of Biblical Literature* 104:297–300.

Batey, R.
1971   *New Testament Nuptial Imagery*. Leiden: Brill.

1984   "Jesus and the Theatre." *New Testament Studies* 30:563–74.

Bauckham, R.
1995   "The Messianic Interpretation of Isa. 10:34 in the Dead Sea Scrolls, 2 Baruch, and the Preaching of John the Baptist." *Dead Sea Discoveries* 2:202–16.

1996   "The Parable of the Royal Wedding Feast (Matthew 22:1–14) and the Parable of the Lame Man and the Blind Man (*Apocryphon of Ezekiel*)." *Journal of Biblical Literature* 115:471–88.

1998   *God Crucified*. Grand Rapids: Eerdmans.

2002   *Gospel Women: Studies of the Named Women in the Gospels*. Grand Rapids: Eerdmans.

Bauckham, R. (ed.)
1998   *The Gospels for All Christians: Rethinking the Gospel Audiences*. Grand Rapids: Eerdmans.

Baudoz, J.-F.
2001   "Les tentations de Jésus." *Christus* 48:37–44.

Bauer, D. R.
1988   *The Structure of Matthew's Gospel*. Journal for the Study of the New Testament: Supplement Series 31. Sheffield: Almond.

1992   "The Major Characters of Matthew's Story." *Interpretation* 46:357–67.

Bauer, D. R., and M. A. Powell (eds.)
1996   *Treasures New and Old: Recent Contributions to Matthean Studies*. Society of Biblical Literature Symposium Series 1. Atlanta: Scholars.

Baum, A. D.
2001   "Ein aramäischer Urmatthäus im kleinasiatischen Gottesdienst: Das Papiaszeugnis zur Entstehung des Matthäusevangeliums." *Zeitschrift für die neutestamentliche Wissenschaft* 92:257–72.

Baum, G.
1965   *Is the New Testament Anti-Semitic?*
2nd ed. Glen Rock, NJ: Paulist Press.

Bauman, C.
1985   *The Sermon on the Mount: The
Modern Quest for Its Meaning.*
Macon, GA: Mercer University Press.

Baumgardt, D.
1991   "Kaddish and the Lord's Prayer."
Jewish Biblical Quarterly 19:164–69.

Baumgarten, A.
1983   "The Name of the Pharisees." *Journal
of Biblical Literature* 102:411–28.
1984   "*Korban* and the Pharisaic
Paradosis." *Journal of the Ancient
Near Eastern Society* 16:5–17.
1987   "The Pharisaic *Paradosis.*" *Harvard
Theological Review* 80:63–77.

Baumgarten, J.
1976   "The Doudecimal Courts of Qumran,
Revelation, and the Sanhedrin."
Journal of Biblical Literature
95:59–78.

Baxter, W. S.
1999   "Mosaic Imagery in the Gospel of
Matthew." *Trinity Journal* 20:69–83.
2004   "The Narrative Setting of the Sermon
on the Mount." *Trinity Journal*
25:27–37.

BDAG   *A Greek-English Lexicon of the New
Testament and Other Early Christian
Literature.* By W. Bauer, F. W. Danker,
W. F. Arndt, and F. W. Gingrich. 3rd
ed. Chicago: University of Chicago
Press, 2000.

BDB   *A Hebrew and English Lexicon of the
Old Testament.* By F. Brown, S. R.
Driver, and C. A. Briggs. Oxford:
Clarendon, 1907.

BDF   *A Greek Grammar of the New
Testament and Other Early Christian
Liteature.* By F. Blass and A.
Debrunner. Translated and revised by
R. W. Funk. Chicago: University of
Chicago Press, 1961.

Beardslee, W.
1979   "Saving One's Life by Losing It."
*Journal of the American Academy of
Religion* 47:57–72.

Beare, F.
1970   "The Mission of the Disciples and
the Mission Charge: Matthew 10
and Parallels." *Journal of Biblical
Literature* 89:1–13.
1981   *The Gospel according to Matthew.*
New York: Harper & Row.

Beasley-Murray, G.
1962   *Baptism in the New Testament.* Grand
Rapids: Eerdmans.
1986   *Jesus and the Kingdom of God.* Grand
Rapids: Eerdmans.
1993   *Jesus and the Last Days.* Peabody,
MA: Hendrickson.

Beaton, R.
1999   "Messiah and Justice: A Key to
Matthew's Use of Isaiah 42:1–4?"
*Journal for the Study of the New
Testament* 75:5–23.
2002   *Isaiah's Christ in Matthew's Gospel.*
Society for New Testament Studies
Monograph Series 123. Cambridge:
Cambridge University Press.

Beck, J. R. , and C. L. Blomberg (eds.)
2001   *Two Views on Women in Ministry.*
Grand Rapids: Zondervan.

Beck, N. A.
1973   *Mature Christianity: The Recognition
and Repudiation of the Anti-Jewish
Polemic in the New Testament.*
Selinsgrove, PA: Susquehanna
University Press.

Becker, H.-J.
1990   *Auf der Kathedra des Mose:
Rabbinisch-theologisches Denken und
anti-rabbinische Polemik in Matthäus
23:1–12.* Berlin: Institut Kirche und
Judentum.

Becking, B.
1994   " 'A Voice Was Heard in Ramah':
Some Remarks on the Structure and
Meaning of Jeremiah 31,15–17."
Biblische Zeitschrift 38:229–42.

Beecher, W. J.
1975   *The Prophets and the Promise.* New
York: Crowell, 1905. Reprinted
Grand Rapids: Baker Academic.

Belkin, S.
1936   "Dissolution of Vows and the
Problem of Anti-social Oaths in
the Gospels and Contemporary
Literature." *Journal of Biblical
Literature* 55:227–34.
1970   "Levirate and Agnate Marriage in
Rabbinic and Cognate Literature."
Jewish Quarterly Review 60:275–329.

Bellinger, W. H., and W. R. Farmer (eds.)
1998   *Jesus and the Suffering Servant:
Isaiah 53 and Christian Origins.*
Valley Forge, PA: Trinity.

Bellinzoni, A. J.
1992   "The Gospel of Matthew in the
Second Century (with Responses)."
Second Century 9:197–275.

Bennett, T.
1987 "Matthew 7:6—a New Interpretation." *Westminster Theological Journal* 49:371–86.

Bennett, W.
1975 "The Son of Man Must . . ." *Novum Testamentum* 17:113–29.

Benoit, P.
1962 "Les outrages à Jésus prophète (Mc xiv 65 par.)." Pp. 92–110 in *Neotestamentica et Patristica: Eine Freundesgabe, Herrn Professor Dr. Oscar Cullmann zu seinem 60. Geburtstag überreicht.* Edited by W. C. van Unnik. Novum Testamentum Supplements 6. Leiden: Brill.

1972 *L'Évangile selon Saint Matthieu.* 4th ed. Paris: Cerf.

1973 *Jesus and the Gospel.* 2 vols. New York: Herder.

Berg, W.
1979 *Die Rezeption alttestamentlicher Motive im Neuen Testament dargestellt an den Seewandelerzählungen.* Freiburg i.B.: Hochschulverlag.

Berger, K.
1972 Die *Gesetzesauslegung Jesu: Ihr historischer Hintergrund im Judentum und im Alten Testament,* vol. 1: *Markus und Parallelen.* Neukirchen-Vluyn: Neukirchener Verlag.

1976 "Volksversammlung und Gemeinde Gottes." *Zeitschrift für Theologie und Kirche* 73:167–207.

1996 "Jesus als Nazoräer/Nasiräer." *Novum Testamentum* 38:323–35.

Bergmeier, R.
1998 "Und deinen Feind hassen." *Theologische Beiträge* 29:41–47.

Berkey, R.
1963 "ΕΓΓΙΖΕΙΝ, ΦΘΑΝΕΙΝ, and Realized Eschatology." *Journal of Biblical Literature* 82:177–87.

Berlin, A.
1983 *The Poetics of Biblical Narrative.* Sheffield: Almond.

Berner, U.
1985 *Die Bergpredigt: Rezeption und Auslegung im 20. Jahrhundert.* 3rd ed. Göttingen: Vandenhoeck & Ruprecht.

Best, E.
1970 "The Camel and the Needle's Eye (Mk 10:25)." *Expository Times* 82:83–89.

Best, E., and R. M. Wilson (eds.)
1979 *Text and Interpretation: Studies in the New Testament Presented to Matthew Black.* Cambridge: Cambridge University Press.

Best, T.
1981 "The Transfiguration: A Select Bibliography." *Journal of the Evangelical Theological Society* 24:157–61.

Betz, H. D.
1967 "The Logion of the Easy Yoke and of Rest (Mt 11,28–30)." *Journal of Biblical Literature* 86:10–24.

1985 *Essays on the Sermon on the Mount.* Translated by L. L. Welborn. Philadelphia: Fortress.

1995 *The Sermon on the Mount: A Commentary on the Sermon on the Mount, Including the Sermon on the Plain (Matthew 5:3–7:27 and Luke 6:20–49).* Edited by A. Y. Collins. Hermeneia. Minneapolis: Fortress.

Betz, O.
1964 "The Dichotomized Servant and the End of Judas Iscariot." *Revue de Qumran* 5:43–58.

Beyschlag, K.
1977 "Zur Geschichte der Bergpredigt in der alten Kirche." *Zeitschrift für Theologie und Kirche* 74:291–322.

Black, D. A.
1988 "Jesus on Anger: The Text of Matthew 5:22a Revisited." *Novum Testamentum* 30:1–8.

1989a "Conjectural Emendations in the Gospel of Matthew." *Novum Testamentum* 31:1–15.

1989b "Remarks on the Translation of Matthew 7:14." *Filologia neotestamentaria* 2:193–95.

Black, D. A., and D. R. Beck (eds.)
2001 *Rethinking the Synoptic Problem.* Grand Rapids: Baker Academic.

Black, M.
1967 *An Aramaic Approach to the Gospels and Acts.* 3rd ed. Oxford: Clarendon.

1969 "The 'Son of Man' Passion Sayings in the Gospel Tradition." *Zeitschrift für die neutestamentliche Wissenschaft* 60:1–8.

1989 "The Use of Rhetorical Terminology in Papias on Mark and Matthew." *Journal for the Study of the New Testament* 37:31–41.

Black, S.
2002   Sentence Conjunctions in the Gospel
        of Matthew. Sheffield: JSOT.
Blair, E. P.
1960   Jesus in the Gospel of Matthew. New
        York: Abingdon.
Blaising, C.
1979   "Gethsemane: A Prayer of Faith."
        Journal of the Evangelical Theological
        Society 22:333–43.
Blaising, C., and D. L. Bock
1993   Progressive Dispensationalism.
        Wheaton, IL: BridgePoint.
Blaising, C., and D. L. Bock (eds.)
1992   Dispensationalism, Israel, and the
        Church: The Search for Definition.
        Grand Rapids: Zondervan.
Blank, S.
1937–38 "The Death of Zechariah in Rabbinic
        Literature." Hebrew Union College
        Annual 12–13:327–46.
Blinzler, J.
1967   Die Brüder und Schwestern Jesu.
        Stuttgart: Katholisches Bibelwerk.
Blinzler, J., O. Kuss, and F. Mussner (eds.)
1963   Neutestamentliche Aufsätze:
        Festschrift für Prof. Josef Schmid zum
        70. Geburtstag. Regensburg: Pustet.
Blomberg, C. L.
1986   "The Legitimacy and Limits of
        Harmonization." Pp. 139–74 in
        Hermeneutics, Authority, and
        Canon. Edited by D. A. Carson and
        J. D. Woodbridge. Grand Rapids:
        Zondervan.
1987a   "Elijah, Election, and the Use of
        Malachi in the New Testament."
        Criswell Theological Review 2:100–
        108.
1987b   The Historical Reliability of the
        Gospels. Leicester, UK: Inter-Varsity.
1990a   Interpreting the Parables. Downers
        Grove, IL: InterVarsity.
1990b   "Marriage, Divorce, Remarriage, and
        Celibacy." Trinity Journal 11:161–96.
1991   "The Liberation of Illegitimacy:
        Women and Rulers in Matthew 1–2."
        Biblical Theology Bulletin 21:145–50.
1992a   Matthew. New American
        Commentary. Nashville: Broadman.
1992b   "On Wealth and Worry: Matt 6:19–
        34—Meaning and Significance."
        Criswell Theological Review 6:73–89.
2002   "Interpreting Old Testament
        Prophetic Literature in Matthew:
        Double Fulfillment." Trinity Journal
        23:17–33.

Blount, B.
1993   "A Socio-Rhetorical Analysis of
        Simon of Cyrene." Semeia 64:171–97.
Boa, K., and W. Proctor
1985   The Star of Bethlehem. Grand Rapids:
        Zondervan.
Böcher, O.
1968   "Wölfe in Schafspelzen: Zum
        religionsgeschichtlichen Hintergrund
        von Mt 7,15." Theologische Zeitschrift
        24:405–26.
Bock, D. L.
1994   Luke 1:1–9:50. Baker Exegetical
        Commentary on the New Testament.
        Grand Rapids: Baker Academic.
1996   Luke 9:51–24:53. Baker Exegetical
        Commentary on the New Testament.
        Grand Rapids: Baker Academic.
Bockmuehl, M.
1989   "Matthew 5:32; 19:9 in the Light
        of Pre-rabbinic Halakhah." New
        Testament Studies 35:291–95.
1998   "'Let the Dead Bury Their Dead'
        (Matt 8:22/Luke 9:60): Jesus and the
        Halakhah." Journal of Theological
        Studies 49:553–81.
Boer, M. C. de
1988   "Ten Thousand Talents? Matthew's
        Interpretation and Redaction of the
        Parable of the Unforgiving Servant
        (Matt 18:23–35)." Catholic Biblical
        Quarterly 50:214–32.
Boismard, M.-É.
1995   "'Notre pain quotidien' (Mt 6,11)."
        Revue biblique 102:371–78.
Bokser, B.
1987   "Was the Lord's Supper a Passover
        Seder?" Biblical Research 3/2:24–33.
Bonnard, P.
1970   L'Évangile selon Saint Matthieu.
        2nd ed. Commentaire du Noveau
        Testament 1. Neuchâtel: Delachaux &
        Niestlé.
1980   Anamnesis: Recherches sur le
        Nouveau Testament. Geneva: Revue
        de Théologie et de Philosophie.
Boobyer, G.
1942   St. Mark and the Transfiguration
        Story. Edinburgh: T&T Clark.
Booth, R.
1986   Jesus and the Laws of Purity.
        Sheffield: JSOT.
Borchert, G. L.
1992   "Matthew 5:48—Perfection and
        the Sermon." Review and Expositor
        89:265–69.

Boring, M. E.
1976   "The Unforgivable Sin Logion."
        Novum Testamentum 18:258–79.
1991   *The Continuing Voice of Jesus:
        Christian Prophecy and the Gospel
        Tradition.* Louisville: Westminster/
        John Knox.
1995   "The Gospel of Matthew." Vol. 8 / pp.
        89–505 in *The New Interpreter's Bible.*
        Edited by L. E. Keck et al. Nashville:
        Abingdon.
Boring, M. E., K. Berger, and C. Colpe (eds.)
1995   *Hellenistic Commentary to the New
        Testament.* Nashville: Abingdon.
Borland, J. A.
1982   "Re-examining New Testament
        Textual-Critical Principles and
        Practices Used to Negate Inerrancy."
        *Journal of the Evangelical Theological
        Society* 25:499–506.
Bornkamm, G.
1970   "The Authority to 'Bind' and 'Loose'
        in the Church in Matthew's Gospel."
        Perspective 11:37–50.
1977–78 "Der Aufbau der Bergpredigt." *New
        Testament Studies* 24:419–32.
Bornkamm, G., G. Barth, and H.-J. Held
1963   *Tradition and Interpretation in
        Matthew.* Philadelphia: Westminster.
Bourke, M. M.
1960   "The Literary Genus of Matthew
        1–2." *Catholic Biblical Quarterly*
        22:160–75.
Bowker, J.
1973   *Jesus and the Pharisees.* Cambridge:
        Cambridge University Press.
Box, G. H.
1922   *Matthew.* New Century Bible. New
        York: Frowde.
Boyer, J. L.
1981   "First Class Conditions: What Do
        They Mean." *Grace Theological
        Journal* 2:75–114.
Bradley, J., and R. Muller
1987   *Church, Word, and Spirit: Historical
        and Theological Essays in Honor of
        Geoffrey W. Bromiley.* Grand Rapids:
        Eerdmans.
Bradshaw, P. F.
1982   *Daily Prayer in the Early Church.*
        London: SPCK.
Brandenburger, E.
1980   *Das Recht des Weltenrichters:
        Untersuchung zu Matthäus 25,31–46.*
        Stuttgart: Katholisches Bibelwerk.

Brandon, S.
1951   *The Fall of Jerusalem and the
        Christian Church.* London: SPCK.
1968   *The Trial of Jesus of Nazareth.* New
        York: Stein & Day.
Brandscheidt, R.
1990   "Messias und Tempel: Die
        alttestamentlichen Zitate in Mt
        21,1–17." *Trierer theologische
        Zeitschrift* 99:36–48.
Brant, J.
1996   "Infelicitous Oaths in the Gospel of
        Matthew." *Journal for the Study of the
        New Testament* 63:3–20.
Bratcher, R.
1981   *A Translator's Guide to the Gospel of
        Matthew.* New York: United Bible
        Societies.
Braude, W.
1940   *Jewish Proselytizing in the First
        Five Centuries of the Common Era.*
        Providence: Brown University Press.
Braumann, G.
1961   "'Dem Himmelreich wird
        Gewalt angetan' (Mt 11,12 par)."
        *Zeitschrift für die neutestamentliche
        Wissenschaft* 52:104–9.
Braun, W.
1989   "Were the New Testament Herodians
        Essenes?" *Revue de Qumran*
        53:75–88.
Brennecke, H. C.
1997   "'Niemand kann zwei Herren dienen':
        Bemerkungen zur Auslegung von Mt
        6,24/Lk 16,13 in der alten Kirche."
        *Zeitschrift für die neutestamentliche
        Wissenschaft* 88:157–69.
Bridges, C. B.
2001   "The Evil Eye in the Sermon on the
        Mount." *Stone-Campbell Journal*
        4:69–79.
Broadus, J.
1886   *Commentary on the Gospel of
        Matthew.* American Commentary.
        Valley Forge, PA: American Baptist
        Publication Society.
Brocke, M., et al. (eds.)
1974   *Das Vaterunser: Gemeinsames im
        Beten von Juden und Christen.*
        Freiburg i.B.: Herald.
Brodie, T.
1992   "Fish, Temple, Tithe, and Remission:
        The God-Based Generosity of
        Deuteronomy 14–15 as One
        Component of Matt 17:22–18:35."
        Revue biblique 99:697–718.

Broer, I.
1980   *Freiheit vom Gesetz und Radikalisierung des Gesetzes: Ein Beitrag zur Theologie des Evangelisten Matthäus.* Stuttgart: Katholisches Bibelwerk.
1986   *Die Seligspreisungen der Bergpredigt.* Bonn: Hanstein.
1993a   "Die Antithesen der Bergpredigt: Ihre Bedeutung und Funktion für die Gemeinde des Matthäus." *Bibel und Kirche* 48:128–33.
1993b   "Redaktionsgeschichtliche Aspekte von Mt. 24:1–28." *Novum Testamentum* 35:209–33.
1993c   "Zur Wirkungsgeschichte des Talio-Verbots in der alten Kirche." *Biblische Notizen* 66:23–31.
1994   "Das Ius Talionis im Neuen Testament." *New Testament Studies* 40:1–21.
1996   "Antijudaism in Matthew's Gospel." *Theology Digest* 43:335–38.

Brooke, G. J.
1989   "The Wisdom of Matthew's Beatitudes (4QBeat and Mt. 5:3–12)." *Scripture Bulletin* 19:35–41.

Brooke, G. J., and F. García Martínez (eds.)
1994   *New Qumran Texts and Studies.* Leiden: Brill.

Brooks, J. A.
1992   "The Unity and Structure of the Sermon on the Mount." *Criswell Theological Review* 6:3–14.

Brooks, O.
1981   "Matthew 28:16–20 and the Design of the First Gospel." *Journal for the Study of the New Testament* 10:2–18.

Brooks, S.
1987   *Matthew's Community: The Evidence of His Special Sayings Material.* Journal for the Study of the New Testament: Supplement Series 16. Sheffield: Sheffield Academic Press.

Brown, C.
1987   "The Gates of Hell and the Church." Pp. 15–43 in *Church, Word, and Spirit: Historical and Theological Essays in Honor of Geoffrey W. Bromiley.* Edited by J. Bradley and R. Muller. Grand Rapids: Eerdmans.

Brown, E.
1998   "The Meaning of Perfection in Matthew." *Unitarian Universalist Christian* 53:24–30.

Brown, J. K.
2002   *The Disciples in Narrative Perspective: The Portrayal and Function of the Matthean Disciples.* Atlanta: Scholars.

Brown, R.
1965   *New Testament Essays.* Milwaukee: Bruce.
1968   *The Semitic Background of the Term "Mystery" in the New Testament.* Philadelphia: Fortress.
1982   "Jesus and the Child as a Model of Spirituality." *Irish Biblical Studies* 4:178–92.
1987   "The Annunciation to Joseph (Matthew 1:18–25)." *Worship* 61:482–92.
1993   *The Birth of the Messiah.* New York: Doubleday.
1994   *The Death of the Messiah.* New York: Doubleday.
1997   *An Introduction to the New Testament.* Garden City, NY: Doubleday.

Brown, R., K. P. Donfried, and J. Reumann (eds.)
1973   *Peter in the New Testament: A Collaborative Assessment by Protestant and Roman Catholic Scholars.* Minneapolis: Augsburg/New York: Paulist Press.
1978   *Mary in the New Testament: A Collaborative Assessment by Protestant and Roman Catholic Scholars.* Philadelphia: Fortress.

Brown, S.
1977   "The Two-Fold Representation of the Mission in Matthew's Gospel." *Studia theologica* 31:21–32.
1978   "The Mission to Israel in Matthew's Central Section." *Zeitschrift für die neutestamentliche Wissenschaft* 69:73–90.
1979   "The Matthean Apocalypse." *Journal for the Study of the New Testament* 4:2–27.
1980   "The Matthean Community and the Gentile Mission." *Novum Testamentum* 22:193–221.
1990   "Faith, the Poor, and the Gentiles: A Tradition-Historical Reflection on Matthew 25:31–46." *Toronto Journal of Theology* 6:171–81.

Bruce, A. B.
1957   "The Gospel according to Matthew." Vol. 1 / pp. 36–43, 61–340 in *The Expositor's Greek Testament.* Reprinted Grand Rapids: Eerdmans.

Bruce, F. F.
1961   "The Book of Zechariah and the
        Passion Narrative." *Bulletin of the
        John Rylands Library* 43:336–53.
1963–65 "Herod Antipas, Tetrarch of Galilee
        and Perea." *Annual of Leeds
        University Oriental Society* 5:6–23.
Bruggen, J. van
1982   "The Lord's Prayer and Textual
        Criticism." *Calvin Theological Journal*
        17:78–87.
Brunec, M.
1967   "De legatione Ioannis Baptistae (Mt
        11,2–24)." *Verbum Domini* 35:193–
        203, 262–70, 321–31.
Bruner, F. D.
1987   *The Christbook: Matthew 1–12.* Waco:
        Word.
1990   *The Churchbook: Matthew 13–28.*
        Waco: Word.
Bruns, J. E.
1961   "The Magi Episode in Matthew 2."
        Catholic Biblical Quarterly 23:51–54.
Buchanan, G.
1991   "Symbolic Money-Changers in the
        Temple?" *New Testament Studies*
        37:280–90.
1996   *The Gospel of Matthew.* 2 vols.
        Lewiston, NY: Mellen.
Buckley, T.
1991   *Seventy Times Seven: Sin, Judgment,
        and Forgiveness in Matthew.*
        Collegeville, MN: Liturgical Press.
Buetubela, B.
1994   "L'universalisme du salut de Mt
        2,1–12." *Revue africaine de théologie*
        18:149–59.
Burchard, C.
1993   "Zu Matthäus 8,5–13." *Zeitschrift für
        die neutestamentliche Wissenschaft*
        84:278–88.
Burger, C.
1970   *Jesus als Davidssohn: Eine
        traditionsgeschichtliche
        Untersuchung.* Göttingen:
        Vandenhoeck & Ruprecht.
1973   "Jesu Taten nach Matthäus 8 und 9."
        Zeitschrift für Theologie und Kirche
        70:272–87.
Burgess, J.
1976   *A History of the Exegesis of Matthew
        16:17–19 from 1781 to 1965.* Ann
        Arbor, MI: Edwards Brothers.
Burkill, T.
1967   "The Historical Development of
        the Story of the Syrophoenician

Woman." *Novum Testamentum*
        9:161–77.
Burnett, F.
1981   *The Testament of Jesus-Sophia:
        A Redaction-Critical Study of the
        Eschatological Discourse in Matthew.*
        Lanham, MD: University Press of
        America.
1983   "Palingenesia in Matt. 19:28:
        A Window on the Matthean
        Community." *Journal for the Study of
        the New Testament.* 17:60–72.
1992   "Exposing the Anti-Jewish Ideology
        of Matthew's Implied Author: The
        Characterization of God as Father."
        Semeia 59:155–92.
Burridge, R. A.
2004   *What Are the Gospels? A Comparison
        with Graeco-Roman Biography.* 2nd
        ed. Grand Rapids: Eerdmans.
Burrows, M.
1940   "Levirate Marriage in Israel." *Journal
        of Biblical Literature* 59:23–33.
Burton, E.
1898   *Syntax of the Moods and Tenses in
        New Testament.* 3rd ed. Edinburgh:
        T&T Clark.
Busse, U.
1996   "In Souveränität- anders Verarbeitete
        Gotteserfahrung in Mt 20,1–16."
        Biblische Zeitschrift 40:61–72.
Butler, B. C.
1951   *The Originality of St. Matthew:
        A Critique of the Two-Document
        Hypothesis.* Cambridge: Cambridge
        University Press.
Byargeon, R. W.
1998   "Echoes of Wisdom in the Lord's
        Prayer." *Journal of the Evangelical
        Theological Society* 41:353–65.
Byrskog, S.
1994   *Jesus the Only Teacher: Didactic
        Authority and Transmission in
        Ancient Israel, Ancient Judaism, and
        the Matthean Community.* Stockholm:
        Almqvist & Wiksell.
1997   "Matthew 5:17–18 in the
        Argumentation of the Context."
        Revue biblique 104:557–71.
2000   *Story as History—History as Story:
        The Gospel Tradition in the Context of
        Ancient Oral History.* Tübingen: Mohr
        Siebeck.
Cadbury, H.
1939   "The Meaning of John 20:23,
        Matthew 16:19, and Matthew

18:18." *Journal of Biblical Literature* 58:251–54.

CAH *Cambridge Ancient History*. Edited by S. A. Cook, F. E. Adcock, and M. P. Charlesworth. 12 vols. Cambridge: Cambridge University Press, 1923–39.

Cahill, L. S.
1987 "The Ethical Implications of the Sermon." *Interpretation* 41:144–56.

Calvin, J.
1960 *Institutes of the Christian Religion*. Edited by J. T. McNeill. Translated by F. L. Battles. 2 vols. Philadelphia: Westminster.
1972 *A Harmony of the Gospels Matthew, Mark, and Luke*. Edited by D. Torrance and T. Torrance. Translated by A. Morrison. 3 vols. Grand Rapids: Eerdmans.

Cameron, P.
1984 *Violence and the Kingdom: The Interpretation of Matthew 11:12*. Frankfurt a.M.: Lang.

Campbell, J.
1948 "The Origin and Meaning of the Christian Use of the Word *Ekklesia*." *Journal of Theological Studies* 49:130–42.

Campbell, K.
1978 "The New Jerusalem in Matthew 5:14." *Scottish Journal of Theology* 31:335–63.

Campbell, K. M.
2005 "What Was Jesus's Occupation?" *Journal of the Evangelical Theological Society* 48:501–19.

Campbell, R. A.
1996 "Jesus and His Baptism." *Tyndale Bulletin* 47:191–214.

Cantwell, L.
1982 "The Parentage of Jesus: Matt. 1:18–21." *Novum Testamentum* 24:304–15.

Capes, D. B.
1999 "Intertextual Echoes in the Matthean Baptismal Narrative." *Bulletin of Biblical Research* 9:37–49.

Capshaw, J.
2004 *A Textlinguistic Analysis of Selected Old Testament Texts in Matthew 1–4*. New York: Lang.

Caragounis, C.
1986 *The Son of Man*. Wissenschaftliche Untersuchungen zum Neuen Testament 38. Tübingen: Mohr.

1989 *Peter and the Rock*. Beihefte zur Zeitschrift für die neutestamentliche Wissenschaft 58. Berlin: de Gruyter.

Cargal, T.
1991 "'His Blood Be upon Us and upon Our Children': A Matthean Double Entendre?" *New Testament Studies* 37:101–12.

Carlisle, C.
1985 "Jesus's Walking on Water: A Note on Matthew 14:22–33." *New Testament Studies* 31:151–55.

Carlston, C. E.
1968 "The Things That Defile (Mark 7:15) and the Law in Matthew and Mark." *New Testament Studies* 15:75–96.
1981 "Parable and Allegory Revisited: An Interpretive Review." *Catholic Biblical Quarterly* 43:228–42.
1985 "Recent American Interpretations of the Sermon on the Mount." *Bangalore Theological Forum* 17:9–22.

Carmichael, D.
1991 "David Daube on the Eucharist and Passover Seder." *Journal for the Study of the New Testament* 42:45–67.

Carmignac, J.
1969 *Recherches sur le "Notre Père."* Paris: Letourzey & Ané.

Carré, P.-M.
2000 "La tentation de Jésus au désert en Matthieu et Luc." *Esprit et vie* 110/21:9–13.

Carroll, K.
1963 "Thou Art Peter." *Novum Testamentum* 6:268–76.

Carson, D. A.
1978 *The Sermon on the Mount*. Grand Rapids: Baker Academic.
1982 "The Jewish Leaders in Matthew's Gospel: A Reappraisal." *Journal of the Evangelical Theological Society* 25:161–74.
1984 "Matthew." Vol. 8. / pp. 1–599 in *The Expositor's Bible Commentary*. Edited by F. E. Gaebelein. Grand Rapids: Zondervan.
1985 "The Ὅμοιος Word-Group as Introduction to Some Matthean Parables." *New Testament Studies* 31:277–82.
1987 *When Jesus Confronts the World*. Grand Rapids: Baker Academic.
1998 *The Inclusive-Language Debate*. Grand Rapids: Baker Academic.

Carson, D. A. (ed.)
1992   *Right with God: Justification in the Bible and the World.* Carlisle, UK: Paternoster/Grand Rapids: Baker Academic.

Carson, D. A., and D. J. Moo
2005   *An Introduction to the New Testament.* Grand Rapids: Zondervan.

Carson, D. A., et al. (eds.)
2001   *Justification and Variegated Nomism,* vol. 1: *The Complexities of Second Temple Judaism.* Grand Rapids: Baker Academic.

Carter, W.
1993   "The Crowds in Matthew's Gospel." *Catholic Biblical Quarterly* 55:54–67.
1994a   *Households and Discipleship: A Study of Matthew 19–20.* Journal for the Study of the New Testament: Supplement Series 103. Sheffield: JSOT.
1994b   *What Are They Saying about Matthew's Sermon on the Mount?* Mahwah, NJ: Paulist Press.
1996   *Matthew: Storyteller, Interpreter, Evangelist.* Peabody, MA: Hendrickson.
1997a   "Matthew 4:18–22 and Matthean Discipleship: An Audience-Oriented Perspective." *Catholic Biblical Quarterly* 59:58–75.
1997b   "Narrative/Literary Approaches to Matthean Theology: The 'Reign of the Heavens' as an Example (Matt. 4:17–5:12)." *Journal for the Study of the New Testament* 67:3–27.
1997c   "'Solomon in All His Glory': Intertextuality and Matthew 6.29." *Journal for the Study of the New Testament* 65:3–25.
2000a   "Evoking Isaiah: Matthean Soteriology and an Intertextual Reading of Isaiah 7–9 and Matthew 1:23 and 4:15–16." *Journal of Biblical Literature* 119:503–20.
2000b   "Matthew 23:37–39." *Interpretation* 54:66–68.

Carter, W., and J. Heil
1998   *Matthew's Parables: Audience-Oriented Perspectives.* Catholic Biblical Quarterly Monograph Series 30. Washington, DC: Catholic Biblical Association.

Casey, M.
1979   *Son of Man.* London: SPCK.
1987   "General, Generic, and Indefinite: The Use of the Term 'Son of Man' in Aramaic Sources and in the Teaching of Jesus." *Journal for the Study of the New Testament* 29:21–56.

Casey, P. M.
1988   "Culture and Historicity: The Plucking of Grain (Mark 2:23–28)." *New Testament Studies* 34:1–23.

Cassidy, R.
1979   "Matthew 17:24–27—a Word on Civil Taxes." *Catholic Biblical Quarterly* 41:571–80.

Catchpole, D. R.
1971a   "The Answer of Jesus to Caiaphas (Matt 26:64)." *New Testament Studies* 17:213–26.
1971b   *The Trial of Jesus: A Study in the Gospels and Jewish Historiography from 1770 to the Present Day.* Leiden: Brill.
1978   "John the Baptist, Jesus, and the Parable of the Tares." *Scottish Journal of Theology* 31:557–70.
1979   "The Poor on Earth and the Son of Man in Heaven: A Re-appraisal of Matthew 25:31–46." *Bulletin of the John Rylands Library* 61:355–97.
1981   "On Doing Violence to the Kingdom." *Irish Biblical Studies* 3:77–91.

Cave, C. H.
1963   "St. Matthew's Infancy Narrative." *New Testament Studies* 9:382–90.

Cerfaux, L.
1954–55   "Les sources scripturaires de Matth. xi.25–30." *Ephemerides theologicae lovanienses* 30:740–46; 31:331–42.

Charette, B.
1990   "A Harvest for the People? An Interpretation of Matthew 9:37f." *Journal for the Study of the New Testament* 38:29–35.
1992a   "To Proclaim Liberty to the Captives: Matthew 11:28–30 in the Light of Old Testament Prophetic Speculation." *New Testament Studies* 38:290–97.
1992b   *The Theme of Recompense in Matthew's Gospel.* Journal for the Study of the New Testament: Supplement Series 79. Sheffield: JSOT.
1996   "'Never Has Anything Like This Been Seen in Israel': The Spirit as Eschatological Sign in Matthew's Gospel." *Journal for Pentecostal Theology* 8:31–51.
2000   *Restoring Presence: The Spirit in Matthew's Gospel.* Sheffield: Sheffield Academic Press.

Charles, J. D.
1992 "The Greatest or the Least in the Kingdom? The Disciple's Relationship to the Law." *Trinity Journal* 13:139–62.

Charlesworth, J. H.
1992a "Jewish Prayers in the Time of Jesus." *Princeton Seminary Bulletin Supplement* 13:36–55.
2000 "The Qumran Beatitudes (4Q525) and the New Testament (Mt 5:3–11, Lk 6:20–26)." *Revue d'histoire et de philosophie religieuses* 80:13–25.

Charlesworth, J. H. (ed.)
1992b *The Lord's Prayer and Other Prayer Texts from the Greco-Roman Era.* Valley Forge, PA: Trinity.
2006 *Jesus and Archaeology.* Grand Rapids: Eerdmans.

Charlesworth, J. H., and L. L. Johns (eds.)
1997 *Hillel and Jesus.* Minneapolis: Fortress.

Chilton, B.
1979 *God in Strength: Jesus's Announcement of the Kingdom.* Freistadt, Austria: Plöchl.
1980 "The Transfiguration: Dominical Assurance and Apostolic Vision." *New Testament Studies* 27:115–24.
1984 *A Galilean Rabbi and His Bible.* Wilmington, DE: Glazier.

Chilton, B., and C. A. Evans (eds.)
1999a *Authenticating the Activities of Jesus.* Leiden: Brill.
1999b *Authenticating the Words of Jesus.* Leiden: Brill.

Christian, P.
1975 *Jesus und seine geringsten Brüder: Mt 25,31–46 redaktionsgeschichtlich Untersucht.* Leipzig: St. Benno.

Clark, K. W.
1947 "The Gentile Bias in Matthew." *Journal of Biblical Literature* 66:165–72.

Clark, R.
1963 "Eschatology and Matthew 10:23." *Restoration Quarterly* 7:73–81.

Clouse, B., and R. G. Clouse (eds.)
1989 *Women in Ministry: Four Views.* Downers Grove, IL: InterVarsity.

Cohen, S. D.
1983 "Conversion to Judaism in Historical Perspective: From Biblical Israel to Postbiblical Judaism." *Conservative Judaism* 36:31–45.

Cohn, H.
1977 *The Trial and Death of Jesus.* New York: Harper & Row, 1971. Reprinted New York: Ktav.

Cohn-Sherbok, D.
1979 "An Analysis of Jesus' Arguments concerning the Plucking of Grain on the Sabbath." *Journal for the Study of the New Testament* 2:31–41.
1981 "Jesus' Defense of the Resurrection of the Dead." *Journal for the Study of the New Testament* 11:64–73.

Collins, A. Y.
1987 "The Origin of the Designation of Jesus as 'Son of Man.'" *Harvard Theological Review* 80:391–407.

Collins, J. J.
1992 "The Son of Man in First Century Judaism." *New Testament Studies* 38:448–66.
1994 "The Works of the Messiah." *Dead Sea Discoveries* 1:98–112.

Comber, J.
1977 "The Composition and Literary Characteristics of Matt 11:20–24." *Catholic Biblical Quarterly* 39:497–504.

Combet-Galland, C.
1987 "La vigne et l'ecriture, histoire de reconaissances." *Études théologiques et religieuses* 62:489–502.

Combrink, H. J.
1977 "Structural Analysis of Mt 9:35–11:1." *Neotestamentica* 11:98–114.
1982 "The Macrostructure of the Gospel of Matthew." *Neotestamentica* 16:1–20.
1983 "The Structure of the Gospel of Matthew as Narrative." *Tyndale Bulletin* 34:61–90.

Comfort, P. W., and D. Barrett
2001 *The Text of the Earliest Greek New Testament Manuscripts.* Wheaton: Tyndale.

Conard, A.
1991 "The Fate of Judas: Matthew 27:3–10." *Toronto Journal of Theology* 7:158–68.

Cook, J.
1988 "The Sparrow's Fall in Matt 10:29b." *Zeitschrift für die neutestamentliche Wissenschaft* 79:138–44.

Cook, M. J.
1983a "Anti-Judaism in the New Testament." *Union Seminary Quarterly Review* 38:125–37.

1983b   "Interpreting 'Pro-Jewish' Passages in Matthew." *Hebrew Union College Annual* 54:135–46.

Copan, P., and R. K. Tacelli (eds.)
2000   *Jesus' Resurrection—Fact or Figment? A Debate between William Lane Craig and Gerd Lüdemann.* Downers Grove, IL: InterVarsity.

Cope, O. L.
1969   "Matthew 25:31–46: 'The Sheep and the Goats' Reinterpreted." *Novum Testamentum* 11:32–44.
1976a   "The Death of John the Baptist in the Gospel of Matthew." *Catholic Biblical Quarterly* 38:515–19.
1976b   *Matthew: A Scribe Trained for the Kingdom of Heaven.* Catholic Biblical Quarterly Monograph Series 5. Washington, DC: Catholic Biblical Association.

Coppens, J.
1981   *La relève apocalyptique du messianisme royale,* vol. 3: *Le fils d'homme néotestamentaire.* Louvain: Louvain University Press.
1983   *La relève apocalyptique du messainisme royale,* vol. 2: *Le fils d'homme vétéro- et intertestamentaire.* Louvain: Louvain University Press.

Coppens, J. (ed.)
1976   *La notion biblique de Dieu.* Gembloux: Duculot.

Cortes Fuentes, D.
2001   "'Not Like the Gentiles': The Characterization of Gentiles in the Gospel according to St. Matthew." *Journal of Hispanic/Latino Theology* 9:6–26.

Cotter, W.
1986   "'For It Was Not the Season for Figs.'" *Catholic Biblical Quarterly* 48:62–66.

Couroyer, B.
1970   "De la mesure dont vous mesurez il vous sera mesuré." *Revue biblique* 77:366–70.

Court, J.
1980   "Right and Left: The Implications for Matthew 25:31–46." *New Testament Studies* 31:223–33.

Cousland, J. R. C.
2002   *The Crowds in the Gospel of Matthew.* Leiden: Brill.

Cox, G. E. P.
1952   *The Gospel of St. Matthew.* Torch Bible Commentary. London: SCM.

Craghan, J. F.
1968   "The Gerasene Demoniac." *Catholic Biblical Quarterly* 30:522–36.

Craig, W. L.
1989   *Assessing the New Testament Evidence for the Historicity of the Resurrection of Jesus.* Toronto: Mellen.

Cranfield, C. E. B.
1962   "The Christian's Political Responsibility according to the New Testament." *Scottish Journal of Theology* 15:176–92.
1994   "Who Are Christ's Brothers (Matthew 25.40)?" *Metanoia* 4/1–2:31–39.

Cranford, L.
1992   "Bibliography for the Sermon on the Mount." *Southwestern Journal of Theology* 35:34–38.

Cremer, F.
1965   *Die Fastenansage Jesu.* Bonn: Hanstein.

Crosby, M. H.
1988   *House of Disciples: Church, Economics, and Justice in Matthew.* New York: Maryknoll, NY: Orbis.
2002   *The Prayer That Jesus Taught Us.* Maryknoll, NY: Orbis.

Cross, F. (ed.)
1968   *Studia Evangelica,* vol. 4: *Papers Presented to the Third International Congress on New Testament Studies Held at Christ Church, Oxford, 1965.* Berlin: Akademie.

Crossan, J.
1973   *In Parables: The Challenge of the Historical Jesus.* New York: Harper & Row.
1983   "Kingdom and Children: A Study in the Aphoristic Tradition." *Semeia* 29:75–95.

Crouzel, H.
1988   "Le sens de 'porneia' dans les incises matthéennes." *La nouvelle revue théologique* 110:903–10.

Culbertson, P.
1988   "Reclaiming the Matthean Vineyard Parables." *Encounter* 49:257–83.

Culliton, J. T. (ed.)
1982   *Non-violence, Central to Christan Spirituality.* Toronto: Mellen.

Cullmann, O.
1950   *Baptism in the New Testament.* London: SCM.
1962a   "Le douzieme apôtre." *Revue d'histoire et de philosophie religieuses* 42:133–40.

1962b   *Peter: Disciple, Apostle, Martyr.*
         Translated by F. Filson. 2nd ed.
         London: SCM.

Cunningham, S., and D. L. Bock
1987   "Is Matthew Midrash?" *Bibliotheca
        sacra* 144:157–80.

Cuvillier, É.
1996   "Chronique matthéenne (II):
        '. . . mais ce n'est pas encore la fin'
        (Mt 24/6b)." *Études théologiques et
        religieuses* 71:81–94.
1997   "Chronique matthéenne (III): '. . . que
        le lecteur comprenne' (Mt 24/15)."
        Études théologiques et religieuses
        72:101–13.
1998   "Chronique matthéenne (IV): 'Vous
        avez entendu qu'il a été dit . . .'
        (Mt 5/27a)." *Études théologiques et
        religieuses* 73:239–56.
1999a   "Chronique matthéenne (V):
        '. . . jusqu'a la fin du monde' (Mt
        28/20)." *Études théologiques et
        religieuses* 74:251–65.
1999b   "La visite des mages dans l'Évangile
        de Matthieu (Matthieu 2,1–12)." *Foi
        et vie* 98:73–85.
2001   "Chronique matthéenne (VI): 'L'un
        de ces plus petits de mes frères . . .'
        (Mt 25/40)." *Études théologiques et
        religieuses* 76:575–98.

Dahl, N. A.
1963   *Das Volk Gottes: Eine Untersuchung
        zum Kirchenbewusstsein des
        Urchristentums.* 2nd ed. Darmstadt:
        Wissenschaftliche Buchgesellschaft.
1976   "The Passion Narrative in Matthew."
        Pp. 37–51 in *Jesus in the Memory
        of the Early Church.* Minneapolis:
        Augsburg.

Dahlberg, B.
1975   "The Typological Use of Jeremiah
        1:4–19 in Matthew 16:13–23." *Journal
        of Biblical Literature* 94:73–80.

Dana, H. E., and J. R. Mantey
1955   *A Manual Grammar of the Greek New
        Testament.* Toronto: Macmillan.

D'Angelo, M.
1992   "'Abba' and 'Father': Imperial
        Theology and the Jesus Tradition."
        Journal of Biblical Literature
        111:611–30.

Daniel, C.
1969   "'Faux prophètes': Surnom des
        Esséniens dans le sermon sur la
        montagne." *Revue de Qumran*
        7:45–79.

Danker, F.
1990   "God with Us: Hellenistic
        Christological Perspectives in
        Matthew." *Currents in Theology and
        Mission* 19:433–39.

Daube, D.
1973   *The New Testament and Rabbinic
        Judaism.* London: University of
        London, Athlone, 1956. Reprinted
        New York: Arno.
1987   *Appeasement or Resistance, and Other
        Essays on New Testament Judaism.*
        Berkeley: University of California
        Press.

Davies, A. (ed.)
1979   *Anti-Semitism and the Foundation of
        Christianity.* New York: Paulist Press.

Davies, M.
1993   *Matthew.* Readings, a New Biblical
        Commentary. Sheffield: JSOT.

Davies, P. R., and R. T. White (eds.)
1990   *A Tribute to Geza Vermes: Essays on
        Jewish and Christian Literature and
        History.* Sheffield: JSOT.

Davies, R. E.
1970   "Christ in Our Place—the
        Contribution of the Prepositions."
        Tyndale Bulletin 21:71–91.

Davies, W. D.
1953   "'Knowledge' in the Dead Sea Scrolls
        and Matthew 11:25–30." *Harvard
        Theological Review* 46:113–39.
1962   *Christian Origins and Judaism.*
        Philadelphia: Westminster.
1964   *The Setting of the Sermon on the
        Mount.* Cambridge: Cambridge
        University Press.
1966   *The Sermon on the Mount.*
        Cambridge: Cambridge University
        Press.

Davies, W. D., and D. Allison Jr.
1988   *A Critical and Exegetical Commentary
        on the Gospel according to Saint
        Matthew,* vol. 1: *Introduction and
        Commentary on Matthew I–VII.*
        International Critical Commentary.
        Edinburgh: T&T Clark.
1991   *A Critical and Exegetical Commentary
        on the Gospel according to Saint
        Matthew,* vol. 2: *Commentary on
        Matthew VIII–XVIII.* International
        Critical Commentary. Edinburgh:
        T&T Clark.
1992   "Matt. 28:16–20: Texts behind
        the Text." *Revue d'histoire et de
        philosophie religieuses* 72:89–98.

1997   *A Critical and Exegetical Commentary on the Gospel according to Saint Matthew*, vol. 3: *Commentary on Matthew XIX–XXVIII*. International Critical Commentary. Edinburgh: T&T Clark.

Davis, C.
1973   "The Fulfillment of Creation: A Study of Matthew's Genealogy." *Journal of the American Academy of Religion* 41:520–35.

Davis, M.
2006   "Matthew 27:57–66." *Interpretation* 60:76–77.

Davison, J.
1985   "*Anomia* and the Question of an Antinomian Polemic in Matthew." *Journal of Biblical Literature* 104:617–35.

Dayton, W.
1945   "The Greek Perfect Tense in Relation to John 20:23, Matthew 16:19, and Matthew 18:18." ThD diss., Northern Baptist Theological Seminary.

Dehandschutter, B.
1979   "La parabole de la perle (Mt 13,45–46) et l'Évangile selon Thomas." *Ephemerides theologicae lovanienses* 55:243–65.

Deines, R., and M. Hengel
1995   "E. P. Sanders' 'Common Judaism,' Jesus, and the Pharisees: A Review Article." *Journal of Theological Studies* 46:1–70.

Delobel, J. (ed.)
1982   *Logia: Les paroles de Jésus*. Louvain: Louvain University Press.

Delorme, J. (ed.)
1989   *Les paraboles évangéliques*. Paris: Cerf.

Deming, W.
1990   "Mark 9.42–10.12, Matthew 5.27–32, and B. Nid. 13b: A First-Century Discussion of Male Sexuality." *New Testament Studies* 36:130–41.

Denaux, A., ed.
1992   *John and the Synoptics*. Louvain: Louvain University Press.

Derickson, G. W.
2006   "Matthew's Chiastic Structure and Its Dispensational Implications." *Bibliotheca Sacra* 163:423–37.

Dermience, A.
1982   "La pericope de la Cananéenne (Mt 15,21–28): Rédaction et théologie." *Ephemerides theologicae Lovanienses* 58:25–49.

1985   "Rédaction et théologie dans le premier évangile: Une perspective de l'exégèse matthéenne récente." *Revue théologique de Louvain* 16:47–64.

Derrett, J. D. M.
1965   "Herod's Oath and the Baptist's Head." *Biblische Zeitschrift* 9:49–59, 233–46.

1970a   "ΚΟΡΒΑΝ, Ο ΕΣΤΙΝ ΔΩΡΟΝ." *New Testament Studies* 16:364–68.

1970b   *Law in the New Testament*. London: Darton, Longman & Todd.

1971   "The Parable of the Two Sons." *Studia theologica* 25:109–16.

1973   "Fig Trees in the New Testament." *Heythrop Journal* 14:249–65.

1974   "Workers in the Vineyard: A Parable of Jesus." *Journal of Jewish Studies* 25:64–91.

1977   "The Zeal of the House and the Cleansing of the Temple." *Downside Review* 95:79–94.

1979a   "Contributions to the Study of the Gerasene Demoniac." *Journal for the Study of the New Testament* 3:2–17.

1979b   "Fresh Light on the Lost Sheep and the Lost Coin." *New Testament Studies* 26:36–60.

1979c   "'Where Two or Three Are Convened in My Name . . .': A Sad Misunderstanding." *Expository Times* 91:83–86.

1980   "Mt 23,8–10: A Midrash on Isa 54,13 and Jer 31,33–34." *Biblica* 62:372–86.

1981   "Why and How Jesus Walked on the Sea." *Novum Testamentum* 23:330–48.

1982   "The Merits of the Narrow Gate (Mt. 7:13–14; Lk. 13:24)." *Journal for the Study of the New Testament* 15:20–29.

1983a   "Binding and Loosing (Matt 16:19; 18:18; John 20:23)." *Journal of Biblical Literature* 102:12–17.

1983b   "The Reason for the Cock-Crowings." *New Testament Studies* 29:142–44.

1983c   "Why Jesus Blessed the Children (Mk 10:13–16)." *Novum Testamentum* 25:1–18.

1984   "Palingenesia (Matt 19:28)." *Journal for the Study of the New Testament* 20:50–58.

1986a   "A Camel through the Eye of a Needle." *New Testament Studies* 32:465–70.

1986b   "Receptacles and Tombs." *Zeitschrift für die neutestamentliche Wissenschaft* 77:255–66.

1988a   "Christ and Reproof (Matthew 7:1–5/ Luke 6:37–42)." *New Testament Studies* 34:271–81.

1988b   "Moving Mountains and Uprooting Trees (Mk 11:22; Mt 17:20, 21:21; Lk 17:6)." *Bibliotheca orientalis* 30:231–44.

1988c   "'Thou Art the Stone, and upon This Stone.'" *Downside Review* 106:276–85.

1997a   "Light on Sparrows and Hairs (Mt 10,29–31)." *Estudios bíblicos* 55:341–53.

1997b   "Shared Themes: The Virgin Birth (Matthew 1:18–2:12)." *Journal of Higher Criticism* 4:57–67.

1998   "Every 'Idle' Word That Men Speak (Mt 12, 36)." *Estudios bíblicos* 56:261–65.

1999   "Hating Father and Mother (Luke 14:26; Matthew 10:37)." *Downside Review* 117:251–72.

2000   "Modes of Renewal (Mk 2:21–22)." *Evangelical Quarterly* 72:3–12.

Desautels, L.
1986   "La mort de Judas (Mt. 27,3–10; Ac 1,15–26)." *Science et esprit* 38:221–39.

Deutsch, C.
1987   *Hidden Wisdom and the Easy Yoke: Wisdom, Torah, and Discipleship in Matthew.* Journal for the Study of the New Testament: Supplement Series 18. Sheffield: JSOT.

1990   "Wisdom in Matthew: Transformation of a Symbol." *Novum Testamentum* 32:13–47.

1992   "Christians and Jews in the First Century: The Gospel of Matthew." *Thought* 67:399–408.

Didier, M. (ed.)
1972   *L'Évangile selon Matthieu: Rédaction et théologie.* Bibliotheca ephemeridum theologicarum lovaniensium 29. Gembloux: Duculot.

Dietzfelbinger, C.
1989   "Das Gleichnis von den anvertrauten Geldern." *Berliner theologische Zeitschrift* 6:222–33.

Dillon, R. J.
1966   "Toward a Tradition-History of the Parables of the True Israel." *Biblica* 47:1–42.

1991   "Ravens, Lilies, and the Kingdom of God (Matt 6:25–33/Luke 12:22–31)." *Catholic Biblical Quarterly* 53:605–27.

Dobbeler, A. von
2000   "Die Restitution Israels und die Bekehrung der Heiden: Das Verhältnis von Mt 10,5b–6 und Mt 28,18–20 unter dem Aspekt der Komplementarität; Erwägungen zum Standort des Matthäusevangeliums." *Zeitschrift für die neutestamentliche Wissenschaft* 91:18–44.

2002   "Die Versammlung 'auf meinen Namen hin' (Mt 18:20) als Identitäts- und Differenzkriterium." *Novum Testamentum* 44:209–30.

Dodd, C. H.
1953   *New Testament Studies.* Manchester: Manchester University Press.

1961   *The Parables of the Kingdom.* Rev. ed. London: Nisbet.

Doeve, J.
1954   *Jewish Hermeneutics in the Synoptic Gospels and Acts.* Assen: Van Gorcum.

Donahue, J.
1971   "Tax Collectors and Sinners: An Attempt at Identification." *Catholic Biblical Quarterly* 33:39–61.

1974   "Recent Studies on the Origin of 'Son of Man' in the Gospels." *Catholic Biblical Quarterly* 48:484–98.

1986   "The 'Parable' of the Sheep and the Goats: A Challenge to Christian Ethics." *Theological Studies* 47:3–31.

Donaldson, J.
1972–73   "The Title Rabbi in the Gospels." *Jewish Quarterly Review* 63:287–91.

Donaldson, T.
1985   *Jesus on the Mountain: A Study in Matthean Theology.* Journal for the Study of the New Testament: Supplement Series 8. Sheffield: JSOT.

Donelson, L. R.
1988   "'Do Not Resist Evil' and the Question of Biblical Authority." *Horizons of Biblical Theology* 10:33–46.

Donfried, K.
1974   "The Allegory of the Ten Virgins (Matt. 25:1–13) as a Summary of Matthean Theology." *Journal of Biblical Literature* 93:415–28.

1975   "The Ten Virgins (Mt. 25:1–13)." *Theology Digest* 2:106–10.

Dormandy, R.
1989   "Hebrews 1.1–2 and the Parable of the Wicked Husbandmen." *Expository Times* 100:371–75.

Dorneich, M. (ed.)
1988   Vater-Unser Bibliographie. 2nd ed. Freiburg i.B.: Herder.

Doty, W.
1971   "An Interpretation: Parable of the Weeds and Wheat." Interpretation 25:185–93.

Doyle, B. R.
1984   "'Crowds' in Matthew: Text and Theology." Catholic Theological Review 6:28–33.
1994   "The Place of the Parable of the Labourers in the Vineyard in Matthew 20:1–16." Australian Biblical Review 42:39–58.
1996   "Positions of Leadership: Some Reflections from Matthew's Gospel." Pacifica 9:135–44.

Draisma, S. (ed.)
1989   Intertextuality in Biblical Writings: Essays in Honour of Bas van Iersel. Kampen: Kok.

Draper, J. A.
1993   "The Development of 'the Sign of the Son of Man' in the Jesus Tradition." New Testament Studies 39:1–21.
1999   "The Genesis and Narrative Thrust of the Paraenesis in the Sermon on the Mount." Journal for the Study of the New Testament 75:25–48.

Dschulnigg, P.
1989   "Gestalt und Funktion des Petrus im Matthäusevangelium." Studien zum Neuen Testament und seiner Umwelt 14:161–83.

Duff, P. B.
1992   "The March of the Divine Warrior and the Advent of the Greco-Roman King: Mark's Account of Jesus' Entry into Jerusalem." Journal of Biblical Literature 111:55–71.

Duke, P. D.
1985   Irony in the Fourth Gospel. Atlanta: John Knox.

Duling, D. C.
1978   "The Therapeutic Son of David: An Element in Matthew's Christological Apologetic." New Testament Studies 24:392–409.
1987   "Binding and Loosing: Matthew 16:19; Matthew 18:18; John 20:23." Forum 3/4:3–31.
1991   "'[Do Not Swear . . .] by Jerusalem Because It Is the City of the Great King' (Matthew 5:35)." Journal of Biblical Literature 110:291–309.

1992   "Matthew's Plurisignificant 'Son of David' in Social Science Perspective: Kinship, Kingship, Magic, and Miracle." Biblical Theology Bulletin 22:99–116.
1997   "'Egalitarian' Ideology, Leadership, and Factional Conflict within the Matthean Group." Biblical Theology Bulletin 27:124–37.
1999   "Matthew 18:15–17: Conflict, Confrontation, and Conflict Resolution in a 'Fictive Kinship' Association." Biblical Theology Bulletin 29:4–22.

Dumais, M.
1995a   Le sermon sur la montagne (Matthieu 5–7). Paris: Cerf.
1995b   Le sermon sur la montagne: État de la recherche, interprétation, bibliographie. Paris: Letouzey et Ané.
1998   "The Sermon on the Mount: An Unattainable Way of Life?" Chicago Studies 37:316–24.

Dungan, D. (ed.)
1990   The Interrelationships of the Gospels. Macon, GA: Mercer University Press.

Dungan, D., and D. Peabody
1996   Beyond the Q Impasse—Luke's Use of Matthew. Valley Forge, PA: Trinity.

Dunn, J. (ed.)
1991   The Parting of the Ways: Between Christianity and Judaism and Their Significance for the Character of Christianity. London: SCM.
1992   Jews and Christians: The Parting of the Ways, AD 70–135. Wissenschaftliche Untersuchungen zum Neuen Testament 66. Tübingen: Mohr Siebeck.

Duplacy, J.
1987   Études de critique textuelle du Noveau Testament. Louvain: Louvain University Press.

Du Plessis, J.
1987   "Pragmatic Meaning in Matthew 13:1–23." Neotestamentica 21:33–56.

Dupont, J.
1958   "Vous n'aurez pas achevé les villes d'Israel avant que le fils de l'homme ne vienne." Novum Testamentum 2:228–44.
1959   Mariage et divorce dans l'évangile: Matthieu 19,3–12 et parallèles. Abbaye de Saint-André: Desclee de Brouwer.
1960   "Le paralytique pardonné (Mt 9,1–8)." Nouvelle revue théologique 82:940–58.

1961 "L'ambassade de Jean Baptiste." *Nouvelle revue théologique* 83:805–21; 943–59.
1964 "Le logion des douze trônes." *Biblica* 45:355–92.
1967 "Le chapitre des paraboles." *Nouvelle revue théologique* 89:800–820.
1968a "La parabole de la brebis perdue." *Gregorianum* 49:265–87.
1968b "Les paraboles du trésor et de la perle." *New Testament Studies* 14:408–18.
1969–73 *Les Béatitudes*. 2nd ed. 3 vols. Paris: Gabalda.
1985a *Études sur les évangiles synoptiques*. Edited by F. Neirynck. 2 vols. Louvain: Peeters.
1985b *Les trois apocalypses synoptiques: Marc 13; Matthieu 24–25; Luc 21*. Paris: Cerf.
1989 *Jésus aux origines de la christologie*. 2nd ed. Louvain: Louvain University Press.

Durston, C.
1988 "Historical Interpretations of the Sermon on the Mount." *Scripture Bulletin* 18:42–49.

Eckstein, H.-J.
2001 "Die 'bessere Gerechtigkeit': Zur Ethik Jesu nach dem Matthäusevangelium." *Theologische Beiträge* 32:299–316.

Edin, M. H.
1998 "Learning What Righteousness Means: Hosea 6:6 and the Ethic of Mercy in Matthew's Gospel." *Word and World* 18:355–63.

Edwards, J. R.
1987 "The Use of *Proserchesthai* in the Gospel of Matthew." *Journal of Biblical Literature* 106:65–74.

Edwards, R. A.
1971 *The Sign of Jonah in the Theology of the Evangelists and Q*. London: SCM.
1985 *Matthew's Story of Jesus*. Philadelphia: Fortress.
1989 "Reading Matthew: The Gospel as Narrative." *Listening* 24:251–61.
1990 "Narrative Implications of Gar in Matthew." *Catholic Biblical Quarterly* 52:636–55.
1997 *Matthew's Narrative Portrait of Disciples: How the Text-Connoted Reader Is Informed*. Harrisburg, PA: Trinity.

Edwards, W. D., W. J. Gabel, and F. E.

Hosmer
1986 "On the Physical Death of Jesus Christ." *Journal of the American Medical Association* 255/11:1455–63.

Eigo, F. A., ed.
1995 *New Perspectives on the Beatitudes*. Villanova, PA: Villanova University Press.

Elbert, P.
1974 "The Perfect Tense in Matthew 16:19 and Three Charismata." *Journal of the Evangelical Theological Society* 17:149–55.

Elliott, J. H.
1992 "Matthew 20:1–15: A Parable of Invidious Comparisons and Evil Eye Accusations." *Biblical Theology Bulletin* 22:52–65.

Elliott, J. K.
1972 "Κηφᾶς: Σίμων Πέτρος: ὁ Πέτρος: An Examination of New Testament Usage." *Novum Testamentum* 14:241–56.
1999 "Six New Papyri of Matthew's Gospel." *Novum Testamentum* 41:105–7.

Elliott, J. K. (ed.)
1976 *Studies in New Testament Language and Text: Essays in Honour of George D. Kilpatrick on the Occasion of His Sixty-fifth Birthday*. Novum Testamentum Supplements 44. Leiden: Brill.

Elliott, M.
2000 *The Survivors of Israel*. Grand Rapids: Eerdmans.

Ellis, E. E.
1999 "The Synoptic Gospels and History." Pp. 49–57 in *Authenticating the Activities of Jesus*. Edited by B. Chilton and C. A. Evans. Leiden: Brill.

Ellis, E. E., and M. Wilcox (eds.)
1969 *Neotestamentica et semitica: Studies in Honour of Matthew Black*. Edinburgh: T&T Clark.

Ellis, P.
1974 *Matthew: His Mind and His Message*. Collegeville, MN: Liturgical Press.

Ellul, D.
1992 "Dérives autour d'un figuier: Matthieu 21:18–22." *Foi et vie* 91:69–76.

Eltester, W.
1962 "'Freund, wozu du gekommen bist' (Mt. xxvi 50)." Pp. 70–91 in *Neotestamentica et Patristica: Eine*

Freundesgabe, Herrn Professor
Dr. Oscar Cullmann zu seinem
60. Geburtstag überreicht. Edited
by W. C. van Unnik. Novum
Testamentum Supplements 6.
Leiden: Brill.

Eltester, W. (ed.)
1960   Judentum–Urchristentum–Kirche.
        Berlin: Töpelmann.

Emerton, J. A.
1962   "Binding and Loosing—Forgiving
        and Retaining." Journal of
        Theological Studies 13:325–31.

Engelbrecht, J.
1990   "The Language of the Gospel of
        Matthew." Neotestamentica 24:199–
        213.
1995   "Are All the Commentaries on
        Matthew Really Necessary? Religion
        and Theology 2:206–15.

Epp, E. J., and G. D. Fee (eds.)
1981   New Testament Textual Criticism: Its
        Significance for Exegesis; Essays in
        Honour of Bruce M. Metzger. Oxford:
        Clarendon.

Erickson, R. J.
1996   "Divine Injustice? Matthew's
        Narrative Strategy and the Slaughter
        of the Innocents (Matthew 2:13–23)."
        Journal for the Study of the New
        Testament 64:5–27.
2000   "Joseph and the Birth of Isaac in
        Matthew 1." Bulletin of Biblical
        Research 10:35–51.

Eskenazi, T. C., et al. (eds.)
1991   The Sabbath in Jewish and Christian
        Tradition. New York: Crossroad.

Evans, C. A.
1985   "On the Isaianic Background of the
        Sower Parable." Catholic Biblical
        Quarterly 47:464–68.
1989a   "Jesus's Action in the Temple:
        Cleansing or Portent of Destruction?"
        Catholic Biblical Quarterly 51:237–70.
1989b   "On the Vineyard Parables of Isaiah
        5 and Mark 12." Biblische Zeitschrift
        28:82–88.
1989c   To See and Not Perceive: Isaiah
        6:9–10 in Early Jewish and Christian
        Interpretation. Sheffield: JSOT.
1992   "Predictions of the Destruction
        of the Herodian Temple in the
        Pseudepigrapha, Qumran Scrolls,
        and Related Texts." Journal for the
        Study of Judaism 10:89–147.
1995   Jesus and His Contemporaries:
        Leiden: Brill.

1996   "Jesus' Parable of the Tenant Farmers
        in Light of Lease Agreements in
        Antiquity." Journal for the Study of
        the Pseudepigrapha 14:65–83.

Evans, C. A., and D. Hagner (eds.)
1993   The New Testament and Anti-
        Semitism. Minneapolis: Fortress.

Evans, C. A., and S. E. Porter (eds.)
2000   Dictionary of New Testament
        Background. Downers Grove, IL:
        InterVarsity.

Evans, C. A., and J. A. Sanders (eds.)
1997   Early Christian Interpretation of
        the Scriptures of Israel. Sheffield:
        Sheffield Academic Press.

Evans, C. A., and W. R. Stegner (eds.)
1994   The Gospels and the Scriptures of
        Israel. Sheffield: JSOT.

Evans, C. A., and W. F. Stinespring (eds.)
1987   Early Jewish and Christian Exegesis.
        Atlanta: Scholars.

Evans, C. F.
1963   The Lord's Prayer. London: SPCK.

Evans, O. E.
1957   "The Unforgivable Sin." Expository
        Times 68:240–44.

Faierstein, M.
1981   "Why Do the Scribes Say That Elijah
        Must Come First?" Journal of Biblical
        Literature 100:75–86.

Falk, Z.
1974   "Binding and Loosing." Journal of
        Jewish Studies 25:92–100.

Farmer, W. R.
1964   The Synoptic Problem. New York:
        Macmillan.
1976   "The Post-sectarian Character of
        Matthew and Its Post-war Setting
        in Antioch of Syria." Perspectives in
        Religious Studies 3:235–47.
1990   "The Passion Prediction Passages
        and the Synoptic Problem." New
        Testament Studies 36:558–70.

Farmer, W. R. (ed.)
1983   New Synoptic Studies. Macon, GA:
        Mercer University Press.
1999   Anti-Judaism and the Gospels. Valley
        Forge, PA: Trinity.

Farnell, F. D.
1999   "The Synoptic Gospels in the
        Ancient Church: The Testimony to
        the Priority of Matthew's Gospel."
        Master's Seminary Journal 10:53–86.

Fascher, E.
1954   "Theologische Beobachtungen zu
        δεῖ." Pp. 228–54 of Neutestamentliche
        Studien. Beihefte zur Zeitschrift für

die neutestamentliche Wissenschaft 21. Berlin: de Gruyter.

Fee, G., and D. Stuart
1993   *How to Read the Bible for All Its Worth.* 2nd. ed. Grand Rapids: Zondervan.

Feiler, P.
1983   "The Stilling of the Storm in Matthew: A Response to Günther Bornkamm." *Journal of the Evangelical Theological Society* 26:399–406.

Feld, H., and J. Nolte
1973   *Wort Gottes in der Zeit.* Düsseldorf: Patmos.

Feldman, L.
1987   "Is the New Testament Anti-Semitic?" *Humanities* 21:1–14.
2003   "Conversion to Judaism in Classical Antiquity." *Hebrew Union College Annual* 74:115–56.

Feldmeier, R.
1987   *Die Krisis des Gottessohnes: Die Gethsemaneerzählung als Schlüssel der Markuspassion.* Tübingen: Mohr.

Feneberg, R.
1988   "Abba-Vater: Eine notwendige Besinnung." *Kirche und Israel* 3:41–52.

Fenton, J. C.
1963   *The Gospel of St. Matthew.* Pelican New Testament Commentaries. New York: Penguin.
1980   "Matthew and the Divinity of Jesus: Three Questions concerning Matthew 1:20–23." Pp. 79–82 in *Studia Biblica 1978: Sixth International Congress on Biblical Studies, Oxford 3–7 April 1978,* vol. 2: *Papers on the Gospels.* Edited by E. A. Livingstone. Journal for the Study of the New Testament: Supplement Series 2. Sheffield: JSOT.

Ferguson, E.
1993   *Backgrounds of Early Christianity.* 2nd ed. Grand Rapids: Eerdmans.

Ferrari d'Occhieppo, K.
1994   *Der Stern von Bethlehem in astronomischer Sicht: Legende oder Tatsache?* 2nd ed. Giessen: Brunnen.

Feuillet, A.
1954   "L'ἐξουσία du fils de l'homme (d'apres Mc. 2.10–28 parr.)." *Recherches de science religieuse* 42:161–92.

1958   "Les perspectives propres à chaque évangéliste dans les récits de la transfiguration." *Biblica* 39:281–301.
1967   "Le logion sur la rançon." *Revue des sciences philosophiques et théologiques* 51:365–402.
1967–68   "Les trois grandes prophéties de la passion et de la résurrection des évangiles synoptiques."*Revue thomiste* 67:533–60; 68:41–74.
1975   "Les deux onctions fautes sur Jésus, et Marie-Madeleine." *Revue thomiste* 75:357–94.
1977   *L'agonie de Gethsémani.* Paris: Gabalda.
1990   "Le Sauveur messianique et sa mère dans les récits de l'enfance de saint Matthieu et de saint Luc." *Divinitas* 34:17–52.

Filson, F.
1960   *A Commentary on the Gospel according to St. Matthew.* Harper's New Testament Commentaries. New York: Harper.

Finkel, A., and L. Frizzell (eds.)
1981   *Standing before God.* New York: Ktav.

Finkelstein, L.
1938   *The Pharisees: The Sociological Background of Their Faith.* 2 vols. Philadelphia: Jewish Publication Society of America.

Finney, P.
1993   "The Rabbi and the Coin Portrait." *Journal of Biblical Literature* 112:629–44.

Fitzer, G.
1957   "Die Sünde wider den Heiligen Geist." *Theologische Zeitschrift* 13:161–82.

Fitzgerald, J. T.
1972   "The Temptation of Jesus: The Testing of the Messiah in Matthew." *Restoration Quarterly* 15:152–60.

Fitzmyer, J.
1959   "The Aramaic Qorban Inscription from Jebel Hallet et-Turi and Mk 7:11/Mt 15:5." *Journal of Biblical Literature* 78:60–65. Reprinted pp. 93–100 in *The Semitic Background of the New Testament.* Grand Rapids: Eerdmans, 1997.
1965   "Anti-Semitism and the Cry of 'All the People' (Mt 27:25)." *Theological Studies* 26:667–71.
1976   "The Matthean Divorce Texts and Some New Palestinian Evidence." *Theological Studies* 37:197–226.

1978   "Crucifixion in Ancient Palestine, Qumran Literature, and the New Testament." *Catholic Biblical Quarterly* 40:493–513.

1985   "More about Elijah Coming First." *Journal of Biblical Literature* 104:295–96.

1997   *The Semitic Background of the New Testament.* Grand Rapids: Eerdmans. This edition combines the previous works *Essays on the Semitic Background of the New Testament,* Missoula, MT: Scholars, 1974; and *A Wandering Aramean,* Missoula, MT: Scholars, 1979.

Fletcher, D.
1964   "Condemned to Die: The Logion on Cross-Bearing." *Interpretation* 18:156–64.

Flusser, D.
1960   "Blessed Are the Poor in Spirit. . . ." *Israel Exploration Journal* 10:1–13.

1961–62   "Matthew 17:24–7 and the Dead Sea Sect." *Tarbiz* 31:150–56.

1975   "Two Anti-Jewish Montages in Matthew." *Immanuel* 5:37–45.

1981   *Die rabbinischen Gleichnisse und der Gleichniserzähler Jesus,* vol. 1: *Das Wesen der Gleichnisse.* Bern: Lang.

1987   *Die Tora in der Bergpredigt: Entdeckungen im Neuen Testament,* vol. 1. Neukirchen: Neukirchener Verlag.

1990   *Das Christentum—ein jüdische Religion.* Munich: Kösel.

1992–93   "'It Is Said to the Elders': On the Interpretation of the So-Called Antitheses in the Sermon on the Mount." *Mishkan* 17–18:115–19.

Fokkelman, J. P.
1999   *Reading Biblical Narrative.* Louisville: Westminster.

Ford, D.
1979   *The Abomination of Desolation in Biblical Eschatology.* Washington, DC: University Press of America.

Fornberg, T.
1995   "The Figure of Peter in Matthew and in 2 Peter." *Indian Theological Studies* 32:237–49.

Fortna, R. T.
1990   "'You Have Made Them Equal to Us!' (Mt 20:1–16)." *Journal of Theology for South Africa* 72:66–72.

1992   "Reading Jesus's Parable of the Talents through Underclass Eyes:

Matt 25:14–30." *Foundations and Facets Forum* 8:211–28.

Fowler, H.
1968   *The Gospel of Matthew.* 4 vols. Bible Study Textbook Series. Joplin, MO: College Press.

Fowler, M.
2001   "City on a Hill: An Interpretation of Matth 5:14b/*GThom* 32." *Journal of Higher Criticism* 8:68–72.

Fowler, R.
1981   *Loaves and Fishes.* Chico, CA: Scholars.

Fox, G. G.
1942   "The Matthean Misrepresentation of Tephilin." *Journal of Near Eastern Studies* 1:373–77.

France, R. T.
1968   "The Servant of the Lord in the Teaching of Jesus." *Tyndale Bulletin* 19:26–52.

1979   "Herod and the Children of Bethlehem." *Novum Testamentum* 21:98–120.

1980–81   "The Formula Quotations of Matthew 2 and the Problem of Communication." *New Testament Studies* 27:233–51.

1982   *Jesus and the Old Testament.* Downers Grove, IL: InterVarsity, 1971. Reprinted Grand Rapids: Baker Academic.

1985   *The Gospel according to Matthew: An Introduction and Commentary.* Tyndale New Testament Commentaries. Leicester, UK: Inter-Varsity/Grand Rapids: Eerdmans.

1989   *Matthew: Evangelist and Teacher.* Grand Rapids: Zondervan.

1990   *Divine Government: God's Kingship in the Gospel of Mark.* London: SPCK.

France, R. T., and D. Wenham (eds.)
1980   *Studies of History and Tradition in the Four Gospels,* vol. 1. Sheffield: JSOT.

1981   *Studies of History and Tradition in the Four Gospels,* vol. 2. Sheffield: JSOT.

Frankemölle, H.
1996   "Johannes der Täufer und Jesus im Matthäusevangelium: Jesus als Nachfolger des Täufers." *New Testament Studies* 42:196–218.

Frankemölle, H., and K. Kertelge (eds.)
1989   *Vom Urchristentum zu Jesus.* Freiburg i.B.: Herder.

Freed, E. D.
1987   "The Women in Matthew's
        Genealogy." *Journal for the Study of
        the New Testament* 29:3–19.
2001   *The Stories of Jesus's Birth: A Critical
        Introduction*. Sheffield: Sheffield
        Academic Press.
Freyne, S.
1980   *Galilee from Alexander the Great to
        Hadrian*. Wilmington, DE: Glazier.
1985   "Vilifying the Other and Defining
        the Self: Matthew's and John's Anti-
        Jewish Polemic in Focus." Pp. 117–43
        in *"To See Ourselves as Others See
        Us": Christians, Jews, "Others" in Late
        Antiquity*. Edited by J. Neusner and
        E. S. Frerichs. Chico, CA: Scholars.
1988a   *Galilee, Jesus, and the Gospels:
        Literary Approaches and Historical
        Investigation*. Dublin: Gill &
        Macmillan.
1988b   "Oppression from the Jews:
        Matthew's Gospel as an Early
        Christian Response." *Concilium*
        200:47–53.
Frickenschmidt, D.
1997   *Evangelium als Biographie: Die
        vier Evangelien im Rahmen antiker
        Erzählkunst*. Tübingen: Francke.
Friedrich, J.
1977   *Gott im Bruder? Eine
        methodenkritische Untersuchung
        von Redaktion, Überlieferung und
        Traditionen in Mt 25,31–46*. Stuttgart:
        Calwer.
Frieling, R.
1969   *Die Verklärung auf dem Berge: Eine
        Studie zum Evangelienverständnis*.
        Stuttgart: Urachhaus.
Fuchs, A.
1990   "Offene Probleme der
        Synoptikerforschung: Zur Geschichte
        der Perikop Mk 2,1–12 par Mt
        9,1–8 par Lk 5,17–26." *Studien zum
        Neuen Testament und seiner Umwelt*
        15:73–99.
1994   "Die Sünde wider den Heiligen Geist:
        Mk 3,28–30 par Mt 12,31–37 par Lk
        12,10." *Studien zum Neuen Testament
        und seiner Umwelt* 19:113–30.
1999   "Die Übereinstimmungen der
        Perikope von der Taufe Jesu:
        Mk 1,9–11 par Mt 3,13–17 par
        Lk 3,21–22." *Studien zum Neuen
        Testament und seiner Umwelt*
        24:5–34.

Fuchs, J.
1991   "Die schwierige goldene Regel."
        Stimmen der Zeit 209:773–81.
Funk, R. W.
1959   "The Wilderness." *Journal of Biblical
        Literature* 78:205–14.
Furnish, V.
1972   *The Love Command in the New
        Testament*. Nashville: Abingdon.
Gaebelein, A. C.
1910   *The Gospel of Matthew*. Wheaton:
        Van Kampen.
Gaechter, P.
1963   *Die literarische Kunst im Matthäus-
        Evangelium*. Innsbruck: Tyrolia.
Gale, A. M.
2005   *Redefining Ancient Borders: The
        Jewish Scribal Framework of
        Matthew's Gospel*. Edinburgh: T&T
        Clark.
Gander, G.
1967   *L'évangile de l'église: Commentaire
        de l'Évangile selon Matthieu*. Aix-en-
        Provence: Faculté Libre de Théologie
        Protestante.
Gardner, R. B.
1991   *Matthew*. Believers Church
        Commentary. Scottdale, PA: Herald.
Garland, D.
1979   *The Intention of Matthew 23*. Studien
        zum Neuen Testament 52. Leiden:
        Brill.
1990   *One Hundred Years of Study on the
        Passion Narratives*. Macon, GA:
        Mercer University Press.
1992   "The Lord's Prayer in the Gospel
        of Matthew." *Review and Expositor*
        89:215–28.
1993   *Reading Matthew: A Literary and
        Theological Commentary on the First
        Gospel*. New York: Crossroad.
Garlington, D.
1995   "Oath-Taking in the Community of
        the New Age (Matthew 5:33–37)."
        Trinity Journal 16:139–70.
Gärtner, B.
1971   *Iscariot*. Philadelphia: Fortress.
Gaston, L.
1962   "Beelzeboul." *Theologische Zeitschrift*
        18:247–55.
1970   *No Stone on Another: Studies in the
        Significance of the Fall of Jerusalem*.
        Novum Testamentum Supplements
        23. Leiden: Brill.
Geist, H.
1986   *Menschensohn und Gemeinde: Eine
        redaktionskritische Untersuchung*

zur Menschensohnprädikation im Matthäusevangelium. Würzburg: Echter.

Genuyt, F.
1991 "Évangile de Matthieu 10,1–42: Le díscours apostolique." *Sémiotique et Bible* 64:3–14.
1993 "Matthieu, chapitre 12,1–21." *Sémiotique et Bible* 70:41–54.
1996 "Matthieu 18." *Sémiotique et Bible* 82:3–15.
1997 "Les Béatitudes selon saint Matthieu (5,3–12)." *Lumière et vie* 47:21–30.
1998 "'Notre-Père' selon saint Matthieu." *Lumière et vie* 48:27–37.

George, A.
1968 "Qui veut sauver sa vie la perdra; qui perd sa vie la sauvera." *Bible et vie chrétienne* 83:11–24.

Gerhardsson, B.
1966 *The Testing of God's Son*. Lund: Gleerup.
1968 "The Parable of the Sower and Its Interpretation." *New Testament Studies* 14:165–93.
1972–73 "The Seven Parables in Matthew 13." *New Testament Studies* 19:16–37.
1979 *The Mighty Acts of God according to Matthew*. Lund: Gleerup.
1981 "Confession and Denial before Men: Observations on Matt. 26:57–27:2." *Journal for the Study of the New Testament* 13:46–66.
1988 "The Narrative Meshalim in the Synoptic Gospels: A Comparison with the Narrative Meshalim in the Old Testament." *New Testament Studies* 34:339–63.
1991 "If We Do Not Cut the Parables out of Their Frames." *New Testatment Studies* 37:321–35.

Gero, S.
1976 "The Spirit as Dove at the Baptism of Jesus." *Novum Testamentum* 18:17–35.

Geyser, A.
1978 "Jesus, the Twelve, and the Twelve Tribes in Matthew." *Neotestamentica* 12:1–19.

Gibbs, J. A.
1987 "Parables of Atonement and Assurance: Matthew 13:44–46." *Concordia Theological Quarterly* 51:19–43.

Gibbs, J. M.
1963–64 "Purpose and Pattern in Matthew's Use of the Title 'Son of David.'" *New Testament Studies* 10:446–62.
1968 "The Son of God as Torah Incarnate in Matthew." Pp. 38–46 in *Studia Evangelica*, vol. 4: *Papers Presented to the Third International Congress on New Testament Studies Held at Christ Church, Oxford, 1965*. Edited by F. L. Cross. Berlin: Akademie.
1973 "The Gospel Prologues and Their Function." Pp. 154–88 in *Studia Evangelica*, vol. 6: *Papers Presented to the Fourth International Congress on New Testament Studies Held at Oxford, 1969*. Edited by E. A. Livingstone. Berlin: Akademie.

Giblin, C.
1968 "Theological Perspective and Matthew 10:23." *Theological Studies* 29:637–61.
1971 "'The Things of God' in the Question concerning Tribute to Caesar." *Catholic Biblical Quarterly* 33:510–27.
1975 "Structural and Thematic Correlations in the Matthean Burial-Resurrection Narrative (Matt xxvii–xxviii 20)." *New Testament Studies* 21:406–20.

Gibson, J. B.
1981 "Hoi Telonai kai hai Pornai." *Journal of Theological Studies* 32:429–33.
1995 *The Temptations of Jesus in Early Christianity*. Sheffield: Sheffield Academic Press.
2001 "Matthew 6:9–13//Luke 11:2–4: An Eschatological Prayer?" *Biblical Theology Bulletin* 31/3:96–105.

Giesen, H.
2001 "Galiläa—mehr als eine Landschaft: Bibeltheologischer Stellenwert Galiläas im Matthäusevangelium." *Ephemerides theologicae lovanienses* 77:23–45.

Gill, D.
1991 "Socrates and Jesus on Non-retaliation and Love of Enemies." *Horizons* 18:246–62.

Ginzel, G. B.
1985 *Die Bergpredigt: Jüdisches und christliches Glaubensdokument*. Heidelberg: Lambert Schneider.

GKC *Gesenius' Hebrew Grammar*. Edited by E. Kautzsch. Revised by A. E. Cowley. 2nd English ed. Oxford: Clarendon, 1910.

Glancy, J. A.
2000   "Slaves and Slavery in the Matthean Parables." *Journal of Biblical Literature* 119:67–90.

Gnilka, J.
1961   *Die Verstockung Israels: Isaias 6,9–10 in der Theologie der Synoptiker.* Munich: Kösel.
1961–62   "Die essenischen Tauchbäder und die Johannestaufe." *Revue Qumran* 3:185–207.
1986–88   *Das Matthäusevangelium.* 2 vols. Freiburg i.B.: Herder.

Gnilka, J. (ed.)
1974   *Neues Testament und Kirche.* Freiburg i.B.: Herder.

Gnuse, R.
1990   "Dream Genre in the Matthean Infancy Narratives." *Novum Testamentum* 32:97–120.

Goedt, M. de
1959   "L'explication de la parabole de l'ivraie." *Revue biblique* 66:32–54.

Goldenberg, R.
1982   "Early Rabbinic Explanations of the Destruction of Jerusalem." *Journal of Jewish Studies* 33:517–25.

Golding, T. A.
2006   "The Imagery of Shepherding in the Bible." *Bibliotheca sacra* 163:18–28, 158–75.

Good, D. J.
1990   "The Verb ἀναχωρέω in Matthew's Gospel." *Novum Testamentum* 32:1–12.
1999   *Jesus the Meek King.* Harrisburg, PA: Trinity.

Goodacre, M.
2002   *The Case against Q: Studies in Markan Priority and the Synoptic Problem.* Harrisburg, PA: Trinity.

Goodblatt, D.
1989   "The Place of the Pharisees in First-Century Judaism: The State of the Debate." *Journal for the Study of Judaism* 20:12–30.

Gooding, D.
1978   "Structure littéraire de Matthieu 13,53 a 18,35." *Revue biblique* 85:227–52.

Goodman, M.
1970   "Proselytising in Rabbinic Judaism." *Journal of Jewish Studies* 40:175–85.

Goodspeed, E. J.
1959   *Matthew: Apostle and Evangelist.* Philadelphia: Fortress.

Goulder, M.
1974   *Midrash and Lection in Matthew.* London: SPCK.

Gourges, M.
1998   "Sur l'articulation des Béatitudes matthéenes (Mt 5.3–12)." *New Testament Studies* 44:340–56.

Grant, R. M.
1978   "The Sermon on the Mount in Earliest Christianity." *Semeia* 12:215–31.

Grassi, J.
1977   "The Last Testament-Succession: Literary Background of Matthew 9:35–11:1 and Its Significance." *Biblical Theology Bulletin* 7:172–76.

Gray, S. W.
1989   *The Least of My Brothers: Matt 25:31–46—a History of Interpretation.* Atlanta: Scholars.

Green, H. B.
1975   *The Gospel according to St. Matthew.* New Century Bible. Oxford: Clarendon.
2001   *Matthew, Poet of the Beatitudes.* Journal for the Study of the New Testament: Supplement Series 203. Sheffield: Sheffield Academic Press.

Green, J. B.
1988   *The Death of Jesus: Tradition and Interpretation in the Passion Narrative.* Tübingen: Mohr Siebeck.

Green, J. B., and S. McKnight (eds.)
1992   *Dictionary of Jesus and the Gospels.* Downers Grove, IL: InterVarsity.

Green, J. B., and M. Turner (eds.)
1994   *Jesus of Nazareth: Lord and Christ.* Grand Rapids: Eerdmans/Carlisle, UK: Paternoster.

Green, M.
1983   "The Meaning of Cross-Bearing." *Bibliotheca sacra* 140:117–33.
1988   *Matthew for Today.* Dallas: Word.

Greenfield, G.
1992   "The Ethics of the Sermon on the Mount." *Southwestern Journal of Theology* 35:13–19.

Grelot, P.
1986   "Michée 7,6 dans les évangiles et dans la litterature rabbinique." *Biblica* 67:363–77.
1989   "L'épreuve de la tentation." *Esprit et vie* 99:280–84.
1995a   "Note sur les propositions du Pr Carsten Peter Thiede." *Revue biblique* 102:589–91.

1995b   "Remarques sur un manscrit de
         l'Évangile de Matthieu." *Recherches
         de science religieuse* 83:403–5.
1995c   "Les tentations de Jésus." *Nouvelle
         revue théologique* 117:501–16.

Griesbach, J. J.
1789–90 *Commentatio qua Marci Evangelium
         totum e Matthaei et Lucae
         commentariis decerptum esse
         monstratur.* 2 vols. Jena.

Griffiths, J.
1970   "The Disciple's Cross." *New Testament
         Studies* 16:358–64.

Grindel, J.
1967   "Matthew 12:18–21." *Catholic Biblical
         Quarterly* 29:110–15.

Grudem, W., et al. (eds.)
2006   *Translating Truth: The Case for
         Essentially Literal Bible Translation.*
         Wheaton: Crossway.

Grundmann, W.
1959   "Die νήπιοι in der urchristlichen
         Paränese." *New Testament Studies*
         5:188–205.
1965–66 "Matth. XI.27 und die johanneischen
         'Der Vater-Der Sohn'-Stellen." *New
         Testament Studies* 12:42–49.
1968   *Das Evangelium nach Matthäus.*
         Berlin: Evangelische Verlagsanstalt.
1975   *Das Evangelium nach Matthäus.*
         4th ed. Berlin: Evangelische
         Verlagsanstalt.

Guardiola-Sanchez, L.
1997   "Borderless Women and Borderless
         Texts: A Cultural Reading of Matthew
         15:21–28." *Semeia* 78:69–81.

Guelich, R.
1973   "Mt 5:22: Its Meaning and Integrity."
         *Zeitschrift für die neutestamentliche
         Wissenschaft* 64:39–52.
1976   "The Matthean Beatitudes: 'Entrance
         Requirements' or Eschatological
         Blessings?" *Journal of Biblical
         Literature* 95:415–34.
1982   *The Sermon on the Mount.* Waco:
         Word.

Guelich, R. (ed.)
1978   *Unity and Diversity in the New
         Testament.* Grand Rapids: Eerdmans.

Guenther, A. R.
2002   "The Exception Phrases: Except
         Πορνεία, Including Πορνεία or
         Excluding Πορνεία? (Matthew 5:32;
         19:9)." *Tyndale Bulletin* 53:83–96.

Guenther, H.
1989   "When 'Eagles' Draw Together."
         Forum 5:140–50.

Guijarro, S.
1999   "The Politics of Exorcism: Jesus's
         Reaction to Negative Labels in the
         Beelzebul Controversy." *Biblical
         Theology Bulletin* 29:118–29.

Gundry, R. H.
1967   *The Use of the Old Testament in St.
         Matthew's Gospel.* Studien zum
         Neuen Testament 18. Leiden: Brill,
         1967.
1994   *Matthew: A Commentary on His
         Literary and Theological Art.* 2nd ed.
         Grand Rapids: Eerdmans.
2000   "In Defense of the Church in
         Matthew as a *corpus mixtum.*"
         *Zeitschrift für die neutestamentliche
         Wissenschaft* 91:153–65.

Gurtner, D. M.
2006   "The Veil of the Temple in History
         and Legend." *Journal of the
         Evangelical Theological Society* 49:97–
         114.

Guyénot, L.
1999   *Jésus et Jean Baptiste: Enquête
         historique sur une rencontre
         légendaire.* Chambéry: Exergue.

Habbe, J.
1996   *Palästina zur Zeit Jesu: Die
         Landschaft in Galilaia als
         Hintergrund der synoptischen
         Evangelien.* Neukirchen-Vluyn:
         Neukirchener Verlag.

Habermas, G. R., and M. Licona
2004   *The Case for the Resurrection of Jesus.*
         Grand Rapids: Kregel.

Häfner, G.
1994   *Der verheissene Vorläufer:
         Redaktionskritische Untersuchung
         zur Darstellung Johannes des Täufers
         im Matthäus-Evangelium.* Stuttgart:
         Katholisches Bibelwerk.

Hagner, D. A.
1984   *The Jewish Reclamation of Jesus:
         An Analysis and Critique of Modern
         Jewish Study of Jesus.* Grand Rapids:
         Zondervan.
1993   *Matthew 1–13.* Word Biblical
         Commentary 33a. Dallas: Word.
1995a   *Matthew 14–28.* Word Biblical
         Commentary 33b. Dallas: Word.
1995b   "Writing a Commentary on Matthew:
         Self-Conscious Ruminations of an
         Evangelical." *Semeia* 72:51–72.
1997a   "Balancing Old and New: The Law
         of Moses in Matthew and Paul."
         Interpretation 51:20–30.

1997b   "Ethics and the Sermon on the
          Mount." *Studia theologica* 51:44–59.
1998a   "Law, Righteousness, and
          Discipleship in Matthew." *Word and
          World* 18:364–71.
1998b   "New Things from the Scribe's
          Treasure Box (Matthew 13:52)."
          Expository Times 109:329–34.
2003   "Matthew: Apostate, Reformer,
          Revolutionary?" *New Testament
          Studies* 49:193–209.
Hahn, F.
1985   "Jesu Wort vom bergeversetzenden
          Glauben." *Zeitschrift für die
          neutestamentliche Wissenschaft*
          76:146–69.
Ham, C. A.
2005   *The Coming King and the Rejected
          Shepherd: Matthew's Reading
          of Zechariah's Messianic Hope.*
          Sheffield: Sheffield Phoenix.
Hamerton-Kelly, R., and R. Scroggs (eds.)
1976   *Jews, Greeks, and Christians.* Leiden:
          Brill.
Hamilton, N.
1964   "Temple Cleansing and Temple
          Bank." *Journal of Biblical Literature*
          83:365–72.
Hampel, V.
1989   "Ihr werdet mit den Städten Israels
          nicht zu Ende kommen: Eine
          exegetische Studie über Matthäus
          10:23." *Theologische Zeitschrift*
          45:1–31.
1990   *Menschensohn und historischer Jesus:
          Ein Rätselwort als Schlüssel zum
          messianischen Selbstverständnis Jesu.*
          Neukirchen-Vluyn: Neukirchener
          Verlag.
Hanson, K. C.
1994   "How Honorable! How Shameful!
          A Cultural Analysis of Matthew's
          Macarisms and Reproaches." *Semeia*
          68:81–111.
Hare, D. R. A.
1967   *The Theme of Jewish Persecution of
          Christians in the Gospel according to
          Matthew.* Society for New Testament
          Studies Monograph Series 6.
          Cambridge: Cambridge University
          Press.
1993   *Matthew.* Interpretation. Louisville:
          John Knox.
1998   "Current Trends in Matthean
          Scholarship." *Word and World*
          18:405–10.

2000   "How Jewish Is the Gospel of
          Matthew?" *Catholic Biblical Quarterly*
          62:264–77.
Hare, D. R. A., and D. J. Harrington
1975   "Make Disciples of All the Gentiles
          (Matthew 28:19)." *Catholic Biblical
          Quarterly* 37:359–69.
Harner, P.
1970   *The "I Am" of the Fourth Gospel.*
          Philadelphia: Fortress.
Harrington, D.
1991   *The Gospel of Matthew.* Sacra Pagina.
          Collegeville, MN: Liturgical Press.
Harris, M. J.
1985   *Raised Immortal: Resurrection and
          Immortality in the New Testament.*
          Grand Rapids: Zondervan.
1990   *From Grave to Glory: Resurrection in
          the New Testament.* Grand Rapids:
          Zondervan.
Harrisville, R.
1966   "The Woman of Canaan: A Chapter
          in the History of Exegesis."
          Interpretation 20:274–87.
Hart, H.
1992   "Hosanna in the Highest." *Scottish
          Journal of Theology* 45:283–301.
Hartin, P. J.
1996   "Call to Be Perfect through Suffering
          (James 1,2–4): The Concept of
          Perfection in the Epistle of James
          and the Sermon on the Mount."
          Biblica 77:477–92.
1998   "Disciples as Authorities in Matthew's
          Christian-Jewish Community."
          Neotestamentica 32:389–404.
Hartman, L.
1966   *Prophecy Interpreted: The Formation
          of Some Jewish Apocalyptic Texts and
          of the Eschatological Discourse of
          Mark 13.* Lund: Gleerup.
1972   "Scriptural Exegesis in the Gospel
          of Matthew and the Problem of
          Communication." Pp. 131–52
          in *L'Évangile selon Matthieu:
          Rédaction et théologie.* Edited by M.
          Didier. Bibliotheca ephemeridum
          theologicarum lovaniensium 29.
          Gembloux: Duculot.
1997   *"Into the Name of the Lord Jesus":
          Baptism in the Early Church.*
          Edinburgh: T&T Clark.
Hasler, V.
1962   "Die königliche Hochzeit, Matth.
          22,1–14." *Theologische Zeitschrift*
          18:25–35.

Hatina, T. R.
2006 "Did Jesus Quote Isaiah 29:13 against the Pharisees? An Unpopular Appraisal." *Bulletin for Biblical Research* 16:79–94.

Haubeck, W., and M. Bachmann (eds.)
1980 *Wort in der Zeit*. Leiden: Brill.

Hauerwas, S.
2006 *Matthew*. Brazos Theological Commentary on the Bible. Grand Rapids: Brazos.

Hawkins, J. C.
1909 *Horae synopticae*. Oxford: Clarendon.

Hawthorne, G.
1991 *The Presence and the Power*. Dallas: Word.

Hawthorne, G., and O. Betz (eds.)
1987 *Tradition and Interpretation in the New Testament*. Grand Rapids: Eerdmans.

Hay, D.
1973 *Glory at the Right Hand: Psalm 110 in Early Christian Literature*. Nashville: Abingdon.

Head, J. P.
1995 "The Date of the Magdalen Papyrus of Matthew (P. Magd. Gr. 17 = P64)." *Tyndale Bulletin* 46:251–85.

Heater, H.
1983 "Matthew 2:6 and Its Old Testament Sources." *Journal of the Evangelical Theological Society* 26:395–97.

Hedrick, C.
1990 "On Moving Mountains." *Forum* 6:219–37.

Heil, J. P.
1979 "Significant Aspects of the Healing Miracles in Matthew." *Catholic Biblical Quarterly* 41:274–87.
1981 *Jesus Walking on the Sea*. Rome: Biblical Institute.
1991a "The Blood of Jesus in Matthew: A Narrative-Critical Perspective." *Perspectives in Religious Studies* 18:117–24.
1991b *The Death and Resurrection of Jesus: A Narrative-Critical Reading of Matthew 26–28*. Minneapolis: Fortress.
1991c "The Narrative Roles of the Women in Matthew's Genealogy." *Biblica* 72:538–45.
1991d "The Narrative Structure of Matthew 27:55–28:20." *Journal of Biblical Literature* 110:419–38.
1993 "Ezekiel 34 and the Narrative Strategy of the Shepherd and Sheep Metaphor in Matthew." *Catholic Biblical Quarterly* 55:698–708.
1998 "The Double Meaning of the Narrative of Universal Judgment in Matthew 25:31–46." *Journal for the Study of the New Testament* 69:3–14.

Hein, K.
1970–71 "Judas Iscariot: Key to the Last-Supper Narratives." *New Testament Studies* 17:227–32.

Helyer, L.
2002 *Exploring Jewish Literature of the Second Temple Period*. Downers Grove, IL: InterVarsity.

Hemer, C.
1984 "Epiousios." *Journal for the Study of the New Testament* 22:81–94.

Hendrickx, H.
1987 *The Miracle Stories of the Synoptic Gospels*. London: Chapman.

Hendriksen, W.
1973 *The Gospel of Matthew*. Grand Rapids: Baker Academic.

Hengel, M.
1968 "Das Gleichnis von den Weingärtnern Mc 12.1–12 im Lichte der Zenonpapyri und rabbinischen Gleichnisse." *Zeitschrift für die neutestamentliche Wissenschaft* 59:1–39.
1977 *Crucifixion in the Ancient World*. Philadelphia: Fortress.
1981 *The Charismatic Leader and His Followers*. Translated by J. Greig. New York: Crossroad.
1985 *Studies in the Gospel of Mark*. Translated by J. Bowden. Philadelphia: Fortress.
1987 "Zur matthäischen Bergpredigt und ihrem jüdischen Hintergrund." *Theologische Rundschau* 52:327–400.
2000 *The Four Gospels and the One Gospel of Jesus Christ*. Harrisburg, PA: Trinity.

Hennig, G.
2001 "Matthäus 28,16–20 aus der Sicht der praktischen Theologie: Beobachtungen und Überlieferungen." *Theologische Beiträge* 32:317–26.

Hermant, D.
1996 "Structure littéraire du 'discours communitaire' de Matthieu 18." *Revue biblique* 103:76–90.
1999 *Matthieu: Un écrivain? Les cinq discours du premier évangile, un corpus organisé*. Lyon: Profac.

Hertig, P.
1998   *Matthew's Narrative Use of Galilee in the Multicultural and Missiological Journeys of Jesus.* Lewiston, NY: Mellen.
2001   "The Great Commission Revisited: The Role of God's Reign in Disciple Making." *Missiology* 29:343–53.

Hester, J.
1992   "Socio-Rhetorical Criticism and the Parable of the Tenants." *Journal for the Study of the New Testament* 45:27–57.

Heth, W.
1987   "Unmarried 'for the Sake of the Kingdom' (Matthew 19:12) in the Early Church." *Grace Theological Journal* 8:55–88.

Heth, W., and G. Wenham
1984   *Jesus and Divorce.* London: Hodder & Stoughton.

Hezser, C.
1990   *Lohnmetaphorik und Arbeitswelt in Mt 20,1–16.* Freiburg, Switz.: Universitätsverlag/Göttingen: Vandenhoeck & Ruprecht.

Hicks, J.
1984   "The Sabbath Controversy in Matthew: An Exegesis of Matthew 12:1–14." *Restoration Quarterly* 27:79–91.

Hiebert, D. E.
1992   "An Expository Study of Matthew 28:16–20." *Bibliotheca sacra* 149:338–54.

Hiers, R.
1973   *The Historical Jesus and the Kingdom of God.* Gainesville: University of Florida Press.
1981   *Jesus and the Future.* Atlanta: John Knox.
1985   "'Binding' and 'Loosing': The Matthean Authorizations." *Journal of Biblical Literature* 104:233–50.

Higgins, A. J. B.
1963   "The Sign of the Son of Man (Matt 24:30)." *New Testament Studies* 9:380–82.
1980   *The Son of Man in the Teaching of Jesus.* Society for New Testament Studies Monograph Series 39. Cambridge: Cambridge University Press.

Higgins, A. J. B. (ed.)
1959   *New Testament Essays.* Manchester: Manchester University Press.

Hill, D.
1964   "*Dikaioi* as a Quasi-Technical Term." *New Testament Studies* 11:296–302.
1972   *The Gospel of Matthew.* New Century Bible Commentary. Grand Rapids: Eerdmans.
1976   "False Prophets and Charismatics: Structure and Interpretation in Matthew 7:15–23." *Biblica* 57:327–48.
1977–78 "The Use and Meaning of Hosea 6:6 in Matthew's Gospel." *New Testament Studies* 24:107–19.
1980   "Son and Servant: An Essay on Matthean Christology." *Journal for the Study of the New Testament* 6:2–16.
1983   "'Our Daily Bread' (Matt 6:11) in the History of Exegesis." *Irish Biblical Studies* 5:2–10.
1984   "The Figure of Jesus in Matthew's Gospel: A Response to Professor Kingsbury's Literary-Critical Probe." *Journal for the Study of the New Testament* 21:37–52.
1986   "The Conclusion of Matthew's Gospel: Some Literary Critical Observations." *Irish Biblical Studies* 8:54–63.
1988   "The Walking on the Water." *Expository Times* 99:267–69.

Hinkle, M. E.
2002   "The Lord's Prayer: Empowerment for Living the Sermon on the Mount." *Word and World* 22:9–17.

Hoch, C.
1995   *All Things New: The Significance of Newness for Biblical Theology.* Grand Rapids: Baker Academic.

Hoehner, H.
1972   *Herod Antipas: A Contemporary of Jesus Christ.* Grand Rapids: Zondervan.
1977   *Chronological Aspects of the Life of Christ.* Grand Rapids: Zondervan.

Hoet, R.
1982   "*Omnes autem vos fratres estis*": *Étude de concept ecclésiologique des "frères" selon Mt 23,8–12.* Rome: Gregorian University Press.

Hoffman, P. (ed.)
1973   *Orientierung an Jesus.* Freiburg i.B.: Herder.

Holmes, M.
1990   "The Text of the Matthean Divorce Passages: A Comment on the Appeal to Harmonization in Textual

Decisions." *Journal of Biblical Literature* 109:651–64.

Holst, R.
1976   "The One Anointing of Jesus: Another Application of the Form-Critical Method." *Journal of Biblical Literature* 95:435–46.

Hooker, M.
1971   "Uncomfortable Words, X: The Prohibition of Foreign Missions (Mt 10.5–6)." *Expository Times* 82:361–65.

Horbury, W.
1982   "The Benediction of the Minim and Early Jewish-Christian Controversy." *Journal of Theological Studies* 33:19–61.
1986   "The Twelve and the Phylarchs." *New Testament Studies* 32:503–27.
1998   *Jews and Christians: In Contact and Controversy.* Edinburgh: T&T Clark.

Horgan, M., and P. Kobelski (eds.)
1989   *To Touch the Text: Biblical and Related Studies in Honor of Joseph A. Fitzmyer.* New York: Crossroad.

Horne, E. H.
1998   "The Parable of the Tenants as Indictment." *Journal for the Study of the New Testament* 71:111–16.

Horsley, G. H. R.
1990   "Tί at Matthew 7:14: 'Because,' Not 'How.'" *Filologia neotestamentaria* 3:141–43.

Horsley, R. A.
1979   "Josephus and the Bandits." *Journal for the Study of Judaism* 10:37–63.
1986   "Ethics and Exegesis: 'Love Your Enemies' and the Doctrine of Non-violence." *Journal of the American Academy of Religion* 54:3–31.
1987   *Jesus and the Spiral of Violence: Jewish Resistance in Roman Palestine.* San Francisco: Harper.
1989   *The Liberation of Christmas: The Infancy Narratives in Social Context.* New York: Continuum.

Horsley, R. A., and J. Hanson
1985   *Bandits, Prophets, Messiahs: Popular Movements in the Time of Jesus.* Minneapolis: Winston.

Houk, C.
1966   "Πειρασμός, the Lord's Prayer, and the Massah Tradition." *Scottish Journal of Theology* 19:216–25.

Houlden, J. L.
1987   *Backwards into the Light: The Passion and Resurrection of Jesus according to Matthew and Mark.* London: SCM.

Howard, G.
1977   "The Tetragram and the New Testament." *Journal of Biblical Literature* 96:63–83.
1986   "Was the Gospel of Matthew Originally Written in Hebrew?" *Bible Review* 2:14–25.
1995   *Hebrew Gospel of Matthew.* 2nd ed. Macon, GA: Mercer University Press.

Howard, T. L.
1986   "The Use of Hosea 11:1 in Matthew 2:15: An Alternative Solution." *Bibliotheca sacra* 143:314–28.

Howell, D.
1990   *Matthew's Inclusive Story: A Study in the Narrative Rhetoric of the First Gospel.* Journal for the Study of the New Testament: Supplement Series 42. Sheffield: Sheffield Academic Press.

Hre Kio, S.
1990   "Understanding and Translating 'Nations' in Mt 28:19." *Bible Translator* 41:230–38.

Huat, T. K.
2000   "Christmas in Isaiah 7:14—*sensus literalis, sensus plenior aut felix culpa?*" *Trinity Theological Journal* 9:5–33.

Hubaut, M.
1976   *La parabole des vignerons homicides.* London: Gabalda.

Hubbard, B. J.
1974   *The Matthean Redaction of a Primitive Apostolic Commissioning: An Exegesis of Matthew 28:16–20.* Missoula, MT: Scholars.

Huber, K.
1996   "Vom 'Weinbergleid' zum 'Winzergleichnis': Zu einem Beispiel innerbiblischer *relecture.*" *Protokolle zur Bibel* 5:71–94.

Huffman, N.
1978   "Atypical Features in the Parables of Jesus." *Journal of Biblical Literature* 97:207–20.

Huggins, R. V.
1992   "Matthean Posteriority: A Preliminary Proposal." *Novum Testamentum* 34:1–22.

Hulse, E. V.
1975   "The Nature of Biblical 'Leprosy' and the Use of Alternative Medical Terms in Modern Translations of the Bible." *Palestine Exploration Quarterly* 107:87–105.

Hultgren, A.
1974   "The Double Commandment of Love in Mt 22.34–40." *Catholic Biblical Quarterly* 36:373–78.
1979   *Jesus and His Adversaries: The Form and Function of the Conflict Stories in the Synoptic Tradition.* Minneapolis: Augsburg.
1997   "Matthew's Infancy Narrative and the Nativity of an Emerging Community." *Horizons in Biblical Theology* 19:91–108.
2000   *The Parables of Jesus: A Commentary.* Grand Rapids: Eerdmans.

Hultgren, A., and B. Hall (eds.)
1990   *Christ and His Communities.* Cincinnati: Forward Movement.

Humbert, A.
1954   "Essai d'une théologie du scandale dans les synoptiques." *Biblica* 35:1–28.

Hummel, R.
1966   *Die Auseinandersetzung zwischen Kirche und Judentum im Matthäusevangelium.* Munich: Kaiser.

Humphrey, H.
1977   *The Relationship of Structure and Christology in the Gospel of Matthew.* Ann Arbor, MI: University Microfilms.

Humphreys, C. J.
1992   "The Star of Bethlehem, a Comet in 5 BC, and the Date of Christ's Birth." *Tyndale Bulletin* 43:31–56.

Hunter, A.
1962   "Crux Criticorum—Matt 11.25–30." *New Testament Studies* 8:241–49.

Hutchinson, J. C.
2001   "Women, Gentiles, and Messianic Mission in Matthew's Genealogy." *Bibliotheca sacra* 158:152–64.
2002   "Was John the Baptist an Essene from Qumran?" *Bibliotheca sacra* 159:187–200.

Hutter, M.
1984   "Ein altorientalischer Bittgestus in Mt. 9,20–22." *Zeitschrift für die neutestamentliche Wissenschaft* 75:133–35.

Hylen, S. E.
2000   "Forgiveness and Life in Community." *Interpretation* 54:146–57.

Immisch, O.
1916   "Matthäus 16:18." *Zeitschrift für die neutestamentliche Wissenschaft* 17:18–26.

Ingelaere, J.-C.
1995   "Universalisme et particularisme dans l'Évangile de Matthieu: Matthieu et le judaïsme." *Revue d'histoire et de philosophie religieuses* 75:45–49.

Ingolfsland, D.
2006   "Jesus Remembered: James Dunn and the Synoptic Problem." *Trinity Journal* 27:187–97.

Instone-Brewer, D.
2002   *Divorce and Remarriage in the Bible.* Grand Rapids: Eerdmans.

Ito, A.
1991   "The Question of the Authenticity of the Ban on Swearing (Matthew 5:33–37)." *Journal for the Study of the New Testament* 43:5–13.
1992   "Matthew and the Community of the Dead Sea Scrolls." *Journal for the Study of the New Testament* 48:23–42.
1994   "Les Sept Montagnes de Jésus dans saint Matthieu." *Lumen vitae* 49:413–23.

Jackson, B.
1975   *Essays in Jewish and Christian Legal History.* Leiden: Brill.

Jackson, G.
2002   *"Have Mercy on Me": The Story of the Canaanite Woman in Matthew 15.21–28.* Sheffield: Sheffield Academic Press.

Jacob, R.
1973   *Les péricopes de l'entrée à Jérusalem et la préparation de la cène.* Paris: Gabalda.

Jahnke, V. J.
1988   "'Love Your Enemies': The Value of New Perspectives." *Currents in Theology and Mission* 15:267–73.

Janzen, D.
2000   "The Meaning of *Porneia* in Matthew 5:32 and 19:9: An Approach from the Study of Ancient Near Eastern Culture." *Journal for the Study of the New Testament* 80:66–80.

Janzen, J.
1987   "The Yoke That Gives Rest." *Interpretation* 41:256–68.

Jastrow, M.
1971   *A Dictionary of the Targumim, the Talmud Babli and Yerushalmi, and the Midrashic Literature.* New York: Judaica.

Jaubert, A.
1965   *The Date of the Last Supper.* Staten Island, NY: Alba House.

Jenks, G.
1991   The Origins and Early Development
        of the Antichrist Myth. Berlin: de
        Gruyter.
Jennings, T. W., Jr., and T.-S. B. Liew
2004   "Mistaken Identities but Model
        Faith: Rereading the Centurion, the
        Chap, and the Christ in Matthew
        8:5–13." Journal of Biblical Literature
        123:467–94.
Jensen, P. F.
1979   "The Age of Immanuel." Catholic
        Biblical Quarterly 41:220–39.
Jeremias, J.
1958   Heiligengräber in Jesu Umwelt
        (Mt. 23,29; Lk 11,47). Göttingen:
        Vandenhoeck & Ruprecht.
1960   Infant Baptism in the First Four
        Centuries. London: SCM.
1962   Jerusalem in the Time of Jesus.
        Translated by F. H. Cave and C. H.
        Cave. London: SCM.
1963   The Sermon on the Mount. Translated
        by N. Perrin. Philadelphia: Fortress.
1966a   The Eucharistic Words of Jesus.
        Translated by N. Perrin. London:
        SCM.
1966b   Jesus's Promise to the Nations. 2nd
        ed. London: SCM.
1967   The Prayers of Jesus. London: SCM.
1971   New Testament Theology. New York:
        Scribner's.
1972   The Parables of Jesus. 2nd rev. ed.
        New York: Scribner's.
Jocz, J.
1979   The Jewish People and Jesus Christ:
        The Relationship between Church and
        Synagogue. 3rd ed. Grand Rapids:
        Baker Academic.
Johner, M.
1998   "L'éthique de Jésus: À propos du
        sermon sur la montagne." Revue
        réformée 29:27–43.
Johnson, L. T.
1989   "The New Testament's Anti-Jewish
        Slander and the Conventions of
        Ancient Rhetoric." Journal of Biblical
        Literature 108:419–41.
Johnson, M. D.
1974   "Reflections on a Wisdom approach
        to Matthew's Christology." Catholic
        Biblical Quarterly 36:44–64.
1988   The Purpose of the Biblical
        Genealogies. 2nd ed. Society for New
        Testament Studies Monograph Series
        8. Cambridge: Cambridge University
        Press.

Johnson, P. E.
1995   Reason in the Balance: The Case
        against Naturalism in Science, Law,
        and Education. Downers Griove, IL:
        InterVarsity.
Johnson, S. E.
1991   The Griesbach Hypothesis and
        Redaction Criticism. Atlanta:
        Scholars.
Johnson, S. L.
1967a   "The Triumphal Entry of Christ."
        Bibliotheca sacra 124:218–29.
1967b   "The Agony of Christ." Bibliotheca
        sacra 124:303–13.
Jones, A.
1965   The Gospel according to St. Matthew.
        New York: Sheed & Ward.
Jones, I. H.
1995   The Matthean Parables: A Literary
        and Historical Commentary. Novum
        Testamentum Supplements 80.
        Leiden: Brill.
Jones, J. M.
1994   "Subverting the Textuality of Davidic
        Messianism: Matthew's Presentation
        of the Genealogy and the Davidic
        Title." Catholic Biblical Quarterly
        56:256–72.
Jospe, R.
1990   "Hillel's Rule." Jewish Quarterly
        Review 81:45–57.
Jourjon, M., et al., eds.
1961   À la rencontre de Dieu. Le Puy:
        Mappus.
Jülicher, A.
1899   Die Gleichnisreden Jesu. 2 vols.
        Freiburg i.B.: Mohr Siebeck.
Kagarise, R. J.
2001   "Divine Sovereignty, Human
        Responsibility, and Jesus's Parables:
        The Structure and Meaning of
        Matthew 13:10–17." Evangelical
        Journal 19:29–41.
Kähler, C.
1994   "Satanischer Schriftgebrauch: Zur
        Hermeneutik von Mt 4,1–11/Lk
        4,1–13." Theologische Literaturzeitung
        119:857–68.
Kaiser, W. C., Jr.
1982   "The Arrival of Elijah in Malachi
        and the Gospels." Grace Theological
        Journal 3:221–33.
1985   The Uses of the Old Testament in the
        New. Chicago: Moody.
1988   "The Promise of Isaiah 7:14 and
        the Single-Meaning Hermeneutic."
        Evangelical Journal 6:55–70.

Kaiser, W. C., Jr., and M. Silva
1994   *An Introduction to Biblical Hermeneutics: The Search for Meaning.* Grand Rapids: Zondervan.

Kalin, E. R.
1988   "Matthew 9:18–26: An Exercise in Redaction Criticism." *Currents in Theology and Mission* 15:39–47.

Kallemeyn, H.
1992   "Un Jésus intolerant? (Matthieu 21:12–17)." *Revue réformée* 43:85–91.

Kampen, J.
1988   *The Hasideans and the Origins of Pharisaism.* Atlanta: Scholars.
1994   "The Sectarian Form of the Antitheses within the Social World of the Matthean Community." *Dead Sea Discoveries* 1:338–63.

Kampling, R.
1986   "Jesus von Nazaret—Lehrer und Exorzist." *Biblische Zeitschrift* 30:237–48.

Katz, S.
1984   "Issues in the Separation of Judaism and Christianity after 70 CE: A Reconsideration." *Journal of Biblical Literature* 103:43–76.

Kayalaparampil, T.
1990   "Passion and Resurrection in the Gospel of Matthew." *Bible Bhashyam* 16:41–51.

Kazmierski, C. R.
1987   "The Stones of Abraham: John the Baptist and the End of Torah (Matt 3,7–10 par. Luke 3,7–9)." *Biblica* 68:22–40.
1996   *John the Baptist: Prophet and Evangelist.* Collegeville, MN: Liturgical Press.

Kealy, S. P.
1997   *Matthew's Gospel and the History of Biblical Interpretation.* Lewiston, NY: Mellen.

Keck, L. E.
1970   "The Spirit and the Dove." *New Testament Studies* 17:41–67.

Kee, A.
1969   "The Question about Fasting." *Novum Testamentum* 11:161–73.
1970   "The Old Coat and the New Wine." *Novum Testamentum* 12:13–21.

Kee, H. C.
1983   *Miracle in the Early Christian World.* New Haven: Yale University Press.
1996   "Jesus: A Glutton and a Drunkard." *New Testament Studies* 42:374–93.

Keegan, T. J.
1982   "Introductory Formulae for Matthean Discourses." *Catholic Biblical Quarterly* 44:415–30.

Keener, C.
1991   *And Marries Another: Divorce and Remarriage in the Teaching of the New Testament.* Peabody, MA: Hendrickson.
1997   *Matthew.* The IVP Commentary Series. Downers Grove, IL: InterVarsity.
1999   *A Commentary on the Gospel of Matthew.* Grand Rapids: Eerdmans.
2005   "'Brood of Vipers' (Matt 3:7; 12:34; 23:33)." *Journal for the Study of the New Testament* 28:3–11.

Kelhoffer, J. A.
2005a   *The Diet of John the Baptist: "Locusts and Wild Honey" in Synoptic and Patristic Interpretation.* Wissenschaftliche Untersuchungen zum Neuen Testament 176. Tübingen: Mohr Siebeck.
2005b   "John the Baptist's 'Wild Honey' and 'Honey' in Antiquity." *Greek, Roman, and Byzantine Studies* 45:59–73.

Kellenberger, E.
1997   "Plädoyer für ein nicht-moralisierendes Verständnis von 'anaw und praus." *Protokolle zur Bibel* 6:81–86.

Kelly, W.
1911   *Lectures on the Gospel of Matthew.* New York: Loizeaux.

Kennard, J.
1948   "Hosanna and the Purpose of Jesus." *Journal of Biblical Literature* 67:171–76.
1949   "The Place of Origin of Matthew's Gospel." *Anglican Theological Review* 31:243–46.
1950   *Render to God: A Study of the Tribute Passage.* New York: Oxford University Press.

Kent, H. A., Jr.
1962   "The Gospel according to Matthew." Pp. 929–85 in *The Wycliffe Bible Commentary.* Edited by C. F. Pfeiffer and E. F. Harrison. Chicago: Moody.

Kerr, A. J.
1997   "Matthew 13:25: Sowing *Zizania* among Another's Wheat: Realistic or Artificial?" *Journal of Theological Studies* 48:108–9.

Kertelge, K. (ed.)
1982   Mission im Neuen Testament.
        Freiburg i.B.: Herder.
1988   Der Prozess gegen Jesu. Freiburg i.B.:
        Herder.
Kessler, C.
1997   "Exégèse juive des Béatitudes
        matthéennes." Lumière et vie
        47:51–61.
Kidder, S. J.
1983   "'This Generation' in Matthew 24:34."
        Andrews University Seminary Studies
        21:203–9.
Kidger, M.
1999   The Star of Bethlehem: An
        Astronomer's View. Princeton:
        Princeton University Press.
Kiilunen, J.
1989   Der Doppelgebot der Liebe
        in synoptischer Sicht: Ein
        redaktionskritischer Versuch über Mk
        12,28–34 und die Parallelen. Helsinki:
        Suomalainen Tiedeakademia.
Kiilunen, J., V. Reikkinen, and H. Räisänen
        (eds.)
1983   Glaube und Gerechtigkeit: In
        memoriam Rafael Gyllenberg
        (18.6.1893–29.7.1982). Helsinki:
        Suomen Eksegeettisen Seuran.
Kik, J.
1948   Matthew Twenty-Four. Philadelphia:
        Presbyterian and Reformed.
Kiley, M.
1984   "Why 'Matthew' in Matt 9:9–13?"
        Biblica 65:347–51.
Kilpatrick, G.
1946   The Origins of the Gospel according to
        St. Matthew. Oxford: Clarendon.
Kim, S.
1983   The Son of Man as the Son of God.
        Grand Rapids: Eerdmans.
Kingsbury, J. D.
1966   "The 'Jesus of History' and the 'Christ
        of Faith' in Relation to Matthew's
        View of Time: Reaction to a New
        Approach." Concordia Theological
        Monthly 37:502–8.
1969   The Parables of Jesus in Matthew 13.
        London: SPCK.
1971   "Major Trends in Parable
        Interpretation." Concordia
        Theological Monthly 42:579–96.
1974   "The Composition and Christology
        of Matthew 28:16–20." Journal of
        Biblical Literature 93:573–84.

1978a   "Observations on the 'Miracle
        Chapters' of Matthew 8–9." Catholic
        Biblical Quarterly 40:559–73.
1978b   "The Verb 'Akoluthein' ("to Follow")
        as an Index of Matthew's View of
        His Community." Journal of Biblical
        Literature 97:56–73.
1979   "The Figure of Peter in Matthew's
        Gospel as a Theological Problem."
        Journal of Biblical Literature
        98:67–69.
1981   Jesus Christ in Matthew, Mark, and
        Luke. Philadelphia: Fortress.
1984   "The Figure of Jesus in Matthew's
        Story: A Literary-Critical Probe."
        Journal for the Study of the New
        Testament 21:3–36.
1985   "The Figure of Jesus in Matthew's
        Story: A Rejoinder to David Hill."
        Journal for the Study of the New
        Testament 25:61–81.
1986a   Matthew. 2nd ed. Proclamation
        Commentaries. Philadelphia:
        Fortress.
1986b   "The Parable of the Wicked
        Husbandmen and the Secret
        of Jesus's Divine Sonship in
        Matthew: Some Literary-Critical
        Observations." Journal of Biblical
        Literature 95:643–55.
1987a   "The Developing Conflict between
        Jesus and the Jewish Leaders in
        Matthew's Gospel: A Literary-Critical
        Study." Catholic Biblical Quarterly
        49:57–73.
1987b   "The Place, Structure, and Meaning
        of the Sermon on the Mount within
        Matthew." Interpretation 41:131–43.
1988a   Matthew as Story. 2nd ed.
        Philadelphia: Fortress.
1988b   "On Following Jesus: The 'Eager'
        Scribe and the 'Reluctant' Disciple."
        New Testament Studies 34:45–59.
1988c   "Reflections on 'the Reader' of
        Matthew's Gospel." New Testament
        Studies 34:442–60.
1989   Matthew: Structure, Christology,
        Kingdom. 1975. Reprinted
        Minneapolis: Fortress.
1992   "The Plot of Matthew's Story."
        Interpretation 46:347–56.
1993   Matthew. Interpretation. Louisville:
        John Knox.
1995   "The Rhetoric of Comprehension
        in the Gospel of Matthew." New
        Testament Studies 41:358–77.

Kingsbury, J. D. (ed.)
1997   *Gospel Interpretation: Narrative-Critical and Social-Scientific Approaches.* Harrisburg, PA: Trinity.

Kinman, B.
1994   "Jesus's 'Triumphal Entry' in the Light of Pilate's." *New Testament Studies* 40:442–48.

Kissinger, W.
1975   *The Sermon on the Mount: A History of Interpretation and Bibliography.* Metuchen, NJ: Scarecrow.
1979   *The Parables of Jesus. A History of Interpretation and Bibliography.* Metuchen, NJ: Scarecrow.

Kitzberger, I. R. (ed.)
2000   *Transformative Encounters: Jesus and Women Re-viewed.* Leiden: Brill.

Klassen, W.
1984   *Love of Enemies.* Philadelphia: Fortress.
1996   *Judas: Betrayer or Friend of Jesus?* Minneapolis: Fortress.

Klauck, H.-J.
1978   *Allegorie und Allegorese in synoptischen Gleichnistexten.* Münster: Aschendorff.
1987   *Judas—ein Jünger des Herrn.* Freiburg i.B.: Herder.

Klein, G.
1961   *Die zwölf Apostel.* Göttingen: Vandenhoeck & Ruprecht.

Klemm, H.
1982   "De censu Caesaris: Beobachtungen zu J. Duncan Derretts Interpretation der Perikope Mk. 12:13–17 par." *Novum Testamentum* 24:234–54.

Klijn, A. F. J.
1959   "Scribes, Pharisees, Highpriests, and Elders in the New Testament." *Novum Testamentum* 3:259–67.
1966   "The Question of the Rich Young Man in a Jewish-Christian Gospel." *Novum Testamentum* 8:149–55.

Knoch, O.
1983   "Die Funktion der Handauflegung im Neuen Testament." *Liturgisches Jahrbuch* 33:222–35.

Knowles, M.
1993   *Jeremiah in Matthew's Gospel.* Journal for the Study of the New Testament: Supplement Series 68. Sheffield: JSOT.

Kodell, J.
1978   "The Celibacy Logion in Matthew 19:12." *Biblical Theology Bulletin* 8:19–23.

1988   *The Eucharist in the New Testament.* Collegeville, MN: Liturgical Press.

Kodjak, A.
1986   *A Structural Analysis of the Sermon on the Mount.* Berlin: de Gruyter, 1986.

Koester, C.
1989   "The Origin and Significance of the Flight to Pella Tradition." *Catholic Biblical Quarterly* 51:90–106.

Köhler, W.-D.
1987   *Die Rezeption des Matthäusevangeliums in der Zeit vor Irenäus.* Tübingen: Mohr Siebeck.

Kollmann, B.
1996   "Das Schwurverbot Mt 5,33–37/Jak 5,12 im Spiegel antiker Eidkritik." *Biblische Zeitschrift* 40:179–93.
1997   "Jesu Verbot des Richtens und die Gemeindedisziplin." *Zeitschrift für die neutestamentliche Wissenschaft* 88:170–86.

Kopas, J.
1990   "Jesus and Women in Matthew." *Theology Today* 47:13–21.

Körtner, U.
1983   *Papias von Hierapolis: Ein Beitrag zur Geschichte des frühen Christentums.* Göttingen: Vandenhoeck & Ruprecht.

Koskenniemi, E., et al.
2005   "Wine Mixed with Myrrh (Mark 15:23) and *crurifragium* (John 19:31–32)." *Journal for the Study of the New Testament* 27:379–91.

Kraemer, R. S.
2006   "Implicating Herodias and Her Daughter in the Death of John the Baptizer: A (Christian) Theological Strategy." *Journal of Biblical Literature* 125:321–49.

Krentz, E.
1964   "The Extent of Matthew's Prologue." *Journal of Biblical Literature* 83:409–15.
1983   "None Greater among Those Born from Women: John the Baptist in the Gospel of Matthew." *Currents in Theology and Mission* 10:333–38.
2006   "'Make Disciples': Matthew on Evangelism." *Currents in Theology and Mission* 33:23–41.

Krieger, K.-S.
1986   "Das Publikum der Bergpredigt (Mt 4,23–25)." *Kairos* 28:98–115.

Kruse, H.
1995 "Gold und Weihrauch und Myrrhe (Mt 2,11)." *Münchener theologische Zeitschrift* 46:203–13.

Kugel, J.
1987 "On Hidden Hatred and Open Reproach: Early Exegesis of Leviticus 19:17." *Harvard Theological Review* 80:43–61.

Kügler, J.
1997 "Gold, Weihrauch und Myrrhe: Eine Notiz zu Mt 2,11." *Biblische Notizen* 87:24–33.

Kuhn, H.-W.
1982 "Die Kreuzesstrafe während der frühen Kaiserzeit." Pp. 648–793 in *Aufstieg und Niedergang der römischen Welt*, part 2: *Principat*, 25.1. Edited by H. Temporini and W. Haase. Berlin: de Gruyter.

Kümmel, W.
1957 *Promise and Fulfillment: The Eschatological Message of Jesus.* Naperville, IL: Allenson.
1978 *Heilsgeschehen und Geschichte.* 2 vols. Marburg: Elwert.

Kupp, D. D.
1996 *Matthew's Emmanuel: Divine Presence and God's People in the First Gospel.* Cambridge: Cambridge University Press.

Kürzinger, J.
1983 *Papias von Hierapolis und die Evangelien des Neuen Testaments.* Regensburg: Pustet.

Kvalbein, H.
1997 "Die Wunder der Endzeit: Beobachtungen zu 4Q521 und Matth 11,5p." *Zeitschrift für die neutestamentliche Wissenschaft* 88:111–25.
1998 "The Wonders of the End-Time: Metaphoric Language in 4Q521 and the Interpretation of Matthew 11.5 par." *Journal for the Study of the Pseudepigrapha* 18:87–110.

Kynes, W. L.
1991 *A Christology of Solidarity: Jesus as the Representative of His People in Matthew.* Lanham, MD: University Press of America.

L&N
Greek-English Lexicon of the New Testament: Based on Semantic Domains. By J. P. Louw and E. A. Nida. 2nd ed. 2 vols. New York: United Bible Societies, 1989.

Laansma, J.
1997 "*I Will Give You Rest*": The "*Rest*" Motif in the New Testament with Special Reference to Matthew 11 and Hebrews 3–4. Tübingen: Mohr Siebeck.

Lachs, S.
1975a "On Matthew 6:12." *Novum Testamentum* 17:6–8.
1975b "On Matthew 23:27–28." *Harvard Theological Review* 68:385–88.
1987 *A Rabbinic Commentary on the New Testament: The Gospels of Matthew, Mark, and Luke.* Hoboken, NJ: Ktav.

Lacy, D. R. de
1992 "In Search of a Pharisee." *Tyndale Bulletin* 43:353–72.

Ladd, G.
1974 *The Presence of the Future.* Grand Rapids: Eerdmans.

LaGrand, J.
1995 *The Earliest Christian Mission to "All Nations": In the Light of Matthew's Gospel.* Atlanta: Scholars.

LaGrange, M.
1948 *Évangile selon saint Matthieu.* Paris: Lecoffre.

Lalleman, P. J.
1997 "Healing by a Mere Touch as a Christian Concept." *Tyndale Bulletin* 48:355–61.

Lambrecht, J.
1977a "Jesus and the Law: An Investigation of Mark 7.1–23." *Ephemerides theologicae lovanienses* 53:24–82.
1977b "Parables in Mt 13." *Tijdschrift voor theologie* 17:25–47.
1980 "'Are You the One Who Is to Come, or Should We Look for Another?'" *Louvain Studies* 8:115–28.
1985 *The Sermon on the Mount.* Wilmington, DE: Glazier.
1987 "The Sayings of Jesus on Non-violence." *Louvain Studies* 12:291–305.
1992 *Out of the Treasure: The Parables in the Gospel of Matthew.* Grand Rapids: Eerdmans.
1994 "Is Nonviolent Resistance Jesus's Third Way? An Answer to Walter Wink." *Louvain Studies* 19:350–51.

Lampe, G.
1972–73 "St. Peter's Denial." *Bulletin of the John Rylands Library* 55:346–68.

Lampe, G., and K. Woollcombe
1957   *Essays on Typology.* Studies in
         Biblical Theology 22. Naperville, IL:
         Allenson.
Landis, S.
1994   *Das Verhältnis des Johannes-
         evangeliums zu den Synoptikern: Am
         Beispiel von Mt 8,5–13; Lk 7,1–10; Joh
         4,46–54.* Berlin: de Gruyter.
Landmesser, C.
2001   *Jüngerberufung und Zuwendung zu
         Gott: Ein exegetischer Beitrag zum
         Konzept der matthäischen Soteriologie
         im Anschluss an Mt 9,9–13.*
         Tübingen: Mohr Siebeck.
Lane, A. N.
2004   "Did the Apostolic Church Baptise
         Babies?" *Tyndale Bulletin* 55:109–30.
Lange, J. (ed.)
1980   *Matthäus-Evangelium.* Darmstadt:
         Wissenschaftliche Buchgesellschaft.
Langley, W.
1996   "The Parable of the Two Sons
         (Matthew 21:28–32) against Its
         Semitic and Rabbinic Backdrop."
         Catholic Biblical Quarterly 58:228–43.
Lanier, D.
1992   "The Lord's Prayer: Matt 6:9–13—a
         Thematic and Semantic-Structural
         Analysis." *Criswell Theological Review*
         6:73–89.
Lapide, P.
1980   "A Jewish Exegesis of the Walking on
         the Water." *Concilium* 138:35–40.
1991   "Das Vaterunser—ein jüdisches oder
         ein christliches Gebet?" *Renovatio*
         47:108–10.
La Potterie, I. de
1966   "Mors Johannis Baptistae." *Verbum
         Domini* 44:142–51.
Lategan, B.
1977   "Structural Interrelations in Matthew
         11–12." *Neotestamentica* 11:115–29.
Latham, J. E.
1982   *The Religious Symbolism of Salt.*
         Paris: Beauchesne.
Law, D. R.
1997   "Matthew's Enigmatic Reference to
         Jeremiah in Matthew 16:14." Pp.
         277–302 in *The Book of Jeremiah
         and Its Reception.* Edited by A. H. W.
         Curtis and T. Römer. Louvain:
         Peeters.
Lawlor, G. L.
1974   *The Beatitudes Are for Today.* Grand
         Rapids: Baker Books.

Légasse, S.
1961   "Scribes et disciples de Jésus." *Revue
         biblique* 68:321–45, 481–506.
1968   "Les faux prophètes: Matth.7, 15–20."
         Études franciscaines 18:205–18.
1969   *Jésus et l'enfant.* Paris: Gabalda.
1972a   "Jésus et l'impôt du temple (Mt
         17,24–27)." *Science et esprit*
         24:361–77.
1972b   "L'épisode de la Canaéenne d'apres
         Mt 15,21–28." *Bulletin de littérature
         ecclésiastique* 73:21–40.
1974   "Approche de l'épisode
         préévangélique des fils de Zébédée
         [Mark x.35–40 par.]." *New Testament
         Studies* 20:161–77.
1983   "Le refroidissement de l'amour
         avant la fin (Mt 24,12)." *Studien zum
         Neuen Testament und seiner Umwelt*
         8:91–102.
1993   "L'arrestation de Jésus d'après Marc
         14:43–52." *Études théologiques et
         religieuses* 68:241–47.
1994   *Le process de Jésus: L'histoire.* Paris:
         Cerf.
1998   "Les généalogies de Jésus." *Bulletin
         de littérature ecclésiastique* 99:443–54.
Legrand, L.
1965   "The Harvest Is Plentiful (Mt 9.37)."
         Scripture 17:1–9.
1987   "The Missionary Command of the
         Risen Lord: Mt 28,16–20." *Indian
         Theological Studies* 24:5–28.
Leitch, J. W.
1966   "Lord Also of the Sabbath." *Scottish
         Journal of Theology* 19:426–33.
Lemcio, E.
1986   "The Parables of the Great Supper
         and the Wedding Feast." *Horizons in
         Biblical Theology* 8:1–26.
Le Moyne, J.
1972   *Les Sadducéens.* Paris: Lecoffre.
Lenski, R.
1961   *The Interpretation of St. Matthew's
         Gospel.* Minneapolis: Augsburg.
Léon-Dufour, X. (ed.)
1977   *Les miracles de Jésus selon le
         Nouveau Testament.* Paris: Seuil.
Levin, Y.
2006   "Jesus, 'Son of God' and 'Son of
         David': The 'Adoption' of Jesus
         into the Davidic Line." *Journal for
         the Study of the New Testament*
         28:415–42.
Levine, A.-J.
1988   *The Social and Ethnic Dimensions
         of Matthean Salvation History:*

"Go Nowhere among the Gentiles."
Lewiston, NY: Mellen.

Levine, A.-J., and M. Blickenstaff (eds.)
2001   *A Feminist Companion to Matthew.*
        Sheffield: Sheffield Academic Press.

Levine, A.-J., and R. Pervo (eds.)
1998   *Jewish Proselytism.* Atlanta: Scholars.

Levine, E.
1975–76 "The Sabbath Controversy according
         to Matthew." *New Testament Studies*
         22:480–83.

Levine, L. I. (ed.)
1992   *The Galilee in Late Antiquity.*
        Cambridge: Harvard University
        Press.

Levin-Goldschmidt, H., and M. Limbeck
1976   *Heilvoller Verrat? Judas im Neuen
        Testament.* Stuttgart: Katholisches
        Bibelwerk.

Lewis, J. P.
1995   "'The Gates of Hell Shall Not Prevail
        against It' (Matt 16:18): A Study
        of the History of Interpretation."
        *Journal of the Evangelical Theological
        Society* 38:349–67.
1999–   "Jamnia after Forty Years."
2000   *Hebrew Union College Annual*
        70–71:233–59.

Lightfoot, J.
1997   *A Commentary on the New Testament
        from the Talmud and Hebraica.*
        4 vols. Reprinted Peabody, MA:
        Hendrickson.

Limbeck, M.
1986   *Matthäus-Evangelium.* Stuttgart:
        Katholisches Bibelwerk.

Lindars, B.
1983   *Jesus Son of Man: A Fresh
        Examination of the Son of Man
        Sayings in the Gospels in the Light
        of Recent Research.* Grand Rapids:
        Eerdmans.

Lindars, B. (ed.)
1988   *Law and Religion: Essays on the
        Place of the Law in Israel and Early
        Christianity.* Cambridge: Clarke.

Lindars, B., and S. S. Smalley (eds.)
1973   *Christ and Spirit in the New
        Testament.* Cambridge: Cambridge
        University Press.

Lindemann, A.
1983   "Die Kinder und die
        Gottesherrschaft." *Wort und Dienst*
        17:77–104.

Linnemann, E.
1992   *Is There a Synoptic Problem?*
        Translated by R. Yarbrough. Grand
        Rapids: Baker Academic.

Linton, O.
1965   "The Demand for a Sign from
        Heaven." *Studia theologica*
        19:112–29.
1976   "The Parable of the Children's
        Game." *New Testament Studies*
        22:159–79.

Lips, H. von
1988   "Schweine füttert man, Hunde
        nicht—ein Versuch, das Rätsel von
        Matthäus 7:6 zu lösen." *Zeitschrift für
        die neutestamentliche Wissenschaft*
        79:165–86.

Liver, J.
1963   "The Half-Shekel Offering in Biblical
        and Post-biblical Literature."
        Harvard Theological Review
        56:173–98.

Livingstone, E. A. (ed.)
1980   *Studia Biblica, 1978,* vol. 2: *Papers
        on the Gospels.* Journal for the Study
        of the New Testament: Supplement
        Series 2. Sheffield: JSOT.

Ljungman, H.
1954   *Das Gesetz erfüllen: Matth. 5,17ff. und
        3,15 untersucht.* Lund: Gleerup.

Llewelyn, S.
1989   "Mt 7:6a: Mistranslation
        or Interpretation?" *Novum
        Testamentum* 31:97–103.

Lloyd-Jones, D. M.
1981   *Studies in the Sermon on the Mount.*
        Grand Rapids: Eerdmans.

Loader, W. R. G.
1982   "Son of David, Blindness, and
        Loyalty in Matthew." *Catholic Biblical
        Quarterly* 44:570–85.
1997   *Jesus's Attitude toward the Law: A
        Study of the Gospels.* Tübingen: Mohr
        Siebeck.

Lochman, J. M.
1990   *The Lord's Prayer.* Translated by G. W.
        Bromiley. Grand Rapids: Eerdmans.

Lodge, J.
1986   "Matthew's Passion-Resurrection
        Narrative." *Chicago Studies* 25:3–20.

Loewe, H.
1940   *"Render unto Caesar": Religious
        and Political Loyalty in Palestine.*
        Cambridge: Cambridge University
        Press.

Lohfink, G.
1988   Wem gilt die Bergpredigt? Beiträge zu
        einer Ethik. Freiburg i.B.: Herder.
Lohfink, N.
1997   "The Appeasement of the Messiah:
        Thoughts on Ps 37 and the Third
        Beatitude." Theology Digest
        44:234–41.
Lohmeyer, E.
1956   Das Evangelium des Matthäus.
        Edited by W. Schmauck. Göttingen:
        Vandenhoeck & Ruprecht.
Lohr, C. H.
1961   "Oral Techniques in the Gospel of
        Matthew." Catholic Biblical Quarterly
        23:403–35.
Lohse, E.
1963   "Hosanna." Novum Testamentum
        6:113–19.
Longenecker, R. N. (ed.)
2000   The Challenge of Jesus' Parables.
        Grand Rapids: Eerdmans.
Longenecker, R. N., and M. C. Tenney (eds.)
1974   New Dimensions in New Testament
        Study. Grand Rapids: Zondervan.
Longstaff, T. R. W., and P. Thomas
1988   The Synoptic Problem: A Bibliography.
        Macon, GA: Mercer University Press.
Loos, H. van der
1965   The Miracles of Jesus. Supplements
        to Novum Testamentum 9. Leiden:
        Brill.
Losie, L.
1984   "The Cleansing of the Temple: A
        History of a Gospel Tradition in
        Light of Its Background in the Old
        Testament and in Early Judaism."
        PhD diss., Fuller Theological
        Seminary.
Lovering, E. (ed.)
1995   Society of Biblical Literature 1995
        Seminar Papers. Atlanta: Scholars.
Lövestam, E.
1968   Spiritus Blasphemia: Eine Studie zu
        Mk 3,28f par Mt 12,31f, Lk 12,10.
        Lund: Gleerup.
1995   Jesus and "This Generation."
        Stockholm: Almqvist & Wiksell.
Lowe, M.
1990   "A Hebraic Approach to the Parable
        of the Laborers in the Vineyard."
        Immanuel 24–25:109–17.
LSJ   A Greek-English Lexicon. By H. G.
        Liddell, R. Scott, and H. S. Jones. 9th
        ed. Oxford: Clarendon, 1968.

Luck, U.
1975   "Weisheit und Christologie in Mt
        11,25–30." Wort und Dienst 13:35–51.
Luck, W. F.
1987   Divorce and Remarriage: Recovering
        the Biblical View. San Francisco:
        Harper.
Luedemann, G.
1995   The Resurrection of Jesus: History,
        Experience, Theology. Minneapolis:
        Augsburg/Fortress.
Lull, D. (ed.)
1990   Society of Biblical Literature 1990
        Seminar Papers. Atlanta: Scholars.
Luomanen, P.
1998a   "Corpus Mixtum—an Appropriate
        Description of Matthew's
        Community?" Journal of Biblical
        Literature 117:469–80.
1998b   Entering the Kingdom of Heaven: A
        Study of the Structure of Matthew's
        View of Salvation. Tübingen: Mohr
        Siebeck.
Luz, U.
1978   "Die Erfüllung des Gesetzes bei
        Matthäus." Zeitschrift für Theologie
        und Kirche 75:398–435.
1989   Matthew 1–7: A Commentary.
        Translated by W. Linss. Minneapolis:
        Augsburg.
1991   "The Primacy Text (Matt 16:18)."
        Princeton Seminary Bulletin 12:41–55.
1992a   "Matthew's Anti-Judaism: Its Origin
        and Contemporary Significance."
        Currents in Theology and Mission
        19:405–15.
1992b   "The Son of Man in Matthew:
        Heavenly Judge or Human Christ?"
        Journal for the Study of the New
        Testament 48:12–16.
1994   Matthew in History: Interpretation,
        Influence, and Effects. Minneapolis:
        Augsburg.
1995   The Theology of the Gospel of
        Matthew. Cambridge: Cambridge
        University Press.
2001   Matthew 8–20. Translated by J. E.
        Couch. Hermeneia. Minneapolis:
        Fortress.
2005   Matthew 21–28. Translated by J. E.
        Couch. Hermeneia. Minneapolis:
        Fortress.
Lybaeck, L.
2002   Old and New in Matthew 11–13:
        Normativity in the Development of
        Three Theological Themes. Göttingen:
        Vandenhoeck & Ruprecht.

Maalouf, T. T.
1999   "Were the Magi from Persia
        or Arabia?" *Bibliotheca sacra*
        156:423–42.
Maccoby, H.
1982   "The Washing of Cups." *Journal
        for the Study of the New Testament*
        14:3–15.
1992   *Judas Iscariot and the Myth of Jewish
        Evil.* New York: Free Press.
MacDonald, D.
1989   "The Worth of the Assarion." *Historia*
        38:120–23.
Machen, J. G.
1930   *The Virgin Birth of Christ.* New York:
        Harper.
Mack, B. L., and V. K. Robbins (eds.)
1989   *Patterns of Persuasion in the Gospels.*
        Sonoma, CA: Polebridge.
Maclaurin, E.
1978   "Beelzeboul." *Novum Testamentum*
        20:156–60.
MacRae, G. (ed.)
1976   *Society of Biblical Literature 1976
        Seminar Papers.* Missoula, MT:
        Scholars.
Maher, M.
1975   "'Take My Yoke upon You' (Matt
        11:29)." *New Testament Studies*
        22:97–103.
Maier, G.
1979–80 *Matthäus-Evangelium.* 2 vols.
        Neuhausen: Hänssler.
Maier, J., and J. Schreiner (eds.)
1973   *Literatur und Religion des
        Frühjudentums.* Würzburg: Echter.
Malina, B.
1987   "Wealth and Poverty in the
        New Testament and Its World."
        Interpretation 41:354–67.
1990   "Jewish Christianity or Christian
        Judaism: Toward a Hypothetical
        Definition." *Journal for the Study of
        Judaism* 7:46–57.
Malina, B., and J. Neyrey
1988   *Calling Jesus Names: The Social Value
        of Labels in Matthew.* Sonoma, CA:
        Polebridge.
Mandell, S.
1984   "Who Paid the Temple Tax When
        the Jews Were under Roman
        Rule?" *Harvard Theological Review*
        77:223–42.
Mann, J.
1924   "Rabbinic Studies in the Synoptic
        Gospels." *Hebrew Union College
        Annual* 1:323–55.

Manns, F.
1988   "Une tradition rabbinique
        réinterprétée dans l'Évangile de
        Mt 22,1–10 et en Rm 11,30–32."
        Antonianum 63:416–26.
1991   "La parabole des talents:
        Wirkungsgeschichte et racines
        juives." *Recherches de science
        religieuse* 65:343–62.
Manor, D.
1982   "A Brief History of Levirate Marriage
        as It Relates to the Bible." *Near
        East Archaeological Society Bulletin*
        20:33–52.
Mans, M. J.
1997   "The Early Latin Church Fathers on
        Herod and the Infanticide." *Harvard
        Theological Studies* 53:92–102.
Manson, T.
1964   *Only to the House of Israel? Jesus and
        the Non-Jews.* Philadelphia: Fortress.
Mantey, J.
1939   "The Mistranslation of the Perfect
        Tense in John 20:23, Matthew 16:19,
        and Matthew 18:18." *Journal of
        Biblical Literature* 58:243–49.
1973   "Evidence That the Perfect Tense
        in John 20:23 and Matthew 16:19
        Is Mistranslated." *Journal of the
        Evangelical Theological Society*
        16:129–38.
1981   "Distorted Translations in John
        20:23; Matthew 16:18–19 and 18:18."
        Review and Expositor 78:409–16.
Marcus, J.
1988a   "Entering the Kingly Power of
        God." *Journal of Biblical Literature*
        107:663–75.
1988b   "The Gates of Hell and the Keys
        of the Kingdom." *Catholic Biblical
        Quarterly* 50:443–55.
Marguerat, D.
1978   "L'église et le monde en Matthieu
        13:36–43." *Revue de théologie et de
        philosophie* 110:111–29.
1981   *Le jugement dans l'Évangile selon
        Matthieu.* Geneva: Labor et Fides.
1995   "Le Noveau Testament est-il anti-
        juif? L'exemple de Matthieu et du
        livres des Actes." *Revue théologique
        de Louvain* 26:145–64.
Marin, L.
1971   "Essai d'analyse structurale d'un
        récit-parabole: Matthieu 13,1–23."
        Études théologiques et religieuses
        46:35–74.

Marshall, I. H.
1970 "Uncomfortable Words, VI: 'Fear Him Who Can Destroy Both Soul and Body in Hell' (Mt 10:28 RSV)." *Expository Times* 81:276–80.
1973 "New Wine in Old Wineskins, V: The Biblical Use of the Word Ἐκκλησία." *Expository Times* 84:359–63.
1978 *Commentary on Luke.* New International Greek Testament Commentary. Grand Rapids: Eerdmans.
1980 *Last Supper and Lord's Supper.* Grand Rapids: Eerdmans.
1994 "The Synoptic 'Son of Man' Sayings in the Light of Linguistic Study." Pp. 72–94 in *To Tell the Mystery: Essays on New Testament Eschatology in Honor of Robert H. Gundry.* Edited by Thomas E. Schmidt and Moisés Silva. Journal for the Study of the New Testament: Supplement Series 100. Sheffield: JSOT.

Martin, B. L.
1983 "Matthew on Christ and the Law." *Theological Studies* 44:53–70.

Martin, F.
1988 "Parole, écriture, accomplissement dans l'Évangile de Matthieu." *Sémiotique et Bible* 50:27–51.
1989 "Mourir: Matthieu 26–28." *Sémiotique et Bible* 53:18–47.
1996 "Parabole des talents: Matthieu 25,14–30." *Sémiotique et Bible* 84:14–24.

Martin, F., and L. Panier
1987 "Devoilement du péché et salut dans le récit de la passion selon saint Matthieu." *Lumière et vie* 36:72–88.

Martin, J.
1986 "Dispensational Approaches to the Sermon on the Mount." Pp. 35–48 in *Essays in Honor of J. Dwight Pentecost.* Edited by S. D. Toussaint and C. H. Dyer. Chicago: Moody.

Martin de Viviés, P. de
1995 *Jesus et le fils de l'homme: Emplois et significations de l'expression 'fils de l'homme' dans les Évangiles.* Lyon: Profac.

Martinez, E.
1961 "The Interpretation of οἱ μαθηταί in Matthew 18." *Catholic Biblical Quarterly* 23:281–92.

Marucci, C.
1986 "Die implizite Christologie in der sogenannten Vollmachtsfrage."

Zeitschrift für katholische Theologie 108:292–300.

Mason, S.
1990 "Pharisaic Dominance before 70 CE and the Gospels' Hypocrisy Charge (Matt 23:2–3)." *Harvard Theological Review* 83:363–81.

Massaux, E.
1990–93 *The Influence of the Gospel of Saint Matthew on Christian Literature before Saint Irenaeus.* Translated by N. Belval and S. Hecht. 3 vols. Macon, GA: Mercer University Press.

Massey, I. A.
1991 *Interpreting the Sermon on the Mount in the Light of Jewish Tradition as Evidenced in the Palestinian Targums of the Pentateuch.* Lewiston, NY: Mellen.

Masson, J.
1982 *Jésus, fils de David, dans les généalogies de saint Mathieu et de saint Luc.* Paris: Tequi.

Masuda, S.
1982 "The Good News of the Miracle of the Bread." *New Testament Studies* 28:191–219.

Matera, F. J.
1964 *The Trial of Jesus.* Toronto: Clark.
1986 *Passion Narratives and Gospel Theologies: Interpreting the Gospels through Their Passion Narratives.* New York: Paulist Press.
1987 "The Plot of Matthew's Gospel." *Catholic Biblical Quarterly* 49:233–53.
1989 "The Ethics of the Kingdom in the Gospel of Matthew." *Listening* 24:241–50.
1991 "The Trial of Jesus." *Interpretation* 45:5–16.

Mathys, H.-P.
1986 *Liebe deinen Nächsten wie dich selbst: Untersuchungen zum alttestamentlichen Gebot der Nächstenliebe (Lev 19:18).* Göttingen: Vandenhoeck & Ruprecht.

Mauser, U.
1961 "Matthew Twists the Scripture." *Journal of Biblical Literature* 80:143–48.
1963 *Christ in the Wilderness.* Studies in Biblical Theology 39. London: SCM.

Mayhue, R. L.
1995 "For What Did Christ Atone in Isa 53:4–5?" *Master's Seminary Journal* 6:121–41.

Maynard, A. H.
1985 "ΤΙ ΕΜΟΙ ΚΑΙ ΣΟΙ." *New Testament Studies* 31:582–86.

McArthur, H.
1987 "Celibacy in Judaism at the Time of Christian Beginnings." *Andrews University Seminary Studies* 25:163–81.

McArthur, H., and R. Johnston
1990 *They Also Taught in Parables: Rabbinic Parables from the First Centuries of the Christian Era.* Grand Rapids: Zondervan.

McCane, B. R.
1990 "'Let the Dead Bury Their Own Dead': Secondary Burial and Matt 8:21–22." *Harvard Theological Review* 83:31–43.

McCartney, D., and P. Enns
2001 "Matthew and Hosea: A Response to John Sailhamer." *Westminster Theological Journal* 63:97–105.

McConnell, R.
1969 *Law and Prophecy in Matthew's Gospel.* Basel: Reinhardt.

McDermott, J.
1984 "Mt 10:23 in Context." *Biblische Zeitschrift* 28:230–40.

McEleney, N. J.
1976 "Matthew 17:24–27—Who Paid the Temple Tax?" *Catholic Biblical Quarterly* 38:178–92.
1979 "The Principles of the Sermon on the Mount." *Catholic Biblical Quarterly* 41:552–70.
1981 "The Beatitudes of the Sermon on the Mount/Plain." *Catholic Biblical Quarterly* 43:1–13.
1985 "Does the Trumpet Sound or Resound? An Interpretation of Matthew 6:2." *Zeitschrift für die neutestamentliche Wissenschaft* 76:43–46.
1990 "Peter's Denials—How Many? To Whom?" *Catholic Biblical Quarterly* 52:467–72.
1994 "The Unity and Theme of Matthew 7:1–12." *Catholic Biblical Quarterly* 56:490–500.

McGing, B.
1991 "Pontius Pilate and the Sources." *Catholic Biblical Quarterly* 53:416–38.

McGuckin, J.
1986 *The Transfiguration of Christ in Scripture and Tradition.* Lewiston, NY: Mellen.

McIver, R. K.
1994 "One Hundred-Fold Yield—Miraculous or Mundane? Matthew 13:8, 23; Mark 4:8, 20; Luke 8:8." *New Testament Studies* 40:606–8.
1995a "The Parable of the Weeds among the Wheat (Matthew 13:24–30, 36–43) and the Relationship between the Kingdom and the Church as Portrayed in the Gospel of Matthew." *Journal of Biblical Literature* 114:643–59.
1995b "The Sabbath in the Gospel of Matthew: A Paradigm for Understanding the Law in Matthew." *Andrews University Seminary Studies* 33:231–43.
1999 "Twentieth-Century Approaches to the Matthean Community." *Andrews University Seminary Studies* 37:23–38.

McKenzie, J. L.
1968 "The Gospel according to Matthew." Pp. 62–114 in *The Jerome Biblical Commentary.* Edited by R. E. Brown et al. Englewood Cliffs, NJ: Prentice-Hall.

McKnight, S.
1986 "New Shepherds for Israel: An Historical and Critical Study of Matthew 9:35–11:1." PhD diss., University of Nottingham.
1991 *A Light among the Gentiles: Jewish Missionary Activity in the Second Temple Period.* Minneapolis: Fortress.
2001 "Jesus and the Twelve." *Bulletin of Biblical Research* 11:203–31.

McKnight, S., and G. R. Osborne (eds.)
2004 *The Face of New Testament Studies: A Survey of Recent Research.* Grand Rapids: Baker Academic.

McNeile, A. H.
1911 "Τότε in Saint Matthew." *Journal of Theological Studies* 12:127–28.
1915 *The Gospel according to St. Matthew.* London: Macmillan.

McRay, J.
2003 *Paul: His Life and Teaching.* Grand Rapids: Baker Academic.

Meadors, G. T.
1985 "The 'Poor' in the Beatitudes of Matthew and Luke." *Grace Theological Journal* 6:305–14.

Meadors, G. T. (ed.)
1991 *New Testament Essays in Honor of Homer A. Kent Jr.* Winona Lake, IN: BMH Books, 1991.

Meeks, W., and R. Wilken
1978 *Jews and Christians in Antioch in the First Four Centuries of the Common Era.* Society of Biblical Literature Sources for Biblical Study 13. Missoula, MT: Scholars.

Meier, J. P.
1976 *Law and History in St. Matthew's Gospel: A Redactional Study of Matt 5:17–48.* Analecta biblica 78. Rome: Biblical Institute Press.

1977a "Nations or Gentiles in Matthew 28:19?" *Catholic Biblical Quarterly* 39:94–102.

1977b "Two Disputed Questions in Matthew 28:16–20." *Journal of Biblical Literature* 96:407–24.

1979 *The Vision of Matthew: Christ, Church, and Morality in the First Gospel.* New York: Paulist Press.

1980a "John the Baptist in Matthew's Gospel." *Journal of Biblical Literature* 99:383–405.

1980b *Matthew.* New Testament Message. Wilmington, DE: Glazier.

1992 "The Brothers and Sisters of Jesus in Ecumenical Perspective." *Catholic Biblical Quarterly* 54:1–28.

1997 "The Circle of the Twelve: Did It Exist during Jesus's Public Ministry?" *Journal of Biblical Literature* 116:635–72.

Menahem, R.
1990 *"Epitropos/Paqid* in the Parable of the Laborers in the Vineyard." *Immanuel* 24/25:118–31.

Menken, M. J.
1984 "The References to Jeremiah in the Gospel according to Matthew." *Ephemerides theologicae lovanienses* 60:5–24.

1997 "The Source of the Quotation from Isaiah 53:4 in Matthew 8:17." *Novum Testamentum* 39:313–27.

1998a "The Quotation from Isaiah 42:1–4 in Matthew 12:18–21: Its Relationship with the Matthean Context." *Bijdragen* 59:251–66.

1998b "The Textual Form of the Quotation from Isaiah 8:23–9:1 in Matthew 4:15–16." *Revue biblique* 105:526–45.

1999a "The Greek Translation of Hosea 11:1 in Matthew 2:15: Matthean or Pre-Matthean?" *Filologia neotestamentaria* 12:79–88.

1999b "The Quotation from Isaiah 42,1–4 in Matthew 12,18–21: Its Textual Form."

Ephemerides theologicae lovanienses 75:32–52.

2001a "The Sources of the Old Testament Quotation in Matthew 2:23." *Journal of Biblical Literature* 120:451–68.

2001b "The Textual Form of the Quotation of Isaiah 7:14 in Matthew 1:23." *Novum Testamentum* 43:144–60.

Menninger, R. E.
1994 *Israel and the Church in the Gospel of Matthew.* New York: Lang.

Merklein, H. (ed.)
1989 *Neues Testament und Ethik.* Freiburg i.B.: Herder.

Merrill, E.
1980 "The Sign of Jonah." *Journal of the Evangelical Theological Society* 23:123–29.

Metzger, B.
1951 "The Formulas Introducing Quotations of Scripture in the New Testament and in the Mishnah." *Journal of Biblical Literature* 70:297–307.

1957 "How Many Times Does 'EPIOUSIOS' Occur outside the Lord's Prayer?" *Expository Times* 69:52–54.

1972 "The Text of Matthew 1:16." Pp. 16–24 in *Studies in New Testament and Early Christian Literature.* Edited by D. Aune. Leiden: Brill.

1994 *A Textual Commentary on the Greek New Testament.* 2nd ed. Stuttgart: Deutsche Bibelgesellschaft.

Meyer, B.
1990 "Many (= All) Are Called, but Few (= Not All) Are Chosen." *New Testament Studies* 36:89–97.

Meyer, P.
1986 "Matthew 21:1–11." *Interpretation* 40:180–85.

Mézange, C.
2000 "Simon le Zélote était-il un révolutionnaire?" *Biblica* 81:489–506.

Michaels, J. R.
1965 "Apostolic Hardships and Righteous Gentiles: A Study of Matthew 25:31–46." *Journal of Biblical Literature* 84:27–37.

1968 "The Parable of the Regretful Son." *Harvard Theological Review* 61:15–26.

Mielziner, M.
1968 *Introduction to the Talmud.* New York: Bloch.

Migliore, D.
1993   *The Lord's Prayer: Principles for Reclaiming Christian Prayer.* Grand Rapids: Eerdmans.

Milavec, A.
1989   "Mark's Parable of the Wicked Husbandmen as Reaffirming God's Predilection for Israel." *Journal of Ecumenical Studies* 26:289–312.
1995   "The Social Setting of 'Turning the Other Cheek' and 'Loving One's Enemies' in Light of the *Didache.*" *Biblical Theology Bulletin* 25:131–43.

Miler, J.
1999   *Les citations d'accomplissement dans l'Évangile de Matthieu.* Rome: Pontifical Biblical Institute.
2001   "Le travail de l'accomplissement: Matthieu et les Écritures." *Foi et vie* 100:13–29.

Milikowsky, C.
1988   "Which Gehenna? Retribution and Eschatology in the Synoptic Gospels." *New Testament Studies* 34:238–49.

Miller, R.
1988   "The Rejection of the Prophets in Q." *Journal of Biblical Literature* 107:225–40.

Mills, W. E.
2000   *Bibliographies on the Life and Teachings of Jesus,* vol. 3: *The Sermon on the Mount/Plain.* Lewiston, NY: Mellen.

Milton, H.
1962   "The Structure of the Prologue to St. Matthew's Gospel." *Journal of Biblical Literature* 81:175–81.

Minear, P. S.
1982   *Matthew: The Teacher's Gospel.* New York: Pilgrim.
1997   "The Salt of the Earth." *Interpretation* 51:31–41.
2000   "The Home of the *Our Father.*" *Worship* 74:212–22.
2002   "But Whose Prayer Is It?" *Worship* 76:324–38.

Mitton, C.
1956–57   "Expository Problems: Present Justification and Future Judgment—a Discussion of the Parable of the Sheep and the Goats." *Expository Times* 68:46–50.
1973   "Leaven." *Expository Times* 84:339–43.

Moffitt, D. M.
2006   "Righteous Bloodshed, Matthew's Passion Narrative, and the Temple's Destruction: Lamentations as a Matthean Intertext." *Journal of Biblical Literature* 125:299–320.

Mohrlang, R.
1984   *Matthew and Paul: A Comparison of Ethical Perspectives.* Society for New Testament Studies Monograph Series 48. Cambridge: Cambridge University Press.

Molldrem, M.
1991   "A Hermeneutic of Pastoral Care and the Law/Gospel Paradigm Applied to the Divorce Texts of Scripture." *Interpretation* 45:43–54.

Moloney, F.
1979   "Matthew 19:3–12 and Celibacy." *Journal for the Study of the New Testament* 2:42–60.

Monsarrat, V.
1977   "Matthieu 24–25." *Foi et vie* 5:67–80.

Montefiore, C., and H. Loewe
1974   *A Rabbinic Anthology.* New York: Schocken.

Montefiore, H.
1963–64   "Jesus and the Temple Tax." *New Testament Studies* 10:60–71.

Moo, D.
1983   *The Old Testament in the Gospel Passion Narratives.* Sheffield: JSOT.
1984   "Jesus and the Authority of the Mosaic Law." *Journal for the Study of the New Testament* 20:3–49.

Moor, J.
1998   "The Targumic Background of Mark 12:1–12: The Parable of the Wicked Tenants." *Journal for the Study of Judaism* 29:63–80.

Moore, G. F.
1921   "Fourteen Generations—490 Years." *Harvard Theological Review* 14:97–113.

Moore, W.
1975   "*Biazo, Arpazo,* and Cognates in Josephus." *New Testament Studies* 21:519–43.
1989   "Violence to the Kingdom." *Expository Times* 100:174–77.

Mora, V.
1983   *Le signe de Jonas.* Paris: Cerf.

Morgan, C., and R. Peterson (eds.)
2004   *Hell under Fire.* Grand Rapids: Zondervan.

Morgan, M. P., and P. J. Kobelski
1989   *To Touch the Text.* New York: Crossroad.

Morosco, R. E.
1979   "Redaction Criticism and the Evangelical: Matthew 10 as a Test Case." *Journal of the Evangelical Theological Society* 22:323–32.
1984   "Matthew's Formation of a Commissioning Type-Scene out of the Story of Jesus' Commissioning of the Twelve." *Journal of Biblical Literature* 103:539–56.

Morrice, W.
1984   "The Parable of the Dragnet and the Gospel of Thomas." *Expository Times* 95:269–73.

Morris, L.
1992   *The Gospel according to Matthew.* Grand Rapids: Eerdmans.

Moses, A. D. A.
1996   *Matthew's Transfiguration Story and Jewish-Christian Controversy.* Journal for the Study of the New Testament: Supplement Series 122. Sheffield: Sheffield Academic Press.

Motte, A.
1981   "La structure du logion de Matthieu, XI,28–30." *Revue biblique* 88:226–33.

Motyer, J. A.
1970   "Context and Content in the Interpretation of Isa 7:14." *Tyndale Bulletin* 21:118–25.

Motyer, S.
1997   *Your Father the Devil? A New Approach to John and the Jews.* Carlisle, UK: Paternoster.

Moulder, W.
1977   "The Old Testament Background and the Interpretation of Mark x.45." *New Testament Studies* 24:120–27.

Moule, C. F. D.
1959   *An Idiom Book of New Testament Greek.* 2nd ed. Cambridge: Cambridge University Press.
1968   "Fulfillment-Words in the New Testament: Use and Abuse." *New Testament Studies* 14:293–320.
1974   "An Unresolved Problem in the Temptation-Clause in the Lord's Prayer." *Reformed Theological Review* 33:65–75.

Moulton, J. H.
1908   *A Grammar of New Testament Greek,* vol. 1: *Prolegomena.* 3rd ed. Edinburgh: T&T Clark.

Moulton, J. H., and W. F. Howard
1920   *A Grammar of New Testament Greek,* vol. 2: *Accidence and Word Formation.* Edinburgh: T&T Clark.

Moulton, J. H., and N. Turner
1963   *A Grammar of New Testament Greek,* vol. 3: *Syntax.* Edinburgh: T&T Clark.
1976   *A Grammar of New Testament Greek,* vol. 4: *Style.* Edinburgh: T&T Clark.

Mounce, R. H.
1985   *Matthew.* Good News Commentary. San Francisco: Harper.

Mowery, R. L.
1990   "Subtle Differences: The Matthean 'Son of God' References." *Novum Testamentum* 32:193–200.
1994   "The Matthean References to the Kingdom: Different Terms for Different Audiences." *Ephemerides theologicae lovanienses* 70:398–405.
2002   "Son of God in Roman Imperial Titles and Matthew." *Biblica* 83:100–110.

Moyise, S. (ed.)
2000   *The Old Testament in the New Testament.* Sheffield: Sheffield Academic Press.

Müller, M.
1992   "The Gospel of Matthew and the Mosaic Law—a Chapter of a Biblical Theology." *Studia theologica* 46:109–20.
1999   "The Theological Interpretation of the Figure of Jesus in the Gospel of Matthew: Some Principal Features of Matthean Christology." *New Testament Studies* 45:157–73.
2001   "The Reception of the Old Testament in Matthew and Luke-Acts: From Interpretation to Proof from Scripture." *Novum Testamentum* 43:315–30.

Müller, P.
1992   *In der Mitte der Gemeinde: Kinder im Neuen Testament.* Neukirchen-Vluyn: Neukirchener Verlag.

Mullins, T. Y.
1991   "Jesus, the 'Son of David.'" *Andrews University Seminary Studies* 29:117–26.

Munck, J.
1962   "Die Tradition über das Matthäusevangelium bei Papias." Pp. 249–60 in *Neotestamentica et Patristica: Eine Freundesgabe, Herrn Professor Dr. Oscar Cullmann zu seinem 60. Geburtstag überreicht.* Edited by W. C. van Unnik. Novum Testamentum Supplement 6. Leiden: Brill.

Murphy-O'Connor, J.
1975   "The Structure of Matthew 14–17."
        Revue biblique 82:360–84.
1987   "What Really Happened at the
        Transfiguration?" *Bible Review*
        3:8–21.
1990   "John the Baptist and Jesus: History
        and Hypothesis." *New Testament
        Studies* 36:359–74.
1999a   "Fishers of Fish, Fishers of Men:
        What We Know of the First Disciples
        from Their Profession." *Bible Review*
        15:22–27, 48–49
1999b   "Triumph over Temptation: The
        Historical Core behind the Testing of
        Jesus." *Bible Review* 15:34–43, 48–49.

Mussner, F.
1959   "Der nicht erkannte Kairos (Mt
        11,16–10; Lk 7,31–5)." *Biblica*
        40:599–612.

NA²⁷   *Novum Testamentum Graece.* Edited
        by [E. and E. Nestle,] B. Aland et
        al. 27th rev. ed. Stuttgart: Deutsche
        Bibelgesellschaft, 1993.

Nagel, D. von
1999   "Das Gleichnis vom Schatz im Acker
        und von der kostbaren Perle." *Erbe
        und Auftrag* 75:234–38.

Nau, A. J.
1992   *Peter in Matthew.* Collegeville, MN:
        Liturgical Press.

Neirynck, F.
1974   *The Minor Agreements of Matthew
        and Luke against Mark with a
        Cumulative List.* Louvain: Louvain
        University Press.
1988   "ΑΠΟ ΤΟΤΕ ΗΡΞΑΤΟ and the
        Structure of Matthew." *Ephemerides
        theologicae lovanienses* 64:21–59.

Nepper-Christiansen, P.
1958   *Das Matthäusevangelium: Ein
        judenchristliches Evangelium?* Århus:
        Universitetsforlaget.
1995   "Math 10,23—Et crux interpretum?"
        Dansk teologisk tidsskrift 58:161–75.

Nettelhorst, R. P.
1988   "The Genealogy of Jesus." *Journal of
        the Evangelical Theological Society*
        31:169–72.

Neudecker, R.
1992   "'And You Shall Love Your Neighbor
        as Yourself—I Am the Lord' (Lev
        19:18) in Jewish Interpretation."
        Biblica 73:496–517.
1994   "Das 'Ehescheidungsgesetz' von Dtn
        24:1–4 nach altjüdischer Auslegung:
        Ein Beitrag zum Verständnis der
        neutestamentlichen Aussagen zur
        Ehescheidung." *Biblica* 75:350–87.

Neugebauer, F.
1986   *Jesu Versuchung: Wegentscheidung
        am Anfang.* Tübingen: Mohr.

Neusner, J.
1973   *From Politics to Piety: The Emergence
        of Pharisaic Judaism.* Englewood
        Cliffs, NJ: Prentice-Hall.
1976   "'First Cleanse the Inside': The
        'Halakhic' Background of a
        Controversy-Saying." *New Testament
        Studies* 22:486–95.

Neusner, J., and E. S. Frerichs (eds.)
1985   *"To See Ourselves as Others See Us":
        Christians, Jews, "Others" in Late
        Antiquity.* Chico, CA: Scholars.

Neville, D.
1994   *Arguments from Order in Synoptic
        Source Criticism.* Macon, GA: Mercer
        University Press.

Newell, J., and R. Newell
1972   "The Parable of the Wicked Tenants."
        Novum Testamentum 14:226–37.

Newman, B. M., and P. C. Stine
1988   *A Translator's Handbook on the
        Gospel of Matthew.* New York: United
        Bible Societies.

Newport, K.
1990   "A Note on the 'Seat of Moses'
        (Matthew 23:2)." *Andrews University
        Seminary Studies* 28:53–58.
1995   *The Sources and Sitz im Leben of
        Matthew 23.* Journal for the Study
        of the New Testament: Supplement
        Series 117. Sheffield: Sheffield
        Academic Press.

Neyrey, J.
1982   "The Thematic Use of Isaiah 42:1–4
        in Matthew 12." *Biblica* 63:457–73.
1998   *Honor and Shame in the Gospel of
        Matthew.* Louisville: Westminster/
        John Knox.

Nickelsburg, G. W. E.
1972   *Resurrection, Immortality, and
        Eternal Life.* Cambridge: Harvard
        University Press.
1981   "Enoch, Levi, and Peter: Recipients
        of Revelation in Upper Galilee."
        Journal of Biblical Literature 100:575–
        600.
2003   *Ancient Judaism and Christian
        Origins.* Minneapolis: Fortress.

Nicoll, W. R. (ed.)
1957   *The Expositor's Greek Testament.*
        5 vols. Reprinted Grand Rapids:
        Eerdmans.

Nida, E. A., and C. R. Taber
1982   *The Theory and Practice of Translation.* Leiden: Brill.
NIDNTT   *New International Dictionary of New Testament Theology.* Edited by C. Brown. 4 vols. Grand Rapids: Zondervan, 1975–85.
Niedner, F. A.
1989   "Rereading Matthew on Jerusalem and Judaism." *Biblical Theology Bulletin* 19:43–47.
2002   "Rachel's Lament." *Word and World* 22:406–14.
Nijman, M., and K. A. Worp
1999   "Ἐπιούσιος in a Documentary Papyrus?" *Novum Testamentum* 41:231–34.
Nineham, D.
1975–76   "The Genealogy in St. Matthew's Gospel and Its Significance for the Study of the Gospel." *Bulletin of the John Rylands Library* 58:421–44.
Nolan, B. M.
1979   *The Royal Son of God: The Christology of Matthew 1–2 in the Setting of the Gospel.* Göttingen: Vandenhoeck & Ruprecht.
Nolland, J.
1995   "The Gospel Prohibition of Divorce: Tradition History and Meaning." *Journal for the Study of the New Testament* 58:19–35.
1996a   "Genealogical Annotation in Genesis as Background for the Matthean Genealogy of Jesus." *Tyndale Bulletin* 47:115–22.
1996b   "No Son-of-God Christology in Matthew 1:18–25." *Journal for the Study of the New Testament* 62:3–12.
1996c   "What Kind of Genesis Do We Have in Matt 1:1?" *New Testament Studies* 42:463–71.
1997a   "The Four (Five) Women and Other Annotations in Matthew's Genealogy." *New Testament Studies* 43:527–39.
1997b   "Jechoniah and His Brothers (Matthew 1:11)." *Bulletin of Biblical Research* 7:169–78.
1998   "The Sources for Matthew 2:1–12." *Catholic Biblical Quarterly* 60:283–300.
2005   *The Gospel according to Matthew.* New International Greek Testament Commentary. Grand Rapids: Eerdmans.

Novakovic, L.
1997   "Jesus as the Davidic Messiah in Matthew." *Horizons in Biblical Theology* 19:148–91.
2003   *Messiah, the Healer of the Sick: A Study of Jesus as the Son of David in the Gospel of Matthew.* Tübingen: Mohr Siebeck.
Oakley, I. J.
1985   "Hypocrisy in Matthew." *Irish Biblical Studies* 7:118–38.
Oakman, D. E.
1993   "Cursing Fig Trees and Robbers' Dens." *Semeia* 64:253–72.
Oberlinner, L., and P. Fiedler (eds.)
1991   *Salz der Erde—Licht der Welt: Exegetische Studien zum Matthäusevangelium.* Stuttgart: Katholisches Bibelwerk.
O'Brien, P. T., and D. G. Peterson (eds.)
1986   *God Who Is Rich in Mercy.* Grand Rapids: Baker Academic.
O'Callaghan, J.
1990   "Fluctuación textual en Mt 20.21, 26, 27." *Biblica* 71:552–58.
Oesterley, W.
1936   *The Gospel Parables in the Light of Their Jewish Background.* London: Macmillan.
Ogawa, A.
1979   "Paraboles de l'Israel véritable? Réconsidération critique de Mt.xxi.28–xxii.14." *Novum Testamentum* 21:121–49.
O'Grady, J. F.
2001   "The Community of Matthew." *Chicago Studies* 40:239–50.
Olmstead, W. G.
2003   *Matthew's Trilogy of Parables: The Nation, the Nations, and the Reader in Matthew 21:28–22:14.* Cambridge: Cambridge University Press.
O'Neill, J. C.
1983   "The Unforgivable Sin." *Journal for the Study of the New Testament* 19:37–42.
1993a   "'Good Master' and the 'Good' Sayings in the Teaching of Jesus." *Irish Biblical Studies* 15:167–78.
1993b   "The Lord's Prayer." *Journal for the Study of the New Testament* 51:3–25.
Orchard, B.
1973   "The Meaning of τὸν ἐπιούσιον (Mt 6:11 = Lk 11:3)." *Biblical Theology Bulletin* 3:274–82.

Orchard, B., and H. Riley
1987   *The Order of the Synoptics: Why Three Synoptic Gospels?* Macon, GA: Mercer University Press.

O'Rourke, J.
1962   "The Fulfillment Texts in Matthew." *Catholic Biblical Quarterly* 24:394–403.

Orton, D.
1989   *The Understanding Scribe: Matthew and the Apocalyptic Ideal.* Sheffield: JSOT.

Osborne, G. R.
1984   *The Resurrection Narratives: A Redactional Study.* Grand Rapids: Baker Academic.
2005   "Historical Narrative and Truth in the Bible." *Journal of the Evangelical Theological Society* 48:673–88.

Osborne, R. E.
1973   "The Provenance of Matthew's Gospel." *Studies in Religion* 3:220–35.

Oster, R.
1985   "'Show Me a Denarius': Symbolism of Roman Coinage and Christian Beliefs." *Restoration Quarterly* 28:107–15.

Ostmeyer, K.-H.
2000   "Der Stammbaum des Verheissenen: Theologische Implikationen der Namen und Zahlen in Mt 1.1–17." *New Testament Studies* 46:175–92.

OTP   *The Old Testament Pseudepigrapha.* Edited by J. H. Charlesworth. 2 vols. Garden City, NY: Doubleday, 1983–85.

Overholt, T.
1982   "Seeing Is Believing: The Social Setting of Prophetic Acts of Power." *Journal for the Study of the Old Testament* 23:3–31.

Overman, J. A.
1990a   "Heroes and Villains in Palestinian Lore: Matthew's Use of Traditional Jewish Polemic in the Passion Narrative." Pp. 592–602 in *Society of Biblical Literature 1990 Seminar Papers.* Edited by D. Lull. Atlanta: Scholars.
1990b   *Matthew's Gospel and Formative Judaism.* Minneapolis: Fortress.
1996   *Church and Community in Crisis: The Gospel according to Matthew.* Valley Forge, PA: Trinity.

Owen-Ball, D.
1993   "Rabbinic Rhetoric and the Tribute Passage (Mt. 22:15–22; Mk. 12:13–17;

Lk. 20:20–26)." *Novum Testamentum* 35:1–14.

Paesler, K.
1999   *Das Tempelwort Jesu: Die Traditionen von Tempelzerstörung und Tempelerneuerung im Neuen Testament.* Göttingen: Vandenhoeck & Ruprechtt.

Paffenroth, K.
1999   "Jesus as Anointed and Healing Son of David in Matthew." *Biblica* 80:547–54.

Pak, C. H.
1997   "Die Arbeiter im Weingerg (Mt 20,1–16)." *Bibel und Kirche* 52:136–37.

Pamment, M.
1980–81 "The Kingdom of Heaven according to the First Gospel." *New Testament Studies* 27:211–32.
1983   "The Son of Man in the First Gospel." *New Testament Studies* 29:116–29.

Panier, L.
1993   "Le fils de l'homme et les nations." *Sémiotique et Bible* 69:39–52.

Pantle-Schieber, K.
1989   "Anmerkungen zur Auseinandersetzung von ekklesia und Judentum im Matthäusevangelium." *Zeitschrift für die neutestamentliche Wissenschaft* 80:145–62.

Pappas, H.
1980   "The Exhortation to Fearless Confession—Mt 10:26–33." *Greek Orthodox Theological Review* 25:239–48.

Park, E. C.
1995   *The Mission Discourse in Matthew's Interpretation.* Tübingen: Mohr Siebeck.

Park, S. J.
2000   "La tempête apaisée: Matthieu 8,23–27." *Semiotique et Bible* 99:33–51.

Parker, D. C.
1999   "Was Matthew Written before 50 CE? The Magdalen Papyrus of Matthew." *Expository Times* 107:40–43.

Parpola, S.
2001   "The Magi and the Star: Babylonian Astronomy Dates Jesus' Birth." *Bible Review* 17/6:16–23, 52, 54.

Parratt, J.
1969   "The Laying on of Hands in the NT: A Reexamination in the Light of the Hebrew Terminology." *Expository Times* 80:210–14.

Pathrapankal, J.
1997   "The Ethics of the Sermon on the Mount: Its Relevance and Challenge to Our Times." *Jeevadhara* 27:389–407.

Patsch, H.
1971   "Der Einzug in Jerusalem." *Zeitschrift für Theologie und Kirche* 68:1–26.

Patte, D.
1983   "Jesus's Pronouncement about Entering the Kingdom as a Child: A Structural Exegesis." *Semeia* 29:3–42.
1987   *The Gospel according to Matthew: A Structural Commentary on Matthew's Faith.* Philadelphia: Fortress.
1988   "Anti-Semitism in the New Testament: Confronting the Dark Side of Paul's and Matthew's Teaching." *Chicago Theological Seminary Register* 78:31–52.
1996   *Discipleship according to the Sermon on the Mount.* Valley Forge, PA: Trinity.

Pautrel, R.
1936   "Les Canons du Mashal rabbinique, I." *Recherches de science religieuse* 26:6–45.
1938   "Les Canons du Mashal rabbinique, II." *Recherches de science religieuse* 28:264–81.

Pawlikowski, J. T.
1989   "Christian-Jewish Dialogue and Matthew." *Bible Today* 27:356–62.

Payne, P. B.
1978   "The Order of Sowing and Ploughing in the Parable of the Sower." *New Testament Studies* 25:123–29.
1980   "The Seeming Inconsistency of the Interpretation of the Parable of the Sower." *New Testament Studies* 26:564–68.

Peabody, D. A.
2002   *One Gospel from Two: Mark's Use of Matthew and Luke.* Valley Forge, PA: Trinity.

Pedersen, S.
1975   "Die Proklamation Jesu als des eschatologischen Offenbarungsträgers (Mt. xvii.1–13)." *Novum Testamentum* 17:241–64.

Peels, H. G.
2001   "The Blood 'from Abel to Zechariah' (Matthew 23:35; Luke 11:50) and the Canon of the Old Testament." *Zeitschrift für die alttestamentliche Wissenschaft* 113:583–601.

Peerbolte, L.
1996   *The Antecedents of Antichrist: A Traditio-Historical Study of the Earliest Christian Views on Eschatological Opponents.* Leiden: Brill.

Pelletier, M.
1990   *Les pharisiens: Histoire d'un parti méconnu.* Paris: Cerf.

Pennington, J.
2003   "'Heaven' and 'Heavens' in the LXX: Exploring the Relationship between *Shamyim* and *Ouranos*." *Bulletin of the International Organization for Septuagint and Cognate Studies* 36:39–59.

Perels, O. (ed.)
1963   *Begründung und Gebrauch der heiligen Taufe.* Berlin: Lutherisches Verlagshaus.

Perkins, L.
1998   "Greater than Solomon (Matt 12:42)." *Trinity Journal* 19:207–17.

Perkins, P.
1982   *Love Commands in the New Testament.* New York: Paulist Press.

Perlewitz, M.
1976   *The Gospel of Matthew.* Wilmington, DE: Glazier.

Perowne, S.
1973   *The Life and Times of Herod the Great.* 1956. Reprinted London: Hodder & Stoughton.
1974   *The Later Herods.* 1958. Reprinted London: Hodder & Stoughton.

Perrin, N.
1963   *The Kingdom of God in the Teaching of Jesus.* Philadelphia: Westminster.

Pesch, R.
1988   *Der Prozess Jesu geht weiter.* Freiburg i.B.: Herder.

Pesch, W.
1963   "Die sogenannte Gemeindeordnung Mt 18." *Biblische Zeitschrift* 7:220–35.
1966   *Matthäus der Seelsorger.* Stuttgart: Katholisches Bibelwerk.
1968   "Levi-Matthäus (Mc 2.14/Mt 9.9; 10.3). Ein Beitrag zur Lösung eines alten Problems." *Zeitschrift für die neutestamentliche Wissenschaft* 59:40–56.
1972   *Der Besessene von Gerasa.* Stuttgart: Katholisches Bibelwerk.

Petersen, W.
1981   "The Parable of the Lost Sheep in the Gospel of Thomas and the

Synoptics." *Novum Testamentum* 23:128–47.

Peterson, D. N.
2006   "Translating Παραλυτικός in Mark 2:1–12: A Proposal." *Bulletin of Biblical Research* 16:261–72.

Peterson, W. L.
1998   "The *Vorlage* of Shem-Tob's 'Hebrew Matthew.'" *New Testament Studies* 44:490–512.

Petrie, C. S.
1967   "The Authorship of 'The Gospel according to Matthew': A Reconsideration of the External Evidence." *New Testament Studies* 14:15–33.

Petrotta, A. J.
1985   "A Closer Look at Matt 2:6 and Its Old Testament Sources." *Journal of the Evangelical Theological Society* 28:47–52.

1990   "An Even Closer Look at Matt 2:6 and Its Old Testament Sources." *Journal of the Evangelical Theological Society* 33:311–15.

Petuchowski, J., and M. Brocke
1978   *The Lord's Prayer and Jewish Liturgy.* New York: Seabury.

Phillips, G.
1985   "History and Text: The Reader in Context in Matthew's Parables Discourse." *Semeia* 31:111–38.

Philonenko, M.
2001   *Le Notre Père: De la prière de Jésus à la prière des disciples.* Paris: Gallimard.

Pilch, J. J.
1981   "Biblical Leprosy and Body Symbolism." *Irish Biblical Studes* 11:108–13.

Piper, J.
1979   *Love Your Enemies.* Society for New Testament Studies Monograph Series 38. Cambridge: Cambridge University Press.

Pixner, B.
1985   "Searching for the New Testament Site of Bethsaida." *Biblical Archaeologist* 48:207–16.

Plummer, A.
1915   *An Exegetical Commentary on the Gospel according to S. Matthew.* London: R. Scott.

Plumptre, E.
1957   *The Gospel according to Matthew.* Reprinted Grand Rapids: Zondervan.

Poelman, R.
1964   *Times of Grace: The Sign of Forty in the Bible.* New York: Herder.

Pope, M.
1988   "Hosanna—What It Really Means." *Bible Review* 4:16–25.

Porter, L. B.
1995   "Salt of the Earth." *Homiletic and Pastoral Review* 95:51–58.

Porter, S. E.
1988   "Vague Verbs, Periphrastics, and Matt 16:19." *Filologia neotestamentica* 1:155–73.

Porter, S. E., and A. R. Cross (eds.)
1999   *Baptism, the New Testament, and the Church.* Sheffield: Sheffield Academic Press.

Porter, S. E., P. Joyce, and D. E. Orton (eds.)
1994   *Crossing the Boundaries: Essays in Biblical Interpretation in Honour of Michael D. Goulder.* Leiden: Brill.

Porter, S. E., and J. T. Reed (eds.)
1999   *Discourse Analysis and the New Testament: Approaches and Results.* Sheffield: Sheffield Academic Press.

Porton, G.
1994   *The Stranger within Your Gates: Converts and Conversion in Rabbinic Literature.* Chicago: University of Chicago Press.

Pöttner, M.
1997   "Metaphern der universalen Liebe (Mt 5,13a. 14a)." *Theologische Literaturzeitung* 122:105–21.

Powell, M. A.
1988   "The Religious Leaders in Matthew: A Literary-Critical Approach." PhD diss., Union Theological Seminary, Richmond, VA.

1990   *What Is Narrative Criticism?* Minneapolis: Fortress.

1992a   "The Plots and Subplots of Matthew's Gospel." *New Testament Studies* 38:198–202.

1992b   "Toward a Narrative-Critical Understanding of Matthew." *Interpretation* 46:341–46.

1994   "Expected and Unexpected Readings of Matthew: What the Reader Knows." *Anglican Theological Review* 48/2:31–52.

1995a   "Do and Keep What Moses Says (Matthew 23:2–7)." *Journal of Biblical Literature* 114:419–35.

1995b   *God with Us: A Pastoral Theology of Matthew's Gospel.* Minneapolis: Fortress.

1996   "Matthew's Beatitudes: Reversals and Rewards of the Kingdom." *Catholic Biblical Quarterly* 58:460–79.

2000   "The Magi as Wise Men: Re-examining a Basic Supposition." *New Testament Studies* 46:1–20.

Poythress, V., and W. Grudem

2004   *The TNIV and the Gender-Neutral Bible Controversy.* Nashville: Broadman & Holman.

Pritz, R.

1988   *Nazarene Jewish Christianity: From the End of the New Testament until Its Disappearance in the Fourth Century.* Studia postbiblica 37. Leiden: Brill.

Pryor, J. W.

1991a   "The Great Thanksgiving and the Fourth Gospel." *Biblische Zeitschrift* 35:157–79.

1991b   "John 3:3, 5: A Study in the Relation of John's Gospel to the Synoptic Tradition." *Journal for the Study of the New Testament* 41:71–95.

Przybylski, B.

1974   "The Role of Mt 3:13–4:11 in the Structure and Theology of the Gospel of Matthew." *Biblical Theology Bulletin* 4:222–35.

1980   *Righteousness in Matthew and in His World of Thought.* New York: Cambridge University Press.

1986   "The Setting of Matthean Anti-Judaism." Pp. 181–200 in *Anti-Judaism in Early Christianity*, vol. 1: *Paul and the Gospels.* Edited by P. Richardson and D. Granskou. Waterloo, ON: Wilfrid Laurier University Press.

Puech, E.

1988   "Un hymne essenien en partie retrouvé et les Béatitudes: 1QH 5:12–6:18 (= col. 13–14:7) et 4QBeat." *Revue de Qumran* 13:59–88.

1991   "4Q525 et les péricopes de Béatitudes en ben Sira et Matthieu." *Revue biblique* 138:80–106.

Puig i Tàrrech, A.

1985   *La parabole des dix vierges (Mt 25,1–13).* Rome: Biblical Institute Press.

Pusey, K.

1984   "Jewish Proselyte Baptism." *Expository Times* 95:141–45.

Quesnel, M.

1991   *Jésus-Christ selon saint Matthieu: Synthèse théologique.* Paris: Desclée.

Quesnell, Q.

1969   *The Mind of Mark: Interpretation and Method through the Exegesis of Mark 6,52.* Analecta biblica 38. Rome: Pontifical Biblical Institute.

Rabbinowitz, N. S.

2003   "Does Jesus Recognize the Authority of the Pharisees and Does He Endorse Their *Halakhah*?" *Journal of the Evangelical Theological Society* 46:423–47.

Rahmni, L.

1990   "Stone Synagogue Chairs: Their Identification, Use, and Significance." *Israel Exploration Journal* 40:192–214.

Raimbault, C.

1998   "Une analyse structurelle de l'adoration des mages in Mt 2, 1–12." *Estudios bíblicos* 56:221–35.

Ramsay, A.

1946   *The Glory of God and the Transfiguration of Christ.* Philadelphia: Westminster.

Rathey, M.

1991   "Talion im NT? Zu Mt 5,38–42." *Zeitschrift für die neutestamentliche Wissenschaft* 82:264–66.

Reeves, K. H.

1993   *The Resurrection Narrative in Matthew: A Literary-Critical Examination.* Lewiston, NY: Mellen.

1998   "They Worshiped Him, and They Doubted: Matthew 28:17." *Bible Translator* 49:344–49.

Refoulé, F.

1993   "Jésus, nouveau Moïse, ou Pierre, nouveau grand prêtre?" *Revue théologique de Louvain* 24:145–62.

Reicke, B.

1986   *The Roots of the Synoptic Gospels.* Philadelphia: Fortress.

Reinhartz, A.

1988   "The New Testament and Anti-Judaism: A Literary-Critical Approach." *Journal of Ecumenical Studies* 25:524–37.

Reiser, M.

1997   *Jesus and Judgment: The Eschatological Proclamation in Its Jewish Context.* Translated by L. M. Maloney. Minneapolis: Fortress.

2001   "Love of Enemies in the Context of Eternity." *New Testament Studies* 47:411–27.

Repschinski, B.
2000   The Controversy Stories in the Gospel
        of Matthew: Their Redaction, Form,
        and Relevance for the Relationship
        between the Matthean Community
        and Formative Judaism. Göttingen:
        Vandenhoeck & Ruprecht.
2006   "'For He Will Save His People
        from Their Sins' (Matthew 1:21):
        A Christology for Christian Jews."
        Catholic Biblical Quarterly 68:248–67.
Resseguie, J.
2005   Narrative Criticism of the New
        Testament. Grand Rapids: Baker
        Academic.
Rhoads, D., and K. Syreeni
1999   Characterization in the Gospels:
        Reconceiving Narrative Criticism.
        Sheffield: Sheffield Academic Press.
Rice, G.
1978   "Neglected Interpretation of the
        Immanuel Prophecy." Zeitschrift für
        die alttestamentliche Wissenschaft
        90:220–27.
Richards, J. (ed.)
1968   Soli Deo Gloria. Richmond: John
        Knox.
Richards, K. (ed.)
1986   Society of Biblical Literature 1986
        Seminar Papers. Atlanta: Scholars.
1987   Society of Biblical Literature 1987
        Seminar Papers. Atlanta: Scholars.
Richards, W.
1978   "Another Look at the Parable of the
        Two Sons." Biblical Research 23:5–14.
Richardson, A.
1955   "The Feeding of the Five Thousand."
        Interpretation 9:144–49.
Richardson, P., and D. Granskou (eds.)
1986   Anti-Judaism in Early Christianity,
        vol. 1: Paul and the Gospels.
        Waterloo, ON: Wilfrid Laurier
        University Press.
Ricoeur, P.
1990   "The Golden Rule: Exegetical and
        Theological Perplexities." New
        Testament Studies 36:393–97.
Ridderbos, H. N.
1962   The Coming of the Kingdom.
        Translated by H. De Jongste.
        Edited by R. Zorn. Philadelphia:
        Presbyterian & Reformed.
1987   Matthew. Bible Student's
        Commentary. Grand Rapids:
        Zondervan.

Rieckert, P.
1982   "The Narrative Coherence of
        Matthew 26–28." Neotestamentica
        16:53–74.
Riesenfeld, H.
1947   Jésus transfiguré. Copenhagen:
        Munksgaard.
Rigaux, B.
1959   "ΒΔΕΛΥΓΜΑ ΤΗΣ ΕΡΗΜΩΣΕΩΣ (Mc
        13,14; Mt 24,15)." Biblica 40:675–83.
1968   The Testimony of St. Matthew.
        Translated by P. J. Oliguy. Chicago:
        Franciscan Herald.
Riley, H.
1992   The First Gospel. Macon, GA: Mercer
        University Press.
Ringshausen, G.
1986   "Die Kinder der Weisheit: Zur
        Auslegung von Mk 10:13–16 par."
        Zeitschrift für die neutestamentliche
        Wissenschaft 77:34–63.
Rist, J. M.
1978   On the Independence of Matthew
        and Mark. Cambridge: Cambridge
        University Press.
Ristow, H., and K. Matthiae (eds.)
1963   Der historische Jesus und der
        kerygmatische Christus: Beiträge zum
        Christusverständnis in Forschung und
        Verkündigung. Berlin: Evangelische
        Verlagsanstalt.
Ritmeyer, K., and L. Ritmeyer
1989   "Reconstructing Herod's Temple
        Mount in Jerusalem." Biblical
        Archaeology Review 15/6:23–42.
Ritt, H.
1979   "Der 'Seewandel Jesu' (Mk 6:45–52
        par.)." Biblische Zeitschrift 23:71–84.
Rivkin, E.
1978   A Hidden Revolution: The Pharisees'
        Search for the Kingdom Within.
        Nashville: Abingdon.
1984   What Crucified Jesus? Nashville:
        Abingdon.
Robbins, V. K.
1983   "Pronouncement Stories and
        Jesus' Blessing of the Children:
        A Rhetorical Approach." Semeia
        29:43–74.
1987   "The Woman Who Touched Jesus'
        Garment: Socio-Rhetorical Analysis
        of the Synoptic Accounts." New
        Testament Studies 33:502–15.
Roberts, C. H.
1953   "An Early Papyrus of the First
        Gospel." Harvard Theological Review
        46:233–27.

Roberts, R.
1963   "An Evil Eye (Matthew 6:23)."
        Restoration Quarterly 7:143–47.
Robertson, A. T.
1934   *A Grammar of the Greek New
        Testament in the Light of Historical
        Research.* Nashville: Broadman.
Robinson, B.
1984   "Peter and His Successors: Tradition
        and Redaction in Matthew 16:17–19."
        *Journal for the Study of the New
        Testament* 21:85–104.
Robinson, J. A. T.
1958   "Elijah, John, and Jesus." *New
        Testament Studies* 4:263–81.
1975   "The Parable of the Wicked
        Husbandmen: A Test of Synoptic
        Relationships." *New Testament
        Studies* 21:443–61.
1976   *Redating the New Testament.* London:
        SCM.
1979   *Jesus and His Coming.* 2nd ed.
        Philadelphia: Westminster.
Robinson, J. M., et al. (eds.)
2000   *The Critical Edition of Q.* Hermeneia.
        Minneapolis: Fortress.
Robinson, T. H.
1928   *The Gospel of Matthew.* Moffatt New
        Testament Commentary. London:
        Hodder & Stoughton.
Rochais, G.
1981   *Les récits de résurrection des
        morts dans le Nouveau Testament.*
        Cambridge: Cambridge University
        Press.
Rogers, C.
1993   "The Promises to David in Early
        Judaism." *Bibliotheca sacra* 150:285–
        302.
Roh, T.
2001   *Die "familia dei" in den synoptischen
        Evangelien: Eine redactions- und
        sozialgeschichtliche Untersuchung
        zu einem urchristlichen Bildfeld.*
        Fribourg, Switz.: Universitätsverlag.
Rohrbaugh, R.
1993   "A Peasant Reading of the Parable
        of the Talents/Pounds: A Text of
        Terror?" *Biblical Theology Bulletin*
        23:32–39.
Röhser, G.
1995   "Der wahre 'Schriftgelehrte':
        Ein Beitrag zum Problem der
        'Toraverschärfung' in den Antithesen
        der Bergpredigt." *Zeitschrift für
        die neutestamentliche Wissenschaft*
        86:20–33.

Roloff, J.
1992   "Das Kirchenverständnis des
        Matthäus im Spiegel seiner
        Gleichnisse." *New Testament Studies*
        38:337–56.
Römelt, J.
1992   "Normativität, ethische Radikalität,
        und christlicher Glaube: Zur
        theologisch-ethischen Hermeneutik
        der Bergpredigt." *Zeitschrift für
        katholische Theologie* 114:293–303.
Roquefort, D.
1983   "Judas: Une figure de la perversion."
        Études théologiques et religieuses
        58:501–13.
Rordorf, W.
1972   "Un chapitre d'éthique judéo-
        chrétienne: Les deux voies."
        Recherches de science religieuse
        60:109–28.
Ross, J.
1978   "Epileptic or Moonstruck?" *Biblical
        Theology* 29:126–28.
1987   "Which Zechariah?" *Irish Biblical
        Studies* 9:70–73.
Roth, C.
1949   "The 'Chair of Moses' and Its
        Survivals." *Palestine Exploration
        Quarterly* 81:100–111.
Rothfuchs, W.
1969   *Die Erfüllungszitate des Matthäus-
        Evangeliums.* Stuttgart:
        Kohlhammer.
Rowdon, H. (ed.)
1982   *Christ the Lord.* Leicester, UK: Inter-
        Varsity.
Ruckstuhl, E.
1965   *Chronology of the Last Days of Jesus.*
        Translated by V. Drapela. New York:
        Desclee.
Rüger, H.
1969   "Mit welchem Mass ihr messt,
        wird euch gemessen werden."
        *Zeitschrift für die neutestamentliche
        Wissenschaft* 60:174–82.
Russell, E.
1982   "The Image of the Jew in Matthew's
        Gospel." Pp. 427–42 of *Studia
        Evangelica,* vol. 7: *Papers Presented
        to the Fifth International Congress on
        Biblical Studies Held at Oxford, 1973.*
        Edited by E. A. Livingstone. Berlin:
        Akademie.
1986   "'Anti-Semitism' in the Gospel of
        Matthew." *Irish Biblical Studies*
        8:183–96.

1989 "The Image of the Jew in Matthew's Gospel." *Proceedings of the Irish Biblical Association* 12:37–57.

Rutgers, L. V., et al. (eds.)
1998 *The Use of Sacred Books in the Ancient World*. Louvain: Peeters.

Ruzer, S.
1996 "The Technique of Composite Citation in the Sermon on the Mount (Matt 5:21–22, 33–37)." *Revue biblique* 103:65–75.
2002 "From 'Love Your Neighbour' to 'Love Your Enemy': Trajectories in Early Jewish Exegesis." *Revue biblique* 109:371–89.

Ryan, T.
1978 "Matthew 15:29–31: An Overlooked Summary." *Horizons* 5:31–42.

Ryken, L.
1984 *How to Read the Bible as Literature and Get More out of It*. Grand Rapids: Zondervan.
1987 *Words of Life*. Grand Rapids: Baker Academic.
2003 *The Word of God in English*. Wheaton: Crossway.

Sabourin, L.
1974 "The Biblical Cloud." *Biblical Theology Bulletin* 4:290–311.
1977 "'You Will Not Have Gone through All the Towns of Israel Before the Son of Man Comes' (Matt 10:23b)." *Biblical Theology Bulletin* 7:5–11.
1978 *L'évangile selon saint Matthieu et ses principaux parallèles*. Rome: Biblical Institute Press.
1982 *The Gospel according to St. Matthew*. 2 vols. Bombay: St. Paul.

Saddington, D. B.
2006 "The Centurion of Matthew 8:5–13: Consideration of the Proposal of Theodore W. Jennings, Jr., and Tat-Siong Benny Liew." *Journal of Biblical Literature* 125:140–42.

Safrai, S.
1987 *The Literature of the Sages*. Philadelphia: Fortress/Assen: Van Gorcum.

Safrai, S., and M. Stern (eds.)
1976 *The Jewish People in the First Century*. 2 vols. Philadelphia: Fortress.

Safrai, Z.
1996 "Gergesa, Gerasa, or Gadara? Where Did Jesus' Miracle Occur?" *Jerusalem Perspective* 51:16–19.

Sailhamer, J.
2001 "Hosea 11:1 and Matthew 2:15." *Westminster Theological Journal* 63:87–96.

Saldarini, A.
1984 *Jesus and Passover*. New York: Paulist Press.
1992a "Delegitimation of Leaders in Matthew 23." *Catholic Biblical Quarterly* 54:659–80.
1992b "The Gospel of Matthew and Jewish-Christian Conflict in the Galilee." Pp. 23–38 in *The Galilee in Late Antiquity*. Edited by L. Levine. Cambridge: Harvard University Press.
1994 *Matthew's Christian-Jewish Community*. Chicago: University of Chicago Press.
1995 "Boundaries and Polemics in the Gospel of Matthew." *Biblical Interpretation* 3:239–65.
1997 "Understanding Matthew's Vitriol." *Bible Review* 13/2:32–39, 45.
2001 *Pharisees, Scribes, and Sadducees in Palestinian Society*. Reprinted with foreword by J. VanderKam. Grand Rapids: Eerdmans.

Sand, A.
1976 *Das Gesetz und die Propheten: Untersuchungen zur Theologie des Evangeliums nach Matthäus*. Regensburg: Pustet.
1983 *Reich Gottes und Eheverzicht im Evangelium nach Matthäus*. Stuttgart: Katholisches Bibelwerk.
1986 *Das Evangelium nach Matthäus*. Regensburg: Pustet.

Sanders, E. P.
1983 "Jesus and the Sinners." *Journal for the Study of the New Testament* 19:5–36.
1985 *Jesus and Judaism*. Philadelphia: Fortress.
1992 *Judaism: Practice and Belief, 63 BCE–66 CE*. London: SCM/Philadelphia: Trinity.

Sanders, E. P. (ed.)
1981 *Jewish and Christian Self-Definition*, vol. 2: *Aspects of Judaism in the Graeco-Roman Period*. London: SCM.

Sanders, J. T.
1992a "Christians and Jews in the Roman Empire: A Conversation with Rodney Stark." *Sociological Analysis* 53:433–45.
1992b "Jewish Christianity in Antioch before the Time of Hadrian: Where

Does the Identity Lie?" Pp. 346–61 in *Society of Biblical Literature 1992 Seminar Papers*. Edited by E. Lovering. Atlanta: Scholars.

1993   *Schismatics, Sectarians, Dissidents, Deviants: The First Hundred Years of Jewish-Christian Relations*. Valley Forge, PA: Trinity.

Sandmel, S.
1971   "The Trial of Jesus: Reservations." *Judaism* 20:69–74.

1978   *Anti-Semitism in the New Testament?* Philadelphia: Fortress.

1987   *Herod: Profile of a Tyrant*. Philadelphia: Lippincott.

Sandt, H. van de
2002   "'Do Not Give What Is Holy to the Dogs' (Did 9:5D and Matt 7:6A): The Eucharistic Food of the Didache in Its Jewish Purity Setting." *Vigiliae christianae* 56:223–46.

Satterthwaite, P. E., R. S. Hess, and G. J. Wenham (eds.)
1995   *The Lord's Anointed: Interpretation of Old Testament Messianic Texts*. Carlisle, UK: Paternoster/Grand Rapids: Baker Academic.

Saucy, R. L.
1993   *The Case for Progressive Dispensationalism*. Grand Rapids: Zondervan.

Scaer, D.
1991   "The Relation of Matthew 28:16–20 to the Rest of the Gospel." *Concordia Theological Quarterly* 55:245–66.

2000   *The Sermon on the Mount: The Church's First Statement of the Gospel*. St. Louis: Concordia.

2004   *Discourses in Matthew*. St. Louis: Concordia.

Schaberg, J.
1982   *The Father, the Son, and the Holy Spirit: The Triadic Phrase in Matthew 28:19b*. Society of Biblical Literature Dissertation Series 61. Chico, CA: Society of Biblical Literature.

1987   *The Illegitimacy of Jesus*. San Francisco: Harper.

1997   "Feminist Interpretation of the Infancy Narrative of Matthew." *Journal of Feminist Studies in Religion* 13:35–62.

Scharbert, J.
1997   "Die Ehescheidung und die 'Unzuchtklauseln' bei Matthäus." *Forum katholische Theologie* 13:106–26.

Schedl, C.
1981   "Die Salbung Jesu in Betanien: Zur Kompositionskunst von Mk 14,3–9 und Mt 26,6–13." *Bibel und Liturgie* 54:151–62.

Schenk, W.
1972   "Tradition und Redaktion in der Epileptiker-Perikope Mk 9:14–29." *Zeitschrift für die neutestamentliche Wissenschaft* 63:76–94.

1983   "Gefangenschaft und Tod des Täufers." *New Testament Studies* 29:453–83.

1987   *Die Sprache des Matthäus: Die Text-Konstituenten in ihre makro- und mikrostrukturellen Relationen*. Göttingen: Vandenhoeck & Ruprecht.

Schenke, L.
1983   *Die wunderbare Brotvermehrung*. Würzburg: Echter.

Schenke, L. (ed.)
1988   *Studien zum Matthäusevangelium*. Stuttgart: Katholisches Bibelwerk.

Schiffman, L.
1981   "Jewish Sectarianism in Second Temple Times." Pp. 1–46 in *Great Schisms in Jewish History*. Edited by R. Jospe and S. M. Wagner. New York: Ktav.

Schiffman, L., and J. VanderKam (eds.)
2000   *Encyclopedia of the Dead Sea Scrolls*. 2 vols. Oxford: Oxford University Press.

Schlatter, A.
1956   *Johannes der Täufer*. Edited by W. Michaelis. Basel: Reinhardt.

1963   *Der Evangelist Matthäus: Sein Sprache, sein Ziel, seine Selbständigkeit*. 6th ed. Stuttgart: Calwer.

Schlosser, J.
1990   "La parole de Jésus sur le fin du temple." *New Testament Studies* 36:398–414.

Schmidt, T. E.
1988   "Burden, Barrier, Blasphemy: Wealth in Matt 6:33, Luke 14:33, and Luke 16:15." *Trinity Journal* 9:171–89.

Schnabel, E. J.
2004   *Early Christian Mission*. 2 vols. Downers Grove, IL: InterVarsity.

Schnackenburg, R.
2002   *The Gospel of Matthew*. Translated by R. Barr. Grand Rapids: Eerdmans.

Schniewind, J.
1956   *Das Evangelium nach Matthäus*. Göttingen: Vandenhoeck & Ruprecht.

Schönle, V.

1982   *Johannes, Jesus und die Juden: Die theologische Position des Matthäus und des Verfassers der Redenquelle im Lichte von Mt. 11.* Frankfurt a.M.: Lang.

Schrage, W.

1963   "'Ekklesia' und 'Synagoge.'" *Zeitschrift für Theologie und Kirche* 60:178–202.

Schrage, W. (ed.)

1986   *Studien zum Text und zur Ethik des Neuen Testaments: Festschrift zum 80. Geburtstag von Heinrich Greeven.* Berlin: de Gruyter.

Schürer, E.

1973   *The History of the Jewish People in the Age of Jesus Christ (175 BC–AD 135).* Revised and edited by G. Vermes et al. 4 vols. Edinburgh: T&T Clark.

Schürmann, H.

1968   *Traditionsgeschichtliche Untersuchungen zu den synoptischen Evangelien.* Düsseldorf: Patmos.

Schwartz, D. R.

1992   *Studies in the Jewish Background of Christianity.* Tübingen: Mohr Siebeck.

Schwarz, G.

1988   *Jesus und Judas.* Stuttgart: Kohlhammer.

1992a   "Ἀνοίξας τὸ στόμα αὐτοῦ (Matthäus 17.27)." *New Testament Studies* 38:138–41.

1992b   "Jesus und der Feigenbaum am Wege (Mk 11,12–14, 20–25/Mt 21,18–22)." *Biblische Notizen* 61:36–37.

1992c   "Τὸ πτερύγιον τοῦ ἱεροῦ (Mt 4,5/Lk 4,9)." *Biblischen Notizen* 61:33–35.

1994a   "'Ein grosses Beben entstand auf dem Meer'? (Matthäus 8,24)." *Biblische Notizen* 74:31–32.

1994b   "'Er berührte ihre Hand'? (Matthäus 8,15)." *Biblische Notizen* 73:33–35.

Schweitzer, A.

1968   *The Quest of the Historical Jesus.* Translated by W. Montgomery. New York: Macmillan.

Schweizer, E.

1972–73   "Formgeschichtliches zu den Seligspreisungen Jesu." *New Testament Studies* 19:121–26.

1975   *The Good News according to Matthew.* Atlanta: John Knox.

Scobie, C. H.

1964   *John the Baptist.* London: SCM.

Scofield, C. I.

1909   *The Scofield Reference Bible.* New York: Oxford University Press.

Scorgie, G., et al. (eds.)

2002   *The Task of Bible Translation.* Grand Rapids: Zondervan.

Scorgie, G., and M. Strauss

2003   *The Challenge of Bible Translation: Communicating God's Word to the World.* Grand Rapids: Zondervan.

Scott, B. B.

1985   "The King's Accounting: Matthew 18:23–34." *Journal of Biblical Literature* 104:429–42.

Scott, J. J.

1990   "Gentiles and the Ministry of Jesus: Further Observations on Matt 10:5–6; 15:21–28." *Journal of the Evangelical Theological Society* 33:161–69.

Scott, J. W.

1985   "Matthew's Intention to Write Story." *Westminster Theological Journal* 47:68–82.

Scott, R.

1965   "The Sign of Jonah." *Interpretation* 19:16–25.

Seeley, D.

1992   "Rulership and Service in Mark 10:41–45." *Novum Testamentum* 35:234–50.

Seeligmann, I. L.

1948   *The Septuagint Version of Isaiah: A Discussion of Its Problems.* Leiden: Brill.

Segal, M.

1927   *A Grammar of Mishnaic Hebrew.* Oxford: Clarendon.

Segbroeck, F. van

1968   "Jésus rejeté par sa patrie (Mt 13,54–58)." *Biblica* 48:167–98.

Segbroeck, F. van, et al. (eds.)

1992   *The Four Gospels, 1992: Festschrift Frans Neirynck.* Bibliotheca ephemeridum theologicarum lovaniensium 100. Louvain: Louvain University Press.

Segovia, F. F. (ed.)

1985   *Discipleship in the New Testament.* Philadelphia: Fortress.

Senior, D.

1975   *The Passion Narrative according to St. Matthew.* Bibliotheca ephemeridum theologicarum lovaniensium 39. Louvain: Louvain University Press.

1977   *Invitation to Matthew.* New York: Doubleday.

1985   *The Passion of Jesus in the Gospel of
        Matthew.* Wilmington, DE: Glazier.
1987   "Matthew's Special Material in the
        Passion Story: Implications for the
        Evangelist's Redactional Technique
        and Theological Perspective."
        Ephemerides theologicae lovanienses
        63:272–94.
1996   *What Are They Saying about
        Matthew?* Rev. ed. New York: Paulist
        Press.
1999   "Between Two Worlds: Gentiles
        and Jewish Christians in Matthew's
        Gospel." *Catholic Biblical Quarterly*
        61:1–23.

Senn, F.
1986   "The Lord's Supper, Not the
        Passover." *Worship* 60:362–68.

Shae, G.
1974   "The Question on the Authority of
        Jesus." *Novum Testamentum* 16:1–29.

Shanks, H.
1974   "Is the Title 'Rabbi' Anachronistic
        in the Gospels?" *Jewish Quarterly
        Review* 53:337–45.

Shepherd, J.
2004   "The Kingdom Suffering Violence:
        Understanding the Violence Logion
        of Matthew 11:12." Master's thesis,
        Grand Rapids Theological Seminary.

Shepherd, M. H., Jr., and E. C. Hobbs (eds.)
1974   *Gospel Studies in Honor of Sherman
        Elbridge Johnson.* Anglican
        Theological Review Supplementary
        Series 3. Evanston, IL: Anglican
        Theological Review.

Shepherd, T.
1993   *Markan Sandwich Stories: Narration,
        Definition, and Function.* Berrien
        Springs, MI: Andrews University
        Press.

Shillington, V. G. (ed.)
1997   *Jesus and His Parables: Interpreting
        the Parables of Jesus Today.*
        Edinburgh: T&T Clark.

Shirock, R.
1992   "Whose Exorcists Are They? The
        Referents of οἱ υἱοὶ ὑμῶν at Matthew
        12,27/Luke 11,19." *Journal for the
        Study of the New Testament* 46:41–51.

Shuler, P.
1982   *A Genre for the Gospels: The
        Biographical Character of Matthew.*
        Philadelphia: Fortress.

Sider, J.
1981   "The Meaning of *Parabole* in the
        Usage of the Synoptic Evangelists."
        Biblica 62:453–70.
1984   "Interpreting the Hid Treasure."
        Christian Scholar's Review 13:360–72.
1985   "Proportional Analogy in the Gospel
        Parables." *New Testament Studies*
        31:1–23.
1995   *Interpreting the Parables: A
        Hermeneutical Guide to Their
        Meaning.* Grand Rapids: Zondervan.

Sigal, P.
1986   *The Halakah of Jesus of Nazareth
        according to the Gospel of Matthew.*
        Lanham, MD: University Press of
        America.

Sim, D.
1990   "The Man without the Wedding
        Garment (Matthew 22:11–13)."
        Heythrop Journal 31:165–78.
1992   "Matthew 22:13a and 1 Enoch 10:4a:
        A Case of Literary Dependence?"
        *Journal for the Study of the New
        Testament* 47:3–19.
1993a   "The 'Confession' of the Soldiers in
        Matthew 27:54." *Heythrop Journal*
        34:401–24.
1993b   "The Meaning of παλιγγενεσία in
        Matthew 19:28." *Journal for the Study
        of the New Testament* 50:3–12.
1995   "The Gospel of Matthew and the
        Gentiles." *Journal for the Study of the
        New Testament* 57:19–48.
1996a   *Apocalyptic Eschatology in the
        Gospel of Matthew.* Society for New
        Testament Studies Monograph
        Series 88. Cambridge: Cambridge
        University Press.
1996b   "Christianity and Ethnicity in the
        Gospel of Matthew." Pp. 171–95 in
        Ethnicity and the Bible. Edited by M.
        Brett. Leiden: Brill.
1998a   "Are the Least Included in the
        Kingdom of Heaven? The Meaning of
        Matthew 5:19." *Harvard Theological
        Studies* 54:573–87.
1998b   *The Gospel of Matthew and Christian
        Judaism.* Edinburgh: T&T Clark,
        1998.
1999a   "Angels of Eschatological
        Punishment in the Jewish and
        Christian Apocalyptic Traditions and
        in the Gospel of Matthew." *Harvard
        Theological Studies* 55:693–718.

1999b "The Magi: Gentiles or Jews?" *Harvard Theological Studies* 55:980–1000.

2000 "The Sword Motif in Matthew 10:34." *Harvard Theological Studies.* 56:84–104.

2001 "The Social Setting of the Matthean Community." *Harvard Theological Studies* 57:268–80.

Simonetti, M.

2001 *Matthew 1–13.* Ancient Christian Commentary on Scripture 1a. Downers Grove, IL: InterVarsity.

2002 *Matthew 14–28.* Ancient Christian Commentary on Scripture 1b. Downers Grove, IL: InterVarsity.

Slater, T. B.

1980 "Notes on Matthew's Structure." *Journal of Biblical Literature* 99:436.

Slingerland, H.

1979 "The Transjordanian Origin of Matthew's Gospel." *Journal for the Study of the New Testament* 3:18–28.

Sloyan, G.

2006 *Jesus on Trial.* 2nd ed. Minneapolis: Fortress.

Smillie, G. R.

2002 "'Even the Dogs': Gentiles in the Gospel of Matthew." *Journal of the Evangelical Theological Society* 45:73–97.

Smit Sibinga, J.

1966 "Ignatius and Matthew." *Novum Testamentum* 8:263–83.

1975 "The Structure of Apocalyptic Discourse: Matthew 24 and 25." *Studia theologica* 29:71–79.

1994 "Exploring the Composition of Matth. 5–7: The Sermon on the Mount and Some of Its 'Structures.'" *Filologia neotestamentaria* 7:175–95.

Smith, C. R.

1997 "Literary Evidence of a Fivefold Structure in the Gospel of Matthew." *New Testament Studies* 43:540–41.

Smith, C. W. F.

1963 "The Mixed State of the Church in Matthew's Gospel." *Journal of Biblical Literature* 82:149–68.

Smith, D.

1982 "Jewish Proselyte Baptism and the Baptism of John." *Restoration Quarterly* 25:13–32.

Smith, D. T.

1989 "The Matthean Exception Clauses in the Light of Matthew's Theology and Community." *Studia biblica et theologica* 17:55–82.

Smith, M.

1968 *Tannaitic Parallels to the Gospels.* Philadelphia: Society of Biblical Literature.

1980 "The Origin and History of the Transfiguration Story." *Union Seminary Quarterly Review* 36:39–44.

Smith, R. H.

1989 *Matthew.* Augsburg Commentary. Minneapolis: Augsburg.

1990 "Matthew 27:25: The Hardest Verse in Matthew's Gospel." *Currents in Theology and Mission* 17:421–28.

1992a "Interpreting Matthew Today." *Currents in Theology and Mission* 19:424–32.

1992b "Matthew's Message for Insiders: Charisma and Commandment in a First-Century Community." *Interpretation* 46:229–39.

1998 "Blessed Are the Poor in (Holy) Spirit (Matthew 5:3)." *Word and World* 18:389–96.

Smyth, H. W.

1956 *Greek Grammar.* Revised by G. M. Messing. Cambridge: Harvard University Press.

Smyth, K.

1975 "Matthew 28: Resurrection as Theophany." *Irish Theological Quarterly* 42:259–71.

1982 "The Structural Principle of Matthew's Gospel." *Irish Biblical Studies* 4:207–20.

Snodgrass, K.

1983 *The Parable of the Wicked Tenants.* Wissenschaftliche Untersuchungen zum Neuen Testament 27. Tübingen: Mohr Siebeck.

1992 "Matthew's Understanding of the Law." *Interpretation* 46:368–78.

1998 "Recent Research on the Parable of the Wicked Tenants." *Bulletin for Biblical Research* 8:187–215.

Soarés-Prabhu, G.

1976 *The Formula Quotations in the Infancy Narratives of Saint Matthew's Gospel.* Rome: Biblical Institute.

Söding, T.

1992 "Die Tempelaktion Jesu." *Trierer theologische Zeitschrift* 101:36–64.

Songer, H. S.

1992 "The Sermon on the Mount and Its Jewish Foreground." *Review and Expositor* 89:165–77.

Sparks, K.
2006   "Gospel as Conquest: Moses Typology
        in Matthew 28:16–20." *Catholic
        Biblical Quarterly* 68:651–63.
Sproul, R. C.
1998   *The Last Days according to Jesus.*
        Grand Rapids: Baker Books.
Sproule, J.
1980   "The Problem of the Mustard Seed."
        Grace Theological Journal 1:37–42.
Stanley, D.
1980   *Jesus in Gethsemane.* New York:
        Paulist Press.
Stanton, G.
1982   "Salvation Proclaimed, X: Matthew
        11:28–30—Comfortable Words?"
        Expository Times 94:3–8.
1984   "The Gospel of Matthew and
        Judaism." *Bulletin of the John
        Rylands Library* 66:254–84.
1985   "The Origin and Purpose of
        Matthew's Gospel: Matthean
        Scholarship from 1945–80." Pp.
        1889–1951 in *Aufstieg und Niedergang
        der römischen Welt,* part 2: *Principat,*
        25.3. Edited by H. Temporini and W.
        Haase. Berlin: de Gruyter.
1989   "'Pray That Your Flight May Not Be
        in Winter or on a Sabbath' (Matthew
        24:20)." *Journal for the Study of the
        New Testament* 37:17–30.
1992a   "The Communities of Matthew."
        Interpretation 46:379–91.
1992b   *A Gospel for a New People: Studies in
        Matthew.* Edinburgh: T&T Clark.
1994   "Revisiting Matthew's Communities."
        Pp. 9–23 in *Society of Biblical
        Literature 1994 Seminar Papers.*
        Edited by E. Lovering. Atlanta:
        Scholars.
1996   "Revisiting Matthew's Communities."
        Harvard Theological Studies
        52:376–94.
Stanton, G. (ed.)
1995   *The Interpretation of Matthew.* 2nd
        ed. Edinburgh: T&T Clark.
Steck, K.
1955   "Über Matthäus 11,25–30."
        Evangelische Theologie 15:343–49.
Steck, O.
1967   *Israel und das gewaltsame Geschick
        der Propheten: Untersuchungen zur
        Überlieferung des deuteronomischen
        Geschichtbildes im Alten Testament,
        Spätjudentum und Urchristentum.*
        Wissenschaftliche Monographien
        zum Alten und Neuen Testament 23.

Neukirchen-Vluyn: Neukirchener
Verlag.
Stegemann, W.
1985   "Die Versuchung Jesu im
        Matthäusevangelium: Mt 4,1–11."
        Evangelische Theologie 45:29–44.
Stegemann, W., et al. (eds.)
2002   *The Social Setting of Jesus and the
        Gospels.* Minneapolis: Fortress.
Stein, R. H.
1976   "Is the Transfiguration (Mark 9:2–8)
        a Misplaced Resurrection-Account?"
        Journal of Biblical Literature
        95:79–96.
1979   "'Is It Lawful for a Man to Divorce
        His Wife?'" *Journal of the Evangelical
        Theological Society* 22:115–21.
2001   *Studying the Synoptic Gospels: Origin
        and Interpretation.* 2nd ed. Grand
        Rapids: Baker Academic.
Steinhauser, M. G.
1990   "The Sayings on Anxieties: Matt
        6:25–34 and Luke 12:22–32." *Forum*
        6/1:67–79.
Stemberger, G.
1995   *Jewish Contemporaries of Jesus:
        Pharisees, Sadducees, Essenes.*
        Translated by A. Mahnke.
        Minneapolis: Fortress.
Stendahl, K.
1962   "Matthew." Vol. 2 / pp. 769–98 in
        Peake's Commentary on the Bible.
        Edited by M. Black and H. H.
        Rowley. London: Nelson.
1968   *The School of St. Matthew and Its
        Use of the Old Testament.* 2nd ed.
        Philadelphia: Fortress.
Stenger, W.
1986   "Die Seligpreisung der Geschmähten
        (Mt 5,11–12; Lk 6,22–23)." *Kairos*
        28:33–60.
1988   *Gebt dem Kaiser, was des Kaisers ist!*
        Frankfurt a.M.: Athenäum.
Sterling, G. E.
1993   "Jesus as Exorcist: An Analysis of
        Matthew 17:14–20; Mark 9:14–29;
        Luke 9:37–43a." *Catholic Biblical
        Quarterly* 55:467–93.
Stern, D.
1991   *Parables in Midrash: Narrative and
        Exegesis in Rabbinic Literature.*
        Cambridge: Harvard University
        Press.
Stern, J.
1966   "Jesus's Citation of Dt 6.5 and
        Lv 19.18 in the Light of Jewish

Tradition." *Catholic Biblical Quarterly* 28:312–16.

Stevens, G. L.
1992   "Understanding the Sermon on the Mount: Its Rabbinic and New Testament Context." *Theological Educator* 46:83–95.

Stewart, R. B. (ed.)
2006   *The Resurrection of Jesus: John Dominic Crossan and N. T. Wright in Dialogue.* Minneapolis: Augsburg/ Fortress.

Stewart-Sykes, A.
1995   "Matthew's 'Miracle Chapters': From Composition to Narrative, and Back Again." *Scripture Bulletin* 25:55–65.

Stock, A.
1978   "Matthean Divorce Texts." *Biblical Theology Bulletin* 8:24–33.
1987   "Is Matthew's Presentation of Jesus Ironic?" *Biblical Theology Bulletin* 17:64–69.
1994   *The Method and Message of Matthew.* Collegeville, MN: Liturgical Press.

Stoldt, H.
1980   *History and Criticism of the Markan Hypothesis.* Translated by D. Niewyk. Macon, GA: Mercer University Press.

Stonehouse, N.
1979   *The Witness of the Synoptic Gospels to Christ.* Reprinted Grand Rapids: Baker Academic.

Stott, J. R. W.
1978   *Christian Counter-Culture.* Downers Grove, IL: InterVarsity.

Strack, H. L., and G. Stemberger
1992   *Introduction to the Talmud and Midrash.* Translated by M. Bockmuehl. Minneapolis: Fortress.

Strange, J., and H. Shanks
1982   "Has the House Where Jesus Stayed in Capernaum Been Found?" *Biblical Archaeology Review* 8:26–37.

Strauss, M. L.
1998   *Distorting Scripture? The Challenge of Bible Translation and Gender Accuracy.* Downers Grove, IL: InterVarsity.

Strawson, W.
1959   *Jesus and the Future Life: A Study in the Synoptic Gospels.* London: Epworth.

Strecker, G.
1966   *Der Weg der Gerechtigkeit: Untersuchung zur Theologie des Matthäus.* 2nd rev. ed. Göttingen: Vandenhoeck & Ruprecht.

1978   "Die Antitheses der Bergpredikt (Mt 5:21–48 par.)." *Zeitschrift für die neutestamentliche Wissenschaft* 69:36–72.
1988   *The Sermon on the Mount: An Exegetical Commentary.* Nashville: Abingdon.

Streeter, B. H.
1924   *The Four Gospels: A Study of Origins.* London: Macmillan.

Strelan, R.
1996   "A Ripping Good Yarn: Matthew 13:24–30." *Lutheran Theological Journal* 30:22–29.

Strickert. F.
1998   *Bethsaida: Home of the Apostles.* Collegeville, MN: Liturgical Press.

Strickland, W. G. (ed.)
1996   *Five Views on Law and Gospel.* Grand Rapids: Zondervan.

Stritzky, M.-B.
1989   *Studien zur Überlieferung und Interpretation des Vaterunsers in der frühchristlichen Literatur.* Münster: Aschendorff.

Stuhlmacher, P.
1986   *Reconciliation, Law, and Righteousness: Essays in Biblical Theology.* Translated by E. Kalin. Philadelphia: Fortress.

Stuhlmacher, P. (ed.)
1991   *The Gospel and the Gospels.* Grand Rapids: Eerdmans.

Suggs, M.
1970   *Wisdom, Christology, and Law in Matthew's Gospel.* Cambridge: Harvard University Press.

Suh, J. S.
2006   "Das Weltgericht und die matthäische Gemeinde." *Novum Testamentum* 48:217–33.

Suhl, A.
1968   "Der Davidssohn im Matthäus-Evangelium." *Zeitschrift für die neutestamentliche Wissenschaft* 59:57–81.

Sukenik, E.
1930   "The Seat of Moses in Ancient Synagogues." *Tarbiz* 1:145–51.
1934   *Ancient Synagogues in Palestine and Greece.* Oxford: Oxford University Press.

Swaeles, R.
1960   "L'orientation ecclésiastique de la parabole du festin nuptial en Mt. XXII,1–14." *Ephemerides theologicae lovanienses* 36:655–84.

1963 "La parabole du festin nuptial (Mt 22:1–14)." *Assemblées du Seigneur* 74:33–49.

Swanson, D. C.
1958 "Diminutives in the Greek New Testament." *Journal of Biblical Literature* 77:134–51.

Swanson, R. J.
1995 *New Testament Greek Manuscripts: Variant Readings Arranged in Horizontal Lines against Codex Vaticanus*, vol. 1: *Matthew*. Sheffield: Sheffield Academic Press.

Syreeni, K.
1990 "Between Heaven and Earth: On the Structure of Matthew's Symbolic Universe." *Journal for the Study of the New Testament* 40:3–13.
1994 "Separation and Identity: Aspects of the Symbolic World of Matt 6.1–18." *New Testament Studies* 40:522–41.
1999 "A Single Eye: Aspects of the Symbolic World of Matt 6:22–23." *Studia theologica* 53:97–118.

Talbert, C. H.
1977 *What Is a Gospel? The Genre of the Canonical Gospels*. Philadelphia: Fortress.
2001 "Indicative and Imperative in Matthean Soteriology." *Biblica* 82:515–38.
2006 *Reading the Sermon on the Mount*. Grand Rapids: Baker Academic.

Talbot, M.
2002 *"Heureux les doux, car ils hériteront la terre" (Mt 5,4[5])*. Paris: Gabalda.

Tannehill, R.
1975 *The Sword of His Mouth*. Philadelphia: Fortress.

Tasker, R. V. G.
1961 *The Gospel according to St. Matthew*. Tyndale New Testament Commentary. Grand Rapids: Eerdmans.

Tavardon, P.
2002 *Les métamorphoses de l'esprit: Une exégèse du logion des deux baptêmes Mt 3:10–12 et parallèles*. Paris: Gabalda.

Taylor, J.
1989 "'The Love of Many Will Grow Cold': Matt 24:9–13 and the Neronian Persecution." *Revue biblique* 96:352–57.
1991 "The Coming of Elijah, Mt 17,10–13 and Mark 9,11–13: The Development of Texts." *Revue biblique* 98:107–19.

Taylor, N. H.
1997 *The Immerser: John the Baptist within Second Temple Judaism*. Grand Rapids: Eerdmans.

2001 "The Temptation of Jesus on the Mountain: A Palestinian Christian Polemic against Agrippa I?" *Journal for the Study of the New Testament* 83:27–49.

TDNT *Theological Dictionary of the New Testament*. Edited by G. Kittel and G. Friedrich. Translated and edited by G. W. Bromiley. 10 vols. Grand Rapids: Eerdmans, 1964–76.

Teeple, H. M.
1957 *The Mosaic Eschatological Prophet*. Journal of Biblical Literature Monograph Series 10. Philadelphia: Society of Biblical Literature.

Telfer, W.
1928 "The Form of a Dove." *Journal of Theological Studies* 29:238–42.

Telford, W.
1980 *The Barren Temple and the Withered Fig Tree*. Sheffield: JSOT.

Temple, P.
1955 "The Rejection at Nazareth." *Catholic Biblical Quarterly* 17:229–42.

Tevel, J. M.
1992 "The Labourers in the Vineyard: The Exegesis of Matthew 20:1–7 in the Early Church." *Vigiliae christianae* 46:356–80.

Thayse, A.
1998 *Matthieu: L'évangile revisité*. Brussels: Racine.

Theissen, G.
1983 *The Miracle Stories of the Early Christian Tradition*. Translated by F. McDonagh. Philadelphia: Fortress.
1991 *The Gospels in Context: Social and Political History in the Synoptic Tradition*. Translated by L. Maloney. Minneapolis: Fortress.

Theobald, C.
1995 "La regle d'or chez Paul Ricoeur: Une interrogation théologique." *Recherches de science religieuse* 83:43–59.

Thiede, C. P.
1995 "Papyrus Magdalen Greek 17 (Gregory-Aland P64): A Reappraisal." *Zeitschrift für Papyrologie und Epigraphik* 105:13–20. Reprinted *Tyndale Bulletin* 46 (1995): 29–42.
1996 "The Magdalen Papyrus: A Reply." *Expository Times* 107:240–41.

Thiede, C. P., and M. D'Ancona
1996   *Eyewitness to Jesus: Amazing New Manuscript Evidence about the Origin of the Gospels.* New York: Doubleday.

Thielman, F.
1999   *The Law and the New Testament: The Question of Continuity.* New York: Crossroad.

Thiemann, R.
1987   "The Unnamed Woman at Bethany." *Theology Today* 44:179–88.

Thiering, B.
1979   "Are the 'Violent Men' False Teachers?" *Novum Testamentum* 21:293–97.

Thimmes, P. L.
1992   *Studies in the Biblical Sea-Storm Type-Scene: Convention and Invention.* San Francisco: Mellen Research University Press.

Thoma, C., and M. Wyschogrod (eds.)
1989   *Parable and Story in Judaism and Christianity.* New York: Paulist Press.

Thomas, J. C.
1993   "The Kingdom of God in the Gospel according to Matthew." *New Testament Studies* 39:136–46.

Thomas, R. L.
1982   "The Rich Young Man in Matthew." *Grace Theological Journal* 3:235–60.
2002   *Three Views on the Origins of the Synoptic Gospels.* Grand Rapids: Kregel.

Thomas, W. H. G.
1961   *Outline Studies in the Gospel of Matthew.* Grand Rapids: Eerdmans.

Thompson, J. W.
1999   "The Background and Function of the Beatitudes in Matthew and Luke." *Restoration Quarterly* 41:109–16.

Thompson, M. M.
1982   "The Structure of Matthew." *Studia biblica et theologica* 12:195–238.

Thompson, W. G.
1970   *Matthew's Advice to a Divided Community: Matthew 17:22–18:35.* Analecta biblica 44. Rome: Biblical Institute.
1971   "Reflections on the Composition of Matthew 8:1–9:34." *Catholic Biblical Quarterly* 33:365–88.
1974   "An Historical Perspective in the Gospel of Matthew." *Journal of Biblical Literature* 93:243–62.
1989a   *Matthew's Jesus.* London: Sheed & Ward.

1989b   *Matthew's Story: Good News for Uncertain Times.* New York: Paulist Press.

Thrall, M. E.
1962   *Greek Particles in the New Testament: Linguistic and Exegetical Studies.* Grand Rapids: Eerdmans.
1970   "Elijah and Moses in Mark's Account of the Transfiguration." *New Testament Studies* 16:305–17.

Tigay, J.
1979   "On the Term Phylacteries (Matt 23:5)." *Harvard Theological Review* 72:45–53.

Tilborg, S. van
1972a   "A Form Criticism of the Lord's Prayer." *Novum Testamentum* 14:94–105.
1972b   *The Jewish Leaders in Matthew.* Leiden: Brill.

Tisera, G.
1993   *Universalism according to the Gospel of Matthew.* Frankfurt a.M.: Lang.

Tödt, H.
1965   *The Son of Man in the Synoptic Tradition.* Philadelphia: Westminster.

Toit, A. B. du
2000   "The Kingdom of God in the Gospel of Matthew." *Skrif en kerk* 21:545–63.

Tolbert, M.
1979   *Perspectives on the Parables: An Approach to Multiple Interpretations.* Philadelphia: Fortress.

Tooley, W.
1964   "The Shepherd and Sheep Image in the Teaching of Jesus." *Novum Testamentum* 7:15–25.

Topel, J.
1998   "The Tarnished Golden Rule (Luke 6:31): The Inescapable Radicalness of Christian Ethics." *Theological Studies* 59:475–85.

Tosato, A.
1979   "Joseph, Being a Just Man (Matt 1:19)." *Catholic Biblical Quarterly* 41:547–51.

Tournay, R. J.
1998   "Ne nous laisse pas entrer en tentation." *Nouvelle revue théologique* 120:440–43.

Toussaint, S.
1980   *Behold the King: A Study of Matthew.* Portland, OR: Multnomah.
2004   "A Critique of the Preterist View of the Olivet Discourse." *Bibliotheca sacra* 161:469–90.

Toussaint, S., and C. Dyer (eds.)
1986   *Essays in Honor of J. Dwight Pentecost.* Chicago: Moody.

Townsend, J. T.
1961   "Matthew 23:9." *Journal of Theological Studies* 12:56–59.

Trainor, M.
1991   "The Beginning of Wisdom: The Teacher and the Disciples in Matthew's Community." *Pacifica* 4:148–64.

Trautman, D.
1966   *The Eunuch Logion of Matthew 19:12: Historical and Exegetical Dimensions as Related to Celibacy.* Rome: Catholic Book Agency.

Trevett, C.
1984   "Approaching Matthew from the Second Century: The Under-used Ignatian Correspondence." *Journal for the Study of the New Testament* 20:59–67.

Trilling, W.
1959   "Die Täufertradition bei Matthäus." *Biblische Zeitschrift* 3:271–89.
1964   *Das wahre Israel: Studien zur Theologie des Matthäus-Evangeliums.* Munich: Kösel.
1981   *The Gospel according to Matthew.* London: Burns & Oates.

Tripp, D. H.
1999   "*Zizania* (Matthew 13:25): Realistic, If Also Figurative." *Journal of Theological Studies* 50:628.

Trites, A.
1979   "The Transfiguration of Jesus: The Gospel in Microcosm." *Evangelical Quarterly* 51:67–79.
1992   "The Blessings and Warnings of the Kingdom (Matthew 5:3–12; 7:13–27)." *Review and Expositor* 89:179–96.

Trummer, P.
1991   *Die blutende Frau: Wunderheilungen im Neuen Testament.* Freiburg i.B.: Herder.
1998   *Dass meine Augen sich öffnen: Kleine biblische Erkenntnislehre am Beispiel der Blindenheilungen Jesu.* Stuttgart: Kohlhammer.

Trunk, D.
1994   *Der messianische Heiler: Eine redactions- und religionsgeschichtliche Studie zu den Exorzismen im Matthäusevangelium.* Freiburg i.B.: Herder.

Tuckett, C. M.
1996   *Q and the History of Early Christianity.* Peabody, MA: Hendricksen.

Tuckett, C. M. (ed.)
1983a   *The Messianic Secret.* Philadelphia: Fortress.
1983b   *The Revival of the Griesbach Hypothesis.* Cambridge: Cambridge University Press.
1984   *Synoptic Studies: The Ampleforth Conferences of 1982 and 1983.* Sheffield: JSOT.
1997   *The Scriptures in the Gospels.* Bibliotheca ephemeridum theologicarum lovaniensium 131. Louvain: Louvain University Press.

Tuñí, J. O.
1972   "La tipología Israel-Jesus en Mt 1–2." *Estudios ecclesiásticos* 47:361–76.

Turner, D. L.
1983   "Evangelicals, Redaction Criticism, and the Current Inerrancy Crisis." *Grace Theological Journal* 4:263–88.
1984   "Evangelicals, Redaction Criticism, and Inerrancy: The Debate Continues." *Grace Theological Journal* 5:37–45.
1989   "The Structure and Sequence of Matthew 24:1–41: Interaction with Evangelical Treatments." *Grace Theological Journal* 10:3–27.
1991   "*Primus inter pares*? Peter in the Gospel of Matthew." Pp. 179–201 in *New Testament Essays in Honor of Homer A. Kent Jr.* Edited by G. T. Meadors. Winona Lake, IN: BMH Books.
1992a   "The New Jerusalem in Revelation 21:1–22:5: Consummation of a Biblical Continuum." Pp. 264–92 in *Dispensationalism, Israel, and the Church: The Search for Definition.* Edited by C. Blaising and D. Bock. Grand Rapids: Zondervan.
1992b   "Whom Does God Approve? The Context, Structure, Purpose, and Exegesis of Matthew's Beatitudes." *Criswell Theological Review* 6:29–42.
2002   "Matthew 21:43 and the Future of Israel." *Bibliotheca sacra* 159/633:46–61.
2004   "Matthew 23 as Jewish Prophetic Critique." *Journal of Biblical Studies* 4/1: §§23–42. http://journalofbiblicalstudies.org/issue9/Critique.pdf.

Turner, N.
1965   *Grammatical Insights into the New Testament.* Edinburgh: Clark.

Twelftree, G.
1993   *Jesus the Exorcist.* Peabody, MA: Hendrickson.
1999   *Jesus the Miracle Worker: A Historical and Theological Study.* Downers Grove, IL: InterVarsity.

Tyson, J. B., and T. R. W. Longstaff
1978   *Synoptic Abstract.* Computer Bible 15. Wooster, OH: Biblical Research Associates.

Tzaferis, V.
1985   "Crucifixion—the Archaeological Evidence." *Biblical Archaeological Review* 11:44–53.

UBS⁴   *The Greek New Testament.* Edited by B. Aland et al. 4th rev. ed. Stuttgart: Deutsche Bibelgesellschaft and United Bible Societies, 1994.

Unnik, W. C. van
1974   "The Death of Judas in Saint Matthew's Gospel." Pp. 44–57 in *Gospel Studies in Honor of Sherman Elbridge Johnson.* Edited by M. H. Shepherd Jr. and E. C. Hobbs. Anglican Theological Review Supplementary Series 3. Evanston, IL: Anglican Theological Review.

Unnik, W. C. van (ed.)
1962   *Neotestamentica et Patristica: Eine Freundesgabe, Herrn Professor Dr. Oscar Cullmann zu seinem 60. Geburtstag überreicht.* Novum Testamentum Supplements 6. Leiden: Brill.

Uprichard, R. E. H.
1981   "The Baptism of Jesus." *Irish Biblical Studies* 3:187–202.

Uro, R.
1987   *Sheep among Wolves: A Study of the Mission Instructions of Q.* Helsinki: Suomalainen Tiedeakatemia.

Vaganay, L.
1953   "Le schématisme du discours communautaire à la lumière de la critique des sources." *Revue biblique* 60:203–44.

Van Aarde, A. G.
1982   "Matthew's Portrayal of the Disciples and the Structure of Mt 13:53–17:27." *Neotestamentica* 16:21–34.
1989   "Resonance and Reception: Interpreting Mt 17:24–27 in Context." *Scripture* 29:1–12.

1997   "The First Testament in the Gospel of Matthew." *Hervormde Teologiese Studies* 53:126–45.

Van Beek, G. W.
1960   "Frankincense and Myrrh." *Biblical Archaeologist* 23:70–94.

Van Zyl, H. C.
1982   "Structural Analysis of Mt 18." *Neotestamentica* 16:35–55.

Vardaman, J., and E. Yamauchi (eds.)
1989   *Chronos, Kairos, Christos: Nativity and Chronology Studies Presented to Jack Finegan.* Winona Lake, IN: Eisenbrauns.

Vargas-Machuca, A.
1969   "El paralitico perdonado en la redación de Mateo (Mt. 9,1–8)." *Estudios bíblicos* 44:15–43.

Venetz, H.-J.
1980   "Bittet den Herrn der Ernte: Überlegungen zu Lk 10.2/Mt 9.37." *Diakonia* 11:148–61.

Vermes, G.
1973   *Jesus the Jew.* London: Collins.
1978   "The Present State of the 'Son of Man' Debate." *Journal of Jewish Studies* 29:123–34.

Verseput, D. J.
1986   *The Rejection of the Humble Messianic King: A Study of the Composition of Matthew 11–12.* Frankfurt a.M.: Lang.
1987   "The Role and Meaning of the 'Son of God' Title in Matthew's Gospel." *New Testament Studies* 33:532–56.
1992   "The Faith of the Reader and the Narrative of Matthew 13.53–16.20." *Journal for the Study of the New Testament* 46:3–24.
1994   "Jesus's Pilgrimage to Jerusalem and Encounter in the Temple: A Geographical Motive in Matthew's Gospel." *Novum Testamentum* 36:109–14.

Via, D.
1971   "The Relationship of Form to Content in the Parable: The Wedding Feast." *Interpretation* 25:171–84.
1987   "Ethical Responsibility and Human Wholeness in Matthew 25:31–46." *Harvard Theological Review* 80:79–100.

Vigne, D.
1992   *Christ au Jourdain: Le baptême de Jesus dans la tradition judéo-chrétienne.* Paris: Gabalda.

Viviano, B.

1979   "Where Was the Gospel according to St. Matthew Written?" *Catholic Biblical Quarterly* 41:533–46.

1989   "The High Priest's Servant's Ear." *Revue biblique* 96:71–80.

1990a   "The Genres of Matthew 1–2: Light from 1 Timothy 1:4." *Revue biblique* 97:31–53.

1990b   "The Gospel according to Matthew." Pp. 630–74 in *The New Jerome Biblical Commentary*. Edited by R. Brown et al. Englewood Cliffs, NJ: Prentice Hall.

1990c   "Social World and Community Leadership: The Case of Matthew 23:1–12, 34." *Journal for the Study of the New Testament* 39:3–21.

1992   "Beatitudes Found among Dead Sea Scrolls." *Biblical Archaeology Review* 18:53–55, 66.

1996   "The Movement of the Star, Matt 2:9 and Num 9:17." *Revue biblique* 103:58–64.

2000   "The Least in the Kingdom: Matthew 11:11, Its Parallel in Luke 7:28 (Q), and Daniel 4:14." *Catholic Biblical Quarterly* 62:41–54.

Vledder, E. J.

1995   "The Social Location of the Matthean Community." *Harvard Theological Studies* 51:388–408.

1997   *Conflict in the Miracle Stories: A Socio-Exegetical Study of Matthew 8–9.* Journal for the Study of the New Testament: Supplement Series 152. Sheffield: Sheffield Academic Press.

Vledder, E. J., and A. Van Aarde

1994   "The Social Stratification of the Matthean Community." *Neotestamentica* 28:511–22.

Vliet, H. van

1958   "No Single Testimony: A Study on the Adoption of the Law of Deut. 19:15 Par. into the New Testament." PhD diss., University of Utrecht.

Vogler, W.

1983   *Judas Iskarioth.* Berlin: Evangelische Verlaganstalt.

Vögtle, A.

1971   *Das Evangelium und die Evangelien.* Dusseldorf: Patmos.

Völkel, M.

1978   "Freund der Zöllner und Sünder." *Zeitschrift für die neutestamentliche Wissenschaft* 69:1–10.

Vorster, W.

1977   "The Structure of Matthew 13." *Neotestamentica* 11:130–38.

1981   *Wat is 'n evangelie?* Pretoria: Kerkboekhandel.

Waetjen, H. C.

1976   "The Genealogy as the Key to the Gospel according to Matthew." *Journal of Biblical Literature* 95:205–30.

Wagner, H. (ed.)

1985   *Judas Iskariot: Menschliches oder heilsgeschichtliches Drama?* Frankfurt a.M.: Knecht.

Wagner, V.

2001   "Mit der Herkunft Jesu aus Nazaret gegen die Geltung des Gesetzes?" *Zeitschrift für die neutestamentliche Wissenschaft* 92:273–82.

Wainwright, E. M.

1988   "God Wills to Invite All to the Banquet." *International Review of Missions* 77:185–93.

1991   *Towards a Feminist Critical Reading of the Gospel according to Matthew.* Beihefte zur Zeitschrift für die neutestamentliche Wissenschaft 60. Berlin: de Gruyter.

1998   *Shall We Look for Another? A Feminist Rereading of the Matthean Jesus.* Maryknoll, NY: Orbis.

2000   "Reading Matthew 3–4: Jesus—Sage, Seer, Sophia, Son of God." *Journal for the Study of the New Testament* 77:25–43.

Walker, R.

1967   *Die Heilsgeschichte im ersten Evangelium.* Göttingen: Vandenhoeck & Ruprecht.

Wallace, D. B.

1995   "The Article with Multiple Substantives Connected by Καί in the New Testament." PhD diss., Dallas Theological Seminary.

1996   *Greek Grammar beyond the Basics.* Grand Rapids: Zondervan.

Waltke, B., and M. O'Connor

1990   *An Introduction to Biblical Hebrew Syntax.* Winona Lake, IN: Eisenbrauns.

Walton, J.

1987   "Isaiah 7:14: What's in a Name?" *Journal of the Evangelical Theological Society* 30:289–306.

Walvoord, J. F.

1974   *Matthew: Thy Kingdom Come.* Chicago: Moody.

1985   "Is a Posttribulational Rapture
        Revealed in Matthew 24?" *Grace
        Theological Journal* 6:257–66.
Walvoord, J. F., and R. B. Zuck
1983   *The Bible Knowledge Commentary.*
        Wheaton: Victor.
Wansbrough, H.
2000   "The New Israel: The Community
        of Matthew and the Community
        of Qumran." *Studien zum Neuen
        Testament und seiner Umwelt*
        25:8–22.
Warden, D.
1997   "The Words of Jesus on Divorce."
        Restoration Quarterly 39:141–53.
Ware, B. (ed.)
2002   "Special Focus on the TNIV."
        *Journal for Biblical Manhood and
        Womanhood* 7/2:1–95.
Warren, A.
1998   "Did Moses Permit Divorce? Modal
        Weqatal as Key to New Testament
        Reading of Deuteronomy 24:1–4."
        Tyndale Bulletin 49:39–56.
Watson, F. (ed.)
1993   *The Open Text: New Directions for
        Biblical Studies?* London: SCM.
Watty, W.
1982   "Jesus and the Temple: Cleansing
        or Cursing?" *Expository Times*
        93:235–39.
Weaver, D. J.
1990   *Matthew's Missionary Discourse: A
        Literary Critical Analysis.* Journal
        for the Study of the New Testament:
        Supplement Series 38. Sheffield:
        JSOT.
1992   "Matthew 28:1–10." *Interpretation*
        46:398–402.
2000   "Rewriting the Messianic Script:
        Matthew's Account of the Birth of
        Jesus." *Interpretation* 54:376–85.
Webb, R. L.
1991a   "The Activity of John the Baptist's
        Expected Figure at the Threshing
        Floor." *Journal for the Study of the
        New Testament* 43:103–11.
1991b   *John the Baptizer and Prophet: A
        Socio-Historical Study.* Sheffield:
        JSOT.
2000   "Jesus's Baptism: Its Historicity and
        Implications." *Bulletin of Biblical
        Research* 10:261–309.
Webb, W. J.
2001   *Slaves, Women and Homosexuals:
        Exploring the Hermeneutics of
        Cultural Analysis.* Downers Grove, IL:
        InterVarsity.
Weber, B.
1993   "Alltagswelt und Gottesreich:
        Überlieferung zum
        Verstehenshintergrund des
        Gleichnisses vom 'Schalksknecht'
        (Matthäus 18,23–34)." *Biblische
        Zeitschrift* 37:161–82.
1994   "Vergeltung oder Vergebung!?
        Matthäus 18,21–35 auf den
        Hintergrund des 'Erlassjahres.'"
        Theologische Zeitschrift 50:124–51.
Weber, H.-R.
1979   *The Cross: Tradition and
        Interpretation.* London: SPCK.
Weber, K.
1995   "Is There a Qumran Parallel to
        Matthew 24,51//Luke 12,46?" *Revue
        de Qumran* 16:657–63.
1997   "The Image of the Sheep and Goats
        in Matthew 25:31–46." *Catholic
        Biblical Quarterly* 59:657–78.
Weder, H.
1978   *Die Gleichnisse Jesu als Metaphern.*
        Göttingen: Vandenhoeck & Ruprecht.
Weeden, T.
1979   "Recovering the Parabolic Intent in
        the Parable of the Sower." *Journal
        of the American Academy of Religion*
        47:97–120.
Wehnert, J.
1991   "Die Auswanderung der Jerusalemer
        Christen nach Pella—historisches
        Faktum oder theologische
        Konstruktion?" *Zeitschrift für
        Kirchengeschichte* 102:321–55.
Weibling, J. M.
2001   "Reconciling Matthew and Mark on
        Divorce." *Trinity Journal* 22:219–35.
Weinfield, M.
1990   "The Charge of Hypocrisy in
        Matthew 23 and in Jewish Sources."
        Immanuel 24/25:52–58.
1997   "The Jewish Roots of Matthew's
        Vitriol." *Bible Review* 13/5:31.
Weiss, H.
1990   "The Sabbath in the Synoptic
        Gospels." *Journal for the Study of the
        New Testament* 38:13–27.
Weiss, H.-F.
2001   "Noch einmal: Zur frage eines
        Antijudaismus bzw. Antipharisäismus
        im Matthäusevangelium." *Zeitschrift
        für Neues Testament* 4:37–41.

Weiss, J.
1971   *Jesus' Proclamation of the Kingdom of God.* Edited and translated by R. H. Hiers and D. L. Holland. Philadelphia: Fortress.

Weiss, W.
1989   *"Eine neue Lehre in Vollmacht."* Berlin: de Gruyter.

Wenham, D.
1973   "The Resurrection Narratives in Matthew's Gospel." *Tyndale Bulletin* 24:21–54.

1974   "The Interpretation of the Parable of the Sower." *New Testament Studies* 20:299–319.

1978–79 "The Structure of Matthew 13." *New Testament Studies* 25:516–22.

1979   "Jesus and the Law: An Exegesis of Matthew 5:17–20." *Themelios* 4:92–96.

1980   "A Note on Matthew 24:10–12." *Tyndale Bulletin* 31:155–62.

1982   "A Note on Mark 9:33–42/Matt 18:1–6/Luke 9:46–50." *Journal for the Study of the New Testament* 14:113–18.

1984   *The Rediscovery of Jesus' Eschatological Discourse.* Sheffield: JSOT.

1995   *Paul: Follower of Jesus or Founder of Christianity?* Grand Rapids: Eerdmans.

Wenham, D., and C. Blomberg
1986   *Gospel Perspectives*, vol. 6. Sheffield: JSOT.

Wenham, G. J.
1984   "Matthew and Divorce: An Old Crux Revisited." *Journal for the Study of the New Testament* 22:95–97.

1986   "The Syntax of Matthew 19:9." *Journal for the Study of the New Testament* 28:17–23.

Wenham, J. W.
1978–79 "How Many Cock-Crowings? The Problem of Harmonistic Text-Variants." *New Testament Studies* 25:523–25.

1982   "Why Do You Ask about the Good? A Study of the Relation between Text and Source Criticism." *New Testament Studies* 28:116–25.

1984   *Easter Enigma.* Exeter, UK: Paternoster.

1991   *Redating Matthew, Mark, and Luke: A Fresh Assault on the Synoptic Problem.* London: Hodder & Stoughton.

1992   *Redating Matthew, Mark, and Luke.* Downers Grove, IL: InterVarsity.

Weren, W. J. C.
1979   *De broeders van de mensenzoon: Mt 25,31–46 als toegang tot de eschatologie van Matteüs.* Amsterdam: Ton Bolland.

1996   "Children in Matthew: A Semantic Study." *Concilium* 2:53–63.

1997   "The Five Women in Matthew's Genealogy." *Catholic Biblical Quarterly* 59:288–305.

1998   "The Use of Isaiah 5:1–7 in the Parable of the Tenants (Mark 12,1–12; Matthew 21,33–46)." *Biblica* 79:1–26.

2006   "The Macrostructure of Matthew's Gospel: A New Proposal." *Biblica* 87:171–200.

Werner, E.
1946   "'Hosanna' in the Gospels." *Journal of Biblical Literature* 65:97–122.

Westcott, B. F.
1895   *An Introduction to the Study of the Gospels.* 8th ed. London: Macmillan.

Westerholm, S.
1978   *Jesus and Scribal Authority.* Lund: Gleerup.

1992   "The Law in the Sermon on the Mount: Matt 5:17–48." *Criswell Theological Review* 6:43–56.

2006   *Understanding Matthew.* Grand Rapids: Baker Academic.

Westermann, C.
1967   *Basic Forms of Prophetic Speech.* Philadelphia: Westminster.

1990   *The Parables of Jesus in the Light of the Old Testament.* Minneapolis: Fortress.

Whelan, C. F.
1993   "Suicide in the Ancient World: A Re-examination of Matthew 27:3–10." *Laval théologique et philosophique* 49:505–22.

White, W.
1979   *The Mind of Matthew.* Philadelphia: Westminster.

Whitters, M.
2006   "Jesus in the Footsteps of Jeremiah." *Catholic Biblical Quarterly* 68:229–47.

Wick, P.
1996   "Die erste Antithese (Mt 5,21–26): Eine Pilgerpredigt." *Theologische Zeitschrift* 52:236–42.

1998   "Der historische Ort von Mt 6,1–18." *Revue biblique* 105:332–58.

Wiebe, P. H.
1989   "Jesus' Divorce Exception." *Journal of the Evangelical Theological Society* 32:327–33.

Wilcox, M.
1975   "Peter and the Rock: A Fresh Look at Matthew 16:17–19." *New Testament Studies* 22:73–88.

Wilkens, W.
1981–82 "Die Versuchung Jesu nach Matthäus." *New Testament Studies* 28:479–89.

Wilkins, M. J.
1988   *The Concept of Disciple in Matthew's Gospel.* Leiden: Brill.
1995   *Discipleship in the Ancient World and in Matthew's Gospel.* 2nd. ed. Grand Rapids: Baker Academic.

Wilkins, M. J., and J. P. Moreland (eds.)
1995   *Jesus under Fire.* Grand Rapids: Zondervan.

Wilkinson, J.
1967   "The Case of the Epileptic Boy." *Expository Times* 79:39–42.
1974   "The Mission Charge to the Twelve and Modern Medical Missions." *Scottish Journal of Theology* 27:313–28.
1975   "The Way from Jerusalem to Jericho." *Biblical Archaeologist* 38:10–24.

Williams, J.
1965   "A Note on the Unpardonable Sin Logion." *New Testament Studies* 12:75–77.

Williams, M. C.
2006   *Two Gospels from One: A Comprehensive Text-Critical Analysis of the Synoptic Gospels.* Grand Rapids: Kregel.

Willis, J. T.
1978   "The Meaning of Isaiah 7:14 and Its Application in Matthew 1:23." *Restoration Quarterly* 21:1–18.

Willis, W. (ed.)
1987   *The Kingdom of God in 20th Century Interpretation.* Peabody, MA: Hendrickson.

Wills, L.
2001   "Scribal Methods in Matthew and Mishnah Abot." *Catholic Biblical Quarterly* 63:241–57.

Wilson, M.
1989   *Our Father Abraham.* Grand Rapids: Eerdmans.

Wilson, R. R.
1977   *Genealogy and History in the Biblical World.* New Haven: Yale University Press.

Wimmer, J. F.
1982   *Fasting in the New Testament: A Study in Biblical Theology.* New York: Paulist Press.

Winer, G.
1882   *A Treatise on the Grammar of New Testament Greek.* 3rd ed., rev. Edinburgh: T&T Clark.

Wink, W.
1968   *John the Baptist in the Gospel Tradition.* Society for New Testament Studies Monograph Series 7. London: Cambridge University Press.
1992   "Beyond Just War and Pacifism: Jesus's Nonviolent Way." *Review and Expositor* 89:197–214.
2002   *The Human Being: Jesus and the Enigma of the Son of Man.* Minneapolis: Fortress.

Winkle, R.
1986   "The Jeremiah Model for Jesus in the Temple." *Andrews University Seminary Studies* 24:155–72.

Winter, B. W.
1991   "The Messiah as the Tutor: The Meaning of Καθηγητής in Matthew 23:10." *Tyndale Bulletin* 42:152–57.

Witherington, B., III
1984   *Women in the Ministry of Jesus: A Study of Jesus' Attitudes to Women and Their Roles as Reflected in His Earthly Life.* Society for New Testament Studies Monograph Series 51. Cambridge: Cambridge University Press.
1985   "Matthew 5:32 and 19:19—Exception or Exceptional Situation?" *New Testament Studies* 31:571–75.
1995   *The Jesus Quest: The Third Search for the Jew of Nazareth.* Downers Grove, IL: InterVarsity.
2000   *Jesus the Sage.* Minneapolis: Augsburg/Fortress.
2006   *Matthew.* Smyth & Helwys Bible Commentary. Macon, GA: Smyth & Helwys.

Wolf, H. M.
1972   "A Solution to the Immanuel Prophecy in Isa. 7:14–8:22." *Journal of Biblical Literature* 91:449–56.

Wolff, C.
1988   "Niedrigkeit und Verzicht im Wort und Weg Jesu und in der

apostolischen Existenz des Paulus."
New Testament Studies 34:183–96.

Wong, E.
1991 "The Matthean Understanding of the Sabbath: A Response to G. N. Stanton." *Journal for the Study of the New Testament* 44:3–18.

Worth, R. H.
1997 *The Sermon on the Mount: Its Old Testament Roots.* New York: Paulist Press.

Woschitz, K.
1985 "Erzähler Glaube: Die Geschichte vom starken Glauben als Geschichte Gottes mit Juden und Heiden (Mt 15,21–28 par)." *Zeitschrift für katholische Theologie* 107:319–32.

Wrembek, C.
1991 "Das Gleichnis vom königlichen Hochzeitsmahl und vom Mann ohne hochzeitliches Gewand." *Geist und Leben* 64:17–40.

Wright, A.
1989 "The Sermon on the Mount: A Jewish View." *New Blackfriars* 70:182–89.

Wright, D. F.
2005 *What Has Infant Baptism Done to Baptism?* Carlisle, UK: Paternoster.

Wright, N. T.
1996 *Christian Origins and the Question of God*, vol. 2: *Jesus and the Victory of God.* Minneapolis: Fortress.
1997 "Thy Kingdom Come: Living the Lord's Prayer." *Christian Century* 114:268–70.
2003 *Christian Origins and the Question of God*, vol. 3 *The Resurrection of the Son of God.* Minneapolis: Augsburg.

Yamasaki, G.
1998 *John the Baptist in Life and Death: Audience-Oriented Criticism of Matthew's Narrative.* Sheffield: Sheffield Academic Press.

Yamauchi, E.
1966 "The 'Daily Bread' Motif in Antiquity." *Westminster Theological Journal* 28:145–56.
1989 "The Episode of the Magi." Pp. 15–39 in *Chronos, Kairos, Christos: Nativity and Chronology Studies Presented to Jack Finegan.* Edited by J. Vardaman and E. Yamauchi. Winona Lake, IN: Eisenbrauns.

Yang, Y.-E.
1987 *Jesus and the Sabbath in Matthew's Gospel.* Sheffield: Sheffield Academic Press.

Yarbrough, R. W.
1983 "The Date of Papias: A Reassessment." *Journal of the Evangelical Theological Society* 26:181–91.
1997 "Eta Linnemann: Friend or Foe of Biblical Scholarship?" *Master's Seminary Journal* 8:163–89.

Yarnold, E.
1968 "*Teleios* in St. Matthew's Gospel." *Studia evangelica* 4:269–73.

Young, B. H.
1989 *Jesus and His Jewish Parables: Rediscovering the Roots of Jesus's Teaching.* New York: Paulist Press.
1995 *Jesus the Jewish Theologian.* Peabody, MA: Hendrickson.

Young, N. H.
1985 "Jesus and the Sinners: Some Queries." *Journal for the Study of the New Testament* 24:73–75.

Young, R.
1994 *Intermediate New Testament Greek: A Linguistic and Exegetical Approach.* Nashville: Broadman.

Zatelli, I.
1991 "Rachel's Lament in the Targum and Other Ancient Jewish Interpretation." *Rivista biblica italiana* 39:477–90.

Zeilinger, F.
2002 *Zwischen Himmel und Erde: Ein Kommentar zur 'Bergpredigt' Matthäus 5–7.* Stuttgart: Kohlhammer.

Zeitlin, S.
1924 "The Halaka in the Gospels and Its Relation to the Jewish Law at the Time of Jesus." *Hebrew Union College Annual* 1:357–73.
1942 *Who Crucified Jesus?* New York: Harper.

Zeller, D.
1977 "Die Bildlogik des Gleichnisses Mt 11,16f./Lk 7,31f." *Zeitschrift für die neutestamentliche Wissenschaft* 68:252–57.

Zerbe, G.
1993 *Non-retaliation in Early Jewish and New Testament Texts.* Sheffield: Sheffield Academic Press.

Zerwick, M.
1963 *Biblical Greek.* Translated by J. Smith. Rome: Pontifical Biblical Institute.

Zias, J., and E. Sekeles
1985   "The Crucified Man from Giv'at
        ha-Mivtar: A Reappraisal." *Israel
        Exploration Journal* 35:22–27.
Ziesler, J. A.
1972–73 "The Removal of the Bridegroom: A
        Note on Mark 2:18–22 and Parallels."
        New Testament Studies 19:190–94.
1984   "Matthew and the Presence of Jesus."
        Epworth Review 11:55–63, 90–97.
Zimmermann, H.
1960   "Das absolute ἐγώ εἰμι
        als die neutestamentliche
        Offensbarungsformel." *Biblische
        Zeitschrift* 4:54–69, 266–76.
Zöckler, T.
2001   "Light within the Human Person: A
        Comparison of Matthew 6:22–23 and
        Gospel of Thomas 24." *Journal of
        Biblical Literature* 120:487–99.

Zolli, E.
2001   "Abermals: Ναζοραῖος in Mt 2,23."
        Theologische Zeitschrift 57:402–5.
Zucker, D. J.
1990   "Jesus and Jeremiah in the Matthean
        Tradition." *Journal of Ecumenical
        Studies* 27:288–305.
Zumstein, J.
1977   *La condition du croyant dans
        l'Évangile selon Matthieu.* Göttingen:
        Vandenhoeck & Ruprecht.
1980   "Antioche sur l'Oronte et l'Évangile
        selon Matthieu." *Studien zum
        Neuen Testament und seiner Umwelt*
        5:22–38.
2001   *Notre Père: La prière de Jésus au coeur
        de notre vie.* Poliez-le-Grand: Moulin.

Index of Subjects

Abraham 59–60, 113
adultery 167–68, 170–71, 459–61
Ahaz 70, 133
allegories 333–34
amillennialism 322
Amos 62
Andrew 136, 265
angelic visits 63, 66–68, 89, 681
anger and abusive speech 167, 168–70
annihilationism 279
anointing 619
Anti-Marcionite Prologues 17
antinomianism 213–23
Antipas 97, 362–65
anti-Semitism 45–46, 562–63, 641, 650–51, 655–56
anxiety 198–202
apostasy 440
apostles 264–65. *See also* disciples and discipleship
apostolic succession 407
Archelaus 97
Asaph 347
Aspah 62
audience and occasion 14–15, 72
authority, conflict over 44–47
authorship 11–13

Balthasar 79
baptism 690
baptism of repentance, John's 105–10
Barabbas 653–54
Bar Kokhba 573
Bartholomew 265
Bathsheba 27, 59, 60
Beatitudes 101, 146–47
Bethany 619
Bethlehem 83–84, 92–95
Bethphage 494

Bethsaida 299–300
betrothal customs 65
blood libel 654, 655–56
Boaz 27
brotherhood 605–6
burial of dead 239–40

Caesarea Philippi 403
Caiaphas 617, 639–41
canonicity 17
Capernaum 133, 232, 248, 300–301, 428, 430
Caspar 79
celibacy 463–64
Chaldeans 79
charity 183–84
chauvinism 671, 680
children 435–40, 464–65, 501
Chorazin 299–300
Christian Jews 3, 45, 159, 269, 563
Christology. *See also specific names for Jesus*
    authority over nature 243–45
    irony of Jesus's crucifixion 610
    Jesus as God-with-us 73
    Jesus's baptism and attestment 122
    Jesus's invitation 304–5
    messianic status 56–57
    names for Jesus 32–37, 231
    trinitarian message of Jesus 303
    worship of Jesus by magi 80–81, 86
church 46–47, 404–6
church discipline 352, 408, 431, 443–47
cleansing rituals 110
commandments 535–37
community 318
compassion 313, 604

conditional immortality 279
continuity *vs.* discontinuity 255–56
covenant theology 4
covetousness 470–71
creation motif 122
cross 661
crowds
    kingdom message to 337, 350, 354–55
    parabolic discourse with 140, 230, 381
crucifixion 482, 660–61, 664–66
Cyrene 659

daily sustenance 188, 193
dating of writings 13–14
David 58, 60, 78, 84, 309–10
dead, raising from 260
Dead Sea Scrolls 146
Decapolis 140
decay 196n5
desert, role of 106, 126
devil/Satan
    encroachment on domain of 294, 322
    position, in temptations 128
    possession by 139–40, 245–47, 261–62, 320–21
dietary laws 383–84
disciples and discipleship
    anxiety of 200–202
    call to discipleship 135–37
    charity practice 183–84
    commission of Twelve 264–65, 268–70
    costs of 239–40
    discipline of sinning 443–47
    distance from Jesus 631
    doubt 688

emulation of God 177–78, 180
essence of 411–14
faith 245, 357–58, 372–73, 376, 393–94, 424–25, 504–5, 688
and family 137, 273–74, 276–77, 330–31
fasting practice 190–91
flight of 637
good works paramount 156, 509–10
Great Commission 689–91
and greed 197–98
higher righteousness of 164
imperception and misunderstanding of 382, 486, 487–88, 504, 619
instruction on support 271–72
and Jesus's absence 357
Jesus's criticism of 400–401
Jesus's ministry as model to 139, 154, 262–63
Jesus warns against Pharisaic practices 545–49
and law 158–59
locus of Jesus's ministry 165
love of enemies 177
loyalty 282–83
mercy 152
opposition to 263, 273–82
orientation to others and service 433, 491–92, 548
and parabolic discourse 338–41
persecution and vindication 273, 275–76, 278–80, 574–75
Peter as representative 376, 644
and Pharisees 382, 394
prayer practice 184–90, 208–10
religious duty performance 180–81
rewards of 283–84, 475–76
sacrifice involved in 352, 469–71
scope of mission 267
as sibling of Jesus in judgment narrative 606–7
status and ambition 487–88
stewardship 598–602
vs. antinomianism 213–23
weakness of 633
dispensationalism 605
divine sovereignty vs. human responsibility 305–6, 621–22, 625, 656
divorce 45, 65–66, 168, 171–72, 459–63
dogs 207
doves, appearance of 120
dreams 653–54

earth, theological significance of 151
earthly treasures 196
earthquakes 573, 667, 670–71, 680–81
Eastern Orthodox Christianity 384
Egypt, escape to and return from 90–91
Elijah 109, 295–96, 403, 417, 421, 422
Elisha 296, 393
encomium genre 5
engagement customs 65
Ephrathah 83
eschatology
  bliss of, with faith 232–33
  coming of the Messiah 569, 578–79, 583–84, 585–86
  eschatological reversal 233, 477–81, 501–2
  faithful stewardship rewarded 601
  heavenly disturbance 582–83
  ignorance of timing of 588–90, 592–93, 595–97
  John's message of 108, 113
  judgment narrative 601–11
  in parables 350–51, 353–54
  table metaphor 389
  women's labor as metaphor for 573
Essenes 112, 217
ethical dualism 213–23
Eucharist 369, 625, 626–27
evangelism, personal 470–71

evil, as part of divine providence 92, 344–45
exorcism 44, 245–47, 261–62, 320–21, 327, 424
eyes/eyesight 197

faith. See also unbelief in face of revelation
  of disciples 245, 357–58, 372–73, 376, 393–94, 424–25, 504–5, 688
  and healing 236, 259, 261
  as overriding 556
false messiahs 573, 578
false prophets 216–20, 578–79
family
  discipleship and 137, 273–74, 276–77, 330–31
  Jesus's teachings on 458–65
famines 573
fasting 190–91
Feast of Unleavened Bread 623, 624
fidelity 574–75
Field of Blood 649
first-class condition (reality) 127–28
flogging 654–55
flute playing 259
forgiveness 448–52
fruit, as metaphor 217, 324, 504–5, 585–86
fulfillment, prophetic
  about 19–25
  baptism of Jesus 118–21
  escape to and return from Egypt 90–91
  healing 235–36, 316–17
  Jesus's arrest and crucifixion 636–37
  Joseph's settlement in Nazareth 98–100
  Judas's suicide 649–50
  Mary's conception and birth of Jesus 68–73
  massacre at Bethlehem 93–95
  Pharisaic hypocrisy 380–81

Gadara 245–47, 250
Galilee 98, 688
gates of hades 405
Gennesaret 375–76
Gentiles
  eschatological fate of 351, 480–81

extension of salvation to 650

mission to 268–69, 393, 671, 689–90

portrayal of 15, 27–28, 133–34, 233, 388

supersession of Israel by 510, 517–19

gentile world mission 46–47

Gerasa 250

Gethsemane 631

gifts of the magi 86

goats 608, 609

God

emulation of 177–78, 180

as Father 186n20

God's love 176–77

sovereignty of, vs. human responsibility 305–6, 621–22, 625, 656

voice of 120, 417–18

Golden Rule 211–12

Golgotha 660

good works 156, 162, 509–10, 604

Gospel genre 4–5

Gospels

historical-theological dichotomy in Gospels 4–5

literary independence 6

literary interindependence 6–7

literary structure 8–10

literary style 10–11

narrative criticism approach to 7–8

Olivet Discourse in 567

parallels 121

Passion treatment 613

Peter's three denials 642

synoptic problem 6–7

grace 168

greed 197–98, 471, 622

gullibility vs. judgmentalism 203–7

Hallel 496

hamotzi 368–69

hand washing 377–79

healing fulfillments 235–36, 316–17. See also sickness

heaven, opening of 119–20

heavenly treasures 196

heavenly voice 120

Hebrew Bible

in crucifixion narrative 663, 665–66

ethical dualism 213–14

in fulfillment quotations 70–72, 107–9

and Jesus's ministry 291

and Matthew's eschatology 581–82

as source 17–19, 212

Herodians 526, 527

Herodias 364

Herod the Great 44, 78–83, 92–95

Herod the tetrarch 362–66

Hillel 460–61

historical-theological dichotomy in Gospels 4–5

hoarding 196

Holy Spirit 114n13, 120, 321, 322–24, 690

hospitality 271–72, 433

hubris 433

human responsibility vs. divine sovereignty 305–6, 621–22, 625, 656

humility 151, 433, 435–36, 495, 497

hypocrisy 501, 553–54

illumination. See light, metaphor

Immanuel (Jesus) 34, 72, 263, 303

infant baptism 465

infidelity 168, 171–72, 461–63

Israel

composition of 68

John's ministry directed to 110

leaders indicted by Jesus 513–19, 524–25

mission to 268–69

primacy of election 389

redemption of, through Jesus 488

rejection of prophets 559

twelve tribes 476

unbelief of 24–25, 286–87

Jacob 58

James 136–37, 265, 486

Jeconiah 59

Jeremiah 93, 403

Jerusalem

as city on the hill 155

destruction of 578

fear at Jesus's birth 81–82

Jesus's entry into 494–97

Jesus. See also Christology; Passion of Jesus

accusations of

collaboration with the devil 245–47, 319, 320–22

anointing 619

association with sinners 296–97

authority of 224–25, 243–46, 508–10

baptism, contrasted with John's 115–16

birth of 63–75

charismatic 135

childhood 105

Christology in Matthew 32–37, 56–57, 73, 239

compassion of 369

conflict over Authority 44–47

cry of abandonment 669

death of 327, 669

divinity vs. humanity of 589, 633

division before harmony in mission 280–81

egalitarianism of 547–48

endorsement by Father 120, 417–18

entry into Jerusalem 494–97

escape to and return from Egypt 90–91, 96–100

eschatology (see eschatology)

genealogy, in Matthew 25–32, 57–62, 67

God's will above 632–33

holistic ministry 139

invitation of 304–6

John's doubts and questions 290–92

and law 157–58, 161–64, 167–68

naming 67

and outsiders 236–37

Pharisaic opposition to 309–14, 318, 320–22, 396–97, 526–29, 535–37

questions Pharisees 540–42

as ransom for many 488

as rejected Prophet 557–58

relationship to Moses 76, 97, 127, 129, 149

resurrection as redemption

682–84
siblings of 74, 360
sinners association 44, 46
sonship 31–32, 34–35, 61,
120–21, 127–28, 373,
376, 662–63
temple confrontation
499–502
transfiguration of 413,
416–20
Jews, Christian 3, 45, 159
Joachim 62
John 136–37, 265, 486
John, Gospel of 54
John the Baptist
ascetic life of 296–97
authority of 508–10
baptism of Jesus 117–23
contrast to ministry of
Jesus 114–16
death of 362–66, 421
diet and clothing 109
disciples and fasting
254–56
doubts and questions Jesus
290–92
fulfillment of prophecy by
107–9
ministry of 54, 106–7
origins of baptism of
repentance 105–10
rebukes Pharisees and
Sadducees 111–14
significance and role 122,
292–96
Jonah 326–27
Joseph (husband of Mary)
angelic visits 63, 66–68, 89,
96–97
genealogy of 30–31, 60–61,
62, 67
obedience of 73–75, 89,
97–98
righteousness 65–66
Joseph of Arimathea 674
Judah 58
Judaism 3, 549, 563
Judas Iscariot 265, 525,
621–22, 625, 644, 648–51
judgmentalism vs. gullibility
203–7
justice 170, 189, 556

Kaddish 186
kingdom of heaven/God
and evil 345
in Matthew 37–44, 107, 473

message to crowds 337,
350, 354–55
in parables 522
Peter and keys to 405,
407–8
status in 433, 434–36
violence, and inauguration
of 294–95
King of Israel (Jesus) 34

Last Supper 369
laudatory biography genre 5
law, disciples and 158–59
law, Jesus and 157–58,
161–64, 165–68
legal experts 355
lepers, cleansing of 230–31
Levi (Matthew). See Matthew
(Levi)
light, metaphor 101, 155–56
literary structure 8–10
literary style 10–11
Lord (Jesus) 35, 231, 491,
540–42
Lord's Supper 625, 626–27
love
of enemies 168, 176–78
as fulfillment of law 159
of God and neighbors
536–37
Luke, Gospel of
characteristics of
beginning 54
Jesus's baptism 121
Jesus's genealogy in 28–32
kingdom use in 39–42
Olivet Discourse in 567
Passion treatment 613
testing of Jesus 124
lust 167–68, 170–71

M, as source 7, 521
Magdalene, Mary 671, 675
Magdalen papyrus 16n23
magi, visit of 76–87
manna 369, 370
Marcion 17
Mark, Gospel of
concision of beginning 54
disciples doubt of Jesus
689
Jesus's baptism 121
kingdom use in 39–42
Markan priority 6–7
Matthew's relation to 3,
357, 393, 614
Olivet Discourse in 567

outline 8–9
Passion treatment 613–14
testing of Jesus 124
marriage 168, 171–72,
459–65, 531–32
Mary (mother of Jesus)
genealogy of 27–28, 61
perpetual virginity 74–75,
330
virgin conception 64–65,
69–70
Mary (mother of James and
Joseph) 671, 675
Matthew, Gospel of
audience and occasion
14–15, 72
authorship 11–13
canonicity 17
Christology 32–37, 56–57,
73
church and gentile world
mission 46–47
conflict over authority
44–47
dating 13–14
fulfillment quotations
19–25
genealogy of Jesus 25–32,
57–62, 67
Hebrew Bible use 17–19
influence on the church
2–3
kingdom of heaven/God
37–44
literary structure 8–10
literary style 10–11
and Mark's account 3, 357,
393, 614
numerical patterning in 11,
25–27, 58, 59n4
outline 10, 47–51
overview of message 1–2
Passion treatment 613–14
Semitisms in 10
source use in 10–11, 13
textual history 15–16
theological emphases
17–47
title 56–57
Matthew (Levi) 12–13, 252
Melchior 79
mercy 139, 152, 253–54, 556
Messiah/Christ (Jesus) 32–33,
57, 406, 540–42
messiahs, false 573, 578–79
miracle meals 392–94
mission

commission of Twelve
264–65, 268–70
division before harmony in
mission 280–81
to Gentiles 268–69, 393,
671, 689–90
Great Commission 689–91
to Israel 268–69
mockery and irony 663–64
Moses 149, 166–67, 255, 393,
417
mountains and mountaintops
129, 149, 230, 416, 417,
688
Mount of Olives 494
mourning 150, 239–40, 259
Muratorian Fragment 17
murder 167, 168–70

narrative criticism approach
about 7–8
literary structure 8–10
literary style 10–11
nature, Jesus's authority over
243–45
Nazarenes 643
Nazareth 96–100, 359–61
Nazirites 99
Noah, days of 588–90
numerical patterning
examples of 11
forty 126–27
fourteen 25–27, 58, 59n4,
61
seven 61
ten 595
twelve 264–65

oaths 168, 172–74, 555
Olivet Discourse 4, 565–67
oral tradition 6

pacifism 636–37
Papias 15–16
parables/parabolic discourse
biblical basis for 346–47
etymology 338
interpretation of 333–34
multiple access points of
341–42
structure of 332–33
parental love 260
Passion of Jesus
betrayal prediction 624–25
first prediction 410, 483–84
foretold in parable of the
tenant farmers 515

fourth prediction 612
narrative commences 612
second prediction 426,
483–84
third prediction 482–84
Passover 612, 623–24, 626–27
Paul 159, 217n5, 220
peace, Jesus and 280–81
peacemakers 152–53
persecution 153–56, 273,
275–76, 278–80
Peter (Simon)
denial prediction 628–29
faith, and doubt, of 373
first disciple called 136,
265
as foundational apostle
406–8
and Jesus's identity 403–5
and Jesus's suffering
410–11
mother-in-law healed 234
three denials 639, 642–44,
650
and transfiguration of
Jesus 417–18
Pharisees
attempts to trap Jesus
526–29, 535–37
charges against Jesus 261
etymology and origins 111
as false prophets 217
fulfilling measure of sin of
ancestors 23
Jesus contrasted with
166–67
Jesus questions 540–42
Jesus rebukes 379–80
and Jesus's meal with
sinners 252–54
Jesus warns against
400–401, 545–49
John rebukes 110–14
opposition to Jesus 309–14,
318, 320–22
plans to destroy Jesus
313–14
request for sign 326–28,
396–97
and ritual purity 377–79
secure tomb of Jesus
676–77
testing of Jesus 459–61,
527–28
woe oracles upon 550–58
Philip 97
piety, inner 556–57

pigs 207, 246–47
Pilate 646, 653–55
poor 619–20
possessions 196–97
poverty 150
prayer 184–90, 208–10
premillennialism 322
priests. See Pharisees; religious leaders
privatism 144
progressive dispensationalism 4
prophecy, predictive 22–25,
565–66
prophets, rejection of 559
Protestant Christianity 384,
406–7
publicity vs. privacy 185
punishment miracle 503n1
purity, inner 44, 152, 155,
253, 381

Q, as source 7, 521
Qumran 110, 112

Rachel 94–95
Rahab 27, 59–60
Ramah 94
redemptive history 91
religious duties
charity 183–84
fasting 190–91
prayer 184–90
right attitude 179–83, 201
religious leaders. See also
Pharisees
and blood libel 656
cover up of resurrection
685–86
plot to kill Jesus 617
secure tomb of Jesus
676–77
temple confrontations
499–502, 508–10,
514–19
remarriage 461–63
repentance, John's baptism of
105–10
resurrection
of Jesus 683–84, 686
marriage in 531–33
of saints at Jesus's death
670–71
retaliation 168, 174–75
revelation
to prideful and humble 303
through dreams 66

unbelief in face of 286–87,
299–301
riches, earthly 469–73
righteousness, teachings on
44
baptism of Jesus 118–19
Joseph's case 65–66
in Sermon on the Mount
151
ritual purity 110, 377–79,
383–84
Roman Catholic Christianity
384, 406–7
Ruth 27, 59

Sabbath observance 44,
309–14
sacrifice 469–71
Sadducees 82
associated with Pharisees
397
etymology and origins
111–12
Jesus warns against
400–401
John rebukes 110–14
and Messiah's coming 82
question Jesus 530–33
salt metaphor 101, 154–55
Samaritans 268–69
Sanhedrin 639
Satan. See devil/Satan
Sea of Galilee 372–73
self-denial 412, 537
Semitisms 10
Sermon on the Mount
analysis 143
Beatitudes 146–47
discipleship vs.
antinomianism
213–23
emphasis in Matthew 2
historicity 141–42
interpretative approaches
4, 143–44
Jesus and the law 157–58,
161–68
literary structure 142–43
love of enemies 176–78
religious duties 179–83,
179–91, 201
as representative ethical

teachings of Jesus
142, 144
sexual ethics 170–72
Shammai 460–61
sheep 608–9
sickness 235, 253, 260. See
also healing fulfillments
Sidon 300
silence, about miracles 231
Simon of Cyrene 659
Simon (Peter). See Peter
(Simon)
Simon the leper 619
Simon the Zealot 265
simplicity vs. verbosity 185
sin
avoidance of 189
enticing believers to
437–38
forgiveness of 44, 67–68,
188–89, 247–49
necessity of forgiveness
448–52
of Pharisees's ancestors 23
sickness, death, and 235,
253
unforgivable 322–24
singleness 463–64
sinners, Jesus's association
with 252–54, 296–97, 430
slander 248, 292, 296, 317,
323, 382
slavery 197–98
Sodom 300
Solomon 60
Son of Abraham (Jesus)
33–34, 57–58
Son of David (Jesus) 33,
57–58, 261, 320, 491, 496,
540–42
Son of God (Jesus) 34–35,
373, 376, 420, 639, 671
Son of Man (Jesus) 36–37,
239, 248–49, 277, 583
sons of the kingdom 233
sources 10–11, 13, 17–19
star, rising 80
status 433, 434–36, 487
stewardship, faithful 598–602
Suffering Servant motif 120
sun, darkened 667, 670
synoptic problem 6–7

Tabernacles, Feast of 417
Tamar 27, 59
taxes 429–30
Teacher (Jesus) 36
temple, destruction of 565,
568–69, 577, 579–80
textual history 15–16
Thaddaeus 265
theological emphases 17–47
Thomas 265
titulus 661
Torah, oral and written
383–84, 469
translation notes 4
trees as metaphor 324, 504
trinity 303, 589, 690
triumphalism 295
truthfulness 168, 172–74
typology 347
Tyre 300

unbelief in face of revelation
286–87, 299–301, 318, 342
unforgivable sin 322–24
unfruitful trees 114

vengeance 383
verbosity vs. simplicity 185
vineyard imagery 513–19
violence 636
violence and inauguration of
kingdom 294–95
virgin and virginity 69–70
vows 168, 172–74, 383

wars 573
wealth as barrier to eternal
life 469–73
wedding banquet imagery
254–55, 594, 596
Wirkungsgeschichte 2
wisdom, personification of
305
withdrawal in face of danger
24, 86n12, 132, 387
women 27–28, 59, 671, 680

Zealots 217
Zechariah 495, 558
Zerah 58

Index of Authors

Abadie, P. 25n27
Abel, E. L. 11n11, 59n4, 529
Abrahams, I. 184n16, 186
Achtemeier, P. 371n1
Adler, N. 511
Adna, J. 247
Agbanou, V. 566n1, 567n3
Agnew, F. H. 181
Aitken, W. 278n6
Aland, B. 16n22, 510, 511
Aland, K. 16n22, 510, 511,
  547n3
Albright, W. 31, 277
Alexander, P. S. 212n1
Alford, H. 413
Allen, L. 143n5
Allen, W. 73n10, 265, 407, 413,
  509n5, 546n1
Allison, D. C. 2, 3, 8, 8n8,
  9n9, 10, 10n9, 11, 11n11,
  12, 12n12, 14n16, 14n18,
  16n21, 16n24, 42, 43n33, 56,
  63, 75n12, 75n13, 76, 79n3,
  80n5, 81, 83, 86, 91, 94, 95,
  97, 99, 99n2, 100, 102, 109,
  110, 112, 113, 114, 115, 117,
  119, 120, 120n4, 121n5, 122,
  123, 127, 135, 136n1, 138,
  139, 142, 142n3, 144n7, 146,
  147n7, 149, 152, 153, 154,
  162, 163n10, 168, 170, 172,
  173, 179n1, 183, 184n16,
  185n17, 186, 186n19, 193,
  195, 197, 197n6, 199, 199n11,
  203, 203n1, 204, 207, 211,
  212, 214, 215, 218, 219, 220,
  227, 230n2, 233, 234, 239n2,
  240n4, 243, 244n2, 245n3,
  246, 254, 256, 259, 260, 262,
  264, 266, 270, 277, 278,
  279, 280, 286, 289, 292, 294,
  294n8, 302n1, 302n2, 310,
  310n6, 316n2, 322, 327, 330,
  332, 333n1, 341, 342, 343,
  346, 352, 353n2, 357, 359,
  360, 361, 365, 369, 369n3,
  376, 377, 382n12, 383, 389,
  392, 393, 397, 398, 401, 402,
  402n1, 404n5, 405n7, 407n14,

408, 411, 413, 415n1, 417,
  418n3, 419, 419n7, 422n13,
  424, 428, 429n2, 430, 432n2,
  435n2, 436, 439, 439n1, 444,
  446, 452, 456, 462, 462n9,
  464n16, 470, 472n3, 480n11,
  482, 487, 488, 493, 495, 496,
  497, 501, 501n5, 502, 503,
  504, 507, 508n3, 509, 509n5,
  512, 517n12, 517n13, 521,
  525, 525n6, 527, 528, 529,
  532, 532n3, 536n5, 537,
  543n3, 546n2, 553, 555, 556,
  557, 558n13, 562, 563, 563n2,
  566, 566n1, 567, 568, 574n6,
  579, 580n5, 581, 583n2, 586,
  587, 588, 590, 599n5, 600,
  601, 603, 604n1, 608n12, 612,
  614, 615, 619, 621, 624, 625,
  627, 629, 634, 643, 649, 650,
  654, 655, 656, 658, 660, 669,
  670, 670n4, 677, 679n1, 682,
  688, 689, 689n2
Alter, R. 8n7
Amaru, B. 559n18
Anderson, J. C. 11n10
Anderson, J. G. 231n6
Anderson, R. 269
Anno, Y. 269
Arav, R. 299
Archbald, P. 354n4
Argyle, A. W. 595n3
Arnott, A. 623
Aune, D. E. 2, 5, 46n35, 53n1,
  214n1, 217n4, 386n2, 388n5,
  519
Aurelius, E. 233n14
Aus, R. 243, 362n2, 364
Aveni, A. F. 80n5

Baarda, T. 250
Bacchiocchi, S. 302n2
Bachmann, M. 480n9
Bacon, B. W. 9
Badia, L. F. 110
Bahat, D. 499
Bahr, G. 184n16, 186, 627n2
Bailey, K. E. 333n1, 334

Bailey, M. L. 37n31, 334, 343n9,
  344, 345n13, 352n1, 353n3,
  354n4, 355n6
Balch, D. 2, 12n12, 13n15,
  14n17, 14n18, 45n34, 443
Ballard, P. 524n4
Bammel, E. 148n7, 277n4,
  428n1, 429, 430, 493n1,
  528n3, 529n5, 638n1, 643
Bandstra, A. J. 191
Banks, R. 158n2, 310, 377n1,
  428n1, 537n8
Barbieri, L. A., Jr. 70, 566,
  605n2
Barclay, W. 90, 249, 369, 388n5,
  408, 413n7, 480, 481, 604n1
Barkay, G. 660
Barnes, A. 30, 70, 566
Barnett, P. 294n8
Barr, D. L. 8n8
Barr, J. 183n14, 186n20
Barrett, C. K. 488, 529n6
Barrett, D. 16n22
Barta, K. A. 266, 280
Barth, G. 2, 217n5, 227n1,
  227n2, 238, 243, 373, 377n1,
  423n1, 492
Bartnicki, R. 277n4, 495n3
Barton, S. C. 330, 441n5
Basser, H. 407n15
Batey, R. 183n14, 595n3
Bauckham, R. 14n19, 27n28,
  106n1, 428, 428n1, 429, 499,
  501n6, 666n4, 671, 682
Baudoz, J.-F. 130n6
Bauer, D. R. 2, 8n8, 9, 10n9,
  11n10, 25n27, 134, 142n3,
  158, 158n2, 259n3, 297, 410,
  428n1, 607n9
Baum, A. D. 16n21
Bauman, C. 143n5
Baumbach, G. 111n9
Baumgardt, D. 186
Baumgarten, A. 111, 377n1,
  380n9
Baumgarten, J. 475
Baxter, W. S. 97, 149
BDF (F. Blass, A. Debrunner, R.
  W. Funk) 21, 28, 59n3, 60n5,

64n2, 65, 66, 66n5, 67, 68, 74,
80, 80n4, 81, 82, 83, 85n9,
85n10, 85n11, 89, 89n2, 89n3,
97, 118, 126, 127, 194n4,
217n3, 223, 258n1, 284n4,
296n11, 302n1, 310n6, 320n1,
365, 388, 389n6, 405n10,
410n2, 418n2, 426n1, 429n3,
434n1, 438n2, 438n3, 475n1,
478n5, 479n6, 481, 495n4,
508n3, 509n5, 535n4, 546n1,
608n11, 643n1, 646n1, 649n1,
669n3
Beardslee, W. 282n15
Beare, F. 2, 5, 79, 81, 93, 108,
150, 233, 267n4, 369, 383,
388n5, 408, 413, 432n2, 480,
517n12, 549, 562, 586, 604,
604n1, 641, 650, 655
Beasley-Murray, G. 37n31,
43n33, 110, 322n8, 413,
465n18, 567n3
Beaton, R. 19n26, 316, 317
Beck, D. R. 6n4
Beck, J. R. 547n4
Becker, H.-J. 549n6
Becking, B. 95
Beecher, W. J. 72n9
Belkin, S. 380n9, 531
Bellinger, W. H. 235n19
Bellinzoni, A. J. 17
Bennett, T. 207n9
Bennett, W. 410n1
Benoit, P. 2, 9n9, 638n1, 649n2
Berg, W. 201
Berger, K. 100n3, 380n9, 404n4
Bergmeier, R. 176
Berkey, R. 321
Berlin, A. 8n7
Berner, U. 143n5
Best, E. 406n12, 472n3
Best, T. 415n1
Betz, H. D. 142n2, 142n3,
143n5, 184n16, 185, 185n17,
188, 188n23, 189, 197, 199,
218n5, 220n14, 221, 302n2,
305
Betz, O. 227n1, 496n6, 537n8,
558, 593, 649n2
Beyschlag, K. 143n5
Birdsall, J. N. 265
Black, D. A. 6n4, 16n24, 215n2
Black, M. 37n30, 109n5, 189,
409, 556, 637n4
Black, M. 16n21
Black, S. 11n10, 89, 89n1
Blaising, C. 4, 633n4
Blank, S. 558n13
Blickenstaff, M. 236n20
Blinzler, J. 329, 497n7

Blomberg, C. L. 2, 5, 7, 10, 14,
26, 27n28, 28, 30, 56, 70, 108,
111, 115, 127, 168, 170, 175,
195, 245, 255, 260n4, 263, 271,
277, 286, 321, 333, 333n1, 334,
376, 383, 387, 391, 392, 400,
407n13, 413, 421n10, 422n13,
424, 428, 428n1, 429, 464n16,
476, 479, 488n5, 490, 500,
504, 516, 523, 532, 535, 543n1,
547n4, 551, 556, 558n13, 565,
566, 574, 575, 580, 584, 586,
594, 598, 605, 605n4, 612, 622,
640, 646, 649, 654, 670, 670n5,
679n1, 680, 681, 688
Blount, B. 659
Boa, K. 80n5
Böcher, O. 79n3, 220n14
Bock, D. L. 4, 5, 32, 124, 141,
142, 146n2, 150n10, 468,
598n1, 640n4
Bockmuehl, M. 172n27, 240n4,
464n16
Boer, M. C. de 450n3
Boismard, M.-É. 188n23
Bokser, B. 627n2
Bonnard, P. 2, 9n9, 432n4
Boobyer, G. 417
Booth, R. 377n1, 380n9
Borchert, G. L. 177
Boring, M. E. 74, 90, 142, 146,
155, 162, 164, 164n12, 165,
166, 177, 180, 193, 203, 206,
211, 214, 227n2, 249, 253, 255,
259, 261, 264, 266, 277n4, 293,
294, 323n9, 333, 347, 352,
369n3, 383, 388n5, 406n11,
413, 419, 421n9, 422, 432n2,
449, 487, 496, 500, 503n1, 506,
517n12, 521, 523n1, 525, 536,
540n3, 543n1, 569n3, 582n1,
592, 593, 602n6, 604, 604n1,
612
Borland, J. A. 62
Bornkamm, G. 2, 142, 142n3,
208, 217n5, 227n1, 227n2,
238, 243, 339n4, 373, 377n1,
407n15, 410, 423n1, 492
Bourke, M. M. 56
Bowker, J. 111n7
Bowman, J. 547n3
Boyer, J. L. 127, 128n4
Bradshaw, P. F. 184n16
Brandenburger, E. 607n9
Brandon, S. 14, 638n1
Brandscheidt, R. 495n3, 496n5,
500, 501
Brant, J. 174n30
Braude, W. 555n7
Braumann, G. 294n8
Braun, W. 527

Brennecke, H. C. 198
Bridges, C. B. 197
Broadus, J. 30, 70, 121, 407,
472n3, 566
Brocke, M. 184n16
Brodie, T. 426
Broer, I. 2, 46n35, 147n7, 174,
567n3, 615n1
Brooke, G. J. 146n6, 172n27,
464n16
Brooks, J. A. 142n3
Brown, C. 405n7
Brown, E. 177
Brown, J. K. 136n2
Brown, R. 6n5, 25n27, 26, 27,
28, 31, 52, 53, 65, 74, 75n13,
87n13, 91n4, 99, 99n2, 136n1,
184n16, 339n4, 407n14,
435n5, 465n20, 615n1, 626,
636n1, 637n4, 641, 644, 646,
664, 664n2, 665
Brown, S. 14n17, 31, 47n36,
59n4, 66, 76, 91, 267n2,
267n4, 567n3, 607n9
Bruce, A. B. 243n2
Bruce, F. F. 362, 495, 529n5
Bruggen, J. van 191
Brunec, M. 290n2
Bruner, F. D. 2, 3, 61, 73, 75,
115, 118, 127, 148n7, 150,
184n16, 203, 236, 237, 249,
272, 301, 330, 407n13, 407n14,
408, 409, 443, 452, 462n10,
465, 472n3, 480, 517n13, 548,
562, 562n1, 604, 636n2, 650
Buchanan, G. 501n6
Büchsel, F. 475n2, 488
Buck, E. 656n5
Buckley, T. 450n3
Buetubela, B. 87n13
Bunyan, J. 323
Burchard, C. 234n16
Burger, C. 227n1, 490n1, 497n7
Burgess, J. 403
Burkill, T. 386n2, 389
Burnett, F. 46n35, 297, 475n2,
567n3
Burridge, R. A. 5n3
Burrows, M. 531
Burton, E. 546n1
Busse, U. 480n9
Butler, B. C. 6n5, 7
Byargeon, R. W. 184n16
Byrskog, S. 5, 157, 547

Cadbury, H. 405
Cahill, L. S. 144n7
Calvin, J. 30, 70, 90, 115, 126,
141, 159n5, 203, 277n5, 294,
302n1, 303, 330, 388, 406,
407, 408, 413n7, 470, 490,

546, 562n1, 612, 626, 636n2, 644, 649
Cameron, P. 294, 294n8
Campbell, J. 404n4
Campbell, K. 155n15
Campbell, K. M. 360
Campbell, R. A. 115
Capes, D. B. 121n5
Caragounis, C. 37n30, 37n31, 43n33, 136n1, 239n2, 404, 406
Carey, W. 598n3
Carlisle, C. 371n1
Carlston, C. E. 143n5, 333, 377n1, 382
Carmichael, D. 627n2
Carmignac, J. 184n16, 189
Carmody, T. 444n2
Carré, P.-M. 130n6
Carson, D. A. 4n2, 7, 9n9, 11n11, 13, 14, 27, 29ne, 31, 32n29, 42, 56, 58, 64n1, 65, 65n3, 68, 70, 71, 81, 89, 91, 95, 99, 102, 108n3, 111n7, 117, 119, 120, 127, 141, 142n2, 148n7, 150, 170, 172n25, 193, 201, 203, 208, 218n5, 247, 264, 267n3, 277, 294, 294n8, 343n10, 347, 354, 383, 388, 391, 407n13, 408, 412n4, 413n7, 417, 420, 421n10, 431, 462n10, 488n5, 504, 517n12, 524, 546, 565, 566, 567n3, 574, 590, 595, 605n4, 612, 650, 677
Carter, W. 8n8, 37n31, 46n35, 134n1, 137n4, 140, 143n5, 200, 223n20, 333n1, 334, 334n4, 450n3, 458, 480n9, 510n8, 517n12
Casey, M. 37n30, 239n2
Casey, P. M. 309
Cassidy, R. 428n1, 429n2
Catchpole, D. R. 234n16, 294n8, 352n1, 493n1, 604n1, 607n9, 638n1
Cerfaux, L. 302n2
Charette, B. 65, 262, 263, 302n2, 305n4
Charles, J. D. 158n2
Charlesworth, J. H. 139n1, 140, 146n6, 184n16, 186n18, 212n1, 261, 299, 478, 499, 531, 617, 646, 650, 659
Chilton, B. 37n31, 139n1, 184n16, 187, 247, 278, 294n8, 322n7, 322n8, 413n6, 415n1, 514n3, 516n8
Christian, P. 604n1, 607n9
Ciampa, R. 140n2
Clark, K. W. 11n11, 12n13, 510
Clark, R. 277n4
Clements, R. E. 550

Clouse, B. 547n4
Clouse, R. G. 547n4
Cohen, S. D. 555n7
Cohn-Sherbok, D. 308n1, 310
Cohn, H. 638n1
Collins, A. Y. 37n30, 239n2
Collins, J. J. 37n30, 239n2, 291, 291n4
Combet-Galland, C. 513n2
Combrink, H. J. 8n8, 266, 267n4
Comfort, P. W. 16n22
Conard, A. 649n2
Cook, J. 279
Cook, M. J. 12n13, 46n35
Copan, P. 679n1
Cope, O. L. 281n11, 355, 362n2, 469
Coppens, J. 37n30, 302n2
Corley, B. 637n4
Cothenet, É. 217, 220n14
Cotter, W. 503n1
Couroyer, B. 207n9
Cousland, J. R. C. 140
Craghan, J. F. 246
Craig, W. L. 533, 679n1, 686
Cranfield, C. E. B. 529n6, 604n1
Cranford, L. 143n5
Cremer, F. 254
Crosby, M. H. 184n16
Cross, F. 557, 690
Crossan, J. 43, 435n5
Crouzel, H. 172n25
Culbertson, P. 480n9
Culliton, J. T. 175n34
Cullmann, O. 118, 136n1, 264n8, 407n14, 465n18
Cuvillier, É. 87n13, 170, 573, 577, 609, 690

Dahl, N. A. 404n4, 615n1
Dahlberg, B. 403n2
Daly, R. J. 175n34
Dana, H. E. 115, 198n9
D'Ancona, M. 16n23
D'Angelo, M. 186n20
Daniel, C. 217, 220n14
Danker, F. 415n1
Daube, D. 428n1, 464n17, 469n2, 508, 510n7, 529n5, 619n1, 627n2, 633n4
Dautzenberg, G. 428n1
Davies, P. R. 183n14, 189
Davies, R. E. 488
Davies, W. D. 2, 3, 8, 9n9, 10, 11, 11n11, 12, 12n12, 14n16, 14n17, 14n18, 16n21, 16n24, 42, 56, 63, 81, 83, 86, 91, 94, 95, 97, 99, 99n2, 100, 102, 109, 110, 112, 113, 114, 115, 117, 119, 120, 120n4, 122, 123, 127, 135, 138, 139, 142, 142n4,

146, 147n7, 153, 154, 162, 163n10, 168, 172, 173, 179n1, 183, 184n16, 185n17, 186, 186n19, 193, 195, 197, 199, 199n11, 203, 203n1, 204, 207, 211, 212, 214, 215, 218, 219, 220, 233, 234, 239n2, 240n4, 243, 244n2, 245n3, 246, 254, 256, 259, 260, 262, 264, 266, 270, 277, 286, 289, 292, 294, 294n8, 302n1, 302n2, 303, 310, 310n6, 316n2, 322, 327, 330, 332, 333n1, 341, 342, 343, 346, 352, 353n2, 357, 359, 360, 361, 365, 369, 369n3, 376, 377, 382n12, 383, 389, 392, 397, 398, 401, 402, 402n1, 404n5, 405n7, 407n14, 408, 411, 413, 415n1, 418n3, 419n7, 424, 428, 429n2, 430, 431, 432n2, 435n2, 436, 439, 439n1, 444, 446, 452, 456, 462, 462n9, 470, 472n3, 480n11, 482, 487, 488, 493, 496, 497, 501, 501n5, 502, 503, 504, 507, 508n3, 509, 509n5, 512, 517n12, 517n13, 521, 525, 525n6, 527, 528, 529, 532, 532n3, 536n5, 537, 543n3, 546n2, 553, 555, 556, 557, 558n13, 562, 563, 563n2, 566, 566n1, 567, 568, 579, 580n5, 581, 583n2, 586, 587, 588, 590, 599n5, 600, 601, 603, 604n1, 608n12, 612, 619, 621, 624, 625, 627, 629, 634, 643, 649, 650, 654, 655, 656, 658, 660, 669, 670, 677, 689, 689n2
Davis, C. 25n27, 59n4
Davis, M. 674
Davison, J. 217, 220
Dayton, W. 405n10
Dean, M. 142n3
Dehandschutter, B. 353n3
Deines, R. 111n7
Delling, G. 79n3, 185n17
Delobel, J. 215, 302n2, 303
Delorme, J. 516n8, 594n1
Deming, W. 171
Denaux, A. 215, 495n3
Dermience, A. 7, 386n2, 389
Derrett, J. D. M. 75n13, 207n9, 215, 246, 256, 280, 281, 324, 362n2, 371n1, 380n9, 407n15, 423n1, 428n1, 441n5, 446, 450n3, 464n16, 465n20, 472n3, 475n2, 480n9, 501n6, 504n3, 510n7, 516n8, 524n4, 529n5, 547, 557, 585, 599n4, 619n1, 643
Desautels, L. 649n2
Descamps, A. 615n1

Deutsch, C. 45n34, 136n2, 239,
296n12, 302n2, 305, 360
Didier, M. 2, 16n24, 17n25,
19n26, 217, 220n14, 227n1,
334n4, 566n1, 615n1
Dietzfelbinger, C. 599n4
Di Lella, A. 147n7
Dillon, R. J. 200n14, 201, 510n8
Dobbeler, A. von 446, 687n1,
689
Dodd, C. H. 42, 159n5
Donahue, J. 37n30, 239n2, 296,
604
Donaldson, J. 547
Donaldson, T. 130n6, 149,
230n2, 390, 391, 393, 415n1,
419, 537n8, 688
Donelson, L. R. 175n34
Donfried, K. 594, 594n1
Dormandy, R. 516n8
Dorneich, M. 184n16
Doty, W. 352n1
Doyle, B. R. 140, 480n9, 488
Draisma, S. 649n2
Draper, J. A. 142n4, 583n2
Dschulnigg, P. 136n1
Duff, P. B. 493n1
Duke, P. D. 664n1
Duling, D. C. 33, 173, 261n5,
320, 407n15, 444n1, 488,
490n1
Dumais, M. 142n2, 143n5,
144n7
Dungan, D. 5n3, 6n4, 6n6
Dunn, J. 45n34, 139n1, 265
Dunne, F. P. 340
Duplacy, J. 423n1, 466
Du Plessis, J. 343n9
Dupont, J. 147n7, 249n6, 277n4,
290n2, 291n5, 309n3, 334n4,
353n3, 435, 435n5, 441n5,
464n16, 475n2, 475n3, 567n3
Durston, C. 143n5
Dyer, C. 38, 43

Eckstein, H.-J. 163
Edin, M. H. 253
Edwards, J. R. 127n3
Edwards, R. A. 8n7, 67n7,
136n2, 137n4, 238, 239,
325n2, 397
Edwards, W. D. 664n2, 665
Eigo, F. A. 147n7
Elbert, P. 405n9
Elliott, J. H. 480n9
Elliott, J. K. 16n24, 249n6,
406n12
Elliott, M. 113n12, 233n14,
381n11, 513n2, 519n18,
525n5, 562n1
Ellis, E. E. 5, 250, 435, 435n5

Ellul, D. 504n3
Eltester, W. 308n1, 636
Emerton, J. A. 407n15
Engelbrecht, J. 3, 10
Enns, P. 91n4
Epp, E. J. 371n1, 398
Erickson, R. J. 75n13, 88
Eshel, E. 140, 261
Eskenazi, T. C. 308n1
Evans, C. A. 46n35, 111n7,
112n9, 130n6, 139n1, 140n2,
169n17, 184n16, 187, 247,
259n3, 278, 322n7, 334n3,
340, 340n6, 343n9, 464n16,
496n5, 500, 501n6, 512n1,
514n3, 515, 515n6, 516n8,
518, 569n2, 595n3, 617, 646,
659
Evans, C. F. 184n16
Evans, O. E. 323n9

Fagen, R. S. 547n3
Faierstein, M. 422n13
Falk, Z. 408
Farmer, W. R. 6n6, 7, 13, 14n18,
37n31, 46n35, 235n19, 483,
519
Farnell, F. D. 6, 12
Fascher, E. 410n1
Fee, G. 90, 371n1, 398
Feiler, P. 243
Feld, H. 278n6
Feldman, L. 555n7
Feldmeier, R. 633n4
Feneberg, R. 186n20
Fenton, J. C. 68, 76, 330
Ferguson, E. 528n3
Ferrari d'Occhieppo, K. 79n3,
80n5
Feuillet, A. 73, 249, 409, 415n1,
489n6, 619n1, 633n4
Fiedler, P. 144n7, 428n1, 432n4
Finkel, A. 184n16, 446
Finkelstein, L. 111n7
Finney, P. 529n5
Fitzgerald, J. T. 130n6
Fitzmyer, J. 148n7, 239n2,
282n14, 380n9, 406n12, 412,
422n13, 464n16, 496n6,
541n4, 664n2
Fletcher, D. 282n15
Flusser, D. 142n4, 150n9, 186,
223n20, 334n3, 428n1
Fohrer, G. 557n11
Fokkelman, J. P. 3, 8n7
Fonrobert, C. 259n3
Ford, D. 580n5
Fornberg, T. 136n1
Fortna, R. T. 480n9, 599n4
Fowler, H. 70, 90, 115
Fowler, M. 155

Fowler, R. 367n1
Fox, G. G. 12n13
France, R. T. 2, 5, 11n11, 17n25,
19n26, 32n29, 37n31, 53n1,
91n4, 93, 95, 141, 141n1, 203,
214, 233, 333n1, 343n9, 362,
388n5, 406, 407n13, 413n7,
476, 488, 488n5, 501n5,
517n13, 546, 566, 579, 584,
594n1, 599n4, 605n4, 607n9,
649n2, 664, 673
Frankemölle, H. 106n1, 114,
176n35, 267n2
Freed, E. D. 27n28, 53n1
Frerichs, E. S. 46n35
Freyne, S. 45n34, 46n35, 98,
134n1
Frickenschmidt, D. 5n3
Friedrich, J. 604n1, 605n4,
607n9
Frieling, R. 415n1
Frizzell, L. 184n16, 446
Fuchs, A. 121n5, 249n6, 323n9
Fuchs, J. 212n2
Funk, R. W. 106
Furnish, V. 534, 537n8

Gaebelein, A. C. 39, 143, 190,
345n14, 353
Gaechter, P. 2, 8n8, 9n9, 439
Gale, A. M. 82n7
García Martínez, F. 172n27,
464n16
Gardner, R. B. 122, 636
Garland, D. 2, 46n35, 165, 173,
184n16, 263, 264, 277, 335,
353, 394, 423, 428n1, 431n1,
432n2, 445, 459n5, 520, 525,
543, 543n3, 544n4, 549, 551,
554, 556, 557, 561, 562, 562n1,
594, 598, 605n4, 608n12, 612,
615n1
Garlington, D. 174n30
Gärtner, B. 622n1
Gaston, L. 278n6, 567n3
Gatzweiler, K. 227n1
Geist, H. 37n30
Genuyt, F. 148n7, 184n16, 266,
308n1, 432n4
George, A. 282n15
Gerhardsson, B. 2, 130n6,
227n1, 333, 333n1, 334,
343n9, 536, 537n8, 638n1
Gero, S. 120n4
Geyser, A. 264n8
Gibbs, J. A. 353n3
Gibbs, J. M. 33, 34, 261n5, 320,
490n1
Giblin, C. 277n4, 529n5, 673
Gibson, J. B. 130n6, 184n16,
509

Giesen, H. 134n1, 139
Gill, D. 175n34
Ginzel, G. B. 142n4
GKC (W. Gesenius, E. Kautzsch, A. E. Cowley) 320n1, 557n11
Glancy, J. A. 450
Gnilka, J. 12, 110, 220n14, 269, 277, 340n6, 362n2, 432n2, 475n3, 599n5, 673
Gnuse, R. 66
Goedt, M. de 352n1
Golding, T. A. 84, 262n6
Good, D. J. 87n12, 305
Goodacre, M. 13
Goodblatt, D. 111n7
Gooding, D. 357n1
Gourges, M. 148n7
Granskou, D. 656n5
Grant, R. M. 143n5
Grassi, J. 267n4
Gray, S. W. 604, 607n9
Green, H. B. 148n7
Green, J. B. 10, 37n31, 43n33, 46, 47n36, 57, 79n2, 82n7, 111n7, 136n2, 139n1, 169n17, 172, 172n25, 173, 261, 415n1, 499n1, 502, 554, 626, 627n2, 637n4, 640n4, 664n2, 666n4, 683n1
Green, M. 282n15, 594
Greenfield, G. 144n7
Greeven, H. 249n6
Grelot, P. 16n23, 130n6, 189, 281n11
Grier, J. 158n2
Griesbach, J. J. 6, 6n6
Griffiths, J. 282n15
Grudem, W. 4n2
Grundmann, W. 2, 142, 303, 410n1
Guelich, R. 5, 5n3, 142, 142n2, 143n5, 147, 148n7, 150n10, 208, 214, 215, 217n5, 232n7
Guenther, A. R. 172n26
Guenther, H. 579
Guijarro, S. 320
Gundry, R. H. 2, 7, 8, 11, 11n11, 14, 14n16, 15, 17n25, 19n26, 26, 42, 66, 70, 79, 89, 91, 93, 95, 98, 99, 107, 120, 127, 146, 150, 203, 208, 217n5, 218n5, 233, 246n5, 272, 277, 291, 303, 310n6, 316n2, 343, 352, 391, 406, 417, 421, 422, 440, 462, 464, 476, 480, 495, 495n3, 496n5, 501n5, 521, 524n2, 525, 525n6, 527, 536n5, 543n1, 558n13, 589, 605n4, 649, 670
Gurtner, D. M. 670
Guyénot, L. 106n1

Habbe, J. 134n1
Habermas, G. R. 679n1
Hachlili, R. 139n1
Häfner, G. 37n30, 106n1
Hagner, D. A. 2, 3, 11, 14, 14n17, 19n26, 46n35, 58n2, 61, 65, 70, 91, 99n2, 136n2, 138, 141, 144n7, 145, 150, 151, 155, 159n5, 165, 168, 172, 197, 203, 208, 214, 217n5, 218n5, 231, 232n7, 233, 234, 239n2, 247, 255, 259, 273, 277, 280, 281n12, 286, 292, 311, 332, 334n4, 344, 354, 355, 355n6, 357, 369, 383, 391, 392, 393, 400, 402n1, 407n13, 408, 413, 417, 421n10, 432, 435, 446, 462, 463, 478, 480, 488n5, 496, 504, 505, 517n13, 521, 524, 532, 534, 537, 543, 543n3, 558n13, 565, 566, 569, 575, 578, 581, 594, 596n4, 603, 606, 608n12, 612, 613, 619, 634, 640, 650, 656, 669, 670, 670n5, 688, 689, 6065n4
Hahn, F. 423n1, 567n3
Hall, B. 188n23
Ham, C. A. 495
Hamerton-Kelly, R. 536, 537n8
Hamilton, N. 499n3
Hampel, V. 37n30, 277n4
Hanson, K. C. 148n7, 573n3, 637n3
Hare, D. R. A. 2, 3, 14n17, 47n36, 90, 150, 153, 165, 269, 383, 384, 406n11, 413, 432, 480, 490, 517n13, 562n1, 594, 599, 689
Harner, P. 373n3
Harrington, D. 2, 8, 14, 47n36, 74, 97, 118, 128n5, 165, 277, 308n1, 330, 383, 432n2, 504, 517n12, 543n3, 558n13, 563n2, 592, 598n2, 605n3, 608n12, 689
Harris, M. J. 115, 260n4, 683n1
Harrisville, R. 386n2, 389
Hart, H. 496n6, 528n3, 529n5
Hartin, P. J. 136n2, 177
Hartman, L. 17n25, 19n26, 567n3, 573, 573n5, 690
Harvey, A. E. 464n16
Hasitschka, M. 130n6
Hasler, V. 524n4
Hatina, T. R. 381
Haubeck, W. 480n9
Hauerwas, S. 2, 27, 167, 323, 407n14, 481, 517, 689n2
Hawkins, J. C. 6n4
Hawthorne, G. 114n13, 227n1, 315n1, 496n6, 537n8, 558, 589

Hay, D. 541n4
Head, J. P. 16n23
Heard, W. J., Jr. 494n2
Heater, H. 84
Hedrick, C. 504n3
Heil, J. P. 27n28, 139, 223n20, 227n1, 245, 333n1, 334, 334n4, 371n1, 372, 373, 450n3, 480n9, 510n8, 607n9, 615n1, 654, 671, 673
Hein, K. 625
Held, H.-J. 2, 217n5, 227n1, 227n2, 238, 243, 373, 377n1, 423n1, 492
Helyer, L. 379n5
Hemer, C. 188, 188n23
Hendrickx, H. 227n2, 314
Hendriksen, W. 8, 59, 61, 70, 86, 150, 221, 277, 294, 407n13, 413n7, 434, 476, 516, 566, 579, 594, 669
Hengel, M. 11, 111n7, 142n4, 239n3, 282n14, 516n8, 664, 664n2
Hennig, G. 687n1
Hermant, D. 11n10, 432n4
Hertig, P. 134n1, 687n1
Herzog, W. R., II 502
Hester, J. 516n8
Heth, W. 462, 464, 464n16
Hezser, C. 480n10
Hicks, J. 308n1
Hiebert, D. E. 687n1
Hiers, R. 322n7, 407n15, 408
Higgins, A. J. B. 37n30, 239n2, 637n4
Hill, D. 9n9, 32n29, 34, 73, 99, 118, 188n23, 208, 217, 218n5, 220n14, 253, 283n2, 371n1, 424, 426, 480, 494, 543, 604n1, 655, 687n1
Hinkle, M. E. 184n16
Hirschfeld, Y. 478
Hirunuma, T. 398
Hoch, C. 475n2
Hoehner, H. 79n2, 79n3, 97, 105, 362, 362n2, 363, 364, 365, 612, 623
Hoet, R. 547
Hoffmann, P. 362n2, 407n14
Holmes, M. 466
Holst, R. 619n1
Hooker, M. 267n2
Horbury, W. 45n34, 264n8, 428n1, 429, 430
Horgan, M. 444n2
Horne, E. H. 516n8
Horsley, G. H. R. 215n2
Horsley, R. A. 28, 79n3, 81, 175n34, 502, 573n3, 637n3
Houk, C. 189

Houlden, J. L. 158n2
Howard, G. 15
Howard, T. L. 91
Howard, W. F. 106, 296n11, 365, 388, 406n10, 546n1
Howell, D. 11n10
Huat, T. K. 70
Hubaut, M. 516n8
Huber, K. 516n8
Huffman, N. 440
Huggins, R. V. 7
Hulse, E. V. 231n6
Hultgren, A. 45n34, 53n1, 188n23, 223n20, 297n12, 308n1, 333n1, 343n9, 344, 346, 352, 352n1, 353n3, 441n5, 450n3, 480n9, 481, 509n5, 510n7, 516n8, 519, 521, 525n6, 537n8, 592, 598n1, 599n4, 604, 607n9
Humbert, A. 411
Hummel, R. 14n17
Humphrey, H. 8n8
Humphreys, C. J. 80n5
Hunter, A. 302n2
Hurtado, L. W. 57
Hutchinson, J. C. 27n28, 106n1, 291n5
Hutter, M. 259n3
Hylen, S. E. 450n3

Immisch, O. 403
Ingelaere, J.-C. 46n35
Ingolfsland, D. 6
Instone-Brewer, D. 172n27, 462n10
Ito, A. 174n30

Jackson, B. 445n4
Jackson, G. 27n28, 386n2
Jacob, R. 497n7
Jahnke, V. J. 176n35
Janzen, D. 172n25
Janzen, J. 305
Jastrow, M. 111, 149n8, 171n22, 198n8, 547, 660
Jaubert, A. 623
Jenks, G. 580n5
Jennings, T. W., Jr. 234n16
Jensen, P. F. 72n9
Jenson, P. P. 84
Jeremias, J. 82n7, 184n16, 186n20, 267n2, 338, 368, 386n2, 387n3, 410, 440n4, 465n18, 488, 509n5, 546, 557, 594, 595, 596n4, 627n2
Johner, M. 144n7
Johns, L. L. 212n1
Johnson, L. T. 46n35, 562
Johnson, M. D. 25n27, 59n4, 297

Johnson, P. E. 533
Johnson, S. E. 7
Johnson, S. L. 497n7, 633n4
Johnston, R. 334n3
Jones, I. H. 223n20, 256, 297n12, 333n1, 334n4, 355n6, 441n5, 450n3
Jones, J. M. 59n4
Jones, R. N. 231n6
Jospe, R. 211
Jourjon, M. 423n1
Jülicher, A. 333

Kagarise, R. J. 341
Kähler, C. 129
Kaiser, W. C., Jr. 71, 72, 72n9, 91, 94, 295, 422, 422n13, 566n2
Kalin, E. R. 260
Kallemeyn, H. 501n6
Kampen, J. 111n7, 167, 172n27, 464n16
Kampling, R. 140
Kayalaparampil, T. 633n4
Kazmierski, C. R. 106n1, 113
Kealy, S. P. 2
Keck, L. E. 120n4
Kee, A. 254
Kee, H. C. 227n2, 296
Keegan, T. J. 149
Keener, C. 2, 14n19, 27, 57, 66, 79n3, 86, 93n2, 107, 112, 113n12, 141, 149, 150, 154, 165, 172, 172n27, 181, 183, 186n20, 203, 208, 209n1, 227, 237, 246, 247, 272, 277, 291, 294, 300, 308n1, 310, 312, 320, 353, 364, 364n5, 368, 388, 407n13, 413, 440, 450, 462, 491, 502, 509, 517n12, 518, 543n1, 548, 555, 556, 562n1, 566, 580n5, 595n3, 598, 604, 605n4, 612
Keesmaat, S. 450n3
Kelhoffer, J. A. 109
Kellenberger, E. 150n10
Kelly, W. 39
Kennard, J. 14n19, 496n6, 529n5
Kerr, A. J. 343n11
Kertelge, K. 176n35, 267n2, 638n1
Kessler, C. 148n7
Kidder, S. J. 586
Kidger, M. 80n5
Kiilunen, J. 308n1, 472n3, 537n8
Kik, J. 566
Kiley, M. 13, 252
Kilpatrick, G. 14
Kim, S. 37n30, 239n2

Kingsbury, J. D. 2, 7, 8n7, 8n8, 9, 10n9, 32n29, 34, 45n34, 53n1, 57n1, 134, 136n1, 136n2, 142n3, 226, 227n1, 238, 243n1, 262, 265n9, 333n1, 334n4, 407, 407n14, 410, 516n8, 517n12, 687n1
Kissinger, W. 143n5, 333, 333n1, 343n9
Kitzberger, I. R. 236n20, 259n3
Klassen, W. 175n34, 622n1, 650
Klauck, H.-J. 333, 622n1
Klein, G. 264n8
Klemm, H. 529n5
Klijn, A. F. J. 82n7, 410, 470
Kloppenborg, J. 139n1
Knoch, O. 464n17
Knowles, M. 93, 95, 137n4, 223n20, 403n2, 480n9, 500n4, 559n18
Kobelski, P. J. 147n7, 444n2
Kodell, J. 464n16, 627n2
Kodjak, A. 142n3
Koester, C. 578
Köhler, W.-D. 12
Kollmann, B. 174n30, 207
Kopas, J. 671
Körtner, U. 16n21
Koskenniemi, E. 660, 665
Kraemer, R. S. 362n2
Krentz, E. 8n8, 56, 106n1, 687n1
Krieger, K.-S. 140
Kruse, H. 86
Kugel, J. 444n2
Kügler, J. 86
Kuhn, H.-W. 176n35, 664n2
Kümmel, W. 290n2, 567n3
Kupp, D. D. 34, 73, 446, 690
Kürzinger, J. 15, 16n21
Kutsko, J. 403
Kvalbein, H. 291
Kynes, W. L. 489n6

Laansma, J. 297, 305, 305n4
Lachs, S. 183, 186n19, 188, 557
Lacy, D. R. de 111n7
Ladd, G. 43, 322, 566, 604
LaGrand, J. 47n36, 575n10, 689
LaGrange, M. 2, 9n9, 217, 310n6
Lalleman, P. J. 234
Lambrecht, J. 142n2, 175n34, 214, 290n2, 333n1, 334n4, 377n1, 566n1
Lampe, G. 643
Landis, S. 234
Landmesser, C. 254
Lane, A. N. 465n18
Lange, J. 106n1, 249n6, 407n14
Langley, W. 510n7
Lanier, D. 184n16

Lapide, P. 184n16, 371n1
La Potterie, I. de 362n2
Lategan, B. 286
Latham, J. E. 155
Law, D. R. 93
Lawlor, G. L. 143n6, 148n7
Le Moyne, J. 112n9
Légasse, S. 220n14, 227n1, 262,
    302n2, 355n6, 386n2, 387,
    428n1, 435n5, 465n20, 489n6,
    574, 594n1, 637n4, 638n1
Legrand, L. 263, 687n1
Leitch, J. W. 308n1
Lenski, R. 406, 579
Léon-Dufour, X. 227n1, 262
Levi, T. 575n10
Levin, Y. 33
Levine, A.-J. 46n35, 47n36,
    236n20, 259n3, 267n3, 269,
    386n2, 388n5, 389, 518, 519,
    555n7, 689
Levine, E. 308n1
Levine, L. I. 45n34, 134n1
Levin-Goldschmidt, H. 622n1
Lewis, J. P. 3, 278n6
Licona, M. 679n1
Liefeld, W. 415n1
Liew, T.-S. B. 234n16
Lightfoot, J. 584
Limbeck, M. 2, 278n6, 622n1
Lindars, B. 37n30, 234n16,
    239n2, 499, 501n6, 606
Lindemann, A. 465n18
Lindeskog, G. 472n3
Linnemann, E. 6
Linton, O. 297n12, 325
Lips, H. von 207n9
Liver, J. 428n1
Livingstone, E. A. 93, 95, 386n2,
    413n6, 594n1
Ljungman, H. 158n2
Llewelyn, S. 207n9
Lloyd-Jones, D. M. 142n2,
    148n7
Loader, W. R. G. 33, 158n2, 247,
    261n5, 320, 490n1
Lochman, J. M. 184n16
Lodge, J. 615n1
Loewe, H. 53, 529n5
Lohfink, G. 144n7, 497n7
Lohfink, N. 151
Lohr, C. H. 10
Lohse, E. 144n7, 308n1, 496n6
Longenecker, R. 223n20, 333,
    333n1, 334n3, 334n4, 339,
    415n1, 441n5, 450n3, 480n9,
    510, 510n8, 524n4, 594n1,
    599n4, 604, 607n9
Longstaff, T. R. W. 6n4, 13,
    13n14

Loos, H. van der 227n1, 227n2,
    367n1, 423n1
Losie, L. 501n6
Love, S. 259n3
Lovering, E. 333n1
Lövestam, E. 296, 323n9, 586
Lowe, M. 480n9
Luck, U. 302n2, 469
Luck, W. F. 172n27
Luedemann, G. 683n1
Lull, D. 537n8
Luomanen, P. 158n2, 164n11,
    217n4, 240n4, 302n2, 352
Lust, J. 84
Luz, U. 2, 11, 11n10, 12n12,
    19n26, 37n30, 46n35, 68, 90,
    99, 115, 121, 136n2, 142n3,
    143n5, 146, 158n2, 169n18,
    172n25, 184n16, 227n1, 233,
    246n5, 247, 252, 261n5, 262,
    277n4, 282n15, 294, 333n1,
    334n4, 338n3, 352, 369n3,
    388, 388n5, 391, 401, 402n1,
    405n7, 407n14, 419n7, 429,
    432, 435n5, 444, 447, 461n6,
    465n18, 471, 475n3, 480n11,
    490, 607n9
Lybaeck, L. 310, 355n6

Maalouf, T. T. 79
Maccoby, H. 556, 651
MacDonald, D. 279
Machen, J. G. 30, 31, 62, 70
Mack, B. L. 308n1
Maclaurin, E. 278n6
MacRae, G. 277n4
Maher, M. 305
Maier, G. 2, 14, 490
Maier, J. 111n9
Maisch, I. 432n4
Malina, B. 470, 473n5
Mandell, S. 428n1
Mánek, J. 606
Mann, C. 31, 277
Manns, F. 524, 524n4, 599n4
Manor, D. 531
Mans, M. J. 95
Manson, T. 267n2
Mantey, J. R. 115, 198n9, 405n9
Marcus, J. 134, 322n7, 407n15
Marguerat, D. 2, 46n35, 220n14,
    233, 301, 352n1, 567n3
Marin, L. 333
Marshall, I. H. 32, 37n30, 278,
    404n4, 627n2
Martens, A. 510, 510n8, 524n4
Martin de Viviés, P. de 37n30
Martin, B. L. 158n2
Martin, F. 19n26, 599n4, 615n1
Martin, J. 143n6
Martin, R. P. 232n7

Martinez, E. 432n4
Martini, C. 16n24
Marucci, C. 510n7
Mason, S. 111n7, 554n6
Massaux, E. 2, 13n15
Massey, I. A. 142n4
Masson, J. 25n27, 31, 490n1
Masuda, S. 367n1
Matera, F. J. 8n8, 144n7, 615n1,
    638n1, 666n4
Mathys, H.-P. 176
Matthiae, K. 264n8
Mauser, U. 106
Mayhue, R. L. 235
Maynard, A. H. 246
McArthur, H. 334n3, 464n16
McCane, B. R. 240n4
McCartney, D. 91n4
McConnell, R. 158n2
McDermott, J. 277n4
McEleney, N. J. 148n7, 183, 208,
    428n1, 642
McGing, B. 646
McGuckin, J. 415n1
McIver, R. K. 14n17, 309n3,
    338n3, 352n1
McKenzie, J. L. 74
McKnight, S. 10, 14n17, 37n31,
    43n33, 46n35, 57, 79n2,
    82n7, 98, 111n7, 139, 139n1,
    169n17, 172, 172n25, 173,
    264, 264n8, 267n4, 277n4,
    278, 333n1, 415n1, 499n1,
    502, 554, 626, 627n2, 637n4,
    664n2, 666n4, 683n1
McNeile, A. H. 74, 93n1, 208,
    388n5, 406, 413, 421n10, 487,
    509n5, 586
McRay, J. 159n3
Meadors, G. T. 150n10, 158n2
Meier, J. P. 2, 9n9, 12n31, 74,
    102, 106n1, 158n2, 189, 221,
    253, 264n8, 291n5, 362n2,
    383, 413, 432n2, 475n3, 496,
    504, 510, 543, 548, 550n2, 562,
    562n1, 597, 604n1
Menahem, R. 480n9
Menken, M. J. 69, 90, 93, 94, 99,
    99n2, 100n3, 134n1, 235n19,
    316n2, 317, 346, 403n2, 495n3
Menninger, R. E. 517n13
Meredith, A. 12, 16n21
Merkel, H. 463
Merklein, H. 247, 534n1, 537n8
Merrill, E. 325n2
Metzger, B. 29na, 62, 75, 95,
    156, 178, 188, 191, 202, 223,
    237, 240, 265, 297, 301, 311,
    348, 361, 365, 374, 384, 385,
    397, 398, 401, 439, 447, 453,
    466, 471, 481, 489, 492, 510,

511, 520, 525, 538, 549, 575,
590, 597, 602, 627, 651, 654,
656, 666, 669n2, 672, 681, 692
Metzler, N. 187
Meyer, B. 524
Meyer, P. 497n7
Meyers, C. 499n1
Meyers, E. M. 139n1
Mézange, C. 265
Michaels, J. R. 511, 605, 607
Michel, O. 687n1
Mielziner, M. 379n5
Migliore, D. 184n16
Milavec, A. 176n35, 516n8
Miler, J. 19n26
Milikowsky, C. 279
Miller, R. 559n18
Mills, W. E. 143n5
Milton, H. 56
Minear, P. S. 155, 184n16,
220n14
Mitton, C. 400, 604
Moffitt, D. M. 663
Mohrlang, R. 159n5
Molldrem, M. 463
Moloney, F. 464n16
Monsarrat, V. 567n3
Montefiore, H. 428n1, 535
Moo, D. 11n11, 13, 17n25,
158n2, 495, 615n1, 649n2
Moor, J. 516n8
Moore, G. F. 25n27
Moore, W. 294n8, 295
Mora, V. 325n2
Moreland, J. 142, 533, 679n1,
686
Morgan, C. 279, 610
Morgan, M. P. 147n7
Morosco, R. E. 267n4
Morrice, W. 354n4
Morris, L. 2, 8, 99, 113, 136n2,
405n9, 407, 407n13, 413n7,
438n3, 509n5, 517n12
Moses, A. D. A. 415n1
Motte, A. 304
Motyer, J. A. 71, 72n9
Motyer, S. 563
Moulder, W. 488
Moule, C. F. D. 19n26, 85n10,
97n1, 158n2, 189, 296n11,
405n10, 428n1, 429, 430,
475n1, 493n1, 528n3, 529n5,
546n1
Moulton, J. H. 85n9, 89n1, 97,
97n1, 106, 106n2, 109, 109n5,
115, 120, 121, 194n4, 198n9,
206, 284n4, 296n11, 296n12,
310n6, 320n1, 325n1, 365,
388, 389n6, 405n9, 405n10,
406n10, 429n3, 434n1, 459n2,

475n1, 481, 495n4, 535n4,
546n1, 625n1
Mounce, R. H. 200
Mowery, R. L. 35, 37n31
Moyise, S. 94
Müller, M. 19n26, 32n29, 158n2
Müller, P. 435n5
Mullins, T. Y. 261n5
Munck, J. 16n21
Murphy-O'Connor, J. 106n1,
130n6, 137n4, 357n1, 362n2,
415n1
Mussner, F. 297n12

Nagel, D. von 353n3
Nau, A. J. 136n1, 265n9, 407n14
Neirynck, F. 6n4, 8n8, 309n3,
410
Nepper-Christiansen, P. 12n13,
277n4
Nettelhorst, R. P. 59n4
Neudecker, R. 460, 469n2,
536n6
Neugebauer, F. 130n6
Neusner, J. 46n35, 111n7, 379,
556
Neville, D. 6n6
Newell, J. 516n8
Newell, R. 516n8
Newport, K. 544n4, 546n2
Neyrey, J. 317
Nickelsburg, G. W. E. 235n18,
235n19, 403, 531
Nida, E. A. 4n1
Niebuhr, K. 291
Niedner, F. A. 46n35, 95
Nijman, M. 188n23
Nineham, D. 25n27, 59n4
Nolan, B. M. 261n5
Nolland, J. 2, 5n3, 11n10, 12,
13, 14, 17n25, 27, 27n28, 34,
56, 60, 73, 87n13, 91, 99, 119,
120, 125, 143n5, 146, 149, 154,
155, 162, 163n10, 164, 165,
172n27, 183, 198n8, 205, 206,
227, 249, 262, 265, 379, 402n1,
516, 562n1, 568, 569, 578, 690
Nolte, J. 278n6
Novakovic, L. 33

Oakley, I. J. 183n14
Oakman, D. E. 184n16
Oakman, D.E. 504n3
Oberlinner, L. 144n7, 428n1,
432n4
O'Brien, P. T. 282n15
O'Callaghan, J. 489n6
O'Collins, G. G. 282n14, 664n2
O'Connor, M. 557n11, 608n11
Oepke, A. 435n5
Oesterley, W. 334n3

Ogawa, A. 510n8
O'Grady, J. F. 14n17
Olmstead, W. G. 421, 509
O'Neill, J. C. 184n16, 323n9,
516n8
Orchard, B. 6n4, 6n6, 188n23
O'Rourke, J. 158n2
Orton, D. 355, 355n6
Osborne, G. R. 5, 14n17, 98,
139, 333n1, 679n1, 683n1
Osborne, R. E. 14n19
Oster, R. 529n5
Ostmeyer, K.-H. 59n4
Overholt, T. 504n1
Overman, J. A. 2, 3, 14, 58, 159,
162, 165, 186n19, 205, 233n14,
317, 333n1, 353, 373, 383,
406n11, 408, 408n16, 429n2,
467, 476, 504, 516, 517n12,
525, 558n13, 563n2, 597, 598,
605n4, 656n5
Owen-Ball, D. 529n5

Paesler, K. 501n6
Paffenroth, K. 33
Page, S. H. T 488n5
Pak, C. H. 480n9
Pamment, M. 37n30, 37n31, 38
Panier, L. 607n9, 615n1
Pantle-Schieber, K. 45n34
Pappas, H. 278
Park, E. C. 267n4
Park, S. J. 245
Parker, D. C. 16n23
Parpola, S. 80n5
Parratt, J. 464n17
Pathrapankal, J. 144n7
Patsch, H. 497n7
Patte, D. 136n2, 239, 432n2,
435n5, 500, 503n1
Pautrel, R. 334n3
Pawlikowski, J. T. 46n35
Payne, P. B. 333n1, 338, 343n9
Peabody, D. A. 6n6
Pedersen, S. 415n1
Peerbolte, L. 580n5
Pelletier, M. 111n7
Pennington, J. 39, 42
Perels, O. 465n18
Perkins, L. 327
Perkins, P. 537n8
Perowne, S. 79n2, 362
Perrin, N. 37n31
Pervo, R. 555n7
Pesch, R. 534n1, 537n8, 638n1
Pesch, W. 246, 432n2, 432n4
Petersen, W. 441n5
Peterson, D. G. 282n15
Peterson, D. N. 140
Peterson, R. 279, 610
Peterson, W. L. 15

Petrie, C. S. 11n11
Petrotta, A. J. 84
Petuchowski, J. 184n16
Phillips, G. 334n4
Philonenko, M. 184n16
Pixner, B. 299
Plummer, A. 181, 406n11, 413
Poelman, R. 127n2
Pope, M. 496n6
Porter, L. B. 155
Porter, S. E. 89, 89n1, 111n7, 112n9, 139n1, 140n2, 158n2, 169n17, 405n9, 595n3, 646, 690
Porton, G. 112n9, 555n7
Pöttner, M. 155n14
Powell, M. A. 3, 7, 8n7, 8n8, 25n27, 79, 142n3, 148n7, 158, 158n2, 259n3, 297, 428n1, 517n12, 546n2, 607n9
Poythress, V. 4n2
Pregeant, R. 297
Proctor, W. 80n5
Pryor, J. W. 303, 436
Przybylski, B. 46n35, 65n3, 151n11, 509n6
Puech, E. 146n6, 531
Puig i Tàrrech, A. 594n1, 599n5
Pusey, K. 110

Quesnel, M. 32n29

Rabbinowitz, N. S. 401, 546, 546n2, 549n6
Rahmni, L. 546n2
Raimbault, C. 87n13
Ramsay, A. 415n1, 419
Rathey, M. 174, 175n34
Reed, J. T. 89, 89n1
Reeves, K. H. 679n1, 688
Refoulé, F. 415n1
Reicke, B. 6n4, 14, 249n6
Reiser, M. 176n35, 233, 301, 567n3
Rengstorf, K. H. 479n8
Repschinski, B. 45n34, 68, 308n1, 314
Resseguie, J. 3, 8n7
Rhoads, D. 8n7, 136n1, 528n4
Rice, G. 72n9
Richards, J. 596n4
Richards, K. 277n4
Richards, W. 510n7
Richardson, A. 367n1
Richardson, P. 656n5
Ricoeur, P. 212, 212n2
Ridderbos, H. N. 37n31, 70, 115, 407n13, 413n7, 421n10
Rieckert, P. 615n1
Riesenfeld, H. 417
Rigaux, B. 264n8, 580n5

Riley, H. 6n4, 6n6
Ringshausen, G. 465n20
Rist, J. M. 6
Ristow, H. 264n8
Ritmeyer, K. 499n1
Ritmeyer, L. 499n1
Ritt, H. 371n1
Rivkin, E. 111n7, 638n1
Robbins, V. K. 259n3, 308n1, 435n5
Roberts, C. H. 16n23
Roberts, R. 197
Robertson, A. T. 495n4, 546n1, 557n11, 669n3
Robinson, B. 408
Robinson, J. A. T. 14, 14n16, 277n4, 422n13, 516n8
Robinson, J. M. 13
Robinson, T. H. 90, 604
Rochais, G. 260n4
Rogers, C. 490n1
Roh, T. 330
Rohrbaugh, R. 599n4
Röhser, G. 167
Roloff, J. 441n5, 480n9
Römelt, J. 144n7
Roquefort, D. 622n1
Rordorf, W. 214n1
Rosenblatt, M. 259n3
Ross, J. 424, 558n13
Roth, C. 546n2
Rothfuchs, W. 17n25
Rowdon, H. 32n29, 586
Ruckstuhl, E. 624
Rüger, H. 207n9
Russell, E. 46n35, 386n2
Rutgers, L. V. 346
Ruzer, S. 169, 176n35
Ryan, T. 390
Ryken, L. 4n2, 333

Sabbe, M. 302n2, 303
Sabourin, L. 277n4, 551, 583
Saddington, D. B. 234n16
Safrai, S. 379n5, 595n3
Safrai, Z. 250
Sailhamer, J. 91n4
Saldarini, A. 2, 3, 14, 45n34, 46n35, 111n7, 112n9, 517n12, 518, 519, 562, 563n2, 627n2, 655
Sand, A. 2, 464n16
Sanders, E. P. 252, 499n1, 502
Sanders, J. A. 130n6, 259n3
Sanders, J. T. 496n5
Sandmel, S. 46n35, 362, 562, 638n1, 655
Sandt, H. van de 206
Satterthwaite, P. E. 84
Saucy, R. L. 4

Scaer, D. 9n9, 142n2, 543n1, 567n3, 687n1
Schaberg, J. 28, 53n1, 65, 690
Scharbert, J. 172n27
Schedl, C. 619n1
Schenk, W. 11n10, 362n2, 423n1
Schenke, L. 2, 6n4, 79n3, 139, 187, 367n1, 435n5, 480n9, 497n7, 567n3, 615n1, 689n2
Schiffman, L. 112n10, 146n6
Schlatter, A. 9n9, 106n1, 291n5, 364
Schlosser, J. 569n2
Schmid, J. 511
Schmidt, T. E. 404n4
Schnabel, E. J. 46, 47n36, 267n2, 389, 687n1
Schnackenburg, R. 2, 79, 99, 155, 246n5, 249, 251, 254n7, 262, 277, 286, 382, 388n5, 392, 408, 413, 435n5, 475n3, 503n1, 504, 517, 525, 539, 604n1, 655n4
Schneider, G. 187
Schoedel, W. R. 13n15
Schönle, V. 290n2
Schrage, W. 404n4, 469
Schreiner, J. 112n9
Schrenk, G. 295
Schürer, E. 186n19, 527
Schürmann, H. 277n4
Schwartz, D. R. 82n7
Schwarz, G. 129, 234, 244, 428n1, 504n3, 625, 644
Schweitzer, A. 42, 143, 370, 408
Schweizer, E. 2, 14n17, 42, 148n7, 208, 221, 246n5, 308n1, 382, 406n11, 432n2, 475n3, 481, 546
Scobie, C. H. 106n1, 291n5
Scofield, C. I. 38, 39, 143
Scorgie, G. 4n2
Scott, B. B. 142n3, 450n3
Scott, J. J. 46, 267n2, 389
Scott, J. W. 5, 8n7
Scott, R. 325n2
Scroggs, R. 536, 537n8
Seccombe, D. 282n15
Seeley, D. 489n6
Seeligmann, I. L. 69
Segal, M. 12n12, 320n1
Segbroeck, F. van 5n3, 8n8, 17n25, 19n26, 137n4, 148n7, 234n16, 238, 247, 359, 361
Segovia, F. F. 136n2
Sekeles, E. 664n2
Senior, D. 14n17, 19n26, 562n1, 615n1, 633n4, 637n4, 666n4
Senn, F. 627n2
Shae, G. 507, 510n7
Shanks, H. 234, 547

Shepherd, J. 294n8, 295
Shepherd, T. 258
Sherriff, J. 594n1
Shillington, V. G. 480n9, 516n8, 599n4
Shuler, P. 2, 5, 5n3, 46n35
Sickenberger, J. 6n4
Sider, J. 333, 333n1, 338
Sievers, J. 446
Sigal, P. 14, 172n27, 309n3, 464n16
Silva, M. 566n2
Sim, D. 2, 3, 14, 14n17, 46, 86, 268, 351, 517n12, 524, 563n2, 689
Slater, T. B. 8n8
Slingerland, H. 14
Sloyan, G. 638n1
Smalley, S. S. 606
Smillie, G. R. 46
Smith, C. R. 9
Smith, C. W. F. 352
Smith, D. 106n1, 110
Smith, D. T. 172n26
Smith, M. 415n1
Smith, R. H. 150n10, 554
Smit Sibinga, J. 13n15, 142n3, 371n1, 566n1
Smyth, H. W. 405n8
Smyth, K. 8n8, 679n1
Snodgrass, K. 158, 158n2, 333n1, 515, 515n6, 516n8
Soarés-Prabhu, G. 17n25, 19n26, 20, 21, 91n4, 99n2, 495n4, 496
Söding, T. 501n6
Songer, H. S. 142n4
Sparks, K. 687n1
Sproul, R. C. 566
Sproule, J. 344
Stählin, G. 411, 438n1
Standaert, B. 8n8
Stanley, D. 633n4
Stanton, G. 2, 5n3, 14, 14n17, 17n25, 19n26, 52, 136n2, 142n3, 143n5, 261, 302n2, 306, 517n13, 562n1, 578, 605n4, 607n9, 687n1
Stark, R. 14n18
Steck, K. 302n2
Steck, O. 154n13, 559n18
Stegemann, W. 130n6, 259n3
Stegner, W. R. 130n6, 464n16
Stein, R. H. 6n4, 13, 172, 172n25, 333, 419, 464n16, 626, 627n2
Steinhauser, M. G. 201
Stemberger, G. 111n7, 112n9, 379n5
Stendahl, K. 10n9, 17n25, 19n26, 52, 316n2, 496, 501n5

Stenger, W. 154, 529n5
Sterling, G. E. 423n1
Stern, D. 334n3, 512n1, 516n8
Stern, J. 537n8
Stern, M. 595n3
Stewart-Sykes, A. 227n1
Stewart, R. B. 679n1
Stinespring, W. F. 496n5
Stock, A. 464n16
Stoldt, H. 7
Stonehouse, N. 11n11, 277
Stott, J. R. W. 142n2, 148n7, 154
Strack, H. L. 379n5
Strange, J. 234
Strauss, M. L. 4n2
Strawson, W. 322n8
Strecker, G. 142n2, 143n5, 205, 210, 211, 214, 217, 537n8
Streeter, B. H. 6n4, 7, 13, 14n18
Strelan, R. 352n1
Strickert, F. 299
Strickland, W. G. 159n5
Stritzky, M.-B. 184n16
Strobel, A. 465n18
Stuart, D. 90
Stuhlmacher, P. 5, 5n3, 488
Suggs, M. 214n1, 297, 302n2
Suh, J. S. 605
Suhl, A. 261n5, 490n1
Sukenik, E. 546n2
Swaeles, R. 524n4
Swanson, D. C. 388
Swanson, R. J. 16n24
Syreeni, K. 8n7, 136n1, 181

Taber, C. R. 4n1
Tacelli, R. K. 679n1
Talbert, C. H. 5, 142n2
Talbot, M. 151
Tannehill, R. 280
Tasker, R. V. G. 95, 99, 189, 566, 584, 594
Tavardon, P. 115
Taylor, J. 106n1, 110, 291n5, 422n13, 574
Taylor, N. H. 130n6
Teeple, H. M. 227
Telfer, W. 120n4
Telford, W. 504, 504n3
Temple, P. 361
Tenney, M. C. 339, 415n1, 604
Tevel, J. M. 480n9
Theissen, G. 227n2, 362n2
Theobald, C. 212n2
Thiede, C. P. 16n23
Thielman, F. 159n5
Thiemann, R. 619n1
Thiering, B. 294n8
Thimmes, P. L. 243
Thoma, C. 334n3, 512n1, 516n8

Thomas, J. C. 6n4, 37n31, 134n1, 322n8
Thomas, R. L. 6, 470
Thomas, W. H. G. 345n14, 470
Thompson, J. W. 148n7
Thompson, M. M. 8n8
Thompson, W. G. 227n1, 426, 431n1, 432, 432n4, 438n3, 440, 443, 444, 567n3
Thrall, M. E. 300n3, 417
Tigay, J. 547n3
Tilborg, S. van 183n14, 185, 510n7, 510n8, 559n18, 649n2
Tilborg, S. van 184n16
Tisera, G. 47, 134n1, 234n16, 267n3, 317
Tödt, H. 37n30, 239n2
Toit, A. B. du 37n31
Tolbert, M. 333, 333n1
Topel, J. 212n2
Tosato, A. 65, 65n3
Tournay, R. J. 189
Toussaint, S. 8, 38, 39, 43, 70, 99–100, 293, 295, 322n7, 334, 339, 345, 345n14, 353, 406, 407, 413, 566, 579, 586, 605n2
Trainor, M. 136n2
Traub, H. 507n1
Trautman, D. 464n16
Trevett, C. 13n15
Trilling, W. 106n1, 291n5, 362n2, 390, 497n7, 516n8, 517n13
Trimaille, M. 516n8
Tripp, D. H. 343n11
Trites, A. 148n7, 220n14, 415n1
Trummer, P. 259n3, 261
Trunk, D. 140, 261
Tuckett, C. M. 6, 6n4, 7, 12, 13, 16n21, 19n26, 84, 130n6, 231, 291, 310, 316
Turner, D. L. 136n1, 146, 148n7, 264, 265n9, 300, 376, 407, 407n14, 438, 510, 516n8, 517n12, 566, 566n2, 567n3, 569, 584, 586, 644
Turner, M. 37n31, 46, 47n36, 136n2, 261, 640n4
Turner, N. 85n9, 89n1, 97, 97n1, 106n2, 109, 109n5, 115, 120, 121, 194n4, 198n9, 206, 284n4, 296n12, 310n6, 320n1, 325n1, 389n6, 405n9, 406n10, 429n3, 434n1, 459n2, 475n1, 481, 495n4, 535n4, 546n1, 625n1
Twelftree, G. 82n7, 139, 169n17, 261, 321, 423n1
Tyson, J. B. 13, 13n14
Tzaferis, V. 664n2

Unnik, W. C. van 649n2
Uprichard, R. E. H. 121n5
Uro, R. 267n4

Vaganay, L. 432n4
Van Aarde, A. G. 14n17, 17n25, 357n1, 428n1
Van Beek, G. W. 86
VanderKam, J. 112n10, 146n6
Van Elderen, B. 59n4, 339
Van Zyl, H. C. 432n4
Vardaman, J. 59n4, 78, 79n3
Vargas-Machuca, A. 249n6
Venetz, H.-J. 263
Vermes, G. 37n30, 186n20, 239n2
Verseput, D. J. 35, 286, 294, 294n8, 297, 308n1, 329, 331, 357n1, 404, 477, 671
Via, D. 524n4, 604, 607n9
Vigne, D. 121n5
Viviano, B. 14, 14n19, 74, 85n10, 139n1, 146n6, 293, 407, 549n6, 636
Vledder, E. J. 14n17, 45n34, 227n1
Vliet, H. van 445n4
Vogler, W. 622n1
Vögtle, A. 290n2, 325n2
Völkel, M. 297n12
Vorster, W. 5n3, 333

Waetjen, H. C. 25n27, 56, 59n4
Wagner, H. 622n1
Wagner, V. 100n3
Wainwright, E. M. 106n1, 236n20, 259n3, 486, 524n4
Wallace, D. B. 28, 61n6, 64n2, 65, 66, 66n5, 67, 67n6, 73n10, 75, 81, 83, 85n9, 85n11, 89n1, 89n3, 97, 106n2, 109, 110, 111, 113n11, 115, 117n2, 118, 120n3, 121, 128n5, 145n1, 163n9, 165, 198n9, 200n16, 201n17, 204n2, 204n3, 209, 209n2, 217n3, 218n7, 218n8, 232n10, 233n12, 234n15, 234n17, 246n4, 255n8, 268n1, 276n2, 280n9, 281n12, 283n1, 290n1, 291n3, 300n2, 309n2, 321n4, 338n1, 339n5, 340n7, 364n3, 364n4, 364n5, 388n4, 389n6, 397n1, 400n1, 406n10, 418n2, 426n4, 430n5, 434n1, 435n4, 438n3, 440n3, 449n1, 459n3, 463n11, 472n1, 475n1, 479n6, 479n7, 486n1, 486n3, 487n4, 491n2, 535n4, 546n1, 553n5, 568n2, 569n3, 583n1, 596n5, 596n6, 602n6, 606n7, 608n11, 608n13, 625n1, 649n1, 677n1, 689n3
Waltke, B. 557n11, 608n11
Walton, J. 71, 72, 72n9
Walvoord, J. F. 38, 39, 70, 143, 190, 334, 339, 345, 345n13, 345n14, 353, 406, 566, 569, 574, 579, 586, 590, 594, 605n2, 690
Wansbrough, H. 14n17, 431
Warden, D. 172n27
Ware, B. 4n2
Warren, A. 172n26
Watson, F. 607n9
Watty, W. 501n6
Weaver, D. J. 53n1, 266, 267n4
Webb, R. L. 106n1, 116, 121n5, 291n5
Webb, W. J. 547n4, 548
Weber, B. 450n3
Weber, H.-R. 666n4
Weber, K. 593, 607n9
Weder, H. 594n1, 597
Weeden, T. 343n9
Wehnert, J. 578
Weibling, J. M. 172n26
Weiss, H. 309n3
Weiss, H.-F. 46n35
Weiss, J. 42, 322n7
Weiss, W. 510n7
Welch, J. 653n1
Wenham, D. 5, 53n1, 159n5, 260n4, 321, 332, 333, 333n1, 343n9, 428, 428n1, 429, 435n5, 488n5, 567n3, 574, 586, 594n1, 596n4, 649n2
Wenham, G. J. 462, 464
Wenham, J. W. 6n4, 6n5, 469, 642, 679n1
Weren, W. J. C. 8n8, 27n28, 465n18, 514, 607n9
Werner, E. 496n6
Westcott, B. F. 6
Westerholm, S. 3, 111n7, 136n2, 158n2
Westermann, C. 334n2, 550
White, W. 14n17, 183n14, 189, 443
Whitters, M. 403n2
Wick, P. 170, 181
Wiebe, P. H. 172n26
Wilckens, U. 554
Wilcox, M. 250, 406, 435, 435n5
Wilkens, W. 130n6
Wilkins, M. 3, 136n2, 142, 239, 533, 679n1, 686, 690
Wilkinson, J. 267n2, 423n1, 491
Williams, J. 323n9
Williams, M. C. 7
Willis, J. T. 72, 72n9
Willis, W. 37n31, 43n33, 134n1

Wilson, M. 651
Wilson, R. M. 406n12
Wilson, R. R. 25n27, 59n4
Wimmer, J. F. 127, 190n25
Winer, G. 293n7, 310n6, 389n6, 406n10, 557n11
Wink, W. 37n30, 106n1, 144n7, 175n34, 291n5, 362n2, 422n13
Winkle, R. 93, 403n2
Winter, B. W. 547
Wise, M. O. 499n1
Witherington, B., III 2, 14, 141, 172n26, 297, 407n14, 462, 462n10, 543n2, 671
Wohlgemut, J. R. 599n4
Wolf, H. M. 72n9
Wolff, C. 464n16
Wong, E. 309n3, 578
Worp, K. A. 188n23
Worth, R. H. 142n4
Woschitz, K. 386n2
Wrede, W. 231
Wrembek, C. 524n4
Wright, D. F. 465n18
Wright, D. P. 231n6
Wright, N. T. 184n16, 322n7, 683n1
Wyschogrod, M. 334n3, 512n1, 516n8

Yamasaki, G. 106n1, 121n5
Yamauchi, E. 59n4, 78, 79n3, 80, 139n1
Yang, Y.-E. 308, 309n3, 314
Yarbrough, R. W. 13, 16n21, 279, 610
Yarnold, E. 469
Young, B. H. 334n3, 334n4, 516n8
Young, N. H. 252
Young, R. 243n2, 406n10
Yri, N. 65n3, 201

Zatelli, I. 94n3
Zeilinger, F. 142n2
Zeitlin, S. 377n1, 638n1
Zeller, D. 297n12
Zerbe, G. 175n34
Zerwick, M. 21, 74, 83, 85n9, 117n1, 120n3, 296n11, 389n6, 406n10, 475n1, 495n4, 546n1, 582n1, 608n11
Zias, J. 664n2
Ziesler, J. A. 254, 446
Zimmerli, W. 148n7
Zimmermann, H. 373n3
Zöckler, T. 197
Zolli, E. 100n3
Zuck, R. B. 70, 345n13, 566, 605n2
Zucker, D. J. 93, 403n2
Zumstein, J. 14n18, 184n16

Index of Greek Words

ἀδελφός 169n19, 605–6, 606n5
ᾅδης 279
ἀμήν 163n10
ἀναπληρόω 21
ἀπόλλυμι 279
ἀπὸ τότε 134
ἀπὸ τότε ἤρξατο ὁ Ἰησοῦς 9
ἁρπάζω 294

βασανίζω 451n6
βασανιστής 451n6
βάσανος 451n6
βασιλεία 43
βασιλεία τοῦ θεοῦ 37, 39–41, 321n6
βασιλεία τῶν οὐρανῶν 37, 39–41, 321n6
Βεελζεβούλ 278n6
βιάζεται 294–95
βιασταί 294
βίβλος γενέσεως 56
βρῶσις 196, 196n5

Γαδαρηνῶν 249–50
γέγραπται 82, 87, 130–31
γέεννα 279
Γερασηνῶν 250

Γεργεσηνῶν 250
γῆ 155n14

δεῖ 410n1
δικαιοσύνη 183

Ἑβραΐδι διαλέκτῳ 15n20
ἐγεννήθη 61
ἐγέννησεν 58
ἐγώ εἰμι 372–73n3
ἔθνος 518
εἰμί 532
ἐκκλησία 404, 404n4
ἐλάχιστος 606, 606n7
Ἐμμανουήλ 72–73
ἐξ ἀνθρώπων 507n1
ἐξ οὐρανοῦ 507n1
ἐπιούσιος 188
ἔρημος 106
ἔφθασεν 107
ἐφ᾽ ὃ πάρει 636n1
ἕως 73–74

ἤγγικεν 107

θλῖψις 574n6

ἰδού 66n4
Ἰησοῦς 67

ἵλεώς σοι 410n2

καὶ ἐγένετο ὅτε ἐτέλεσεν ὁ Ἰησοῦς 9, 134
καταλύω 162
κόσμος 155n14
κρίνω 475n3
κυνάριον 388
κύων 388

λαός 68, 655n4
λέγων 66n5

Μαθθαῖον 13
μακάριος 146, 149
μεταμέλομαι 649
μετανοέω 649
μὴ φοβηθῇς 67n6
μικροί, οἱ 606
μυστήριον 339n4

Ναζαρέτ 99
Ναζωραῖος 99
νήπιος 606n6

ὀλιγόπιστος 244
οὐκ ἐγίνωσκεν 73n10
ὀφειλήματα 188
ὄχλος 655n4

παιδίον 606n6

παῖς 606n6
παλιγγενεσία 475n2
παρθένος 69
πέτρα 406
Πέτρος 406
πληρόω 20, 23, 82
πληρωθῇ 19, 20
πληρωθῶσιν 21
πληρῶσαι 157–58
πορνεία 171, 172n25, 462
προσκυνέω 376, 486n2
πρῶτον 239n3

σαπρός 218n9
σεισμός 244
σκανδαλίζω 360n1
σῴζω 259

τέλειος 177
τελῶναι 176–77n37

υἱός 78, 557n10
ὕπαγε ὀπίσω μου 411n3
ὕπαγε, σατανᾶ 411n3
ὗς 78

Φιλίππου 365

Χριστός 56–57, 57n1

Index of Scripture and Other Ancient Writings

Old Testament *781*
New Testament *791*
Old Testament Apocrypha *818*
Old Testament Pseudepigrapha *820*
New Testament Apocrypha *822*
Rabbinic Writings *822*

Targums *824*
Qumran / Dead Sea Scrolls *824*
Josephus *825*
Philo *827*
Classical Writers *827*
Church Fathers *827*

Old Testament

Genesis

1–2 461, 461n6, 465
1:2 120, 122
1:27 18, 459, 459n3, 459n4, 461
1:27 LXX 465
1:28 464
2:2 305
2:4 56
2:24 18, 459, 459n3, 461, 462, 462n9
3 235, 249
3:1 112, 128, 275
4:1 73
4:1–16 170
4:8–10 558
4:8–16 558
4:15 449, 449n2
4:17 73
4:23–24 174
4:24 449, 449n2
4:25 73
5:1 56
5:2 18, 461
5:28–10:32 588
6–7 221n16
6:5 171
6:5–7:24 589
6:5–8:22 588
6:9 56, 177n38
7:4 126n2, 127
7:7 589
7:16 596
8:10 120
8:21 171
9:6 636n2

10:1 56
11:10 56
11:27 56
11:29 27
12 34
12–50 59
12:1–3 54, 57, 59
12:2 516n7, 518
12:2–3 269
12:3 389, 689
13:13 300n4
14:22 172
15:12 419n5
15:16 558n12
16 66
16:1–16 63
16:11 67
17:1 177n38
17:1–8 404n5
17:3 631n2
17:15 404n5
17:17 631n2
17:19 67
18–19 272, 272n3
18:1–8 609
18:19 220n13
18:20–19:28 300n4
18:32 595n2
20:17 176
21:24 172
22 34
22:1 126
22:2 120, 122, 123
22:5 631
22:13 LXX 488
22:17 222
22:20–24 27

23 78
24:16 69
24:43 69
25:12 56
25:19 56
26:29 272n2
28:17 419n5
31:54 LXX 378n2
32:22–32 404n5
32:28–29 187n22
34:1–31 174
34:3 LXX 70
35:18 669
35:19 83, 94
35:22–26 27
36:1 56
36:9 56
37:2 56
37:5–7 66
37:25 86
37:28 621
37:29 641n5
38:6–30 59, 531
38:8 LXX 531n1
38:26 73
40:19 365n6
42:17–18 327
43:11 109
43:23 LXX 410n2
43:27 177
43:30 LXX 185
44:7 LXX 410n2
44:17 LXX 410n2
45:22 524n2
45:23 595n2
46 89
46:3 518n15

47:31 172
48:7 83, 94
48:14 170, 464n17
48:14–15 464
49:10 59, 83
50:5 239, 240
50:20 306, 576

Exodus

1:17 529n6
1:22 76
2:8 69
2:15 76
2:20 LXX 378n2
2:23 76
3 66
3:1 512n1
3:6 19, 34, 530, 532
3:8 109
3:13–14 187n22
3:14 372n3
3:15 19
4:19 97
4:19–20 76
4:22 122
4:22–23 91, 120
4:30–31 326
5:1 393
6:12 418n3
7:11 219n12, 578
7:22 219n12
7:28 LXX 185
8:3 Eng 185
8:7 219n12
8:18 219n12
10:22 668–69

12:1–20 624
12:11 623
12:13 623
12:15 623
12:15–20 345
12:18–20 624
12:19 522
12:21 623
12:21–27 625
12:27 623
12:29–30 LXX 596
12:37 369
12:42 631
12:43 623
13:2 500
13:9 547
13:12 500
13:16 547
13:21–22 583
14:10–15:21 372, 373
14:24 LXX 372
14:31 373
15:1 501n5
15:2 501n5
16 369, 393, 400
16:7–12 481
16:29 578
16:31 268n1
16:32 589n2
16:35 126, 126n2
17:2 396, 538n2
17:7 129, 396, 538n2
18:1 509
18:7 LXX 177
19–20 149
19:4 561
19:6 379n3, 516n7, 518
19:16 579, 583n3, 584
19:20 417
19:21 440
20:2 537, 599n5
20:2–3 470
20:4 538
20:5 198n8
20:7 172, 323n9
20:10 309n3
20:10–11 305
20:12 18, 239, 240,
  274, 379, 379n7
20:12–16 18, 469
20:13 18, 168, 650
20:13–17 382
20:14 18, 170
20:16 174
20:17 168, 381, 382,
  470
20:20 126
21:1 536n7
21:12 169
21:16 LXX 380n8
21:17 18, 274, 379,
  379n7
21:24 18, 174
21:32 614, 621
21:35 176
22:2 313
22:3 450n4

22:21–22 176
22:23 365n6
22:25–26 175
22:25–27 175
23:4–5 174n31, 176,
  212
23:9 176
23:15 623
23:20 87
24:1 416, 419
24:2 372
24:4 624
24:8 625
24:12 419
24:12–18 416
24:15–18 419
24:16 419
24:16–17 418
24:18 126n2, 127
26:31–35 670
26:37 670
28:41 32, 57
29:32 369
29:37 207
30:11–16 429, 500
30:12 488
30:17–21 379
30:19 654
30:21 654
30:23 86
30:34–38 86
30:35 154
31:14 309n5, 312, 314
31:15 305
31:18 416
32 130
32:10 518n15
32:30–34 372
33:7–11 416, 417
33:13 518n16
33:14 305, 305n4
33:18–34:9 419n7
33:20 152
34 149
34:14 198n8
34:18 623
34:21 309n3
34:25 345
34:28 126n2, 127, 190,
  595n2
34:29 LXX 230n2
34:29–30 419
34:29–35 416, 418
34:30 419n5
34:35 419
35:2 305
38:18 670
38:25–26 429
40:31 654
40:34–38 418
40:35–38 583

Leviticus

1:2 380
1:3 380
1:10 380

2:1 380
2:1–2 86
2:3 207
2:5 380
2:11 345
2:13 154
2:14–16 86
4:2 512n1
4:7–35 625
5:3 231
5:7 500
5:11 500
6:14–18 86
7:13–14 345
10:6 268n1
11 383
11:4 556
11:7 207, 246
11:15 199
11:20–23 109
11:23 556
11:41 556
11:44–45 157
12:2–8 98
12:6 500
12:8 500
12:20 463n12
13–14 231, 231n5, 259
13:45–46 231
13:47–59 230
13:49 229
14:2 229
14:2–57 231
14:22 500
15:11 379, 379n3
15:14 500
15:25–33 259
16:2 670
16:14 449n2
16:19 449n2
16:34 254
18 462
18:3 512n1
18:5 469
18:16 364
18:16–18 172n25
18:21 187n22
19 536
19:2 177
19:9–10 309
19:9–15 149n8
19:12 18, 172
19:13 271, 479
19:14 437n1
19:15 475n3
19:15–18 444n2
19:17 LXX 444
19:17–18 445
19:18 18, 19, 174, 176,
  212, 469, 469n2, 534,
  536, 536n6, 537, 610
19:32–33 149n8
19:33–34 176, 536
19:34 212
20:9 274, 379, 379n7,
  654n2
20:9 LXX 380n8

20:21 364
21:2 239
21:3 69
21:7 461
21:11 239
21:13 69
21:14 69
21:18–19 500
22:24 463n12
22:32 187n22
23:4–8 624
23:5–6 612
23:17 345
23:42–43 417
24:5–9 309
24:7 86
24:8 309, 310
24:14 515n5
24:16 641
24:20 18, 174
24:23 515n5
25:18–22 195
25:35–55 175
26:18 449n2
26:21 449n2
26:24 449n2
26:28 449n2
27:30 556

Numbers

3:1 56
3:26 670
5:11–31 66
6 24
6:2 99
6:3 669
6:6–7 239
6:6–8 557n8
6:13 99
6:14 380
6:15 369
6:18–21 99
9:1–14 624
11 393
11:13 368
11:21–22 368
12:5–9 417
12:10–15 231n5
12:13 176
14:5 631n2
14:12 518n15
14:22 538n2, 595n2
14:27 424, 481
14:33 126, 126n2
15:30–31 323
15:33 312
15:36 515n5
15:37–39 547
15:38–39 259n2
17:25 557n10
18:19 154
18:31 271
19:11–12 557n8
21:7 176
21:29 300
22 217n4

22–24 80
23:7 338
23:18 338
23:19 36
24:17 79, 80, 87,
    557n10
25:11 265
27:17 217, 262n6
27:18–23 464n17
28:9–10 309n5, 310
28:16–17 612
28:17 624
29:7–11 254
30:1–5 380n9
30:2 18
30:3–15 172
31:50 380
32:13 126n2
35:30 445n4

Deuteronomy

1:16 176
1:16–17 475n3
1:27 426n3, 481
1:35 326
2:7 126, 126n2
4:6–8 518n15
4:10 LXX 404n4
4:13 595n2
4:23–24 198n8
4:29 209
4:32 582
4:33 419n5
4:34 518n16
5:6 537
5:8 538
5:8–9 198n8
5:12–15 309n3
5:16 18, 239, 240, 274,
    379, 379n7
5:16–20 18, 469
5:17 18, 169
5:17–21 382
5:18 18, 170
5:21 382
5:26 404n3
6 130
6–8 126
6:4 418, 418n3, 445n3,
    469, 536, 537
6:4–5 130
6:5 19, 534, 536, 537
6:8 547
6:12–14 130
6:13 18, 87, 130, 131,
    173, 198, 486n2
6:14–15 198n8
6:16 18, 87, 129, 131,
    396, 528n2
7:2 176
7:7 LXX 518n14
7:12–13 473
8:2 126, 126n2
8:3 18, 87, 128, 128n5,
    129, 131, 369, 400
8:4 126

8:5 128
8:16 369, 400
9:9 127
9:9–10:10 126n2
9:14 518n16
10:4 595n2
10:12 536n5
10:16 LXX 461n7
10:18 551n4
10:18–19 176
10:20 173
11:18 547
11:26 213
12:10 305n4
13:1–2 574n8
13:1–5 219n12, 220,
    320, 578
13:1–8 217n4
14 383
14:4–20 207
14:8 246
14:14 199
14:22–23 556
14:29 551n4
15 620
15:1–2 620
15:4 149n8, 620
15:6 620
15:7 149n8
15:7–10 620
15:7–11 175, 183n13
15:9 197, 479, 606
15:10 620
15:11 149n8, 619, 620
15:14 620
15:18 620
16:1–2 623
16:1–8 624
16:3–8 623
16:16 623
16:18 169, 475n3
17:5 515n5
17:6 445n4, 639
17:8–13 169
17:10 546
18:9–22 574n8
18:13 177, 177n38
18:14–22 217n4, 220
18:15 37, 417, 418,
    418n3, 445n3
18:15–18 403
18:15–19 162n8, 417,
    418
18:16 LXX 404n4
18:18–19 418n3
19:10 654n2
19:15 18, 491, 639
19:21 18, 174
20:16 176
21:1–9 379, 654
21:22–23 666, 674, 683
21:23 482
22:4 313
22:12 259n2, 547
22:14 69
22:19 69
22:20 69

22:23–24 65
22:23–27 66
22:27 MT 461n8
22:28 MT 461n8
23:1 463n12
23:3–6 176
23:10 MT 461n8
23:11 MT 461n8
23:18 649
23:21–23 172, 380n9
23:23 173
23:23 MT 461n8
23:24–25 308
23:25 309, 310
23:25 MT 461n8
24 461
24:1 18, 66, 171,
    171n22, 171n23,
    171n24, 459, 461,
    461n6
24:1–3 172
24:1–4 171, 460, 461,
    461n8
24:3 171, 171n22
24:5 MT 461n8
24:7 MT 461n8
24:10 LXX 188
24:10 MT 461n8
24:12–13 175
24:15 271, 479
24:19 MT 461n8
24:20 MT 461n8
24:21 MT 461n8
25:2 557n10
25:4 271
25:5 19, 530, 531,
    531n1
25:5–6 531, 531n1
25:5–10 31, 531
25:19 305n4
26:5 518n15
27:15 163n10, 550
27:16 379n7
27:19 176, 551n4
27:25 649
28:1 509
28:1–2 221
28:1–14 473
28:15 221
28:15–46 559
28:24 221
28:29 669
28:30 221, 221n15
28:45 221
28:53–57 577
28:54 197
28:56 197
28:58 221
29:5 126, 126n2
29:18–20 323
29:23 272n3, 300n4
30:4 582
30:6 184
30:10 536n5
30:15 213
30:19 213
31:30 LXX 404n4

32:4 177n38, 222
32:5 326, 424
32:9 512n1
32:10–11 561
32:13 109
32:18 222
32:20 424
32:28 518n16
32:31 222
32:32 272n3, 300n4
32:35 174, 175
32:39 372n3
32:44–45 612
33:9 330n1
33:29 146n3
34:9 464n17

Joshua

1:13 305n4
2 59
2:1–21 59
2:6 578
2:12 172
2:19 654n2
2:24 426n3
3:17 LXX 518n14
4:1 LXX 518n14
5:6 126, 126n2, 518n16
5:8 518n16
5:13–15 439n1
6:5 583n3
6:17 59
6:22–25 59
7:20–21 189
7:21 171
7:24 654
10:13 518n16
12:1 429n4
15:8 279n7
18:16 279n7
19:15 83
19:32–29 133
22:4 305n4
22:5 536
23:1 305n4
24:14 177n38
24:16 LXX 410n2

Judges

1:8 523
2:14 426n3
2:20 518n16
3:10 475n3
3:11 126n2
4:4–5 475n3
5:10 494
5:31 126n2, 351
6 66
6:11–12 135
6:23 272n2
8:28 126n2
9:7–15 218, 344n12
9:45 154
10:4 494
10:14 557n11

11:39 73
12:13–14 494
13:1 126n2
13:2–25 63
13:5 22, 99
13:5–7 24
13:7 22, 99
14:8 109
14:12 524n2
16:17 99
17:7–9 83
18:6 272n2
18:7 133
18:28 133
19:1–2 83
19:18 83
19:20 272n2
19:24 69
19:25 73

Ruth

1:1 475n3
1:1–2 83
2:10 631n2
2:12 561
2:14 669
3–4 531
3:13–18 27
4:2 595n2
4:11 83
4:18–22 59, 60

1 Samuel

1:1 258n1
1:8 595n2
1:11 99
1:19 73
2:2 222
3:14 323n9
4:18 126n2
4:21–22 568
6:7 258n1
7:3 268n1
7:5–6 190n25
9:3–5 494
9:15–16 32, 57
9:21 495
9:25 578
10:1 32, 57
10:2 94, 494
10:12 338
11:2 170
14:25 109
14:45 280
14:45 LXX 410n2
14:52 557n10
15:22 169, 253
15:27–28 641n5
15:28 LXX 516
16:1 82
16:3 32, 57
16:12–13 32, 57
16:14–23 321n5
17:12 82, 83
17:15 82

17:16 126n2
17:26 404n3
17:43 207
18:5 84
18:13 84
18:16 84
20:34 LXX 378n2
21 310
21:1–6 309
22:2 450n4
22:18–19 502n7
24:6 32, 57
24:15 258n1
24:17–19 176
25:21–35 292
25:25 67
25:30 84
26:16 557n10
29:3 LXX 450
29:9 532n3
30:1 327
30:12–13 327
30:15 426n3

2 Samuel

1:1 84
1:14 32, 57
1:16 654n2
1:17–27 561
2:3–4 84
2:11 84
3:34 557n10
5 84
5:2 82, 84, 87, 262n6
5:4 126n2
5:5–10 84
5:8 500
5:11 300n1
7:1 305n4
7:3 518
7:5–16 122
7:7–8 440
7:8–16 54
7:11 305n4
7:11–16 57
7:12–14 540n2
7:12–16 496, 640n3
7:13–14 120
7:14 404, 639
7:14–15 91
7:14–16 33
7:18–19 495
7:20 220n13
7:23 516n7
8:17 112
9:6 631n2
9:7 LXX 378n2
10:4 523
11 27
11–12 60
11:2 171, 578
12:1–15 205
12:6 449n2
12:20 191n26
13:2 69
13:18 69

13:29 494
14:2 191n26
14:4 496n6
14:11 280
14:17 532n3
15:5 LXX 373
15:7 126n2
15:24 112
15:30 494n2
16:9 365n6
17:23 648, 649
18:33 561
19:4 561
19:6 176
19:27 532n3
20:20 LXX 410n2
22:3 LXX 405n8
22:24 177n38
22:31 177n38
23:3–4 351
23:17 LXX 410n2
24:17 608n14

1 Kings

1:4 73
1:32–40 493n1, 495, 496
1:33 494
1:34 112
1:48 393
2:11 126n2
2:19 608
2:22 557n11
3:9 475n3
3:11 176
3:13 200
4:20–34 200
4:30 Eng 168n15
4:32 Eng 338
5:1 300n1
5:4 305n4
5:10 LXX 168n15
5:12 LXX 338
7:1–51 200
7:51 LXX 499n3
8:13 278n6
8:30 507n1
8:31–32 172
8:46–53 559
8:56 305n4
9:7–8 562
9:11–12 300n1
10 80, 325
10:1–13 327
10:8 146n3
10:14–29 200
11:4 LXX 469
11:7 494n2
11:42 126n2
13:1–6 312
13:15 LXX 378n2
17:2–6 106
17:8–16 367n1, 370, 393
17:9–24 283
17:12 368

17:16 369
17:17–24 260
18–19 559
18:4 515n4
18:14 154n13
18:19 217n4
18:26–29 185
18:27 557n11
18:39 631n2
18:40 265
19:4 292
19:8 126n2, 127, 190
19:8–14 417
19:10 154n13, 265
19:19–21 135, 239
20:29 327
20:35 321n3, 557n10
21:10 515n5
21:13 515n5
21:19 207
21:29 495
22 559
22:6 217n4
22:15 557n11
22:17 262, 262n6
22:18–20 495
22:19 608

2 Kings

1:2 278n6
1:3 278n6
1:6 278n6
1:8 109, 293
1:16 278n6
2:3 321n3
2:5 321n3
2:7 321n3
2:9–15 296
2:11 417
2:12 547
2:15 321n3
2:19–22 154
4:1 321n3, 450n4
4:1–7 367n1, 370, 393
4:2 368
4:6–7 369
4:9–37 283
4:17–37 260
4:18–37 424
4:33 185
4:38 321n3
4:38–44 393
4:42 368
4:42–44 367n1, 370
4:44 369
5 231n5
5:5–6 LXX 450
5:13 547
5:22 321n3
6:1 321n3
6:1–2 106
6:21 547
6:26 496n6
6:30–33 365n6
8:24 60
9:1 321n3

9:13 496
9:32 463n12
10:6–8 365n6
12:10–15 558n12
13:14 547
15:29 133
17:13 162n8
17:24–27 133
18:15 LXX 499n3
18:37–19:1 641n5
19:4 404n3
19:21 495
20:18 463n12
21:14 426n3
22–23 501
23:9 623
23:10 279
23:13 494n2
23:25 536n5
24:3–4 654
24:10–15 577
24:16 60n5
25:29 524n2

1 Chronicles

2:3–15 59
2:18–21 27
2:24 27
2:34 27
2:46–49 27
3:10–14 27, 60
3:11 60
3:14 LXX 62
3:15–16 62
3:16 59
3:19 60
4:4 83
5:22 60n5
7:24 27
11:2 84
11:19 LXX 410n2
12:29 112
14:1–2 300n1
16:36 393
17:11–14 540n2
17:13 404
17:18 220n13
17:21 518
24:19–21 409
25:2 346
28:2 LXX 404n4
28:8 LXX 404n4
29:3–7 450
29:11–13 189
29:22 32, 57

2 Chronicles

1:10 475n3
2:3 300n1
2:11 300n1
3:14 670
9 80, 325
9:1–12 327
9:7 146n3
10:5 327

10:12 327
13:5 154
18:16 262n6
19:5 169
22:1 60
22:11 60
24:17–22 559n14
24:19–21 515n4
24:20 379, 558n13
24:21 558
24:27 60
25:16 559n14
26 231n5
28:3 279, 279n7
28:11 418n3
29:3–11 501
29:30 346, 348
30:10 515n4
30:18–20 381
33:6 279
35:25 259
36:15–16 154n13, 409,
    559n14
36:16 362, 515n4
36:22 523

Ezra

3:2 60
3:8 60
4:14 154
5:2 60
6:9 154
7:11 355n5
9:7 429n4

Nehemiah

1:4 190n25
4:2 LXX 535n3
5:1–13 450n4, 473n5
5:6 LXX 451n5
5:13 163n10, 272
6:2 LXX 535n3
8:2 LXX 404n4
8:6 163n10
9:20 369
9:21 126, 126n2
9:26 154n13, 162n8,
    559n14
9:26–30 515n4
9:30 559n14
10:32–33 429
11:30 279n7
12:1 60
12:14 LXX 499n3
13:4–9 LXX 499n3
13:5 86
13:9 86
13:15–22 309n3

Esther

1:11 364
2:9 364
2:12 86
3:8 LXX 445n3

4:1–4 300
4:16–5:1 327
4:17 LXX 219
5:3 364
5:6 364
6:8–9 524n2
7:2 364
9:16 305n4
10:2 434

Job

1 126
1:20 641n5
4:8 263n7
4:19 196
5:5 263n7
5:17 146n3
6:6 154
8:15 222
9:8 372, 373
11:18–19 244
16:10 175
18:5 596
19:3 595n2
19:25–27 531
20:8 372
22:6–7 609
24:6 263n7
24:13 509n6
26:11–12 373, 376
28:18 352
31:29 176
31:29–30 174n31
31:32 609
31:40 338
32:19 255
33:15–17 66
33:23 439n1
38:3 557n11
38:16 373
38:17 405
38:41 199
39:6 154
39:12 322
40:10 557n11
42 150
42:6 107

Psalms

1:1 146n3
1:1–6 213
1:3 113, 515
1:4 114, 115
1:6 220n13, 596
2 33, 93, 120, 123,
    640n3
2:2 32, 57, 535
2:2 LXX 535n3
2:6–7 91
2:6–8 404
2:7 34, 119, 120, 122,
    123, 417–18, 639
2:9 541, 658
2:10 475n3
2:12 91, 146n3, 404

3 631
3:5–6 244
3:7 175
6 631
6:8 220, 609
6:9 MT 220
7:3–5 176
7:15 382
8 501
8:2 498, 501, 502
8:3 18, 501n5
8:3 LXX 501n5
8:4 36
9:13 405
9:14 495
11:6 222, 486, 631n1
12:3 184n15
15 146n6
15:2 177n38
16:2 469
17:8 561
18:2 222
18:15–16 LXX 373
18:25–26 205
18:30 Eng 177n38
18:31 MT 177n38
18:31 222
18:46 222
21:23 LXX 404n4
22 410n1
22:1 19, 657, 663, 666,
    667, 669, 669n2
22:6–8 99
22:7 482, 658, 662, 663
22:8 614, 663
22:8–9 663
22:13 99
22:16 207
22:17 663
22:18 660, 661, 663
22:22 Eng 404n4
23 84, 440
23:2 368
23:3 509n6
23:5 191n26
24:3–4 152, 381
26:4–5 176
26:6 654
27:5 222
28:4 412
28:5 381
29:1 501n5
31 631
32:1 146n3
32:2 146n3
33:12 146n3, 516n7,
    518
33:18–19 278
34:7 439n1
34:9 146n3
34:18 LXX 404n4
34:19–22 410n1
35:18 Eng 404n4
35:23 244
36:7 561
37:2 200
37:6 150n9

37:7 151
37:9 151
37:10–17 149n8
37:11 150n9, 151
37:18 220n13
40:5 146n3
40:6–8 253
41:2 146n3
41:9 636
41:13 393
42 631
42:2 404n3
43:1 518n16
44:23–24 244
45:6–7 541
45:8 86
45:12 300n1
48:2 38, 79, 173
49:7–9 312, 488
49:14 Eng 278n6
49:15 MT 278n6
50 62
50:14 172
50:16–23 554n6
51:2–3 381
51:6 381
51:6–9 110
51:10 152, 381
51:12 632
51:16–17 381
52:1 184n15
57:1 561
57:2 475n3
58:4 112
59:4 244
59:5 393
59:17 501n5
61:4 561
62:12 412
62:13 414
63:7 561
65:5 146n3
65:7 244, 373, 376
66:10–12 221n16
68:25 Eng 69
68:26 MT 69
68:34 501n5
68:35 393
69:1–3 372, 373
69:6 393
69:8 99
69:11 300
69:13–15 372
69:14–15 373
69:20–21 99
69:21 660, 663, 669
69:33 609
71:2 475n3
71:4 475n3
72:1 91
72:10–12 86
72:18 393
73–83 62
73:1 152
73:13 654
75:8 486, 631n1
76:12 429n4

77:19 372
78 346n15, 347, 348
78:2 18, 22, 24, 346, 346n15, 347, 348, 350
78:4 346, 347
78:4–7 346
78:7 347
78:8 346
78:11 346
78:11–12 347
78:12–16 346
78:15–16 346n15
78:17–22 346
78:18 346n15, 528n2
78:21 346
78:23 346n15
78:23–29 346
78:24 346n15, 369
78:24–25 346n15
78:27 222
78:31 346n15
78:31–34 346
78:32 347
78:32–33 346
78:35 346n15
78:36–37 346, 346n15, 380, 554n6
78:37 346n15, 381
78:38–39 346
78:39–42 346
78:41 396, 528n2
78:42–43 347
78:42–55 346
78:44 346n15
78:45 346n15
78:52 217
78:56 396, 528n2
78:56–58 346
78:59–64 346
78:65–72 346
78:70 346n15
78:70–72 84
78:71–72 346n15
79:11 557n10
80:8–13 344n12, 513n2
81:3 583n3
81:16 109
83:15 222
84:2 404n3
84:5 146n3
84:6 146n3
84:13 146n3
87:4 300n1
89 33, 540n2
89:3 122
89:8–9 244
89:9–10 373, 376
89:16 146n3
89:20 122
89:23 557n10
89:26–27 122, 639
89:26–37 91
89:27 34, 120
89:27–29 404
89:38–45 410n1
90:5–6 200
91 57, 129

91:1–4 561
91:7 595n2
91:11–12 18, 87, 129, 130, 131, 439n1
94:6 176
94:12 146n3
95:7–8 461n7
95:7–11 129
95:9 528n2
95:10 126, 126n2
96:7 501n5
100:3 217
101:23 LXX 535n3
102:11 200
102:21 557n10
103:3 249
103:15–16 200
104:2 416
104:7 244
104:12 344n12
104:15 191n26
104:27–30 199
105:4 209
106:3 146n3
106:5 518n16
106:14 528n2
106:41 426n3
106:48 163n10, 393
107:3 232
107:5 151
107:9 151, 370
107:10 133
107:18 405
107:23–32 244, 372, 373
107:29 373, 376
107:31–32 373
107:34 154
108:21 LXX 219
109:1 LXX 540n3
109:25 662
110 540, 540n3, 541n4
110:1 19, 33, 35, 526, 539, 540, 541, 640
110:1 MT 540n3
110:2 658
110:3 86
110:4 540n3
110:5 540n3
112:1 146n3
113–18 496
115–18 626
117:25 LXX 496n5
117:26 LXX 496n5
118:10–25 410n1
118:19–20 215
118:22 515, 515n6
118:22–23 19, 37
118:25 MT 496n5
118:25 496n6
118:25–26 18, 33, 45, 493, 515, 563
118:26 19, 290n1, 422n12, 501, 544, 561, 562, 569
118:26 MT 496n5
119 594

119:1 146n3, 177n38
119:2 146n3
119:29–32 213
119:89 585
119:105 594
119:115 220
119:176 440
123:1 368n2
126:5–6 338
127:1 221n15
127:2 195
127:5 146n3
128:1 146n3
128:2 146n3
130:8 67, 68
132:2 LXX 619
132:13–18 370
133:1 223
133:2 Eng 619
137:5 170
137:7–9 176
137:8 146n3
137:9 146n3
139:17 223
139:18 222
139:19 220
139:19–22 176
139:24 213
140:8 LXX 219
141:2 500
144:7 LXX 373
144:15 146n3
145:9 177
146:5 146n3
146:9 176
147:9 199
147:14 370
147:20 518n16
148:1 496
149:2 LXX 254n6

Proverbs

1:20–23 303
1:28 209
1:31 113
2:4 352
2:5 253n2
2:20 509n6
3:6 536n7
3:12 444n2, 445
3:13 146n3
3:15 352
3:24–26 244
4:23–27 438
6:6 LXX 601
6:6–9 602
6:9 LXX 601
6:20 379n7
8:1–21 305
8:1–36 303
8:11 352
8:15 529n6
8:17 209
8:20 509n6
8:32 146n3
8:32–36 305

8:34 146n3
9:4–6 305
9:9 602
10:18 444n2
10:19 LXX 185n17
10:25 221, 221n15
11:20 177n38
11:30 113
12:7 221n15, 222
12:10 313
12:28 509n6
13:9 596
14:2 213
14:11 221n15, 222
14:21 146n3, 152
14:34 518n16
15:16–17 470n3
15:25 551n4
16:7 509n6
16:18–19 149n8
16:20 146n3
16:31 509n6
17:5 LXX 152
17:20 LXX 461n7
18:24 330n1
19:17 606, 609
20:7 146n3
20:22 174
20:26 115
20:27 594
21:16 509n6
21:21 509n6
22:4 473
22:16 473
22:22 473
22:22–23 473n5
23:6 197, 479
23:10–11 473n5
23:22 379n7
24:3 221n15
24:12 412
24:16 449n2
24:17–18 174n31, 176
24:29 174, 176
25:9–10 444, 444n2, 445
25:21–22 174, 175, 176
26:4–5 444n2
26:27 382
27:1 201
27:5–6 444n2, 445
28:6 213
28:14 146n3
28:18 177n38, 213
28:22 197, 479
28:24 379n7
29:7 183n13
29:18 146n3
30:8–9 199
30:19 69
31:5 557n10
31:6 660
31:8–9 475n3

Ecclesiastes

1:3 412

4:1 184n15
5:2 185
5:4–5 173
5:5 184n15
7:19 595n2
9:2 173
9:8 191n26
10:17 146n3

Song of Songs

1:3 69
1:13 86
3:6 86
3:11 595
6:8 69

Isaiah

1:4 516n7, 518
1:5 235n19
1:8 495
1:9 525n5
1:9–10 272n3, 300n4
1:10 517n9
1:10–17 253
1:10–18 169
1:11 253n2
1:15 185
1:21 517n10
1:23 476n3, 551n4
1:23–26 517n9
1:25 115
2:2–3 233
2:2–4 575n10
2:2–5 155n15
2:11–12 588n1
2:20 219n11
3:9 272n3
3:9–11 300
3:10 113
3:12 382
3:14 382
4:2 99
4:4 110, 115
5 514
5:1 514n3, 515, 557n10
5:1–2 334n2, 512, 514, 514n3
5:1–7 113, 480, 513, 514
5:2 218n6, 514n3
5:4 218n6
5:7 218n6, 268n1, 514, 514n3
5:8 550n1, 551n4
5:8–10 473n5
5:11 550n1
5:18 550n1
5:20 550n1
5:21 550n1
5:22 550n1
5:24 114
5:24–25 523
6 150, 339
6:9 557n11
6:9–10 18, 22, 24, 339

6:9–10 LXX 339n6
6:9–10 340, 340n6, 341n8, 346
6:10 339n6, 382
6:11 424
7 72
7–8 72
7–9 72, 133
7:2 70, 72
7:3 404n5
7:11 71
7:13 70, 72
7:14 18, 22, 23, 34, 52, 53, 63, 69, 70, 71, 72, 72n9, 99, 133, 690
7:14–16 72
7:15–17 71
7:16 70
8:1–4 504
8:3–4 72, 404n5
8:8 18, 34, 72, 133
8:8 LXX 72
8:9–10 557n11
8:10 18, 34, 72, 133
8:10 LXX 72
8:14 411, 515
8:14–15 516
8:17 LXX 405n8
8:18 71
9:1 133
9:1–2 18, 22, 24, 98, 102, 132, 133, 688
9:1–7 72
9:2 155
9:2 LXX 518n14
9:3 263n7
9:6 404n5, 541
9:6–7 24, 33, 133, 134n1
9:7 72, 272n2
9:16 382
10:5–11 523
10:6 518n16
10:15–19 114
10:20 219n11
10:20–22 525n5
10:22 222
11:1 22, 24, 52, 99, 119, 540n2, 541
11:1–2 119
11:1–5 33, 72
11:6 LXX 435n3, 606n6
11:10 540n2, 541
11:10–12 583n2
13:6 585
13:8 573n4
13:10 582
13:14 322
13:19 272n3, 300n4
13:21 327
14:3 305n4
14:13–15 300
14:15 301
14:29 112
16:1 495
17:5 263n7

18:2 583n2
18:4 263n7, 3350
19:2 573
19:8 LXX 353
19:20 71
20:3 71
22:15 407
22:22 405, 407, 596
23:1–4 387
23:1–8 300n1
24:13 263n7
24:15 393
24:18 382
24:19 670n4
24:23 582
25:6–9 233
25:6–10 254
26:2 516n7, 518
26:15 518n16
26:17 573n4
26:19 291, 531
26:20 185
27:2 513n2
27:2–6 514
27:12 350
27:12–13 263n7
27:13 582, 583n3
28:2 221n16
28:7 502n7
28:12 205n4
28:15–18 222
28:15–19 405
28:16 515
28:17 221n16
28:24–26 338n2
29:1 554
29:2 554
29:6 221n16, 670n4
29:7 554
29:9 557n11
29:10 554
29:10–12 554
29:13 18, 380, 380n10, 381, 384, 554
29:14 554
29:15 554
29:18 291
29:20–21 554
29:23 187n22, 393
30:6 112
30:10 559n14
30:18 146n3
30:27–30 115, 221n16
30:33 609
31:5 561
31:9 146n3
32:15 115
32:17 195
32:20 146n3
34:4 504, 582
34:14 327
35:5 291
35:5–6 260, 261, 291, 393
35:6 291
37:16 393
37:22 495

37:30　71
38:7　71
38:9–10　405
38:22　71
39:7　463n12
40　121
40–66　108
40:3　18, 35, 101, 102, 108, 121, 293, 421
40:3–5　108, 425
40:5　108
40:6–8　200, 200n14
40:8　585
40:11　322, 440
41:4　372n3
41:14–16　115
42　24, 120, 123, 155n15, 317n7
42:1　34, 37, 119, 120, 122, 123, 303, 316n3, 317, 317n7, 321, 418
42:1–4　18, 22, 24, 72, 108, 231, 261, 315, 316, 488, 665, 690
42:2　430
42:2–3　316n4
42:3　316n5
42:3–42:4　316n5
42:4　316n5, 317
42:4 LXX　316n6
42:4 MT　316n6
42:6　155
42:7　291
42:18　291
43:1–2　372, 373n3
43:1–13　373n3
43:5　372, 373n3
43:5–6　232
43:6　583
43:10　317n7, 372n3
43:13　372n3
43:16　372
44:1　123
44:3　110, 115
44:28　523
45:1　32, 523
45:6　233
45:20–22　575n10
46:4　372n3, 424
47:12　557n11
47:13–15　79
48:1–2　554n6
49　155n15
49:6　155, 575n10
49:7　99
49:11　425
49:12　232
49:15　210
50:1　450n4
50:4–9　174, 641
50:6　174, 175, 641, 658
50:9　196
51:1　196n5
51:1–2　404n5
51:1–5　151
51:3　196n5
51:4　196n5

51:4–5　155
51:6　196n5
51:7　196n5
51:8　196, 196n5
51:9　244
51:9–10　244, 372
51:17　486, 631n1
51:22　486, 631n1
52–53　410n1
52:6　152, 187n22, 373n3
52:13　235, 317n7
52:15　108
53　235, 235n18, 235n19
53:1　235n18
53:2　99, 235n18
53:2–3　99
53:3–6　666
53:4　18, 22, 24, 108, 229, 235, 236, 488, 625
53:4–6　235
53:5　235n18
53:6　268, 387, 440
53:7　108, 235, 235n18, 639, 653
53:7–8　235n18
53:8　99, 235, 255
53:9　235n18, 663, 674
53:10　625
53:10–12　488
53:11　118, 235
53:11–12　235
53:12　235n18, 625, 662, 663
53:12 LXX　488
54　155n15
54:4–6　596
54:5　326
54:5–6　255
54:5–8　524
54:9　589
54:10 LXX　410n2
54:10　425
55:5　575n10
55:10–11　338
55:13　71
56:2　146n3, 309n3
56:3–5　463n12
56:4　309n3
56:6　309n3
56:6–8　575n10
56:7　18, 87, 131, 498, 500, 505
56:7 LXX　500n4
56:11　262n6
57:3　326
57:15　150, 186, 436
58:1　183
58:1–5　554n6
58:2　518n16
58:3–7　190
59:19　233
60　155n15
60:1–6　86
60:3–4　233

60:6　86
60:11　215
60:16　152
60:18　215
60:21　381
60:22　518n16
61　151
61:1　119, 149, 291
61:1–2　149n8, 150, 151
61:2　588n1
61:3　381
61:3–11　151
61:6　379n3
61:10　525n6
62:1　579
62:4–5　255, 524
62:5　596
62:10　215, 583n2
62:11　18, 22, 24, 34, 494
62:11 LXX　494n3
63:7　268n1
63:10　323
63:15　278n6
64:1　119
64:6　525n6
64:10–11　562
65:1　209, 518n16
65:4　246
65:13–14　232
65:17　108
65:24　185
66:1　173
66:1–2　150, 302
66:2　436
66:3　246
66:7–8　573n4
66:8　518n16
66:16　281n13
66:17　246
66:18 LXX　608n12
66:19　71
66:22　108

Jeremiah

1:5　220n13
1:10　381
2:2　326
2:3　263n7
2:21　218n6, 513n2
3:8　171n22
3:9–10　326
3:10　554n6
3:15　262n6
3:19　122
4:3　338n2
4:4 LXX　461n7
4:11–14　110
4:13　582, 583
4:14　517n10
4:21　583n2
4:31　495, 573n4
5:4–5　517n9
5:5　305n3
5:6　217
5:9　518n16

5:21　24
5:21–23　340
5:28　476n3
5:29　518n16
5:30–31　517n9
6:2　495
6:7　235n19
6:11　169n18
6:13　217n4, 502n7
6:16　304, 305
6:20　86, 253n2
6:24　573n4
7　253
7:1–11　517n11
7:4–11　554n6
7:5–6　176
7:8–15　569n2
7:11　87, 131, 498, 500, 500n4
7:21　557n11
7:21–22　253n2
7:22–23　253
7:25–26　515n4, 559n14
7:28　518n16
7:31–32　279
7:32　279n7
8:5　517n10
8:6　107
8:8–12　217n4
8:13　504
8:20　263n7
9:8 LXX　518n14
9:9 Eng　518n14
9:10–11　569n2
9:17–22　259
10:1–2　79
10:2　396, 397
10:10　670n4
10:19　235n19
10:21　262n6
11:16　114
11:17　381
12:2　554n6
12:7　562, 568
12:10　262n6, 480, 513n2
12:13　263n7
12:16　405n6
13　504
13:27　561
14:11–12　190
14:14　219
15:2　636n2
15:7　116
15:17　169n18
16:7　259, 631n1
16:16　136
17:6　154
17:9　171
18:2　649
18:2–6　24
18:7　381
18:9　405n6
18:16　662
19　504, 650
19:1–13　24, 649
19:2–9　279

20 559
20:1–2 515n4
20:1–6 404n5
20:14–18 292
21:8 213
22:3 176
22:5 564
22:13–14 221n15
22:15–17 149n8
22:18 550
22:23 573n4
23 84, 440, 517n9
23:1–4 262n6
23:2 217, 322, 553
23:2–3 268
23:3–4 608n14
23:4–5 440
23:5 57
23:5–6 33, 540n2, 541
23:6 404n5
23:13–22 217n4
23:14 272n3, 300n4
23:28 557n11
24:1–10 504
24:6 381
24:7 152
25:4 515n4, 559n14
25:15 631n1
25:15–17 486
25:22 300n1, 387
26:1–11 502
26:5 559n14
26:6 562, 569n2
26:11 154n13
26:15 654n2
26:18 569n2
26:20–23 559
26:21–23 515n4
26:23 154n13
27–28 504
27:3 300n1
27:5–11 529n6
27:15 219
28:15 217n4
29:2 463n12
29:4–14 94
29:7 176
29:9 219
29:13 209
29:31 217n4
30:3 94
30:5–6 573n4
30:7–8 588n1
30:8–9 94
30:22 94
31 94, 95
31:1 94
31:2 94
31:4 94, 381, 405n6
31:7 94
31:9 91, 94, 122
31:10 440
31:13 94
31:15 18, 22, 23, 52,
    53, 93, 94, 95
31:15 MT 94
31:15 LXX 94

31:17 94
31:20 91, 94, 122
31:21 94
31:28 381
31:29 654
31:31 94, 248
31:31–34 152, 625
31:32 94, 596
31:33 94
31:34 94
31:36 516n7, 518,
    518n16
32:6–9 19, 22, 648, 649
32:35 279
32:41 381n11
33:7 405n6
33:14–15 94
33:15 57, 540n2
33:15–16 541
33:17 94
33:24 518n16
34:19 463n12
36:26 355n5
36:32 355n5
37–38 559
38:7 463n12
38:15 LXX 95
40:1 94
41:16 463n12
42:10 381, 405n6
44:25 557n11
45:4 381
46:10 588n1
46:22 112
47:4 300n1
48:17 658
48:36 259
48:41 573n4
48:44 382
49:12 631n1
49:18 272n3, 300n4
50:6 268, 387, 440
50:40 272n3, 300n4
51:7 486
51:27 583n2
51:33 116, 263n7, 350
51:35 654n2
51:46 573
51:63–64 437

Lamentations

1–5 517n10
1:6 495
2:14 217n4
2:15 662, 663
3:30 174, 175
4:6 272n3
4:7 MT 99
4:12 429n4
4:13 517n9
4:21 557n11
5:7 654

Ezekiel

1:1 119

1:4 418
1:28–2:2 419n5
3:1 268n1
3:1–3 504
3:7 LXX 461n7
3:20 183n12
3:27 557n11
4:1–5:17 504
4:6 126n2, 127
6:9 171
7:10–19 588n1
8 517n11
8–10 502n7
8:12 568
9:8–9 517n10
9:9 568
10:4 418
11:23 494n2, 568
12:5 196
12:7 196
12:11 60n5
12:22 593
12:27 LXX 397n2
13:2–16 217n4
13:8–16 221n15
13:10–16 221n16
14:3 437n1
14:7 437n1
16 517n10
16:4 154
16:7–8 524
16:7–22 596
16:32 326
16:46–56 272n3, 300n4
16:49 183n13
17:2 338
17:23 344n12
18:2 654
18:13 654n2
18:19–32 654
18:21 107
18:23 107
18:27 107
18:28 107
18:30 437n1
18:30–32 107
19:10–14 513n2
20:13 309n3
20:39 557n11
21:5 338
22 517n10
22:7 176, 379n7
22:27 275
22:27–28 217
22:28 217n4
22:29 176
23:31 486
23:38–39 517n11
24:3 338
24:6–9 300
24:17 259
24:22 259
26:20 300
27:17 109
27:33 429n4
28:2 300n1
28:12 300n1

28:21 300n1
29:11–13 126n2
30:3 585, 588n1
31:6 344n12
31:12 218
31:14 300
32:7 582
32:18 300
32:24 300
33:3–6 583n3
33:4 654n2
33:13 183n12
33:30–33 554n6
34 84, 440, 517n9
34:2–8 553
34:5 262, 262n6
34:6 608n14
34:10–12 440
34:11–12 268
34:11–16 440
34:13 322
34:15 387
34:15–16 440
34:16 268, 440
34:17–22 608
34:23 440
34:23–24 540n2
34:31 268
36:9 338n2
36:17 259
36:20 187n22
36:23 187n22
36:24–27 110
36:25–27 115
36:33 562n1
37:1–14 670
37:12 667
37:13 670
37:14 115
37:22 516n7, 518
37:23 115
37:24 540n2
38:22 221n16
39:29 115
40–48 502
40:3 439n1
43:7 446
43:24 154
44:6–14 517n11
44:22 461
44:24 476n3
47:22–23 176

Daniel

1:1–2 538, 577, 579
1:2 523, 529n6
1:3 463n12
1:4 79
1:12 595n2
2 66
2:2 79
2:18–19 39, 339n4
2:19 42
2:21 529n6, 538
2:27–30 339n4
2:28 39, 42, 507n1

2:28–29 573
2:34–35 516
2:35 114, 116
2:37 39, 42, 523
2:37–38 529n6, 538
2:44 39, 42, 516
2:44–45 37, 516
2:45 573
2:47 339n4
3:6 351
3:16–18 529n6
4:6 339n4
4:7 79
4:10–12 344n12
4:14 218
4:17 293
4:21 344n12
4:26 42, 107, 186n21
4:31 42
4:34–35 39
4:37 39, 42
5:1–4 579
5:2–4 577
5:7 79
5:22–23 577, 579
5:23 39, 42
6:6–10 529n6
6:15 LXX 451n5
6:17 677
6:27 42
7 46, 47, 66, 219n10,
410n1, 581, 689
7:2 582, 583
7:9 476, 581, 681
7:9–14 219n10
7:10 583
7:13 19, 32, 35, 36,
57n1, 277, 290n1,
583, 638, 640
7:13–14 32, 34, 37,
239, 248, 389, 476,
541, 582, 584, 608n10,
658, 689, 689n2, 691
7:13–27 610
7:18 476, 689, 691
7:21 573
7:22 219n10, 476, 689,
689n2, 691
7:25 397n2
7:25–27 689n2
7:27 219n10, 476, 516,
689, 691
8:13 577
8:17 36
8:17–18 419n5, 681
8:23 558n12
9:3 190, 190n25
9:6 362, 515n4, 559n14
9:7 517n10
9:10 362, 515n4,
559n14
9:12 476n3, 517n10
9:16 517n10
9:18 183n12
9:20 517n10
9:24 57, 517n10,
558n12

9:25–27 290n1
9:26 99, 222, 573
9:27 397n2, 565, 577
10:3 191n26
10:6 416, 681
10:8–9 6681
10:8–12 419n5
10:10–14 439n1
10:12 185
10:15 681
11:11 426n3
11:14 LXX 397n2
11:31 565, 577
11:33–34 488
11:44 573
12:1 439n1, 565,
574n6, 578, 578n2,
582
12:2 259, 260, 279,
531, 610, 684
12:3 155, 351, 417, 684
12:10 488, 577n1
12:11 565, 577
12:12 146n3
12:17 39

Hosea

1–3 326
1:2–9 504
1:4–9 404n5
1:5 219n11
1:6–7 91
1:10 91
2:1 91
2:9 263n7
2:10 559n16
2:12 504
2:14 253n2
2:16 524, 596
2:16–23 255
2:19 596
2:21 253n2
2:23 91
3:1 524
3:4 253n2
3:5 91, 253n2
4:1 253n2
4:4–6 502n7, 517n9
4:4–10 253n2
4:13–14 253n2
4:19 253n2
5:13 235n19
6 253n2
6:1–3 253n2
6:4 253n2
6:5 253n2
6:6 18, 152, 169, 251,
253, 253n2, 281n11,
309, 310, 381, 500,
556
6:9 253n2
6:11 116, 263n7, 350
7:11 91
7:16 91
8:11–13 253n2
8:13 91, 253n2

9:4 253n2, 259
9:6 91
10:1 113, 513n2
10:1–2 253n2
10:12 253n2
10:12–13 113
11:1 18, 22, 23, 34, 52,
53, 90, 91, 91n4, 122
11:2 253n2
11:5 91
11:8 91
11:8–11 253n2
12:1 91
12:6 253n2
12:10 253n2
12:12 253n2
13:3 114, 116
13:4 91
13:5 220n13
13:13 573n4
14:1 253n2

Joel

1:7 504
1:14 190
1:15 585, 588n1
2:1 183, 583n3, 585
2:1–2 588n1
2:2 565, 574n6, 578n2,
669
2:10 573, 573n5, 582,
670n4
2:13 641n5
2:15 183, 190
2:27 446
2:28 66
2:28–29 115
2:31 582, 669
3:2 608n12
3:4–8 300n1
3:11–12 608n12
3:13 116, 263n7, 350
3:14 588n1
3:15 582

Amos

2:6 450n4
2:6–8 149n8
2:10 126, 126n2
2:11–12 99
2:12 559n14
3:2 220n13
4:4–5 557n11
4:11 300n4
5:5 557n11
5:10 177n38
5:11–12 473n5
5:16 259
5:18 550n1
5:18–20 588n1
5:20 582
5:22 253n2
5:25 127n2
6:1 550n1
6:4 550n1

7:10–17 515n4, 559
7:12–13 559n14
7:14 557n10
7:14–15 135
8:6 450n4
8:8 670n4
8:9 219n11, 582, 663,
667, 669
9:8–12 562n1
9:11 219n11, 405n6
9:13–15 263n7

Jonah

1–2 244
1:1–16 372
1:4–2:10 373
1:9 555
1:15 373, 376
1:16 373
1:17 18, 325, 326
2:2–9 373
3:2 327
3:4 127, 127n2
3:5 190, 190n25, 300
4:4 LXX 451n5
4:9 451n5
4:10–11 176

Micah

2 440
2:1–3 280n11
2:8–9 280n11
2:12–3:3 84
3:1–4 280n11
3:1–5 517n9
3:5–7 217n4
3:8–12 281n11
3:9–10 517n10
3:9–12 280n11
3:11 502n7, 554n6
3:12 569n2
4:1–2 233
4:1–3 575n10
4:1–8 281n11
4:7 518n16
4:8 495
4:9–10 573n4
4:10 495
4:12–13 116
4:13 495
5:2 18, 52, 53, 76, 78,
82, 83, 84, 87, 131
5:3 573n4
6:6 253n2
6:6–8 152, 169
6:8 152, 436, 468, 535,
556
6:9–12 280n11
7:3 280n11
7:5–6 280n11
7:6 18, 276, 280,
280n11

Nahum

1:5　670n4
1:7　220n13
3:14–15　557n11

Habakkuk

1:6　523
2:3　593
2:4　536
2:6　550n1
2:9　550n1
2:12　550n1
2:12–13　550n1
2:15　550n1
2:16　486
2:17　550n1
2:19　550n1
2:19–20　550n1
3:11　278n6
3:15　372
3:16　574n6

Zephaniah

1:3　351
1:4　517n10
1:4–13　517n11
1:7　585, 588n1
1:10　219n11
1:12　517n10
1:14　585, 588n1
1:15　219n11, 574n6,
　582
1:16　583n3
2:1　518n16
2:9　154, 272n3

2:9 LXX　518n14
3:1　517n10
3:3–4　217, 517n9
3:4　502n7, 517n11
3:8　608n12
3:14　495

Haggai

1:1　60
1:12　60
1:14　60
2:2　60
2:6　555, 573, 573n5,
　582, 670n4
2:14　518n16
2:21　555
2:23　60

Zechariah

1:1　558, 558n13
1:12–17　495
2:2–5　495
2:6　582
2:6 LXX　583
2:10　495
2:10–11　446
2:12　495
3:2　495
3:3–5　524n2
4:14　557n10
6:12　404n5
7:4–14　190
7:9　475n3
7:9–10　176, 556
7:12　162n8
8:3–8　495

8:17　172
8:19　190
8:20–23　233
8:23　259n2, 595n2
9–14　495
9:1–4　300n1
9:9　18, 22, 24, 38, 493,
　494, 495, 496
9:9 LXX　494n3
9:11　495, 625
9:14　579
10:2　262
10:2–3　262n6
11　650
11:7　650
11:12　495, 614
11:12–13　19, 22, 24,
　495, 558n13, 621, 648,
　649, 650, 651
11:13　650
11:16　262n6
11:17　170, 550n1
12:2　486
12:2–9　495
12:3　219n11
12:10　541, 582, 583
12:12　582
13:1　110, 219n11, 495
13:2–4　217n4
13:4　109
13:7　19, 25, 87, 131,
　268, 495, 541, 629,
　637
13:7–9　322, 410n1
13:9　115
14:1　588n1
14:2　608n12
14:2–8　495

14:3　573
14:4　219n11, 494n2,
　504n2, 569
14:4–5　495, 573n5,
　670n4
14:5　412, 573, 608n10,
　670
14:5 LXX　608
14:10　425
14:16–21　417
14:21　495, 499n2, 501,
　502

Malachi

1:6–14　554n6
1:6–2:9　517n11
1:11　233
2:10–16　459n4
2:14–16　168, 463
2:16　461
3:1　18, 87, 108, 121,
　131, 290n1, 292, 293,
　295, 502
3:1–3　115
3:1–4　502
3:2　588n1
3:2–4　501
3:5　176
3:9　518n16
3:22–23 LXX　421
4:1　115
4:5　109, 403
4:5–6　295, 296, 417,
　421, 422n12, 669
4:5–6 Eng　421
4:6　281

New Testament

Matthew

1　16, 52, 75, 236
1–2　19, 23, 28, 52, 73,
　100, 101, 102, 105,
　347
1–4　16, 244
1–25　667
1:1　33, 38, 52, 54,
　56, 57, 57n1, 58, 59,
　64, 73, 75, 78, 120,
　261n5, 269, 320, 346,
　387, 389, 404, 490n1,
　491, 496, 540n2, 541,
　640, 689
1:1–6　26
1:1–11　102
1:1–17　11, 26, 47, 52,
　54, 64
1:1–25　56
1:1–2:23　8, 10, 47,
　52, 56
1:1–4:16　9, 102

1:2　26, 29, 33, 57, 59,
　169n19, 605
1:2–3　83
1:2–6　26, 30, 54, 58, 59
1:2–16　58, 61, 62
1:2–17　29, 52, 53, 54,
　56, 57
1:2–25　52, 56
1:3　15, 29, 30, 46, 58,
　59n3, 133, 207, 317,
　386, 531, 671, 691
1:3–4　59
1:3–5　233n14
1:3–6　59, 60
1:4　59
1:5　15, 29, 46, 58,
　59n3, 386, 531, 691
1:5–6　133, 207, 317,
　671
1:6　15, 29, 30, 33, 38,
　46, 54, 57, 58, 59,
　59n3, 78, 79, 691
1:6–11　26, 54, 58, 60
1:6–16　30

1:7　29
1:7–8　62
1:7–10　60
1:8　29, 60
1:9　29
1:10　29, 62
1:11　29, 59, 60, 60n5,
　62, 169n19, 605
1:11–12　559
1:12　29, 29nb, 30, 60,
　60n5
1:12–15　60
1:12–16　26, 54, 58, 60
1:13　29
1:13–15　60
1:14　29
1:15　29
1:16　26, 29, 30, 31, 38,
　56, 57, 58, 59, 59n3,
　60, 61, 62, 63, 70, 73,
　78, 120, 329, 495
1:16–17　32, 541
1:16–18　404

1:17　26, 33, 38, 54, 56,
　57, 58, 60n5, 61, 64,
　74n11, 78, 559, 689
1:18　32, 56, 59n3, 61,
　63, 64, 64n2, 65, 66,
　67, 70, 73, 75, 78,
　114n13, 126, 276, 321,
　329, 595n3
1:18–19　63
1:18–25　47, 52, 53, 61,
　62, 63, 75n13, 80, 88,
　120, 329
1:18–2:23　60
1:19　61, 63, 64, 65,
　117n1, 118, 151,
　151n11, 152, 183n12,
　462
1:19–20　73
1:20　33, 38, 52, 57,
　57n1, 59n3, 61, 64,
　64n2, 66, 70, 73, 78,
　78n1, 86, 89, 113n11,
　114n13, 119, 126,
　163n9, 204n2, 276,

320, 321, 387, 490n1, 491, 541, 653, 681
1:20–21 63, 66
1:20–24 493
1:21 57n1, 63, 67, 68, 75, 91, 235, 248, 259, 410, 459n3, 473, 475, 488, 611, 614, 625, 641, 645, 663, 665, 669, 683, 689
1:22 19, 20, 21, 23, 25, 66n5, 68, 69, 75, 82, 90, 93, 98, 100, 162
1:22–23 23, 63, 68, 637
1:23 18, 22, 34, 52, 57n1, 66n4, 69, 71, 72n9, 99, 109, 133, 246, 303, 419, 420, 446, 541, 541n5, 640, 669, 690, 692
1:24 61, 66, 73, 89, 97, 222, 495
1:24–25 63, 73
1:25 57n1, 73, 73n10, 74, 74n11, 75, 330, 615
2 34, 44, 52, 76, 92, 94, 95, 119, 236, 362
2–3 16
2:1 38, 57, 64n2, 66n4, 76, 78, 80, 85, 133, 363, 378, 492
2:1–2 77, 78, 317
2:1–11 519
2:1–12 46, 47, 52, 53, 76, 88, 92, 233n14, 294, 389
2:1–23 56
2:2 38, 66n5, 76, 79, 81, 86, 259, 281n12, 376, 486n2, 609, 682, 689
2:2–12 207
2:3 38, 76, 81, 85, 378, 492, 496
2:3–4 77, 81
2:4 56, 68, 76, 81, 82n7, 85, 110, 225, 239, 355n5, 404, 482, 500
2:4–6 22, 76
2:5 82, 87, 131
2:5–6 76, 77, 82, 92
2:6 18, 37, 52, 59, 68, 76, 83, 99, 100, 263, 606
2:7 76, 78, 92, 93n1
2:7–8 76, 77, 84, 85
2:8 81, 84n8, 89n2, 259, 376, 382n12, 486n2
2:8–21 435
2:9 38, 66n4, 74n11
2:9–10 85
2:9–11 76, 77, 85
2:10 238n1, 353

2:11 76, 81, 86, 259, 317, 376, 486n2, 495, 682
2:11–13 61
2:12 66, 76, 77, 86, 86n12, 89, 368, 653
2:12–14 132, 315, 387
2:12–23 85
2:13 52, 61, 64n2, 66, 66n4, 66n5, 74n11, 86, 86n12, 88, 89, 89n1, 96, 97, 106, 117n2, 284n4, 412n5, 455, 653
2:13–15 47, 52, 53, 63, 73, 76, 88, 91, 92, 96
2:13–23 52, 76, 88
2:14 86n12, 97, 368
2:14–15 88, 89
2:15 18, 20, 21, 22, 23, 25, 34, 52, 57n1, 66n5, 69, 74n11, 88, 90, 91n4, 93, 94, 98, 100, 120, 133, 162, 246, 373, 376, 404, 541n5, 640
2:16 78, 84, 84n8, 86, 92, 93n1, 232n7, 238n1, 306, 312, 382n12, 606n6
2:16–18 47, 52, 53, 76, 88, 91, 92, 95, 294, 615
2:17 20, 21, 23, 25, 93, 93n1, 98, 100, 107, 133, 162
2:17–18 23, 92, 93
2:18 18, 22, 52, 94, 95
2:19 52, 61, 64n2, 66, 66n4, 82, 86, 89, 89n1, 96, 653, 681
2:19–20 91, 96
2:19–21 63, 73
2:19–23 47, 52, 53, 76, 88, 96
2:20 66n5, 96, 97, 198n10, 488
2:21 91
2:21–23 91, 96, 97
2:22 66, 86, 86n12, 97n1, 105, 132, 315, 368, 387, 488
2:22–23 118
2:23 18, 20, 21, 22, 23, 24, 25, 52, 72, 87, 96, 98, 99, 100n3, 105, 119, 133, 162, 235n18, 359, 496, 643
2:41 685
3 16, 122
3–4 102
3–7 103, 142
3–25 142
3:1 89n1, 105, 118, 126
3:1–2 104, 107
3:1–6 102, 104, 105
3:1–12 47, 104, 118

3:1–15 291n5
3:1–4:11 8
3:1–4:16 102, 105
3:1–4:25 10, 47, 101, 102, 103
3:1–7:29 10, 47, 101
3:2 37, 38, 39, 43, 44, 66n5, 106, 107, 122, 132, 134, 139, 144, 147, 150, 188, 253, 256, 268, 269, 293, 321, 334, 362, 523, 574, 649, 665
3:3 18, 35, 66n5, 100, 104, 106, 107, 293, 387, 421
3:4 75, 104, 109, 254, 293
3:5 73n10, 93n1, 281n11, 378, 492
3:5–6 104, 109, 119
3:6 67, 110, 117, 248, 645
3:7 104, 110, 111n6, 205, 238n1, 306, 313, 324, 396, 397, 423, 558
3:7–8 109, 401
3:7–9 115
3:7–10 6, 324
3:7–12 44, 102, 104, 110, 291, 559
3:8 104, 106, 113, 117, 156, 218n6, 222, 514, 523, 574n9, 649
3:8–9 113
3:8–10 33, 218, 263, 341, 342, 650
3:9 33, 57, 59, 59n3, 104, 110, 112, 113, 114, 128, 269, 388, 404n5
3:9–10 233n14
3:10 104, 113, 120n3, 156, 218n6, 222, 318, 381, 480, 504, 514
3:10–12 290, 292, 438
3:11 64, 75, 104, 106, 110, 114n13, 121, 232, 276, 290n1, 422n11, 422n12, 496, 649
3:11–12 114
3:12 104, 113, 114, 115, 116, 263, 322, 343, 350, 351, 417, 504, 514, 583, 590, 609, 610
3:13 89n1, 93n1, 105, 117, 284n4
3:13–14 114
3:13–15 102, 118
3:13–17 47, 117, 121n5, 290, 291
3:14 65, 66n5, 73n10, 104, 117, 118, 296n11
3:14–15 117, 118, 121

3:15 23, 25, 65n3, 93n1, 118, 151, 151n11, 154, 162, 183n12
3:16 64, 66n4, 72, 119, 122, 248, 276, 315n1, 589
3:16–17 102, 117, 118, 119, 126, 690
3:16–4:1 321
3:17 34, 42, 57n1, 66n4, 66n5, 73, 119, 121, 122, 123, 186, 219, 246, 303, 315, 316, 329, 373, 376, 402, 404, 415, 417, 418, 418n4, 541, 541n5, 639, 640, 663, 669
4 16, 124, 138
4–10 292
4:1 64, 93n1, 106, 114n13, 120, 124, 126, 126n1, 127, 128, 189, 248, 276, 284n4, 306, 396, 397n1, 589
4:1–2 124, 125, 126
4:1–11 44, 47, 102, 118, 124, 139, 189, 303, 455, 528, 576, 578, 632, 663, 691
4:2 126, 127n2, 190, 190n25, 503, 589
4:3 34, 57n1, 120, 127, 127n3, 128n4, 209, 246, 281n11, 373, 376, 396, 404, 541n5, 640, 662
4:3–4 125, 127, 400
4:4 18, 87, 128, 130, 131, 199, 685
4:5 89n1, 93n1, 126n1, 129
4:5–7 125, 129
4:6 18, 34, 57n1, 87, 89n1, 120, 128n4, 129, 130, 131, 246, 373, 376, 404, 541n5, 636, 640, 662
4:7 18, 87, 129, 131, 236, 387, 396, 459n3, 528n2
4:8 37, 39, 80, 89n1, 126n1, 149, 155n14, 230, 412, 688
4:8–9 129, 411
4:8–10 125, 129, 411
4:9 86, 486n2
4:9–10 81, 682
4:10 18, 87, 89n1, 93n1, 126n1, 130, 131, 198, 205, 387, 411, 411n3, 459n3, 486n2, 609
4:11 66n4, 89n1, 93n1, 124, 125, 126n1, 127n3, 130, 589, 636

4:12 86n12, 101, 124, 132, 290, 291, 315, 368, 387, 426n2, 574n6
4:12–13 132
4:12–16 98
4:12–17 47, 132
4:12–25 101, 102, 124
4:12–15:20 8
4:13 100, 133, 232, 248, 288, 300, 359, 360
4:14 20, 21, 23, 24, 25, 66n5, 100, 108, 162
4:14–16 132, 133, 688
4:14–17 291
4:15 57, 98, 133, 140, 454, 518
4:15–16 18, 22, 72, 233n14, 317
4:16 68, 155, 233
4:17 9, 37, 38, 40, 43, 44, 93n1, 102, 106, 107, 122, 124, 132, 134, 139, 144, 147, 150, 188, 253, 256, 268, 269, 293, 321, 334, 362, 410, 523, 574, 612, 649, 665, 684
4:17–16:20 9, 102
4:18 135, 136, 136n1, 169n19, 265, 265n9, 406, 430, 605, 619
4:18–20 135, 136
4:18–21 354
4:18–22 47, 135, 137, 137n4, 244, 252, 264, 416
4:19 89n1, 114, 135, 136, 140, 305, 354
4:19–25 252n1
4:20 135, 136, 136n2, 243n1, 353, 430, 602
4:21 135, 140, 169n19, 265, 430, 486, 605
4:21–22 135, 136, 382
4:22 135, 136n2, 330, 353, 470, 602, 2434n1
4:23 37, 38, 40, 68, 101, 106, 138, 140, 142, 224, 246, 262, 284, 290, 291, 300, 315, 341, 574, 690
4:23–24 226, 227, 235, 264, 368, 375, 391, 607
4:23–25 38, 47, 138, 139, 261, 454
4:23–5:1 231
4:23–5:2 262
4:23–9:35 138
4:24 139, 140, 205, 219, 232, 245, 248, 260, 261, 387, 424, 451n6, 464, 609n16
4:24–25 140

4:25 136n2, 140, 224, 230, 230n3, 243n1, 290, 317, 378, 454, 491, 492
4:25–5:2 224
5 16, 177
5–7 4, 102, 138, 142, 223, 224, 226, 262, 355, 611
5–9 229, 262, 263
5:1 64n2, 127n3, 140, 224, 230, 230n3, 238n1, 337, 391, 416, 569, 688
5:1–2 141, 142, 143, 148, 149, 372
5:1–16 47, 145
5:1–7:29 10, 47, 101, 103, 141
5:2 66n5, 690
5:3 37, 38, 40, 43, 44, 145, 149, 150, 156, 188, 291, 303, 351, 353, 471, 472
5:3–4 150
5:3–6 147, 148, 149, 152
5:3–9 43
5:3–10 153, 154, 196, 201
5:3–11 146n4, 592
5:3–12 101, 143, 146, 292n6, 404, 533n5, 540, 550n2, 573n1, 609
5:3–16 143
5:3–7:27 138
5:4 145, 150, 156, 233
5:4–5 156
5:4–9 150, 584
5:5 145, 151, 156, 305, 316, 317, 351, 434, 486, 495, 497, 584, 609
5:5–6 281n11
5:6 65n3, 145, 149, 151, 152, 183n12, 187, 188
5:6–7 145n1
5:7 145, 151, 152, 203, 253, 316, 317, 491, 607
5:7–10 148, 152, 156
5:7–12 147
5:8 145, 150, 151, 152, 155, 191, 196, 452, 557
5:9 145, 145n1, 150, 152, 177, 186, 272n2, 281, 429, 495, 636
5:10 37, 38, 40, 43, 44, 65n3, 145, 146, 150, 151, 151n11, 153, 183n12, 351, 576
5:10–12 147, 150, 193, 202, 215, 294, 306,

359, 455, 497, 581, 615
5:10–16 206, 207
5:11 153, 156, 180n3, 359, 574, 607
5:11–12 145, 146, 148, 153, 154, 278, 341, 409, 689n2
5:11–16 148, 153
5:12 23, 42, 153, 183, 218, 220, 283, 362, 515n4, 523, 559, 684
5:13 151, 154, 209
5:13–16 101, 143, 148, 153, 154
5:14 155
5:15 69, 594, 602
5:15–16 155
5:16 42, 162, 164, 183, 186, 191, 218, 276n3, 507n1
5:17 17, 23, 25, 143, 144, 157, 161, 162, 163, 163n9, 166, 211, 212, 222, 281, 281n12, 295n9, 313, 417
5:17–18 161n6
5:17–20 143, 157, 158, 158n2, 160, 161, 162, 191, 212, 220, 256, 355, 461n6, 690
5:17–48 15, 47, 142, 157, 203, 217, 253, 305, 310, 311, 313, 354, 383, 394, 401, 418, 469, 470, 518, 534, 670, 690
5:17–7:12 101, 143
5:18 74, 74n11, 151, 155n14, 157, 161, 161n6, 162n8, 163, 163n10, 166n13, 424, 475, 475n2, 568n2, 585, 689n2
5:18–19 163
5:18–20 23
5:19 37, 38, 40, 43, 157, 161, 163, 218, 222, 434, 535n4, 606
5:19–20 44, 158, 161n6
5:20 37, 38, 39, 40, 65n3, 82, 82n7, 111n6, 147, 151, 151n11, 157, 161n6, 162, 163, 164n11, 166, 166n13, 167, 177, 178, 179, 183, 183n12, 191, 201, 205, 211, 225, 239, 263, 290, 305, 355n5, 435, 527n1, 546, 557, 568n2
5:20–22 152
5:20–6:18 44
5:21 18, 164, 166, 168, 169, 172, 179, 208, 211, 212, 459n3
5:21–22 168, 446, 546

5:21–26 157, 160, 167, 168, 170, 203, 205, 382n12, 447, 449
5:21–32 157, 191
5:21–48 143, 147, 158, 160, 162, 164, 165, 166, 172n25, 177, 178, 179, 191, 212, 224, 383, 395, 469
5:22 114, 164, 166n13, 178, 191, 222, 279, 279n7, 351, 438, 555, 557, 558, 596, 639
5:22–24 206, 444, 444n1, 606, 606n5
5:23 222
5:23–24 169, 170, 189, 190
5:23–26 164
5:24 93n1, 239n3
5:25 74n11, 574n6
5:25–26 170, 451
5:26 74, 74n11, 163n10, 568n2
5:27 18, 164, 165, 166, 179, 383, 459n3
5:27–28 152, 170, 382, 383, 546
5:27–30 157, 160, 168, 170
5:27–32 382n12
5:28 152, 164, 166n13, 170, 179n2, 191, 196, 383, 452, 557
5:29 128n4, 170, 279n7, 360n1, 558, 628
5:29–30 164, 170, 240, 279, 292, 437, 437n1, 438, 440, 555, 574n7
5:29–39 394
5:30 128n4, 170, 279n7, 360n1, 558
5:31 18, 164, 165, 166, 171, 179, 459, 462
5:31–32 157, 160, 164n12, 168, 171, 172n27, 173, 174, 459, 460
5:32 75n12, 164, 164n12, 166n13, 170, 172, 172n25, 178, 459, 462, 466
5:33 18, 157n1, 164, 165, 166, 168, 172, 179, 459n3
5:33–34 172, 383
5:33–37 157, 160, 166, 168, 172, 174n30, 551, 555, 643
5:33–48 157, 172, 191
5:34 42, 164, 165, 166n13, 172, 173, 555, 608
5:34–35 689n2
5:34–36 173, 173n28
5:34–37 164

5:35   38, 79, 151,
  155n14, 378, 492, 524
5:37   126n1, 130, 173,
  191, 350, 383
5:38   18, 164, 165, 166,
  174, 179, 205
5:38–39   174, 383
5:38–42   157, 160, 168,
  174, 615, 636, 641
5:38–48   150, 170, 189,
  203, 205, 294, 449
5:39   126n1, 164, 165,
  166n13, 174, 175,
  175n33, 540
5:39–42   164, 175, 193
5:40   175, 175n33,
  475n3
5:41   175, 175n33, 659
5:42   175, 175n33
5:43   18, 67, 164, 165,
  166, 179, 459n3,
  469n2, 536
5:43–44   176
5:43–47   205
5:43–48   153, 157, 160,
  168, 176, 205
5:44   153, 164, 165,
  166n13, 177, 178,
  193, 540
5:45   42, 65n3, 151,
  151n11, 153n12, 176,
  177, 186, 200, 276n3,
  429, 524
5:45–47   164, 176, 177
5:45–48   212
5:46   154, 177n37, 178,
  183, 209, 252
5:46–47   176, 445
5:47   133, 169n19, 177,
  177n37, 178, 185, 200,
  209, 606, 607
5:48   42, 157, 176, 177,
  179, 180, 186, 191,
  200, 222, 276n3, 441,
  459n3, 469
6   194, 201
6–24   16
6:1   42, 65n3, 151,
  151n11, 179, 179n2,
  180, 180n6, 181, 182,
  183, 186, 191, 200,
  217, 276n3, 281n12,
  557
6:1–2   380
6:1–18   47, 142, 143,
  154, 178, 179, 181,
  184, 185, 190, 191,
  194, 201, 203, 212,
  305, 547
6:2   139, 163n10, 179,
  180, 180n3, 180n4,
  180n5, 180n9, 205,
  206, 222, 528, 553,
  554, 593, 600
6:2–4   152, 179, 181,
  182, 183, 185, 191

6:2–18   179, 180,
  180n6, 181, 183
6:3   64n2, 179, 180,
  180n7, 608
6:4   179, 180, 180n9,
  180n10, 186, 191, 192,
  200, 210, 276n3, 684
6:5   139, 163n10, 179,
  180, 180n3, 180n4,
  180n5, 180n9, 183,
  190n24, 205, 206,
  380, 459n3, 528, 553,
  554, 593
6:5–6   184, 185
6:5–8   181, 185
6:5–15   179, 181, 182,
  184, 191
6:6   180, 180n3, 180n7,
  180n9, 180n10, 186,
  191, 192, 200, 210,
  276n3, 579
6:6–8   281n11
6:7   179, 180, 180n3,
  185n17, 200, 209,
  600, 685
6:7–8   179, 180n4, 184,
  185
6:8   186, 191, 193, 200,
  209, 210, 222, 276n3,
  504
6:9   42, 180, 180n7,
  184, 185, 191, 200,
  209, 210n3, 218, 222,
  276n3, 429, 507n1
6:9–10   181, 184, 185,
  187, 196, 295, 583
6:9–13   11, 142, 180,
  208, 210, 504
6:9–15   181, 184, 185
6:10   38, 40, 42, 43,
  144, 149, 151, 155n14,
  184, 187, 189, 201,
  219, 249, 351, 445,
  463, 584, 631, 632,
  640n3, 684, 689n2,
  691, 692
6:11   184, 188, 193,
  201, 400
6:11–13   181, 184, 188
6:11–15   184
6:12   169, 177, 184,
  188, 189, 203, 205,
  248, 449
6:12–15   203
6:12–8:3   276
6:13   38, 40, 126n1,
  130, 173n29, 184, 188,
  189, 191, 350
6:13–14   639
6:13–15   191, 193
6:14   191, 192, 276n3,
  281n11, 441, 452, 453
6:14–15   169, 181, 184,
  186, 188, 189, 203,
  205, 449, 452
6:15   192, 200, 276n3

6:16   163n10, 179, 180,
  180n3, 180n5, 180n9,
  183, 191, 205, 206,
  254, 380, 528, 553,
  554, 593
6:16–18   181, 182, 185,
  190, 191, 241, 255,
  425
6:17   179, 180, 180n7
6:18   179, 180, 180n9,
  180n10, 186, 191, 192,
  200, 210, 254, 276n3
6:19   151, 155n14, 193,
  194, 194n1, 196
6:19–20   193, 196n5,
  591, 689n2
6:19–21   86, 147, 193,
  194, 195, 196, 203,
  470, 622, 684
6:19–24   193, 195, 196,
  198, 412
6:19–34   47, 143, 178,
  190, 193, 194, 198,
  201, 203, 212, 341,
  342, 352
6:19–7:6   208
6:19–7:12   142, 203,
  208
6:19–7:27   142
6:20   42, 193, 194n2,
  196
6:20–21   194
6:21   152, 196, 452, 470
6:21–24   193
6:22   222, 594
6:22–23   193, 194, 195,
  197, 203
6:22–24   152, 194
6:23   128n4, 197,
  197n6, 222, 479
6:24   193, 194, 195,
  196, 197, 198, 203,
  205, 470, 470n3, 473,
  622
6:25   188, 193, 194,
  194n3, 194n4, 198,
  199, 200, 201, 202,
  276, 400, 488
6:25–26   198
6:25–27   195, 198,
  204n2, 209
6:25–31   194
6:25–33   201
6:25–34   193, 195, 198,
  203
6:26   65, 114, 117n1,
  186, 194, 194n4, 198,
  199, 199n11, 200,
  239, 263, 276n3, 280,
  296n11, 343, 429, 441
6:26–27   194, 198
6:26–30   193, 209, 313
6:27   194n4, 198, 199
6:28   193, 194, 200n14,
  202
6:28–29   194, 200
6:28–30   195, 198, 199

6:29   232n11
6:30   128n4, 194,
  194n4, 198, 199,
  199n11, 200n14, 218,
  232, 244, 373, 400,
  423, 424, 505, 633,
  688, 691n4
6:31   66n5, 193, 194,
  194n3, 198, 200, 201,
  202, 222, 276, 400
6:31–32   194, 200
6:31–34   195, 200
6:32   133, 185, 193,
  210, 276n3, 441, 518
6:32–33   193
6:33   37, 38, 40, 42, 43,
  44, 65n3, 147, 151,
  151n11, 183n12, 193,
  194, 194n2, 200, 202,
  239n3, 471, 684
6:33–34   194, 200
6:34   188, 193, 194,
  194n1, 194n3, 198,
  201, 222, 276
7   213
7:1   204, 205
7:1–2   203, 204n3, 208,
  475n3, 684
7:1–5   203, 204, 206,
  207, 208
7:1–6   47, 143, 203,
  204, 207n9, 208, 212
7:1–11   203
7:1–12   194, 203
7:2   204, 205
7:3   205, 206, 206n7
7:3–4   206, 208, 209
7:3–5   169n19, 203,
  204, 205, 206n7, 438,
  444n1, 606, 606n5
7:4   66n4, 206, 206n7
7:5   93n1, 183, 206,
  206n7, 209, 239n3,
  528, 553, 593
7:6   203, 204, 204n2,
  205, 206, 206n8, 207,
  208, 247, 260, 272,
  306, 340, 352, 382,
  388, 406
7:7   208, 209
7:7–8   208, 209, 209n1,
  210
7:7–11   47, 143, 203,
  208, 210, 212, 504
7:8   209, 209n2, 210,
  581
7:9   129, 210n3, 400
7:9–10   208, 209, 368
7:9–11   209, 210
7:11   42, 128n4, 186,
  200, 208, 209, 210,
  210n3, 212, 222,
  276n3, 313, 601
7:12   47, 143, 144, 162,
  162n8, 203, 205, 208,
  211, 212, 215, 218,
  222, 295n9, 313, 417,

451, 469n2, 534, 536, 610
7:12–14 500n4
7:13 164n11, 215, 215n2, 219, 222, 223
7:13–14 101, 143, 147, 213, 214, 215, 216, 221, 299, 524
7:13–27 47, 143, 212, 213, 214
7:14 215, 215n2, 223, 469, 581
7:15 214, 216, 217, 221, 268, 275, 351, 574n8
7:15–17 283
7:15–20 214, 219
7:15–23 101, 143, 213, 214, 216, 220, 220n14, 525
7:15–27 523
7:16 69, 205, 214, 216, 217, 218, 219, 318, 514
7:16–18 218
7:16–19 219
7:16–20 113, 156, 216, 219, 324, 341, 342, 504, 514, 650
7:17 216, 218, 218n7, 218n9
7:17–18 218, 218n7
7:17–19 214, 218
7:18 216, 218, 218n7, 218n9
7:19 114, 214, 215, 216, 218, 221, 480
7:20 205, 214, 216, 217, 219, 581
7:20–27 574n9
7:21 37, 37n32, 38, 39, 40, 42, 43, 164n11, 186, 219, 276, 276n3, 280, 329, 351, 422, 435, 510, 541n5, 684
7:21–22 35, 218, 387, 491
7:21–23 43, 107, 191, 204, 205, 214, 216, 218, 219, 224, 240, 273n1, 352, 497, 524, 569, 596, 601
7:21–27 509, 573n1, 690
7:22 214, 219, 219n11, 221, 245, 581, 588, 611
7:22–23 147, 214, 351, 541, 557, 640n3
7:23 93n1, 214, 215, 219, 220, 221, 351, 574, 609
7:24 4, 221, 221n17, 222, 223, 276, 296n10, 343n10, 406, 418n3, 445n3, 477n4, 592, 596

7:24–25 221, 222, 581
7:24–27 101, 143, 156, 213, 214, 221, 222, 223n20, 224, 284, 337, 339, 597
7:25 222
7:26 147, 215, 221, 221n17, 222, 223, 296n10, 343n10, 418n3, 445n3, 477n4, 596
7:26–27 106, 155, 221, 222, 691
7:27 142, 215, 581
7:28 9, 134, 142, 224, 224n1, 244, 266, 284, 290, 360, 454, 532, 612
7:28–29 44, 47, 101, 142, 143, 224, 229, 246, 248, 262, 263, 264
7:28–8:1 141, 149, 224
7:29 82n7, 138, 166, 224, 225, 228, 232, 242, 244, 290, 355n5, 508, 689, 690
8 236
8–9 138, 142, 226, 227, 228, 245, 246, 248, 262, 269, 286, 358
8–10 142
8:1 64n2, 136n2, 140, 229n1, 230, 230n2, 230n3, 232, 243n1, 245, 252n1, 261, 262, 290, 317, 418n2, 491
8:1–4 229, 230, 231, 233
8:1–15 236
8:1–17 47, 227, 228, 229, 238, 247, 253
8:1–22 47, 228
8:1–9:34 138, 224
8:1–10:4 10, 47, 227
8:1–10:42 101
8:1–11:1 10, 47, 226
8:2 35, 66n4, 66n5, 80, 127n3, 149, 230, 236, 259, 261, 291, 376, 387, 486n2, 619, 681, 682
8:2–3 231n5
8:2–4 230, 259
8:2–25 491
8:2–9:34 227
8:3 219, 258, 491, 495, 602
8:3–4 70, 72, 231
8:4 89n1, 229, 231, 261, 315, 406, 490
8:5 57, 64n2, 127n3, 133, 149, 229n1, 245, 248, 418n2, 671
8:5–6 232

8:5–13 229, 232, 234n16, 389, 394, 424, 691
8:6 35, 66n5, 232, 248, 387, 389, 451n6, 681
8:7 89n1, 139
8:7–9 232
8:8 35, 70, 231, 232, 235, 387, 389, 671, 681
8:8–9 166, 262
8:9 101, 138, 142, 224, 225, 226, 228, 229, 242, 246, 248, 264, 508, 689
8:9–13 38
8:10 15, 70, 72, 77, 81, 136n2, 163n10, 207, 237, 252n1, 389, 423
8:10–11 232
8:10–12 33, 46, 133, 205, 229, 234, 317, 395, 481, 522, 671
8:11 37, 40, 43, 57, 58, 59, 80, 187, 232, 253, 268, 269, 293, 370, 389, 486, 524, 533n5, 596, 601, 625
8:11–12 254, 263, 267, 273n1, 317, 351, 524, 573n1
8:12 38, 40, 153n12, 233, 269, 350, 351, 555, 557n10, 593, 602, 610
8:13 219, 232n7, 234, 261, 671
8:14 136n1, 229n1, 232n9, 245, 337
8:14–15 229, 234, 261
8:14–17 229, 233
8:15 258, 260, 491
8:16 64n2, 139, 140, 219, 226, 232, 234, 245, 261, 375, 391, 418n2, 464, 609n16
8:16–17 229, 234, 253
8:17 18, 20, 21, 22, 23, 24, 25, 66n5, 75, 98, 108, 162, 229, 235, 236, 249, 259, 488
8:18 70, 72, 140, 230n3, 231, 238, 240, 243, 245, 290
8:18–20 238, 240
8:18–22 48, 137, 227, 228, 238, 240, 241, 247, 263
8:19 36, 82n7, 127n3, 136, 136n2, 149, 239, 243n1, 252n1, 258n1, 326, 355n5, 429, 469, 531, 643n1
8:19–20 238
8:19–22 243

8:20 36, 57n1, 89n1, 99, 136, 199, 239, 248, 306, 497
8:21 35, 240, 243n1, 523, 681
8:21–22 137, 238, 239, 464
8:22 89n1, 136, 136n2, 330, 470
8:22–23 252n1, 495
8:23 136n2, 243, 243n1, 243n2, 245
8:23–27 73, 137, 242, 243, 245, 371, 372, 373, 376
8:23–9:8 48, 227, 238, 241, 242, 247
8:23–9:17 48, 241
8:24 66n4, 75, 573n5, 596
8:24–25 244
8:25 35, 66n5, 67, 127n3, 245, 259, 373, 387, 681
8:25–26 243, 419n5
8:26 89n1, 93n1, 200, 232, 241, 244, 357, 371, 373, 400, 423, 424, 505, 633, 688, 691n4
8:27 66n5, 244, 371, 373, 538
8:28 64n2, 140, 245, 245n3, 249, 261, 418n2
8:28–29 246
8:28–32 245
8:28–34 139, 242, 243, 245, 247, 261, 391, 455, 609n16
8:29 34, 57n1, 66n4, 66n5, 139, 246n5, 373, 376, 404, 451n6, 541n5
8:30–32 246
8:31 66n5, 128n4, 219, 245
8:32 66n4, 207, 639
8:33 245, 261
8:33–34 245, 247
8:34 66n4, 238n1, 241, 245n3, 306, 359
9:1 232, 245, 247, 288, 300, 360
9:1–3 248
9:1–6 401
9:1–8 44, 242, 243, 245, 247, 249n6, 251, 253, 507
9:2 66n4, 67, 190, 232, 232n9, 247, 248, 250, 259, 261, 372, 464
9:3 66n4, 82n7, 241, 247, 248, 249, 263, 290, 306, 322, 355n5, 359, 396, 507, 639

9:4　152, 238n1, 250, 342, 382n12, 429
9:4–5　247, 248
9:4–6　248
9:5　67, 190
9:6　36, 57n1, 67, 89n1, 93n1, 101, 138, 151, 155n14, 166, 190, 219, 225, 228, 229, 239, 242, 246, 259, 260, 262, 269, 299, 303, 323, 369, 420, 425, 508, 615
9:6–7　247
9:6–8　38, 142, 224, 226, 232, 264, 397, 689
9:7　249
9:7–8　249
9:8　140, 156, 225, 230n3, 238n1, 244, 247, 250, 290, 508
9:9　12, 89n1, 135, 136, 136n2, 141, 243n1, 245, 251, 252, 252n1, 264, 265, 353, 470, 495
9:9–11　430
9:9–12　68
9:9–13　12, 44, 251, 254, 479
9:9–17　48, 227, 241, 247, 251, 263
9:10　64n2, 66n4, 245, 251, 296, 429, 624
9:10–11　177n37, 252, 509
9:10–13　166, 204, 251, 252, 445, 510, 524
9:11　36, 111n6, 238n1, 252, 290, 296, 306, 313, 326, 359, 396, 429, 527n1, 531
9:12　306
9:12–13　152, 251, 253, 303, 500
9:13　18, 65n3, 85n9, 106, 151n11, 152, 248, 252, 253n4, 256, 281n11, 281n12, 309, 310, 381, 534, 546, 556, 559, 607, 656
9:14　66n5, 89n1, 93n1, 102, 111n6, 127n3, 190, 245, 256, 291, 322, 365
9:14–15　190, 190n25, 254
9:14–17　6, 251, 254, 255
9:15　37, 93n1, 180n3, 233, 254, 255, 426, 522, 524, 557n10, 581, 594, 620
9:15–17　337, 339
9:16　23, 255

9:16–17　254, 255, 255n8, 354
9:17　69, 255
9:18　64n2, 66n4, 66n5, 80, 245, 258, 259, 376, 464n17, 486n2, 643n1, 682
9:18–19　257, 258
9:18–26　227, 260, 291, 424
9:18–34　227, 257, 258, 261
9:18–10:4　48, 257
9:19　136n2, 259
9:20　66n4, 127n3, 175, 259, 264, 547
9:20–21　375
9:20–22　227, 257, 258, 259
9:21　259
9:21–22　67
9:22　219, 232, 238n1, 248, 250, 259, 260, 261, 372, 388
9:23　238n1, 250
9:23–24　259
9:23–25　261
9:23–26　257, 258
9:24　86n12, 259, 315, 596
9:24–25　364
9:25–26　260
9:26　261
9:27　33, 38, 57, 57n1, 66n5, 136n2, 152, 154, 244n2, 245, 252n1, 320, 387, 490n1, 491, 492, 496
9:27–28　260, 291, 500, 540n2
9:27–31　257, 260, 490, 491
9:28　89n1, 127n3, 244n2, 349, 360, 387, 491, 681
9:29　66n5, 93n1, 232, 234, 388
9:29–30　491
9:29–31　261
9:30　66n5, 231, 315, 406, 490
9:31　260
9:32　64n2, 66n4, 245, 261, 291, 387, 418n2, 464
9:32–33　291
9:32–34　139, 140, 231, 245, 257, 260, 261, 319, 609n16
9:33　64n2, 66n5, 224, 230n3, 244, 290, 418n2, 538
9:33–34　219
9:34　44, 111n6, 139, 248, 249, 263, 265, 278, 290, 294, 306, 313, 320, 322, 323,

330, 359, 360, 362n1, 396, 401, 455, 507, 527n1
9:35　38, 40, 101, 106, 138, 139, 142, 224, 226, 235, 245, 262, 264, 269, 284, 300, 315, 341, 375, 391, 454, 574, 690
9:35–36　84, 368, 389
9:35–38　227, 257, 261, 262, 263, 266
9:35–10:4　227, 257, 262
9:35–10:5　266
9:36　37, 84, 140, 152, 217, 230n3, 236, 238n1, 246, 260, 262, 263, 264, 267, 268, 346, 369, 387, 392, 440, 450, 476, 491, 561, 608n14, 629, 641, 656
9:37　89n1, 93n1, 350, 422n11, 478
9:37–38　216, 263, 264
9:38　263, 478
9:41–42　507
10　16, 226, 262, 263, 267, 277, 355, 611
10–11　16
10:1　101, 138, 139, 166, 219, 220, 225, 229, 235, 246, 264, 266, 268, 284, 327, 370, 373, 484, 487, 508, 647, 689
10:1–4　252, 257, 261, 262, 264, 548
10:1–8　519n17
10:2　64, 136, 136n1, 264, 265n9, 406, 486, 605, 619
10:2–4　12, 264, 268
10:2–5　266
10:3　12, 177n37, 252, 265, 445
10:3–4　265
10:4　265, 426n2, 574n6, 619, 621
10:5　66n5, 207, 264, 269, 271, 454, 484, 518
10:5–6　133, 236, 267, 267n3, 268, 389, 689, 2247
10:5–8　48, 266, 267, 268
10:5–10　266
10:5–16　266n1
10:5–42　137, 257, 264, 268
10:5–11:1　10, 48, 266
10:6　139, 217, 220, 268n1, 387, 440, 476, 608n14

10:7　37, 38, 40, 43, 44, 66n5, 106, 107, 139, 268, 269, 321, 334, 373, 408, 523, 574
10:7–8　138, 266, 425
10:8　139, 140, 219, 220, 231, 231n5, 245, 246, 260n4, 268, 269, 270, 271, 291, 424, 425
10:9–10　271
10:9–15　48, 267, 271
10:10　175, 478
10:10–11　523
10:11　74n11, 217, 264, 271
10:11–13　266, 271, 272
10:11–14　436
10:12–4　271
10:13　153, 281, 422n11, 523
10:13–15　247, 273
10:13–17　205
10:14　222, 264, 276, 418n3, 445n3
10:14–15　266, 272
10:14–39　306, 359
10:14–42　263
10:15　163n10, 219n11, 271, 300, 300n3
10:16　66n4, 207, 217, 218, 222, 268, 275, 440, 592, 596, 608n14
10:16–17　249
10:16–18　273
10:16–20　273, 274, 275, 692
10:16–23　215, 273, 274, 275
10:16–25　341
10:16–33　255, 558
10:16–39　48, 202, 206, 266, 267, 273, 294, 409, 615
10:16–42　44, 150, 153, 576
10:17　139, 169n17, 217, 275, 294, 426n2, 574n6, 639
10:17–18　275, 529n6
10:17–22　540
10:17–23　574
10:17–25　266n1
10:17–42　689n2
10:18　38, 153, 231, 247, 264, 267, 268, 275, 317, 335, 518, 574, 607, 671
10:18–19　609
10:19　180n3, 199, 426n2, 574n6, 588
10:19–20　273, 276
10:20　64, 248, 276, 276n3, 279
10:21　137, 273, 276, 280, 330, 410, 426n2, 483, 574n6, 605

10:21–22 276
10:21–23 273, 274, 276
10:22 154, 156, 259, 264, 267, 279, 280, 473, 574, 597, 607
10:22–23 273, 575
10:23 36, 57n1, 74, 74n11, 163n10, 180n3, 276, 277, 277n4, 282, 413, 568n2, 569, 573n1, 581, 583, 689, 691
10:24–25 35, 36, 264, 273, 274, 278, 335, 387, 483, 491
10:24–33 247, 273, 274, 278, 576
10:25 73, 126n1, 128n4, 154, 261, 278n6, 320, 322, 323, 360, 362n1, 477, 574, 591, 607
10:26 267, 278, 280
10:26–27 273, 274, 278
10:26–33 278
10:26–42 266n1
10:27 106, 139, 278
10:28 267, 278, 279, 280, 410, 440, 483, 555, 558, 574
10:28–31 278
10:28–33 273, 274, 278, 529n6
10:29 65, 117n1, 276n3, 279, 296n11
10:29–30 280n10
10:29–31 279
10:31 199, 278, 279, 280n10, 313
10:32 42, 280, 280n10, 329, 611
10:32–33 219, 219n10, 264, 276n3, 280, 303, 351, 574, 574n9, 644
10:33 42, 276n3, 279, 280, 412
10:34 151, 153, 155n14, 271, 272, 280
10:34–35 281n12
10:34–36 274, 280
10:34–37 137
10:34–39 240, 273, 274, 276, 280, 318, 329, 540
10:35 280n11
10:35–36 18, 276, 280
10:35–37 330
10:37 197, 240, 281n11
10:37–38 272n1, 523
10:37–39 274, 281, 283
10:38 114, 136, 136n2, 243n1, 255, 410, 411, 412, 426, 435, 482, 483, 574, 659
10:38–39 485, 537, 663, 665, 666, 683

10:39 153, 264, 284, 412, 487
10:39–42 611
10:40 73, 264, 303, 514, 606, 609
10:40–41 437
10:40–42 266, 271, 283, 295, 436, 603, 606
10:40–11:1 48, 267, 283
10:41 65n3, 151n11, 154n13, 217, 220, 283, 351, 609
10:41–42 154, 182, 183, 351, 475, 559
10:42 163n10, 283n1, 284, 303, 306, 437, 465, 501, 568n2, 606, 609
11 16, 284, 286, 306, 309
11–12 16, 286, 307, 330, 334, 342, 358
11–13 142, 354
11:1 9, 106, 134, 139, 142, 224n1, 226, 264, 266, 284, 300, 322, 335, 360, 454, 484, 612, 690
11:1–6 335, 345, 411
11:1–16 286
11:1–20 615
11:2 37, 56, 289, 297, 365, 404
11:2–3 32, 289, 290
11:2–6 235, 288, 289, 290, 292
11:2–14 102
11:2–19 48, 102, 286, 288, 289, 306
11:2–30 48, 288
11:2–12:50 10, 48, 285, 286, 307
11:2–13:52 48, 285
11:2–13:53 10
11:3 422n12, 496
11:4 85n9
11:4–5 219, 291
11:4–6 289, 290, 291
11:5 149, 150, 151, 231, 231n5, 261n5, 289, 291, 322, 500, 619
11:6 146n4, 171n21, 290, 292, 360n1, 381, 437n1, 592, 628
11:7 64n2, 106, 140, 230n3, 293n7
11:7–8 293
11:7–9 109, 293, 293n7
11:7–10 289, 292
11:7–15 288, 289, 292, 508
11:7–18 559
11:7–19 292
11:7–24 319

11:8 38, 66n4, 109, 293n7
11:9 283, 293, 293n7, 295, 297, 364
11:9–10 293n7
11:10 18, 66n4, 87, 131, 289, 295, 403
11:10–14 420
11:11 37, 40, 122, 163n10, 293, 300, 365, 434, 437, 606
11:11–12 44
11:11–13 102, 340, 354
11:11–15 289, 292, 293
11:12 4, 37, 40, 43, 44, 74n11, 281, 286, 293, 294, 306, 359
11:13 74n11, 162n8, 295
11:14 75, 109, 128n4, 290n1, 295, 296, 417, 421, 422, 422n12, 669n2
11:14–15 295
11:15 295, 297, 338, 347, 350, 351, 355, 418n3, 463n13
11:16 222n18, 223, 343n10, 424, 435, 477n4, 478, 479n8, 558, 586, 636
11:16–19 99, 288, 289, 292, 296, 299, 326, 337, 339
11:16–24 44, 286, 306, 423
11:17 259, 296, 297
11:17–19 296n11
11:18 109, 245, 254, 296
11:18–19 99, 132, 133, 296, 362, 363
11:18–24 286
11:19 36, 57n1, 66n4, 119, 151n11, 177n37, 248, 252, 289, 292, 296, 297, 305, 479, 509
11:19–24 359
11:20 93n1, 106, 298, 299
11:20–21 649
11:20–22 288, 299
11:20–24 48, 249, 273n1, 286, 288, 298, 299, 306, 360, 455
11:21 106, 298, 300, 438, 550n1, 553
11:21–22 299
11:21–23 322
11:21–24 298, 327
11:22 219n11, 298, 300, 351, 387, 640n2
11:22–24 271, 573n1
11:23 74n11, 133, 232, 279n8, 298, 300, 300n2, 301, 686

11:23–24 288, 299, 300
11:24 219n11, 272n3, 298, 300, 300n3, 351, 640n2
11:25 42, 151, 155n14, 185, 187, 302, 327, 465, 497, 501, 606n6, 689n2
11:25–26 372
11:25–27 87, 276n3, 288, 302, 303, 305, 318, 339, 340, 361, 376, 402, 404, 406, 525, 541n5
11:25–30 48, 152, 286, 288, 302, 306, 625
11:26 303, 440n4
11:27 35, 57n1, 73, 219, 219n10, 303, 304, 306, 329, 340, 351, 373, 404, 524, 562, 578, 669, 689
11:28 304, 561
11:28–29 87
11:28–30 288, 302, 304, 305, 340, 361
11:29 99, 150, 151, 152, 154, 304, 305, 316, 317, 435, 452, 495, 540
11:29–30 311
11:30 304, 305, 546
12 16, 286, 292, 308n1, 323, 324, 339, 394
12:1 284, 302n1, 307, 338
12:1–2 308, 309
12:1–4 541
12:1–8 48, 204, 286, 307, 308, 308n1, 309
12:1–12 309n3
12:1–14 44, 319, 330, 534
12:1–19 276
12:1–21 48, 306, 307
12:1–45 394
12:1–52 332
12:2 66n4, 111n6, 238n1, 249, 286, 306, 322, 359, 396, 401, 527, 527n1
12:2–14 459
12:3 38, 261, 309, 309n2, 309n4, 310, 327, 331, 496, 501, 515
12:3–4 308, 309
12:3–5 508
12:3–8 308, 309
12:4 311, 400, 527
12:5 309, 309n4, 501
12:5–6 308, 309, 310
12:6 79, 232n11, 309, 310, 327, 331, 429, 502, 507, 541, 667
12:7 18, 152, 253, 281n11, 300n2, 310,

313, 381, 500, 534, 546, 556, 559, 607
12:7–8 308, 309, 310
12:8 35, 36, 57n1, 309, 310, 311, 331, 387, 491, 507, 541
12:9 139
12:9–10 312
12:9–14 48, 286, 307, 312, 314
12:10 66n4, 66n5, 139, 249, 286, 306, 312, 322, 359, 396, 527, 639
12:11 210n3, 382, 508, 592
12:11–12 268, 312, 313, 440
12:12 199, 280
12:13 89n1, 93n1, 322
12:13–14 312, 313
12:14 111n6, 249, 286, 294, 310, 312, 331, 335, 359, 394, 396, 400, 401, 455, 459, 483, 516, 527, 527n1, 615, 617, 646, 646n1
12:14–21 665
12:15 86n12, 132, 136n2, 139, 230n3, 252n1, 317, 368, 387, 454
12:15–16 315
12:15–21 48, 231, 261, 286, 307, 315, 317, 361, 578
12:16 231, 261, 406
12:17 20, 21, 23, 25, 66n5, 108, 162
12:17–18 316
12:17–21 24, 286, 315, 316, 331, 690
12:18 37, 64, 66n4, 114n13, 119, 120, 123, 232n7, 276, 303, 315n1, 316, 321, 322, 373, 518, 589
12:18–19 503
12:18–21 18, 22, 72, 108, 123, 151, 488, 497, 540
12:19 99, 345, 429, 430
12:19–21 316
12:20 74, 74n11, 119, 316n5, 317
12:21 316n6, 518
12:22 93n1, 139, 140, 245, 261, 291, 318, 319, 322, 387, 464, 500
12:22–23 261n5, 319, 320
12:22–24 231
12:22–29 264, 327, 609n16
12:22–32 44, 139

12:22–37 48, 261, 286, 318, 319
12:22–50 48, 306, 318
12:23 33, 38, 57, 57n1, 140, 230n3, 244, 318, 320, 323, 387, 490n1, 491, 496
12:24 111n6, 126n1, 140, 245, 248, 249, 260, 261, 265, 278n6, 285, 286, 306, 313, 317, 318, 319, 320, 322, 323, 326, 360, 396, 401, 455, 459, 507, 527n1, 639
12:24–29 219
12:24–32 324, 330
12:24–45 359
12:25 37, 40, 248, 321, 324, 429
12:25–26 321
12:25–27 319, 320
12:25–28 318
12:25–37 318, 320
12:26 37, 40, 126n1, 128n4, 508
12:26–28 321n4
12:27 126n1, 128n4, 245, 278n6, 321, 557n10
12:27–28 140
12:28 37, 38, 40, 42, 43, 64, 107, 114n13, 119, 120, 128, 128n4, 245, 246, 248, 276, 294, 295, 321, 321n4, 323, 334, 362n1, 389, 397, 438n3, 473, 507, 523, 589
12:28–29 130, 235, 319, 322
12:28–30 319, 321
12:29 93n1, 239n3, 321, 323, 337, 339, 345, 591, 646
12:29–30 318
12:30–37 319
12:31 67, 248, 323
12:31–32 190, 276, 285, 317, 318, 322, 323, 382n12
12:31–37 319, 322
12:32 36, 57n1, 155n14, 163, 273n1, 323, 351, 622, 643
12:33 113, 114, 156, 218n6, 218n9, 324, 337, 339, 341, 342, 514
12:33–37 318, 324, 574n9
12:34 112, 152, 342, 452, 557, 558
12:34–35 324
12:34–37 173
12:35 354
12:36 232n11, 324

12:37 65n3, 151n11, 324
12:38 36, 66n5, 82, 82n7, 93n1, 111n6, 127, 239, 249, 286, 318, 324, 325, 326, 355n5, 378, 396, 401, 459, 469, 507, 527n1, 531, 546, 639
12:38–39 361
12:38–40 255, 396, 483, 613, 676
12:38–42 44, 325
12:38–45 48, 286, 318, 325
12:39 296, 325, 326, 347, 382n12, 424, 558, 578, 582n1, 586
12:39–40 397, 615
12:39–41 318, 325, 326
12:39–42 423
12:39–45 318, 325, 326
12:40 18, 36, 57n1, 328, 410, 426, 600, 629, 681, 683
12:40–41 326, 397
12:41 66n4, 106, 115, 309, 327, 351, 541, 558, 649
12:41–42 273n1, 286, 296, 309, 310n6, 325, 331, 347, 586
12:42 66n4, 79, 80, 281n12, 296, 309, 318, 325, 327, 558
12:43 65, 126, 180n3, 296n11
12:43–45 235, 246, 318, 325, 327, 337, 339, 609n16
12:44 89n1, 93n1
12:45 93n1, 296, 325, 424, 558, 586, 656
12:46 64n2, 66n4, 74, 140, 230n3, 331, 337
12:46–47 169n19, 318, 329, 605
12:46–50 48, 61, 137, 186, 240, 274, 276, 286, 318, 329, 331, 335, 360, 361, 464, 624
12:47 66n4, 329, 331
12:48 329, 330
12:48–50 169n19, 318, 329, 330, 606
12:49 66n4, 329
12:49–50 682
12:50 42, 75, 206, 219, 222, 276n3, 329, 444n1, 548n5
13 10, 11, 38, 44, 286, 333, 334, 334n4, 339, 353, 354, 357, 375, 543, 611
13–14 16, 394

13:1 105, 337, 349, 360, 429, 569
13:1–2 149, 332, 335, 337, 350
13:1–9 332, 333
13:1–23 342
13:1–33 335
13:1–35 48, 335
13:1–52 10, 285, 355, 394
13:2 230n3, 231, 317, 491
13:2–35 346
13:3 66n4, 66n5, 284n4, 337, 338
13:3–9 335, 337
13:3–33 332, 349
13:3–52 287, 332
13:3–53 335
13:4 361, 422n11
13:4–7 338
13:4–8 338
13:5 222, 602
13:5–6 338
13:6 64n2
13:7 344
13:8 113, 156, 218n6, 338, 353, 422n11, 514
13:8–9 338
13:9 295, 297, 337, 338, 347, 350, 351, 355, 418n3, 463n13
13:10 127n3, 335, 338, 354, 355, 434
13:10–12 339
13:10–13 205, 350
13:10–17 285, 303, 332, 333, 335, 338, 404, 406
13:10–23 332, 335, 338, 381, 382
13:11 37, 38, 40, 339n5, 347, 353, 355, 361
13:11–12 341, 346
13:11–15 340
13:12 339n5, 602
13:13 338, 339, 347
13:13–15 24, 339, 341, 382, 418n3
13:14 21, 22, 23, 25, 108, 341n8, 568n2
13:14–15 18, 339, 339n6, 346, 559
13:15 68, 152, 339n6, 342, 452
13:16 146n4, 592
13:16–17 340
13:17 65, 65n3, 151n11, 163n10, 283, 293, 296n11
13:18 338
13:18–22 341
13:18–23 333, 335, 337, 338, 340, 341, 360, 504, 594

13:19 38, 40, 64n2, 106, 126n1, 130, 139, 152, 173n29, 222, 269, 285, 286, 334, 341n8, 343, 344, 347, 351, 361, 445n3, 452, 574
13:19–21 44
13:19–22 287, 423
13:19–23 286, 335, 337, 341, 408, 524
13:20 222, 353
13:20–21 597
13:20–22 155
13:20–23 523, 574n9
13:21 64n2, 150, 153, 171n21, 215, 276, 292, 342, 360n1, 437n1, 574, 574n6, 574n7, 628
13:22 155n14, 222, 323, 342, 344, 353, 470, 470n3
13:23 113, 156, 222, 287, 335, 341, 341n8, 342, 345, 353, 422n11, 514, 598
13:24 37, 38, 40, 43, 66n5, 222n18, 296n10, 338, 344, 350, 354, 450, 477n4, 522, 595
13:24–26 335, 343
13:24–30 219, 332, 335, 343, 349, 353, 381n11
13:24–33 333, 342
13:25 286, 341, 596
13:25–26 523
13:26 93n1, 113, 156, 218n6, 514
13:27 127n3, 278, 477, 591
13:27–30 335, 343
13:28 89n1, 206, 286, 341
13:28–30 322
13:30 74n11, 114, 163, 179n2, 239n3, 246, 263, 287, 335, 382
13:31 37, 38, 39, 40, 66n5, 222n18, 296n10, 343n10, 354, 425, 450, 477n4, 522, 595
13:31–32 335, 344, 473n4
13:31–33 39, 332, 349, 352, 353, 355, 585
13:32 180n3, 199, 344n12, 422n11, 437
13:33 37, 38, 40, 74, 74n11, 222n18, 296n10, 335, 343n10, 344, 354, 400, 450, 477n4, 522, 595
13:33–36 338
13:34 230n3, 690

13:34–35 332, 333, 335, 346
13:34–36 543
13:34–43 332
13:35 18, 20, 21, 22, 23, 24, 25, 66n5, 98, 162, 346, 348
13:36 66n5, 93n1, 127n3, 230n3, 337, 350, 354, 355, 360, 424, 429, 448
13:36–39 350
13:36–43 204, 219, 332, 333, 335, 342, 343, 344, 349, 350, 353, 573n1
13:36–52 48, 332, 349
13:36–53 340, 346
13:37 36, 57n1, 351
13:37–39 354
13:37–42 684
13:37–43 187, 333, 350, 381n11, 504, 594, 692
13:38 38, 40, 126n1, 130, 153n12, 155n14, 156, 173n29, 233, 318, 352, 524, 557n10, 578
13:38–39 44, 351
13:38–40 650
13:38–43 43
13:39 126n1, 130, 163, 206, 263, 286–87, 323, 334, 341, 417, 480, 514
13:39–40 155n14, 569, 690
13:39–43 287, 347
13:40 163, 218, 323, 600, 610
13:40–32 569
13:40–41 412, 413
13:40–42 287, 350, 524, 583
13:40–43 188, 335, 350, 533n5, 584
13:41 36, 38, 40, 57n1, 130, 171n21, 217, 220, 292, 351, 422, 437n1, 438, 541, 557, 574, 608, 608n10, 636
13:41–42 351, 523, 525, 581, 590
13:41–43 219n10, 273n1, 351, 497, 574n9, 640n3
13:42 114, 218, 233, 593, 602, 609
13:43 38, 40, 65n3, 93n1, 151n11, 260, 276n3, 295, 297, 334, 335, 338, 350, 351, 353, 354, 355, 417, 463n13, 519n17, 592, 609, 684
13:43–45 38
13:43–46 287

13:44 37, 40, 196, 222n18, 296n10, 343n10, 349, 352, 353, 354, 477n4, 522, 595, 601
13:44–46 332, 349, 353n3, 355, 470, 585
13:44–48 333
13:45 37, 40, 168n16, 222n18, 296n10, 343n10, 352, 354, 450, 477n4, 522, 595
13:45–46 152, 207, 349, 352
13:47 37, 38, 40, 43, 168n16, 222n18, 296n10, 343n10, 354, 430, 450, 477n4, 595, 608n12
13:47–48 353
13:47–50 136, 204, 219, 332, 349, 353, 354n4, 573n1
13:48 23, 218n9, 524
13:48–49 287
13:48–50 583
13:49 65n3, 130, 151n11, 155n14, 163, 334, 351, 352, 569, 601, 608, 609, 611, 690
13:49–50 287, 333, 335, 353, 354, 523, 594
13:50 114, 218, 233, 351, 593, 602, 609, 610
13:51 89n1, 332, 382, 394, 421
13:51–52 205, 285, 287, 332, 333, 347, 349, 354, 355n6, 400
13:52 37, 38, 40, 82n7, 196, 222n18, 225, 239, 278, 296n10, 332, 343n10, 354, 477, 477n4, 522, 591, 595, 626
13:53 9, 134, 142, 224n1, 266, 284, 338, 359, 360, 430, 454, 612
13:53–58 44, 48, 335, 357, 359, 361, 375
13:53–14:12 362
13:53–14:13 132
13:53–14:36 394
13:53–17:27 10, 48, 356, 357, 357n1, 358, 359, 360, 425
13:53–19:2 10, 48, 356
13:54 139, 224, 296, 359, 361, 363, 431, 496, 532
13:54–56 359, 360
13:54–58 105, 358, 359, 360, 361, 391

13:55 57n1, 61, 74, 169n19, 221, 361, 605, 619, 671
13:55–56 74, 329, 360
13:56 74, 330, 361
13:57 37, 171n21, 292, 320n1, 359, 361, 364, 381, 394, 437n1, 496, 628
13:57–58 359, 360
13:58 423
14 375, 376
14–17 362n2
14–18 142
14:1 302n1, 365
14:1–2 362, 363
14:1–12 44, 48, 102, 132, 291n5, 294, 296, 357, 358, 362, 362n2, 365, 375
14:1–13 615
14:2 75, 134, 232n7, 364, 403
14:3 365, 606, 646
14:3–5 363, 364
14:3–6 382n12
14:3–12 362, 363, 364
14:4 459, 495, 527
14:5 230n3, 293, 361, 364n5, 495, 508
14:5–21:46 364n5
14:6–8 364
14:6–11 363, 364
14:7 173, 643
14:8 89n1, 364
14:9 38, 173, 362, 365, 495, 643
14:9–11 364
14:10 382n12, 394
14:11 364
14:12 127n3, 363, 365, 366, 394
14:12–13 410
14:13 81, 86n12, 132, 136n2, 231, 243n1, 252n1, 315, 365, 371, 372, 387, 390, 491, 631
14:13–14 367, 368, 375, 390
14:13–15 230n3, 691n4
14:13–21 48, 357, 358, 367, 367n1, 369, 390, 392, 394, 400
14:13–33 376
14:14 84, 139, 140, 240, 262, 369, 375, 390, 391, 392, 450, 454, 491, 561, 619
14:14–12 607
14:14–21 389
14:15 64n2, 66n5, 127n3, 357, 368, 372, 376, 387
14:15–16 367, 394
14:15–17 390n1
14:15–18 367, 368, 390

14:15–21   367, 375
14:16   390, 609
14:16–17   368, 495
14:16–21   424, 425
14:17   89n1, 320n1,
   376, 390, 400, 569
14:17–20   367
14:18   390
14:18–19   390n2
14:19   230n3, 369, 390,
   400, 625
14:19–20   242, 390
14:19–21   367, 368
14:20   23, 264, 369, 390
14:20–21   390
14:21   367, 369, 390,
   435
14:22   74, 74n11, 375,
   602
14:22–23   230n3, 371,
   372
14:22–33   48, 242, 357,
   358, 371, 371n1, 375
14:23   64n2, 149, 230,
   231, 368, 391, 631,
   688
14:24   244, 372n2, 374,
   451n6
14:24–25   371
14:24–27   371, 372
14:26   66n5, 238n1
14:26–27   371, 419n5,
   424
14:26–31   425
14:27   66n5, 259
14:28   35, 128n4,
   136n1, 387, 449, 477,
   491, 681
14:28–29   265n9
14:28–30   376
14:28–31   371, 373,
   424, 629
14:29   136n1, 374
14:30   35, 66n5, 244,
   249, 259, 374, 387,
   425, 681
14:31   89n1, 200, 232,
   244, 357, 371, 400,
   423, 425, 505, 569,
   602, 633, 687, 688,
   691n4
14:31–33   376
14:32   64n2
14:32–33   371, 373
14:33   34, 57n1, 66n5,
   81, 246, 259, 371, 376,
   388, 404, 425, 486n2,
   682
14:34   375
14:34–36   48, 357, 358,
   375, 391
14:35   464
14:35–36   375
14:36   259, 547
15   393, 394
15–28   16

15:1   66n5, 81, 82,
   82n7, 89n1, 93n1,
   111n6, 127n3, 355n5,
   394, 396, 459, 492,
   527n1, 546
15:1–2   254, 377, 378,
   401
15:1–9   166, 330, 377,
   378, 394
15:1–12   507
15:1–14   391, 400, 641
15:1–20   44, 48, 111,
   152, 357, 358, 377,
   377n1, 383, 387, 393,
   394, 534, 546
15:2   82n7, 180n3, 252,
   377, 383, 394, 400,
   401, 410, 527n1
15:3   305, 310, 380,
   384, 508
15:3–6   377, 379, 383
15:3–7   339
15:3–9   305, 377, 379,
   546
15:3–20   305
15:4   18, 21, 69, 166,
   239, 379, 380n8, 384
15:4–5   380
15:4–6   240, 274, 555
15:5   379, 380, 384, 554
15:6   305, 380, 384,
   554, 568n2
15:7   21, 66n5, 69, 108,
   183, 206, 313, 528,
   553, 593
15:7–8   99, 554
15:7–9   377, 380, 554,
   557, 559
15:8   68, 152, 342,
   346n15, 452
15:8–9   18
15:9   384
15:10   230n3, 382
15:10–11   377, 381, 394
15:10–20   387
15:11   324, 377, 381,
   382, 383, 384
15:11–20   554
15:12   89n1, 93n1,
   111n6, 127n3,
   171n21, 222, 231,
   313, 360n1, 401, 424,
   430, 434, 437n1, 459,
   527n1, 628
15:12–14   377, 381,
   382, 394
15:12–20   357, 377,
   381, 395
15:13   219, 276n3, 381
15:13–14   400
15:14   205, 313, 382,
   385, 396, 397, 555
15:15   136n1, 338,
   373n4, 376, 381, 382,
   385, 404, 407, 475,
   569
15:15–16   265n9

15:15–20   355, 377, 382
15:16   424, 425
15:16–18   599
15:16–20   382
15:17   382, 383
15:17–20   196
15:18   152, 342, 382,
   452
15:18–20   438
15:19   152, 171, 324,
   382, 383, 452, 557
15:19–29   384
15:20   377, 383
15:21   87n12, 132, 231,
   300n1, 315, 368, 386,
   387, 390, 391
15:21–28   48, 232,
   233n14, 300, 357, 358,
   386, 386n1, 386n2,
   387, 394, 424, 430,
   487, 671, 691
15:21–18:35   8
15:22   33, 35, 38, 57,
   57n1, 66n4, 66n5,
   152, 154, 245, 261,
   261n5, 320, 389,
   490n1, 491, 496,
   609n16, 681
15:22–23   386, 387
15:22–28   139, 140,
   317, 481
15:23   66n5, 111,
   127n3, 357, 386n1,
   387, 394, 424, 425,
   691n4
15:23–24   386, 387
15:24   133, 207, 268,
   268n1, 320n1, 386,
   386n1, 387, 388, 393,
   440, 476, 514, 608n14
15:24–27   689
15:25   35, 66n5, 80,
   259, 376, 486n2, 681,
   682
15:25–26   386, 388
15:26   386n1, 388, 400
15:26–27   207, 389,
   394, 522
15:27   35, 388, 681
15:27–28   386, 388
15:28   15, 46, 77, 93n1,
   133, 207, 232, 234,
   316, 317, 386n1,
   388n6, 389, 395
15:29   149, 230, 342,
   390, 416, 569, 688
15:29–31   390, 391, 394
15:29–32   424
15:29–39   48, 357, 358,
   390, 400
15:30   127n3, 139, 140,
   317, 390, 491
15:30–31   291, 367,
   375, 390, 391, 454,
   500
15:30–32   368
15:30–33   230n3

15:31   140, 156, 225,
   391, 392, 395, 538
15:32   84, 140, 262,
   369, 390, 440, 450,
   487, 491, 561, 609
15:32–33   367, 387,
   390n1, 691n4
15:32–34   390, 392
15:32–38   400
15:32–39   367, 389,
   393, 394, 397
15:33   89n1, 106, 357,
   368, 390, 391, 392,
   394, 424, 425, 569
15:33–34   400
15:34   89n1
15:34–37   367
15:35   390
15:35–36   230n3, 390,
   390n2, 392
15:35–37   390
15:36   390, 394, 400,
   625
15:36–37   242
15:37   23, 369, 390, 392
15:37–38   390, 392
15:38   367, 369, 390,
   435
15:39   230n3, 390, 391,
   392, 395, 400, 403
16   413
16–28   410
16:1   42, 111, 111n6,
   127, 127n3, 231, 254,
   326, 392, 396, 397,
   401, 459, 459n1, 507,
   527, 527n1, 528, 535,
   639
16:1–2   535
16:1–4   44, 48, 326,
   357, 358, 396, 399,
   578
16:1–12   413
16:2   64n2
16:2–3   397
16:2–4   339, 396, 397
16:3   246, 398, 422n11
16:4   231, 296, 326,
   396, 397, 410, 426,
   483, 558, 586, 613,
   615, 676
16:5   399, 400, 403,
   424, 425
16:5–11   393
16:5–12   44, 49, 357,
   358, 396, 399, 400,
   569, 691n4
16:6   111, 111n6, 217,
   231, 313, 345, 396,
   397, 399, 401, 527n1,
   535
16:6–7   399, 400
16:6–11   399, 400
16:7   66n5, 400n1
16:8   200, 232, 244,
   315n1, 373, 394, 413,

423, 425, 505, 633, 688, 691n4
16:8–11 399, 400
16:8–12 400
16:9 421
16:9–10 370
16:11 111, 111n6, 397, 399, 401
16:11–12 217, 345, 527n1, 535
16:12 93n1, 111, 111n6, 397, 399, 401, 421
16:13 57n1, 66n5, 402, 403, 408, 426
16:13–14 36, 402, 403, 424
16:13–16 357
16:13–19 402
16:13–20 49, 357, 358, 396, 402
16:13–28 136, 357
16:14 37, 93, 102, 295, 363, 404, 422n11, 425, 496, 669n2
16:15 89n1, 402
16:15–16 402, 403
16:15–17 340
16:15–19 519n17
16:16 32, 33, 35, 56, 57n1, 136n1, 246, 265n9, 373n4, 376, 382, 402, 403, 404, 405, 406, 407, 408, 425, 449, 475, 477, 541, 541n5, 639, 669
16:16–17 136, 406, 619
16:16–18 413
16:16–19 265, 408
16:17 42, 146n4, 219, 276n3, 329, 402, 404, 411, 562, 592
16:17–18 136, 404
16:17–19 376, 402, 403, 404, 434
16:18 12, 46, 67, 136n1, 222, 265n9, 279n8, 404, 406, 409, 411, 445, 633, 670, 683
16:18–19 43, 68, 516, 690
16:18–20 405
16:19 37, 40, 42, 44, 106, 151, 155n14, 249, 405, 405n10, 408, 445, 445n6, 689n2
16:19–40 276
16:20 32, 56, 75, 93n1, 231, 315, 402, 404, 406, 408, 415, 420
16:21 9, 81, 82, 82n7, 87n12, 93n1, 102, 255, 312, 313, 327, 355n5, 356, 357, 378, 400, 409, 410, 413, 418n4, 426, 452, 455,

457, 483, 484, 492, 494, 501, 512, 519, 527n1, 569, 612, 613, 615, 629, 676, 679, 681, 683
16:21–22 418
16:21–23 409, 629
16:21–25 317
16:21–26 130, 357
16:21–27 295
16:21–28 49, 127, 357, 358, 396, 409, 434, 435
16:21–28:20 9, 102
16:22 35, 66n5, 136n1, 357, 410, 424, 425, 426, 431, 449, 477, 568n2, 569, 628, 633, 681
16:22–23 35, 265n9, 409, 410, 691n4
16:23 126n1, 127, 131, 136n1, 171n21, 292, 409, 411, 411n3, 430, 438n1, 609
16:24 93n1, 114, 128n4, 136, 136n2, 243n1, 252n1, 409, 411, 411n3, 412, 412n4, 435, 465, 482, 659
16:24–25 240, 282, 412n4, 497, 537, 666
16:24–26 4, 342, 470, 485, 537, 663, 665, 683
16:24–28 356, 409, 411, 414, 476, 689n2
16:25 153, 201, 259, 412, 473, 487
16:25–26 353
16:25–27 412
16:25–28 409, 412
16:26 155n14, 412, 488
16:26–27 412n4
16:27 57n1, 93n1, 130, 183, 191, 219n10, 273n1, 276n3, 352, 365, 411, 412, 414, 417, 418, 422, 475, 477, 497, 533n5, 541, 569, 583, 592, 608, 636, 640n3, 684, 692
16:27–28 36, 188, 204, 410, 412n4, 431, 434, 573n1, 583, 584, 608n10
16:28 38, 40, 57n1, 74, 74n11, 80, 163n10, 269, 277, 412, 412n5, 413, 416, 568n2
17 418n2, 430
17:1 89n1, 136, 136n1, 149, 230, 265, 265n9, 391, 413, 415, 416, 419, 425, 434, 482, 486, 606–1, 631, 688

17:1–2 413
17:1–3 415, 416
17:1–8 225, 372, 418n3, 689
17:1–13 49, 357, 358, 415
17:2 351, 413, 415, 416, 419, 419n7, 422, 679
17:3 66n4, 415, 417, 669n2
17:4 35, 128n4, 136n1, 265n9, 373n4, 407, 415, 417, 422, 424, 425, 475, 477, 681, 691n4
17:4–5 429
17:4–6 357
17:4–8 415, 417
17:5 57n1, 64n2, 66n4, 66n5, 119, 120, 121, 219, 246, 303, 315, 316, 373, 376, 402, 413, 415, 417, 418n2, 419, 420, 445n3, 541, 640, 663, 669
17:6 81, 85n11, 249, 419, 631
17:6–8 415, 416, 418
17:7 127n3, 372, 419
17:8 320n1, 419n6
17:9 36, 57n1, 64n2, 66n5, 74, 74n11, 230, 231, 261, 313, 315, 327, 357, 406, 410, 415, 418n2, 420, 425, 679, 681, 683
17:9–13 102, 132, 255, 291n5, 295, 415, 420, 422n13, 615
17:10 66n5, 82n7, 295, 355n5, 410, 410n1, 415, 420, 569
17:10–11 424, 425
17:10–13 109, 281, 357, 403, 417, 669n2
17:11 295, 352, 421, 422, 422n11, 431, 434
17:11–12 415, 421, 422n11
17:12 36, 44, 57n1, 122, 133, 232n11, 296, 312, 313, 357, 361, 363, 365, 368, 394, 412n5, 421, 426, 559, 613, 650
17:12–13 134, 362
17:13 93n1, 415, 421, 421n9
17:14 127n3, 140, 230n3, 418n2
17:14–16 423, 424
17:14–18 423, 424
17:14–20 691n4
17:14–21 49, 357, 358, 423

17:15 35, 66n5, 152, 154, 491, 681
17:16 139, 261, 357, 423, 424, 464
17:17 73, 74n11, 296, 326, 423, 424, 425, 558, 586
17:17–18 423, 424
17:18 139, 140, 232n7, 244, 245, 423, 424
17:19 93n1, 127n3, 261, 423, 424, 434, 569
17:19–20 357, 504
17:19–21 423, 424
17:20 89n1, 163n10, 200, 230, 232, 244, 344, 400, 423, 424, 425, 435, 505, 633, 688
17:20–21 423, 424, 4423
17:21 425
17:22 36, 57n1, 64n2, 313, 412n5, 418n2, 426, 427, 574n6
17:22–23 49, 255, 312, 327, 356, 357, 358, 409, 410, 426, 457, 483, 484, 512, 519, 569, 612, 613, 615, 676
17:23 357, 426, 431, 569, 629, 679, 681, 683
17:24 36, 64n2, 127n3, 133, 136n1, 232, 254, 265n9, 326, 418n2, 434, 449, 450, 477, 531
17:24–25 428, 429
17:24–27 49, 357, 358, 376, 428, 431n1, 500, 527
17:25 38, 89n1, 136, 357, 407, 440, 509, 619
17:25–26 428, 429
17:26 64n2, 219, 265n9, 418n2, 428, 430, 541n5
17:26–27 428
17:27 171n21, 219, 292, 360n1, 428, 429, 437, 437n1, 438
18 355, 357, 431, 452, 456, 611
18–19 16
18:1 37, 40, 66n5, 127n3, 430, 431, 434, 691n4
18:1–4 436, 481, 486
18:1–5 49, 152, 431, 434, 435n2, 437, 548
18:1–6 501
18:1–10 306, 439

18:1–14 49, 432, 433, 448, 464, 487
18:1–20 432
18:1–35 432n4
18:1–19:2 10, 49, 356, 431
18:2 431, 433, 435
18:2–4 435
18:2–5 432, 434, 435, 435n3, 437, 606n6
18:3 37, 40, 163n10, 164n11, 435n2, 439, 555, 568n2, 601
18:3–4 39, 44, 435
18:3–5 464
18:4 37, 41, 433, 435n2, 497, 548
18:4–5 440
18:4–6 437
18:5 433, 435n2, 436, 446, 606
18:5–6 465n19
18:5–9 441
18:5–10 452
18:6 169, 284, 303, 306, 360n1, 432, 433, 435n3, 437, 437n1, 444, 446, 536, 574n7, 606, 629
18:6–7 431
18:6–9 49, 171n21, 292, 437, 452
18:6–10 433, 436, 439
18:6–14 431, 446
18:7 155n14, 171n21, 300, 411, 433, 438, 438n1, 438n2, 550n1, 553, 640n2
18:7–9 170, 437
18:8 128n4, 279, 360n1, 433, 437n1, 438, 609, 625n1, 629
18:8–9 114, 164n11, 215, 218, 273n1, 351, 432, 438, 469, 574n7, 609, 610
18:9 128n4, 279, 279n7, 360n1, 437n1, 438, 555, 558
18:10 42, 130, 169, 219, 276n3, 284, 329, 432, 435n3, 437, 439, 444, 606
18:10–11 439
18:10–14 49, 432, 439
18:11 36, 57n1, 439, 441, 473
18:12 268, 387, 433, 440, 440n2, 444, 509, 592, 608n14
18:12–13 432, 439, 440, 446
18:12–14 437, 452
18:12–17 169
18:12–20 205
18:13 163n10, 440n2

18:14 42, 276n3, 284, 432, 432n3, 435n3, 437, 439, 440, 441, 442, 465, 606
18:15 169n19, 206, 432, 438, 443, 444, 444n1, 445, 445n3, 446, 447, 449, 606, 606n5
18:15–16 418n3
18:15–17 169, 352, 432, 443, 444, 446, 449
18:15–20 49, 73, 205, 206, 431, 432, 442, 443, 446, 447, 448, 452, 519n17
18:15–35 49, 432, 442
18:16 18, 443, 444, 445, 454, 639
18:17 46, 177n37, 252, 404, 443, 444, 445, 445n3, 600
18:17–20 690
18:18 163n10, 249, 405, 405n8, 407, 408, 445, 446, 447
18:18–19 151, 689n2
18:18–20 432, 443, 445, 689n2, 690
18:19 42, 163n10, 168n16, 209, 219, 249, 276n3, 329, 432, 446, 447, 504
18:19–20 444, 446, 447
18:20 34, 446, 692
18:21 35, 74n11, 93n1, 127n3, 136n1, 169n19, 206, 265n9, 373n4, 376, 407, 431, 432, 444, 444n1, 446, 447, 448, 449, 477, 569, 606, 606n5, 633, 681, 691n4
18:21–22 205, 448, 449, 467
18:21–25 189
18:21–35 49, 152, 169, 352, 431, 432, 442, 446, 448, 452, 463, 476
18:22 74n11, 89n1, 448, 449, 450
18:23 37, 38, 41, 222n18, 296n10, 343n10, 449, 450, 477n4, 522, 595, 601
18:23–25 602
18:23–27 448, 449, 450
18:23–35 448, 449, 450, 467
18:24 64n2, 418n2, 451, 600
18:24–27 450
18:25 64n2, 418n2

18:26 66n5, 80, 81, 86, 376, 451, 452, 453, 486n2, 682
18:27 561
18:28 66n5, 128n4, 478, 538, 600
18:28–30 448, 449, 450
18:28–33 593
18:29 66n5, 432, 453
18:30 74n11, 451
18:31 238n1, 432
18:31–34 448, 449, 451
18:32 89n1, 93n1, 188, 451
18:32–35 190, 205
18:33 152, 262, 432, 491, 561
18:34 74, 74n11, 426n2, 451, 523
18:35 152, 169n19, 206, 276n3, 432, 432n3, 442, 444n1, 446, 448, 449, 450, 451, 453, 459, 557, 606, 606n5, 611
19 16, 454, 469, 477
19–20 456
19–23 456
19–25 142
19:1 9, 134, 140, 142, 224n1, 266, 284, 360, 431, 452, 455, 456, 459, 477, 492, 494, 519, 612
19:1–2 49, 454, 457
19:1–9 166
19:1–12 464n16
19:1–22 534
19:1–20:34 8
19:2 136n2, 139, 140, 230n3, 243n1, 252n1, 317, 391, 456, 477, 482, 491
19:2–20:16 459n5
19:3 66n5, 111n6, 127, 127n3, 254, 396, 397n1, 401, 455, 458, 459, 462, 464, 469, 469n1, 477, 527, 527n1, 528, 535, 639
19:3–6 459
19:3–9 45, 172, 457, 458, 459, 463n11
19:3–12 174
19:3–15 49, 457, 458, 465
19:3–20:28 456
19:3–20:34 49, 455, 457
19:3–23:9 456
19:3–23:39 10, 49
19:3–26:2 10, 455
19:4 309n4, 465, 475, 501, 515
19:4–5 18, 508
19:4–6 459
19:4–9 339

19:7 18, 89n1, 171, 171n22, 458, 459, 466
19:7–9 460, 461
19:8 89n1, 168, 459, 462, 463, 475
19:8–9 274
19:9 75n12, 170, 172, 232n11, 382n12, 459, 462, 466
19:10 89n1, 128n4, 458, 463, 463n11, 464, 466, 468, 477, 569
19:10–12 457, 458, 463, 464
19:10–20:28 456
19:11 463, 466
19:11–12 462
19:12 37, 41, 59n3, 463, 463n13
19:13 93n1, 458, 569, 633
19:13–14 435, 606n6
19:13–15 152, 436, 457, 458, 464, 465, 465n20
19:14 37, 39, 41, 44, 452, 464, 465n19, 473n4, 497, 501
19:14–15 464, 468
19:15 445
19:16 36, 66n4, 127n3, 239, 469n1, 471, 473, 531, 610
19:16–17 215, 468, 469, 470, 473
19:16–22 49, 457, 467, 468, 470, 477
19:16–26 137
19:16–30 472
19:16–20:16 49, 457, 467
19:16–20:28 467
19:17 128n4, 164n11, 435, 469, 471, 479
19:17–22 339
19:18 89n1, 170, 459n3
19:18–19 18, 468
19:18–20 469
19:19 211, 240, 274, 313, 330, 379, 470, 536, 610
19:20 89n1, 471
19:20–22 468
19:21 86, 128n4, 136, 136n2, 196, 243n1, 252n1, 470, 473, 475, 485, 619
19:21–22 353, 469, 674
19:22 81, 222, 471
19:22–26 198n8
19:23 37, 41, 163n10, 342, 472, 472n1
19:23–24 39, 41, 42, 164n11, 215, 435, 468, 472, 473
19:23–26 49, 457, 467, 472, 674

19:23–29 477
19:23–26:2 49
19:24 37, 38, 41, 42, 166n13, 168n16, 215, 321n6, 472, 472n3, 473
19:25 66n5, 81, 224, 259, 473, 477, 532, 569
19:25–26 468, 473
19:26 471–1
19:27 66n4, 93n1, 136n1, 136n2, 243n1, 265n9, 373n4, 404, 407, 474, 477, 480, 629, 691n4
19:27–28 252n1, 475
19:27–29 182, 353, 411, 467, 684
19:27–30 137, 352, 474, 475, 584
19:27–20:15 477
19:27–20:16 49, 457, 467, 474
19:28 4, 36, 57n1, 58, 80, 108, 122, 136n2, 149, 163, 163n10, 180n3, 191, 204, 219n10, 233, 235, 239, 243n1, 264, 269, 370, 412, 421, 422, 463, 475n3, 476, 486, 487, 497, 516, 519n17, 531n2, 533n5, 548, 569, 584, 608, 637, 640, 640n3, 671, 683, 691, 692
19:28–29 151, 201, 273n1, 479, 576, 582, 592, 633
19:28–30 68, 188, 474, 573n1
19:29 137, 153, 183, 215, 240, 274, 330, 469, 473, 476, 481, 606, 609, 610
19:29–30 476
19:30 239n3, 476, 477, 478, 479, 480, 486, 487
19:30–20:16 467, 478
20 492
20–21 16
20:1 37, 41, 222n18, 278, 296n10, 343n10, 354, 450, 476, 477, 591, 595
20:1–2 477, 478
20:1–7 477, 478
20:1–15 476, 509
20:1–16 263, 474, 476, 477
20:2 279, 429, 450, 451, 479, 538
20:3 478, 668n1
20:3–5 478
20:4 65n3

20:5 478, 668n1
20:6 89n1, 478
20:6–7 478
20:7 89n1
20:8 64n2, 74n11, 89n1, 183, 188, 474, 478, 480
20:8–12 479
20:8–15 477, 478
20:9 429, 450, 451
20:9–10 538
20:10 429, 450, 451, 481
20:11 591
20:11–12 480
20:12 66n5
20:13 429, 450, 451, 479, 524, 538, 636
20:13–15 479
20:14 479
20:15 197, 469, 479, 481
20:16 239n3, 476, 477, 478, 479, 480, 481, 486
20:17 264, 456, 482, 484, 492, 519
20:17–18 81, 378, 615
20:17–19 49, 357, 410, 456, 457, 477, 482, 483, 484, 485, 486, 613, 676
20:18 36, 57n1, 66n4, 81, 82, 82n7, 313, 355n5, 482, 492, 501, 519, 527n1, 624
20:18–19 312, 409, 426, 426n2, 482, 487, 494, 512, 569, 574n6, 612, 646
20:19 276, 482, 483, 518, 629, 654, 658, 679, 681, 683
20:20 80, 93n1, 127n3, 136, 265, 376, 682
20:20–21 475n3, 486, 671
20:20–23 457, 485, 486
20:20–24 490
20:20–28 49, 411, 431, 434, 435, 452, 467, 477, 480, 481, 485, 487, 489n6, 519n17, 606, 691n4
20:21 38, 41, 80, 89n1, 149, 430
20:22 89n1, 489, 631, 633
20:22–23 486, 625, 631n1
20:23 89n1, 149, 219, 276n3, 329, 422n11, 486, 489, 558, 608, 609, 662, 665
20:24 81, 486, 569, 606, 619
20:24–28 457, 485, 486

20:25 434, 485, 487, 518, 548
20:25–26 487
20:25–28 317, 481, 548
20:26 459n3, 489, 497
20:26–27 240, 485, 487
20:26–28 497, 537, 665, 683
20:27 239n3, 459n3, 480
20:27–28 441
20:28 36, 57n1, 68, 198n10, 235, 248, 255, 281n12, 353, 410, 430n5, 435, 459, 475, 485, 487, 488, 488n5, 489, 490, 492, 548, 600, 611, 614, 615, 625, 641, 645, 663, 665, 669
20:29 64n2, 136n2, 230n3, 243n1, 252n1, 418n2, 454, 456, 477, 482, 490, 492, 496, 519
20:29–30 491
20:29–31 490, 491
20:29–34 49, 260, 457, 490
20:29–21:22 456
20:30 38, 57, 57n1, 66n4, 66n5, 152, 261n5, 291, 492, 500, 540n2, 681
20:30–31 33, 35, 154, 320, 387, 490, 492, 496
20:30–34 38
20:31 38, 57, 57n1, 66n5, 230n3, 464, 492, 681
20:32–34 490, 491
20:33 35, 486n3, 681
20:34 136n2, 234, 252n1, 262, 392, 450, 456, 490, 491, 561, 602
21 16, 79, 514n3
21–22 456, 520
21–23 339, 498, 613
21–28 613
21:1 81, 93n1, 107, 378, 456, 457, 492, 493, 494
21:1–5 493, 494
21:1–6 623
21:1–11 49, 345, 493, 493n1, 497n7, 538
21:1–23:39 455
21:1–27:66 8
21:2 66n5, 602
21:2–3 248, 493, 624
21:2–6 493
21:3 35, 67, 459n3
21:4 20, 21, 23, 25, 66n5, 68, 162
21:4–5 22, 24, 493

21:4–9 495
21:5 18, 22, 34, 38, 66n4, 80, 85n11, 99, 119, 151, 497, 540, 609
21:6–7 493
21:6–9 493, 495
21:7 495
21:8 240, 496
21:8–9 230n3, 491, 492, 493
21:8–17 45
21:9 18, 33, 37, 38, 57, 57n1, 66n5, 136n2, 230, 252n1, 261, 261n5, 290n1, 320, 387, 422n12, 490, 490n1, 491, 492, 493, 496, 496n5, 501, 515, 540n2, 544, 561, 562, 563, 654
21:9–11 637
21:10 64n2, 66n5, 81, 378, 418n2, 456, 492
21:10–11 493, 496
21:11 37, 100, 133, 230, 230n3, 231, 359, 403, 425, 496, 497, 516, 654
21:12 498, 499, 502, 544, 545
21:12–13 429, 495, 498, 499, 639
21:12–14 498
21:12–16 508
21:12–17 49, 498, 501n6, 519, 544
21:12–22:46 401
21:12–23:39 456
21:13 18, 87, 89n1, 131, 498, 500, 500n4, 505, 559, 562, 637n3
21:14 127n3, 139, 291, 456, 498, 500
21:14–15 499
21:15 33, 38, 57, 57n1, 66n5, 81, 82, 82n7, 232n7, 238n1, 261, 261n5, 320, 355n5, 387, 401, 490n1, 491, 492, 515, 527n1, 540n2, 542, 543, 606n6, 619, 637
21:15–16 436, 465, 490, 498, 504
21:15–17 498, 500, 506
21:16 18, 89n1, 254, 303, 309n4, 498, 502, 515, 544, 559, 606n6
21:16–17 498
21:17 456, 498, 568, 619, 626
21:18 378, 456, 589
21:18–19 503
21:18–22 49, 503, 504n3, 519

21:19 89n1, 113, 114, 218n6, 238n1, 242, 250, 258n1, 320n1, 341, 342, 509, 514, 643n1
21:20 66n5, 238n1, 244, 434, 538
21:20–22 503, 504
21:20–26 384
21:21 163n10, 230, 232, 425
21:22 209
21:23 64n2, 66n5, 68, 82, 82n7, 127n3, 254, 396, 401, 410, 418n2, 456, 477, 506, 507, 508, 509n4, 512, 527n1, 539, 544, 637, 689, 690
21:23–24 225
21:23–27 45, 264
21:23–32 49, 102, 507, 510n7
21:23–44 519
21:23–22:14 526, 542, 544
21:23–22:46 49, 456, 506
21:24 508
21:24–27 506, 507, 508, 519
21:24–22:46 506
21:25 42, 66n5, 107, 507, 544
21:26 230n3, 293, 364, 403, 516, 617, 637, 654
21:27 75, 225, 508, 509n4
21:27–28:31 276
21:28 127n3, 239n3, 440, 478, 480, 509, 513, 522, 544, 592
21:28–30 509, 544
21:28–31 507
21:28–32 506, 507, 509, 510n8, 519
21:28–44 45
21:29 519, 649
21:29–30 510
21:29–31 510
21:30 127n3, 521
21:31 37, 38, 41, 42, 77, 89n1, 163n10, 219, 233n14, 239n3, 321n6, 382n12, 473, 508, 509, 511, 515, 544, 656
21:31–32 177n37, 241, 252, 479, 509, 524
21:32 65n3, 118, 151n11, 238n1, 284n4, 296, 423, 507, 509, 521, 559, 649
21:33 278, 334n2, 338, 354, 478, 512, 513,

522, 544, 559, 591, 600
21:33–34 514
21:33–39 544
21:33–41 35, 480
21:33–44 113, 264, 509, 519
21:33–46 49, 409, 506, 509, 510n8, 512, 514, 518, 519, 538
21:34 107, 218n6, 263, 341, 342, 504, 514, 515
21:34–35 512, 514
21:34–36 154n13, 512, 514
21:34–39 23
21:35 422n11, 523, 574
21:35–39 293, 517, 521
21:36 512, 514, 523
21:37 66n5, 113, 376, 521, 541
21:37–38 57n1
21:37–39 456, 512, 513, 514, 515, 541n5, 615
21:38 238n1, 313
21:38–39 312, 613
21:38–44 569
21:39 357, 520, 523
21:39–41 478
21:40 180n3, 544
21:40–41 512, 513, 515
21:41 89n1, 156, 218n6, 341, 342, 397n2, 508, 509, 514, 519, 593
21:41–45 523
21:41–46 497
21:42 19, 89n1, 113, 501, 515, 517, 521, 544, 559
21:42–43 515
21:42–44 37, 512, 513, 515
21:43 4, 37, 38, 41, 42, 68, 106, 133, 218n6, 233n14, 268, 269, 321n6, 341, 342, 473, 476, 510, 514, 515, 516, 517, 518
21:44 516, 517, 520
21:45 82n7, 111n6, 338, 410, 514, 517, 527, 527n1, 544, 676
21:45–46 45, 512, 513, 516, 519
21:46 37, 230n3, 313, 364, 508
22 45, 519, 542
22:1 66n5, 302n1, 338, 520, 521
22:1–3 521, 522
22:1–4 510n8
22:1–13 352

22:1–14 49, 232, 253, 506, 509, 521, 524n4, 544, 594, 596
22:2 37, 38, 41, 57n1, 222n18, 296n10, 343n10, 376, 450, 477n4, 522, 541, 541n5, 569, 601, 625
22:2–3 521
22:2–13 521
22:2–14 35, 596
22:3 562
22:3–7 521
22:4 66n4, 66n5, 305, 370, 609
22:4–6 521, 523
22:5 422n11, 525
22:6 154n13, 515n4, 525, 574
22:7 38, 521, 523, 541, 562, 615
22:8 89n1, 93n1, 272n1, 281, 422n11
22:8–10 77, 521, 523
22:9 133, 268, 317
22:9–10 354, 519
22:10 524, 525, 601
22:10–13 521
22:10–14 521, 598
22:11 38, 624
22:11–13 521, 522, 524, 525
22:11–14 352, 596, 597
22:12 89n1, 479n8, 535n2, 636
22:13 38, 93n1, 233, 351, 521, 525n6, 593, 602, 610, 646
22:14 481, 521, 522, 524, 578
22:15 93n1, 111n6, 127, 312, 313, 396, 477, 507, 520, 526, 527n1, 535, 617, 646, 646n1
22:15–16 401, 526, 527
22:15–17 526, 527
22:15–22 49, 429, 430, 506, 526, 529n5, 544
22:15–40 542
22:16 36, 66n5, 89n1, 239, 254, 326, 526, 527, 529, 531, 535
22:16–17 527
22:17 429, 440, 459, 509, 544
22:17–18 526
22:18 127, 183, 206, 248, 315n1, 459, 527, 528, 535, 544, 553, 554
22:18–22 526, 527
22:19 429, 451, 478, 526
22:19–22 174n32, 538
22:20 89n1, 544
22:20–21 526

22:21 89n1, 93n1, 508, 526, 529
22:22 225, 526, 537
22:23 66n5, 111n6, 127n3, 254, 396, 401, 526, 527n1, 530, 533
22:23–28 530
22:23–33 49, 112, 401, 506, 526, 530, 544, 676
22:24 19, 36, 66n5, 239, 530, 531
22:24–25 352, 606
22:24–28 530
22:25–27 530
22:25–28 531
22:26 74n11
22:28 530, 544, 593
22:29 530, 531
22:29–30 531
22:29–32 530, 573n1
22:29–33 530, 531
22:30 42, 130, 530, 531, 532, 533
22:30–32 352
22:31 66n5, 309n4
22:31–32 530, 532
22:32 19, 34, 57, 372n3, 533, 544
22:33 140, 224, 230n3, 530, 537
22:34 111n6, 313, 396, 526, 527n1, 532, 534, 535
22:34–35 111n6, 401
22:34–40 49, 159, 166, 167, 211, 506, 526, 534, 537n8, 574
22:34–46 544
22:35 127, 254, 397n1, 459, 459n1, 477, 527, 528, 538
22:35–36 534, 535
22:35–40 159
22:36 239, 326, 469, 531, 544
22:36–40 211, 310
22:37 19, 152, 452, 459n3, 534, 544, 557
22:37–40 147, 534, 535, 536
22:38 239n3, 534
22:39 19, 222n18, 459n3, 469n2, 477n4, 534, 544, 610
22:39–40 313, 536
22:40 162n8, 295n9, 534
22:41 64n2, 111n6, 401, 418n2, 527n1, 539, 539n1, 542
22:41–42 32, 539, 540
22:41–45 33, 310, 320, 537
22:41–46 50, 254, 309, 490n1, 496, 506, 526, 539, 542

22:42 56, 57, 57n1, 66n5, 261, 261n5, 387, 404, 440, 491, 508, 539, 544
22:42–43 38
22:43 21, 64, 66n5, 69, 89n1, 261, 261n5, 541, 544
22:43–44 273n1
22:43–45 539
22:43–46 539, 540
22:44 19, 74n11, 149, 343, 544, 569, 608
22:45 35, 38, 57, 57n1, 128n4, 261, 261n5, 376, 541, 544
22:46 508, 537, 539, 539n1, 542, 544
23 9, 15, 16, 456, 504, 508, 520, 538, 542, 543, 543n1, 543n2, 543n3, 544, 544n4, 546, 550n2, 559, 562, 563, 564
23–25 543
23:1 93n1, 230n3, 543
23:1–2 545
23:1–3 545
23:1–7 205
23:1–12 45, 50, 305, 543, 543n3, 544, 545, 548, 549n6
23:1–39 50, 456, 543
23:2 66n5, 82, 82n7, 111n6, 149, 355n5, 527n1, 546, 569
23:2–3 239, 545, 546
23:2–7 545
23:2–12 549
23:2–33 401
23:2–36 166
23:3 545, 546, 548, 549, 554
23:3–4 546
23:4 305, 545, 546, 548, 549
23:4–7 545, 546
23:5 179n2, 259, 547
23:5–7 185, 545, 547, 548
23:6 139, 547
23:7 478, 547
23:7–8 636
23:8 36, 169n19, 278, 330, 404, 429, 444n1, 606, 682
23:8–10 545, 547, 548, 606
23:8–11 276
23:8–12 497, 545, 547, 563, 671, 691n4
23:9 42, 151, 155n14, 276n3, 549, 689n2
23:9–12 519n17
23:10 32, 56, 404
23:11–12 487, 545, 548
23:12 683

23:13 37, 41, 82, 82n7, 111n6, 164n11, 233n14, 239, 408, 435, 517, 527n1, 528, 543, 551, 552, 553, 559, 593
23:13–15 183, 206, 355n5, 380, 546, 553
23:13–16 300, 438
23:13–28 543n3
23:13–30 380
23:13–33 543n3
23:13–36 45, 50, 543, 544, 549, 550, 551, 561
23:13–39 299
23:14 551n3, 551n4, 553, 554, 559
23:15 82, 82n7, 111n6, 153n12, 180n3, 233, 233n14, 239, 279, 279n7, 350, 527n1, 528, 551, 552, 553, 554, 557n10, 558
23:16 188, 382, 551, 553, 555
23:16–19 555
23:16–22 168, 173, 174, 551, 552, 555, 643
23:16–24 305, 552, 555
23:17 222, 555, 560, 596
23:17–22 551
23:18 188, 555
23:18–19 555
23:19 555, 560
23:20 555
23:20–22 555
23:21 555
23:22 42, 555, 608
23:23 82, 82n7, 111n6, 152, 163, 206, 232, 239, 310, 380, 384, 527n1, 528, 534, 536, 546, 548, 551, 553, 560, 593, 641, 649
23:23–24 167, 551, 552, 556
23:23–29 300, 438
23:24 382, 472n2, 551, 555, 556
23:25 82, 82n7, 111n6, 206, 239, 380, 527n1, 528, 546, 553, 560, 593
23:25–26 551, 552, 556
23:25–28 152, 552, 556
23:26 111n6, 152, 527n1, 551, 560
23:27 82, 82n7, 111n6, 206, 239, 380, 422n11, 527n1, 528, 546, 553, 557, 593
23:27–28 551, 552, 556

23:28 65n3, 151n11, 183, 217, 220, 351, 422n11, 551, 574
23:29 65n3, 82, 82n7, 111n6, 151n11, 206, 239, 380, 527n1, 528, 546, 553, 593, 676
23:29–30 552, 557
23:29–31 559
23:29–36 23, 154n13, 326, 523, 543, 551, 552, 557
23:29–37 362, 515n4
23:29–39 154, 409, 497, 515, 543n3
23:30 300n2
23:30–32 313
23:31 153n12
23:31–32 153
23:31–33 552, 557
23:31–36 551
23:32 23, 25, 162, 362, 456, 613, 615
23:32–39 543n3
23:33 112, 113, 279, 279n7, 324, 423, 555, 558
23:34 66n4, 82n7, 139, 150, 217, 220, 225, 239, 276, 283, 294, 305, 354, 355, 355n5, 482, 519n17, 548, 558, 574, 607, 689n2
23:34–35 206, 382n12
23:34–36 267, 341, 552, 558
23:35 65n3, 74n11, 151n11, 558, 558n13, 559, 650, 684
23:35–36 558, 654
23:36 163n10, 239n3, 296, 328, 423, 586, 656
23:37 81, 233n14, 378, 492, 522, 539, 551, 561, 563, 568
23:37–29 562n1
23:37–39 50, 543, 544, 561
23:38 66n4, 106, 543, 562, 564, 577
23:38–39 562
23:38–24:1 501
23:39 19, 37, 74, 74n11, 273n1, 290n1, 496, 496n5, 502, 543, 544, 561, 562, 562n1, 563, 568n2, 569, 573n1, 583
24 16, 581, 584
24–25 4, 13, 14, 355, 456, 543, 543n2, 544, 610, 611, 613
24:1 127n3, 397, 544, 568
24:1–2 568

24:1–3 50, 455, 456, 543, 562, 565, 567, 568, 626
24:1–31 584
24:1–35 565, 566
24:1–26:2 10, 50, 565
24:2 162, 163n10, 502, 516, 523, 568, 572, 639, 670
24:2–3 544
24:3 64n2, 66n5, 127n3, 149, 155n14, 163, 230, 323, 326, 337, 418n2, 434, 494n2, 543, 566, 568, 569, 571, 572, 577, 583, 584, 585, 587, 594, 597, 603, 610, 688, 690
24:4 565, 610
24:4–5 565, 572, 573, 578
24:4–14 50, 565, 567, 571, 572, 573, 575
24:4–28 585
24:4–35 50, 455, 565, 570, 571, 610
24:4–25:31 455
24:4–25:46 50, 568, 570
24:5 56, 66n5, 214, 404, 574, 643
24:6 410, 410n1, 412n5, 565, 572, 575, 578
24:6–7 565, 573
24:6–8 572, 573
24:7 37, 41, 244, 565, 575, 584, 670n4
24:8 565, 572, 573, 575
24:9 44, 93n1, 150, 154, 206, 207, 215, 267, 294, 518, 565, 574n6, 608n12
24:9–10 426n2, 574
24:9–11 525
24:9–12 572, 574
24:9–13 202, 341, 543
24:9–14 153, 266n1
24:9–31 689n2
24:10 93n1, 171n21, 292, 341, 360n1, 437n1, 565, 574n6, 629
24:10–11 438
24:10–12 155, 352, 574, 598
24:10–14 597
24:11 214, 217, 217n4, 218, 219, 565, 578
24:11–12 217, 220, 574
24:12 217, 351, 557
24:12–13 525
24:13 156, 259, 276, 533n5, 574, 597
24:13–14 565, 572, 574, 610

24:14 38, 41, 93n1, 106, 132, 133, 134, 139, 163, 187, 231, 233n14, 237, 267, 268, 269, 276, 317, 321, 334, 341, 352, 389, 455, 518, 519n17, 572, 575, 584, 608n12, 671, 691
24:14–30 604
24:15 523, 543, 562, 565, 576, 577, 579
24:15–16 523
24:15–28 50, 565, 567, 571, 576, 581, 582
24:16 93n1, 230, 565, 577
24:16–20 576, 577
24:17–18 577
24:18 175
24:19 219n11, 300, 438, 550n1, 553, 577
24:20 309n3, 313, 577
24:21 74n11, 93n1, 155n14, 215, 565, 568n2, 574n6
24:21–22 543, 576, 578, 584
24:22 67, 105, 219n11, 259, 300n2, 524, 525, 574, 583, 589
24:23 56, 66n4, 93n1, 404, 578, 610
24:23–25 578
24:23–26 32, 219n12, 574
24:23–27 573
24:23–28 576, 578
24:24 214, 217, 217n4, 218, 408, 524, 525, 573n2, 574n8, 578, 583
24:25 66n4
24:26 66n4, 106, 185, 578, 610
24:26–28 578
24:27 36, 57n1, 74n11, 80, 397, 582, 583, 584, 600
24:28 579
24:29 105, 215, 219n11, 565, 574n6, 578n2, 581, 582, 583, 590, 602, 668
24:29–31 50, 219n10, 497, 533n5, 565, 567, 571, 581, 582, 584, 603
24:30 19, 36, 57n1, 93n1, 151, 204, 277, 326, 397, 418, 422, 541, 543, 581, 582, 640, 640n3
24:30–31 42, 273n1, 412, 413, 584
24:31 74n11, 130, 350, 524, 525, 578, 581,

582, 583, 584, 590, 596, 608, 608n10
24:31–25:13 611
24:32 180n3, 338, 585
24:32–33 585
24:32–35 50, 565, 571, 585
24:32–41 567
24:32–25:13 604, 610
24:33 180n3, 533n5, 585, 586, 596, 610
24:34 74, 74n11, 163n10, 296, 326, 423, 558, 568n2, 584, 585, 586
24:34–35 163, 585
24:35 151, 155n14, 475, 475n2, 568n2, 585, 689n2
24:36 105, 130, 219n11, 486, 541n5, 565, 583, 587, 588, 589, 590, 593, 594, 597
24:36–37 588, 610
24:36–42 50, 565, 586, 587, 588, 591
24:36–44 569, 597
24:36–51 593
24:36–25:13 565
24:36–25:31 455
24:36–25:46 50, 565, 566, 570, 587, 610
24:37 36, 57n1, 543, 583, 588, 600
24:37–39 587
24:37–42 594
24:38 164n11, 219n11, 589, 590, 595
24:38–39 588, 589, 590, 594
24:39 36, 74, 74n11, 221n16, 543, 583, 593, 597
24:39–41 588
24:39–42 610
24:40 93n1
24:40–41 583, 584, 589, 592
24:40–42 589, 590
24:41–42 583
24:42 35, 533n5, 543, 583, 588, 590, 593, 597
24:42–43 632
24:42–44 567, 583, 587, 597
24:43 196, 278, 300n2, 372, 478, 591, 594, 596
24:43–44 50, 565, 587, 591
24:44 36, 57n1, 277, 543, 583, 588, 590, 591, 593, 597, 610
24:44–47 533n5

24:45 222, 284n4, 596, 601
24:45–47 592
24:45–51 50, 565, 567, 587, 591, 592, 594, 600
24:45–25:46 567, 569
24:46 146n4, 583, 587
24:47 163n10, 601
24:48 342, 452, 557, 583, 596, 597, 601
24:48–51 592
24:49 451
24:50 291n3, 583, 587, 588, 597
24:50–51 273n1
24:51 183, 206, 233, 351, 524, 538, 553, 602
25 16, 593
25–26 16
25–28 16
25:1 37, 38, 41, 43, 69, 93n1, 222n18, 223, 296n10, 343n10, 450, 477n4, 524, 595, 597
25:1–5 595
25:1–10 522
25:1–12 65
25:1–13 44, 50, 253, 565, 567, 587, 591, 592, 594
25:2 222
25:2–5 596
25:3 222, 602
25:4 222
25:5 64n2, 572, 592, 596, 597, 601
25:6 66n4, 543, 583
25:6–10 595, 596
25:7 69, 93n1
25:8 222
25:9 66n5, 222, 568n2
25:10 164n11, 232, 370, 601, 625
25:10–12 595, 596, 602
25:11 66n5, 69, 219, 601
25:11–12 598
25:12 163n10, 219
25:13 57n1, 533n5, 543, 583, 587, 588, 593, 594, 595, 597, 610, 632
25:14–15 514, 599, 600
25:14–30 50, 565, 567, 587, 592, 598, 599, 610, 611
25:14–46 273n1
25:15 422n11, 598, 599, 601, 602
25:15–16 602
25:16 599
25:16–18 599, 601
25:17 599
25:18 599, 601
25:19 89n1, 543, 583

25:19–23 599, 601
25:19–30 599, 601
25:20 66n5, 127n3
25:20–21 599
25:21 164n11, 419n7, 435, 581, 592, 599
25:21–29 183
25:22 127n3
25:22–23 599
25:23 164n11, 419n7, 435, 581, 592, 599
25:24 127n3, 263, 601
25:24–27 601, 602
25:24–30 599, 601
25:25 352
25:26 263, 451, 601
25:28–29 601, 602n6
25:28–30 602
25:29 339, 533n5, 592, 602n6
25:30 233, 351, 524, 593, 608, 610
25:30–31 475
25:31 34, 36, 43, 57n1, 93n1, 107, 130, 149, 180n3, 205, 239, 277, 412, 413, 419n7, 422, 486, 541, 543, 569, 583, 610, 636, 640, 640n3, 684
25:31–32 584, 664
25:31–33 350, 603, 604, 607, 608
25:31–40 295, 684
25:31–46 50, 84, 150, 219n10, 497, 537, 565, 567, 587, 590, 603, 604, 606, 610, 611, 692
25:32 37, 263, 317, 322, 518, 587, 600, 604, 605n3
25:32–33 268, 440, 604
25:33 217, 422n11
25:34 34, 38, 41, 43, 80, 93n1, 107, 151, 155n14, 183, 188, 219, 276n3, 329, 419n7, 533n5, 583, 592, 609, 610
25:34–36 603
25:34–40 471, 543, 603, 604, 607, 609
25:35–36 606, 607
25:35–40 436
25:35–45 559
25:37 35, 65n3, 66n5, 93n1, 151n11, 183n12, 351
25:37–39 603
25:40 38, 73, 163n10, 169n19, 284, 303, 306, 437, 444n1, 465, 501, 603, 604, 606, 607, 682
25:40–41 34

25:41   93n1, 114,
126n1, 130, 218, 220,
246, 246n5, 279, 438,
593, 609, 610
25:41–43   603
25:41–45   603, 604,
607, 609
25:44   35, 66n5, 93n1,
603
25:45   73, 93n1,
163n10, 284, 306, 437,
465, 501, 603, 604,
606, 607
25:46   65n3, 151n11,
215, 279, 351, 419n7,
469, 533n5, 583, 584,
593, 603, 604, 607,
610
26   16, 621, 644, 645
26–28   613, 667
26:1   9, 134, 142,
224n1, 266, 284, 360,
454, 611, 612
26:1–2   50, 410, 426,
455, 612, 614, 616
26:1–5   621
26:1–46   613
26:2   36, 57n1, 410,
426n2, 482, 483, 484,
569, 574n6, 611, 612,
613, 617, 624, 633,
635, 644
26:2–3   619
26:2–5   313
26:3   68, 82, 82n7,
93n1, 410, 484, 508,
527n1, 617
26:3–4   97, 617
26:3–5   45, 50, 516,
542, 616, 617, 644
26:3–46   50, 616
26:3–28:20   10, 50, 613
26:4   312
26:4–35   628
26:5   68, 617, 621, 637,
654
26:6   64n2, 231n5, 501,
623
26:6–7   618, 619
26:6–13   50, 471, 616,
618, 619n1, 644, 648,
677, 691n4
26:7   64n2, 127n3,
191n26, 624, 680
26:8   66n5, 238n1
26:8–9   618, 619, 631
26:9   643
26:10   315n1, 429, 633
26:10–13   618, 619
26:11   183n13, 255,
619, 620
26:12   179n2, 410, 569,
615, 644
26:13   106, 139,
155n14, 163n10,
573n1, 574

26:14   82n7, 93n1, 264,
265, 484, 527n1, 636
26:14–16   50, 313, 516,
542, 616, 617, 621,
624, 644
26:15   574n6, 614, 621
26:15–16   426n2, 495
26:16   93n1, 574n6
26:17   66n5, 127n3
26:17–19   616, 623, 624
26:17–29   644
26:17–30   50, 623
26:18   36, 255, 621,
623, 624, 635
26:19   495
26:20   64n2, 264, 484,
627, 646, 649
26:20–22   624
26:20–25   616, 621,
623, 624
26:20–29   369
26:20–32   410
26:20–35   648
26:21   64n2, 163n10,
426n2, 573n1, 574n6,
612, 636, 644
26:21–25   516
26:22   35, 426, 621, 681
26:23–24   644
26:23–25   426n2,
574n6, 625
26:24   36, 57n1, 87,
131, 235n18, 300,
438, 525, 550n1, 553,
621, 625n1, 635, 636,
645, 650
26:24–25   644
26:25   37, 89n1, 265,
429, 547, 614, 636,
640, 653, 691n4
26:26   64n2, 368, 400
26:26–18   615
26:26–29   475, 495,
522, 623, 625
26:26–30   68
26:26–46   616
26:27   66n5, 627
26:27–28   95
26:27–29   683
26:28   67, 235, 248,
292, 353, 488, 611,
614, 625, 627, 641,
644, 645, 663, 665,
669
26:29   38, 41, 43, 74,
74n11, 105, 107,
180n3, 219, 219n11,
232n11, 253, 276n3,
352, 370, 389, 519n17,
533n5, 541n5, 568n2,
573n1, 601, 625, 627
26:30   230, 494n2, 623,
626, 688
26:30–35   495
26:31   19, 25, 37, 84,
87, 89n1, 93n1, 131,
171n21, 217, 263,

268, 292, 322, 360n1,
437n1, 440, 525,
608n14, 612, 621,
628, 635, 637, 645,
674, 681
26:31–32   628, 683
26:31–33   628
26:31–35   50, 628, 633,
642, 644, 680
26:31–46   644
26:32   482, 519n17,
628, 643, 644, 679,
681, 682, 683, 688
26:33   128n4, 136n1,
171n21, 265n9, 292,
360n1, 373n4, 437n1,
628, 629
26:33–35   407, 449,
477, 632, 644, 691n4
26:34   163n10, 628, 643
26:34–35   412, 628, 629
26:35   89n1, 136n1,
265n9, 373n4, 486,
568n2, 628, 629, 631,
632, 635, 643
26:36   50, 74, 74n11,
89n1, 93n1, 630, 631
26:36–44   372
26:36–46   50, 154, 488,
613, 630
26:37   136, 136n1,
265n9, 416, 426, 482,
486
26:37–38   630, 631
26:37–39   633
26:37–41   50, 630, 631
26:38   74n11, 89n1,
93n1
26:38–46   596
26:39   66n5, 128n4,
219, 276n3, 300n3,
329, 486, 541n5, 625,
630, 631, 632, 635,
636, 640n2, 645, 662
26:39–41   631
26:40   89n1, 136n1,
265n9, 477, 630, 631,
632, 691n4
26:40–41   630, 632
26:41   422n11, 632
26:42   66n5, 128n4,
219, 276n3, 329, 525,
541n5, 614, 630, 631,
633, 635, 636, 645,
662
26:42–43   50, 630, 632
26:43   630, 631, 691n4
26:44   630, 631, 633,
645, 663
26:44–46   50, 630, 632
26:45   36, 57n1, 66n4,
89n1, 93n1, 252, 588,
630, 631, 632, 644,
691n4
26:45–46   107, 426n2,
574n6, 612
26:46   66n4, 630

26:46–56   516
26:47   64n2, 66n4, 68,
82, 82n7, 140, 230n3,
264, 265, 281, 410,
484, 508, 527n1, 628,
634, 637
26:47–50   635, 636
26:47–56   45, 50, 542,
613, 617, 621, 635,
637n4, 644
26:47–68   483
26:47–27:26   50, 634
26:48   66n5, 75, 426n2,
574n6
26:49   37, 127n3, 265,
547, 602, 636
26:50   93n1, 127n3,
479n8, 524, 612, 614
26:51   66n4, 82n7,
527n1
26:51–52   636
26:51–54   635, 636
26:51–55   281
26:52   89n1, 93n1, 665
26:52–54   614
26:53   130, 219, 264,
276n3, 329, 541n5,
610
26:53–54   631, 636
26:54   21, 22, 23, 25,
98, 162, 410, 410n1,
525, 573, 612, 621,
635, 644, 645
26:54–56   25
26:55   140, 230n3, 500,
662, 690
26:55–56   635, 637
26:56   21, 22, 23, 25,
68, 93n1, 98, 162,
410n1, 525, 612, 621,
633, 635, 636, 645,
691n4
26:57   82, 82n7, 276,
355n5, 410, 527n1,
663
26:57–58   638, 639
26:57–65   527n1
26:57–68   45, 50, 613,
638, 644, 648
26:58   74n11, 136n1,
136n2, 252n1, 265n9,
477, 642
26:59   82n7, 169n17,
276, 312
26:59–61   382n12, 638,
639
26:59–65   507
26:60   65, 127n3,
296n11, 445n4
26:61   162, 568, 635,
662
26:62   82n7, 653
26:62–63   542
26:62–64   638, 639, 640
26:63   35, 56, 57n1,
82, 82n7, 108, 173,

235n18, 376, 404, 541n5, 614, 663
26:63–64 32, 33, 541
26:64 19, 33, 34, 36, 57n1, 89n1, 149, 205, 219n10, 239, 277, 300n3, 412, 413, 418, 497, 508, 540n3, 541, 573n1, 583, 608, 608n10, 625, 638, 640, 644, 645, 653, 670, 689
26:65 66n5, 82n7, 93n1, 248
26:65–68 638, 640
26:66 440, 482
26:67 93n1, 175, 235n18, 615
26:67–68 483, 658
26:68 32, 56, 66n5, 82, 404, 614, 642, 658
26:69 66n5, 127n3, 136n1, 258n1, 265n9, 614
26:69–70 642, 643
26:69–75 51, 477, 613, 632, 639, 642, 644, 646, 648, 691n4
26:70 66n5
26:70–75 412
26:71 89n1, 100, 359, 645
26:71–72 642, 643
26:72 614
26:73 127n3, 136n1, 265n9
26:73–74 642, 643
26:74 93n1, 173, 602
26:75 136n1, 265n9, 628, 629, 642, 643, 650
27 79, 678
27:1 64n2, 68, 82, 82n7, 312, 313, 410, 483, 508, 527n1, 614, 646n1, 678
27:1–2 51, 613, 646, 648, 655
27:1–7 527n1
27:1–10 483, 644
27:2 276, 483, 516, 647, 653
27:2–4 426n2, 574n6
27:2–37 482
27:3 82n7, 93n1, 238n1, 265, 410, 508, 527n1, 644, 650
27:3–4 678
27:3–5 648, 649
27:3–8 648
27:3–10 51, 495, 622, 648, 650, 6113
27:4 66n5, 67, 151n11, 154, 459n3, 651, 678
27:5 86n12
27:6 82n7, 152, 380, 459, 527

27:6–8 648, 649
27:7 313, 478n5, 646, 646n1
27:8 74n11, 686
27:9 20, 21, 23, 25, 66n5, 93, 93n1, 153n12, 162, 651
27:9–10 19, 22, 24, 558n13, 648, 649, 651
27:10 651
27:11 34, 38, 66n5, 80, 82, 276, 542, 609, 625, 637, 652, 653, 669
27:11–13 175
27:11–14 652, 653
27:11–26 45, 51, 613, 648, 652
27:11–37 483
27:12 82n7, 235n18, 410, 483, 508, 527n1, 646n1, 649, 652, 663
27:12–14 652, 653
27:13 89n1, 93n1, 542
27:14 108, 235n18, 639
27:15 230n3, 643n1, 655n4
27:15–16 652
27:15–19 653
27:15–26 403, 652, 653
27:16 93n1, 656
27:16–17 654, 656
27:17 32, 56, 64n2, 82, 404, 614, 656
27:17–18 653
27:17–20 652
27:18 314, 426n2, 574n6
27:18–19 678
27:18–24 365
27:19 64n2, 65n3, 66, 66n5, 151n11, 154, 614, 652, 656
27:20 82n7, 140, 230n3, 312, 410, 483, 496, 508, 527n1, 649, 653, 655n4, 656, 678
27:20–23 654
27:20–25 655
27:20–26 516
27:21 652
27:22 32, 56, 82, 89n1, 404, 614
27:22–23 482
27:22–26 483
27:23 66n5, 652
27:23–24 678
27:24 66n5, 140, 151n11, 230n3, 238n1, 276, 459n3, 617, 649, 656
27:24–25 230, 382n12, 614, 652
27:24–26 410, 654
27:25 68, 655, 655n4, 656
27:26 93n1, 276, 426n2, 482, 652

27:26–31 483
27:27 93n1, 658, 659, 671, 677
27:27–31 657, 658, 664
27:27–32 51, 658
27:27–37 658, 662
27:27–56 51, 613, 657
27:28 659
27:28–29 653
27:28–31 615, 658
27:29 34, 38, 66n5, 80, 82, 482, 609, 637, 659, 661
27:31 482, 483
27:31–32 482, 658
27:32 175, 282, 619, 657, 659
27:32–44 45
27:33 657, 660
27:33–37 51, 660
27:34 657, 663
27:34–36 660
27:35 175, 482, 483, 615, 657, 661, 663
27:36 657, 663
27:37 34, 38, 80, 82, 609, 614, 653, 657, 661, 665
27:37–38 637
27:38 93n1, 235n18, 482, 488, 500, 608, 637n3, 662, 663
27:38–40 662
27:38–44 51, 657, 659n1, 662
27:39 615, 660, 663
27:39–40 657, 662, 663
27:39–44 658
27:40 35, 57n1, 66n5, 128n4, 162, 259, 376, 404, 482, 541n5, 568, 578, 614, 639, 662, 666, 678
27:41 82n7, 355n5, 410, 482, 527n1, 615
27:41–43 483, 657, 662, 663, 678
27:41–44 663
27:42 34, 38, 80, 259, 482, 609, 637, 653, 661, 662, 666
27:43 35, 57n1, 128n4, 376, 404, 541n5, 614, 663, 678
27:44 500, 615, 637n3, 657, 662, 663, 664, 667
27:45 74n11, 663, 667, 668
27:45–46 478
27:45–49 403
27:45–56 51, 657, 667
27:46 19, 66n5, 541n5, 632, 663, 665, 667, 668, 669, 669n2
27:46–49 668, 669
27:47 295

27:47–49 667
27:48 602, 660
27:49 259, 295, 672
27:50 667, 668, 669
27:51 66n4, 74n11, 222, 244, 488, 667, 670
27:51–53 495, 614, 667, 668, 670, 678, 680, 684
27:52 259, 260
27:52–53 670, 671
27:53 129, 670, 670n6
27:54 15, 35, 46, 57, 57n1, 66n5, 85n11, 232n8, 233n14, 238n1, 246, 249, 316, 317, 373, 376, 404, 483, 541n5, 573n5, 638, 659, 667, 668, 671, 678, 2207
27:55 136n2, 243n1, 252n1
27:55–56 667, 668, 671
27:55–57 664
27:56 136, 265, 486, 675, 680
27:57 64n2, 75, 471, 473, 614, 663, 674
27:57–61 51, 365, 613, 673, 674
27:57–66 51, 673
27:58 93n1, 127n3
27:58–60 674
27:59 619
27:60 222, 663
27:61 671, 675, 679, 680
27:62 82n7, 111n6, 516, 527n1, 535, 678
27:62–64 676
27:62–66 51, 312, 483, 614, 673, 676
27:62–28:15 613
27:63 66n5, 482
27:63–64 629, 685
27:64 68, 74n11, 382n12, 677
27:65 677, 685
27:65–66 483, 681
28 673, 678, 679n1
28:1 309n3, 674, 680
28:1–2 681
28:1–7 51, 680
28:1–10 671, 673, 675, 679
28:1–15 51, 679
28:1–20 8
28:2 66n4, 127n3, 244, 573n5, 610, 670n4, 679
28:2–3 680
28:3 416
28:4 419n5, 680, 681, 685
28:5 372, 482
28:5–7 680, 681

28:6   482, 629, 679,
   681, 682
28:6–7   679
28:7   66n4, 98, 454,
   519n17, 628, 629, 643,
   682, 683
28:8   353, 419n5, 679,
   684
28:8–9   682
28:8–10   51, 682
28:9   66n4, 66n5, 81,
   127n3, 376, 486n2,
   677, 682, 684, 688
28:9–10   615, 679
28:10   89n1, 93n1,
   169n19, 330, 372,
   444n1, 606, 628, 629,
   643, 644, 681, 682,
   683, 688
28:11   64n2, 66n4,
   82n7, 527n1, 679, 686
28:11–12   685
28:11–15   45, 51, 312,
   328, 483, 615, 640,
   673, 676, 677, 679,
   685
28:12   82n7, 313, 410,
   527n1, 646
28:12–13   677
28:13   66n5
28:13–15   685
28:14   677
28:15   686
28:16   98, 149, 230,
   629, 643, 681, 688
28:16–17   688, 691
28:16–20   51, 133,
   519n17, 613, 615,
   628, 673, 679, 683,
   687, 687n1
28:17   81, 238n1, 373,
   376, 486n2, 677, 688
28:18   32, 34, 42,
   66n5, 80, 127n3, 151,
   155n14, 166, 187,
   219n10, 249, 264, 303,
   419, 508, 541, 633,
   640, 664, 679, 687,
   688, 689
28:18–19   303
28:18–20   37, 43, 46,
   47, 73, 216, 225, 267,
   269, 276, 304, 317,
   334, 373, 389, 408,
   420, 575, 644, 650,
   671
28:19   15, 46, 57n1, 65,
   85n9, 108, 119, 132,
   133, 134, 233n14, 237,
   268, 334, 352, 376,
   384, 404, 518, 541n5,
   548, 584, 619, 640,
   678, 687, 688, 689
28:19–20   207, 347,
   354, 384, 611, 687
28:20   34, 66n4, 74n11,
   155n14, 163, 187, 233,

350, 352, 419, 475n2,
   497, 533n5, 569, 612,
   633, 687, 688, 690,
   692
45:20   546
53:12   235n18

Mark

1:2   121
1:2–3   108
1:8   121
1:9   54
1:9–11   117
1:12–13   124
1:14–20   138
1:15   40
1:17   136
1:29   265
1:29–31   234
1:32–34   235
1:35   185
1:39   138
1:40–42   231n5
1:40–44   230
2:1–12   242, 247, 248
2:4   578
2:13–17   12
2:14   12, 252
2:14–22   251, 252
2:18   256, 527n1
2:18–20   190n25
2:18–22   6, 254
2:19   254n6
2:23–28   308
2:26   311
2:27   310
3:1–6   312
3:6   527
3:8   140
3:13–19   264
3:16–19   12, 264
3:17   557n10
3:18   12
3:20   378n2
3:20–30   320
3:21   329, 330
3:22   265, 278n6, 378
3:24   40
3:28   557n10
3:31   329
3:31–32   74
3:31–35   329
4:1–2   337
4:1–9   337
4:3–9   338
4:9   297
4:10–12   339
4:11   40, 339, 339n4,
   340
4:13–20   341
4:17   437n1
4:23   297, 338
4:26   40
4:29   263n7
4:30   39, 40
4:30–32   344, 473n4

4:33–34   346
4:35–41   242, 243
5:1   245, 249, 250
5:1–20   242, 245
5:6   81
5:7   451n6
5:20   140
5:22   258n1
5:22–43   257
5:34   272n2
6:1–6   360
6:3   74, 221, 360, 361,
   437n1
6:5   464n17
6:7–13   264
6:8–9   271
6:8–11   266n1, 271
6:10–12   272
6:11   272
6:14–29   363
6:19   364
6:20   364n5
6:23   41
6:32–44   367
6:34   262
6:41   185
6:45   375
6:45–51   372
6:46   185
6:47   374
6:48   451n5
6:53–56   375
7   391
7:1–23   378
7:3–4   379
7:10   384
7:11   380
7:13   385
7:16   297
7:19   383
7:22   197, 479
7:24–30   386, 387
7:30   232n9
7:31   140, 391
7:31–37   391
7:31–8:10   390
7:32   464n17
7:34   368n2
8:1–10   367, 393
8:10   392, 395
8:11–12   326
8:11–13   396
8:13–21   400
8:15   363
8:23   464n17
8:25   464n17
8:27   408
8:27–30   402
8:31–9:1   409, 410
8:33   131
9:1   40
9:2–13   415
9:5   422, 547
9:14–29   423
9:29   190n25, 425
9:30–32   426
9:33–37   434

9:37–41   266n1
9:38   321n5
9:42–47   437, 437n1
9:43   279n7
9:45   279n7
9:47   41, 279n7
9:50   154
10:1   140
10:1–12   459
10:4   171n22, 466
10:11   172
10:11–12   171
10:13–16   464
10:14   39, 41, 473n4
10:15   41
10:17   471
10:17–22   468
10:18   471
10:20   471
10:23   41
10:23–27   472
10:25   41, 473
10:29   481
10:30   475n2, 481
10:32   484
10:32–34   482
10:35–45   486
10:37   41
10:38   489
10:40   489
10:43   489
10:45   488
10:46–52   490
10:47   492
10:47–48   261n5
11–16   613
11:1   494, 501
11:1–11   494
11:7   495, 496
11:10   41
11:11   499
11:11–12   501
11:12–14   503
11:13   503n1
11:15   502
11:15–18   499
11:15–19   503
11:20–24   503
11:21   547
11:27–33   507
12:1–12   512, 513
12:8   520
12:13–17   526
12:18–27   530
12:23   531n2
12:27   533
12:28–34   534, 535
12:30   536n5
12:34   41
12:35–37   539
12:36   540n3
12:38–39   545
12:38–40   545–46
12:40   559
12:41   499n3
12:41–44   181, 499
12:43   499n3

13   567
13:1   568n1
13:1–4   567, 568
13:3   265
13:5–13   567, 573
13:7   575
13:8   41, 573n4
13:9–13   266n1, 275
13:11–13   276
13:13   606n8
13:14–23   567, 576, 577
13:22   217n4
13:24–27   567, 582
13:28–31   585
13:28–32   567
13:32   588, 589, 590
13:33–37   567
13:34   598n1
13:35–36   596
13:36   596
14:1–2   612, 617
14:3   231n5, 501
14:3–9   618, 619
14:10–11   621
14:12–26   623
14:17   627
14:23   627
14:24   627
14:25   41
14:27   437n1
14:27–31   628
14:29   437n1
14:32–42   185, 630
14:38   189
14:43–52   635
14:45   547
14:53–65   638
14:61   404
14:62   540n3
14:65   175
14:66–72   642
14:69   645
14:70   643
15:1   646, 647
15:1–15   652
15:16–41   657
15:17   659
15:19   81
15:21   175
15:23   86
15:33–41   667
15:42–47   673
15:43   41, 674
16:1   619, 680
16:1–7   680
16:8   684, 688
16:8–11   682
16:11   688
16:13–14   688
16:14   461n7
16:15–18   687
16:19   540n3

Luke

1   105
1:1   6

1:1–4   6, 54
1:5   82
1:5–25   63, 118
1:6   65
1:8   82
1:11   681
1:13   67, 372, 681
1:15   67n8, 99, 254
1:17   295, 421, 422
1:19   439n1
1:26   78, 681
1:26–27   98
1:27   64, 69, 541
1:30   372, 681
1:31   67
1:32   31, 541, 608
1:32–33   640n3
1:33   41
1:34   73
1:34–35   70
1:35   67n8, 120, 420
1:39–56   118
1:41   67n8
1:45   146n4
1:67   67n8
1:68   393, 488
1:69   541
1:76   293
1:79   133, 272n2
2   98
2:1–5   527
2:1–7   78, 98
2:4   78, 541
2:5   64
2:7   75, 86
2:8–20   79
2:9   681
2:10   372, 681
2:11   78, 541
2:14   152, 272n2, 281,
   303, 496
2:21–38   98
2:22   89
2:22–24   500
2:24   93
2:25–38   105
2:26   67n8
2:32   269
2:36   69
2:37   190n25, 499, 500
2:38   488
2:39   98
2:40   105
2:46–47   105
2:48–49   105
2:52   105
3:1   97, 363, 646, 647
3:1–2   105, 121
3:1–22   102
3:4–6   108
3:5–6   121
3:7–9   6
3:10–15   121
3:11   183n13
3:12–13   252
3:16   121
3:19–20   363

3:21   122
3:21–22   117
3:22   31, 589
3:23   29, 30, 31, 105,
   118
3:23–28   54
3:23–38   28, 29, 58
3:24   29
3:24–31   30
3:25   29
3:26   29
3:27   29, 29nb, 30
3:28   29
3:29   29
3:30   29
3:31   29, 30
3:32   29
3:32–34   30
3:33   29, 30
3:34   29
3:35   29
3:36   29
3:37   29
3:38   29, 31
4:1   31, 120, 589
4:1–13   124
4:2   127
4:3   31
4:5   39
4:7   81
4:8   81
4:9   31
4:13   130
4:14   31, 589
4:14–15   138
4:16–28   139
4:16–30   133, 360
4:18   31, 120, 291, 589,
   619
4:25–26   669n2
4:27   231n5
4:38–39   234
4:40   464n17
4:40–41   235
4:43   41
4:44   138
5:4–9   353
5:12   631n2
5:12–13   231n5
5:12–14   230
5:16   185, 372
5:17–26   242, 247, 248
5:27   252
5:27–32   12
5:27–39   251, 252
5:29   252
5:32   253n4, 256
5:33   256
5:33–39   254
5:34   254n6
6:1–5   308
6:4   311
6:6–11   312
6:12   185, 372
6:12–16   264
6:14–16   12, 264
6:15   12, 538n4

6:17–49   141
6:20   40, 146n4, 150
6:20–26   146n2
6:21   146n4, 233
6:22   146n4, 156
6:24–26   550n1
6:25   233
6:26   217n4
6:27–28   176, 178
6:29   175
6:29–30   174
6:31   211
6:34–35   175
6:35   177
6:36   452
6:37–38   203, 205
6:39   382
6:40   278
6:41–42   203, 206
6:42   206
6:43–44   218
6:43–46   214, 216
6:46   219
6:47–49   214, 221
7:1–10   232
7:2   232n8
7:6   232n8
7:9   237
7:11–17   260n4
7:18   297
7:18–23   291
7:18–35   289, 291
7:22   231n5
7:23   146n4, 437n1
7:24–35   292
7:28   40
7:31   223
7:32   297
7:32–35   296
7:35   297
7:45   636
7:46   191n26
7:50   272n2
8:1   40
8:2–3   671
8:3   363, 471
8:4   337
8:4–8   337
8:5–8   338
8:8   297
8:9–10   339
8:10   40, 339, 339n4
8:11–15   341
8:19–20   74
8:19–21   329
8:21   222
8:22–25   242, 243
8:26   245, 249, 250
8:26–39   242, 245
8:28   451n6
8:41   258n1
8:41–56   257
9:1–6   264
9:2   40
9:3   271
9:3–5   266n1, 271
9:5   272

9:7   363
9:7–10   363
9:8   168n15, 669n2
9:10–17   367
9:11   41
9:18   185, 372, 408
9:18–21   402
9:22–27   409, 410
9:27   40
9:28–29   185, 372
9:28–36   415
9:31   417
9:32   412–13
9:33   422
9:37–43   423
9:43–45   426
9:46–48   434
9:51–53   454
9:51–55   219n12
9:57–60   238
9:57–62   523
9:60   41
9:62   41
10:2   263
10:4–12   271
10:5   272n2
10:5–6   272
10:5–15   266n1
10:7   271
10:9   41
10:10–11   272
10:11   41, 272
10:15   279n8, 301
10:16   606
10:20   219n12
10:21   302, 440n4
10:21–22   303
10:23   146n4
10:25   535, 538
10:25–28   534
10:25–29   469
10:25–37   176
10:26   162n8
10:27   536n5
10:41   199
11:1   185, 372
11:1–4   185
11:2   40, 185n17
11:3   188
11:4   188, 189
11:9–13   208
11:11–12   209
11:14–23   320
11:15   265, 278n6
11:15–26   326
11:17   40
11:18   40, 278n6
11:19   278n6
11:20   40
11:24–26   325
11:27   146n4
11:27–28   329
11:28   146n4
11:29–32   326
11:34–36   197
11:38   378
11:39–41   556

11:42   556
11:43   547
11:44   556
11:45   535
11:46   305, 546, 549
11:47–48   557
11:50   609n15
11:52   405, 408, 535
12:1   401
12:2–9   278
12:2–12   266n1
12:3   185
12:5   279n7
12:8–9   280
12:10   320
12:11   199
12:13–21   412
12:16–21   196
12:22   199, 202
12:22–23   198n10
12:22–31   198
12:24   185
12:26   199
12:27   202
12:30   185
12:31   40
12:32   41
12:33   469
12:33–34   196
12:35–40   597
12:37   146n4
12:38   592
12:39–40   591
12:42   598
12:42–46   592
12:42–48   592
12:43   146n4
12:46   593
12:47–48   300
12:48   602
12:49   223
12:50   489
12:51   280
12:52   405n8
12:54–56   396, 397, 398
12:57–59   170
13:1   646
13:1–2   643
13:1–5   249
13:6–9   218
13:14   312
13:18   40, 223
13:18–19   473n4
13:18–21   344
13:20   40
13:20–21   344
13:24   214, 215
13:25   596
13:25–27   219
13:27   220
13:29   40, 41, 522
13:31–32   363
13:34–35   561
13:35   564
14:1   378n2
14:3   535
14:7–11   547

14:8–10   489
14:14   531n2
14:15   41, 146n4, 389
14:15–16   232
14:15–24   521
14:26   197
14:34   154
14:34–35   154
14:35   297, 338
15:1–2   204
15:3–7   440
15:15   246
15:18   39, 42, 107, 186n21, 196, 507n1
15:19   272n1, 281
15:21   39, 42, 107, 281
15:22   524n2
16:8   233, 557n10
16:9   198n8
16:10   601
16:11   198n8
16:13   197, 198n8
16:16   40, 294, 295n9
16:17   162n8, 163
16:18   171, 172
16:19–31   532, 609
16:20   232n9
16:21   388
16:23   279n8, 451n6
16:27–31   328
16:31   397, 677, 685
17:1   438n1
17:1–2   437
17:2   437n1
17:3   447
17:4   449
17:6   504
17:12   231, 231n5
17:14   231
17:16   631n2
17:20   41
17:21   41
17:23–24   579
17:26–30   589
17:31   219n11, 577
17:34–35   589
17:37   579
18:1–8   388
18:9–14   177n37, 204
18:10   500
18:10–11   499
18:12   190, 190n25, 254
18:13   368n2
18:15–17   464
18:16   39, 41, 473n4
18:17   41
18:18   471
18:18–23   468
18:19   471
18:21   471
18:24   41
18:24–27   472
18:25   41, 473
18:29   41, 481
18:30   481
18:31   484
18:31–34   482

18:33   654n3
18:35–43   490
18:37   643
18:38   492
18:38–39   261n5
19–24   613
19:1–10   177n37, 253
19:2   471
19:8   470n3
19:8–9   471
19:10   441
19:11   41
19:12   41
19:12–27   598
19:13   600, 602
19:15   41
19:17   601
19:20   601
19:26   602
19:29   494, 501
19:29–44   494
19:32–34   495
19:35   495, 496
19:38   152, 272n2, 496
19:45   502
19:45–48   499
20:1–8   507
20:9–19   512, 513
20:15   520
20:18   516
20:20–26   526
20:27–40   530
20:33   531n2
20:34   557n10
20:35   531n2
20:36   557n10
20:41–44   539
20:42–43   540n3
20:45–46   545
20:45–47   546
20:46   547
20:47   559
21   567
21:1   499n3
21:1–4   181, 619
21:5–7   567, 568
21:8–19   567, 573
21:9   575
21:10   41
21:11   575
21:12–17   276
21:12–19   266n1
21:18   280
21:20   516, 523
21:20–24   567, 576, 577
21:24   281n13, 397n2
21:25–27   567, 582
21:28–33   567
21:29–33   585
21:31   41
21:34   219n11
21:34–36   567, 593
21:35   608n12
21:37–22:2   612, 617
22:3   622
22:3–6   621
22:7–20   623

22:16 41
22:18 41
22:19 625
22:20 625, 627
22:24–30 486
22:27 487
22:29 41
22:30 41, 475, 476
22:37 235n18
22:40 628
22:40–46 630
22:43 589
22:47–53 635
22:50–51 636
22:54–55 638
22:55–62 642
22:59 643, 645
22:63–71 638
22:66–23:1 646
22:67 404
22:69 540n3
22:70 404
23:1 647
23:1–14 314
23:1–25 652
23:6 643
23:7–12 363
23:14 676
23:15 363
23:16 654n3
23:26–49 657
23:28–31 578
23:29 146n4
23:34 176
23:39–43 663
23:41–51 105
23:42 41
23:44–49 667
23:47 232n8
23:50–56 673
23:51 41
24:1 619
24:1–8 680
24:4 532n3
24:9–12 682
24:13 372n2
24:13–53 687
24:17 191
24:26–27 410
24:27 71
24:30 368
24:36 272n2
24:39 665
24:44 162n8, 295,
    295n9
24:44–45 71
24:46–49 687
24:49 120
24:50 501
24:52 81
24:53 499

John

1:1–18 54
1:4–5 155
1:14 303, 420, 446

1:18 303, 420
1:19 378
1:19–34 102
1:21 295, 296, 403,
    421, 669n2
1:25 403, 669n2
1:27 281
1:28 140
1:32 589
1:32–34 120
1:35–42 136, 137n3
1:35–44 265, 265n9
1:38 547
1:39 668n1
1:42 406n12
1:43–48 265
1:45 162n8, 295n9, 359
1:46–47 100
1:49 404, 547
1:51 119, 640
2:6 378
2:12 74
2:14–22 502
2:15 654n3
2:18–22 639
2:20 568n1
3:2 547
3:3 39
3:3–5 436
3:5 39
3:13 589
3:18 323
3:19–21 155
3:26 140, 547
3:27 507n1
3:29 255, 594
3:34 120, 248, 589
3:35 219n10, 303
4:1–42 470
4:3–4 454
4:6 589, 668n1
4:9 454
4:20–24 81
4:22 269, 389, 519
4:31 547
4:32 196n5
4:34 128
4:35 350
4:35–38 263n7
4:45 643
4:46–53 234
4:52 668n1
5:7–9 312
5:19–29 219n10
5:22 608
5:25–29 260
5:27 608, 608n10
5:28–29 533n5, 610
5:29 279, 531n2
5:39 71
6:1–13 367
6:5–7 265
6:8 265
6:11–13 369
6:14 422n12
6:14–15 299, 403
6:16–21 372

6:19 372n2
6:25 547
6:26 397
6:26–27 299
6:27 196n5
6:30 326
6:30–59 369
6:31 346, 346n15
6:35 128
6:55 196n5
6:61 437n1
6:63 404
6:65 404
6:68 265n9
6:69 404
6:70 622, 650
6:70–71 265
6:71 265
7:1–5 330
7:3 74
7:3–9 274
7:5 74
7:10 74
7:12 676
7:15 360
7:23 310
7:39 640
7:40 403
7:41–42 100
7:42 78, 540n2
7:47 676
7:52 100, 643
8:2–3 499
8:12 155
8:17 445n4
8:20 499n3
8:44 173, 350
8:52 413n6
8:56 340
9:1 500
9:2 547
9:2–3 249
9:8 183n13
9:38 81
10 440, 608n14
10:1–30 217
10:4 629
10:11–16 84
10:12 217, 275, 322
10:14 220n13
10:16 269, 519
10:18 634
10:33 248
10:34 162n8
10:40 140
11 671
11:1 501, 619
11:11 670n7
11:11–12 259
11:11–14 259
11:16 265
11:18 372n2, 501, 619
11:24–25 531n2
11:27 404, 422n12
11:41 368n2
11:41–42 185
11:43–44 260n4

11:45–53 617, 677
11:49 617
11:55 612
12–21 613
12:1 501
12:1–11 618, 619
12:3 619
12:4 265
12:4–6 622
12:6 430
12:9–11 677
12:12–19 494
12:14 496
12:14–15 494
12:20 81
12:21–22 265
12:22 265
12:23 640
12:31 140, 322
12:32–33 640
12:34 36, 162n8, 540n3
12:36 557n10
12:37 299
12:38 235n18
12:39–40 339
12:40 340n6
12:47 222
13 690
13:1 612
13:2 265, 622
13:6–37 265n9
13:12–17 222, 487
13:17 690
13:18 636
13:20 436, 437, 606
13:21–30 623
13:23 11
13:26 265, 625
13:27 636
13:29 265, 430
13:31–38 628
13:34 212, 469n2
13:34–35 537
14:5 265
14:6–9 303
14:8–9 265
14:9 424
14:15–31 276
14:21–24 212
14:30 320n2
15:2–8 218n6
15:6 218
15:8 156
15:16 135, 218n6
15:18 606n8
15:20 278
15:20–21 606n8
15:25 162n8
15:26–16:31 276
16:1 437n1
16:9 323
16:11 140, 320n2, 322
16:20–22 573n4
16:23–24 208
16:33 574n6, 576
17:1 368n2
17:1–5 589

17:1–8   303
17:4–5   419, 640
17:12   557n10, 621, 644
17:14   606n8
17:15   173n29, 189
17:18   606n8
17:24   419, 609n15
17:26   212
18:2–12   635
18:3   596n4
18:5   643
18:7   625, 643
18:10   636
18:10–27   265n9
18:11   486
18:12   636
18:13–14   617, 683
18:15–16   644
18:19–24   638
18:22–23   175
18:24   617
18:25–27   642
18:28   617, 624, 646
18:28–19:16   652
18:29   647
18:31   482, 646
18:36   39
18:36–37   653
19:2   659
19:3   175
19:11   529n6
19:12   314, 527
19:12–16   655
19:17   515n5, 520
19:17–37   657
19:19   643
19:19–22   661
19:20   515n5, 520
19:24   660, 661
19:25   671
19:26   11
19:27   330
19:28   589
19:28–37   667
19:31–33   665
19:31–42   673
19:34   672
19:37   583
19:38   674
19:38–40   619
19:38–42   674
19:39   86
20:1   680
20:1–2   686
20:2   11
20:2–6   265n9
20:2–18   682
20:19   272n2
20:19–21:23   687
20:21   272n2
20:21–23   687
20:22   120
20:23   405, 445
20:24–28   265
20:25   665
20:26   272n2
20:29   146n4

20:30–31   5
21:2   265
21:2–21   265n9
21:6–8   353
21:7   11
21:9–10   368
21:15–17   650
21:15–19   628
21:15–22   643
21:16   346n15
21:20   11
21:20–23   486
21:24   11

Acts

1:1   388n6
1:1–11   687
1:2   120
1:3   127, 127n2
1:3–11   677
1:5   120
1:6   421
1:6–7   583, 597
1:6–8   572
1:7   397n2, 589
1:8   120, 687
1:9–11   583, 671
1:10   681
1:11   643
1:12   578
1:13   12, 264, 528n4
1:13–15   265n9
1:14   74
1:15–22   650n3
1:16   21, 265, 540
1:16–20   644, 648
1:18–19   648
1:19   649
1:25   265
2   406
2:3   115
2:4   120
2:7   643
2:10   659
2:11   554
2:14–38   265n9
2:14–39   650n3
2:15   668n1
2:16   108
2:17   66
2:20   582
2:22   248, 359, 643
2:23   306, 426n2, 621, 637
2:24   326, 677
`2:24–36   482
2:27   279n8
2:29   557n9
2:30   540
2:31   279n8
2:32   326, 684n2
2:32–33   640
2:33   120
2:34–35   540n3
2:36   268n1, 326
2:38   649

2:38–39   120
2:41–47   677
2:42   626
2:43–47   469
2:46   170
3:1   170, 500, 668n1
3:1–2   500
3:1–10   183n13
3:1–12   265n9
3:1–26   650n3
3:6   269, 359, 643
3:13   232n7, 426n2
3:13–18   637
3:15   326, 482, 677, 684n2
3:20   397n2
3:21   421, 475n2
3:22–23   418
3:25   321n3
3:26   232n7, 684n2
4:1–2   527n1
4:1–22   276
4:2   684n2
4:7   508
4:8   276
4:8–12   650n3
4:8–19   265n9
4:10   359, 482, 643, 684n2
4:11   515
4:13   276, 643
4:19–20   529n6, 650n3
4:24–28   93
4:25   21, 541
4:26   535, 535n3
4:27   232n7, 363, 646, 647
4:27–28   576, 621
4:29   276
4:30   232n7
4:31   276
4:32–5:11   269
4:33   684n2
4:34–37   471
4:35   183n13
4:36   12, 252, 557n10
5:1–4   473
5:1–11   650n3
5:3–29   265n9
5:4   471
5:6   674
5:9   528n2
5:10   674
5:12   170
5:17–18   527n1
5:17–41   276
5:27   275
5:28   654n2
5:29   529n6
5:29–32   650n3
5:30   482, 666, 684n2
5:32   276
5:33–40   207
5:36–37   573n3
5:37   643
5:38–39   508
5:42   170

6:2–3   183n13
6:5   276, 554
6:6   464n17
6:7   677
6:8–8:3   207
6:9   659
6:10   276
6:11–14   641
6:12   275
6:14   359, 568, 643
7:2   547
7:30–42   127n2
7:35   346n15
7:36   126
7:38 LXX   404n4
7:42   268n1
7:44   106
7:49   173, 302
7:51   276, 323, 562
7:52   154n13, 515n4, 558, 558n12
7:55   276
7:56   120
7:57–58   641
7:58   515n5
7:60   176, 259, 670n7
8:1   404
8:2   674
8:9   79
8:9–24   219n12
8:14   407
8:14–15   268
8:14–20   265n9
8:14–24   650n3
8:17–19   464n17
8:18–20   269
8:19   508
8:20   271
8:21   346n15
8:26–40   463n12
8:30   219
8:32–33   235n18
9:4   606n8
9:12   464n17
9:17   464n17
9:31   677
9:32–43   265n9
9:36   183n13
10   406
10:1   232n8
10:1–11:18   650n3
10:2   183n13, 554
10:4   440n4
10:5–46   265n9
10:9   578, 668n1
10:10–14   246
10:10–16   384
10:12–14   207
10:20   578
10:22   232n8, 554
10:28   232, 384
10:30   668n1
10:31   185
10:35   554
10:36   152
10:38   120, 248, 359, 589

10:39 666
10:40 482, 677, 684n2
10:42 219n10
10:44–11:18 159
11:1–18 268, 407
11:2–13 265n9
11:3 232
11:3–18 384
11:19 574n6
11:20 659
11:27–30 573
11:29 183n13
12:1 363
12:1–2 486
12:1–3 558
12:2 265, 365n6
12:3–17 650n3
12:4 677
12:5–18 265n9
12:6 244
12:15 439n1, 532n3
12:20 300n1
13:1 659
13:2–3 190, 190n25
13:3 464n17
13:5 159n4
13:6 79, 217n4, 574n8
13:6–12 219n12
13:8 79
13:9 276
13:10 350
13:15 159n4, 162n8, 295n9
13:16 554
13:18 127n2
13:21 127n2
13:25 281
13:26 159n3, 554
13:28 661
13:29 666
13:30 482, 677
13:30–37 684n2
13:32 159n3
13:33–37 482, 640
13:36 259, 670n7
13:37 326
13:43 554
13:44–51 207
13:46–47 159n3
13:48 306
13:50 554
13:51 272
14:4 641n5
14:8–18 200
14:15 404n3
14:17 177
14:22 574n6, 576
14:23 190, 190n25, 404
15 162, 268, 407
15:1–5 159
15:7 265n9
15:7–11 650n3
15:10 305, 408, 528n2, 546
15:12–18 269
15:19–29 159
15:20 211

15:20–29 172n25
15:28 546
15:33 272n2
16:14 554
16:19–40 207
16:26 573n5
16:36 272n2
17:1 159n4
17:4 554
17:10 159n4
17:13 277
17:17 554
17:18 684n2
17:27 209
17:30 649
17:30–31 533n5, 640n3
17:31 219n10, 260, 326, 609, 677, 684, 684n2
17:32 531n2
18:1–3 269
18:4 159n4
18:6 272, 654n2
18:7 554
18:9 292
18:12–17 207
18:18 99, 159n4
19:4 290n1
19:6 464n17
19:13–14 321n5
19:13–17 219n12
19:23–41 207
20:7–12 626
20:8 596n4
20:9–12 259
20:17–26 159n4
20:23 574n6
20:26 654n2
20:28 404
20:29 217, 275
20:29–30 574n8
20:33–35 269
20:35 183n13
21:9 69, 463
21:20 528n4, 677
21:20–21 159
21:20–26 218n5
21:21 159, 162
21:23–24 99
21:26 170
21:27–44 207
21:28 159
21:32 232n8
21:38 106, 528n4, 573n3, 579n3
21:39 159n3
22:1 547
22:3 159n3, 159n4
22:4 574n6
22:7 606n8
22:8 359, 643
22:14 159n3
22:17 159n4, 170
22:24–25 654n3
22:25 232n8
22:26 232n8
23:1–6 159n4

23:2–3 175
23:3 556
23:5–6 159n3
23:6 531n2, 684n2
23:6–9 676
23:6–10 527n1, 677
23:8 530
23:21 190n25
23:23 668n1
23:28 661
24:5 100, 359, 643
24:11–21 159n3, 159n4
24:12 170
24:14 162n8, 295n9, 519
24:14–18 159
24:15 279, 531n2, 677
24:17 183n13
24:18 170
24:21 531n2, 677, 684n2
24:23 232n8
25:8 159, 159n4, 170
25:19 677, 684n2
25:23 275
26:4–8 159n3
26:8 677, 684n2
26:9 359
26:14 606n8
26:18 155, 322, 508
26:20–23 159n4
26:21 170
26:22–23 159n3
26:23 677, 684n2
27:1 232n8
27:4 372
27:6 232n8
27:11 232n8
27:26 410n1
27:27 596
27:31 232n8
27:34 280
27:43 232n8
28:1–6 200
28:8 464n17
28:14–31 677
28:16 232n8
28:17 159, 159n3
28:18 661
28:19–20 159n3
28:20 159n4, 519
28:23 159, 159n3, 162n8, 295n9
28:25 21
28:26–27 339, 340n6

Romans

1:1 346n15
1:1–2 159n3
1:2 21
1:3 57, 540n2
1:4 683, 684n2
1:7 191
1:16 269
1:18 186n21
1:29–31 382n12

1:30 379n7
2:1 205, 388n6
2:3 388n6
2:5 540n3
2:6 412
2:9 574n6
2:13 220
2:16 219n10
2:19 155, 382
2:21–24 546, 554
2:28–29 184
3:1–8 162
3:1–4:15 113
3:8 218n5, 220
3:19 162n8
3:21 162n8, 295n9
3:24–26 666n3
3:31 162, 218n5
4 389
4:4 188
4:7 146n4
4:8 146n4
4:9–17 57
4:20 504
4:25 426n2, 683, 684n2
5:1–2 151
5:10 200n15
5:12 249
5:12–6:11 666
5:15 200n15, 488
5:17 200n15
5:19 488
6:1 218n5
6:1–11 683
6:1–23 537
6:2–11 412n4
6:4–5 684n2
6:14 158
6:14–15 162
6:15 218n5
6:19 632
7:1–6 158
7:4 218n6
7:12 159
7:14 159
8:1–4 159
8:4 159
8:4–17 632
8:11 533, 684n2
8:18 411, 576
8:18–23 475, 475n2
8:18–25 476
8:23 235
8:25 220
8:28–39 576
8:29 682
8:32 426n2
8:34 540n3
8:35 281n13, 574n6, 609
9–11 342, 651
9:1–3 563
9:1–5 561
9:1–11:32 113
9:3 159n3
9:6 476, 525n5
9:20 388n6

9:23   609
9:26   404n3
9:27   222
9:29–31   525n5
9:33   438n1
10:1   561
10:4   158, 159
10:9   684n2
10:16   235n18
11:1   159n3
11:1–2   562
11:1–5   525n5
11:2   669n2
11:8   340n6
11:9   438n1
11:11–12   562
11:11–24   666
11:15   562
11:16–24   269, 519, 561
11:17   389
11:18–23   510
11:22   220
11:23–27   562
11:25   339n4
11:29   540n3
12:2   416
12:6   602
12:6–8   598
12:9–10   469n2
12:11   601
12:12   574n6, 574n9
12:14–21   175
13:1–7   430, 529, 529n6
13:7   429
13:7–8   188
13:8–9   212
13:8–10   159, 537
13:9   469n2
13:9–10   534
13:11–14   438, 632
13:14   220
14:2–3   384
14:3   439
14:6   384
14:10   205, 439
14:10–12   609
14:12   412
14:13   438n1
14:13–23   430
14:14–15   384
14:15   439
14:17   196n5, 272n2
14:22   146n4
15:7–12   389, 666
15:7–13   159n3, 269, 519
15:12   540n2
16:2   272n1
16:16   636
16:17   438n1
16:19   275
16:20   272n2

1 Corinthians

1:2   404
1:12   406n12, 650

1:18   661
1:18–25   684
1:22   326, 328, 396
1:23   438n1
1:23–24   666n3
1:23–25   661
1:26   471
1:26–29   470n3, 674
3:6–9   338
3:9–15   405n6
3:10   406
3:10–15   221n15, 412
3:22   650n3
4:2   592
4:5   205, 246
4:8–13   609
4:11   609
5:1   172n25, 462
5:1–6:11   445n5
5:3   476n3
5:4   446
5:6–8   345
5:7   612, 627
5:9–10   254
5:12   205, 476n3
6:2   476
6:2–3   476n3
6:7–8   175
6:9–10   382n12
6:16   461
7:1–2   463
7:3   188
7:5   126, 528
7:7   598
7:7–9   463
7:25   69–70
7:26   578
7:28   70
7:32–34   199
7:32–38   463
7:34   70
7:36   70
7:37   70
7:39   670n7
8:3   220n13
8:4   196n5
8:9–9:1   430
8:12   606n8
8:13   437n1
9:5   234, 463, 650n3
9:9   271
9:14   271
9:16   550n1
9:18   269
9:19–23   159, 430
10:1–11   404
10:3   346n15
10:4   346n15
10:5   126, 346n15
10:9   129, 346n15, 396–97, 528n2
10:13   189, 576
11:20–22   626
11:22   439
11:23   426n2, 574n6
11:23–26   625
11:24–25   625

11:25   625, 627
11:26   370, 389, 626
11:30   249, 259, 670n7
11:31   206
12–14   219n12
12:4–7   598
12:7   602
12:13   666
12:22   200n15
12:25   199
12:26–27   606n8
12:28   404
13:2   425, 504
13:3   469
13:5   449
14:4–5   405n6
14:12   405n6
14:16   368
14:21   162n8
14:25   631n2
15   684n2
15:4–28   482
15:5   650n3
15:5–8   677
15:6   259, 670n7
15:9   606n7
15:12–13   531n2
15:16–19   683
15:18   259, 670n7
15:20   259, 667
15:20–22   666
15:20–28   303, 640n3, 670
15:22   249
15:23   579, 667
15:25   540n3
15:27   501
15:35–39   532
15:42   531n2
15:50–55   671
15:51   670n7
15:51–57   609
15:51–58   533
16:11   272n2
16:13   590, 633
16:22   187

2 Corinthians

1:4   574n6
1:6   574n6
1:8   292, 574n6
1:20   63, 163n10
2:5–11   445n5
3:3   404n3
3:7–18   418
3:9   200n15
3:11   200n15
3:12–18   419
3:18   416, 419n7
4:1–2   598
4:5   487
4:7   264
4:7–10   317
4:8   292
4:10   684n2
4:14   684n2

5:10   219n10, 412, 608, 609
5:17   462, 537
5:21   666n3, 669
6:1–10   609
6:16   404n3
7:8   649
9:10   196n5, 263n7
10:1   487
11:2   70, 255, 524, 595n3
11:7   269
11:12–15   217n4
11:15   412
11:20   175
11:23–25   276
11:27   609
11:29   437n1
12:7   609n16
12:8   632
12:9–10   317, 487
12:11   606n7
12:14–18   269
12:20   382n12
13:1   445n4
13:1–2   445n5
13:4   684n2

Galatians

1:1   684n2
1:6–9   159
1:18   406n12, 650n3
2:1–10   218n5
2:7   265n9
2:7–15   650n3
2:10   183n13, 471
2:11–14   407
2:13   183n14
2:20   412n4, 537, 666
3:1   159
3:1–3   159
3:6–14   57
3:13   482, 666, 683
3:14   159
3:23–25   159
3:28   671
3:29   57
4:9   220n13
4:14   606
4:17   159
4:19   573n4
4:27   573n4
5:1   305
5:1–4   159
5:6   220
5:9   345
5:11   438n1
5:12   159
5:13–14   159
5:14   212, 469n2, 534, 537
5:15   207
5:16–24   632
5:19–21   382n12
5:22   218n6
6:1   205, 206, 438

6:1–5   445n5
6:1–6   548
6:10   471, 607
6:12–13   159
6:14   537, 666, 684
6:15   159

Ephesians

1:4   609n15
1:5   303
1:9   303
1:9–10   303
1:10   397n2
1:20   540n3, 684n2
1:20–23   689
1:22   404, 501
2:1–6   322, 666
2:2   320n2
2:2–3   557n10
2:5   684n2
2:10   220
2:11–12   666
2:11–13   269
2:11–22   389, 462, 519
2:14–18   152
2:17   272n2
2:19–20   405n6
2:20   404, 406, 407
3:4   339n4
3:4–5   340
3:8   606n7
3:20   504
4:7   602
4:7–8   598
4:10   684n2
4:11–16   548
4:17   220
4:17–24   537
4:22–24   666
4:28   183n13
4:29   218n9
4:31–5:2   176n36, 177, 190, 452
5:3–5   382n12
5:8   155
5:9   218n6
5:14   633
5:21–6:4   464
5:21–6:9   458, 548n5
5:25   404
5:25–32   255
5:27   594
5:28–29   537
5:31   461
6:1–3   379n7
6:11–17   322
6:16   173n29

Philippians

1:11   218n6
1:12–18   276
2:5–11   419, 435, 487
2:6–8   589
2:6–11   689
2:8–9   684n2

2:9–11   219n10, 640, 658
2:12   200n15
2:13   303
2:15   155, 275
2:20   199
3:2   207, 388
3:6   469
3:11   531n2
3:17–19   218n5
3:21   501
4:6   199
4:6–7   195
4:10–18   269

Colossians

1:6   218n6
1:10   218n6
1:12–13   155
1:13   322
1:15–20   689
1:16–19   419
1:23   220
1:24   435
2:8–15   666
2:9   419
2:12   684n2
2:14   665
2:16   196n5, 384
2:22   381
3:1   540n3
3:1–4   537, 666, 684n2
3:3   412n4
3:5   382n12
3:5–8   171
3:6   557n10
3:8   382n12
3:9–11   666
3:13   190
3:14   534
3:18–21   464
3:18–4:1   458, 548n5
3:20   379n7
4:2   633
4:6   154

1 Thessalonians

1:9   404n3
1:10   219n10
2:14–16   558n12
2:15   154n13, 277, 515n4
2:19   579
3:5   528
3:13   579
4:13   259
4:13–14   670n7
4:13–18   590
4:14   684n2
4:15   579
4:16   583n3
4:17   583
5:1–2   397n2
5:1–3   593
5:2   591

5:2–6   597
5:3   573n4
5:5   557n10
5:6   590, 596
5:6–8   633
5:7   593
5:9   574
5:12–13   548
5:15   175
5:20   217n4

2 Thessalonians

1:4   574n6
1:6–9   574n6
1:6–10   583, 590
1:7   608n10
1:8   610
1:9   279
2:2   588n1
2:2–3   572
2:3   557n10, 573
2:3–4   579
2:4   577, 580
2:7   339n4
2:8   574
2:8–12   573n2
2:9   578
2:9–10   219n12
2:10   574
3:3   189
3:6   445n5
3:14–15   445n5

1 Timothy

1:9–10   382n12
1:15   606n7
2:1–2   185, 529n6
2:5   589
2:6   487, 488, 666n3
2:8   185
2:9   352
3:2   548
3:15   404n3, 405n6
3:16   684n2
4:1   397n2
4:1–5   574n7
4:10   404n3
4:12   439
4:14   464n17
5:1–2   548
5:1–4   379n7
5:10   609
5:17   548
5:18   271, 478
5:19   445n4
5:19–20   445n5
5:20   444n2
5:22   464n17
6:6–10   195
6:6–19   412
6:9–10   471
6:10   470n3, 473
6:11   388n6
6:13   644, 646, 647
6:14–15   397n2

6:17–19   471, 674
6:18–19   196
6:20   388n6

2 Timothy

1:6   464n17
2:3   574n9
2:10   306, 574, 574n9
2:12   220n13, 280, 574n9, 576
2:18   531n2
2:19   220n13
3:1–13   574n7
3:2   379n7
3:2–8   382n12
3:4   574
3:12   576
3:16   21, 69, 444n2
4:1   219n10
4:2   444n2, 445n5
4:8   219n10, 219n11
4:14   412
4:18   189
21:11–13   411

Titus

1:6   548
1:7   598
1:14   381
2:7   220
2:14   220, 488
2:15   445n5
3:3   382n12
3:5   475n2
3:8   220
3:10   445n5
3:10–11   207
3:14   220

Hebrews

1:1–4   419
1:3   446, 540n3, 684n2
1:13   540n3
1:14   439, 574
2:6–9   501
2:9   413n6, 666n3, 684
2:11   682
2:12 LXX   404n4
2:13   405n8
2:14   140, 684
2:14–15   666n3
2:14–18   633
2:17–18   606n8
2:18   189
3–4   67
3:1–6   405n6
3:7–11   461n7
3:7–19   129
3:9   127n2, 528n2
3:11   305n4
3:12   404n3
3:15   461n7
3:17   127n2
3:18   305n4

4:1 305n4
4:3 609n15
4:7 461n7
4:14–16 633
4:15 189, 528
5:6 540n3
5:7–8 292
5:7–10 633
5:10 540n3
6:2 531n2
6:6 323
6:18 445n4
6:20 540n3
7:3 540n3
7:11 540n3
7:14 59
7:15 540n3
7:17–21 540n3
7:21 649
7:26–27 666n3
8:1 540n3
8:8 268n1
8:10 268n1
9:11–12 666n3
9:12 488
9:12–14 684
9:14 404n3
9:19–22 625
9:26 609n15
9:28 574, 666n3
10:4–9 253
10:12 666n3, 684n2
10:12–13 540n3
10:28 445n4
10:29 625
10:31 279, 404n3
10:32–34 207
10:32–38 435
10:34 609
10:37 290n1, 422n12
11:4 558
11:13 340
11:16 155n15
11:31 59
11:32–38 558n12
11:32–39 515n4
11:35 531n2, 533n5
11:37 109
11:38 106, 281, 577
11:39–40 340
12:1 684n2
12:2 540n3, 601
12:16 196n5
12:18–24 404
12:18–29 224
12:19 583n3
12:22 155n15, 404n3
12:23 404
12:25 200n15
13:2 609
13:3 609
13:5 195
13:12 515n5, 520
13:15 218n6
13:17 548
13:20 625

James

1:6 504
1:9–11 471, 548n5, 674
1:10–11 200
1:11 338
1:12 146n4, 574n9
1:12–18 189
1:13–15 189
1:22–25 222
1:27 551n4
2 162
2:1–4 547
2:1–17 471
2:5 149n8
2:8 469n2, 534, 537
2:13 205, 452
2:14–26 218n5
2:16 272n2
2:19 246
2:20 388n6
2:25 59
3:6 279n7
3:9–10 534
3:10–12 218n6
3:12 218
3:17–18 152
3:18 113, 152, 218n6
4:4 326
4:7 322
4:11–12 205, 206
4:12 279
4:13–15 201
5:1–6 473n5
5:2–3 196
5:4 478
5:7 579
5:8 585
5:9 205, 585
5:10 154n13, 515n4
5:11 574n9
5:12 172
5:15 249
5:16–18 292
5:17 669n2

1 Peter

1:1 265n9
1:5 574
1:9 574
1:10–12 340, 411
1:12 589n2
1:14–25 177
1:16 157
1:17 412
1:18 488
1:18–19 488
1:19 627, 684
1:20 609n15
1:21 684n2
1:23 404n3
1:24–25 200
2:5 379n3, 405n6
2:7 515
2:8 438n1
2:9 379n3, 516n7, 518

2:12 156
2:13–17 430, 529, 529n6
2:20 574n9
2:21–25 435
2:22 235n18
2:23 175
2:24 666
2:25 440
3:14 153, 278
3:18 666n3
3:18–22 684n2, 689
3:20 588
3:22 501
4:3 382n12
4:10 598, 602
4:15–16 156
4:17 405n6
5:2 217
5:4 219n10, 407
5:7 195
5:8 345, 590, 633
5:8–9 322
5:14 636

2 Peter

1:1 265n9
1:10–11 574
1:16–18 413
1:16–19 418
1:19–21 21, 69
2:1 217n4, 574n8, 578
2:4 610
2:5 588, 589
2:6 272n3, 300n4
2:9 189, 576
2:13 626
2:14 170
2:15–16 217n4
2:17 233n13, 524n3
2:22 207, 388
3:4 579, 593, 670n7
3:5–7 588
3:6 589
3:7 610
3:8–9 292
3:10 588n1, 591
3:11–14 533n5
3:12–14 291n3
3:13 475n2
3:15 292

1 John

1:8 177
2:4–11 212
2:10 438n1
2:13 173n29
2:16 170
2:17 471
2:18 573n2, 578, 579
2:22 573n2, 579
2:26 573
2:28 579
3:2 152
3:8 140, 322

3:10 350
3:11–18 212
3:12 558
3:13–17 534
4:1 217n4, 574n8, 578
4:3 573n2, 579
4:7–12 177, 212
4:11 452
4:19–21 212, 534, 537
5:3 305, 546
5:16 323, 445n5
5:18–19 173n29

2 John

7 573, 573n2, 579
10 217, 445n5
10–11 436

3 John

5–8 606
5–10 436
6 272n1, 606
7 217
10 445n5

Jude

4 217
6 609n16, 610
7 272n3, 300n4, 610
11 550n1
12 626
13 233n13, 524n3, 610
17–19 574n7
20–23 445n5

Revelation

1:1 410n1, 573
1:3 146n4
1:4 290n1, 404
1:5 429n4, 667, 684n2
1:7 583, 640n3
1:8 290n1
1:9 435, 574n9
1:10 583n3
1:12–13 594
1:16 416
1:17 372, 419n5, 681
1:18 279n8, 405, 407, 684
2:1 439n1
2:4 574
2:7 295, 338
2:8 439n1, 684n2
2:9–10 574n6
2:10 278, 528, 595n2
2:11 295
2:12 439n1
2:14 438n1
2:17 295, 370
2:18 439n1
2:20 217n4, 573n2
2:22 232n9, 574n6
2:26 476n3

2:26–27 476, 640n3, 684
2:26–28 576
2:28 476n3
2:29 295
3:1 439n1
3:2–3 590
3:3 591
3:4–5 416, 417, 525n6
3:6 295
3:7 405, 407, 439n1, 596
3:10 189, 574n9
3:12 155n15
3:13 295
3:14 163n10, 439n1
3:17 470n3
3:17–18 412
3:18 525n6
3:20 585
3:21 476, 476n3, 540n3, 608, 684
3:21–22 576
3:22 295
4–5 187
4:1 120, 346n15, 573, 583n3
4:5 596n4
5:1–14 689
5:5 140, 345, 540n2
5:5–10 640
5:6 684
5:6–10 684n2
5:6–14 419
5:9 684
5:9–10 666n3
5:10 576
6:1–11 575
6:4 281n13
6:8 279n8, 573
6:9–11 684
6:10–11 558n12
6:12 573n5, 670n4
6:12–13 582
6:15 429n4
7:1 583
7:2 404n3

7:4–8 370
7:9 416, 417
7:11 631n2
7:12 163n10
7:14 565, 574n6, 578n2
8:2 439n1, 583n3
8:5 573n5, 670n4
8:6–13 583n3
8:10 596n4
8:12 582
8:13 550n1
9:1 583n3
9:1–6 407
9:5 451n6
9:12 550n1
9:13–14 583n3
9:20–21 382n12
10:1 416, 681
10:7 583n3
11:1–2 580
11:3 445n4, 515n4
11:3–6 422, 669n2
11:8 300n4
11:10 451n6
11:13 573n5, 670n4
11:14 550n1
11:15 583n3, 640n3
11:16 631n2
11:19 573n5, 670n4
12:1 397
12:2 451n6, 573n4
12:3 397
12:6 106
12:7 609n16
12:7–10 140
12:9 573n2, 609n16
12:12 550n1
12:14 397n2
13:3 578
13:4 573n2
13:8 573n2, 579, 609n15
13:9 338
13:10 574n9, 636n2
13:11–18 574n7
13:13–15 219n12
13:14 573n2

14:4 70, 595n3
14:7 279
14:10 279, 451n6, 610, 631n1
14:11 451n6
14:12 574n9
14:13 146n4
14:14–20 116, 350
14:15 263n7
14:15–19 350
14:20 372n2
15:6 681
15:7 404n3
16:4 346n15
16:13 217n4, 346n15, 574n8
16:15 146n4, 590, 591
16:18 573n5, 578n2, 670n4
16:19 631n1
17:4 352, 631n1
17:8 609n15
18:6 631n1
18:8 573
18:10 451n6, 550n1, 561
18:12 352
18:15 451n6
18:16 352, 550n1, 561
18:18–19 561
18:19 550n1
18:21 437
18:22 259
19:7 255, 524, 594, 601
19:7–9 625
19:7–10 596
19:8 524n2, 525n6
19:9 146n4, 232, 370, 522, 524, 594
19:11 219n10
19:11–16 640n3
19:17–18 579
19:20 217n4, 573n2, 574n8, 578, 609, 610
20 322
20–22 322
20:1–3 407

20:1–10 140, 322
20:3 246n5, 322, 573n2
20:4 365n6, 476n3, 576
20:4–6 640n3
20:5–6 531n2
20:6 146n4, 476, 476n3
20:8 222, 573n2
20:9 346n15
20:10 217n4, 246n5, 279, 451n6, 573n2, 574n8, 609, 610
20:11–15 609
20:12 412
20:13 279n8
20:14–15 246n5, 610
20:15 279
21–22 475n2
21:2 255
21:2–27 155n15
21:4 233, 235
21:8 279, 382n12, 610
21:9 255
21:12 475, 519
21:12–13 215
21:12–14 269, 370, 637
21:14 404, 406, 407
21:15 215
21:16 372n2
21:16–17 370
21:21 215
21:24–26 86
21:25 215
22:2 476n3
22:4 152
22:5 476n3
22:6 410n1
22:7 146n4
22:11 557n11
22:12 412
22:14 215, 525n6
22:15 207, 388
22:16 540n2
22:17 255
22:20 163n10, 187

Old Testament Apocrypha

Baruch

3:11 279n8
3:19 279n8
3:32 303
4:37 232
6:66–67 397

1 Esdras

3:20 LXX 188
4:21 669
4:58 186n21, 368n2
6:21 476n3
6:22 Eng 476n3

9:47 LXX 163n10

2 Esdras

2:16–18 403n2
2:20–23 609
3:20 113
3:25–27 502n7
4:11 419n5
4:26–27 350
4:26–32 338
4:26–40 263n7
4:37 397n2
4:42 573n4
4:52 589n2

5:1–2 574n7
5:4 397
5:4–5 582
5:6 579
5:9 281
5:14–15 419n5
5:21–40 523
5:46 595n2
6:1 609n15
6:13–16 573n5, 670n4
6:22 573
6:24 281
6:25 574n9
6:26 413n6, 421
7 532

7:3–9 213
7:6–9 215
7:27 574n9
7:36 351
7:37 608n12
7:39–40 397
7:75 475n2
7:93 233n13
7:97 417
7:106 272n3
7:113 350
8:1 524
8:3 524
8:41 338
8:55 524

8:60   609
9:3   573n5, 670n4
9:7–8   574n9
9:15   524
9:17   350
9:31–37   338
10:25–59   580n4
10:30   419n5
10:38   339n4
12:36–37   339n4
13:8–11   115
13:16   550n1
13:19   550n1
14:5   339n4
14:50   355n5
15:20   429n4

Judith

2:28   300n1
6:19   186n21
8:5   190
8:35   272n2
9:12 LXX   302
9:13   562
10:22   596n4
11:19   262n6
12:7   378
12:16   170n20
14:19   641n5
16:7–8   191n26
16:17   550n1

1 Maccabees

1:43   309n3
1:45   309n3
1:47   246
1:54   577
1:59   577
2:7   550n1
2:21 LXX   410n2
2:28   577, 578
2:31   577
2:32–41   309n3
2:39–41   309n5
2:44   169n18
2:58   417
3:6   220
3:18   186n21
3:47   191
3:50   186n21
3:60   186n21
4   501
4:2   254n6
4:24   186n21
4:30   426n3
4:59 LXX   404n4
5   133
5:4   411
5:15   300n1
5:28   523
5:45–54   493n1, 496
6:7   577
6:54   573
7:8   434
9:27   578n2

9:37–42   595
9:56   451n6
9:73   476n3
10:31   429
10:68 LXX   451n5
11:1   222
11:33   476n3
11:34   674
11:35   429
11:71   641n5
13:27–30   557n9
13:49–53   493n1
13:51   496
14:16 LXX   451n5
14:49 LXX   499n3
15:8 LXX   188

2 Maccabees

2:8   418
3:1–6 LXX   499n3
3:24 LXX   499n3
3:28 LXX   499n3
3:40 LXX   499n3
4:21–22   493n1
5:27   109
6:1–5   577
6:11   577
6:14   558n12
6:18–23   247
6:30   278
7:9   153, 532
7:9–11   531
7:13   451n6
7:17   451n6
7:36   532
10   501
10:6   577
10:7   496
10:26   500
10:35   169n18
11:6   440n1
11:25   476n3
11:36   476n3
12:45   670n7
13:12   190n25
14:33   569n2
14:38   153
15:12–16   403n2

3 Maccabees

2:4   589
2:5   272n3
4:21   186n21
5:21–24   660
5:51   215, 405
6:18–19   440n1
6:30   476n3
7:6   186n21
7:23   163n10

4 Maccabees

4:11   419n5
4:17–18   146n5
6:5   451n6

6:17   57
6:22   57
7:19   532
8–18   531
9:6   451n6
9:29   153
11:2   451n6
13:13–15   278
13:15   379
13:17   532
15:17   388n6
16:24   379
16:25   532
18:1   57
18:3   153
18:24   163n10

Sirach

1:2   222
1:6–9   303
1:22   169n18
1:29   183n14
2:12   213
2:12–14   550n1
3:7–8   379n7
3:12–15   379n7
3:30   183n13
4:1–8   183n13
4:9   476n3
4:17   451n6
6:23–31   305
7:14   185
7:35   609
9:5   437n1
9:8   170n20
11:18–19   412
12:1–3   183n13
13:3–4   473n5
13:15   469n2
14:1 LXX   146n3
14:2 LXX   146n3
14:8–10   479
14:20 LXX   146n3
14:20–27   146n6
15:1–10   146n6
15:11–17   213
15:11–20   189
16:7   589
16:9–10   461n7
17:22   183n13
18:20   205
19:13–20:2   444n2
20:30   352
21:10   213
22:16–18   221n15
23:6   170n20
23:9   173
23:25   113
24:5–6   372
24:19   305
24:19–22   303
25:8 LXX   146n3
25:9 LXX   146n3
25:16–26   463
25:21   170, 437n1
25:26   462n9

26:1 LXX   146n3
26:9   170
27:6   218n6, 324
28:1–8   174n31
28:19 LXX   146n3
29:8   183n13
29:10   601
31:5–7   470n3
31:7   471, 473
31:8 LXX   146n3
31:8–11   198n8
31:15   211
32:15   183n14
33:2   183n14
34:7   437n1
34:15 LXX   146n3
34:20–26   473n5
34:31   190
35:24   412
38:16   239
39:1   168n15
39:1–3   355n5
39:30   281n13
41:8   550n1
41:14   156n16
41:21   170n20
42:8   476n3
43:23   373, 376
44   547
46:19   670n7
48:10   295, 421
48:11 LXX   146n3
48:13   670n7
50:6–7   155
50:7   351
50:28 LXX   146n3
51:14   500
51:23–27   305
51:23–30   303

Tobit

1:3   183n13, 509n6
1:16–20   365
1:17–20   674
2:2   183n13
2:3–8   674
2:3–9   365
2:14   183n13
3:4   445n3
3:7–8   531
3:10   279n8
3:10 LXX   451n5
3:17   321
4:3   239
4:3–4   365, 674
4:5   379
4:5–6   183n12
4:5–11   469
4:7   479
4:7–11   183n13
4:10   184
4:15   211
5:15   478
6:14   674
7:17 LXX   302
8:1–3   321n5

8:3   321
8:8   163n10
8:9   674
10:13   186n21
12:8   182n11, 183,
    183n12, 184, 190n25
12:8–9   183n13
12:12–14   365
12:13   674
12:15   440n1
12:17   272n2, 419n5
13:6   562n1
13:14 Eng   146n3

13:14   150
13:15–16 LXX   146n3
13:16–18   580n4
14:5   397n2, 580n4
14:10   184, 233n13
14:10–12   365
14:11–13   674

Wisdom of Solomon

1:1   476n3

2:1–5   532n4
2:18–20   663
3:8   476, 476n3
3:9   525n5
3:13   146n3
3:14   463n12
4:15   525n5
5:5   532n3
5:6–7   213
5:20   281n13
8:4   303
9:1–18   303
10:10   303

12:21   172
14:2–4   372, 373
14:11   411
14:25–26   382n12
14:28   172
16:13   405
16:13–14   278
17:20   524n3
17:21   233n13

Old Testament Pseudepigrapha

Ahiqar
8.38   593

Apocalypse of Abraham
13   341
25.1–6   502n7
27.1–7   502n7
29   525n5

Apocalypse of Elijah
2.41   577
4.1–6   580n4
4.21   577

Apocalypse of Moses
16.3   343n11

Apocalypse of Peter
78.23   233

Apocalypse of Sedrach
14.2   631n2

Assumption of Moses
1.14   609n15
7   554n6
7.3–10   382n12
7.5–10   556
10.4   670n4

2 Baruch
1.1–5   502n7
6.7–9   352
7.1   523
8.1–2   568
8.2   562
10.13–14   578
10.18   405, 502n7
13.1–2   419n5
13.3   350
13.4   502n7
19.5   350

20.1–2   578
21.8   350, 589n2
21.17   609
27.5   281n13
27.6   573
27.15   350
29.3–8   255
30.2   479
32.1–6   475n2
38.1   339
40.1   281n13
40.1–3   579
41.3   305n3, 574n7
41.4   561
44.12   475n2
44.15   524
48.2–3   339n4
48.3   589n2
48.26   185
48.34   573n2
48.38   574n7
51.1–3   417
51.4   339
51.5   532n3
51.6   610
51.10   215, 417, 532n3
51.12   417
51.15   412
52.6   153
53.7–12   221n16
54.1   578, 589n2
57.2   475n2
64.6   568
66.1   536n5
66.4   217n4
70.1–2   350
70.2   263n7
70.3   281
70.8   573, 670n4
70.9   317n7, 574n9
72.1–6   605n2
72.2   608n12
80.3   523
81.4   339n4
83.1   578

3 Baruch
11.2   405
12–16   599n5

4 Baruch
1.1–8   559n15
4.3–8   502n7
4.4   405
9.5   405
9.19–31   559n15

1 Enoch
1.3–9   670n4
1.6–7   573n5
1.8   372
1.9   608n10
5.1–9   525n5
6.2   186n21
10.4   321
10.4–5   524
10.4–6   246
10.4–7   322
10.11–13   321
10.12–13   246
10.13   609
10.15–16   246
10.16   381n11, 513n2
12.3–4   355n5
13.1   321
13.8   186n21
14.13–14   419n5
14.21   440n1
15–16   246
15.1   355n5
16.1   350
16.3   461n7
19.1   246
20.5   440n1
20.8   532
22.1–14   532
22.3   609
22.6–7   558
38.2   625
38.4   417
39.7   351, 561
40.6   440n1
40.9   440n1
45.3   219n11, 413
45.3–5   475n2
48.4   429n4
48.4–5   575n10
54.1–2   609

54.4–6   322
54.6   350
55.4   413
56.7   281
58.2   146n5
60.3–4   419n5
60.8   532
61.8   413, 608n10
61.12   187n22
62.1–5   608n10
62.2   413
62.4   573n4
62.5   640
62.12   281n13
62.14   255
62.15   532
62.15–16   525n6
63.1   350
63.6   233n13
63.10   198n8
63.11   281n13
63.15–16   416
67.8   170n20
67.10   589
67.13   609
68.5   339n4
69.27–29   608n10
69.28   246, 321
69.29   413
71.1   416
71.2–3   419n5
72.1   475n2
80.4   582
81.4   146n5
82.4   146n5, 509n6
83–90   502n7
83.9   186n21
84.6   381n11, 513n2
89   512n1
89–90   217
89.42   207
89.56   514n3, 562
89.66–67   514n3
89.73   514n3
90.6   608n14
90.19   281n13
90.20–36   6008n10
90.22–27   574n7
90.28–29   580n4

90.30 608n14
90.32 608n14
91.7 186n21, 574n7
91.11–12 281n13
92–105 473n5
92.3 509n6
93.2 381n11
93.5 381n11
93.9 574n7
93.10 381n11
94.1 509n6
94.6–95.7 550n1
94.7 222
94.8 198n8
96.4 198n8
96.4–8 550n1
97.8 198n8
98.9–99.2 550n1
99.10 146n5, 509n6
100.1–2 281
100.7–9 550n1
102.2 573n5
102.5 279n8
102.6–11 532n4
103.2 339n4
103.5 146n5
103.7 233n13, 279n8
104.1 440n1
104.1–6 532n3
104.2 351, 417
108.3 233
108.10 412
108.14 233n13

2 Enoch
1.8 419n5
9.1 609
10.2 233n13
10.4–6 609
13.64–70 550n1
20.2 419n5
21.2–3 419n5
22.4–5 419n5
29.4–5 609n16
30.15 213
40.12 233
41.1 146n5
42.6–14 146n5
42.10 213
42.14 217n6
44.4 146n5
48.9 146n5
50.3–4 174n31
50.4 175
51.1–2 [J text] 601
52.1–14 146n5
61.1 211
61.3 146n5
62.1 146n5
64.5 355n5
66.7 146n5

3 Enoch
1.7–9 419n5
18.18 405

4 Ezra
See 2 Esdras under OT
Apocrypha

Greek Apocalypse of Ezra
1.9 550n1
1.24 550n1
2.19 300n4
4.38 524n3
7.12 300n4

Joseph and Aseneth
2.6 595
6.4 410n2
8–11 555n7
14.4 631n2

Jubilees
1.9 437n1
1.12–14 559n15
1.15–16 536
1.15–18 562n1
1.16 381n11, 513n2
1.20 509n6
1.27 580n4
1.29 475n2
2.2 439n1
2.17–23 309n3
2.18 439n1
4.3 558
5.6 246
5.10 246
7.20 379n7, 469n2
7.34 381n11
10.7 321
10.8–9 246
11.11 338n2
11.11–12 341
14.16 558n12
15.34 323
16.5 300n4
16.25 536
19.8 595n2
19.31 536
20.2 469n2
20.5–6 589
20.6 300n4
21.2–3 219
21.23 219
23.11–31 531
23.14 326
23.14–17 574n7
23.16 281
23.19 281
23.19–21 379
23.21 502n7
23.26 509n6
23.29 322
25.15 509n6
29.14–20 379n7
31.14 439n1
35.1–6 379n7
35.11–13 379n7
36.4 469n2
36.8 469n2
36.24 536

48.15 320n2
50.10–11 309n5
50.12 309n3

Letter of Aristeas
1 6
8 6
26 601
159 547n3
204–5 198n8
207 211
228 379n7
229 534n1
238 379n7
305–6 378
322 6

Life of Adam and Eve
33.1 440n1

Lives of the Prophets
1–3 559n15
4.2 463n15
6–7 559n15
10.10–11 326
15 559n15
23 559n15

Martyrdom and Ascension of Isaiah
in toto 559n15
2.12–15 217n4
3.10 300n4
4.3 381n11

Psalms of Solomon
1.8 502n7
2.3–5 502n7
2.16 412
4.1–5 556
4.6 183n14
4.19–20 554n6
4.20 183n14
4.23 411
5.3 322
5.9–10 199
7.9 305n3
8.11–13 502n7
14.2–3 344n12, 381n11
14.3–4 513n2
14.9 233n13, 524n3
15.10 233n13
16.2 405
16.7–8 170
17.8–10 412
17.15 557n10
17.17 106
17.21 589n2
17.21–43 540n2
17.28 476n3
18.7–9 540n2

Pseudo-Philo
Liber antiquitatum biblicarum
3.9 573
3.10 412, 475n2
4.11 532
6.1 281
6.6 449n2
12.1 416
15.5 440n1
16.2 558
19.2 568
23.4 404n5
26.13 558n12
51.4 155
60.3 246

Questions of Ezra (Recension A)
3 524n3

Sibylline Oracles
3.263–64 338n3
3.371–72 146n5

Testament of Asher
1.3–5 213
1.7 381
6.4 609n16
7.5 379

Testament of Benjamin
2.2–4 654n3
3.3–4 469n2
7.4 449
9.2 608n12

Testament of Dan
5.3 534n1
5.6 320n2

Testament of Gad
4 444n2
4.2 469n2
6.3–5 444n2

Testament of Issachar
5.2 469n2, 534n1
7.6 534n1

Testament of Jacob
5.9 233

Testament of Job
9.7–8 184n15
17.3 412

Testament of Judah
10.4 531n1
19.1–2 470n3

Testament of Levi
3.5 440n1

5.6 440n1
10.2 573n2
14.1–8 502n7
14.4 379
15.1 577
16.4 569n2
17.11 382n12, 502n7
18.5–9 575n10
18.12 321, 408
18.40 416

Testament of Moses
5.3–6.1 502n7
7.4 573n2
7.8–10 502n7
8.1 578n2
8.1–5 579
10.5 582

Testament of Naphtali
1.6 211

Testament of Reuben
3.3–6 382n12
6.9 469n2

Testament of Simeon
2.11–14 312

Testament of Solomon
1.14 408
22.8 129
23.1 425

Testament of Zebulun
9.8 322

New Testament Apocrypha

Acts of John
109 353n2

Acts of Peter
20 353n2

Gospel of Thomas
5 182
6 211
8 295

9 337
14 182, 190
16 281
20 338n2, 344
21 295
22 435
24 295
36 199
40 381
41 602

45 218n6, 324
46 435
57 343, 343n11
64 295
65 295, 512
76 352
89 556
93 206
96 295, 344
104 190

107 440
109 352

Protevangelium of James
9.2 74
23–24 558n13

Rabbinic Writings

'Abot de Rabbi Nathan
4 253n5
5 379n6
14a 599n5
24a 221
39 323n9
43 317n7
121B 317n7

Babylonian Talmud
'Abodah Zarah
18a 529n6
'Arakin
10a 496
Baba Batra
3b 425
9b 184n15
10a 469
10a–b 184n15
60b 190n25
Baba Meṣi'a
38b 472n2
42a 601
Baba Qamma
113a 528n4
Berakot
6b 183
11b 601
28a 184n15, 556
28b 214
55a 602

55b 472n2
56b 494
60b 189
63a 536n7
64a 425
'Erubin
43b 421
Giṭṭin
57b 559n17
60b 379n4
90b 460
Ḥagigah
3b 408n16
Ketubbot
7b 595n2
Makkot
23b–24a 535
Megillah
6b 169n18
20a 182
Menaḥot
35a 547n3
Mo'ed Qaṭan
16b 184n15
Nedarim
22a 173
62a 184n15
Pesaḥim
110a 320n2
112b 528n4
113a 184n15

113b 554n6
Qiddušin
66a 111n8
Šabbat
8b 547n3
12b 580n4
13a 111n8
31a 211, 536, 536n7, 555n7
35b 183
102b 601
152b 599n5
Sanhedrin
4a 425
14b 494
35a 183
43a 12, 660
90b 532n4
93b 463n15
96b 559n17
98a 494
118a 421
152a 463n12
Soṭah
9b 425
20a–22b 111n8
22b 111, 181, 184n15, 554n6
41b–42a 184n15, 554n6
Sukkah
30a 252
41a 580n4
49b 253n5

51b 568n1
Yebamot
48b 436
61b–64b 464
79a 184n15
80b 463n12
Yoma
72b 556
78b 413n6
86b–87a 449

Deuteronomy Rabbah
3.17 417
on Deut. 28:1 509

Ecclesiastes Rabbah
3.16 559n17
on Eccles. 4:1 184n15
on Eccles. 5:5 184n15
10.4 559n17

Esther Rabbah
1.17 554n6

Exodus Rabbah
on Exod. 3:1 512n1
on Exod. 12:19 522
on Exod. 18:1 509
on Exod. 21:1 536n7

Lamentations Rabbah
proem 5 559n17
proem 23 559n17
1.16.51 559n17
2.2.4 559n17
2.20.23 559n17
4.13.16 559n17

Leviticus Rabbah
on Lev. 4:2 512n1
on Lev. 18:3 512n1

Mekilta
on Exod. 15:1 501n5
on Exod. 16:32 589n2
on Exod. 19:21 440
on Exod. 20:2 599n5
on Exod. 20:7 323n9
on Exod. 20:24 446
on Exod. 21:35 176
on Exod. 22:2 313
on Exod. 22:23 365n6
on Exod. 31:14 309n5

Midrash Tanḥuma
Ki Tassa §17 379n4
on Lev. 4:1 559n17
on Deut. 15:9 606

Mishnah
'Abot
1.1 111, 225, 546, 555n7
1.1–3 379
1.2 142, 253n5
1.3 186n21, 269, 481
1.3–4 546
1.5 183n13
1.6 135, 205, 546
1.8 546
1.10 546
1.11 186n21
1.12 152, 536, 546, 555n7
1.13 184n15, 269, 481
2.1 163
2.2 186n21
2.5 205
2.7 636n2
2.8 546
2.9 214, 253n3, 381, 479
2.11 479
2.12 186n21, 197
2.12–13 214
2.15 197
2.15–16 480n10
2.17 198n8
3.1 436
3.2 446
3.3 446
3.5 305n3
3.6 446
3.11 435n5
3.12 436
3.18 163
4.1 163

4.2 601
4.4 436
4.5 269, 481
4.9 198n8
4.10 436
4.17 412
5.1–6 595n2
5.13 183n13, 184n15
5.16 197
5.22 197
6.1 436
6.11 535

Baba Batra
10.8 451

Baba Meṣi'a
1.8 421
2.8 421
3.4–5 421

Baba Qamma
4.4 435n5
6.2 435n5
6.4 435n5
7.7 247
8.6 175
10.1 183n13

Bekorot
4.6 269

Berakot
1.1–2 536
2.2 305n3
3.1 239
3.3 547n3
3.5 185
4.4 185
6.1 369, 627
9.5 569

Beṣah
3.4 313n1

Demai
2.3 173

'Eduyyot
8.7 421

'Erubin
in toto 578
3.2 435n5

Giṭṭin
9.1–3 462
9.10 66, 171, 171n23, 171n24, 460

Ḥagigah
1.1 500
2.5 378

Kelim
1.4 557n8
25.1–9 556

Kerithot
1.7 500, 502n7

Ketubbot
in toto 462
4.4 259
5.2 65
7.6 460

Ma'aśer Šeni
4.10–11 380
5.1 557n8

Makkot
3.16 535

Menaḥot
5.1–2 344

Middot
2.4 569

Mo'ed Qaṭan
1.2 557n8

Nedarim
in toto 555
1.2–4 380
1.3 173
3.11 310, 380
4.7–8 380n9
5.6 380
9.1 380, 380n9
9.7 380
10.5 65
11.12 461

Nega'im
in toto 231n5

Niddah
in toto 259
4.2 112
5.2 344

'Oholot
17.1–18.6 557n8

Parah
3.7 112

Pe'ah
2.1 338
2.7–8 309

Pesaḥim
in toto 624
6.1–2 309n5, 310
10 623, 626
10.3 625, 626
10.4–5 625
10.6 580n4
10.6–7 626
10.7 626

Šabbat
6.10 664n2
7.2 309n3, 338n2
16.1–7 309n5
18.3 309n5
19.1–3 309n5
22.6 313
23.4 259

Sanhedrin
in toto 169n17
1.1 446
3.2 173
4–7 641
4.1 646
7.1 365n6
7.1–4 482
7.3 365n6
7.5 641n5

10.1 381, 525, 532n4
10.2 649
11.3 547n3

Šebi'it
in toto 639
4.13 173
9.1 556

Šebu'ot
3.8 547n3
3.11 547n3

Šeqalim
1–2 429
1.1 557n8
1.3 183, 435n5
1.6 499
2.1 183
2.5 421
5.6 184n15, 499, 499n3
6.1–5 183
6.5 499n3

Soṭah
1.7 205
2.5 163n10
3.8 450n4
5.1 461
9.11 169n17
9.15 154, 281, 574n7

Sukkah
2.8 435n5
3.10 435n5

Ta'anit
1.4–5 191n26
1.4–7 190n25
2.1 190n25
2.5 183
2.9 190n25
4.8 525n6

Ṭoharot
8.8 344

Yadayim
in toto 379
1.1 378
4.6–7 112

Yebamot
in toto 531
2.8 461
6.6 464
8.4 463n12

Yoma
8.6 309n5, 313
8.9 449

Zabim
2.1 463n12
5 259

Numbers Rabbah
149a 253n3

Palestinian/ Jerusalem Talmud
Berakot
2.8 480n10
4.7b 185

14b 111n8, 184n15,
  554n6
Ḥagigah
2.76c 401n2
Pesaḥim
6.1.33a 225
Soṭah
5.4 501n5
19a 111n8
20c 111n8, 184n15,
  554n6
22b 184n15
Ta'anit
69a 559n17
Yoma
45c 445

Psalms Rabbah
on Ps. 12:3 184n15
on Ps. 52:1 184n15

Seder Eliyahu
Rabbah
18 253n3

Seder Eliyahu Zuta
2 379n4

Shemoneh Esreh
benediction 1 302–3
benediction 10 583n3

Sipra
on Lev. 19.1–4 469n2
on Lev. 19:18 176,
  469n2, 536

on Lev. 29:6 480n10

Sipre Deuteronomy
on 11:26 214
on 32:9 512n1

Sipre Numbers
on 15:33 312

Song of Songs
Rabbah
1.10.1 379n4
7.14.1 599n5

Tosefta
Me'ilah
1.16 514n3

Menaḥot
13.18–22 502n7
Pesaḥim
8.8 494
Šabbat
1.15 111n8
Soṭah
6.4 501n5
Sukkah
3.15 514n3
Yoma
5.12 554n6
5.13 449
Zebaḥim
11.16–17 502n7

Targums

Targum Jonathan
on Isa. 42:1 317n7
on Isa. 43:10 317n7
on Isa. 52:13 317n7

Targum on Isaiah
on 5:1 514n3
on 5:11 515
on 42:1 123
on 50:11 636n2

Targum
on Lamentations
on 2:20 559n17

Targum on Psalms
on 18:14 573n4
on 118:22 515, 515n6

Qumran / Dead Sea Scrolls

CD
1.1 183n12
1.7 381n11
1.9–11 382
1.16 183n12, 509n6
1.18–19 546
2.15 177n38
2.16 170n20
3.15 303
3.15–16 219
3.18–4.10 405n6
4–5 379
4.12–5.17 259
4.17 183n12, 198n8
4.17–5.6 459n4
4.19 221n15
4.21 459n4
4.21–5.2 171n24
5.20 573n2
6.15 557n10
6.18–20 469n2
6.20–21 536
7.2–3 444n2
7.5 177n38
7.17 404
7.17–18 559n16
7.21 573n2
8.7 198n8
8.8 323
8.12 221n16
8.18 221n16

9.2–8 431, 444n2
9.3–6 174n31
9.16–22 444n2
9.17–23 445n4
10.14–11.18 309n3,
  310n7
10.18–19 310n7
11.12–14 313n1
11.21–22 183
11.22 404
12.3–6 436
12.6 404
13.9–10 408n16
14.3–6 436
14.13–16 183n13
14.20 198n8
14.21 431
15 555
15.1–5 173
15.5–6 173
15.15–17 436, 500
16.6–12 555
16.14–15 380
19.24 221n16
19.31 221n16

1Q27
frg. 1.2.5 198n8

1QapGen
20.29 321n5

22.16 302
22.21 302

1QH
2.13–14 583n2
3.7–10 573n4
3.12–13 573, 573n5
3.14 221n16
3.21–23 532n3
4.14–15 379n6
4.16 217n4
4.32–33 303
5.9 183n12
5.13–14.3 150n9
6.13 439n1, 532n3
6.13–16 146n6
6.14–16 344n12
6.15 381n11
6.22–25 373
6.34–35 583n2
7.14 509n6
8.4–8 344n12
8.21 115n14
13.11–12 475n2
14.24 405
15.14 183n12
15.17 183n12

1QM
1.1 351, 557n10
1.5 610

1.9–14 578n2
2.16–3.11 583n3
3.13–14 583n2
4.10 404
7.3–4 500
9.5–6 610
11.9 150n9
11.13 150n9
12.5 186n21
13.5–6 155
13.14 150n9
13.14–15 155
14.7 150, 150n9
15.5–6 320n2
17.8 233
18.14 303

1QpHab
in toto 108n3
2.1–10 574n7
7.1–14 593
8.8–13 502n7
9.3–7 502n7
9.4–5 499n3
10.5–6 550n1
11.2 550n1
11.7–8 437n1
12.3 150n9, 405n6
12.5 550n1
12.6 150n9
12.10 150n9

12.14–15 550n1

1QS
1–9 330n1
1.1–17 330n1
1.3–4 176
1.5 183n12
1.6–7 170n20
1.8 177n38
1.10–11 176
1.11–13 470
2.2 177n38
2.5–9 550n1
2.12 437n1
2.15 610
2.19–25 436
2.24–3.1 330n1
3.1 183n12
3.3 155
3.6–9 381
3.7–9 115n14
3.13–4.26 213
3.19–22 155
3.20–26 351
3.24 437n1
4.2 509n6
4.9–11 382n12
4.10 170n20, 554n6
4.13 233n13
4.21 115n14
4.25 475n2
5.5–7 405n6
5.7–8 173
5.11–12 339
5.13 610
5.13–14 381
5.23 436
5.24–6.1 444n2
5.25 469n2
5.25–6.1 431
6.1 488
6.2 198n8
6.4 436
6.4–5 370
6.7–8 488
6.8–13 436
6.19–22 470
6.22 436
6.27 173
6.27–7.2 173
7.6–7 470

7.15–17 323
7.22–23 323
7.24–25 470
8.1 177n38
8.2 183n12
8.4–10 405n6
8.5 381n11
8.14 108n4
8.20–21 177n38
9.2 436
9.3–6 405n6
9.5 183n12
9.8–9 470
9.15 146n6
9.16 436
9.16–18 444n2
9.17 339n4
9.19–20 108n4
9.22 470
10.17–19 174n31
10.18–19 198n8
10.19–20 175
11.1–2 175
11.2 198n8
11.7–8 532n3
11.8 381n11
11.18 303

1QSa
2.4 404
2.8–9 500
2.11–22 370
2.17–22 255

1QSb
3.7 326
4.25 532n3
4.25–26 439n1

4Q159
in toto 309
frg. 1.2.6–7 429

4Q164
in toto 405n6

4Q166
frg. 1.2.1–6 559n16

4Q169
in toto 108n3

frgs. 3–4.1.11 499n3
frgs. 3–4.2.1–11 550n1

4Q171
col. 1, frg. 1.1.21 150n9
col. 2, frg. 1.2.10 150n9

4Q174
1.10–14 540n2
3.17 183n12

4Q179
frg. 1.1.4 550n1
frg. 1.2.1 550n1

4Q184
frg. 1.10 405
frg. 1.16 183n12

4Q185
frgs. 1–2.1.9 550n1

4Q266
frg. 3.2.18–19 559n16
frg. 10.1.14 198n8

4Q274
frg. 1.1.9 557n8

4Q286
frg. 7.2.2–12 550n1

4Q381
15.4 373

4Q385
frg. 3.2–5 578

4Q387
frg. 3.2.13–14 558n12

4Q390
in toto 502n7
frg. 2.1.5 559n16

4Q394
frg. 2.18–19 500

4Q397–99
2.80–82 557n8

4Q398
14–17 536n5

4Q400
1.1.4 439n1
frg. 1.1.16 303

4Q500
2–7 514n3

4Q510
1.7 610

4Q511
2f.35 449n2
frg. 35 532n3
frgs. 63–64.3.5 550n1

4Q525
2.2.1–6 146n6

4QFlor
1.1–3 580n4
1.8 350
1.10–14 540n2
4.3–4 577n1

4QMMT
in toto 379n6
frg. 2.18–19 500

4QOrdinances
frg. 1.2.6–7 429

11QT
15.3 369
29.8–10 580n4
46.12 446
48.15–17 259
53–54 173
54.4 459n4
54.8–18 217n4
57.17–19 171n24
59.8–9 558n12
61.1–5 217n4
61.6–7 445n4
64.6–13 664n2
64.8–9 445n4

Josephus

Against Apion
1.55 6
1.166–67 380
1.290 82n6
2.44 659
2.76–77 528
2.84 555
2.190 536
2.199–204 464
2.205 557n8

2.206 379n7
2.210 555n7

Jewish Antiquities
1.53 558
1.72–76 589
1.179 272n2
1.218 669
1.252 388n6
1.331–33 372
2.20 426n3

2.70 450
2.105 451n6
2.200 639
2.317 623
2.333 425
3.108 600
3.212 436
3.213 534n1
3.294 183
4.72–73 380
4.212–13 547n3

4.219 445n4
4.231–39 309
4.244–59 460
4.253 171n23, 461
4.254–56 531
4.291 463n12
4.326 418
5.147 669
5.213 372
5.342 674
6.38 646n1

6.120 82n6
6.166 541
6.305 388n6
6.332 279n8
7.110 82n6
7.130 170
7.171 168n15
7.293 82n6
7.319 82n6
7.364 82n6
7.369 479
7.379 430
7.390–92 557n9
8.45–49 321n5
8.165–73 327
8.236 217n4
8.318 217n4
8.320 300n1
9.71 344
9.85 344
9.101 451n6
9.164 82n6
9.178 609
9.209 232n9
9.263–66 523
10.11 631n2
10.51 379
10.55 82n6
10.58 82n6
10.94 82n6
10.95 82n6
10.149 82n6
10.186 463n15
10.249 577n1
10.258 677
11.22 82n6
11.26 82n6
11.29 82n6
11.66 475n2
11.68 6
11.83 410
11.128 82n6
11.140 163
11.145 639
11.162 368n2
11.248 82n6
11.250 82n6
11.272 82n6
11.287 82n6
11.325–29 493n1
11.340–45 493n1
12.32 601
12.141 429
12.142 82n6
12.175–76 450
12.255 451n6
12.285 12, 252
12.302 636
12.348–49 493n1
12.406 410
12.413 168n15, 451n6
12.430 669
13.20 595
13.127 674
13.171–73 112
13.241 451n6
13.249 557n9
13.297 379, 379n6
13.297–98 112
13.304–6 493n1

13.379–83 664n2
13.399–404 381
13.408 379
14–18 78n2
14.22–24 559n15
14.34–36 555
14.63 310
14.69 232n8
14.72 555
14.89–91 169n17
14.105 499n3
14.106 555
14.107 488
14.110 499n3, 555
14.114–18 659
14.125 365n6
14.159–62 637n3
14.167–80 169n17
14.369 669
14.471 573
15.7 573
15.95 300n1
15.205–7 593
15.228–29 593
15.231 93n2
15.363–64 403
15.391–402 568n1
15.395 555
15.411–12 129
15.415 372n2
16.3 450n4
16.12–15 493n1
16.160 659
16.172 429
16.232 451n6
16.245 451n6
16.319 82n6
16.392–94 93n2
17.41 379
17.42 111
17.74 388n6
17.168–81 96
17.180–87 93n2
17.188 97, 363
17.193 93n2
17.193–205 493n1
17.213 623
17.271–85 573n3
17.282 232n8
17.311–17 97
17.320 450
17.341 364
17.342–44 97
18.2 646
18.4–10 528n4
18.11 112
18.12–17 530
18.14 676
18.16 676
18.16–17 112
18.23–25 528n4
18.27 363
18.35 12, 252, 617, 646
18.55–62 646
18.60 372n2
18.63–64 664n2
18.85 326
18.85–89 646
18.95 12, 252
18.102 363, 528n4

18.108 557n9
18.109 363
18.116–19 364
18.117 109, 115, 381
18.118 109, 508
18.122 363
18.136–37 364, 365
18.240–56 363
18.312 429
18.342 6
19.125 6
19.239 619
19.294 499n3
20.17 555n7
20.34–48 555n7
20.95 557n9
20.97 326
20.97–99 573n3, 579n3
20.106 623
20.160–67 637n3
20.160–72 573n3
20.167–72 219n12, 579n3
20.169 494n2
20.170 326
20.179–81 502n7
20.188 573n3, 579n3
20.189 106
20.196 12, 252
20.200–201 574
20.204–7 502n7
20.208–9 82n6
20.213 502n7
20.220 479

Jewish War
1.12 578n2
1.97–98 664n2
1.110–12 381
1.111 408n16
1.154 527
1.370 573n5
1.404–6 403
1.479 82n6
1.529 82n6
1.532 82n6
1.551 93n2
1.596 279n8
1.629 232n9
1.635 451n6
2.63 232n8
2.116 364
2.118 527, 528n4
2.119 536
2.120–58 330n1
2.121 170
2.129 524n2
2.131 524n2
2.135 173
2.139 173, 176
2.142 173
2.162–66 530
2.163 676
2.164–66 112
2.165 676
2.168 403
2.169–77 646
2.253–54 637n3
2.258–63 579n3
2.259–62 106

2.262 494n2
2.280 623
2.306 654n3
2.308 654n3
2.316 641n5
2.403–5 527
2.409–10 529n6
2.433 527, 528n4
2.481–83 593
3.47 191
3.124 232n8
3.320 573
3.369 649
3.374 532
3.432 6
3.437 259
3.446 140
3.509–15 403
3.516–21 375
4.286 573n5
4.317 674
4.334–44 558n13
4.504 637n3
4.531–32 557n9
5.99 623
5.120 429
5.184–226 568n1
5.192 372n2
5.200 499n3
5.201–10 555
5.222 555
5.377 175
5.449 654n3
5.449–51 282n14, 664, 664n2
6.43 595n2
6.282 499n3
6.285 217n4
6.285–87 574n8
6.288 573n2
6.288–322 568
6.300–309 502, 569n2
6.301–11 550n1
6.304 654n3
6.353–55 523
6.363 523
6.406–8 523
6.423–24 623
6.426 259
7.1–4 568
7.114–15 352
7.185 321n5
7.200–202 654n3
7.203 664n2
7.218 429
7.218–29 429n2
7.253–57 528n4
7.284 372n2
7.438 574n8

Life
9.42 245, 250
11 109
49 445n4
62 169n17
193–96 502n7
204 379n7
256 445n4
341 140
426 461

Philo

Against Flaccus
10.75 654n3
72.84–85 664n2
96 451n6

On Drunkenness
17 379n7

On Flight and Finding
1.3 464

On the Contemplative Life
66 368n2

On the Decalogue
18–19 469n2
20 534n1
50–51 534n1
84 173
106 534n1

108–10 534n1
121 469, 534n1
154 534n1

On the Embassy to Gaius
299–305 646

On the Life of Abraham
96 451n6
208 534n1

On the Life of Moses
1.57 416
1.70 416
1.96 595n2
2.22 309n3
2.65 475n2
2.68–9 463n15

On the Migration of Abraham
69 463n12

On the Posterity of Cain
17.61 664n2
52 382n12

On the Sacrifices of Cain and Abel
32 382n12

On the Special Laws
1.1 469n2
1.76–77 429
1.305 461n7
2.1 173
2.15 536
2.63 534n1, 536
2.184–85 345

2.203 190n25
2.234–36 379n7
3.30 461
3.31 169n18
3.79–82 461
4.82 451n6

On the Virtues
51 534n1

That Every Good Person Is Free
35 479
83 534n1
87 379n7
108 451n6

That the Worse Attacks the Better
176 463n14

Who Is the Heir?
181 168n15

Classical Writers

Artemidorus Daldianus
Onirocritica
2.56 659n2

Cicero
In Verrem
2.5.63 664n2
2.5.66 664n2
2.5.163–70 664n2
Pro Rabirio Perduellionis Reo
16 664n2

Dio Cassius
Roman History
57.18.5 555n7
69.12.1–2 579

Dionysius of Halicarnassus
Roman Antiquities
7.69 654–55

Herodotus
History
1.126 664n2
3.132 664n2
3.159 664n2

Horace
Satires
1.4.141–44 555n7

Macrobius
Saturnalia
2.4.11 78

Plato
Gorgias
473b–c 282n14

Plautus
Miles gloriosus
2.359–60 659n2

Pliny the Elder
Natural History
16.49 504
18.21.94–95 338n3
18.176 338n2
18.180–81 338n2
31.73–92 154–55

Plutarch
De sera numinis vindicta
9 659n2

Seneca
Ad Lucilium
101 282n14

Ad Marciam de consolatione
20.3 664n2

Strabo
Geography
15.3.11 338n3

Suetonius
Tiberius
8 97

Tacitus
Annales
2.42 527
15.44 574, 646
15.44.4 282n14
Historiae
2.72.1–2 664n2
5.5 555n7
5.8 568n1

Church Fathers

Athanasius
Festal Letters
39 17

Augustine
City of God
19.14 537

21.24 323
Harmony of the Gospels
1.1.1–4 6n5
1.3.6 6n5
1.4.7 6n5
2.4.9 26

4.10.11 6n5
Homilies on the Gospels
37 481
Sermon on the Mount
2.24.87 221

Barnabas
1.4 509n6
4.3 397n2, 578
5.5 609n15
16.1–5 514n3
16.3–4 580n4
18.1 214

Chromatius
Tractate on Matthew
3.1 74

1 Clement
11.1 300n4

**Clement
of Alexandria**
Paedagogus
2.12 353n2
3.7.39 294
Stromata
3.13 17

Cyprian
Epistles
73.10 17

Cyril of Jerusalem
Catechesis
14 12

Didache
1.1 213
1.2 211, 469n2, 536
1.3 190n25
1.4–5 175
1.6 183n13
2.2 213
5.1 213, 382n12
7 109
7.1 690
7.4 190n25
8 186
8.1 190n25, 254
8.2 185, 188
9–10 626
9.5 206, 388
10.6 496n6

11–12 217n4
11.3–12 269
11.7 323
11.11 168n15
13.1 272n1
14.1 626
16 579
16.3–4 217n4
16.4 578
16.5 574n9
16.6 583n3

Epiphanius
*Refutation
of All Heresies*
30.3 12

Eusebius
*Demonstration
of the Gospel*
3.2 419
*Ecclesiastical
History*
2.23.11 129
3.5.3 578
3.24.6 15n20
3.25.1 17
3.39 12
3.39.1 168n15
3.39.15 7
3.39.16 15
5.8.2 12
5.10.3 15n20
6.8 463n14
6.14 12
6.25.3 17
6.25.4 12, 15n20
Onomasticon
74.13 250

**First Council
of Nicea**
canon 1 463n14

Hilary of Poitiers
On Matthew
1.1 30

Ignatius
To the Ephesians
19 13n15
To the Smyrnaeans
1 13n15

Irenaeus
Against Heresies
3.1.1 12, 15n20
3.11.8 17
3.11.9 323
4.26.1 353n2
4.36.7 481
4.37.7 294
5.30.4 580n4

Jerome
Epistles
108.12 494
Prologue to Matthew
in toto 12

John Chrysostom
*Homiliae
in Matthaeum*
5.3 74
57.1 422
64.2 475n3
67.2 510
70.2 529n6

Justin Martyr
*Dialogue
with Trypho*
43.5–8 69
84.1–4 69
108.2 686
First Apology
29 463n14

Origen
*Commentary
on John*
5.41 250
*Commentary
on Matthew*
13.14 434
Contra Celsum
1.60 86
First Principles
1.3.7 323
Prayer
27.7 188
29–30 189

**Shepherd
of Hermas**
Similitude
5.2 512n1

Tertullian
Against Marcion
4.2 11
4.19 330
On Baptism
12 245
18 465
The Flesh of Christ
7 330